March 10–14, 2019
Glasgow, Scotland UK

Association for
Computing Machinery

Advancing Computing as a Science & Profession

CHIIR'19

Proceedings of the 2019 Conference on
Human Information Interaction and Retrieval

Sponsored by:

ACM SIGIR

In Cooperation with:

ACM SIGCHI

Association for
Computing Machinery

Advancing Computing as a Science & Profession

The Association for Computing Machinery
2 Penn Plaza, Suite 701
New York, New York 10121-0701

ISBN: 978-1-4503-6025-8 (Digital)

ISBN: 978-1-4503-6738-7 (Print)

Additional copies may be ordered prepaid from:

ACM Order Department
PO Box 30777
New York, NY 10087-0777, USA

Phone: 1-800-342-6626 (USA and Canada)
+1-212-626-0500 (Global)
Fax: +1-212-944-1318
E-mail: acmhelp@acm.org
Hours of Operation: 8:30 am – 4:30 pm ET

CHIIR 2019 Chairs' Welcome

It is our great pleasure to welcome you to Glasgow and to the *Fourth ACM SIGIR Conference on Information Interaction and Retrieval (CHIIR'19).* The number of contributed papers and short papers, and the number of conference attendees, clearly demonstrate the value of this unique forum for researchers and students interested in the user-centered aspects of information interaction and information retrieval. We are very pleased to see a great range of topics and institutions represented in the programme for this edition of the CHIIR conference series.

We would like to thank the people and institutions who have contributed to making CHIIR'19 a success. We first thank the authors for providing the content of the conference program. The three Program chairs, Hideo Joho, Vanessa Murdock and Pernilla Qvarfordt invested a huge amount of time and effort in organizing the paper reviewing and selection process for the full and short papers, and in putting together a very interesting program, with the help of the Senior Program Committee and the Program Committee. We are grateful for the efforts of the Tutorial Chair, Catherine L. Smith, the Workshops Chairs, Stephann Makri and Suzan Verberne, the organizers of the Doctoral Consortium, Yashar Moshfeghi and Heather O'Brien, the Demos and Resources Chairs, Jiyin He and Frank Hopfgartner, the Publicity Chair, Diane Pennington, and the Publications Chair, Craig Macdonald. We also very grateful to Mateusz Dubiel and Sylvain Daronnat, for leading the student volunteers and for all their support with our webpages.

Finally, we thank the hosting organization, the University of Strathclyde, for their practical support we could wish for, our colleagues at the Technology and Innovation Centre for help with all the logistics of the conference, and the City of Glasgow for inviting us into the City Chambers for the welcome reception. We hope that you will find the program interesting and thought-provoking and the interaction with old and new friends and colleagues engaging and stimulating, - and that you will enjoy the city of Glasgow!

Leif Azzopardi
General Co-chair
University of Strathclyde

Martin Halvey
General Co-chair
University of Strathclyde

Ian Ruthven
General Co-chair
University of Strathclyde

CHIIR 2019 Program Overview

We are delighted to welcome you to the Fourth ACM SIGIR Conference on Human Information Interaction and Retrieval (CHIIR), held in Glasgow, UK from March 10 to March 14, 2019. As information systems become more embedded in our day-to-day experiences, it becomes increasingly important to understand how people interact with information and the consequences of those interactions in our personal and professional lives as well as for our communities. CHIIR provides a unique forum for the dissemination and discussion of research on the user-centered aspects of information interaction and information retrieval.

The CHIIR 2019 program includes different tracks to allow our research community to experience both the breath and the depth of Human Information Interaction and Retrieval. The Full Papers allows systematic and methodological sound research to advance our field. The Perspective Papers brings reflection of our fundamental concepts and methodologies to the program. The Short Papers and Demonstrations tracks are a venue for emerging ideas. We received a total of 56 Full Paper and 7 Perspective Paper submissions, of which 21 were accepted for publication in the proceedings, resulting in an acceptance rate of 33.3%. A total of 47 Short paper submissions and 8 Demo submissions was received, out of which 23 (48.9%) Short Papers and 13 Demos were accepted. Full papers are allocated a 30-minute presentation slot in the program. Short papers are presented as posters along with Demonstrations during a special evening session. Best papers were selected by the Best paper committee consisting of Irene Lopatovska (Pratt Institute, USA, Chair), Nim Dvir (University of Albany, Canada), Ying-Hsang Liu (Charles Sturt University, Australia), and Dan Russell (Google, USA). Nomination was made by the Program Chairs, reviewers and Senior Program Committee members.

In addition to contributed papers and demonstrations, the CHIIR program features two keynotes by prominent researchers, Ranjitha Kumar (University of Illinois at Urbana-Champaign, USA) and Daniela Petrelli (Sheffield Hallam University, UK). We thank the keynote speakers for their inspiring talks and for sharing their insights and wisdom with the conference attendees. CHIIR 2019 also features three Practitioner talks, creating opportunity for an exchange of ideas and experience between academia and industry, two Workshops, one Tutorial, and a Doctoral Consortium.

We would like to acknowledge the tremendous work of the Organizing Committee for putting together this technical program, including the Demo Chairs Jiyin He (Singal, the Netherlands) and Frank Hopfgartner (University of Sheffield, UK), the Doctoral Consortium Chairs Heather O'Brien (University of British Columbia, Canada) and Yashar Moshfeghi (University of Strathclyde, UK), and the Workshops Chairs Suzan Verberne (Leiden University, the Netherlands) and Stephann Makri (University of London, UK), Tutorial Chair Catherine L. Smith (Kent State University, USA) and Publication Chair Craig Macdonald (University of Glasgow) as well as the 15 Senior Program Committee members and 67 Program Committee members who reviewed submissions. The credit for creating a high quality technical program goes to them.

We would also like to thank the general chairs, Martin Halvey (University of Strathclyde, UK), Ian Ruthven (University of Strathclyde, UK) and Leif Azzopardi (University of Strathclyde, UK), for their insights, advice and friendly reminders all along the way. Finally, we are grateful to the authors and attendees, whose support and enthusiasm are what make this conference a success.

We hope that you find the CHIIR 2019 program interesting and thought-provoking. Our goal was not only to create the opportunity for researchers and practitioners from around the world to share their research and experiences, but also to foster new user-centered research and innovation in information interaction and information retrieval.

Vanessa Murdock
Program Co-chair
Amazon, USA

Pernilla Qvarfordt
Program Co-chair
pxq Labs, USA

Hideo Joho
Program Co-chair
University of Tsukuba, Japan

Table of Contents

Session 5: Information Interests & Needs

Session 6: Search in Context

Session 7: Search Interactions

Session 8: Search in Context

Poster Session

Demo Papers

Tutorial

Workshops

Doctorial Consortium

CHIIR 2019 Conference Organization

General Chairs: Leif Azzopardi *(University of Strathclyde, UK)*
Martin Halvey *(University of Strathclyde, UK)*
Ian Ruthven *(University of Strathclyde, UK)*

Program Chairs: Hideo Joho *(University of Tsukuba, Japan)*
Vanessa Murdock *(Amazon, USA)*
Pernilla Qvarfordt *(pxq Labs, USA)*

Demos and Resources Co-Chairs: Jiyin He *(Signal Media, UK)*
Frank Hopfgartner *(University of Sheffield, UK)*

Doctoral Consortium Co-Chairs: Yashar Moshfeghi (*University of Strathclyde, UK)*
Heather O'Brien *(University of British Columbia, Canada)*

Workshops Co-Chairs: Stephann Makri *(University of London, UK)*
Suzan Verberne *(Leiden Institute of Advanced Computer Science, NL)*

Tutorial Chair: Catherine L. Smith *(Kent State University, USA)*

Publicity Chair: Diane Pennington *(University of Strathclyde, UK)*

Proceedings Chair: Craig Macdonald *(University of Glasgow, UK)*

Student Volunteering Co-Chairs: Mateusz Dubiel (*University of Strathclyde, UK)*
Sylvain Daronnat (*University of Strathclyde, UK)*

Senior Program Committee: Ioannis Arapakis *(Telefonica Research, Spain)*
Katriina Byström *(Oslo Metropolitan University, Norway)*
Robert Capra *(University of North Carolina at Chapel Hill, USA)*
Abdigani Diriye *(IBM Research Africa, Kenya)*
David Elsweiler *(University of Regensburg, Germany)*
Henry Field *(Endicott College, USA)*
Claudia Hauff *(Delft University of Technology, The Netherlands)*
Orland Hoeber *(University of Regina, Canada)*
Joemon Jose *(University of Glasgow, UK)*
Jaana Kekäläinen *(University of Tampere, Finland)*
Diane Kelly *(University of Tennessee, USA)*
Irene Lopatovska *(Pratt Institute, USA)*
Daniel Russell *(Google, USA)*
Catherine Smith *(Kent State University, USA)*
Mark Smucker *(University of Waterloo, Canada)*

Best Paper Committee Chair: Irene Lopatovska *(Pratt Institute, USA)*

Best Paper Committee: Nim Dvir *(University of Albany, Canada)*
Ying-Hsang Liu *(Charles Sturt University, Australia)*
Daniel Russell *(Google, USA)*

Program Committee: Nicholas Belkin *(Rutgers University, USA)*
Klaus Berberich *(Max Planck Institute for Informatics, Germany)*
Gerd Berget *(Oslo Metropolitan University, Norway)*
Nilavra Bhattacharya *(The University of Texas at Austin, USA)*
Ralf Bierig *(Maynooth University, Ireland)*
Dania Bilal *(University of Tennessee, USA)*
Lennart Björneborn *(University of Copenhagen, Denmark)*
Toine Bogers *(Aalborg University Copenhagen, Denmark)*
Pia Borlund *(Oslo Metropolitan University, Norway)*
Pavel Braslavski *(Ural Federal University, Russia)*
Kathy Brennan *(The University of British Columbia, Canada)*
Ashlee Edwards *(Instagram, USA)*
Marc Bron *(Yahoo Labs, UK)*
George Buchanan *(The University of Melbourne, Australia)*
Yung-Sheng Chang (*The University of Texas at Austin, USA*)
Charles Cole *(Colemining Inc., Canada)*
Kevyn Collins-Thompson *(University of Michigan, USA)*
Arjen de Vries *(Radboud University, The Netherlands)*
David Ellis *(Aberystwyth University, UK)*
Nicola Ferro *(University of Padova, Italy)*
Luanne Freund *(The University of British Columbia, Canada)*
Ingo Frommholz *(University of Bedfordshire, UK)*
Norbert Fuhr *(University of Duisburg-Essen, Germany)*
Hua Guo *(Twitter Inc., USA)*
Jacek Gwizdka *(The University of Texas at Austin, USA)*
Matthias Hagen *(Martin-Luther-Universität Halle-Wittenberg, Germany)*
Morgan Harvey *(Northumbria University, UK)*
Morten Hertzum *(University of Copenhagen, Denmark)*
Jeff Huang *(Brown University, USA)*
Hugo Huurdeman *(University of Amsterdam, The Netherlands)*
Isto Huvila *(Uppsala University, Sweden)*
Sampath Jayarathna *(Old Dominion University, USA)*
Gareth Jones *(Dublin City University, Ireland)*
Jaap Kamps *(University of Amsterdam, The Netherlands)*
Makoto P. Kato *(Kyoto University, Japan)*
Markus Kattenbeck *(University of Regensburg, Germany)*

Program Committee, cont.

Claus-Peter Klas *(GESIS – Leibniz Institute for Social Sciences, Germany)*
Andreas Komninos *(University of Patras, Greece)*
Udo Kruschwitz *(University of Essex, UK)*
Sanna Kumpulainen *(University of Tampere, Finland)*
Dirk Lewandowski *(University of Applied Sciences, Germany)*
Christina Lioma *(University of Copenhagen, Denmark)*
Florian Meier *(Aalborg University Copenhagen, Denmark)*
Chang Liu *(Peking University, China)*
Jingjing Liu *(University of South Carolina, USA)*
Ying-Hsang Liu *(The Australian National University, Australia)*
Andreas Lommatzsch *(TU Berlin, Germany)*
Andrew Macfarlane *(City, University of London, UK)*
Thomas Mandl *(University of Hildesheim, Germany)*
Stephann Makri *(City, University of London, UK)*
Dana McKay *(The University of Melbourne Australia)*
Peter Mutschke *(GESIS – Leibniz Institute for the Social Sciences, Germany)*
Heather O'Brien *(University of British Columbia, Canada)*
Alexandra Papoutsaki *(Pomona College, USA)*
Edie Rasmussen *(The University of British Columbia, Canada)*
Diane Rasmussen Pennington *(University of Strathclyde, UK)*
Soo Young Rieh *(University of Michigan, USA)*
Tuukka Ruotsalo *(Aalto University, Finland)*
Tony Russell-Rose *(UXLabs, UK)*
Alan Said *(University of Gothenburg, Sweden)*
Abhishek Singh *(LinkedIn, USA)*
Eero Sormunen *(Tampere University, Finland)*
Damiano Spina *(RMIT University, Australia)*
Max L. Wilson *(University of Nottingham, UK)*
Christa Womser-Hacker *(University of Hildesheim, Germany)*
Iris Xie *(University of Wisconsin-Milwaukee, USA)*
Takehiro Yamamoto *(Kyoto University, Japan)*
Yusuke Yamamoto *(Shizuoka University, Japan)*
Jie Yang *(University of Fribourg, Switzerland)*
Amy Zhang *(Massachusetts Institute of Technology, USA)*
Yan Zhang *(The University of Texas at Austin, USA)*
Ziqi Zhang *(Sheffield University, UK)*

Sponsor: SIGIR Special Interest Group on Information Retrieval

In-cooperation with: SIGCHI

Data-Driven Design: Beyond A/B Testing

Ranjitha Kumar
University of Illinois at Urbana-Champaign
ranjitha@illinois.edu

ABSTRACT

A/B testing has become the de facto standard for optimizing design, helping designers craft more effective user experiences by leveraging data. A typical A/B test involves dividing user traffic between two experimental conditions (A and B), and looking for statistically significant differences in performance indicators (e.g., conversion rates) between them. While this technique is popular, there are other, powerful data-driven methods — complementary to A/B testing — that can tie design choices to desired outcomes.

Mining data from *existing designs* can expose designers to a greater space of divergent solutions than A/B testing [1, 4]. Since companies cannot predict a priori if the engineering effort for creating alternatives will be commensurate with a performance increase, they often test small changes, along gradients to local optima. With the millions of websites and mobile apps available today, it is likely that almost any UX problem a designer encounters has already been considered and solved by someone. The challenges are finding relevant existing solutions, measuring their performance, and correlating these metrics with design features. Recent systems that capture and aggregate interaction data from third-party Android apps — with zero code integration — open-source analytics that were previously locked away in each app, allowing designers to test and compare UI/UX patterns found in the wild [2, 3].

Lightweight prototypes with tight user feedback loops, or *experimentation engines*, can bootstrap product design involving technologies that are actively being developed (e.g., artificial intelligence, virtual/augmented reality), where both use cases and capabilities are not well-understood [5]. These systems afford staged automation: initially, "Wizard of Oz" techniques can scaffold needfinding, and eventually be replaced with automated solutions informed by the collected data. For example, a chatbot deployed on social media can serve as an experimentation engine for automating fashion advice [7]. At first, a pool of personal stylists can power the chatbot to collect organic conversations revealing common fashion problems, effective interaction patterns for addressing them, and design considerations for automation. Once technologies are developed to scale useful interventions [8, 9], the chatbot platform provides a testbed for iteratively refining them.

Generative models trained on a set of effective design examples can support predictive workflows that allow designers to rapidly prototype new, performant solutions [6]. Models such as generative adversarial networks and variational autoencoders can produce designs based on high-level constraints, or complete them given partial specifications. For example, a mobile wireframing tool backed by such a model could suggest adding "username" and "password" input fields to a screen with a centrally placed "login" button.

CHIIR '19, March 10–14, 2019, Glasgow, Scotland Uk

ACM ISBN 978-1-4503-6025-8/19/03.
https://doi.org/10.1145/3295750.3300046

CCS CONCEPTS

• **Human-centered computing → Interaction design process and methods; Systems and tools for interaction design.**

KEYWORDS

data-driven design, design mining, UI/UX, mobile apps, fashion

ACM Reference Format:

Ranjitha Kumar. 2019. Data-Driven Design: Beyond A/B Testing. In *2019 Conference on Human Information Interaction and Retrieval (CHIIR '19), March 10–14, 2019, Glasgow, Scotland Uk.* ACM, New York, NY, USA, 2 pages. https://doi.org/10.1145/3295750.3300046

BIOGRAPHY

Ranjitha Kumar is an Assistant Professor in the Department of Computer Science at the University of Illinois at Urbana-Champaign (UIUC), where she leads the Data-Driven Design group. She is the recipient of a 2018 NSF CAREER award, and UIUC's 2018 C.W. Gear Outstanding Junior Faculty Award. Her research has won best paper awards/nominations at premier conferences in HCI, and is supported by grants from Google, Amazon, and Adobe. She received her PhD from the Computer Science Department at Stanford University in 2014, and was formerly the Chief Scientist at Apropose, Inc., a data-driven design company she founded that was backed by Andreessen Horowitz and New Enterprise Associates.

REFERENCES

[1] Biplab Deka, Zifeng Huang, Chad Franzen, Joshua Hibschman, Daniel Afergan, Yang Li, Jeffrey Nichols, and Ranjitha Kumar. 2017. Rico: A Mobile App Dataset for Building Data-Driven Design Applications. In *Proc. UIST.* 845–854.

[2] Biplab Deka, Zifeng Huang, Chad Franzen, Jeffrey Nichols, Yang Li, and Ranjitha Kumar. 2017. ZIPT: Zero-Integration Performance Testing of Mobile App Designs. In *Proc. UIST.* 727–736.

[3] Biplab Deka, Zifeng Huang, and Ranjitha Kumar. 2016. ERICA: Interaction Mining Mobile Apps. In *Proc. UIST.* 767–776.

[4] Ranjitha Kumar, Arvind Satyanarayan, Cesar Torres, Maxine Lim, Salman Ahmad, Scott R. Klemmer, and Jerry O. Talton. 2013. Webzeitgeist: Design Mining the Web. In *Proc. CHI.* 3083–3092.

[5] Ranjitha Kumar and Kristen Vaccaro. 2017. An Experimentation Engine for Data-Driven Fashion Systems. In *Proc. AAAI Spring Symposium.*

[6] Jerry Talton, Lingfeng Yang, Ranjitha Kumar, Maxine Lim, Noah Goodman, and Radomír Měch. 2012. Learning Design Patterns with Bayesian Grammar Induction. In *Proc. UIST.* 63–74.

[7] Kristen Vaccaro, Tanvi Agarwalla, Sunaya Shivakumar, and Ranjitha Kumar. 2018. Designing the Future of Personal Fashion. In *Proceedings of the 2018 CHI Conference on Human Factors in Computing Systems (CHI '18).* 627–627.

[8] Kristen Vaccaro, Sunaya Shivakumar, Ziqiao Ding, Karrie Karahalios, and Ranjitha Kumar. 2016. The Elements of Fashion Style. In *Proc. UIST.* 777–785.

[9] Mariya I Vasileva, Bryan A Plummer, Krishna Dusad, Shreya Rajpal, Ranjitha Kumar, and David Forsyth. 2018. Learning Type-Aware Embeddings for Fashion Compatibility. *Proc. ECCV,* 405–421.

From Delivering Facts to Generating Emotions: The Complex Relationship between Museums and Information

Daniela Petrelli
Art & Design Research Centre
Sheffield Hallam University
153 Arundel Street, Sheffield S1 2NU, UK
d.petrelli@shu.ac.uk

ABSTRACT

Motivation: The past 25 years have seen a constant increase in the use of information technology to deliver digital content in cultural heritage settings. Museums have experimented with multimedia PCs, PDAs and phones, table-tops, Google Glass and now VR. The aim has always been to provide more information despite the fact that only a minority of visitors consumes the information on offer. Failing to engage visitors should direct our concerns on the 'receiving' side rather than on the 'delivering' side, that is to say to look at the visitors' experience rather than the technology [1].

Problem statement: The problem lays in the way the interactive experience is designed: too often it is as an 'add on' to the physical exhibition rather than an integral part of the experience. The emerging Internet of Things bridges the gap between the physical and the digital and enables to seamless integrate the digital content with the material collection or the historical space. Via embedded technology it is possible to collect and exploit visitors' data opening up new possibilities to create engaging and personalised visitors' experiences onsite and online.

Approach: Using a number of case studies of exhibitions and installations used by over 20,000 visitors across Europe, I will show how the interaction with information can be designed as part of multisensory exhibitions that engages the visitor at many levels and generate emotion. The approach is collaborative and requires the equal contribution of technologists, designers and content experts throughout the whole process, from early conception to the final implementation. The response of the visitors goes well beyond expectations opening up new opportunities for long-term visitors' engagement.

CCS Concepts/ACM Classifiers

• Human-centered computing~HCI design and evaluation methods • Human-centered computing~Mixed / augmented reality • Human-centered computing~Empirical studies in interaction design

Author Keywords

Tangible and embodied interaction; Internet of Things; cultural heritage; museum; multisensory; affective interaction

BIOGRAPHY

Dr Daniela Petrelli started working on technologies for cultural heritage in 1996 designing the first context-sensitive personalised interactive mobile guide. Recently she led the European project meSch that explored tangible and embodied interactions in museums and heritage sites. meSch has received international awards and is the first to use the Internet of Things and Cloud Computing in museums. Dr Petrelli's other research interests include personal and family memories, data visualisation, multimedia and multilingual information access. In her career, she has published over 100 international peer-reviewed contributions and received 12 awards both from academia and industry. Dr Petrelli is Professor of Interaction Design and director of the Digital Materiality Lab, an interest group looking into new digital-material hybrids.

REFERENCE

1. Beverly Serrell and Britt Raphling. 1992. Computers on the Exhibti Floor. Curator – The Museum Journal, 35 (3).

ACM ISBN 978-1-4503-6025-8/19/03.
https://doi.org/10.1145/3295750.3300047

Learning About Work Tasks to Inform Intelligent Assistant Design

Johanne R. Trippas
Damiano Spina
Falk Scholer
johanne.trippas@rmit.edu.au
damiano.spina@rmit.edu.au
falk.scholer@rmit.edu.au
RMIT University
Melbourne, Australia

Ahmed Hassan Awadallah
Peter Bailey
Paul N. Bennett
Ryen W. White
hassanam@microsoft.com
pbailey@microsoft.com
pauben@microsoft.com
ryenw@microsoft.com
Microsoft
Redmond, USA

Jonathan Liono
Yongli Ren
Flora D. Salim
Mark Sanderson
jonathan.liono@rmit.edu.au
yongli.ren@rmit.edu.au
flora.salim@rmit.edu.au
mark.sanderson@rmit.edu.au
RMIT University
Melbourne, Australia

ABSTRACT

Intelligent assistants can serve many purposes, including entertainment (e.g. playing music), home automation, and task management (e.g. timers, reminders). The role of these assistants is evolving to also support people engaged in work tasks, in workplaces and beyond. To design truly useful intelligent assistants for work, it is important to better understand the work tasks that people are performing. Based on a survey of 401 respondents' daily tasks and activities in a work setting, we present a classification of work-related tasks, and analyze their key characteristics, including the frequency of their self-reported tasks, the environment in which they undertake the tasks, and which, if any, electronic devices are used. We also investigate the cyber, physical, and social aspects of tasks. Finally, we reflect on how intelligent assistants could influence and help people in a work environment to complete their tasks, and synthesize our findings to provide insight on the future of intelligent assistants in support of amplifying personal productivity.

ACM Reference Format:
Johanne R. Trippas, Damiano Spina, Falk Scholer, Ahmed Hassan Awadallah, Peter Bailey, Paul N. Bennett, Ryen W. White, Jonathan Liono, Yongli Ren, Flora D. Salim, and Mark Sanderson. 2019. Learning About Work Tasks to Inform Intelligent Assistant Design. In *2019 Conference on Human Information Interaction and Retrieval (CHIIR '19), March 10–14, 2019, Glasgow, United Kingdom.* ACM, New York, NY, USA, 10 pages. https://doi.org/10.1145/3295750.3298934

1 INTRODUCTION

Intelligent assistants such as Amazon Alexa or Microsoft Cortana provide a useful way for people to manage many of their tasks, including personal and work-related activities. In recent years, there has been growing interest in applications of these assistants in workplaces to empower employees, through offerings such as Alexa for Business[1] and Cortana Skills Kit for Enterprise.[2] Despite the potential for these assistants to help people complete their work tasks (at work, at home, or on-the-go), penetration of these assistants in workplaces is limited [19], and task support is restricted to low-level tasks such as controlling devices, seeking information, or entertainment [26]. In work settings in particular, intelligent assistants are mostly used for basic tasks such as voice dictation, calendar management, and customer/employee support [19]. To increase the uptake of intelligent assistants for work tasks, a better understanding of the tasks that people perform, and how next-generation intelligent assistants could support them, is needed.

There are many ways to understand tasks and activities, including diary studies [17], naturalistic field studies [32], and lifelog analysis [13]. A commonly used way to characterize tasks and activities is through statistical time-use surveys [6], enabling an understanding of which activities people are engaging in and for how long. Examples include the average number of hours that individuals spend on activities including traveling, working in paid and unpaid jobs, social life, and personal care. However, these surveys do not provide a fine-grained understanding of how these tasks and activities are completed. Understanding how people complete activities—including important aspects such as the devices used and the involvement of other individuals—can provide insights into how to support these activities with digital assistants. Other studies have examined daily information needs [8], tasks in communications [4], or information-seeking [16, 22]. Recently, the influences of cyber, physical, and social behaviors were used to analyze information-seeking activities indoors [29, 30]. However, these studies do not focus on work tasks, including the impact of task properties (cyber, physical, or social factors), or the support that intelligent assistants can offer to help workers complete their tasks.

To inform the design of intelligent assistants to support work tasks, we developed a survey to better understand people's everyday tasks and task performance. We focus on information workers, since their activities frequently require digital support. We distributed the survey broadly and received around 400 responses. In this paper,

CHIIR '19, March 10–14, 2019, Glasgow, United Kingdom

ACM ISBN 978-1-4503-6025-8/19/03...$15.00
https://doi.org/10.1145/3295750.3298934

[1] https://aws.amazon.com/alexaforbusiness/
[2] https://blogs.microsoft.com/ai/cortana-for-enterprise/

we focus on tasks described by survey respondents as *work-related.* We apply thematic and quantitative analysis to provide deep insight and understanding into the work tasks that people perform. The main contributions of this paper are:

- A comprehensive classification of work-related tasks.
- An analysis of the key characteristics of tasks, focusing primarily on temporal aspects such as task duration.
- An investigation of the cyber, physical, and social (CPS) properties of tasks, including device usage.
- Design recommendations for how intelligent assistants could support work tasks, both on demand and proactively, drawing on insights from the survey.

The remainder of the paper is structured as follows. In Section 2, we describe related work, including task taxonomies, intelligent assistants, and tasks and activities in email and search. Section 3 describes the survey methodology, including the pilot survey. Section 4 describes the results of the analysis. We discuss the results and their implications in Section 5 and conclude in Section 6 with a summary of our findings and potential avenues for future work.

2 RELATED WORK

In this research, we characterize tasks performed by information workers and examine opportunities for intelligent assistants to support them.

2.1 Task Taxonomies

Previous work on understanding human activities has attempted to build taxonomies of tasks and human activities. Kahneman et al. [17] used a Day Reconstruction Method (DRM) to assess how people spend their time and how they experience various activities in their lives. They asked study participants to construct a short diary by segmenting their day into episodes and assigning a name, a start time, and an end time for each episode. They used this information to construct an activity taxonomy (e.g. socializing, eating, working, commuting, etc.) and interaction partners (e.g. friends, relatives, co-workers, etc.). This taxonomy was used in defining activities for activity identification in lifelog data [13].

Time-use surveys have been carried out at different levels for many decades [6]. A time-use survey is a statistical survey that aims to report data on how people spend their time. They typically characterize time spent in different categories such as paid work, unpaid work (e.g. domestic work, voluntary work, etc.), social life and leisure (e.g. sports, mass media, etc.), and personal care (e.g. sleeping, eating, etc.) [6]. The objective is to identify, classify and quantify the main types of activity that people engage in which has implications on a wide range of policy concerns [38].

Other research has focused on characterizing tasks carried out in team settings [40]. The study noted the increased use of team-based work structure and suggested that studying work tasks should take team characteristics into account. Different types of tasks such as managing others, advising others, problem solving, and social interaction were considered. Analysis showed that different types of teams engage in multiple types of tasks to accomplish their mission.

Other studies have focused on specific types of tasks. For example, Church et al. [8] studied the daily information needs of people through a large-scale, in-depth, quantitative investigation. They conducted a study spanning a three-month period and involving more than 100 users. The study gathered in situ insights into the types of needs that occur from day to day, how those needs are addressed, and how contextual, technological, and demographic factors impact on those needs. They showed that there are recurring daily information needs such as finding availability and information about people. They also showed that people employ two main modalities for satisfying daily information needs (Internet access and asking others for help). Similar work has focused on understanding mobile information needs [9, 34] and found that the majority of such needs happen where people are away from their familiar contexts and that geographical needs were very popular.

Our research also aims to characterize tasks, but we focus on understanding everyday work-related tasks and task performance with the objective of informing the design of intelligent assistants to support work tasks. We also examine cyber, physical, and social aspects of these tasks. Finally, we examine the tools currently used by information workers to accomplish these tasks and identify opportunities for intelligent assistants to provide support.

2.2 Intelligent Assistants

Intelligent digital assistants on mobile devices, personal computers, and smart speakers have recently gained considerable attention as increasing number of users interact with them to fulfill their information needs and complete their tasks. This has motivated work on user interaction studies to characterize the usage of these assistants. Mehrotra et al. [26] investigated the different use cases of a desktop-based digital assistant. The analysis reveals that, given the conversational nature of user interactions, longer sessions (i.e. sessions with a large number of queries) are more common than in the traditional web search paradigm. Exploring the different use cases, they observed that users go beyond general search and use a digital assistant to accomplish several tasks such as time management (setting reminders and meetings), entertainment (e.g. playing music), communication (e.g. sending text messages), etc.

The interest in new form factors for intelligent assistants, such as smart speakers, motivated new studies of the most common use cases for intelligent assistants on these devices. A recent report [19] focused on studying how people use smart speakers. The findings showed that the living room has become the most common location choice at 46% for smart speaker owners, closely followed by the kitchen (41%) and bedrooms (37%). Trailing far behind is the work office at 2.7%, indicating that such assistants still have a long way to go to penetrate the workspace. They report that listening to music is the top use case, followed by checking the weather, asking questions, and setting timers and alarms. Other interesting use cases include calling and messaging, and smart home control.

Understanding how intelligent assistants are used in a workplace setting is less studied and not very well understood. A recent report [37] focused on this angle by conducting a survey of over 500 people from different industries and organization sizes. The study showed that the penetration of intelligent assistants in the workplace is still limited, and that they are mostly used for basic tasks such as voice dictation or calendar management.

These studies highlight two important aspect that motivate this work. The first is that intelligent assistant usage for work-related tasks is rather limited, and developers of intelligent assistants have a considerable challenge in order to penetrate the workspace. The second is that the current tasks being supported by intelligent assistants are limited in scope, with basic question answering, device control, and calendar management being the most frequent use cases. This highlights the need for a detailed study of tasks performed by information workers, and the potential for intelligent assistants to support users with these tasks.

2.3 Tasks in Email and Web Search

Web search and email have been extensively used to understand what tasks users are engaged with—even though both give only a partial view of tasks and activities. Prior research has treated emails as a communication tool for workplace activities or a task management resource [4]. Kushmerick and Lau [21] formalized e-commerce activities as finite-state automata, where transitions among states represent messages sent between participants. Dredze and Wallach [12] used user-generated activity labels and classified emails into activities using overlapping participants and content similarity. Shen et al. [33] predicted tasks associated with an incoming email by leveraging email sender, recipients and distinct subject words. Dredze and Wallach [12] and Qadir et al. [28] used approaches inspired by topic modeling to use content, people and thread information to identify different activities in email.

Tasks and activities have also been extensively studied in the context of Web search. Kelly and Belkin [18] conducted a longitudinal study to elicit tasks that were of current interest, or that were expected to be of interest, to subjects doing web search. Subjects were asked to think about their online information-seeking activities in terms of tasks and to create personal labels for each task. They used this information to produce the following nine task groupings: *Academic Research, Entertainment, News and Weather, Personal Communication, Shopping and Selling, Teaching, Hobbies and Personal Interests, Travel,* and *Jobs/Career.* Using that data, White and Kelly [39] developed different implicit feedback models for each task grouping. Other work focused on extracting tasks from search logs [16, 24], identifying cross-session search tasks [1, 20] or supporting complex search tasks that are composed of several smaller sub-tasks [14]. Research on developing taxonomies of information needs in web search [5], understanding searchers' information goals [31], and understanding tasks via action-topic pairs over both search and browsing logs [3] is also relevant in this context.

While we consider communication and information seeking, our objective is to come up with a broader characterization of tasks that covers several additional task types. Additionally, we do not consider how to improve task support in email clients or search engines but rather focus on characterizing the opportunities for intelligent assistants to provide more comprehensive task support to their users.

3 METHODOLOGY

We conducted an online survey[3] using Qualtrics[4] to gather information about tasks which are carried out in a work context. The survey consisted of both open-ended and multiple-choice questions, as well as screener questions such as age, location, employment status, and highest completed education.

The aim of the survey was to understand task behaviour in daily (work) life by capturing the range of tasks and sub-tasks that people perform, and their motivation, task duration, or task regularity. We then analyzed which tasks are completed most often, interruptions while performing the task, CPS (Cyber-Physical-Social) activities involved, and which planning tools are used.

Participation was voluntary and anonymous. Our call for participation informed participants[5] that the survey was titled "Exploration of Human Tasks in Daily Life".

3.1 Survey

An initial pilot survey was conducted with a panel constrained to participants located in Australia, using a sampling approach that followed national demographics based on participant age. Further restrictions were based on gender and population distribution according to states and territories in Australia. People in the Qualtrics database meeting these criteria were randomly selected and emailed an invitation for participating in the online survey.

Pilot data was collected from 106 participants; analysis of the responses helped to estimate the quality of the data collected, and to revise and extend the set of questions. For instance, we revised the survey to include further questions about tasks such as their regularity, interruptions that occur while performing the task, and which planning tools are used.

Moreover, the analysis of the initial pilot showed that respondents were often not employed or retired, and often had a high school degree as the highest level of education. Since respondents were allowed to provide tasks from their everyday life, it meant that many of the tasks were short and household-related. As a result, participation restrictions were developed for the main survey, requiring that respondents:

- Were between 25–59 years old;
- Were employed or self-employed;
- Had completed a bachelor's degree or higher.

For the main survey, the panel was constrained to participants located in Australia, the United Kingdom, and the United States. People in the Qualtrics database meeting the above criteria were randomly selected and emailed an invitation to participate in the online survey. The survey was conducted from May 17 to July 2 2018, and sent out to 833 individuals. 410 respondents completed the survey: a 49% response rate. The completed responses were manually checked, and 9 were identified as invalid, leaving a final number of 401 respondents, whose data is analyzed in this paper.

Overall, participants were required to supply information about four tasks, each of which took a different duration (less than 30 minutes; 30 minutes to two hours; two hours to a day; more than a day). The survey questions are attached in Appendix A. In the online setup, the same questions were displayed for each of the four tasks that participants supplied, and the word "task" was automatically replaced with their corresponding answers for Question 1.

While the definition of *information worker* is not agreed upon in the literature, by sampling from professionals with a degree, we aim

[3]Survey reviewed and approved by the Human Research Ethics Committee at RMIT University (SEHAPP 11-18).

[4]https://www.qualtrics.com/

[5]We use *respondents* and *participants* interchangeably.

to characterize the tasks of people whose work commonly requires digital information support.

3.2 Categorization of Free Text Results with a Thematic Analysis Approach

Thematic analysis involves identifying, analyzing, and reporting patterns (themes) within the qualitative data [10, 11]. This method allows for analyzing qualitative data in an accessible and theoretically flexible manner and is often seen as a fundamental technique for analysing qualitative data [10]. We adopted the six-step process as outlined by Clarke and Braun [11]: (Step 1) familiarizing self with data; (Step 2) generating initial codes; (Step 3) searching for themes; (Step 4) reviewing themes; (Step 5) defining and naming themes; and (Step 6) producing the report.

The first pass of steps 1–3 were completed by one author, leading to an initial list of detailed low-level categories and a set of candidate themes. Steps 4 and 5 were then iterated over by a group of authors. The potential merging of categories, and alternative categories, were proposed and discussed; if agreement was reached, the proposed changes were introduced. The final set of higher level categories are the result of an iterative process and in-depth discussions among the assessors. All categories were developed only from the specific task description that respondents entered in response to Survey Question 1 ("List a task that you carried out in a work setting"). A task was allocated to a single category; if a multi-faceted task was specified (e.g. "write an email to advance a project") then only the first facet was used to determine the category (in this case, *Communication*). The final categorization scheme, consisting of 14 task categories, is presented in detail in Section 4.2.

4 RESULTS

In this section we report the tasks that respondents performed in a work context based on our categorization scheme. We further analyze the tasks based on time-use categories; duration, continuity and regularity; and Cyber-Physical-Social aspects.

4.1 Demographics

We collected a total of 401 individual responses to the survey, originating from people living in Australia (139 respondents), the United Kingdom (133 respondents), and the United States (129 respondents). A total of 221 respondents identified as being female, 179 respondents identified as being male, and 1 respondent preferred not to answer this question. Respondents cover the entire spectrum of ages we aimed to target (25–59 years old), balanced across the three countries, with a small skew towards younger age brackets: 25–29 years old (72 respondents); 30–34 (77); 35–39 (66); 40–44 (61); 45–49 (63); 50–54 (41); and 55–59 (21). According to the time-tracking system embedded in Qualtrics, participants spent a median of 16 minutes to complete the survey.

We used occupation categories taken from the Australian Bureau of Statistics [2] for respondents to identify their occupation. All eleven occupation categories were covered at least by 4 respondents. The majority of respondents (166) identified as being a *qualified professional*, followed by *clerks, skilled office, sales and service staff* (54); *senior management in large business organizations* (51); and *associate professionals* (47).

The respondents provide a broad view of professionals that are currently working, of an age consistent with primary career years, and having at least a bachelor's degree. These professionals are likely to perform substantial (and diverse) digital information work.

4.2 Characterizing Information Workers' Tasks

All respondents were asked *"List a task you carried out in a work setting"*. Respondents had to describe four different tasks they carried out depending on the length of time it took them to complete the task (less than 30 minutes, longer than 30 minutes, longer than two hours, and more than a day). We classified all free text input for the question according to the method described in Section 3.2, to obtain the following categories:

Communication. This category consists of tasks related to individuals exchanging information directly, either synchronously or asynchronously, e.g. calling (phone or online), emailing, face-to-face meetings (direct or via an online meeting platform). The emailing section of the communication category consists of many subgroups which can be divided into the action people are taking, such as replying, reading, sending, checking, and deleting.

Documentation. This category consists of tasks related to creating or refining written documents. Many respondents described compiling or writing different types of reports: annual, weekly, etc. Many other respondents described actions such as typed, designed, or edited without specifying a document type. Some responses included in this category indicated they made "notes". Thus, this category is focused on documents. We do not include emails in this category since the primary purpose of email message creation is generally *communication.*

Admin and Management. This is a broad category covering tasks to operate a workplace: recruitment and staff inductions, management of people, management of files including printing, copying or scanning a document, and general paperwork.

Planning. This category consists of tasks which are related to preparing, engineering, planning, or booking items such as arranging events, meeting preparation, booking travel, etc. Some of these tasks include immediate and precise planning such as "arrange a meeting with an international client" or "created plan and agenda for an upcoming meeting with participants in person and via skype", as well as broader future planning such as "monthly planning".

Education. This category consists of two major subgroups: teaching and learning. Common examples of the first subgroup include "teaching a class" or "training new employees". Examples of the second subgroup include "undertook a training course" or "attending training". A third minor subgroup is marking work which is mostly undertaken in an educational setting such as grading assessments, papers, or exams.

IT. This category consists of software- or hardware-related tasks. Software-related tasks include maintaining websites, writing and designing software, or setting up databases. The hardware-related tasks include fixing computers or printers.

Finance. This category includes monitoring and recording expenditures; bookkeeping tasks such as tax, bills, and payroll; as well as budgeting and invoicing.

Physical. This category consists of three subgroups: cleaning, sporting activities, and physical labour. All three require physical activity in order to complete the task.

Problem solving. This category is associated with respondents who carry out research: e.g. conduct, collate, or analyze input, which includes searching and researching.

Low-level. This category consists of data entry tasks: gathering, collection, or importing. Other responses which are also related to this low-level grouping are tasks related to spreadsheets such as creating, filling out, or updating a spreadsheet.

Project. This category consists of responses which explicitly mentioned making progress or working on a project such as collaborating, completing, or finalizing a project.

Customer care. This category groups responses which relate to helping clients or customers (patients are considered customers in this setting). Responses include dealing with, serving, or taking care of customers.

Meals and breaks. This category has two major subgroups: one related to sustenance and one describing the act of pausing. Examples of the first subgroup include: breakfast, eating lunch, or making a meal. Such responses were often seen as a break in a work setting. Therefore we grouped these tasks with the second subgroup, "having a break".

Travel. This category includes tasks related to transit such as flying to a client, driving to an interview, or transporting goods, and are all categorized as travel.

Invalid. As a result of the annotation process, a total of 1,035 responses have been classified to one of the task categories described above. The remaining 569 (35.5% of original) have been categorized as *Invalid*. These include responses explicitly indicating that no task was completed for a particular time length; generic responses (e.g. "work in progress"); responses that were not clear (e.g. "desk job work") or not applicable (e.g. "all the details").

4.3 Tasks According to Time-use Survey

In order to understand the different kind of tasks respondents completed, participants categorized their own tasks according to the time-use survey categories [38].[6] This survey is designed to understand how people behave in a 24-hour period and provide a starting point to an existing classification schema since no existing categorization schema exists specifically for tasks.

The three most commonly reported categories on which time was spent were *Working and work-related activities* (540 tasks, 52.2%), *Educational activities* (152 tasks, 14.7%), and *Professional and personal care services* (110 tasks, 10.6%). Together, these three covered 77.5% of the annotated tasks (802 out of 1,035 tasks).

[6]https://unstats.un.org/unsd/gender/timeuse/

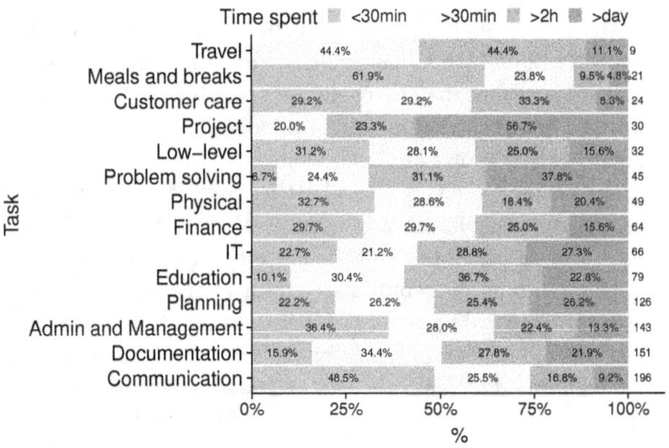

Figure 1: Tasks reported by respondents, sorted by frequency. For consistency, we maintain this sort order for the figures shown in the remainder of the paper.

4.4 Task Duration, Continuity and Regularity

The amount of time that it takes to complete a task is likely to have implications for the kind of support that can be offered, and a fundamental consideration of the survey design was therefore to gather information about tasks of different durations. For example, longer tasks may provide an opportunity for task support such as: assisting in remembering the state for incomplete tasks, assisting in breaking the task into smaller portions, resuming the task on another digital device, or leveraging idle time to perform other work if the task does not require full attention. Likewise, tasks which are interrupted are opportunities for assisting resuming the task. Therefore we ask:

- What is the distribution of task duration among task types? To answer this, we characterize task types in terms of those where more than one third of the responses indicated the task took at least two hours. We then give examples of particular responses where digital support is more likely and those where the benefit of digital support seems less obvious.
- What types of tasks are interrupted most frequently? To answer this, we characterize interruptions by quantifying the blocks of time needed to complete the task and again report example responses where digital support is more or less likely.
- Are tasks performed regularly? To answer this, we look at the responses of Questions 14 and 15 of the survey (see Appendix A).

Figure 1 shows the duration of different type of tasks. The graph shows that all the task types besides *Meals and breaks*, and perhaps *Communication*, include instances that take a considerable amount of time. *Project* tasks are typically long: 56.7% take more than a day and no responses indicated less than 30 min. Digital support would be useful in tasks such as "collaborating on a project" or "working on a new business project". Travel tasks reported in the survey also take at least more than half an hour. An intelligent assistant is not necessarily useful in this particular type of task (e.g. "transporting goods"), unless it is part of a larger task (e.g. "travelled to client"). *Problem solving* tasks are also typically long (37.8% more than a day; 31.1% more than 2 hours). In tasks such as "searching for a resolution to a problem", "data analysis" or "inventory analysis", an intelligent assistant may be useful by providing access to search, recommendation and summarization tools.

Figure 2 (left) shows how many blocks of time the participants spent to complete the task. For all categories, the majority of tasks were reported as completed in a single block of time, without interruptions. In particular *Breaks and meals* and *Travel* were all completed with no interruptions. Responses also suggest that it is not straightforward to quantify blocks of time: the "More than 5 blocks of time" option is typically preferred to indicate interruptions. *Planning, Problem solving* and *Low-level* are the tasks that have more interruptions (e.g. "preparing financial budget", "planning for teaching", "research", or "data collection"). *Planning* and *Problem solving* are typically long duration tasks. *Education* tasks are also long, but often taken in a continuous block of time (e.g. "lecturing"). *Low-level* tasks have interruptions, but are not necessarily long (e.g. "data entry").

Figure 2 (right) shows the regularity of tasks that are atomic or part of a larger tasks or goals (*subtasks*). Most of the tasks are performed regularly (86.7% for subtasks; 69.9% for atomic tasks; 79.6% in total). This suggests that an intelligent assistant may *see* multiple instances of a task, and therefore has more chances to identify patterns and respond proactively (e.g. suggest to perform a task, see Section 5). The figure also shows that tasks that are part of a larger task or goal (subtasks) are very likely to be tasks carried out regularly (86.7%).

4.5 Cyber-Physical-Social Aspects of Tasks

Cyber (Electronic Devices and Online Activities to Perform Tasks). Of the 1,035 tasks categorized in the taxonomy described in Section 4.2, in 71.9% (744) involve the use of electronic devices to complete a task, while 29.1% (291) of the time no electronic devices are used to complete a task. The leftmost bar chart in Figure 3 shows the number of devices used for each task category. The chart shows that devices are used less when performing *Physical* and *Meals and breaks* tasks. On the other hand, *Problem solving, Customer care,* and *Planning* tasks involve the use of multiple devices at least 25% of the time.

Respondents had a free text field to indicate which electronic devices they used to complete the task. We categorized these devices into a set of categories including *Desktop, Laptop, Phone, Tablet, Specialized equipment, Copier/Printer/Scanner* and *Other.* From the tasks that identified the use of electronic devices, personal computers are used most of the time (92.7%), with desktops (54.0%) being more widely used than laptops (37.7%). However, no physical tasks are performed with desktops and laptops. People also tend not to do complex tasks with their phones and tablets, e.g. tasks associating with other devices, such as *Documentation, IT, Finance,* and *Project* tasks. The *Specialized equipment* category includes devices such as carpet shampoo machines, dryers, electronic tills, or soldering irons. Categories which received less than 1% of the responses include instances such as "computer databases", "cloud computing", or "servers".

If the participants indicated the use of a device, we also asked whether they include any online activities to complete the task. We asked them to choose any combination of: Web browsing, Web searching, performing online transactions, using a specific app, online chatting, e-mailing, using a digital assistant, or other.

Figure 3 (right) shows the number of online activities for the different tasks. Most of the tasks involved some type of online activity, being *Physical, Meals and breaks,* and *Travel* the ones that involved the lowest. *Project* tasks involve multiple online activities: Web browsing (12), Web searching (14), e-mailing (12), and online chatting (10). Web browsing, Web searching and e-mailing are also the main online activities involved in other tasks, especially in *Documentation, Communication, Planning,* and *Problem solving.*

For *Low-level* and *Finance* tasks, "other" and "using a specific app" were the most reported online activities, respectively.

Physical. Respondents answered a question "*Did you engage in any physical activities in order to complete the task?*". If they answered negatively, they skipped ahead to the next questions. However, the respondents who answered affirmatively (18.1%) were asked a follow-up question about which kind of physical activity they performed.

As seen in Figure 4 (left) the categorization provides us with an overview of which tasks required physical activity in order to be completed. As may be expected, the *Physical* tasks category has the highest percentage of all categories which involved physical activity (69.4%); the key subcategories inside this grouping include cleaning and other physical work.

The *Physical* category is followed by *Meals and breaks* (61.9%) and *Travel* (55.6%). The rest of the categories only involve physical activities a third of the times or less. If we compare the low proportion of physical activity with the high proportions we have seen in the cyber dimension, we can envisage opportunities to provide support with intelligent assistants.

Social. The social aspect of the self-reported tasks was asked in the question "*Did you engage in any social interactions in order to complete the task?*". If respondents answered affirmatively, they were also asked what kind of social interactions they engaged in.

Figure 4 (right) shows the percentage of tasks that involve social interactions, for each category. Overall, around 40% of the tasks reported involve social interactions. *Customer care* tasks involve social interactions 75% of the time, substantially more than the others. Around half of the tasks categorized as *Project, Problem solving, Planning, Communication,* and *Meals and breaks* involve social interaction. The categories that are less likely to involve social interactions are *Low-level* and *Finance* (both around 19%).

4.6 Supporting Information Workers' Tasks

Currently used tools. Responses for Question 19 show that the most common tool is a digital calendar, used by nearly half of our respondents; this is followed in popularity by non-digital tools such as paper lists, post-it notes, and a paper calendar, which together correspond to 48% of the tools reported by the participants. Other digital tools that can assist in task planning, completion and tracking—such as digital lists, alarm clocks or productivity platforms—were less commonly used.

Opportunities for intelligent assistants. We also asked participants to describe the features or capabilities that they would want

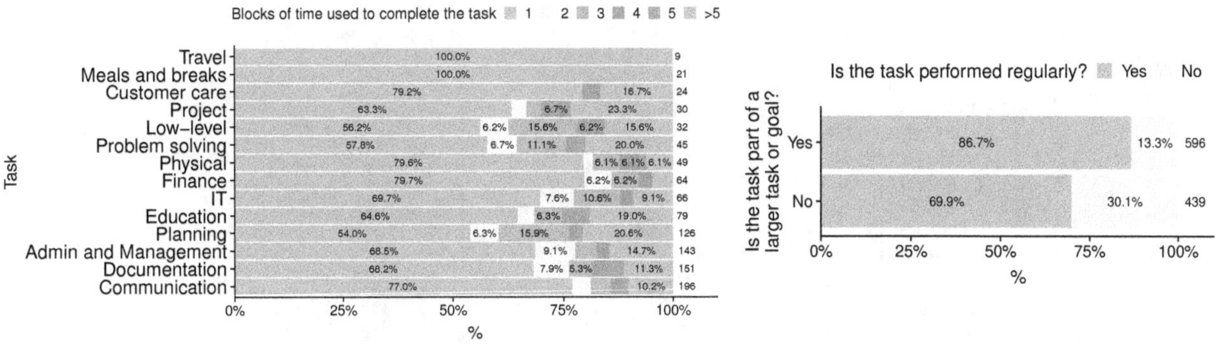

Figure 2: Task continuity (left) and task regularity (right).

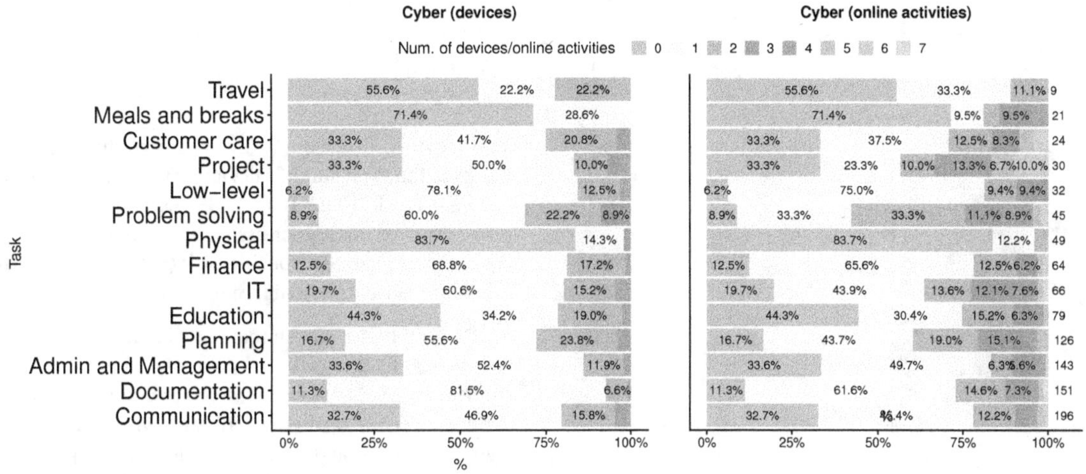

Figure 3: Devices and online activities (cyber). Respondents could indicate both multiple devices and online activities used to complete a task.

to have in a hypothetical new piece of technology. Figure 5 shows the features reported.

Many participants (46.9%) do not report a particular feature (or report they do not need any). Most wanted features related to more effective task management: reminders, calendars or task scheduling. Other features are related to: assisting with the organization of information (automatic sorting, listing, etc.); the need for technology that allows access to information from multiple devices and synchronizes the content in a common place (*ubiquitous access*); and tracking of task progression and completion. The long tail of features includes: voice-enabled interaction; capabilities to adapt to the context of the user; assistance with collaboration; taking notes; searching while the user is performing a task.

5 DISCUSSION AND IMPLICATIONS

The analysis of the survey responses shows that information workers perform a broad range of tasks. A substantial number of tasks take more than two hours to complete. We found that tasks categorized as *Planning*, *Problem solving*, and *Low-level* are more likely to be interrupted. We also found that most of the tasks are performed regularly. Our analysis of CPS aspects showed that multiple devices are used simultaneously to complete tasks to perform online activities such as Web browsing, search and, e-mailing. Tasks that involve physical activities typically involve less device usage. In terms of the social aspect, 40% of the tasks involve social interactions. We also found that, although non-digital tools such as paper lists, post-it notes, and paper calendars are heavily used, participants desired features for more effective task management.

The analysis allows us to better understand how people perform tasks in work settings, and reveals that there are several ways in which intelligent assistants can support information workers:

Task identification. The characteristics of tasks observed in our analysis can be used to automatically identify the current task; user activity can also help [35]. For instance, if the user is performing simultaneous online activities using multiple devices, without social interactions, and for a long period of time, it is likely that the user is performing a *Planning* or *Problem solving* task. Intelligent assistants may engage with users (e.g. asking questions via voice [36]) to help manage uncertainty regarding any task inferences.

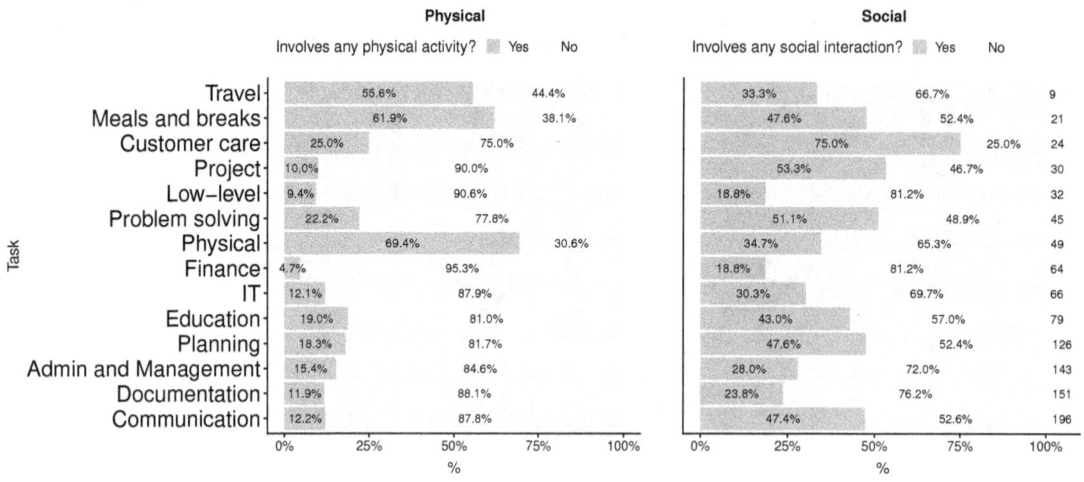

Figure 4: Physical and social activities.

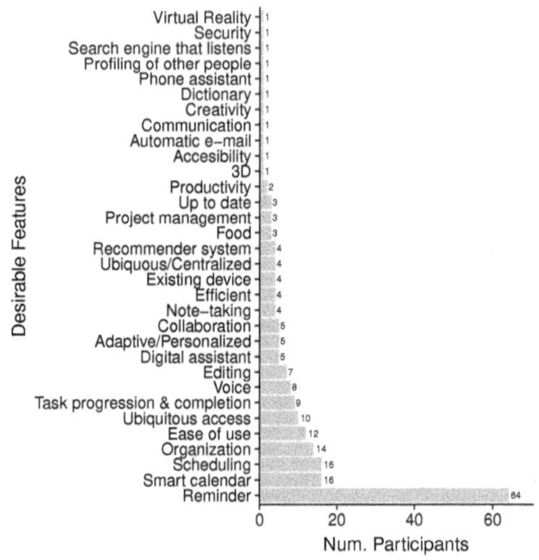

Figure 5: Desirable features for an imaginary new piece of technology as reported by participants.

Task progression and completion. Similarly, task characteristics such as duration or interruptions can be used to track progress and completion of tasks. We found that the majority of tasks are performed regularly and (as Figure 5 shows) reminders were the most requested feature from respondents. It should be feasible to apply data mining and machine learning methods to identify patterns in the behaviours pertaining to task activities and their progression over time, as shown in other domains, e.g. medicine [27].

Task recommendation and automatic scheduling. CPS signals may help generate contextual recommendations about when and where users can complete tasks. Support for organization, scheduling, and calendering were also among the most requested features (Figure 5). The assistant may find time (from duration estimates) to complete pending tasks, set agendas (from time, TO-DOs, and task dependencies), or divide tasks into microtasks [7].

Task resumption. Our analysis showed that many tasks spanned blocks of time and multiple devices. This increases the need for tools to support task resumption [15, 25]. Keeping track of interruptions may allow an intelligent assistant to proactively indicate that it is timely to resume a specific task (e.g. continuing the task on a different device or in a different context).

Multi-step tasks. Given that tasks are likely to be part of a larger task or goal (58% of tasks per Figure 2), an intelligent assistant may support multi-step tasks by recommending content, resources, or actions relevant to the current step with knowledge of already-completed steps (and where possible, what steps are still to come).

The analysis presented in this paper has some limitations. Although a broad number of tasks have been identified, our analysis is based on a survey of a specific cohort (currently employed, older than 25 years old, and from a set of English-speaking countries). There are aspects of the responses that have also not been analyzed herein (e.g. locations or task difficulty) and will be in future work.

6 CONCLUSIONS AND FUTURE WORK

This work aimed to better understand the completion of tasks in work settings. We analyzed the responses of around 400 participants to a survey that capture the range of tasks and sub-tasks people perform. Our thematic and quantitative analysis derived a characterization of work tasks. An investigation of task duration, continuity, and regularity, as well as a detailed analysis of cyber-physical-social aspects, allowed us to provide design recommendations for how intelligent assistants could support work tasks, both on-demand and proactively. Future plans include running user studies to collect cyber-physical-social aspects from mobile devices in-situ during information work [23]. Sensors in these devices will record human activities and routines, to be associated with task progression. Consequently, we will explore how these data could be used for task identification, tracking, and recommendation.

ACKNOWLEDGMENTS

This research was partially supported by Microsoft Research. Any opinions, findings and conclusions expressed in this paper are those of the authors and do not necessarily reflect those of the sponsor.

REFERENCES

[1] Eugene Agichtein, Ryen W. White, Susan T. Dumais, and Paul N. Bennett. 2012. Search, Interrupted: Understanding and Predicting Search Task Continuation. In *Proc. SIGIR.* ACM, 315–324.

[2] Australian Bureau of Statistics. 2013. Directories, Classifications and Manuals by Topic. http://www.abs.gov.au/ausstats/abs@.nsf/ViewContent?readform&view=DirClassManualsbyTopic&Action=Expand&Num=6.1.3 Accessed on 15-01-2019.

[3] Peter Bailey, Liwei Chen, Scott Grosenick, Li Jiang, Yan Li, Paul Reinholdtsen, Charles Salada, Haidong Wang, and Sandy Wong. 2012. User Task Understanding: A Web Search Engine Perspective. In *NII Shonan Meeting on Whole-Session Evaluation of Interactive Information Retrieval Systems.*

[4] Victoria Bellotti, Nicolas Ducheneaut, Mark Howard, and Ian Smith. 2003. Taking Email to Task: The Design and Evaluation of a Task Management Centered Email Tool. In *Proc. CHI.* ACM, 345–352.

[5] Andrei Broder. 2002. A Taxonomy of Web Search. *ACM SIGIR Forum* 36, 2 (2002), 3–10.

[6] Jacques Charmes. 2015. Time Use across the World: Findings of a World Compilation of Time-Use Surveys. *Background paper for Human Development Report* (2015).

[7] Justin Cheng, Jaime Teevan, Shamsi T. Iqbal, and Michael S. Bernstein. 2015. Break It Down: A Comparison of Macro- and Microtasks. In *Proc. CHI.* ACM, 4061–4064.

[8] Karen Church, Mauro Cherubini, and Nuria Oliver. 2014. A Large-Scale Study of Daily Information Needs Captured In Situ. *ACM Trans. on Computer-Human Interaction* 21, 2, Article 10 (Feb. 2014), 46 pages.

[9] Karen Church and Barry Smyth. 2009. Understanding the Intent Behind Mobile Information Needs. In *Proc. IUI.* ACM, 247–256.

[10] Victoria Clarke and Virginia Braun. 2006. Using Thematic Analysis in Psychology. *Qual. Res. Psychol.* 3, 2 (2006), 77–101.

[11] Victoria Clarke and Virginia Braun. 2013. *Successful Qualitative Research: A Practical Guide for Beginners.* Sage.

[12] Mark Dredze and Hanna Wallach. 2008. User Models for Email Activity Management. In *IUI Workshop on Ubiquitous User Modeling.*

[13] Cathal Gurrin, Hideo Joho, Frank Hopfgartner, Liting Zhou, Rashmi Gupta, Rami Albatal, Dang Nguyen, and Duc Tien. 2017. Overview of NTCIR-13 Lifelog-2 Task. In *Proc. NTCIR.*

[14] Ahmed Hassan Awadallah, Ryen W. White, Patrick Pantel, Susan T. Dumais, and Yi-Min Wang. 2014. Supporting Complex Search Tasks. In *Proc. CIKM.* ACM, 829–838.

[15] Shamsi T. Iqbal and Eric Horvitz. 2007. Disruption and Recovery of Computing Tasks: Field study, Analysis, and Directions. In *Proc. CHI.* ACM, 677–686.

[16] Rosie Jones and Kristina Lisa Klinkner. 2008. Beyond the Session Timeout: Automatic Hierarchical Segmentation of Search Topics in Query Logs. In *Proc. CIKM.* ACM, 699–708.

[17] Daniel Kahneman, Alan B. Krueger, David A. Schkade, Norbert Schwarz, and Arthur A. Stone. 2004. A Survey Method for Characterizing Daily Life Experience: The Day Reconstruction Method. *Science* 306, 5702 (2004), 1776–1780.

[18] Diane Kelly and Nicholas J. Belkin. 2004. Display Time as Implicit Feedback: Understanding Task Effects. In *Proc. SIGIR.* ACM, 377–384.

[19] Bret Kinsella and Ava Mutchler. 2018. *Smart Speaker Consumer Adoption Report.* https://voicebot.ai/wp-content/uploads/2018/03/smart_speaker_consumer_adoption_report_2018.pdf Accessed on 15-01-2019.

[20] Alexander Kotov, Paul N. Bennett, Ryen W. White, Susan T. Dumais, and Jaime Teevan. 2011. Modeling and Analysis of Cross-Session Search Tasks. In *Proc. SIGIR.* ACM, 5–14.

[21] Nicholas Kushmerick and Tessa Lau. 2005. Automated email activity management: an unsupervised learning approach. In *Proc. IUI.* ACM, 67–74.

[22] Yuelin Li and Nicholas J. Belkin. 2008. A Faceted Approach to Conceptualizing Tasks in Information Seeking. *Inf. Proc. & Man.* 44, 6 (2008), 1822–1837.

[23] Jonathan Liono, Johanne R. Trippas, Damiano Spina, Mohammad S. Rahaman, Yongli Ren, Flora D. Salim, Mark Sanderson, Falk Scholer, and Ryen W. White. 2019. Building a Benchmark for Task Progress in Digital Assistants. In *Proc. WSDM'19 Task Intelligence Workshop (TI@WSDM19).*

[24] Claudio Lucchese, Salvatore Orlando, Raffaele Perego, Fabrizio Silvestri, and Gabriele Tolomei. 2011. Identifying Task-Based Sessions in Search Engine Query Logs. In *Proc. WSDM.* ACM, 277–286.

[25] Gloria Mark, Victor M. Gonzalez, and Justin Harris. 2005. No Task Left Behind?: Examining the Nature of Fragmented Work. In *Proc. CHI.* ACM, 321–330.

[26] Rishabh Mehrotra, Ahmed Hassan Awadallah, Ahmed E. Kholy, and Imed Zitouni. 2017. Hey Cortana! Exploring the Use Cases of a Desktop Based Digital Assistant. In *Proc. 1st International Workshop on Conversational Approaches to Information Retrieval (CAIR'17).*

[27] Michael J. Paul, Ryen W. White, and Eric Horvitz. 2016. Search and Breast Cancer: On Episodic Shifts of Attention over Life Histories of an Illness. *ACM Transactions on the Web (TWEB)* 10, 2 (2016), 13.

[28] Ashequl Qadir, Michael Gamon, Patrick Pantel, and Ahmed Hassan Awadallah. 2016. Activity Modeling in Email. In *Proc. NAACL.* 1452–1462.

[29] Yongli Ren, Martin Tomko, Flora D. Salim, Jeffrey Chan, Charles L.A. Clarke, and Mark Sanderson. 2018. A Location-Query-Browse Graph for Contextual Recommendation. *IEEE Trans. Know. Data Eng.* 30, 2 (Feb 2018), 204–218.

[30] Yongli Ren, Martin Tomko, Flora D. Salim, Kevin Ong, and Mark Sanderson. 2017. Analyzing Web Behavior in Indoor Retail Spaces. *JASIST* 68, 1 (2017), 62–76.

[31] Daniel E. Rose and Danny Levinson. 2004. Understanding User Goals in Web Search. In *Proc. WWW.* ACM, 13–19.

[32] Miamaria Saastamoinen and Kalervo Järvelin. 2017. Search Task Features in Work Tasks of Varying Types and Complexity. *JASIST* 68, 5 (2017), 1111–1123.

[33] Jianqiang Shen, Lida Li, Thomas G. Dietterich, and Jonathan L. Herlocker. 2006. A Hybrid Learning System for Recognizing User Tasks from Desktop Activities and Email Messages. In *Proc. IUI.* ACM, 86–92.

[34] Timothy Sohn, Kevin A. Li, William G. Griswold, and James D. Hollan. 2008. A Diary Study of Mobile Information Needs. In *Proc. CHI.* ACM, 433–442.

[35] Simone Stumpf, Xinlong Bao, Anton Dragunov, Thomas G. Dietterich, Jon Herlocker, Kevin Johnsrude, Lida Li, and JianQiang Shen. 2005. Predicting User Tasks: I Know What You're Doing. In *AAAI'05 Workshop on Human Comprehensible Machine Learning.*

[36] Johanne R. Trippas, Damiano Spina, Lawrence Cavedon, Hideo Joho, and Mark Sanderson. 2018. Informing the Design of Spoken Conversational Search. In *Proc. CHIIR.* ACM, 32–41.

[37] Peter Tsai. 2018. *AI Chatbots and Intelligent Assistants in the Workplace.* https://community.spiceworks.com/blog/2964-data-snapshot-ai-chatbots_and-intelligent-assistants-in-the-workplace Accessed on 15-01-2019.

[38] United Nations. Statistical Division. 2007. *Guide to Producing Statistics on Time Use: Measuring Paid and Unpaid Work.* United Nations Publications.

[39] Ryen W. White and Diane Kelly. 2006. A study on the effects of personalization and task information on implicit feedback performance. In *Proc. CIKM.* ACM, 297–306.

[40] Jessica L. Wildman, Amanda L. Thayer, Michael A. Rosen, Eduardo Salas, John E. Mathieu, and Sara R. Rayne. 2012. Task Types and Team-Level Attributes: Synthesis of Team Classification Literature. *Human Resource Development Review* 11, 1 (2012), 97–129.

A QUESTIONNAIRE

(1) List a task that you carried out in a work setting and
   (a) took less than 30 minutes.
   (b) took longer than 30 minutes.
   (c) longer than 2 hours.
   (d) more than a day.
(2) Where did you carry out the task?
(3) When did you carry out the task?
(4) Was the task completed in one continuous block of time? (how many?)
(5) What tools, mechanisms or processes did you use to remind yourself to continue the task?
(6) In which context did you compete the task? (Time-used categories)
(7) Did you use electronic devices in order to complete the task? (which?)
(8) Did you do any of the following online activities in order to complete the task? (web browsing, web searching, performing online transactions, using a specific app, online chatting, emailing, using a digital assistant, other)
(9) Did you engage in any physical activities? (which one?)
(10) Did you engage in any social interactions in order to complete the task? (which one?)
(11) I wanted to do the task.
(12) The task was easy.
(13) Are there triggers that lead you to work on the task? (Which?)
(14) Is it a regular task?
(15) Is the task part of a larger goal? (which?)
(16) List the steps to complete the task
(17) Was there anything you did before initiating the task?
(18) Was there anything you did after initiating the task?
(19) Which tools do you currently use to help you plan, complete or keep track of tasks?
(20) Imagine there is a new piece of technology, what features or capabilities would you want it to have?

Embedding Search into a Conversational Platform to Support Collaborative Search

Sandeep Avula[1], Jaime Arguello[1], Robert Capra[1], Jordan Dodson[1], Yuhui Huang[1], Filip Radlinski[2]
[1]University of North Carolina at Chapel Hill, [2]Google
{asandeep,jarguello,rcapra}@unc.edu,{jojordan,yuhui97}@live.unc.edu,filiprad@google.com

ABSTRACT

Popular messaging platforms such as Slack have given rise to thousands of applications (or bots) that users can engage with individually or as a group. In this paper, we study the use of searchbots (i.e., bots that perform specific types of searches) during collaborative information-seeking tasks mediated through Slack. We report on a user study in which 27 pairs of participants were exposed to three searchbot conditions (a within-subjects design). In the first condition, participants completed the task by searching independently and coordinating through Slack (no searchbot). In the second condition, participants could only search inside of Slack using the searchbot. In the third condition, participants could both search inside of Slack using the searchbot and outside of Slack using their own independent search interfaces. We investigate four research questions focusing on the influence of the searchbot condition on outcomes associated with: (RQ1) participants' levels of workload, (RQ2) collaborative awareness, (RQ3) experiences interacting with the searchbot, and (RQ4) search behaviors. Our results suggest opportunities and challenges in designing searchbots to support collaborative search. On one hand, access to the searchbot resulted in more collaborative awareness, ease of coordination, and fewer duplicated searches. On the other hand, forcing participants to share the querying environment resulted in fewer overall queries, fewer query refinements by individuals, and greater levels of effort. We discuss the implications of our findings for designing effective searchbots to support collaborative search.

KEYWORDS

Searchbots; collaborative search; search behavior

ACM Reference Format:

Sandeep Avula, Jaime Arguello, Robert Capra, Jordan Dodson, Yuhui Huang, Filip Radlinski. 2019. Embedding Search into a Conversational Platform to Support Collaborative Search. In *2019 Conference on Human Information Interaction and Retrieval (CHIIR'19), March 10-14, 2019, Glasgow, Scotland, UK.* ACM, NY, NY, USA, 9 pages. https://doi.org/10.1145/3295750.3298928

CHIIR '19, March 10–14, 2019, Glasgow, Scotland Uk

ACM ISBN 978-1-4503-6025-8/19/03...$15.00
https://doi.org/10.1145/3295750.3298928

1 INTRODUCTION

Messaging platforms such as Slack and Microsoft Teams have become increasingly common and allow users to collaborate remotely on work-related and personal tasks. These new messaging platforms differ from older ones (e.g., IRC) in their aesthetics and ability to integrate with third-party applications (or "bots") that users can interact with directly from the communication channel. For example, Slack currently has third-party bots that perform services such as scheduling, cloud storage, version control, video conferencing, and other e-commerce services (e.g., travel booking, food delivery, and ride sharing). Additionally, so-called "searchbots" have been designed to perform specific types of searches (e.g., search for weather, news, and social media content). Currently, users mostly interact with searchbots by sending explicit requests (e.g., "@weatherbot new york city"), answering follow-up questions initiated by the searchbot, and interacting with the search results directly inside of the communication channel.

To date, much of the consideration of searchbots (and bots in general) has focused on their use by *individuals*. However, searchbots are also well-positioned to support *multiple* users working collaboratively on information-seeking tasks. Within information retrieval, the goal of *collaborative search* is to understand how people collaborate on information-seeking tasks and to design systems to support such collaborations. The most prominent approach has been to develop *dedicated* systems to support collaborative search [4, 8, 23, 25, 30, 33]. These systems have been designed with the search engine as the centerpiece component, but include peripheral tools for collaborators to communicate, share information, and gain awareness of each other's activities.

Dedicated systems for collaborative search have been found to provide benefits for users [4, 23, 25, 32]. However, in spite of these findings, stand-alone systems have not gained widespread adoption. In fact, research suggests that while people frequently engage in collaborative search, they do so using non-integrated tools—independent search systems and communication tools such as instant messaging, email, and phone [5, 21, 22]. Morris [22] and Hearst [11] highlighted these findings as a rationale to develop *lightweight search tools that can be integrated directly into existing communication platforms.* Our research is an answer to this call.

Within the context of collaborative search, integrating search tools into a communication platform such as Slack may provide benefits, but also introduce challenges. In terms of benefits, embedded search tools may help collaborators gain awareness of each other's activities and avoid duplicated work. In terms of challenges, sharing the *same* search environment may also prevent collaborators from effectively implementing "division of labor" strategies that require both joint and *independent* work. To gain insights into this novel design space, in this paper we evaluated two different searchbot designs, and compared them against a baseline scenario in which collaborators must search independently (no searchbot).

We report on a laboratory study in which 27 pairs of participants collaborated on three information-seeking tasks using the Slack messaging platform and were exposed to three searchbot conditions (a within-subjects design). In the *browser_only* condition, participants could *only* search using their own individual search interfaces. In this condition, we simulate the baseline scenario in which collaborators must search independently and use the messaging platform to share their findings and coordinate. In the *slack_only* condition, participants could *only* issue queries inside of Slack. We instrumented a searchbot that allowed participants to issue queries from Slack and returned search results directly in the Slack channel. Finally, in the *slack_browser* condition, participants were able to issue queries inside of Slack and also issue queries independently using their own individual search interfaces.

Our study investigated the following *four* research questions, in which the *searchbot condition* was the independent variable.

RQ1: What is the effect of the searchbot condition on participants' level of workload during the task? We used the NASA TLX [1] to measure different aspects of workload.

RQ2: What is the effect of the searchbot condition on participants' collaborative experience? We asked participants about their level of collaborative awareness, effort, and enjoyment.

RQ3: What is the effect of the searchbot condition on participants' experiences while interacting with the searchbot inside of Slack (only for the *slack_only* and *slack_browser* conditions)? We asked participants about gains obtained from the searchbot and their experiences coordinating their use of the searchbot.

RQ4: What is the effect of the searchbot condition on participants' search behaviors during the task? We investigated this question from three perspectives. First, we report on measures derived from the participant pair (e.g., total number of queries issued). Second, we report on the extent to which both participants issued queries with the same search intent versus engaging in "division of labor" strategies. Third, we report on the extent to which participants issued queries with the same intent as a previous query from the same participant (i.e., evidence of individual query refinement).

2 RELATED WORK

Our work builds upon two areas of prior research: (1) collaborative search and (2) shared control of devices.

Collaborative Search: The goal of collaborative search is to understand how people work together on information-seeking tasks and to develop systems to support such collaborations. Collaborative search has been studied in situations in which collaborators are co-located versus remote, and working synchronously versus asynchronously [31]. In this paper, we focus on remote and synchronous collaborations mediated through a messaging platform.

Many dedicated systems have been developed to support collaborative search, including SearchTogether [23], CoSense [25], Coagmento [30], CollabSearch [33], Querium [8], ResultsSpace [4], and SearchX [28]. All of these stand-alone systems include a search interface, as well as peripheral tools for collaborators to communicate, share information, and gain awareness of each other's activities.

Prior studies have found that dedicated systems can provide a wide-range of benefits for users. For example, tools to help users gain awareness of each other's activities have been found to help collaborators learn from each other [14, 23], avoid duplicated work [23, 28, 32], review each other's work [14], hand-off work to each other [25], and track their progress [32]. Capra *et al.* [4] found that awareness features also allowed participants to implement different collaborative strategies: (1) maximizing group precision by evaluating each other's findings and (2) maximizing group recall by *avoiding* each other's search paths.

While dedicated systems have been found to provide benefits, they have not gained widespread adoption. In a survey by Morris [22], about 50% of respondents reported performing collaborative searches at least once a week. In spite of this, respondents reported mostly using non-integrated search and communication tools. Interestingly, respondents also reported frustration with the lack of awareness associated with non-integrated tools, which can lead to duplicated work. Morris concluded by arguing that future research should develop "glue systems" that offer integration between existing search and communication tools.

A few systems evaluated in prior work resemble the types of "glue systems" proposed by Morris. The SearchBuddies system was developed to automatically embed search results in response to questions posted on Facebook [12]. A qualitative analysis of people's reactions to the SearchBuddies system suggests opportunities and challenges for "socially-embedded search systems". For example, some users found the embedded search results useful when they were complementary to answers provided by other "real" users. On the other hand, other users responded negatively when the embedded search results were relevant, but also obvious.

In a Wizard of Oz study, Avula *et al.* [3] explored searchbots that automatically intervened in Slack conversations centered around collaborative search. The authors evaluated two types of interventions: (1) intervening and asking questions about the needed information before providing search results and (2) intervening by "inferring" the needed information and directly providing search results. Both conditions improved participants' collaborative experience compared to a *no searchbot* condition.

Shared Control: Based on prior work on collaborative search, embedding search technology into communication platforms may provide benefits to collaborators (e.g., raising collaborative awareness). However, it may also introduce challenges associated with shared control (i.e., the need for collaborators to coordinate their use of the tool in the same workspace). Prior research has studied how *groups* coordinate their use of interactive systems, including desktop search interfaces [2], tabletop search interfaces [24], large screen applications [15, 29], mobile phone applications [18, 19], and voice-enabled personal assistants such as Siri [27]. While these studies have focused on co-located collaborations, their findings may also generalize to remote collaborations over a messaging platform. Studies have found that shared control introduces several challenges. Through a series of semi-structured interviews, Amershi and Morris [2] found that co-located web search can result in: (1) imbalanced participation, (2) pacing issues (i.e., one collaborator setting the pace for the others), and (3) difficulties implementing "division of labor" strategies (i.e., performing sub-tasks in parallel). Furthermore, studies have also found that group members often *self-select* when deciding who will interact with the system at a particular point in time [27, 29]. Self-selected (versus negotiated) interactions can lead to sub-optimal group outcomes and imbalanced engagement among collaborators. Finally, sharing a physical or virtual workspace can also be distracting when the awareness of others' activities is not beneficial [2, 24].

Prior research on group dynamics suggests that people working together tend to transition between periods of tightly coupled *group* work and more loosely coupled *individual* work (e.g., completing sub-tasks in parallel) [6, 9, 20]. More closely related to collaborative search, the CoSearch system was developed to support group searching as well as parallel searching by co-located individuals. Amershi and Morris [2] evaluated the CoSearch system against two other conditions: sharing a single computer and parallel searching on different computers. Participants reported greater awareness and sense of teamwork in the CoSearch and "shared" conditions as compared to the parallel condition. Additionally, participants reported greater ease in implementing "division of labor" strategies with the CoSearch system as compared to the shared condition.

3 METHODS

To investigate our four research questions, we conducted a laboratory study with 27 pairs of participants (44 female and 10 male). Participants were undergraduate students from our institution and were recruited in pairs. Each participant pair collaborated on three tasks that required searching for information. In this study, we did not investigate task effects. Therefore, to keep our search tasks as consistent as possible, we designed three *comparative* tasks to use in the study (Section 3.2). Participants were seated in different rooms and were each given access to three resources to use during the tasks. Resource 1: During all tasks, participants used the Slack messaging platform to communicate. Resource 2: During all tasks, participants used a shared Google Spreadsheet to create a joint written response for the task. Resource 3: For each of the three different tasks, participants were given a configuration of search tools to search for information.

The configuration of search tools available to participants varied based on our three *searchbot conditions* (Section 3.3). In the *browser_only* condition, participants were each given their own search interface to search independently. In the *slack_only* condition, participants were only able to issue queries inside of the shared Slack channel. Finally, in the *slack_browser* condition, participants were able to query the searchbot inside of Slack and also use their own independent search interface. All search tools used the same back-end system (i.e., the same document collection, retrieval model, and snippet-generation algorithm). All tools searched the New York Times (NYT) Corpus, which contains about 1.8 million NYT articles from 1987-2007.[1] As described in Section 3.2, our tasks were contextualized with this archival news collection in mind. All search tools were implemented using Lucene (v5.3.1) for retrieval and snippet-generation. For retrieval, we used Lucene's implementation of the query-likelihood model with Dirichlet smoothing and the default parameter values.

3.1 Study Protocol

Participants started the experiment by completing a demographic questionnaire. Then, they completed three search tasks, each associated with a different searchbot condition (Section 3.3). Each search task followed the same protocol. First, both participants came into the same room and the moderator explained the searchbot condition associated with the task (e.g., "In the next task, you will only be able to search inside of Slack using the searchbot"). Then, the moderator gave the participants a demonstration of how to interact with the available systems in the condition. Following this demonstration, the moderator read the search task to the participants and gave each a printed copy. Next, participants each went to their separate rooms to complete the task. Participants were given 15 minutes to complete each task. After completing each task, each participant completed a series of post-task questionnaires (Section 3.4). We used Camtasia software to record both participants' screens and Slack's API to log their communication. Additionally, we logged all query and click events inside and outside of Slack. Each participant was given $20 USD for participating in the study.

3.2 Search Tasks

Participants completed three *comparative* search tasks that we designed for the study. A comparative task is one that requires comparing different *items* (or alternatives) along different *dimensions* (or criteria). For example, a comparative "shopping task" might require comparing different products along dimensions such as their price, quality, and durability.

During each task, participants were asked to: (1) choose *three* items to consider, (2) compare the items along *three* dimensions, and (3) make a final item selection. Participants were given the exact three dimensions to consider, but *not* the items. Therefore, as part of the task, participants had to find (and agree upon) three candidate items. To compare the items (before making a selection), participants were asked to complete a 3x3 table representing the items (three rows) and dimensions (three columns). The 3x3 table was provided as a shared Google Spreadsheet. Participants were instructed to use the available search tools to find information and complete the 3x3 table (i.e., find information for each item-dimension pair). After completing the table, participants were instructed to mark their final item selection and provide a justification.

Participants completed three comparative tasks: (1) a sports personality task, (2) a lawsuits against Apple task, and (3) a sci-fi movie task. Each task included a background story (to contextualize the task) and an objective statement. Participants were assigned gender-neutral names during the experiment: Jamie and Taylor. The sports personality task had the following background story and objective:

Background: "Jamie and Taylor are journalism students and have been paired to work together on a class assignment. For this assignment, they need to write about an interesting sports personality covered in the New York Times from 1987-2007."

Objective: "Your goal is to compare/contrast THREE different sports personalities across the following THREE dimensions: (1) type of sport, (2) achievements, and (3) scandals. After completing the 3x3 table, please select the personality who you both think is the most interesting to write about based on the dimensions. Once you've made your choice, write a brief justification below the table."

Our other two tasks had the following three dimensions: Apple lawsuits task (company involved, subject of the lawsuit, outcome) and sci-fi movie task (plot, director, overall review).

[1] https://catalog.ldc.upenn.edu/ldc2008t19

Figure 1: Searchbot query and results inside of Slack.

3.3 Searchbot conditions

Participants in our study experienced three searchbot conditions: *browser_only*, *slack_only*, and *slack_browser*. These conditions varied based on the search tools available to the participants.

In the *browser_only* condition, participants each used out-of-channel search tools. The goal of this condition was to simulate a scenario in which collaborators must use their own independent systems to search and use the messaging platform to coordinate and share their findings.

In the *slack_only* condition, participants could only issue queries inside of Slack. Participants could submit queries to the searchbot using the "@bot" preamble (e.g., "@bot Roger Federer"). We used Slack's API to instrument a searchbot that was able to automatically respond to queries and embed its search results directly inside of Slack. As shown in Figure 1, the searchbot embedded the top-three search results inside of Slack and also included a "click here for more" hyperlink that opened an independent (i.e., not shared) pop-up browser window with additional results. The pop-up window included pagination controls and displayed 10 results per page. In the *slack_only* condition, the pop-up window did *not* include a search box and participants were therefore not able to issue subsequent queries from their own independent pop-up windows. In other words, participants were forced to issue all queries by invoking the searchbot from the shared Slack channel.

Finally, in the *slack_browser* condition, participants could issue queries inside and outside of Slack. Participants had to issue the first query against the searchbot inside of Slack. However, after clicking the "click here for more" hyperlink, the browser pop-up with additional search results *also* included a search box that participants could use to search independently. In other words, participants were free to search inside of Slack by using the searchbot or to search independently from their own independent pop-up windows (after the initial searchbot query).

Participants were exposed to all three searchbot conditions and all three search tasks. We used two Latin Squares to counterbalance the presentation of searchbot condition and search task, for a total of 9 treatment orders that were repeated 3 times across our 27 participant pairs.

3.4 Post-task Questionnaires

At the end of each task, participants completed a series of post-task questionnaires. Two of these were designed by us and are provided in the appendix. First, participants completed the 6-item NASA-TLX questionnaire [1], which measures six aspects of workload: (1) mental demand, (2) physical demand (3) temporal demand, (4) failure, (5) effort, and (6) frustration.

Second, participants completed a 10-item questionnaire about their collaborative experience during the task (Table 2). We designed this questionnaire to capture three different aspects of participants' collaborative experience: (1) level of awareness of each other's activities (4 items), (2) level of collaborative effort (4 items), and (3) level of collaborative enjoyment (2 items).

Finally, in the *slack_only* and *slack_browser* conditions, participants completed a 6-item questionnaire about their experiences interacting with the searchbot inside of Slack (Table 3). This questionnaire measured two aspects of participants' experiences with the searchbot: (1) gains obtained from the searchbot (2 items) and (2) ease of coordinating the use of the searchbot (4 items).

In all three questionnaires, participants responded using a seven-point scale. For all NASA-TLX questions *except* for the failure question, participants responded using a seven-point scale, from "very low" (1) to "very high" (7). For the NASA-TLX question on failure, participants rated their performance from 'perfect' (1) to 'failure' (7). Thus, for all NASA-TLX questions, higher response values indicate higher workload. For the other two questionnaires, participants responded to agreement statements using a seven-point scale, from "strongly disagree" (1) to "strongly agree" (7). Except for the bot_part_distract item, high response values for these two questionnaires indicate positive experiences (i.e., high collaborative awareness and ease of coordinating the use of the searchbot).

3.5 Search Behaviors

As part of RQ4, we investigated whether participants exhibited different search behaviors across searchbot conditions. In this section, we describe novel measures developed for this study.

Query Intent Overlap: Our *query intent overlap* measure considers the degree of overlap between the search intents of both participants. Our goal was to measure the extent to which participants searched for the same types of information (high overlap) or engaged in more "division of labor" strategies (low overlap).

To compute this measure, we performed a qualitative analysis of all queries issued by participants (inside or outside of Slack). As previously mentioned, our tasks required participants to compare items along three dimensions. We manually coded participants' queries based on the item(s) and dimension(s) mentioned in the query (i.e., a two-dimensional coding scheme). The items and dimensions were indexed based on their order of appearance in the joint query stream from both participants.

To illustrate, Table 1 shows the first four queries from a query stream and their respective item and dimension codes. The first query is coded as (*,*) because it mentions no items and dimensions. The second query is coded as (1,*) because it mentions the first item in the stream and no dimension. The third query is coded as (*,1) because it mentions the first dimension in the steam and no item. Finally, the fourth query is coded as (2,2) because it mentions the second item and dimension in the query stream.

Table 1: Example item/dimension codes

Query	Item Code	Dimension Code
sci-fi movies	*	*
ET movie	1	*
sci-fi movie reviews	*	1
the matrix director	2	2

To test the reliability of our coding scheme, two of the authors coded 10% of all query streams. The Cohen's Kappa agreement for the item and dimension codes was $\kappa = 0.989$ and $\kappa = 0.917$, respectively. Given these levels of "near perfect agreement" [17], one of the authors coded the remaining 90% of all query streams.

Given our coding of all queries, we computed the following query intent overlap measure. Let $(I, D)_1$ denote the set of item-dimension codes associated with one participant's queries and let $(I, D)_2$ denote the set of item-dimension codes associated with the *other* participant's queries. We define our query intent overlap (QIO) measure as:

$$\text{QIO} = \frac{(I,D)_1 \cap (I,D)_2}{(I,D)_1 \cup (I,D)_2}$$

QIO is in the range [0,1], with high values indicating a high search intent overlap based on the item-dimension pairs explicitly mentioned in participants' queries.

Repeated Intent: We computed one measure that considered the degree to which participants re-issued queries with the same intent as another query from the *same* participant. To this end, we used the two-dimensional coding scheme described above. Our *repeated intent* (RI) measure considers the percentage of a participant's queries that had the same item-dimension codes as another query from the *same* participant. Again, RI is in the range [0,1], with high values indicating a high degree of query reformulation with the same intent (i.e., evidence of individual query refinement).

3.6 Data Analysis

For RQ1-RQ4, we investigate the effects of the searchbot condition on different outcomes. We used mixed-effects regression models to analyze the effect of the searchbot condition on each outcome. Using mixed-effect models provided two advantages. First, in a few instances, participants did not answer every questionnaire item, resulting in imbalanced data. Mixed-effects models are well-suited for imbalanced repeated measures data [10]. Second, using mixed-effects models allowed us to account for random variations due to the search task ($n = 3$), the participant pair ($n = 27$), and the participant ($n = 54$). For outcome measures at the participant-pair level (e.g., total queries issued), we included task ID and the participant-pair ID as random effects. For outcome measures at the participant level (e.g., mental demand), we included as random effects the task ID and the participant ID nested within the participant-pair ID. We tested the statistical significance of each mixed-effects model by computing the χ^2 statistic using the likelihood-ratio test against a null model (i.e., one without the searchbot condition as a co-variate). To compare between all pairs of searchbot conditions, we ran analyses using the *browser_only* and *slack_only* conditions as baselines, and used a Holm-Bonferroni correction [13].

4 RESULTS

In the following sections, we present our results for RQ1-RQ4. In Section 5, we discuss the main trends and implications.

4.1 RQ1: Workload

To investigate RQ1, we analyzed participants' post-task responses to the NASA-TLX questionnaire, which measured six aspects of workload: (1) mental demand, (2) physical demand, (3) temporal demand, (4) failure, (5) effort, and (6) frustration. Figure 2 shows the means and 95% confidence intervals of participants' responses across searchbot conditions. Searchbot condition had a significant effect for effort ($\chi^2(2) = 11.757, p < 0.01$). Participants reported greater levels of effort during the *slack_only* ($\beta = 0.574$, S.E. $= 0.220$, $p < 0.01$) and *slack_browser* condition ($\beta = 0.741$, S.E. $= 0.220$, $p < 0.01$) as compared to the *browser_only* condition. One possible explanation is that the novelty of the searchbot required participants to expend more effort than when completing the task using familiar, non-integrated tools. Our results for RQ2-RQ4 provide insights about *why* the *slack_only* and *slack_browser* conditions required more effort.

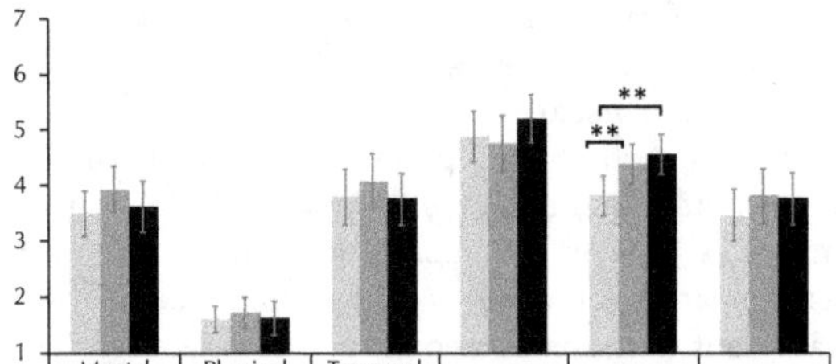

	Mental Demand	Physical Demand	Temporal Demand	Failure	Effort	Frustration
browser_only	3.500	1.592	3.796	4.870	3.814	3.462
slack_only	3.925	1.703	4.074	4.759	4.388	3.814
slack_browser	3.629	1.611	3.759	5.185	4.555	3.759

Figure 2: Post-task responses about workload across the searchbot conditions. '' denotes significant differences at $p < .01$ level.**

4.2 RQ2: Collaborative Experience

To investigate RQ2, we analyzed participants' responses to our post-task questionnaire about their collaborative experience: (1) awareness of each other's activities; (2) ease of collaboration (sharing information, coordinating, communicating, reaching consensus); and (3) enjoyment. Figure 3 shows the means and 95% confidence intervals of participants' responses about their collaborative experience across searchbot conditions.

Collaborative Awareness: Searchbot condition had a significant effect for three measures of awareness: (1) aware_partner ($\chi^2(2) = 19.718, p < 0.001$), (2) aware_self ($\chi^2(2) = 15.035, p < 0.001$), and (3) aware_part_info ($\chi^2(2) = 9.545, p < 0.01$).

In terms of aware_partner, participants reported greater awareness of their partner's activities in the *slack_only* ($\beta = 0.907$, S.E. $= 0.210$, $p < 0.001$) and *slack_browser* condition ($\beta = 0.778$, S.E. $= 0.210$, $p < 0.001$) as compared to the *browser_only* condition. In terms of aware_self, participants reported greater confidence that their partner was aware of their own activities in the *slack_only* ($\beta = 0.740$, S.E. $= 0.207$, $p < 0.001$) and *slack_browser* condition ($\beta = 0.704$, S.E. $= 0.207$, $p < 0.001$) as compared to the *browser_only* condition. Finally, in terms of aware_part_info, participants reported greater confidence that their partner was considering useful information in the *slack_only* condition as compared to the *browser_only* ($\beta = -0.463$, S.E. $= 0.148$, $p < 0.01$) and *slack_browser* condition ($\beta = -0.296$, S.E. $= 0.148$, $p < 0.05$).

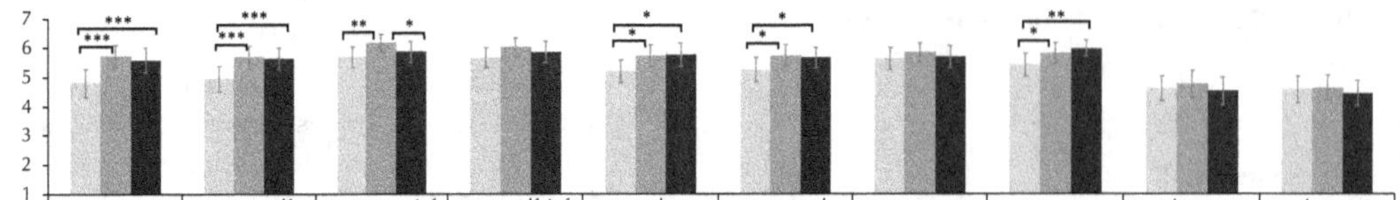

	aware_partner	aware_self	aware_part_info	aware_self_info	ease_share	ease_cord	ease_comm	ease_cons	enjoy_me	enjoy_part
browser_only	4.814	4.944	5.703	5.667	5.203	5.259	5.629	5.425	4.611	4.574
slack_only	5.722	5.685	6.166	6.037	5.740	5.740	5.833	5.814	4.759	4.629
slack_browser	5.592	5.648	5.870	5.851	5.759	5.667	5.698	5.981	4.537	4.444

Figure 3: Post-task responses about collaborative experience across the searchbot conditions. '*', '', and '***' denote significant differences at $p < .05$, $p < .01$ and $p < .001$ level.**

Collaborative Effort: Searchbot condition had a significant effect for three measures of collaborative effort: (1) ease_share ($\chi^2(2) = 8.987, p < 0.05$), (2) ease_cord ($\chi^2(2) = 7.712, p < 0.05$), and (3) ease_cons ($\chi^2(2) = 9.447, p < 0.01$).

In terms of ease_share, participants reported greater ease in sharing information in the *slack_only* (β = 0.537, S.E. = 0.206, $p < 0.05$) and *slack_browser* condition (β = 0.556, S.E. = 0.206, $p < 0.05$) as compared to the *browser_only* condition. In terms of ease_cord, participants reported greater ease in coordinating with their partner in the *slack_only* (β = 0.482, S.E. = 0.183, $p < 0.05$) and *slack_browser* condition (β = 0.407, S.E. = 0.183, $p < 0.05$) as compared to the *browser_only* condition. Finally, in terms of ease_cons, participants reported greater ease in reaching consensus with their partner in the *slack_only* (β = 0.389, S.E. = 0.184, $p < 0.05$) and *slack_browser* condition (β = 0.571, S.E. = 0.184, $p < 0.01$) as compared to the *browser_only* condition.

Collaborative Enjoyment: Searchbot condition did not have a significant effect on either measure of collaborative enjoyment (enjoy_me, enjoy_part).

4.3 RQ3: Searchbot Experience

To investigate RQ3, we analyzed participants' responses to our post-task questionnaire about their experiences using the searchbot. This 6-item questionnaire was only given to participants in the *slack_only* and *slack_browser* conditions, and focused on two main themes: (1) ease of coordinating the use of the searchbot and (2) gains obtained from the searchbot. Figure 4 shows the means and 95% confidence intervals of participants' responses for the *slack_only* and *slack_browser* conditions.

Coordinating Searchbot Use: Searchbot condition had a significant effect on three measures associated with participants' experiences coordinating the use of the searchbot: (1) bot_part_intent ($\chi^2(1) = 4.676, p < 0.05$), (2) bot_part_info ($\chi^2(1) = 7.744, p < 0.01$), and (3) bot_part_distract ($\chi^2(1) = 7.884, p < 0.01$).

In terms of bot_part_intent, participants reported greater awareness of their partner's goals when interacting with the searchbot in the *slack_only* versus *slack_browser* condition (β = 0.463, S.E. = 0.209, $p < 0.05$). In terms of bot_part_info, participants reported greater awareness of the information their partner was requesting from the searchbot in the *slack_only* versus *slack_browser* condition (β = 0.759, S.E. = 0.263, $p < 0.01$). In terms of bot_part_distract, participants reported being more distracted by their partner's interactions with the searchbot in the *slack_only* versus *slack_browser* condition (β = 0.574, S.E. = 0.197, $p < 0.01$).

Gains: Searchbot condition did not have a significant effect on the gains from the searchbot (bot_useful_info, bot_saved_time).

4.4 RQ4: Search Behaviors

In RQ4, we investigate whether participants exhibited different search behaviors across searchbot conditions. We approach this question from three different perspectives. First, we consider measures that combine the activities of *both* participants (e.g., the total number of queries issued). Second, we consider the extent to which both participants issued queries with the same search intent. Third, we consider the extent to which individual participants issued queries with the same intent as a previous query from the *same* participant (i.e., evidence of individual query refinement).

Aggregate Measures: We investigate the effect of the searchbot condition on four aggregate measures: (1) total number of queries, (2) abandoned queries, (3) clicks, and (4) clicks per query. As shown in Figures 5a-5d, searchbot condition had a significant effect on three measures: (1) queries ($\chi^2(2) = 10.837, p < 0.01$), (2) abandoned queries ($\chi^2(2) = 14.581, p < 0.001$), and (3) clicks per query ($\chi^2(2) = 6.673, p < 0.05$).

In terms of queries, participants issued fewer queries in the *slack_only* condition as compared to the *browser_only* (β = 2.481, S.E. = 1.042, $p < 0.05$) and *slack_browser* condition (β = 3.519, S.E. = 1.042, $p < 0.01$). Similarly, participants had fewer abandoned queries in the *slack_only* condition as compared to the *browser_only* (β = 2.111, S.E. = 0.754, $p < 0.05$) and *slack_browser* condition (β = 3.00, S.E. = 0.754, $p < 0.001$). In terms of clicks per query, participants had more clicks per query in the *slack_only* condition as compared to the *browser_only* (β = 0.476, S.E. = 0.235, $p < 0.05$) and *slack_browser* condition (β = 0.593, S.E. = 0.235, $p < 0.05$).

Query Intent Overlap: Our query intent overlap (QIO) measure considered the extent to which both participants issued queries with same search intent or engaged in more "division of labor" strategies. As shown in Figure 6, searchbot condition had a significant effect on QIO ($\chi^2(2) = 12.983, p < 0.01$). Participants' queries had a greater intent overlap in the *browser_only* condition as compared to the *slack_only* (β = 0.162, S.E. = 0.045, $p < 0.001$) and *slack_browser* condition (β = 0.133, S.E. = 0.045, $p < 0.01$).

Repeated Intent queries: Our repeated intent (RI) measure considered the extent to which individual participants issued queries with the same search intent (i.e., same item-dimension codes) as another query issued by the same participant, which we treat as evidence of individual query refinement. As shown in Figure 7, searchbot condition had a significant effect on RI ($\chi^2(2) = 14.966, p < 0.01$). Participants issued a greater percentage of queries with the same intent as another query in the *browser_only* (β = 0.167, S.E. = 0.053, $p < 0.001$) and *slack_browser* condition (β = 0.198, S.E. = 0.053, $p < 0.001$) as compared to the *slack_only* condition.

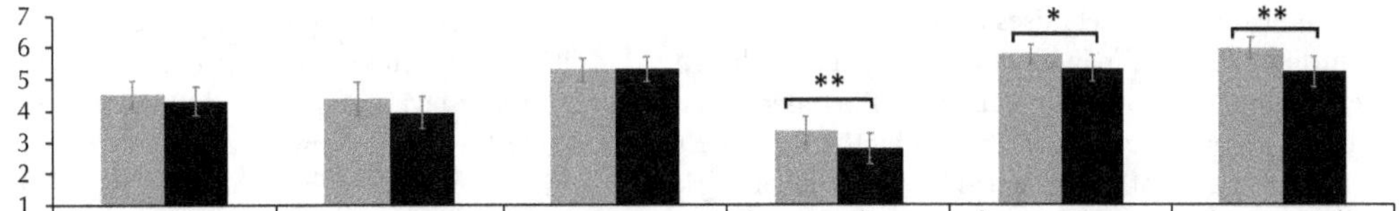

	bot_useful_info	bot_saved_time	coordinate_bot_use	bot_part_distract	bot_part_intent	bot_part_info
slack_only	4.518	4.388	5.296	3.351	5.778	5.962
slack_browser	4.314	3.944	5.296	2.778	5.314	5.203

Figure 4: Post-task responses about participants' experiences with the searchbot in the *slack_only* and *slack_browser* conditions. '*' and '' denote significant differences at $p < .05$, and $p < .01$ level.**

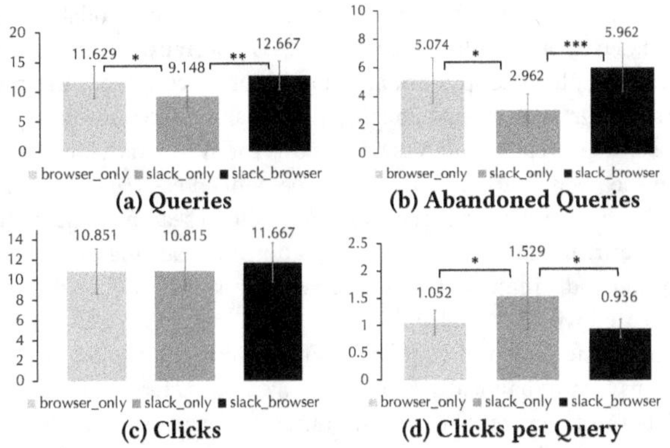

Figure 5: Aggregate measures across searchbot conditions. '*', '', and '***' denote significant differences at $p < .05$, $p < .01$, and $p < .001$ level.**

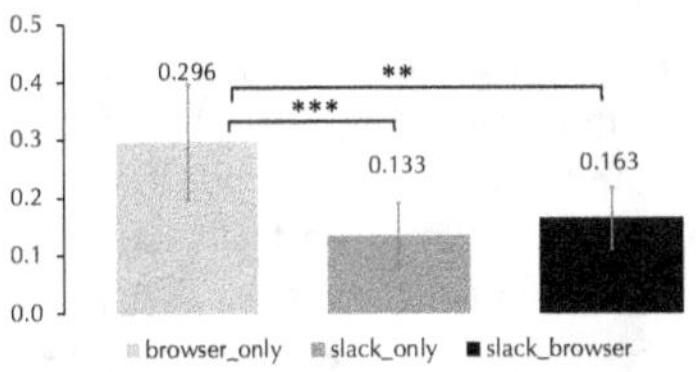

Figure 6: Query Intent Overlap. '' and '***' denote significant differences at $p < .01$ and $p < .001$ level.**

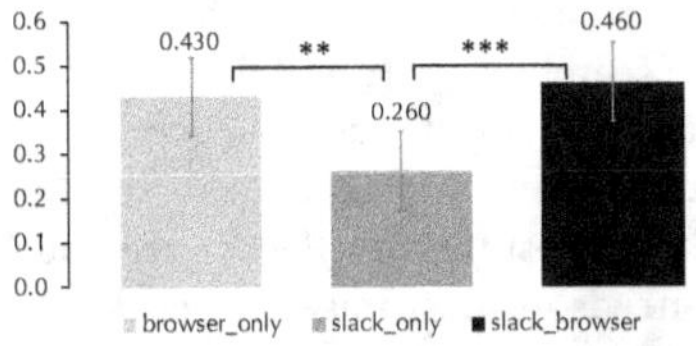

Figure 7: Repeated Intent (RI). '' and '***' denote significant differences at $p < .01$ and $p < .001$ level.**

5 DISCUSSION

Our goal in this study was to investigate different ways of embedding search tools into a communication platform (i.e., Slack). We investigated three conditions: *browser_only*, *slack_only*, and *slack_browser*. Here, we discuss our findings and implications.

RQ1: In terms of workload, participants reported greater effort in the *slack_only* and *slack_browser* conditions as compared to the *browser_only* condition (Figure 2). In other words, participants reported the least amount of effort in the condition where they completed the task using familiar, non-integrated tools (i.e., searching independently and coordinating through Slack). One possibility is that the novelty of the searchbot caused participants to expend more effort. Additionally, our results for RQ2-RQ4 (discussed below) provide insights as to *how* participants expended more effort in the *slack_only* and *slack_browser* conditions.

RQ2: Our results suggest that the searchbot improved participants' collaborative awareness and experience (Figure 3). In terms of awareness, participants reported significantly greater awareness of their partner's activities and greater confidence that their partner was aware of their own activities in the *slack_only* and *slack_browser* conditions. Between these two conditions, awareness was slightly greater in the *slack_only* condition. Specifically, participants reported greater confidence that their partner was searching for valuable information in the *slack_only* condition. In terms of their collaborative experience, participants reported significantly greater ease in sharing information, coordinating, and reaching consensus in the *slack_only* and *slack_browser* conditions. In relation to RQ1, these results suggest that the effort increase in the *slack_only* and *slack_browser* conditions did *not* originate from communication and coordination efforts.

Our RQ2 results suggest that integrating search tools into communication channels such as Slack provides some of the same benefits as standalone collaborative search systems [4, 8, 23, 25, 30, 33]. These findings are also consistent with prior work on searchbots that intervene in collaborations [3]. In that study, the searchbot raised collaborators' awareness of their activities and made it easier to share information, coordinate, and reach consensus.

RQ3: In terms of participants' experiences with the searchbot, our results suggest two main trends (Figure 4). First, in the *slack_only* condition, participants reported greater awareness of their partner's motivations for interacting with the searchbot. Most likely, this greater awareness came from participants being forced to share the same querying environment.

Second, in the *slack_only* condition, participants reported being more distracted by their partner's interactions with the searchbot. This result resonates with prior research on group dynamics and shared control of devices. Prior work shows that teamwork involves periods of tightly coupled *group* work and loosely coupled *individual* work [6, 9, 20]. Furthermore, prior studies have found that being aware of other's activities can be burdensome at times when it is not beneficial (e.g., during periods of individual work) [2, 24]. Our RQ3 results suggest that forcing users to search within the communication channel raises awareness, but can also be distracting during periods of individual work. Again, in relation to RQ1, our results suggest a possible source of effort associated with the searchbot—participants were distracted by their partner's interactions with the searchbot during periods of individual work.

RQ4: Our results suggest that the searchbot condition had an effect on participants' behaviors, both as partners and individual searchers. First, based on our qualitative coding of all queries issued, participants' search intents had less overlap in the *slack_only* and *slack_browser* conditions (Figure 6). One possibility is that the greater awareness in these two conditions allowed participants to avoid searching for the same information. Capra *et al.* [4] also observed that awareness features in a dedicated collaborative search system allowed participants to avoid each other's search paths.

Second, in the *slack_only* condition, participants issued significantly fewer queries, had fewer abandoned queries, and more clicks per query than in the other two conditions (Figures 5). One possibility is that participants in the *slack_only* condition issued fewer queries to avoid distracting their partners. As a negative outcome of issuing fewer queries, individual participants in the *slack_only* condition issued fewer queries with a repeated intent (Figure 7). This result points to another source of effort introduced by the searchbot (RQ1)—participants in the *slack_only* condition tried to do more with fewer (potentially sub-optimal) queries. Greater levels of query refinement in the *browser_only* and *slack_browser* conditions might have led to better search results and less effort.

Summary and Implications: Our results for RQ1-RQ4 suggest opportunities and challenges for designing search tools that can be embedded into communication channels such as Slack.

In terms of opportunities, access to the searchbot provided several benefits. When given access to the searchbot, participants reported greater awareness of each other's activities and less effort in sharing information, coordinating, and reaching consensus. Moreover, the increased awareness from the searchbot may have allowed participants to avoid searching for the same type of information (i.e., avoiding duplicated work).

In terms of challenges, access to the searchbot also had negative consequences. First, in some cases, participants found their partner's interactions with the searchbot to be distracting. Based on prior work, these distractions probably occurred at times when participants were engaged in individual work and the awareness of their partner's activities was not beneficial [2, 24]. Second, our results suggest that participants in the *slack_only* condition completed the task using fewer queries that were possibly sub-optimal. Participants in the *slack_only* condition (vs. both other conditions) issued fewer queries, had fewer abandoned queries, more clicks per query, and fewer query-reformulations with the same intent (i.e., less query refinement). Finally, the novelty of the searchbot might have also added some overhead for participants. Participants reported the least amount of overall effort in the baseline condition, in which they had to search independently (no searchbot).

Overall, our results suggest that the *slack_browser* condition provided important benefits compared to the other two conditions. Compared to the *slack_only* condition, individual participants in the *slack_browser* condition issued more queries with a repeated intent, which possibly led to better search results. Compared to the *browser_only* condition, participants in the *slack_browser* condition reported greater awareness, lower coordination effort, and had lower levels of query intent overlap (i.e., less duplicated work). While the *slack_browser* condition provided benefits, it also required more effort than the *browser_only* condition. Future work should build on this design and identify sources of effort that can be alleviated.

The increasing popularity of messaging platforms such as Slack is an opportunity to develop lightweight search tools that users can interact with directly from the platform. Tools such as searchbots are not only well-positioned to assist individual users, but also *multiple* users collaborating on tasks involving search. Our results have implications for designing searchbots to support collaborative search. First, our results suggest that it is important to support *both* tightly coupled group work and more loosely coupled individual work. In our case, forcing collaborators to share the same querying environment resulted in less trial-and-error at the individual work level (i.e., less individual query refinement). Less trial-and-error may have negative consequences—sub-optimal search results in the short-term and lower levels of exploration and learning in the long-term. Second, greater collaborative awareness has benefits (e.g., less duplicated work), but also comes at a cost (e.g., can be distracting at times when it is not beneficial). Future research should develop systems that dynamically adjust their awareness features based on collaborators' current activities. In this respect, a system might be able to adjust the *amount* of collaborative awareness provided (i.e., which activities are communicated), how *saliently* the awareness is communicated, and whether the awareness is provided in real-time versus "cached" for collaborators to use later.

6 CONCLUSION

We reported on a study that investigated different ways of integrating search tools into messaging platforms such as Slack. Specifically, we investigated different searchbot designs. In our study, 27 participant-pairs collaborated on tasks using Slack and were exposed to three searchbot conditions: (1) only searching independently outside of Slack, (2) only searching inside of Slack using the searchbot, and (3) searching both inside of Slack (using the searchbot) and outside of Slack (using independent interfaces).

Our results suggest opportunities and challenges in designing searchbots to support collaborative search. In terms of opportunities, access to the searchbot increased participants' awareness of each other's activities, made it easier to communicate and coordinate, and resulted in fewer duplicated searches. In terms of challenges, our results suggest that an effective searchbot design must satisfy different needs. It must raise awareness of collaborators' activities in cases where the awareness is beneficial. Additionally, the design must allow users to pursue their individual low-level strategies without intruding on each other's "space". In our study, forcing participants to share the same querying environment (only using the searchbot) resulted in fewer queries with the same intent (i.e., less query refinement) and possibly sub-optimal search results and task outcomes.

Outside of IR, the CSCW community has also identified collaborative agents (e.g., personal assistants, bots, and embodied robots) as an important area for future research [7, 16, 26]. Our findings may help inform the design of search-based agents that support remote or co-located synchronous collaborations.

7 ACKNOWLEDGEMENTS

This work was supported in part by NSF grants IIS-1451668 and IIS-1552587. Any opinions, findings, conclusions, and recommendations expressed in this paper are the authors' and do not necessarily reflect those of the NSF.

REFERENCES

[1] National Aeronautics and Space Administration Human Systems Integration Division. 2016. TLX NASA Ames. (2016).

[2] Saleema Amershi and Meredith Ringel Morris. 2008. CoSearch: a system for co-located collaborative web search. In *CHI*. ACM, 1647–1656.

[3] Sandeep Avula, Gordon Chadwick, Jaime Arguello, and Robert Capra. 2018. SearchBots: User Engagement with ChatBots During Collaborative Search. In *CHIIR*. ACM, 52–61.

[4] Robert Capra, Annie Chen, Katie Hawthorne, Jaime Arguello, Lee Shaw, and Gary Marchionini. 2012. Design and Evaluation of a System to Support Collaborative Search. In *ASIST*. Wiley.

[5] Robert Capra, Gary Marchionini, Javier Velasco-Martin, and Katrina Muller. 2010. Tools-at-hand and Learning in Multi-session, Collaborative Search. In *CHI*. ACM, 951–960.

[6] Mary Elwart-Keys, David Halonen, Marjorie Horton, Robert Kass, and Paul Scott. 1990. User interface requirements for face to face groupware. In *CHI*. ACM, 295–301.

[7] Lia Emanuel, Joel Fischer, Wendy Ju, and Saiph Savage. 2016. Innovations in Autonomous Systems: Challenges and Opportunities for Human-agent Collaboration. In *CSCW*. ACM, 193–196.

[8] Gene Golovchinsky, Jeremy Pickens, and Abdigani Diriye. 2011. Designing for Collaboration in Information Seeking. In *HCIR*.

[9] Roberto Gonzales-Ibanez, Muge Haseki, and Chirag Shah. 2013. Let's search together, but not too close! An analysis of communication and performance in collaborative information seeking. *Information Processing & Management* 49, 5 (2013), 1165 – 1179.

[10] Ralitza Gueorguieva and John H Krystal. 2004. Move over anova: progress in analyzing repeated-measures data andits reflection in papers published in the archives of general psychiatry. *Archives of general psychiatry* 61, 3 (2004), 310–317.

[11] Marti A. Hearst. 2014. What's Missing from Collaborative Search? *Computer* 47, 3 (2014).

[12] B. Hecht, J. Teevan, M.R. Morris, and D. Liebling. 2012. SearchBuddies: Bringing Search Engines into the Conversation. In *ICWSM*. AAAI, 138–145.

[13] Sture Holm. 1979. A simple sequentially rejective multiple test procedure. *Scandinavian journal of statistics* (1979), 65–70.

[14] Nyi Nyi Htun, Martin Halvey, and Lynne Baillie. 2017. How Can We Better Support Users with Non-Uniform Information Access in Collaborative Information Retrieval?. In *CHIIR*. ACM, 235–244.

[15] Shahram Izadi, Harry Brignull, Tom Rodden, Yvonne Rogers, and Mia Underwood. 2003. Dynamo: a public interactive surface supporting the cooperative sharing and exchange of media. In *UIST*. ACM, 159–168.

[16] Malte F. Jung, Selma Šabanović, Friederike Eyssel, and Marlena Fraune. 2017. Robots in Groups and Teams. In *CSCW*. ACM, 401–407.

[17] J Richard Landis and Gary G Koch. 1977. The measurement of observer agreement for categorical data. *biometrics* (1977), 159–174.

[18] Andrés Lucero, Jussi Holopainen, and Tero Jokela. 2012. MobiComics: collaborative use of mobile phones and large displays for public expression. In *MobileHCI*. ACM, 383–392.

[19] Andrés Lucero, Jaakko Keränen, and Hannu Korhonen. 2010. Collaborative use of mobile phones for brainstorming. In *MobileHCI*. ACM, 337–340.

[20] Munir Mandviwalla and Lorne Olfman. 1994. What do groups need? A proposed set of generic groupware requirements. *TOCHI* 1, 3 (1994), 245–268.

[21] Meredith Ringel Morris. 2008. A Survey of Collaborative Web Search Practices. In *CHI*. ACM, 1657–1660.

[22] Meredith Ringel Morris. 2013. Collaborative Search Revisited. In *CSCW*. ACM, 1181–1192.

[23] Meredith Ringel Morris and Eric Horvitz. 2007. SearchTogether: An Interface for Collaborative Web Search. In *UIST*. ACM, 3–12.

[24] Meredith Ringel Morris, Andreas Paepcke, and Terry Winograd. 2006. Teamsearch: Comparing techniques for co-present collaborative search of digital media. In *TABLETOP*. IEEE.

[25] Sharoda A. Paul and Meredith Ringel Morris. 2009. CoSense: Enhancing Sensemaking for Collaborative Web Search. In *CHI*. ACM, 2007–2012.

[26] Martin Porcheron, Joel E. Fischer, Moira McGregor, Barry Brown, Ewa Luger, Heloisa Candello, and Kenton O'Hara. 2017. Talking with Conversational Agents in Collaborative Action. In *CSCW*. ACM, 431–436.

[27] Martin Porcheron, Joel E. Fischer, and Sarah Sharples. 2017. "Do Animals Have Accents?": Talking with Agents in Multi-Party Conversation. In *CSCW*. ACM, 207–219.

[28] Sindunuraga Rikarno Putra, Felipe Moraes, and Claudia Hauff. 2018. SearchX: Empowering Collaborative Search Research. In *SIGIR*. ACM, 1265–1268.

[29] Daniel M Russell, Clemens Drews, and Alison Sue. 2002. Social aspects of using large public interactive displays for collaboration. In *UbiComp*. Springer, 229–236.

[30] Chirag Shah. 2010. Coagmento-a collaborative information seeking, synthesis and sense-making framework. In *CSCW*. ACM, 6–11.

[31] Chirag Shah. 2012. *Collaborative Information Seeking: The Art and Science of Making the Whole Greater Than the Sum of All*. Springer.

[32] Chirag Shah. 2013. Effects of awareness on coordination in collaborative information seeking. *JASIST* 64, 6 (2013).

[33] Zhen Yue, Shuguang Han, and Daqing He. 2012. An investigation of search processes in collaborative exploratory web search. In *ASIST*. Wiley.

8 APPENDIX

Table 2: Post-task questions about collaborative experience.

Theme	Tag	Description
Awareness	aware_partner	During the task, I had a pretty good idea about what my partner was doing.
	aware_self	During the task, I think my partner had a pretty good idea about what I was doing.
	aware_part_info	During the task, I was confident that my partner was looking at information I would find valuable for completing the task.
	aware_self_info	During the task, I was confident that I was looking at information my partner would find valuable for completing the task.
Effort	ease_share	It was easy to share information with my partner during the task.
	ease_coord	It was easy for my partner and I to coordinate our efforts during this task.
	ease_comm	It was easy to communicate with my partner during this task.
	ease_cons	It was easy for my partner and I to reach consensus during this task.
Enjoyment	enjoy_me	I enjoyed completing this task.
	enjoy_part	I think my partner enjoyed completing this task.

Table 3: Post-task questions about the searchbot.

Theme	Tag	Description
Gains	bot_useful_info	The *Searchbot* provided us with useful information.
	bot_saved_time	The *Searchbot* saved me and my partner some time.
Coordination	coordinate_bot_use	It was easy for me and my partner to coordinate our use of the *Searchbot* during this task.
	bot_part_distract	I found my partner's interactions with the *Searchbot* to be distracting.
	bot_part_intent	I always knew why my partner was interacting with the *Searchbot*.
	bot_part_info	I always knew what information my partner was requesting from the *Searchbot*.

User Intent Prediction in Information-seeking Conversations

Chen Qu
University of Massachusetts Amherst
chenqu@cs.umass.edu

Liu Yang
University of Massachusetts Amherst
lyang@cs.umass.edu

W. Bruce Croft
University of Massachusetts Amherst
croft@cs.umass.edu

Yongfeng Zhang
Rutgers University
yongfeng.zhang@rutgers.edu

Johanne R. Trippas
RMIT University
johanne.trippas@rmit.edu.au

Minghui Qiu
Alibaba Group
minghui.qmh@alibaba-inc.com

ABSTRACT

Conversational assistants are being progressively adopted by the general population. However, they are not capable of handling complicated information-seeking tasks that involve multiple turns of information exchange. Due to the limited communication bandwidth in conversational search, it is important for conversational assistants to accurately detect and predict user intent in information-seeking conversations. In this paper, we investigate two aspects of user intent prediction in an information-seeking setting. First, we extract features based on the content, structural, and sentiment characteristics of a given utterance, and use classic machine learning methods to perform user intent prediction. We then conduct an in-depth feature importance analysis to identify key features in this prediction task. We find that structural features contribute most to the prediction performance. Given this finding, we construct neural classifiers to incorporate context information and achieve better performance without feature engineering. Our findings can provide insights into the important factors and effective methods of user intent prediction in information-seeking conversations.

KEYWORDS

User Intent Prediction; Information-seeking Conversations; Conversational Search; Multi-turn Question Answering

ACM Reference Format:

Chen Qu, Liu Yang, W. Bruce Croft, Yongfeng Zhang, Johanne R. Trippas, and Minghui Qiu. 2019. User Intent Prediction in Information-seeking Conversations. In *2019 Conference on Human Information Interaction and Retrieval (CHIIR '19), March 10–14, 2019, Glasgow, Scotland Uk.* ACM, New York, NY, USA, 9 pages. https://doi.org/10.1145/3295750.3298924

1 INTRODUCTION

Many companies have launched conversational assistants (CA) such as Amazon Echo, Google Home, Microsoft Cortana, etc. These devices allow users to issue voice commands to the CA for goal oriented tasks or to conduct simple question answering (QA) tasks, such as adding calendar events or asking for news. This trend has led many researchers in the information retrieval (IR) and natural language processing (NLP) community to pay more attention to conversational search. For examples, SIGIR'18, ICTIR'17, and EMNLP'18 all have workshops[1,2,3] on conversational search.

However, most CAs are not yet capable of handling multi-turn information-seeking conversations, where users have multiple rounds of information exchange with CAs to retrieve or specify answers. One reason is the difficulty to model the conversation about the information need both before and after an answer has been given. Thus an important step in modeling conversational interactions is to accurately detect and predict user intent in this interactive information-seeking process. More specifically, CAs should be capable of improving previous answers if they can correctly process critical information provided by the users, such as relevance judgments (feedback) and clarifications of the information need. Thus, CAs need to elicit more information proactively when they are not confident, before providing an answer [24].

The Learn-IR workshop[4] at WSDM'18 highlighted the significant research need for user intent analysis and prediction in an interactive information-seeking process. To address this research demand, we conducted experiments on user intent prediction using the MSDialog [19] data. This data collection consists of multi-turn information-seeking dialogs in the technical support domain. The dialogs are typically initiated by an information seeker who asks technical issues about Microsoft products, such as "How do I downgrade from Windows 10 to Windows 7?". This kind of question is non-factoid and often requires multiple rounds of conversational interactions. The answers are provided by Microsoft staff and other experienced product users such as "Microsoft Most Valuable Professionals" (MVPs). These human agents (information providers) also explicitly ask for feedback on their provided answers and thus keep the users engaged. The MSDialog data is annotated with a set of 12 *user intent types* [2, 19]. There are different definitions of "user intent" in our field. In this paper, user intent refers to a taxonomy of utterances in information-seeking conversations (Table 1). Each utterance of the MSDialog was annotated with the user intent types using Amazon Mechanical Turk (MTurk)[5]. MSDialog provides a high-quality resource to show how information-seeking conversations are structured between humans. In addition to MSDialog, we also used a portion of Ubuntu Dialog Corpus (UDC) [14] which was annotated with the same user intent types in [19] to further validate our findings.

CHIIR '19, March 10–14, 2019, Glasgow, Scotland Uk

ACM ISBN 978-1-4503-6025-8/19/03...$15.00
https://doi.org/10.1145/3295750.3298924

[1] https://sites.google.com/view/cair-ws/cair-2018
[2] http://sigir.org/ictir2017/sessions/search-oriented-conversational-ai-scai/
[3] https://scai.info/ [4] https://task-ir.github.io/wsdm2018-learnIR-workshop/
[5] https://www.mturk.com/

The purposes of user intent prediction are threefold. First, it is necessary for CAs to accurately identify user intent in information-seeking conversations. Only in this way can CAs process the information accordingly and use it to provide answers and adjust previous answers. Similar to customer service over phones, routing user questions to different sub-modules in a conversational retrieval system is only possible if the user intent is correctly identified. Second, the CAs need to learn and imitate the behavior of human agents. By identifying user intent in information-seeking conversations, we expect the CA to learn the use of different intent and when to issue requests for more information or details spontaneously. Finally, user intent prediction models can be used to automatically annotate more dialog utterances for data analysis and other tasks such as conversational answer finding.

Previous work typically focused on dialog act classification for open-domain conversations [9, 13, 22]. In human-computer chitchat, the goal of the CA is to generate responses that are as realistic as possible with the primary purpose of entertaining. In contrast to chatting, users initiate information-seeking conversations for specific information needs. Human behaviors in chatting and information-seeking conversations can be very different due to the fundamentally distinct purposes. In addition, the Dialog State Tracking Challenges (DSTC)[6] focus on goal oriented conversations. These tasks are typically tackled with slot filling [27, 31]. In information-seeking conversations, slot filling is not suitable because of the diversity of information needs. User intent analysis and prediction are needed for an information-seeking setting.

We conduct experiments using two different approaches to predict user intent in information-seeking conversations. Firstly, we extract rich features to capture the content, structural, and sentiment characteristics of utterances and learn models with traditional machine learning (ML) methods. Secondly, we use the implicit representation learning in neural architectures to predict user intent without feature engineering. We then incorporate context information into neural models for enhanced performance.

Our contributions can be summarized as follows. (1) We extract rich features including feature groups related to content, structures, and sentiment to predict user intent in information-seeking conversations. We perform an in-depth feature importance analysis on both group and individual level to identify the key factors in this task. (2) We design several variations of neural classifiers to predict user intent without explicit feature engineering. We show that neural models can achieve comparable performance compared to feature engineering based methods. Moreover, neural models achieve statistically significant improvements over traditional methods after incorporating context information. (3) Our experiments show that the trained model achieves good generalization performance on another open benchmark information-seeking conversation dataset (UDC). The code of the implemented user intent prediction models will be released to the research community.[7]

The rest of our paper is organized as follows. In Section 2, we present related work regarding utterance type classification, conversational search, and multi-turn question answering. In Section 3, we formulate the research question of user intent prediction in information-seeking conversations. We also describe the data creation and annotating process. In Section 4, we extract rich features and learn traditional ML models for user intent prediction. We also perform feature importance analysis in this section. In Section 5, we introduce various enhanced neural classifiers for user intent prediction. Section 6 presents the conclusion and future work.

2 RELATED WORK

Our work is closely related to utterance classification, conversational search, and multi-turn question answering.

Utterance Classification. Utterance classification is well studied in the NLP and IR domain. Many different classification techniques such as statistical approaches [22], SVM, or Hidden Markov Models [23] have been used for different applications including human-human chatting [22], student's utterance [17], or forum post classifications [2]. However, recent advances in deep learning allow us to use neural architectures for utterance classification both on the word [10] and character level [32]. These new deep learning techniques have been applied in medical dialog systems [4]. In this paper, we focus on user intent prediction in information-seeking conversations. This specific utterance classification task presents unique challenges because of the complexity and diversity of human information-seeking conversations.

Conversational Search. Searching via conversational interactions with IR systems is an increasingly popular research topic in both industry and academia [3, 21, 33]. Oddy [16] introduced man-machine IR through dialogs without explicitly formulating queries. Belkin et al. [1] modeled the human-computer interaction in information-seeking as dialogs. Moreover, information-seeking via conversations is especially important in exploratory search [15, 25], where users are unfamiliar with the domain they are searching and would rely on effective interactions with retrieval systems. More recently, Radlinski and Craswell [20] identified key properties in conversational IR systems. Trippas et al. [24] conducted lab-based observational studies on conversational search and identified that it is more interactive than traditional search and new information-seeking models are needed. In our work, we focus on an essential study in conversational search, which is to predict user intent in this information-seeking setting. Our findings can help build conversational search systems that can provide enhanced searching experience using predicted user intent.

Multi-turn Question Answering. Early research on multi-turn question answering dates back to AutoTutor [6], which can simulate human tutors to assist college students to learn computer science. Recent work has focused on single turn QA on factoid questions [30] and other open-domain questions (e.g. WikiQA [29]). The Ubuntu Dialog Corpus [14] and MSDialog [19] provide large scale multi-turn QA dialogs in the technical support domain. Wu et al. [26] and Yang et al. [28] used these datasets to perform conversation response ranking for non-factoid questions. Our work focuses on a specific research need for multi-turn QA in the information-seeking setting. The performance of multi-turn QA could be improved if the user intent is correctly identified.

[6] https://www.microsoft.com/en-us/research/event/dialog-state-tracking-challenge/
[7] https://github.com/prdwb/UserIntentPrediction

3 TASK DEFINITION AND DATASET

3.1 Task Definition

The research problem of user intent prediction in information-seeking conversations is defined as follows. The input of the system is an information-seeking dialog dataset $\mathcal{D} = \{(\mathcal{U}_i, \mathcal{Y}_i)\}_{i=1}^{N}$ and a set of user intent labels $\mathcal{L} = \{l_1, l_2, \ldots, l_c\}$. A dialog $\mathcal{U}_i = \{u_i^1, u_i^2, \ldots, u_i^k\}$ contains multiple turns of utterances. u_i^k is the utterance at the k-th turn of the i-th dialog. $\mathcal{Y}_i$ consists of annotated user intent labels $\{\mathrm{y}_i^1, \mathrm{y}_i^2, \ldots, \mathrm{y}_i^k\}$, where $\mathrm{y}_i^k = \{y_i^{k(1)}, y_i^{k(2)}, \ldots, y_i^{k(c)}\}$. Here $y_i^{k(m)}, \ldots, y_i^{k(n)} = 1$ denotes that the utterance u_i^k in dialog $\mathcal{U}_i$ is labeled with user intent $\{l_m, \ldots, l_n\}$. Given an utterance u_i^k and other utterances in dialog $\mathcal{U}_i$, the goal is to predict the user intent $\mathcal{Y}_i$ of this utterance. The challenge of this task lies in the complexity and diversity of human information-seeking conversations, where one utterance often expresses multiple user intent [24].

3.2 Dataset

We use the MSDialog dataset that consists of technical support dialogs for Microsoft products. The data was crawled from the well-moderated Microsoft Community forum[8] which contains high-quality technical support dialogs between users and agents. The agents include Microsoft staff, community moderators, MVPs, or other experienced product users. Very rich structured data were collected with the dialogs, including the question popularity, answer vote, affiliation of information providers, etc. We choose this dataset because of its information-seeking nature and the well annotated user intent. Although MSDialog has limitations such as a narrow subject domain and forum-style language, no other openly available dialog datasets with the same detailed annotation exist. We believe this should be a first step to predict user intent in an information-seeking setting.

The dataset contains two sets, a complete set that consists of all the crawled dialogs and a labeled subset that contains only dialogs with user intent annotation. A taxonomy of 12 labels presented in Table 1 were developed in Qu et al. [19] based on work by Bhatia et al. [2] to characterize the user intent in information-seeking conversations. We also present the user intent distribution in Table 1. The complete set consists of 35,000 multi-turn QA dialogs in the technical support domain. Over 2,000 dialogs were selected for user intent annotation on MTurk with the following criteria: (1) With 3 to 10 turns. (2) With 2 to 4 participants. (3) With at least one correct answer selected by the community. (4) Falls into one of the categories of following major Microsoft products: Windows, Office, Bing, and Skype. The inter-rater agreement score was used to ensure the annotation quality. One utterance can be labeled with more than one user intent. A comparison of statistics between the complete set and the labeled subset is presented in Table 2.

In order to test the generalization performance of our findings, we use a small portion of UDC that is annotated with the same user intent types. This dataset also consists of multi-turn information-seeking conversations in a technical support domain between an information seeker and provider. However, UDC is generated from internet relay chat (IRC) and contains a significant amount of typos, Internet language, and abbreviations. In addition, UDC contains shorter utterances and more turns per dialog. This part of experiment is presented in Section 5.3.

[8] https://answers.microsoft.com

Table 1: User intent taxonomy and distribution in MSDialog

Code	Label	Description	%
OQ	Original Question	The first question from the user to initiate the dialog.	13
RQ	Repeat Question	Other users repeat a previous question.	3
CQ	Clarifying Question	User or agent asks for clarifications.	4
FD	Further Details	User or agent provides more details.	14
FQ	Follow Up Question	User asks for follow up questions about relevant issues.	5
IR	Information Request	Agent asks for information from users.	6
PA	Potential Answer	A potential answer or solution provided by agents.	22
PF	Positive Feedback	User provides positive feedback for working solutions.	6
NF	Negative Feedback	User provides negative feedback for useless solutions.	4
GG	Greetings/Gratitude	Greetings or expressing gratitude.	22
JK	Junk	No useful information in the utterance.	1
O	Others	Utterances cannot be categorized using other classes.	1

Table 2: Statistics of MSDialog (complete & labeled subset)

Items	Complete set	Labeled subset
# Dialogs	35,000	2,199
# Utterances	300,000	10,020
# Words (in total)	24,000,000	653,000
Avg. # Participants	3.18	2.79
Avg. # Turns Per Dialog	8.94	4.56
Avg. # Words Per Utterance	75.91	65.16

3.3 Data Preprocessing

The purpose of this classification task is to identify and predict user intent so that CAs can process the information accordingly to satisfy the users' information needs. However, utterances which were labeled *Greetings/Gratitude*, *Junk*, and *Others* do not contribute to the purpose of providing information about QA related user intent. Therefore, we remove occurrences of these labels. Note that we only remove these labels if there are more than one label of the given utterance. For example, if the annotation for the given utterance is *GG+OQ*, we transform the annotation into *OQ*. If the annotation is just *GG*, no transformation is needed. This reduces the number of unique label combinations from 316 to 152.

In addition, some label combinations of user intent labels are quite rare in the data. As indicated in Figure 1a, the top frequent label combinations have hundreds of occurrences in the data (e.g. *PA*, *OQ*, *PF*, *FD+PA*, *FD*), while the least frequent labels only have exactly one occurrence (e.g. *CQ+FD+IR+RQ*, *CQ+FD+FQ+PF*). These rare label combinations are very likely due to minor annotation errors or noise with MTurk. Annotation quality assurance was performed based on the dialog-level inter-rater agreement [19] to keep the complete dialog intact and thus may result in minor noise on an utterance level. We also plot the cumulative distribution of label combinations for better illustration in Figure 1b. The most frequent 32 label combinations constitute 90% of total label combination occurrences as marked in the figure. All 12 user intent labels are individually present in these 32 most frequent combinations except for *Others*. For the rest of the label combinations, we randomly sample one of the labels from each combination as the user intent label for the given utterance. For example, if the annotation for the given utterance is *CQ+FD+IR+RQ*, we transform it into a single label by randomly sampling one of the four labels, such as *CQ*. Therefore, the total number of label combinations in the data was reduced to

33 (including *Others*). We adopted this setting since these rare label combinations are very likely due to minor annotation errors. In addition, it would be very difficult to learn a prediction model for these label combinations with few instances.

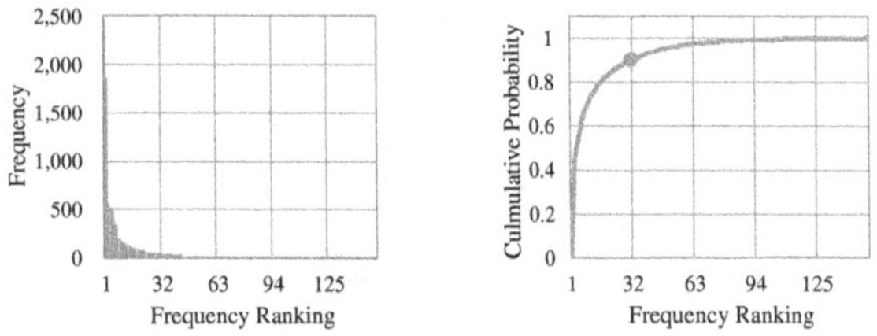

(a) Label combination occurrence from the most frequent to the least frequent.

(b) Cumulative occurrence probability added from the most frequent to the least frequent. The marked point is (32, 0.9).

Figure 1: Label combination distribution

For UDC, we observe a similar label combination distribution. So we preprocess the data in the same way. We have 34 label combinations for the UDC with 27 of them overlapping with MSDialog.

4 BASELINES AND FEATURE ANALYSIS

In this section, we extract several features following previous work [2, 5] and adopt different ML methods to build baseline models. In addition to reporting baseline performance, we also perform feature importance analysis to identify key factors in user intent prediction.

4.1 Features

We extract three groups of features to detect user intent in information-seeking conversations, including content, structural, and sentiment features. An overview of the features is provided in Table 3. Although MSDialog is derived from forum data, it is considered as a dialog dataset [19]. Thus, we refrain from developing features that can only be extracted from the metadata of the forum, such as user authority level or answer votes, so that our method can be applicable to dialog systems. The features are designed to capture the content and sentiment characteristics of the utterances as well as the structural information of the dialogs.

Content features. We build a TF-IDF representation of utterances and compute the cosine similarity of the given utterance with the dialog initial utterance (which typically is the question that initiates the QA dialog), and the entire dialog. These features are meant to capture the relevance level of the given utterance to the dialog in a general way. In addition, the presence of question marks is a strong indicator that the current utterance contains a question. Moreover, we assume that 5W1H keywords (what, where, when, why, who, and how) can suggest the type of the question.

Structural features. The position of an utterance in a dialog can reveal crucial information about user intent. Intuitively, answers tend to be at even number positions in a dialog, while user feedback and follow up questions tend to be at odd number positions. In addition, we include the utterance length with and without duplication removal and stemming. We analyzed the data and found that utterances containing positive feedback are relatively short, while utterances containing questions or answers tend to be long as they typically contain details. Finally, if the given utterance is generated by the information seeker (dialog starter), it is more likely to contain user related questions or user feedback. The structural features not only provide individual characteristics for utterances, but also evaluate the utterances on a dialog level.

Sentiment features. We expect sentiment features to be useful in identifying user feedback and gratitude expressions. In information-seeking conversations, positive and negative sentiments do not necessarily determine the feedback type. However, we expect them to be correlated to some extent. We also include classic indicators of sentiment, such as the presence of "thank", "does not/did not" and exclamation marks. In addition, we use VADER [8] to compute the positive/negative/neutral sentiment scores. We also count the number of positive and negative words using an opinion lexicon [12].

4.2 Methods and Evaluation Metrics

4.2.1 Methods. For each utterance, we extract a set of features as described in Section 4.1. To apply traditional ML methods with features to this task, we need to transform this multi-label classification problem to multi-class classification. Three transformation strategies are typically used: binary relevance, classifier chains, and label powerset. Binary relevance does not consider the label correlations and label powerset generates new labels for every label combination. So we choose classifier chains as the transformation strategy for traditional ML methods. This strategy performs binary classifications for each label and take predictions for previous labels as extra features. This transformation strategy is the best fit for our task as it considers the label dependency without explicitly generating new labels for every label combination. We adopt classic ML methods, including Naive Bayes classifier, SVM, random forest, and AdaBoost as baseline classifiers. In addition, we use ML-kNN, which supports multi-label classification by nature.

4.2.2 Metrics. Due to the nature of the intent prediction task, we adopt metrics suitable for multi-label classification problems.

Accuracy (Acc). It is known as the intersection over the union (IoU) in the multi-label classification settings. Accuracy is defined as the number of correctly predicted labels divided by the union of predicted and true labels for every utterance. For example, if the model predicts "*PA+CQ*" for the given utterance while the ground truth is "*PA+IR*", then the accuracy is $\frac{1}{3}$. The reported performance is the average metric over all utterances.

Precision, recall and F1 score. Precision is defined as the number of correctly predicted labels divided by predicted labels. Recall is defined as the number of correctly predicted labels divided by true labels. F1 is their harmonic mean. These metrics provide an overall performance evaluation for all utterances.

4.3 Main Experiments and Results

4.3.1 Experimental Setup. We split the labeled subset of MSDialog into training, validation, and test sets. Table 4 gives the statistics of the three sets. We have to point out that although this dataset is not that large, the annotation cost for such fine-grained user intent in conversations is quite high (estimated around \$1,700 on MTurk according to [19]). This dataset size is also larger than the data used in related work [2, 23]. The models are trained with

Table 3: Features extracted for user intent prediction in information-seeking conversations.

Feature Name	Group	Description	Type
Initial Utterance Similarity	Content	Cosine similarity between the utterance and the first utterance of the dialog	Real
Dialog Similarity	Content	Cosine similarity between the utterance and the entire dialog	Real
Question Mark	Content	Does the utterance contain a *question mark*	Binary
Duplicate	Content	Does the utterance contain the keywords *same, similar*	Binary
5W1H	Content	Does the utterance contain the keywords *what, where, when, why, who, how*	One-hot vector
Absolute Position	Structural	Absolute position of an utterance in the dialog	Numerical
Normalized Position	Structural	Normalized position of an utterance in the dialog (AbsPos divided by # utterances)	Real
Utterance Length	Structural	Total number of words in an utterance after stop words removal	Numerical
Utterance Length Unique	Structural	Unique number of words in an utterance after stop words removal	Numerical
Utterance Length Stemmed Unique	Structural	Unique number of words in an utterance after stop words removal and stemming	Numerical
Is Starter	Structural	Is the utterance made by the dialog starter	Binary
Thank	Sentiment	Does the utterance contain the keyword *thank*	Binary
Exclamation Mark	Sentiment	Does the utterance contain an *exclamation mark*	Binary
Feedback	Sentiment	Does the utterance contain the keyword *did not, does not*	Binary
Sentiment Scores	Sentiment	Sentiment scores of the utterance computed by VADER [8] (positive, neutral, and negative)	Real
Opinion Lexicon	Sentiment	Number of positive and negative words from an opinion lexicon	Numerical

scikit-multilearn[9] and scikit-learn[10] on the training set. We tune the hyper-parameters on the validation set based on accuracy and report the performance on the test set.

Table 4: Statistics of training, validation, and testing sets

Item	Train	Val	Test
# Utterances	8,064	986	970
Min. # Turns Per Dialog	3	3	3
Max. # Turns Per Dialog	10	10	10
Avg. # Turns Per Dialog	4.58	4.48	4.43
Avg. # Words Per Utterance	70.42	67.53	68.64

4.3.2 *Baseline Results.* The baseline results are presented in Table 5. Two ensemble methods, random forest and AdaBoost achieve the best overall performance of all baseline classifiers. AdaBoost achieves the best accuracy while random forest achieves the best F1 score. Surprisingly, ML-kNN performs relatively poorly despite its nature of an adapted algorithm for multi-label classification.

Table 5: Experiment results for baseline classifiers

Methods	Acc	Precision	Recall	F1
ML-kNN	0.4715	0.6322	0.4471	0.5238
NaiveBayes	0.4870	0.5563	0.4988	0.5260
SVM	0.6342	0.7270	0.5847	0.6481
RandForest	0.6268	**0.7657**	0.5903	**0.6667**
AdaBoost	**0.6399**	0.7247	**0.6030**	0.6583

4.4 Additional Feature Importance Analysis

4.4.1 *Feature Group Analysis.* We use one of the best baseline classifiers, random forest, and different combinations of feature groups to analyze the feature importance on a group level. The hyper-parameters are set to the best ones tuned on all features .

For using a single feature group, structural features is the most important feature group as presented in Table 6. Structural features and content features are significantly more important than sentiment features. We expect the sentiment features to capture the sentiment in user feedback but they might not be able to effectively discriminate other user intent. Structural features provide better performance than content features. We believe that this can be explained by the fact that hand-crafted content features cannot capture the complex user intent dynamics in human information-seeking conversations.

Table 6: Experiment results for different feature groups

Group(s)	Acc	Precision	Recall	F1
Content	0.5272	0.6097	0.4821	0.5384
Structural	**0.5809**	**0.6871**	**0.5434**	**0.6068**
Sentiment	0.3306	0.4087	0.3222	0.3603
Con+Str	0.6081	0.7393	0.5640	0.6399
Con+Sen	0.5577	0.6523	0.5179	0.5774
Str+Sent	**0.6110**	**0.7569**	**0.5672**	**0.6485**
All	**0.6268**	**0.7657**	**0.5903**	**0.6667**

For combinations of two feature groups, content+structural features and structural+sentiment features achieve comparable results. However, structural+sentiment features achieve slightly higher results on all metrics. The performance of using two groups of features is higher than using one of these two feature groups individually. Thus, combining structural features with another feature group boosts the performance of using structural features alone. Interestingly, content+sentiment features is unable to outperform the structural features alone. The results of using all features is the highest among all settings, confirming that all feature groups contribute to the performance of user intent prediction.

4.4.2 *Feature Importance Scores.* In the previous section, we evaluated the feature importance on a group level. In this section we focus on individual features to provide a more fine-grained analysis. We use random forest to output individual feature importance scores.[11] As described in Section 4.2, we used classifier chains to transform this multi-label classification problem. This method expands the feature space by including previous label predictions as new features for the current label prediction. This makes it not appropriate to evaluate original features. Thus, we use the Label Powerset method as the data transformation strategy for this section. The relative feature importance scores are presented in Table 7. This analysis can identify key factors in user intent prediction.

We summarize our observations as follows: (1) Structural features including "Absolute Position", "Normalized Position", "Is Starter" are ranked in the top-5 in terms of feature importance. Moreover,

[9] http://scikit.ml/ [10] http://scikit-learn.org/stable/

[11] https://scikit-learn.org/stable/auto_examples/ensemble/plot_forest_importances.html

Table 7: Individual feature importance from a random forest classifier with relative importance scores. "Str", "Con", "Sen" refer to "Structural", "Content", "Sentiment" respectively.

Rank	Feature	Group	Impt	Rank	Feature	Group	Impt
1	AbsPos	Str	1.0	13	Lex(Pos)	Sen	0.2814
2	InitSim	Con	0.9745	14	Lex(Neg)	Sen	0.2337
3	NormPos	Str	0.8684	15	Thank	Sen	0.1607
4	Starter	Str	0.8677	16	How	Con	0.08074
5	DlgSim	Con	0.6778	17	Dup	Con	0.06908
6	SenScr(Neu)	Sen	0.6465	18	What	Con	0.06576
7	SenScr(Pos)	Sen	0.5601	19	ExMark	Sen	0.06424
8	Len	Str	0.5335	20	When	Con	0.05989
9	LenUni	Str	0.4381	21	Feedback	Sen	0.02859
10	LenStem	Str	0.4354	22	Where	Con	0.02356
11	SenScr(Neg)	Sen	0.3495	23	Why	Con	0.0232
12	QuestMark	Con	0.3003	24	Who	Con	0.01423

other structural features, such as various forms of utterance length are observed to be relatively informative in general. This confirms the results in Section 4.4.1 that the structural feature group is the most important one. (2) "Initial Utterance Similarity" and "Dialog Similarity" are content features that can be highly informative for identifying user intent. Both features are indicators of how closely the utterance connects with the information-seeking process. Other content features, such as "5W1H", however, contribute little to predicting user intent. (3) Some sentiment features are relatively important in identifying user intent, such as positive and neutral sentiment scores. However, some other sentiment features contribute little to the task, such as the existence of exclamation marks and "thank". (4) We observe that features ranked from the 15th to the last one in Table 7 are all "keyword features". These features are based on a simple rule that whether the given utterance contains pre-defined keywords. For example, the "5W1H" feature looks for "what/where/when/why/who/how" in the given utterance and the "Feedback" feature looks for "did not/does not". The major drawback of manual feature engineering is amplified in this task due to the complexity and diversity of human information-seeking conversations.

5 ENHANCED NEURAL CLASSIFIERS

We expected the content of an utterance to be a good indicator of user intent types compared to other features. However, as shown in Section 4.4, the hand-crafted content features are unable to capture the complex characteristics of human information-seeking conversations. Thus, in this section we adopt neural architectures to automatically learn representations of utterances without feature engineering.

5.1 Our Approach

5.1.1 Base Models. Given the previous success in modeling text sequences using CNN and bidirectional LSTM (BiLSTM) [7], we choose these two architectures as our base models. Although utterances are grouped as dialogs, the base models consider utterances independently.

Given an utterance $u_i^k = \{w_1, w_2, \ldots, w_m\}$ (the k-th utterance in the i-th dialog) that contains m tokens, we first transform the sequence of tokens into a sequence of token indices $S = \{s_1, s_2, \ldots, s_m\}$. Then we pad the sequence S to a fixed length n (the max sequence length). Both CNN and BiLSTM start with an embedding layer initiated with pre-trained word embeddings. Preliminary experiments indicated that using MSDialog (complete set) to train word embeddings is more effective than using GloVe [18] in terms of final model performance. The embedding layer maps each token in the utterances to a word embedding vector with a dimension of d.

We focus on the CNN model following previous work [10] here, because it achieves better performance in our experiments. After the embedding layer, filters with the shape (f, d) are applied to a window of f words. f is also referred to as the filter size. Concretely, a convolution operation is denoted as

$$c_i = \sigma(\mathbf{w} \cdot \mathbf{e}_{i:i+f-1} + b) \tag{1}$$

Where c_i is the feature generated by the i-th filter with weights $\mathbf{w}$ and bias b. This filter is applied to an embedding matrix, which is the concatenation from the i-th to the $(i + f - 1)$-th embedding vectors. An non-linearity function (ReLU) is also applied. This operation is applied to every possible window of words and generates a feature map $\mathbf{c} = \{c_1, c_2, \ldots, c_{n-f+1}\}$. More filters are applied to extract features of the utterance content. Max pooling are applied to select the most salient feature of a window of f' features by taking the maximum value $\hat{c_i} = max\{\mathbf{c}_{i:i+f'-1}\}$. f' denotes the max pooling kernel size. A dropout layer is applied after the pooling layer for regularization.

After the last convolutional layer, we perform global max pooling by taking the maximum value $\hat{c} = max\{\mathbf{c}\}$ for the feature map $\mathbf{c}$ at this step. This operation reduces the dimension of the tensor to one. This tensor is further transformed to an output tensor of shape $(1, l)$, where l is the number of user intent labels (12 for our task). Sigmoid activation is applied to each value of the output tensor to squash the value to a confidence level between 0 and 1. A threshold is chosen to determine whether the given label present in the final prediction. If the model is not confident of predicting any label, the label of the highest confidence level is the prediction. We tuned the threshold with the validation data.

5.1.2 Incorporate Context Information. As shown in the previous work [19], user intent follows clear flow patterns in information-seeking conversations. The user intent of a given utterance is closely related to the utterances around it, which compose the *context* for the given utterance. Incorporating context information into neural models is easier compared to that for traditional ML methods shown in Section 4. We consider two ways as follows.

Direct Expansion. The most straightforward way to incorporate context information is to expand the given utterance with its context. Concretely, the expanded utterance for u_i^k is $\hat{u}_i^k = u_i^{k-1} \oplus u_i^k \oplus u_i^{k+1}$, where $\oplus$ is the concatenate operator. $\hat{u}_i^k$ is considered as the given utterance in base models.

Context Representation. Given an expanded utterance $\hat{u}_i^k$ as input, the neural architecture first segments it into three original utterances of u_i^{k-1}, u_i^k, and u_i^{k+1}. We apply convolution operations and max pooling to the utterances separately as shown in Figure 2a. After global pooling following the last convolutional layer, the three one-dimensional tensors are concatenated for final predictions. This approach extracts features from the given utterance and its context separately. Thus, we are able to learn the importance of the given utterance and its context by tuning context-specific hyper-parameters, such as the number of filters for context utterances.

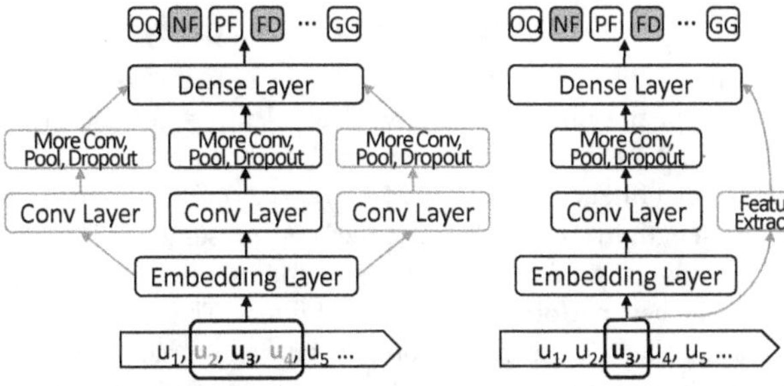

(a) CNN-Context-Rep (b) CNN-Feature

Figure 2: Architectures for enhanced neural classifiers. Components marked orange are extra information incorporated into the base CNN model (black). The utterance in bold is the current utterance. Predicted labels are marked blue.

5.1.3 Incorporate Extra Features. We found many useful features for user intent prediction such as structural features in the feature importance analysis in Section 4.4. However, nearly half of the features can not be exploited by only looking at a single utterance. For example, normalized/absolute utterance position and utterance similarity with the dialog/initial utterance cannot be captured without a holistic view over the entire dialog. Some of the uncaptured features are highly informative. This motivates us to incorporate hand-crafted features into the neural architectures. As shown in Figure 2b, all hand-crafted features described in Section 4.1 are incorporated into neural architectures at the last dense layer. The feature vector is concatenated with the neural representation of the utterance before making final predictions.

Finally, we combine two base models with various extra components to produce several systems for comparison as follows:

- **CNN**. The base CNN model that consists of three convolutional layers with the same filter size.
- **CNN-Feature**. The CNN model that incorporates extra hand-crafted features at the last layer.
- **CNN-Context**. The CNN model that incorporates context information with direct expansion.
- **CNN-Context-Rep**. The CNN model that incorporates context information with context representation.
- **BiLSTM**. The BiLSTM model that represents the given utterance both in the ordinary order and the reverse order.
- **BiLSTM-Context**. The BiLSTM model that incorporates context information with direct expansion.

5.2 Experiments and Evaluation

5.2.1 Neural Baselines. In addition to the base model of **BiLSTM** and **CNN**, we further introduce two commonly used neural models for text classification as baselines. For both new baselines, we modify the models to generate multi-label predictions.

CNN-MFS. The CNN model with multiple filter sizes as described by Kim [10] is a pioneer model to apply neural networks to text classification. This model uses different filter sizes of 3, 4, and 5 to generate feature maps of different window sizes.

Char-CNN. Zhang et al. [32] introduced a character-level CNN for text classification. There are two variants of the model, a large one and a small one, depending on the numbers of convolutional filters and dense layer units. We report the performance on the small model as it achieves better results in our task.

5.2.2 Experimental Setup. We use the same data and metrics as in baseline experiments in Section 4. All models are implemented with TensorFlow[12] and Keras[13]. Hyper-parameters are tuned with the validation data. We found that setting (convolutional filters, dropout rate, dense layer units, max sequence length, convolutional filters for context, and dense layer units for context) to (1024, 0.6, 256, 800, 128, 128) respectively turned out to be the best setting for our best performing model CNN-Conext-Rep. The convolutional filter size and pooling size are set to (3, 3). All models are trained with a NVIDIA Titan X GPU using Adam [11]. The initial learning rate is 0.001. The parameters of Adam, β_1 and β_2 are 0.9 and 0.999 respectively. The batch size is 128. For the word embedding layer, we trained word embeddings with Gensim[14] with CBOW model using MSDialog (complete set). The dimension of word embedding is 100. Word vectors are set to trainable.

5.2.3 Evaluation Results. We select the two strongest feature based classifiers from Section 4 as feature based baselines in addition to neural baselines. They are random forest with the best F1 score and AdaBoost with the best accuracy. The performance comparison of models is presented in Table 8.

Table 8: Results comparison. The significance test can only be performed on accuracy. In a multi-label classification setting, accuracy gives a score for each individual sample, while other metrics evaluate the performance over all samples. ‡ means statistically significant difference over the best baseline with $p < 10^{-4}$ measured by the Student's paired t-test.

Method Types	Methods	Accuracy	Precision	Recall	F1
Feature based Baselines	Random Forest	0.6268	**0.7657**	0.5903	**0.6667**
	AdaBoost	**0.6399**	0.7247	**0.6030**	0.6583
Neural Baselines	BiLSTM	0.5515	0.6284	0.5274	0.5735
	CNN	**0.6364**	0.7152	**0.6054**	**0.6558**
	CNN-MFS	0.6342	**0.7308**	0.5919	0.6541
	Char-CNN	0.5419	0.6350	0.4940	0.5557
Neural Classifiers	BiLSTM-Context	0.6006	0.6951	0.5640	0.6227
	CNN-Feature	0.6509	0.7619	0.6110	0.6781
	CNN-Context	0.6555	0.7577	0.6070	0.6740
	CNN-Context-Rep	**0.6885‡**	**0.7883**	**0.6516**	**0.7134**

The base CNN model without feature engineering achieves similar results with the strongest feature based baselines. The performance of the base CNN model is better than the base BiLSTM model. CNN-MFS takes advantage of different filter sizes and also achieves comparable results. Char-CNN, however, performs poorly in this task. Char-CNN does not use pre-trained word embeddings because it learns features from a character-level which would require much more training data.

BiLSTM performs poorly in this task. Even though BiLSTM-Context has a major improvement over BiLSTM, it has inferior results compared to the base CNN model. Compared to non-factoid question answering or chatting, utterances in information-seeking conversations tend to be longer. BiLSTM(-Context) tries to model a

[12] https://www.tensorflow.org/ [13] https://keras.io/
[14] https://radimrehurek.com/gensim/

holistic sequence dependency and thus performs poorly on handling these long utterances.

The best result of the feature based baselines is slightly higher than neural baselines. This can be accounted for by the lack of information in neural models. Even though we assume that most of the content and sentiment features can be learned by neural models, the neural models have no access to most of the structural features. Thus, we incorporate all the features to neural models to produce CNN-Feature model. This model outperforms all baseline classifiers. This confirms that incorporating dialog-level information can be beneficial to predicting user intent.

Both CNN-Context and CNN-Context-Rep outperform baseline models and CNN-Feature without explicit feature engineering. These results demonstrate the effectiveness of the implicit feature learning of neural architectures. CNN-Context-Rep performs better than CNN-Context. This indicates that incorporating high-level features of context information learned by neural architectures is better than directly capturing the raw context information. In a multi-label classification setting, accuracy produces a score for each individual sample, while precision/recall/F1 evaluate the performance over all samples. Thus, accuracy is the only metric that is suitable for significance tests. Our best model, CNN-Context-Rep achieves statistically significant improvement over the best baseline with $p < 10^{-4}$ measured by the Student's paired t-test.

5.3 Generalization on Ubuntu Dialogs

In this section, we would like to evaluate the generalization performances of different methods on other data in addition to MSDialog. We train different models on MSDialog and test them on the Ubuntu Dialog Corpus (UDC). We select the two best performing feature based classifiers (random forest and AdaBoost) and the best neural model (CNN-Context-Rep) to test the generalization performance. Although the number of annotated Ubuntu dialogs is limited, it is sufficient to demonstrate the predicting performance. We split the annotated UDC data into validation and test sets with an equal size. We train the model on MSDialog data only and tune the hyper-parameters on the UDC validation set. The performance on the UDC test set is presented in Table 9.

Table 9: Testing performance on UDC of different models trained with MSDialog. The significance test can only be performed on accuracy. ‡ means statistically significant difference over both strongest feature based baselines with $p <$ 0.01 measured by the Student's paired t-test.

Methods	Accuracy	Precision	Recall	F1
Random Forest	0.4405	**0.6781**	0.4077	0.5092
AdaBoost	0.4430	0.5913	0.4187	0.4902
CNN-Context-Rep	**0.4708**‡	0.5647	**0.5129**	**0.5375**

The generalization results on UDC are not as good as MSDialog. Although MSDialog and UDC both consist of multi-turn information-seeking dialogs from the technical support domain, the drastically different language style adds difficulty for model generalization and transferring. In this challenging setting, CNN-Context-Rep still achieves statistically significant improvement over both baselines in terms of accuracy with $p < 0.01$ measured by the Student's paired t-test.

5.4 Hyper-parameter Sensitivity Analysis

We further analyze the impact of two hyper-parameters on CNN-Context-Rep: the number of convolutional filters for the given utterance and the max sequence length. The choices for number of convolutional filters are (64, 128, 256, 512, 1024). We tune the max sequence length in (50, 100, 200, ..., 1000). As presented in Figure 3, the performance gradually increases as the number of filters increases. The best performance is at 1,024 filters. This confirms our expectation that more convolutional filters can extract richer features and thus produce better results. In addition, the performance fluctuates as the max sequence length increases. Performance with larger ($\geqslant$ 800) max sequence length are better in general.

5.5 Case Study

Table 10 gives examples of the predictions that different systems fail to make. In the first utterance, the agent asks for the user's iOS version before providing a potential answer, which is a very common pattern of agents' responses. Our CNN-Context-Rep is able to identify the *Information Request* in the utterance while AdaBoost cannot. In the second utterance, both models fail to predict the *Negative Feedback*. This might be due to the fact that the feedback is not explicitly expressed. In addition, it could be relevant that the number of feedback utterances in the training data is relatively limited compared to questions and answers, which makes it more difficult to predict positive/negative feedback.

Table 10: Two utterances with their ground-truth and predicted user intent labels. Bold font indicates mispredicted content or labels. "Ours" refers to CNN-Context-Rep.

Hello. Welcome to Skype Community! **Please provide us the iOS version of your iPad.** The required iOS version for iPad is iOS 8 or higher and for the new Skype on iOS requires iOS 9 or higher. For more information, click here. Hope this helps. Let me know if you need further assistance. Thank you!			
Ground truth: **IR**, PA	Ours: **IR**, PA	AdaBoost: PA	Actor: agent
After modified the Windows entry, value of regedit, **the error also happened.** When I use C++ for creating another new Microsoft::Office::Interop::PowerPoint:: Application instance, the COMException is throwed.			
Ground truth: FD, **NF**	Ours: FD	AdaBoost: FD	Actor: user

6 CONCLUSIONS

In this paper, we studied two approaches to predict user intent in information-seeking conversations. First we use different ML methods with a rich feature set, including the content, structural, and sentiment features. We perform thorough feature importance analysis on both group level and individual level, which shows that structural features contribute most in this prediction task. Given findings from feature analysis, we construct enhanced neural classifiers to incorporate context information for user intent prediction. The enhanced neural model without feature engineering outperforms the baseline models by a large margin. Our findings can provide insights in the important factors of user intent prediction in information-seeking conversations. Future work will consider other methods for user intent prediction. Utilizing the predicted user intent to rank or generate conversation responses in an information-seeking setting is also interesting to explore.

ACKNOWLEDGMENTS

This work was supported in part by the Center for Intelligent Information Retrieval and in part by NSF IIS-1715095. Any opinions, findings and conclusions or recommendations expressed in this material are those of the authors and do not necessarily reflect those of the sponsor.

REFERENCES

[1] N. J. Belkin, C. Cool, A. Stein, and U. Thiel. Cases, Scripts, and Information-Seeking Strategies: On the Design of Interactive Information Retrieval Systems. 1970.
[2] S. Bhatia, P. Biyani, and P. Mitra. Classifying User Messages For Managing Web Forum Data. In *WebDB '12*, 2012.
[3] W. B. Croft and R. H. Thompson. I3R: A New Approach to the Design of Document Retrieval Systems. *J. Am. Soc. Inf. Sci.*, 1987.
[4] D. Datta, V. Brashers, J. Owen, C. White, and L. E. Barnes. A Deep Learning Methodology for Semantic Utterance Classification in Virtual Human Dialogue Systems. In *IVA '16*, 2016.
[5] S. Ding, G. Cong, C. Lin, and X. Zhu. Using Conditional Random Fields to Extract Contexts and Answers of Questions from Online Forums. In *ACL '08*, 2008.
[6] A. C. Graesser, K. Wiemer-Hastings, P. Wiemer-Hastings, and R. Kreuz. AutoTutor: A simulation of a human tutor. *Cognitive Systems Research*, 2001.
[7] A. Graves and J. Schmidhuber. Framewise phoneme classification with bidirectional lstm and other neural network architectures. *Neural Networks*, 2005.
[8] C. J. Hutto and E. Gilbert. VADER: A Parsimonious Rule-Based Model for Sentiment Analysis of Social Media Text. In *ICWSM '14*, 2014.
[9] H. Khanpour, N. Guntakandla, and R. D. Nielsen. Dialogue Act Classification in Domain-Independent Conversations Using a Deep Recurrent Neural Network. In *COLING '16*, 2016.
[10] Y. Kim. Convolutional Neural Networks for Sentence Classification. In *EMNLP '14*, 2014.
[11] D. P. Kingma and J. Ba. Adam: A Method for Stochastic Optimization. In *ICLR '15*, 2015.
[12] B. Liu, M. Hu, and J. Cheng. Opinion Observer: Analyzing and Comparing Opinions on the Web. In *WWW '05*, 2005.
[13] Y. Liu, K. Han, Z. Tan, and Y. Lei. "Using Context Information for Dialog Act Classification in DNN Framework". In *EMNLP '17*, 2017.
[14] R. Lowe, N. Pow, I. Serban, and J. Pineau. The Ubuntu Dialogue Corpus: A Large Dataset for Research in Unstructured Multi-Turn Dialogue Systems. In *SIGDIAL '15*, 2015.
[15] G. Marchionini. Exploratory Search: From Finding to Understanding. *Commun. ACM*, 2006.
[16] R. N. Oddy. *Information Retrieval through Man-Machine Dialogue.* 1977.
[17] A. Olney, M. Louwerse, E. Matthews, J. Marineau, H. Hite-Mitchell, and A. Graesser. Utterance Classification in AutoTutor. In *HLT-NAACL-EDUC*, 2003.
[18] J. Pennington, R. Socher, and C. D. Manning. GloVe: Global Vectors for Word Representation. In *EMNLP '14*, 2014.
[19] C. Qu, L. Yang, W. B. Croft, J. R. Trippas, Y. Zhang, and M. Qiu. Analyzing and Characterizing User Intent in Information-seeking Conversations. In *SIGIR '18*, 2018.
[20] F. Radlinski and N. Craswell. A Theoretical Framework for Conversational Search. In *CHIIR '17*, 2017.
[21] S. Shiga, H. Joho, R. Blanco, J. R. Trippas, and M. Sanderson. Modelling information needs in collaborative search conversations. In *SIGIR '17*, 2017.
[22] A. Stolcke, N. Coccaro, R. Bates, C. Van Ess-Dykema, C. Van Ess-Dykema, K. Ries, E. Shriberg, D. Jurafsky, R. Martin, and M. Meteer. Dialogue act modeling for automatic tagging and recognition of conversational speech. *Comput. Linguist.*, 2000.
[23] D. Surendran and G. A. Levow. Dialog act tagging with support vector machines and hidden markov models. In *ICSLP '06*, 2006.
[24] J. R. Trippas, D. Spina, L. Cavedon, H. Joho, and M. Sanderson. Informing the Design of Spoken Conversational Search: Perspective Paper. In *CHIIR '18*, 2018.
[25] R. W. White and R. A. Roth. *Exploratory Search: Beyond the Query-Response Paradigm.* Synthesis Lectures on Information Concepts, Retrieval, and Services. 2009.
[26] Y. Wu, W. Wu, C. Xing, M. Zhou, and Z. Li. Sequential Matching Network: A New Architecture for Multi-turn Response Selection in Retrieval-Based Chatbots. In *ACL '17*, 2017.
[27] Z. Yan, N. Duan, P. Chen, M. Zhou, J. Zhou, and Z. Li. Building Task-Oriented Dialogue Systems for Online Shopping. In *AAAI '17*, 2017.
[28] L. Yang, M. Qiu, C. Qu, J. Guo, Y. Zhang, W. B. Croft, J. Huang, and H. Chen. Response Ranking with Deep Matching Networks and External Knowledge in Information-seeking Conversation Systems. In *SIGIR '18*, 2018.
[29] Y. Yang, W. T. Yih, and C. Meek. WikiQA: A Challenge Dataset for Open-Domain Question Answering. In *EMNLP '15*, 2015.
[30] J. Yin, X. Jiang, Z. Lu, L. Shang, H. Li, and X. Li. Neural Generative Question Answering. In *IJCAI '15*, 2015.
[31] X. Zhang and H. Wang. A joint model of intent determination and slot filling for spoken language understanding. In *IJCAI '16*, 2016.
[32] X. Zhang, J. J. Zhao, and L LeCun. Character-level Convolutional Networks for Text Classification. In *NIPS '15*, 2015.
[33] Y. Zhang, X. Chen, Q. Ai, L. Yang, and W. B. Croft. Towards conversational search and recommendation: System ask, user respond. In *CIKM '18*, 2018.

A ADDITIONAL FIGURE

We include an additional figure to illustrate our findings from above. Figure 3 shows the results of the hyper-parameter sensitivity analysis.

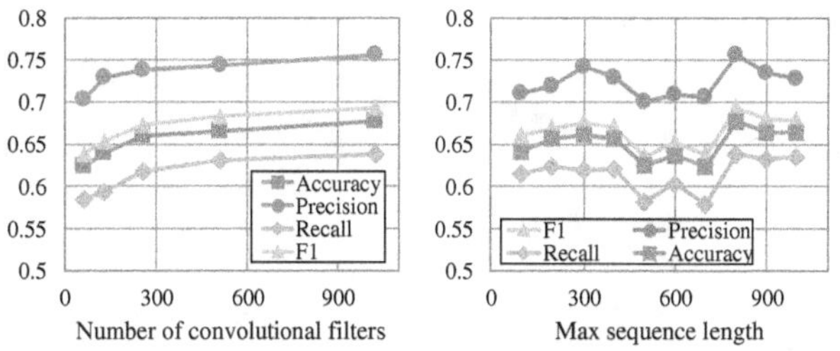

Figure 3: Performance of CNN-Context-Rep with different number of convolutional filters and max sequence length.

Interacting with Digital Documents

A Real Life Study of Historians' Task Processes, Actions and Goals

Laura Korkeamäki†
Faculty of Information Technology and Communication Sciences, Tampere University
Tampere, Finland
laura.korkeamaki@tuni.fi

Sanna Kumpulainen
Faculty of Information Technology and Communication Sciences, Tampere University
Tampere, Finland
sanna.kumpulainen@tuni.fi

ABSTRACT

The aim of this study was to find out what is historians' task-based information interaction like in digital environments. The study was based on TBII framework [20]. The research was conducted in real-life setting using interview and shadowing. The following task process types were identified: (i) searching secondary sources, (ii) reading and making notes, (iii) collecting and processing data, (iv) analyzing and (v) writing. We found that IR interfaces were not always optimal for historians' use, and that the interfaces should support the expression of information needs better. The data processing consumes a lot of historians' time and they could benefit from designing better tools. We also found out that task process types have an effect on how digital tools or data are being used. Therefore, the context in which the tool or data is being used, should be taken into account when designing tools for historians.

CCS CONCEPTS

• Information systems~Users and interactive retrieval

KEYWORDS

Information interaction, Task-based studies, User studies, Ethnographic methods

ACM Reference format:

Laura Korkeamäki and Sanna Kumpulainen. 2019. Interacting with Digital Documents: A Real Life Study of Historians' Task Processes, Actions and Goals. In *Proceedings of ACM SIGIR Conference on Human Information Interaction and Retrieval (CHIIR' 19). 10-14 March, 2019, Glasgow, Scotland, UK.* ACM, New York, NY, USA, 9 pages. https://doi.org/10.1145/3295750.3298931

†Corresponding author

CHIIR '19, March 10–14, 2019, Glasgow, Scotland UK

ACM ISBN 978-1-4503-6025-8/19/03...$15.00
https://doi.org/10.1145/3295750.3298931

1 INTRODUCTION

People interact with information in work and leisure contexts, and the goal is often to use that information in real-life tasks [4]. Much of the information interaction takes place in a digital environment because technology is becoming ubiquitous in people's lives. A digital environment can be defined as "a context, or a 'place', that is enabled by technology and digital devices, often transmitted over the internet, or other digital means, e.g. mobile phone network" [33]. In this research, we aim at studying historians' information interaction during work task performance in digital environments. We focus on historians' task processes and, more precisely, on historians' task goals and actions.

As early as 1990, Bates argued that people want more control over search process, and information retrieval (IR) systems should support the search strategies of people's own choosing – not the other way around [2]. Although digital technology and IR systems have developed vastly since then, we are still dealing with the same issues. Especially for historians, it is vital to build contextual knowledge around the research questions [12]. Therefore, it is not enough for historians to form search queries and trust the algorithms to do their magic. Instead, historians have a habit of combining several search strategies [1, 9, 11, 31].

Information interaction happens in all parts of the research process, not just during information searching. In this research, we use task-based information interaction (TBII) framework presented by Järvelin et al. [20] including activities from task planning to synthesizing and reporting. Studying information interaction is important because digital environments and tools can change how people interact with information [4]. For example, when new digital tools are created for historians, the designs can have an effect on how data can be viewed and what kind of connections historians can see in the data [14]. Consequently, digital tools affect what kind of history research can be made.

In this research, we focus on historians' goals and actions during work task performance. The goals within the tasks can change and alter the task process, even when the task itself remains the same [34]. Therefore, it is important to study task goals and related actions in order to support researchers' work.

2 BACKGROUND

2.1 History as a Domain

History research helps to understand the present based on previous experiences. In information studies, information seeking of humanities and history scholars have been a long-lasting interest [3, 13]. As an academic domain, history is sometimes connected to humanities and sometimes to social sciences [5]. There are many subfields in history, e.g., political, social and culture history.

Historians study the past by exploring various kinds of primary sources, such as letters, diaries, newspapers, magazines and official reports. Works published by other researchers (e.g. books, essays, articles) are considered secondary sources [7]. Searching for primary materials may require a trip to an archive, although historians are increasingly relying on digital primary sources [9, 30]. The varied information environment, the use of primary sources and the emerging digital methods makes history a very timely and interesting research domain in information interaction.

According to Brundage [7], history should not be viewed as a static concept, because "historians constantly search for fresh sources, approaches, methodological tools, and interpretations, in an effort to offer an ever-new past to whatever the present is". In addition, Cullen [10] pointed out that the ability to form good questions, while writing an essay or doing research is particularly important in history. These ways of working require interacting with information, which is the focus of our research.

There are several studies concerning historians' search for primary sources [1, 9, 31]. Dalton and Charnigo [11] covered both primary and secondary sources. Duff and Johnson [12] studied historians' information seeking behavior. In addition, Martin and Quan-Haase [24-26] have written several research papers of historians' information behavior and serendipity in historical research. There are also studies of historians' [30] and humanists' [18] research practices in digital environments. However, information interaction research in the domain of history is lacking. Although Freund and Toms [16] studied how genealogists and historians interacted with archival finding aids, their research was conducted in a laboratory-like setting. Here we address historians' information interaction in real world settings.

2.2 Conceptual Framework

In this research, we use the following task-related concepts: *activity, task process, action* and *task goal.*

Firstly, by using the term *activity* we refer specifically to the activities presented in *TBII framework* [20]. TBII framework focuses on cognitive and behavioral aspects in human performance divided into five generic activities (Figure 1). The first activity is *task planning and reflective assessment,* which is viewed as a meta-activity, ongoing through the whole task process. It includes e.g., setting goals, making plans and altering them if necessary.

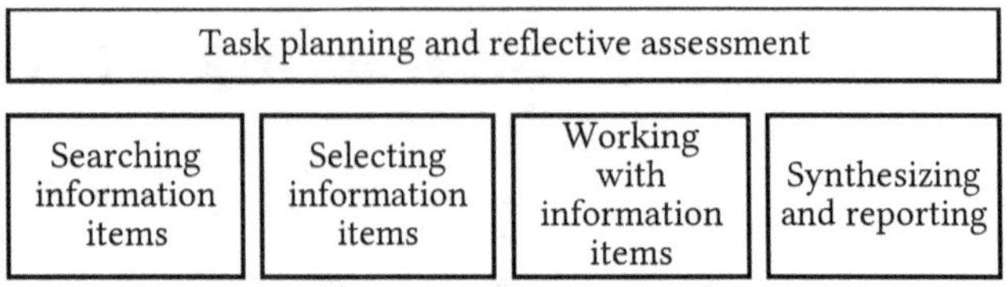

Figure 1: Five activities in TBII framework [20]

Searching information items is a relatively brief and possibly a repeated activity. The purpose of this activity is to find information items to be used in the task process. The term *information item* refers to books, articles, paragraphs, pictures, videos etc. In the activity of *selecting information items* focus is put on deciding which information items are relevant in performing the task. *Working with information items* includes e.g., reading the information items, organizing them, making analysis or converting them into more suitable formats. *Synthesizing and reporting* involves e.g., writing research articles, making conclusions and presenting the results to others.

Secondly, according to Byström and Hansen [8], *a task process* means different kinds of *actions* that an individual performs over time in order to reach a goal. These actions can be cognitive, behavioral or affective [21].

Thirdly, the importance of understanding people's *task goals* and activities has been widely recognized. For example, Blandford and Attfield [4] noted, "information is only useful when it is interpreted and applied by people in the context of their goals and activities". With the help of Daniels' classification of goals, Xie [34] proposed four levels of user goal types: long-term goal, leading search goal, current search goal and interactive intention. It is important to be aware of that task goals can differ depending on how general or specific they are. In our research, the term *goal* refers to participants' perceived task goals.

Lastly, the concept *action* can be described at different levels. For example, Bates [2] introduced the following concepts related to search tasks: moves, tactics, stratagems and strategies. However, Bates' definition of the term "move" would be too specific for the purpose of this research. Hence, we use the term "action" in a broader sense. A set of one or several actions form a task process.

3 RESEARCH DESIGN

3.1 Research Questions

We aim at studying historians' task-based information interaction in digital environments by utilizing the TBII framework [20]. Digital environment was seen relevant, because the use of various types of digital sources have gained increasing attention among historians.

We study the activities from TBII model as task performance processes. The research questions are derived from the view presented by Byström and Hansen [8], who suggested that task processes consist of certain goals and actions. Historians' task-based information interaction in digital information environments is studied by addressing the following research questions:

RQ1. What are *the task process types* of historians?

RQ2. What kinds of *goals* are included in the different task process types?

RQ3. What kinds of *actions* are included in the different task process types?

3.2 Methods

We used a qualitative research setting that is discussed next. This is a naturalistic field study. The data collection methods were interview and shadowing, which were conducted in the premises of three universities in Finland. Data was collected between January and March 2018.

3.2.1 Recruitment and participants

The participants were selected by purposive sampling. The criteria for sampling were the following: (i) participants should use digital primary sources in their research projects, (ii) they should include experienced and less experienced researchers, (iii) they should include representatives from different subfields in history, and (iv) they should be located geographically close enough because conducting the study required travelling from the researcher.

At first, participants for this study were sought by checking ongoing research projects in digital history from Finnish universities' web pages. Participants were first contacted by email. During recruitment, also snowball sampling was used, meaning that historians were asked to recommend suitable participants for this study. Participants were recruited also from a digital history seminar (organized early 2018), where it was possible to meet historians in person.

This study included five historians (Table 1) who met the criteria of purposive sampling. The participants were doctoral students or postdoctoral researchers. They had worked as researchers approximately from 1 to 12 years, which indicates various levels of expertise. The participants' research topics were related to one or several subfields, i.e., conceptual or cultural history, digital humanism, history of authorship, intellectual, labor or social history.

Table 1: Participants' research experience

Participant	Career stage	Years working as a researcher*
P1	PhD student	1
P2	PhD student	3
P3	Postdoc	12
P4	Postdoc	7
P5	Postdoc	7

*after master's degree

3.2.2 Interview

Written consent was obtained for the interview and shadowing. Semi-structured interviews were conducted in person. Each of the participants was interviewed once before shadowing (Table 2). Interviews lasted 49 min–1.5 h each. By meeting the participants before shadowing the researcher gained better understanding of the participants' research topics and information environment. Interviews were audio recorded and later transcribed.

Table 2: Interviews and shadowing sessions

Participant	No. of interviews	No. of shadowing sessions	Avg. duration of a shadowing session (min)
P1	1	4	140
P2	1	4	73
P3	1	0	0
P4	1	3	151
P5	1	4	127

3.2.3 Shadowing

Shadowing is a research method, where shadowees are observed while doing their real-life work tasks. Shadower can also ask questions from the shadowees during the sessions if needed [27]. Shadowing reveals information that shadowees forgot to mention during interviews or didn't consider worth mentioning. However, it should be noted that the data collected by shadowing is selective regarding time and place. [28] Four of the participants were shadowed three to four times. Each shadowing session lasted about one to three hours. The shadowing sessions included usually one or two task sessions. Data was collected by handwritten field notes and by video recordings of conversations and participants' computer screens during shadowing sessions.

3.2.4 Data processing and analysis

Table 3 shows an overview of the data collected. The analysis was qualitative because in that way it was possible to gain a holistic view on the historians' task processes, goals and actions. First, the historians' different task process types were identified from the shadowing data (cf. RQ1). In this research, different task processes were assigned to different types according to their qualitative features. In other words, *a task process type* refers to a group of similar sequences of performed activities that are clearly observable or can be expressed in words by the participants, when asked to describe their task performance. The task process types were formed pragmatically. For example, one historian was reading a scientific article and making notes for future use. These types of task processes were labeled as "reading and making notes".

Table 3: Material collected and processed for this research

5 interviews	5 h 40 min of audio recordings and 55 pages of word by word transcriptions
15 shadowing sessions	49 pages of transcribed field notes, 30 h 10 min of video recordings and 48 pages of transcribed video material*

*Only relevant parts of the videos were transcribed

Secondly, the goals and actions of each task process type were analyzed (cf. RQ2 and RQ3). In the beginning of the shadowing sessions, the historians were asked to tell the goals of their current tasks and how they were going to reach those goals. The identifications of the goals and actions were supported by observations, additional questions asked during the shadowings, and by the spontaneous conversations with the historians. For example, one historian's goal for reading an article was to increase basic understanding of a topic. This goal was labeled as "learning". During the shadowing session, the historian read the article linearly (labeled as "reading"), saved article's reference information to a reference management program (labeled as "organizing notes and citations"), and wrote notes on paper and to the reference management program (labeled as "making notes"). In addition, the historian noticed that one in-text citation was mentioned several times in the article, and decided to look that source more closely (labeled as "following citations"). The historian explained that getting to know the conversations is helpful when the topic is unfamiliar (labeled as "learning").

The analysis of the shadowing data was complemented by the data from the interviews. The interviews were analyzed on the parts that were related to the task process types identified from the shadowing data.

We focused on three TBII activities: searching information items, working with information items, and synthesizing and reporting. In this research, selecting information items was considered a part of searching process and was not analyzed separately. Järvelin et al. [20] noted also that selecting information items is interleaved with the searching activity. Therefore, we combined these TBII activities into one category – searching and selecting information items.

Planning and reflective assessment was not the focus in this research because there were relatively few and brief actions observed (e.g., checking to do -lists, keeping a research diary, thinking of a time-effective solution to a task) related to this activity.

4 RESULTS

All historians used digital documents (digital primary and secondary sources) in their work. Some of the historians also used digital research methods. Because many of the historians were currently working with multiple research projects the shadowing data included work tasks from different projects and project stages. Overall, five task process types were identified from the shadowing data (Table 4).

The task process types were partially overlapping. For example, historians often worked with primary sources throughout the research process.

> [...] This is that sort of history research that doesn't divide clearly into those kinds of stages where you first search the primary sources, then you get to know them, sit down and start writing. Instead, you work with the primary sources all the way. (P1, interview)

Table 4: Task process types according to activities in TBII framework

Searching and selecting information items	Working with information items	Synthesizing and reporting
(i) Searching secondary sources	(ii) Reading and making notes (iii) Collecting and processing data (iv) Analyzing	(v) Writing

The search and selection of primary sources were not studied in this research because historians had already collected them for their studies or they knew where to refind them if needed. Therefore, the first (i) task process type in Table 4 concerned only secondary sources, such as books and articles. The task process types three (iii) and four (iv) concerned mainly primary sources. Reading (ii) and writing (v) included interaction with both primary and secondary sources.

4.1 Searching and Selecting Information Items

Historians searched for secondary sources (e.g. scientific articles) using information retrieval systems (e.g. Ebsco, JSTOR, Google Scholar and Finna, which is a Finnish search portal). The goal for searching secondary sources was to support the writing process. Sometimes, at the early stages of the writing process, the information need was vague. Historian P4 said that while searching new information the goal was also finding better focus for the article.

> [...] it could be beneficial to this work [writing an article] to do kind of wider searches [...] that in a certain way you also try to find focus for the work. (P4, shadowing)

Historian P5 did complementary literature searches for the current writing task, but was not satisfied with the search results. P5 hoped for more options for expressing ones' information needs by, e.g., narrowing down the search to the domain of history or to a certain historical era.

> It feels like that if the [historical era] is in the headline of a book or an article, then one might be able to find [relevant books or articles] with a bit of luck. [...] one old [library search portal] had it like as an index term, like history in general or a certain [century]. It would help finding. (P5, shadowing)

In general, historians felt that following leads was a good way to find secondary sources. For historian P3 following citations was maybe even more important search strategy than using information retrieval systems.

> I do not remember the last time I searched for some library database [...] at least compared to that I just read what other people are referring to. [...] Then the question is how the newest literature comes to my attention. Maybe it is more like those email lists and Facebook [...]. One just sort of intuitively picks what is relevant. (P3, interview)

Historians found secondary sources also in conversations with other researchers and by attending conferences and seminars. In addition, historians browsed sometimes books in libraries. Historian P4 mentioned keeping an eye on secondary sources also for future needs and for personal collections.

During shadowing sessions, selecting information items happened in iterative circles. As participants searched secondary sources, their understanding of the literature improved which helped them identify relevant secondary sources. For example, while using Google Scholar, historian P4 noticed a familiar book and that the author might have other interesting works. Therefore, P4 continued using the author's name as search terms.

> I realized that [...] That [the author] is such that appears in several places and who has written interesting stuff. So I just realized that, aa, I should also take these into considerations. (P4, shadowing)

It remained unclear how many of the items the participants selected during literature searches would end up in their final work. For example, at the end of one shadowing session, P5 assessed some of the items potentially useful.

> Maybe I did find a few, but then they didn't contain very useful things I needed here. At least to that one footnote I didn't get anything more. But otherwise maybe some details that I can add there and compare. (P5, shadowing)

4.2 Working with Information Items

4.2.1 Reading and making notes

At the beginning of a shadowing session, historian P1 stated that the goal for reading an article was to increase basic understanding on a particular topic. For the same reason, P1 also followed citations during reading. Historians followed citations during reading also because in that way they were able to find more secondary sources.

> [the topic of the article] is a bit unfamiliar to me, so I have to check a bit what are the conversations that they are referring to. (P1, shadowing)

> Then of course, if I find some new citations [while reading books], perhaps I will also google and save them for myself. (P5, shadowing)

Historians read both electronic and printed secondary sources. For example, one historian preferred reading electronic sources with reader software, because it enabled to write notes directly into the software and save them later in Word format. Some historians preferred printing interesting articles.

Historians made notes for writing tasks. One historian used footnotes in the note making in such a way that they could be easily moved into drafts. Another historian chose to write notes directly into the draft presentation. Sometimes notes were made with regard to future use. For example, historian P5 anticipated future needs.

> Then I'll have these notes for the rest of my life. Then I won't have to go back reading these books. And then I can use them while I write my own stuff. (P5, shadowing)

Historians used different kinds of tools in note making, such as note-taking software, reference management software or word-processing programs. Some historians chose also to use cloud-based file storage services (e.g. Google Drive, Evernote, Dropbox) because then the notes could be accessed from any computer. Some also felt that electronic notes were easier to store and refind. On the other hand, the traditional note making method with paper and pencil was still in use. For example, one historian wrote notes in a physical notebook, or wrote comments on sticky notes and attached them on book pages and later transcribed them using word-processing program. Organizing notes was also an essential part of reading and note making.

4.2.2 Collecting and processing data

Historians' goal was to collect and process data for analysis. If primary sources existed only in physical form, they had to be digitized first. Some of the historians digitized the data themselves. They had visited in archives and taken pictures of primary sources with digital cameras. In some cases, the primary sources were already in digital form and accessed or downloaded using digital archives.

Digital primary sources sometimes needed further processing in order to be analyzed, e.g., by optical character recognition (OCR) or transcribing digital handwritten documents. In some cases, digital archive provided materials both in digital images and in OCR-format.

Two of the historians constructed databases manually. They first retrieved the digital primary sources either from their own collections or from digital archives. Then they started reading through the digital documents and collected information items into databases that they had created using a spreadsheet or a database management program. They also added new fields into databases when necessary.

> Now I'm going to continue building this database [...] I insert here my original sources. And then I have created here a template, so I can later find the results easier and process them and make comparisons. (P5, shadowing)

Historian P1 was building a database from digital primary sources using programming (e.g. "R"). P1 wrote down the steps needed in performing the task, either to sticky notes or to some digital document. From time to time P1 used Google to solve the problems that arose during the programming and often ended up on Q&A programming websites and found answers quickly.

Historians' goal was to collect data in such a way that the information loss on the relevant data would be minimal. Historian P3 told that it was important to see whether the page numbers were in Roman or Arabic numerals. For another example, historian P5 wrote words to a database in their original language, when it was difficult to come up with a suitable translation. Historians also collected "address information" (e.g. web addresses or headlines of digital primary sources) to locate the origin of data fragments. This information was useful if they needed to go back to the original primary sources.

Some of the historians worked a lot with OCR-texts. Although the OCR-text was very useful, it caused a lot of extra work during data collecting and processing.

> [...] it is worth checking out the actual OCR from the original source, because they often go page by page, and it might be that the article continues to the next page, and if you want the whole OCR from it. (P4, interview)

Sometimes OCR-text contained misidentified characters, and sometimes words or paragraphs had switched places. For example, while building a database, historian P4 had to compare a digital image and its OCR-text with each other and correct the OCR-text. Historian P2 thought that it would be useful if for example editorials or advertisements could be separated from the rest of the data automatically.

Some archives offered primary sources as downloadable data packages. Historians considered this very useful. If data packages were not available, the digital documents had to be retrieved from the archives one by one. This made the use of primary materials difficult. Historians generally used e.g., txt- and csv-files. Sometimes files had to be named in a certain way in order to be used as input to the programs. Historian P2 processed the data for computer-aided analysis programs and at the same time tried to figure out the fastest ways to do the processing.

> Hopefully [the digital primary sources] will be in such a format that they can be analyzed with [computer-aided] programs that I can do the actual analysis. This is like preprocessing. (P2, shadowing)

At least two historians were planning to deposit the data to an open access data archive for future use. One historian wrote a description of the dataset, for example, how data was collected and processed, and what possible problems it contained. Writing the description was considered important, because otherwise it would be hard for other researchers to use the data.

4.2.3 Analyzing

The main goal for analysis was understanding the phenomenon, although historians had more specific goals for analysis relating to their own studies. One way of understanding the phenomenon was asking questions. Historian P4 wrote down questions that arose while interacting with primary sources.

> I'm sort of writing down the questions for myself and wondering if this could relate to this thing or not. It is kind of thinking aloud. [...] sometimes the questions that arise aren't relevant. But sometimes they are the ones that push the research forward. (P4, interview)

Some historians used or planned to use computer-aided programs in analyzing big data by calculating (e.g. word frequencies) or visualizing (e.g. geographical locations in a map). However, the work processes were not always ideal, e.g., an analysis program processed data longer than expected or did not provide the data in preferred format. In addition, poor OCR quality was a problem during the analyzing. One historian considered using alternative data because of the poor OCR quality. Especially when using big data, historians had to evaluate the impact of the noisy OCR on the results and if the analysis is worth doing.

When asked whether they primarily used traditional or computer-aided research methods, historian P5 mentioned using only traditional methods during the research process, although P5 used some digital tools in analysis (e.g. spreadsheet) to make it easier to do comparisons and graphs. Historian P1 described using primarily computer-aided methods because of the vast amount of coding during the research process. Most historians combined traditional and computer-aided methods. Historian P4 described using computer-aided research methods during research process as follows:

> On some parts, computer-aided methods are being used, but the whole process isn't algorithmic so that we could do a bigger analysis just on algorithms and could continue on making a historical analysis, but actually we use them in certain points of the work process. (P4, interview)

Historians worked to interpret the results. When the computer-aided analysis is done and the data is visible on the screen, the actual interpretation is based on the context of the data. Historian P2 described using analysis programs and making interpretations as follows:

> When talking about digital history, the best presentations that I have seen have not been that miraculous in a methodological sense. They have been [...] for example calculating words. But then what has been great, is how the researcher has explained the contexts [...]. (P2, shadowing)

Seeing the original context was important also in the analysis stage. Therefore, historians went back to the primary sources for close reading. One historian explained that it was important to see if a news article was on the first or the last page of a newspaper, or what the other articles told about the era. Close reading was also a way to find quotations. Primary sources were retrieved for close reading from their own collections or from digital archives. In case of primary sources being big data, there was considerably less need for close reading but it was still a fundamental stage in the research process.

4.3 Synthesizing and Reporting

The main goal for writing was to produce a monograph, an article or a conference paper. Historians had sub goals, e.g., writing one chapter to a monograph or find a better focus for an article. Historians' writing was also connected to analyzing.

> I feel like there is still a lot to do in terms of finding the final focus for the article. [...] But on the other hand, the focus cannot be reached until you have gone through these [primary sources] and then read more literature. Now I'm like in this vague state in this regard. (P4, shadowing)

> But what I'm doing right now and what I should be doing is analyzing. In other words, to write, write and write. (P2, interview)

Text style, publication channel and target audience affected on what kind of texts the historians were writing. For example, one historian had a goal to write an international scientific article.

Historian P5 was working on with a current draft in order to shorten it and make it more readable. Historians had also time-related goals, for example, when the texts were supposed to be finished.

Historians writing styles varied. For example, historian P5 had a straightforward writing style, whereas historian P4 processed text little by little towards the final draft. Historian P1 started by drafting a general framework of the text which helped keeping the writing process on the right track.

> [...] I will make a kind of a plan about the whole structure and then I'll start writing, and then of course it changes along the way. (P1, interview)

In the case of two historians (P2 and P4), the writing of the first version of a text seemed similar. Historian P2 described the writing process as follows:

> [...] you write the first version, look all the notes that you have related to the topic from the notebooks and other notes. And maybe the preliminary results. And you put them all to the same Word-file. And then you check what you have. And then you start arranging what things are related to each other. And when you have written the first version, it's useful to take comments. (P2, interview)

Similarly, P4 combined different texts into an article draft and added citations from a reference management program. P4 told that, at first, the text file grows enormous but eventually the text narrows down as the focus of the text clarifies.

Actions related to writing were also locating the information needed for writing and using writing-support tools. Historians searched for information (e.g. notes, secondary sources, primary sources) from their own collections by browsing the file structures on their computers or using computers' own search fields. Historians made searches also from individual documents' text content. They searched information from reference management software, note-taking software and from library databases. For example, historian P5 used a note-taking software as a sort of a road map in order to locate the right document from personal collections.

> [...] I have rarely put all my notes from the sources to [the note-taking software]. I have the longer versions of the notes in different files, but eventually [the note-taking software] is the help finding the right Word document. (P5, interview)

While processing big text files, it was important for one historian to be able to move quickly to a specific part of the text. Historian P4 made use of the headlining of the Microsoft Word text processing program.

> [...] with the help of these [headlines] it is sort of easier to go from a part of the text to another when you are moving the text blocks into their right places. (P4, shadowing)

Reference management was an integral part of the writing process for historians. Some historians used reference management programs and some historians also maintained notes on the things they had not written yet on their texts. They updated these notes during the writing for example by putting a check mark next to the note they had already added.

4.4 Summary of Results

Altogether, we identified five task process types that were included in the following activities in the TBII model: searching and selecting information items, working with information items, and synthesizing and reporting. Table 5 shows the TBII activities on the left column, and the task process types with related goals and actions are on the right.

Table 5: Goals and actions in different task process types

TBII activity		Task process type
SEARCHING AND SELECTING INFORMATION ITEMS		SEARCHING SECONDARY SOURCES
	Goals:	Acquire secondary sources (e.g. books and articles)
		Gaining a better focus for a writing task
	Actions:	Using information retrieval systems
		Following citations
		Having conversations with colleagues
		Browsing library books
		Keeping an eye on interesting literature
WORKING WITH INFORMATION ITEMS		READING AND MAKING NOTES
	Goals:	Learning (e.g. improving the basic understanding of the current topic)
		Making notes for future use
	Actions:	Reading
		Following citations
		Making notes
		Organizing notes and citations
		COLLECTING AND PROCESSING DATA
	Goals:	Collecting and processing data for analysis
		Depositing data to an open access archive
	Actions:	Digitizing primary sources
		Building databases
		Preparing data for analysis
		Writing a description of a dataset
		ANALYSING
	Goals:	Understanding phenomenon (e.g. describing it, comparing, detecting similarities and differences)
	Actions:	Writing down questions
		Using analysis programs
		Interpreting data from databases or from results obtained using analysis programs
		Close reading of digital primary sources
SYNTHESIZING AND REPORTING		WRITING
	Goals:	Finishing a writing work (main goal)
		Finding a focus for an article
		Writing for certain audience and forum
		Scheduling the writing process
	Actions:	Writing and processing text
		Locating information items for writing
		Using tools to support writing

5 DISCUSSION

In this research, we used TBII model [20] as a framework for task process types. We studied information interaction of historians with the focus on the use of digital primary sources. Further, we examined task goals and actions during the real-life task processes by interviewing and shadowing the participants.

The task process types are similar to the scholarly primitives in [32]. The action types during the task process type Searching secondary sources corroborate the findings in previous studies [11], although many of them concentrated on finding primary sources, not necessarily their use [1, 9, 31].

In case of the secondary sources, we found that some historians felt that following citations was a better way of finding them than using information retrieval systems. Citations provide context to the research and help finding information efficiently. This is similar to Bates' *footnote chasing* and *citation searching* [2]. This action was also important during reading and making notes. Therefore, it should be as smooth as possible. Links across information items is already an existing feature of exploratory search functionalities in some digital libraries [17]. However, the links should cover also different types of information allowing citation following from primary to secondary sources. This means integration of heterogeneous information resources [22]. In the future, time spent reading in digital environments will increase and therefore it requires more attention from system designers [15].

Whereas following citations was a principal action in searching secondary sources, historians also considered IR systems useful. In our study, IR systems were used to find a better focus for a writing task. This is an example of an exploratory search, where the goal is about learning rather than fact-finding [23]. However, the existing IR interfaces show results in lists and do not adequately support exploration. Systems helping to understand connections between information items, e.g., by topical exploration as suggested by [29], may better support this action. However, this support should also be expanded across varying types of sources.

It became evident that the information needs in search tasks are more versatile and dynamic than the systems expect them to be. For example, one historian searched literature to support the writing process. While the main goal of finding useful secondary sources remained the same, there were changes in the sub goals during the task. In some points, literature was searched with a sharp focus to find a helpful reference, and occasionally, the aim was to find literature more generally. We did not study this in detail because our focus was broader and its study requires more focused research setting. However, the changes in sub goals described above are similar to shifts of interactive intentions presented by Xie [34]. Historians lack support from IR interfaces in expressing their information needs. Huurdeman [19] suggested that at the beginning of a writing process people need low-level support such as input and control features, e.g., word clouds. Yet we found that even the simplest input or control features were missing. For example, one historian noted that some IR interfaces lacked possibilities to narrow down the search to the sub-field of history or to a specific historical era.

Further, we found that motivations in accessing the information resources were depended on the task process type. In case of the primary sources, historians preferred to download data packages when collecting and processing data. By downloading bulks of data, they saved time instead of downloading items one by one. On the other hand, in the analysis phase they wanted to examine individual documents in detail to confirm the context of the data, and retrieved the documents for close reading. These kinds of different uses of information items should be designed into digital archives and tools to help the historians work tasks.

Historians wanted to save time during collecting and processing data because of time consuming analyzing and writing phase. As Given and Willson [18] noted, data preparation phase is often overlooked when talking about research practices of digital humanities researchers. Because of its time-consuming nature, instead of just providing digital primary sources to be clicked and opened one by one, the data should be accessible also as data packages and in different formats.

Similar to Given and Willson's [18] study, we discovered that historians used different kinds of tools to support their writing, e.g, note-taking or reference management software. In addition, we noticed that writing was a part of analyzing, a way of making connections and developing new ideas. Accordingly, Brockman et al. [6] found humanities scholars' writing as a uniting activity for many other activities e.g., reading and studying primary sources.

Considering the limitations of this study, the presence of the researcher may have affected how the historians worked during the shadowing, e.g., they may have selected simpler and more focused task and not all possible task process types are included. Furthermore, the shadowing was limited to situations where the historians were working alone at their computers. However, it became evident that they worked in co-operation with other researchers. Further historians conducted self-chosen real tasks during the shadowing. Although we studied few historians' performance and the results may not be generalizable to larger population, we believe that observing real world situations give rich view on information interactions that cannot be captured by any other means.

6 CONCLUSION

The purpose of this research was to find out what is historians' information interaction like in digital environments. As a conclusion, we argue that historians need better support for expressing their information needs in information retrieval systems. Furthermore, the IR systems need features that support exploratory searching. The task processes have an effect on how the digital tools are being used. This should be noted when designing digital tools for historians. Further, data processing is a time-consuming task, which could be supported better with automated tools and digital archive design.

ACKNOWLEDGMENTS

This research was supported by the Academy of Finland grant number 310278.

REFERENCES

[1] I. G. Anderson. 2004. Are you being served? Historians and the search for primary sources. Archivaria, 58(Fall 2004), 81-129.

[2] M. J. Bates. 1990. Where should the person stop and the information search interface start? Information Processing & Management, 26(5), 575-591.

[3] M. J. Bates, D. N. Wilde and S. Siegfried. 1993. An analysis of search terminology used by humanities scholars: The Getty Online Searching Project Report Number 1. The Library Quarterly, 63(1), 1-39.

[4] A. Blandford and S. Attfield. 2010. Interacting with information. Morgan & Claypool, San Rafael.

[5] C. L. Borgman. 2007. Scholarship in the digital age: information, infrastructure, and the Internet. MIT Press, Cambridge, Mass.

[6] W. S. Brockman, L. Neumann, C. L. Palmer and T. J. Tidline. 2001. Scholarly work in the humanities and the evolving information environment. Digital Library Federation. Council on Library and Information Resources. Washington, D.C. Retrieved from https://www.clir.org/pubs/reports/pub104/.

[7] A. Brundage. 2017. Going to the sources: A guide to historical research and writing. (6th ed.). John Wiley & Sons, Incorporated, Hoboken, NJ.

[8] K. Byström and P. Hansen. 2005. Conceptual framework for tasks in information studies. Journal of the American Society for Information Science and Technology, 56(10), 1050-1061. DOI: 10.1002/asi.20197.

[9] A. Chassanoff. 2013. Historians and the use of primary source materials in the digital age. The American Archivist, 76(2), 458-480. DOI: //doi.org/10.17723/aarc.76.2.lh76217m2m376n28.

[10] J. Cullen. 2017. Essaying the past: How to read, write, and think about history. (3rd ed.). John Wiley & Sons, Incorporated, Chichester, UK; Hoboken, NJ.

[11] M. S. Dalton and L. Charnigo. 2004. Historians and their information sources. College & Research Libraries, 65(5), 400-425. DOI: 10.5860/crl.65.5.400.

[12] W. M. Duff and C. A. Johnson. 2002. Accidentally found on purpose: Information-seeking behavior of historians in archives. The Library Quarterly, 72(4), 472-496. DOI: 10.1086/lq.72.4.40039793.

[13] D. Ellis. 1993. Modeling the information-seeking patterns of academic researchers: A grounded theory approach. The Library Quarterly, 63(4), 469-486. DOI: 10.1086/602622.

[14] A. T. Erickson. 2013. Historical research and the problem of categories: reflections on 10,000 digital note cards. In K. Nawrotzki and J. Dougherty (Eds). *Writing history in the digital age.* University of Michigan Press, Ann Arbor, MI. DOI: //dx.doi.org/10.3998/dh.12230987.0001.001.

[15] L. Freund, R. Kopak and H. O'Brien. 2016. The effects of textual environment on reading comprehension: Implications for searching as learning. Journal of Information Science, 42(1), 79-93. DOI: 10.1177/0165551515614472

[16] L. Freund and E. G. Toms. 2016. Interacting with archival finding aids. Journal of the Association for Information Science and Technology, 67(4), 994-1008. DOI: 10.1002/asi.23436.

[17] N. Fuhr, C. Klas, A. Schaefer and P. Mutschke. 2002. Daffodil: An integrated desktop for supporting high-level search activities in federated digital libraries. In M. Agosti and C. Thanos (Eds). *Research and Advanced Technology for Digital Libraries.* (6th European Conference, ECDL 2002, Rome, Italy, September 16–18, 2002). Springer, Berlin, Heidelberg, 597-612.

[18] L. M. Given and R. Willson. 2018. Information technology and the humanities scholar: Documenting digital research practices. Journal of the Association for Information Science and Technology, 69(6), 807-819. DOI: 10.1002/asi.24008.

[19] H. C. Huurdeman. 2018. Supporting the complex dynamics of the information seeking process. Ph.D. Dissertation. University of Amsterdam, The Netherlands. Retrieved from http://hdl.handle.net/11245.1/1e3bf31a-0833-4ead-a00c-4cb1399d0216.

[20] K. Järvelin, P. Vakkari, P. Arvola, F. Baskaya, A. Järvelin, J. Kekäläinen, H. Keskustalo, S. Kumpulainen, M. Saastamoinen, R. Savolainen and E. Sormunen. 2015. Task-based information interaction evaluation: The viewpoint of program theory. ACM Transactions on Information Systems, 33, 1, Article 3 (March 2015), 30 pages. DOI: //dx.doi.org/10.1145/2699660.

[21] C. C. Kuhlthau. 1993. A principle of uncertainty for information seeking. Journal of Documentation, 49(4), 339-355. DOI: //doi.org/10.1108/eb026918.

[22] S. Kumpulainen and K. Järvelin. 2010. Information interaction in molecular medicine: integrated use of multiple channels. In N. Belkin & al. (Eds.), Proceedings of the Information Interaction in Context conference (IIiX 2010), New Brunswick, NJ, August 2010. ACM, New York, NY, USA (pp. 95-104.) DOI: 10.1145/1840784.1840800.

[23] G. Marchionini. 2006. Exploratory search: From finding to understanding. Communications of the ACM, 49(4), 41-46. DOI: 10.1145/1121949.1121979.

[24] K. Martin and A. Quan-Haase. 2013. Are e-books replacing print books? Tradition, serendipity, and opportunity in the adoption and use of e-books for historical research and teaching. Journal of the American Society for Information Science and Technology, 64(5), 1016-1028. DOI: 10.1002/asi.22801.

[25] K. Martin and A. Quan-Haase. 2016. The role of agency in historians' experiences of serendipity in physical and digital information environments. Journal of Documentation, 72(6), 1008-1026. DOI: 10.1108/JD-11-2015-0144.

[26] K. Martin and A. Quan-Haase. 2017. "A process of controlled serendipity": An exploratory study of historians' and digital historians' experiences of serendipity in digital environments. In S. Erdelez & N. K. Agarwal (Eds.), Proceedings of the Association for Information Science and Technology (pp. 289–297.) Hoboken, NJ: Wiley. DOI: 10.1002/pra2.2017.14505401032.

[27] S. McDonald. 2005. Studying actions in context: a qualitative shadowing method for organizational research. Qualitative research, 5(4), 455-473. DOI: 10.1177/1468794105056923.

[28] S. McDonald and B. Simpson. 2014. Shadowing research in organizations: the methodological debates. Qualitative Research in Organizations and Management: An International Journal, 9(1), 3-20. DOI: 10.1108/QROM-02-2014-1204.

[29] T. Ruotsalo, G. Jacucci, P. Myllymäki and S. Kaski. 2015. Interactive intent modeling: Information discovery beyond search. Communications of the ACM, 58(1), 86-92. DOI: 10.1145/2656334.

[30] J. Rutner and R. C. Schonfeld. 2012. Supporting the changing research practices of historians. Final Report from ITHAKA S+R. DOI: //doi.org/10.18665/sr.22532.

[31] H. R. Tibbo. 2003. Primarily history in America: How U.S. historians search for primary materials at the dawn of the digital age. The American Archivist, 66(Spring/Summer 2003), 9-50.

[32] J. Unsworth. 2000. Scholarly primitives: What methods do humanities researchers have in common, and how might our tools reflect this. *Symposium on Humanities Computing: Formal Methods, Experimental Practice.* (King's College, London, May 13, 2000).

[33] R. Vuorikari, Y. Punie, S. Carretero Gomez and G. Van den Brande. 2016. DigComp 2.0: The Digital Competence Framework for Citizens. Update Phase 1: The Conceptual Reference Model. Luxembourg Publication Office of the European Union. EUR 27948 EN. DOI: 10.2791/11517. Retrieved from https://publications.europa.eu/en/publication-detail/-/publication/bc52328b-294e-11e6-b616-01aa75ed71a1/language-en#.

[34] H. Xie. 2000. Shifts of interactive intentions and information-seeking strategies in interactive information retrieval. Journal of The American Society for Information Science, 51(9), 841-857.

Take Me Out: Space and Place in Library Interactions

George Buchanan†
Melbourne iSchool
University of Melbourne
Melbourne, Australia
george.buchanan@unimelb.edu.au

Dana McKay
Melbourne iSchool
University of Melbourne
Melbourne, Australia
danamckay@gmail.com

Stephann Makri
Centre for HCI Design
City, University of London
London, United Kingdom
stephann@city.ac.uk

ABSTRACT

Information interactions are strongly affected by the place where they occur. Specific locations are often associated with searches on particular topics, and individual users perform different tasks in habituated places. A classic example of habituated space is the commuter who regularly reads the news on the train. This paper investigates these associations through four user studies that examine different uses of place in information interaction. Through this, we reveal the ways in which the location of information interactions makes them effective or ineffective. This extends our interpretation of the role of place in information interaction beyond established foci such as location-based search.

CCS CONCEPTS

• Human-centered computing~Empirical studies in HCI
• Human-centered computing~Ubiquitous and mobile computing theory, concepts and paradigms

KEYWORDS

Digital libraries, space and place, information interaction.

ACM Reference format:
George Buchanan, Dana McKay and Stephann Makri. 2019. Take Me Out: Space and Place in Library Interactions. In *Proceedings of ACM Conference on Human Information Interaction and Retrieval (CHIIR'19). March 10–14, 2019, Glasgow, Scotland UK.* ACM, New York, NY, USA, 9 pages. https://doi.org/10.1145/3295750.3298935

1 Introduction

Information users' current location often influences their goals and behaviour when interacting with information. At a museum, for example, users often will search online for ideas inspired by the artefacts in front of them. However, location can have more subtle effects, such as a user searching for information on a hobby while having their morning coffee. For the average person, that coffee shop will have no particular association with crochet, but for the person who regularly reads up about their hobby, there will be.

Location and place are often used interchangeably, but in human-computer interaction, there is a conceptual distinction between space and place [1]. Space is 'real-world' three-dimensional space, and its arrangement and shape can inhibit or enable behaviours. Place, on the other hand, is a concept drawn from architecture: the expected role and function of a particular location. Adapting the well-known adage, a house is just a space, but a home is one's own place.

Location-based search is a well-established tool in information retrieval. Researchers have abstracted beyond specifics of location such as longitude and latitude. A search for a restaurant can draw from GPS data to name the current location, or calculate distance. Previous activity in a location can aggregate to reveal something of its meaning and associations with the searches done there. Both named and GPS locations can also be semantically mapped to particular meanings through a variety of methods of reasoning.

However, there are gaps between the IR use of location and the HCI understanding of place. In IR 'place' is sometimes used to describe semantic associations with a location [2] In this case, place influences the search algorithm, and what material it reports to the user. Interaction designers consider place not only as an influence on the best outcome of a task, but as adjusting the structure of the task, or even the choice of task to do. In information interaction, both approaches have to be considered.

Libraries are long-established as a place for discovering and working with information. They are typically physical, but for the last twenty years have also existed in digital form. The conception of place from architecture has been applied to libraries to understand social uses of library buildings [3]. However, this sheds little light on how information work is done.

Digital content has and is transforming the use of libraries—e.g. nearly all journal articles are accessed online. Libraries are also investing heavily in digital content; the proportion of books in UK libraries in digital form has increased from 20 to 30 percent since 2014; in Australia over 90% of university library book holdings are now ebooks. There is considerable ignorance of and resistance to the use of digital resources though, some of which is related to the physical realities of the library. Digital books are difficult to browse, and invisible to the 50% of information seekers who use shelf-browsing as part of their information seeking. Digital content is convenient however, and where information seekers do access it, the library expands both in space and time.

ACM ISBN 978-1-4503-6025-8/19/03 ... $15.00
https://doi.org/10.1145/3295750.3298935

This paper reflects on four studies that have sought to use the physical space of the library in combination with mobile devices to support users' interactions with information. Libraries are still well-used in universities as places of study, and the physical space is still strongly influenced by print holdings. Our studies span a seven-year period, and highlight a range of issues of space and place in libraries. The paper proceeds as follows: first we recap related literature from interaction design, library science, information retrieval and information interaction; we summarise four studies before describing them in chronological order; then, we synthesise the findings of the four studies, and contrast our insights with the existing literature. Finally, we conclude with a summary of our contribution and a consideration of future work.

2 Background

Space and place have long interactions with HCI, libraries, information interaction and information retrieval. This section discusses space and place in each domain, drawing first on HCI.

2.1 Space and Place in Interaction Design

Paul Dourish has been the main proponent of the understanding of place and space in interaction. In 1996, Harrison and Dourish introduced the concepts in the context of HCI [1]. Ten years later, Dourish reflected on the earlier paper [4], specifically addressing the need to reconsider the concepts after the emergence of mobile computing. In particular, Dourish then argued 'against the simple dualism' that he felt had emerged in the use of the two terms—that place often was constructed from the practiced use of particular space, and that space was also often created to make a place for particular uses, saying 'Place and space are both products of social practice, albeit different systems of practice'.

Dourish noted the temptation and potential value of typologies in combining space and place, particularly citing [5]. His main concern was that this stemmed from a 'separation of space and place into two different domains'.

Despite Dourish's concerns about the terms he helped introduce, others have adopted or extended the approach. Recently, for example, the theory of proxemics has been used to complement the space/place concept [6].

2.2 Place and Space in the Library

One of the fundamental features of the library is its location as a place in the shared social consciousness. However, what a library 'means' has moved over time.

The 'Carnegie model' of libraries (see [7]) now frames what most people experience as the norm of libraries. Open-stack shelving means that readers can physically browse at least the most active parts of the library's holding. This proved a powerful improvement over older closed-stack libraries, where a reader had to consult card indexes and request a known item.

This model is badly disrupted by digital technologies. In principle, readers of a university library can take out ebooks at any time in any location: everywhere is now an 'open-stack'. While library users praise this convenience [8; 9], ebook uptake is slow and reluctant [10]. The reasons readers give for not using ebooks include intrusive digital rights management, bad support for annotation, poor reading experience, lack of serendipitous discovery when using online materials and an overall preference for print [8; 9; 11-13]. These limitations mean that the 'online place' of the digital library does not serve its users as well as the physical counterpart; in turn interactions with it will look very different than physical interactions.

The key value of open-stack browsing was identified as early as 1969, when Levine referred to shelf browsing as a 'pleasurable process of exploration' [14]. Later studies have confirmed shelf browsing as a valuable activity, painting the library stacks as sources of information and inspiration [9; 15-17]. The shelves support discovery so well, in fact, that they have been described as a 'browsing engine' [18].

Academics value libraries as places to work without distraction, even going so far in one case as to refer to them as 'sacred' [10; 17]. Student use of libraries also places a heavy emphasis on quiet, solo study [19; 20]. This view of libraries may seem anachronistic, but it is recently supported (2017) by Warwick who notes that elements of the physical library experience are 'wonderous': e.g. 'an intense sense of fascination and attraction that strikes a visitor when they walk through the door to the actual resource'. (p. 11) [21]. Library spaces are well designed to support such solo activities.

In contrast to the social ideal of libraries as places of quiet, solo reflection and individual serendipitous discovery, modern academic libraries host significant group and social activity [20; 22]. This activity is sometimes purely academic, sometimes purely social, and sometimes a mix of the two [23]. It is a clear expectation, though, particularly among students, that the library should support group work, and their space should offer a distinction between group and solo use [20; 23; 24]. This is not the only tension between the library as place—the concept of the library—and the library as space. A recent study notes the two in direct conflict, with the silence and scholarliness of the place interfering with the ability to browse, and so limiting the functionality of the space [25].

What is noticeably absent from all these discussions of library space and place, though, is a consideration of online resources or materials. While there has been some argument for the consideration of online resources as part of both library space and place (e.g. [26; 27]), digital resources are notable for the absence of any hint of their existence in the physical space of the vast majority of libraries.

2.3 Place and Space in Information Retrieval

As noted in the introduction, space and place have in various ways been considered in information retrieval. Some recent work on mobile IR has started to fuse elements of the understanding of place in HCI with traditional concerns IR. Karen Church's recent work [28], includes an analysis of both where mobile information work, particularly searches, occurred and the social context in which they occurred. This revealed that search is often done, for example, at home in the presence of family, and individuals have established routines. While this has not yet led to novel algorithms, the fusion of social, personal, chronological and location information in that analysis is very close to HCI's understanding of place, rather than traditional location-based IR.

Other researchers have established that geographical locations can particularly trigger searches based on the real-world role of those places. For example, museums often provoke incidental searches based on their artefacts [29].

2.4 Place and Space in Information Interaction

There have been some—albeit limited—attempts to blend physical and digital information spaces in libraries. Kleiner et al's Blended Shelf [18] offers a virtual library shelf browsing experience which aims to augment physical shelf browsing. Blended Shelf incorporates real-world attributes of books, such as size and availability, but allows users to dynamically sort items on the shelf by a range of attributes e.g. title or subject. Martin et al [30] present a conceptual app design STAK (Serendipitous Tool for Augmenting Knowledge). The app aims to allow users to access digital material to complement what they see on the library shelves. Based on user modelling, STAK infers user interest by tracking when user linger in a particular location, then uses user modelling to recommend nearby items of interest.

Blended spaces have the potential to both leverage libraries' investments in online resources and improve library user experience. Even so, blending physical and digital spaces should be approached with caution, Warwick [21] notes the 'danger of technocratic arrogance if we assume everything can be modelled digitally and thus improved' (p. 11). She further argues that a purely 'digital library' seems a misguided goal. Rather than reproduce a physical library in digital form, designers should aim to create useful digital resources that can be used in physical libraries. This paper reports on a number of attempts to do exactly that, further it notes some commonalities in what they reveal not just about space and place in the library, but about how mobile services in particular can improve them.

2.5 Summary

We have examined the ways in which space and place have been considered in interaction design. While the concepts are well-cited and used in interaction design overall, they have received surprisingly little consideration in information interaction. Location- and context aware systems address some of the same concerns, but they typically avoid the physical internal architecture associated with spaces, and the social construction of places. Typical location- and context-aware information finding tools align, in most cases, with Harrison and Dourish's conception of space—i.e. a physical location. The social construction of place is, however, more complex than simple geography.

In the context of libraries, there are many ways in which space and place are connected. This almost exactly mirrors the caution urged for by Dourish not to split the two as a duality. At the same time, this co-location of the two in traditional libraries allows us to understand the two as disparate lenses to understand a user's interaction with the space, a mobile device or mobile service.

The main body of this paper uses this approach, taking four studies of prototype mobile systems that are located in library spaces. Each is intended to enhance the user's engagement with library holdings—in some cases print books, in others online journals. Some have been reported elsewhere, focusing on the design and development processes. Here we focus on how each system uses physical space, and then in turn on how place influences the type and level of benefit each mobile app provides. Finally, we discuss how the responses to each prototype can inform how we consider place in the context of mobile interaction.

3 Programme of Research

We report four studies of different prototype systems, each of which uses space to improve the user experience of libraries.

The first study used observations and interviews in university libraries to gather requirements for a location- and context-aware mobile system. This system used a user's location within the library (space) and the context of the books on their desks (information place) to focus and filter catalogue search. This study—and the observations and interviews that were its cornerstone—informed the rest of the program of research.

The second study aimed to address low awareness of, and difficulties in accessing, online databases amongst library users. This system used the large displays in libraries as a means of transmitting information, but relied on users' mobile phones to allow them to capture the information and take it with them.

The third study built on the first two—adjusting the focus on finding ebooks of potential interest rather than whole collections. This used print books of interest as a proxy for physical space, resulting in an intriguing divergence of space and place.

Finally, we used a digital app space to address one of the problems of library space: books on a similar topic shelved at a geographic distance due to the vagaries of classification schemes.

4 Study 1: Using Space to Focus Search

Our first study sought to use the library space as a clue to the reader's topical interests. The primary approach was to filter by topic the content of the library's online catalogue. A search done on 'resilience' would produce different results for users in the psychology and engineering sections. The two disciplines use the same term in sharply differing ways, and filtering avoided distracting 'false positive' matches. We were thus using space as place to refine the user's interaction with the library catalogue.

4.1 Design

The design focussed on the use of laptops and smartphones. The location sensing in the building was done using Bluetooth beacons, and the reader's location was resolved to a physical space and topical place (e.g. 2nd floor, west wing, history section).

After initial pilot work the design was refined for testing. Full details are available in [31]. The final functions included the following changes to the library catalogue interface: 1) restricting search results to topics near the user's location; 2) highlighting online databases on the topics near the user's location(e.g. the ACM library in computer science, or Early English Books online in English Literature) by a panel to the right of the usual search display; 3) the ability to scan a book's RFID tag to trigger a search on the book's topic in the library catalogue.

The pilot study provided insights into the use of space—most users of the library adopted particular locations in the building, and were repeatedly seen at the same location on different days. The books piled on a reader's desk (often two or more in total) suggested their task, and those who worked remotely from the shelves for their topic more often had larger numbers of books—quite possibly to save repeated journeys across the library [31]. Interviews revealed that those working away from their topic location did so for privacy or silence—e.g. one graduate student said 'I really need somewhere quiet I can concentrate in', while a faculty member said 'it's good to be away from where people expect to find me—I don't get interrupted'.

The design drew on these observations, providing RFID scanning to allow the user to prime the topic of interest from the books on their desk, and their location to identify online content and focus their search results. As users in most cases used space near their area of interest, suggesting related material would focus their search results on books that would more likely be useful.

4.2 User Study

We recruited ten participants who used the prototype in situ, using a provided laptop computer. The participants completed chosen tasks that they chose themselves in advance of the session. Subjective feedback favoured specific features: using a single book to trigger a search was preferred, due to a greater sense of control. Knowledge of the library space or place led to users explicitly adjusting their plans: e.g. one participant said of a book 'Oh, that's not on this floor—it's downstairs. It may be useful but I'd have to be sure to take the trip'. This was typical of the seven participants who looked at a book's topic headings, six of whom rejected a book due to its topic seeming too marginal, or the distance to it being too great.

Eight participants explored the related online resources lists, and all of those found one or more new sources of information that they rated 'useful' or 'very useful'. One comment was that 'I wouldn't need this every time, but I'm finding stuff that I'm sure I've missed for years'. As this adjustment was a simple panel on their library search screen, it suggests that users were able to discern relatively minor adjustments to a familiar digital place.

4.3 Summary

This study showed that most users followed the library's design of place by using the areas where the books on their topic resided. A minority chose a distant writing location, and used a bigger pile of books to save time fetching books. The content of the reader's desk was a more reliable indication of their interests than their physical location. Users could adopt their own regular 'place' for study away from their topic shelves, and would repeatedly be seen at the same location, suggesting a personally rehearsed combination of space and place. The study directly informed two following studies, that each focussed on different elements of the initial prototype.

5 Study 2: Promoting Online Collections

Our second study deployed a public electronic display in a library, to promote the availability of online databases (primarily, but not exclusively, of journals) to the library's readers. It is a common problem in libraries that electronic holdings are used much less than expected. Users are unaware of the range of material available, and electronic databases are invisible in the main library catalogue.

This design was independent of the first study. In concert with the subject librarians at a research-focussed London university, we identified a number of under-used online databases that were understood to be of potential value to students. An initial survey of 108 library users, revealed that only 19 (18%) had any awareness of the university's main electronic holdings. As the university was in the process of reorienting the physical space away from library books and toward study space due to overwhelming demand, this issue was of immediate concern. Printed posters promoting the material appeared to have little effect, based on informal feedback from library staff, which was confirmed by our survey results.

Library staff were keen to use QR codes to provide URLs. However, our survey also revealed that then (2012), users often did not have QR reader software on their phone (68/108) and of those that did, most reported not using it regularly (26/40) and finding the experience unrewarding (31/40). This discounted the likelihood of a QR-based approach proving helpful.

There were two recently-installed large displays that carouselled through several screens about the library. Each screen appeared for 12 seconds, and there was no way of capturing the screen, other than photographing it. We initially considered the snap-and-grab approach of Maunder et al [32]. However, that is based on Bluetooth and at the time users often had Bluetooth turned off to save battery, and the standard was unreliable. The approach of capturing the content from a large display appeared to have promise, as users did notice the displays, and over two thirds (73/108) reported seeing some material of interest, but even they had problems in following it up.

Following the survey, two prototypes were constructed using a participatory design method with a panel of two library staff and six students. A pilot-study with ten users tested both designs, and that evaluation strongly favoured one, that we now describe.

5.1 Design

The host library provided subject lists for 14 different domains (incl. business studies, music, computer science and electrical engineering). Each listed up to ten online sources, including ebook collections and, more commonly, journal databases.

The app, when used near the library's two electronic displays, allowed the user to 'capture' the current subject (e.g. electronic engineering) on display. This would open a webpage with links to the relevant subject materials (e.g. the IEEE digital library) available through the library. The links would only required the student's login to get full-text access. The subject web page would appear if the app was opened outside the library. We simply used network time to identify the currently displayed subject, and presumed no 'capture' would occur within the first second of a page's display, without referring in fact to the previous page.

This 'portable' web-page addressed the primary problem that emerged during the design process—that users found even short URLs hard to type in. One design participant had photographed the content of slides from the existing displays, but even that did not directly solve the issue—e.g. 'typing it [a URL] in when the phone keeps blanking is a pain'. The page could also be emailed to the student's university email account, for convenience.

5.2 User Study

The prototype was tested in a three-week trial. There were 113 recorded installations of the app in the first week, followed by a further 72. All but 24 were through a pop-up information stand at the library In total, there were 93 uses of the app's capture feature. We recruited twelve participants who used the app, and conducted a brief diary study, with entry and exit interviews.

The twelve participants included seven female and five male students. Ten were undergraduates, and two graduates (both female). Each participant was asked about the digital resources available for their discipline. Only three were able to name one online resource, though ten reported being aware that there were resources (e.g. P1, 'I...ugh...I know there is stuff, just I'm not sure what there is' and P9 'I know I should have but I'm not sure I have time'. These responses reflected the experience of the library staff. Interviews covered thirty library-related questions, covering borrowing rates, times of use of the library, use of inter-library loans, etc. This was done to gather more information on the participants, while not exposing the main purpose of the study.

In their exit interviews, participants named 23 resources in total, and thirteen could name at least one resource. All had used the app at least once. All but one had used the app within four days of starting the study, and only two used it in the three days before the end of the study. Despite the obvious risk of priming from the app's function, the length of intervening period (on average just over 10 days from the last use), makes it unlikely that participants would have taken care to remember specific details.

However, it was also clear that few participants would have installed the app just to gain this information. To quote P6 'Honest, I'm not sure I'd have bothered. I try not to have too many apps.' The weak maturity of web apps at the time circumscribed the implementation, but now a web-app would be easily made. The current version includes subject-specific library information on electronic holdings which can be texted or emailed to the user.

Another issue was the role of the displays in the library. P4 noted, 'I often ignore them. The content is ... I don't find it useful?' and P6 said 'You pass them, but too often they're just blank or telling you the opening hours, which... well, if you're in there, it's open?!'. This explained the limited number of installations via the displays: users had learned to ignore them. In contrast, direct recruitment produced many more installations. This ignoring of a regular feature of the space is analogous to banner-blindness in web usability [33], where users consistently ignore heading content on web pages, due to it often containing little useful information. While webpages have no physical form, expectations of place can lead to inaction, as well as action.

5.3 Summary

Superficially, this design was effective. Readers captured information on digital library offerings via their mobile phones; and then accessed those holdings outside the library—e.g. at home. The app thus expanded the library place beyond the building. The most interesting finding in terms of space and place, though, is that library users learned to ignore the library's digital displays—an element of space—to the detriment of their uptake of new books and systems, i.e. use of the library as a place. This demonstrates an interesting challenge for libraries as currently physical displays of new books are heavily used as sources of discovery [34; 35].

6 Study 3: From Print Books to Ebooks

This 2017 study addressed the problem that libraries' main textbook holdings are increasingly digital, but seldom visible in the library itself, and use is often low [36].

As noted in Study 2, one approach has been to put up signs that tell users the availability of the electronic holdings, but this has not proven effective in widespread use. We now took a different approach. Rather than highlighting the general availability of ebook collections, we focused the reader's attention on specific ebooks related to a print book they chose. We planned to use location as the key, but this proved impracticable. Instead, we allowed readers to scan barcodes of books of interest, then showed related ebooks.

6.1 Design

The host library provided two complete catalogues: first, their traditional print book holdings, and second, their main ebook collection. Both collections were uploaded into a database and indexed. Where the catalogue data allowed, the electronic form of print holdings was identified, and for electronic holdings, any print copies were noted. However, few books were held in both forms. Almost every book (over 99%), print and electronic, had one or more Dewey Decimal Classification numbers, and these were used to identify related books that shared the same topic.

We did not have access to the full text of either collection, so full-text search could not be used. Words from the book's title were used to find and rank potentially relevant documents. Some books shared no non-stop words with other books in their classification topic. In such exceptional cases a random choice of all documents was made. Normally, a random selection was taken from the top 10 ranked documents. Pilot tests led to showing three sample books to the user, as this fitted on a single screen.

We rejected the use of location within the library in this app for three reasons: 1) it was not practicable to provide the number of Bluetooth beacons needed for the whole library; 2) a low density of hubs meant WiFi could not be used for fine-grained location data; 3) Apple and Google had restricted the ability of apps to use network data to identify a user's location.

Instead, books' ISBN numbers were captured using the phone's camera. The ISBN was validated and then used to identify the (print) book being scanned, and related ebooks were found in the database, before being presented to the reader. Clicking on an ebook would open its online page on the user's web browser.

When a reader scanned a (valid) book, the app queried the database for three best matches for display. The request and the response were logged on the server, with any selection of books by the user. The user's geolocation, if available, was also recorded.

6.2 User Study

We deployed the prototype on the personal mobile phones of seventeen volunteers who agreed to have their usage of the app tracked over two weeks. In addition, participants could indicate if the content suggested to them was useful, partly useful or not useful, and provide brief diary-like commentary after each use.

The study design was approved by the University of Melbourne Human Ethics Approval Group. No personally identifying material was recorded. The cohort contained 7 female, 10 male undergraduate students. Where two or more scans occurred within ten minutes, the scans formed a multi-scan session. Other scans were in single sessions.

6.3 Results

There were 61 logged uses of the app, though the records of 8 were incomplete due to the user dismissing the feedback step. In four of these eight cases, the scan was immediately followed by another scan. We found that 29 (14 pairs, and one set of three) scans occurred as part of a scan session (see above for definition). Thus, there were 15 multiple scan sessions, and 32 single scans.

6.3.1 Location

Nine sessions took place outside of the university. Four took place at the bookshop of another university, one at a large public library, and four at other locations that appear to be domestic. One certainly was, the diary entry simply saying 'scanned at home'. Three other sessions took place at the university bookshop, close by the library. These different sessions included 7 users—so almost half used the app outside the library, which we hadn't foreseen.

Study instructions presupposed location within the library. Without prompting, the app was used in other book-related places. It is likely that had the participants been briefed to use the app more widely, there would been more use outside the library. This shows that even in a brief deployment, users will experiment with a mobile service in locations where similar activities occur.

6.3.2 Feedback

The success of individual recommendations varied. The system made a total of 183 recommendations (three per scan), obtaining quantitative feedback on 58 items. Forty-one were rated useful, eleven partly useful, and six not useful. All but six of these items were clicked on for reading—two of each rating type. The unrated items likely contain a higher proportion of not useful and partly useful ratings. As many choices were necessarily random, this is a credible outcome, when contrasted with the selection rate for search result lists [37; 38].

Two participants, P4 and P9, both scanned the same book (on Python). They saw the same recommendation—an ebook of a Python textbook by another author. They rated the ebook highly, P9 noting 'nice to get an ebook too'. An accounting book was scanned and an alternative ebook resulted in P3 recording 'didn't know we had this—no need to carry it. Took the book too.' These responses suggest that at least three participants ended up using an ebook in addition to a text they borrowed from the library.

Four participants provided feedback that there was a missing feature in the app. To quote P3:'You can't scan a book that isn't there', and P12 noted 'wanted to scan a missing book—used another'. This points out an, in retrospect, obvious problem: absent books cannot be scanned. For context, the university has few books that are held in both digital and print form—so the feature would seldom reveal an immediate digital equivalent.

All but one of the participants reported the app as useful. This was corroborated by usage: while individual matches varied in usefulness, 49 (of 61) scans logged one or more viewed matches. and 47 scans included one or more positively rated matches.

6.4 Summary

This study revealed that even when an app is expected to be grounded in a particular space, users will rather associate it with the place's function, than location. Our users exploited the app in other reading places, not simply the intended location of use.

Engagement with the app's recommendations was good, and resulted in the discovery of new material. As with Study 1, users engaged well with book-focussed recommendations, which contrasted with the lower engagement seen with more abstract collections in Studies 1&2. Where digital places are unfamiliar, users struggle to identify a meaning and purpose to them.

7 Study 4: Connecting distant print books

The final study addresses a limitation of physical space in libraries: two books on the same topic may be shelved at distant locations, due to the vagaries of classification. Savvy readers often exploit the library's organization by browsing books nearby one of known relevance [39]. Separating related texts thus limits the opportunity for serendipitous encounters.

Documents do not have the same constraints online. Ebooks can be classified 'polyhierarchically', with the same book appearing under multiple topics. A greater quantity of related books can then appear together. The presentation of a digital library can be also re-arranged at will, e.g. to highlight recommended material. However, the digital experience has limitations: readers usually scan fewer books, lowering the chance of experiencing serendipitous encounters. We developed an iPad app to bring remote, but related, material into the user's hands.

7.1 Design

The design was of a tablet-based (iPad) application, we needed the larger display space for content. Readers photographed textbook covers, whereupon Amazon recommendations for related books would be used to find, books elsewhere in the library. The app also displayed the Amazon description of the book, its reviews, and its library shelf mark.

A first-cut design prototype was created and tested with six users in a pilot test, and initial usability issues addressed. In the revised prototype, display functions were implemented using inVision, and the book-cover detection replicated by a wizard-of-oz method [40]. While textbook cover identification is a tractable problem, it was outside the projects' research goals.

7.2 User Study

The pilot was followed with a full study involving fourteen students in the library of a research-focussed university in London, UK. Participants were asked to browse a given set of bookshelves, select any book of interest to them, then to make use of the mobile app (to view the book's description, reviews and other recommended books available within the library). These books could be shelved anywhere in the library (i.e. all recommended books in the library were catalogued, including those not on the given set of shelves). After interacting with the prototype, and any movement across the library to examine the other books recommended by it, participants were asked about their experiences of the prototype in a semi-structured interview.

Our interest was in the overall benefit of providing a digitally unified space of related books, where the physical books were spread across the library, of bringing reviews to the shelves to inform and supplement a reader's book choices and of recommending books that may not be proximally located.

7.3 Results

Amazon recommendations influenced the readers' confidence in their book choices, unless there were already strong reasons for examining a book, such as prior experience of the book or strong recommendations by lecturers: e.g. P5 explained 'I will definitely borrow and read this book because obviously people are saying that it's not only a foundational book, but also a great book.' Seven readers rejected one or more recommendations at first glance, four on the basis of the review content being substantially irrelevant, and three on the basis of the content being generally relevant, but lacking key material that they sought.

Participants provided favourable qualitative feedback on books they would otherwise have not encountered (or rejected)—e.g. P3 took a recommended book from a bottom shelf, which they said they would normally not do. (this is a common behaviour, [19; 41]). Others reflected on the limitations of keyword search, explaining that 'I don't think I would find it without this app, because if I'm searching for books on data visualization, but the title of this book doesn't have "data" or other similar keywords' (P5). Thus, the digital place of the catalogue and the physical place of the shelves would both have negated the chances of this information encounter.

Ten participants encountered useful material from at least one recommendation. P10 commented 'I would not have searched for these four books... if I didn't have these suggestions. I would only look at the section based on the shelfmark and look at books around it'. P4, who rejected three of their four recommendations, said of the fourth 'I wasn't expecting that. I wasn't looking for it. It's relevant to what I'm looking for. It was so good and has everything I wanted. .... I'm happy with the content'.

Participants appreciated being shown the location of recommended books. P6 said 'it's giving me location, which is good because I could explore books based on proximity [to each other].'

7.4 Summary

Temporarily using digital space, to harness information not available in the physical space (in this case Amazon reviews and recommendations) successfully encouraged participants to examine books they might not otherwise have looked at. This is likely due to the fact the prototype app shifted the focus back to the physical space, by guiding participants to the recommended or reviewed books on the library shelves. We consider this an example of blending the physical and digital library spaces in a complementary way that may encourage physical library use.

As with our first study, we found that users' decisions to pursue a recommendation was influenced by perceived topic relevance and the distance within the library to fetch a book. However, the presence of the digital place within their interaction was much more successful than with the use of digital collections, as seen in Study 2. Participants leveraged their knowledge of the library as place, helping them make book selection judgments. As the entire interaction with content continued in one place, the library, there was no need to grasp an understanding of a second place, and all interaction was with physical books.

8 Overall Insights

As noted in the introduction, the idea of the library as a rehearsed place that is well understood by users is widely accepted. We've deployed four mobile systems that leverage the library space in different ways. The variable results of our investigations shed some light on the ways in which space and place affect interactions—positively and negatively—dependent on context.

The existence of banner blindness on web pages is well known [33]. We have not encountered previous literature that raises a similar expectation with space. We saw that users learn to ignore content in a space that they frequently use, where the place is repeatedly used for content of little relevance to them.

There were also problems in introducing new collections of digital material—users struggled to connect their general library knowledge of place to digital venues where scope and structure were unclear, adding considerably to their cognitive effort.

These two negative points contrast with the success we have had with book-focussed enhancements—users would use book-focussed apps in reading places beyond the library, and happily adopted book-focussed mobile services. Congruence with the utility of the place, and its content, led to effective interactions.

Similarly, allowing the user to craft a personal signal of place, through the contents of their desk, proved highly effective, particularly as the user controlled this cue.

9 Discussion

Previous researchers have endeavoured to use physical space as a lever to assist in information interaction [18; 31; 42]. These met with mixed results. There were no clear signs across that work of how space or place influenced the success or failure of these systems. This earlier work, however, did not assess the influence of space and place on their effectiveness. Our own research suggests that relative success and failure are not simply ascribed to the physicality of the interaction, or well-established issues in information interaction.

Previous information interaction research has suggested incongruity with place is a barrier to adoption. In [42] users rejected a new library interface as being "gimmicky'—e.g. one saying 'I don't want to play some games' (in the library). Participants suggested that the new interface, which was seen as 'playful' should only be in a children's library. The disjunct between these users' concept of the library as place, and the presentation offered in this app resulted in user rejection.

Those who have argued for the use of space and place in HCI and CSCW have produced guidance on how they can explain the effectiveness of existing designs, and might be leveraged to develop new, effective interactions. However, one major caveat regarding that guidance is that much of it dates to before the mass adoption of mobile technologies (e.g. the classic Harrison and Dourish paper [1] dates from 1996), and even the later revision [4] arrived a year before the release of the first iPhone and the arrival of the mass-market smartphone. That event disrupted much of the experiences with earlier mobile phones, and no major reflection on the concepts of space and place has been offered since. While mobile technologies might seem incongruous with libraries, a number of previous studies have noted their ubiquity in library settings [23; 43; 44]; the sense of appropriate use of mobiles in the library has changed, but it met initial resistance. As with the playful interface that users resisted, the introduction of new technologies is disruptive, and the sense and use of place is defended by library readers [42]. The importance of place-consistency is by far the most relevant concept [1] from early place work.

Brown and Perry emphasised the problems of place. In contrast, we demonstrate the advantages of place-knowledge. Users appropriated a library-focussed tool to use in book-related places in general, and were quickly able to use place-based knowledge to make information about new electronic books and unseen print books. Setting a place-based frame for design is quite likely useful in designing mobile apps, and may indeed explain the relative success of interactive navigation [45], where a little local knowledge may be boosting user performance in ways we don't currently grasp. Likewise, it may be playing a key role in the demand for, and effectiveness of, guidance and explanation on interpreting local landmarks [45; 46]. Local guides are a foundational interest in mobile HCI [47], and it is surprising that we lack research that examines their utility from a place-based perspective.

Libraries represent a specifically organised and structured physical location, but other buildings share similar properties–most directly museums, for example. We would expect our initial insights into how place impacts on usability to recur in such cases, and further work to explore that is certainly needed.

Designers should consider space and place carefully when designing mobile experiences, reflecting on our existing assumptions and preconceptions to design experiences that combine the best of both the physical environment and digital technologies. Just as it is naïve to assume that we should try to digitally recreate aspects of the physical library, and vice-versa, it is also over-simplistic to consider space and place as combined concepts; we should instead unbundle them and consider how to support different combinations of space and place in a particular work or everyday-life context (in this case the library as an effective learning environment). Reflecting on how we can 'add value' by augmenting the physical environment through mobile design is important. We need to engage with design not just for the sake of novelty, but also for the sake of usefulness—and the sort of reflection we encourage hopes to engender the next generation of truly useful mobile tools, in libraries and elsewhere.

10 Conclusions

The library is a well-rehearsed place, with a range of meanings to users. The space is more contested, with study spaces competing for space with books, and silent spaces competing with social spaces. The rehearsed uses of the space—for example browsing the shelves—limit possible uses of the full offerings of the library, both in terms of the limitations of the physical space for presenting polyhierarchical information, and in terms of the massively increasing online offerings of the library.

This paper presented four systems that each leverage the space of the library to afford further interactions with the library as place. Some interventions were more successful than others: e.g. inferring too much about a reader's interest from their location, was not always successful, but examining the information place they had built for themselves was more likely to meet their needs.

Merging the digital with physical spaces was especially valuable to readers. Once the utility of these systems was grasped, they used them to expand the place of the library beyond its walls: we recorded a number of uses of systems outside the library. Equally, supporting the information available at the shelves with digital information about other offerings and recommendations and ratings improved the utility of the space.

Perhaps the most astonishing finding though, was the discovery of physical 'banner blindness' to the digital displays in the library. This (lack of) interaction with physical space revealed a surprising analogue between physical and digital space.

Overall, though, we have demonstrated a number of ways in which digital information interactions can support users of a physical space in expanding the rehearsed place of the library. These interactions afford a number of opportunities for increased access to information, and better information decision making.

There is further scope in information interaction for leveraging space to support place, particularly, we suspect, in GLAM institutions. How best to identify these opportunities and offer interesting and relevant information to meet a user's space and place remains an avenue for future work.

ACKNOWLEDGMENTS

We thank the Joint Information Systems Council and the Australian Research Council each for the support of part of this work, and our various participants for their time and enthusiasm.

REFERENCES

[1] Harrison, S. and Dourish, P., 1996. Re-place-ing space: the roles of place and space in collaborative systems. In (Boston, Massachusetts, USA), ACM, 67-76. DOI= http://doi.org/10.1145/240080.240193.

[2] Jones, C.B., Alani, H., and Tudhope, D., 2001. Geographical Information Retrieval with Ontologies of Place. In *Proc COSIT 01* (Berlin, Heidelberg), Springer, 322-335. DOI= http://doi.org/10.1007/3-540-45424-1_22.

[3] Given, L.M. and Leckie, G.J., 2003. "Sweeping" the library: Mapping the social activity space of the public library. *Lib and Inf Sci Res 25*, 4 (2003/12/01/), 365-385. DOI= http://doi.org/https://doi.org/10.1016/S0740-8188(03)00049-5.

[4] Dourish, P., 2006. Re-space-ing place: "place" and "space" ten years on. In *Proc CSCW 06* (Banff, Alberta, Canada), ACM, 299-308. DOI= http://doi.org/10.1145/1180875.1180921.

[5] Jones, Q., Grandhi, S.A., Whittaker, S., Chivakula, K., and Terveen, L., 2004. Putting systems into place: a qualitative study of design requirements for location-aware community systems. In *Proc CSCW 04* (Chicago, Illinois, USA), ACM, 202-211. DOI= http://doi.org/10.1145/1031607.1031640.

[6] Krogh, P.G., Petersen, M.G., O'hara, K., and Groenbaek, J.E., 2017. Sensitizing Concepts for Socio-spatial Literacy in HCI. In *Proc CHI 17* (Denver, Colorado, USA), ACM, 6449-6460. DOI= http://doi.org/10.1145/3025453.3025756.

[7] Petroski, H., 1999. *The Book on the Bookshelf.* Random House, New York.

[8] Rowlands, I., Nicholas, D., Jamali, H.R., and Huntington, P., 2007. What do faculty and students really think about e-books? *Aslib Proceedings 59*, 6, 489-511. DOI= http://doi.org/10.1108/00012530710839588.

[9] Makri, S., Blandford, A., Gow, J., Rimmer, J., Warwick, C., and Buchanan, G., 2007. A library or just another information resource? A case study of users' mental models of traditional and digital libraries: Research Articles. *JASIST 58*, 3, 433-445. DOI= http://doi.org/10.1002/asi.v58:3.

[10] Buchanan, G., Mckay, D., and Levitt, J., 2015. Where My Books Go: Choice and Place in Digital Reading. In *Proc JCDL 15* (Knoxville, Tennessee, USA), ACM, 17-26. DOI= http://doi.org/10.1145/2756406.2756917.

[11] Shelburne, W.A., 2009. E-book usage in an academic library: User attitudes and behaviors. *Libr Collect Acquis 33*, 2-3, 59-72.

[12] Li, C., Poe, F., Potter, M., Quigley, B., and Wilson, J., 2011. *UC Libraries Academic e-Book Usage Survey.* University of California, Springer, California Digital Libraries.

[13] Thayer, A., Lee, C.P., Hwang, L.H., Sales, H., Sen, P., and Dalal, N., 2011. The imposition and superimposition of digital reading technology: the academic potential of e-readers. In *Proc CHI 11* (Vancouver, BC, Canada), ACM. DOI= http://doi.org/10.1145/1978942.1979375.

[14] Levine, M.M., 1969. An Essay on Browsing. *RQ 9*, 1, 35-93.

[15] Cooksey, E.B., 2004. Too Important to Be Left to Chance—Serendipity and the Digital Library. *Science & Technology Libraries 25*, 1-2 (2004/11/29), 23-32. DOI= http://doi.org/10.1300/J122v25n01_03.

[16] Mckay, D., 2011. A jump to the left (and then a step to the right): reading practices within academic ebooks. In *Proc OzCHI 11* (Canberra, Australia), ACM, 202-210. DOI= http://doi.org/10.1145/2071536.2071569.

[17] Engel, D. and Antell, K., 2004. The life of the mind: A study of faculty spaces in academic libraries. *C&RL 65*, 1, 8-26.

[18] Kleiner, E., Rädle, R., and Reiterer, H., 2013. Blended shelf: reality-based presentation and exploration of library collections. In *Proc CHI 13* (Paris, France), ACM, 577-582. DOI= http://doi.org/10.1145/2468356.2468458.

[19] Buchanan, G.R. and Mckay, D., 2017. Something is Lost, Something is Found: Book Use at the Library Shelves. In *Proc CHIIR 17* (Oslo, Norway), ACM, 37-46. DOI= http://doi.org/10.1145/3020165.3020187.

[20] Fried Foster, N. and Gibbons, S., 2007. *Studying Students: The Undergraduate Research Project at the University of Rochester.* Association of College and Research Libraries, Rochester, NY.

[21] Warwick, C., 2017. Beauty is truth: Multi-sensory input and the challenge of designing aesthetically pleasing digital resources. *Digital Scholarship in the Humanities 32*, suppl_2, ii135-ii150. DOI= http://doi.org/10.1093/llc/fqx036.

[22] Bryant, J., Matthews, G., and Walton, G., 2009. Academic libraries and social and learning space. *J Libr Inf Sci 41*, 1 (March 1, 2009), 7-18. DOI= http://doi.org/10.1177/0961000608099895.

[23] Mckay, D. and Buchanan, G., 2014. On the other side from you: how library design facilitates and hinders group work. In *Proc OzCHI 14* (Sydney, New South Wales, Australia), ACM, 97-106. DOI= http://doi.org/10.1145/2686612.2686625.

[24] Cocciolo, A., 2010. Alleviating physical space constraints using virtual space?: A study from an urban academic library. *Library Hi Tech 28*, 4, 523-535.

[25] Waugh, S., Mckay, D., and Makri, S., 2017. 'Too Much Serendipity': The Tension between Information Seeking and Encountering at the Library Shelves. In *Proc CHIIR 17* (Oslo, Norway), ACM, 277-280. DOI= http://doi.org/10.1145/3020165.3022132.

[26] Pomerantz, J. and Marchionini, G., 2007. The digital library as place. *J Doc 63*, 4, 505-533.

[27] Mckay, D., 2013. Thinking inside the box: The library website as space. *InCite 34*, 6/7, 24.

[28] Church, K. and Oliver, N., 2011. Understanding mobile web and mobile search use in today's dynamic mobile landscape. In *Proc Mobile HCI 11* (Stockholm, Sweden), ACM, 67-76. DOI= http://doi.org/10.1145/2037373.2037385.

[29] Arter, D., Buchanan, G., Jones, M., and Harper, R., 2007. Incidental information and mobile search. In *Proc Mobile HCI 07* (Singapore), ACM, 413-420. DOI= http://doi.org/10.1145/1377999.1378047.

[30] Kim Martin , B.G., Anabel Quan-Haase, 2017. STAK - Serendipitous tool for augmenting knowledge: A conceptual tool for bridging digital and physical resources. *Digital Studies*, 9.

[31] Buchanan, G.R., 2010. The fused library: integrating digital and physical libraries with location-aware sensors. In *Proc JCDL 10* (Gold Coast, Queensland, Australia), ACM, 273-282. DOI= http://doi.org/10.1145/1816123.1816165.

[32] Maunder, A.J., Marsden, G., and Harper, R., 2008. SnapAndGrab: accessing and sharing contextual multi-media content using bluetooth enabled camera phones and large situated displays. In *Proc CHI 08* (Florence, Italy), ACM, 2319-2324. DOI= http://doi.org/10.1145/1358628.1358677.

[33] Benway, J.P., 1998. Banner Blindness: The Irony of Attention Grabbing on the World Wide Web. *HFESA Proceedings 42*, 5, 463-467. DOI= http://doi.org/10.1177/154193129804200504.

[34] Saarinen, K. and Vakkari, P., 2013. A sign of a good book: readers' methods of accessing fiction in the public library. *J Doc. 69*, 5, 736-754. DOI= http://doi.org/10.1108/JD-04-2012-0041.

[35] Ooi, K., 2008. How Adult Fiction Readers Select Fiction Books in Public Libraries: A Study of Information Seeking in Context. In *School of Information Management* Victoria University of Wellington, Wellington, New Zealand.

[36] Buczynski, J.A., 2010. Library eBooks: Some Can't Find Them, Others Find Them and Don't Know What They Are. *Library eBooks: Some Can't Find Them, Others Find Them and Don't Know What They Are 15*, 1 (2010/02/26), 11-19. DOI= http://doi.org/10.1080/10875300903517089.

[37] White, R.W. and Drucker, S.M., 2007. Investigating behavioral variability in web search. In *Proc WWW 07* (Banff, Alberta, Canada), ACM, 21-30. DOI= http://doi.org/10.1145/1242572.1242576.

[38] Craswell, N., Zoeter, O., Taylor, M., and Ramsey, B., 2008. An experimental comparison of click position-bias models. In *Proc WSDM 08* (Palo Alto, California, USA), ACM, 87-94. DOI= http://doi.org/10.1145/1341531.1341545.

[39] Marchionini, G., 1995. *Information seeking in electronic environments.* Cambridge University Press.

[40] Kelley, J.F., 1983. An empirical methodology for writing user-friendly natural language computer applications. In *Proc CHI 83* (Boston, Massachusetts, USA), ACM, 193-196. DOI= http://doi.org/10.1145/800045.801609.

[41] Fussler, H.H. and Simon, J.L., 1969. *Patterns in the use of books in large research libraries.* University of Chicago Press, Chicago, IL.

[42] Hinrichs, U., Butscher, S., M, J., #252, Ller, and Reiterer, H., 2016. Diving in at the Deep End: The Value of Alternative In-Situ Approaches for Systematic Library Search. In *Proc CHI 16* (San Jose, California, USA), ACM, 4634-4646. DOI= http://doi.org/10.1145/2858036.2858549.

[43] Buchanan, G. and Mckay, D., 2016. But what's here is mine: materialities of physical personal workspaces. In *Proc OzCHI 16* (Launceston, Tasmania, Australia), ACM, 115-124. DOI= http://doi.org/10.1145/3010915.3010946.

[44] Bailin, K., 2011. Changes in Academic Library Space: A Case Study at UNSW. *AA&RL 42*, 342-359. DOI= http://doi.org/10.1080/00048623.2011.10722245.

[45] Schöning, J., Krüger, A., Cheverst, K., Rohs, M., Löchtefeld, M., and Taher, F., 2009. PhotoMap: using spontaneously taken images of public maps for pedestrian navigation tasks on mobile devices. In *Proc Mobile HCI 09* (Bonn, Germany), ACM, 1-10. DOI= http://doi.org/10.1145/1613858.1613876.

[46] Davies, N., Cheverst, K., Dix, A., and Hesse, A., 2005. Understanding the role of image recognition in mobile tour guides. In *Proc Mobile HCI 05* (Salzburg, Austria), ACM, 191-198. DOI= http://doi.org/10.1145/1085777.1085809.

[47] Cheverst, K., Davies, N., Mitchell, K., Friday, A., and Efstratiou, C., 2000. Developing a context-aware electronic tourist guide: some issues and experiences. In *Proc CHI 00* (The Hague, The Netherlands), ACM, 17-24. DOI= http://doi.org/10.1145/332040.332047.

Knowledge-Context in Search Systems: Toward Information-Literate Actions

Catherine L. Smith
School of Information
Kent State University
Kent Ohio USA
csmit141@kent.edu

Soo Young Rieh
School of Information
University of Michigan
Ann Arbor Michigan USA
rieh@umich.edu

ABSTRACT

In this perspectives paper we define knowledge-context as meta information that searchers use when making sense of information displayed in and accessible from a search engine results page (SERP). We argue that enriching the knowledge-context in SERPs has great potential for facilitating human learning, critical thinking, and creativity by expanding searchers' information-literate actions such as comparing, evaluating, and differentiating between information sources. Thus it supports the development of learning-centric search systems. Using theories and empirical findings from psychology and the learning sciences, we first discuss general effects of Web search on memory and learning. After reviewing selected research addressing metacognition and self-regulated learning, we discuss design goals for search systems that support metacognitive skills required for long-term learning, creativity, and critical thinking. We then propose that SERPs make both bibliographic and inferential knowledge-context readily accessible to motivate and facilitate information-literate actions for learning and creative endeavors. A brief discussion of related ideas, designs, and prototypes found in prior work follows. We conclude the paper by presenting future research directions and questions on knowledge-context, information-literate actions, and learning-centric search systems.

CCS CONCEPTS

• Information systems~Information retrieval

• Information systems~Users and interactive retrieval

KEYWORDS: searching as learning; search interaction; information literacy; metacognition; transactive memory; learning-centric search

ACM Reference format:

Catherine L. Smith and Soo Young Rieh. 2019. Knowledge-Context in Search Systems: Toward Information-Literate Actions. In *CHIIR '19: 2019 Conference on Human Information Interaction & Retrieval March 10–14, 2019, Glasgow, United Kingdom.* ACM, New York, NY, USA, 9 pages. https://doi.org/10.1145/3295750.3298940

CHIIR '19, March 10–14, 2019, Glasgow, United Kingdom

ACM ISBN 978-1-4503-6025-8/19/03...$15.00
https://doi.org/10.1145/3295750.3298940

1 Introduction

In modern Web search systems, users interact with search engine results pages (SERPs) that combine precise and decontextualized factual information with access to underlying information sources and their content. Although searchers with information literacy skill may investigate and evaluate the information presented in a SERP, many trust that the facts are accurate, or when investigating sources simply click results at the top of the list with little effort to take *information-literate action* (ILA) such as comparing, evaluating, and differentiating between sources. SERPs provide minimal structure or support for ILA, so even information literate searchers must devise or learn an approach for enriching the limited information provided. Searchers with limited information literacy are, by definition, unlikely to initiate ILA on their own, and the system provides them little or no support for developing or learning a process for ILA and gaining its value.

Task-centric [58] and answer-centric [15] views of predictive retrieval system design [54] suggest optimal systems accurately and reliably compare, evaluate, and differentiate between sources on behalf of their users, that is, they unburden the searcher from the subtask of these judgments to minimize or eliminate search interaction [27]. These views suggest that the information found is for use in task completion or question answering; there is little or no focus on designing to support a searcher's possible need to retain and integrate information in long-term memory.

Traditionally, Web SERPs have supported these views by conveying meta-information users easily understand in forms such as list order, cue-laden item content summaries (title, url, snippet), entity cards, dictionary definitions, images, video links, news item headlines, items for sale, suggested queries, and extracted facts or answers. Explicit answers are identified directly as such. Increasingly, Web SERPs also include metadata such as dates of publication, author, publisher, other source attributions, and source-specific metadata such as categories for comic book and movie trivia. All these forms of information comprise the *knowledge-context* searchers use when making sense of the information displayed on and accessible from the SERP. In a task or answer-centric system, knowledge-context may be designed not only to enable the searcher's selection of the most relevant and useful results, but also to positively influence the searcher's confidence in the accuracy and reliability of the system's comparison, evaluation, and differentiation of the answers, information, and sources presented.

In this perspectives paper we raise questions about how the knowledge-context in SERPs affects searchers' proclivities in the use of ILA and present evidence from recent research in the learning sciences and cognitive psychology that informs theory and research approaches on these questions. Based on this we present a vision for research and design initiatives focused on developing an extended and enriched knowledge-context that enables and motivates users' development and use of ILA. Such a system would optimize not just for accuracy and reliability of results, but also for the development of human learning and information literacy.

Knowledge-context is an important concept in the field of human information interaction and retrieval because it expands our perspective on the problems we are trying to solve in the design of search and retrieval systems. Of late, our CHIIR-related research agenda has tended to focus on systems designed with the assumption that interaction involves a set of achievable sub-goals, with precise factual answers and efficient task completion as criteria for success. As suggested above, these designs reflect an implicit assumption that the system has little or no reason to support users in remembering information beyond completion of a sub-goal or task. We know that people may learn when they search (for example, vocabulary terms [44, 48]), but an answer-oriented task focus can treat human learning as a secondary objective. Also, search system designers often seek explicitly to avoid impediments to task progress such that the system must engender a high degree of confidence in retrieved information [54]. Indeed, the use of ILA may be seen as an indicator that the system is not sufficiently optimized. Assuming that task and answer-centric design priorities are important, what might be gained by designing for knowledge-context that induces a user to take information-literate action? In this paper we take a new perspective on learning-centric design priorities in which knowledge-context facilitates individual human learning and creative endeavors.

2 Knowledge-Context and Information-Literate Actions

In order to learn, understand, and gain confidence in their knowledge, information literate people ask and answer questions about the information they encounter. Information literacy is one of a larger group of literacies that extend from the traditional scope of locating, accessing, and using information to higher order thinking skills and related literacies for technology, visual information, media, and online social engagement [28, 41]. In this paper, we propose that knowledge-context affects ILA associated with learning goals such as the need to remember and synthesize information. For example, an information literate person differentiates multiple sources of information on the basis of characteristics such as attribution (who made this claim), the provenance of an information source (e.g., its author, publisher, website owner), the oeuvre of an author, or referents to and from a source (e.g., citations, links, quotations). ILA is motivated by the need to make independent judgments about a source such as its authenticity, authority, or recency and the need to make sense of information that conflicts with prior knowledge or expectations. Thus ILA is part of the broader concept of sense-making [31]. It is also related to the concept of exploratory search in that it supports learning and investigation [30]. Knowledge-context is readily accessible meta-information, organized and displayed for searchers to use during information seeking. It can be designed to prompt and support ILA, which in turn supports exploration, sense-making, and learning.

Unfortunately, when using a search system designed to impart a high level of confidence in the accuracy and reliability of retrieved information, users may judge that the value of ILA is not sufficient to warrant its cost in cognitive load and time. Indeed, studies of U.S. university students find that even those who learn about the value and skills of ILA may rarely use it [5], and that this may have deleterious effects on learning [6].

ILA and its resulting judgments are a form of *self-regulated learning* (discussed below), guided by internal standards, monitoring skills, and plans. Development and use of these metacognitive skills depend on, among other things, the ability to accurately monitor and differentiate between what one already knows and what one does not know. This "knowledge of knowledge" (*metacomprehension* [12]) guides attention and action during reading and learning. We suggest that the knowledge-context accessible to a learner provides cues that can prompt or inhibit constructive questions about information.

3 Effects of Web search on Metacognition

A recent and growing body of literature in psychology and the learning sciences reports findings on general effects of search engine interaction on memory and learning. Much of this work uses *transactive memory* as a key theoretical construct [53]. A long, broad, and deep literature on this subject finds transactive memory among married couples [52] and within systems of shared human and machine cognition [22]. Transactive memory exists when people split responsibility for remembering parts of the information required to complete a task cooperatively, such as a medical procedure or running a household [33]. Evidence is emerging that people use Web search as a form of transactive memory [13, 16, 17, 20, 36, 42, 51, 53]. Key results have been replicated and extended using a variety of related constructs including: the accuracy, strength, and accessibility of information in memory; people's judgments about whether they know something; and how accurately people can recognize correct information. These studies compare measures of cognition and metacognition in situations where participants expect information to be saved vs. not saved on a computer, or where Web search is accessible vs. inaccessible, or used vs. not used. This section of the paper reviews selected studies from this literature.

In an often-cited early study, Sparrow, Liu and Wegner [42] had people type trivia statements into a computer. Researchers told some participants the computer would save the statements and others that they would be erased. The latter group were more likely to remember the information. The former group were more likely to remember where the information was saved than the information itself. The authors also found evidence that people think of a Web search engine, putatively *where* they can find information, when asked a trivia question they cannot answer. This result is directly related to the construct *feeling-of-knowing*, a subjective judgment that one knows something well enough to be able to recall or recognize it in the future [26]. Research on metacognition in learning and psychology often uses feeling-of-knowing as a measure.

In research comparing question-answering among people with and without access to a Web search engine, Ferguson, McLean, and Risko [16] found that the feeling-of-knowing an answer is lower when a Web search engine is accessible than when it is not. Lower feeling of knowing is associated with a lower propensity to answer a question from memory. Further, Risko, Ferguson, and McLean [36] sought to understand associations between feeling-of-knowing and the decision to search for information on the Web, which they hypothesized was related to a *feeling-of-findability*. When people didn't know the answer to a question but then found the correct information by searching, feeling-of-findability correlated well with elapsed time used to search but not with feeling-of-knowing prior to searching. Feeling-of-findability did correlate well with independent judgements on query formulation difficulty and the frequency of a topic among Web searches. The authors found that low feeling-of-findability was associated with less likelihood of persistence and success in a search.

Related research has investigated how the use of Web searching affects metacognition, including the accuracy of memory recall, judgements of recall accuracy, and judgments of cognitive ability such as the feeling of being good at thinking, of having a good memory, and of knowing where to find information. In a study that compared situations where Web search was used or not used, Fisher et al. [17] found that the use of Web search affected people's judgments of what they knew such that they overestimated their own knowledge of information that may be found on the Web (i.e., there is no overestimation for knowledge of one's own private personal history). Surprisingly, overestimation is independent of whether searching returns the information sought, or any results at all. It is also independent of the Web search provider used. The authors suggested that the process of querying the search system may cause the overconfidence. People confuse the feeling that they can find information with their own actual internal knowledge of the information. This finding is echoed in measures of cognitive self-esteem, which are higher when Web search is used, and are affected by the type of device used for searching (e.g., smartphone vs. laptop), independent of the accuracy of the information found when searching [20].

In summary, when people believe information will be stored on a computer they are less likely to remember the information, and more likely to remember where the information has been saved. When people feel they don't know something, they are mentally primed to search the Web. People make accurate predictions on how easily they can find information on the Web and tend to give up sooner or fail to find what they seek when they foresee difficulty. For topics where information can be found on the Web, the use of Web search leads people to overestimate how much they know, and to generally inflate their judgments on the quality of their own memories and cognitive skills, and on knowing where to find information. These findings have important implications for learning in our Web-centric society. Next, we discuss general findings on the role of metacognition in learning and some possible implications that provide guidance in considering designs for learning-centric search systems.

4 Metacognitive Strategies for Self-regulated Learning

This section follows a line of research that addresses metacognition in learning for the long-term, where people store information in memory such that they can use it in generating new ideas and to solve complex or novel problems. One of the fundamental concepts of memory theory is that our memories form and learning occurs when we use what we know by recalling it from our internal memory and actively engaging it in thinking [1]. One of the precepts of designing for learning is the idea that passive exposure to information greatly diminishes the likelihood that people will remember it and be able to use it beyond the short term [7]. That is, the acquisition of information with little or no cognitive effort generally results in little or no learning.

Metacognitive skill involves controlling what one thinks about through planning and monitoring. It allows people to tell the difference between what they have and have not learned and stored in long-term memory. People build metacognitive skills during childhood development and through education [39]. *Self-regulated learning* is a metacognitive skill that enables an engaged learner to adjust plans and attention to meet the needs of an unfolding complex learning task or problem [57]. Poor metacognition degrades the learning process when people can't tell the difference between what they know and what they don't yet know [12]. The subjective feeling-of-knowing affects learning because it guides further metacognition, attention, and subsequent learning. Metacognitive strategies enable internal regulation of attention, which is essential for successful self-regulated learning [4].

Above we have reviewed studies on the distorting effects of Web search on feeling-of-knowing and effects on search behavior related to feeling-of-findability. These findings raise important questions on whether and how the ubiquitous and transactive-memory-like nature of Web search affects metacognitive skills and self-regulated learning. The questions have two types. The first concerns whether an inflated feeling-of-knowing and inaccurate metacognition interferes with a learner's metacognitive control of attention to information found during search. The second type addresses the extent to which access to the Web's transactive memory supplants educational goals in general knowledge such that students commit to memory less than is necessary for successful active integration, constructive inference, and interactive co-inference in learning [7] and creative problem solving [38]. The findings discussed below address these types of questions.

Metacognitive strategies can help reduce overestimation of knowing and increase the cognitive engagement required for learning. Several strategies with high efficacy involve actively summarizing newly learned information after a delay (long enough to reduce activation in short-term memory) [12]. Simply writing five keywords that label what has been learned improves the accuracy for memory of learning (metacomprehension judgements; knowing that you know), as well as for the content of that learning [47]. In task and answer-centric search system designs, ubiquitous, precise, and easy access to general knowledge may obviate the value of learning gained by restating newly learned information using notes or labels. Another highly efficacious metacognitive strategy involves spacing and interleaving during learning, where each iteration between related focal topics requires a shift in attention and recall of the information to be learned. This strategy slows learning in the short term but enhances long-term retention, possibly drawing attention to associations among topics for greater synthesis [2]. The ubiquitous precision of retrieval results, frequent decontextualization of facts as answers presented in the SERP, and the speed of system latency on revised queries may inhibit iterations over new information and resulting productive transitions in attention that facilitate metacomprehension and self-regulated learning.

System designs that involve restating what users can easily find [23] or interleaving less precise (intrinsically diverse) search results [8] may seem incompatible with the goals of task and answer-centric search. We claim this view is limited because it prioritizes the short-term value of retrieved information. A design that prioritizes long-term learning does not necessarily impede efficient task-fulfilment [43]. We propose that access to learning-centric knowledge-context would facilitate self-regulated learning.

5 Learning-Centric Knowledge-Context

The findings discussed above motivate consideration of the goals and priorities of alternative designs for Web search systems. Figure 1 sketches the theoretical relations between the concepts we have introduced above. We propose that precise, easy, and ubiquitous search systems can also be designed to better facilitate long-term learning and creative endeavor. The remainder of the paper addresses concepts for the design of learning-centric search systems.

A learning-centric search system supports knowledge-context as a central design priority. In such a system, searchers encounter an enriched knowledge-context that prompts and facilitates metacognitive engagement, including the metacognitive strategies of information literacy and information literate action. This in turn supports active engagement with information and resulting long-term learning and the metacomprehension needed for successful self-regulated learning. In this section we focus on the specific metacognitive strategies of information literacy involved in comparing, evaluating, and differentiating information, which require engagement with knowledge-context.

Information literate searchers tend to ask a series of questions, such as "Who said that?"; "When did they say it?"; "How have others used it?"; and "How does it compare with statements elsewhere?" The results above suggest that those with access to highly reliable transactive Web memory are likely to trust the Web search system as a source of valid information, believing it obviates any need to ask such questions. In a system designed to impart high levels of confidence, a SERP with minimal knowledge-context provides few if any cues to possible problems with routine, undifferentiated trust in the system and its sources. Hence it offers little that might prompt ILA.

Using such a system, information literate searchers may use iterative exploratory search to take actions such as comparing multiple information sources, critically evaluating information, and differentiating to extract information from sources. Readily accessible and navigable knowledge-context facilitates these actions. For instance, a searcher may pay attention to an author or publisher name to make judgments about a source's authority or credibility. A scholar may judge information credibility by the number and quality of citations to a scholarly article. A student may check their understanding by reviewing documents that present the same information at different reading levels. A journalist may read multiple documents written in the same era in order to examine contrasting viewpoints about a topic. In all of these cases, the searcher seeks to make sense of information by using additional contextual information associated with a source and its content. Assessing credibility, checking understanding, and comparing multiple viewpoints are examples of ILA that knowledge-context can promote and facilitate.

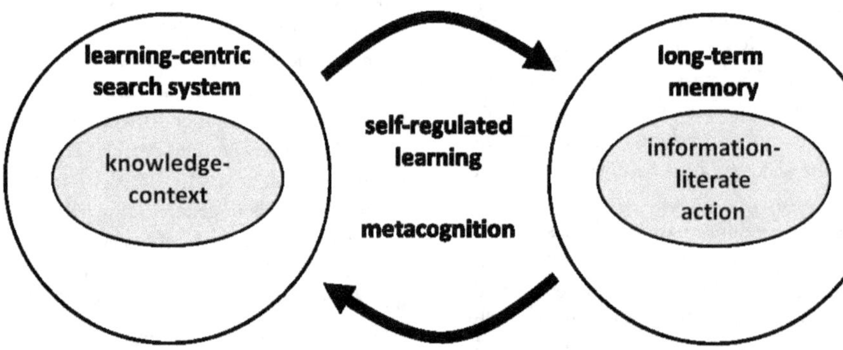

Figure 1. Framework supporting self-regulated learning through information literate action motivated and facilitated by knowledge-context.

Our concept of information literacy extends past the traditional set of information skills for locating, accessing, evaluating, and using information to higher-order thinking processes such as critical thinking [32, 56] and creative problem solving [38] that rely on retention and integration of information in long-term memory. Information literacy involves the capacity to evaluate critically the system itself and take control of learning by asking and answering questions actively [14]. Information literacy involves not just active engagement with information but also a comprehensive understanding of it [28]. From the viewpoint of information literacy, SERPs enriched with knowledge-context offer rich cues about information from multiple dimensions, allowing searchers to engage deeply with information. In our view, knowledge-context serves as more than raw material and metadata "out there to be accessed efficiently" [14].

Critical thinking is a self-directed thought process that improves an individual's ability to uncover the deep structure of knowledge by recognizing the relationships between concepts [32]. In fact, the ability to identify and articulate inferential connections between multiple pieces of information is a core concept of critical thinking. Although there are numerous definitions of critical thinking, most concur that it is a higher-order cognitive process that leads to actions such as discovering, sorting, distinguishing, contrasting, integrating, aggregating, synthesizing, and generating [35]. We believe that readily available knowledge-context in SERPs would motivate and facilitate development of critical thinking as searchers engage with information more actively and critically.

Knowledge-context is also important to the creativity process Sawyer describes [38]. In his definition, creative thinking involves recognizing a problem or anomaly, active learning of new information, time for new associations to strengthen in memory, and the generation of ideas. Learning and idea incubation result in a final external expression of a solution or decision. Easy, reliable access to enriched knowledge-context, along with appropriate cues, are likely to provide opportunities for searchers to comprehend multiple aspects of information.

For purposes of our argument, we divide knowledge-context into two types: *bibliographic knowledge-context* and *inferential knowledge-context*. The first type focuses on sources, with the goal of using features such as authorship, publisher, affiliation, and type of source to determine information credibility [34]. The bibliographic knowledge-context needed to differentiate, organize, and encode on this basis is associated with the information source and does not change after a source is created.

The second type of knowledge-context pertains to the characteristics of information content, and how content connects one source to another, or affects past or current meanings of a source. The goal of ILA with this context is understanding of *what* was said and its meaning in the context of other possibly conflicting or supporting information sources. Inferential knowledge-context is not static but dynamic in that it changes as the searcher uses a source and as other sources and uses alter its contextual meaning. For example, over time a pattern of citations to a text enables inference about changes to the meaning, relevance, or influence of the text. Inferential knowledge-context includes objective information such as citation and access patterns, and associations with other sources, people, organizations, places, etc. (i.e., abstract and concrete entities). For an information literate person, inferential knowledge-context has a subjective component in that it is always contingent on new information, divergent thinking, novel associations, and use in creativity.

We argue that a learning-centric search system must support and facilitate access and use for both types of knowledge-context. Table 1 lists examples of both types. We propose that interaction with knowledge-context would help people integrate information into long-term memory, resulting in enriched learning experiences in which they may generate new ideas and solutions difficult to imagine under the current design of SERPs.

6 Components of a Learning-Centric Search System

In this section we briefly present selected research on search behavior, system prototypes, and design ideas that inform our vision for learning-centric search systems. Figure 2 depicts a simple schematic for key components of such systems.

Table 1: Examples of bibliographic and inferential knowledge-context

Bibliographic Knowledge-Context	Inferential Knowledge-Context
• Assigned subject, topic category, or classification	• Queries that return the source
• Publisher name and location	• Other documents retrieved with source (SERP)
• Publisher/producer's audience classification (children, teens, adults, experts, etc.)	• Author's other works
• Publisher/producer's genre classification (poetry, novel, non-fiction, history, biography, etc.)	• Publisher's catalog of works and authors
• Original publication date and time	• Citation count; link direction/degree
• Reading level scores	• Description of readership/audience
• Author name(s)	• Genre (opinion, fiction, fact, advertising)
• Author affiliation(s)	• Number of similar documents (any criterion)
• Form (text, image, video, audio, data, etc.)	• History, trend, or aggregation on a criterion
• Contemporaneous sources (published at same time)	• Valence (hateful, bigoted, racist, sexist, erroneous, ironic, humorous, propaganda)
• Language(s) of creation or translation	• Citations to and from the work or the author
• Entities mentioned or represented	• Version, revision date/time; prior versions
	• User history of interaction with and saving the source

Desirable difficulties and slow interaction. Vakkari and Huuskonen's [49] longitudinal study of search and long-term learning among medical students informs our perspective. The study demonstrated advantages due to *desirable difficulties* [2]: the idea that productive engagement with information requires expenditure of effort to handle difficult thinking [25]. Vakkari and Huuskonen's examination of student essays revealed that the precision of search results correlated negatively with long-term learning. Students who tended to use the system's advanced search features in more frequent search sessions experienced lower retrieval precision but learned more than students who used more precise general search features in fewer sessions. Students whose essays reflected greater knowledge chose the desirable difficulty of more complex searching, in effect, slowing the pace of their learning over more search sessions interleaved with reading and deep engagement with the information they found [2]. Importantly, the successful students had sufficient background to gain the advantages of the difficulties [3].

Intentionally slow technologies have been proposed to prioritize time for a user's reflection and learning [19]. Slow search technology has been conceptualized variously as a means of providing greater precision of results [46] or to support search on slow network connections [45]. Dörk [10] envisions slow technology as an opportunity to design new interfaces and visualizations that facilitate the use of knowledge-context in activities such as orienteering, exploration, browsing, and the collection of information for later use. Specific design goals in this work focus on intuitive visualizations that integrate explicit and implicit relations in a navigable structure [11]. These goals and concepts fit well with the needs of a system that makes knowledge-context recognizable and usable for ILA. Further, we envision a mixed-initiative artificial intelligence that facilitates the desirable difficulty of ILA in slow search interaction [21, 37].

Knowledge organization for knowledge-context. Two recent papers express other ideas that parallel our conception of a learning-centric search system and knowledge-context. In a straightforward example of knowledge-context, Fuhr et al. [18] proposed a set of computable evaluative measures and criteria for metadata describing characteristics of textual news sources: factuality, readability, virality, emotion (valence), opinion, controversy, authority/credibility/trust, technicality, and topicality. They proposed the measures as descriptions of computational characteristics and judgments for a source. The authors present a schema in the style of a nutrition label that would be accessible alongside a source. Accessing and reading the label would be an information-literate action.

In an inferential form of knowledge-context, Voskarides et al. [50] generated rankings for entities associated on a knowledge graph, with the goal of organizing relevant factual associations and entities for navigation of a large, complex graph. As knowledge-context, the rankings are useful for presenting entity cards relevant to an initial query or search session. Once ranked, the cards may be presented or organized for browsing. We envision a system designed to facilitate interaction with contextualized entity cards and the creation of personal entity cards that restate newly learned information in a personal knowledge-context, discussed next.

Recent work on a learning-centric search system prototype, SearchAssist [23], draws attention to the need for two sources for knowledge-context: a public knowledge-context derived from external information sources accessed via the Web, and a private knowledge-context derived from internal information sources comprising a user's personal information management (PIM) space [9, 55]. We propose that a complete knowledge-context includes a user's PIM space, where they store interim and final products of information-literate-actions and make them accessible for future sensemaking and learning.

In summary, knowledge-context is more than metadata or a knowledge-graph. It is also an organizing schema that makes knowledge structures useful for learning.

Interface design. In addition to Dörk's [11] visualization concepts, our ideas on interface design spring from three examples. Marchionini, et al.'s Agileviews [29] framework defines a set of orienting constructs for navigation of complex information spaces.

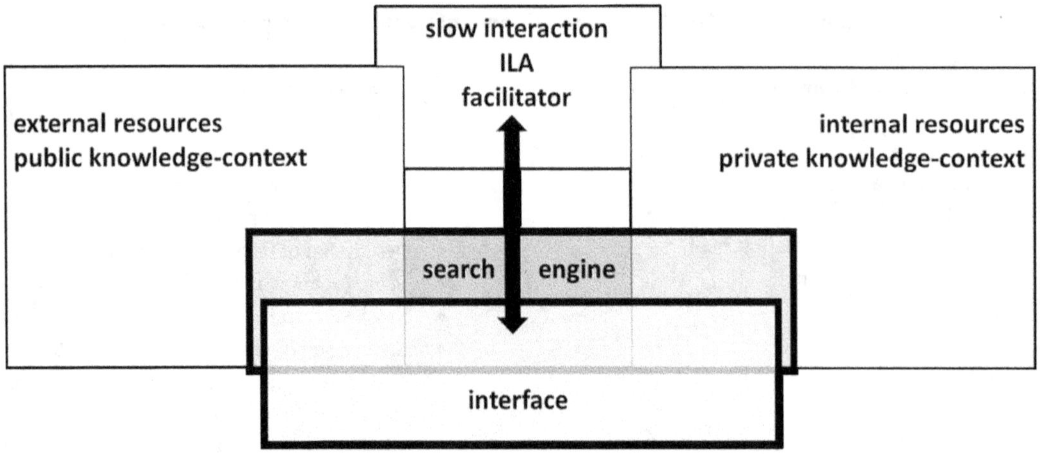

Figure 2. Components of a hypothetical learning-centric search system.

These include preview, primary view, overview, and review, with look ahead, peripheral, and shared views. The design objective was to guide visual attention during partition, exploration, and sensemaking for a large corpus. The complexity of Agileviews stands in stark contrast with the simplicity of a ranked list, and indeed, in a review of prototype projects the authors opined that "One challenge ... is how to show context without complicating the screen display." For us, the compelling idea in Agileviews is the prospect of gaining a traversable overview that enables visualization of selected associations that form usable partitions within and across forms of knowledge-context.

Marchionini's idea is simplified in designs that present labeled topic clusters, such as the structure-aware TopicFlower visualization [40]. A TopicFlower is generated by extracting topics from text, prioritizing them relative to the salient structure and content of the corpus, and organizing topics for display using labels for topic clusters and associations. The eventual goal is to make topics and their associations navigable for exploration and discovery, an objective included in our vision of a navigable representation of knowledge-context structure.

Navigating a knowledge-context requires metacognitive skills. Encounters with the intrinsic diversity of knowledge-context may engender some of the advantages of spacing and interleaving topics during learning. More active metacognitive engagement is likely to come from a process of restating newly learned information in notes, summaries, or keywords. These more deliberate constructive activities require an interface that supports integration with a user's PIM space [24]. The SearchAssist interface [23] provides a mechanism for searchers to categorize saved search results using a simple label in a simple list that remains visible throughout a task, similar to a visual bookmark. Other than querying and using the results list, the saved, labeled, and organized list of sources was the most used and subjectively useful feature in the interface, particularly in the final stages of an experimental essay task. Qualitative data indicated that searchers recognized how active engagement with this element of the interface affected their metacognitive actions (planning and monitoring) as well as ILA with respect to differentiation and evaluation of sources.

7 Conclusion and Future Research Directions

In recent years there have been several workshops, special journal issues, and publications regarding conceptualizing *searching as learning*. This paper makes a contribution to the field of human information interaction and retrieval, as well as searching as learning, by proposing a new perspective in which we emphasize the importance of enriching the knowledge-context of retrieval results. Our focus has been on evidence that current task and answer-centric designs may impede important components of learning. We have proposed, discussed, and described our proposals for an enriched knowledge-context, designed to facilitate learning and creativity. Specifically, we have described two forms of knowledge-context, which we propose are necessary to prompt and facilitate ILA, more useful metacognitive strategies, and more effective learning. This perspective suggests the following future research questions.

- Does the use of knowledge-context and ILA improve metacomprehension, metacognitive skill, and long-term memory for needed information?
- What specific forms of knowledge-context motivate searchers to engage in ILA?
- Which specific forms of knowledge-context are fundamental and which others are most salient for specific tasks, learning objectives and stages?
- How can a system scaffold productive ILA so that searchers learn and gain the long-term value of ILA along with a set of functional metacognitive skills that become routine?

One of our objectives in presenting our perspective has been to bring recent literature on transactive memory and metacomprehension to the ideas and goals of search system design. The problem of how to design for productive cognitive load that enhances long-term and deep human learning is difficult, particularly when the goal has been designs that get out of the way to speed up interaction and minimize load.

To make more than a series of marginal improvements to existing systems, collaborative, interdisciplinary research programs on retrieval and interaction design as well as controlled experimental research on the above questions and hypotheses are essential. Such studies require experimental systems and both laboratory and longitudinal research designs. The object of this work is not improved system performance but a system that reflects psychological factors that affect and are affected by knowledge organization, interface design, and the role of speed in interaction. Progress on these complex questions depends on a shared infrastructure that enables development of four key architectural components of an experimental system for basic research in human computer interaction and information retrieval: a knowledge structure for integrating external public and internal private knowledge-context; a search engine that integrates bibliographic and inferential knowledge-context; interfaces and visual representations of knowledge-context in search results; and an artificial intelligence that facilitates development of metacognitive skills and the use of ILA. In addition to controlled experiments, a grounded understanding of how people use search systems to support their own self-directed learning in formal and informal learning situations is essential. System designers must recognize the role of reflection in self-regulation and metacognition during search. It is time to consider and respond to the effects of ubiquitous, precise, easy and passive information access with the goal of supporting learning, critical thinking, and creativity.

ACKNOWLEDGMENTS

We thank the anonymous reviewers for their helpful comments, reactions, ideas, and suggestions for extending the paper.

REFERENCES

[1] J.R. Anderson. 2000. Learning and memory: An integrated approach. John Wiley & Sons Inc., Annapolis, MD.

[2] E. Bjork and R. Bjork. 2011. Making things hard on yourself, but in a good way: Creating desirable difficulties to enhance learning. In Psychology in the real world, Worth, New York, NY.

[3] R.A. Bjork. 2018. Being Suspicious of the Sense of Ease and Undeterred by the Sense of Difficulty: Looking Back at Schmidt and Bjork (1992). Perspectives on Psychological Science, 13(2), 146–148.
[4] R.A. Bjork. J. Dunlosky, and N. Kornell. 2013. Self-regulated Learning: Beliefs, Techniques, and Illusions. Annual Review of Psychology. 64, 417–444.
[5] B.S. Bloom and M. Deyrup. 2012. The truth is out: How they really search. In Proceedings of the 32nd Annual Charleston Conference (2012). Purdue University Press, West Lafayette, IN. DOI: http://dx.doi.org/10.5703/1288284315103.
[6] M.J. Carlozzi. 2018. They Found It–Now Do They Bother? An Analysis of First-Year Synthesis. College & Research Libraries, 79(5), 659-670.
[7] M.T. Chi. and R. Wylie 2014. The ICA Framework: Linking Cognitive Engagement to Active Learning Outcomes. Educational Psychologist, 49(4), 219–243.
[8] K. Collins-Thompson, S.Y. Rieh, C.C. Haynes, and R. Syed. 2016. Assessing Learning Outcomes in Web Search: A Comparison of Tasks and Query Strategies. In Proceedings of the 2016 ACM on Conference on Human Information Interaction and Retrieval (CHIIR '16). ACM, New York, NY, USA, 163-172.
[9] E. Cutrell, S.T. Dumais, and J. Teevan. 2006. Searching to Eliminate Personal Information Management. Communications of the ACM, 49(1), 58–64.
[10] M. Dörk, P. Bennett, and R. Davies. 2013. Taking our sweet time to search. In Proceedings of CHI 2013 Workshop on Changing Perspectives of Time in HCI .
[11] M. Dörk, S. Carpendale, and C. Williamson. Visualizing Explicit and Implicit Relations of Complex Information Spaces. Information Visualization, 11(1), 5–21.
[12] J. Dunlosky and A.R. Lipko. 2007. Metacomprehension: A Brief History and how to Improve its Accuracy. Current Directions in Psychological Science, 16(4), 228–232.
[13] T.L. Dunn, C. Gaspar, D. McLean, D.J. Koehler, and E.F. Risko. 2018. Distributed Metacognition: Examining the Metacognitions Associated with Retrieval from Internal and External Stores. Prepublication.
[14] J. Elmborg. 2006. Critical Information Literacy: Implications for Instructional Practice. The Journal of Academic Librarianship, 32(2), 192–199.
[15] O. Etzioni. 2011. Search Needs a Shake-up. Nature, 476(7358), 25-26.
[16] A.M. Ferguson, D. McLean, and E.F. Risko. 2015. Answers at Your Fingertips: Access to the Internet Influences Willingness to Answer Questions. Consciousness and Cognition, 37, 91–102.
[17] M. Fisher, M.K. Goddu, and F.C. Keil. 2015. Searching for Explanations: How the Internet Inflates Estimates of Internal Knowledge. Journal of Experimental Psychology: General, 144(3), 674–687.
[18] N. Fuhr, A. Giachanou, G. Grefenstette, I. Gurevych, A. Hanselowski, K. Jarvelin, R. Jones, et al.. 2018. An Information Nutritional Label for Online Documents. ACM SIGIR Forum, 51(3), 46–66.
[19] L. Hallnäs and J. Redström. 2001. Slow Technology–designing for Reflection. Personal and Ubiquitous Computing. 5(3), 201–212.
[20] K.A. Hamilton and M.Z. Yao. 2018. Blurring Boundaries: Effects of Device Features on Metacognitive Evaluations. Computers in Human Behavior, 89, 213–220.
[21] E. Horvitz. 1999. Uncertainty, Action, and Interaction: In Pursuit of Mixed-initiative Computing. IEEE Intelligent Systems, 14(5), 17–20.
[22] E. Hutchins. 1995. How a Cockpit Remembers its Speeds. Cognitive Science, 19(3), 265–288.
[23] H.C. Huurdeman, M.L. Wilson, and J. Kamps. 2016. Active and Passive Utility of Search Interface Features in Different Information Seeking Task Stages. In Proceedings of the 2016 ACM on Conference on Human Information Interaction and Retrieval (CHIIR '16). ACM, New York, NY, USA, 3-12.
[24] H.C. Huurdeman. 2017. Dynamic compositions: Recombining search user interface features for supporting complex work tasks. In CHIIR Workshop on Supporting Complex Search Tasks, Oslo, Norway, 21-24. http://ceur-ws.org/Vol-1798/paper5.pdf
[25] M. Kapur. 2016. Examining Productive Failure, Productive Success, Unproductive Failure, and Unproductive Success in Learning. Educational Psychologist, 51(2), 289–299.
[26] A. Koriat. 1996. Memory's Knowledge of Its Own Knowledge: The Accessibility Account of Feeling of Knowing, Metacognition: Knowing about knowing, The MIT Press, Cambridge, MA.
[27] D.J. Liebling, P.N. Bennett, and R.W. White. 2012. Anticipatory search: using context to initiate search. In Proceedings of the 35th international ACM SIGIR conference on Research and development in information retrieval (SIGIR '12). ACM, New York, NY, USA, 1035-1036.
[28] T.P. Mackey and T.E. Jacobson. 2010. Reframing Information Literacy as a Metaliteracy. College & Research Libraries, 72(1), 62–78.
[29] G. Marchionini, G. Geisler, and B. Brunk. 2000. Agileviews: A human-centered framework for interfaces to information spaces. In Proceedings of the Annual Conference of the American Society for Information Science. 271-280.
[30] G. Marchionini. 2006. Exploratory Search: From Finding to Understanding. Communications of the ACM, 49(4), 41–46.
[31] G. Marchionini. Search, Sense Making and Learning: Closing Gaps. Information and Learning Sciences. Prepublication.
[32] J.W. Mulnix. 2012. Thinking Critically about Critical Thinking. Educational Philosophy and Theory, 44(5), 464–479.
[33] V. Peltokorpi. 2008. Transactive Memory Systems. Review of General Psychology, 12(4), 378-394.
[34] S.Y. Rieh. 2002. Judgment of Information Quality and Cognitive Authority in the Web. Journal of the American Society for Information Science and Technology, 53(2), 145–161.
[35] S.Y. Rieh, K. Collins-Thompson, P. Hansen, and H-J. Lee. 2016. Towards Searching as a Learning Process: A Review of Current Perspectives and Future Directions. Journal of Information Science, 42(1), 19–34.
[36] E.F. Risko, A.M. Ferguson, and D. McLean. 2016. On Retrieving Information from External Knowledge Stores: Feeling-of-findability, Feeling-of-knowing and Internet Search. Computers in Human Behavior, 65, 534–543.
[37] T. Ruotsalo, J. Peltonen, M. JA Eugster, D. Głowacka, P. Floréen, P. Myllymäki, G. Jacucci, and S. Kaski. 2018. Interactive Intent Modeling for Exploratory Search. ACM Transactions on Information Systems (TOIS), 36(4), 44-46.
[38] R.K. Sawyer. 2011. Explaining creativity: The science of human innovation. Oxford University Press, New York, NY.
[39] W. Schneider. 2008. The Development of Metacognitive Knowledge in Children and Adolescents: Major Trends and Implications for Education. Mind, Brain, and Education, 2(3), 114–121.
[40] J. Singh, S. Zerr, and S. Siersdorfer. 2017. Structure-Aware Visualization of Text Corpora. In Proceedings of the 2017 Conference on Conference Human Information Interaction and Retrieval (CHIIR '17). ACM, New York, NY, USA, 107-116.
[41] C.L. Smith and M.L. Matteson. 2018. Information Literacy in the Age of Machines that Learn: Desiderata for Machines that Teach. Libri, 68(2), 71–84.
[42] B. Sparrow, J. Liu, and D.M. Wegner. 2011. Google Effects on Memory: Cognitive Consequences of Having Information at our Fingertips. Science, 333(6043), 776-778.
[43] R. Syed and K. Collins-Thompson. 2018. Exploring Document Retrieval Features Associated with Improved Short- and Long-term Vocabulary Learning Outcomes. In Proceedings of the 2018 Conference on Human Information Interaction & Retrieval (CHIIR '18). ACM, New York, NY, USA, 191-200.
[44] R. Syed and K. Collins-Thompson. 2017. Retrieval Algorithms Optimized for Human Learning. In Proceedings of the 40th International ACM SIGIR Conference on Research and Development in Information Retrieval (SIGIR '17). ACM, New York, NY, USA, 555-564.
[45] J. Teevan, K. Collins-Thompson, R.W. White, and S. Dumais. 2014. Slow Search. Communications of the ACM, 57(8), 36–38.
[46] J. Teevan, K. Collins-Thompson, R.W. White, S.T. Dumais, and Y. Kim. 2013. Slow Search: Information Retrieval without Time Constraints. In Proceedings of the Symposium on Human-Computer Interaction and Information Retrieval (HCIR '13). ACM, New York, NY, USA.
[47] K.W. Thiede, J. Dunlosky, T.D. Griffin, and J. Wiley. 2005. Understanding the Delayed-keyword Effect on Metacomprehension Accuracy. Journal of Experimental Psychology: Learning, Memory, and Cognition, 31(6), 1267-1280.
[48] P. Vakkari. 2016. Searching as Learning: A Systematization Based on Literature. Journal of Information Science, 42(1), 7–18.
[49] P. Vakkari and S. Huuskonen. 2012. Search Effort Degrades Search Output but Improves Task Outcome. Journal of the American Society for Information Science and Technology, 63(4), 657–670.
[50] N. Voskarides, E. Meij, R. Reinanda, A. Khaitan, M. Osborne, G. Stefanoni, P. Kambadur, and M. de Rijke. 2018. Weakly-supervised Contextualization of Knowledge Graph Facts. In The 41st International ACM SIGIR Conference on Research & Development in Information Retrieval (SIGIR '18). ACM, New York, NY, USA, 765-774.
[51] A.F. Ward. 2013. Supernormal: How the Internet is Changing Our Memories and Our Minds. Psychological Inquiry, 24(4), 341–348.
[52] D.M. Wegner. 1987. Transactive Memory: A Contemporary Analysis of the Group Mind. Theories of group behavior. Springer, New York, NY.
[53] D.M. Wegner and A.F. Ward. 2013. How Google is Changing Your Brain. Scientific American, 309(6), 58–61.
[54] R.W. White. 2016. Interactions with search systems. Cambridge University Press, New York, NY.
[55] R. Whitham and L. Cruickshank. 2017. The Function and Future of the Folder. Interacting with Computers, 29(5), 629–647.
[56] S. Wineberg. 2016. Why Historical Thinking is not about History. History News, Spring 2016, 13-16.
[57] P.H. Winne and R. Azevedo. 2005. Metacognition. The Cambridge handbook of the learning sciences, Cambridge University Press, New York, NY.
[58] Y. Zhang et al. 2011. User-click modeling for understanding and predicting search-behavior. In Proceedings of the 17th ACM SIGKDD international conference on Knowledge discovery and data mining (KDD '11). ACM, New York, NY, USA, 1388-1396.

Measuring Learning During Search: Differences in Interactions, Eye-Gaze, and Semantic Similarity to Expert Knowledge

Nilavra Bhattacharya
School of Information
The University of Texas at Austin
nilavra@ieee.org

Jacek Gwizdka
School of Information
The University of Texas at Austin
chiir2019@gwizdka.com

ABSTRACT

We investigate the relationship between search behavior, eye-tracking measures, and learning. We conducted a user study where 30 participants performed searches on the web. We measured their verbal knowledge before and after each task in a content-independent manner, by assessing the semantic similarity of their entries to expert vocabulary. We hypothesize that differences in verbal knowledge-change of participants are reflected in their search behaviors and eye-gaze measures related to acquiring information and reading. Our results show that participants with higher change in verbal knowledge differ by reading significantly less, and entering more sophisticated queries, compared to those with lower change in knowledge. However, we do not find significant differences in other search interactions like page visits, and number of queries.

CCS CONCEPTS

• **Human-centered computing → Empirical studies in HCI**; *Web-based interaction.*

KEYWORDS

search as learning; measuring knowledge change; human information behavior; eye-tracking

ACM Reference Format:
Nilavra Bhattacharya and Jacek Gwizdka. 2019. Measuring Learning During Search: Differences in Interactions, Eye-Gaze, and Semantic Similarity to Expert Knowledge. In *2019 Conference on Human Information Interaction and Retrieval (CHIIR '19), March 10–14, 2019, Glasgow, Scotland, UK.* ACM, New York, NY, USA, 9 pages. https://doi.org/10.1145/3295750.3298926

1 INTRODUCTION

We investigate the relationship between search behavior, eye gaze, and learning. Marchionini described information seeking as "a process, in which humans purposefully engage in order to change their state of knowledge" [19]. Thus information search is driven by higher-level human needs. We can consider information seeking as a process that changes the state of a searcher's knowledge. This consideration points us to works that draw upon strong ties between information search and learning. For example, exploratory search has been described as search as learning [20]. More recently, Jansen et al. [16] noted that "a learning theory may better describe the information searching process than more commonly used paradigms of decision making or problem solving". I-LEARN model created by Neuman, from the learning theory perspective, attempts to connect learning theory with information science perspectives [22]. The model posits "the use of information as the fundamental building block for learning". If we consider learning as an integral part of information search process, the challenge then is how to measure learning. We can turn to the educational psychology literature, but we should first note that measuring a searcher's learning is actually not new in our field. For example, Pirolli et al. [26] measured user learning in their evaluation of Scatter/Gather exploratory search interface. Learning was assessed by examining gains in a user's understanding of the topic structure, and in a user's ability to formulate effective queries. Possible operationalizations of learning measurement include measures of a user's ability to formulate more effective queries, a user's familiarity with concepts, and relationships between concepts.

Our interest is in the learning that takes place at the bottom level of the modified Bloom's taxonomy – the remembering and factual knowledge level [1]. Therefore, we operationalize learning as changes in verbal knowledge [17] from before to after a search session. One goal of our work is to construct learning measures that require minimal input from users, and, for example, do not require users to answer topic-specific comprehension tests. We use two types of learning measures, a simple topic-independent measure, and a measure based on semantic similarity with expert vocabulary. Our expectation is that searchers who invest more search-effort, and who consume more result pages, learn more. In other words, their topical vocabulary improves and becomes more similar to expert vocabulary. Search-effort is conceptualized as a two part, multiple-component construct: (a) search interaction (i.e., visiting SERPs and result pages, entering queries); and (b) acquiring text from web pages by reading (i.e., number and duration of reading fixations, length of reading sequences, number and length of eye regressions).

2 BACKGROUND

Learning, in the context of interactive information retrieval, is interesting for a few reasons. Assessment of learning outcomes resulting from search, are a good candidate for more comprehensive, user-oriented evaluation measure of information retrieval systems. In particular, the need to perform evaluations that go beyond individual query interaction has been noted by many researchers, and some approaches have been proposed (e.g., most recently by Raman

CHIIR '19, March 10–14, 2019, Glasgow, Scotland, UK

ACM ISBN 978-1-4503-6025-8/19/03...$15.00
https://doi.org/10.1145/3295750.3298926

et al. [27]). Measuring learning on whole, or multiple-session search offers one possible approach.

However, assessing learning typically requires collecting explicit (knowledge-based) responses from users. Collecting such responses may be disruptive, and while it works well in controlled research conditions, it is hard to transfer this approach to the field. Two questions arise: 1) which implicit measurement techniques of learning could be used; and 2) which techniques work outside the laboratory.

With recent technological advances in (psycho-physiological and brain) sensing techniques, tools that enable implicit assessment of changes in a user's cognitive state are now more readily available. One such tool is eye-tracking. Prior work [4] demonstrates feasibility of using eye gaze patterns to assess differences in the levels of users' domain knowledge (at least for text search). This work indicates a possibility of using eye tracking to measure changes in a searcher's learning. One advantage of using measurement techniques based on eye tracking is the possibility of scaling up to larger numbers of users. If the current trend in dropping eye tracker prices continues, we can expect that in-not-so-distant-future, eye trackers will become a selectable option for many computers, just like getting a larger hard drive. (A reasonably good, but slow, eye tracker currently costs few hundred USD). This line of research is still in early development and we need more studies to confirm reliability and to examine validity of using eye gaze patterns in measuring learning. Our work aims to contribute to these developments.

Past efforts have tried to gauge the existing domain knowledge or expertise of a user from interaction features. Wildemuth [30] observed that with change in expertise, novices tend to replicate the search tactics employed by domain experts. White et al. [29] predicted domain expertise from interaction measures like website visits, dwell time, focusing on single vs. multiple topics on search engine result pages (SERPs), etc. Cole et al. [4] identified that behavioral features were topic-agnostic predictive cues of a user's domain knowledge. Further, Zhang et al. [33] identified a separate set of features, like the rank of search-result rank considered relevant, and average query length, as being predictive of a user's knowledge. Other works have tried to measure the change in knowledge over a task-span, and correlate it with interaction measures. Collins-Thompson et al. [6] observed that diversity in a user's queries is an indicator of increased knowledge gain. Eickhoff et al. [7] studied correlations between search interactions, visited SERP features, and learning needs related to declarative or procedural knowledge. Vakkari [28] presented a set of features that are predictive of knowledge change during searches.

With the advent of the 'Search-as-Learning' (SAL) sub-field, new research has also investigated the measurement of knowledge change during online information search tasks [11, 12, 31, 32]. For instance, Gadiraju et al. [11] and Yu et al. [32] measured pre- and post-task knowledge levels using online tests, where participants had to choose between 'True', 'False' and 'I don't know' options for a series of factual questions related to the topic of the search task. Knowledge change was quantified as the difference between the pre- and post-task scores. Yu et al. [32] also proposed an automated system to predict this differential knowledge-change measure using a variety of interaction features as predictors. However, the drawbacks of this approach are that (a) it requires creation of domain specific knowledge-tests, (b) users get exposed to the topics of the task before searching starts, which may interact with the pre-task knowledge levels, and (c) in multiple-choice questions, users may select the correct answers by guessing. Ghosh et al. [12] takes a different approach for pre- and post-task assessments, by asking the participants about their perceived levels of existing knowledge, task difficulty, newly gained knowledge, and interest in the topic, all measured using five-point Likert scales. Knowledge change was operationalized as a paired sample t-test to determine if self-perceived existing knowledge and self-perceived new knowledge differ significantly. Although this approach avoids the need of domain specific tests, and exposing users to task-topics, it relies heavily on the user's perception of his/her own knowledge change. Such perceived measures are subjective to users, and may not provide a truly quantifiable indication of knowledge change.

In light of the above, we see that past works have either studied a limited range of learning objectives, or considered limited predictive features. Many of them required domain-specific information as well. In this work, we aim to contribute by investigating knowledge-change assessment metrics that (a) do not require domain-specific comprehension tests, (b) do not expose the user to the topic of the search in the pre-task assessment, and (c) attempt to assess a user's true knowledge-level (with respect to expert knowledge) with minimal scope for guessing or subjective differences.

3 METHOD

3.1 Experimental Design

We conducted a controlled, within-subject user study with 30 participants (16 females; mean age 24.5 years), who were asked to search for health-related information on the internet. We pre-screened our participants for (a) native-level English familiarity (to minimize influence of varied levels of English familiarity on their eye movements and fixations), (b) non-expert topic familiarity (so that they did not have extensive prior knowledge of the topic for which we were trying to measure their learning on search), and (c) uncorrected 20/20 vision (to minimize problems with eye-tracking). In the pre-screening survey, all participants reported using the internet for longer than an hour everyday, and daily usage of Google search engine. The majority of the participants had been using Google for longer than seven years, and considered themselves proficient in searching for information online.

3.2 Task Description

To investigate changes in vocabulary knowledge, each participant performed two information search tasks on health-related topics in counterbalanced order. These two tasks simulated a work-task approach by triggering realistic information-need for participants [2], as they were asked to find useful information for helping a family member and a friend. The tasks were designed to be complex, and contained multiple facets. The prompts for each task are:

Task 1: *Vitamin A: Your teenage cousin has asked your advice in regard to taking vitamin A for health improvement purposes. You have heard conflicting reports about the effects of vitamin A, and you want to explore this topic to help your cousin. Specifically, you want to know:*

(i) What is the recommended dosage of vitamin A for underweight teenagers?
(ii) What are the health benefits of taking vitamin A? Please find at least 3 benefits and 3 disadvantages of vitamin A.

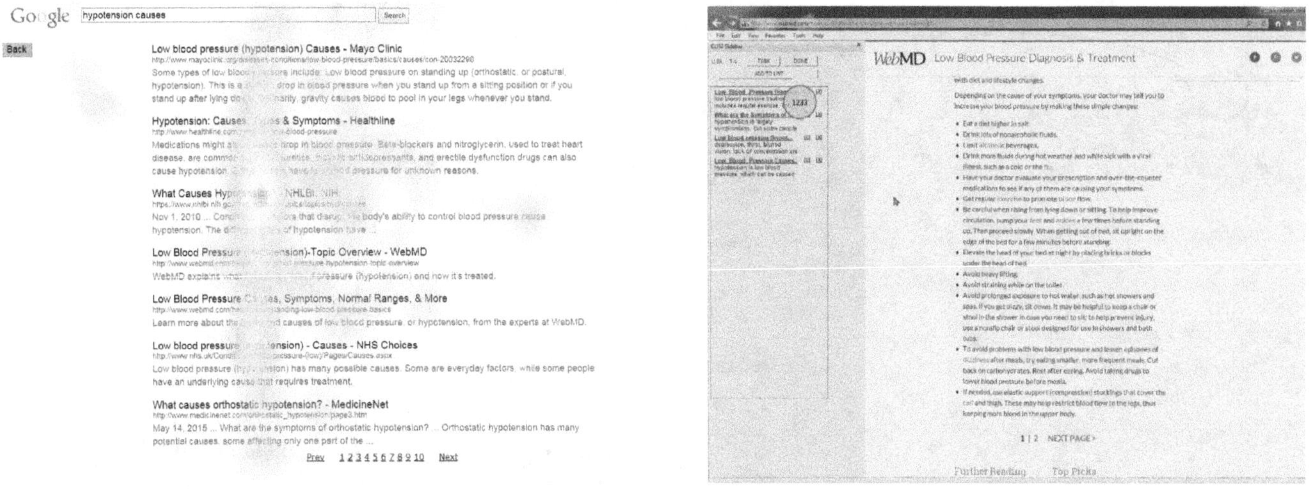

(a) (b)

Figure 1: Screenshots of our system: (a) Customized Google SERP, with 7 results per page, and no advertisements. (b) A 'CONTENT' page showing our customized left-sidebar, for viewing the task-prompt, creating bookmarks and taking notes. Green/yellow patches in (a) are eye-tracking fixation heatmaps. The circle with number in (b) is an eye-fixation with duration.

(iii) *What are the consequences of vitamin A deficiency or excess? Please find 3 consequences of vitamin A deficiency and 3 consequences of its excess.*
(iv) *Please find at least 3 food items that are considered as good sources of vitamin A.*

Task 2: *Hypotension: Your friend has hypotension. You are curious about this issue and want to investigate more. Specifically, you want to know:*

(i) *What are the causes of hypotension?*
(ii) *What are the consequences of hypotension?*
(iii) *What are the differences between hypotension and hypertension in terms of symptoms? Please find at least 3 differences in symptoms between them.*
(iv) *What are some medical treatments for hypotension? Which solution would you recommend to your friend if he/she also has a heart condition? Why?*

3.3 Apparatus

The main search tasks were performed using Internet Explorer. The tasks started from a customized version of the Google search engine interface (Fig. 1a), and the browser had an additional sidebar on the left (Fig. 1b). In our custom-written search engine interface, search results were retrieved from Google in real-time in the background by a proxy server. A search engine result page (SERP) controlled the display of the search results, by showing only seven results per page. This ensured that eye fixations were accurately tracked on each individual result in the SERP, and no advertisements could distract our participants. We chose seven results per page as this allowed the search results to have an optimum increased font size (and thereby increased visual angle), so that we could track eye-movements at the level of individual elements of search results surrogates. All other webpages (which we call 'CONTENT' pages) were displayed in their true form.

The sidebar on the left showed (on demand) the current search task prompt on the top, and had bookmarking and note-taking sections below. Bookmarking allowed the participants to save the URLs of webpages they opened and considered relevant. The list of bookmarked pages were available on the sidebar all throughout a search-task session, and a bookmarked page could be re-opened instantly by clicking the bookmark. The note-taking feature allowed participants to write and / or copy-paste relevant text from the webpages they visited. When the participants were performing the search tasks, we recorded their interactions with the computer system. This included eye gaze, keystrokes, mouse clicks, and other activities like bookmarks, notes, search queries, URLs of pages visited, etc., as well as the timing and duration of these activities. Eye gaze was captured using a Tobii TX-300 eye-tracker (Tobii Technology AB, Sweden) controlled by iMotions software (iMotions A/S) that also captured all user interactions.

3.4 Procedure

Each experimental session started with the assessment of participant's working memory capacity (WMC) using memory span task [8] and health literacy using the eHealth Literacy Scale (eHEALS) [23]. Next, the participants performed a training task to familiarize themselves with the custom user interfaces (bookmarking and note-taking), and the study procedure. After the training, participants started the main search tasks. Task steps are illustrated in Fig. 2.

Each task started with a Pre-task knowledge assessment, to gauge the existing or initial knowledge of the participant for the task (Fig. 2a). The prompt for the pre-task assessment was as follows:

Think of what you already know on the topic of this search and list as many phrases or words as you can that come to your mind. For example, if you know about side effects, please do not just type the phrase "side effects", but rather type "side effects" and then list the specific side effects you know about. Please list only one word or phrase per line and end each line with a comma.

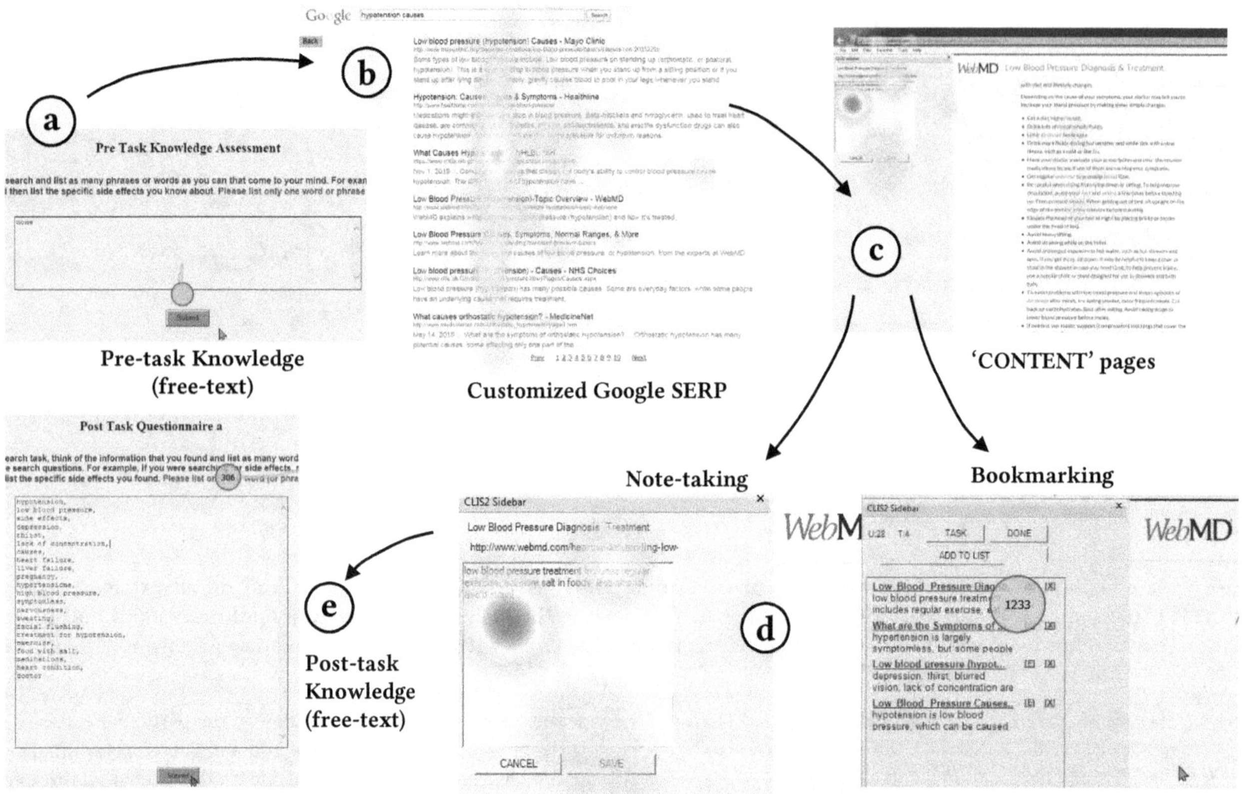

Figure 2: Procedure for each of the search tasks: (a) pre-task knowledge assessment, (b) searching for information using Google, (c) visiting search result webpages, (d) bookmarking webpages that contain relevant information, and also taking notes, and (e) assessing the knowledge change through a post-task questionnaire.

After the pre-task assessment, the online searching started. Participants searched for, and visited publicly available webpages using Google. We asked them to bookmark a webpage if they considered it relevant to their task, and (optionally) to take notes of the information found on the webpage with respect to information need prompted by a task scenario. The bookmarking and note-taking features were mechanisms to help participants engage more in the simulated tasks in the lab (motivating task scenarios, as discussed in [2]). Since the tasks motivated the participants to find information for helping their friends and family, the notes were meant to help them remember and share the information they found.

We classified each visited webpage as a 'SERP' (Search Engine Result Page) or a 'CONTENT' page, based on whether it was a Google SERP, or any other page, respectively. A CONTENT page was further marked as 'RELEVANT', if the participant bookmarked the page.

At the end of each task, the participants completed a Post-task knowledge assessment. This served as the final check of the participant's knowledge for the topic of the search session. The prompt for the post-task assessment was as follows:

Now that you have completed this search task, think of the information that you found and list as many words or phrases as you can on the topic of the search task. This will be short ANSWERS to the search questions. For example, if you were searching for side effects, please do not just type the phrase "side effects", but rather type "side effects" and then list the specific side effects you found. Please list only one word (or phrase) per line and end each line with a comma.

After the Post-task assessment for each task, participants were presented with the NASA-TLX (Task Load Index) [15], which measured their perceived workload invested in the search task.

A key difference of our study from recent works like [11, 32] is that we aimed to capture knowledge change in the form of free-recall from memory, so that it is independent of the task topic. (Although participants took notes while searching, they were not allowed to consult these notes during the post-task assessment, as we were trying to capture how much of the information they learnt, and remembered). There was no time-limit on any portion of the task, including the Pre- and Post-task knowledge assessments. A session typically lasted for 1.5 to 2 hours. On completion of the entire study session, each participant received $25.

4 MEASURES

We have calculated our variables for each search task separately. We argue that for a user having minimal topical expertise, knowledge of disparate topics (e.g. Vitamin A vs. hypotension) are independent of each other. Therefore, a *user-task pair* is our unit of analysis, and all the measures described below are calculated for each of such user-task pairs.

4.1 Knowledge Change Measures (KC)

Our aim was to measure the difference in a user's knowledge of vocabulary on a searched topic, before and after a search task. So we needed two measurement points, and deliberated on a variety of possibilities for assessing participants' knowledge levels. Fact-checking questions before a task were considered inappropriate, as we wanted to avoid exposing the participant to the topic's content before they start the search. Since the tasks were conducted on the open web, we could not use methods like Sentence Verification Technique (SVT) [10], which requires creation of questions for each document. Our participants were not experts on the topics, hence concept maps and mind-mapping were deemed inappropriate, as they are particularly difficult to score for non-experts. Thus we settled for the Pre- and Post-Task knowledge assessments, where participants were asked to free-recall as many words or phrases on the topic of the task as they could, without time limit.

4.1.1 Simple Knowledge Change Measure: Our first knowledge change measure, *KC_Simple*, is a simple, topic-independent measure. It was calculated as the relative difference in the number of items (words or phrases) entered by users before and after each task.

4.1.2 Expert Knowledge Creation: In order to support more sophisticated measure of knowledge change, we created a vocabulary of expert words and phrases on the search task topics. The vocabulary was crowd-sourced on the Amazon Mechanical Turk (AMT) platform, and then verified in consultation with a medical doctor. A separate question for each facet of our search tasks was administered on AMT. The questions asked crowd-workers to enter as many words or phrases as they could on the topic of a task facet, along with providing links to web-sources for this information. We received responses from 156 and 91 crowd-workers on Task 1 and 2, respectively. The responses yielded 474 and 171 words / phrases on the topics of Task 1 and 2. After removing duplicates, the lists were reviewed and cleaned in consultation with a medical doctor. The final result was two lists of 115 and 105 words or phrases, for Task 1 and 2, respectively.

4.1.3 Semantic Similarity with Expert Knowledge: Semantic similarity between two pieces of text (words / phrases / sentences / documents) measures how similar the two texts are, in terms of their meaning, rather than their syntactical representation (e.g. their string format) [14]. To measure the knowledge-change of our participants, we calculated how much their Pre- and Post-task free-recall entries were semantically similar to our curated expert vocabulary. For this purpose we used the state-of-the-art Universal Sentence Encoder [3] from Google's TensorFlow Hub, which encodes natural texts into a 512-dimensional embedding vector. We did not use popular word-embedding models like word2vec [21] and GloVe [25] because they are more suited for single word comparisons, while we were measuring similarity between phrases and/or sentences. The universal sentence encoder is pre-trained and optimized for greater-than-word length text, like sentences, phrases or short paragraphs. Before encoding our texts (participant input or expert knowledge) into sentence embedding vectors, we removed stopwords from the text using the English stopword list from the popular python package, Scikit-Learn [24]. Instead of using the raw cosine value of similarity between two sentence embedding vectors **u** and **v** as a measure of their semantic similarity, we used the angular similarity between the vectors, sim(**u**, **v**) (Eqn. 1), as it provides better discrimination power than the raw cosine value.

$$sim(\mathbf{u}, \mathbf{v}) = \left(1 - \arccos\left(\frac{\mathbf{u} \cdot \mathbf{v}}{\|\mathbf{u}\| \, \|\mathbf{v}\|}\right) / \pi\right) \tag{1}$$

First we calculated angular similarity between Pre-task entries and expert vocabulary $pre\_exp\_sim = sim(\mathbf{pre\_task}, \mathbf{expert})$, and angular similarity between Post-task entries and expert vocabulary $post\_exp\_sim = sim(\mathbf{post\_task}, \mathbf{expert})$,. Then we calculated our knowledge change measures by taking the difference (*KC_Sem_Diff*) between them (Eqn. 2), as well as their ratio (Eqn. 3) (*KC_Sem_Ratio*).

$$KC\_Sem\_Diff = post\_exp\_sim - pre\_exp\_sim \tag{2}$$

$$KC\_Sem\_Ratio = \frac{post\_exp\_sim}{pre\_exp\_sim} \tag{3}$$

4.2 Eye-tracking Measures (ET)

The eye-tracking variables we use reflect the process of reading. We calculated them on SERPs and CONTENT pages, and separately, on CONTENT pages relevant to a task, since we assume that participants learn most from reading such web pages. We label eye fixations as "reading", when a person is reading words sequentially in a horizontal line on a web page (in contrast with scanning text, when eyes are being fixated on isolated words) [4, 5], and we use only "reading fixations" in our measures.

We calculated total duration, and count of fixations on all pages of given a type, as well per page. We also calculated total length of reading sequences (in pixels), number of eye regressions (when eyes are moving back to fixate on a previously seen word), and the length of regressions (in pixels).

4.3 Search Interaction Measures (SI)

Search behavior was characterized by typical measures that included number of visited SERPs and CONTENT pages (we counted visits as well as revisits that were longer than 300ms and associated with at least two fixations), dwell time on pages by their type, number of queries, type of query reformulations [18], and commonality of words used in queries. This commonality was measured as the harmonic mean of the word usage-frequencies (obtained from the Google Web Trillion Word Corpus [9] which contains approximately 13.5 mln. unique words) of the words used in queries, with a lower number indicating that less common, or more specialized words were used in queries.

Search-effort is operationalized as a two part, multiple-component construct, composed of the above two groups of measures, SI and ET: (a) search interaction (i.e., visiting SERPs, clicking links and visiting content pages (result pages), entering queries); and (b) acquiring text from web pages (i.e., number and duration of reading fixations, length of reading sequences, number and length of eye regressions).

Table 1: Selected results showing differences in the search-interactions (SI) and Eye-tracking (ET) variables, for the HI and LO knowledge-change groups based on our proposed knowledge-change (KC) measures. More differences were observed in ET measures, and less for SI measures.

Category	*Measure Name*	*KC_Simple* LO: Mean (SD)	HI: Mean (SD)	M-W |z|	*KC_Sem_Ratio* LO: Mean (SD)	HI: Mean (SD)	M-W |z|	*KC_Sem_Diff* LO: Mean (SD)	HI: Mean (SD)	M-W |z|	*Description*
Participant	*eHEALS*	36.56 (5.8)	38.25 (4.58)	1.40	36 (6.65)	38.83 (2.66)	1.50	36.72 (5.77)	38.08 (4.68)	1.04	eHealth Literacy Score of each participant
	WMC	4.78 (.94)	4.85 (1.1)	0.11	4.84 (1.04)	4.79 (1)	0.20	4.86 (1.02)	4.77 (1.03)	0.32	Working Memory Capacity (WMC) for remembering long and short words
Webpage (SI)	*pg_n*	24.72 (14.77)	28.62 (14.18)	1.07	26.8 (16.67)	26.45 (12.1)	0.46	26.52 (16.78)	26.75 (11.95)	0.71	Total number of webpages visited
	pg_serp_n	11.8 (6.25)	11.66 (7.87)	0.38	12.48 (7.93)	10.95 (5.98)	0.33	12.44 (7.93)	11 (5.99)	0.27	Number of SERPs
	pg_content_n	11.52 (9.17)	15.33 (9.37)	1.54	12.88 (9.9)	13.91 (8.97)	0.50	12.64 (10.05)	14.16 (8.76)	0.81	Number of CONTENT pages
	pg_content_rel_n	9.72 (13.67)	8.33 (5.25)	0.46	10.32 (13.85)	7.7 (4.45)	0.07	10.08 (13.93)	7.95 (4.34)	0.39	Number of CONTENT pages bookmarked (i.e. considered relevant)
Query (SI)	*query_n*	6.04 (3.36)	6.12 (3.62)	0.15	6.08 (3.76)	6.08 (3.18)	0.25	6.12 (3.78)	6.04 (3.15)	0.19	Number of queries entered
	qr_new_n	0.6 (1.25)	0.83 (.96)	1.49	.48 (.82)	.95 (1.33)	1.35	.4 (.76)	1.04 (1.33)	*1.95^*	Query reformulations: number of new queries
	search_effectiveness	1.63 (1.49)	2.1 (2.81)	0.06	1.77 (1.63)	1.95 (2.75)	0.31	1.74 (1.65)	1.98 (2.73)	0.17	Ratio of RELEVANT CONTENT pages visited to number of queries entered
	q_words_freq	9,203k (14,126k)	8,141k (12,601k)	0.78	10,325k (14,079k)	6,973k (12,442k)	*1.76^*	10,845k (14,087k)	6,431k (12,255k)	**2.16 ***	Harmonic mean of usage-frequencies of words (from Google n-gram corpus [9]) used in queries. Lower number means less common (more specialized) words were used in queries.
Eye-tracking (ET)	*rseq_len*	107k (50k)	80k (37k)	**2.08 ***	106k (50k)	80k (37k)	**2.06 ***	106k (50k)	81k (37k)	**1.98 ***	Total length of scan-paths obtained by joining 'reading' fixation points (in k-pixels)
	regr_n	199.52 (94.05)	156.58 (78.42)	1.63	202.28 (96.99)	153.7 (72.72)	*1.75^*	202.08 (97.24)	153.91 (72.53)	*1.71^*	Number of backward regressions
	regr_len	43k (20k)	31k (15k)	**2.04 ***	42k (20k)	31k (15k)	*1.80^*	42k (20k)	31k (15k)	*1.78^*	Total length of regressions (in k-pixels)
	fix_dur_content_sum	475451 (170890)	439282 (212973)	1.32	490878 (166768)	423212 (212294)	**2.00 ***	483675 (177089)	430715 (205695)	*1.78^*	Total duration of reading fixations on CONTENT pages, summed across all such pages (in ms)
	fix_dur_content_avg	25673 (22351)	15607 (9774)	**2.02 ***	22908 (18316)	18486 (17615)	*1.80^*	22698 (18450)	18706 (17523)	1.54	Total duration of reading fixations on CONTENT pages, averaged across all such pages (in ms)
	fix_n_content_avg	92.05 (81.38)	56.57 (31.46)	*1.90^*	82.32 (67.59)	66.71 (60.6)	*1.74^*	82.29 (67.61)	66.75 (60.58)	*1.72^*	Number of reading fixations per CONTENT page, averaged across pages visited
	pRR_serp	.29 (.1)	.23 (.11)	**2.10 ***	.28 (.1)	.23 (.12)	1.50	.28 (.1)	.23 (.12)	1.60	Probability of continuing to read on SERPs, averaged across SERPs visited
	pRR_content	.3 (.06)	.34 (.12)	0.54	.3 (.07)	.34 (.11)	0.64	.3 (.07)	.34 (.11)	1.02	Probability of continuing to read on CONTENT pages, averaged across pages visited
Workload	*NASA_TLX*	2.98 (.7)	3.25 (.7)	1.18	2.87 (.62)	3.36 (.71)	**2.16 ***	2.88 (.62)	3.36 (.72)	**2.11 ***	NASA Task Load Index average score

For Mann Whitney (M-W) statistics, (green cells with *) indicates $p < .05$, and (yellow cells with ^) indicates approaching .05 significance ($.05 \leq p < .1$).

5 RESULTS

In the context of our research questions, the ET and SI measures are our dependent variables, The three KC measures constructed from Pre- and Post-task responses are our independent variables. We calculated these variables separately for each task, because we argue that knowledge of disparate topics are independent of each other, and that task-topics can interact with participants' knowledge, and motivate their cognition differently. So we consider a user-task pair to be our unit of analysis. Since 30 participants performed two tasks each, there were 60 user-task pairs. Due to technical difficulties during the study (computer crash, noisy eye-tracking data, etc.) some data had to be discarded, and usable data is available for 49 user-task pairs (26 for Task 1 and 23 for Task 2). The analysis reported in this section are performed on these 49 units of analysis.

For each of the three KC measures, we partitioned the user-tasks into a LO group and a HI group, based on median-split of the particular KC score. Thus, we had three LO groups and three HI groups in total, corresponding to each KC measure.

Since our knowledge change measures are new, we do not fully know their properties. So we checked in how many instances the same user-task pair was placed in different groups (LO vs HI) by the different KC measures. We saw that the LO and HI groups were nearly identical for the two semantic similarity measures (*KC_Sem_Diff* and *KC_Sem_Ratio*) and differed only in 2/49 cases, while they were slightly different when semantic similarity measures were compared with the simple measure (*KC_Simple*) (9/49 cases). We conclude that our KC measures assess changes in topic vocabulary in similar way.

Since the measures were not normally distributed, we used non-parametric Mann-Whitney U tests to compare differences between the groups reflected in the ET and SI measures described in previous section. The results and test statistics are reported in Table 1, where the significant results are marked.

There were no differences between the eHEALS and WMC scores for the LO and HI groups, and there were no differences between the groups for most search interaction measures. LO and HI users visited about the same number of SERPs, and CONTENT pages, and marked about the same number of the latter as relevant. There was also no difference in time spent on both types of pages (total and average), no difference in the number of queries entered, and no difference in search effectiveness (number of relevant pages found per query). However, the LO group entered fewer new queries in reformulations (significant difference for *KC_Sim_Diff*, and approaching significance for *KC_Sim_Ratio*), and they used more common (or less specialized) words in their queries (*q_words_freq*). The commonality of words was measured using word-usage frequency in English, from the Google Web Trillion Word Corpus [9] (Sec. 4.3).

On CONTENT pages, LO group fixated more, had higher duration of reading fixations, and higher duration of fixations per page. In particular, on relevant CONTENT pages, the LO group had longer overall reading sequences and more eye regressions in reading. But there were no such differences in reading SERPs. On the other hand, LO users reported lower workload than HI users.

We note that these differences generally have similar pattern for our simple knowledge change measure (*KC_Simple*), as well as for our more sophisticated measure based on semantic similarity (*KC_Sem_Diff* and *KC_Sem_Ratio*).

In addition to examining differences between groups based on knowledge change measures, we separately examined differences between the two groups split based on the semantic similarity of their Post-task entries to expert vocabulary (*post_exp_sim*). This measurement, taken at one point in time after each task, represents assessment of similarity of users' vocabulary to that of experts. The results are in Table 2. The LO group visited fewer CONTENT pages, but about the same number of SERPs. LO found fewer relevant CONTENT pages, but entered about the same number of queries and used much fewer new queries in their reformulations: thus the LO group had lower search effectiveness. This group also reported lower mental workload on search tasks (approaching significance). The LO tended to continue reading on SERPs (*pRR_serp*), but had lower probability of reading on CONTENT pages (*pRR_content*). In contrast the HI group had higher probability to continue reading CONTENT pages but lower on SERPs. LO group had longer total fixation duration and more fixations on SERPs, but no such difference was found for CONTENT pages.

We did not analyze the content of the notes taken by the participants, as we saw that most of the notes were directly copy-pasted from the webpages they visited, rather than their own assimilation of the information they found.

Table 2: Selected results showing differences in some search-interactions (SI) and Eye-tracking (ET) variables, for the HI and LO groups based on similarity of post-task to expert knowledge.

Measure Name	*post_exp_sim*		
	LO: Mean (SD)	HI: Mean (SD)	M-W |z|
pg_n	24.44 (15.5)	28.91 (13.24)	*1.65^*
pg_serp_n	12.48 (7.73)	10.95 (6.25)	0.55
pg_content_n	10.4 (8.6)	16.5 (9.29)	**2.71***
pg_content_rel_n	8.16 (13.64)	9.95 (5.29)	**2.68***
qr_new_n	.28 (.79)	1.16 (1.23)	**3.29***
search_effectiveness	1.38 (1.47)	2.36 (2.75)	**2.19***
fix_dur_serp_avg	3356.92 (1408.21)	2681.13 (1377.82)	*1.72^*
fix_n_serp_avg	12.51 (5.4)	9.94 (5.25)	*1.78^*
pRR_serp	.3 (.11)	.22 (.1)	**2.39***
pRR_content	.27 (.06)	.37 (.1)	**3.37***
NASA_TLX	2.98 (.73)	3.25 (.67)	1.35

For Mann Whitney (M-W) statistics, (*) indicates $p < .05$, and (^) indicates approaching .05 significance ($.05 \le p < .1$).

6 DISCUSSION

The observed differences between LO and HI groups do not seem to be related to differences in their health literacy or working memory capacity. The measured knowledge change was based on lower-level vocabulary change and was assessed only during a relatively short duration of experimental session. This may be a reason why we did not observe effects of literacy in the general search-task-area (health literacy) on knowledge change. It is also plausible that our participant sample was too uniform to observe effects of their general mental capacity, such as working memory capacity (WMC).

The difference in reading behavior between LO and HI groups on CONTENT pages is in an unexpected direction. The LO group generally spent more time on reading CONTENT pages, and moved their eyes backward in reading sequences more often, and by a longer distance than the HI group. Thus, as reflected in ET measures, the LO group put more effort into reading on the tasks, yet our KC measures indicate that they learned less. This is a likely indication that Lo group had more difficulty in acquiring information, and that in spite of investing more effort, they learned less.

Queries entered by HI group contained more specialized vocabulary than LO group. This evidence, taken together with ET measures, show that difficulty experienced by LO group in acquiring information may be indicative of lower general verbal skill of LO group. We have not measured this individual difference in the current study.

The higher mental workload reported by HI group may be, in part, a result of higher effort needed to produce more specialized queries. Prior work showed that query production is associated with higher levels of cognitive load in web search [13].

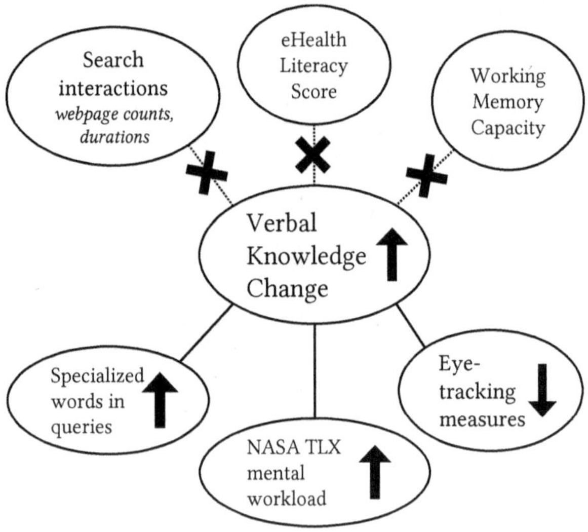

Figure 3: Summary of our findings. Arrows represent directions of relationship between measurement categories, while crosses represent no relationship.

Our findings in this work are in line with what was observed in past efforts to measure knowledge change. For instance, Yu et al. [32] observed that the total, average and maximum time spent on webpages have the highest predictive power for measuring knowledge change. Similarly, we also report significant differences in (a) *fix_dur_content_sum* between HI and LO groups of *KC_Sem_Ratio*, and (b) *fix_dur_content_avg* between HI and LO groups of *KC_Simple*. However, interestingly for us, the direction of difference in our study is opposite to intuition, i.e. users with higher knowledge gain spent less time on reading in CONTENT pages. It is important to remember however, that KC measure of Yu et al. [32] was based on a series of factual questions related to the topic of the search task, whereas ours is a topic-independent measure. Yu et al. [32] further observed that count of unique terms used in queries was the only query-related feature that showed predictive power. This is also corroborated by our finding that *q_word_freq* differs significantly for HI and LO groups based on *KC_Sem_Diff*, and is tending towards significance for *KC_Sem_Ratio* groups. In other words, people with increased knowledge change used less frequent words to perform their searches, which indicates that they were using specialized vocabulary. Similar to Yu et al's [32] random forest model showing that counts and percentages of webpages and SERPs visited are very weak predictors of knowledge change, our results also show no significant differences in number of visited SERPs and CONTENT pages between people who learned more and learned less.

The one-point measure of semantic similarity between participant's post-task free-recall and expert vocabulary (*post_exp_sim*) showed interesting relationships between LO/HI groups, and the SI and ET measures. The LO group were SERP readers who opened fewer CONTENT pages, found fewer relevant pages, and acquired less vocabulary. They entered about the same number of queries and thus visited about the same number of SERPs as HI group. But the LO group took more time to read the SERPs rather than investing more time in reading CONTENT pages, which is what HI group did. The LO group was apparently unable to identify more relevant results in-spite of investing effort in reading SERPs. The result was that words and phrases produced by HI group in free-recall were semantically closer to expert vocabulary than free-recall entries produced by LO group. Thus we could plausibly speculate that reading CONTENT pages rather than SERPs positively affects gaining more specialized vocabulary.

Fig. 3 highlights the findings of our study: users who scored higher on our knowledge change measure used less frequent / uncommon words in their queries, did lesser amount of reading on webpages, and reported higher mental workload, than those who scored less. No significant differences were found between groups w.r.t. search interactions, online health literacy, and working memory capacity.

7 CONCLUSION

Our new measures of knowledge change are related to differences in reading and querying behavior. But they uncovered some unexpected relationships, and plausibly tapped into interaction effects of search behavior, and reading with individual differences (such as, verbal ability), which were not measured.

Limitations of our work include using only two search tasks that were of similar nature (limited to health related topics), performing data analysis at the task level, a relatively uniform group of participants, and a short-time frame of experimental session. In future we plan to use a wider range of tasks, more diverse participant samples, additional individual difference tests, such as assessment of verbal skills, and conduct multiple-session study so that learning could be measured over a longer period of time.

ACKNOWLEDGEMENTS

We thank Dr. Andrzej Kahl, our medical doctor consultant for helping to review and clean the crowd responses during expert knowledge corpus creation; and Yinglong Zhang, for contributing to experimental data collection, and crowdsourcing of expert vocabulary. We also thank An Thanh Nguyen for suggesting the Universal Sentence Encoder from TensorFlow Hub.

The research described in this paper was partially funded by IMLS Award #RE-04-11-0062-11 to Jacek Gwizdka. We also gratefully acknowledge the ACM SIGIR Student Travel Grant awarded to Nilavra Bhattacharya.

REFERENCES

[1] Lorin W. Anderson, David R. Krathwohl, and Benjamin Samuel Bloom. 2001. *A Taxonomy for Learning, Teaching, and Assessing: A Revision of Bloom's Taxonomy of Educational Objectives*. Longman. 08901.

[2] P. Borlund. 2003. The IIR Evaluation Model: A Framework for Evaluation of Interactive Information Retrieval Systems. *Information Research* 8, 3 (2003), paper no. 152.

[3] Daniel Cer, Yinfei Yang, Sheng-yi Kong, Nan Hua, Nicole Limtiaco, Rhomni St John, Noah Constant, Mario Guajardo-Cespedes, Steve Yuan, Chris Tar, and others. 2018. Universal Sentence Encoder. *arXiv preprint arXiv:1803.11175* (2018).

[4] Michael J. Cole, Jacek Gwizdka, Chang Liu, Nicholas J. Belkin, and Xiangmin Zhang. 2013. Inferring User Knowledge Level from Eye Movement Patterns. *Information Processing & Management* 49, 5 (Sept. 2013), 1075–1091.

[5] Michael J. Cole, Jacek Gwizdka, Chang Liu, Ralf Bierig, Nicholas J. Belkin, and Xiangmin Zhang. 2011. Task and User Effects on Reading Patterns in Information Search. 23, 4 (2011), 346–362. https://doi.org/10.1016/j.intcom.2011.04.007 0016.

[6] Kevyn Collins-Thompson, Soo Young Rieh, Carl C Haynes, and Rohail Syed. 2016. Assessing learning outcomes in web search: A comparison of tasks and query strategies. In *Proceedings of the 2016 ACM on Conference on Human Information Interaction and Retrieval*. ACM, 163–172.

[7] Carsten Eickhoff, Jaime Teevan, Ryen White, and Susan Dumais. 2014. Lessons from the journey: a query log analysis of within-session learning. In *Proceedings of the 7th ACM international conference on Web search and data mining*. ACM, 223–232.

[8] Greg Francis, Ian Neath, and Daniel R. VanHorn. 2008. *CogLab on a CD*. Wadsworth/Thomson Learning. 00019.

[9] Alex Franz and Thorsten Brants. 2006. All Our N-Gram Are Belong to You. *Google Machine Translation Team* 20 (2006).

[10] Luanne Freund, Rick Kopak, and Heather O'Brien. 2016. The Effects of Textual Environment on Reading Comprehension: Implications for Searching as Learning. *Journal of Information Science* 42, 1 (Feb. 2016), 79–93. 00001.

[11] Ujwal Gadiraju, Ran Yu, Stefan Dietze, and Peter Holtz. 2018. Analyzing Knowledge Gain of Users in Informational Search Sessions on the Web. In *Proceedings of the 2018 Conference on Human Information Interaction&Retrieval (CHIIR '18)*. ACM, New York, NY, USA, 2–11. https://doi.org/10.1145/3176349.3176381

[12] Souvick Ghosh, Manasa Rath, and Chirag Shah. 2018. Searching As Learning: Exploring Search Behavior and Learning Outcomes in Learning-Related Tasks. In *Proceedings of the 2018 Conference on Human Information Interaction&Retrieval (CHIIR '18)*. ACM, New York, NY, USA, 22–31. https://doi.org/10.1145/3176349.3176386

[13] Jacek Gwizdka. 2010. Distribution of Cognitive Load in Web Search. *Journal of the American Society for Information Science and Technology* 61, 11 (2010), 2167–2187. https://doi.org/10.1002/asi.21385

[14] Sébastien Harispe, Sylvie Ranwez, Stefan Janaqi, and Jacky Montmain. 2015. Semantic similarity from natural language and ontology analysis. *Synthesis Lectures on Human Language Technologies* 8, 1 (2015), 1–254.

[15] Sandra G Hart and Lowell E Staveland. 1988. Development of NASA-TLX (Task Load Index): Results of empirical and theoretical research. In *Advances in psychology*. Vol. 52. Elsevier, 139–183.

[16] Bernard J. Jansen, Danielle Booth, and Brian Smith. 2009. Using the Taxonomy of Cognitive Learning to Model Online Searching. *Information Processing & Management* 45, 6 (Nov. 2009), 643–663. https://doi.org/10.1016/j.ipm.2009.05.004

[17] Kurt Kraiger, J. Kevin Ford, and Eduardo Salas. 1993. Application of Cognitive, Skill-Based, and Affective Theories of Learning Outcomes to New Methods of Training Evaluation. *Journal of Applied Psychology* 78, 2 (1993), 311–328.

[18] Chang Liu, Jacek Gwizdka, Jingjing Liu, Tao Xu, and Nicholas J. Belkin. 2010. Analysis and Evaluation of Query Reformulations in Different Task Types. In *Proceedings of the 73rd ASIS&T Annual Meeting on Navigating Streams in an Information Ecosystem - Volume 47 (ASIS&T '10)*. American Society for Information Science, Silver Springs, MD, USA, 17:1–17:10. https://doi.org/10.1002/meet.14504701214

[19] Gary Marchionini. 1997. *Information Seeking in Electronic Environments*. Cambridge University Press. Cited by 1717.

[20] Gary Marchionini. 2006. Exploratory Search: From Finding to Understanding. *Commun. ACM* 49, 4 (April 2006), 41–46. https://doi.org/10.1145/1121949.1121979

[21] Tomas Mikolov, Ilya Sutskever, Kai Chen, Greg S Corrado, and Jeff Dean. 2013. Distributed representations of words and phrases and their compositionality. In *Advances in neural information processing systems*. 3111–3119.

[22] Delia. Neuman. 2011. *Learning in Information-Rich Environments: I-LEARN and the Construction of Knowledge in the 21st Century*. Springer, New York. 00011.

[23] Cameron D Norman and Harvey A Skinner. 2006. eHEALS: the eHealth literacy scale. *Journal of medical Internet research* 8, 4 (2006).

[24] F. Pedregosa, G. Varoquaux, A. Gramfort, V. Michel, B. Thirion, O. Grisel, M. Blondel, P. Prettenhofer, R. Weiss, V. Dubourg, J. Vanderplas, A. Passos, D. Cournapeau, M. Brucher, M. Perrot, and E. Duchesnay. 2011. Scikit-learn: Machine Learning in Python. *Journal of Machine Learning Research* 12 (2011), 2825–2830.

[25] Jeffrey Pennington, Richard Socher, and Christopher Manning. 2014. Glove: Global vectors for word representation. In *Proceedings of the 2014 conference on empirical methods in natural language processing (EMNLP)*. 1532–1543.

[26] Peter Pirolli, Patricia Schank, Marti Hearst, and Christine Diehl. 1996. Scatter/Gather Browsing Communicates the Topic Structure of a Very Large Text Collection. 213–220.

[27] Karthik Raman, Paul N. Bennett, and Kevyn Collins-Thompson. 2013. Toward Whole-Session Relevance: Exploring Intrinsic Diversity in Web Search. In *Proceedings of the 36th International ACM SIGIR Conference on Research and Development in Information Retrieval (SIGIR '13)*. ACM, New York, NY, USA, 463–472. https://doi.org/10.1145/2484028.2484089 Cited by 0000.

[28] Pertti Vakkari. 2016. Searching as learning: A systematization based on literature. *Journal of Information Science* 42, 1 (2016), 7–18.

[29] Ryen W. White, Susan T. Dumais, and Jaime Teevan. 2009. Characterizing the Influence of Domain Expertise on Web Search Behavior. In *Proceedings of the Second ACM International Conference on Web Search and Data Mining - WSDM '09*. ACM Press, Barcelona, Spain, 132.

[30] Barbara M. Wildemuth. 2004. The Effects of Domain Knowledge on Search Tactic Formulation. *Journal of the American Society for Information Science and Technology* 55, 3 (Feb. 2004), 246–258.

[31] Ran Yu, Ujwal Gadiraju, and Stefan Dietze. 2018. Detecting, Understanding and Supporting Everyday Learning in Web Search. *arXiv:1806.11046 [cs]* (June 2018). arXiv:cs/1806.11046

[32] Ran Yu, Ujwal Gadiraju, Peter Holtz, Markus Rokicki, Philipp Kemkes, and Stefan Dietze. 2018. Predicting User Knowledge Gain in Informational Search Sessions. In *The 41st International ACM SIGIR Conference on Research & Development in Information Retrieval (SIGIR '18)*. ACM, New York, NY, USA, 75–84. https://doi.org/10.1145/3209978.3210064

[33] Xiangmin Zhang, Michael Cole, and Nicholas Belkin. 2011. Predicting users' domain knowledge from search behaviors. In *Proceedings of the 34th international ACM SIGIR conference on Research and development in Information Retrieval*. ACM, 1225–1226.

Reading Protocol: Understanding what has been Read in Interactive Information Retrieval Tasks

Daniel Hienert*, Dagmar Kern*, Matthew Mitsui+, Chirag Shah+, Nicholas J. Belkin+

*GESIS – Leibniz Institute for the Social Sciences
Cologne, Germany
{firstname.lastname}@gesis.org

+School of Communication & Information
Rutgers University
New Brunswick, NJ, USA
{mmitsui, chirags, belkin}@rutgers.edu

ABSTRACT

In Interactive Information Retrieval (IIR) experiments the user's gaze motion on web pages is often recorded with eye tracking. The data is used to analyze gaze behavior or to identify Areas of Interest (AOI) the user has looked at. So far, tools for analyzing eye tracking data have certain limitations in supporting the analysis of gaze behavior in IIR experiments. Experiments often consist of a huge number of different visited web pages. In existing analysis tools the data can only be analyzed in videos or images and AOIs for every single web page have to be specified by hand, in a very time consuming process. In this work, we propose the reading protocol software which breaks eye tracking data down to the textual level by considering the HTML structure of the web pages. This has a lot of advantages for the analyst. First and foremost, it can easily be identified on a large scale what has actually been viewed and read on the stimuli pages by the subjects. Second, the web page structure can be used to filter to AOIs. Third, gaze data of multiple users can be presented on the same page, and fourth, fixation times on text can be exported and further processed in other tools. We present the software, its validation, and example use cases with data from three existing IIR experiments.

CCS CONCEPTS

• **Information systems~Users and interactive retrieval**

KEYWORDS

Eye Tracking; Reading Behavior; Task

ACM Reference format:

Daniel Hienert, Dagmar Kern, Matthew Mitsui, Chirag Shah, Nicholas J. Belkin. 2019. Reading Protocol: Understanding what has been Read in Interactive Information Retrieval Tasks. In Proceedings of the 2019 Conference on Human Information Interaction and Retrieval (CHIIR '19), March 10–14, 2019, Glasgow, Scotland Uk. ACM, New York, NY, USA, 9 pages. DOI: 10.1145/3295750.3298921

ACM ISBN 978-1-4503-6025-8/19/03...$15.00
https://doi.org/10.1145/3295750.3298921

1 INTRODUCTION

A significant part of research in Interactive Information Retrieval (IIR) is to study user behavior in the context of search tasks. Therefore, in IIR experiments, the user's interaction with the system is recorded by capturing keyboard, mouse and browser actions, but also by recording the user's gaze motion on the monitor with eye tracking. This allows the analyst to understand which regions the user has looked at. In (I)IR, interesting findings between gaze behavior and concepts such as relevance [2, 18], user interest [1, 16], knowledge level [13] or task types [15] has been found.

Eye tracking software records the stimulus data (what is shown on the monitor) as images and videos with the benefit of simple data collection. However, the disadvantages become apparent later during data analysis: Gaze data can be shown and analyzed again only on images and videos, e.g. as gaze plots or heat maps. Thereby, the underlying website structure and the visible text can be accessed only with great effort, e.g. by manual inspection of the videos or by drawing areas of interest (AOI) manually on the stimuli images.

In this paper, we introduce the reading protocol tool. The software exploits the idea of mapping gaze data down to the textual level. As a result, it gives the analyst much more possibilities for analyzing eye tracking data. It can be directly seen over tens or hundreds of stimuli pages what has been viewed and read by the subjects on the text level. The whole data set can be immediately filtered down to certain participants, stimuli pages and areas of interest. Fixation times for all this data can be exported and further processed in other tools. In the context of IIR, this gives much more possibilities to understand what has actually been viewed and read by users within a search task.

In the following, we will present related work in the areas of IIR, eye tracking, and reading behavior. We will then present the reading protocol tool, its validation and will show its capabilities with data from three existing IIR experiments and will then discuss the pros and cons of the tool.

2 RELATED WORK

2.1 The Task in IIR

The *task* plays an important role in the IIR search process. The need to conduct a task arises from a *problematic situation* in which a user realizes that she lacks knowledge about a specific problem, topic or situation [3]. A search task is then the activity to accomplish the *goal* of receiving information about the specific issue [35]. An overall goal can be divided into several sub-goals which are processed by a user with different *information seeking strategies* (ISS) [4]. Models in IIR put these basic concepts into an overall system. As a turning point in IR research, the classical laboratory framework has been extended by Ingwersen & Järvelin [21] with the seeking-, work-task-, socio-organizational and cultural context. Borlund [9] proposes an IIR evaluation model with the help of the simulated work task. This can be used to evaluate IIR systems as realistically as possible, but also relatively controlled. Another framework is the usefulness evaluation model [12] which tries to measure the usefulness on the entire seeking episode, on each interaction, and on the system support level. In order to study different task characteristics, it can be differentiated between different *task types*. Kellar et al. [24], for example, differentiate between fact finding, information gathering, browsing and transactions. Li & Belkin [26] apply a faceted task classification system to describe a task on facets such as the source of task, task doer, time, action, product, and goal. Recently, in IIR, the role of *learning* in the search process has become more prominent [34]. This view tries to understand how the interaction with information leads to the modification of a searcher's knowledge structure.

2.2 Eye Tracking in IR

Eye tracking as a method to capture the user's gaze is used in different disciplines such a Marketing, Psychology or HCI. It is also used as a method to study user behavior in information search, e.g. for general web search [17] or over different task types [23]. On a more conceptual level, gaze data can also be used as a source for implicit user feedback. For example, a number of research works [e.g. 2, 18] try to find relationships between gaze behavior and the concept of *relevance*. Other research uses gaze data to identify the search *interest* [1] or the *intention* of the current search query [33]. Gaze data can also be used proactively for *re-ranking* and *query expansion* [10]. Specifically, in IIR eye tracking data has been used to predict the user's knowledge level [13] or to discriminate between different task types [15], also in relation to task facets [14].

The idea of mapping eye tracking data to the Document Object Model (DOM) of a web page and to the web page text has already been applied in earlier systems. After an eye tracking experiment, WebEyeMapper and WebLogger [27] can be used to map eye tracking data and cached web pages to specific HTML elements and their text content. The results are stored in a database. WebGazeAnalyzer [5] uses the same basic process but also allows to analyzes reading behavior on web pages with metrics such as reading coverage, regressions and reading speed. Unfortunately, these earlier research systems seem to be discontinued and not publically available. More recent research uses eye tracking data on the word level e.g. for the analysis of topical interests [16] or for showing multimedia content based on the read word [6].

Gaze data can be visualized with a number of visualizations such as gaze plots or heat maps, a recent overview of visualization types is given in [7]. However, most visualization techniques are focused on showing the overall gaze behavior on the whole stimulus page. More specialized visualization techniques for reading behavior are presented in applications such as EyeMap [32] or GazePlot [31] which show fixations and saccades at the word level.

2.3 Reading Behavior

A common model for the human reading process is the E-Z reader model [28]. This model assumes that reading is a serial process in which the reader fixates one word at a time (fixation) and then shifts to the next word (saccade). The fixation is divided into two stages: L1 - the basic word identification ("familiarity check") and L2 understanding the meaning ("lexical access"). In reading tasks fixation times can be e.g. 122ms for L1 and between 151ms and 233ms for L1+L2 depending on word length, word frequency and the word/text difficulty [28]. In non-reading tasks, e.g. the visual search of target words, fixation times can differ [29]. Reading behavior can also differ much in real-world settings [22] on the different levels of reading words and sentences, whole text comprehension and the integration over multiple documents. Reading behaviour is also influenced by the reader with different expertise, knowledge, attitude, ability and especially the task one is doing.

3 THE READING PROTOCOL TOOL

In this section, we present the reading protocol tool. We first outline the main concept, give an overview of the user interface, describe the needed input data and explain briefly the computation of word-eye-fixations.

3.1 Main Idea

Eye tracking data in all common analysis software is most often visualized as (gaze)-videos, heat maps or gaze plots ([7] gives an overview). This makes the analysis process costly because video- and image-based data needs to be inspected manually by the data analyst. The connection between gaze data and underlying data such as the website structure or the text is lost and cannot be further processed. The reading protocol tool maps eye tracking data down to the word level of the website's textual content. In reading protocol's user interface the gaze data is then shown on the textual level what gives the analyst much more possibilities for the analysis.

3.2 User Interface

The user interface of reading protocol mainly consists of three different components: (1) the filter menu, (2) the stimulus section and (3) the overall data table. An instance of reading protocol can be found under the address www.vizgr.org/reading_protocol.

The filter menu (Fig. 1a) contains a number of filters with which the analyst can filter down the data set of the whole IIR experiment. There are filters for subjects, stimuli pages, and AOIs described by Cascading Style Sheets (CSS) labels. The filtered data set is then shown accordingly in the stimulus section and in the overall data table. There are three sliders to control the coloring behavior of fixated words and for hiding non-fixated text sections.

The stimulus section (Fig. 1b) shows per default for every subject each stimulus in chronological order. Words which have been fixated are coded along a cold (blue) to hot (red) color scale. Words and text passages which has been viewed longer (e.g. 122ms and above) can be identified easily by their more hot-

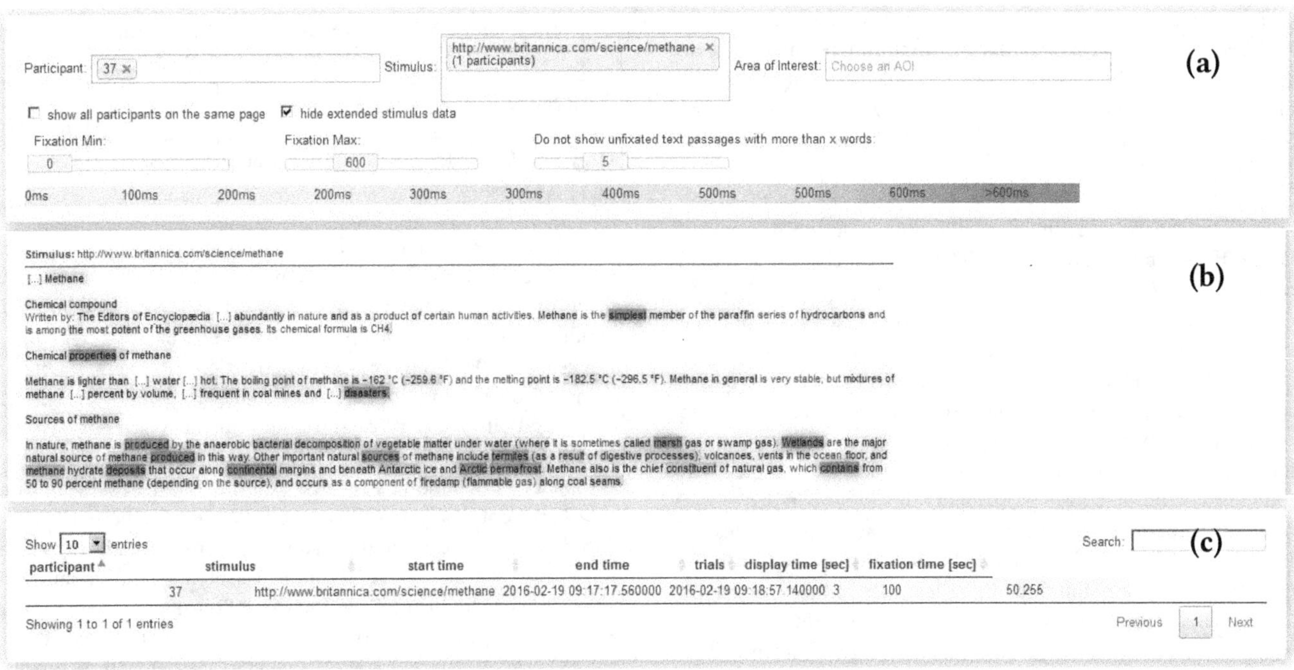

Figure 1: Reading protocol's user interface

colored backgrounds. Words and text passages that have been viewed only by scanning (e.g. everything under 122ms) are only slightly cold color-coded in violet.

The data table (Fig. 1c) then contains all information in a table format which can be either sorted and searched or copied to external tools.

3.3 Input Data

Reading protocol needs two input data sets: (1) raw eye gaze data from the eye tracking software. This can normally be exported as CSV from the eye tracking software. (2) the stimuli pages as HTML. These can either (a) be recorded live in new experiments with a number of browser plugins, (b) be taken from existing experiments if recorded or (c) be transformed from existing stimuli images of existing experiments via OCR. Compare the reading protocol software page for details[1]. Reading protocol then processes this data and builds the word-eye-fixations object. This is a JSON structure which contains every word from the stimulus page that has been viewed by the participant identified by the eye tracking x, y coordinates. For every word, there is the word position (based on the web page as text), the aggregated fixation time, and a timestamp for the first and last time the user has viewed this word.

3.4 Computing Word-Eye-Fixations

To compute eye fixations on words, the algorithm first opens the stimuli web page in a browser in the original layout. Raw gaze coordinates are loaded from the database. Fixations and saccades are separated with an I-DT algorithm [30]. For each fixation coordinate we use a browser-specific method (e.g. *caretPositionFromPoint* in Firefox) to determine the word under these coordinates. Fixation times, time stamps, word position and other information are collected for each individual word over all coordinates and are later saved in the database. For more details on the algorithm check the code in the repository[1].

[1] The reading protocol software is open source and can be found under https://git.gesis.org/iir/reading-protocol

4 EXAMPLE DATASETS

To demonstrate the tool's functionality in the following section, we use three existing datasets from IIR experiments. Two come from domain-specific literature search in the social sciences, and one dataset derives from web search in the area of journalism.

(1) The first dataset comes from a lab study with two groups of 16 subjects each. All subjects worked in different fields of the social sciences. The first group consisted of bachelor and master students; the other group was built from postdoctoral researchers. The students were between 22 and 35 years old (m=26.38; 12 female, 4 male) and the postdocs were between 30 and 62 years old (m=40.19; 8 female, 8 male). All subjects were recruited via e-mail and personal recommendation. All subjects were given the same document about "education inequality". Their task was to find similar documents in the social science literature portal Sowiport [20]. They were free to use different search strategies like author or keyword search, and they had ten minutes time to solve the task. The main research question was to find out which search strategies users would apply.

The subjects used a keyboard, a mouse and a 22″-monitor connected to a laptop. The laptop display served as an observation screen for the interviewer who was with the subject in the same room during the study. For tracking their eye movements, a remote eye tracking device SMI iView RED 250 was used with a 0.4 degree gaze position accuracy. It has been attached to the bottom side of the stimulus monitor. The eye tracker was calibrated with each subject using a 9-point calibration with a sampling frequency of 250Hz. More details on the experiment and the results can be found in [11]. We refer to this experiment as the "search strategies"-experiment.

Eye tracking data for this experiment was exported with the SMI BeGaze tool as CSV and imported into the reading protocol database (~3 million rows). Subjects viewed altogether 511 detailed record pages which were downloaded from the Sowiport portal including all JS and CSS and stored in the reading protocol database.

(2) The second dataset consists of data recorded during another lab study with the same literature portal Sowiport but with different tasks and subjects. The 25 researchers in the field of social science (16 female, 9 male, age ranging from 23 to 45 years, 14 held a bachelor degree, 10 a master degree and one is a postdoctoral researcher) were recruited through the IIRpanel[2], mailing lists, and posters at the local university. Participants were asked in simulated work task scenarios to search for and to bookmark relevant publications either to a topic they are familiar with or to an unfamiliar topic. The topic was individually chosen by the participants themselves. In this study, two different conditions of representing an abstract were tested. In one case, the 20% most important keywords (based on tf-idf calculations) were highlighted in yellow. The other case served as a baseline with no highlighted words. With this study, we wanted to find out how abstract with highlighted words affect the information search behavior.

In single sessions, participants set in front of a 22″ monitor, connected to a laptop that ran the eye tracking software form SMI and used keyboard and mouse to perform their tasks. The eye gazes were recorded by remote eye tracking device SMI iView RED 250 using a sampling rate of 60Hz. The interviewer was observing the screen and gaze activities in a different room. Results on this experiment can be found in [25]. We refer to this experiment as the "highlighting"-experiment. Here again, eye tracking data was transferred from the SMI BeGaze tool to reading protocol via CSV (~2.6 million rows). Subjects looked at 1,272 detailed record pages which have been downloaded from Sowiport with JS and CSS and stored in the reading protocol database.

(3) For the third experiment, we use study data from a lab study with 40 undergraduate students from undergraduate journalism courses having completed at least one course in news writing. Subjects had to perform two different search tasks on two different search topics. For this work, we use only data for the topic: "Methane Clathrates and global warming". There were four different search tasks to choose from, but in this experiment, we only use two. The first task was Copy Editing (CPE): subjects had 20 minutes time to check the accuracy of six italicized statements from a given text. They should find and save web pages that confirm or disconfirm the statements. For this task, we have valid eye tracking data for 9 subjects (from 19 years to 21 years; m=20.33; 7 female, 2 male). The second task was Story Pitch (SP): subjects should find and save web pages that contain the six most interesting facts about the world economic impact of global warming on the Arctic Region. Here, we have valid eye tracking data from 7 subjects (from 20 years to 23 years; m=21.14; 4 female, 3 male). Both tasks have the same topic, but can be characterized by different task facets [26] as shown in table 1.

[2] https://multiweb.gesis.org/iirpanel/?en

Table 1: Task facets in the journalism experiment

	Task Facets			
Task Name	**Product**	**Level**	**Goal**	**Named Items?**
Copy Editing (CPE)	Find facts	Segment	Specific	Yes
Story Pitch (SP)	Find facts	Segment	Amorphous	No

Subjects here used a keyboard, a mouse and a 24″ monitor (1920x1080 pixels). Their activity was recorded with the Firefox browser plugin Coagmento and Morae[3]. Eye tracking was conducted with a GazePoint GP3 tracker, a 60 Hz bright pupil tracker with 0.5-1 degree accuracy. Participants were calibrated using 9-point calibration. Details on the experiment design can be found in [19]. We refer to this experiment as the "journalism"-experiment.

The eye tracking data for this experiment was exported from the GazePoint Analysis software to CSV. Because here, the eyes' coordinates were stored absolute to the monitor, before importing, we added the scrolling offset and additionally the browser's header offset. For CPE (Copy Editing), we have around 850,000 rows, for SP (Story Pitch) around 550,000 rows. Within the experiment, the pure HTML code of the viewed web pages was saved by Coagmento. Before importing to reading protocol, the corresponding JS and CSS files were crawled from the Wayback Machine[4]. All pages were then manually verified with the gaze videos for their original layout as in the experiment. For CPE we have 73 content pages, for task SP we have 70 pages.

5 Tool Validation

Building the word-eye-fixations object has a number of issues which needs to be addressed and validated. Eye tracking coordinates can be either absolute to monitor or relative to the browser's viewport. In the first case, the user's scrolling behavior needs to be taken into account. The stimulus page has to be in the original layout as it has been shown in the experiment when building word-eye-fixations from existing experiments. As a first attempt, we compared visually heat and gaze maps from existing software to the ones created with reading protocol. Figure 2 shows an example from the highlighting experiment: (a) a heat map of the stimulus page from the original eye tracking software (SMI BeGaze), (b) rendered eye-tracking points with the reading protocol script, (c) the textual view in reading protocol.

Figure 2: Comparing eye tracking coordinates: (a) a heat map from SMI BeGaze, (b) rendered eye-tracking points with reading protocol, (c) the textual view in reading protocol

[3] https://www.techsmith.de/morae.html
[4] https://archive.org/web/

A second validation was done by comparing fixation times in AOIs of the same dataset between BeGaze and the reading protocol. In the highlighting experiment (cp. section 4.2) subjects had to search and bookmark documents to a topic they are either familiar or unfamiliar with. In BeGaze we manually drew AOIs over all record sections (the document's metadata + abstract) and abstract sections in n=990 stimuli and exported the AOI fixation times. Both AOIs differ in size and the abstract AOI also differs in its position on the page. Similarly, in reading protocol we filtered all stimuli pages to the record and the abstract section and exported fixation times. Note that the algorithm in BeGaze for computing fixations differs from the one in reading protocol: in reading protocol we only count eye tracking coordinates over words, not in white spaces. However, by comparing the data, we found a correlation between the two approaches. Table 2 shows the exact results. As expected, the mean fixation times of reading protocol (RP) are a bit under those of BeGaze, because of the fact that the reading protocol does not consider whitespaces. We found a very strong Pearson correlation between both data rows of 0.912 for the record AOI and of 0.957 for the abstract AOI (both with $p<0.0001$). Figure 3 shows the graph of fixation times over all stimuli pages. It can be seen that the reading protocol curve (blue in Fig. 3) tracks the BeGaze curve (red in Fig 3) accurately.

Table 2: Fixation times in sec. comparison between data analyzed with BeGaze and with the Reading Protocol (RP)

AOI	Tool	Max	Mean	SD	Pearson
Record	BeGaze	113.245	13.873	15.399	**0.912**
	RP	92.446	11.468	13.149	
Abstract	BeGaze	95.032	9.248	13.346	**0.957**
	RP	87.070	7.730	11.792	

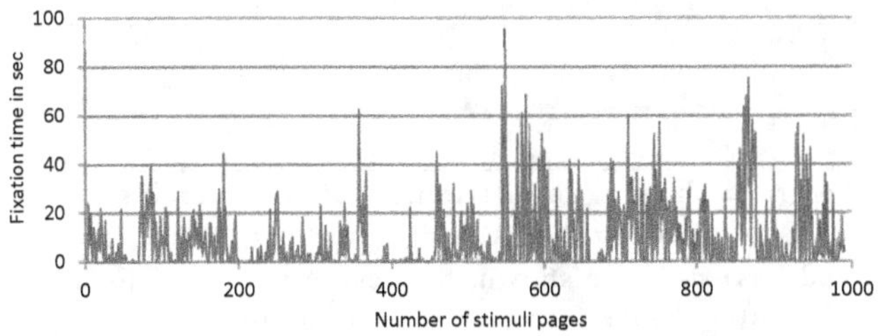

Figure 3: Fixation times in sec over all stimuli for the AOI Abstract. Reading Protocol is in blue and BeGaze in red.

6 USAGE OF THE READING PROTOCOL

In this section, we show how the reading protocol tool can be used to analyze data sets from IIR experiments. We will show the functionality and application with the help of the example datasets described above. We do not want to give a full-scale analysis on reading behavior in web search here but we want to give examples how reading protocol can support analyzing data from different experiments.

6.1 From Gaze Images/Videos to the Text Level

Existing eye tracking analysis software provide a number of visualization techniques to analyze gaze data (cp. [7]). For example, the user's scan path can be replayed as an overlay on stimulus images or videos. Or the fixations are shown as a heat map over the stimulus image. In common for all different visualizations is that the gaze data is shown over stimulus images/videos to let the analyst understand where exactly and for how long a subject has looked at on a stimulus. However, the underlying text can only inspected manually – so the analyst has to check which regions are hot-colored and has then to extract manually from the image/video what is the text underneath.

In reading protocol, we transfer from stimulus images and videos to the textual level. This has some advantages which are shown in this and the next paragraphs. However, the core idea is to understand what has been viewed and read on the textual level in the context of an IIR task.

For every stimulus page, gaze data is encoded as colored backgrounds of the words in the sense of a heat map. Words with only slight fixations times (0 to 100ms) are colored in light-violet, words with higher fixations times (>100ms) are colored from blue over green/yellow/orange to red. This way, the analyst can instantly see which stimuli pages have only be scanned and which passages have been viewed and read more intensively.

To allow an even better overview on the stimuli level, we use two techniques: (1) with two sliders the analyst can control the coloring behavior. "Fixation min" sets the starting point, "fixation max" the end point of the color scale. For example, one can color only words with more than 122ms fixation time ("lexical access") and above. (2) The analyst can control with another slider how many consecutive words are hidden that have not been fixated at all. This hides larger text passages from the page which have not been viewed and let the stimuli collapse. Figure 4 shows a stimulus page from the journalism task Story Pitch where the subject has inspected the Wikipedia page for "Methane Clathrates".

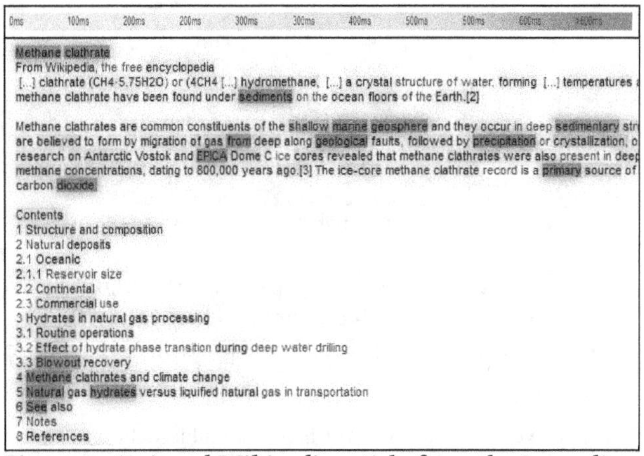

Figure 4: A viewed Wikipedia article from the journalism task Story Pitch. The first paragraph has been only scanned; parts of the first paragraph are collapsed in "[...]". The second paragraph has been extensively read. Note, how the subject is also interested in the "Methane clathrates and climate change" line in the list of contents.

6.2 Task-based experiments

The task is an important concept in IIR (see Section 2.1) and also the starting point of many experiments conducted in IIR. A lot of data is collected within such experiments such as log data with user actions, keyboard and mouse data, questionnaires, but also eye tracking data. Often research in IIR tries to find correlations between user behavior and recorded data. Existing eye tracking analysis software take into account the concept of the task only by labeling the task type to subjects. However, for further analysis, visualizations techniques from the analysis software have to be used or raw gaze data has to be exported and further processed in other statistical software.

Reading protocol supports the concept of the task in different ways. First, stimuli pages in reading protocol are arranged in chronological order in the task so that an analyst can see which pages have been viewed and which text has been viewed and read by the user. All stimulus pages are shown on the same user interface and can be overviewed by scrolling. If the amount of data is too much, it can be filtered by participant, stimuli and additionally by areas of interest. This allows a quick overview of the data and the reading behavior. Second, task-related data and data from other resources can be additionally shown per stimulus and in the data table. For example, one can add information for the task type (A or B), the task topic, the perceived task difficulty from the questionnaire and information such as the stimuli's usefulness rated by the user. Figure 5 shows a stimulus page from the highlighting experiment with extensive annotated task and stimulus data. This example also shows that an analyst can easily see whether correlations exist between the words read and the additional displayed annotated task and stimulus data. One can see, e.g., that words with longer fixation times refer to the topic on which the participant was looking for, in this case, "well-being of migrants".

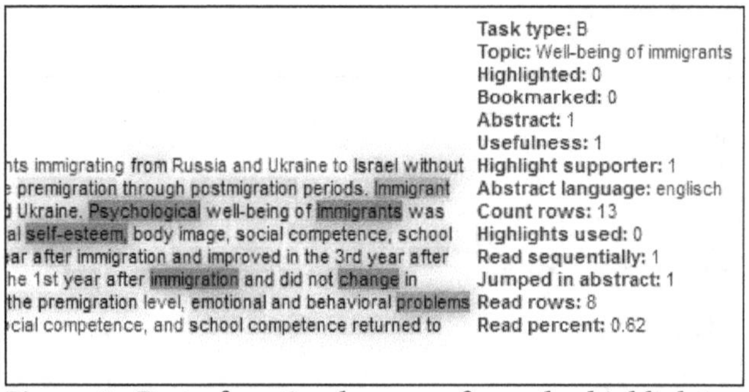

Figure 5: Part of a stimulus page from the highlighting experiment with extensive annotated task and stimulus data on the right side.

6.3 Areas of Interest

Existing eye tracking software holds stimulus data as images. Each stimulus which has been viewed by a subject (e.g. a web page) is saved as a separate screenshot. Often analysts are only interested in certain parts of the stimulus because the experiment focuses on it. For example, in literature search one can ask what the influence of the title vs. the abstract section is.

In existing analysis software areas of interest have to be created manually by the analyst as stimulus data are images. AOIs have to be created manually for each stimulus. Therefore, the analyst has to draw the AOIs on the stimulus image with forms such as rectangles, polygons or ellipses. This has to be done for each stimuli-subject combination. In large experiments with hundreds and thousands of stimuli pages, this is very time-consuming. Additionally, AOIs can change over time, for example, when websites are changing their appearance with dynamic elements.

In reading protocol the analyst can filter all stimuli pages to certain AOIs with a mouse click. Within the rendering process reading protocol extracts all CSS IDs and class information of the stimuli pages. In the user interface, the analyst can choose one or more labels from the filter menu and all stimuli pages are filtered to these elements. Additionally, the fixation time, number of words and characters fixated and the percentage of words fixated for the chosen AOIs are shown in the page information and in the data table.

Example Search Strategies: In the search strategies experiment it is interesting to understand for the analyst which document sections such as title, authors, keywords etc. has been viewed and which has been used for browsing in the document collection in the sense of the task. For users, there are several possibilities, e.g. browsing by author names, category, keywords, related entries, references, citations etc. The analyst can filter down to these areas of interest, can view and compare reading times. Figure 6 shows stimuli pages from this experiment showing only the AOIs title, authors, source, category, and keywords.

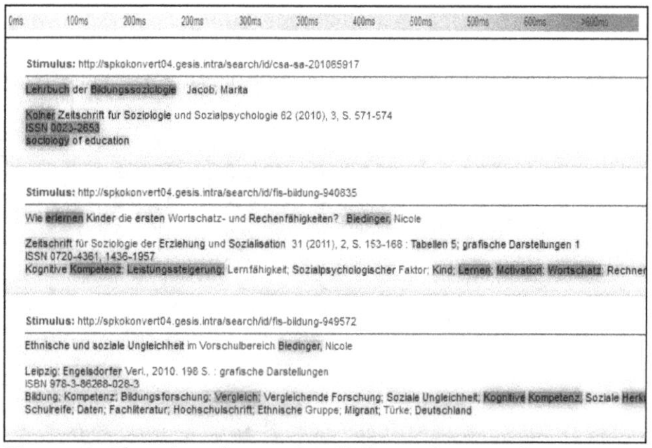

Figure 6: Showing three stimuli from the search strategies experiment. Only the AOIs title, authors, source, category and keywords are shown, the rest is hidden. This user is inspecting document keywords very intensively.

6.4 Multiple users

In existing analysis software, it is possible to integrate eye tracking data of multiple users. For example, in SMI BeGaze a heat map visualization can show the accumulated data of multiple users. Fixations for all users are summed up and shown on the same stimulus page. With this, the analyst can identify what are hot regions on the same stimulus page over all subjects.

However, this approach has certain limitations: first, data on a stimulus can only be aggregated if the stimulus is exactly the same. But, web pages' layout can change because of dynamic elements such as news tickers or advertisements. Also, if experiments are conducted over a longer time period, web pages can slightly change, e.g. because of a new design. In such cases, for each layout version, a new stimulus image is created and the data of different users cannot be shown anymore on the same stimulus page. Second, eye tracking data is again only shown on

Table 3: Statements extracted from the task description which has to be confirmed in the Copy Editing task of the journalism experiment

A	The researchers estimate that the climate effects of the release of this gas could cost *$60 trillion, roughly the size of the global economy in 2012.*
B	Large amounts of methane are concentrated in the frozen Arctic tundra *but are also found as semi-solid gas hydrates under the sea.*
C	*Scientists have found plumes of gas up to a kilometer in diameter rising from these waters.*
D	It is thought that *up to 30% of the world's undiscovered gas and 13% of undiscovered oil lie in the waters.*
E	According to Lloyds of London, *investment in the Arctic could reach $100 billion within ten years.*
F	When you look at satellite imagery, for instance the MeToP satellite, *that's gone up significantly in the last three years and the place where the increase is happening most is over the Arctic.*

images. So, stimuli pages cannot be filtered down to certain regions, fixation data for these regions are missing, and viewed text cannot be extracted and further processed.

In reading protocol, it is easy to see which stimuli pages have been seen by multiple users. In the selection menu for stimuli pages, it is annotated how many subjects have visited this page. By choosing one stimulus, the page is shown for the different users. With a tick on "show all participants on the same page" word-eye-fixations for all subjects are merged and then shown on a single stimulus page. Because reading protocol operates on the textual level, different layout versions of a stimulus can also be integrated. Therefore, within the process of merging word-eye-fixations of different users the algorithm looks, if the word cannot be found on the exact same position if it can be found in the near context of about 50 characters before or after. This way, layout variations of the same stimulus are handled more flexible and word-eye-fixations of multiple users can be integrated for one design variation. Additionally, the stimulus page can be filtered to certain AOIs and fixation data can be computed for these areas.

Showing data of multiple users on the same stimuli makes sense when they conduct the same task. We want to show examples from the search strategies- and the journalism experiment.

Example Search strategies: In the search strategies experiment all 32 subjects started from the same page to find related publications on the topic "education inequality". The analyst can now view these pages separated by subjects to study which page segments has been read by each user. With a click on "show all participants on the same page" the page is shown with the integrated data over all subjects. Playing around with the min fixation time slider reveals that users have read with highest fixation times the title and authors of the article (around 28sec in sum), followed by the DOI (~25sec), the tab label "References" and the category information (~23sec), then source and keywords (~15sec) and the tab label "Citations" (~12sec). This could be a starting point to compare this pattern to other pages in this experiment.

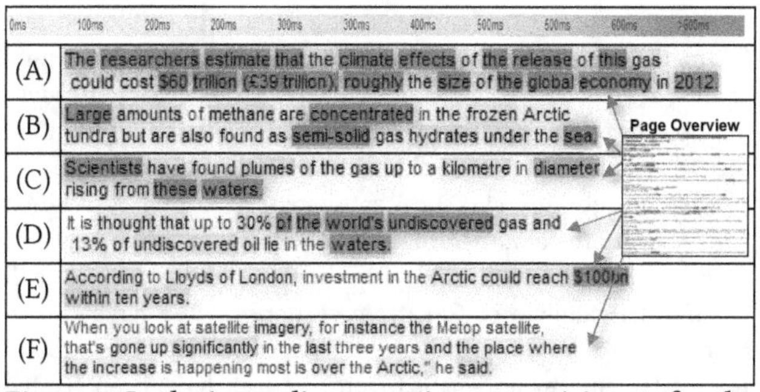

Figure 7: In the journalism experiment participants for the Copy Editing task have found the statements A-F from Table 3 on one BBC web page. The processed reading protocol page shows that the text fragments have been read extensively with a lot of fixations over 600ms. Fixation times differ because not all participants have searched or found all statements on this page.

Example Journalism CPE: In the Copy Editing task of the journalism experiment subjects were asked to verify statements from a given text by bookmarking web pages that confirm or disconfirm these statements. Table 3 shows the statements from the task description in isolation. The analyst can now check in reading protocol which web pages have been viewed by most participants in the stimuli menu. For example, the page "https://www.bbc.com/news/science-environment-23432769" has been viewed by 6 of 9 subjects. With a click, the data set is filtered to only this page showing for each subject the individual gaze behavior on it. The analyst can now check which text fragments have been read by the individual users. With a click on "show all participants on the same page" all gaze data is shown on the same page. This stimulus page is also a good example of a page that has changed its appearance in the time of the experiment because of different advertisements and news. On the textual level reading protocol can integrate the different word-eye-fixations so that we are able to see all subjects on the same stimuli. Figure 7 then shows that all verifications for this task from A) to F) can be found on the BBC web page. Showing gaze data of all subjects on the same page let the statements appear in highly red, especially the first one. This reading behavior can be found for the Copy Editing (CPE) task, but not for Story Pitch (SP) where the fixation times are higher over larger segments of the stimuli pages. Both task types have the task facets *product=find_facts* and *segment=level* in common, but differ in *goal=specific vs amorphous* and *named-items=yes vs. no* (cp. Table 1). In [14] it was found that CPE tasks have a high number of Scan-to-Read and Read-to-Scan transitions. It differs from other task types by the *level=segment* facet in opposite to *level=document.* Here we found more specifically, that for two task types with *level=segment* the one with *named-items=yes* shows a specific reading behavior with high fixation times over the single statements.

6.5 Further Processing

Reading Protocol provides three different mechanisms for further processing of the data. (1) A CSV table of the word-eye-fixations object can be copied for each stimulus by clicking on the button "Copy Word-Eye-Fixations as CSV to Clipboard". This table can then be used to analyze eye fixations on the word level in any other tool. (2) Processed and colored text or filtered text fragments can be easily copied from the user interface and analyzed further, e.g. by comparing read text fragments over multiple pages in isolation (3) The data table with information on task data, eye-fixations, filter for certain AOIs can be copied and pasted into any statistical software, e.g. to find correlation between certain columns.

Example Journalism CPE: To show an example, we will resume the example of CPE from section 6.4. We have shown that an analyst can instantly see by the hot-colored background that statements to be verified from the task have been fixated longer than the other text on the stimulus page. With the BBC web page, we already have found a good example showing this behavior. The next step would be to analyze exact fixation times for each statement and each subject.

Therefore, the analyst can copy word-eye-fixations for each subject for this stimulus from the reading protocol user interface to a statistical tool like Excel. Then word-eye-fixations for the specific statements can be separated from the rest, and by summing up a table can be generated that shows fixation times for each statement over all subjects (see Table 4). This table gives now a formal representation of the stimuli visualization that has been shown in reading protocol.

Table 4: Fixation times in ms for each statement

Subject # / Statement	13	32	61	66	7	83
A	2562.4	4219	5998.9	8312.7	1972.9	4992.8
B	2318.6	472.3	1134	114.7	2726.1	1050.4
C	2412.3	262.8	82.2	0	1128.2	988
D	5240.8	0	0	0	1120.2	1477.8
E	2323.3	0	0	0	743.8	312.6
F	723.4	0	32.7	0	49.6	362.6

The question of who has read which statement can now be answered more easily. Statement A has been read by all subjects and subject 13 has read all statements on the page. Inversely, fixation times with zero or up to 100ms indicate that the user has not read the statement.

We could go on with that analysis. However, we only want to show how word-eye-fixations can be exported and further processed in other tools to understand on a statement or text passage basis what has been read and what not, with exact fixation values.

7 DISCUSSION & CONCLUSION

In this section, we want to discuss the pros and cons of reading protocol and ideas for future work.

The last section showed that reading protocol provides a number of advantages for analysts of IIR experiments: (1) they can see over the whole task which pages have been scanned, which text sections have been read and for how long. (2) Viewing and reading behavior can be brought into relation with other task-data such as task types, questionnaire data and so on. (3) The whole dataset can be easily filtered to certain AOIs in order to prevent information overflow. (4) Gaze data of multiple users can be shown on the same page which helps to identify important text passages. (5) All fixation times on the word level and other task attributes can easily be exported and further analyzed in other tools. All in all, reading protocol helps to circumvent the manual inspection over dozens or hundreds of single images and videos in standard eye tracking analysis software.

However, there are also certain aspects an analyst has to be aware of when using the reading protocol software. In Web search, users are not only looking at HTML web pages but also at other media types such as images, videos, PDFs, presentations and so on. Reading protocol can only map eye tracking data to the text level when the HTML DOM is available, so other media types are ignored in the user interface. An analyst should be aware that within the search process, information read by the subjects can also come from other media types and one has to check e.g. the gaze videos or log protocols in addition.

Eye tracking data has a certain inaccuracy depending on factors such as hardware, software, calibration process and individual participant. Eye tracking hardware, for example, has a certain accuracy that is measured in degrees of visual angle, e.g. between 0.5-1 degree. One degree corresponds to a mean error of 11mm with a screen distance of 65cm. This error can even increase if the calibration process was poor; subjects are moving too much or wearing eye glasses, contact lenses or jewelry. All these factors sum up to a certain inaccuracy of the gaze data. This can be especially critical in reading situations with small-sized text [8]. This effect is the same for original eye tracking analysis software as for reading protocol; so, an analyst should take care of good gaze data quality. However, in the sections 6.4 and 6.5 we showed that eye tracking data can be good enough to recognize read statements within a web page, especially if we aggregate data over multiple users.

An aspect of future work is the aspect of learning in the search process. Vakkari [34] describes learning as changing one's knowledge structure by changes in concepts and their relations. He states: "Titles, abstracts and text passages browsed include possible ideas for restructuring her conceptual understanding of the topic". This is exactly what is processed and visualized by reading protocol. The exact fixation times are stored per single word and can be further processed per stimulus, per sentence or text passage and over the whole task. This can be a formal description of what comes to a user's mind from the system side within the search task and what can be one source of learning.

Understanding what participants have read at each point within a search task is the key to understand what might be the next action step or what they have learned. So far, with image- and video-based analysis software it is hard to track fixation times on text over the whole search process. Reading protocol automates this activity and lets the analyst understand what has been read in the search task, even over multiple participants and in specific areas of interest. In IIR experiments this will give the analyst an additional data stream that helps to understand, for example, what are the effects of the task type and task topic on reading behavior.

Acknowledgements This work was partly funded by the NSF grant no. IIS-1423239.

REFERENCES

[1] Ajanki, A., Hardoon, D.R., Kaski, S., Puolamäki, K. and Shawe-Taylor, J. 2009. Can eyes reveal interest? Implicit queries from gaze patterns. *User Modeling and User-Adapted Interaction.* 19, 4 (Oct. 2009), 307–339. DOI:https://doi.org/10.1007/s11257-009-9066-4.

[2] Balatsoukas, P. and Ruthven, I. 2012. An Eye-tracking Approach to the Analysis of Relevance Judgments on the Web: The Case of Google Search Engine. *J. Am. Soc. Inf. Sci. Technol.* 63, 9 (Sep. 2012), 1728–1746. DOI:https://doi.org/10.1002/asi.22707.

[3] Belkin, N.J. 1980. Anomalous states of knowledge as a basis for information retrieval. *Canadian Journal of Information Science.* 5 (1980), 133–143.

[4] Belkin, N.J., Cool, C., Stein, A. and Thiel, U. 1995. Cases, Scripts, and Information-Seeking Strategies: On the Design of Interactive Information Retrieval Systems. *EXPERT SYSTEMS WITH APPLICATIONS.* 9, (1995), 379–395.

[5] Beymer, D. and Russell, D.M. 2005. WebGazeAnalyzer: A System for Capturing and Analyzing Web Reading Behavior Using Eye Gaze. *CHI '05 Extended Abstracts on Human Factors in Computing Systems* (New York, NY, USA, 2005), 1913–1916.

[6] Biedert, R., Buscher, G. and Dengel, A. 2010. The eyeBook – Using Eye Tracking to Enhance the Reading Experience. *Informatik-Spektrum.* 33, 3 (2010), 272–281.

[7] Blascheck, T., Kurzhals, K., Raschke, M., Burch, M., Weiskopf, D. and Ertl, T. Visualization of Eye Tracking Data: A Taxonomy and Survey. *Computer Graphics Forum.* 36, 8, 260–284. DOI:https://doi.org/10.1111/cgf.13079.

[8] Blignaut, P., Holmqvist, K., Nyström, M. and Dewhurst, R. 2014. Improving the Accuracy of Video-Based Eye Tracking in Real Time through Post-Calibration Regression. *Current Trends in Eye Tracking Research.* M. Horsley, M. Eliot, B.A. Knight, and R. Reilly, eds. Springer International Publishing. 77–100.

[9] Borlund, P. 2003. The IIR evaluation model: a framework for evaluation of interactive information retrieval systems. *Information Research: an international electronic journal.* (2003).

[10] Buscher, G., Dengel, A. and van Elst, L. 2008. Query Expansion Using Gaze-based Feedback on the Subdocument Level. *Proceedings of the 31st Annual International ACM SIGIR Conference on Research and Development in Information Retrieval* (New York, NY, USA, 2008), 387–394.

[11] Carevic, Z., Lusky, M., Hoek, W. van and Mayr, P. 2017. Investigating exploratory search activities based on the stratagem level in digital libraries. *International Journal on Digital Libraries.* (2017), 1–21.

[12] Cole, M., Liu, J., Belkin, N., Bierig, R., Gwizdka, J., Liu, C., Zhang, J. and Zhang, X. 2009. Usefulness as the criterion for evaluation of interactive information retrieval. *Proceedings of the Workshop on Human-Computer Interaction and Information Retrieval* (2009), 1–4.

[13] Cole, M.J., Gwizdka, J., Liu, C., Belkin, N.J. and Zhang, X. 2013. Inferring User Knowledge Level from Eye Movement Patterns. *Inf. Process. Manage.* 49, 5 (Sep. 2013), 1075–1091. DOI:https://doi.org/10.1016/j.ipm.2012.08.004.

[14] Cole, M.J., Gwizdka, J., Liu, C., Bierig, R., Belkin, N.J. and Zhang, X. 2011. Task and user effects on reading patterns in information search. *Interacting with Computers.* 23, 4 (2011), 346–362.

[15] Cole, M.J., Hendahewa, C., Belkin, N.J. and Shah, C. 2014. Discrimination Between Tasks with User Activity Patterns During Information Search. *Proceedings of the 37th International ACM SIGIR Conference on Research & Development in Information Retrieval* (New York, NY, USA, 2014), 567–576.

[16] Eickhoff, C., Dungs, S. and Tran, V. 2015. An Eye-Tracking Study of Query Reformulation. *Proceedings of the 38th International ACM SIGIR Conference on Research and Development in Information Retrieval* (New York, NY, USA, 2015), 13–22.

[17] Granka, L.A., Joachims, T. and Gay, G. 2004. Eye-tracking Analysis of User Behavior in WWW Search. *Proceedings of the 27th Annual International ACM SIGIR Conference on Research and Development in Information Retrieval* (New York, NY, USA, 2004), 478–479.

[18] Gwizdka, J. 2014. Characterizing Relevance with Eye-tracking Measures. *Proceedings of the 5th Information Interaction in Context Symposium* (New York, NY, USA, 2014), 58–67.

[19] Hienert, D., Mitsui, M., Mayr, P., Shah, C. and Belkin, N.J. 2018. The Role of the Task Topic in Web Search of Different Task Types. *Proceedings of the 2018 Conference on Human Information Interaction & Retrieval* (New York, NY, USA, 2018), 72–81.

[20] Hienert, D., Sawitzki, F. and Mayr, P. 2015. Digital Library Research in Action - Supporting Information Retrieval in Sowiport. *D-Lib Magazine.* 21, 3/4 (2015). DOI:https://doi.org/http://dx.doi.org/10.1045/march2015-hienert.

[21] Ingwersen, P. and Järvelin, K. 2007. On the Holistic Cognitive Theory for Information Retrieval: Drifting Outside the Border of the Laboratory Framework. *Studies in the Theory of Information Retrieval (ICTIR 2007). Budapest, Hungary: Foundation for Information Society* (2007), 135–147.

[22] Jarodzka, H. and Brand-Gruwel, S. Tracking the reading eye: towards a model of real-world reading. *Journal of Computer Assisted Learning.* 33, 3, 193–201. DOI:https://doi.org/10.1111/jcal.12189.

[23] Jiang, J., He, D. and Allan, J. 2014. Searching, Browsing, and Clicking in a Search Session: Changes in User Behavior by Task and over Time. *Proceedings of the 37th International ACM SIGIR Conference on Research & Development in Information Retrieval* (New York, NY, USA, 2014), 607–616.

[24] Kellar, M., Watters, C. and Shepherd, M. 2007. A Field Study Characterizing Web-based Information-seeking Tasks. *J. Am. Soc. Inf. Sci. Technol.* 58, 7 (May 2007), 999–1018. DOI:https://doi.org/10.1002/asi.v58:7.

[25] Kern, D., Hienert, D., Angerbauer, K., Tilman, D. and Borlund, P. Lessons Learned from Users Reading Highlighted Abstracts in a Digital Library. *CHIIR '19 Proceedings of the 2019 Conference on Human Information Interaction & Retrieval.*

[26] Li, Y. and Belkin, N.J. 2008. A faceted approach to conceptualizing tasks in information seeking. *Information Processing & Management.* 44, 6 (2008), 1822–1837. DOI:https://doi.org/https://doi.org/10.1016/j.ipm.2008.07.005.

[27] Reeder, R.W., Pirolli, P. and Card, S.K. 2001. WebEyeMapper and WebLogger: Tools for Analyzing Eye Tracking Data Collected in Web-use Studies. *CHI '01 Extended Abstracts on Human Factors in Computing Systems* (New York, NY, USA, 2001), 19–20.

[28] Reichle, E.D., Pollatsek, A. and Rayner, K. 2006. E-Z Reader: A Cognitive-control, Serial-attention Model of Eye-movement Behavior During Reading. *Cogn. Syst. Res.* 7, 1 (Mar. 2006), 4–22. DOI:https://doi.org/10.1016/j.cogsys.2005.07.002.

[29] Reichle, E.D., Pollatsek, A. and Rayner, K. 2012. Using E-Z Reader to simulate eye movements in nonreading tasks: a unified framework for understanding the eye-mind link. *Psychological review.* 119, 1 (Jan. 2012), 155–185. DOI:https://doi.org/10.1037/a0026473.

[30] Salvucci, D.D. and Goldberg, J.H. 2000. Identifying Fixations and Saccades in Eye-tracking Protocols. *Proceedings of the 2000 Symposium on Eye Tracking Research & Applications* (New York, NY, USA, 2000), 71–78.

[31] Špakov, O., Siirtola, H., Istance, H. and Räihä, K.-J. 2017. Visualizing the Reading Activity of People Learning to Read. *Journal of Eye Movement Research.* 10, 5 (2017).

[32] Tang, S., Reilly, R.G. and Vorstius, C. 2012. EyeMap: a software system for visualizing and analyzing eye movement data in reading. *Behavior Research Methods.* 44, 2 (Jun. 2012), 420–438. DOI:https://doi.org/10.3758/s13428-011-0156-y.

[33] Umemoto, K., Yamamoto, T., Nakamura, S. and Tanaka, K. 2012. Search Intent Estimation from User's Eye Movements for Supporting Information Seeking. *Proceedings of the International Working Conference on Advanced Visual Interfaces* (New York, NY, USA, 2012), 349–356.

[34] Vakkari, P. 2016. Searching as learning: A systematization based on literature. *Journal of Information Science.* 42, 1 (2016), 7–18.

[35] Vakkari, P. 2003. Task-based information searching. *Annual Review of Information Science and Technology.* 37, 1 (2003), 413–464. DOI:https://doi.org/10.1002/aris.1440370110.

HAIR: Towards Developing a Global Self-Updating Peer Support Group Meeting List Using Human-Aided Information Retrieval

Sabirat Rubya
University of Minnesota
Minneapolis, MN, USA
rubya001@umn.edu

Xizi Wang
University of Michigan
Ann Arbor, MI, USA
xiziwang@umich.edu

Svetlana Yarosh
University of Minnesota
Minneapolis, MN, USA
lana@umn.edu

ABSTRACT

Alcoholics Anonymous (AA) is the largest grassroots peer support group for any health condition. While AA meeting attendance is particularly important for people who are newly sober, newcomers often have trouble finding meetings because of a lack of global up-to-date meeting list due to preference for regional autonomy in AA's organizational structure. Detection of regional webpages containing meetings and extraction of day, time, and address of meetings from those pages are essential steps in making the information available and up-to-date in a global meeting list. However, varied structure of the webpages and the meetings pose challenges in achieving the goal with traditional information retrieval methods. In this paper we propose HAIR: a semi-automated human-aided information retrieval technique and explore its potential to solve this problem. We describe future directions in developing this critical tool and discuss major implications of our work in pointing to the importance of context-specific rather than context-agnostic semi-automated information retrieval techniques by conceptualizing the proposed methods and results in a broader context.

CCS CONCEPTS

• Information systems → Information retrieval → Users and interactive retrieval • Human-centered computing → Collaborative and social computing

KEYWORDS

Alcoholics Anonymous; Peer support; Classification; Information Retrieval; Human Computation; Crowdsourcing.

ACM Reference format:

Sabirat Rubya, Xizi Wang and Svetlana Yarosh. 2019. HAIR: Towards Developing a Global Self-Updating Peer Support Group Meeting List using Human-Aided Information Retrieval. In *Proceedings of the ACM SIGIR Conference on Human Information Interaction and Retrieval (CHIIR'19). Glasgow, Scotland, UK,* ACM, New York, NY, USA, 10 pages. https://doi.org/10.1145/3295750.3298933

CHIIR '19, March 10–14, 2019, Glasgow, United Kingdom

ACM ISBN 978-1-4503-6025-8/19/03...$15.00
https://doi.org/10.1145/3295750.3298933

1 INTRODUCTION

Jane just got out of a rehab. As a next step, her counselor has suggested that she attend multiple AA meetings per week in her first year of recovery. She finds a meeting finder app, installs it on her phone, and searches for a nearby meeting. She drives for 30 minutes only to find out that the meeting is not happening there anymore (turns out the meeting information in the app was gathered over a year ago)! Frustrated and confused, Jane even thinks that maybe it's a "sign" that she should go back to drinking. Luckily, she doesn't give up, after some more search, calling a hotline, and finding an updated webpage of meetings in her town she is finally able to find and attend another meeting. "How many people aren't as lucky?" she thinks.

Alcohol Use Disorder (AUD) is a prevalent and high-impact health condition. It is estimated to cost the United States $249 billion per year, with 6.2% of Americans developing an AUD [50]. Treatments for recovery from AUD are most effective when clinical intervention is coupled with long-term maintenance programs [19]. Alcoholics Anonymous (AA) is one of the most effective and popular maintenance programs [12]. It is a free peer-based social support program that offers over fifty thousand face-to-face group meetings worldwide for people struggling with AUD. While AA meetings have the potential for positive impact on people's chances of long-term recovery [31], the illustrative scenario above depicts a critical problem that could be encountered by anyone new to recovery or new to a geographic location. There is evidence that approximately 90% of alcoholics are likely to experience at least one relapse over the 4-year period following treatment [3], and Jane could have easily been one of them if she had given after being misdirected with outdated meeting data.

Individual AA groups value autonomy, and they typically operate at a local level (e.g. county, city, town, etc.). One consequence of this level of autonomy is inconsistency in how local groups make their meeting information available (e.g., different regional AA websites contain meeting information in different formats and structures) and a lack of a national or global meeting list [36,48]. Designing a static meeting finder will not solve the problem since it would soon become outdated whenever any of the regional websites updates any meeting details. Our long-term goal is to create and maintain a searchable global "self-

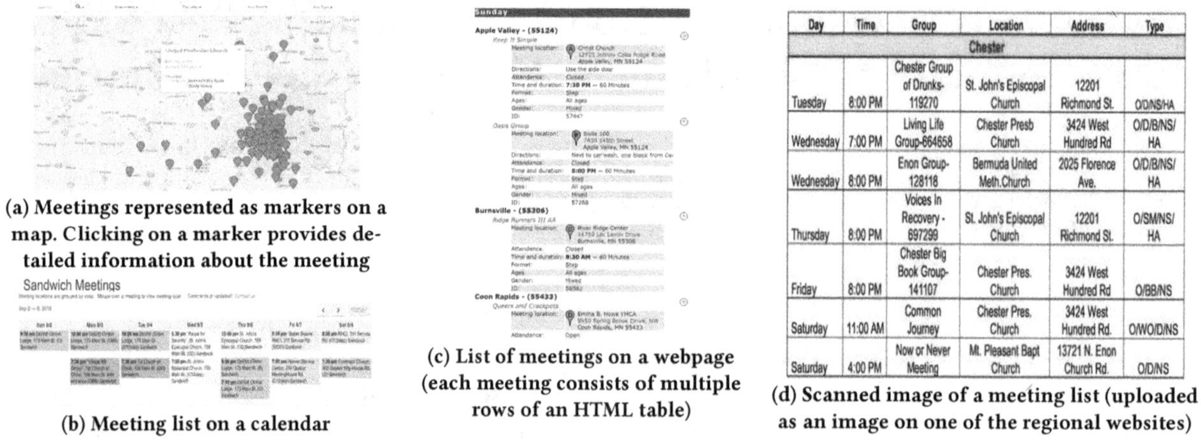

(a) Meetings represented as markers on a map. Clicking on a marker provides detailed information about the meeting

(b) Meeting list on a calendar

(c) List of meetings on a webpage (each meeting consists of multiple rows of an HTML table)

(d) Scanned image of a meeting list (uploaded as an image on one of the regional websites)

Figure 1: Different structures of meeting pages on different regional domains

updating" AA meeting list by retrieving meeting information from all the regional websites, making it available in a searchable format, and having a systematic way for the list to self-update automatically at a regular interval.

In this paper, we approach the technical challenges in extracting meeting information from all regional websites to achieve this goal. Although there has been extensive research on information retrieval from heterogeneous unstructured sources, the automated techniques may fall short in this context due to the diversity in the format and structure of the regional websites. Additionally, retrieving complete information often requires contextual knowledge. Integration of human computation (crowdsourcing) with automated IR approaches have produced better-quality results in knowledge acquisition tasks, and thus have the potential to be applied in solving the problem under consideration. In this paper we investigate the following research questions:

RQ1: What are the information retrieval challenges of developing a global self-updating AA meeting list?

RQ2: How can we combine human computation with existing IR algorithms to provide a more accurate and scalable solution to develop the list?

We answer these questions by proposing and evaluating a semi-automated **Human-Aided Information Retrieval (HAIR)** approach to information retrieval in community contexts like AA, that may empower the members of the community to work in concert with automated classification and retrieval algorithms.

2 RELATED WORK

The process of retrieving meetings from regional AA websites includes classification to identify webpages that contain meeting lists and information retrieval to extract meeting details. We incorporated human computation techniques with the automated processes of classification and information retrieval. In this section, we describe relevant research in these three fields (classification, information retrieval, and human computation), and situate the opportunities for expanding on and combining these approaches in a single solution.

2.1 Classification of Webpages

Our proposed method includes classifying a regional AA website page as a "meeting page" (a page containing information about one or more AA meeting) or a "non-meeting page" (a page that does not).

There have been extensive investigations in classifying different types of webpages using machine learning [29,43]. Most common models built to identify, categorize, and filter information from webpages use supervised learning techniques (neural networks [2], support vector machines [18,38], etc.). In service of better online search and web content management, researchers constructed features based on the text content of URL addresses [11], structure and content of webpages (e.g., [6,34]), and aspects of neighboring pages [33,41]. We primarily followed methods from the first two categories to generate features for our machine learning model, as those are more relevant in this context. For the classification task (i.e., distinguishing a webpage containing a meeting list from a page that does not) we applied Random Forest with Bagging, since research suggests that this might be the most accurate technique in this kind of imbalanced binary classification problems [1].

However, applying these techniques off-the-shelf is unlikely to provide expected accuracy in developing a self-updating global meeting list due to two reasons. The first reason is the diversity in the structure of local AA websites. There are many different examples of structures, such as regional AA domains having seven different meeting pages (one for each day of the week) that need to be classified correctly to get a complete set of meeting pages for that area. However, these pages may seem dissimilar when fed to a model for classification, since there may be a day with dozens of meetings versus another day with just one or two meetings. The second reason involves contextual challenges in identifying meeting pages. AA meetings are not the only type of information page that includes addresses and times[1] (e.g., office hours, non-recurring organizational meetings which are not

[1] Example: http://www.utahaa.org/calendar/calendar.php

open to all, etc.). Automated processes do not contain domain knowledge and may fail to classify these pages accurately.

2.2 Information Extraction from Unstructured and Semi-Structured Sources

To extract meeting information (e.g., day, time, address) from meeting pages, we build on prior work from Information Retrieval (IR), particularly pattern detection techniques. Regional pages vary drastically in the type and structure of meetings on them (see Figure 1 for examples), necessitating our work to be situated in research on IR techniques from heterogenous unstructured sources.

Previously researchers have used natural language processing (NLP) [14], pattern matching [28], and machine learning [5,13,22], etc. for extracting data from heterogeneous semi-structured or unstructured sources. Popular applications of these techniques, "named entity recognition" [30] and "temporal information extraction [26]," are relevant here, since we want to extract specific temporal entities (i.e., address, day, and time) associated with each AA meeting. Researchers have recently used natural language to extract temporal information (e.g., events) from unstructured text in social networking sites [35] or Wikipedia [20,44]. We followed and extended a modified version of the algorithm developed by Chang *et al.* [5], in which the treelike structure of webpages and repetitive patterns were utilized to extract multiple records of similar type.

The above techniques may be used as a potential solution for retrieving meeting information, however two challenges reduce the success of off-the-shelf solutions. The first challenge is in the diversity in the format structures of each "meeting page." Meetings may be represented in different structures on different pages, such as an HTML table row or combination of table rows, an event on a calendar, or even text on a scanned image. Automated algorithms may struggle to find and relate the correct details to a specific meeting. The second challenge involves the role of context. Complete retrieval often depends on knowing how the page was accessed. For instance, some meeting pages provide an option of a dynamic search; relevant information about a meeting (e.g., time, area, type, etc.) may come from a selected option of a dropdown list. Existing methods may fail to understand this context.

2.3 Combining Human & Machine Intelligence

Due to the limitations discussed in the previous subsections, we propose to combine human computation and machine intelligence to get a better result than either could achieve alone. To leverage the "wisdom of the crowd," we suggest recruiting crowd workers from a crowdsourcing marketplace to verify both the classified webpages and the automatically extracted meeting information and to identify missing information [39].

Human computation is a computer science technique in which a computational process performs its function by outsourcing certain steps to humans [46]. Recent research has been particularly interested in systems that leverage human and machine intelligence independently and/or in sequence, combining results from both sources [40,47]. For example in the field of machine learning, crowd workers have been employed to generate ground truth data and features and to validate results after classification [7,9]. Alternatively, other systems have utilized machine learning and classification techniques to filter low quality crowdsourced data [25,42,45]. However, it is not until recently that crowdsourcing has been combined with machine computations to improve accuracy of tasks that are difficult for either to perform independently [10]. This combination has been proved efficient in solving problems like video-captioning [16], cheating detection [24], acquiring street-level accessibility information [15], and building intelligent environments [21]. Researchers have also considered utilizing crowdsourcing to improve results in solving problems like data wrangling [17], collating data from multiple sources [8], and knowledge acquisition [27,47]. This process of pipelining computation results with human verification is similar to the concept of "centaur chess" where each human player reviews possible results of candidate moves generated by a machine intelligence "teammate" before making the final decision and selecting the team's move [4]. Centaur chess teams outperform both humans and computers acting alone.

The limitations of existing automated IR techniques make our problem a good fit for combining human computing with machine intelligence. Classifying webpages and retrieving information from probable meeting pages through algorithms may not always provide accurate and expected results, when such information is crucial. Moreover, incorporating human input with machine results has proven effective in cases where contextual knowledge is important. Therefore, we propose HAIR: a human-aided information retrieval technique to address information retrieval challenges in the context of developing a global self-updating peer support meeting list for AA.

3 HAIR: HUMAN-AIDED INFORMATION RETRIEVAL

In this section, we describe the process of obtaining the initial dataset (i.e., pages from regional AA websites), followed by the two steps of HAIR to develop the meeting list: classification of pages and retrieval of meeting records from meeting pages.

3.1. Obtaining the Initial Webpages

The official website of AA lists the homepage URLs for all regional AA domains by the US state names [51]. Each of these domains usually consists of pages describing the AA program, weekly meetings in that region, non-recurring events, resources for newcomers in recovery, etc. We wrote a web scraping script using the Python Selenium library that:

1. Extracts homepage URLs of the regional websites
2. Recursively traverses through the links referenced by each homepage using depth-first search up to three levels. By manual inspection, we determined that meeting pages appeared within three levels of the homepage

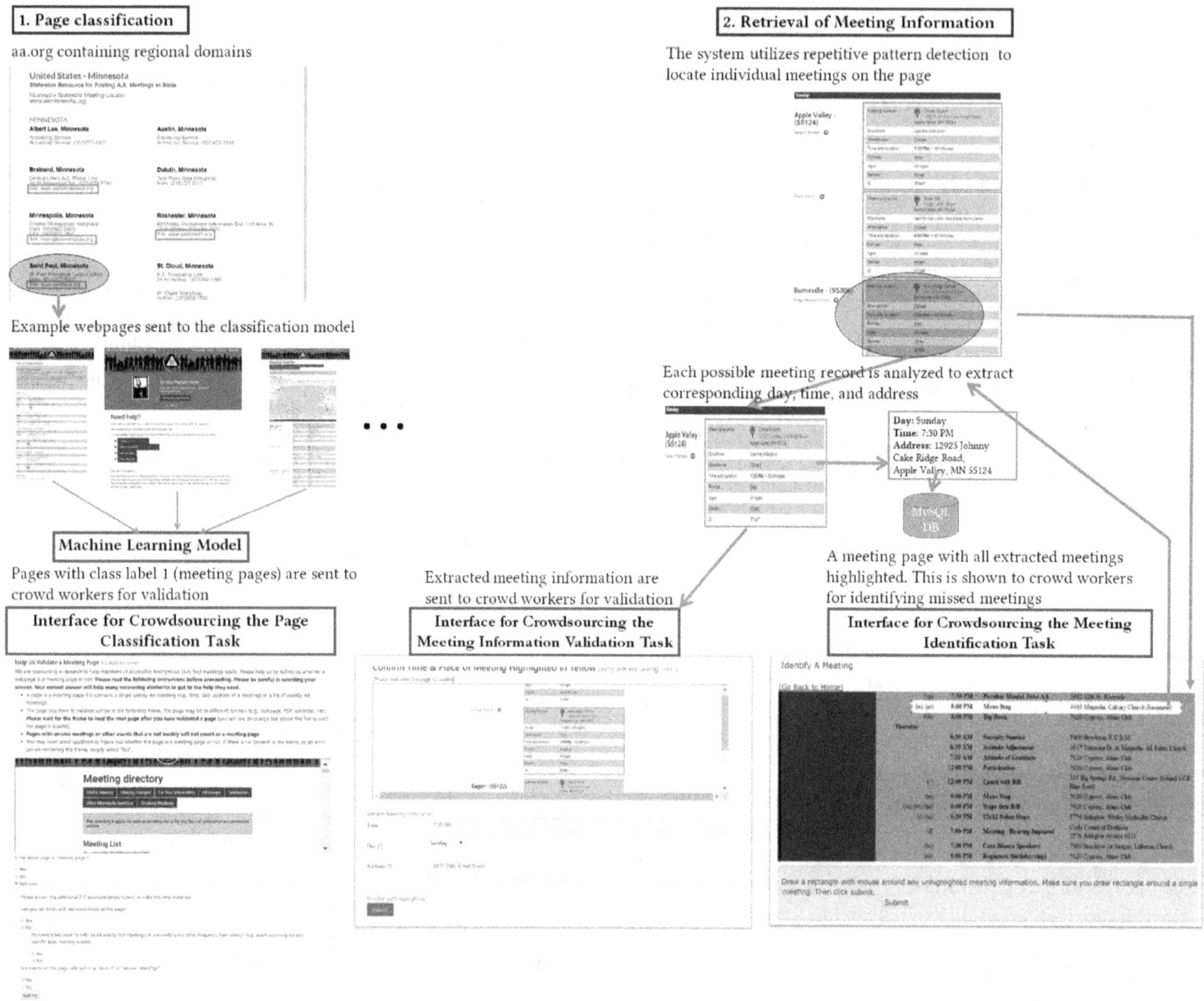

Figure 2: Pipeline of HAIR (the page classification phase is on left, and the meeting information retrieval phase is on right)

3. Determines the MIME type for each of the pages and saves the URLs along with their types in a MySQL database

Following this method, we obtained over 10,000 URLs by scraping 385 domains. This number does not match with the total number of AA regions throughout the US, since 207 regions listed their hotline numbers only. After filtering and removal of duplicates, we ended up with 9468 pages in total.

3.2 Classification of Pages

This phase consists of automatic classification of pages as "meeting page" or "non-meeting page" using a machine learning classifier and integrating human computation with the output of the classification model.

3.2.1 Classification of Pages using Machine Learning

Since AA websites contain other resources for recovery, only a small subset of the extracted URLs would refer to a meeting list. In order to efficiently reduce the number of pages to look for meeting records we developed a binary classification model.

Ground Truth and Features. We selected a random subset containing 642 pages to train the classifier, making sure to pick at least one page from each regional domain. Each page was classified manually and independently by at least two researchers, with a 0 (non-meeting page) or a 1 (meeting page) value as the class. Cases of disagreement were discussed among researchers until consensus was reached. 452 and 190 pages were classified as nonmeeting pages and meeting pages respectively.

From our experience of manually classifying hundreds of pages, we developed a list of possible page features to use in the classification. The set of final features included:

- presence of the word "meeting" in the URL (e.g., http://aaminneapolis.org/meetings)
- number of occurrences of word "meeting" in the text
- proportion of occurrences of text structured as a time
- proportion of occurrences of text structured as an address
- number of occurrences of weekday names in the text

We considered the proportions of days, times, and addressed since meeting pages often contain a larger number of times and addresses than the non-meeting pages regardless the format of the page. We considered proportions instead of raw numbers since number of meetings on a page can vary from very few to a few hundreds. A Python script extracted these features from the 9468 pages and saved them in the database. We applied appropriate methods for scraping different formats of webpages based on the MIME type. We considered eight different formats: HTML, PDF, Google Calendar, Google Map, Document (.doc, .docx, .xls, or .xlsx), Google doc, Google sheet, and images.

Classification. This is an imbalanced classification problem [23] and we determined that the *recall* of the model is more important to consider in this context than precision. Misclassifying a meeting page may result in multiple meetings missing in the final global list. If a meeting page is misclassified with a high confidence (more on section 3.2.2), this page will not further be sent for crowdsourcing and hence this error cannot be recovered in latter stages of the pipeline. On the other hand, a misclassified non-meeting page will be either sent to crowd workers (if confidence is low) or checked for presence of meetings in the next stage and eventually removed from consideration. Therefore, we cannot overlook the cost of misclassifying the meeting pages which are a small subset of the test instances. We tried out several classification algorithms [1] using the Python WEKA wrapper to determine which one performs better with respect to recall and overall F1 score, selecting random bagging with forest.

3.2.2 Integrating Human Computation

Determining Which Pages to Send to Crowd Workers. We used a prediction margin with each classified instance, rating the confidence of the classifier associated with that prediction. We selected a cutoff value where the set of instances below the margin were sent for crowdsourcing and the remaining were accepted as correct classification. We sorted the pages by prediction margin, inspected them to determine a threshold confidence that minimizes both the size of the set below the threshold (needing crowdsourcing) and the number of errors above the threshold (number of missed meetings), and selected the cutoff to be 90%.

Interface of the Page Classification Task. We created a HIT (Human Intelligence Task) on Amazon Mechanical Turk (mTurk) [52], a crowdsourcing internet marketplace. The HIT description included instructions, examples of meeting and non-meeting pages, and a link to the web interface that we developed for the crowd workers to label meeting pages (see the interface for page classification task in Figure 2). The web interface was developed using the Python Flask framework. For each HIT, it showed 20 random pages sequentially and asked the worker if it was a meeting page with "yes", "no", and "not sure" options. If workers selected "not sure," they had to answer two or three additional questions to help us determine the label.

Recruiting Workers and Filtering Results. We conducted several pilot experiments (both with mTurkers and non-mTurkers who were undergraduate students) to refine the task design and description, to determine the pay per task, and to define a reasonable minimum time of task completion.

Based on the number of pages needing to be crowdsourced (section 4.1), we had 971 assignments of the task. Each HIT had a payment of 50 cents to fulfill the minimum state wage requirement. We followed the majority voting scheme, with five different workers labeling each page to determine the final class [10]. For ensuring label quality, we used best practices from previous work [49]. We only accepted answers from workers with greater than 50% accuracy. Additionally, we considered the amount of time (a minimum of 120 seconds based on the pilot experiments) a worker took to complete a HIT to avoid answers from untrustworthy workers. We disregarded and reassigned 51 HITs that did not meet this requirement.

3.3 Retrieval of Meeting Information

This phase consists of an automated pattern detection approach to retrieve meeting records from the pages obtained from the previous phase and crowdsourcing to identify missed meetings if any and to validate the retrieved meetings.

There is an absence of confident ground truth of meeting records for the global list, since there are about 60 thousand meetings overall. As a proof of concept, we applied the retrieval and crowdsourcing to the meeting pages from five different regional websites in Minnesota. The ground truth consisted of 1892 meetings from eight meeting pages in these domains.

3.3.1. Automated Approaches for Meeting Retrieval

We applied a pattern detection-based approach for identifying meeting location on meeting pages and a regular expression approach to extract corresponding meeting records.

Identification of Meeting Location on Meeting Pages. We used a combination of pattern detection techniques from existing Python libraries and from prior literature. This step was necessary for pinpointing individual meeting records in a list of meetings. For the webpages identified as meeting pages, we applied repetitive pattern detection technique described in [5]. The HTML content of the webpages was represented as a tree of HTML tags and similar patterns were extracted. About 60% of the meeting pages were of this type. For PDFs we used the Python PDFMiner library to determine text segments along with their coordinates. Any other types of document files were converted to PDF and the same approach was followed. We utilized the Calendar API to extract multiple events from the meeting pages where a Google Calendar was located. We analyzed the image files using the Python Tesseract library and extracted coordinates of text segments along with their content.

Extraction of Meeting Information. We checked for presence of regular expressions of time, day, or address in the repetitive patterns. If any of these aspects was missing from a pattern (e.g., the page may be accessed by selecting a particular day from a dropdown and we have to associate the day record with each of the meetings on the page), we searched that aspect in the siblings and then in the parent of that pattern recursively in the pattern tree. All events from Google Calendars were initially considered as meetings. The text segments were checked with regular expressions from PDFs and images. We considered the coordinates of the neighboring text segments for missing aspect and assigned it from the segment that is in nearest (Euclidean) distance. All records were saved in the database.

3.3.2 Integrating Human Computation

We integrated crowdsourcing to edit incorrectly fetched information by the automated approach (validation) and to retrieve

	Accuracy (%)	Recall (%)	F1 score (%)	#of meeting pages
ML	68	90.5	73.8	4268
ML+HC	80.4	94	77.8	1275

Table 1: Performance of the page classification

	Classification Result	<90% Confidence
Meeting pages	4268	3569
Non-meeting pages	4558	312

Table 2: Number of pages needing human input

meetings that were not detected (identification). We created two different HITs on mTurk and developed corresponding interfaces using the Python Flask framework.

Meeting Validation. The interface sequentially showed 10 random meetings highlighted in yellow on corresponding webpages and asked the worker if it was a meeting record, with "yes" and "no" options (Figure 2). If workers selected "no" for a meeting, they were advanced to the next record. Otherwise, they were prompted to edit the automatically extracted details of the meeting if these did not match with highlighted record.

Meeting Identification. The interface sequentially showed 20 random meeting pages with the retrieved meetings highlighted in yellow and asked the workers if they noticed any meeting as not highlighted, with "yes" and "no" options. If workers selected "no" for a page, they were advanced to the next page. Otherwise, they would be asked to select a rectangle around any un-highlighted single meeting. We then retrieved corresponding information from the answers and fed this record to the validation task. Therefore, the next worker who seeing this page would have this meeting highlighted. We continued the task until three workers had selected "no" for all the meeting pages, meaning all meetings on those pages were retrieved.

Recruiting Workers and Filtering Results. After a round of pilot experiments we established the pay per task to be 60 cents for both types of HIT, and the minimum HIT completion time to accept an answer to be 150 seconds for the meeting validation HIT and 120 seconds for the meeting identification HIT. We had 410 assignments of the meeting validation HIT and 75 assignments for the meeting identification HIT. We followed majority voting scheme where three different workers labeled each meeting. However, for edited meeting information from the validation task, we considered both majority votes and completeness (e.g., a meeting address with vs without a zip). We had to disregard and reassign answers from 20 validation HIT and 31 identification HIT that did not meet this requirement.

4 Results

We discuss the results of classification of pages and retrieval of meeting information and compare the results before and after enhancing with crowdsourcing. Additionally, we explain the results in terms of the effects in the context of AA.

4.1 Classification of Pages

The classifier reduced the number of pages to send to the crowd workers for meeting retrieval, while crowdsourcing substantially improved the accuracy of the classifier.

	Accurately Identified Meetings	Meetings identified with partially correct info (e.g., wrong time, day, or address)	Unidentified Meetings
IR	72.2 (1366)	10.9 (206)	16.9 (320)
IR+HC	94.8 (1794)	3.2 (60)	2.0 (38)

Table 3: % (number) of meetings from the Minnesota domains

We classified 8826 test pages (since 642 of the 9468 pages were used as training instances) with the supervised machine learning model (ML). The classifier output 4268 pages as "meeting pages" (with ≥90% confident about 699 pages). The accuracy of the model is not as high as recall since we tried to maximize recall. Similarly, the classifier labels pages as non-meeting with more confidence so that there is a very low probability of misclassifying a meeting page (Table 2). Nonetheless, when we looked for sources of errors we noticed that many of the misclassified meeting pages had very few meeting records and the proportions of time and address present in the text content of those pages were lower compared to other meeting pages. Moreover, non-meeting pages listing events or other details that look like meetings (e.g., office hours) were misclassified as meeting pages.

For enhancing the model with human computation (HC), we selected the 3569 meeting pages and 312 non-meeting pages for which the classifier's confidence was less than 90%. We noticed that the "not sure" option was very infrequent in the answers and we did not observe any cases where we had to consider this option. After filtering the crowdsourced answers, the number of total meeting pages was reduced to 1275. Therefore, the workers labeled 576 pages out of 3881 pages as meeting pages. The performance of the combined approach showed significantly better results in terms of recall and F1 score (see Table 1). However, we found out that the list of meeting pages still included pages with non-recurring organizational event pages, or statistics. Possible reasons for this are workers not being enough careful, or their lack of contextual knowledge.

There was a synergistic effect of combining the ML and HC. First, the automated classification reduced the number of pages needing human input from 8826 to 3881 (by about 56%), thus reduced the cost of crowdsourcing. If we reduced the confidence threshold, there would be even fewer pages, however, we may have missed more meeting pages. Second, the ML only approach would result in misclassification of more than 30% of the pages, resulting in missing a relatively high number of meetings.

Explanation in terms of the Context of Recovery

The ML only approach would have missed more than 800 meeting pages, completely making their meetings unavailable to people who need the help desperately. Although these pages usually consist of relatively small number of meetings, even pages with one meeting is important since it might be the only meeting happening in a rural area. Crowdsourcing helped identify many of these pages. On the other hand, many non-meeting pages were misclassified with ML only approach, potentially confusing, frustrating, and misdirecting people at a critical stage of their recovery. Crowdsourcing reduced this impact substantially by detecting 2993 such non-meeting pages.

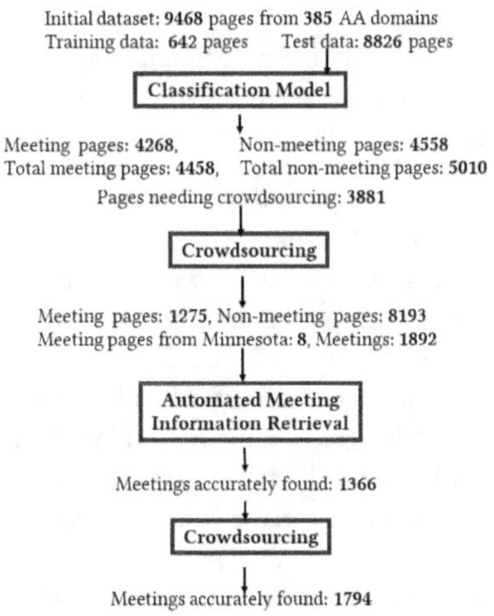

Figure 3: Summary of results

4.2 Retrieval of Meeting Information

We applied pattern-detection- and regular-expression-based approaches to identify and retrieve meeting records from pages obtained from the previous phase. Crowdsourcing complemented the automated approaches by validating information and identifying missed records.

Websites of the five regions from Minnesota had almost same variety in format of pages as the set of all pages and thus can be considered as a representative sample. Page classification phase produced 11 meeting pages from these five. However, while extracting ground truth meetings, we discarded three pages that had zero meetings. The pattern detection approach (IR) was able to detect 1572 meetings (correctly or with partially correct information) out of 1892 meeting records. However, while looking for sources of probable errors, we noticed that in the cases of attaching information present in nearby co-ordinates or in a neighboring node in the HTML tree (e.g., meetings listed by days on a page) the pattern detection often failed resulting in 16.9% of the meetings unidentified (Table-3).

Due to the variety in representation of time, day, and address and due to meetings with incomplete address information or simply listing a church as the address, regular expression did not work accurately in every case, resulting the number of correctly identified meetings to be 1365. Although only 11% of the meetings fell in the category of partially identified, it is very high if considered in the context of recovery, which we describe shortly.

Human computation (HC) substantially improved the percentage of correctly identified meetings by recognizing 282 additional meetings and reduced the percentage of meetings with wrong information by updating 146 meeting records (see the bottom row of Table 3).

There was a synergistic effect of combining the two techniques. First, the results from the combined techniques could enhance the accuracy of the page classification step. For example, there were pages where no record was marked in the IR or HC as meeting information. Clearly these are misclassified meeting pages and there is a potential for feeding the pages back to the previous phase. Second, the IR only approach would have missed relatively high number of meetings and included many meetings with potentially wrong information.

Explanation in terms of the Context of Recovery

The 3rd column of Table 3 may be considered as the most important metrics to evaluate the proposed approach in terms of effect on people in recovery. For example, the unidentified meetings could include the only meeting or a very popular meeting in a particular area and failure to find that is frustrating. However, the 2nd column refers to the fact that, after automated extraction about 11% meetings would consist of wrong information, creating confusion and potentially sending people to a location where there is no meeting. In other words, going back to the hypothetical example that we started with, this result implies that Jane has a good chance of ending up in a wrong location regardless. The results from both phases are summarized in Figure 3.

5 DISCUSSION

In this section, we conceptualize this work in a broader IR context and discuss future directions towards developing the global self-updating meeting list.

5.1 Leveraging the Specifics of Context

Prior work has investigated different IR techniques that consider human-in-the-loop (e.g., [8,27]). However, most work takes a context-agnostic approach to include human computation and make decisions about information retrieval strategies. In contrast, recovery is a high-impact context where specific decisions and approaches may lead to significant positive or negative impact on people's lives. We considered the context in:

Prioritizing errors. The classification model was selected to prioritize recall over precision. This idea is espoused in many imbalanced classification problems particularly involving fraud detection (e.g., [32]). In the context of AA, obtaining all the meeting pages was essential, even though it added extra pages to send for human input. We designed the latter phases in a way that eventually discarded those misclassified non-meeting pages.

Additionally, we considered what the percentage of unidentified meetings and the percentage of meetings identified with partially correct information would mean to someone in recovery. The latter one (while conceptually "partially correct") may have a bigger negative impact on members of AA, since it might send someone at a time or to a place where there is no meeting. That is why we took both into consideration and designed the "meeting validation" and the "meeting identification" tasks separately to ensure correctness of the extracted meetings as well as to minimize the number of unidentified meetings.

Designing for eventual user value. Our long-term goal is to provide substantial value to AA members. While in a less critical context, it would be reasonable to simply identify and catalog local pages, that may not provide sufficient value for newcomers who may already be experiencing information overload [37]. Our motivation for including the meeting retrieval phase is to produce a complete list of searchable meetings and to present them in a navigational interface that provides information in a more scalable, geographically, and temporally relevant way.

Overall, this points to the idea of moving away from context-agnostic IR methods towards ones bespoke to work better in this specific high-impact context. Building on this design insight, we plan to involve people in recovery instead of mTurk workers for human computation. One significant source of error in page classification was both the classifier and the mTurkers failing to distinguish organizational (area) meetings and the actual weekly AA meetings. Since people in recovery are more familiar with the distinction between these two, involving them will potentially improve the performance of the crowdsourcing step.

5.2 Assumptions about Ground Truth

Currently, we assume that the meeting information on any regional website is accurate, while reality may not reflect this. One possible future direction to solve this problem is to extend the human-in-the loop part of the HAIR into the physical world. Although this paper does not focus on the sustainability of the developed meeting list (more in next section), we hope to develop a meeting finder app from the extracted meetings and make it public and available for use by people in recovery. We will then have opportunities to send the app users on physical world "mission" in their local area to identify and modify possible inaccuracies on regional pages. For instance, while periodically extracting meeting information, we may note that a page has not been updated in over six months, pointing to the possibility of the page being outdated. The app may ask users searching for meetings in that area to volunteer to validate information by going to a listed meeting and confirming if that is still existent. The idea of this future work implies that human-aided information retrieval can be implemented not only online but also in the real world.

5.3 Sustainability of HAIR

This work focuses on the technical challenges of developing the meeting list. However, in future, we need to consider the sustainability of the obtained list since we are not only interested in getting a snapshot of meetings at a single point in time, but also plan to enable it to sustainably self-update.

5.3.1 Future Direction in Allowing the List to "Self-update"

To make the list self-updating one approach is to automatically run the proposed methods in a regular interval and obtain the most recent version of the meetings. We plan to update the meeting information once a month by applying the following approaches that reduce the cost of crowdsourcing:

1. Instead of classifying all webpages, we will first look for new pages added to the regional websites and pages that have changed since the last update, and send only those pages to the ML model.
2. Instead of all the pages from the previous version of the list, we will now send only the set of pages for crowdsourcing that are obtained from step 1 above.
3. After automated extraction of meeting records we will match with crowd answers from the previous version and select appropriate subset to crowdsource.
4. Before crowdsourcing, we will check the day, time, address of all meetings in a region to remove possible duplicates.

Additionally, to make information more accessible, we have developed a web API that external applications or websites can send request to fetch the set of current meeting pages and the extracted meetings from the database.

5.3.2 Consequences of Self-Updating

Some errors may disappear with time when continual updates are performed (e.g., if the crowd workers identify a wrong meeting page or a wrong meeting once, the next time the same page or meeting will possibly be evaluated by a different set of workers, creating a probability of amending the error). On the contrary, if a meeting page remains unidentified and does not change frequently, we will not consider it in subsequent self-updating processes, and the error will compound.

As we transition to involve volunteers (AA members) in crowdsourcing reducing the monetary cost to zero, the projected cost must be calculated in terms of human time. If we continue to update the list in a one-month interval, considering the current average task completion time of mTurkers, the cost would be about 96 hours human-time per update. However, it will be significantly reduced when we incorporate the steps described above in subsequent updates. AA members who have many years in recovery perform service work for the community, which creates opportunities for us to offer the crowdsourcing as a service that could enhance their recovery while also providing valuable information for newcomers.

6 CONCLUSION

Due to tradition of regional autonomy in its organizational structure, AA currently lacks a global or national meeting list. This makes it difficult for newcomers in recovery or people traveling to a new area to find the support they need. With a goal of creating a navigational meeting finder app which includes all AA meetings throughout the United States, we propose HAIR: a semi-automated information retrieval approach that classifies webpages of different structures and formats and extracts meeting information from them combining machine learning, pattern detection, and crowdsourcing techniques. We conclude that crowdsourcing has potential to be applied in concert with IR techniques in this high-impact context, as it substantially improves the accuracy of the automated approaches by being able to identify many meeting pages and to modify wrong meeting information. Additionally, a major implication of our work is pointing to the importance of context-specific rather than context-agnostic semi-automated IR methods.

ACKNOWLEDGMENTS

We would like to thank Thomas Crumrine for helping us develop the machine learning model. We also thank Zachary Levonian and Loren Terveen for their useful feedback on the paper. This work was funded by the NSF grant (1464376 and 1651575).

REFERENCES

[1] Ansam A. AbdulHussien. 2017. Comparison of Machine Learning Algorithms to Classify Web Pages. *International Journal of*

Advanced Computer Science and Applications (ijacsa) 8, 11. https://doi.org/10.14569/IJACSA.2017.081127

[2] Anagnostopoulos, C. Anagnostopoulos, V. Loumos, and E. Kayafas. 2004. Classifying Web pages employing a probabilistic neural network. *IEE Proceedings - Software* 151, 3: 139–150. https://doi.org/10.1049/ip-sen:20040121

[3] Howard C. Becker. 2008. Alcohol dependence, withdrawal, and relapse. *Alcohol Research & Health* 31, 4: 348–361.

[4] Mike Cassidy. 2014. Centaur Chess Shows Power of Teaming Human and Machine. *Huffington Post.* Retrieved August 13, 2018 from https://www.huffingtonpost.com/mike-cassidy/centaur-chess-shows-power_b_6383606.html

[5] Chia-Hui Chang and Shao-Chen Lui. 2001. IEPAD: Information Extraction Based on Pattern Discovery. In *Proceedings of the 10th International Conference on World Wide Web* (WWW '01), 681–688. https://doi.org/10.1145/371920.372182

[6] Michael Chau and Hsinchun Chen. 2008. A Machine Learning Approach to Web Page Filtering Using Content and Structure Analysis. *Decis. Support Syst.* 44, 2: 482–494. https://doi.org/10.1016/j.dss.2007.06.002

[7] Yinlin Chen, Paul Logasa Bogen II, Haowei Hsieh, Edward A. Fox, and Lillian N. Cassel. 2012. Categorization of Computing Education Resources with Utilization of Crowdsourcing. In *Proceedings of the 12th ACM/IEEE-CS Joint Conference on Digital Libraries* (JCDL '12), 121–124. https://doi.org/10.1145/2232817.2232840

[8] Zhe Chen. 2014. A Semiautomatic Approach for Accurate and Low-Effort Spreadsheet Data Extraction.

[9] Justin Cheng and Michael S. Bernstein. 2015. Flock: Hybrid Crowd-Machine Learning Classifiers. In *Proceedings of the 18th ACM Conference on Computer Supported Cooperative Work & Social Computing* (CSCW '15), 600–611. https://doi.org/10.1145/2675133.2675214

[10] Ed H. Chi. 2017. Technical Perspective: Humans and Computers Working Together on Hard Tasks. *Commun. ACM* 60, 9: 92–92. https://doi.org/10.1145/3068614

[11] M. I. Devi, R. Rajaram, and K. Selvakuberan. 2007. Machine Learning Techniques for Automated Web Page Classification Using URL Features. In *International Conference on Computational Intelligence and Multimedia Applications (ICCIMA 2007)*, 116–120. https://doi.org/10.1109/ICCIMA.2007.342

[12] M. Ferri, L. Amato, and M. Davoli. 2006. Alcoholics Anonymous and other 12-step programmes for alcohol dependence. *The Cochrane Database of Systematic Reviews*, 3: CD005032. https://doi.org/10.1002/14651858.CD005032.pub2

[13] Dayne Freitag. 2000. Machine Learning for Information Extraction in Informal Domains. *Machine Learning* 39, 2–3: 169–202. https://doi.org/10.1023/A:1007601113994

[14] F. S. Gharehchopogh and Z. A. Khalifelu. 2011. Analysis and evaluation of unstructured data: text mining versus natural language processing. In *2011 5th International Conference on Application of Information and Communication Technologies (AICT)*, 1–4. https://doi.org/10.1109/ICAICT.2011.6111017

[15] Kotaro Hara and Jon E. Froehlich. 2015. Characterizing and Visualizing Physical World Accessibility at Scale Using Crowdsourcing, Computer Vision, and Machine Learning. *SIGACCESS Access. Comput.*, 113: 13–21. https://doi.org/10.1145/2850440.2850442

[16] Yun Huang, Yifeng Huang, Na Xue, and Jeffrey P. Bigham. 2017. Leveraging Complementary Contributions of Different Workers for Efficient Crowdsourcing of Video Captions. In *Proceedings of the 2017 CHI Conference on Human Factors in Computing Systems* (CHI '17), 4617–4626. https://doi.org/10.1145/3025453.3026032

[17] Zhongjun Jin, Michael R. Anderson, Michael Cafarella, and H. V. Jagadish. 2017. Foofah: Transforming Data By Example. In *Proceedings of the 2017 ACM International Conference on Management of Data* (SIGMOD '17), 683–698. https://doi.org/10.1145/3035918.3064034

[18] Thorsten Joachims. 1998. Text categorization with Support Vector Machines: Learning with many relevant features. In *Machine Learning: ECML-98*, Claire Nédellec and Céline Rouveirol (eds.). Springer Berlin Heidelberg, Berlin, Heidelberg, 137–142. https://doi.org/10.1007/BFb0026683

[19] Herbert D. Kleber, Roger D. Weiss, Raymond F. Anton, Tony P. George, Shelly F. Greenfield, Thomas R. Kosten, Charles P. O'Brien, Bruce J. Rounsaville, Eric C. Strain, Douglas M. Ziedonis, Grace Hennessy, Hilary Smith Connery, John S. McIntyre, Sara C. Charles, Daniel J. Anzia, Ian A. Cook, Molly T. Finnerty, Bradley R. Johnson, James E. Nininger, Paul Summergrad, Sherwyn M. Woods, Joel Yager, Robert Pyles, C. Deborah Cross, Roger Peele, John P. D. Shemo, Lawrence Lurie, R. Dale Walker, Mary Ann Barnovitz, Sheila Hafter Gray, Sunil Saxena, Tina Tonnu, Robert Kunkle, Amy B. Albert, Laura J. Fochtmann, Claudia Hart, Darrel Regier, Work Group on Substance Use Disorders, American Psychiatric Association, and Steering Committee on Practice Guidelines. 2007. Treatment of patients with substance use disorders, second edition. American Psychiatric Association. *The American Journal of Psychiatry* 164, 4 Suppl: 5–123.

[20] Erdal Kuzey and Gerhard Weikum. 2012. Extraction of Temporal Facts and Events from Wikipedia. In *Proceedings of the 2Nd Temporal Web Analytics Workshop* (TempWeb '12), 25–32. https://doi.org/10.1145/2169095.2169101

[21] Gierad Laput, Walter S. Lasecki, Jason Wiese, Robert Xiao, Jeffrey P. Bigham, and Chris Harrison. 2015. Zensors: Adaptive, Rapidly Deployable, Human-Intelligent Sensor Feeds. In *Proceedings of the 33rd Annual ACM Conference on Human Factors in Computing Systems* (CHI '15), 1935–1944. https://doi.org/10.1145/2702123.2702416

[22] Wendy Lehnert, Stephen Soderland, David Aronow, FangFang Feng, and Avinoam Shmueli. 1995. Inductive text classification for medical applications. *Journal of Experimental & Theoretical Artificial Intelligence* 7, 1: 49–80. https://doi.org/10.1080/09528139508953800

[23] Camelia Lemnaru and Rodica Potolea. 2012. Imbalanced Classification Problems: Systematic Study, Issues and Best Practices. In *Enterprise Information Systems* (Lecture Notes in Business Information Processing), 35–50.

[24] Xuanchong Li, Kai-min Chang, Yueran Yuan, and Alexander Hauptmann. 2015. Massive Open Online Proctor: Protecting the Credibility of MOOCs Certificates. In *Proceedings of the 18th ACM Conference on Computer Supported Cooperative Work & Social Computing* (CSCW '15), 1129–1137. https://doi.org/10.1145/2675133.2675245

[25] Henry Lieberman, Karthik Dinakar, and Birago Jones. 2013. Crowdsourced Ethics with Personalized Story Matching. In *CHI '13 Extended Abstracts on Human Factors in Computing Systems* (CHI EA '13), 709–714. https://doi.org/10.1145/2468356.2468481

[26] Xiao Ling and Daniel S. Weld. 2010. Temporal Information Extraction. In *Twenty-Fourth AAAI Conference on Artificial Intelligence.* Retrieved September 21, 2018 from https://www.aaai.org/ocs/index.php/AAAI/AAAI10/paper/view/1805

[27] Huaxi Liu, Ning Wang, and Xiangran Ren. 2015. CrowdSR: A Crowd Enabled System for Semantic Recovering of Web Tables. In *Web-Age Information Management* (Lecture Notes in Computer Science), 581–583.

[28] Brian McLernon and Nicholas Kushmerick. 2006. *Transductive Pattern Learning for Information Extraction.* UNIVERSITY COLL DUBLIN (IRELAND), UNIVERSITY COLL DUBLIN (IRELAND). Retrieved August 19, 2018 from http://www.dtic.mil/docs/citations/ADA456766

[29] Dunja Mladenic. 1998. *Turning Yahoo into an Automatic Web-Page Classifier.*

[30] Raymond J. Mooney and Razvan Bunescu. 2005. Mining Knowledge from Text Using Information Extraction. *SIGKDD Explor. Newsl.* 7, 1: 3–10. https://doi.org/10.1145/1089815.1089817

[31] Rudolf H. Moos and Bernice S. Moos. 2006. Participation in Treatment and Alcoholics Anonymous: A 16-Year Follow-Up of Initially Untreated Individuals. *Journal of clinical psychology* 62, 6: 735–750. https://doi.org/10.1002/jclp.20259

[32] Clifton Phua, Damminda Alahakoon, and Vincent Lee. 2004. Minority Report in Fraud Detection: Classification of Skewed Data. *SIGKDD Explor. Newsl.* 6, 1: 50–59. https://doi.org/10.1145/1007730.1007738

[33] Xiaoguang Qi and Brian D. Davison. 2006. Knowing a Web Page by the Company It Keeps. In *Proceedings of the 15th ACM International Conference on Information and Knowledge Management* (CIKM '06), 228–237. https://doi.org/10.1145/1183614.1183650

[34] Xiaoguang Qi and Brian D. Davison. 2009. Web Page Classification: Features and Algorithms. *ACM Comput. Surv.* 41, 2: 12:1–12:31. https://doi.org/10.1145/1459352.1459357

[35] Alan Ritter, Mausam, Oren Etzioni, and Sam Clark. 2012. Open Domain Event Extraction from Twitter. In *Proceedings of the 18th ACM SIGKDD International Conference on Knowledge Discovery and Data Mining* (KDD '12), 1104–1112. https://doi.org/10.1145/2339530.2339704

[36] Sabirat Rubya. 2017. Facilitating Peer Support for Recovery from Substance Use Disorders. In *Proceedings of the 2017 CHI Conference Extended Abstracts on Human Factors in Computing Systems* (CHI EA '17), 172–177. https://doi.org/10.1145/3027063.3048431

[37] Sabirat Rubya and Svetlana Yarosh. 2017. Video-Mediated Peer Support in an Online Community for Recovery from Substance Use Disorders. In *Proceedings of the 2017 ACM Conference on Computer Supported Cooperative Work and Social Computing* (CSCW '17), 1454–1469. https://doi.org/10.1145/2998181.2998246

[38] E. Saraç and S. A. Özel. 2013. Web page classification using firefly optimization. In *2013 IEEE INISTA*, 1–5. https://doi.org/10.1109/INISTA.2013.6577619

[39] Thimo Schulze, Simone Krug, and Martin Schader. 2012. Workers' Task Choice in Crowdsourcing and Human Computation Markets. *ICIS 2012 Proceedings.* Retrieved from http://aisel.aisnet.org/icis2012/proceedings/ResearchInProgress/40

[40] Vinay Shashidhar, Nishant Pandey, and Varun Aggarwal. 2015. Spoken English Grading: Machine Learning with Crowd Intelligence. In *Proceedings of the 21th ACM SIGKDD International Conference on Knowledge Discovery and Data Mining* (KDD '15), 2089–2097. https://doi.org/10.1145/2783258.2788595

[41] Wongkot Sriurai, Phayung Meesad, and Choochart Haruechaiyasak. 2010. Hierarchical Web Page Classification Based on a Topic Model and Neighboring Pages Integration. *arXiv:1003.1510 [cs].* Retrieved August 13, 2018 from http://arxiv.org/abs/1003.1510

[42] Chong Sun, Narasimhan Rampalli, Frank Yang, and AnHai Doan. 2014. Chimera: Large-scale Classification Using Machine Learning, Rules, and Crowdsourcing. *Proc. VLDB Endow.* 7, 13: 1529–1540. https://doi.org/10.14778/2733004.2733024

[43] Makoto Tsukada, Takashi Washio, and Hiroshi Motoda. 2001. Automatic Web-Page Classification by Using Machine Learning Methods. In *Proceedings of the First Asia-Pacific Conference on Web Intelligence: Research and Development* (WI '01), 303–313. Retrieved January 11, 2017 from http://dl.acm.org/citation.cfm?id=645960.673927

[44] Yafang Wang, Mingjie Zhu, Lizhen Qu, Marc Spaniol, and Gerhard Weikum. 2010. Timely YAGO: Harvesting, Querying, and Visualizing Temporal Knowledge from Wikipedia. In *Proceedings of the 13th International Conference on Extending Database Technology* (EDBT '10), 697–700. https://doi.org/10.1145/1739041.1739130

[45] 4Shomir Wilson, Florian Schaub, Rohan Ramanath, Norman Sadeh, Fei Liu, Noah A. Smith, and Frederick Liu. 2016. Crowdsourcing Annotations for Websites' Privacy Policies: Can It Really Work? In *Proceedings of the 25th International Conference on World Wide Web* (WWW '16), 133–143. https://doi.org/10.1145/2872427.2883035

[46] Yang Yang, Bin B. Zhu, Rui Guo, Linjun Yang, Shipeng Li, and Nenghai Yu. 2008. A Comprehensive Human Computation Framework: With Application to Image Labeling. In *Proceedings of the 16th ACM International Conference on Multimedia* (MM '08), 479–488. https://doi.org/10.1145/1459359.1459423

[47] Dahai Yao, Hailong Sun, and Xudong Liu. 2015. Combining Crowd Contributions with Machine Learning to Detect Malicious Mobile Apps. In *Proceedings of the 7th Asia-Pacific Symposium on Internetware* (Internetware '15), 120–123. https://doi.org/10.1145/2875913.2875941

[48] Svetlana Yarosh. 2013. Shifting Dynamics or Breaking Sacred Traditions?: The Role of Technology in Twelve-step Fellowships. In *Proceedings of the SIGCHI Conference on Human Factors in Computing Systems* (CHI '13), 3413–3422. https://doi.org/10.1145/2470654.2466468

[49] D. Yue, G. Yu, D. Shen, and X. Yu. 2014. A Weighted Aggregation Rule in Crowdsourcing Systems for High Result Accuracy. In *2014 IEEE 12th International Conference on Dependable, Autonomic and Secure Computing,* 265–270. https://doi.org/10.1109/DASC.2014.54

[50] Alcohol Facts and Statistics | National Institute on Alcohol Abuse and Alcoholism (NIAAA). Retrieved September 6, 2018 from https://www.niaaa.nih.gov/alcohol-health/overview-alcohol-consumption/alcohol-facts-and-statistics

[51] Alcoholics Anonymous : A.A. Near You. Retrieved September 23, 2018 from https://www.aa.org/pages/en_US/find-aa-resources

[52] Amazon Mechanical Turk. Retrieved September 23, 2018 from https://www.mturk.com/

Experimental Methods in IIR: The Tension between Rigour and Ethics in Studies Involving Users with Dyslexia

Gerd Berget
Dep. of Archivistics, Library and Information Science
Oslo Metropolitian University
Oslo, Norway
gerd.berget@oslomet.no

Andrew MacFarlane
Centre for HCI Design
City, University of London
London, UK
a.macfarlane@city.ac.uk

ABSTRACT

Designing user studies in the interactive information retrieval (IIR) paradigm on people with impairments may sometimes require different methodological considerations than for other users. Consequently, there may be a tension between what the community regards as being a rigorous methodology against what researchers can do ethically with their users. This paper discusses issues to consider when designing IIR studies involving people with dyslexia, such as sampling, informed consent and data collection. The conclusion is that conducting user studies on participants with dyslexia requires special considerations at all stages of the experimental design. The purpose of this paper is to raise awareness and understanding in the research community about experimental methods involving users with dyslexia, and addresses researchers, as well as editors and reviewers. Several of the issues raised do not only apply to people with dyslexia, but have implications when researching other groups, for instance elderly people and users with learning, cognitive, sensory or motor impairments.

CCS CONCEPTS

Information systems→Information retrieval→Users and interactive retrieval→Search interfaces • Human-centred computing→Accessibility→Empirical studies in accessibility

KEYWORDS

Interactive information retrieval; User studies; Dyslexia; Impairments

ACM Reference format:
Gerd Berget, and Andrew MacFarlane. 2018. Experimental Methods in IIR: The Tension Between Rigour and Ethics in Studies Involving Users with Dyslexia. In *Proceedings of the 2019 Conference on Human Information Interaction and Retrieval (CHIIR'19), March 10-14, 2018, Glasgow, UK.* ACM, New York, NY, USA, 9 pages. https://doi.org/10.1145/3295750.3298939

ACM ISBN 978-1-4503-6025-8/19/03...$15.00
https://doi.org/10.1145/3295750.3298939

1 INTRODUCTION

Over the past two decades, an increasing number of user studies on information retrieval have addressed people with impairments [21]. In the last ten years or so, we have conducted several studies within the field of IIR with a focus on users with dyslexia [3-5; 28-30]. Through these studies we have experienced many methodological issues where there is a mismatch between rigorous methodology and what you can actually do in experiments regarding people with impairments. In this perspective paper we will discuss some of these issues, and suggest alternative methodological approaches and considerations. The main focus is on laboratory evaluations of the interaction between users and systems. However, several issues apply to other research methods, for instance sampling, informed consent, how to document diagnoses and reporting results. Our aim is to outline the best practice for undertaking IIR experiments involving users with dyslexia, in the light of particular ethical issues which arise with this user group.

Dyslexia is a cognitive impairment with an estimated prevalence of around 7% of the world population [42]. Although dyslexia is mainly characterised by reading and writing difficulties, the cognitive profile is often quite complex and typically includes impaired short-term memory [41], reduced rapid naming skills [39] and concentration difficulties, especially when focusing on a task for a long time [33]. Moreover, it has been reported that people with dyslexia have challenges with mental organisation [24].

Reduced self-esteem is another well-documented characteristic related to dyslexia, in addition to anxiety and fear of failure, among others caused by negative experiences at school [40]. Comorbidity with other diagnoses is also quite common. A total of 18-20% of the dyslexic population also have ADHD or ADD [15]. Prevalence with other diagnoses is also frequently reported, such as the writing impairment dysgraphia [37], the mathematical disorder dyscalculia [27] and dyspraxia, an impairment in the organization of movement [16].

Detailed knowledge about the cognitive and physical abilities of the participants is a very important aspect of designing studies involving users with impairments. For instance, the cognitive profile of people with dyslexia affects the ability to read and understand written information and the capability to complete comprehensive tasks in long-lasting sessions. We will revisit these challenges and present alternative procedures for conducting experiments involving this user group in the following sections.

The paper is structured as follows: firstly, we set the scene by outlining the issue of vulnerable groups and ethical concerns. In the light of these we address standard experimental methods in IIR, with a focus on the topics that are most relevant for users with impairments, namely sampling, informed consent, method of data collection and reporting results, outlining problems at each stage. We then suggest revised experimental methods in the areas addressed. A set of recommendations for researchers undertaking work involving users with dyslexia is then provided, together with a concluding statement on prospects in the field as a whole.

2 VULNERABLE USER GROUPS

Many studies today on users with impairments are conducted within the universal design paradigm, where the main goal is to design systems that can be used by all people, regardless of cultural background, gender, age and physical and mental abilities [47]. However, while there is an increasing awareness that people with impairments need to be included in research, there has been little focus on the experimental design of such studies.

Much IIR experimentation has focused on the general population, with very little work until recently on users with cognitive issues such as dyslexia [3-5; 28-30]. Therefore, little attention has been paid to the differences these users have with the general population and the impact this impairment may have on the result of any experiment conducted. In order to address the issues of concern regarding users with specific impairments, more focus on ethical issues is required. This is because such users (including people with dyslexia) are regarded as being vulnerable. For people with dyslexia, vulnerability takes a number of forms including a lack of self-esteem [35; 49], a tendency to become tired after significant intellectual effort [33] and anxiety [9; 40].

Ethical panels require researchers to give extra consideration to vulnerable groups, over and above what would be expected with the general population. For example, at City, University of London researchers are specifically asked to identify the given vulnerable group and identify a specific strategy to ensure their well-being, they do not feel pressured to take part and are free to withdraw at any time from the study [10]. Approval for the study is only granted if the ethics panel consider these issues fully addressed and the participants are treated in an appropriate ethical manner. For users with dyslexia IIR researchers have a clear responsibility to ensure that users' self-esteem is not reduced further, they do not put together an experiment which will tire out the users or make them feel anxious whilst undertaking it. In this light we examine the standard methods for experimentation in IIR.

3 EXPERIMENTAL METHODS IN IIR

In IIR studies, researchers address the interaction between users and information systems. A challenge within the field of IIR has been to create experimental situations that consider individual factors, while at the same time makes it possible to establish causal relationships. According to Kelly [25], there has been little guidance on experimental frameworks and there has been a lack of well-established methods in IIR.

The experimental setting often used for the evaluation of IIR systems typically consists of three components: users, information needs and relevance judgements [6]. An important topic for IIR is whether people can actually use the system in question. We argue that studies on people with impairments need to follow the cognitive user-centred approach as described by Borlund [6], and not a system-driven approach. Users with impairments have specific issues that can only be addressed through a user centred approach, and the focus of experiments needs to be on the users rather than the system.

3.1 Sampling

Sampling is much discussed in methodological literature. According to standard textbooks, the sampling frame, a complete list of sampling units, is an important starting point when recruiting participants to ensure a representative population [14]. However, lists of people with impairments are not accessible to researchers, for ethical reasons, since such diagnoses represent highly sensitive information. Ethics panels will not allow researchers to use prior diagnosis without explicit consent from the user (which may not be forthcoming as the user may not wish to disclose sensitive personal information). Consequently, the sampling process must rely on volunteering participants, making it challenging to assemble a balanced sample.

Classic experimental design often involves two comparable groups: one experimental group and one control group, where only the independent variable should differ between the two groups. In the context of dyslexia, the control group should therefore consist of people without this diagnosis. According to Mortimore and Crozier [33] adults may not always be aware of their dyslexia. Consequently, researchers may potentially include people with undiagnosed dyslexia in the control group, weakening the validity of the experimental design.

3.2 Informed consent

According to Frankfort-Nachmias, Nachmias and DeWaard [14], informed consent is the most important tool to ensure the welfare and rights of participants. Informed consent ensures that the participants have received a fair explanation of the study and been informed that they can discontinue participation and withdraw the consent at any time.

Demands for informed consent are now included in various national and federal legislations. Official rules are typically set out by national data inspectorates or research ethics committees concerning content and form of such documents. Consent documents are therefore usually comprehensive to cover ethical guidelines and will often require extensive reading. However, the main challenge for people with dyslexia regards reading and word decoding, which typically causes slower reading rates and/or decoding errors [20]. Consequently, researchers do not know whether the participant has comprehended all the written information before signing, which may cause serious violation of research ethics. Reduced short-term memory may also be a challenge, because participants may quickly forget information they were given at the beginning of a session.

3.3 Method of data collection

In IIR experiments the common procedure is as follows:

- Pre-experiment survey,
- Training for the system,
- Searching system with the given information needs and
- Post-experiment survey.

Most of these procedures, apart from searching the system, are optional depending on the experimental research question but do require thought. The issue raised above in terms of accessibility of documents applies to any survey carried out during the experiment. The key issue is the tasks the users will undertake whilst doing the experiment, and what data will be collected. Users' search behaviour can be logged [23] and eye-tracking can be used [17] in order to collect quantitative data about their activities. Participants must of course be fully appraised of the data being collected about them and why.

The task itself will have a significant impact on the variable used. IIR experiments typically require that at least two topics are used, to ameliorate the topic effect as they can vary in complexity and scope. Experiments often use many more, e.g. the TREC-6 Interactive track [50] used six topics in the experiments. However, presenting too much information to people with dyslexia is problematic (for reasons stated above). Presenting as many as six topics to a user with dyslexia will undoubtedly impact on short term memory capacity and lead to tiredness very quickly. Senior members of the IIR community raised this issue with one author when the idea of experimenting with users with dyslexia was first mooted [31]. For this reason, it is better to use one topic, but this means the topic effect needs to be addressed in a different way (this cannot be ignored due to its importance). This issue also affects the randomization of tasks. If a between subject experiment is carried out then the experimenter needs to ensure that topics are balanced between users in the dyslexia group and the control group. Finally, the experimenter needs to think about the total time for experiments, due to tiredness the user group feels when undertaking intellectually intensive activities.

3.4 Reporting results

There are clear rules both in research ethics and methodology to anonymise data when reporting results. However, there are no guidelines regarding how to refer to participants. There are different practises on how to refer to such user groups, often related to which model of disability that is used, for instance the medical model, social model or the gap-model [18] and terminology often change over time. It is always good practice to anonymise the participants of the study, but often participants in the control group and dyslexia group will be labelled differently so that contrasts can be made in between subject designs.

Another key issue is to keep the participants informed of the results. Although this might be standard procedure, it is particularly important that vulnerable user groups understand that their activities have real worth.

4 REVISED METHODS IN IIR

In this section we suggest some revised methods in IIR to deal with the key issues presented above. According to Newell et al. [36] studies on marginalised groups, for instance people who are elderly or have an impairment, require a different approach than traditional user studies. It is argued that designers need to develop an empathetic relationship with the users rather than treating them as "test subjects". Newell, Gregor, Morgan, Pullin and Macaulay [36] claim that building such a relationship is not always possible in traditional laboratories, where experimenters observe participants from a distance. This approach is referred to as User-Sensitive Inclusive Design [36]. Empathy is an important aspect of all user studies, especially when the test group comprise vulnerable users, and is important in all phases of user studies, from the planning, initial contact with participants and referral of results.

4.1 Sampling

Ethically, it is favourable that researchers are not allowed access to lists of people with impairments. Consequently, it is not possible to use sampling frames or statistical methods to get a random, representative sample of people with dyslexia. The researchers have to rely solely on recruitment by people volunteering, which may cause sample bias. It is therefore important to consider where and how information about the study is given. One solution is for instance cooperation with user organisations, for instance the British Dyslexia Association [7], students disability services at universities or social media such as Facebook groups that are particularly relevant for the target group.

Balancing the participant group according to variables such as gender and age is also important. For instance, dyslexia is more prevalent among males than females [43], and this imbalance should be reflected in the sample. However, in our experiences and as reported by other researchers [26], females are more likely to volunteer for studies than males. As a consequence, there is a risk of an unequal gender distribution, which may be particularly skewed since the sample should consist of a higher portion of males than females.

4.2 Informed consent

Informed consent implies that participants have read, understood and signed comprehensive documents describing the study. However, reading difficulties can cause decoding errors. Moreover, reduced reading speed can make reading recruitment letters a time-consuming and potentially exhausting activity. As a consequence, some participants may sign consent forms without comprehending the actual content of the document. Conducting a study where participants have signed consent forms without reading and / or fully understanding the content would be a serious violation of research ethics. The experimenter therefore needs to ensure that the participant has comprehended all the information provided.

Difficulties with informed consent have been reported for other vulnerable user groups, such as elderly people with dementia [1] or participants with severe cognitive impairments [8; 38]. Astell, Alm, Gowans, Ellis, Dye and Vaughan [1] suggest that experiments undertaken with users who have dementia should first send out letters about the study to give them time to understand its purpose, then repeat the information later verbally and have the participants consent with a neutral third-party present.

In three of the studies we conducted [3-5], additional verbal information was provided at the start of the experimental session to ensure that the participants had received and comprehended all the necessary information. The use of accessible technologies such as screen-readers can also be used to read out materials, since multimodal communication can assist users with dyslexia in understanding [32]. Another option is to make a short sound recording or movie that can be transmitted to the participants.

Researchers have reported that text format may affect the reading process [12; 32; 44]. Consequently, the researchers have to consider the use of font types, font sizes, spacing between letters and lines and the use of colours, to support the readers with dyslexia to the largest possible extent.

Reduced short-term memory of people with dyslexia is another potential challenge. There is a risk that users may not remember all the information they have been given, for example that they can discontinue participation and withdraw the consent at any time. Consequently, it might be necessary to consider repeating the most important information, especially if the participants are involved in several sessions over time.

4.3 Method of data collection

There are several issues related to methods for data collection. In this section we address diagnoses and the experimental design of topics and tasks.

4.3.1 Diagnosis. Diagnostic papers are highly sensitive, and potential participants may avoid volunteering for studies where they need to share such information with outsiders. A solution to this issue is to rely solely on self-reporting of diagnoses or the researchers conduct screening tests themselves. There are two main issues with self-reporting: does the participant actually have a valid diagnosis, and if control users are included, are the experimenters sure that none of these participants have dyslexia? The first issue might be especially important if the participants are given remuneration, since there is a risk of people volunteering simply to receive the payment. Further, people may think they have a diagnosis, but without proper evaluation it is not possible to ensure that the right diagnosis has been set.

The second issue with self-reporting of dyslexia concerns the control users. It is crucial to ensure that the control participants do not have any degree of dyslexia, since the presence or absence of this diagnosis is typically the controlled variable. It is reported that people may not be aware of their dyslexia, and undiagnosed adults is not uncommon [51]. Since people may not be aware of their dyslexia diagnosis, there is a need for screening tests of the control group as well as the self-reported users with dyslexia. In one of our studies [2] several control users had to be excluded due to low scores on the screening tests, confirming the need for screening all participants.

Another concern is how to deal with the test scores of control users. According to International Test Commission [22], researchers should provide users with feedback of test results. We argue that this is especially important if the test scores for control users are indicative of dyslexia, where the participants may need further diagnostic tests conducted by professionals to receive a proper diagnosis. For example, with student participants the researcher should know the relevant student support services and direct the participant to the relevant person in that service.

One quick way to test whether a person might have dyslexia or not is to use the Adult Dyslexia Checklist developed by the British Dyslexia Association [46]. This screening test does not provide enough information for diagnostic assessment, but may indicate assessment needs. The test contains 15 questions related to typical issues associated with dyslexia, for example whether the person confuses words, have difficulties reading out loud and have trouble telling left from right. This test is no substitution for a diagnosis from a qualified psychologist, but might be a helpful screening tool.

Word Chain tests are also widely used in research [11], and is based on word recognition skills. The procedure is as follows: the participant is presented with a certain amount of word chains, where several words are put together without blank space. The task is to divide the word chain into the proper words by marking the white space, and the user is given a certain amount of time to complete the task. Points are given based on the number of correct word chains completed on time, and normative data exists for different age ranges. These tests are quick to complete, easy to evaluate and are developed in several languages and variations [11]. However, this test must also be regarded as a screening tool, and not a diagnostic test.

Dual diagnosis represents another challenge. It might be difficult to investigate the effect of dyslexia on information searching in contexts with a presence of other diagnoses such as ADHD or dyscalculia. Depending on the research aim, it may be necessary to remove such participants from the study results. Moreover, dyslexia occurs in different degrees and with variations. Consequently, a thorough psychological evaluation of each participant may be necessary to have a proper understanding of the cognitive profile of each user. Examples of characteristics to test are decoding skills, concentration skills, reduced short-term memory capacity and rapid naming skills, all of which may affect the ability to search for information.

There are a number of relevant tests available that are relatively easy to conduct [19; 48; 53]. A widely used test is the open source Victoria Stroop test, that may provide data on concentration and rapid naming skills [48]. Memory capacity tests may also be useful, for instance a Digit span test [52] or a Corsi Block-tapping test [48]. Both of these memory tests are freely available in the open source software "PEBL: The Psychology Experimental Building Language" [34].

Overall, it is important to only include tests that are necessary, explain to the participants why they are conducted and to complete them according to ethical guidelines. When working with vulnerable user groups, it is especially important to reduce the test-takers anxiety and avoid creating unnecessary anxiety [22].

Another general issue is that some researchers combine users with very different diagnoses in one study, for instance autism, dyslexia and ADHD without discussing the potential problems concerning the inclusion of users with needs that differ substantially or are conflicting. We recommend focusing on one diagnosis at a time whenever possible. Otherwise, it should be clearly stated and discussed that several diagnoses are studied, and results should be isolated for each user group and compared to see whether there are differences according to diagnosis.

4.3.2 Experimental tasks. As stated in Section 3.3, care must be taken to ensure participants are treated ethically and fairly e.g. not tiring them out. Firstly, the users should not be involved in long sessions with many topics. In MacFarlane, Al-Wabil, Marshall, Albrair, Jones and Zaphiris [28] and MacFarlane, Albrair, Marshall and Buchanan [29] experiments were restricted to around 1 hour, with actual searching time approximately 30 minutes. Two topics can be used in the experiment, but each user only gets one. The topics are split in both the dyslexia and control group, but both get the same topics (see Table 1). Topics should be split amongst each type of user as evenly as possible (e.g. round robin, so that users do not all start with the same topic), and the balance between types of users should nearly be equal (e.g. C should be around the same size as D).

Randomization of tasks is not always possible. In Berget and Sandnes [4] and Berget and Sandnes [5] users were asked to solve search tasks with various degrees of difficulty. The tasks were formulated quite specifically, often including relevant search terms, because the purpose was to test how reduced spelling skills caused by dyslexia may affect query formulation. The study was divided into two sessions conducted some months apart, with searching times of approximately 20 minutes for each session. Each participant solved the same 10 tasks, but were given a different set for the two sessions. The varying difficulty levels of the tasks combined with the vulnerability of participants with dyslexia made it impossible to randomize the tasks. Consequently, all participants solved the tasks in the same order, starting with a very simple task to provide a sense of coping. This was followed by tasks that were increasingly difficult. An easier task was given in the middle of the session with the purpose to encourage the participants, while the most difficult task was solved last. Several participants commented after the experiment that if the most difficult task had been presented first, they would have lost confidence and terminated the session. These attitudes confirm the need to consider the vulnerability and feeling of coping of the participants over rigid methodological procedures concerning randomization of tasks. However, the researcher needs to be aware of the consequences of this methodological choice.

Table 1: Topic distribution (C=Control users, D=Users with Dyslexia)

User Type	Topic A	Topic B
Control	C/2	C/2
Dyslexia	D/2	D/2

4.4 Reporting results

Here we report best practice when dealing with the data collected in experiments involving users with dyslexia.

4.4.1 Diagnosis. Experimenters should be clear about what (if any) procedure they used to ensure the controls and users with dyslexia are distinct groups, their strategy with dealing with participants with undiagnosed dyslexia and how they deal with them in the study. Given that dyslexia describes a spectrum of cognitive abilities, the researcher should provide an overview of the profile of the cohort and provide some idea as to how the participants match the overall population of people with dyslexia. In cases where the difference between various types of participants with dyslexia is examined (e.g. severe vs mild forms), then the cognitive profile differences need to be clearly explained and again the research needs to justify the placement of users into the particular groups. In such cases, the screening tests described in Section 4.3.1 can be useful to get an indication of the severity of the dyslexia for each person. Diagnosis can also be used when examining experimental results. Moreover, dual diagnoses need to be addressed, as discussed in Section 4.3.1, and preferably statistical tests should be run with and without dual diagnosis participants (and their controls if applicable).

4.4.2 Experimental results. Variables collected when examining the cognitive profile can be used in statistical analysis with search variables (e.g. such as number of iterations in a session, number of terms per query or time spent per query) and correlations can be particularly useful. For example MacFarlane, Albrair, Marshall and Buchanan [29] took one variable (documents judged irrelevant) and did correlations with the cognitive variables. In this case Digit Span (a measure of short-term memory capacity) showed a strong correlation with that search variable. We concentrated on this search variable as it was the only one in which the difference between the dyslexia group and the control group was significant.

Our advice would be to identify an initial variable or variables that have demonstrated significant difference and focus on these. However, what must be done is to ensure that there is a real difference between the two groups, and there is no topic effect i.e. topic effects are considered to be important in the field and variables have to be cross checked accordingly. The design of the experiment outlined in section 4.3.1 is therefore critical, and an orthogonal topic comparison is necessary (as per Table 1).

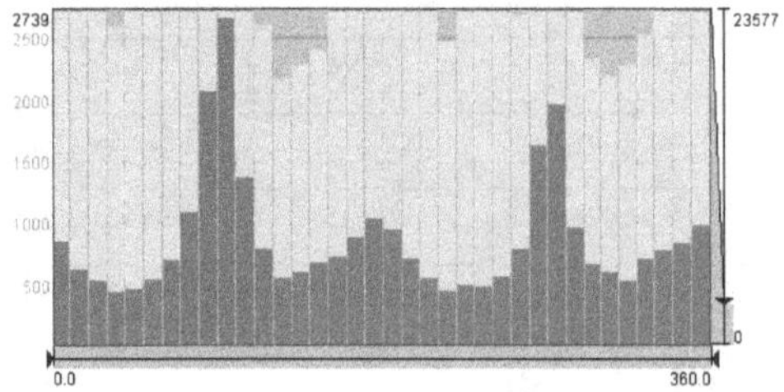

Figure 1 – Control group frequency distribution of eye movements

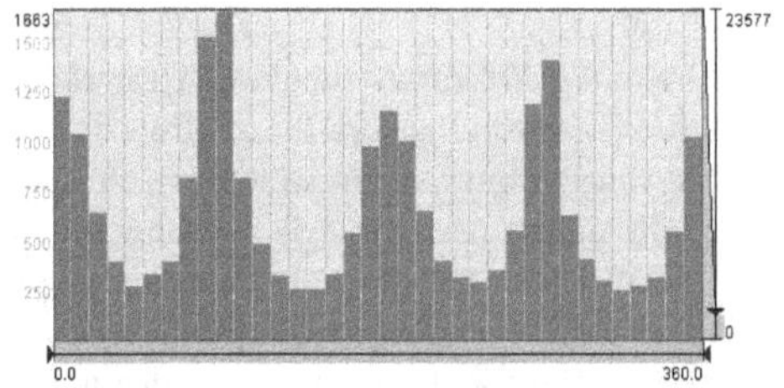

Figure 2 – Dyslexia group frequency distribution of eye movements

In MacFarlane, Albrair, Marshall and Buchanan [29] the only statistically significant variable showed no topic effect i.e. there was no significant difference between the topics. Thus, if no topic effect is demonstrated on a given variable (documents judged irrelevant), then any difference from other comparisons is real i.e. the difference between controls and users with dyslexia on that variable. This is the key way to ensure that users are treated ethically and some rigour in the experimental results is adhered to.

Comparing search variables between the two user groups may also be purposeful. In the context of search variables, users with dyslexia and the control group can be compared with for example t-tests to get a better understanding of which parts of the search process that are most affected by the impairment. These types of comparisons may be useful to apply to different types of search systems. For instance, Berget and Sandnes [4], found that there were significant differences between users with dyslexia and control users in misspellings, search times and number of queries needed to solve a task in a system with no query-building aids and a high demand for correct spelling. In another experiment using a system with query-building aids and a higher tolerance for misspellings, Berget and Sandnes [5] found that the differences in spelling skills did not affect the overall performance due to a higher tolerance for errors implemented in the system. Consequently, analysing several variables and including different types of systems may demonstrate the potential in UI design to counteract or entirely remove the potentially negative effect of an impairment on search performance.

Methodological choices are also, as in any experiment, important. Regarding dyslexia, eye-tracking has proven especially useful, since the eye-movements may reveal certain search behaviours that are not directly visible in variables such as search times or misspellings. For instance, MacFarlane, Buchanan, Al-Wabil, Andrienko and Andrienko [30] found that people with dyslexia backtracked when viewing results and documents during search, which is probably caused by short-term memory challenges (forgetting and looking back as a reminder).

Using visualisations (see Figure 1 and 2) can provide very useful contrasts on different users' interaction behaviours. For instance, a comparison of figures 1 and 2 show change of eye direction on the UI, compiled in a histogram from 0^0 to 360^0. In these examples eye movements at $0^0/360^0$ and 180^0 are more frequent indicating more vertical eye movements in users with dyslexia than control users. In a study by Berget and Sandnes [5], eye data revealed that people with dyslexia did not look at the suggestions provided by the autocomplete function as extensively as the control users, due to an intense focus on the keyboard during query input.

4.4.3 Referring to users. The strategy for referring to people with impairments have varied over time, and has among other factors been closely related to the dominating model on disability. According to Grue [18], an especially discussed topic has been the impairment/disability dichotomy. It is now a common view that a person has an impairment, not a disability. In contrast, a disability is something that occurs when there is a mismatch between the demands from the society and the person's abilities. Moreover, a basic rule seems to be referring to people first, and not the disability, for instance "person with a cognitive impairment", not "cognitively disabled" or "cognitively impaired". In this case we would recommend using phrases such as 'person with dyslexia'.

Another issue is how one refers to the control group. In some contexts, the words neurotypical is used for the control users, in other cases one simply uses "control group" or "participants without dyslexia". It is important to avoid using "normal" as a measurement, thus implying that the participants who diverge from the "standard" are "not normal". It is also important to be aware of terminology changes over time. For instance, the phrase "word blindness" has been replaced by "dyslexia" [45], and should not be used, since it may give a wrong impression of the aetiology of the diagnosis. Consequently, when referring to older studies researchers cannot always uncritically adopt the same terminology applied there, they must ensure that they use current terminology from recent literature.

5 SUMMARY OF RECOMMENDATIONS

Our stated aim was to provide some ideas for best practice in conducting IIR experiments involving users with dyslexia, and the many issues with the standard form of experimentation that researchers must consider if they are to undertake the work ethically. The key issue is that these users are regarded as being a vulnerable group, due to low self-esteem, tendency to tiredness and anxiety. The standard IIR experimental method must be adapted to ensure that ethical considerations are adhered to, but also ensuring that the methods used are rigorous and the results produced are useful and transferable to the IIR community either for undertaking further experimentation with the group or to inform system design, or both. We have not addressed the issue of naturalistic studies, but many of the ideas here in terms of sampling and informed consent do also apply to such contexts.

User studies on various impairments have revealed important design issues in search user interfaces, and topics that need to be addressed by the research community. In accordance with the universal design perspective, several of these issues would be problematic for other users as well, and measures to make the systems more accessible would also be beneficial for people without impairments.

We summarise our recommendations based on our prior experience outlined above in the following sub-sections with a particular focus on undertaking research involving users with dyslexia (we assume the standard IIR experimental procedure).

5.1 Experimental Design

When considering study design there are a number of key issues around users and topics that need to be considered. Researchers should be clear about how they will distinguish between the users with dyslexia and the control group, and if necessary, between different types of dyslexia, e.g. mild vs severe forms. Given the ethical issues with requesting prior diagnosis, we strongly recommend that researchers consider the use of a wide variety of psychological tests which are freely available [34; 46; 48]. Researchers should put in place strategies to deal with undiagnosed users with dyslexia in the control group i.e. where to get advice and who to contact for a full diagnostic evaluation. The user should be provided with a full profile of their diagnostic test results if required. This is a significant ethical issue, which researchers must think carefully about when for example completing ethics panel applications. Other variables such as the gender balance should be considered given the prevalence of dyslexia in the male population.

Once the researchers have a clear focus on the type of user with dyslexia they will work with, various aspects of the study design need to be considered carefully. In terms of topics and/or tasks, a limited number should be selected, but should not be restricted to just one type of task or one topic – the task/topic effect is too profound. At least two topics should be chosen, but should be balanced out to ensure that equal number of topics are distributed to users in both the dyslexia group and the control group (see Table 1). If necessary, distribute the topics within each group based on gender. Researchers need to think about the complexity of the topics and its potential effect on for instance tiredness and self-esteem of users with dyslexia. If tasks rather than topics are used, a limited number should be utilized, and the researcher should think about the balance between complexity and number (many simple tasks vs. fewer complex tasks). All sub groups should be as balanced as possible within the sampling constraints.

Next the researcher needs to think about the materials to be used in the experiment. What type of survey instruments will be used e.g. questionnaires, interviews, observations? Logging of the searches may also be considered [28; 29]. How will informed consent be obtained from the user, and how will all materials be presented in an accessible way?

Researchers should not only think about the form of information sheets, consent forms and questionnaires (e.g. clear wording without excessive text) but the type of accessible technology that may be required by the users (e.g. screen readers and colour schemes on the user interface). Before proceeding, ethical approval for the study must be obtained from an appropriate panel.

5.2 Experimental conduct

Once the experiment has been designed and appropriate ethical approval has been obtained the work can be carried out and participants recruited for the study. Informed consent must be given by the user before the experiment is started. At any stage in the experiment, the researcher should be prepared to step in and give the user appropriate assistance (e.g. with assistive technologies). Also, the researcher should keep in mind that the participant might have forgotten information given at the beginning of the experiment, and consider repeating the most fundamental issues, especially if the experiment is conducted over more than one session.

Before starting the experiment properly, it is important to carry out any diagnostic process beforehand. All users must be subject to the same tests (useful for analysis later on), the type depending on the aims of the study. If control users are recruited, and found to have a similar profile to users with dyslexia, provide them with advice on what to do next together with the data collected so that a professional therapist can provide them with the appropriate help. In terms of the experiment itself, we strongly recommend that they are removed from the study and not placed in the dyslexia group. Users with dyslexia have had a full diagnostic assessment, whereas undiagnosed participants do not, and putting them into that group introduces uncertainty, impacting on the reliability of the study. However, the undiagnosed user should be allowed to complete the experiment for their own interest, and to obtain the appropriate reward (in having volunteered for the study in the first place).

Once the diagnostic test has been carried out the experiment can be done in earnest. This may well start with a pre-experiment survey, collecting demographic information e.g. gender, age and perhaps the level of prior experience with the type of search system being investigated. Accessible technology should be used where necessary e.g. screen readers for questionnaires. After this a short training session should take place to familiarise the user with the system, either with a test topic or with the users' own information need. This should be long enough for the user to learn how to use the system, but should not over burden the user cognitively (taking into account the work they will undertake in the main experiment).

The main experiment should then take place. We recommend restricting the experiment to no more than one hour, with around 30 or so minutes devoted to the main searching task. Researchers should think clearly about the balance between the different elements of the IIR process. Researchers should be ready to step in when participants are having problems, and if it is clear that the users struggle due to the system itself (e.g. the UI causes visual problems), then the researcher should be prepared to either make changes or in extreme cases stop the experiment. In such cases user's data should be omitted from the study.

When the experiment is completed, any post experiment survey can be carried out, using the same strategy and methods as with any pre-experiment survey. The researcher should take time to wrap up and reassure the participant if and when required. It may be appropriate to return to the issue of informed consent to ensure the user fully understood the purpose and rationale of research carried out. For participants who have struggled and showed frustration and/or anxiety about the performance, the researcher should take the time to explain that the study was not about performing at a certain level, but to rather understand how the UI design can be changed to better accommodate their search behaviour. Consequently, the participant will hopefully feel less frustrated and that the effort was purposeful.

5.3 Reporting and dissemination of results

A key issue with the analysis stage is putting thought into the analysis of variables collected. The first thing to do is to examine the cognitive variables and undertake a statistical analysis on group membership – in particular to ensure that control participants are not undiagnosed users with dyslexia. Typically, comparisons between participants with dyslexia and the control users or users with severe and mild dyslexia will be carried out, both on the cognitive variables and the search variables. Correlations between cognitive and search variables can be usefully carried out. Any demographic information e.g. gender can also be used as an extra dimension of analysis.

One key issue must be addressed in the analysis – that of task or topic. For example, the variables used to examine the differences between users with dyslexia and the controls can also be subject to a topic comparison (as per Table 1). The class of tasks can be treated in a similar way. If any significant difference is found on a given variable on the topic, then there is a clear topic effect to factor into the analysis. For example, in cases where a topic effect is demonstrated on a variable, statistical significance on comparisons between users in the dyslexia group and the control group on that variable need to be treated with care – i.e. the effect of dyslexia is not conclusively demonstrated. Further analysis may be necessary to make conclusive statements – one strategy is to reject any significant differences on the cognitive variable if a topic effect is shown [28; 29]. A further method which can prove useful is the application of multiple regression analysis [13], which can be used to demonstrate which variables are the most significant. Researchers should consider different visualisation techniques for the display of aggregate data, for example the eye tracking examples provided in figures 1 and 2. More examples can be found in MacFarlane, Buchanan, Al-Wabil, Andrienko and Andrienko [30].

If literals have been collected in the pre and post experiment survey, then various forms of qualitative analysis can be carried out for example discourse analysis. Mixed method approaches can be a very useful strategy in the domain. We argue that any statistical analysis of the user behaviour and cognitive profile can be enhanced by the examination of user views of the search experience, picking up issues on usability and accessibility that cannot be detected by quantitative methods alone.

Finally, when writing up the results, researchers should think clearly about how they refer to their participants – particularly given that the users recruited may wish to see the published article.

6 CONCLUSION

In this paper we argue for the use of a revised IIR approach, that builds on the knowledge already gained in the area over many years. In our experience this has yielded positive results, and we have been able to make contributions to knowledge through the methodology. A question to be raised is whether this methodology is generalizable to other types of impairments. In the authors view, this needs to be considered on a case by case basis – it is entirely possible that some impairments put serious constraints on the IIR methodology making it unusable, in which case a different approach is required. We hope this paper is the start of a serious examination of the issue of impairments and methods in the IIR community.

REFERENCES

[1] A. Astell, N. Alm, G. Gowans, M. Ellis, R. Dye and P. Vaughan. 2008. Involving older people with dementia and their carers in designing computer based support systems: Some methodological considerations. *Universal Access in the Information Society*, 8(1), 49.

[2] G. Berget. 2016. *Search and find?: An accessibility study of dyslexia and information retrieval.* University of Oslo, Oslo, Norway.

[3] G. Berget, F. Mulvey and F. E. Sandnes. 2016. Is visual content in textual search interfaces beneficial to dyslexic users? *International Journal of Human-Computer Studies, 92-93*, 17-29.

[4] G. Berget and F. E. Sandnes. 2015. Searching databases without query-building aids: Implications for dyslexic users. *Information Research, 20*(4), paper 689.

[5] G. Berget and F. E. Sandnes. 2016. Do autocomplete functions reduce the impact of dyslexia on information-searching behavior?: The case of Google. *Journal of the Association for Information Science and Technology, 67*(10), 2320-2328.

[6] P. Borlund. 2000. Experimental components for the evaluation of interactive information retrieval systems. *Journal of Documentation, 56*(1), 71-90.

[7] British Dyslexia Association, 2018. *British Dyslexia Association.* Retrieved from https://www.bdadyslexia.org.uk/.

[8] L. Cameron and J. Murphy. 2007. Obtaining consent to participate in research: The issues involved in including people with a range of learning and communication disabilities. *British Journal of Learning Disabilities, 35*(2), 113-120.

[9] J. M. Caroll. and J. E. Iles, 2006. An assessment of anxiety levels in dyslexic students in higher education. *British Journal of Educational Psychology, 76*(3), 651-662.

[10] City University of London, 2018. *Research ethics City University, London.* Retrieved from https://www.city.ac.uk/department-computer-science/research-ethics.

[11] A. E. Dahle and A.-M. Knivsberg, 2014. Internalizing, externalizing and attention problems in dyslexia. *Scandinavian Journal of Disability Research, 16*(2), 179-193.

[12] L. Evett and D. Brown, 2005. Text formats and web design for visually impaired and dyslexic readers: Clear text for all. *Interacting with Computers, 17*(4), 453-472.

[13] A. Fourney, M. R. Morris, A. Ali and L. Vonessen, 2018. Assessing the readability of web search results for searchers with dyslexia. In *Proceedings of the The 41st International ACM SIGIR Conference on Research & Development in Information Retrieval.* ACM, New York, NY, USA, 1069-1072.

[14] C. Frankfort-Nachmias, D. Nachmias and J. Dewaard, 2015. *Research methods in the social sciences.* Worth, New York, NY, USA.

[15] E. Germanò, A. Gagliano and P. Curatolo, 2010. Comorbidity of ADHD and dyslexia. *Developmental Neuropsychology, 35*(5), 475-493.

[16] J. Gibbs, J. Appleton and R. Appleton, 2007. Dyspraxia or developmental coordination disorder?: Unravelling the enigma. *Archives of Disease in Childhood, 92*(6), 534-539.

[17] J. H. Goldberg, M. J. Stimson, M. Lewenstein, N. Scott and A. M. Wichansky, 2002. Eye tracking in web search tasks: Design implications. In *Proceedings of the Proceedings of the 2002 symposium on Eye tracking research & applications, New Orleans, Louisiana 2002.* ACM, New York, NY, USA, 51-58.

[18] J. Grue, 2011. Discourse analysis and disability: Some topics and issues. *Discourse & Society, 22*(5), 532-546.

[19] J. Hatcher, M. J. Snowling and Y. M. Griffiths, 2002. Cognitive assessment of dyslexic students in higher education. *British Journal of Educational Psychology, 72*(1), 119-133.

[20] M. Hebert, X. Zhang and W. Parrila, 2018. Examining reading comprehension text and question answering time differences in university students with and without a history of reading difficulties. *Annals of Dyslexia, 68*(1), 15-24.

[21] H. Hill, 2013. Disability and accessibility in the library and information science literature: A content analysis. *Library & Information Science Research, 35*(2), 137-142.

[22] International Test Commission, 2001. International Guidelines for Test Use. *International Journal of Testing, 1*(2), 93.

[23] B. J. Jansen, 2006. Search log analysis: What it is, what's been done, how to do it. *Library & Information Science Research, 28*(3), 407-432.

[24] S. Jeffries and J. Everatt, 2004. Working memory: Its role in dyslexia and other specific learning difficulties. *Dyslexia,* 10(3), 196-214.

[25] D. Kelly, 2009. Methods for evaluating interactive information retrieval systems with users. *Foundations and Trends® in Information Retrieval, 3*(1–2), 1-224.

[26] S. E. Kelly, T. D. Spector, L. F. Cherkas, B. Prainsack, and J. M. Harris, 2015. Evaluating the consent preferences of UK research volunteers for genetic and clinical studies. *PLOS ONE, 10*(3), e0118027.

[27] K. Landerl, B. Fussenegger, K. Moll, and E. Willburger, 2009. Dyslexia and dyscalculia: Two learning disorders with different cognitive profiles. *Journal of Experimental Child Psychology, 103*(3), 309-324.

[28] A. MacFarlane, A. Al-Wabil, C. R. Marshall, A. Albrair, S. A. Jones and P. Zaphiris, 2010. The effect of dyslexia on information retrieval: A pilot study. *Journal of Documentation, 66*(3), 307-326.

[29] A. MacFarlane, A. Albrair, C. R. Marshall and G. Buchanan, 2012. Phonological working memory impacts on information searching: An investigation of dyslexia. In *Proceedings of the Proceedings of the 4th Information Interaction in Context Symposium, Nijmegen, The Netherlands, 2012.* ACM, New York, NY, USA, 27-34.

[30] A. MacFarlane, G. Buchanan, A. Al-Wabil, G. Andrienko and N. Andrienko, 2017. Visual analysis of dyslexia on search. In *Proceedings of the Proceedings of the 2017 Conference on Conference Human Information Interaction and Retrieval, Oslo, Norway, 2017.* ACM, New York, NY, USA, 285-288.

[31] A. MacFarlane, H., Petrie and S. A. Jones, 2005. A user study on the effect of dyslexia on information retrieval. In *Proceedings of COLIS 2005 Workshop on Evaluating User Studies in Information Access,* 31-38.

[32] J. E. McCarthy and S. J. Swierenga, 2010. What we know about dyslexia and Web accessibility: A research review. *Universal Access in the Information Society, 9*(2), 147-152.

[33] T. Mortimore and W. R. Crozier, 2006. Dyslexia and difficulties with study skills in higher education. *Studies in Higher Education, 31*(2), 235-251.

[34] S. T. Mueller, and B. J. Piper, 2014. The Psychology Experiment Building Language (PEBL) and PEBL Test Battery. *Journal of Neuroscience Methods, 222,* 250-259.

[35] B. A. Nalavany, L. W. Carawan, and L. J. Brown, 2011. Considering the role of traditional and specialist schools: Do school experiences impact the emotional well-being and self-esteem of adults with dyslexia? *British Journal of Special Education, 38*(4), 191-200.

[36] A. F. Newell, P. Gregor, M. Morgan, G. Pullin and C. Macaulay, 2011. User-Sensitive Inclusive Design. *Universal Access in the Information Society, 10*(3), 235-243.

[37] R. I. Nicolson and A. J. Fawcett, 2011. Dyslexia, dysgraphia, procedural learning and the cerebellum. *Cortex, 47*(1), 117-127.

[38] M. Nind, 2008. *Conducting qualitative research with people with learning, communication and other disabilities: Methodological challenges.* National Centre for Research Methods, University of Southampton, Southampton, United Kingdom.

[39] E. S. Norton and M. Wolf, 2012. Rapid automatized naming (RAN) and reading fluency: Implications for understanding and treatment of reading disabilities. *Annual Review of Psychology, 63*(1), 427-452.

[40] S. Novita, 2016. Secondary symptoms of dyslexia: A comparison of self-esteem and anxiety profiles of children with and without dyslexia. *European Journal of Special Needs Education, 31*(2), 279-288.

[41] T. M. Perez, M. Poncelet, E. Salmon and S. Majerus, 2015. Functional alterations in order short-term memory networks in adults with dyslexia. *Developmental Neuropsychology, 40*(7-8), 407-429.

[42] R. L. Peterson and B.F. Pennington, 2015. Developmental Dyslexia. *Annual Review of Clinical Psychology, 11*(1), 283-307.

[43] J. M. Quinn and R. K. Wagner, 2015. Gender differences in reading impairment and in the identification of impaired readers: Results from a large-scale study of at-risk readers. *Journal of Learning Disabilities, 48*(4), 433-445.

[44] L. Rello and R. Baeza-Yates, 2017. How to present more readable text for people with dyslexia. *Universal Access in the Information Society, 16*(1), 29-49.

[45] T. A. Serry and L. Hammond, 2015. What's in a word? Australian experts' knowledge, views and experiences using the term dyslexia. *Australian Journal of Learning Difficulties, 20*(2), 143-161.

[46] I. Smythe and J. Everatt, 2001. *Adult checklist.* Retrieved from https://www.bdadyslexia.org.uk/common/ckeditor/filemanager/userfiles/Adult-Checklist.pdf.

[47] M. F. Story, 1998. Maximizing usability: The principles of universal design. *Assistive Technology, 10*(1), 4-12.

[48] E. Strauss, E. M. S. Sherman and O. Spreen, 2006. *A compendium of neuropsychological tests: Administration, norms, and commentary.* Oxford Press, Oxford, United Kingdom.

[49] M. M. Terras, L. C. Thompson and H. Minnis, 2009. Dyslexia and psycho-social functioning: An exploratory study of the role of self-esteem and understanding. *Dyslexia, 15*(4), 304-327.

[50] Text Retrieval Conference, n.d. *TREC-6 interactive track specifications.* Retrieved from https://trec.nist.gov/data/t6i/trec6spec

[51] M. Warmington, S. E. Stothard and M. J. Snowling, 2013. Assessing dyslexia in higher education: The York adult assessment battery-revised. *Journal of Research in Special Educational Needs, 13*(1), 48-56.

[52] D. Wechsler, 1997. *Wechsler Adult Intelligence Test.* The Psychological Corporation, San Antonio, TX, USA.

[53] G. S. Wilkinson and G. J. Wilkinson, 2006. *Wide Range Achievement Test.* Psychological Assessment Resources, Florida, USA.

NotifyMeHere: Intelligent Notification Delivery in Multi-Device Environments

Abhinav Mehrotra
University College London, UK
a.mehrotra@ucl.ac.uk

Robert Hendley
University of Birmingham, UK
r.j.hendley@bham.ac.uk

Mirco Musolesi
University College London, UK
The Alan Turing Institute, UK
m.musolesi@ucl.ac.uk

ABSTRACT

Personal interactions and information access are happening more and more through the mediation of computing devices of various types all around us. In our daily life we use many computing devices running different versions of the same application such as email clients or social media platforms, which alert users about a new piece of information or event on all devices. In this paper wefi rst present a study investigating the factors influencing users' decisions in handling notifications in a multi-device environment. We collected 57,242 *in-the-wild* notifications from 24 users over a period of 21 days. We found that users' decisions in handling notifications are impacted by their physical activity, location, network connectivity, application category and the device used for handling the previous notification. Finally, we show that an individualized model can predict the device on which the user will handle a notification in the given context with 82% specificity and 91% sensitivity.

CCS CONCEPTS

• **Human-centered computing** → *HCI design and evaluation methods*; *Empirical studies in ubiquitous and mobile computing*;

KEYWORDS

Mobile Sensing, Multi-device Notifications, Interruptibility, Context-aware Computing

ACM Reference Format:
Abhinav Mehrotra, Robert Hendley, and Mirco Musolesi. 2019. NotifyMeHere: Intelligent Notification Delivery in Multi-Device Environments. In *2019 Conference on Human Information Interaction and Retrieval (CHIIR '19), March 10–14, 2019, Glasgow, United Kingdom.* ACM, New York, NY, USA, 9 pages. https://doi.org/10.1145/3295750.3298932

1 INTRODUCTION

Cross-platform applications leverage notifications to trigger real-time alerts for steering users' attention towards newly available information through auditive, visual and haptic signals. Indeed, these notifications are beneficial to users for proactive personalized information delivery about a variety of events such as travel update information or a new comment on a social network post [8, 43]. However, notifications sometimes arrive at inappropriate moments and, for this reason, they can have an adverse impact on the execution of the ongoing tasks [7, 10, 11] and even on the affective state of users [5, 6]. The problem is exacerbated by the fact that cross-platform applications prompt users on *multiple devices at the same time*, which makes these notifications even more disruptive and annoying [39]. In light of this, a recent study shows that users prefer to receive notifications on specific devices based on their situation [42].

Until now, previous interruptibility management studies have used notification and contextual information to infer opportune moments for delivering mobile notifications (e.g., [19, 21, 25, 35, 36, 40]) and to learn the types of notifications users prefer to receive in different situations (e.g., [22, 30]). In this work, to the best of our knowledge, for thefi rst time we try to address the problem of delivering notifications *on the right device* in different contexts. It is very difficult to define the concept of *right* device, but as afirst approximation, it can be seen as the device on which users prefer to handle a specific notification given their context.

In order to design a solution for intelligent cross-platform notification delivery, wefi rst conduct an in-situ study to investigate the contextual factors impacting users' decisions for handling notifications on specific devices. In particular, in this paper we investigate how users behave in different contexts when they receive a notification on their mobile phone as well as on a generic alternative device (i.e., any alternative computing device that runs a version of applications that are also available for mobile phones) at the same time. Through a passive logging smartphone application we collected 57,242 in-the-wild notifications from 24 users over a period of 21 days. Out of these notifications, around 44.8% of them (i.e., 25,677) were triggered by cross-platform applications. We found that 28.59% of notifications that are triggered by cross-platform applications are handled on an alternative device (i.e., not handled on the mobile phone). Our results show that users' decisions for handling notifications on a mobile or an alternative device are associated with their physical activity, location, application category and network connectivity.

Starting from this analysis, in this paper we present the design, implementation and evaluation of NotifyMeHere, a solution for intelligent notification delivery in multi-device environments. The design is based on a prediction component based on a model of user interaction with notifications on a mobile or an alternative device in different sensed contexts. NotifyMeHere can be implemented as a cross-platform application's server component that is aware of all devices of each user that have subscription to the application.

ACM ISBN 978-1-4503-6025-8/19/03...$15.00
https://doi.org/10.1145/3295750.3298932

In order to assess NotifyMeHere, we implemented and evaluated predictors by using a series of machine learning algorithms including AdaBoost [34], Random Forest [9] and Recursive Partitioning [17]. Our results show that predictors are more accurate when they are trained using data of each user (with 75% specificity and 90% sensitivity) compared to generic predictors trained on data related to a set of users. In fact, the latter achieves only 37% specificity and 90% sensitivity.

2 RELATED WORK

The effects of interruptions caused by notifications occurring at inopportune moments have been investigated thoroughly in the past (see, for example, [10, 11]). Studies have demonstrated that interrupting users engaged in tasks has considerable negative impact on task completion time [10, 11], error rate [7], and affective state [5, 6].

In order to address these issues, many previous mobile interruptibility studies have investigated how users perceive notifications [31, 38] and the factors involved in users' receptivity [14, 16, 23, 26, 27]. At the same time, the advances in the area of machine learning have enabled us to model users' interruptibility by exploiting their historical notification interaction data [24]. Previous studies have proposed various mechanisms for modeling interruptibility that can be used by applications to deliver notifications at the inferred opportune moments by means of users' contextual information [15, 18–20, 29, 35, 37], the notification content [22, 25] or the prospective information [21]. In a seminal paper [19] Ho and Intille suggested that the transition between two physical activities (such as sitting and walking) can be used as an opportune moment for delivering notifications. Similarly, Fischer et al. [15] showed that users react faster to notifications that are delivered immediately at the end of a task, such as afterfi nishing a phone call or reading a text message. In [37] Rosenthal et al. proposed a mechanism that relies on experience sampling to learn users' preferences for ringer mode settings and to predict when to mute a phone to prevent interruptions caused by notifications. Pielot et al. [32] proposed a model that can predict whether a user will view a notification within a few minutes with a precision of approximately 81%. Pejovic and Musolesi [29] proposed a mechanism that relies on contextual information (including activity, location and time of the day) to predict opportune moments for delivering notifications. Mehrotra et al. [25] designed a mechanism that relies on both contextual information and the notification content for modeling interruptibility. In a further study, Mehrotra et al. [22] proposed an interruptibility management mechanism that learns users' preferences for receiving notifications based on the automatic extraction of rules by mining their interaction with mobile notifications. The goal of their system is to be intelligible to users: for this reason, it makes the discovered rules transparent so that users can decide whether to accept or discard them at run-time.

3 DATA COLLECTION

To investigate the factors that determine users' decisions about handling notifications on specific devices in different situations, we conducted afi eld study to collect data through the real-world deployment of an Android app. As shown in Table 1, the app passively collects information about *in-the-wild* notification handling and context information (including physical activity, location and network connectivity).

Group	Features
Notification	Arrival time, removal time and sender application name.
Context	Physical activity, location and network connectivity.
Phone Usage	Foreground application (including home screen) usage, lock/unlock, screen change and click events with timestamp.

Table 1: Description of features from the dataset.

Our application relies on Android's Notification Listener Service [2] to log users' interaction with notifications and uses Google's Activity Recognition API [3] to obtain the information about user's physical activities classified as *walking, bicycling, commuting in-vehicle* or *still.* The application samples GPS data in an adaptive sensing fashion as described in [25]. Furthermore, the application relies on the NetworkInfo API [1] to get notified in real-time about network connectivity changes.

The Android application also collected additional data about other phone's and contextual attributes, such as ringer mode, call and SMS logs. However, we do not discuss those aspects of the data because they are not used for the analysis presented in this paper.

3.1 Recruitment of the Participants

We published the application on the Google Play Store and made it available to the general public for free. We advertised the application through different channels: academic mailing lists, Twitter, Facebook and Reddit.

In order to ensure privacy compliance, our application goes through a two-stage user agreement to access user's critical data. Firstly, a user has to give explicit permission as required by the Android operating system for capturing application usage, notifications and user's interaction with the mobile phone (such as clicks and screen changes). Secondly, the application shows a list of information that is collected and asks for user consent. It is worth noting that the study was done in accordance with our institution's ethical research procedure and the consent form itself for the data collection was reviewed by its Ethics Review Board.

4 DATASET

From 4th January to 1st June 2016, our application was installed by 87 participants from the Google Play Store. However, many users did not keep the application running actively and/or uninstalled it after a few days. Therefore, we selected a subset of the data for the analysis by considering only the users who kept the application running for at least 21 days. There are 26 users who satisfied this constraint. We also found that these users contribute minimum 80 notifications for each day. Note that we do not have information about the demographics of these participants because it was not asked during the study for privacy reasons following our institution's Ethics Board review. Ourfi nal dataset (i.e., the subset of active users) comprises 57,242 notification instances, 8.19 million phone usage events and 1.9 million context samples.

4.1 Identifying Devices on Which Notifications are Handled

First of all, we would like to underline the fact that in this work we predict the device on which a notification will be handled by the user but for only two classes of devices: personal phones and alternative devices (i.e., any device other than their phone). However, the proposed model is highly generalizable to the case of multiple classes of devices.

In order to infer whether a notification is handled or not (i.e., handled on some other device), we assume that a notification is automatically removed from the notification bar (or from the lock screen) of the phone if it was delivered on some other device and the user has already interacted with it on other device. More specifically, our assumption is that a notification is handled on a mobile phone only if the user has interacted with the phone between its arrival time (t_a) and its removal time (t_r). If there was no phone interaction logged in the interval between the time t_a and t_r, we assume that the user handled the notification on an alternative device. In fact, for instance, if a user receives a travel update notification on her phone as well as laptop, but she views and clicks the notification on her laptop then the corresponding application running on the phone automatically removes the notification from the notification bar. Therefore, to check the user's interaction during the interval between t_a and t_r, we use the phone usage data collected by our application (see Table 1). As discussed earlier, this data contains the logs for clicks, changes in the foreground and lock/unlock events.

4.1.1 Issues with Long Response Time. A recent study on mobile notifications [25] pointed out that some applications automatically kill the notifications that they generated and are not handled by the user within 30 minutes from their arrival time. This shows that some notifications can be automatically removed from the phone without being handled on an alternative device and, therefore, the notification response labels might not be correct in these cases. For this reason, we check notifications of which apps never have the value of $t_r - t_a$ more than 30 *min* andfi lter out all notifications of these apps that have $t_r - t_a = 30\ mins$.

4.1.2 Removing Notifications of Active Apps. Some apps such as instant messengers could generate continuous notifications even when the corresponding app is already in foreground (i.e., actively in use). However, such notifications are not of interest for us as it is very likely that users will handle these notifications on the same device on which they are interacting with the corresponding app. Therefore, on arrival of a notification the data collection app checked whether the corresponding app is in use or not, and in case the app is in foreground the response time of the notification is set to 0. In the analysis for this study we discarded all these notifications.

4.1.3 Removing Stacked Notifications. Another issue with the data is the duplicate entries introduced by "stacked" notifications (i.e., multiple notifications from the same applications getting displayed in the notification bar). In the Android operating system, these stacked notifications are aggregated into a single notification presenting the summary of all stacked notifications. However, fortunately, the Android Notification Listener API triggers a new notification event for stack notification update and, thus, our application collected them as separate notifications.

Tofi nd the stacked notifications we iterate through each notification and check if any other notification from the same application arrived between t_a and t_r of another notification. Since all notifications stacked together receive the same response (i.e., click or dismiss) at the same time, in a sense they represent duplicate entries and are not useful for quantifying users' reactions in that specific context. Therefore, from each group of stacked notifications we keep the notification that arrivedfi rst and drop out the remaining ones.

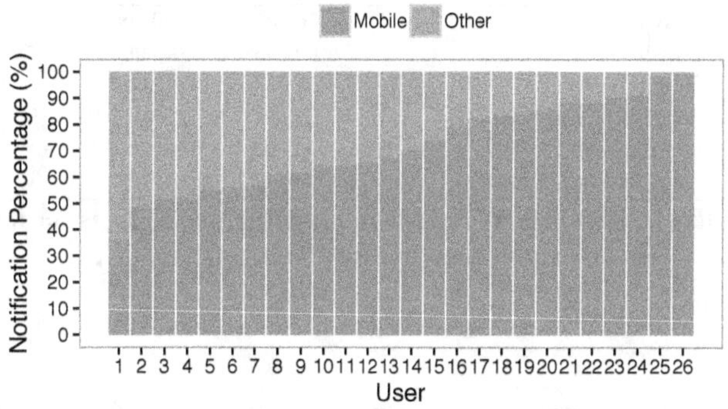

Figure 1: Percentage of notifications handled on mobile and other devices by the users.

4.1.4 Notification Distribution. In Figure 1 we show the percentage of notifications that are handled on mobile phones and alternative devices by each user. The results show that a few users handle 50% or above of the overall notifications on alternative devices, whereas a few users interact with nearly all notifications through their mobile phones. Overall, there are 71.41% notifications that are handled on mobile phones and the remaining on alternative devices.

For the evaluation of NotifyMeHere, we consider only users that handle notifications on multiple devices. Indeed, the limit (and, in a sense, trivial) case of a user interacting with a single device can be addressed simply by delivering all the notifications only on it without any prediction. Therefore, for fairness, we discard two users (users 25 and 26 in Figure 1) as they handle almost all the notifications (close to 100%) on the phone. As a result, we only consider the 24 users who satisfy this constraint. Finally, the dataset contains 69.18% notifications that are handled on mobile phones.

5 IMPACT ON NOTIFICATION HANDLING BEHAVIOR IN A MULTI-DEVICE ENVIRONMENT

In this section we investigate the effect of different factors on users' behavior with respect to notification handling in a multi-device environment.

Feature	χ^2	p-value
Activity	163.05	<0.005
Location	694.55	<0.005
Time Interval	6.14	0.1047
Network Connectivity	158.64	<0.005
App Category	792.93	<0.005
Previous Click	6465.40	<0.005

Table 2: Analysis of factors influencing users' decision for handling cross-platform notifications.

In order to perform this analysis, we link notifications to contextual and notification-based features that include:

Activity: physical activity as inferred through phone sensors. As discussed earlier, the application relies on the Google Activity Recognition API to log the information about users' physical activities classified as *walking*, *cycling*, *commuting in-vehicle* or *still*. However, we merge *walking* and *cycling* together as the *moving* activity, because we assume that while moving (i.e., either walking or cycling) users interact only with their phone rather than other devices such as their laptop. We are aware that it is unlikely that users interact with the mobile phone while biking. However, in case they want to interact with notifications in such a context, it is very likely that they will use a mobile phone rather than other devices (such as a laptop).

Location: semantic location (e.g., home, work, other). In order to cluster the GPS data we apply the clustering algorithm presented in [41]. For each clustered location we assign one of the following labels: *home*, *work* or *other*. We assign the *home* label to the place where a user spends the majority of the night hours (from 20:00 to 08:00). We generically refer to *work* as the second most significant place (i.e., the place where users spend most of their time apart from home). We are aware that this generic label might not be correct in some cases. The labeling might be improved by using geo-spatial data, but this is outside the scope of this paper. All other places are labeled as *other*.

Time Interval: time at which the notification arrived. We split a day into six time intervals: early morning (05:00-08:00), morning (08:00-12:00), afternoon (12:00-16:00), evening (16:00-20:00), night (20:00-23:00) and late night (23:00-05:00).

Network Connectivity: type of network (i.e., mobile data, WiFi or none) the phone is connected to.

Previous Click: the device on which the previous notification was handled (i.e., mobile or other).

App Category: the category of app that triggered the notification. Since the categories defined by the Google Play Store are too generic, we manually categorize the apps. Here we consider only the cross-platform applications and our categories include: *chat*, *email* and *social*.

We compute the effect of each of the above contextual and notification-based metrics (i.e., independent variables or IVs) on the user's behavior in terms of handling notifications in a multi-device environment (i.e., dependent variable or DV). Since they contain categorical values, we use Pearson's Chi-squared test [28] to investigate if there is a statistically significant relationship between the DV and IVs. In Table 2 we present the results of our analysis. We observe that there is a significant relationship between the user's behavior in terms of handling notifications and several factors, including activity, location, network connectivity, application category and the device used for attending to the previous notification. However, there is no significant impact of the time interval on the user's notification handling behavior.

The association with users' activity can be due to the fact that when users are moving they usually do not carry and interact with multiple devices. Indeed, there is the possibility that interactions with multiple devices happen while users travel for example on public transit (e.g., a train). Similarly, the association with location indicates that people do not carry multiple devices everywhere. For instance, we might carry multiple devices while at home, workplace or in a coffee shop, but not for example inside a gym. At the same time, the association with the app category indicates that people tend to handle some types of notifications on specific devices. For instance, we tend to chat more on phones but read emails more frequently on laptops due to usability factors.

6 PREDICTING THE RIGHT DEVICE ON WHICH TO DELIVER NOTIFICATIONS

In this section we discuss the implementation and evaluation of our proposed approach for predicting the device on which a notification will be handled by a user. We build two types of prediction models: (i) *individualized models* that are trained with the portion of data of a single user, i.e., the owner of the device, and (ii) *generic models* that are trained with the entire dataset containing data about all users.

As discussed above, users' notification handling behavior is not influenced by all features. Therefore, we build a prediction model that exploits only a subset of features. In particular, we only use activity, location, network connectivity, application category and the device on which the previous notification was acted upon for constructing the prediction model.

Both of these models are built by using three machine learning algorithms: AdaBoost [34], Random Forest [9] and Recursive Partitioning [17]. We evaluate these models for predicting the device on which the user will handle a notification in different contexts by using the k-fold cross validation approach with the value of k as 10. Moreover, we use the default parameters for all models available in the *scikit-learn* package [4].

In order to assess the performance of these models, we chose to compare the predicted response with the actual response (i.e., the ground truth) and compute the accuracy in terms of:

- *Sensitivity*: ratio between the number of notifications that are correctly predicted as handled on the mobile device and the total number of notifications that are actually handled on it.
- *Specificity*: ratio between the number of notifications that are correctly predicted as handled on an alternative device and the total number of notifications that are actually handled on an alternative device.

It is worth noting that we use the 10-fold cross validation approach for computing the mean and the standard-error with a 95% confidence interval of sensitivity and specificity for both models.

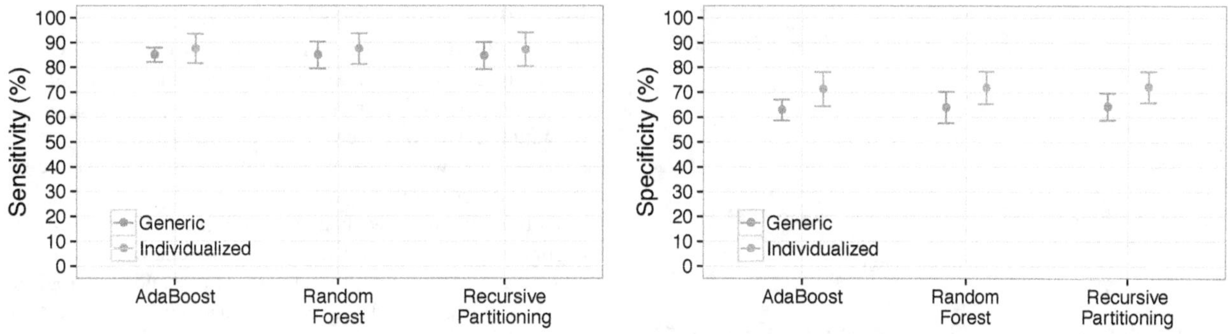

Figure 2: Prediction results for individualized and generic models using three different machine learning algorithms.

In Figure 2 we present the prediction results for individualized and generic models. The results show that for all machine learning algorithms the performance of both individual-based and generic models is similar. Both of these models achieve 85-89% sensitivity and 65-71% specificity.

6.1 Why are the Performance Results of the Individualized and Generic Models Similar?

In order to investigate why there are small differences in the performance of individualized and generic models, we explore the *importance* (based on the Gini index [9]) for each of the independent variables. It is worth noting that studies have demonstrated that the Gini index and Information Gain are the best metrics for the selection of features and there are no significant differences in their performances [33]. We opted for the Gini index as it is used internally in many classifiers, including those used in our analysis.

As shown in Table 3, the Gini index of the variable *previous click* dominates over the others (i.e., more than 20 times bigger compared to the other variables). In other words, this indicates that the *previous click* is the most important feature for the prediction of the device on which the next notification will be handled. This is due to the fact that most of the notifications are handled on the same device as their preceding notification and, thus, both models can achieve high accuracy by using solely the "previous click" feature.

Feature	Gini index
Activity	51.31
Location	79.57
Network Connectivity	21.31
App Category	89.49
Previous Click	1610.11

Table 3: Gini index of the features used for training prediction models.

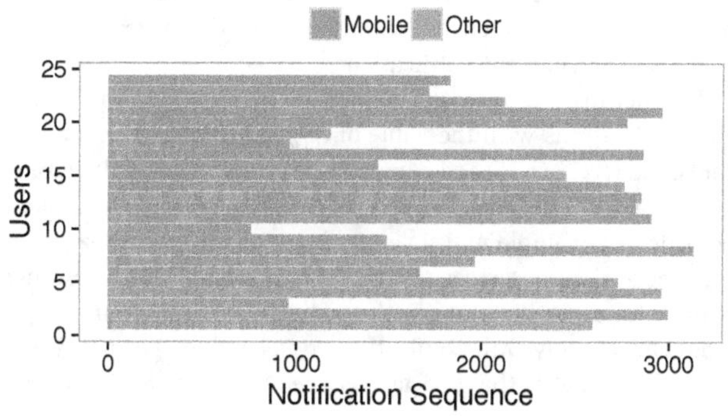

Figure 3: Sequence of notifications handled by users on mobile and other devices.

6.2 Analyzing Notification Handling Sequence

In order to understand users' behavior for handling notifications over time and to confirm that most of the notifications are handled on the same device as their preceding notification, we plot the sequence of notifications along with the device on which they are handled. As shown in Figure 3, most users handle a sequence of notifications on the same device. This demonstrates that once individuals start handling notifications on a device they keep on handling the subsequent notifications on the same device for a certain amount of time. Indeed, users do not switch devices very frequently; rather, they have a fairly prolonged interaction with a single device, especially in the case of mobile phones [13]. For instance, if a user starts chatting with a friend on her laptop then with a high probability they will continue to chat on that device instead of switching to their phone.

6.3 Impact of Time Elapsed between Subsequent Notifications

Thefi ndings presented above demonstrate that the *previous click* feature is an important variable that can solely predict the device on which the notification will be handled. This is probably due to the fact that it is very likely that a user will act upon the current notification on the same device on which the previous one was handled. However, the temporal dimension (i.e., the time elapsed between the last and current notification) might also play a key

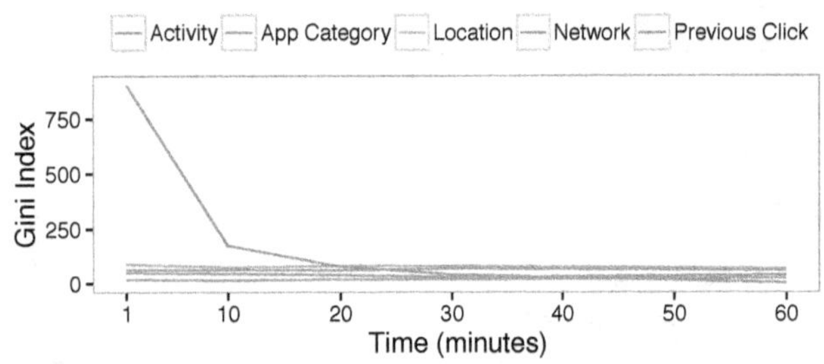

Figure 4: Importance of variables for predicting the right device.

role here since a user's context may change after some time. Indeed, after a certain time, when users move to a new environment, they might want to receive notifications on a different device that is now available to them. A recent study has shown that users' preferences for receiving notifications on a specific device changes when they switch their context [42]. Therefore, it is very important to investigate a critical question: *is the previous click feature still sufficiently informative if there is a long time between two consecutive notifications?*

For this reason, we investigate the optimal value of the time elapse (t_{elapse}) until which the *previous click* feature can be solely used for predicting the device on which a notification will be handled. Here, t_{elapse} refers to the time difference between the arrival of the last and current notifications.

In order to investigate the optimal value of t_{elapse}, wefi lter out the notifications with the value of t_{elapse} greater than a certain threshold ($t_{threshold}$) and compute the importance of all variables based on the Gini index. To better understand thisfi ltering, let us consider an example withfi ve notifications (n_1, n_2, n_3, n_4 and n_5) arriving at times t, $t + 20s$, $t + 70s$, $t + 100s$, and $t + 200s$. Now, if we want tofi lter notifications with $t_{threshold}$ equal to 1 minute, we would be left only with notifications n_1, n_3 and n_5. The notification n_2 isfi ltered out as the time gap between n_1 and n_2 is 20s (which is less than $t_{threshold}$). However, n_3 is notfi ltered because the time gap between n_1 and n_3 is 70s (here n_1 is considered as a preceding notification because n_2 is discarded). Similarly, n_4 is dropped as the time gap between n_3 and n_4 is below $t_{threshold}$. It is worth noting that we use the k-fold cross validation approach (with k equal to 10) while computing the variable importance to ensure that the variable importance is computed only with the training data.

Finally, we compute the variable importance by setting the value of $t_{threshold} \in [1, 10, 20, 10, 30, 60]$ minutes. As shown in Figure 4, the *previous click* feature dominates over all other features only for the $t_{threshold}$ of up to 10 minutes. *Therefore, we can conclude that the previous click feature can be used solely for predicting the device for delivering notifications but only when the preceding notification has arrived approximately within 10 minutes.* We observe that this result is essentially valid for this set of users (i.e., we are not making any claim about its universality), but we believe that the methodology described above can be applied to any population in order to estimate the optimal threshold.

6.4 Modeling Context Change

We now discuss how the performance of our model can be improved by introducing additional temporal-based features. Since the *previous click* feature is not reliable for predicting the device on which a user will receive a notification after 10 minutes, we introduce a new feature, namely *time elapsed - notification* (since the last notification).

At the same time, we believe that users' preferences might not change immediately after the context switch. Instead they would take some time to adjust to the new context and thus, their preferences would change after a certain adjustment period. Consider for example a scenario where Alice switches context between "commute" and "workplace". She uses a mobile phone during the commute and on reaching the workplace she might start using her laptop/desktop and want to get notifications on that device. However, she would not immediately start using those devices, rather she might still be receptive to notifications on her mobile phone for some time even after the context switch. Therefore, it is of fundamental importance for the prediction model to have the knowledge about when a context change happened (and, most critically, how long ago).

To provide such information to the prediction model, we introduce three more features that inform the model about the time elapsed since the switch in each context modality (i.e., activity, location and network connectivity). We name these features *time elapsed - activity, time elapsed - location* and *time elapsed - network* for the time passed since the previous switch in activity, location and network connectivity, respectively. These features can be exploited to learn how long it takes for users to change their notification handling behavior once they switch to a new context. For instance, in the example above, Alice reaches her office (which corresponds to a change in activity, location and network connectivity) but she might not start using her laptop until after a certain amount of time.

6.5 Exploiting Context Change Features to Improve the Prediction Models

We build both individualized and generic models by using the same three machine learning algorithms: AdaBoost, Random Forest and Recursive Partitioning. All models are built using the following features: *activity, location, network connectivity, app category, previous click, time elapse - activity, time elapse - location, time elapse - network* and *time elapse - notification.*

In Figure 5 we present the prediction results for both individualized and generic models. The results show that for all machine learning algorithms the individual-based models outperform the generic models in terms of specificity, but there is no significant difference in terms of sensitivity. The individual-based models achieve around 91% sensitivity and 82% specificity. However, the generic models could obtain only 90% sensitivity and 68% specificity. Overall, all models built by using time-dependent features could successfully outperform the frequency-based model that we use as the benchmark.

These results demonstrate that by introducing new features both the sensitivity and specificity of the individualized models improve by 2% and 11% respectively. On the other hand, the sensitivity and

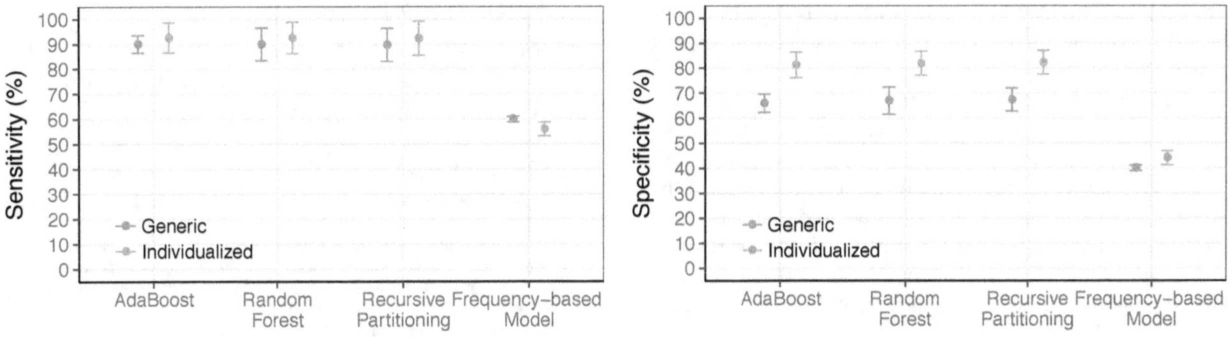

Figure 5: Prediction results for individualized and generic models built on three different machine learning algorithms by using time-dependent features and the frequency-based model (used as a baseline).

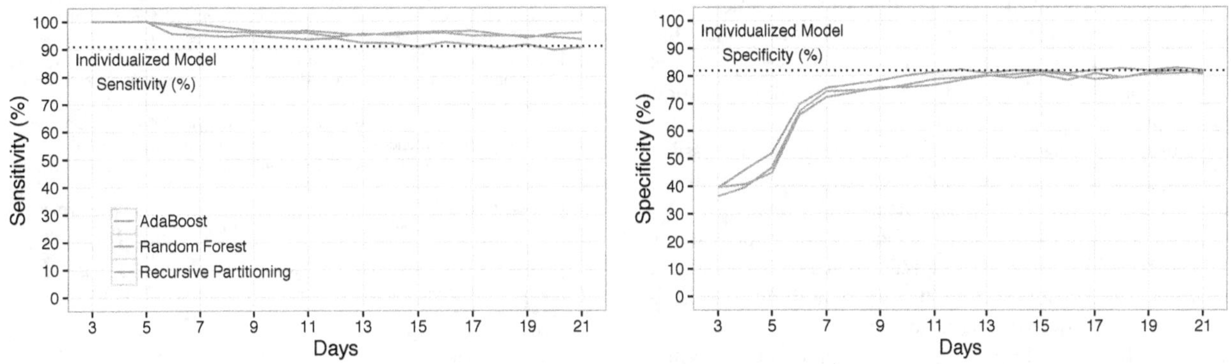

Figure 6: Prediction results for the online learning approach.

specificity of the generic models with new features increase by only 5% and 3% respectively.

7 ONLINE LEARNING APPROACH

In the previous section we have discussed and evaluated the prediction models by using a batch learning method based on "static" data, which is collected, stored and only then processed. However, this approach has two key drawbacks when used on mobile phones *in-the-wild*. Firstly, in a real world scenario the training data is not initially available; it rather becomes available gradually as new notifications arrive. Therefore, an individualized model cannot be constructed until a sufficient amount of data is available. This is known as the *bootstrapping problem* [12]. Another limitation is that the model cannot adapt when users change their behavioral patterns and, thus, the prediction accuracy might be dramatically reduced.

To overcome these issues it is possible to adopt an online learning approach in which a model is periodically trained with the available data that is collected gradually. Although this approach does not solve the issue of initial bootstrapping completely, it still enables relatively fast learning, adaptation to the potential changes in the user's behavior and improvement of the performance over time (i.e., the average prediction accuracy can be enhanced gradually as more and more training data becomes available). We construct individualized models with the same three algorithms: AdaBoost, Random Forest and Recursive Partitioning. We iteratively train the models with all the notifications collected by the end of each day and evaluate these models by using the notifications of the following day. More formally, on day D a model is built by using notifications from day 1 to day $D - 1$ and it is evaluated by using the notifications from day D.

Figure 6 presents the prediction accuracy of the models with increasing number of days. The best achievable performance of the individualized prediction model trained with the batch learning approach is 82% specificity and 91% sensitivity (as discussed in the previous section). The results demonstrate that in just seven days all models become stable achieving a specificity of more than 70% and sensitivity of more than 95%.

8 DISCUSSION AND LIMITATIONS

According to the results, in our dataset around 44.8% of notifications are triggered by cross-platform applications and 28.59% of these notifications are handled on an alternative device (i.e., not handled on the mobile phone). However, this is not consistent for all users.

Instead, some users interact with notifications solely on their mobile phones, whereas others tend to use multiple devices for handling notifications.

The results also demonstrate that users' decisions in terms of handling notifications on a mobile or an alternative device are associated with their physical activity, location, application category, network connectivity and the device on which they handled the preceding notification. These features can be used to model users' behavior in terms of their interaction with notifications in multi-device environments. However, we have shown that it is more effective to train such models on individual data rather than on the entire set of users' data.

The main limitation of this work resides in the fact that we do not have data for each device accessed by a user but only for two classes of devices: personal phones and alternative devices (i.e., any device other than the phone). At the same time, the proposed model is highly generalizable to the case of multiple classes of devices. We would also like to point out that, from a practical point of view, it might be very difficult to deploy a real-world system that is able to capture *all* the interactions of a user with *all* the devices they access. Indeed, it might not be feasible to install notification loggers for privacy, legal or technical reasons (e.g., on workstations in companies, etc.). Moreover, we believe that this would be possible only for a subset of devices (or, more precisely, operating systems) for which a specific version of the application is available.

We would also like to underline the fact that some applications might be affected by a delay with respect to syncing cross-platform notifications (i.e., a delay between the user's handling of a notification in one of the devices and its automatic removal in all the other ones). The overall impact is probably negligible, but when this happens, we might fail to account for multiple interactions with duplicate notifications. Indeed, in the current study, it was not possible to identify such duplicate interactions as we do not have a notification interaction logger on all devices accessed by users.

9 CONCLUSIONS

In this paper we have presented a novel solution for intelligent notification delivery in multi-device environments by analyzing previous notification response behavior and a series of features that describe the user's context. In particular, we have shown that there is a significant relationship between user's behavior in terms of handling notifications and several contextual dimensions, including activity, location, network connectivity, application category and the device used for attending to the previous notification.

We have constructed and evaluated a set of prediction models, considering both generalized and personalized training approaches. We have shown that an individualized model is characterized by better prediction performance (i.e., 82% specificity and 91% sensitivity). We have also discussed the implementation of an online predictor that achieves a specificity of 70% and a sensitivity of 95% in just seven days.

The proposed mechanism could be considered as a building block for intelligent notification delivery in multi-device environments. The mechanism can be implemented as a server component that should be aware of all devices of each user that have subscripted to a given cross-platform application.

ACKNOWLEDGEMENTS

This work was supported through the EPSRC grants EP/L018829/2 and EP/P016278/1 at UCL and by The Alan Turing Institute under the EPSRC grant EP/N510129/1.

REFERENCES

[1] 2016. Android's NetworkInfo API. https://developer.android.com/reference/android/net/NetworkInfo.html.
[2] 2016. Android's Notification Listener Service. http://developer.android.com/reference/android/service/notification/NotificationListenerService.html.
[3] 2016. Google's Activity Recognition Application. http://developer.android.com/training/location/activity-recognition.html.
[4] 2018. Scikit-learn Package. https://scikit-learn.org.
[5] Piotr D Adamczyk and Brian P Bailey. 2004. If not now, when?: the effects of interruption at different moments within task execution. In *CHI'04*.
[6] Brian P Bailey and Joseph A Konstan. 2006. On the need for attention-aware systems: Measuring effects of interruption on task performance, error rate, and affective state. *Computers in Human Behavior* 22, 4 (2006), 685–708.
[7] Brian P Bailey, Joseph A Konstan, and John V Carlis. 2000. Measuring the effects of interruptions on task performance in the user interface. In *SMC'00*.
[8] Nicholas J Belkin and W Bruce Croft. 1992. Informationfi ltering and information retrieval: Two sides of the same coin? *Commun. ACM* 35, 12 (1992), 29–38.
[9] Leo Breiman. 2001. Random forests. *Machine Learning* 45, 1 (2001), 5–32.
[10] Edward Cutrell, Mary Czerwinski, and Eric Horvitz. 2001. Notification, disruption, and memory: Effects of messaging interruptions on memory and performance. In *Interact'01*.
[11] Mary Czerwinski, Edward Cutrell, and Eric Horvitz. 2000. Instant messaging and interruption: Influence of task type on performance. In *OZCHI'00*.
[12] Bradley Efron and Robert J Tibshirani. 1994. *An introduction to the bootstrap*. CRC press.
[13] Hossein Falaki, Ratul Mahajan, Srikanth Kandula, Dimitrios Lymberopoulos, Ramesh Govindan, and Deborah Estrin. 2010. Diversity in smartphone usage. In *MobiSys'10*.
[14] Adrienne Porter Felt, Serge Egelman, and David Wagner. 2012. I've got 99 problems, but vibration ain't one: a survey of smartphone users' concerns. In *SPSM'12*.
[15] Joel E Fischer, Chris Greenhalgh, and Steve Benford. 2011. Investigating episodes of mobile phone activity as indicators of opportune moments to deliver notifications. In *MobileHCI'11*.
[16] Joel E Fischer, Nick Yee, Victoria Bellotti, Nathan Good, Steve Benford, and Chris Greenhalgh. 2010. Effects of content and time of delivery on receptivity to mobile interruptions. In *MobileHCI'10*.
[17] Jerome H Friedman. 1976. A recursive partitioning decision rule for nonparametric classification. *IEEE Trans. Comput.* 26, 4 (1976), 404–408.
[18] Sukeshini A Grandhi and Quentin Jones. 2009. Conceptualizing interpersonal interruption management: A theoretical framework and research program. In *HICSS'09*.
[19] Joyce Ho and Stephen S. Intille. 2005. Using Context-Aware Computing to Reduce the Perceived Burden of Interruptions from Mobile Devices. In *CHI'05*.
[20] Eric Horvitz, Paul Koch, and Johnson Apacible. 2004. BusyBody: creating and fielding personalized models of the cost of interruption. In *CSCW'04*.
[21] Jimmy Lin, Salman Mohammed, Royal Sequiera, and Luchen Tan. 2018. Update Delivery Mechanisms for Prospective Information Needs: An Analysis of Attention in Mobile Users. In *SIGIR'18*.
[22] Abhinav Mehrotra, Robert Hendley, and Mirco Musolesi. 2016. PrefMiner: Mining User's Preferences for Intelligent Mobile Notification Management. In *UbiComp'16*.
[23] Abhinav Mehrotra, Sandrine R. Müller, Gabriella M. Harari, Samuel D. Gosling, Cecilia Mascolo, Mirco Musolesi, and Peter J. Rentfrow. 2017. Understanding the role of places and activities on mobile phone interaction and usage patterns. *IMWUT* 1, 3 (2017).
[24] Abhinav Mehrotra and Mirco Musolesi. 2017. Intelligent Notification Systems: A Survey of the State of the Art and Research Challenges. *arXiv preprint:1711.10171* (2017).
[25] Abhinav Mehrotra, Mirco Musolesi, Robert Hendley, and Veljko Pejovic. 2015. Designing Content-driven Intelligent Notification Mechanisms for Mobile Applications. In *UbiComp'15*.
[26] Abhinav Mehrotra, Veljko Pejovic, Jo Vermeulen, Robert Hendley, and Mirco Musolesi. 2016. My Phone and Me: Understanding People's Receptivity to Mobile Notifications. In *CHI'16*.
[27] Abhinav Mehrotra, Fani Tsapeli, Robert Hendley, and Mirco Musolesi. 2017. MyTraces: Investigating Correlation and Causation between Users' Emotional States and Mobile Phone Interaction. *IMWUT* 1, 3 (2017).
[28] Karl Pearson. 1900. On the criterion that a given system of deviations from the probable in the case of a correlated system of variables is such that it can

be reasonably supposed to have arisen from random sampling. *The London, Edinburgh, and Dublin Philosophical Magazine and Journal of Science* 50, 302 (1900), 157–175.
[29] Veljko Pejovic and Mirco Musolesi. 2014. InterruptMe: designing intelligent prompting mechanisms for pervasive applications. In *UbiComp'14*.
[30] Martin Pielot, Bruno Cardoso, Kleomenis Katevas, Joan Serrà, Aleksandar Matic, and Nuria Oliver. 2017. Beyond interruptibility: Predicting opportune moments to engage mobile phone users. *IMWUT* 1, 3 (2017), 91.
[31] Martin Pielot, Karen Church, and Rodrigo de Oliveira. 2014. An in-situ study of mobile phone notifications. In *MobileHCI'14*.
[32] Martin Pielot, Rodrigo de Oliveira, Haewoon Kwak, and Nuria Oliver. 2014. Didn't you see my message?: predicting attentiveness to mobile instant messages. In *CHI'14*.
[33] Laura Elena Raileanu and Kilian Stoffel. 2004. Theoretical comparison between the gini index and information gain criteria. *Annals of Mathematics and Artificial Intelligence* 41, 1 (2004), 77–93.
[34] Gunnar Rätsch, Takashi Onoda, and K-R Müller. 2001. Soft margins for AdaBoost. *Machine Learning* 42, 3 (2001), 287–320.
[35] Adam Roegiest, Luchen Tan, and Jimmy Lin. 2017. Online in-situ interleaved evaluation of real-time push notification systems. In *SIGIR'17*.
[36] Adam Roegiest, Luchen Tan, Jimmy Lin, and Charles LA Clarke. 2016. A platform for streaming push notifications to mobile assessors. In *SIGIR'16*.
[37] Stephanie Rosenthal, Anind K Dey, and Manuela Veloso. 2011. Using decision-theoretic experience sampling to build personalized mobile phone interruption models. In *PerCom'11*.
[38] Alireza Sahami Shirazi, Niels Henze, Tilman Dingler, Martin Pielot, Dominik Weber, and Albrecht Schmidt. 2014. Large-scale assessment of mobile notifications. In *CHI'14*.
[39] Alireza Sahami Shirazi and Niels Henze. 2015. Assessment of Notifications on Smartwatches. In *MobileHCI'15 Adjunct*.
[40] Luchen Tan, Adam Roegiest, Jimmy Lin, and Charles LA Clarke. 2016. An exploration of evaluation metrics for mobile push notifications. In *SIGIR'16*.
[41] Fani Tsapeli and Mirco Musolesi. 2015. Investigating causality in human behavior from smartphone sensor data: a quasi-experimental approach. *EPJ Data Science* 4, 1 (2015), 1–15.
[42] Dominik Weber, Alexandra Voit, Philipp Kratzer, and Niels Henze. 2016. In-situ investigation of notifications in multi-device environments. In *UbiComp'16*.
[43] Dominik Weber, Alexandra Voit, Huy Viet Le, and Niels Henze. 2016. Notification dashboard: enabling reflection on mobile notifications. In *MobileHCI'16 Adjunct*.

Searching for Old News: User Interests and Behavior within a National Collection

Tessel Bogaard
Centrum Wiskunde & Informatica
Amsterdam, The Netherlands
Tessel.Bogaard@cwi.nl

Laura Hollink
Centrum Wiskunde & Informatica
Amsterdam, The Netherlands
L.Hollink@cwi.nl

Jan Wielemaker
Centrum Wiskunde & Informatica
Vrije Universiteit Amsterdam
Amsterdam, The Netherlands
J.Wielemaker@cwi.nl

Lynda Hardman
Centrum Wiskunde & Informatica
Universiteit Utrecht
Amsterdam/Utrecht, The Netherlands
Lynda.Hardman@cwi.nl

Jacco van Ossenbruggen
Centrum Wiskunde & Informatica
Vrije Universiteit Amsterdam
Amsterdam, The Netherlands
Jacco.van.Ossenbruggen@cwi.nl

ABSTRACT

Modeling user interests helps to improve system support or refine recommendations in Interactive Information Retrieval. The aim of this study is to identify user interests in different parts of an online collection and investigate the related search behavior. To do this, we propose to use the metadata of selected facets and clicked documents as features for clustering sessions identified in user logs. We evaluate the session clusters by measuring their stability over a six-month period.

We apply our approach to data from the National Library of the Netherlands, a typical digital library with a richly annotated historical newspaper collection and a faceted search interface. Our results show that users interested in specific parts of the collection use different search techniques. We demonstrate that a metadata-based clustering helps to reveal and understand user interests in terms of the collection, and how search behavior is related to specific parts within the collection.

CCS CONCEPTS

• **Information systems → Digital libraries and archives**; *Clustering*; *Query log analysis*; *Search interfaces*;

KEYWORDS

User interest; Search behavior; Digital libraries; Metadata; Log analysis; Clustering

ACM Reference Format:

Tessel Bogaard, Laura Hollink, Jan Wielemaker, Lynda Hardman, and Jacco van Ossenbruggen. 2019. Searching for Old News: User Interests and Behavior within a National Collection. In *2019 Conference on Human Information Interaction and Retrieval (CHIIR '19), March 10–14, 2019, Glasgow, United Kingdom.* ACM, New York, NY, USA, 9 pages. https://doi.org/10.1145/3295750.3298925

CHIIR '19, March 10–14, 2019, Glasgow, United Kingdom

ACM ISBN 978-1-4503-6025-8/19/03...$15.00
https://doi.org/10.1145/3295750.3298925

1 INTRODUCTION

Understanding user interests and related search behavior can reveal the different types of system support users need. Collections are not always homogeneous and users may have different information needs depending on which parts of a collection they are interested in. This begs the question of how we can identify different "parts" of a collection – for example through different usage patterns and/or by professionally curated categorizations of the documents in the collection. If we are able to identify different usage patterns corresponding to identifiable parts of the collection then we can better help collection owners in providing support for these.

The research questions addressed in this paper are thus:

- (RQ1) What are the user interests in terms of the different parts of a collection? How can we detect these?
- (RQ2) What is the related search behavior within these parts?

Understanding the answers to these questions may lead to more targeted search interfaces, better search algorithms, and a fine-tuning of strategies for collection management.

In a digital library or archive, metadata categorizations of the documents are often reflected in facets, allowing the user to filter the search results. We use the metadata of facets selected and of documents clicked to detect user interests. As we do not know in advance in which (combinations of) metadata categories users are interested, we apply a data-driven partitioning of sessions: a clustering of sessions based on the metadata features of both search (selected facet values) and clicks (document metadata) in each session, and we analyze the behavior in the resulting clusters.

Evaluating the resulting clustering is nontrivial, for different reasons: first, an interpretation of the results is subjective, and second, we have no ground truth available in the data as a way to measure the "correctness" of the clustering. Nevertheless, as we are interested in stable clusters that reappear over different periods, we test the stability of the clusters in each month over a six-month period and interpret stability as an indicator of the quality of the clustering, similar to the cluster stability measured between two periods in [3].

We apply our approach to data from the National Library of the Netherlands, a digital library with a richly annotated historical newspaper collection spanning 400 years, and a faceted search interface. The library has granted us access to both user logs[1] and the metadata descriptions of the documents in the collection.

Our results show that the detected user interests are stable, and that the related search behavior varies within the different parts of the collection. Examples of user interests are: specific types of news items, such as family announcements (relating to births, marriages, deaths), specific periods, such as 1930-49 (including the Great Depression and World War II), or specific regions, such as Suriname (one of the former Dutch colonies). We observe users focusing exclusively on specific parts of the collection, in some parts spending less time and few search techniques, in other parts spending a lot of time and a variety of search techniques. As a result this approach can help to find and investigate these highly-focused users. This can inform the design of more targeted user interfaces, or help to improve search systems or collection management. We contribute to the research field by demonstrating that a partitioning of sessions into clusters based on the metadata of a collection and an investigation of related search behavior reveals specific user needs in specific parts of a collection, where in an overall analysis these patterns would disappear.

2 RELATED WORK

To answer our research questions, definitions of user interests and sessions are needed. Additionally, we need a method to group the sessions. In this section we discuss relevant literature with respect to how to detect user interests, define sessions, and what methods can be used to group the identified sessions.

Detecting user interests. User interests are frequently derived from queries, for example by categorizing user queries in [15], or finding search topics by semantic linking of user queries [10]. Alternatively, interests can be detected in logs using the context of search [23], or search histories [24]; and in [9] mouse hovering is used to help understand user interests within a digital library, in combination with query analysis and the (analyzed) metadata of document clicks in a statistical analysis.

Similar to this research, we use a form of categorization to identify user interests, and similar to [9], we make use of the metadata categories of the collection. However, we use the metadata directly as found in facets selected and documents clicked, rather than the query input, to identify user interests, as we aim for a definition of user interests in terms of parts of the collection.

Defining sessions. Search behavior is often interpreted using a bounded sequence of search actions by a user [12]. Sessions have been studied to understand search in context and to evaluate it in terms of success or failure [12]. Sessions help to provide information about repeated visits [13], to examine query modification [10], to obtain information about learning in search [5], or to find patterns in search behavior [3, 19].

We use sessions to put user interactions in a context and so to enable the detection of user interests and behavior. This requires a computational method for specifying the beginning and end of a session. Sessions can be specified based on query boundaries using the IP address as identifier. For example, in [7] a session is defined as a search query and the following clicks until the next query, and in [11] a session is bounded by the presence of overlapping terms in successive queries until there is no more common term. Sessions are frequently bounded by a timeout, a period of inactivity by a user, e.g. [2, 5, 10, 12]. In the context of studying web navigation, the concept of a *clickstream* is more often used, as in [22]. A clickstream is the navigational path a user follows, consisting of consecutive HTTP requests from a single IP address. We adopt this definition of a session, as it enables the identification of multiple users behind a single IP and we want to avoid breaking up longer sessions by using a timeout.

Grouping user logs. Several approaches exist to group user logs in order to find patterns, for example logs can be classified or clustered. To classify different types of behavior, queries have been grouped into *why* versus *what* questions [5], into DBpedia concepts [16], or into categorizations based on a thesaurus related to the collection [11]. Alternatively, Niu and Hemminger have provided an analysis of faceted versus non-faceted search, grouping the logs based on user actions, showing in their work that facets play an important role in search [18]. In our study, we not only include the facets, we also enrich the clicked documents with their metadata descriptions, and use this metadata explicitly to group the user logs for the detection of user interests.

Clustering techniques can also be used to detect patterns in logs. For example, Wang et al. use unsupervised hierarchical clustering to detect user behavior patterns in social networks [22]. In our work, we also use unsupervised clustering and not supervised classification, for similar reasons: we do not have a ground truth available in the data, nor do we know in advance which patterns we want to detect. However, since our data is skewed we use a different algorithm that is more robust to outliers.

Clustering techniques have been used before in the context of a digital library. Chen and Cooper applied a hybrid clustering technique to detect different types of users in the logs, combining an initial clustering using k-means with hierarchical clustering to get to the final clusters [3]. In this research, sessions are represented using a set of features based on user interactions with the search system. More recently, Niu and Hemminger have reproduced this research with an added focus on the facets present in more recent search interfaces [19]. In our study the goal is different, as we aim to find the user interests in terms of the collection and relate these user interests to search behavior. Nevertheless, we use a similar clustering technique and a similar representation of the sessions to be clustered as in [3] and [19], even though we focus exclusively on the bibliographic metadata features of search and clicks.

To evaluate the clustering we look at stability [21], similar to the approach in [3]. This approach was more recently investigated as a validation method for a clustering in a log analysis of a digital library in [6].

3 METHOD

In this study we use a clustering algorithm to detect the user interests and investigate the relation between these user interests and

[1] Logs collected from the search platform http://www.delpher.nl, access granted under a strict confidentiality agreement.

search behavior in the collection. For the clustering of the sessions, we base the features on the metadata of facets and clicked documents (the metadata of the facets are the selected values used in search). To do this we need both user logs and metadata records of the collection being searched.

3.1 Session Identification and Representation

We identify sessions in the logs based on a *clickstream* model, using the IP address as identifier and connecting sequential HTTP requests to follow the user navigating the search platform.

We represent the sessions based on the metadata values of the search interactions, where available in the facets selected, and clicked documents, linked to the metadata records of the collection. We include all values of the (main) categories in the metadata (such as publication date, origin or type of document). These values are proportional to the number of search interactions or the number of clicked documents per session, and are used as features for the clustering.

To detect the user interests, we apply a clustering algorithm representing the sessions using a metadata feature set. As the features are likely to be correlated, principal component analysis is applied for dimensionality reduction before clustering with a standardized feature set. We retain the principal components with a standard deviation equal to or higher than 1 for the clustering.

In addition, we collect interaction variables based on user interactions within the search interface to analyze the search behavior. These variables include typical variables, such as the total duration of a session, the number of HTTP requests, the proportions of actions that are search or clicks, and specific variables dependent on the search interface, such as facets or reordering of results.

3.2 Clustering

We use an unsupervised clustering algorithm, as we have no ground truth available and do not know in advance what kind of patterns are present in the data. Since we cannot assume the data adheres to a normal distribution, we have chosen a k-medoids method [14], partitioning the data into k clusters, as k-medoids is more robust against outliers than k-means is, it is to k-means what the median is to the mean. As we have a high number of sessions and many dimensions in the clustering, we apply the CLARANS algorithm[17], a k-medoids variant optimized for large datasets. We use the Manhattan distance as distance metric for the clustering, because it is suitable for data represented in a high dimensional space [1]. To choose the number of clusters k, we apply the silhouette method [20], which measures the separation between the clusters with values ranging from -1 to 1, the higher values indicating a better clustering. We cluster the sessions repeatedly with different values for k and select the k with highest average silhouette width. We use a statistical summary of user behavior in each resulting cluster to analyze differences in behavior between the clusters based on the user interests.

3.3 Evaluation of Clustering

Our goal is to find stable patterns that reoccur in different period, so we evaluate the stability of the clustering over time, using this as an indication for clustering quality [21]. For this purpose, we cluster logs collected in separate periods, similar to the approach in [3]. We use a six-month period as it is the maximum period user logs can be retained according to Dutch law and as is common practice to protect the privacy of users. The size of each period is a month, as the sample size used in the collection of the logs was a month and some sessions have a duration longer than two weeks (12% of the sessions).

The stability of the clusters between two periods, the previous period and the target period, is measured as follows:

(1) We cluster the sessions in the previous period using the same value for k as was used for the target period.

(2) For each cluster in the previous period we determine a "center" by taking the original metadata features of the sessions and computing the median for each feature, resulting in a set of medians.

(3) For each session in the target period, we compute the Manhattan distance to each of the centers in the previous period based on the original metadata features.

(4) We assign each session in the target period to the cluster from the previous period with the shortest Manhattan distance, the nearest "center".

(5) For each of the k clusters in the target period, we compute the percentage of sessions in each of the k clusters of the previous period, resulting in k x k percentages .

(6) We define the stability of a cluster in the target period as the highest of the k percentages, the best match.

(7) The stability of a clustering as a whole is the average stability of all its clusters, weighted by cluster size.

We inspect in detail the overlap between the clusters between two periods. We do this with a "stability matrix", that shows the amount of matching (i.e. the percentages per cluster as assigned in step 5) between each of the clusters of the two periods. In the stability matrix, the clusters of the target period are the columns (percentages in the columns sum to 100%), and the previous period the rows.

We remark that cluster stability and silhouette widths measure different things: the first consistency between clusterings over time and the second consistency within a clustering.

4 THE NATIONAL LIBRARY OF THE NETHERLANDS

We apply our method to a library that is representative for digital libraries in general, with a richly annotated collection of digitized historical documents and a faceted search interface. The National Library of the Netherlands has granted us access to user logs from their search platform[2], our focus is on the historical newspaper collection, amounting to more than 90% of all HTTP page requests to the library's search platform.

From this collection, users can retrieve full newspaper issues, pages, or individual items on a newspaper page. The documents in the collection are annotated with bibliographic metadata records, including a publication date, distribution zone and type of newspaper item. The distribution zone of a document is the geographical region where the newspaper was distributed, and can be one of

[2] http://www.delpher.nl provides access to collections from the National Library of the Netherlands and other heritage institutions, comprising newspapers, magazines, radio bulletins, and books.

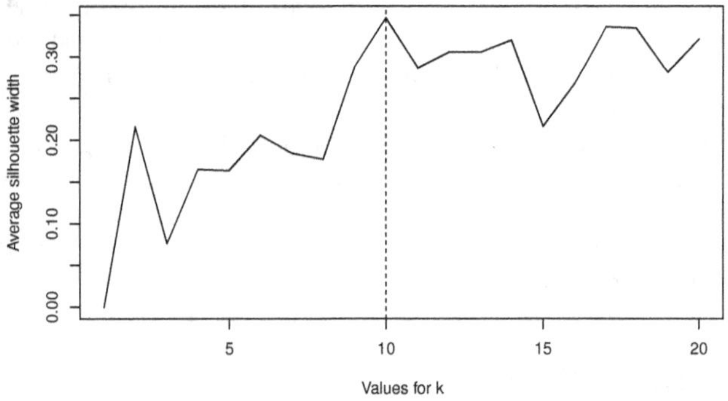

Figure 1: Average silhouette widths for k in March

the following values: "local", "national", one of the former Dutch colonies ("Indonesia", "Suriname", or the "Antilles"), or, in a few cases, "unknown". The available newspaper item types are: news articles, advertisements, announcements (relating to births, marriages, deaths) or images (illustrations or photographs, search on the caption text). Table 2 shows the percentages for each metadata value in the collection.

The search interface combines full-text search with facets. The facets are filters based on the metadata attributes of the collection, and include time facets, indicating the publication date, item type facets, and distribution zone facets. In addition, users may change the relevance ranking of the results on a results page to alphabetical or chronological ordering. From a results page, a user can click on a document and, after viewing a document, download it.

The logs used in this experiment were collected between October 2015 and March 2016 (raw data 200M records). In addition, we received the full text digitalization and metadata records of the historical newspaper collection (103M documents at the time), making it possible to link the clicked documents in the logs to the metadata records of all the documents in the collection.

4.1 Session Identification and Representation

The user logs contain all HTTP requests to the server. This includes the requested URL, the referrer URL (the origin of the request), the IP address of the client, the browser agent and a timestamp.

We identified sessions from these logs using a *clickstream* model, following the navigational path of a user on the search platform. We removed all logs stemming from web crawlers based on browser agents or a request for robots.txt, redirects, and the loading of style sheets and images. Sequential requests for the same URL right after each other are removed as well, as these are likely reloads of the browser and do not represent a new user interaction.

We group the records by IP address, using the referrer URL to link subsequent requests. Since we are interested in search behavior in relation to the metadata of facets used and documents clicked, we kept only sessions where the sequence consists of more than one search interaction or clicked document in the newspaper collection. This brings the total number of sessions to 255,175 in six months.

For the clustering we create a feature set relating to the metadata values of (i) the clicked documents and of (ii) the facets used in search (Table 1), proportional to the number of clicks or search interactions in that session. For the time facets and publication dates of clicked documents, we split the values into four bins based on equal proportions over all clicked documents and rounded to decades. This leads to a single bin for the period before 1900 and three bins in the 1900-1995 period (Table 2 for the distribution of these values within the collection). The values for the time facets are based on dates within the indicated years, using the same bins as for clicks. We add an extra time facet for the period 1900-1995 to capture those facets that cross the boundaries of the bins in the period 1900-1995.

We define additional session variables influenced by the user interactions in the search interface, and not used for clustering; these are the duration of a session, the number of search interactions and clicks, the use of facets or multiple facets in an interaction, the

Table 1: Session features based on metadata

	Publication date clicks
1	percentage of clicks published between 1600 and 1899
2	percentage of clicks published between 1900 and 1929
3	percentage of clicks published between 1930 and 1949
4	percentage of clicks published between 1950 and 1995
	Item types clicks
5	percentage clicked articles
6	percentage clicked family announcements
7	percentage clicked advertisements
8	percentage clicked images
	Distribution zone clicks
9	percentage of clicks with a local distribution zone
10	percentage of clicks with a national distribution zone
11	percentage of clicks with an Indonesian distribution zone
12	percentage of clicks with a Suriname distribution zone
13	percentage of clicks with a Antilles distribution zone
14	percentage of clicks with an unknown distribution zone
	Search with time facets
15	percentage of search with time facets
16	percentage of search with time facets within 1600 and 1899
17	percentage of search with time facets within 1900 and 1995
18	percentage of search with time facets within 1900 and 1929
19	percentage of search with time facets within 1930 and 1949
20	percentage of search with time facets within 1950 and 1995
	Search with item facets
21	percentage of search with item facets
22	percentage of search with article facets
23	percentage of search with family announcement facets
24	percentage of search with advertisement facets
25	percentage of search with image facets
	Search with distribution zone facets
26	percentage of search with distribution zone facets
27	percentage of search with local facets
28	percentage of search with national facets
29	percentage of search with Indonesian facets
30	percentage of search with Suriname facets
31	percentage of search with Antilles facets
32	percentage of search with unknown facets

Table 2: Collection metadata

Publication date	**Percentage**
between 1600 and 1899	12%
between 1900 and 1929	27%
between 1930 and 1949	26%
between 1950 and 1995	35%
Item type	
articles	67%
family announcements	2%
advertisements	29%
images	2%
Distribution zone	
local	40%
national	45%
Indonesia	12%
Suriname	1%
Antilles	2%
unknown	0.05%

use of quotes in queries and the reranking of the results by time. We compute these variables – except the total duration and length (number of interactions) – proportional to the length of the session or the number of search interactions.

4.2 Clustering Sessions

We applied principal component analysis on the metadata features in each month separately, in March this led to 15 principal components with an explained variance in the data of 75%. These 15 principal components are used for the clustering, reducing the number of dimensions for the clustering from 32 to 15. We have chosen the number of clusters k based on the average silhouette widths for this month, the highest average silhouette width under twenty is for k equals 10 with a value of 0.35, the first silhouette width above 0.3 (not a high silhouette width but this is not unexpected considering the 15 dimensions – the principal components – used to cluster). We have clustered the sessions from the month March (45,845 sessions) into ten clusters, and using the same value for k as for March we have also clustered the sessions from the previous months to evaluate the stability of the patterns found in March.

5 RESULTS

We describe the resulting ten clusters from March ($k = 10$ based on the average silhouette widths as mentioned in section 4.2) in terms of the original values of the metadata features used for clustering, and investigate the stability of this clustering over time. Then, we analyze the search behavior within the clusters.

5.1 Clusters

We have labeled the clusters using the most distinctive values of the session features present in a cluster (Table 3), and provided short descriptions of the clusters. The clusters show focused sessions centered around dedicated metadata categories.

For example, one of the larger clusters, the *recent national* cluster (16%), is exclusively centered around the recent national documents in the collection. In most sessions in this cluster, all the clicked documents are published between 1950-95 and have a national distribution zone. Similarly, most sessions in the *recent local* cluster (16%) contain only clicked documents with a local distribution zone of which the large majority is published between 1950-95. This indicates that users searching in the recent parts of the collection are mainly searching for documents with either a local or a national distribution zone and not both, resulting in two separate clusters.

Other clusters are likewise focused, either on a specific period, such as the *1930-49* cluster (15%) with the clicks on documents published during the Great Depression and World War II in the Netherlands, the *1900-29* and the *historical* cluster; or on a specific item type, such as the *family* cluster, where in addition to a majority of announcement clicks most sessions also include announcement facets, and the *article* cluster. For the two smallest clusters, based on a distribution zone, the *Suriname* cluster and the *Antilles* cluster, most sessions include the distribution zone facet next to a majority of clicks from the distribution zone.

The largest cluster (19%), however, is the cluster with sessions without distinct metadata, labeled *no metadata*. Despite leaving out the sessions of length 1 in the data preparation, there is still a relatively large cluster of sessions where hardly any facets are used or documents clicked, leading to a sessions without any representative metadata values.

5.2 Cluster Stability

To evaluate the clustering, we check the stability of the clusters, matching the sessions in the clusters to the cluster centers of the previous five months. Table 4 shows, per cluster and for all clusters combined, the percentage of sessions in the clusters of March that falls in the highest matching cluster of each of the previous months.

We observe that overall the clustering is stable, with an average stability of 73%. In particular, the *recent national*, *historical* and *family* clusters are stable every month, as is the *no metadata* cluster. (Note that, even while the percentage of family announcements in the collection is low at 2% (Table 2), there is stable user interest in this part.) Nevertheless, not all clusters in March can be traced back in the previous months. For example, the two smallest clusters in March, *Suriname* and the *Antilles*, do not match well in most of the previous months. Furthermore, the *1930-49* and *1900-29* clusters match well in most but not all months.

The silhouette widths (measuring the consistency within and between the clusters) of the clusters show no direct connection to whether a cluster is stable over time. The *family* cluster, for example, has a relatively high silhouette width of 0.62, but the *historical* cluster, similarly stable, has a lower silhouette width of 0.19. On the other hand, the *Suriname* cluster also has a relatively high silhouette width of 0.64 but a low stability, as for the *Antilles* cluster, both the silhouette width and the stability are low. This can be explained by the fact that cluster stability and silhouette width measure different things: consistency between clusterings over time and consistency within a clustering respectively.

To better understand the stability measurements in detail, we show a single month of the stability results in Figure 2, comparing March 2016 to February 2016. The clusters in February (on the rows) have been labeled in the same manner as the clusters in March.

Table 3: Clusters March

Number of sessions	Silh. width	Label	Description
8667 (19%)	0.66	no metadata	Sessions with little to no metadata values.
7238 (16%)	0.42	recent national	At least half the sessions include 100% clicks between 1950-95 with a national distribution zone. About 25% sessions additionally include other clicks.
7549 (16%)	0.25	recent local	At least half the sessions include 100% local clicks, of which 85% or more are between 1950-95. About 25% sessions additionally include other clicks.
6837 (15%)	0.13	1930-49	At least half the sessions in this cluster include 100% clicks between 1930-49. About 25% of sessions additionally include clicks after 1949.
5537 (12%)	0.02	1900-29	At least half the sessions include 100% clicks between 1900-29. In the sessions more clicks have a national distribution zone than a local one. About 25% of sessions additionally include a minority of clicks between 1930-49s.
4156 (9%)	0.19	historical	At least 75% sessions include facets or (a majority of) clicks from before 1900. About half the sessions also include clicks on adverts, about 25% clicks on announcements. There are more clicks in the sessions on documents with a local distribution zone than with a national one.
2701 (6%)	0.62	family	At least 75% sessions include announcement facets and a majority of clicks on announcements. In addition, more clicks in the sessions are local than national, and published in the 20th century. About 25% of sessions additionally include clicks on adverts; 25% include clicks on Indonesian documents; 25% clicks on pre-1900 documents; and 25% include time facets or distribution zone facets.
2101 (5%)	0.37	article	All sessions include item facets. At least 75% include article facets, 25% advertisement facets. Most of the sessions include a majority of article clicks; some sessions additionally include advertisement clicks. About 25% include time facets between 1900-95; and 25% include national distribution zone facets.
850 (2%)	0.64	Suriname	At least 75% sessions include a majority of Suriname clicks, and about half the sessions include Suriname facets. Additionally, about half the sessions include clicks between 1950-95; and about 25% sessions include announcement facets; 25% include some announcement clicks; and 25% include some advertisement clicks.
208 (0.5%)	0.0	Antilles	All sessions include Antilles facets; at least 75% sessions also a majority of Antilles clicks.

Table 4: Stability testing over time (March)

clusters	freq	Oct	Nov	Dec	Jan	Feb
combined	100%	74%	68%	75%	72%	75%
no metadata	19%	93%	96%	95%	96%	97%
recent national	16%	80%	78%	81%	75%	80%
recent local	16%	60%	62%	63%	59%	66%
1930-49	15%	72%	49%	77%	50%	48%
1900-29	12%	58%	26%	79%	67%	81%
historical	9%	82%	82%	68%	81%	83%
family	6%	88%	86%	86%	84%	85%
article	5%	61%	69%	19%	67%	66%
Suriname	2%	49%	55%	54%	38%	49%
Antilles	0.5%	35%	29%	27%	30%	33%

Here we observe good matching scores on the diagonal for the *no metadata, recent national, recent local, 1900-29, historical, family* and *article* clusters. The *1930-49* cluster, however, does not match to a single cluster, but to two with 48% in one and 28% in another cluster of February. A closer inspection shows that in February the period 1930-49 is split up into two separate clusters, one with mainly local clicks, and a second cluster with mainly national clicks within the same time period. On the other hand, the smallest clusters, the *Suriname* and *Antilles* clusters, have no good match in February at all. The highest matches here are with the *no metadata* cluster. This is because frequently for these sessions the Manhattan distance to the *no metadata* cluster is smaller than to the other clusters, resulting in these cases in an assignment to the *no metadata* cluster.

5.3 Search Behavior

We observe a split between the first five clusters in March (*no metadata, recent national, recent local, 1930-49* and *1900-29*), and the last five clusters (*historical, family, article* and *Suriname* and *Antilles*) in Table 5. The first five clusters are shorter, use fewer advanced search techniques, and – with the exception of the first cluster – are more click-oriented; the last five clusters are much longer in time spent and pages visited, and use more advanced search techniques such as facets or reranking of results.

Among the first five clusters, the *no metadata* cluster is different. The sessions in this cluster are the shortest, with the majority less than 2 minutes, and consist of only search interactions, no clicks. Nevertheless, users do spend time and effort (median of 5 interactions), possibly we observe users that completed their search using only the snippets on the results page, or these might be

no metadata 8667	recent national 7238	recent local 7549	1930–49 6837	1900–29 5537	historical 4156	family 2701	article 2101	Suriname 850	Antilles 208	February / March
97.08	8.57	15.6	6.23	5.69	9.14	0.22	6.14	48.82	32.69	no metadata 8178
0.48	80.44	6.35	1.02	1.41	1.66	1.04	8.66	11.65	30.29	recent national 7252
0.09	1.08	65.73	3.25	1.17	0.96	1.44	3.24	2.82	8.65	recent local 7153
0.24	0.06	1.95	47.64	1.28	0.46	0.7	3.71	3.88	5.29	1930–49, local 4206
0.52	2.78	3.05	4.45	81.18	1.52	0.15	2.71	7.88	1.44	1900–29 5442
0.12	0.28	1.15	1.43	2.29	82.72	1	2.95	8.71	3.85	historical 3918
0.13	1.93	1.92	1.78	1.97	1.06	85.12	1.38	9.65	6.73	family 2954
0.28	0.3	1.79	1.08	1.39	0.67	0.07	65.83	3.18	7.69	article 2405
0.85	1.08	2.38	4.72	1.37	1.3	9.55	2.81	1.18	1.92	Indonesia 1189
0.21	3.5	0.08	28.39	2.24	0.51	0.7	2.57	2.24	1.44	1930–49, national 3045

Figure 2: Stability matrix, tracing how the sessions in the clusters of March (columns, next to the label the size of the cluster is given) are matched to the cluster centers of February (rows, next to the label the size of the February cluster is given). The percentages in the columns (each column totaling 100 percent) signify the percentages of sessions in the March cluster closest to a February cluster in the rows (distance measured using the Manhattan distance of the metadata features for each session in March to the median values of the metadata features of the clusters of February).

Table 5: Search behavior in metadata clusters March

clusters	duration	length	search	clicks	facets		multiple facets		quotes	reranking results
	median	median	median	median	median	q3*	median	q3*	q3*	q3*
combined	00:13:22	16	81%	18%	0%	46%	0%	3%	0%	0%
no metadata	00:01:43	5	100%	0%	0%	33%	0%	0%	0%	0%
recent national	00:13:30	17	68%	29%	0%	7%	0%	0%	0%	0%
recent local	00:13:16	17	71%	25%	0%	16%	0%	0%	0%	0%
1930-49	00:18:04	20	75%	23%	0%	39%	0%	0%	0%	0%
1900-29	00:17:17	16	71%	25%	0%	31%	0%	0%	0%	0%
historical	00:44:02	36	84%	15%	43%	67%	0%	13%	0%	3%
family	46:07:41	70	83%	17%	52%	77%	9%	36%	29%	19%
article	01:14:03	41	82%	17%	48%	85%	13%	59%	0%	17%
Suriname	00:39:27	30	80%	19%	38%	68%	0%	29%	0%	0%
Antilles	01:03:30	40	81%	18%	61%	87%	11%	48%	0%	28%

* q3, or third quartile, is the middle value between the median and maximum

examples of failed search. Of the four more click-oriented clusters, all focus on documents published in the 20th century, with the *recent national* on average the highest percentage of clicks per session. The majority of sessions in these clusters does not make much use of the facets or other more advanced search techniques, but show a more "browsing" behavior where users click through results instead of refining their search. This could in part be explained by the collection, these clusters represent larger parts of the collection (Table 2), the digitization of these documents is likely better (the paper of the newspapers are not aged as much, the language in the documents easier to digitize), and fewer search techniques may be needed to find the desired document.

Next, we have five clusters where users spend a long time and visit many pages. The sessions in these clusters contain a lower percentage of clicks, and the majority of the sessions uses facets. Note that, apart from the *article* cluster, these clusters correlate with smaller parts of the collection (Table 2), and thus likely require more effort from the user. Of these, the *family* cluster contains on average the longest sessions, the majority is longer than a day and the number of interactions is by far the highest, in line with previous research into genealogists and family historians [4], and this cluster likely represents in large part this user group. (Sessions longer than a day are unlikely to be sessions where a user continuously searches, but sessions where a user returns to the same search a day later.) This cluster contains just 6% of the number of the sessions in the month, but the number of interactions is high with a median of 70, resulting in a lot of traffic on the search platform even while the percentage of announcements in the collection is just 2%, and suggesting the users in this cluster are highly engaged in their search. In this cluster we also observe the most frequent use of quotes for the queries, this is not unexpected as search within the family announcements are likely to include search for personal names with respect to genealogy and family histories.

6 DISCUSSION

Our results demonstrate that patterns of user behavior can be correlated with document metadata in a way that provides clusters that can be described in a meaningful way to collection curators.

Metadata Dependency. Our clustering using the metadata of search and clicks is dependent on by the existing metadata categories the curators have given; however, this is inherent to any curated online collection. It is possible to (additionally) use query analysis and link the query to the metadata of the collection, for example by using a relevant ontology or thesaurus as was done in [10, 11]. Query analysis, however, suffers from several disadvantages: queries can be ambiguous as they form an uncontrolled vocabulary, and queries may include privacy-sensitive information.

Session Identification. To identify the sessions to be clustered we have chosen a clickstream model, as it can help to split possible multiple users behind a single IP address, and to find complete searches. This approach leads in some cases to shorter or longer sessions than when a timeout is used, think for example when a user continues their search in a new tab thereby breaking off a clickstream-based session, or the opposite case when a user continues the next day with their search, this would lead to a break in a timeout-based session. For example, the sessions in the *family* cluster last for longer than a day in the clickstream-based sessions, when using the timeout-based session definition these sessions would be broken up into multiple sessions. An alternative to a purely clickstream-based session definition could be a combination of clickstream and query-term overlap, even though query analysis can introduce another sort of bias, and also for this reason we have chosen to keep the session definition simple.

Exploring k. We have clustered the sessions into ten clusters based on the best average silhouette width under twenty, however, the number of clusters k can also be used as a parameter of how fine-grained the analysis of the user interests is going to be. As the average silhouette widths for k values under twenty illustrate (Fig. 1), higher values of k can have similar average silhouette widths, making it possible to first set k low for an overview, and then higher to investigate more detailed user interests. The extent to which the value of k should be manipulated is dependent on, among other things, the existing metadata categories and the level of detail deemed appropriate by curators. Also, a higher value for k, might solve the disappearance of clusters like the *Suriname* and *Antilles* clusters in previous periods, which in the stability matrix merged into the *no metadata* cluster in the month of February (Fig. 2).

Fuzzy Clustering. Even though the large majority of sessions in each cluster are highly focused, we do find sessions on the edges of the clusters that are a bit more "mixed" with respect to user interests, such as the *1900-29* cluster where some of the sessions also include a minority of clicks from between 1930-49 (Table 3). The clustering algorithm we applied, however, is binary, in the sense that a session belongs to a single cluster, even if in some cases it is possible that it has characteristics matching more than one. For future work, it could be interesting to look into more fuzzy or soft clustering techniques, where a session can belong to multiple clusters.

Clustering Search Behavior. It is possible to cluster the same sessions using interaction features describing search behavior, such as session duration or number of clicks. These "behavior" clusters can then be mapped to the identified user interests, as opposed to a simple statistical summary, making it possible to find more than a single search pattern for each user interest. However, a first attempt using the same clustering method but with interaction features based on the search interface did not lead to more detailed insights than the statistical analysis provided: the overall overview remained the same. Possibly a search task analysis, such as presented in [8] is more effective here.

7 CONCLUSION

By applying a clustering algorithm we were able to identify user interests and investigate the relation between them and search behavior within the historical newspaper collection of the National Library of the Netherlands. The user interests we identified are stable over a six-month period. Our approach can be used to find relations between user interests and behavior in any collection described by metadata, such as digital libraries and archives.

Using the clustering based on the metadata features of search and clicks, we were able to observe users focusing on specific parts of the collection, in some parts spending less time and few search techniques, in other parts spending a large amount of time and a variety of search techniques. This method can help to find and investigate these highly-focused users. These findings can inform the design of more targeted user interfaces providing better access to specific parts of the collection, or help to improve search systems or collection management.

ACKNOWLEDGMENTS

We would like to thank the National Library of the Netherlands for their support. This research is partially supported by the VRE4EIC project, a project that has received funding from the European

Union's Horizon 2020 research and innovation program under grant agreement No 676247.

REFERENCES

[1] Charu C. Aggarwal, Alexander Hinneburg, and Daniel A. Keim. 2001. On the surprising behavior of distance metrics in high dimensional space. *Database Theory âĂŞ ICDT 2001* (2001). https://doi.org/10.1007/3-540-44503-X{_}27

[2] Olivier Chapelle and Ya Zhang. 2009. A Dynamic Bayesian Network Click Model for Web Search Ranking. In *Proceedings of the 18th International Conference on World Wide Web (WWW '09)*. ACM, New York, NY, USA, 1–10. https://doi.org/10.1145/1526709.1526711

[3] Hui Min Chen and Michael D Cooper. 2001. Using clustering techniques to detect usage patterns in a Web-based information system. *Journal of the American Society for Information Science and Technology* 52, 11 (2001), 888–904. https://doi.org/10.1002/asi.1159

[4] Paul Darby and Paul D Clough. 2013. Investigating the information-seeking behaviour of genealogists and family historians. *J. Information Science* 39, 1 (2013), 73–84. https://doi.org/10.1177/0165551512469765

[5] Carsten Eickhoff, Jaime Teevan, Ryen White, and Susan Dumais. 2014. Lessons from the Journey: A Query Log Analysis of Within-session Learning. In *Proceedings of the 7th ACM International Conference on Web Search and Data Mining (WSDM '14)*. ACM, New York, NY, USA, 223–232. https://doi.org/10.1145/2556195.2556217

[6] Daniel Grech and Paul Clough. 2016. Investigating Cluster Stability when Analyzing Transaction Logs. In *Proceedings of the 16th ACM/IEEE-CS on Joint Conference on Digital Libraries (JCDL '16)*. ACM, New York, NY, USA, 115–118. https://doi.org/10.1145/2910896.2910923

[7] Fan Guo, Chao Liu, and Yi Min Wang. 2009. Efficient Multiple-click Models in Web Search. In *Proceedings of the Second ACM International Conference on Web Search and Data Mining (WSDM '09)*. ACM, New York, NY, USA, 124–131. https://doi.org/10.1145/1498759.1498818

[8] Jiyin He, Pernilla Qvarfordt, Martin Halvey, and Gene Golovchinsky. 2016. Beyond actions: Exploring the discovery of tactics from user logs. *Information Processing & Management* 52, 6 (2016), 1200 – 1226. https://doi.org/10.1016/j.ipm.2016.05.007

[9] Daniel Hienert and Dagmar Kern. 2017. Term-Mouse-Fixations As an Additional Indicator for Topical User Interests in Domain-Specific Search. In *Proceedings of the ACM SIGIR International Conference on Theory of Information Retrieval (ICTIR '17)*. ACM, New York, NY, USA, 249–252. https://doi.org/10.1145/3121050.3121088

[10] Vera Hollink, Theodora Tsikrika, and Arjen P de Vries. 2011. Semantic search log analysis: A method and a study on professional image search. *Journal of the American Society for Information Science and Technology* 62, 4 (6 2011), 691–713. https://doi.org/10.1002/asi.21484

[11] Bouke Huurnink, Laura Hollink, Wietske Den Van Heuvel, and Maarten De Rijke. 2010. Search Behavior of Media Professionals at an Audiovisual Archive: A Transaction Log Analysis. *Journal of the American Society for Information Science and Technology* (2010). https://doi.org/10.1002/asi.21327

[12] Bernard J. Jansen and Amanda Spink. 2006. How are we searching the World Wide Web? A comparison of nine search engine transaction logs. (2006). https://doi.org/10.1016/j.ipm.2004.10.007

[13] Steve Jones, Sally Jo Cunningham, Rodger Mcnab, and Stefan Boddie. 2000. A Transaction Log Analysis of a Digital Library. *International Journal on Digital Libraries* 3, 2 (2000), 152–169. https://doi.org/10.1007/s007999900022

[14] L Kaufman and P J Rousseeuw. 1987. Clustering by means of medoids. (1987).

[15] Fang Liu, Clement Yu, and Weiyi Meng. 2002. Personalized Web Search by Mapping User Queries to Categories. In *Proceedings of the Eleventh International Conference on Information and Knowledge Management (CIKM '02)*. ACM, New York, NY, USA, 558–565. https://doi.org/10.1145/584792.584884

[16] Edgar Meij, Marc Bron, Laura Hollink, Bouke Huurnink, and Maarten de Rijke. 2011. Mapping queries to the Linking Open Data cloud: A case study using DBpedia. *Web Semantics: Science, Services and Agents on the World Wide Web* 9, 4 (2011), 418 – 433. https://doi.org/10.1016/j.websem.2011.04.001

[17] Raymond T Ng and Jiawei Han. 2002. CLARANS: A Method for Clustering Objects for Spatial Data Mining. *IEEE Trans. Knowl. Data Eng.* 14, 5 (2002), 1003–1016. https://doi.org/10.1109/TKDE.2002.1033770

[18] Xi Niu and Bradley Hemminger. 2015. Analyzing the interaction patterns in a faceted search interface. *Journal of the Association for Information Science and Technology* (2015). https://doi.org/10.1002/asi.23227

[19] Xi Niu and Bradley M. Hemminger. 2010. Beyond text querying and ranking list: How people are searching through faceted catalogs in two library environments. In *Proceedings of the ASIST Annual Meeting*. https://doi.org/10.1002/meet.14504701294

[20] Peter J Rousseeuw. 1987. Silhouettes: A graphical aid to the interpretation and validation of cluster analysis. *J. Comput. Appl. Math.* 20, Supplement C (1987), 53 – 65. https://doi.org/10.1016/0377-0427(87)90125-7

[21] Robert Tibshirani and Guenther Walther. 2005. Cluster Validation by Prediction Strength. *Journal of Computational and Graphical Statistics* 14, 3 (2005), 511–528. http://www.jstor.org/stable/27594130

[22] Gang Wang, Xinyi Zhang, Shiliang Tang, Haitao Zheng, and Ben Y Zhao. 2016. Unsupervised Clickstream Clustering for User Behavior Analysis. In *Proceedings of the 2016 CHI Conference on Human Factors in ComputingSystems, San Jose, CA, USA, May 7-12, 2016*, Allison Druin and, Cliff Lampe and, Dan Morris and, Juan Pablo Hourcade and, and Jofish Kaye (Eds.). ACM, 225–236. https://doi.org/10.1145/2858036.2858107

[23] Ryen W White, Peter Bailey, and Liwei Chen. 2009. Predicting User Interests from Contextual Information. In *Proceedings of the 32Nd International ACM SIGIR Conference on Research and Development in Information Retrieval (SIGIR '09)*. ACM, New York, NY, USA, 363–370. https://doi.org/10.1145/1571941.1572005

[24] Ryen W White, Wei Chu, Ahmed Hassan, Xiaodong He, Yang Song, and Hongning Wang. 2013. Enhancing Personalized Search by Mining and Modeling Task Behavior. In *Proceedings of the 22Nd International Conference on World Wide Web (WWW '13)*. ACM, New York, NY, USA, 1411–1420. https://doi.org/10.1145/2488388.2488511

Task, Information Seeking Intentions, and User Behavior: Toward A Multi-level Understanding of Web Search

Jiqun Liu, Matthew Mitsui, Nicholas J. Belkin, Chirag Shah
School of Communication & Information
Rutgers University
New Brunswick, NJ, USA, 08901
{jl2033,mmitsui,belkin,chirags}@scarletmail.rutgers.edu

ABSTRACT

According to the cognitive viewpoint of information retrieval (IR) research, a search task can be conceptualized as a sequence of information seeking intentions which both motivate and are influenced by search behaviors. While the behavioral effects of task features have been thoroughly discussed in a large body of literature, how different information seeking intentions in query segments serve as bridges between task and Web search behavior still remains unexplored. To develop a more comprehensive, multi-level (i.e., task level, intention level, and behavior level) understanding of Web search, the authors analyzed intention and search behavior data collected from 693 query segments generated by 40 participants in a controlled lab setting, seeking to answer two main research questions: 1) *from task to intention*: how do different task features affect users' information seeking intentions at different stages of a search session? 2) *from intention to behavior*: How is a user's search behavior associated with their information seeking intentions in the current and next query segments respectively? The results demonstrate that: 1) Task features significantly affected the frequency of occurrence of most of the information seeking intentions, and these effects gradually faded away as search sessions proceeded; 2) The presences of a variety of intentions in both current and subsequent query segments were connected with and detectable by different subsets of behavioral measures. This study contributes to the understanding of the connections between task, intentions in query segments, and search behavior, and thereby has implications for designing system affordances for supporting different intentions and search activities in various task stages and contexts.

CCS CONCEPTS

• **Information systems → Users and interactive retrieval.**

KEYWORDS

Information seeking intention; task; interactive IR

CHIIR '19, March 10–14, 2019, Glasgow, United Kingdom

ACM ISBN 978-1-4503-6025-8/19/03...$15.00
https://doi.org/10.1145/3295750.3298922

ACM Reference Format:
Jiqun Liu, Matthew Mitsui, Nicholas J. Belkin, Chirag Shah. 2019. Task, Information Seeking Intentions, and User Behavior: Toward A Multi-level Understanding of Web Search. In *2019 Conference on Human Information Interaction and Retrieval (CHIIR '19), March 10–14, 2019, Glasgow, United Kingdom.* ACM, New York, NY, USA, 10 pages. https://doi.org/10.1145/3295750.3298922

1 INTRODUCTION

During an information seeking episode, people often engage in a series of information behaviors with various goals and intentions which emerge from characteristics of their tasks and problematic situations. In the context of interactive information retrieval (IIR), a user's information seeking tactics are generally motivated and heavily influenced by their *information seeking intentions* [19]. Previous research has shown that people intend to achieve different goals and thereby adopt different search strategies at different stages during the course of information search [22, 27]. To design an adaptive IR system and to support users' interactions with information, IR researchers need to embrace a comprehensive understanding of how search task and search behaviors are connected to information seeking intentions at different stages of a search session.

According to the cognitive viewpoint of IR research, a search task can be conceptualized as a sequence of information seeking intentions which both motivate and are influenced by Web search behaviors. Previous IR literature on Web search has discussed the effects of task features on users' search behavior and experience (e.g., [1, 10, 16, 17]). While the findings from this line of research imply the cognitive changes behind the tasks and behavioral variations in search, the relationships between task, information seeking intentions, and user behavior still remain unexplored. To address this research gap and to model the interactions between different levels (i.e., task level, intention level, and behavior level) of Web search, IR researchers need to directly collect data on the various goals that users attempt to achieve in local steps (i.e., query segment) of task-based information seeking and search session, and to analyze: 1) how users' information seeking intentions vary across different query segments and task types; 2) how users' information seeking intentions are associated with their Web search behaviors.

To address this issue, the authors conducted a controlled lab study in which participants were assigned two different work tasks, and to accomplish a specific, different search task for each. After each search session, a recording of the session was played back, and participants were asked to explicitly annotate their information seeking intentions for *each query segment.* In this study, query segment is defined as *a search session segment which starts from one issued query and ends at the next query.* Based on the data collected from 693 query segments generated by 40 participants in 80 search sessions, the authors analyzed the effects of search task features on the frequency of occurrence of information seeking intentions in different query segments/stages of search, and also examined the relationships between Web search behavior and information seeking intentions in current and subsequent query segments respectively.

This study has multiple contributions: 1) Overall, this study reveals the connections between task, information seeking intentions, and user behavior in Web search and enriches the multi-level understanding of users' interaction with IR systems. 2) With respect to the effects of task features, this study offers direct evidence on the variations in users' information seeking intentions in tasks of different types and demonstrates that some of the task effects on intentions vary significantly across different query segments within a search session. 3) Regarding the relationships between intention and user behavior, this study indicates that the presences of a variety of information seeking intentions in both current and subsequent query segments are closely connected with and detectable by different subsets of behavioral measurements. 4) From the IIR system design and evaluation perspective, this work has implications for system designers on how to better support different information seeking intentions and facilitate users' interactions with information at different stages of search and in different task scenarios. Also, this study encourages future researchers to develop new evaluation metrics and frameworks tailored to different types of intentions.

2 BACKGROUND

2.1 Information Seeking Intentions

Search task is a complex, multidimensional concept. To decompose search task, prior studies mainly focused on a set of widely-discussed search task features (e.g., task complexity, task difficulty, task type) and their connections to the variations in Web search behavior (e.g., [1, 12]). Regarding the cognitive space and intention aspect of users, however, information seeking intentions in query segments as cognitive-level components of search task have been scarcely studied. As a result, although users often navigate to useful information with small, local steps under the influence of search tasks [25], it is still unclear how their information seeking intentions in local steps (i.e., query segments) are connected to low-level search behavior and high-level, global context (i.e., search task).

Some early theoretical research on classifying search sessions could be thought of as applicable to information seeking intentions. For instance, Broder [3] argued that Web searches in terms of information seeking and search intention could be classified into three categories: navigational, transactional, and informational. Aiming to build a more detailed scheme of intentions, Kellar, Watters, and Shepherd [11] proposed a new typology of user intentions generated in search, which includes fact finding, information gathering, browsing, and transactions. These classifications, as is some later work discussed below, were built upon analysis of queries that initiated search sessions and did not take into account the search actions within query segments. Also, these early theoretical classifications only identified broad intention categories and ignored the nuance between different specific intentions within each category.

Besides the theoretical speculation on the classification of intentions, according to Rha et al. [22], Xie [27] is the only example of an empirically-based classification of intentions which motivate people to engage in different interactions with search engines. Nevertheless, other similar research on users' goals, knowledge gap, and search intent can also be of help to understand users' intention in information seeking and search episodes. For example, Rose and Levinson [23] analyzed a set of queries randomly selected from AltaVista query logs and proposed a hierarchical typology of users' search goals. Similarly, drawing on the ideas of the Sense-Making approach [7], Savolainen and Kari [24] revealed the discontinuous and dynamic nature of Web searching episodes and developed a conceptual framework of knowledge gaps faced by searchers as well as the corresponding gap-bridging strategies. Jansen and Booth [9] developed a three-level hierarchy of user intent to automatically classify Web search queries based on the information seeking intentions behind these queries. They found that users' query intent (i.e., informational, navigational, transactional) varies by different search topics. In recent research on information seeking intention, Mitsui, Shah, and Belkin [21] developed a set of information seeking intentions based on Xie [27]'s initial typology of interactive intentions and empirically investigated the distributions of different intentions in search tasks of different types. Rha et al. [22] studied how different types and states (i.e., satisfied or unsatisfied) of information seeking intentions lead to different query reformulation strategies. Despite the increasing attention to the role of user intentions, the connections between task, information seeking intentions, and user behavior still has not been systematically studied.

2.2 Task and User Behavior in Web Search

In much of previous research which uses the concept of task, a task was conceptualized either as an abstract construction or as a concrete sequence of actions [4]. Following this line of thought, a large body of IIR research has explored the relationships between task level and behavior level of Web search and investigated the behavioral effects of various task features which include both objective task facets (e.g., task goal, task product) as well as user-task combined features (e.g., perceived task difficulty, topic familiarity). For instance, Jiang, He, and Allan [10] examined the associations between user behaviors (i.e., searching, browsing and clicking) and objective task features (i.e., task product, task goal, task type) and discussed to what extent these behavioral features can help disambiguate search tasks of different types. Capra et al. [5] found that manipulating task priori determinability via modifying task items and dimensions can significantly affect users' task perceptions and choices of search strategies. Similarly, Liu et al. [17] indicates that some whole-session behavioral metrics and eye movement features can serve as useful indicators of search task traits.

With respect to task-user combined features (i.e., users' knowledge and perception concerning tasks at hand), Wildemuth [26] argues that in task-based information search, users' search tactics are influenced by their domain knowledge related to the task topics. Liu, Gwizdka, Liu, and Belkin [18] demonstrates that both whole-session level and within-session level behaviors are affected by task difficulty, and that the dynamic relationships between search behavior and task perception are subject to the influence of task type (i.e., single fact-finding, multiple fact-finding, and multiple-piece information gathering). Similarly, Aula, Khan, and Guan [1] also investigated search behavioral variations under task of different levels of difficulty. By conducting both a lab study and a large-scale online study, they found that when performing difficult search tasks, users tend to issue more diverse queries (have a more unsystematic query refinement process), use advanced operators more frequently, and spend longer time on search engine result pages (SERPs) during their search processes. With respect to the facet of time pressure, Liu and Wei [15] found that users tend to become more selective in examining search results when searching under time pressure.

In addition to the explorations on task-behavior interactions, IR researchers also sought to develop user models based on large-scale behavior log data (e.g., clickstream data, query logs). For example, Borisov et al. [2] constructed a click sequence model (CSM) to predict the order in which a user will interact with the search results on SERPs. Hassan, Jones, and Klinkner [8] conducted behavior analysis based on 1000 user sessions extracted from Yahoo! search engine logs and found that user behavior can serve as a better predictor than document relevance on predicting search success.

Although the previous research discussed above enriched our understanding of Web search interaction and its associations with the overarching tasks, it did not offer us a more holistic understanding of the relationships between task as global context, information seeking intentions in local steps, and user behavior. Especially, the role of intentions in bridging global search context and local search tactics still remains ambiguous.

3 RESEARCH QUESTIONS

To address the research gaps discussed above and to develop a multi-level understanding of Web search, this work reports on a controlled-lab-based study which investigated information seeking intentions and search activities in query segments generated by forty participants in tasks of different types. The authors sought to answer the following research questions (RQs):

- **RQ1a**: What are the effects of task features on the frequency of occurrence of different information seeking intentions in query segments?
- **RQ1b**: To what extent do the frequency of occurrence of different information seeking intentions vary across different stages (query segments) of a search session?
- **RQ1c**: To what extent do the effects of task features vary across different stages of a search session?
- **RQ2a**: How is a user's search behavior associated with her information seeking intentions in the same query segment?
- **RQ2b**: How is a user's search behavior in the current query segment associated with her information seeking intentions in the next/subsequent query segment?

Among the RQs above, RQ1a-c speak to the effects of task features on information seeking intentions in query segments, and RQ2a-b were proposed to examine the relationships between Web search behavior and information seeking intentions at different stages. The lab study designed for answering the research questions is described in detail in the following methodology section.

4 METHODOLOGY

4.1 Information Seeking Intentions

To classify users' information seeking intentions in Web search query segments, this research used the typology of search intentions which was developed and elaborated by Rha et al. [22] based on a subset of Xie [27]'s classification of interaction intentions. The authors gave a description of this typology to the participants before their search sessions were replayed for intention annotation. Then, participants were asked to identify their information seeking intention(s) for *each query segment* based on the typology. Participants could identify multiple intentions in the cases where they tried to accomplish multiple things within a single query segment. Therefore, the intentions identified in our study are not mutually exclusive and should be considered as different variables. Details regarding the intention annotation process are provided in "Procedures" section below. The twenty information seeking intentions are listed in Table 1.

4.2 Search Task and Participants

To control the task context, the authors designed four work tasks within the domain of journalism: Copy editing (CPE), Story pitch (STP), Relationships (REL), and Interview preparation (INT). Forty undergraduate students majoring in journalism were recruited as participants from a research university. To ensure that the participants have a certain level of familiarity with journalism tasks, only upper-division undergraduates who have completed either one journalism writing or reporting class were selected.

The four different search tasks types were defined using four task facets extracted from the task classification scheme proposed by Li and Belkin [14], as modified by Cole et al. [6]: Product, Goal, Level, and Named. With respect to task Product, intellectual task refers to a task which produces new ideas or findings, whereas factual information task refers to a task locating facts, data, or other similar information objects in IR systems. Regarding task Goal, task with specific goal refers to a task with a goal that is explicit and measurable. By contrast, task with amorphous goal is defined as a task with a goal that has no explicitly defined outcome which cannot be measured in a quantitative sense. In terms of Level, a task can be classified into two categories: 1) document-level task: a task for which a document as a whole is judged; 2) segment-level task: a task for which a part or parts of document are judged. The Named facet refers to whether what is to be found is explicitly named; its values are true or false, named or not named. The values of each value for each of the task types are shown in Table 2.

Each of the four task types has two specific versions, which differ from one another in topic (i.e., coelacanths; methane clathrates and global warming). These two topics were selected to control the variable of participant familiarity with the task topic, as our participant population was thought likely to not be familiar with either. Table 2 shows the four specific tasks for the topic of coelacanths; "methane clathrates and global warming" was substituted for "coelacanth" to generate four more specific tasks. Each of the participants was asked to do two tasks of different topics and types, in Latin Square design, pairing CPE with INT, and STP with REL, to balance tasks by topic, and by the values of Product, Level and Named facets.

Table 1: Information seeking intentions and the associated acronyms used in Table 6, 8 and 9

Intention Type	Information Seeking Intentions
Keep record	Keep record of a link (KR)
Identify search information	Identifying something to start (IS); Identify something more to search (IM)
Learn	Learn domain knowledge (LK); Learn database content (LD)
Find	Find known item(s) (FK); Find specific information (FS); Find items sharing a named feature (FN); Find items without predefined criteria (FW)
Access item(s)	Access a specific item (AS); Access items with common characteristics (AC); Access a website/homepage or similar (AW)
Evaluate	Evaluate correctness of an item (EC); Evaluate usefulness of an item (EU); Pick best items from all the useful ones (EB); Evaluate specificity of an item (ES); Evaluate duplication of an item (ED) (i.e., determine whether the information in one item is the same as in others)
Obtain	Obtain specific information to highlight or copy (OS); Obtain part of an item (OP); Obtain a whole item(s) (OW)

Table 2: Tasks assigned in lab study

Task Type	Task Descriptions
Copy Editing (Factual Specific Segment Named True)	Assignment: You are a copy editor at a newspaper and you have only 20 minutes to check the accuracy of six italicized statements in the excerpt of a piece of news story below. Task: Please find and save an authoritative page that either confirms or disconfirms each statement.
Story Pitch (Factual Amorphous Segment Named False)	Assignment: You are planning to pitch a science story to your editor and need to identify interesting facts about the coelacanth ("see-la-kanth"), a fish that dates from the time of dinosaurs and was thought to be extinct. Task: Find and save Web pages that contain the six most interesting facts about coelacanths and/or research about their preservation.
Relationship (Intellectual Amorphous Document Named True)	Assignment: You are writing an article about coelacanths and conservation efforts. You have found an interesting article about coelacanths but in order to develop your article you need to be able to explain the relationship between key facts you have learned. Task: In the following, there are five italicized passages, find an authoritative Web page that explains the relationship between two of the italicized facts.
Interview Preparation (Intellectual Amorphous Document Named False)	Assignment: You are writing an article that profiles a scientist and their research work. You are preparing to interview Mark Erdmann, a marine biologist, about coelacanths and conservation programs. Task: Identify and save authoritative Web pages for the following: Identify two (living) people who likely can provide some personal stories about Dr. Erdmann and his work. Find the three most interesting facts about Dr. Erdmann's research. Find an interesting potential impact of Dr. Erdmann's work.

4.3 Procedure

The lab study started with a demographic questionnaire and a tutorial video on the additional browser interface features our plug-in provided for participants in information search sessions. Participants were free to search anywhere on the web, with the only restriction being to conduct their interactions within the supplied browser, which logged their search behaviors, and provided the ability to save and unsave web pages. The participants then went through the task description (see Table 2) and answered a short questionnaire on task familiarity/experience, topic familiarity, and anticipated task difficulty. They then had up to 20 minutes to complete the first assigned search task, by searching anywhere on the Web, with any search facilities that they wished, but could choose to finish early if they completed it to the best of their ability. Participants' search activities (e.g., query, timestamp, URLs, page type) were recorded with a Firefox browser plugin and Morae (https://www.techsmith.de/morae.html).

Afterwards, participants were asked to finish a post-search questionnaire on search task difficulty and self-reported search experience. At this point, they were asked to read a guidance of the intention annotation task and to watch a video explicating how to annotate search intention in each query segment. The authors then replayed the entire search, query segment by query segment, asking for intention annotation for each segment, in sequence. In our study the intention annotation task had no time limit. For the intention annotation task, participants were asked to select which intentions applied to each query segment in the search session. Within each query segment, participants could choose any number of intentions from the list. Participants could choose "other" if their intention did not match the 20 intentions provided. Participants repeated this selection process for each query segment during the course of intention annotation. The same procedure was then followed for the second search task, and the study session ended with an exit interview with questions related to participants' experience of performing the two search tasks. The entire process took about two hours for each participant.

4.4 Measurements and Data Analysis

With respect to task-intention connection, to answer RQ1a, the authors defined the binary status (i.e., present or absent) of information seeking intentions as dependent variables and employed task type (i.e., copy editing, story pitch, relationship, interview preparation) and task-user combined features (i.e., task familiarity, topic familiarity, perceived task difficulty, time condition/perceived time pressure) as independent variables and built logistic regression models for different information seeking intentions respectively. Data concerning the independent variables was collected via pre- and post-search questionnaires. To clarify the actual meaning of these variables, this section lists the specific questions corresponding to the independent variables in Table 3.

In addition to the task variables, to answer RQ1b, the logistic regression models also include *query percent* (QE) (query percent = n/N, where n is the sequence number of the query segment (nth query segment)) within the corresponding search session and N represents the total number of query segments within the search session) as an independent variable to describe the sequential aspect of query segments. Query percent was measured at the end of each query segment and indicates the stage that the user was in within a given search session. For example, in a search session consisting of four queries, the query percent value of the first and second

Table 3: Task-user combined features

Variables	Questions and Scales
Task familiarity	How much experience do you have with this kind of assignment? 1 (not at all)-7 (extremely) - pre-search
Topic familiarity	How familiar are you with the topic of this assignment? 1 (not at all) - 7 (extremely) - pre-search
Task difficulty	How difficult was it to find the information you need for this assignment? 1 (not at all) - 7 (extremely) - post-search
Time condition	Did you have enough time to complete the assignment successfully? 1 (far too little), 2 (too little), 3 (barely enough), 4 (enough), 5 (more than enough) - post-search

query segments are 0.25 and 0.5 respectively. However, in a search session consisting of only two queries, the query percent of the first and second query segments are 0.5 and 1 respectively. Using query percent instead of the sequence number of a query can make two distinct query segments from different sessions more comparable.

To answer RQ1c, the authors included the interaction between query percent and the other independent variables in the regression models, aiming to examine to what extent the effects of those variables on users' intentions change across different query segments.

To answer RQ2a and RQ2b, this study employed seven Web search behavioral measurements calculated based on the search log data, addressing different aspects of Web search (see Table 4). This study used Mann-Whitney U test to examine intention-behavior connection as none of the search behavior data was normally distributed. The statistical test for each intention-behavior pair was conducted between intention selected group and the entire sample. Specifically, in data analysis, for each type of intention, the authors first statistically tested the difference between the mean of value ranks of each search behavior data of users who had the intention in *current query segment* and that of the same search behavior of the entire sample (RQ2a). Similarly, to respond RQ2b, the authors also tested the difference between the mean of value ranks of each search behavior data of users who had the intention in the *next/subsequent query segment* and the mean of value ranks of the corresponding search behavior of the entire sample in current query segment, aiming to test the connection between current search behaviors and subsequent intentions.

Table 4: Behavioral measurements

Type	Behavioral Measurements
Query behavior	query length (number of terms)
Browsing behavior	number of clicks, number of sources (i.e. unique Internet domains) visited, number of pages (i.e., including repeated pages) viewed
Dwell time (second)	mean dwell time on each SERP, mean dwell time on each content page
Useful judgment	number of bookmarks

5 RESULTS

5.1 Descriptive Statistics

To answer the research questions proposed in previous sections, the authors conducted statistical analysis based on the intention and search behavior data collected from 693 query segments generated by 40 participants in tasks of four different types. For each intention, Figure 1 reports the proportions of query segments in which the intention was selected by users (which means the users had this intention in the corresponding query segments). The result shows that except for the intention of finding specific information, for almost every information seeking intention, the proportions of query segments where the intention was selected is smaller than that of the opposite cases (only three intentions appeared in more than 30% of query segments). This result indicates that there is no ubiquitous information seeking intention in Web search. Instead, the presences of most information seeking intentions may depend on a series of contextual factors and restrictions (e.g., stage of search, task type, users' perception of task). To test the effects of task features (including both objective task type and subjective task-user combined features) on information seeking intentions and to answer RQ1a-c, the authors conducted logistic regression analyses and the results are reported in the following section.

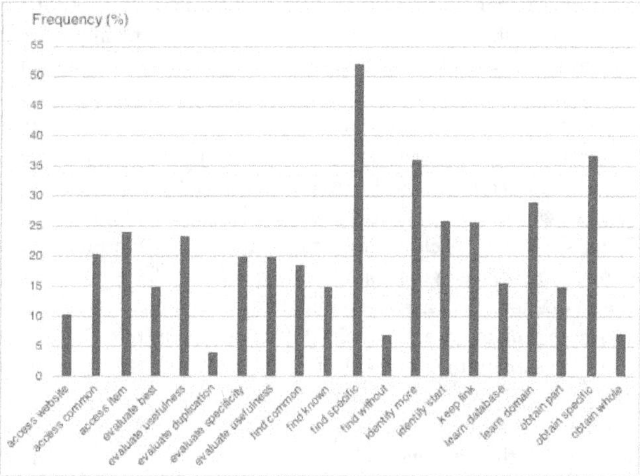

Figure 1: Intention selected in 693 query segments (%)

Table 5: Descriptive statistics of independent variables

Variable	Mean	S.D.	Min.	Max.
Session length	8.66	5.83	2	29
Task familiarity (TE)	3.04	1.67	1	7
Topic familiarity (TF)	1.88	1.34	1	6
Task difficulty (TD)	2.66	1.58	1	7
Time condition (TC)	4.18	.93	2	5

With respect to other independent variables included in logistic regressions, Table 5 reports the descriptive statistics of search session length (measured by number of queries) and task-user combined features. Search sessions which include 3-7 query segments appeared more frequently than other search sessions of other lengths. The relatively large variance in search session length (Mean = 8.66, S.D.=5.83) across different sessions demonstrate that query segments with the same sequence number may represent largely different stages of their respective sessions. Thus, compared to the sequence number of query segments, *query percent* may be a better measurement to describe which search stage a user was in.

For task familiarity (TE), topic familiarity (TF), and task difficulty (TD) measures, the mean values are more closer to the left ends of the scales. Particularly, for topic familiarity measure, the mean value is quite low and in more than 60 of 80 sessions participants identified their level of topic familiarity as 1, indicating that most of the participants were not familiar with the topics at all. This result demonstrates that the topic selection was successful and served the original purpose. The mean value of time condition (TC) score is relatively high, indicating that most of the participants had enough time to complete their tasks. In this time-sufficient setting, participants were more likely to behave in their natural manner.

5.2 From Task to Intention: RQ1a-c

To answer RQ1a-c, this section presents the results of logistic regression analysis for every information seeking intention. Tables 6 report the coefficients of different independent variables (IVs) (task type, task-user combined features, query percent, and interaction terms) in each logistic regression model. This model included three binary variables (STP, REL, INT) to represent the categorical variable task type. The copy editing task (CPE) was not explicitly included and thus was used as a baseline against which the other task were compared because CPE as a factual specific task has a lower level of cognitive complexity compared to other task types [12]. Thus, CPE as a baseline can better help explain the underlying connection between the cognitive demands of different tasks and the frequency of occurrence of different intentions.

Among the reported coefficients, the coefficients of task features can help explain the effects of these variables on the frequency of occurrence of different information seeking intentions (RQ1a). The coefficients of query percent and interaction terms can clarify to what extent the frequency of occurrence of intentions and the main effects of task type and task-user combined features varied across different query segments in search sessions (RQ1b and RQ1c).

According to the results reported in Table 6, the coefficient of query percent is negative and statistically significant in the "AW" column, indicating that as search session proceeded, participants became less likely to directly go to a website or homepage. This result suggests that participants tended to access a known website or homepage at early stage of search session as it could be an easy and useful way to start searching and dealing with the anomalous state of knowledge at the beginning stage. The results in the "AC" column demonstrate that participants with higher level of topic familiarity were more likely to access items with common characteristics. This may be because high level of topic familiarity decreased the difficulty and cognitive load of finding items with common features, and thereby encouraged participants to seek similar items for resolving the tasks. The results reported in the "AS" column indicate that participants accessed specific known item less frequently in story pitch tasks than in copy editing tasks, indicating that it might be difficult (or not necessary) for participants to use a known item(s) in a factual task without a clearly defined goal.

With respect to the intentions under *Evaluate* category, because of the nature of story pitch task (find webpages which contain the most interesting facts about the topic), participants who conducted this task tended to spend more query segments on picking best item(s) from all the useful ones. The intention of evaluating correctness of an item was affected by both the main effects of task features and an interaction term (task familiarity x query percent). Specifically, when participants were conducting story pitch and interview preparation tasks, they were less likely to evaluate the correctness of retrieved items in query segments as these tasks were open-ended and did not require participants to confirm or disconfirm any statement. Interestingly, the results indicate that higher task familiarity led participants to use significantly more query segments in evaluating correctness. However, as the search sessions proceeded, the effect of task familiarity decreased over time (the coefficient of the interaction term is a negative value). Despite the positive effect on the frequency of occurrence of the intention of evaluating correctness, higher task familiarity was associated with significantly lower frequency of evaluating duplication of the retrieved items. The intention of evaluating specificity appeared less frequently in the story pitch task compared to the "baseline" copy editing task as participants needed to find plenty of relevant, specific items to finish copy editing tasks (confirm or disconfirm the given statements). The results presented in "EU" column indicate that participants' intention of evaluating usefulness was affected by both task type and task-user combined features (topic familiarity and task difficulty). Whereas the positive effect of relationship task increased as the search session proceeded, the effects of both topic familiarity and task difficulty gradually decreased over time.

With respect to the intentions under the *Find* category, the frequencies of occurrence of different intentions were associated with different sets of factors. When a participant was more familiar with the task at hand, he or she was less likely to spend time on finding items with something in common. This may be because when performing familiar tasks, participants preferred to search for more diversified results and do more explorations, instead of relying on similar websites and documents. In contrast, a high level of topic familiarity encouraged participants to seek similar items. However, this positive effect of topic familiarity decreased as the search session proceeded. When under less time pressure (having enough time to complete the tasks), participants were more likely to spend time on seeking known items. Similar to the aforementioned effect of topic familiarity, this positive effect of time condition also decreased over time (the coefficient of the interaction term TC*QP is a negative value). In terms of the intention of finding specific items, compared to the copy editing task which requires more specific, predefined information, interview preparation as an open-ended task were associated with significantly lower frequency of seeking a predetermined piece of information. In addition, a higher level of task familiarity also was associated with a decrease in the occurrence of the intention of finding specific items. The intention of finding items without predefined criteria frequently happened in tasks with a high level of difficulty as difficult tasks involved more exploratory search activities (without predetermined guidance). In addition, participants who had sufficient time to work on their tasks

Table 6: The effects of task type and task-user combined features on intentions: Logistic regressions (*p<.05, **p<01. light grey: positive effect. dark grey: negative effect. white: no significant effect). IV (independent variable) definitions are in the Appendix Table 7; Table 1 gives the meaning of the intention acronyms (column labels).

IVs	AW	AC	AS	EB	EC	ED	ES	EU	FC	FK	FS	FW	IM	IS	KR	LD	LK	OP	OS	OW
STP	-1.1	-.97	-1.6*	.83*	-.14*	.87	-1.3*	-.33	.03	.10	-.62	.46	.28	-.05	-.68	-.52	.57	-.78	-1.5*	.02
REL	-.28	.84	.22	-.01	-.04	.28	.02	1.1*	1.1	.26	-.14	-.05	1.2*	-.05	-.13	-1.2	1.1*	-.13	-.37	.14
INT	-.84	.12	-.01	-.16	-2.6**	-.58	-.26	-.96	.73	-.36	-.11*	-.50	1.1*	.31	-.69	-.67	.55	-.09	-.76	-.65
QP	-1.9*	.81	1.3	.30	1.3	2.7	1.4	.05	.76	3.5	-3.9	3.5	-.31	-.98*	-.94	-8.6**	2.1	-3.9	3.4	-5.6
TE	.09	-.26	.13	-.04	.45**	-.48**	-.01	.17	-.42**	.03	-.26**	.06	-.47	-.34**	-.17	-.18	-.17	-.22	.07	-.27*
TF	.08	.30*	.09	.02	-.23	.18	.04	-.26*	.53**	.26	.17	-.12	.12	-.29*	.22	.14	.41**	.48**	-.13	-.14
TD	.17	.23	.25	-.14	.35	.29	.22	.33*	.23	.10	.08	.53*	-.01	.09	.36*	-.33	.25	.20	.43**	-.32
TC	.34	.40	.46	.26	.18	.57	.37	.42	.20	.51*	.18	.92*	.15	.21	.52*	-.59	.76**	.49	.69**	.06
STP*QP	.72	.71	1.0	-.85	-.27	-1.7	.83	1.5	-.27	-1.7	-.12	3.9	.14	-1.7	.99	.25	-.58	1.0	1.2	1.5
REL*QP	.79	.57	-.64	.16	-1.1	-.78	.33	2.5*	-.17	-.36	-.03	3.1	-1.5	-.66	-.02	2.2	-.52	.28	.20	.65
INT*QP	.08	.41	-.46	.79	.93	.10	-.07	3.2	-.52	-.28	1.3	4.5	-1.0	-2.1	.90	-.44	-.82	-.42	.15	1.1
TE*QP	-.01	.31	.13	.11	-.61*	.79	-.13	-.45	.34	.48	.19	-.18	.28	-.57	-.17	.17	.09	.30	.05	.67
TF*QP	.25	-.19	.15	.28	.57*	-.36	.22	.64*	-.73*	-.24	-.09	.05	-.13	.61	.06	.04	-.46	-.11	.26	.24
TD*QP	.01	-.74	-.52	-.41	.35	-.79	-.61	-.78*	-.65	-.33	.14	-1.2*	-.13	-.01	-.55	.29	-.09	.25	-.77*	.42
TC*QP	.19	.01	-.04	-.23	.15	-.51	.01	.17	.44	-1.0*	.64	-1.1	.031	.29	.24	1.6	-.34	.36	-.64	.01

were more likely to do exploratory searches and seek for useful webpages without predetermined features. Again, this main effect gradually decreased as the search session proceeded.

In terms of the intentions under *Identify search information* category, participants were more likely to identify something more to search and to explore a topic more broadly in the two open-ended tasks (relationship task and interview preparation task) than in the copy editing task. With respect to the intention of identifying something to get started (e.g., find good query terms), it appeared more frequently in the earlier stages than in the later stages (the coefficient of query percent is a negative value). Besides, high levels of task familiarity and topic familiarity significantly decreased the frequency of occurrence of this intention, indicating that when a participant was familiar with the task or topic, he or she was more likely to quickly find useful documents and thus did not need to frequently try and restart new search paths.

Based on results in the "KR" column, when a participant was performing a difficult task or having sufficient time in search, he or she tended to save more useful items to look at later. Regarding the intentions under the *Learn* category, participants tended to learn more about the types of available resources at particular websites in the early stages of search than in later stages. Participants usually spent more query segments on learning domain knowledge in the relationship task than in the copy editing task. Besides, having high level of topic familiarity or sufficient time in search usually led to higher frequency of seeking domain knowledge.

With respect to the intentions under the *Obtain* category, when a participant was familiar with the topic of the assigned task, he or she was more likely to seek for parts of relevant items to highlight or copy. A possible reason is that the familiarity of topic could help participants to easily locate useful pieces of information within retrieved items. Compared to the baseline situation (copy editing task), participants who were doing the story pitch task were less likely to seek for specific information to highlight or copy. Participants tended to seek specific known items when they experienced higher task difficulty or had relatively sufficient time in search. However, the positive effect of task difficulty tended to decay over time in search sessions. Participants who were doing familiar tasks were less likely to seek for a whole item to highlight or copy. This may be because obtaining a whole item is an inefficient way of seeking useful information and thus participants who were familiar with their tasks preferred to avoid this inefficient approach.

5.3 From Intention to Behavior: RQ2a-b

To answer RQ2a-b, this section presents the results of Mann-Whitney U test for each intention-behavior pair (see Table 8 and 9 in the Appendix). Specifically, Table 8 illustrates the connection between current search behaviors and current information seeking intentions (RQ2a), and Table 9 shows the relationship between current search behaviors and information seeking intentions in the next/subsequent query segment (RQ2b). Note that we did not employ Kruskal-Wallis test or the associated post hoc pairwise tests (e.g., Bonferroni test) here as the information seeking intentions were not mutually exclusive (i.e. users can select multiple intentions for the same query segment if applicable).

Overall, according to the results in Table 8, all intentions identified were significantly associated with at least one aspect of Web search in current query segment, indicating that information seeking intentions were connected to and reflected by Web search behavior in various ways. For intentions under *Access* and *Evaluate* categories, they were mostly correlated with click activity, dwell time on SERP, and usefulness judgment behavior. Specifically, when participants had intention(s) related to accessing item(s) or evaluating obtained information, they tended to be more active in browsing, page viewing, and judging usefulness of gathered information. In particular, when the identified intention(s) was concerned with comparisons between different results (e.g., access items with common features), participants spent more time on evaluating the results on SERPs visited. As a result, in "AC" and "EB" columns, SERP dwell time was significantly higher than the average level of the sample.

In contrast, intention under *Find* category did not show any unified pattern in intention-behavior connection. In other words, different specific intentions in this group were associated with different intentions. For example, the intention of finding information with common features was positively associated with SERP dwell time as this intention involves evaluating and comparing results on

SERPs. However, the intention of finding specific information was more closely correlated with content page viewing and usefulness judgment behaviors. With respect to the *Identify* category, participants tended to leave SERPs earlier when they merely wanted to identify something more to search, rather than dig deep into the results. When participants sought to identify a starting point for Web search, they were more active in content page reading and clicking, but less patient with SERP viewing and visiting more pages.

Similar to the intentions in *Access* and *Evaluate* groups, most of the intentions under *Keep, Learn* and *Obtain* categories were also closely related to clicking, content page viewing, and bookmarking behaviors, indicating that intentions under these categories could lead to similar search tactics. Among these intentions, when participants sought to learn domain knowledge, they tended to spend less time on browsing SERPs but much longer time on carefully reading the clicked content pages. The intentions of learning database information and obtaining a whole item(s) were only associated with one of the search behaviors, suggesting that their connections to Web search might be loose. Another possible reason is the small scale of sample size. Neither of these two intentions occurred frequently in the collected query segments (frequencies were both lower than 15%). Consequently, the limited sample size may not be able to fully picture the connections between intentions and behaviors.

With respect to the RQ2b, compared to the rich connections between search behavior and current intentions, fewer significant associations were found between search behavior and subsequent intentions (see Table 9). Among all types of intentions, seven intentions (i.e., access specific item(s), evaluate correctness, evaluate duplication, find specific information, learn database information, obtain specific information, obtain a whole item to highlight or copy) had no significant connection with search behavior. This result indicates that some of the intentions were more closely restricted to the local steps or micro-situation (i.e., query segment) and were loosely connected (if not totally disconnected) with previous actions. For other intentions, most of them were positively associated with click activity and usefulness judgments (i.e. bookmarking) behaviors. For example, when participants were active in clicking results and seeking useful webpages, in the subsequent query segment they were more likely to engage in a series of intentions concerning with accessing item, evaluating information, keeping records of useful links, and learning domain knowledge. In addition, when users issued a short query and had a relatively broad search scope in the current query segment, they tended to continue their exploratory search intentions in the subsequent query segments, such as evaluating specificity of obtained items, identifying more relevant information to continue search, and seeking information without predefined criteria. The intentions of finding information with common features and finding known item(s) were only associated with clicking, suggesting that active clicking in current query segment as sunk cost could encourage participants to seeking more gains (i.e., finding more information) in the next round.

6 DISCUSSION AND CONCLUSION

To explore the connections between global contexts and local steps in IIR and to develop a multi-level understanding of Web search, this study examined the effects of task features on information seeking intentions at different stages of search (RQ1a-c) and investigated the connections between search behavior and intentions in both current and subsequent query segments (RQ2a-b). With respect to the research questions, the authors have following answers.

In terms of the effects of task features on user intentions, for RQ1a, our results demonstrate that search task types and user characteristics significantly affected the frequency of occurrence of 18 out of 20 information seeking intentions (excluding only access website and learn database). It is worth noting that task type and task-user combined features (i.e. topic familiarity, perception of task) generated different effects on different information seeking intentions. These results supplement the findings on search behaviors from previous IIR research (e.g., [10, 17]) by confirming the effects of task features on information search at intention level.

To answer the RQ1b, the authors examined the main effect of query percent on the occurrence of different intentions. As search sessions proceeded, participants became less likely to access a particular website or homepage, identify something to start searching, or learn about the resources in databases. For other intentions, the main effect of query percent was not significant, meaning that the local context of search did not significantly affect these intentions. These results enrich our understanding of the cognitive variations in Web search and empirically confirm the classical arguments that users have different intentions at different stages of information search process [13]: for instance, users tend to do more exploratory searches at the beginning and then decrease these open-ended attempts once they formulate their search focuses.

For the RQ1c, results indicate that as the search sessions proceeded, many of the main significant effects of task features gradually faded away. This finding suggests that the main effects of task features are usually stronger at the early stages (the initial query segments) of search. Thus, early stages of a search session can be a good time for task prediction. This result has implications for task modeling and helped explain Mitsui, Liu, and Shah [20]'s findings: first query measures can be at least as good as, and sometimes better than, whole session measures for task type predictions.

With respect to RQ2, aside from clarifying the connections between intentions and search behavior, the results summarized in Table 8 and 9 also have implications for prediction analysis. Each column represents a vector of significant correlations associated with the corresponding intention. For instance, the behavioral vector for the current intention of identifying something to start is $[clicks = above, sources = below, pages = below, SERP = below, content = above]$. To accurately identify users' intentions in the current query segment and more importantly to predict their intentions in the subsequent query segment, the ideal situation is that we could find a unique vector of behavioral measures for each information seeking intention. In this study, the authors identified unique behavioral vectors for 9 current intentions and 7 subsequent intentions. Future studies need to include more behavioral measures and identify unique behavioral vectors for other intentions.

With respect to IIR system design and evaluation, by highlighting the role of information seeking intentions in connecting task features and search behaviors, this study calls for future research efforts on designing new system affordances and identifying more fine-grained system evaluation metrics tailored to different types of intentions in different search stages and task contexts.

7 ACKNOWLEDGEMENTS

This work is supported by the National Science Foundation (NSF) grant IIS-1423239.

REFERENCES

[1] Anne Aula, Rehan M Khan, and Zhiwei Guan. 2010. How does search behavior change as search becomes more difficult?. In *Proceedings of the SIGCHI Conference on Human Factors in Computing Systems*. ACM, 35–44.

[2] Alexey Borisov, Martijn Wardenaar, Ilya Markov, and Maarten de Rijke. 2018. A Click Sequence Model for Web Search. *arXiv preprint arXiv:1805.03411* (2018).

[3] Andrei Broder. 2002. A taxonomy of web search. In *ACM Sigir forum*, Vol. 36. ACM, 3–10.

[4] Katriina Byström and Preben Hansen. 2005. Conceptual framework for tasks in information studies. *Journal of the American Society for Information science and Technology* 56, 10 (2005), 1050–1061.

[5] Robert Capra, Jaime Arguello, Heather O'Brien, Yuan Li, and Bogeum Choi. 2018. The Effects of Manipulating Task Determinability on Search Behaviors and Outcomes. In *The 41st International ACM SIGIR Conference on Research & Development in Information Retrieval*. ACM, 445–454.

[6] Michael J Cole, Chathra Hendahewa, Nicholas J Belkin, and Chirag Shah. 2015. User activity patterns during information search. *ACM Transactions on Information Systems (TOIS)* 33, 1 (2015), 1.

[7] Brenda Dervin. 1998. Sense-making theory and practice: an overview of user interests in knowledge seeking and use. *Journal of knowledge management* 2, 2 (1998), 36–46.

[8] Ahmed Hassan, Rosie Jones, and Kristina Lisa Klinkner. 2010. Beyond DCG: user behavior as a predictor of a successful search. In *Proceedings of the third ACM international conference on Web search and data mining*. ACM, 221–230.

[9] Bernard J Jansen and Danielle Booth. 2010. Classifying web queries by topic and user intent. In *CHI'10 Extended Abstracts on Human Factors in Computing Systems*. ACM, 4285–4290.

[10] Jiepu Jiang, Daqing He, and James Allan. 2014. Searching, browsing, and clicking in a search session: changes in user behavior by task and over time. In *Proceedings of the 37th international ACM SIGIR conference on Research & development in information retrieval*. ACM, 607–616.

[11] Melanie Kellar, Carolyn Watters, and Michael Shepherd. 2007. A field study characterizing Web-based information-seeking tasks. *Journal of the American Society for Information Science and Technology* 58, 7 (2007), 999–1018.

[12] Diane Kelly, Jaime Arguello, Ashlee Edwards, and Wan-Ching Wu. 2015. Development and evaluation of search tasks for IIR experiments using a cognitive complexity framework. In *Proceedings of the 2015 international conference on the theory of information retrieval*. ACM, 101–110.

[13] Carol Collier Kuhlthau. 1999. The role of experience in the information search process of an early career information worker: Perceptions of uncertainty, complexity, construction, and sources. *Journal of the American Society for information Science* 50, 5 (1999), 399–412.

[14] Yuelin Li and Nicholas J Belkin. 2008. A faceted approach to conceptualizing tasks in information seeking. *Information Processing & Management* 44, 6 (2008), 1822–1837.

[15] Chang Liu and Yiming Wei. 2016. The impacts of time constraint on users' search strategy during search process. In *Proceedings of the 79th ASIS&T Annual Meeting: Creating Knowledge, Enhancing Lives through Information & Technology*. American Society for Information Science, 51.

[16] Jingjing Liu and Nicholas J Belkin. 2010. Personalizing information retrieval for multi-session tasks: The roles of task stage and task type. In *Proceedings of the 33rd international ACM SIGIR conference on Research and development in information retrieval*. ACM, 26–33.

[17] Jingjing Liu, Michael J Cole, Chang Liu, Ralf Bierig, Jacek Gwizdka, Nicholas J Belkin, Jun Zhang, and Xiangmin Zhang. 2010. Search behaviors in different task types. In *Proceedings of the 10th annual joint conference on Digital libraries*. ACM, 69–78.

[18] Jingjing Liu, Jacek Gwizdka, Chang Liu, and Nicholas J Belkin. 2010. Predicting task difficulty for different task types. In *Proceedings of the 73rd ASIS&T Annual Meeting on Navigating Streams in an Information Ecosystem-Volume 47*. American Society for Information Science, 16.

[19] Matthew Mitsui, Jiqun Liu, Nicholas J Belkin, and Chirag Shah. 2017. Predicting Information Seeking Intentions from Search Behaviors. In *Proceedings of the 40th International ACM SIGIR Conference on Research and Development in Information Retrieval*. ACM, 1121–1124.

[20] Matthew Mitsui, Jiqun Liu, and Chirag Shah. 2018. How Much is Too Much?: Whole Session vs. First Query Behaviors in Task Type Prediction. In *The 41st International ACM SIGIR Conference on Research & Development in Information Retrieval*. ACM, 1141–1144.

[21] Matthew Mitsui, Chirag Shah, and Nicholas J Belkin. 2016. Extracting Information Seeking Intentions for Web Search Sessions. In *Proceedings of the 39th International ACM SIGIR conference on Research and Development in Information Retrieval*. ACM, 841–844.

[22] Eun Youp Rha, Matthew Mitsui, Nicholas J Belkin, and Chirag Shah. 2016. Exploring the relationships between search intentions and query reformulations. *Proceedings of the Association for Information Science and Technology* 53, 1 (2016), 1–9.

[23] Daniel E Rose and Danny Levinson. 2004. Understanding user goals in web search. In *Proceedings of the 13th international conference on World Wide Web*. ACM, 13–19.

[24] Reijo Savolainen and Jarkko Kari. 2006. Facing and bridging gaps in Web searching. *Information Processing & Management* 42, 2 (2006), 519–537.

[25] Jaime Teevan, Christine Alvarado, Mark S Ackerman, and David R Karger. 2004. The perfect search engine is not enough: a study of orienteering behavior in directed search. In *Proceedings of the SIGCHI conference on Human factors in computing systems*. ACM, 415–422.

[26] Barbara M Wildemuth. 2004. The effects of domain knowledge on search tactic formulation. *Journal of the american society for information science and technology* 55, 3 (2004), 246–258.

[27] Hong Xie. 2002. Patterns between interactive intentions and information-seeking strategies. *Information Processing and Management* 38, 1 (2002), 55–77.

8 APPENDIX

Table 7: Acronyms of the independent variables in the logistic regressions and the definitions

Acronym	Definition
IV	Independent variable
STP	Story pitch task (binary, Y=1, N=0)
REL	Relationship task (binary, Y=1, N=0)
INT	Interview preparation task (binary, Y=1, N=0)
QP	Query percent
TE	Task familiarity/experience
TF	Topic familiarity
TD	Task difficulty
TC	Time condition
STP*QP	The interaction term between STP and QP
REL*QP	The interaction term between REL and QP
INT*QP	The interaction term between INT and QP
TE*QP	The interaction term between TE and QP
TF*QP	The interaction term between TF and QP
TD*QP	The interaction term between TD and QP
TC*QP	The interaction term between TC and QP

Table 8: Median of behavioral measure when the intention was selected in *current* query segment. (Mann-Whitney test. light grey: above the mean of total ranks. dark gray: below the mean of total ranks. white: no significant difference.)

Behavior	AW	AC	AS	EB	EC	ED	ES	EU	FC	FK	FS	FW	IM	IS	KR	LD	LK	OP	OS	OW
query	4	4	4	4	4	3	4	3	4	4	4	3	4	4	4	4	4	4	4	4
click	4	3	4	5	3	6	4	4	3	4	3	3	3	3	4	3	3	4	3	3.5
source	4	4	4	4	4	5	4	4	4	4	4	4	4	4	5	4	4	4	4	4
page	5	5	5	5	5	8	5	5	5	5	5	5	5	4	6	5	5	5	5	5
SERP	8.2	9.5	7.1	7.9	9.1	4.8	8.4	8.1	7.7	6.2	8.8	7.3	6.7	7.4	8.8	7.5	7.3	12.4	9.6	6.8
content	11.4	11.6	11.8	11.9	11.8	17.7	13.2	13.9	9.5	10.7	11.5	14.0	9.9	11.7	13.9	7.7	12.8	12.4	13.4	14.6
bookmark	1	1	1	1	1	1	1	1	0	1	1	1	0	0	1	0	1	1	1	1

Table 9: Median of behavioral measure when the intention was selected in *next* query segment. (Mann-Whitney test. light grey: above the mean of total ranks. dark gray: below the mean of total ranks. white: no significant difference.)

Behavior	AW	AC	AS	EB	EC	ED	ES	EU	FC	FK	FS	FW	IM	IS	KR	LD	LK	OP	OS	OW
query	4	4	4	4	4	4	3	4	4	4	4	3	4	4	4	4	4	4	4	4
click	3	3	3	3.5	3	2	3	3	3	3	3	3	3	3	3	4	4	4	4	4
source	4	4	4	4	4	4	4	4	4	4	4	4	4	5	4	4	4	4	4	4
page	5	5	5	5	5	5	5	5	5	5	5	5	5	5	5	5	5	5	5	5
SERP	6.5	6.8	7.0	5.8	7.1	9.2	6.2	6.3	7.1	6.0	6.9	7.4	5.6	6.0	6.8	6.7	5.8	6.9	7.3	6.0
content	12.1	10.2	11.1	10.5	11.3	7.2	10.5	10.7	10.1	9.1	10.3	15.3	9.7	12.2	11.9	9.4	11.3	11.3	11.3	13.7
bookmark	1	1	1	1	1	0	0	1	1	0	0	1	0	1	1	1	1	1	0	1

Understanding Context for Tasks and Activities

Jan R. Benetka
NTNU
benetka@pm.me

John Krumm
Microsoft Research
jckrumm@microsoft.com

Paul N. Bennett
Microsoft Research
pauben@microsoft.com

ABSTRACT

Human activity is one of the most important pieces of context affecting an individual's information needs. Understanding the relationship between activities, time, location, and other contextual features can improve the quality of various intelligent systems, including contextual search engines, task managers, digital personal assistants, chat bots, and recommender systems.

In this work, we propose a method for extraction of an extensive set of open-vocabulary activities from social media. In particular, we derive tens of thousands of *ongoing* activities from Twitter, where people share information about their past, present, and future events and, using attached metadata, we establish spatiotemporal models of these activities at the time of posting. While public Twitter content is subject to self-censorship (not all activities are tweeted about), we compare extracted data with unbiased survey data (ATUS) and show evidence that for *activities which are tweeted about*, the underlying spatiotemporal profiles correctly capture their real distributions of activity conditioned on time and location. Next, to better understand the set of activities present in this dataset (and what role self-censorship may play), we perform a qualitative analysis to understand the activities, locations, and their temporal properties. Finally, we go on to solve predictive tasks centered on the relationship between activity and spatiotemporal context that are aimed at supporting an individual's information needs. Our predictive models, which incorporate text, personal history and temporal features, show a significant performance gain over a strong frequency-based baseline.

ACM Reference Format:
Jan R. Benetka, John Krumm, and Paul N. Bennett. 2019. Understanding Context for Tasks and Activities. In *2019 Conference on Human Information Interaction and Retrieval (CHIIR '19), March 10–14, 2019, Glasgow, Scotland Uk.* ACM, New York, NY, USA, 10 pages. https://doi.org/10.1145/3295750.3298929

1 INTRODUCTION

It has been shown that human activity plays a major role in affecting what information needs people have. A study by Sohn et al. [34] recognized activity among four most frequent contextual triggers of information needs, which is in line with findings by other authors [9, 15]. While the majority of context-related prior work concentrates on time and location [1, 4, 36], activity as a higher-level driver of information needs remains relatively unexplored with only a handful of publications dedicated to it [3, 10, 23, 37]. In the following two examples of potential context-aware applications, which lead us to investigate the underlying predictive technology, we illustrate how including activity as context would impact a user's information access:

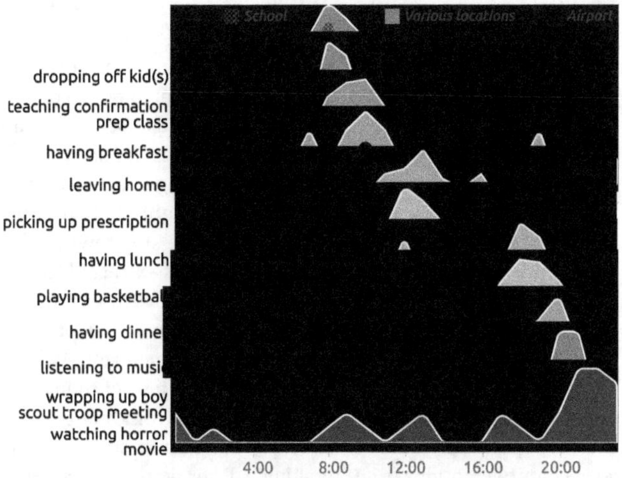

Figure 1: Sample of human activities extracted from Twitter demonstrating the dependencies between activities, time and selected locations (school, airport, various locations).

a) Activity-aware reminder system. Reminder systems allow users to set notifications for future tasks, events or activities to avoid forgetting about them. The notifications are typically invoked when a predefined date/time is met or a specified location boundary is crossed. However, Rong et al. [32] discovered that 40% of people cannot or prefer not to identify a precise time of their tasks/to-do items. This is one reason why an intelligent reminder system should not rely solely on hard-coded conditions. Instead, it should recognize activities mentioned in the reminder message (e.g., *read the article*) and proactively notify the user at any location and time when such an activity has a chance of being performed (e.g., in a *café* during the morning or at *home* in the evening).

b) Activity recommender. Many applications would benefit from a model that takes the user's location and time as input and returns a list of activities ranked according to the probability of being performed. Two such examples could include an automatic suggestion of a person's activity for a status update on a social network (e.g., *Enjoying coffee @ Café Lyst*) or recommendation of activities for a user's upcoming trips (e.g., *Lake Como: cycling*).

In both scenarios, as well as in similar activity-aware systems, the underlying models would be expected to capture the spatiotemporal dependencies of a wide range of open-domain activities. Ideally, the set of recognized activities should cover all activities a person might wish to be recommended or reminded about. In

CHIIR '19, March 10–14, 2019, Glasgow, Scotland Uk

ACM ISBN 978-1-4503-6025-8/19/03...$15.00
https://doi.org/10.1145/3295750.3298929

the long-term, a predictive model between open-domain activities, locations, and time provides a simple foundation for commonsense reasoning about the world – long a goal of AI. That is, the implicit knowledge that certain activities, locations, and times correspond with each other (e.g., breakfast happens in the morning; work usually happens between 9-5 on weekdays but can be observed at other times; at a restaurant one eats but one also meets friends and celebrates milestones). We leave how to leverage these models in more general intelligence as future work and focus here solely on understanding and predicting activities in a spatiotemporal context.

However, such an endeavor requires a large dataset of human activities. This lack of a large-scale set of activities has been one of the impediments to advancing our understanding of activities and their contextual setting as well as how they might relate to tasks and information needs. In this work, we take a step toward alleviating this lack by demonstrating that activities extracted from a large-scale publicly available text source (Twitter) correspond with time and location patterns of activities reported in an independent broad survey. In contrast to surveys with predefined activity categories, textual sources can hold descriptions for tens of thousands of activities from an open vocabulary, ranging from fine-grained and very specific physical actions (e.g., "fixing a bike seat") to high-level cognitive notions (e.g., "thinking"). Prior work has proposed a number of methods for activity extraction from various textual sources [11, 13, 16, 27]. None of them, however, proceeds to jointly model the relation between activities, locations and time (e.g., "*dropping off kid(s)*" example in Fig. 1). In order to extract activities along with these two dimensions, i.e., location and time, reliable in-the-moment activity reports are necessary. ATUS[1], a survey-driven dataset with detailed records about activities of American citizens, on its own, provides rich and credible information. The taxonomy of activities it uses, however, is limited in size and would hardly cover many real scenarios. A shortage of variety is by no means a problem of microblogging platforms such as Twitter, where millions of people share updates about what they do [29].

In this work, we leverage the fact that people have become self-reporters of their own activities on social media, indirectly providing context and expressing their activities with terms that are not limited to any predefined taxonomy. We harvest Twitter for rich textual representations of tens of thousands of activities and simultaneously model their temporal and spatial dimensions by capturing timestamps and geospatial tags at the time of posting. To demonstrate the reliability of in-the-moment reports on Twitter, we are the first to report evaluation against an externally collected large-scale survey, ATUS.

We address the following research questions:

- **RQ1 What are the activities that people perform? How can we obtain an extensive set of them?** We propose a method for extraction of activities that people engage in. We demonstrate the suitability of Twitter as a self-reporting platform for extraction of reliable spatiotemporal properties. (§3)
- **RQ2 When and where do people engage in these activities?** We analyze temporal and spatial profiles of extracted activities to reveal the underlying patterns. (§4)
- **RQ3 Given an activity of a person (and possibly other context), can we predict where it is likely to happen?** We propose and evaluate a model that leverages (personalized) spatiotemporal patterns of activities in order to predict semantic location. This relates to the 'task reminder' scenario. (§5)
- **RQ4 Given a location (and possibly other context), can we predict what activities people will engage in there?** We pose an inverted problem to the one in *RQ*3, addressing the 'activity recommender' scenario. (§5)

In short, this paper makes the following novel contributions:

- Establishes an extensive set of human daily activities;
- Separates ongoing activities from future or past activities in social network posts;
- Profiles the spatial and temporal aspects of ongoing activities;
- Evaluates a sample of these activities against an external survey of activity and spatiotemporal context;
- Proposes several predictive tasks centered on activity and inspired by real-life scenarios, where using activity as additional context would make a profound difference;
- Proposes and evaluates predictive models for the aforementioned tasks.

2 RELATED WORK

Our aim is to profile and predict activities of all complexities while using social media as our source of evidence. Here, we review relevant prior work.

Activity recognition. In contrast to the traditional AI view of activity recognition using wearable/wireless sensors [8] or video [21], widespread connected mobile devices allow for collecting large amounts of contextual data about people's daily activities in a non-intrusive way. Java et al. [18] and Naaman et al. [29] have shown that users of microblogging platforms primarily post updates about their daily routines and experiences, which makes social networks by far the most scalable and diverse source of in-situ information about people's daily activities. Alternative large-scale sources of data that facilitate activity extraction [11, 27] are community-authored reviews of places (e.g., Yelp). While the reviews provide a means for mapping activities to locations, they cannot make a similar relation with time due to the ex post nature of reviews.

Methods to extract activities from textual sources range from manual curation of lists or taxonomies [19, 20, 33], through various supervised machine learning [16] or language modeling [13] techniques, to the application of natural language processing (NLP) [11, 27]. The high quality of manually crafted taxonomies [33], driven by the expertise of their curators, is counterweighted by the limited scalability of human labor involved in the process. Approaches relying on machine learning methods [16] require labeled instances of data and unsupervised language or topical models [13, 40, 41] are robust, nevertheless, they represent latent activities as a probabilistic distribution of words or concepts instead of assigning a concrete label to each activity. Finally, methods based on NLP techniques interpret the concept of activity [11, 27] or a task [12] as a verb-noun phrase pairs (e.g., *drinking coffee*), which they extract using a pattern-based paradigm. These methods are scalable and precise, however, they fail to capture expressions that are not covered by predefined patterns.

[1] American Time Use Survey (12 years, 170K participants)

Activity classification and prediction. A parallel line of literature focuses on activity classification, where a target set of activities already exists. Zhu et al. [42] train a model to label geo-located tweets with top-level activity classes from the ATUS hierarchy [33]. Their approach relies on crowdsourced annotations and contextual features from location-based social networks (LBSN) that include check-in time, venue name and venue category. A similar approach is adopted by Beber at al. [2] with the goal of inferring activities of moving objects based on their trajectories. In addition, the authors profile typical durations of activities, which is a feature of the work by Melià-Seguí et al. [28]. A more user-centric approach that learns activity expressions for individual users and simultaneously transfers training instances between classifiers to fight data sparsity is presented by Song et al. [35]. Weerkamp and de Rijke [38] extend the pool of microblog prediction problems with the task of activity prediction. In their pilot study, which has elements of event-extraction techniques, the authors suggest mining of likely near-future activities from the Twitter stream using a set of user-defined keywords and timeframes.

Activity and location. Arguably, activities that are typically performed at a location define its meaning to some degree [10] (e.g., *café* is a place where people *drink coffee*). Therefore, in some literature, activities and locations are used jointly [5] or interchangeably [17]. A common practice is to use semantic location labels as a proxy to high-level activities (e.g., *office* → *working*) [3, 23, 39]. Given the fact that detecting dominant functional places such as *home* or *work* from people's daily routines is feasible [22], such an approach is an understandable simplification. Nevertheless, a considerable number of locations can be a scene of more than one activity at the same moment [2] (*"Airport"* location in Fig. 1), and one activity can be characteristic of various locations (e.g., *"taking picture"*).

In our work, we use large volumes of tweets that are interlinked with Foursquare check-ins. This allows us to benefit from the text-to-location mapping as in [11, 27]. While Twitter users share information about past, current and future events, we only focus on messages that provide in-the-moment reports (contrary to [38] who target future activities). We extract a multitude of fine-grained activities at each location type, as opposed to [3, 39]. With respect to our data source, we use scalable NLP methods for activity extraction, and we evaluate our results against data from a handcrafted taxonomy of activities and locations (ATUS) [33]. In contrast to the activity classification literature [2, 42], we represent activities with their textual footprint, not with an abstract high-level class. We aim for establishing an extensive set of activities, answering the call by Brush et al. [7].

3 ACTIVITY EXTRACTION

Apart from time and location, human activity is one of the most influential cues affecting the information needs of an individual [15, 34]. While the values of time and location are known and inherently predefined (e.g., units of time, geo-coordinates, semantic labels of locations), the same cannot be said about human activities. The abstraction, ambiguity and variety of activities make it challenging to establish an exhaustive list of them. Yet, our first objective (*RQ*1) is to frame the notion of a *daily activity* and to create an extensive set of the most common activities that people perform and report on a daily basis. Let us first define the key concepts and describe our dataset before proceeding to the actual activity extraction methods:

Definition 3.1. **Human activity**, in the context of this work, is a real-world physical or cognitive activity of a person that she performs in space and time. The level of activity abstraction can vary from low-level (e.g., *moving*), through a more fine-grained activity expression (e.g., *riding on a bike*) to a very abstract notion (e.g, *enjoying the day*).

Definition 3.2. **Activity descriptor**, or simply **activity**, is a textual surface form (e.g., the actual text 'writing a report') referring to any activity that satisfies the definition of human activity.

Definition 3.3. **Temporal profile of an activity** is a histogram of activity observations over a specified temporal interval. In this work, we construct normalized daily and weekly profiles.

Definition 3.4. **Spatial profile of an activity** is a distribution capturing the normalized frequency of activity occurrences across a selected set of location categories. We work with location categories rather than individual locations to focus on patterns that generalize.

3.1 Data

Social networks can be seen as large crowdsourcing platforms with the potential to reveal the global picture of human activity behavior. While any social network that generates textual posts with time and location metadata could be used for our task, we found most reasons to use Twitter data: firstly, it is a widely used and well-researched microblogging platform; secondly, with the exception of our proprietary spam score weighting[2] all data is publicly accessible; finally, it has been shown that people tend to post updates that relate to their state or activity [29]. In our experiments, we operate with a sample of $6,641,503$ geo-tagged Twitter posts that are restricted to the approximated region of the 48 contiguous states of the USA between January 1st 2016 and May 31st 2017. Further, we filter for tweets that are written in English, have a spam score below 0.5 and are cross-posted exclusively via the Foursquare application. Foursquare is a location-based social network, which is used by people to search for, retrieve details about and comment on nearby points of interest (POIs). Users can explicitly mark their visit to a POI by performing a *check-in* within the application, and many people choose to share this activity publicly via Twitter. These are the tweets that we benefit from in this work because they give us a means to pinpoint the user's precise location to the building, business or venue, and, importantly, the location's category. Locations on Foursquare are categorized in a multi-level hierarchy, where the top level has 10 categories (e.g., *Shop & Service*), the second level has 448 (e.g., *Bike Shop*).

3.2 Methods

Importantly, Twitter posts may express information about past, current, or future activity. We now present a simple and effective method for extraction of ongoing activities with their context.

[2]The spam score is an internally determined value that our organization applies to tweets. It is a strong function of the tweet's associated Twitter account.

3.2.1 Preprocessing. Twitter content is noisy, and the language is specific with heavy use of abbreviations and special characters such as emojis [14]. For that reason, we apply several preprocessing steps to minimize the noise in the data:

Content cleaning - we remove URLs, hashtags, and special characters (apostrophes, spurious white spaces, etc.).

Foursquare pointer - when a person checks in using the Foursquare mobile application with the sharing option switched on, the application automatically appends a string to the tweet with user's current location (e.g., `(@ Rolling Hills, CA)`). We remove these suffixes.

Duplicate removal - we consider two tweets to be duplicates when they are posted by the same author, have identical content (after preprocessing steps), and belong to the same Foursquare category.

Timezone inference - in order to calculate the local time of a tweet from its server publication time, we infer the tweet's timezone from its geo-coordinates using *timezonefinder*[3] and apply the time difference to get the local time.

3.2.2 Activity Extraction. Verbs or verb phrases are, by definition, sentence constituents that introduce an action (e.g., feed, go to). Nouns or noun phrases, on the other hand, typically fulfill the role of verbs' arguments (e.g., ducks, popular cafe). To extract activity descriptors from free text, we isolate the linguistically natural structure of *verb+noun* pairs (alternatively *verb phrase+noun phrase*, or combination) using a syntactic parser and a part-of-speech [6] grammar[4]. We denote the verb part as the *activity head phrase* (e.g., feed, go) and the complete pair as the *full activity descriptor* (e.g., feed ducks, go to popular café). Since we are interested in activities that take place at the time of their reporting, we only extract verbs in the present progressive tense, i.e., heuristically identified as verbs ending with '*-ing*' (e.g., feeding, going). In terms of generality, many languages contain tense markers or grammatical constructions that could be leveraged similarly (e.g., Romance or Slavic languages, Chinese, Japanese, Hindi). Future work could use tense as a weak label to bootstrap an in-progress activity descriptor extractor which could then be refined through label supervision to handle less common cases. Below, we provide an extraction example:

<activity>

<verb phrase> <noun phrase>

Picking up my **4K TV** at #BestBuy! GTA will look insane!

After extraction, articles and possessive *s*'s are removed, and the activity text is lemmatized in order to normalize the slight morphologic variations. Several activity examples are displayed in Figure 1 with the activity surface forms as labels on the y-axis. We note that a similar verb-noun extraction technique has been relied on in prior work [11, 12, 27], although, it is only our work that specializes in exclusive extraction of ongoing events.

[3] https://github.com/MrMinimal64/timezonefinder

[4] For the sake of reproducibility, the grammar is available in the Appendix (§A.3).

3.2.3 Extraction Analysis. To verify extraction precision, the first author conducted an evaluation by manually extracting verb+noun phrases that would be naturally understood as valid activity descriptors from 500 tweets, where activity was identified using our extraction algorithm. After comparing these results for an *exact match* with the method's output, we find that the precision is 73.6%. In the vast majority of these cases, the error does not mean that we extract activity from a tweet where there is none. The usual extraction errors are related to misspelling (e.g., *being niceâ*), not capturing the whole activity descriptor (e.g., *trying michelin* instead of *trying michelin starred sushi place*), or inclusion of extraneous text (e.g., *catching pokemon today*). False positives only account for 16% errors and are mostly caused by incorrect part of speech (POS) tagging due to limited context, which leads to the confusion of noun phrases with noun+verb phrases (e.g., *driving distance*).

3.2.4 Semantic Location Extraction. All tweets in our dataset come from the Foursquare mobile application and contain metadata about users' check-ins. We leverage timestamps of check-ins and their location, which, rather than by exact coordinates, are represented by the venue category (e.g., Grocery Store). The categories reflect semantic function of places [3, 39] and also increase generalizibility of our spatiotemporal profiles.

3.3 Results of Activity Extraction

We extracted 226,859 spatiotemporally anchored activities from which 101,869 are unique instances. The number of observations per activity follows a long-tail distribution with 82% of activities appearing only once in the whole dataset and only 2.2% of activities that are repeated ten or more times. These activities were reported by 33,116 users from which 62% performed more than one activity, though only 5% of users are associated with 25 or more activity records. The complexity and the abstraction level of extracted activities vary from very short and general (e.g., *running*) to lengthy and specific (e.g., *practicing egg drop soup delivery skill*). The most selective part of the extraction pipeline is the '*-ing*' filtering step which removes 71.5% of tweets. We would like to stress that our goal in this work is not to extract every activity mentioned in Twitter (high recall); rather we aim for precise extraction of activities that people are engaged in at the time of reporting. Also, we realize that people have individual preferences for when and where they tweet about which activities; however, in aggregate, we demonstrate in our evaluation that we collect a diverse sample that allows us to build reliable models. To aid reproducibility, the Appendix discusses the details of the extraction steps.

3.4 Evaluation: Comparison with ATUS

A primary research question, when deciding to work with the Twitter dataset, is whether and to which degree the microblog posts with their metadata can be trusted to reflect the true relationship between spatiotemporal context and each activity that is found there. We evaluated this by comparing the temporal profiles of certain Twitter activities with results of a large-scale survey of people's time use (ATUS) [33]. This comparison was designed to see if the Twitter profiles were relatively close to ground truth, helping to justify our deeper analysis in the remainder of the paper. ATUS (*American Time Use Survey*), a dataset which we use as our

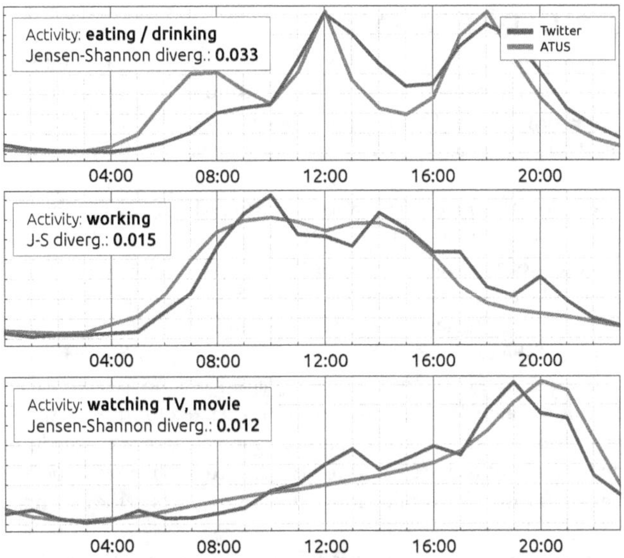

Figure 2: Temporal profiles (normalized) of selected activities in ATUS (red) and Twitter (blue) and their divergence.

ground truth, is an ongoing effort of the U.S. Census Bureau to collect detailed information about the ways Americans spend their time. The survey is conducted by telephone, and participants are asked to describe their day, locations they visited (26 categories), and their activities (17/105/438 categories in top 3 levels). In our study, we used data spanning from 2003 to 2015 which contain 3.35M observations from 170, 842 participants.

Evaluation method. The difference in activity vocabularies between ATUS (limited hierarchy) and Twitter (open vocabulary) poses a challenge for direct comparison of counterpart activities. Therefore, we propose a set of evaluation approaches from the perspective of activities or locations that can be aligned manually in a straightforward way. The evaluation methods are:

A) Quantitative (activity) - Temporal profiles of selected activities are constructed using data from both datasets and the difference between two distributions is computed;

B) Qualitative (activity) - Typical activity locations in both datasets are compared and followed by discussion of differences;

C) Quantitative (location) - We compare temporal profiles of locations, for which all underlying activities are aggregated.

Table 1: Activity comparison.

ATUS	Kahneman	Twitter (example)	D_{JS}
Socializing and communicating	*Socializing*	*visiting friend, …*	0.008
Television and movies	*Watching TV*	*seeing movie, …*	0.012
Relaxing, thinking	*Housework*	*listening to music, …*	0.014
Work, main job	*Working*	*doing work, …*	0.015
Shopping (exc. groceries/gas/food)	*Shopping*	*doing shopping, …*	0.016
Eating and drinking	*Eating*	*eating lunch, …*	0.033
Interior cleaning	*Housework*	*doing laundry, …*	0.041
Travel related to working	*Commuting*	*heading to work, …*	0.048
Physical care for children	*Taking care of ch.*	*picking up baby, …*	0.130
Food and drink preparation	*Preparing food*	*making dinner, …*	0.134

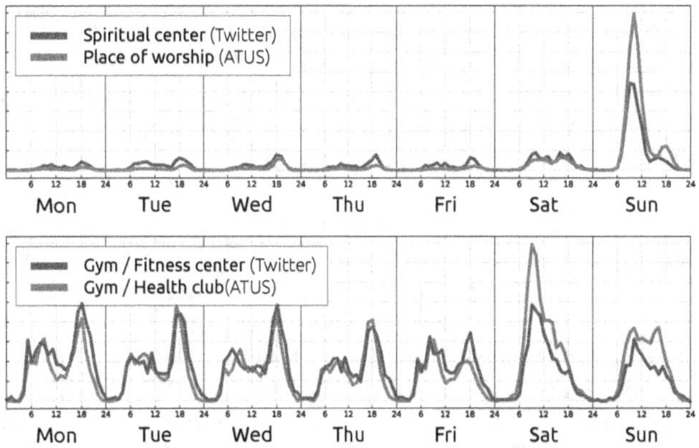

Figure 3: Weekly activity distributions at *Spiritual center/Place of worship* and *Gym* according to Twitter and ATUS data. High correlation confirms credibility of Twitter as a source of self-reported activities.

A. Activity comparison (quantitative). We compared the 15 most frequent activities [5] reported by ATUS survey participants with a study by Kahneman et al. [20] and identified 10 common activities (Table 1). In order to map ATUS activities to those from Twitter, two human assessors manually judged semantic similarity of the top 500 most frequent Twitter activities and, when possible, established a link to the corresponding ATUS activity (inter-rater agreement as Cohen's kappa: $\kappa = 0.79$). To quantify the similarity of the ATUS activities with their Twitter counterparts, we compare the temporal profiles of these activities and express the difference by calculating their Jensen-Shannon divergence (D_{JS}). The results indicate very high similarity for six activities ($D_{JS} \leq 0.035$), high similarity for two ($D_{JS} \approx 0.05$), and low for another two activities ($D_{JS} \geq 0.13$). The weaker correlation in the last two cases (i.e., *'Food and drink preparation'*, *'Physical care for children'*) is caused by relatively lower popularity of Twitter posts containing reference to these activities and consequent low diversity of related activities in rather limited test selection (i.e., 500 most frequent Twitter activities). For instance, all activities in the test set related to food preparation are concerned with dinner, which makes the profile skewed towards later time of the day.

With ATUS as ground truth, this comparison gives us confidence that reported activities in Twitter tend to reflect the actual timing of real activities. In Fig. 2, we depict evaluation plots of the three most frequent ATUS activities: (*'Eating and Drinking'*, *'Work, main job'*, and *'Television and movies'*), which amount for 34% of all activities in ATUS and on average occupy up to 11.4h of one's day [20].

B. Activity comparison (qualitative). Both activities extracted from Twitter and activities reported by participants of the survey are classified into categories of locations (e.g., spiritual center, gym). That leads us to study the typical locations of selected activities, and we find some interesting insights. The characteristic locations of majority of activities are very similar in both datasets. For instance, the activity of *'commuting'* happens in various means of transport (train, car, etc.) in both datasets; *'working'* mostly falls into the category of *respondent's workplace* in ATUS, in Twitter it is *professional*

[5] We exclude *'sleeping'* since it is impossible to tweet about it while performing it.

& other places (which can be considered an equivalent location). To highlight some differences, we observe that some daily activities that often take place at home according to ATUS (*'watching a movie'*, *'eating and drinking'*) are more likely to be tweeted about when performed at out-of-home places (i.e., cinema, restaurant).

C. Location comparison (quantitative). Apart from individual activity comparison, we construct aggregated temporal profiles for all underlying activities that happen at a location. Given that each activity has a specific temporal profile, potential differences of these aggregates in ATUS and Twitter could indicate bias of certain activities that are more or less talked about on Twitter. Despite non-compatible categorization systems of locations in ATUS and Foursquare (via Twitter), we were able to find location equivalents to 11 (out of 26) ATUS categories in Foursquare. We rendered daily and weekly temporal profiles of the location activity aggregates and in Fig. 3, on two examples, we demonstrate good alignment of extracted data with the ground truth. In Fig. 4, we use the weekly profiles to calculate the distribution divergence (D_{JS}) across all 11 location categories, and present the results in the form of a matrix heatmap. The low D_{JS} values on the diagonal indicate positive correlation of aggregated location profiles in Twitter (y-axis) and ATUS locations (x-axis).

The evaluation, in which we compared the temporal and spatial aspects of activities from Twitter and ATUS, suggests a high correlation between the extracted activities and the ground truth in both dimensions. Based on these findings, we conclude that with respect to time and location the activities extracted from Twitter using the proposed techniques are a good representative of people's true activity behavior.

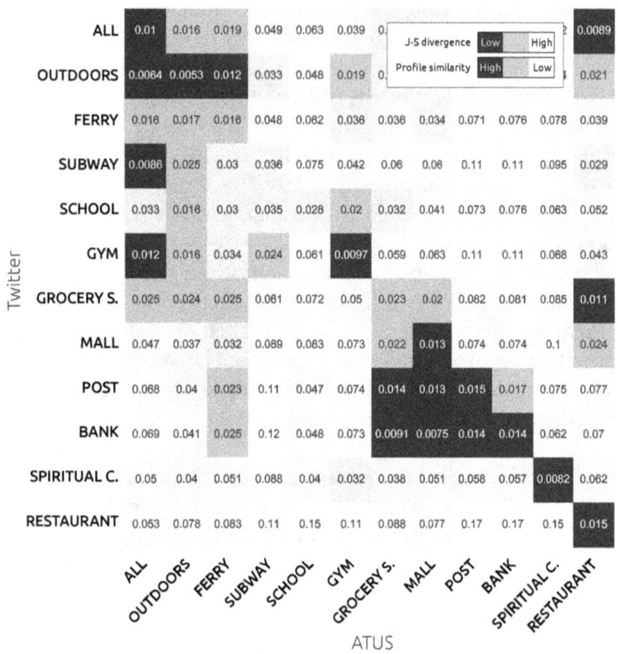

Figure 4: Comparison of 11 counterpart ATUS and Twitter top-level location categories. The difference is expressed as Jensen-Shannon divergence between temporal profiles of location activity aggregates.

4 ACTIVITY ANALYSIS

Assured that Twitter indeed provides a reliable window into activity spatiotemporal profiles, in this section, we address *RQ2* by inspecting what activities are the ones that people report on the most and where and when they tend to happen.

What are the most common activities? Being aware that social networks are subject to self-censorship [26], we studied which are the most common activities that people are willing to tweet about. The most common head phrase is, by a large margin, the verb *'getting.'* This phenomenon can be explained by the polymorphous nature of the verb: it is a constituent of many verbal constructions with a range of different meanings (*getting hair done, getting food, getting up*, etc.). We identified activities related to transportation (e.g., *heading home*), eating and drinking (e.g, *having lunch*) or entertainment (e.g., *celebrating birthday*) to be the most reported ones on Twitter. We list the most common activities in the appendix.

Where do activities take place? Spatially, activities from Twitter are unevenly distributed into location categories with strong bias towards food- or shop-related venues. An underrepresented category of locations are event venues (e.g, *conference room*). The relation between some activities and certain locations is very strong. The conditional probability of *cutting hair* being done in *Salon / Barbershop*, *having ramen* in *Asian Restaurant* or *worshiping* in *Spiritual Center* is 1.0 in all these cases. (We chose activities with 10+ observations.) On the other side of the probability spectrum we find activities such as *killing time* which is almost equally likely to happen in 120 different locations including *Beach, Winery, Zoo, Racetrack*, and *Bookstore.*

When do activities happen? Inspired by the finding of Noulas et al. [30], we inspected the aggregated temporal dynamics of users' activity patterns over the course of a day and a week (Fig. 5). We find that the most active days are Saturday and Friday, while Monday to Wednesday are almost equally quiet. We split the day into four habitual parts: morning (6:00-12:00), afternoon (12:00-18:00), evening (18:00-24:00) and night (00:00-6:00) to find that 43% of activities are reported during the afternoon, and only less than 3% reported at night. Further, when analyzing the temporal scope of various activities individually, we generate profiles of these activities to visually examine their temporal footprints, e.g., see Fig. 1. The plot depicts a sample of temporal distributions that belong to eleven activities, which are selected so that their peak hours are spread out over the timespan of a day. It should be mentioned that the underlying data originate in the US and culture dissimilarities in other regions may lead to different activity profiles.

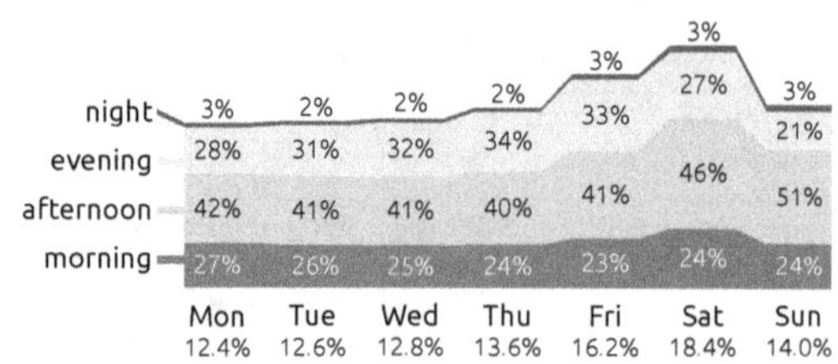

Figure 5: Frequency of reported activities during four periods of day and on different days of the week.

The analysis revealed interesting facts: 1) the distributions of activities and their locations are top-heavy with only a fraction of activities that re-appear frequently, 2) people often report on activities related to their journey, eating/drinking or entertainment, which were recognized as enjoyable activities according to Kahneman et al. [20], and, 3) the most active reporting periods are Friday-Saturday afternoons (which might be partially influenced by the *"Twitter social jet lag"* [24]).

5 PREDICTIONS

The previous section uncovered patterns of human activities. Referring back to our main task, which is to propose models that embrace human activity as a contextual feature, we go on and use the newly acquired insights in two prediction tasks, respectively:

RQ3 Given an activity of a person (and possibly other context), can we predict where it is likely to happen?

RQ4 Given a location (and possibly other context), can we predict what activities people will engage in there?

5.1 Methods

We cast each prediction task in this paper as a ranking problem, where a list of items i is ordered by a ranking score S_i, which reflects its probability $P(i|c)$ of being relevant to a given context c.

In RQ3, the task is to return a ranked list of top- and/or second-level location categories given a full activity and other relevant context on the input. The ranking order reflects the probability of the activity taking place at the location. We denote this model as ***activity-to-location*** (A2L). The problem in RQ4 is reversed, i.e., given a top- or second-level location category (and other relevant context), the goal is to rank activities according to the likelihood of them happening at the given location. We denote this model as ***location-to-activity*** (L2A).

Evaluation metrics. We are primarily focused on precision of our predictions in this work; therefore, we use traditional binary-relevance ranking metrics: mean reciprocal rank (MRR) and precision at a cut-off position $P@k$. We evaluate results for $k = \{1, 3\}$.

Dataset. For the experiments, we chronologically split the Twitter sample of more than $6.5M$ tweets into an initial 90% of training data from the beginning (D_{TR}) and 10% of evaluation data (D_{EV}).

5.2 Baseline

An intuitive and strong baseline ranks items according to their conditional probability computed from the training dataset D_{TR}. In the ***activity-to-location*** task, the probability $P(l|a)$ of location l is proportional to the number of cases the activity a is observed at location l in the training dataset D_{TR}. In ***location-to-activity***, activities are ranked according to the probability $P(a|l)$, which is given by the frequency of activity a at given location l. We discovered that time, and especially the *period of day*, is a strong predictor. Therefore, we include another baseline, BL-*temp*, where the probability is also conditioned on the period of day t, i.e., $P(l|a, t)$ or $P(a|l, t)$.

5.3 Predictive Approach

We operate with a diverse set of features, which, when combined, generate a long feature vector with binary, numerical ($x \in (0, 1) \subset \mathbb{R}$) or categorical values. Below, we discribe their types and, in Table 2, their usage. Ensemble models have proven to be robust and well-performing. Considering their ability to handle large feature spaces with categorical values, we opted for a random forests classifier as the machine learning algorithm of choice.

Textual features. We extract unigrams from activity surface forms and transform them into a feature matrix. Weights of the terms in the matrix are calculated using Tf-Idf to ensure higher values of informative terms.

Temporal features are inferred from the activity timestamp (local time). We extract hour of day (0-23), part of the day as in Section 4, day of week, month, and timezone.

Spatial / Activity prior features. Spatial prior features capture the prior probability of top- and second-level location categories in the training dataset for a given activity a. The activity prior feature contains the prior probability of activities given a top- or second-level location category.

Personal features encode a user's past behavior as observed in the training dataset. In *RQ*3, the behavior is represented by a feature vector that consists of binary flags indicating activities that user performed in the past. In *RQ*4, analogously, the sparse vector marks locations previously visited by the user.

Table 2: Overview of features and their usage in *activity-to-location* (A2L) and *location-to-activity* (L2A) models.

Feature	Feature type	Value type	*A2L*	*L2A*
Activity descriptor unigrams	*Textual*	*Numerical*	✓	
Hour of day	*Temporal*	*Categorical*	✓	✓
Period of day	*Temporal*	*Categorical*	✓	✓
Day of week	*Temporal*	*Categorical*	✓	✓
Month of year	*Temporal*	*Categorical*	✓	✓
Timezone id	*Temporal*	*Categorical*	✓	✓
General location category prior	*Spatial prior*	*Numerical*	✓	
General activity prior	*Activity prior*	*Numerical*		✓
User's location category prior	*Personal*	*Binary*	✓	
User's activity prior	*Personal*	*Binary*		✓

5.4 Experimental Setup

We compare our models with all features (*All*) against the baselines (*BL*). In addition to that, we investigate the influence of types of feature sets by applying a leave-one-out strategy. Specifically, we train with all feature sets except one: activity textual features (*w/o Text.*), temporal features (*w/o Temp.*), prior features (spatial in *RQ*3 (*w/o Spat.*), activity in *RQ*4 (*w/o Act.*)), or personal features (*w/o Pers.*). For brevity, we only display the feature set analysis for one of the datasets (H), however, the pattern is similar in all other cases.

We observed that number of records per user, activity or category (entities) follows the power-law distribution. In order to mitigate data sparsity and study its influence on prediction performance, we propose three filtering approaches. The most aggressive strategy only keeps the *head* (H) of the dataset, i.e., the 100 most frequent users, 20 categories and 100 activities. The more relaxed variants expand the data with the *body* (H+B): 1000 most frequent users, 50 categories and 500 activities; and the *tail* fraction (H+B+T) of the dataset: 5000 most frequent users, 100 categories and 1000 activities.

Table 3: Prediction results of *activity-to-location* model.

Data	Model	MRR	Impr.	P@1	Impr.	P@3	Impr.
H	BL	0.59		0.45		0.68	
	All	**0.70**	**18.6%**	**0.54**	**20.4%**	**0.82**	**20.9%**
	w/o Text.	0.62	4.8%	0.45	0.4%	0.72	5.9%
	w/o Temp.	0.39	-33.2%	0.16	-63.6%	0.49	-27.9%
	w/o Spat.	0.61	3.6%	0.44	-2.7%	0.71	4.7%
	w/o Pers.	0.52	-12.4%	0.32	-29.8%	0.65	-5.0%
H+B	BL	0.47		0.34		0.53	
	All	**0.59**	**26.2%**	**0.44**	**29.7%**	**0.66**	**23.5%**
H+B+T	BL	0.43		0.31		0.49	
	All	**0.52**	**21.3%**	**0.37**	**20.6%**	**0.57**	**16.9%**

Table 4: Prediction results of *location-to-activity* model.

Data	Model	MRR	Impr.	P@1	Impr.	P@3	Impr.
H	BL-*temp*	0.34		0.21		0.42	
	All	**0.45**	**32.8%**	**0.36**	**70.6%**	**0.53**	**26.5%**
	w/o Temp.	0.41	20.2%	0.29	37.4%	0.48	14.5%
	w/o Act.	0.31	-10.3%	0.22	13.7%	0.35	-15.6%
	w/o Pers.	0.28	-17.0%	0.18	-12.8%	0.34	-17.8%
H+B	BL-*temp*	0.25		0.15		0.27	
	All	**0.32**	**29.2%**	**0.25**	**66.7%**	**0.37**	**39.6%**
H+B+T	BL-*temp*	0.21		0.13		0.23	
	All	**0.23**	**9.9%**	**0.18**	**41.5%**	**0.26**	**13.00%**

5.5 Results and Discussion

Tables 3 and 4 present prediction results of *activity-to-location* and *location-to-activity* models, respectively. Location in both cases refers to the second-level categories, which offer an order of magnitude more location categories than the top-level categories. The tables contain results for each filtering strategy ('Data' column) and compare values with the best-performing baseline (BL or BL-*temp*).

The evaluation results in Table 3 show the superiority of the ***activity-to-location*** model over the baseline by up to 26.2% in MRR for the H+B dataset. The significant improvement in MRR is accompanied by precision increase at the cut-off points of 1 and 3 by up to 29.7% and 23.5%, respectively. We see that the model benefits the most from the temporal features *(Temp.)*, suggesting that given we know which activity a person is occupied with, her location strongly depends on time. The *textual features (Text.)*, apart from enhancing the results, ensure generalizability of the model to unseen activities by leveraging prior knowledge about linguistically similar activities.

The task of predicting activity for a given location (***location-to-activity*** model) is a relatively more difficult problem, which is noticeable from the baseline (BL-*temp*) numbers in Table 4. Our technique, however, consistently outperforms the strongest baseline, achieving performance improvement of up to 32.8% in MRR and 70.6% and 39.6% in P@1 and P@3, respectively. While user's historical data *(Pers.)* have a significant impact on the predictive performance in both tasks, it is the activity prediction where knowing user's past behavior (i.e., past activities at given location) is crucial. We observed that as the datasets get sparser, the benefit of personal data grows stronger.

Strengths. Some human activities tend to happen at a very limited number of location types irrespective of personal preferences (*depositing check* - Bank, *waiting to board a flight* - Airport), and even simple modeling technique can capture these regularities. On the other end of the spectrum lie activities that are very general and whose entropy w.r.t. location categories is high, e.g., *'enjoying night'* that was observed 45 times in 21 distinct categories. The benefit of our models over probabilistic baselines is in their ability to handle activities whose typical location changes in time and is rather user-specific. We illustrate the temporal dependence of an activity on *'dropping off kid'* in Figure 6. We see how the probability of activity location changes over the course of a day (Thu). The probabilities depend on historical behavior of each user, and, in this particular case, our model improves the MRR by 0.51.

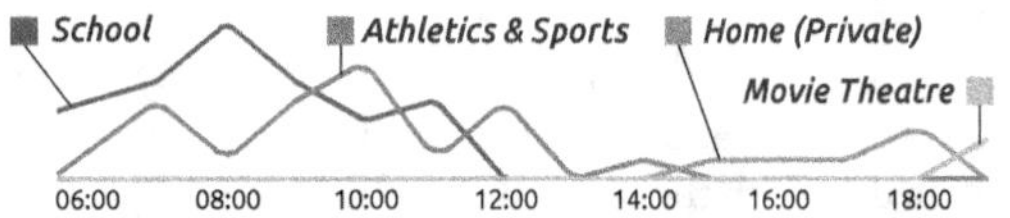

Figure 6: Relative location probabilities changing in time for '*dropping off kid*' activity as returned by our model.

Implications. The negative correlation between prediction performance and data sparsity confirms our hypothesis that restriction of the dataset to the most frequent entities leads to more accurate predictions. The obvious explanation is that the task becomes relatively simpler, since the number of classes drops. We note that the ultimate goal is to support prediction into a rich open-set of activities and, while our model performs well there, it leaves a research opportunity for further improvements that generalize to the tail.

6 CONCLUSIONS AND FUTURE WORK

Human activity is clearly one of the major drivers that influence information needs of people. In this paper, we have shown that large amounts of open-domain activities are self-reported by users in their social media posts. While not all activities that people perform are tweeted about (due to self-censorship [31]), by focusing on extraction of ongoing activities present on Twitter, we are able to reliably model spatial and temporal aspects of thousands of activities that do get published. We demonstrate reliability by contrasting the extracted spatiotemporal profiles with real-life distributions captured in an independent large-scale survey of people's daily routines, ATUS. Our work was primarily motivated by two context-aware applications (i.e., reminder and recommender), which would greatly benefit from reliable activity–location prediction models. To address that, we pose two tasks: 1) prediction of locations for a given activity and 2) prediction of activities for a given location. In both of them, a proposed model outperforms a strong frequency-based baseline by a significant margin of 26.2% and 32.8% MRR improvement, in respective order.

In order to preserve variety in this initial study, we did not consider resolution of synonym activities, nor did we cluster activities into categories. Future work could try to increase the robustness of learned models by learning an embedding of activities to support synonymy. Another interesting direction for follow-up research, since we now have a good understanding of spatiotemporal patterns of various activities, would be to use them to identify web searches that are related to these activities.

To conclude, this work provides a significant step toward a probabilistic model of common-sense that enables context-aware systems to reason about the connections between location, time, and natural language descriptions of activity. Furthermore, there is an exciting opportunity for further research given both the public nature of the data source and unexplored modeling choices.

REFERENCES

[1] Gediminas Adomavicius and Alexander Tuzhilin. 2015. Context-aware recommender systems. In *Recommender systems handbook*. Springer, 191–226. https://doi.org/10.1145/1454008.1454068

[2] Marco Aurelio Beber, Carlos Andres Ferrero, Renato Fileto, and Vania Bogorny. 2016. Towards activity recognition in moving object trajectories from Twitter data. In *Proc. of GeoInfo*. 68–79.

[3] Jan R Benetka, Krisztian Balog, and Kjetil Nørvåg. 2017. Anticipating Information Needs Based on Check-in Activity. In *Proc. of WSDM*. https://doi.org/10.1145/3018661.3018679

[4] Paul N Bennett, Filip Radlinski, Ryen W White, and Emine Yilmaz. 2011. Inferring and using location metadata to personalize web search. In *Proc. in SIGIR*. ACM, 135–144. https://doi.org/10.1145/2009916.2009938

[5] Frank R Bentley and Crysta J Metcalf. 2008. Location and activity sharing in everyday mobile communication. In *CHI Extended Abstracts*. ACM, 2453–2462. https://doi.org/10.1145/1358628.1358702

[6] Kalina Bontcheva, Leon Derczynski, Adam Funk, Mark A. Greenwood, Diana Maynard, and Niraj Aswani. 2013. TwitIE: An Open-Source Information Extraction Pipeline for Microblog Text. In *Proc. of RANLP*. Association for Computational Linguistics.

[7] AJ Bernheim Brush, John Krumm, James Scott, and T Scott Saponas. 2011. Recognizing activities from mobile sensor data: Challenges and opportunities. In *Proc. of Ubicomp*.

[8] Liming Chen, Jesse Hoey, Chris D Nugent, Diane J Cook, and Zhiwen Yu. 2012. Sensor-based activity recognition. *IEEE Trans. on SMC* 42, 6 (2012), 790–808. https://doi.org/10.1109/TSMCC.2012.2198883

[9] Karen Church and Barry Smyth. 2009. Understanding the intent behind mobile information needs. In *Proc. of IUI*. ACM, 247–256. https://doi.org/10.1145/1502650.1502686

[10] David Dearman, Timothy Sohn, and Khai N Truong. 2011. Opportunities exist: continuous discovery of places to perform activities. In *Proc. of CHI*. ACM, 2429–2438. https://doi.org/10.1145/1978942.1979297

[11] David Dearman and Khai N Truong. 2010. Identifying the activities supported by locations with community-authored content. In *Proc. of Ubicomp*. ACM, 23–32. https://doi.org/10.1145/1864349.1864354

[12] David Graus, Paul N Bennett, Ryen W White, and Eric Horvitz. 2016. Analyzing and Predicting Task Reminders. In *Proc. of UMAP*. ACM, 7–15. https://doi.org/10.1145/2930238.2930239

[13] Nir Grinberg, Mor Naaman, Blake Shaw, and Gilad Lotan. 2013. Extracting Diurnal Patterns of Real World Activity from Social Media. In *Proc. of ICWSM*.

[14] Bo Han and Timothy Baldwin. 2011. Lexical normalisation of short text messages: Makn sens a# twitter. In *Proc. of HLT*. Association for Computational Linguistics, 368–378.

[15] Annika M Hinze, Carole Chang, and David M Nichols. 2010. Contextual queries express mobile information needs. In *Proc. of MobileHCI*. ACM, 327–336. https://doi.org/10.1145/1851600.1851658

[16] Nabil Hossain, Tianran Hu, Roghayeh Feizi, Ann Marie White, Jiebo Luo, and Henry Kautz. 2016. Inferring fine-grained details on user activities and home location from social media: Detecting drinking-while-tweeting patterns in communities. *arXiv preprint arXiv:1603.03181* (2016).

[17] Giovanni Iachello, Ian Smith, Sunny Consolvo, Gregory Abowd, Jeff Hughes, James Howard, Fred Potter, James Scott, Timothy Sohn, Jeffrey Hightower, et al. 2005. Control, deception, and communication: Evaluating the deployment of a location-enhanced messaging service. *Proc. of UbiComp*, 903–903. https://doi.org/10.1007/11551201_13

[18] Akshay Java, Xiaodan Song, Tim Finin, and Belle Tseng. 2009. Why we twitter: An analysis of a microblogging community. *Advances in Web Mining and Web Usage Analysis* (2009), 118–138. https://doi.org/10.1145/1348549.1348556

[19] F Thomas Juster and Frank P Stafford. 1985. *Time, goods, and well-being.*

[20] Daniel Kahneman, Alan B Krueger, David A Schkade, Norbert Schwarz, and Arthur A Stone. 2004. A survey method for characterizing daily life experience: The day reconstruction method. *Science* 306, 5702 (2004), 1776–1780. https://doi.org/10.1126/science.1103572

[21] Shian-Ru Ke, Hoang Le Uyen Thuc, Yong-Jin Lee, Jenq-Neng Hwang, Jang-Hee Yoo, and Kyoung-Ho Choi. 2013. A review on video-based human activity recognition. *Computers* 2, 2 (2013), 88–131. https://doi.org/10.3390/computers2020088

[22] John Krumm, Dany Rouhana, and Ming-Wei Chang. 2015. Placer++: Semantic place labels beyond the visit. In *Proc. of PerCom*. IEEE, 11–19. https://doi.org/10.1109/PERCOM.2015.7146504

[23] Michael G Lamming and William M Newman. 1992. Activity-based Information Retrieval: Technology in Support of Personal Memory. In *IFIP Congress (3)*, Vol. 14. 68–81.

[24] Eugene Leypunskiy, Emre Kıcıman, Mili Shah, Olivia J Walch, Andrey Rzhetsky, Aaron R Dinner, and Michael J Rust. 2018. Geographically Resolved Rhythms in Twitter Use Reveal Social Pressures on Daily Activity Patterns. *Current Biology* 28, 23 (2018), 3763–3775. https://doi.org/10.1016/j.cub.2018.10.016

[25] Mitchell P Marcus, Mary Ann Marcinkiewicz, and Beatrice Santorini. 1993. Building a large annotated corpus of English: The Penn Treebank. *Computational linguistics* 19, 2 (1993), 313–330.

[26] Alice E Marwick and Danah Boyd. 2011. I tweet honestly, I tweet passionately: Twitter users, context collapse, and the imagined audience. *New media & society* 13, 1 (2011), 114–133. https://doi.org/10.1177/1461444810365313

[27] Sahisnu Mazumder, Dhaval Patel, and Sameep Mehta. 2014. Actminer: Discovering location-specific activities from community-authored reviews. In *Proc. of DaWaK*. Springer, 332–344. https://doi.org/10.1007/978-3-319-10160-6_30

[28] Joan Melià-Seguí, Rui Zhang, Eugene Bart, Bob Price, and Oliver Brdiczka. 2012. Activity duration analysis for context-aware services using foursquare check-ins. In *Proc. of Self-IoT*. ACM, 13–18. https://doi.org/10.1145/2378023.2378027

[29] Mor Naaman, Jeffrey Boase, and Chih-Hui Lai. 2010. Is it really about me?: message content in social awareness streams. In *Proc. of CSCW*. ACM, 189–192.

[30] Anastasios Noulas, Salvatore Scellato, Cecilia Mascolo, and Massimiliano Pontil. 2011. An Empirical Study of Geographic User Activity Patterns in Foursquare. In *Proc. of ICWSM*.

[31] Alexandra Olteanu, Emre Kiciman, and Carlos Castillo. 2018. A Critical Review of Online Social Data: Biases, Methodological Pitfalls, and Ethical Boundaries. In *Proc. of WSDM*. 785–786. https://doi.org/10.1145/3159652.3162004

[32] Xin Rong, Adam Fourney, Robin N Brewer, Meredith Ringel Morris, and Paul N Bennett. 2017. Managing Uncertainty in Time Expressions for Virtual Assistants. In *Proc. of CHI*. ACM, 568–579. https://doi.org/10.1145/3025453.3025674

[33] Kristina J Shelley. 2005. Developing the American time use survey activity classification system. *Monthly Lab. Rev.* 128 (2005), 3.

[34] Timothy Sohn, Kevin A Li, William G Griswold, and James D Hollan. 2008. A diary study of mobile information needs. In *Proc. of CHI*. https://doi.org/10.1145/1357054.1357125

[35] Yangqiu Song, Zhengdong Lu, Cane Wing-ki Leung, and Qiang Yang. 2013. Collaborative boosting for activity classification in microblogs. In *Proc. of SIGKDD*. ACM, 482–490. https://doi.org/10.1145/2487575.2487661

[36] Jaime Teevan, Amy Karlson, Shahriyar Amini, AJ Bernheim Brush, and John Krumm. 2011. Understanding the importance of location, time, and people in mobile local search behavior. In *Proc. of MobileHCI*. ACM, 77–80. https://doi.org/10.1145/2037373.2037386

[37] Sergey Volokhin and Eugene Agichtein. 2018. Understanding Music Listening Intents During Daily Activities with Implications for Contextual Music Recommendation. In *CHIIR*. https://doi.org/10.1145/3176349.3176885

[38] Wouter Weerkamp, Maarten De Rijke, et al. 2012. Activity prediction: A twitter-based exploration. In *Proc. of TAIA*.

[39] Dingqi Yang, Daqing Zhang, Vincent W. Zheng, and Zhiyong Yu. 2015. Modeling User Activity Preference by Leveraging User Spatial Temporal Characteristics in LBSNs. *IEEE Trans. on SMC* 45, 1 (2015), 129–142. https://doi.org/10.1109/TSMC.2014.2327053

[40] Chao Zhang, Mengxiong Liu, Zhengchao Liu, Carl Yang, Luming Zhang, and Jiawei Han. 2018. Spatiotemporal Activity Modeling Under Data Scarcity: A Graph-Regularized Cross-Modal Embedding Approach. AAAI.

[41] Chao Zhang, Keyang Zhang, Quan Yuan, Fangbo Tao, Luming Zhang, Tim Hanratty, and Jiawei Han. 2017. React: Online multimodal embedding for recency-aware spatiotemporal activity modeling. In *SIGIR*. https://doi.org/10.1145/3077136.3080814

[42] Zack Zhu, Ulf Blanke, and Gerhard Tröster. 2016. Recognizing composite daily activities from crowd-labelled social media data. *Pervasive and Mobile Computing* 26 (2016), 103–120. https://doi.org/10.1016/j.pmcj.2015.10.007

A APPENDIX

A.1 Activity Phrases

We computed the most common activity head phrases found in Twitter, including their relative frequencies and some example noun phrases for each one, shown in Table A1. We see that each verb phrase can introduce a variety of activities, whose ambiguity is only resolved by the following noun phrase.

Table A1: Most common activity head phrases with a sample of related common full activities.

#	Activity head phrase Verb phrase	 Freq.	Full activity Noun phrases (most common)
1.	*getting*	11.8%	...*hair (done), stuff, lunch, food, gas,* ...
2.	*picking up*	5.6%	...*dinner, lunch, thing, med, car, food, load,* ...
3.	*having*	4.3%	...*lunch, dinner, fun, breakfast, time, drink,* ...
4.	*watching*	3.6%	...*game, movie, TV, football, girl, fireworks,* ...
5.	*going*	3.3%	...*home, to be day, to bed, to work, to gym,* ...
6.	*trying*	3.3%	...*place, something, out place, spot, out spot,* ...
7.	*celebrating*	2.6%	...*birthday, year, life, day, anniversary, bday,* ...
8.	*heading*	2.5%	...*home, to airport, to work, to bed, downtown,* ...
9.	*checking*	2.3%	...*(out) place, out spot, thing, out location,* ...
10.	*enjoying*	2.2%	...*day, weather, lunch, dinner, time, view,* ...
11.	*taking*	2.2%	...*care, break, advantage, tour, mom, picture,* ...
12.	*doing*	1.9%	...*thing, laundry, work, shopping, something,* ...
13.	*making*	1.7%	...*money, friend, round, time, dinner, progress,* ...
14.	*seeing*	1.6%	...*friend, movie, show, doctor, deadpool, girl,* ...
15.	*grabbing*	1.5%	...*lunch, dinner, bite, breakfast, food, coffee,* ...
16.	*visiting*	1.4%	...*friend, mom, dad, family, grandma, aunt,* ...
17.	*dropping*	1.4%	...*kid, off donation, off car, off load, off passenger,* ...
18.	*eating*	1.4%	...*lunch, dinner, breakfast, food, pizza, supper,* ...
19.	*working*	1.2%	...*today, night, hour, way, prayer, shift,* ...
20.	*starting*	1.2%	...*day, week, weekend, year, morning, trip,* ...
21.	*playing*	0.9%	...*game, pokemon, tune, tourist, music, golf,* ...
22.	*buying*	0.9%	...*stuff, grocery, food, thing, car, book,* ...
23.	*opening*	0.7%	...*day, night, ceremony, weekend, account, session,* ...
24.	*being*	0.7%	...*tourist, home, adult, kid, fatty, friend,* ...
25.	*drinking*	0.6%	...*beer, coffee, wine, water, tea, brew,* ...

A.2 Overview of the Tweet-filtering Process

Filtering tweets down to activity assertions takes 10 steps, as outlined in Table A2. Our goal was to create a precise set of relevant activity tweets, but not to necessarily find all relevant tweets.

A.3 Activity Extraction Grammar

For completeness and reproducibility purposes, we present the complete grammar we used for extraction of *verb+noun* pairs (i.e., <VPNP>) after the text was tokenized and tagged with parts of speech [6]. We refer the reader to the Penn Treebank POS tagset [25] for a full overview of the POS tags.

```
NPS: {<NNS>* <NN>* <POS>? <FW>* <NNS>* <NN>*}
JX:  {<JJ>* <JJS>* <JJR>* <,>?}
NP:  {<DT>? <CD>? <NNP>* <NNPS>* <JX>*
     (<DT> <VBG>)? <CD>? <NPS>}
VP:  {<VBG> <RP>* (<JJ> <TO>)? <TO>? <VB>*}
VPNP:{<VP> <PRP$>* <NP>}
```

For a better idea about how the extraction grammar works, we display a parse tree of an example phrase:

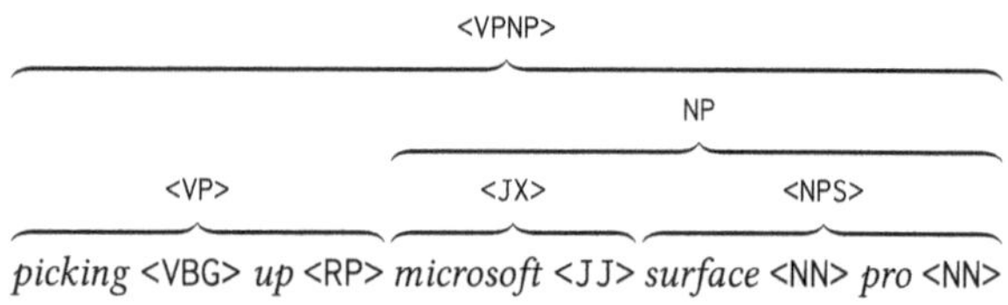

Table A2: Filtering of tweets during the activity extraction process. Along with description of each step, the table displays a number of remaining tweets after the step is performed and the percentage of the original volume of tweets that it represents.

#	Processing step	Number of tweets	Percentage
1.	Tweets from US region (in English) originating from Foursquare app	6 641 503	100%
2.	Removal of duplicate tweets (based on TweetID)	5 845 289	88.0%
3.	Filtering of corrupted records (due to parsing)	5 845 108	88.0%
4.	Filtering for tweets by users with spamScore < .5	5 841 176	87.9%
5.	Filtering for tweets with spamScore < .5	5 788 598	87.2%
6.	Filtering for tweets containing '-ing'	1 044 127	15.7%
8.	Content cleaning for tweets (removal of tweets that become empty after this step)	544 762	8.2%
9.	Duplicate filtering (based on User ID, Text & Category)	518 368	7.8%
10.	Activity extraction (filtering for tweets containing $\geq$ 1 activities)	193 219	2.9%

Understanding Mobile Search Task Relevance and User Behaviour in Context

Mohammad Aliannejadi
Università della Svizzera italiana (USI)
mohammad.alian.nejadi@usi.ch

Morgan Harvey
Northumbria University
morgan.harvey@northumbria.ac.uk

Luca Costa
Università della Svizzera italiana (USI)
luca.costa@usi.ch

Matthew Pointon
Northumbria University
m.pointon@northumbria.ac.uk

Fabio Crestani
Università della Svizzera italiana (USI)
fabio.crestani@usi.ch

ABSTRACT

Improvements in mobile technologies have led to a dramatic change in how and when people access and use information, and is having a profound impact on how users address their daily information needs. Smart phones are rapidly becoming our main method of accessing information and are frequently used to perform "on-the-go" search tasks. As research into information retrieval continues to evolve, evaluating search behaviour in context is relatively new. Previous research has studied the effects of context through either self-reported diary studies or quantitative log analysis; however, neither approach is able to accurately capture context of use at the time of searching.

In this study, we aim to gain a better understanding of task relevance and search behaviour via a task-based user study (n=31) employing a bespoke Android app. The app allowed us to accurately capture the user's context when completing tasks at different times of the day over the period of a week. Through analysis of the collected data, we gain a better understanding of how using smart phones on the go impacts search behaviour, search performance and task relevance and whether or not the actual context is an important factor.

KEYWORDS

mobile search; context; user study; field study

ACM Reference Format:
Mohammad Aliannejadi, Morgan Harvey, Luca Costa, Matthew Pointon, and Fabio Crestani. 2019. Understanding Mobile Search Task Relevance and User Behaviour in Context. In *2019 Conference on Human Information Interaction and Retrieval (CHIIR '19), March 10–14, 2019, Glasgow, United Kingdom.* ACM, New York, NY, USA, 9 pages. https://doi.org/10.1145/3295750.3298923

1 INTRODUCTION

Recent years have seen the ever-increasing use of mobile devices, such as smartphone and tablets, to search the web for information, to the extent that, as of 2016, more searches are performed on mobile devices than on more "traditional" desktop computers [17]. Mobile devices can be readily used in many situations that a desktop computer cannot and, since they are carried constantly on one's person, at most of the times of the day and night. As such, searching is now performed in a larger range of contexts than ever before and, often, contemporaneously with other tasks [19].

Context refers to the the circumstances that form the setting for an event (e.g. location, time or current activity) and can have a profound effect on task relevance and on people's information needs, their search behaviour and ultimate success [10, 21]. Research shows that mobile users search throughout most of the day [34] - often from immediately after waking in the morning until falling asleep at night - and in many different locations [19, 23], including when "on the go" walking down the street, in pubs and restaurants and on public transport.

Previous research has investigated how context affects mobile search task relevance, search behaviour, performance and success typically by means of either self-reported diary studies (e.g. [10, 21, 27]) or through the quantitative analysis of large-scale search logs (e.g. [24]). While both approaches can provide useful insights to better understand and improve mobile search, neither is able to accurately capture the context of the user at the time of searching. Log studies are unable to easily capture user's opinions and feelings regarding the task and self-reported diary studies rely on the ability of the user to accurately and honestly report on the context and on their own searching behaviour.

In this work we seek to gain a more complete understanding of task relevance and search behaviour by means of a task-based user study. Our main research questions, therefore, are:

- **RQ1:** Which kinds of task do people prefer to complete on mobile devices and what impact does time have on this?
- **RQ2:** How does perceived task relevance vary by temporal context and what impact does this variation have on user behaviour and performance?
- **RQ3:** What effect does situational context (activity) have on performance?

To this end, we have developed a bespoke Android application (aka. app), called *Omicron*, that prompts the participants to complete a given search task at a specific time window. The participants were asked to keep Omicron running on their phones for a period of one week. During this week, a background service kept collecting useful information about the participants context as well as their

CHIIR '19, March 10–14, 2019, Glasgow, United Kingdom

ACM ISBN 978-1-4503-6025-8/19/03...$15.00
https://doi.org/10.1145/3295750.3298923

interactions with their device, while searching. We have made Omicron open source to facilitate research on mobile search[1].

The remainder of the paper is structured as follows: In section 2 we consider related work on the topics of query log analysis, mobile search interaction and interaction with mobile devices in general; section 3 describes our research methodology including the user studies we performed; sections 4 describes the results of the user studies in detail; section 5 discusses how the results relate to the existing literature and suggests reasons and intuition behind them; and section 6 concludes the paper with suggestions for potential future work.

2 RELATED WORK

Research on human interaction with mobile devices has been growing in recent years. One of the main focuses in this field of research has been to understand how users interact with search engines on mobile devices [15]. In this section, we start with brief overview of studies that analyse mobile query logs. We then consider those that analyse human interaction when performing mobile search and, finally, we summarise studies that try to understand human interaction with mobile devices thorough various methods of study.

2.1 Query log analysis

Studying large-scale query logs gives researchers crucial information on how people translate their information needs in the form of queries. Kamvar and Baluja [24] conducted one of the earliest studies, analysing a large-scale mobile search query log and found that mobile queries were less diverse than desktop queries and that the distribution over task types varied between desktop and mobile search. Crestani and Du [14] compared spoken and written queries in a lab study with 12 users. They found that spoken queries are longer and closer to natural language. Church et al. [13] analysed six million search queries in a period of one week to understand the click-through rate and found that users generally focused only on the first few search results. Later, Song et al. [34] studied a commercial search log and found significant difference in search patterns dependent on the devices used (between iPhone, iPad, and desktop). For instance, they found that query length on mobile devices were longer. However, they suggested that the query length continues to change and this could be a sign of evolving mobile usage patterns. Also, query categories, usage time, and location of usage were different among different devices. More recently, Guy [18] analysed 500,000 spoken queries from a commercial mobile search app, submitted via a voice interface. The analyses showed that voice queries are longer on average and are closer to natural language. Moreover, they are more focused on multimedia content and require less interaction with the device's touchscreen.

2.2 Mobile search interaction

Understanding human interaction while doing mobile search has become an area of interest since mobile devices are constantly evolving [34]. For this reason, many researchers have conducted user studies to understand various aspects of user behaviour and interaction in relation to mobile search. Sohn et al. [33] conducted a two-week diary study from 20 participants in which they found that contextual features such as activity and time influence 72% of mobile information needs. Kaikkonen [23] asked 390 mobile Internet users to fill an online survey, followed by 23 face-to-face interviews and analysed the impact of location and Web page design on mobile phone browsing behaviour. Similar to the results of [24], the author found that there was a considerable difference between the tasks that mobile and desktop users conducted and that location was an important factor in determining what people wanted to search for using their mobile devices.

Church and Smyth [12] studied the intent behind mobile information needs of twenty users over four weeks via a diary study. They observed significant differences between mobile and desktop information needs. In particular, they found that users had many non-informational information needs, with geographical and personal information needs being popular. Later, Church and Oliver [11] carried out another diary and interview study to understand the shift of mobile information needs at the time of the study. The study was done over a four-week period with 18 active mobile users, discovering that the popularity of stationary mobile Web access was increasing. In another attempt to understand users' information needs, Church et al. [10] conducted a large-scale *snippet-based diary* [8] study with 100 participants throughout a three-month period. This technique allowed users to capture moments in-situ and send them via SMS or MMS. Later, they could access a Web site in which they would review the messages and provide more details about their context. They found significant differences in terms of information needs and how they were addressed depending on user gender, device and location.

Other studies have aimed to analyse touch-screen gestures [35], the effect of searching on-the-go [19], the effect of result snippets [26] as well as users' perception of result usefulness [28]. Williams et al. [35] conducted a lab study with 60 participants, focusing on the analysis of user gesture interactions, such as touch actions, and their relation with good search abandonment on mobile search. They showed that the time spent interacting with answers on a SERP is positively correlated with good abandonment and satisfaction. Through another lab study with 72 participants, Ong et al. [30] observed different patterns in user behaviour while doing mobile and desktop search as the amount of information scent was altered. They found that users' behaviour differ significantly on mobile: for instance, desktop users preferred SERPs with a higher number of relevant search results; whereas this preference was not observed in the mobile environment. Kim et al. [26] conducted a lab study with 24 participants and analysed the effect of snippet size on mobile search time and accuracy. They found that, for informational tasks on mobile devices, longer snippets lead to longer search times with no better search accuracy.

2.3 Situational context

Since mobile devices can be used in many different contexts (e.g. when walking on when on public transport), researchers have considered what impact these situations have on users as they go about various tasks. Bragdon et al. [7] conducted a lab study with 15 participants and found that, in the presence of environmental distractions, touch-screen gesture design leads to significant performance gain and reduced cognitive load, as opposed to soft buttons.

[1]Available at https://github.com/aliannejadi/Omicron

In another lab study of 13 participants, Mizobuchi et al. [29] analysed the speed and accuracy of text input on mobile devices under various situational contexts. They found that texting whilst walking resulted in either a significant decrease in input speed or walking pace, indicating that the mental workload of performing both tasks simultaneously results in the user prioritising one over the other.

Barnard et al. [5] investigated reading comprehension and word search when walking and found that contextual variations can have large effects on user behaviour by impairing performance and increasing user workload. Harvey and Pointon [19] recruited 24 participants and conducted a lab study where they found that fragmented attention of users while searching on-the-go affects their search objective and their perception of task difficult and of their own performance. Hoggan et al. [22] considered the effect of using public transport while performing simple touchscreen typing tasks. Participants performed the tasks on a noisy and bumpy subway and were found to perform progressively worse as the noise level and bumpiness of the ride increased. Harvey and Pointon [20] confirmed this finding in a lab study by simulating noisy everyday situations. In this work participants were asked to complete search tasks and those subjected to the noisy conditions were found to perceive more stress and time pressure, leading to a reduced ability to identify task-relevant documents and a compulsion to finish the search task more quickly.

2.4 Limitations of prior research

Although previous research has studied mobile search and the effect of context in various aspects, it has been done via lab-based, self-reporting and/or diary studies. Each of these study settings introduce specific limitations. In particular, a lab study does not capture users' interactions in-situ, as users' attention varies dramatically depending on their context. Moreover, self-report and diary studies highly depend on participants' willingness to report their context and details of their searches and on their ability to accurately recall and describe their interaction and behaviour. Therefore, many contextual information would be missing in situations when users are distracted. In this study, we perform a task-based field study, aiming to understand the impact of context on users' behaviour in-situ. This enables us to examine users' willingness to complete various mobile search tasks as well as their engagement, interaction, behaviour and performance under various contexts.

3 METHOD

To achieve our aims we conducted a task-based user study in which participants were asked to complete a number of search tasks based on a pre-defined schedule over the period of a week (from Monday through to Sunday). Each participant was randomly assigned to one of three "groups", each of which had a different schedule of times and days when they would be issued with tasks. Table 1 shows an example group schedule. The schedules were designed such that, over the groups, tasks were evenly balanced over all time slots and such that users received a maximum of two task notifications per weekday and only one on Saturday and Sunday. This was to ensure that participants were not overloaded and would thus be more likely to complete all of the tasks when scheduled. The 5 time periods were intended to capture different temporal contexts during the user's day, for example the "Early morning" period (between 8AM and 10AM) should capture the context of the user either preparing to go to work, walking to work or just starting work in the morning.

Table 1: Example group task schedule.

	Mon	Tue	Wed	Thur	Fri	Sat	Sun
Early morning	x			x			
Late morning			x		x		x
Early afternoon	x	x		x			
Late afternoon			x		x		
Evening		x				x	

Participants were required to install Omicron on their mobile phones for the duration of the study. The app alerted users to new tasks, allowed them to complete tasks by searching and indicating relevant documents, presented users with questionnaires and logged interactions and various other sensor data. Data collected included: acceleration and gyroscopic sensor data (which could be used to infer activity), battery level, GPS location and light level. Activities included in vehicle, walking, on bicycle, running and still and were inferred based on accelerometer and gyroscope data by Google's Activity Recognition Transition API [2]. All collected data was automatically uploaded to a secure server for analysis; a data recovery system was implemented to ensure that all recorded data reached the remote server, even if there were times when no connection was available.

The 5 search tasks were designed to conform to the kinds of tasks people have been shown to frequently conduct on mobile devices [9, 34]. Some task types are further delineated into individual "one-shot" tasks (i.e. those that a single user could only be given once) and "multi-use" tasks. The tasks were as follows:

(1) Entertainment (multi-use)
You are feeling a bit bored. Find a film you would like to watch.
(2) Restaurant/local (multi-use)
You are feeling hungry. Find a restaurant you want to go to to eat.
(3) Shopping/cooking (multi-use) Find a recipe you'd like to cook for your dinner tonight.
(4) Information look-up (single-use)
  (a) Find out what the latest headlines are in *XX*.
  (b) You are looking for a new car. Find out what electric vehicles are available in your country.
  (c) You are soon off on holiday to *XX*. Find some fun/interesting things to do there.
(5) Transport (single-use)
  (a) Find a cheap way to get to *XX* from *YY*.
  (b) You fancy some exercise. Find a nice walk from where you are to *XX*.
  (c) You are planning a bike ride around the city. Where can you hire a bike?

Tasks were automatically sent to participants' phones based on their own group-based schedules and in a random order (see Figure 1a). Once a new task was received by the device, a system prompt would appear and persist in the system notification tray

[2]https://developer.android.com/guide/topics/location/transitions

until either actioned or dismissed. Participants could choose to dismiss a task, in which case it would be scheduled to reappear at a later time slot, unless there was another task scheduled for that period, in which case the delayed task would appear directly after the new task. Once assigned a new task, participants were able to use the app's own search interface to search for, read and bookmark relevant documents (see Figure 1b). Search was implemented by using the Bing search API and displayed short snippets for each result. Participants could indicate relevance by tapping star icons next to each search result. Note that participants were given a test task after installing the app and were given a tutorial explaining the interface.

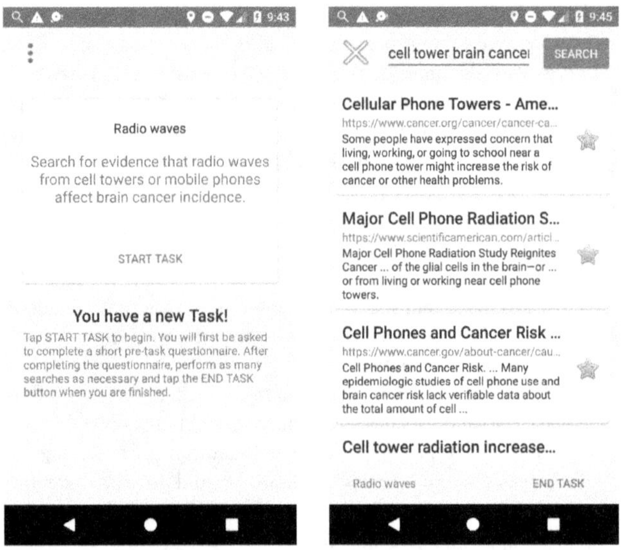

(a) New task notification. (b) App search interface.

Figure 1: Interface screenshots.

Before and after completing each task participants were asked to complete short questionnaires, which appeared automatically within Omicron and were administered by Qualtrics[3]. The pre-task questionnaire asked participants about their prior knowledge of the given task, how difficult they expected it to be, whether or no the task was clear and their level of interest in the task. After completing the task they were asked about how stressed and distracted they were feeling, how difficult they found the task, how relevant the task was the them personally, how relevant it was to the current context (time of day) and how often they perform such a task. Additionally, after installing the app on their device, participants completed a short pre-study questionnaire about their demographic details and mobile device usage.

4 RESULTS

4.1 Participants

Participants were recruited by researchers from both collaborating institutions in Switzerland and the UK. In total 31 people took part in the study, of whom 21 were male and who had a median age range of 25 to 34 years (only 3 participants were younger than this and only 2 older). Participants were generally well-educated - 23% held Bachelor's degrees, 58% Master's and 6% doctorates - and 74% described their English language ability as advanced or better; there were 6 native speakers. 14 participants stated that they most often use their mobile phones to connect to the Internet, 11 use a laptop and 6 most often use a desktop machine. 13 reported using their mobile device between 1 and 2 hours per day on average, 9 used theirs between 2 and 3 hours, and 8 said they use their phone for more than 3 hours per day; only a single participant reported using their device for less than an hour per day.

[3]https://www.qualtrics.com

4.2 Task completion

Each participant was assigned a total of 12 tasks to complete over the week: 2 per weekday and 1 each on Saturday and Sunday. Of the 31 participants, only 5 completed all 12 tasks, with a median completion rate of 9 tasks per participant. Out of a total of 372 assigned tasks, participants rescheduled 123.

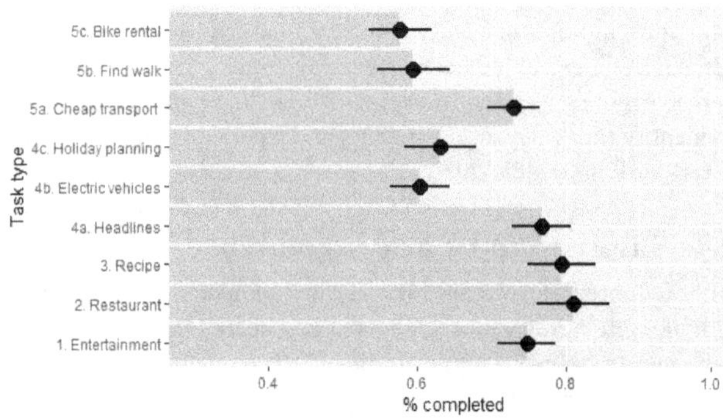

Figure 2: Completion rate by task.

Completion rates varied considerably by task type. Figure 2 shows the completion rate by type of task (and 95% confidence interval[4]; please refer to Section 3 for expanded task descriptions). Although linear modelling did not demonstrate task to be a significant predictor of completion rate, it does appear that the task had some effect. Participants seemed to be more willing to complete tasks relating to food, eating and news headlines (tasks 2, 3 and 4a) than on bike rental and electric cars. This may be because cuisine and news are topics relevant to almost everyone, while cycling and automotive subjects may only be relevant to a smaller number of people. It may also be that people perceived the food-related tasks to be easier to complete or more interesting.

Analysis of the pre-task questionnaire data confirms some of these inferences. There was a moderate positive correlation between average completion rate and the mean response to the question of how knowledgeable participants were about the task ($\rho(9) = 0.536, p = 0.137$), a strongly (and significant) negative correlation with how difficult participants expected the task to be ($\rho(9) = -0.821, p = 0.007$; the more difficult the task was perceived to be, the less likely it was that it would be completed), and a moderate positive correlation between completion rate personal interest in the task ($\rho(9) = 0.379, p = 0.314$).

[4]Estimated via empirical analysis of a Bootstrap sampling with 1,000 resamples.

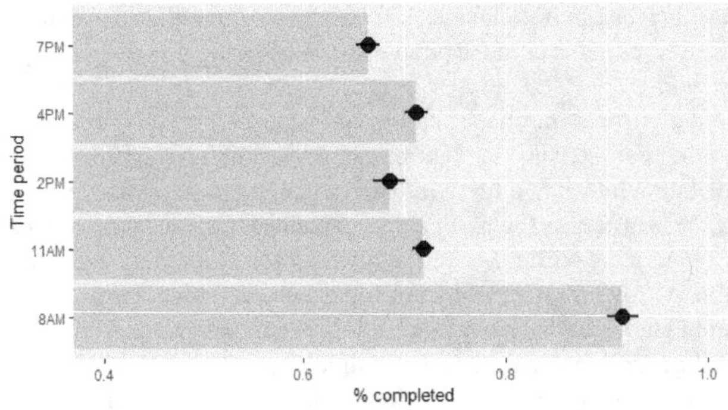

Figure 3: Completion rate by scheduled time period.

Completion rates also varied quite considerably depending on the time period in which the task was given to the user. Figure 3 shows the completion rates and 95% confidence intervals[4] over all participants by time period. This demonstrates that users were much more likely to accept and complete a task in the morning but that this willingness to engage reduced as the day went on with almost half of all tasks assigned at 7PM being ignored. Logistic regression modelling shows that the time period is a significant predictor of completion ($\beta = -.11, t(372) = -3.65, p \ll 0.01$).

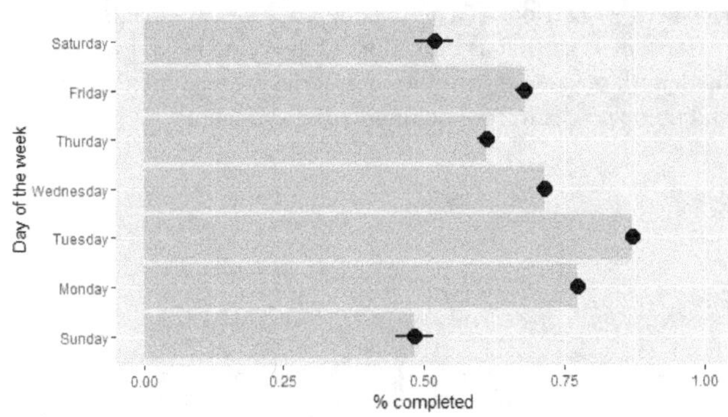

Figure 4: Completion rate by weekday.

As shown in Figure 4, the weekday on which the task was assigned has a large impact on completion rate. Perhaps unsurprisingly, the completion rate is worst on weekends, very good on the first couple of days of the study (i.e. Monday and Tuesday) and middling in later weekdays. The weekday is also a significant predictor of completion rate ($\beta = -.1, t(372) = -1.87, p = 0.031$).

4.3 Pre-task perception

Before completing each task, participants filled in a set of four pre-task questions to gauge their prior knowledge of, and interest in the topic, how difficult they expected the task to be and how clear they felt the task was. Responses to the questions on prior knowledge and difficulty varied little by either weekday or allocation time, although there was a trend of expected difficulty monotonically increasing from a low on Mondays (mean = 1.92) through to a high on Saturdays (mean=2.43). Linear modelling showed the weekday to be a significant predictor of expected difficulty ($\beta = 0.09, t(526) = 3.59, p \ll 0.01$), perhaps suggesting that the cumulative impact of

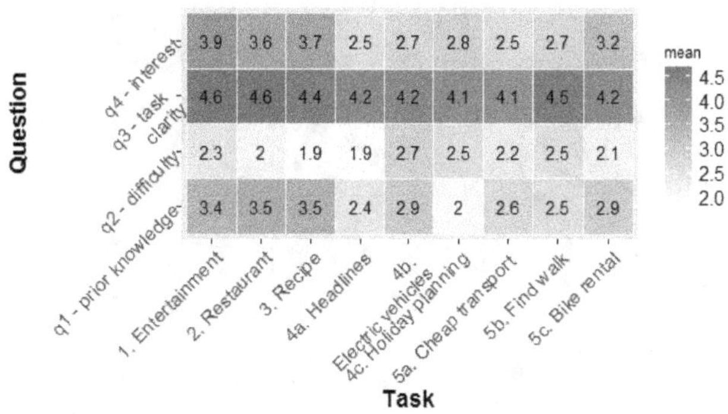

Figure 5: Mean response to pre-task questionnaire by task type.

work over the week can make people feel less able to complete the tasks well. Neither task clarity nor interest showed any noticeable patterns by either weekday or start time.

Figure 5 shows how responses to these questions varied by task type. It seems that participants found all of the tasks to be clear and straightforward, with only very small variations in reported task clarity (Q3). Prior knowledge (Q1) varied quite considerably: participants were quite knowledgeable about the cuisine- and entertainment-based tasks but reported knowing less about news headlines and planning a trip to Slovenia. There was some variation in task interest, which has a similar pattern to that of prior knowledge (i.e. users tend to prefer tasks they feel they are knowledgeable about); responses to these two questions were significantly positively correlated ($\rho(526) = 0.499, p \ll 0.01$).

Difficulty (Q2) was generally assessed to be quite low, although the questions on electric vehicles and holiday planning were expected to be most difficult. We can compare the expected difficulty of tasks from the pre-task questionnaire with the responses to the same question on difficulty in the post-task questionnaire. In doing so we find that most tasks were actually easier than participants expected, those tasks that were expected to be most difficult (4b and 4c). The only exception was task 5c, which participants rated as being more difficult to complete than they had expected.

4.4 Task relevance and post-task perception

Figure 6 shows the mean post-task questionnaire responses by task. Participants did not generally find the tasks to be too difficult, with the possible exception of *question 5b*. Interestingly, the level of perceived stress and distraction does seem to have been somewhat dependent on the task, with the transport-related tasks generally producing more feelings of stress. The first 3 tasks - on entertainment and eating - were deemed to be the most personally relevant on average, while the question on electric cars was generally the least personally relevant. We further investigate temporal relevance in the next subsection.

Interestingly, question 4 (interest in topic) from the pre-task questionnaire is a significant predictor of questions 4, 5 and 6 in the post-task questionnaire (all p-values $\ll 0.001$). This indicates that pre-task interest and temporal and personal relevance are strongly related and that those tasks that a user performs frequently are judged to be more interesting.

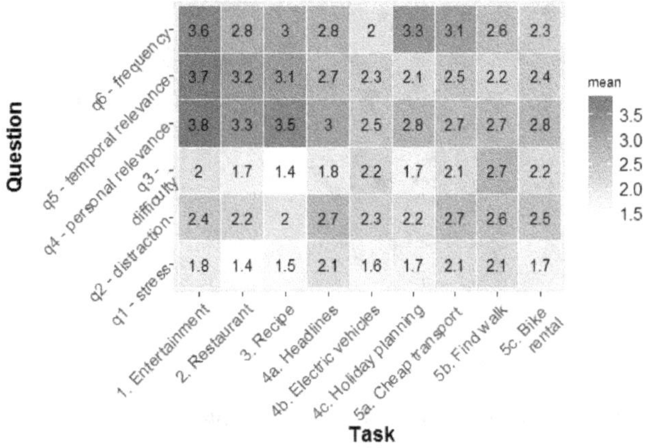

Figure 6: Mean response to post-task questionnaire by task type.

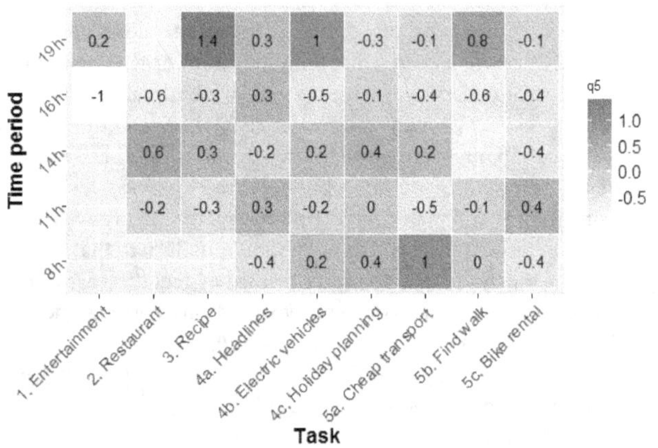

Figure 7: Temporal relevance by scheduled time period (normalised by the mean response for each task).

It is interesting to consider how the combination of task and time period affects participants' perceptions of task relevance. As part of the post-task questionnaire, we asked participants to rate the temporal relevance of the task (original question: "How relevant did you find this task to your current context (time of day)?") from 1 - extremely irrelevant to 5 - extremely relevant. We also asked participants to comment on their rating. Figure 7 shows the mean response by task type and time period (note that task and time period combinations with fewer than 3 responses are left blank and that the responses have been normalised by subtracting the mean response for each task).

The entertainment task appears to be more relevant in the evening than in the mid-afternoon (where participants found it to be very non-relevant), perhaps because people are at work in the mid-afternoon and, as such, are not able to relax by watching a film, while in the evening they can. The food tasks are thought to be more relevant when they are assigned nearer to the times that people generally eat. This is particularly clear from the recipe task, which is much more relevant in the evening and early afternoon time periods than during other times of the day. The transport finding task is much more relevant in the early morning than it is later in the day, perhaps because people are considering how they will get to work.

If a participant chose the lowest response for the question on contextual relevant (i.e. "extremely irrelevant") we asked them to explain why using a textbox. This happened for 32 tasks. In many of these instances the participants explained that they were at work or were busy with other tasks, for example: "I am busy right now and ate my lunch at 3:30 want focus on my work", "I am at work and i [sic] usually check this [sic] things in the evening" and "I'm still at work so searching for holiday activities is a distraction". On 6 occasions participants indicated a lack of relevance of the cycling/bike-related tasks due to a lack of interest, for example: "Because i [sic] almost never ride bikes", "I have no intention of going for a bike ride! Ever!"; or because cycling was not relevant to them at that time: "I'm having lunch, don't care about biking now" and "I'm about to drive into work so don't have time to go fir [sic] a bike ride...". Users also sometimes showed a lack of interest in the topic of electric cars: "I'm not buying an electric car now ", "I don't want to buy an electric car, and it's not a task related to the time".

4.5 Searching behaviour and performance

As we allowed participants to search on the open web, we do not have any relevance judgements available for the tasks we set them. However, we can look at a number of proxy measurements to search performance, as well as indicators of querying behaviour, such as the length of queries, number of queries issued, documents read and number of starred (bookmarked) documents.

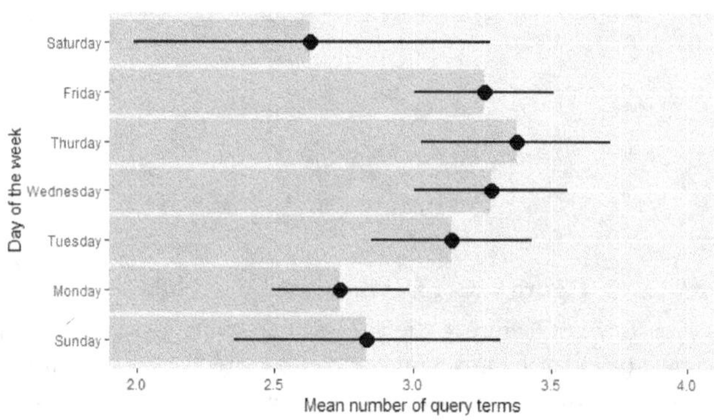

Figure 8: Average (mean) query length in terms by weekday.

The queries submitted were generally quite long at an average length of 3.09 terms and 19.91 characters. Perhaps surprisingly, participants submitted queries of approximately the same length, regardless of the time of day, varying from an average of 2.9 terms in the late afternoon (between 4 and 7PM) to 3.4 in the late morning (between 11AM and 1PM). People tended to spend less time reading search results in the early morning and afternoon (median = 25.5 and 27s) than they did during the rest of the day (median between 31.5 and 36.5s). There was a much larger variation in query length by day of the week. As shown in Figure 8, it seems that (with the exception of Monday) queries submitted during the week were considerably longer than those submitted over the weekend. We

Table 2: Various querying statistics on a per-task basis (q=query; t=task).

Task	Terms/q	Reading time	Bookmarks/t	q/t
1. Entertainment	2.68	46	3.95	2.55
2. Restaurant	3.05	36	2.55	2
3. Recipe	2.92	38	2.64	1.52
4a. Headlines	2.59	25	3.48	1.86
4b. Electric vehicles	3.24	28	3.5	2.83
4c. Holiday planning	3.07	29.5	3.17	1.67
5a. Cheap transport	3.31	23	2.83	2.67
5b. Find walk	3.89	39.5	1.59	2.24
5c. Bike rental	3.14	33	3	2.53

observed a similar temporal effect on result reading time - participants tended to spend more time reading documents on weekdays than during the weekend.

Table 2 shows querying statistics aggregated by task type. Participants tended to submit much longer queries for certain tasks than others: those submitted to tasks 5b and 5c were significantly longer than those submitted to tasks 1, 3 or 4a [5]. Reading time was broadly similar across tasks, although it was highest for question 1, perhaps because people spent more time reading the synopses of films to decide which they found interesting. Reading time was very low for task 5a, suggesting that, once a suitable query had been generated, it was quite easy to identify relevant documents.

It seems that the tasks deemed to be easiest in the post-task questionnaires (tasks 2, 3 and 4c) required the least amount of query modification, with all 3 of them requiring fewer than 2 queries on average to be completed. Some of the more difficult tasks, on the other hand (e.g. tasks 4b and 5c) required considerably more queries - more than 2 and a half on average. There was also quite a lot of variation in the average number of bookmarks submitted by task. Task 5b had the lowest average (only 1.59), while task 1 had the highest (3.95); there was a significant difference between these two ($p= 0.03$). Perhaps many participants only felt they needed to find a single walk, while for the film choosing task, despite the fact that the task was to find "a film you would like to watch", they wanted to make sure they had alternatives. It may also be because the participants found task 5b to be one of the least interesting and also one of the most difficult.

4.6 The effect of situational context

A key advantage to conducting the study through a bespoke Android app and in a naturalistic setting is that we are able to gain insights into how search behaviour and performance is affected by context and, particularly, the situation in which they perform the search. We logged data from each device's accelerometers and gyroscopes and, using Google's Activity Recognition API, were able to infer from these the activity the user was performing when completing the tasks. Note that in doing so we record the closest recognised activity prior to the submission of queries as being the activity state of the user on query submission. In a small number of cases this state was recorded a considerable amount of time before the queries were submitted and, as such, may be erroneous. To account for this, we only calculate statistics for instances where the queries were submitted within an hour of the closest prior activity.

[5] Based on Tukey multiple comparisons of means.

Table 3: Various querying statistics by activity type (q=query; t=task). * indicates a significant difference compared to the *At rest* condition.

Task	Instances	Terms/q	Reading time	Bookmarks/q	q/t
At rest	186	3.1	74	1.46	2.03
Walking	27	2.3*	48*	1.63	1.9
After walking	11	3.27	50	2.55*	1.54
On transport	28	2.71	68	0.7*	3.11

Table 3 shows the activities inferred by the API (walking, on transport, at rest and after walking) and statistics of the querying behaviour exhibited by participants in these situations. There appears to be considerable difference in a number of querying behaviour metrics depending on the condition. When walking, participants submitted significantly shorter queries than when at rest ($p \ll 0.01$) and spent considerably less time reading search results. These results agree with those of Harvey and Pointon [19], who observed similar differences in their more artificial, lab-based study and suggest similar causes - i.e. the distractions and attention shifts caused by walking have a deleterious effect on querying behaviour.

When on transport - a difficult condition to accurately simulate in a laboratory - users tended to submit shorter queries, bookmarked significantly fewer relevant documents per query, although reading time was similar to the *at rest* condition and they submitted more queries per topic on average. These shorter queries, the tendency to bookmark fewer documents per query and increase in number of queries submitted may be due to the noisy and bumpy conditions experienced when travelling by vehicle. Previous work [20, 22] has shown that such conditions can induce a feeling of time pressure and reduce a user's ability to judge the relevance of documents. The increase in number of queries suggests that the users in this condition may be seeking to explore the document space more thoroughly, rather than deeply investigating the documents on each result page.

5 DISCUSSION

This work aims to answer three main research questions in relation to the impact of context on user behaviour and task relevance. In this section, we address each of the research questions in turn.

RQ1: Which kinds of task do people prefer to complete on mobile devices and what impact does time have on this? Our results suggest that users prefer to complete tasks on their mobile devices based primarily on two factors: (i) tasks on which they have more prior knowledge and/or interest; (ii) tasks that are more relevant to their current context. We do not expect users to look for absolutely new information while on the go, unless it is highly relevant to their context. For instance, assume a scenario where a user is having lunch with colleagues and they happen to discuss about the effect of cell towers on brain cancer. The user, presumably, has no prior knowledge about this topic. However, given that he/she is seated (situational context) and seeks to find the answer for the colleagues, it is highly probable that the user completes such a difficult task. Users do not tend to complete search tasks that they perceive to be more difficult, suggesting that they need more attention and time; probably preferring to complete such a task later, either on a desktop or in another context [23], perhaps where they can better concentrate on it [33]. This supports the results of previous work, which showed that users are more engaged with the tasks in which they have more prior knowledge and interest [16].

Our results show that users behave differently at different times of the day as well on different days of the week. In particular, users completed more tasks in the early hours of a day (8AM-11AM) and were typically much less engaged during weekends, similar to the findings of Pielot et al. [31]. It is likely easier for users to engage in a search while their minds are fresh in the morning and less so in the evenings, when other tasks may take priority [33].

RQ2: How does perceived task relevance vary by temporal context and what impact does this variation have on user behaviour and performance? For most of the tasks, the perceived temporal relevance varied based on the time of day. This is more evident for time-dependent tasks such as finding a dinner recipe, which may also be affected by others contextual factors, such as location [33]. Although intuitive, this result is interesting when studied together with search performance, which also varied over the different time periods. Users tended to submit longer queries during weekdays and perform more search tasks in the morning, a result which contrasts with the results of previous research (e.g. Guy [18]). The result also suggest that, while some tasks have more general temporal relevance and, as such, do not vary much in perceived relevance over time, others exhibit much more time-constrained relevance. Such tight constraints on temporal relevance and interest are not generally found in analyses of desktop search log, where querying frequency over the day was much more uniform [6]. Perhaps in a mobile setting, where users require more attention to understand and complete a given task, they exhibit more variation in their behaviour and are more acutely aware of temporal relevance.

Our results provide useful insights to inform the design of future mobile search features considering both temporal and situational contexts. More specifically, a system should be able to provide query suggestion based on users' past queries at the same time or at the same situation. For instance, assume a user commutes every day on train and needs to check the train schedule and delays on a daily basis. A mobile search system should be able to identify this regular pattern and be able to provide the user with suggested queries [4] or information cards [3, 32].

RQ3: What effect does situational context (activity) have on performance? We observed substantial variation in behaviour and search performance by situational contexts. Users completed most of the tasks while they were at rest, suggesting that they dismissed the tasks mostly when they were not at rest and waiting until their situational context was more amenable to searching. According to prior research, using mobile devices while walking requires both cognitive and motor abilities [25]; and thus users' attention is fragmented [19]. For this reason, we observed less task engagement, a decrease in participant attention, reduced reading time and a significant reduction in query length whilst walking.

Our results suggest similar behaviour when users are on transport, although, this context had a much stronger negative impact on a user's ability to assess relevance (as indicated by a significant reduction in number of bookmarks), even more so that observed in a lab setting by Harvey and Pointon [20]. The differences in engagement level under these situational contexts indicates that current search features and mobile interfaces do not facilitate search on the go. In spite of the fact that mobile devices are meant to be accessible in almost all situations, users still appear to prefer searching while they are at rest. This suggests that a more dynamic and smart search UI could improve user experience as they walk or are on transport. For example, more voice-based interaction could be adopted, more robust ways of input such as gesture-based input [7] could be used or the interface could be made to dynamically adapt to context [19].

6 CONCLUSIONS AND FUTURE WORK

The main goal of this study was to understand how temporal and situational contexts affect user behaviour and search performance on mobile devices when performing Web search tasks. We carried out a task-based field study consisting of 31 participants and 12 search tasks in a period of 7 days. We developed Omicron, a bespoke Android app, for this study, enabling us to capture various aspects of users' context and behaviour. The participants were given a maximum of two tasks per day at predefined time slots. Randomly distributing the tasks, we were able to cover all different time slots, for different search tasks, on different days. This enabled us to conduct a thorough analysis on the impact of temporal and situational contexts on user behaviour and performance.

Our results indicate that more dynamic interfaces should be designed to encourage users to search while walking or on transport. Also, we observed substantial variation in user behaviour and performance at various times, suggesting that the UI must be aware of the temporal context of the user. Moreover, we saw that users are more willing to complete new search tasks - which presumably require more attention - during early hours of the day. This suggests the need for a more proactive search interface that could provide information cards or suggested queries based on users' regular querying patterns.

As future work we plan to conduct a follow-up study, focusing on user behaviour as they search in various apps. Recent research has shown that users submit most of their queries within multiple apps [1, 2]. Therefore, it would be interesting to see how users interact with the search engine designed in different apps, under various temporal and situational contexts. Also, as discussed in other studies, user behaviour in terms of app usage vary before, during, and after a search session [9]. It would also be interesting to study the effect app usage before a search session has on the results that users scan or bookmark. For example, if a user spends a considerable amount of time on YouTube, is he/she more likely to interact with results from http://www.youtube.com or not?

ACKNOWLEDGMENTS

This research was partially funded by the RelMobIR project of the Swiss National Science Foundation (SNSF). We would like to thank the participants who patiently helped us in this study.

REFERENCES

[1] Mohammad Aliannejadi, Hamed Zamani, Fabio Crestani, and W. Bruce Croft. 2018. In Situ and Context-Aware Target Apps Selection for Unified Mobile Search. In *Proceedings of the 27th International Conference on Information and Knowledge Management, CIKM '18, Turin, Italy.* ACM, 1383–1392.

[2] Mohammad Aliannejadi, Hamed Zamani, Fabio Crestani, and W. Bruce Croft. 2018. Target Apps Selection: Towards a Unified Search Framework for Mobile Devices. In *Proceedings of the 41st International ACM SIGIR Conference on Research and Development in Information Retrieval, SIGIR '18, Ann Arbor, Michigan, USA.* ACM, 215–224.

[3] Seyed Ali Bahrainian and Fabio Crestani. 2018. Augmentation of Human Memory: Anticipating Topics that Continue in the Next Meeting. In *Proceedings of the 3rd Conference on Human Information Interaction and Retrieval, CHIIR '18, New Brunswick, New Jersey, USA.* ACM, 150–159.

[4] Seyed Ali Bahrainian, Fattane Zarrinkalam, Ida Mele, and Fabio Crestani. 2019. Predicting the Topic of Your Next Query for Just-In-Time IR. In *Proceedings of the 41st European Conference on IR Research, ECIR '19, Cologne, Germany.* Springer.

[5] Leon Barnard, Ji Soo Yi, Julie A Jacko, and Andrew Sears. 2007. Capturing the effects of context on human performance in mobile computing systems. *Personal and Ubiquitous Computing* 11, 2 (2007), 81–96.

[6] Steven M Beitzel, Eric C Jensen, Abdur Chowdhury, Ophir Frieder, and David Grossman. 2007. Temporal analysis of a very large topically categorized web query log. *Journal of the American Society for Information Science and Technology* 58, 2 (2007), 166–178.

[7] Andrew Bragdon, Eugene Nelson, Yang Li, and Ken Hinckley. 2011. Experimental analysis of touch-screen gesture designs in mobile environments. In *Proceedings of the 2011 CHI Conference on Human Factors in Computing Systems, CHI '11, Vancouver, British Columbia, Canada.* ACM, 403–412.

[8] Joel Brandt, Noah Weiss, and Scott R. Klemmer. 2007. txt 4 l8r: lowering the burden for diary studies under mobile conditions. In *Extended Abstracts Proceedings of the 2007 CHI Conference on Human Factors in Computing Systems, CHI '07, San Jose, California, USA.* ACM, 2303–2308.

[9] Juan Pablo Carrascal and Karen Church. 2015. An in-situ study of mobile app & mobile search interactions. In *Proceedings of the 2015 CHI Conference on Human Factors in Computing Systems, CHI '15, Seoul, Republic of Korea.* ACM, 2739–2748.

[10] Karen Church, Mauro Cherubini, and Nuria Oliver. 2014. A large-scale study of daily information needs captured in situ. *ACM Transactions on Computer-Human Interaction (TOCHI)* 21, 2 (2014), 10.

[11] Karen Church and Nuria Oliver. 2011. Understanding mobile web and mobile search use in today's dynamic mobile landscape. In *Proceedings of the 13th Conference on Human-Computer Interaction with Mobile Devices and Services, MobileHCI '11, Stockholm, Sweden.* ACM, 67–76.

[12] Karen Church and Barry Smyth. 2009. Understanding the intent behind mobile information needs. In *Proceedings of the 14th International Conference on Intelligent User Interfaces, IUI '09, Sanibel Island, Florida, USA,.* ACM, 247–256.

[13] Karen Church, Barry Smyth, Keith Bradley, and Paul Cotter. 2008. A large scale study of European mobile search behaviour. In *Proceedings of the 10th Conference on Human-Computer Interaction with Mobile Devices and Services, MobileHCI '08, Amsterdam, the Netherlands.* ACM, 13–22.

[14] Fabio Crestani and Heather Du. 2006. Written versus spoken queries: A qualitative and quantitative comparative analysis. *JASIST* 57, 7 (2006), 881–890.

[15] Fabio Crestani, Stefano Mizzaro, and Ivan Scagnetto. 2017. *Mobile Information Retrieval.* Springer.

[16] Ashlee Edwards and Diane Kelly. 2017. Engaged or Frustrated?: Disambiguating Emotional State in Search. In *Proceedings of the 40th International ACM SIGIR Conference on Research and Development in Information Retrieval, SIGIR '17, Tokyo, Japan.* ACM, 125–134.

[17] StatCounter GlobalStats. 2016. Mobile and tablet internet usage exceeds desktop for first time worldwide. *http://gs.statcounter.com/press/mobile-and-tablet-internet-usage-exceeds-desktop-for-first-time-worldwide* (2016).

[18] Ido Guy. 2016. Searching by Talking: Analysis of Voice Queries on Mobile Web Search. In *Proceedings of the 39th International ACM SIGIR conference on Research and Development in Information Retrieval, SIGIR '16, Pisa, Italy.* ACM, 35–44.

[19] Morgan Harvey and Matthew Pointon. 2017. Searching on the go: the effects of fragmented attention on mobile web search tasks. In *Proceedings of the 40th International ACM SIGIR Conference on Research and Development in Information Retrieval, SIGIR '17, Tokyo, Japan.* ACM, 155–164.

[20] Morgan Harvey and Matthew Pointon. 2018. Noisy Signals: Understanding the Impact of Auditory Distraction on Web Search Tasks. In *Proceedings of the 3rd Conference on Human Information Interaction and Retrieval, CHIIR '18, New Brunswick, New Jersey, USA.* ACM, 241–244.

[21] Annika M Hinze, Carole Chang, and David M Nichols. 2010. Contextual queries express mobile information needs. In *Proceedings of the 12th International Conference on Human Computer Interaction with Mobile Devices and Services, MobileHCI '10, Lisbon, Portugal.* ACM, 327–336.

[22] Eve Hoggan, Andrew Crossan, Stephen A Brewster, and Topi Kaaresoja. 2009. Audio or tactile feedback: which modality when?. In *Proceedings of the 2009 CHI Conference on Human Factors in Computing Systems, CHI '09, Boston, Massachusetts, USA.* ACM, 2253–2256.

[23] Anne Kaikkonen. 2008. Full or tailored mobile web-where and how do people browse on their mobiles?. In *Proceedings of the 5th International Conference on Mobile Technology, Applications, and Systems, MobiSys '08, Yilan, Taiwan.* ACM, 28:1–28:8.

[24] Maryam Kamvar and Shumeet Baluja. 2006. A large scale study of wireless search behavior: Google mobile search. In *Proceedings of the 2006 CHI Conference on Human Factors in Computing Systems, CHI '06, Montréal, Québec, Canada.* ACM, 701–709.

[25] Shaun K. Kane, Jacob O. Wobbrock, and Ian E. Smith. 2008. Getting off the treadmill: evaluating walking user interfaces for mobile devices in public spaces. In *Proceedings of the 10th Conference on Human-Computer Interaction with Mobile Devices and Services, MobileHCI '08, Amsterdam, the Netherlands.* ACM, 109–118.

[26] Jaewon Kim, Paul Thomas, Ramesh Sankaranarayana, Tom Gedeon, and Hwan-Jin Yoon. 2017. What Snippet Size is Needed in Mobile Web Search?. In *Proceedings of the 2nd Conference on Conference Human Information Interaction and Retrieval, CHIIR '17, Oslo, Norway.* ACM, 97–106.

[27] Daijiro Komaki, Takahiro Hara, and Shojiro Nishio. 2012. How does mobile context affect people's web search behavior?: A diary study of mobile information needs and search behaviors. In *Proceedings of the 26th International Conference on Advanced Information Networking and Applications, AINA '12 , Fukuoka, Japan.* IEEE, 245–252.

[28] Jiaxin Mao, Yiqun Liu, Noriko Kando, Cheng Luo, Min Zhang, and Shaoping Ma. 2018. Investigating Result Usefulness in Mobile Search. In *Proceedings of the 40th European Conference on IR Research, ECIR '18, Grenoble, France.* Springer, 223–236.

[29] Sachi Mizobuchi, Mark H. Chignell, and David Newton. 2005. Mobile text entry: relationship between walking speed and text input task difficulty. In *Proceedings of the 7th Conference on Human-Computer Interaction with Mobile Devices and Services, MobileHCI '05, Salzburg, Austria.* ACM, 122–128.

[30] Kevin Ong, Kalervo Järvelin, Mark Sanderson, and Falk Scholer. 2017. Using Information Scent to Understand Mobile and Desktop Web Search Behavior. In *Proceedings of the 40th International ACM SIGIR Conference on Research and Development in Information Retrieval, SIGIR '17, Tokyo, Japan.* ACM, 295–304.

[31] Martin Pielot, Karen Church, and Rodrigo de Oliveira. 2014. An in-situ study of mobile phone notifications. In *Proceedings of the 16th international Conference on Human-Computer Interaction with Mobile Devices and Services, MobileHCI '14, Toronto, Ontario, Canada.* ACM, 233–242.

[32] Milad Shokouhi and Qi Guo. 2015. From Queries to Cards: Re-ranking Proactive Card Recommendations Based on Reactive Search History. In *Proceedings of the 38th International ACM SIGIR Conference on Research and Development in Information Retrieval, SIGIR '15, Santiago, Chile.* ACM, 695–704.

[33] Timothy Sohn, Kevin A. Li, William G. Griswold, and James D. Hollan. 2008. A diary study of mobile information needs. In *Proceedings of the 2008 CHI Conference on Human Factors in Computing Systems, CHI '08, Florence, Italy.* ACM, 433–442.

[34] Yang Song, Hao Ma, Hongning Wang, and Kuansan Wang. 2013. Exploring and exploiting user search behavior on mobile and tablet devices to improve search relevance. In *Proceedings of the 22nd international conference on World Wide Web, WWW '13, Rio de Janeiro, Brazil.* ACM, 1201–1212.

[35] Kyle Williams, Julia Kiseleva, Aidan C. Crook, Imed Zitouni, Ahmed Hassan Awadallah, and Madian Khabsa. 2016. Detecting Good Abandonment in Mobile Search. In *Proceedings of the 25th International Conference on World Wide Web, WWW '16, Montréal, Québec, Canada.* ACM, 495–505.

Understanding How People use Search to Support their Everyday Creative Tasks

Yinglong Zhang
School of Information and Library Science
yinglongz@unc.edu

Robert Capra
School of Information and Library Science
rcapra@unc.edu

ABSTRACT

Creativity is an essential part of people's daily life and work across a range of everyday tasks. However, little prior work has explored how people use search engines and information resources as part of their creative processes, and how systems might better support users working on creative tasks. In this paper, we conducted an online survey with 175 participants to explore how people use search engines and online resources (e.g., images, videos, and social media) to support their creative tasks. Our participants reported information seeking to support a broad range of everyday creativity including tasks in arts, writing, crafts, and technical projects. Our findings show that participants' tasks included multiple stages of creative processes (e.g., creating ideas, combining ideas, executing plans) and that participants reported using search engines along with other tools (such as images and videos) to facilitate their creative process. By using Bayesian random effects regression models, we found that different stages of the creative process influence participants' use of tools. For example, for tasks that involved creating ideas, participants were more likely to use images and social sites, and when needing to put ideas into practice they were more likely to use videos. We also found differences in users' satisfaction with using the tools for different creative stages. Based on our findings, we provide recommendations for supporting users' information seeking needs during creative tasks.

KEYWORDS

Search engines, information search, creativity, creative process

ACM Reference Format:
Yinglong Zhang and Robert Capra. 2019. Understanding How People use Search to Support their Everyday Creative Tasks. In *2019 Conference on Human Information Interaction and Retrieval (CHIIR '19), March 10–14, 2019, Glasgow, Scotland Uk.* ACM, New York, NY, USA, 10 pages. https://doi.org/10.1145/3295750.3298936

1 INTRODUCTION

Creativity and innovation are highly valued characteristics by societies and individuals. From a societal perspective, it has been argued that creativity will become increasingly important because of increased global competitiveness, decreasing numbers of jobs that do not involve aspects of creativity, and growing demand for products of creative industries [50]. In addition to these social dimensions, creativity has been considered as a universal quality that helps individuals survive and is a component of many everyday activities. As Richards highlights, "Throughout our day, whether at home or at work, we humans adapt and innovate, improvise flexibly... Our creativity may involve anything from making breakfast to solving a major conflict with one's boss" [46, p.190].

The importance of supporting humans' creativity through the use of technologies has been recognized by scholars over the past decades. In 1999, Shneiderman [51] emphasized the significance of developing user interfaces that support creativity and highlighted opportunities to facilitate the creative process by using search engines. More recently, in the field of information retrieval, White [64, p.137] has pointed out the need for additional research to investigate ways that information systems can support creativity.

To the best of our knowledge, however, very few efforts have been made to investigate how to design search systems for supporting creativity. With this goal in mind, we must first understand what kinds of creative tasks people perform in their life and work, how they conduct the tasks, and what opportunities there are for search systems to support their needs. In this study, we are particularly interested in understanding people's *everyday creativity*, which Richards defines based on two crucial criteria: originality and meaningfulness [46]. Incorporating these two criteria in the context of information searching, we broadly define *creative tasks* as tasks in which people attempt to use information technology to create something original and meaningful. This definition has an intentionally broad scope, with the "something" being able to refer to both physical and non-physical things (e.g., an idea or a project).

To gain a better understanding of how people use search engines and information tools to support their creative process, we conducted an online survey (N=175) using the Amazon Mechanical Turk (MTurk). Our survey asked participants to think of a time recently when they were trying to create something and went online to look for useful resources or information. We asked participants to type a detailed description of their task, to indicate what computing devices they used as part of the task, what information tools they used, and to indicate which (from a list of) creative process stages (e.g., figuring out goals, creating ideas, combining ideas, etc.) were involved in their task. We also asked about their satisfaction using particular tools to support particular creative process stages.

We grounded our survey questions and analysis in prior research on creativity. One way that creativity has been studied is in terms of different *domains*. We analyzed the participants' responses using a set of everyday creativity domains developed by Jauk et al. [27]: visual arts, performing arts, music, literature/writing, arts & crafts, cooking, and science & engineering.

CHIIR '19, March 10–14, 2019, Glasgow, Scotland Uk

ACM ISBN 978-1-4503-6025-8/19/03...$15.00
https://doi.org/10.1145/3295750.3298936

Creativity is also understood to be a process that involves multiple *stages*. We used a set of creative process stages identified by Sawyer [50]: find goals, look-up information, explore, create ideas, combine ideas, select ideas, and put ideas into practice (execute).

In this paper, we present the results of our survey and address the following research questions:

- **RQ1: What kinds of creative tasks do people perform in their everyday life and work?** To address this, we analyzed participants' task descriptions and categorized them based on a set of *creativity domains* from prior work [27].
- **RQ2: How are computing devices and information tools used by people to support their creative tasks?** For devices, we report on participants' use of desktop/PCs, smartphones, tablets, and other devices to support their tasks. For information tools, we report on the use of search engines, images, videos, and social media sites.
- **RQ3: How is information search used as a part of a creative process?** We examine how seven different creative process stages (e.g., find goals, create ideas, combine ideas, etc.) identified from prior work [50] were involved in our participants' tasks, and show how different information resources and tools were used to support each stage.
- **RQ4: What are the opportunities for search engines to support the creative process?** We present Bayesian regression models to investigate: how the domain of the task influenced the creative stages involved, how the creative stages influenced the resources/tools used, and how satisfied participants' were using particular tools to support creative stages.

Based on our results, we present a set of implications about how IR systems can better support users engaged in creative tasks.

2 RELATED WORK

In this section, we review related work on creativity, information seeking, and tools to support creative tasks.

Definitions of creativity: For the past several decades, different definitions have been proposed to characterize the nature of creativity. In the *sociocultural* approach ("big-C"), scholars attempt to understand creative genius and identify which creative works might last forever [53]. Whereas the sociocultural approach ("big-C") assumes that only certain people can be creative, the *individual* approach ("little-c") looks more at everyday creativity which is seen as central to human survival and must be found in everyone [46]. In the perspective of individualists, creativity is defined as "a new mental combination that is expressed in the world" [50, p.7]. In the work presented here, we focus on everyday creativity ("little-c"). Everyday creativity has been considered along four levels: doing, adapting, making, and creating (the highest level) [48].

Creative process: Despite some disagreements on the definitions of creativity, there is a general agreement that creativity is a *process*. In 1926, Wallas [61] created one of the earliest creative process models by examining four different stages: preparation, incubation, illumination, and verification. Inspired by Wallas' work, other models emerged including Amabile's five-stage model [1], the Geneplore model [16], and Mumford's eight-stage model [42].

In a more recent work, Sawyer developed an integrated framework based on models proposed in previous studies. We used Sawyer's framework in our survey questions. This framework includes eight stages, including [50, p.90]: (1) find and format the problem, (2) acquire knowledge relevant to the problem, (3) gather a broad range of potentially related information, (4) take time off for incubation, (5) generate a large variety of ideas, (6) combine ideas in unexpected ways, (7) select the best ideas, applying relevant criteria, (8) externalize the idea using materials and representations.

There are several important aspects in Sawyer's framework. First, the creative process begins with finding a problem. Previous research on creativity has found that finding and formatting a problem is extremely important [11]. Second, gaining deep knowledge of a domain is crucial in a creative process. Third, different from the aforementioned models, Sawyer's framework considers the stage of externalizing the idea. Previous studies have shown that most creative people externalize their ideas before they are fully formed, and this often results in follow-on ideas [50]. We note that search systems have a role to play in supporting each of these stages.

Domains of creativity: A prevailing view is that people may not be creative in a universal way, but rather are creative in particular domain(s) [12]. In creativity research, many efforts have been made to quantify the domains of creativity. For example, Carson and his colleagues [8] identified three types of creativity: expressive creativity (visual arts, writing, and humor), performance creativity (dance, drama, and music), and scientific creativity (invention, science, culinary). To characterize everyday creative activities, Jauk et al. proposed eight domains, including literature, music, arts & crafts, creative cooking, sports, visual arts, performing arts, and science & engineering [27]. In our analysis, we adapted Jauk et al.'s set of eight domains of creativity (see Section 4).

Information seeking: Information seeking and searching have been explored extensively in the fields of information science (IS) and information retrieval (IR). In previous work, models of information seeking have been developed to describe an interaction cycle that starts with identifying an information need, followed by searching, examining the results, and if necessary, adjusting goals and iterating through the entire process again [38, 40, 57]. Work has also explored how a person's information seeking process and goals evolve over time [35]. Researchers have also considered different characterizations of information seeking tasks. Especially relevant to our work are *exploratory search* tasks, in which a searcher seeks to explore and learn about a topic. Exploratory searches often involve investigation and synthesis [39, 65], which can also be stages of a creative process [50]. Prior work has also examined people's everyday information seeking behaviors [49] and their information behaviors in the context of leisure activities [24, 55, 56].

Also related to our work are efforts to understand and design ways to deliberately induce *serendipity* in search systems. Toms [58] proposed several approaches to supporting serendipitous retrieval (e.g., attempting to enhance the chance of serendipity by randomness, leveraging user profiles, and using relaxed similarity measures). Several efforts have investigated tools to encourage serendipity (e.g., [4], [44]). However, some have argued that focusing on the "chance encounters" aspect of serendipity will not necessarily support creativity [2]. As André, schraefel, Teevan, and Dumais noted in their paper, "Discovery is never by chance" [2], a system could increase users' chances of encountering "dots" of information, but knowing how to connect these dots is a different story.

Information seeking and artists: In the area of library science, efforts have been made to understand artists' information seeking behaviors. For example, by interviewing four artists (a sculptor, painter, fiber artist, and metalsmith), Cobbledick [9] found that these artists had different kinds of information needs (e.g., inspiration, technical information, specific visual information, information about trends and events in the art world, and business information). Inspired by Cobbledick's work, other similar studies have been conducted to investigate the information seeking behaviors of artists [10, 18, 60] and art librarians [36, 54].

Creativity Support Tools (CST): Outside of information search, researchers in human-computer interaction and other fields have explored ways to understand creativity and to design creativity support tools (CSTs). In the past decades, several theories have been developed to inform the design of CSTs [13, 14, 52] and tools have been developed to support crowd ideation [3, 17, 22, 23, 25], to stimulate creative thinking [15, 32, 45, 63], and to support design processes [33, 37, 43].

However, as Frich and his colleagues [19] note, much of the existing creativity-related HCI research has focused on new tools, often developed by the researchers themselves, and investigated in controlled experiments. To address this issue, the authors suggest "shifting our efforts to studying in-vivo use of creativity support tools, not just the ones we build ourselves, but the ones that most creative practitioners employ in practice" [19, p. 1243]. The study presented here is an effort to better understand the types of information seeking tools and strategies that people currently use in practice when they engage in tasks that involve everyday creativity.

3 METHODOLOGY

To explore how people use search engines and online resources to support their everyday creative tasks, we conducted an online survey. In this section, we describe how we recruited our participants and give details about our survey.

3.1 Participants and Recruiting

We recruited participants to complete our survey by posting Human Intelligence Tasks (HITs) to the Amazon Mechanical Turk (MTurk) crowdsourcing platform. To encourage a diverse sample, we used several techniques. First, we posted our recruitment HITs in small batches on different days and times across a one week period. Second, when posting different batches, we included different terms in the "keywords" field of the HIT (for keyword list, see **Appendix A**). The HIT keywords are often used by MTurk workers to search for HITs to work on, so by using different terms we hoped to attract a more diverse sample of participants who were doing tasks that involved creativity. Each day, we posted five groups, each of which included nine HITs. Each group was posted using a different set of keywords, but the survey itself was identical for all participants.

We posted our HITs with the following requirements for the MTurk workers: (1) location in the United States, (2) HIT approval rate greater than or equal to 95%; and (3) age > 18. We configured MTurk and our survey software (Qualtrics) to prevent participants from taking the survey more than once. Participants who completed the survey and entered a valid completion code into the HIT were paid $1.50 USD through the MTurk platform.

3.2 Survey Design

The survey began with a brief demographic questionnaire (e.g., age, gender, education, field of employment). Then participants responded to the main part of the survey – the creative task questionnaire. At the end of the survey, we also included a creative achievement questionnaire that is not analyzed in this paper.

Creative task questionnaire: We asked participants to think of a time recently when they were trying to create something and went online to look for useful resources or information. Focused on this task, we asked participants a series of questions (for full text, see **Appendix B**):

Q.1: Describe the task – We asked participants to type a written description of the task into a textbox. Also as part of Q.1, we asked participants to categorize the domain(s) of the task they described. To make it easier for participants to identify categories, instead of showing the eight high-level domains identified by Jauk et al. [27], we showed participants a list of 18 more specific categories[1] derived based on previous research [8, 27, 28] as well as from our own pilot testing. Participants were instructed to select all categories that applied to characterize their task.

Q.2: Describe how they approached the task – Using another open-ended question, we asked participants to describe how they approached the task (e.g., how they started, what resources they used, what strategies they used to find information).

Q.3: Indicate computing devices used for the task – To gain insight about what different computing devices were involved, we asked them to indicate if they used any of the following: desktop/PC, smartphone, tablet, smart TV, voice assistant (e.g., Siri, Alexa, Google Home), or other (please specify).

Q.4: Indicate information resources/tools used – We also asked which of the following information resources were used to support their task: search engines, videos, images, social sites (e.g., Pinterest, Instagram, etc.), other (please specify).

Q.5: Creative processes stages – Based on the answers to Q.4, we created a loop in the survey that dynamically asked a set of questions to capture the relationship between each information resource and stages of the creative process outlined by Sawyer [50, p.90]:

> For which of the reasons below did you use *<option selected in Q.4>* in the task (choose all that apply, or not applicable):
> - **Find goals**: figure out my goal (what I want to create/design or which problem I want to address/solve)
> - **Look up**: look up information relevant to my goal
> - **Explore**: explore (gather a broad range of potentially related information) about my goal
> - **Create ideas**: create a large variety of ideas that may achieve my goal
> - **Combine ideas**: combine some ideas that I have already had
> - **Select ideas**: select the best ideas from all the new ideas that I have created
> - **Execute**: figure out how to put my ideas into practice to achieve my goal

For example, if in Q.4 a participant chose both search engines and social sites they would see two separate **Q.5** questions, one asking about the reasons for using search engines and another asking about

[1] Visual arts, music, dance, sports, education, architectural design, entrepreneurial ventures, creative writing, humor, inventions, scientific inquiry, theater & film, culinary arts, crafts, product design, presentation, report writing, graphic design, and other.

the reasons for using social sites. Throughout the paper, we will refer to the creative process stages as: find goals, lookup, explore, create ideas, combine ideas, select ideas, and execute.

Q.6: Satisfaction/experience with information resources for each stage – We embedded a second-level loop in the survey to investigate participants' satisfaction with each information tool used for each creative stage. For example, we asked: "How satisfied were you with using *images* to *create ideas*?" Participants were asked to evaluate a resource/tool only when they reported using it.

4 DATA ANALYSIS

Qualitative coding: In the survey, we asked participants to select from 18 domains to categorize their creative task. We thought that providing a large set of 18 domains would help participants identify relevant categories. However, in some cases there was variation in how participants interpreted and applied the categories. For our analysis, we decided to re-categorize the data using eight domains we adapted from Jauk et al. [27] (shown in Table 1). The two authors independently reviewed participants' responses to Q.1 and Q.2 and assigned one of the eight domains. After this initial round of coding, the Cohen's Kappa for inter-coder agreement was $\kappa = 65.9\%$. After this, the authors independently re-coded the 47 responses they had disagreed on in the first round. The overall inter-coder agreement after the second round was 85.2%. Following Bradley's suggestion [6], we resolved the remaining 15 cases by discussion and consensus.

Quantitative analyses: Following the call of Tetsuya Sakai [47] at SIGIR 2017 and Kay et al. [29] at CHI 2016 advocating the use of Bayesian statistics, all the statistical inferences in our study are based on Bayesian inference. In our Bayesian analysis, a No-U-Turn sampler [26] was used; in each model, we ran Stan (http://mc-stan.org/) with six chains, each of which had 8000 iterations. Details of our Bayesian analysis are provided in Appendix C.

Responses and data quality: Based on our MTurk HITs, a total of 175 participants provided responses to our survey (86 female, 86 male, 2 other, 1 no answer). The age ranges of our participants varied broadly: "18-24 years old" (n=20), "25-34 years old" (n=75), "35-44 years old" (n=48), "45-54 years old" (n=19), "55-64 years old" (n=9), and "65-74 years old" (n=3). Most of our participants were employed (n=151, 86%) and came from 22 different fields.

Before we conducted our data analysis, we checked the quality of the survey data. Our manual review showed that all participants provided thoughtful responses to Q.1 and Q.2. The total length of Q.1 and Q.2 ranged from 22 words to 624 words (M = 138.09). Across all the questions, participants spent on average 24.31 minutes completing the survey. Based on our review, participants spent sufficient effort on the survey and we did not omit any responses.

5 RESULTS

5.1 Descriptive statistics

Recall that our survey questions asked participants to describe a particular creative task they had done recently and to answer questions about the domain of the task, the devices used, the information resources/tools used, and the creative process stages that were involved. In this section, we present descriptive statistics about the participants' responses to these questions.

Table 1: Activities and domains of the creative tasks

Domains (count)	Task activities (count)
Visual arts (35)	Painting/sculpture (4), Photography design (1), Interior design/renovation (14), Graphic design (10), Character/logo design (5), Architectural design (1).
Perform arts (2)	Making movie/film (2).
Music (5)	Making music (5).
Literature (15)	Nonfiction writing (5), Fiction writing (10).
Arts and Crafts (54)	Making tools (5), Making cards (5), Making furniture (13), Making jewelry (4), Making decoration or gift (11), Clothing (8), Gardening/landscape work (4), Craft other (4).
Cooking (16)	Cooking (16)
Science & engineering (28)	Academic writing (2), Technical problem solving (14), Programming (5), Website development (4), Building a scientific product (3).
Everyday/other (20)	Learning how to do/use something (5), Non-technical problem solving (15).

Creative task domains: As shown in Table 1, in response to Q.1 and Q.2, the everyday creativity tasks that participants described were distributed across the eight domains we examined. The variety and richness of participants' task descriptions was particularly striking and illustrates the complex information seeking that is required to support everyday creative tasks.

Devices used: In Q.3, participants noted the use of (possibly multiple) computing devices in their creative tasks. Desktop/PC was the most frequently used platform (163 of 175 responses, 93%), followed by smartphones (n=70, 40%), and then tablets (n=26, 15%). Devices such as Google Home (n=3) and Smart TVs (n=2) were mentioned by only a few participants. Using Bayesian logistic regression models, we examined whether this distribution differed based on task domain and did not find any notable differences.

We also investigated different *combinations* of platforms that participants reported using. The most common scenario was that a desktop/PC was the only platform used for a task (n=92, ~53%). However, scenarios that included combinations of two and three devices were very common, being reported in 74 of the 175 responses (~42%). The frequencies included: desktop only (92), desktop + smartphone (46), desktop + smartphone + tablet (12), desktop + tablet (8), other combinations (8), smartphone only (7), tablet only (2). These results suggest that task resumption across devices and sessions [62] is an important part of supporting creative tasks.

Resources/tools used: In Q.4, participants indicated the (possibly multiple) tools and information resources (search engines, images, videos, social sites) they used to accomplish their creative tasks. Figure 1 shows how frequently each tool was used for tasks in each domain. Overall, search engines were the most frequently reported tools. Videos were also frequently used, especially in arts & crafts tasks. Images were commonly used in both visual arts and

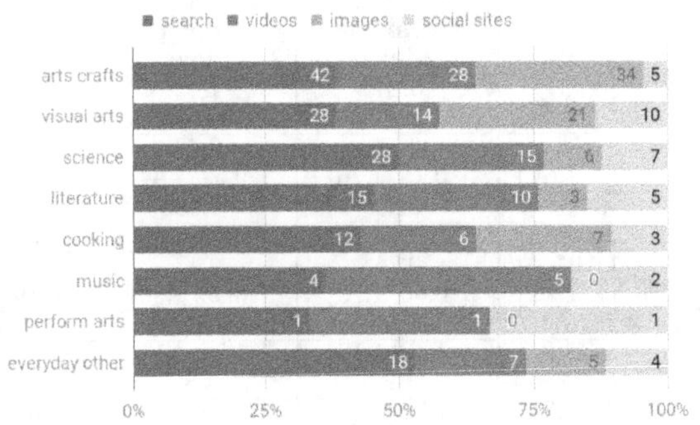

Figure 1: Use of tools across different domains.

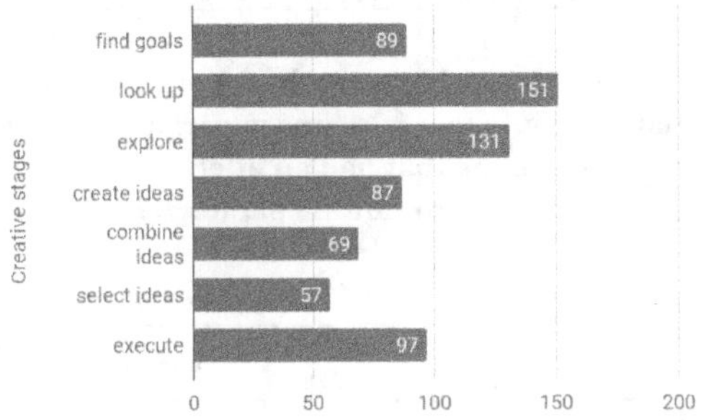

Figure 2: Creative process in creative tasks.

arts & crafts tasks. We also note that tools were used in combinations; approximately 69% of participants used at least two different tools in their creative tasks.[2]

Creative stages involved: Figure 2 shows the creative stages that participants reported as being part of their tasks (from Q.5). Among the stages, **look up** (look up information relevant to the goal, (n=151, 86%)) and **explore** (gather a broad of range of potentially related information about the goal, (n=131, 75%)) were the most frequently involved stages in our participants' creative tasks. However, all stages were commonly used, with even the least frequent (**select ideas**) being used by 33% (n=57) of our participants. These results show the complexity of creative tasks and illustrate how they may differ from fact-finding and comparative search tasks. Similar to exploratory search, the creative tasks reported by our participants involved exploration, learning, and synthesis.

Descriptive statistics summary: Our results show that participants reported tasks that involved multiple creative process stages, and that they used multiple information resources/tools and computing devices to support their tasks. These results also suggest that the participants used resources/tools differently when doing tasks in different domains. To explore these potential differences, we conducted a set of regression analyses (Section 5.2).

[2]The frequencies of tools reported included: search only (39), search + videos (32), search + images (27), search + videos + images (19), search + videos + social (14), search + videos + images (9), images only (8), videos only (7), videos + images (5), search + social (4), images + social (4), search + images + social (4), social only (2).

5.2 Relationships of Domain, Stage, and Tools

In this section, we explore relationships between the task domains, resources/tools used, and the creative stages. We present analyses of (1) how different task domains involve different creative stages, (2) how different creative stages involve the use of different resources/tools, and (3) users' satisfaction using different resources/tools to support particular stages.

5.2.1 How different task domains involve different creative stages. We wanted to investigate how different task domains (e.g., arts & crafts) might involve different creative stages (e.g., create ideas, look up). To investigate this, we developed seven Bayesian logistic regression models (see Equation 1 in Appendix C), one for each creative stage. In each model we included eight dummy variables corresponding to the task domain (e.g., visual arts, cooking, etc.) as predictors. The predicted (binary) outcome for each model was whether that particular stage was included in the task (1) or not (0).

The results of the Bayesian logistic regression analysis are shown in Table 2. Each **column** shows results for one of the models. Following Kruschke's [34] suggestion, we report the *mode* and 95% *high-density interval (HDI)* for each parameter. In Bayesian regression the *mode* indicates the log odds increase or decrease and the *HDI* provides a function similar to a confidence interval in null hypothesis testing (but must be interpreted differently; see details in **Appendix C**). In Bayesian inference, there is no *p*-value; instead, *to interpret the results, the null value (zero) of a coefficient is rejected if its 95% HDI excludes zero* [34]. In other words, when the HDI of a coefficient does not include zero, then we have high confidence that this variable has an effect on the model.

In Table 2, the domains (e.g., visual arts, cooking, etc.) that had an effect in a model are shown in bold and marked with a "*". For each model (stage), the highlighted domains are the ones that were more predictive of that stage. The estimated potential scale reduction factors ($\hat{R}$) of all the models were less than 1.1 for all the parameters, which indicates that the Bayesian models converged well [7].

Description of the results – Three of the models in Table 2 show interesting results (Models 2, 3 and 4). There is evidence that (1) the look-up stage was less likely to be included in arts & crafts tasks (log odd decreased 1.37 in Model 2); (2) the explore stage was less likely be included in everyday/other tasks (log odds decreased 1.06 in Model 3); and the creating ideas stage was more likely to be involved in tasks related to visual arts and arts & crafts (log odds increased 0.85 and 1.10, respectively in Model 4).

5.2.2 How different creative stages involve the use of different resources/tools. To understand whether the creative stages (e.g., find goals, look-up) could be used to predict the use of specific tools, we created four Bayesian random effects logistic regression models, one for each tool (search, videos, images, social sites). In each model, the predicted outcome is a binary variable that indicates whether the particular tool was used in the task. The predictor variables are seven binary variables corresponding to the seven creative stages (e.g., find goals, look-up, etc.). Also in each model, we included random effects to control for the influence of domains on the use of a tool (for instance, images might be generally more likely to be used in the domain of visual arts than in other domains).

		Model 1: Find goals	Model 2: Look up	Model 3: Explore	Model 4: Create ideas	Model 5: Combine ideas	Model 6: Select ideas	Model 7: Execute
Intercept	**Mode**	-0.02	**2.59***	**1.26***	-0.35	**-0.87***	**-1.17***	0.03
	HDI	[-0.56, 0.44]	**[1.74, 3.82]**	**[0.65, 2.19]**	[-0.91, 0.14]	**[-1.77, -0.23]**	**[-2.07, -0.55]**	[-0.48, 0.52]
Visual Arts	**Mode**	0.04	-0.80	-0.18	**0.85***	0.75	0.47	0.20
	HDI	[-0.74, 0.76]	[-2.26, 0.42]	[-1.31, 0.71]	**[0.09, 1.67]**	[-0.15, 1.76]	[-0.52, 1.44]	[-0.48, 1.01]
Cooking	**Mode**	0.08	-1.01	0.09	-0.08	0.33	0.86	-0.27
	HDI	[-0.92, 1.02]	[-2.68, 0.43]	[-1.13, 1.48]	[-1.15, 0.86]	[-0.78, 1.57]	[-0.19, 2.13]	[-1.24, 0.71]
Arts crafts	**Mode**	0.43	**-1.37***	0.02	**1.10***	0.76	0.47	0.52
	HDI	[-0.25, 1.09]	**[-2.67, -0.29]**	[-1.03, 0.89]	**[0.33, 1.77]**	[-0.06, 1.75]	[-0.32, 1.50]	[-0.19, 1.17]
Literature	**Mode**	-0.85	-0.05	-0.39	0.28	-0.13	-0.18	-0.68
	HDI	[-2.09, 0.10]	[-1.84, 2.21]	[-1.53, 0.99]	[-0.81, 1.22]	[-1.32, 1.17]	[-1.50, 1.13]	[-1.71, 0.37]
Music	**Mode**	0.40	0.61	1.39	-0.95	-1.72	-1.57	-0.24
	HDI	[-1.14, 1.99]	[-1.95, 6.27]	[-0.78, 7.16]	[-2.96, 0.84]	[-7.72, 0.47]	[-7.29, 0.73]	[-2.04, 1.18]
Perform arts	**Mode**	-0.01	0.42	-0.85	0.27	0.62	0.79	-0.11
	HDI	[-2.42, 2.39]	[-2.85, 5.72]	[-3.66, 1.53]	[-2.11, 2.74]	[-1.86, 3.31]	[-1.62, 3.61]	[-2.36, 2.47]
Science & engineering	**Mode**	0.36	-0.13	-0.06	-0.23	0.73	0.22	0.43
	HDI	[-0.47, 1.15]	[-1.63, 1.65]	[-1.13, 1.06]	[-1.07, 0.61]	[-0.20, 1.83]	[-0.74, 1.36]	[-0.37, 1.26]
Everyday/other	**Mode**	-0.29	0.15	**-1.06***	-0.94	-0.36	-0.26	0.17
	HDI	[-1.26, 0.57]	[-1.47, 2.43]	**[-2.24, -0.05]**	[-2.09, 0.08]	[-1.70, 0.73]	[-1.38, 1.02]	[-0.72, 1.08]

Note: * indicates that the null value (zero) is rejected.

Table 2: Creative process stages across different domains of creative tasks. Each column shows results for one Bayesian logistic regression model with the eight domains as predictor variables. The predicted outcome is a binary variable that indicates whether the stage was included in the task or not. Cells marked in bold show domains that had an effect in that model. The mode values show the log odds increase/decrease. $\hat{R}$ of all the models were less than 1.1 for all the parameters.

		Intercept	Find goals	Look up	Explore	Create ideas	Combine ideas	Select ideas	Execute	σ
Model 1: search	**Mode**	0.33	-0.97	**2.03***	0.58	0.68	-0.52	-0.18	0.33	**1.01***
	HDI	[-1.52, 2.24]	[-2.01, 0.09]	**[0.95, 3.30]**	[-0.52, 1.71]	[-0.41, 1.75]	[-1.58, 0.54]	[-1.32, 1.00]	[-0.71, 1.45]	**[0.04, 3.49]**
Model 2: Videos	**Mode**	**-1.30***	0.19	1.06	-0.07	0.14	0.02	-0.43	**0.82***	**0.33***
	HDI	**[-2.61, -0.06]**	[-0.50, 0.88]	[-0.02, 2.08]	[-0.89, 0.73]	[-0.59, 0.88]	[-0.67, 0.78]	[-1.23, 0.41]	**[0.09, 1.57]**	**[0.01, 1.63]**
Model 3: Images	**Mode**	**-1.54***	0.45	**-1.27***	**1.66***	**0.93***	0.36	-0.48	-0.01	**0.84***
	HDI	**[-3.39, -0.11]**	[-0.27, 1.26]	**[-2.50, -0.24]**	**[0.63, 2.70]**	**[0.12, 1.73]**	[-0.44, 1.18]	[-1.40, 0.39]	[-0.84, 0.85]	**[0.19, 2.59]**
Model 4: Social sites	**Mode**	**-2.72***	0.04	0.11	0.37	**0.98***	0.57	0.13	0.36	**0.69***
	HDI	**[-4.56, -1.09]**	[-0.86, 0.90]	[-1.23, 1.63]	[-0.77, 1.51]	**[0.07, 1.98]**	[-0.30, 1.53]	[-0.80, 1.09]	[-0.56, 1.33]	**[0.08, 1.8]**

Note: * indicated the null value (zero) is rejected

Table 3: Use of tools to support the creative process. Each row shows results for one Bayesian regression model with the seven creative stages as predictor variables. The predicted outcome is a binary variable that indicates whether the tool was used in the task or not. Cells marked in bold show stages that had an effect in that model. The mode values show the log odds increase/decrease. $\hat{R}$ of all the models were less than 1.1 for all the parameters.

The results of the random effects logistic regression models are shown in Table 3. In Table 3, each **row** shows results for one of the models. According to the results, there is evidence that (1) when participants were doing tasks that included the need to *look-up* relevant information, the log odds of using search engines increased 2.03 in Model 1, whereas the log odds of using images dropped 1.27 in Model 3; (2) when participants tried to *explore* potentially relevant information, the log odds of using images increased 1.66 in Model 3; (3) when participants attempted to create ideas, the log odds of using images and of using social sites increased 0.93 in Model 3 and 0.98 in Model 4, respectively; and (4) when participants attempted to put ideas into practice (*execute*), the log odds of using videos increased 0.82 in Model 2.

These results show that participants used different resources and tools to support different stages of their creative processes and provide practical data about what types of information may be most useful to users during different creative stages. While it is not surprising that users would make use of different tools for different stages, our results show *which* specific tools were the most relevant to specific stages. These findings suggest opportunities for search systems to predict a users' stage and use this information to help show specific types of content (for example, to use queries and interaction history to determine domains and possible stages).

5.2.3 Users' satisfaction of tools to support stages. To investigate participants' satisfaction with using each tool for different stages (Q.6), we developed seven Bayesian random effects ordered probit regression models, one for each stage (e.g., find goals, look-up, etc.). Ordered probit regression is recommended when the outcome is ordinal values, especially when the values are not normally distributed [34]. In each model, the predicted variable is an ordinal variable that indicates the satisfaction score of the tool. The predictors of each model are dummy variables corresponding to the tool that was evaluated. In addition to including the random effects associated with domains, we also included random effects in each

		Model 1: Find goals	Model 2: Look up	Model 3: Explore	Model 4: Create ideas	Model 5: Combine ideas	Model 6: Select ideas	Model 7: Execute
Intercept	Mode	6.53	6.21	6.26	6.05	6.04	6.15	6.34
	HDI	[6.07, 7.04]	[5.87, 6.56]	[5.86, 6.72]	[5.4, 6.74]	[5.57, 6.50]	[5.44, 6.82]	[5.62, 7.1]
Search	Mode	0.27	**0.50***	0.15	0.20	0.00	0.17	-0.04
	HDI	[-0.18, 0.77]	**[0.16, 0.79]**	[-0.22, 0.52]	[-0.39, 0.81]	[-0.47, 0.43]	[-0.56, 0.79]	[-0.55, 0.53]
Videos	Mode	0.36	0.32	**0.46***	0.61	0.08	0.29	0.46
	HDI	[-0.31, 0.96]	[-0.05, 0.72]	**[0.03, 0.97]**	[0.00, 1.47]	[-0.43, 0.64]	[-0.47, 1.10]	[-0.07, 1.01]
Images	Mode	0.38	0.08	0.06	0.47	**0.54***	-0.48	0.18
	HDI	[-0.21, 0.96]	[-0.39, 0.54]	[-0.35, 0.49]	[-0.22, 1.09]	**[0.04, 1.11]**	[-1.29, 0.22]	[-0.43, 0.89]
Social sites	Mode	**-0.94***	**-0.84***	**-0.75***	**-1.35***	-0.65	-0.03	-0.69
	HDI	**[-1.74, -0.27]**	**[-1.42, -0.30]**	**[-1.23, -0.17]**	**[-2.34, -0.37]**	[-1.33, 0.03]	[-1.20, 1.31]	[-1.44, 0.10]
σ_υ	Mode	**1.01***	**0.91***	**1.31***	**1.38***	**0.64***	**0.95***	**1.73***
	HDI	**[0.23, 1.55]**	**[0.54, 1.3]**	**[0.88, 1.77]**	**[0.88, 2.01]**	**[0.01, 1.09]**	**[0.07, 1.50]**	**[1.22, 2.34]**
σ_ω	Mode	0.06	0.05	0.05	**0.09***	0.07	0.11	0.11
	HDI	[0, 0.73]	[0, 0.48]	[0, 0.61]	**[0.01, 1]**	[0, 0.72]	[0, 1.03]	[0, 1.24]

Note: * indicated the null value (zero) is rejected

Table 4: Satisfaction with using each tool in different creative process stages. Each column shows results for one Bayesian ordered probit regression model with the four resources/tools as predictor variables. The predicted outcome is an ordinal variable that indicates satisfaction score of the tool. Cells marked in bold show recourses/tools that had an effect in that model. The mode values show the latent variable, μ increase/decrease (see Equations 3 in Appendix C). $\hat{R}$ of all the models were less than 1.1 for all the parameters.

model to control the impacts of repeated measurements (different tools could be evaluated by the same participant multiple times).

The results of the ordered probit regression models are shown in Table 4. Each **column** shows results for one of the models. The results of the table show that *across different domains and different participants* there is evidence that participants were likely to feel more satisfied with (1) using search engines when they attempted to look up information (Model 2), (2) using videos to explore potentially relevant information (Model 3), and (3) using images to help combine their ideas (Model 5). Based on the results of Model 1, 2, 3, and 4, we also found that people were likely to feel less satisfied with using social sites across several creative process stages (finding goals, look-up, explore, and create ideas). The findings in Table 4 also suggest that there were random effects that resulted from the repeated measurements by participants (σ_υ). This is not surprising, and indicates expected individual biases in using ratings. Table 4 also shows that the random effects associated with the domains of the creative tasks (σ_ω) were very weak, indicating little overall effects of domains on satisfaction with the tools.

6 DISCUSSION

In this paper, we used well-established psychology-based creativity research to ground definitions of creativity, creative processes, and creative tasks in the context of information search. Our findings provide insights about (1) how people use search engines and information resources to support their everyday creativity tasks, (2) the ways that creative process stages that are involved in their tasks, and (3) how they use different information resources to support different creative stages. In this section, we summarize our findings and discuss implications for future research.

With respect to **RQ1** (What types of tasks?), we found that participants looked for information to support a wide range of creative tasks (see Table 1), suggesting many opportunities (and challenges) for search systems to support everyday creativity. Considering **RQ2** (What computing platforms and information tools were used?), we found that in 42% of the tasks (n=74), combinations of devices were used, illustrating the importance of cross-session and cross-device search task resumption [62] in order to support creative tasks. Search engines were frequently used in all the task domains and images played a frequent role in arts & crafts and visual arts tasks. Videos were also commonly used, especially in arts & crafts, science, and literature/writing.

RQ3 addressed the creative process stages involved in our participants' creative tasks. For this question, our results show several interesting findings. First, we found that all of the creative stages we investigated were commonly involved in our participants' tasks. The look-up and explore stages were involved in 86% and 75% of tasks respectively, and even the least common stage (select ideas) was reported in 33% of the tasks. Second, we found that most of our participants' tasks involved *multiple* creative stages – 73% involved at least three different stages.[3] Consistent with prior work on task-based search [30], these results indicate that system awareness of the searcher's ongoing task and task-stage is important for search systems to provide stage-appropriate information.

RQ4 considered the relationships between task domain, creative process stages, and information resources/tools. Our Bayesian logistic regression models found that the look-up stage was less likely to be included in arts & crafts tasks, the explore stage was less likely in everyday/other tasks, and that the creating ideas stage was more likely in visual arts and arts & crafts tasks. Second, we examined whether different stages involved the use of different information resources/tools. Our regression models found that when doing tasks that involved the look-up stage, participants were more likely to use search engines and less likely to use images; that the explore stage increased the use of images, and that the creating ideas stage increased the likelihood of using images and social sites. Finally, we examined participants' satisfaction using different tools to support different stages. Our results showed that participants were likely

[3]**Number of stages included in a task (number of unique tasks)**: one-stage (18), two-stages (29), three-stages (34), four (29), five (21), six (17), and seven-stages (25).

to be more satisfied with using search engines to look-up information, using videos to explore potentially relevant information, and using images to help combine ideas. Participants were less satisfied with using social sites across several stages (finding goals, look-up, explore, create ideas). These results illustrate the importance of understanding users' current tasks and task stages, and point to *specific opportunities* for task-aware search systems to assist users with task- and stage-appropriate information in creative tasks.

Creative tasks: In the most of the tasks we analyzed, searching for information was not the ultimate goal, but was part of a process to achieve the creative goals of the task. Several of the creative stages we investigated are components of other types of information seeking tasks (e.g., look-up). However, several stages are more characteristic of creative tasks (e.g., create ideas, combine ideas). In this sense, creative tasks may be viewed as different from "regular" problem solving tasks. For example, Mumford et al. has concluded that creative tasks may differ from standard problem-solving tasks in that they require both convergent and divergent thinking, more cognitive effort, and may involve combining/reorganzing existing knowledge [42]. Based on these perspectives, we see opportunities for future IR research to address users' needs in different creative stages (e.g., see work on "create" tasks by Kelly et al. [31]).

7 IMPLICATIONS

Below we discuss implications of our work in terms of developing search systems to support creative tasks and future research.

(1) Systems should support cross-device search. In our survey, 47% of the creative tasks were performed across different platforms, suggesting the importance of support for continuing searches across devices. One possible way to support cross-platform creative tasks is to facilitate rich history-keeping and re-finding. Although many search engines currently support cross-platform history features, there are still challenges about how best to support users. For instance, most existing browsers display search history in chronological order, which may make it difficult for users to uncover and make sense of relationships between the information encountered, different creative stages, and keep track of different creative tasks that may be worked on in parallel. Future work should explore approaches to support making use of search history and saved content across different platforms, stages, and projects.

(2) Images and videos play important roles. Our results show that images and videos were an important resource for many creative searches and that they were frequently used in conjunction with search engines. In addition, our results show that the use of resources/tools differs across creative process stages (Table 3). This suggests that creativity can be supported through a better understanding of how to mix and rank different types of vertical content on a search result page based on users' task domain and creative process stage. For instance, in our study, participants were more likely to use videos in the execute stage (figure out how to put my ideas into practice to achieve my goal). One possible reason is that for many people, it is easier to learn procedural knowledge from videos than from textual materials. This is consistent with prior work that has shown that participants searched for videos to learn procedural knowledge about craft techniques and skills [59]. Furthermore, research from learning science has suggested that some types of knowledge are easier to learn with certain media formats than others (e.g., introducing complex topics is easier to learn with videos) [5, 41]. Future research should explore how search engines can better support users to learn different types of knowledge (e.g., declarative vs. procedural knowledge) by optimizing multimedia search results. Our results suggest that users search for information that is not only relevant, but also easy to learn and apply.

(3) There are specific opportunities for task- and stage-aware support. Our results show that for particular creative stages, participants were more likely to use certain tools (e.g., there was increased use of images for the creating ideas stage). In addition, participants had a higher probability of feeling satisfied using certain tools for particular creative stages (e.g., using images to help combine ideas). These findings illustrate opportunities for systems to support users' in particular types of creative tasks and stages.

Interestingly, Table 4 (Model 3) shows that no specific tool was preferred for the "explore" stage. Shneiderman suggested that faceted search interfaces, dynamic queries, and rich mechanisms for organizing search results are possible approaches to supporting users in exploration stages [52]. In addition to supporting the "look up" and "explore" stages, tools could be designed to integrate with search processes to support ideation. For example, Kerne et al. [32] created a novel tool that enables users to collect multimedia content (such as text, images, and videos) as they search.

As our findings suggest, creative tasks are often longitudinal, multi-stage, and multi-session tasks. Search system support for these tasks may benefit not only from traditional methods for session identification, but also from *stage identification* to understand and classify the users' current creative stage. Moreover, information needs may change as users move from one task stage to another. Future work is needed to better understand the relationships of users' information needs across different creative stages.

8 CONCLUSION

In this study, we explored the role that information search plays in supporting everyday creativity. We observed that people engage in information seeking to support an array of creative tasks across different domains and that they often use multiple devices and information resources/tools to support these activities. Our participants' tasks involved multiple creative stages that involved different, more divergent needs (e.g., create ideas) than other types of directed, convergent searching (e.g., find information). We found that search engines and other information resources/tools (e.g., images, videos, social media) are strategically used by people to support their creative processes, but there are opportunities to provide better support. Our findings provide insights into the relationships between creative task domains, creative stages, and information tools to support these activities. These results highlight particular challenges and opportunities for task- and stage-aware search systems to support users working on creative tasks and provide a foundation for future research to investigate ways to design search engines to better support users' creative processes.

Acknowledgements – This work was supported in part by NSF grant IIS-1552587. Any opinions, findings, conclusions, and recommendations expressed in this paper are those of the authors and do not necessarily reflect the views of the NSF.

REFERENCES

[1] T. M. Amabile. 1988. A model of creativity and innovation in organizations. *Research in organizational behavior* 10, 1 (1988), 123–167.

[2] P. André, m. schraefel, J. Teevan, and S. T. Dumais. 2009. Discovery is never by chance: designing for (un) serendipity. In *Proceedings of C&C' 2009*. ACM, 305–314.

[3] S. Bailin. 2012. *Achieving extraordinary ends: An essay on creativity*. Springer Science & Business Media.

[4] R. Beale. 2007. Supporting serendipity: Using ambient intelligence to augment user exploration for data mining and web browsing. *INT J HUM COMPUT INTERACT* 65, 5 (2007), 421–433.

[5] R. A. Berk. 2009. Multimedia teaching with video clips: TV, movies, YouTube, and mtvU in the college classroom. *IJTTL* 5, 1 (2009).

[6] E. H. Bradley, L. A. Curry, and K. J. Devers. 2007. Qualitative data analysis for health services research: developing taxonomy, themes, and theory. *Health services research* 42, 4 (2007), 1758–1772.

[7] S. P. Brooks and A. Gelman. 1998. General methods for monitoring convergence of iterative simulations. *J. computational and graphical stats.* 7, 4 (1998), 434–455.

[8] S. H. Carson, J. B. Peterson, and D. M. Higgins. 2005. Reliability, Validity, and Factor Structure of the Creative Achievement Questionnaire. *Creativity Research Journal* 17, 1 (2005), 37–50.

[9] S. Cobbledick. 1996. The information-seeking behavior of artists: Exploratory interviews. *The Library Quarterly* 66, 4 (1996), 343–372.

[10] S. Cowan. 2004. Informing visual poetry: Information needs and sources of artists. *Art Documentation: Journal of the Art Libraries Society of North America* 23, 2 (2004), 14–20.

[11] M. Csikszentmihalyi. 1996. *Flow and the psychology of discovery and invention*. Harper Collins, New York.

[12] M. Csikszentmihalyi. 2014. Society, culture, and person: A systems view of creativity. In *The Systems Model of Creativity*. Springer, 47–61.

[13] N. Davis, H. Winnemöller, M. Dontcheva, and E. Y.-L. Do. 2013. Toward a cognitive theory of creativity support. In *Proceedings of C&C'2013*. ACM, 13–22.

[14] A. de Rooij, P. J. Corr, and S. Jones. 2015. Emotion and Creativity: Hacking into Cognitive Appraisal Processes to Augment Creative Ideation. In *Proceedings of C&C'2015*. ACM, 265–274.

[15] G. Dove and S. Jones. 2014. Using data to stimulate creative thinking in the design of new products and services. In *Proceedings of DIS'2014*. ACM, 443–452.

[16] R. A. Finke, T. B. Ward, and S. M. Smith. 1992. *Creative cognition: Theory, research, and applications*. The MIT Press, Cambridge, MA, US.

[17] Fran, 231, o. Guimbreti, and others. 2001. Fluid interaction with high-resolution wall-size displays. In *Proceedings of the 14th annual ACM symposium on User interface software and technology*. ACM, Orlando, Florida, 21–30.

[18] P. Frank. 1999. Student artists in the library: an investigation of how they use general academic libraries for their creative needs. *The Journal of Academic Librarianship* 25, 6 (1999), 445–455.

[19] J. Frich, M. Mose Biskjaer, and P. Dalsgaard. 2018. Twenty Years of Creativity Research in Human-Computer Interaction: Current State and Future Directions. In *Proceedings of DIS'2018*. ACM.

[20] A. Gelman. 2006. Prior distributions for variance parameters in hierarchical models. *Bayesian Analysis* 1, 3 (2006), 515–533.

[21] A. Gelman, A. Jakulin, M. G. Pittau, and Y.-S. Su. 2008. A weakly informative default prior distribution for logistic and other regression models. *The Annals of Applied Statistics* (2008), 1360–1383.

[22] R. Gumienny, L. Gericke, M. Wenzel, and C. Meinel. 2013. Supporting creative collaboration in globally distributed companies. In *Proceedings of CSCW'2013*. ACM, San Antonio, Texas, USA, 995–1007.

[23] J. Hailpern, E. Hinterbichler, C. Leppert, D. Cook, and B. P. Bailey. 2007. TEAM STORM: demonstrating an interaction model for working with multiple ideas during creative group work. In *Proceedings of C&C' 2007*. ACM, Washington, DC, USA, 193–202.

[24] J. Hartel. 2003. The serious leisure frontier in library and information science: hobby domains. *Knowledge organization* 30, 3/4 (2003), 228–238.

[25] O. Hilliges, L. Terrenghi, S. Boring, and others. 2007. Designing for collaborative creative problem solving. In *Proceedings of C&C' 2007*. ACM, Washington, DC, USA, 137–146.

[26] M. D. Hoffman and A. Gelman. 2014. The No-U-turn sampler: adaptively setting path lengths in Hamiltonian Monte Carlo. *JMLR* 15, 1 (2014), 1593–1623.

[27] E. Jauk, M. Benedek, and A. C. Neubauer. 2014. The road to creative achievement: A latent variable model of ability and personality predictors. *European journal of personality* 28, 1 (2014), 95–105.

[28] J. C. Kaufman and J. Baer. 2005. The amusement park theory of creativity. *Creativity across domains: Faces of the muse* (2005), 321–328.

[29] M. Kay, G. L. Nelson, and E. B. Hekler. 2016. Researcher-centered design of statistics: Why Bayesian statistics better fit the culture and incentives of HCI. In *Proceedings of CHI'2016*. ACM, 4521–4532.

[30] D. Kelly, J. Arguello, and R. Capra. 2013. NSF workshop on task-based information search systems. In *ACM SIGIR Forum*, Vol. 47. ACM, 116–127.

[31] D. Kelly, J. Arguello, A. Edwards, and W.-c. Wu. 2015. Development and Evaluation of Search Tasks for IIR Experiments Using a Cognitive Complexity Framework. In *ICTIR*. ACM, 101–110.

[32] A. Kerne, N. Lupfer, R. Linder, and others. 2017. Strategies of Free-Form Web Curation: Processes of Creative Engagement with Prior Work. In *Proceedings of C&C'2017*. ACM, 380–392.

[33] J. Kim, M. Agrawala, and M. S. Bernstein. 2017. Mosaic: Designing Online Creative Communities for Sharing Works-in-Progress. In *Proceedings of CSCW'2018*. ACM, 246–258.

[34] J. Kruschke. 2014. *Doing Bayesian data analysis: A tutorial with R, JAGS, and Stan*. Academic Press, Inc., Orlando, FL, USA.

[35] C. C. Kuhlthau. 1991. Inside the search process: Information seeking from the user's perspective. *JASIST* (1991).

[36] S. S. Layne. 1994. Artists, art historians, and visual art information. *The reference librarian* 22, 47 (1994), 23–36.

[37] K. Luther, J.-L. Tolentino, W. Wu, and others. 2015. Structuring, aggregating, and evaluating crowdsourced design critique. In *Proceedings of CSCW' 2015*. ACM, 473–485.

[38] G. Marchionini. 1989. Information-seeking strategies of novices using a full-text electronic encyclopedia. *JASIST* 40, 1 (1989), 54.

[39] G. Marchionini. 2006. Exploratory search: from finding to understanding. *Commun. ACM* 49, 4 (2006), 41–46.

[40] G. Marchionini and R. White. 2007. Find What You Need, Understand What You Find. *INT J HUM COMPUT INTERACT* 23, 3 (2007), 205–237.

[41] R. E. Mayer and R. Moreno. 2003. Nine ways to reduce cognitive load in multimedia learning. *Educational psychologist* 38, 1 (2003), 43–52.

[42] M. D. Mumford, M. I. Mobley, R. Reiter Palmon, C. E. Uhlman, and L. M. Doares. 1991. Process analytic models of creative capacities. *Creativity Research Journal* 4, 2 (1991), 91–122.

[43] K. Nakakoji, Y. Yamamoto, and A. Aoki. 2002. Interaction design as a collective creative process. In *Proceedings of C&C'2002*. ACM, 103–110.

[44] A. Rahman and M. L. Wilson. 2015. Exploring opportunities to facilitate serendipity in search. In *Proceedings of SIGIR'2015*. ACM, 939–942.

[45] M. Resnick. 2007. All I really need to know (about creative thinking) I learned (by studying how children learn) in kindergarten. In *Proceedings of C&C'2007*. ACM, 1–6.

[46] R. Richards. 2010. Everyday creativity: Process and way of life—Four key issues. In *The Cambridge handbook of creativity*. Cambridge University Press, New York, NY, US, 189–215.

[47] T. Sakai. 2017. The Probability that Your Hypothesis Is Correct, Credible Intervals, and Effect Sizes for IR Evaluation. In *Proceedings of SIGIR'2017*. ACM, 25–34.

[48] L. Sanders and P. J. Stappers. 2012. *Convivial design toolbox: Generative research for the front end of design*. BIS.

[49] R. Savolainen. 1995. Everyday life information seeking: Approaching information seeking in the context of "way of life". *Library & information science research* 17, 3 (1995), 259–294.

[50] R. K. Sawyer. 2011. *Explaining creativity: The science of human innovation*. Oxford University Press, New York, NY, US.

[51] B. Shneiderman. 1999. User interfaces for creativity support tools. In *Proceedings of C&C'1999*. ACM, 15–22.

[52] B. Shneiderman. 2007. Creativity support tools: Accelerating discovery and innovation. *Commun. ACM* 50, 12 (2007), 20–32.

[53] D. K. Simonton. 2000. Creativity. Cognitive, personal, developmental, and social aspects. *Am Psychol* 55, 1 (Jan. 2000), 151–158.

[54] D. C. Stam. 1995. Artists and art libraries. *Art libraries journal* 20, 2 (1995), 21–24.

[55] R. A. Stebbins. 2001. Serious leisure. *Society* 38, 4 (2001), 53–57.

[56] R. A. Stebbins. 2009. Leisure and its relationship to library and: information science: bridging the gap. *Library trends* 57, 4 (2009), 618–631.

[57] A. Sutcliffe and M. Ennis. 1998. Towards a cognitive theory of information retrieval. *Interacting with Computers* 10, 3 (1998), 321–351.

[58] E. G. Toms. 2000. Serendipitous Information Retrieval. In *DELOS Workshop: Information Seeking, Searching and Querying in Digital Libraries*. Zurich, 17–20.

[59] C. Torrey, E. F. Churchill, and D. W. McDonald. 2009. Learning how: the search for craft knowledge on the internet. In *Proceedings of CHI'2009*. ACM, 1371–1380.

[60] C. Van Zijl and E. M. Gericke. 2001. Methods used by South African visual artists to find information. *Mousaion* 19, 1 (2001), 3–24.

[61] G. Wallas. 1926. *The art of thought*. J. Cape, London.

[62] Y. Wang, X. Huang, and R. W. White. 2013. Characterizing and supporting cross-device search tasks. In *Proceedings of WSDM'2013*. ACM, 707–716.

[63] H. Wei and B. Durango. 2017. Beyond Level Blueprints: Visualizing the Progression of Emotion and Narrative Driven Games. In *Proceedings of C&C'2017*. ACM, 171–183.

[64] R. W. White. 2016. *Interactions with Search Systems*. Cambridge University Press, New York, NY, US.

[65] R. W. White and R. A. Roth. 2009. Exploratory search: Beyond the query-response paradigm. *Synth. lectures on info. concepts, retrieval, and services* 1, 1 (2009), 1–98.

A KEYWORDS OF MTURK HIT GROUPS

Keywords used in the posting of Amazon Mechanical Turk (MTurk) HIT groups:

- **Group 1**: crafts, architectural design, culinary arts;
- **Group 2**: humor, theater, film;
- **Group 3**: invention, entrepreneurial ventures, product design;
- **Group 4**: visual arts, interaction design, visual design, graphic design;
- **Group 5**: writing, presentation, report writing, creative writing.

B SURVEY QUESTIONS

Q.1. For this set of questions, please think about a time recently when you went online to look for useful resources or information to help you create something. For example: designing something, coming up with a solution to a problem, brainstorming for a project, creating a new recipe, working on a writing project, remodeling your house, and so on.

Q.2. Still focusing on the task you just described, please tell us about your creative process in the task. For example, you can tell us how you started this task, what sites or resources did you use, your strategies to find information or resources, and so on.

Q.3. Which of the following did you use to look for information in this task? Choose all that apply:

- Desktop or PC,
- Smartphone,
- Tablet,
- Smart TV (Apple TV, Roku, Play TV, etc.),
- Google Home or Alexa,
- other (please specify)

Q.4. Which of the following tools did you use as part of your search? Choose all that apply:

- Search engines (Google, Bing, Yahoo, etc.)
- Videos (Youtube, Vimeo, ect.)
- Images (Pinterest, Instagram, Tumblr, Flickr, etc.)
- Social sites (Facebook, Twitter, Reddit, Google+, etc.)
- Other (please specify)

Q.5. For which of the reasons below did you use *<option selected in Q.4>* in the task (Choose all that apply):

- **Figure goals**: figure out my goal (what I want to create/design or which problem I want to address/solve)
- **Look up**: look up information relevant to my goal
- **Explore**: explore (gather a broad of range of potentially related information) about my goal
- **Create ideas**: create a large variety of ideas that may achieve my goal
- **Combine ideas**: combine some ideas that I have already had
- **Select ideas**: select the best ideas from all the new ideas that I have created
- **Execute**: figure out how to put my ideas into practice to achieve my goal
- Not applicable

Q.6. How satisfied were you with using *<option selected in Q.4>* to: *<option selected in Q.5>*

C BAYESIAN ANALYSIS

In the Bayesian models, we adopted Gelman et al.'s suggestions by setting Cauchy distributions as the default weakly informative priors for **intercept** (β_0) and **coefficients** (β_j) [21]. The half-Cauchy distribution is used as the default prior for **scale parameters** (σ) [20]. Normal distribution is used as the priors for **random effects** (ω and υ).

High-density interval (HDI) is recommended to be used for the credible interval in Bayesian analysis [34, p.89]. 95% HDI includes all the most credible values (ones with highest probability density) of the parameter. It should be noted that HDI is different by definition from the CI, which is a limit that provides no distributional information about the parameter values [34].

C.1 Logistic Regression Model

$$\begin{aligned} \mu_i &= logistic\,(\beta_0 + \sum_j \beta_j x_{ij}) \\ y_i &\sim Bernoulli\,(\mu_i) \\ \beta_0 \sim Cauchy\,(0, 10);\ & \beta_j \sim Cauchy\,(0, 2.5) \end{aligned} \tag{1}$$

The sum-to-zero constraint ($\sum_j \beta_j = 0$) is added in the model.

C.2 Rand. Effects Logistic Regression

$$\begin{aligned} \mu_i &= logistic\,(\beta_0 + \omega_{[domain[i]]} + \sum_j \beta_j x_{ij}) \\ y_i &\sim Bernoulli\,(\mu_i) \\ \omega \sim Normal\,(0, \sigma_\omega);\ & \sigma_\omega \sim Cauchy^+\,(0, 5) \\ \beta_0 \sim Cauchy\,(0, 10);\ & \beta_j \sim Cauchy\,(0, 2.5) \end{aligned} \tag{2}$$

ω is the random effects in the model. The *domain*[i] refers to the domain of the task that participant i conducted (*domain*[i] = 1,...,8).

C.3 Rand. Effects Ordered Probit Regression

$$\begin{aligned} \mu_i &= \beta_0 + \upsilon_{[user.id[i]]} + \omega_{[domain[i]]} + \sum_j \beta_j x_{ij} \\ p(y_i = k \mid \mu_i, \boldsymbol{\theta}) &= \phi(\theta_k - \mu_i) - \phi(\theta_{k-1} - \mu_i) \\ \upsilon \sim Normal\,(0, \sigma_\upsilon);\ & \omega \sim Normal\,(0, \sigma_\omega) \\ \sigma_\upsilon, \sigma_\omega &\sim Cauchy^+\,(0, 5) \\ \beta_0 \sim Cauchy\,(0, 10);\ & \beta_j \sim Cauchy\,(0, 2.5) \\ \theta_k &\sim Normal(k + 0.5, 0.25) \end{aligned} \tag{3}$$

In the model, it is assumed that there is a latent variable (μ_i) influencing participant's responses to an ordinal variable, y_i, through some "threshold concepts" that are modeled by a series of threshold values ($\theta_1, \theta_2, ..., \theta_{K-1}$, where K equates the number of ordered options in the ordinal variable). In the model, υ and ω are the random effects. ϕ refers to the cumulative distribution function. $Normal(k + 0.5, 0.25)$ is used as the prior for each threshold values ($k = 2, .., K - 2$) [34]. To make the model determined, the two extreme thresholds are fixed to meaningful values on the outcome scale [34]: $\theta_1 \equiv 1 + 0.5$ and $\theta_{K-1} \equiv K - 0.5$. The sum-to-zero constraint ($\sum_j \beta_j = 0$) is added to the model.

Making Meaning: A Focus for Information Interactions Research

Ian Ruthven
Department of Computer and Information Sciences
University of Strathclyde
Glasgow, United Kingdom
ian.ruthven@strath.ac.uk

ABSTRACT

In this perspectives paper, I discuss meaning-making as an information seeking and interaction enterprise. I present meaning-making as a vital human reaction to significant life changes and present indicative evidence of how people go about gathering information for making meaning within their lives. I discuss some of the various forms of information that can be used for meaning-making, why it is an information seeking task that is different to those we are used to in information seeking research, and motivate meaning-making as a new focus for information seeking and information interactions research.

ACM Reference format:
Ian Ruthven. 2019. Making Meaning: a Focus for Information Interactions Research. In *Proceedings of the Fourth ACM Conference on Human Information Interactions and Retrieval (CHIIR'19), March 10-14, 2019, Glasgow, United Kingdom.* ACM, New York, NY, USA, 9 pages. https://doi.org/10.1145/3295750.3298938

1 INTRODUCTION

We typically motivate research into information seeking by the reasons for which information is sought. Often these are expressed as problem-solving reasons, e.g. [1, 2], in which information helps us complete a task or resolve some uncertainty about the world. Sometimes these reasons are work-based, e.g. [3], other times they are based on everyday concerns, e.g. [4], including our leisure and hobby activities, e.g. [5]. Reasons can also be based on thematic areas of life, e.g. tackling health concerns [6] or seeking refuge [7] or based on interactions with specific types of information [8]. Here, I discuss a new perspective based on seeking information that helps us make *meaning* in problematic areas of life: information that helps us make sense of our lives.

Sense-Making, arising from Brenda Dervin's substantive body of work [9], is a more widely used term than meaning-making within Information Science whereas other disciplines, such as museum studies, favour meaning-making as a term to cover both processes [10].

ACM ISBN 978-1-4503-6025-8/19/03...$15.00 https://doi.org/10.1145/3295750.3298938

There is, however, value in differentiating the process of '*seeking comprehensibility*' of information (sense-making) from understanding its '*existential significance*' (meaning-making) [11]. That is, investigating the space beyond understanding information to exploring how people seek information to understand their own lives and how their lives may be lived differently. This may result in concrete decisions, e.g. to change a job or leave a marriage, or simply result in a new awareness of one's own life and its relationship to others'.

In this paper, I aim to show that there is distinct area of information activity about the most profound nature of our existences and to explore the challenges of this area for information seeking and interaction research. In section 2, I shall present background material to meaning-making. In section 3, I shall attempt to motivate meaning-making as an information seeking and interaction problem and, in section 4, I shall discuss what types of information supports the process of meaning-making. In section 5, I shall present some challenges for the information seeking and interaction research community to support meaning-making and conclude in section 6.

2 MEANING-MAKING

Searching for meaning is a common reaction to a significant life event. Some events seem to carry their own meaning – the birth of a child is often claimed to give 'meaning' to someone's life – or loss of meaning – bereavement often being accompanied by feelings that life has lost its meaning. Meaning-making literature focusses on the process of developing a new understanding of one's own life and a new sense of purpose for that life [12].

The literature also deals with wider groupings and how they create meaning from the information that they possess with McAdam, for example, arguing that meaning-making can occur at different levels: personal, community and national levels [13]. Chatman in her seminal studies of small worlds within prisons pointed to the meaning-making aspect of discourses regarding highly important topics, '*It is this system of common ideas about a shared experience that allows meaning to occur*' [14]. As will be explained in section 4.4, our ideas of the possible ways in which we might live our lives are constrained, to a degree, by the information environments that provide the raw materials for our meaning-making activities. Meaning-making therefore has multiple aspects, including the perceived purpose of our lives and, at a wider level, an understanding of how things work within the cultures in which we live that life and which support our drive towards a life that is meaningful to us.

In the meaning-making literature from outside Information Science, there are two bodies of literature to explain meaning-making. One views meaning-making as a process that happens in *reaction* to an event such as redundancy or illness, section 2.1. The other sees meaning-making as occurring due to a gradual *awareness* that a current existence is not meaningful anymore and a new way of living may be required, section 2.2.

2.1 Significant events

In a review of meaning-making, Park focusses on the importance of meaning-making in response to difficult life events [15]. Her research distils into the following proposition: people possess '*global meaning*' systems that orientate them in the world and are used to make meaning about the world. Any dissonance caused by violations of this global meaning causes distress and sets in course a chain of meaning-making to restore balance and '*a sense of the world as meaningful and their own lives as worthwhile*' [15].

Global meaning systems are schemas, feelings, and perceptions about how the world operates combined with global goals relating to desired states around interactions with the world and a subjective sense of purpose in life that corresponds to the feeling that ones' life has meaning. These form the backdrop of how we interpret new events and situations, [15]. Some aspects of global meaning schemas are very strong. Wu et al., for example, investigate the 'General Belief in a Just World' (GBJW) – the belief that the world is generally a fair place and people tend to get the outcomes they deserve [16]. They demonstrate that this is a stable construct across cultures and a core human belief.

Of course it is not true and most of us realise it is not true whilst still holding onto it in order to feel there is some sense in our interactions with the world. A continuing belief in the GBJW, despite considerable personal difficulty, can be associated with better coping abilities, however an undeserved event such as significant illness can challenge such beliefs and a sense of perceived injustice can block positive adjustments to a life event.

Park's specific contribution is the proposal that new events cause us to appraise the discrepancy between the event and our sense of global meaning [15]. The degree to which an event violates our sense of meaning is directly related to the amount of distress we feel and this distress leads to the need for meaning-making. In Park's model, meaning-making is not problem-solving or emotional coping but an attempt to resolve a dissonance between what we believed about the world and the event that has occurred.

This may not only change our beliefs about the world but also our goals and perceived ability to reach these goals, leading to a loss of purpose and meaning. Park notes a large body of empirical work showing that successful meaning-making can lead to better psychological adjustment and improved well-being [15].

Her approach might be criticised for its emphasis on negative life events that cause 'distress' as meaning-making may follow positive life events or simply confusion after a discovery that ones' life is not what we thought it to be. Genealogy and ancestry tourism, for example, often have strong elements of meaning-making by helping people contextualise their ancestor's lives and sense of where they come from [17]. Bruner's concept of '*turning-points*' in people's own life stories – the events in our lives that we use to distinguish what is important or significant about our lives compared to others' – also play an important role in our meaning-making about our own identities and our process of '*self-making*' [18]. However, Park's framework is useful in thinking about why people seek information during difficult life changes.

Heintzelman and King argue that meaning-making is an instinctive human act: we all have a tendency to make meaning and seek coherence in everyday life [19]. They propose an intuitive response to a lack of coherence corresponding to a 'feeling' that stimuli are not coherent which drives us towards making meaning and 'feeling' better. Park also describes this discrepancy as a '*highly uncomfortable state*' [20]. This 'feeling' is separate to our emotional responses, maybe explaining why only some people seek meaning, as they 'feel' the need to do so.

Meaning-making is not always successful and meaning may never be fully recovered. Neither does successful meaning-making necessarily make someone better off than someone who does not attempt meaning-making. However the literature generally agrees with [21] that '*more coherent narratives were related to more effective problem solving, communication, affective responsiveness, and overall general family functioning*' arguing that the outcomes from successful meaning-making (a greater sense of coherence and purpose in one's life) is better than its absence.

2.2 Gradual awakenings

Other life changes that lead to meaning-making are not the result of significant events such as illness but rather from reorientations of our lives. These reorientations result from a growing awareness that our lives are not working, leading to the desire to belong to a new community or social grouping that is a better fit to how we wish to live our lives in a more 'meaningful' way.

Straus [22] proposed a three-stage model to outline how such change can occur, using the term 'seeker', more or less synonymously with 'information seeker'. Straus's model focussed on religious conversion but the findings generalise to life changes.

In his model, the seeker starts by going through social networks, chance encounters and any available sources of information for leads to possible sources of help. Like most authors, Straus posits that religious conversion starts with a significant life event, such as bereavement, that encourages thoughts on whether a new way of life might be a better fit. Information seekers here are looking for progressive definitions as the basis for understanding (what does it mean to be gay/Muslim/divorced/etc.) and display few concrete strategies in order to find information; rather they act by '*groping through opportunities as they turn up*'. Information seekers may not see themselves as active seekers but rather as people who are receptive to information on a particular theme.

As seekers gradually become aware of their own needs, based on interactions with people and literature, they become increasingly strategic in their information seeking, focussing on good sources of information and interactions with formal groups. Here, there is often a process of learning social norms and practices for conversion and belonging. Although many religious texts emphasise single moments of enlightenment and put forward role models such as St Paul who exemplify sudden moments of divine change, for most people this stage is experimental in nature, testing out belonging with new communities and new ways of living.

Finally, seekers move into a deeper maintenance phase of belonging, understanding practices and reflecting on the experience of a new lived identity. Rules and practice of religion are important to construct a framework for this new identity and we see active information use in the form of reading scripture, for example, to ensure that the new mode of living is '*experientially real*'[22]. Reinforcement and support is a key need in this phase with [23] pointing to re-finding known religious information being a key activity many religious people .

Each stage involves information seeking from initial tentative information encountering to more formalised information interactions. This pattern of moving from initial receptivity to information moves into an active seeking phase and then to a state with a high level of domain knowledge about information sources and practices is also found in other areas of life such as coming-out as LGBT [24, 25] and joining new social groupings [26].

This model is in contrast with a more traditional passive model of identity change that presents individuals as 'being' converted or 'being' radicalised into new identities; rather individuals actively seek meaning by interacting with others who represent a '*collectivity*'[22] and who are prime agents in their own change.

3 MEANING-MAKING AS AN INFORMATION PROBLEM

Meaning does not happen easily; usually it must be sought and constructed. We can find evidence for information seeking and information interactions to support meaning-making where people ask for information, hold discussions about important topics or talk about their lives and their search for understandings. In this section, I provide indicative evidence of Internet tools being used by those in the process of making-meaning about their lives.

3.1 Search Engine Logs

Internet search engines are now a common way of finding information. Meaning is not something we can ask for directly. However, we can see people trying to orientate their lives in different direction and asking for information to do that. A glimpse at the AOL search logs [27] show people trying to gain information to (1) move their lives into better places, e.g. *how do you get over mourning a loss one, how to get over losing my boyfriend, how to get over a broken heart, how does one get over grief, how to deal with death, how to deal with schizophrenia,* (2) understand challenging life situations, e.g. *childless not by choice, am I depressed, how will I know I am starting perimenopause,* or (3) understand what it might take to change a life, e.g. *steps to transition from male to female, steps to getting a divorce, 7 steps to stop addictive behaviour.* Finding information on these topics is easy, but as will be discussed in section 5, finding the right information is not simple.

3.2 Internet Forums

We can find evidence for information seeking and information interactions to support meaning-making in online forums as well. These interactive spaces have the advantage that other people can contribute to understanding a situation and contributing ideas or experiences to help a person make sense of their life. Online groupings can create common understandings of a condition or situation that help people orientate themselves and provide a vocabulary for their own experiences, section 4.3.2.

On social Q&A sites we can see people asking questions such as '*Was I really molested or was it my fault*[1], '*I think I want to start by knowing whether or not it was rape*[2] or '*am I depressed or just pregnant*[3] where they are seeking definitional information about their lives to start the sense-making process that leads to meaning-making. These definitions help orientate people, provide a basis for thinking about their lives and how they should act to change their lives. We also see people asking questions about how to change an unsatisfactory existence such as '*how do I become a better person*'[4], or '*how can I behave better*'[5]. These are not simple questions and often mark the start of a process of change.

3.3 Epistolary Forms

Meaning-making can be an active process that goes beyond accessing information to creating information as a way of understanding one's situation. Self-expression can be a process of bringing something deep and personal out into the open for examination. Alternatively, as the old joke has it, '*I don't know what I think until I hear it come out of my mouth*'.[6] One person's account of their meaning-making journey can be useful to others who are at earlier stages of their meaning-making process.

Sites such as *https://blog.feedspot.com* host hundreds of blogs on topics such as widowhood, pregnancy, divorce, and other significant life areas. Some of these blogs are pure self-expression providing accounts of personal journeys, some are interactive providing a focus for discussions and shared experiences and some are in the 'agony aunt' advice columnist mode where people can interact with an 'expert' on a topic. Expert here often means someone who has experience of the topic rather than professional training or expertise. For those undergoing a significant life change, though, experiential information is often highly valued.

We can also see meaning-making through self-expression occur in narrative forms such as diaries or archives. Archives such as the UK Mass Observation archive[7], a record of everyday life in the UK

[1] https://answers.yahoo.com/question
[2] https://www.thestudentroom.co.uk
[3] https://www.mumsnet.com
[4] https://uk.answers.yahoo.com/question/index?qid=20170615100410AA2ONvh&guc
[5] https://uk.answers.yahoo.com/question/index?qid=20130423095722AALlMX8
[6] More formally, this can be viewed as Discovery Writing. See, for example, https://ore.exeter.ac.uk/repository/handle/10871/13802.
[7] http://www.thekeep.info/collections/mass-observation-archive/

between 1937 and 1955 or the US National Archives[8], are rich sources for examination how people use the act of writing as a means of self-understanding. Oral histories can also form a useful source of information on how individuals have made meaning.

Such self-expression can even rise to the status of art. Oscar Wilde's De Profundis, for example, talks about his process of working through disgrace and imprisonment to a psychological state where he can recreate his life: '*the ultimate discovery at which I have arrived, the starting-point for a fresh development. It has come to me right out of myself, so I know that it has come at the proper time ...My nature is seeking a fresh mode of self-realisation*'. In such cases, we see how *active* is the process of meaning-making involving strong cognitive and emotional work.

4 WHAT SUPPORTS MEANING-MAKING?

People who engage in meaning-making are setting out on a psychological discovery process without a clear idea of where they may end up. The result of meaning-making may differ markedly for different people but information in various forms is usually critical for this process. In this section, I discuss some core types of information that the literature has identified as being useful in the meaning-making process. The major theme in this article is an individual's search for meaning, and meaning-making is a personal journey, however the meaning that can be made is typically shaped by our social settings and what meanings have already been made by those around us.

4.1 Factual Information

Meaning-making often occurs in response to a new life event and new events typically require new information. Some of this information will be information on how to define the event; to help us appraise the event and decide how (and if) to act [28]. As Russell et al. note, even a diagnosis of a serious illness can be positive in that it may clear up severe uncertainty and rule out alternative, worse diagnoses [29].

Sometimes, meaning-making takes the form of meaning-focussed coping: an appraisal-based coping process in which people draw on their beliefs, values or goals to maintain their well-being during and strengthen their coping abilities during stressful life events [30, 31]. Park suggests that meaning-making can involve the search for a more favourable interpretation of current events [32] and therefore a more positive interpretation of the future. However, the key tasks in most accounts of coping are to understand what it is we are facing and how, then, can we deal with it. The 'what it is we are facing' is close to sense-making - making sense of a new situation - whilst the 'how can we deal with it' moves into meaning-making as the 'dealing' involves decisions about how we live our lives and how we respond to the new situation. Both these stages require information.

Some events can, such as bereavement, can be a time of personal information seeking (from the person we are about to lose) or, following a death, leads to a process of information seeking to understand previous generations better and make meaning about our family history. This can be a time where we uncover new information that forces questions about our immediate family history. Stalfa introduced the theoretical concept of '*posthumous disillusionment*' or what he refers to as '*an identity crisis in the midst of grief*' sparked by revelations about the deceased [33]. This can be especially pertinent to suicide, leading to the presence of unanswerable questions (why did I not realise there was a problem?). These unanswered questions may lead therefore to information seeking to restore some kind of balance in understanding who we have lost. Bogensperger and Lueger-Schuster's examination of meaning-making after a bereavement show that information seeking on the death itself may be important [34] to lay the basis for how we make meaning about the event. Was a death an unfortunate accident or Act of God? Different answers can lead to different kinds of meaning e.g. are we a victim of some random event or part of some greater plan?

A particular focus when considering factual information during meaning-making is on what is 'normal' [35] and many authors talk about '*shifting normalities*' [36] during significant life changes including trying to predict what new lives will be like, both '*Heading toward the new normal*' [37] and '*constructing a new conception of self*' [38]. The search for normality requires searching for information to develop an interpretive repertoire about one's life: to be able to tell what about a new situation (one that may or may not feel 'normal') requires attention and concern. Brashers et al. [39], for example, observed how people with chronic illness, over time, can develop strong abilities to 'read' their own bodies and detect the significance of physical signs which may or may not indicate a health concern.

4.2 Spiritual Information

As noted in section 2.1, meaning-making can be necessary because our sense of global meaning has been disrupted and this sense of global meaning is often a religious framework for understanding our lives [20]. People with religious perspectives cope better over longer periods and adapt better to negative life changes even if they may encounter more distress in the initial period after a negative event, [20, 40]. The conclusion being that religious belief may make an initial trauma worse but spiritual belief can act as a coping mechanism for longer-term recovery.

One starting place for the process of religious change is recovery from trauma and there is a large body of literature on this topic. Decker argues that traumatic change necessitates some change in life and the sense of self can lead to seeking higher level meaning and even in the most extreme traumas people can seek positive life changes as result [40]. Conversely, trauma can cause religious disillusionment. The dark night of the soul – a period of religious estrangement, a condition that causes much distress to religious people - is often caused by some traumatic event [41].

Religious information seeking during conversion to a religious life or conversion from one religion to another involves learning new facts, such as on the practices of a new faith group, but also information seeking as a process of understanding a new way of

[8] https://www.archives.gov/

living and there is a heavy emphasis in the literature on personal narratives. Narratives are heavily used by information providers as well as information seekers. Religious literature, in the form of parables, prayers, stories of admirable lives, etc. offers ways of examining one's own life in comparison with others through stories and experiences in a similar way to how modern-day biographies offer comparisons. Highly significant figures such as patron saints who 'understand' our situation are commonly sought out in times of distress. Hess notes that people can often find comfort in religious ritual as *'Rituals provide structure and reliability that counters the chaos and randomness of trauma'* [42].

4.3 Other people

During a period of meaning-making, other people are vitally useful: from being initial sources of information to becoming guides in how to live with a new identity within a new community. Often during these times, we seek 'wise' people: people who have extensive experience and insight into a particular area of life and who can guide us in unfamiliar territory. These come in two forms: professionals whose role is to provide support in life changes and volunteer community members who provide support, often without training or accountability.

4.3.1 Professionals

Within the professional literature of numerous disciplines, there are many discourses around meaning-making, even if not all use that phrase. For example, Transitions Theory, coming from nursing practice, focuses on the role of professionals in supporting successful transitions from one stage in life to another [43]. Many transitions are expressed as entering a state (becoming a widow/cancer patient/mother) but the exit from states can also be important (leaving a marriage, recovering from treatment, retiring) and the ending of roles is often the first stage in taking on new roles. The starting and ending of life roles can be challenging or liberating depending on the types of roles being left and the nature of that leaving.

Transitions Theory uses roles to shape the idea of a successful mastery of that role. The concept of role insufficiency is important: sometimes we cannot act a role successfully and this manifests in negative symptoms such as depression or anxiety or as a sense of powerlessness. One of the core contributions of Transitions Theory is the idea of role supplementation, the professional responsibility of nurses to identify where people are failing to take on new roles successfully and support them in this. Formally, role supplementation is *'further defined as the conveying of information or experience necessary to bring the role incumbent and significant others to full awareness of the anticipated behaviour patterns, units, sentiments, sensations and goals involved in each role'* [44]. This emphasizes that role comprehension, understanding a new life role, can be planned for and that nurses can support role changes.

Lloyd's notion of transition from novice to expert with the *'ability to access information through the lived experiences of practice'* and the *'cognitive scaffolding'* she describes by which experts support literacies of novices within new roles is an important part of meaning-making [45]. Professionals provide information, ways to learn about what to expect from a new life change and how others can dealt with changes. Both Transitions Theory and Lloyd emphasize the experiential nature of this information; not just passing on facts but helping people learn from other's experience.

4.3.2 Community

Some transitions are supported by professionals; in other life transitions, there is no professional support and therefore any support is informally arranged through non-governmental agencies, churches, charities or community members. Here, communities often provide their own intermediaries and mentors, who can be positive and supportive or negative and manipulative.

Yeh [24], for example, examining the identify formation of gay men and lesbians in Taiwan, emphasised the role of mentoring as an important, but not universal, stage in connecting with homosexual communities. One critical role of mentors is in explaining social norms of those communities in order to be accepted and, therefore, become able to access information. Kubiek et al. [25] also mention the valuable role that non-sexual mentors can play in the initial stages of coming out.

Harviainen looked at information practices within the BDSM community [26] and the importance of mentors, not a term Harviainen uses but which fits the role, in joining a new community. Importantly, he noted that the initial phase of joining a new community, and the relief from stigma that can be associated with this stage, can lower an individual's information literacies leading to an over-belief in the information provided. Once an individual is established within a community, they can then develop more critical approaches to information.

Transitions that are viewed negatively by one's social network can lead to people being more vulnerable when transitioning to a new life and mentors can have a very dark side: Knowles for example [46] showing that rape and sexual assaults in prison are often highly planned and based on grooming techniques from those posing as mentors. Those who are more familiar with prison environments or who have social groupings that they can access can become aware of such techniques; those without such informational support are more likely to end up as victims. Kubiek et al. [25] is one of the few papers to mention the role of sexual partners as a source of information on social norms, pointing out the often manipulative nature of such information.

Seeking out those who can aid us in understanding a life change, though, is a natural response. Buunk and Gibbons, reviewing the literature on Social Comparison Theory, suggest that fear-based life changes lead to seeking those in similar situations as do life changes that have a great deal of uncertainty, such as disability [47]. This accords with theory of Davison et al. and their claim that affiliative behaviours – looking for people who are similar – often increases during times of anxiety as we look for people who are similar for understanding and to judge normality and that the shared experiences of others can be more important than professional information structures. The support gained form others' experiences are part of the reason that support groups for things like diet and smoking cessation are common [48].

In health situations, social groupings also help *'paint a portrait of diagnosis'* by developing a collective understanding of disease. Conditions that are socially stigmatising, embarrassing or disfiguring can lead to alienation from normal social support groups [48] and therefore moving outside of our normal social circles to aid understanding and meaning-making. Similarly, the social support systems we normally rely on may not have experience of certain life events and therefore need to seek out others to help with meaning-making. In such events, we are more likely to seek those who have been in similar situations rather those about to face them. i.e. want information and to reduce stress rather than share it [47].

4.4 Narratives

People can be of direct use for advice, information or support during times of change. People can also be of indirect help by providing narratives that can inspire or demonstrate new ways of living a life and examining how other people have lived their lives can be a way of understanding how we can live ours. Adams and Pierce, Trevor and Boddy, and Taylor all discuss the role that literature, in particular autobiographical and fiction, play as a means of understanding a life change [49-51]. These narrative forms help us understand the possibilities for our life, as Singer notes *'The stories that individuals create [of their own identity] draw from the existing repertoire of cultural narratives based in myth, fable, literature, popular entertainment and ethnic family history that define the meaning making parameters of their lives'*. We create and tell stories about ourselves to express the meaning we have made about our lives [52] and we use existing literature to help us create these stories. Some works are particularly powerful, as noted by Ferrari et al. *'Some works of literary fiction and historical narratives become canonical for the exact reason that they model or portray a generally accepted ideology that is abstracted into a master narrative. Cultural master narratives are sense-making structures available to individuals, effectively guiding and shaping the stories they tell to others and themselves.'* [53].

In the case of marginalized groups, literature and mass media may be the only way for people to access representations of their own lives. Visual representation of same-sex attraction, which may often be missing in everyday life, was previously only to be found on mass media and formed an important method of passive information seeking about life's possibilities [54].

Mass media can also provide factual information that forms part of a background knowledge about life. Rothbauer [55], Pecosksie [56] and Liming [57] all point to literature forming an important source of support for identity formation and communication of sexual identities, with literature being especially used during early stages of understanding one's own sexual identities. They also show that fiction often to be read between the lines or 'against' the text to uncover possibly hidden meanings that can be 'read' by a gay/lesbian reading perspective. In Liming's study she uncovered many subtleties in reading patterns to search for lesbian narratives within 'heterosexual' texts and changes in reading habits to 'protect' these interpretations.

Not everyone reads fiction of course and these studies often point to the need by participants to hide such literature to allow safe exploration. However, the power of literature cannot be under-stated and is reflected in the strong attachment of readers to fiction that was important to their understanding of their identity. Even in literature some groups are under-represented, with Waite, and Adams and Peirce [49, 58] noting that portrayals of transgendered characters are not always positive and, compared to LGB characters, appear far less often and less centrally.

Discussion forums are a place where anyone can provide a narrative of their own life and can been seen as a form of what Veinot refers to as collaborative information behaviour with communities sharing their own experience and personal knowledge, [59]. Straus states that *'[the] collective organisation and employment of ritual and other institutions has some direct, practical value in participants' endeavours to create and maintain orderliness and meaningfulness in their lives.'* [22]. That is, communities can create structure and meaning that lead individuals to feeling that they have some coherence to their own existence. This links strongly to the underlying principles of Everyday Life Information Seeking and its concept of mastery of life in which we feel some control over own existence [4].

A core theme in meaning-making is the need to develop understandings of a new situations, such as widowhood, recovery from addiction or parenthood, and what they mean in the sense of what are their characteristics, potentials and limits. These are not quick fix tasks that can be answered during a single search engine session, rather they often seem to be a longer-term, almost meditative process of uncovering a new existence.

A common source of inspiration for this are self-help books and material. Self-help has as its core this aim of understanding life events through sharing lived experiences and talking through significant life events. As a genre, self-help ranges widely in quality and tone but many contained distilled, popularized scientific understandings of an area of life that can help explain a situation a person has entered or give them a way of understanding how they came to a particular point in their own life. The use of narratives, also common to recovery from addiction [60], is common to people trying to find a new way of living rather than incorporating a change into an existing life.

5. INFORMATION INTERACTIONS

As noted in Section 1, the reasons we engage in an information search are often based on problem-solving or task-based understandings. The task of meaning-making is to reconstruct a sense of identity and purpose within our lives. Such understandings are not problems in the sense that information retrieval typically understands; they may come from problematic situations that can, but do not always, benefit from information. However, meaning-making is very subjective: what works for one person may not work for another. It is also an area in which filling cognitive gaps alone is not sufficient; information has to speak to the whole person, including their desires, beliefs, and motivations. Sometimes the right information may be a patchwork of sources or it may be a single object that provides a flash of particular insight. However, we can start to map out how information interaction and retrieval can approach meaning-making as a concept. I will present the discussion under two headings: what interactive techniques may support meaning-making and how do we evaluate support for meaning-making processes?

5.1 Interactive support

Meaning-making may require different kinds of interactive system support, each of which can present new challenges for information interactions research. Some options include:

- **Recommendations**. Many sources of information are associated with user-generated content in the form of recommendations, reviews, and personal experiences. These can help an individual make decisions about what information to use, what books to buy or what sources of support to seek. They can be used to create reading lists and support repositories. Not all sources are equally useful and some may be more useful than others. As noted above, in some areas of life there are canons of books, including biography and fiction, which communities use as sources of particular inspiration and understanding. The question is then how to detect from this content which information is useful for the particular purpose of meaning-making as opposed to other uses: what films, books, essays, etc. change lives as opposed to simply being enjoyable or interesting?
- **Articulating sources of support**. As noted in section 4.3, people can offer useful support during a life change, explaining new experiences and offering support. Those in the early stages of experiencing a problematic information are often unable to express precisely what they want and benefit from interactions with sympathetic and knowledgeable peers [61, 62]. Expertise finding is an established information retrieval task but less common is recommending *groups* of people, either in the form of official support services or also forums and discussion groups. How to identify the best sources for meaning-making is not clear. Issues such as topical expertise are naturally important but people who are sought out for support during meaning-making need to have credibility so issues of trust, empathy and accessibility become important. How can we operationalise such attributes in order to recommend groups to people in search of support?
- **Structuring support**. As described above, whether meaning-making occurs in response to an external life event or an awareness that a life needs change, there are distinct phases of adaptation. We are used in interactive information seeking and retrieval to thinking about phases, e.g. in Kuhlthau's information search process or Taylor's four levels of information need [63, 64] but it is far less common in interactive research to see support for different phases. There are also indications from the meaning-making literature that the right information presented at the wrong time will not be recognised as useful. Therefore, considering what information is most appropriate for different stages of meaning-making is crucial. Early stage support could focus on sense-making information, later stages on coping and adaptation information for example. Meaning-making literature shows that people use different information seeking strategies at different phases of a meaning-making journey, e.g. [22], but we lack detail on how systems could provide different information, or provide information in different ways, for people at each stage.
- **Narratives and possibilities**. As outlined in section 4.4 narratives are very useful in thinking about new possibilities for our lives after a change in our circumstances. Sometimes these narratives may involve leading very different lives with different purposes. A novel search task may then be how to retrieve narratives: how to retrieve fictional or factual accounts of lives that may provide inspiration for how to live our lives?

5.2 How to evaluate meaning-making?

Meaning-making is often stimulated by a range of sources including discussions, narratives, and dedicated resources. Sometimes meaning-making can occur rapidly and without (much) new information but, as indicated in section 2, it is most commonly a process of adjustment, one of change minimization to retain as much as possible of our current beliefs and ways of living, then adjustment to a new mode of living and understanding. This adjustment may be preceded by a phase of negative emotions such depression, uncertainty, confusion, arising from the need for change and uncertainty about how to change. Meaning-making often happens after this, as a process of exploration, testing, and learning being played out.

The information required for meaning-making is unlikely to be obtained through a single search session. Neither can we evaluate it as a collection of topically relevant information. That is not to say that we cannot judge some information as being more useful than others for meaning-making, a point I shall return to later.

The meaning that is made through meaning-making can vary drastically between people after the same life event and so we cannot prescribe what meaning is and evaluate it against a known ideal outcome. However, we can investigate the *process* of meaning-making and how information has contributed to this process. One source of inspiration is Transitions Theory, section 4.3.1, a theory arising from nursing that has a strong emphasis on life roles and how we enter and exit life roles [65]. Transitions Theory has been used across a range of life transitions including changes in job roles [66], personal changes such as menopause [67], becoming a care-giver [68], and illness diagnoses [69].

Transitions theory uses the idea of roles to shape the idea of a successful mastery of a life role. This speaks to Savoilainen's concept of '*mastery of life*', or '*one's pervasive and relatively enduring feeling of confidence that the stimuli deriving from internal and external environments are structured, predictable, and explicable; that one has adequate resources to meet the demands posed by these stimuli, and that these demands are meaningful and worthy of engagement.*' [4]. Savoilainen defines mastery of life as aiming at '*[the] at elimination of continual dissonance between perceptions of "how things are at this moment" and "how they should be."*' This is similar to how we characterized meaning-making: a process of regaining mastery of our own existence, necessary due to a perceived discrepancy between our world as it was and how the world is now.

The concept of role insufficiency is important: sometimes we cannot act a role successfully and this manifests in negative symptoms such as depression or anxiety. One of the core contributions of Transitions Theory is the idea of role supplementation, the professional responsibility of nurses to identify where people are failing to take on new roles successfully and support them in this. Formally, role supplementation is '*the conveying of information or experience necessary to bring the role incumbent and significant others to full awareness of the anticipated behaviour patterns, units, sentiments, sensations and goals involved in each role*' [44]. Ultimately it is this sense of control and that '*demands are meaningful and worthy of engagement*' [4] are what meaning-making is heading for and how it should be evaluated.

In terms of meaning-making we can think of measuring the degree to which a person has identified useful sources, developed an understanding of their new live and its potentials and feels happy with new life changes. We can also try to measure the degree to which they have obtained information to help this support. This is not trivial– and may require new evaluation approaches – but it is how the practice of information provision in operational environments such as hospitals or care centres is typically performed and colleagues in these services may have useful ideas on how to evaluate our solutions.

Sense-making and meaning-making are related. This paper has taken the view that sense-making leads into meaning-making and what sense has been made directs what meaning can be made: knowing the likelihood of cancer returning or how a traumatic situation could have been avoided does make differences in terms of the meanings that can be made from these situations. This does not imply a strictly linear relationship; rather, more likely, with life changes there are iterative episodes of sense-making, meaning-making and information use. Creating a more nuanced way of separating and relating sense-making and meaning-making can also help with creating new evaluation approaches.

At the document or object level we may also think about what relevance means in terms of meaning-making. Saracevic defined motivational relevance as the highest level of relevance and that '*Satisfaction, success, accomplishment, and the like are criteria for inferring motivational relevance*' [70]. These criteria go beyond simply solving problems, rather they suggest that information at the highest level of relevance, information needs to speak to a whole person and their feelings about what they have achieved. In meaning-making there is a similar perspective, that the information has to resonate with a person and speak to a deeper need for transformational change. In a sense, this is what is critical for meaning-making, to find information that religious writers often call '*revelatory knowledge*', information that goes beyond simply providing factual information but promotes a deeper sense of understanding. Can such information be automatically detected? This seems a major challenge for information retrieval.

6. CONCLUSIONS

The literature on meaning-making generally follows the line offered by McAdams, '*that making personal meaning out of life stories typically involves drawing semantic conclusions out of episodic events*' [13]. That is, we use events that happen to us to create a sense of meaning and purpose for our lives. Sometimes these events are unexpected: settled lives may become unsettled or require reconfiguring, resulting in information needs about many areas of life that were previously unproblematic.

Meaning-making does not occur instantaneously and Horowitz has suggested that information avoidance behaviours could be sign that individuals are trying to incorporate information about events that is incompatible with previously held beliefs [71]. Where information professionals can be of use is in appropriate interventions. For Kuhlthau, meaning is the motive for information interactions and she called for collaborative work between information professionals and lay people on how to create meaning, stressing the important role of helping people make meaning out of events and information [63].

Other authors have shown that appropriate intervention can be useful to avoid negative conditions, such as depression, resulting from poor adjustments to life changes. Another useful role of information intermediaries, including systems, can be to help recover identity [72]. The end results of meaning-making can be concrete and measurable, e.g. in terms of having a concrete vocabulary to talk through experiences and feelings [73].

Information science has not dealt as fully with meaning-making compared to sense-making although it is a rich area for study. This perspectives paper proposes meaning-making as a new focus for information-centred research. It is a challenging area as meaning can be difficult to capture and robustly investigate. However, meaning-making is one of the most psychologically important tasks of being human and an area where information interactions research could make significant and profound changes to how we live our lives.

ACKNOWLEDGEMENTS

I am deeply grateful to Dr Rebekah Willson for organizing a silent writing workshop, without which this paper would not have been completed. I am also very grateful indeed to the anonymous reviewers from the CHIIR community for their very insightful comments and suggestions, these have improved both this paper and my own thinking on this topic.

REFERENCES

[1] Savolainen, R. Source preferences in the context of seeking problem-specific information. *Inform Process Manag*, 44, 1 (2008), 274-293.
[2] Belkin, N. J., Oddy, R. N. and Brooks, H. M. ASK for information retrieval: Part I. Background and theory. *J Doc*, 38, 2 (1982), 61-71.
[3] Byström, K., Ruthven, I. and Heinström, J. Work and information: which workplace models still work in modern digital workplaces? *Information Research*, 22, 1 (2017).
[4] Savolainen, R. Everyday Life Information-Seeking - Approaching Information-Seeking in the Context of Way of Life. *Libr Inform Sci Res*, 17, 3 (1995), 259-294.
[5] Hartel, J. The serious leisure frontier in library and information science: hobby domains. *Knowledge organization*, 30, 3-4 (2003), 228-238.
[6] Genuis, S. K. and Bronstein, J. Looking for "normal": Sense making in the context of health disruption. *Journal of the Association for Information Science and Technology*, 68, 3 (2017), 750-761.
[7] Oduntan, O. and Ruthven, I. Investigating the information gaps in refugee integration. *Proceedings of the Association for Information Science and Technology*, 54, 1 (2017), 308-317.
[8] Jones, W. Personal information management. *Annual review of information science and technology*, 41, 1 (2007), 453-504.

[9] Dervin, B., Foreman-Wernet, L. and Lauterbach, E. *Sense-making methodology reader: Selected writings of Brenda Dervin*. Hampton Pr, 2003.

[10] Silverman, L. H. Visitor Meaning-Making in Museums for a New Age. *Curator: The Museum Journal*, 38, 3 (1995), 161-170.

[11] Dransart, D. A. C. From sense-making to meaning-making: Understanding and supporting survivors of suicide. *British Journal of Social Work*, 43, 2 (2013), 317-335.

[12] Lichtenthal, W. G., Currier, J. M., Neimeyer, R. A. and Keesee, N. J. Sense and significance: a mixed methods examination of meaning making after the loss of one's child. *Journal of clinical psychology*, 66, 7 (2010), 791-812.

[13] McAdams, D. P. *The Redemptive Self: Stories Americans Live By-Revised and Expanded Edition*. Oxford University Press, 2013.

[14] Chatman, E. A. A theory of life in the round. *J Assoc Inf Sci Tech*, 50, 3 (1999), 207-217.

[15] Park, C. L. Making sense of the meaning literature: an integrative review of meaning making and its effects on adjustment to stressful life events. *Psychological Bulletin*, 136, 2 (2010), 257-301.

[16] Wu, M. S., Yan, X., Zhou, C., Chen, Y., Li, J., Zhu, Z., Shen, X. and Han, B. General belief in a just world and resilience: Evidence from a collectivistic culture. *European Journal of Personality*, 25, 6 (2011), 431-442.

[17] Alexander, M., Bryce, D. and Murdy, S. Delivering the Past Providing Personalized Ancestral Tourism Experiences. *Journal of Travel Research*, 56, 4 (2016), 543-555.

[18] Bruner, J. Self-Making and World-Making. *Journal of Aesthetic Education*, 25, 1 (1991), 67-78.

[19] Heintzelman, S. J. and King, L. A. (The feeling of) meaning-as-information. *Personality and Social Psychology Review*, 18, 2 (2014), 153-167

[20] Park, C. L. Religion as a meaning-making framework in coping with life stress. *Journal of social issues*, 61, 4 (2005), 707-729.

[21] Fiese, B. H. and Wamboldt, F. S. Coherent accounts of coping with a chronic illness: Convergences and divergences in family measurement using a narrative analysis. *Family Process*, 42, 4 (2003), 439-451.

[22] Straus, R. A. Religious conversion as a personal and collective accomplishment. *Sociology of Religion*, 40, 2 (1979), 158-165.

[23] Wan-Chik, R. Z. *Religious information seeking on the Web: A study of Islamic and Qur'anic information searching*. University of Sheffield, 2013.

[24] Yeh, N.-C. The social constructionist viewpoint on gays and lesbians, and their information behaviour. *Information Research*, 13, 4 (2008).

[25] Kubicek, K., Beyer, W. J., Weiss, G., Iverson, E. and Kipke, M. D. In the dark: Young men's stories of sexual initiation in the absence of relevant sexual health information. *Health Educ Behav*, 37, 2 (2010), 243-263.

[26] Harviainen, J. T. Information Literacies of Self-Identified Sadomasochists: An Ethnographic Case Study. *J Doc*, 71, 3 (2015).

[27] Bar-Ilan, J. *Position paper: Access to query logs—an academic researcher's point of view*. City, 2007.

[28] Sweeny, K. Crisis decision theory: Decisions in the face of negative events. *Psychological Bulletin*, 134, 1 (2008), 61-76.

[29] Russell, C. S., White, M. B. and White, C. P. Why me? Why now? Why multiple sclerosis?: Making meaning and perceived quality of life in a Midwestern sample of patients with multiple sclerosis. *Families, Systems, & Health*, 24, 1 (2006), 65.

[30] Folkman, S. and Moskowitz, J. T. 12 Positive affect and meaning-focused coping during significant psychological stress. *The Scope of Social Psychology: Theory and Applications: Essays in Honour of Wolfgang Stroebe* (2007), 193-208.

[31] Folkman, S. The case for positive emotions in the stress process. *Anxiety, stress, and coping*, 21, 1 (2008), 3-14.

[32] Park, C. L. The meaning making model: A framework for understanding meaning, spirituality, and stress-related growth in health psychology. *The European Health Psychologist*, 15, 2 (2013), 40-47.

[33] Stalfa, F. J. "Posthumous disillusionment" as a type of complicated grief. *Journal of Pastoral Care & Counseling*, 64, 2 (2010), 1-8.

[34] Bogensperger, J. and Lueger-Schuster, B. Losing a child: Finding meaning in bereavement. *European Journal of Psychotraumatology*, 5, 1 (2014), 22910.

[35] Genuis, S. K. and Bronstein, J. Looking for "normal": Sense making in the context of health disruption. *J Assoc Inf Sci Tech*, 68, 3 (2016), 750–761

[36] Sanderson, T., Calnan, M., Morris, M., Richards, P. and Hewlett, S. Shifting normalities: interactions of changing conceptions of a normal life and the normalisation of symptoms in rheumatoid arthritis. *Sociology of health & illness*, 33, 4 (2011), 618-633.

[37] Martell, L. K. Heading Toward the New Normal: A Contemporay Postpartum Experience. *Journal of Obstetric, Gynecologic & Neonatal Nursing*, 30, 5 (2001), 496-506.

[38] Abrams, L. S. and Curran, L. Maternal Identity Negotiations Among Low-Income Women With Symptoms of Postpartum Depression. *Qualitative Health Research*, 21, 3 (2011), 373-385.

[39] Brashers, D. E., Neidig, J. L., Haas, S. M., Dobbs, L. K., Cardillo, L. W. and Russell, J. A. Communication in the management of uncertainty: The case of persons living with HIV or AIDS. *Commun Monogr*, 67, 1 (2000), 63-84.

[40] Decker, L. R. The role of trauma in spiritual development. *Journal of Humanistic Psychology*, 33, 4 (1993), 33-46.

[41] Durà-Vilà, G., Dein, S., Littlewood, R. and Leavey, G. The dark night of the soul: Causes and resolution of emotional distress among contemplative nuns. *Transcultural psychiatry*, 47, 4 (2010), 548-570.

[42] Hess, C. *Sites of violence, sites of grace: Christian nonviolence and the traumatized self*. Lexington Books, 2008.

[43] Meleis, A. I. *Transitions theory: Middle range and situation specific theories in nursing research and practice*. Springer publishing company, 2010.

[44] Meleis, A. I. and Swendsen, L. A. Role supplementation: an empirical test of a nursing intervention. *Nursing Research*, 27, 1 (1978), 11-17.

[45] Lloyd, A. Information literacy landscapes: An emerging picture. *Journal of Documentation*, 62, 5 (2006/09 2006), 570-583.

[46] Knowles, G. J. Male Prison Rape: A Search for Causation and Prevention. *The Howard Journal of Criminal Justice*, 38, 3 (1999), 267-282.

[47] Buunk, A. P. and Gibbons, F. X. Social comparison: The end of a theory and the emergence of a field. *Organizational Behavior and Human Decision Processes*, 102, 1 (2007), 3-21.

[48] Davison, K. P., Pennebaker, J. W. and Dickerson, S. S. Who talks? The social psychology of illness support groups. *American Psychologist*, 55, 2 (2000), 205-217.

[49] Adams, S. S. and Peirce, K. *Is there a transgender canon?: Information seeking and use in the transgender community*. City, 2013.

[50] Trevor, M. and Boddy, J. Transgenderism and Australian social work: A literature review. *Australian Social Work*, 66, 4 (2013), 555-570.

[51] Taylor, J. K. Targeting the information needs of transgender individuals. *Current Studies in Librarianship*, 26, 1/2 (2002), 85-109.

[52] Singer, J. A. Narrative identity and meaning making across the adult lifespan: An introduction. *Journal of personality*, 72, 3 (2004), 437-460.

[53] Ferrari, M., Weststrate, N. M. and Petro, A. *Stories of wisdom to live by: Developing wisdom in a narrative mode*. Springer, City, 2013.

[54] Hamer, J. S. Coming-out: Gay males' information seeking. *School Libraries Worldwide* (2003), 73-89.

[55] Rothbauer, P. M. *"People Aren't Afraid Anymore, But It's Hard to Find Books": Reading Practices That Inform the Personal and Social Identities of Self-Identified Lesbian and Queer Young Women*. City, 2013.

[56] Pecoskie, J. J. Reading in the "Grafted Space": Public/Private Pleasure Reading and Sexual Identity. *Mémoires du livre/Studies in Book Culture*, 3, 2 (2012).

[57] Liming, S. *"Reading for It:" Lesbian readers constructing culture and identity through the textual experience*. Palgrave MacMillan, City, 2007.

[58] Waite, J. *To What Extent Do Public Libraries in the UK Provide Adequate Resources for Trans People*. A study submitted in partial fulfilment of the requirements for the degree of Master of Arts in Librarianship. Sheffield iSchool. The University of Sheffield. Sheffield, City, 2013.

[59] Veinot, T. C. Interactive acquisition and sharing: Understanding the dynamics of HIV/AIDS information networks. *J Am Soc Inf Sci Tec*, 60, 11 (2009), 2313-2332.

[60] Weegmann, M. and Piwowoz-Hjort, E. 'Naught but a story': Narratives of successful AA recovery. *Health Sociology Review*, 18, 3 (2009), 273-283.

[61] Ruthven, I., Buchanan, S. and Jardine, C. Relationships, environment, health and development: The information needs expressed online by young first-time mothers. *J Assoc Inf Sci Tech*, 69, 8 (2018), 985-995.

[62] Ruthven, I., Buchanan, S. and Jardine, C. Isolated, overwhelmed, and worried: Young first-time mothers asking for information and support online. *J Assoc Inf Sci Tech*, 69, 9 (2018), 1073-1083.

[63] Kuhlthau, C. C. Seeking meaning. *Norwood, NJ: Ablex* (1993).

[64] Taylor, R. S. Question-negotiation and information seeking in libraries. *College & research libraries*, 29, 3 (1968), 178-194.

[65] Meleis, A. I. Role insufficiency and role supplementation: a conceptual framework. *Nursing research*, 24, 4 (1975), 264-271.

[66] Meleis, A. I. The undeaning transition: Toward becoming a former dean. *Nursing Outlook*, 64, 2 (3// 2016), 186-196.

[67] Marnocha, S. K., Bergstrom, M. and Dempsey, L. F. The lived experience of perimenopause and menopause. *Contemporary Nurse*, 37, 2 (2011), 229-240.

[68] Duggleby, W. D., Swindle, J., Peacock, S. and Ghosh, S. A mixed methods study of hope, transitions, and quality of life in family caregivers of persons with Alzheimer's disease. *BMC geriatrics*, 11, 1 (2011), 1.

[69] Hanna, K. M. A framework for the youth with type 1 diabetes during the emerging adulthood transition. *Nursing Outlook*, 60, 6 (11// 2012), 401-410.

[70] Saracevic, T. *Relevance reconsidered*. ACM New York, City, 1996.

[71] Horowitz, M. J. Stress-response syndromes: A review of posttraumatic and adjustment disorders. *Psychiatric Services*, 37, 3 (1986), 241-249.

[72] Mokros, H. B. and Aakhus, M. From Information-Seeking Behavior to Meaning Engagement Practice. *Hum Commun Res*, 28, 2 (2002), 298-312.

[73] Hoeybye, M. T. Storytelling of breast cancer in cyberspace. *Online Counteractions to the Isolation and Demeaning of Illness Experience. Copenhagen, Denmark: University of Copenhagen* (2002).

An Interactive Image Retrieval Approach to Searching for Images on Social Media

Manali Gaikwad
Department of Computer Science
University of Regina
Regina, SK, Canada
gaikwadm@uregina.ca

Orland Hoeber
Department of Computer Science
University of Regina
Regina, SK, Canada
orland.hoeber@uregina.ca

ABSTRACT

Searching for images posted within social media services such as Twitter relies on matching textual queries to the contents of the posts that include the images. Unfortunately, social media posts may not always provide accurate or meaningful descriptions of the contents of the embedded images, making searching for images a challenging task. In this research, we augment the textual contents of the posts with new information extracted from the images using image processing and deep learning methods, and provide a visual interface to enable interactive image retrieval. A user study was conducted with 28 participants to collect evidence on how our approach was used in relation to Vakkari's three-stage model of information seeking. We also analyzed participants' perceptions of usefulness, ease of use, and satisfaction in comparison to a common grid-based image search interface. The results from this study highlight the value of providing visual and interactive features to enable searchers to discover images from social media sources.

KEYWORDS

Image search, interactive image retrieval, information seeking, search visualization

ACM Reference Format:
Manali Gaikwad and Orland Hoeber. 2019. An Interactive Image Retrieval Approach to Searching for Images on Social Media. In *2019 Conference on Human Information Interaction and Retrieval (CHIIR '19), March 10–14, 2019, Glasgow, Scotland UK.* ACM, New York, NY, USA, 9 pages. https://doi.org/10.1145/3295750.3298930

1 INTRODUCTION

Over the last decade, we have experienced a rapid growth of social media use due to the development and ongoing refinement of multimedia, networking, and mobile technologies. This technology has changed the way people collect, share, search for, and learn from the information available to them. Social media services such as Twitter have emerged as powerful tools for not only sharing personal opinions and staying informed about friends and family, but also as a source for the discovery of information [12].

CHIIR '19, March 10–14, 2019, Glasgow, Scotland UK

ACM ISBN 978-1-4503-6025-8/19/03...$15.00
https://doi.org/10.1145/3295750.3298930

While the textual aspects of social media continue to be important, embedded media (e.g., images) are becoming increasingly popular. The methods for searching within the image content are not well supported within social media services themselves, nor within other interactive search and exploration tools [7]. Most interfaces that do support image search (e.g., the photos tab of the Twitter search interface) provide a grid-based representation and an implied relevance ranking, supporting visual scanning and scrolling as the primary interactive mechanisms, with little support for interactive exploration and sensemaking.

Image search is an important special case of information seeking, with two specific aspects that make image search challenging: (1) it is common for the searcher to have an under-specified information need [16], and (2) searchers have difficulty textually describing what it is they are seeking [11]. As a result, the traditional targeted-search approach to search interface design (e.g., query box and search results list or grid) may not be sufficient to support the search tasks necessary to find relevant images. Our research approaches this problem from two directions: extracting useful information from the images to augment the social media posts; and developing a visual and interactive image retrieval interface that leverages this extracted information to organize the images and support exploratory search [23] and sensemaking [18] within the context of Vakkari's three-stage model of information seeking [20].

To evaluate our approach to supporting image search tasks, we have developed prototype software called ImgSEE. A controlled laboratory study was conducted to study how participants use ImgSEE in relation to the specific stages of information seeking specified in Vakkari's model. The study also had participants conduct similar search tasks using a common grid-based interface, allowing us to compare how they perceived the interfaces in terms of usability for the intended tasks. The results of this study provide evidence of the benefit of augmenting social media posts with supplemental information from the embedded images, and the value of using this information within a visual interface that supports interactive engagement with the search process.

The remainder of this paper is organized as follows. Section 2 provides an overview of the key literature that has informed this research. Section 3 presents the details of the design and implementation of ImgSEE. Section 4 explains the methodology and results of the user study. The paper concludes with a summary of the primary contributions of this research.

2 RELATED WORK

This work was informed by prior research in the domains of interactive information retrieval, information visualization, and image search. In this section, relevant work from these areas are presented and discussed in the context of interactive image retrieval from social media sources.

2.1 Interactive Information Retrieval

Information retrieval focuses on the process of obtaining relevant information objects to a user's information needs. The traditional approach has changed over time to support users in accomplishing the goal interactively, enabling them to engage in information seeking processes [2]. Information seeking is a problem-solving task that consists of recognizing and understanding the problem, creating a plan for the search, conducting the search, evaluating the results, and repeating the process as required. In order to develop an interactive search interface to support users' information seeking goals, it is important to understand the strategies people use while searching for information.

Vakkari's three-stage model of information seeking [20] is particularly relevant to image retrieval, given the underspecified nature of image search tasks. During the pre-focus stage, a searcher may undertake a series of broad searches in order to assess the breadth of images that are present in the collection. In the focus formulation stage, a searcher may refine the goal of the search activity, and seek relevant images. In the post-focus stage, a searcher may collect, organize, and make use of the found images. Exploratory search processes [23] may occur during the pre-focus and focus formulation stages, as the searcher moves from a broad exploration to a focused search. Sensemaking [18] may occur throughout this exploratory search process, and may also be present during the post-focus stage, as the searcher seeks to organize and manage the images found.

Information foraging theory [17] explains processes associated with people searching for information. An important part of this theory is the concept of information scent [5], which describes a mechanism by which people interpret the information available to them to decide where to direct their efforts. An interactive image retrieval interface may be designed to enable information scent, by providing visual cues that afford the searcher with information regarding the makeup of the image collection and the ability to predict the results of their interaction with the search interface.

2.2 Information Visualization

Information visualization deals with the presentation and communication of abstract data using graphical representations [22]. A visual representation can be processed more quickly compared to a similar amount of text, leveraging the human ability to perceive, interpret, and make sense of visual stimuli. While precision may be lost while visualizing information, what is gained is the ability to assess similarities and relationships among a large amount of data with minimal effort.

The visual encoding of information is a fundamental concern within information visualization. While there are a wide range of visual variables that can be manipulated to encode information (e.g., position, shape, size, brightness, hue, orientation, texture, motion [22]), of particular importance is how colour is used to convey information.

The Opponent Process Theory of Colour [9] explains how humans perceive colour stimuli. This theory suggests that humans can readily see differences in colour across three channels: red-green, yellow-blue, and luminance (black-white). This theory provides a logical organization of colour in a circle, with red and green opposite, yellow and blue opposite, the saturation as the radius from the centre, and the luminance (brightness) as an orthogonal dimension. This organization of colour features prominently in the HSB colour model [4].

Although images are inherently visual, their complexity makes them difficult process in the same way as well-designed information visualizations. With some careful design, it may be possible to leverage the elements of the human visual processing systems to convey meaningful information about images to a user.

2.3 Interactive Image Search

Although image search interfaces have been studied for many years, much of the focus has been on how to organize images in a meaningful order or structure. Common approaches are grid representations [14], hierarchical structures [10], and multi-layered clusters [19]. They often employ a combination of visual and semantic similarity when choosing how to group the images, and limit the interactivity to scrolling, pan & zoom, and the selection of images.

Others have discussed the importance of considering the intent of the image retrieval activity [11], and have identified unique characteristics of image retrieval beyond traditional search settings [1]. A noteworthy approach that is consistent with these works is CIDER [8], which uses automatic query expansion to promote diversification of the image search results, and then interactive visual exploration within the image space to allow searchers to focus on the aspect of the query relevant to their needs and intentions. Our work is inspired by this level of interactivity, but with a focus on enabling the searchers at each stage of Vakkari's three-stage model of information seeking.

3 IMGSEE

In order to address the challenges of searching for images within social media data, we have developed ImgSEE (Image SEarch and Exploration) with a goal of enabling interactivity during the image retrieval process. Necessary first steps are to collect the image data and augment it with supplemental information, which are described in the following two subsections. The ImgSEE interface is described in detail in the subsequent subsection. The final subsection provides a brief overview of an image search scenario, and a link to a video illustrating how ImgSEE may be used to support image seeking tasks.

3.1 Data Collection

Using a set of user-specified harvest queries, data is collected in real-time using the Twitter Streaming API (https://developer.twitter.com). The Apache Spark API provides the core stream processing framework (https://spark.apache.org). The incoming tweets are filtered to remove retweets, duplicate images, and tweets that do not contain image content. The remaining tweets are stored in an instance of Elasticsearch (https://www.elastic.co/products/elasticsearch), serving as the source for the data augmentation stage.

3.2 Data Augmentation

Although the raw tweet data provides a wealth of meta-data about the tweet and author, little information is included about the image embedded within the tweet. In this step, the goal is to augment the collected data with new information extracted from the image. The first step is to download the image and store it for use in these data augmentation steps, as well as for use by the search interface.

A simple image processing algorithm that uses the HSB colour model as its basis provides the average hue, saturation, and brightness over the entire image. In addition, two classes of textual descriptors are extracted from the image contents. Optical character recognition using the Tesseract OCR API (https://github.com/tesseract-ocr/tesseract) identifies explicit textual information from within the images themselves. The semantic contents of the images are identified using DeepDetect (https://deepdetect.com), which uses a deep learning approach trained to classify images based on 1000 generic tags.

This new information is added to the Elasticsearch index for each image on a batch basis, in order to ensure that it does not conflict with the real-time processing of the Twitter data collection. The augmented data records serve as the basis for the interactive image search interface.

3.3 ImgSEE Interface

Vakkari's three-stage model of information seeking [20] (pre-focus, focus formulation, post-focus) served as a guide in the design of the ImgSEE interface. Exploration of the image collection during the pre-focus stage is enabled by textual querying within the contents of the tweets and the new information added in the data augmentation step. In the focus formulation stage, further exploration is enabled through pan & zoom within the dynamic image space, filtering the images based on associated hashtags, and filtering the images based on the timestamp of the tweet. A workspace is provide to support sensemaking and interactive grouping of selected images, which is of use during the post-focus stage.

The core interface was implemented using the Angular library (https://angularjs.org); the visualization features were implemented using D3 (https://d3js.org). A screenshot of the core interface is provided in Figure 1, showing a search for "adventure" among the tweets collected over seven days in September 2017. Here, the searcher has filtered the search results to be those that use the hashtags #summer and #travel. The searcher has also saved some images in the workspace, and organized these into three categories. Each of the core features of ImgSEE are explained in more detail in the subsections below.

3.3.1 Pre-focus: Querying. After a specific image dataset has been selected (based on the harvest queries used to generate the collection), the searcher can issue textual queries to isolate subsets of images from the underlying collection. By default, this search is performed within the textual contents of the tweets. The user can also specify searching within the supplemental information added to the tweet: the text embedded in the images or the semantic descriptions of the images. Such pre-focus querying can allow searchers to quickly experiment with various topics of interest, and visually inspect the search interface (image space, hashtags, and timeline, as shown in Figure 1) to assess the general make-up of the image collection.

3.3.2 Focus Formulation: Image Space Exploration. While many image search interfaces developed within the research community use the visual features of the images to cluster or organize the search results (e.g., self-organizing maps), the visual structures in which the images are organized are dynamically determined by the search results sets. As a result, each search organizes the images differently, and the searcher has to re-learn these structures with each new query.

Our goal was to provide a static organizational structure that would remain constant regardless of the query and the search results set. Doing so promotes learnability and memorability. Leveraging knowledge of the Opponent Process Theory of Colour and the HSB colour space, we use a disc to represent the image space. Hue is represented in the angle in the disc, preserving opposite colours (red vs. green; yellow vs. blue). A combination of saturation and brightness is represented in the radius from the centre. Mapping images to their corresponding locations within this disc results in visually similar images (in terms of colour) being close to one another, and visually different images being distant from one another.

This image space provides a visual overview of the search results, which can be useful for quickly assessing the makeup of the search results as part of the focus formulation stage. Interactive exploration within this image space using pan & zoom operations allow regions that contain many visually similar images to be expanded and inspected, and potentially relevant images to be identified and selected.

Of note is that there may not be any direct correlation between the colour-based distribution of the images and the semantic meaning of the images. The semantics may be explored through interactive querying (previous section) and hashtag filtering (next section). Here, the goal is to provide a logical organization of the images that is easy to interpret (visual similarity of overall colour), and which may be used to isolate relevant images from irrelevant ones (e.g., zooming into a region of adventure images where the colour is predominantly blue can allow the searcher to find images of water-based adventures even if the terms that describe this concept do not appear in the original posts that included the images).

3.3.3 Focus Formulation: Hashtag Filtering. Given the underspecified nature of image queries, it is useful to provide mechanisms to help searchers to understand the makeup of the search results, and interactive features to support query refinement. ImgSEE extracts and presents the top hashtags associated with the search result set, and uses a small-multiples approach to show where the associated images for each of these hashtags exist within the image space framework. Given the small size of these micro-visualizations, each image is represented as a dot, rather than in detail. Selecting any of these hashtags automatically filters the search results to only show those images associated with any of the selected hashtags.

The micro-visualizations support searchers in making visual comparisons of the locations of the images within the image space. This, coupled with the detailed view of the image space, provide information scent, enabling the searcher to observe the potential outcome of selecting a specific hashtag as part of their exploratory search process. In addition, this feature of ImgSEE supports the

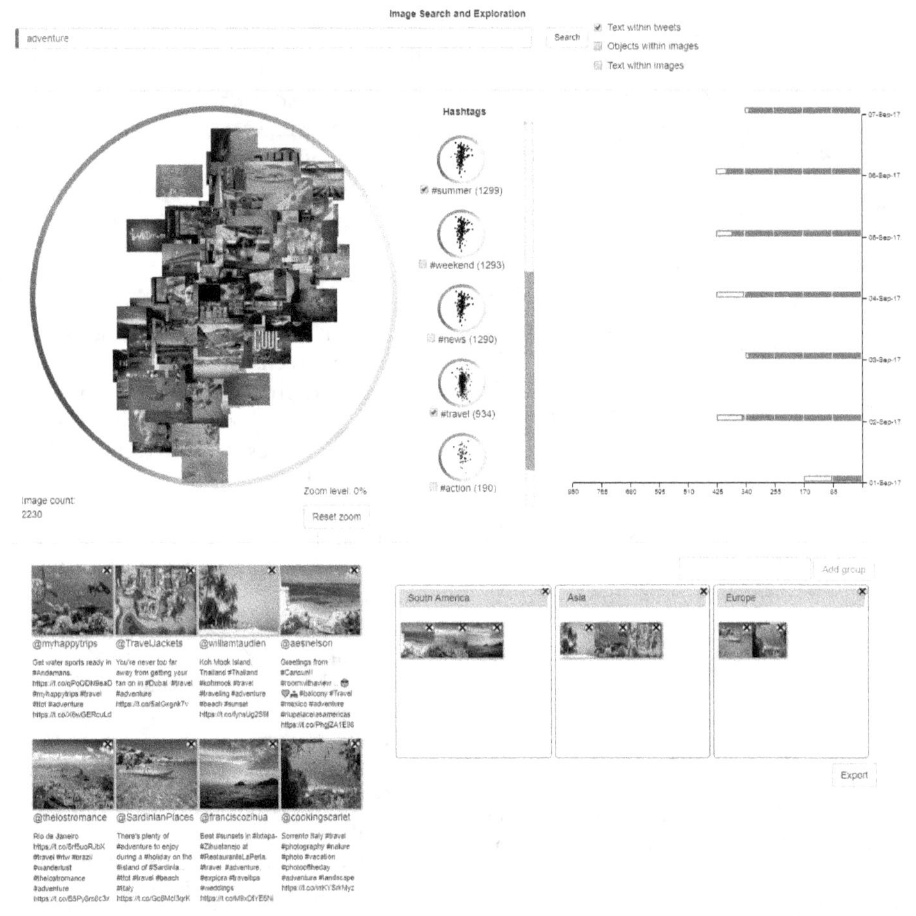

Figure 1: The core interface features of ImgSEE are the image space (left), top hashtags and micro-visualizations (middle), timeline (right), and workspace (bottom).

recognition of relevant information, rather than requiring that it be recalled, enabling searchers to filter the search results to more accurately reflect the information being sought.

3.3.4 Focus Formulation: Temporal Filtering. The timeline visualization provides an overview of temporal patterns of image-based posts, allowing searchers to quickly identify and compare these patterns. Since images are discrete data, a discrete timeline is used [3]. The size of the discrete bins is dynamically determined based on the temporal extent and size of the search results set. Partial bins are represented as partially-filled blocks. This binned approach makes it easy for the searcher to make comparisons and estimate the number of images on a given day.

The timeline supports interactive filtering of the search results, which is reflected in the other interface features (operating as multiple coordinated views). Selecting a specific day filters the search results to only include the images posted on that day. Similarly, selecting or unselecting individual bins further filters the search results. For example, a searcher may choose all images posted on September 5, 2017, and then further filter the timeline to only show those images taken earlier on that day.

Given the importance of temporal information in social media posts, providing searchers with an overview and interactive control over this element of their search activity is valuable. During the focus formulation stage, an overview of the temporal pattern can help the searcher make sense of the relationship between the images being posted and real-world events that have inspired people to post to social media.

3.3.5 Post-focus: Workspace Grouping. While many image search interfaces provide features that support exploratory search, and enable tasks that are useful for the pre-focus and focus formulation information seeking stages, few provide support for the post-focus stage. Given the dynamic nature of image search, it is beneficial to provide features that allow searchers to save, organize, and do something useful with the images discovered.

When a specific image is found to be relevant or useful, it can be selected from the image space, which will automatically copy it to the workspace. Images in the workspace are presented in a grid-based structure, with the most recent additions at the bottom of the grid. Searchers are able to dynamically create and name groups within the workspace, and images can be dragged into these groups. Since mutually exclusive groups would limit the utility of this feature, images may be dragged into multiple groups as needed. Clicking the export button automatically creates a directory structure based on the groups, adds the images to their respective directories, zips these directories into a single file, and initiates a download to the searcher's computer for further use as needed.

3.4 Image Search Scenario

In order to illustrate how ImgSEE can support image retrieval tasks, we have prepared a video [1] of an search scenario where the searcher is seeking images as inspiration for planning an adventure holiday. This scenario includes elements of what makes image search challenging: an under-specified information need and a difficulty in describing what is being sought. The video illustrates how the key interactive features of ImgSEE support the searcher in each stage of Vakkari's three-stage model of information seeking: conducting broad searches and assessing features of the image sets in the pre-focus stage; refining the search goal and seeking relevant images in the focus formulation stage; and collecting, organizing, and using the images in the post-focus stage.

4 EVALUATION

Although the features of ImgSEE were designed to support interactive image retrieval, conducting a controlled laboratory evaluation can provide insight regarding how the approach can be used in relation to Vakkari's three-stage model of information seeking, and the participants' perceptions of usefulness, ease of use, and satisfaction in comparison to a traditional grid-based approach. In order to support this evaluation, we implemented a common grid-based image search interface modelled on the photos tab provided by Twitter's search interface. We call this baseline comparison interface Grid.

4.1 Methodology

The specific methodology for this evaluation was designed to enable answering four research questions:

> **RQ1:** How does the search stage (pre-focus, focus formulation, post-focus) influence the use of the different features of ImgSEE?
> **RQ2:** In comparison to Grid, how useful did participants find ImgSEE?
> **RQ3:** In comparison to Grid, did the participants find ImgSEE easy to use?
> **RQ4:** In comparison to Grid, how satisfied were participants with using ImgSEE?

Two specific image search tasks were devised that each had a degree of under-specification and for which there may not be an obvious query that would lead to a precise set of relevant images. A starting query was used to collect and pre-process the images following the process outlined in Sections 3.1 and 3.2. For each task, the participants used ImgSEE as the image search interface. These tasks were interleaved with using the Grid image search interface on similar tasks. In order to address learning effects, the order of the tasks and the order of the search interface were varied using a Latin square. A fifth task was performed at the end only using ImgSEE on a topic provided by the participants in advance. Participants in the study were given brief instructions to guide them through Vakkari's three-stage model of information seeking. The specific details of these tasks are provided in Table 1.

The data for this study was collected using two primary instruments. To support answering RQ1, the ImgSEE interface was instrumented such that each interaction with the interface was logged. To support answering RQ2, RQ3, and RQ4, a post-study questionnaire based on the Technology Acceptance Model (TAM2) [21] was administered to collect perceptions of usefulness (three questions), ease of use (four questions), and satisfaction (one question). While some have suggested using usefulness as a key criteria when evaluating interactive information retrieval interfaces [6], including ease of use and satisfaction are important when the search interfaces under investigation are novel or somewhat complex to operate, as they provide a more comprehensive view of the participant's experiences during the study.

The study procedure followed the normal pattern for controlled laboratory evaluations. Each session began with an overview of the study process and verification of informed consent. A pre-study questionnaire was administered to measure demographic information and image search experience. A training video was shown for each of the two interfaces, illustrating how they can be used to support image seeking activities at the pre-focus, focus formulation, and post-focus stages. Two laptop computers were used in this study. One was used to manage the study process, administering the pre-study questionnaire, providing instructions to guide the participants through each of the tasks, and administer the post-study questionnaire; the other was pre-loaded with the ImgSEE interface and was used to conduct each of the search tasks.

Each study session took approximately 60 minutes. Participants (n=28) were recruited among our university's student body, and were entered into a draw for a 50% chance to win a $20 gift card.

4.2 Analysis

Because of differences in each of the image seeking tasks, the data on how ImgSEE was used were analyzed and are reported separately. The average number of interactions with each of the core ImgSEE features (RQ1) are presented in a graphical format using standard error of the mean as a measure of variability. These are organized by information seeking stage (pre-focus, focus formulation, post-focus). Using ANOVA, statistically significant differences in the use of the features between the three information seeking stages are noted in a table. In the case of statistically significant differences, post-hoc ANOVA of the two stages with the greatest number of interactions was conducted. If a statistically significant difference was found between these two, the one with the most frequent interaction is reported as the significant stage for the feature. If no statistically significant difference was found, both were reported as the significant stages for the feature. In either case, the mean number of interactions is also reported for these significant stages.

For the overall perceived usefulness (RQ2) and overall perceived ease of use (RQ3) questions, the data was collected using a set of five-point Likert scale measures (three and four questions, respectively). The average of the scores for each of these high-level constructs is provided in graphical format for each interface. Because the distances between these scale levels are not equal, applying statistical

[1] http://www.cs.uregina.ca/~hoeber/download/2018-chiir-imgsee-video.mp4

Introduction	Pre-Focus	Focus Formulation	Post-Focus	Tweets/ Images	Period
Adventure Task: You are in the process of making preliminary plans for an upcoming holiday with a group of friends. You have each decided to find sets of pictures of the places that you want to visit and activities that you want to undertake. You have decided that you want to focus on pictures that other people have posted to Twitter from their adventure vacations.	Using the provided application, start the search session using the keyword "adventure". Explore among the images to find those related to various locations and activities of interest to you.	Select one of the locations or activities you identified in the previous step and find more images relevant to this topic.	Among the images you found in the previous step, organize the images into some logical structure and then export them for sharing them with your friends.	4,883	7 days
Restaurant Task: Imagine you are a food blogger and you are looking to find images of food that other people are tweeting about right now. Your goal is to collect images that will give you ideas on the types of restaurants you might want to visit soon for your own food blog.	Using the provided application, start the search session using keyword "restaurant". Explore among the images to find what the latest trend is.	Select a specific type of food or restaurant that will be the focus of your next food blog and find more images related to this topic.	Among the images you found in the previous step, organize the images into some logical structure and then export them for use when you are writing your blog post.	3,781	15 days
Self-Selected Task: Your final task is to use ImgSEE to search for images related to one of the general topics you provided when you were recruited for this study. We have chosen the topic based on the one that had most images posted to Twitter in the last week. The topic along with the initial query is provided on the paper that the investigator has placed beside the computer.	Find images related to a small set of subtopics you find interesting.	Narrow this down to a single topic and find more images related to it.	Among the images you found in the previous step, organize the images into some logical structure and then export them to complete the task.	3,115 (average)	8 days (average)

Table 1: Tasks, phase instructions, and image collection properties.

measures such as ANOVA directly is not recommended. However, summing the set of Likert scale scores that measure the same underlying phenomenon can allow ANOVA to be used [13]. We follow this advice, using one-way ANOVA within-subjects analysis since all participants were exposed to both interfaces.

For the perceived satisfaction measure (RQ4), one question was asked and data was collected using a five-point Likert scale. As with the other data regarding the perceptions of the participants, the average of this score is presented in graphical format for each interface. Since just one question was asked about this high-level construct, a chi-squared test was used to analyze this measure.

4.3 Results

4.3.1 RQ1: Search Stage and Feature Use. For each of the three search tasks conducted using ImgSEE, the number of interactions with each of the core ImgSEE features were analyzed across each of the three information seeking stages. Figure 2 shows the mean number of such interactions. The general pattern across all tasks was for the querying to be used during the pre-focus and focus formulation stages; the image space exploration to be used extensively during focus formulation, but also somewhat during the pre-focus stage; the hashtag filtering to be used lightly during the pre-focus and focus formulation stages; and the workspace grouping to be used primarily during the post-focus stage. The temporal filtering features were used sporadically across the three stages, and with a high degree of variability among the participants (as shown with the relatively large standard error compared to the low interaction means).

Analysis of this data revealed statistically significant differences in which stage participants interacted with most of the ImgSEE features (see Table 2). The obvious features of Figure 2 were statistically significant (i.e., image space exploration is primarily used during the focus formulation stage and workspace grouping is primarily used during the post-focus stage). Less obvious are the statistically significant differences in which stages the querying and hashtag filtering features were used (both pre-focus and focus formulation stages, but not the post-focus stage). The temporal filtering feature was not used much, and there was no significant differences in how it was used across the stages.

While there were very little differences between the tasks themselves, it is worth examining the participants' self-selected tasks in more detail. Given their personal interest and prior knowledge

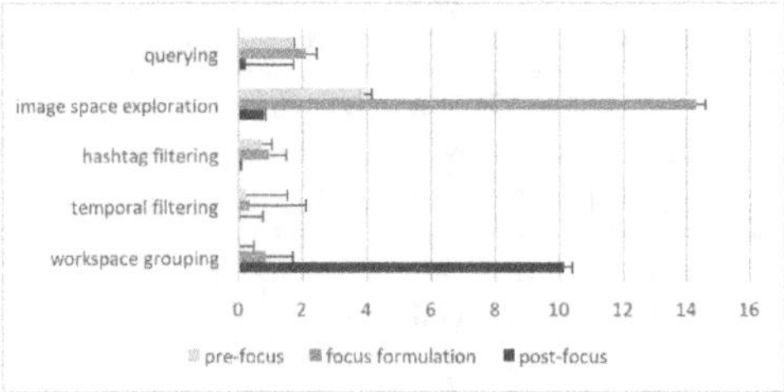

(a) Adventure Task

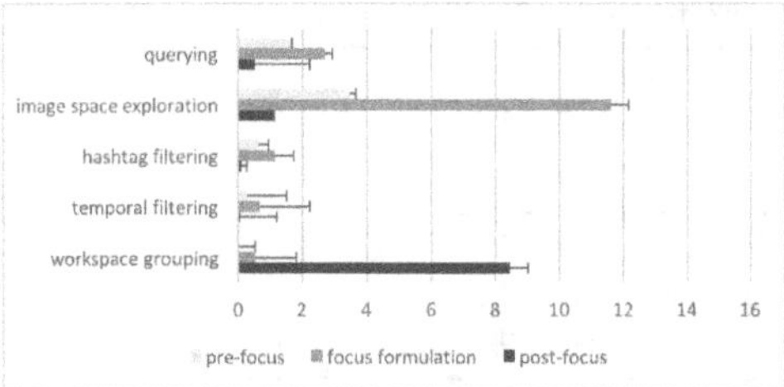

(b) Restaurant Task

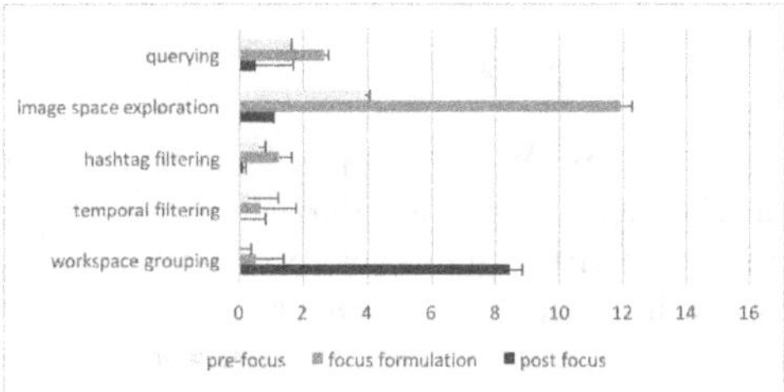

(c) Self-Selected Task

Figure 2: Frequency of interaction with each of the core ImgSEE features during each of the stages of information seeking. Error bars represent the standard error of the mean.

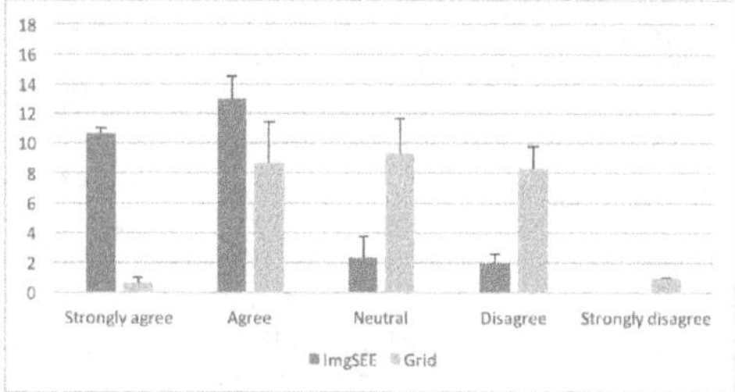

(a) Overall usefulness of the two interfaces.

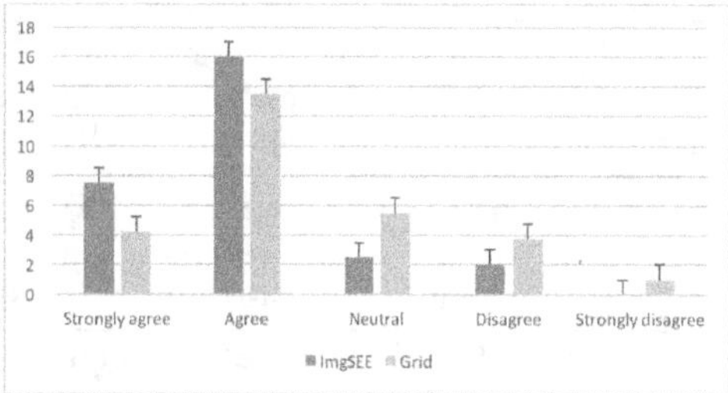

(b) Overall ease of use of the two interfaces.

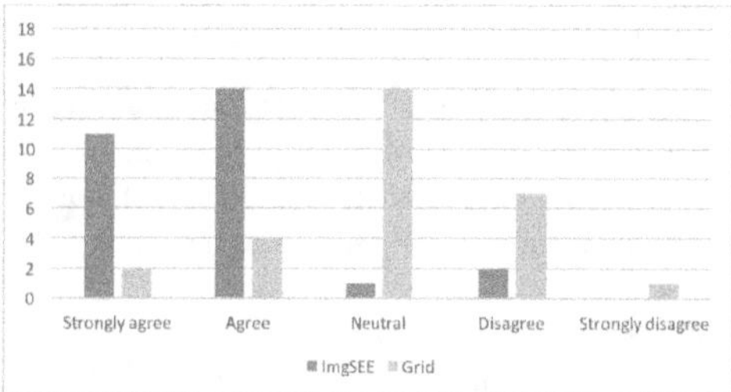

(c) Overall satisfaction with using the two interfaces.

Figure 3: Responses to questions regarding the overall usefulness, ease of use, and satisfaction with using ImgSEE and Grid. Error bars represent the standard error of the mean.

of this task, many participants moved quickly through the pre-focus stage, issuing one to two queries, using the hashtag filtering perhaps once, and interacting with the image space about four times. When in the focus formulation stage, the participants used each of these features more extensively, issuing up to three queries, using the hashtag filtering once, and interacting with the image space about twelve times. After entering the post-task phase, the workspace grouping became the primary interface element that was used, although some participants used the querying and image space exploration features as well. We view this self-selected task as providing the most realistic view of how ImgSEE might be used, since it was based on each participants' specific image seeking interests, and was performed last in the study (after the participants would have gained some experience in using the interface).

When designing ImgSEE, we used Vakkari's three-stage model of information seeking as a guide for developing visual and interactive features that support the searcher throughout the stages. More specifically, we hypothesized that the querying feature would primarily support pre-focus activities, that the image space exploration, hashtag filtering, and temporal filtering would support focus formulation activities, and that workspace grouping would support post-focus activities. While findings partially validate those hypotheses, it is clear that there is not a 1:1 correspondence between interface feature and information seeking stage. During the pre-focus stage, not only did participants issue queries, they also engaged with the exploratory search features to some degree (image space exploration and hashtag filtering). During the focus formulation stage, these same exploratory search features became the dominant mechanism for interaction, although there was also an increase in querying as a mechanism for focusing the search. The post-focus stage found participants primarily using the sensemaking features provided by the workspace grouping, although some querying and image space exploration was done, which indicates that some participants may have temporarily return to the focus formulation stage. This last point is noteworthy, since it provides evidence that Vakkari's model may be cyclical, rather than linear.

4.3.2 RQ2-4: Participant Perceptions of Usability. The validity of the results presented in the previous section can be enhanced by

Feature	Task	ANOVA Across Stages	Stage(s) of Significant Interaction
	adventure	$F(2,81) = 6.27, \mathbf{p < 0.005}$	pre-focus (m=1.7) & focus formulation (m=2.1)
	restaurant	$F(2,81) = 3.32, \mathbf{p < 0.05}$	pre-focus (m=1.7) & focus formulation (m=2.7)
querying	self-selected	$F(2,81) = 5.02, \mathbf{p = 0.01}$	pre-focus (m=1.4) & focus formulation (m=3.2)
	adventure	$F(2,81) = 55.45, \mathbf{p < 0.0001}$	focus formulation (m=14.1)
	restaurant	$F(2,81) = 35.83, \mathbf{p < 0.0001}$	focus formulation (m=11.6)
image space exploration	self-selected	$F(2,81) = 42.34, \mathbf{p < 0.0001}$	focus formulation (m=13.4)
	adventure	$F(2,81) = 3.37, \mathbf{p < 0.05}$	pre-focus (m=0.7) & focus formulation (m=0.9)
	restaurant	$F(2,81) = 3.58, \mathbf{p < 0.05}$	pre-focus (m=0.6) & focus formulation (m=1.1)
hashtag filtering	self-selected	$F(2,81) = 4.15, \mathbf{p < 0.05}$	pre-focus (m=0.6) & focus formulation (m=1.0)
	adventure	$F(2,81) = 0.95, p = 0.391$	
	restaurant	$F(2,81) = 1.86, p = 0.162$	
temporal filtering	self-selected	$F(2,81) = 1.74, p = 0.182$	
	adventure	$F(2,81) = 75.45, \mathbf{p < 0.0001}$	post-focus (m=9.9)
	restaurant	$F(2,81) = 46.46, \mathbf{p < 0.0001}$	post-focus (m=8.4)
workspace grouping	self-selected	$F(2,81) = 76.00, \mathbf{p < 0.0001}$	post-focus (m=9.3)

Table 2: Statistical analysis (ANOVA) of the frequency of feature use across the three stages of information seeking. Statistically significant results are in bold, and indicate that feature was used more frequently in one or more stages than the others. For the stages with significant interaction using a given feature, the mean number of interactions are reported.

studying how the participants perceived the usability of ImgSEE in comparison to the more common grid-based approach to image retrieval interfaces. If the participants found ImgSEE useful, easy to use, and satisfying, this not only speaks to the quality of the implementation of the approach, but also enhances the trustworthiness of the findings on how the approach enabled the participants to undertake interactive image retrieval processes.

Overall, participants in this study reported more positive perceptions of the usefulness (RQ2), ease of use (RQ3), and satisfaction (RQ4) after using ImgSEE in comparison to Grid. The average number of responses at each level of the Likert scales for each of these high-level constructs are illustrated in Figure 3.

The participants' degree of agreement to statements regarding the usefulness of the Grid interface was evenly distributed between agree, neutral, and disagree, whereas for ImgSEE, the participants strongly agreed or agreed with these statements. For ease of use, there was a similar pattern of agreeing with the statements for both interfaces, but with a positive bias for ImgSEE. Participants were primarily neutral in terms of satisfaction with Grid, whereas most strongly agreed or agreed with the statement about satisfaction when considering their use of ImgSEE.

Analyses of these data revealed statistically significant differences across all three measures. Single factor ANOVA of the usefulness and ease of use data resulted in $F(1,54) = 28.94, \mathbf{p < 0.0001}$ and $F(1,54) = 5.78, \mathbf{p < 0.05}$, respectively. A chi-squared test of independence of the data for the satisfaction question resulted in $X^2(4,56) = 26.83, \mathbf{p < 0.0001}$. In all cases, participants reported more positive responses regarding ImgSEE than Grid.

5 CONCLUSIONS

To the best of our knowledge, this is the first study that has used Vakkari's three-stage model of information seeking in the context of interactive image retrieval. We employed it as both a design guide, and as a mechanism for controlling the laboratory-based evaluation. This model is synergistic with exploratory search and sensemaking processes, which are especially useful for image search tasks where the information need may be under-specified and the searcher may be challenged in describing what they are seeking.

This paper provides examples of how information visualization techniques can enhance interactive information retrieval processes under the special constraints of image search. The study showed that the participants were able to follow the three stages of information seeking and make use of most of the features provide to support these stages. Of note is that the most frequently used features were those that provided the images themselves as the primary interaction elements (image space exploration and workspace grouping). As a result, for future image search interfaces, we suggest ensuring that the images themselves remain visible, rather than being abstracted away as in the hashtag filtering and temporal filtering features.

A final observation from this study was that some participants seemed to return to the focus formulation stage after entering the post-focus stage. For complex search tasks that have under-specified information needs like image search tasks, the search process may be more cyclical than linear. For future research, studying image search in the context of non-linear information seeking models such as Meho & Tibbo's model of digital library search [15] may provide further insight into how interactive information retrieval approaches can be designed to enhance image search tasks.

ACKNOWLEDGMENTS

We acknowledge the support of the Natural Sciences and Engineering Research Council of Canada (NSERC), through the Discovery Grant held by the second author (RGPIN-2017-06446).

REFERENCES

[1] Paul André, Edward Cutrell, Desney S. Tan, and Greg Smith. 2009. Designing Novel Image Search Interfaces by Understanding Unique Characteristics and Usage. In *Proceedings of the IFIP TC 13 International Conference on Human-Computer Interaction (INTERACT)*. Springer, Berlin, Heidelberg, 340–353. https://doi.org/10.1007/978-3-642-03658-3_40

[2] Nicholas J. Belkin. 2016. People, interacting with information. *ACM SIGIR Forum* 49, 2 (2016), 13–27. https://doi.org/10.1145/2888422.2888424

[3] Matthew Brehmer, Bongshin Lee, Benjamin Bach, Nathalie Henry Riche, and Tamara Munzner. 2017. Timelines revisited: A design space and considerations for expressive storytelling. *IEEE Transactions on Visualization and Computer Graphics* 29, 9 (2017), 2151–2164. https://doi.org/10.1109/TVCG.2016.2614803

[4] Nilgün Camgöz, Cengiz Yener, and Dilek Güvenç. 2004. Effects of hue, saturation, and brightness: Part 2: Attention. *Color Research & Application* 29, 1 (2004), 20–28. https://doi.org/10.1002/col.10214

[5] Ed H. Chi, Peter Pirolli, Kim Chen, and James Pitkow. 2001. Using information scent to model user information needs and actions and the web. In *Proceedings of the SIGCHI Conference on Human Factors in Computing Systems*. ACM, New York, USA, 490–497. https://doi.org/10.1145/365024.365325

[6] M. Cole, J. Liu, N. Belkin, R. Bierig, J. Gwizdka, C. Liu, J. Zhang, and X. Zhang. 2009. Usefulness as the Criterion for Evaluation of Interactive Information Retrieval. In *Proceedings of the Workshop on Human-Computer Interaction and Information Retrieval*. 1–4.

[7] Orland Hoeber, Larena Hoeber, Maha El Meseery, Kenneth Odoh, and Radhika Gopi. 2016. Visual Twitter analytics (Vista): Temporally changing sentiment and the discovery of emergent themes within sport event tweets. *Online Information Review* 40, 1 (2016), 25–41. https://doi.org/10.1108/OIR-02-2015-0067

[8] Enamul Hoque, Orland Hoeber, and Minglun Gong. 2013. CIDER: Concept-based image diversification, exploration, and retrieval. *Information Processing & Management* 49, 5 (2013), 1122–1138. https://doi.org/10.1016/j.ipm.2012.12.001

[9] Leo M. Hurvich and Dorothea Jameson. 1957. An opponent-process theory of color vision. *Psychological Review* 64, 6, Pt.1 (1957), 384–404. https://doi.org/10.1037/h0041403

[10] Yushi Jing, Henry Rowley, Jingbin Wang, David Tsai, Chuck Rosenberg, and Michele Covell. 2012. Google image swirl: A large-scale content-based image visualization system. In *Proceedings of the International Conference on World Wide Web*. 539–540. https://doi.org/10.1145/2187980.2188116

[11] Christoph Kofler, Martha Larson, and Alan Hanjalic. 2016. User Intent in Multimedia Search: A Survey of the State of the Art and Future Challenges. *Comput. Surveys* 49, 2 (2016), 36:1–36:37. https://doi.org/10.1145/2954930

[12] Haewoon Kwak, Changhyun Lee, Hosung Park, and Sue Moon. 2010. What is Twitter, a social network or a news media?. In *Proceedings of the International Conference on World Wide Web*. ACM, New York, USA, 519–600. https://doi.org/10.1145/1772690.1772751

[13] Bjorn Lantz. 2013. Equidistance of Likert-type scales and validation of inferential methods using experiments and simulations. *The Electronic Journal of Business Research Methods* 11, 1 (2013), 16–28.

[14] Mathias Lux, Michael Riegler, Pål Halvorsen, Konstantin Pogorelov, and Nektarios Anagnostopoulos. 2016. LIRE: Open source visual information retrieval. In *Proceedings of the International Conference on Multimedia Systems*. ACM, New York, USA, 30:1–30:4. https://doi.org/10.1145/2910017.2910630

[15] Lokman I. Meho and Helen R. Tibbo. 2003. Modeling the Information-Seeking Behavior of Social Scientists: Ellis's Study Revisited. *Journal of the American Society for Information Science and Technology* 54, 6 (2003), 570–587.

[16] Vicki L. O'Day and Robin Jeffries. 1993. Orienteering in an information landscape: How information seekers get from here to there. In *Proceedings of the INTERCHI Conference on Human Factors in Computing Systems*. ACM, New York, USA, 438–445. https://doi.org/10.1145/169059.169365

[17] Peter Pirolli and Stuart Card. 1999. Information foraging. *Psychological Review* 106, 4 (1999), 643–675. https://doi.org/10.1037/0033-295X.106.4.643

[18] Peter Pirolli and Daniel M. Russell. 2011. Introduction to this special issue on sensemaking. *Human-Computer Interaction* 26, 1-2 (2011), 1–8. https://doi.org/10.1080/07370024.2011.556557

[19] Grant Strong, Orland Hoeber, and Minglun Gong. 2010. Visual image browsing and exploration (Vibe): User evaluations of image search tasks. In *International Conference on Active Media Technology*. Springer, Berlin, Heidelberg, 424–435. https://doi.org/10.1007/978-3-642-15470-6_44

[20] Pertti Vakkari. 2003. Task-based information searching. *Annual Review of Information Science and Technology* 37, 1 (2003), 413–464. https://doi.org/10.1002/aris.1440370110

[21] Viswanath Venkatesh and Fred D. Davis. 2000. A theoretical extension of the technology acceptance model: Four longitudinal field studies. *Management Science* 46, 2 (2000), 186–204. https://doi.org/10.1287/mnsc.46.2.186.11926

[22] Matthew O. Ward, Georges Grinstein, and Daniel Keim. 2015. *Interactive Data Visualization: Foundations, Techniques, and Applications* (2nd ed.). A. K. Peters, Ltd., Natick, MA, USA.

[23] Ryen W. White and Resa A. Roth. 2009. *Exploratory Search: Beyond the Query-Response Paradigm*. Morgan & Claypool Publisher, San Rafael, CA. https://doi.org/10.2200/S00174ED1V01Y200901ICR003

A Rank-biased Neural Network Model for Click Modeling

Hai-Tao Yu*
yuhaitao@slis.tsukuba.ac.jp
Y-lab, University of Tsukuba, Japan

Adam Jatowt
adam@dl.kuis.kyoto-u.ac.jp
Kyoto University, Japan

Roi Blanco†
roiblan@amazon.com
Amazon Research, Spain

Joemon M. Jose
Joemon.Jose@glasgow.ac.uk
University of Glasgow, UK

Ke Zhou
Ke.Zhou@nottingham.ac.uk
University of Nottingham, UK

ABSTRACT

Query logs contain rich feedback information from a large number of users interacting with search engines. Various click models have been developed to decode users' search behavior and to extract useful knowledge from query logs. Although the state-of-the-art neural click models have been shown to be very effective in click modeling, the input representations of queries and documents rely on either manually crafted features or on automatic methods suffering from the high-dimensionality issue. Moreover, these neural click models are still rather restrictive when coping with commonly biased user clicks. In this paper, we investigate how to effectively deploy a neural network model for decoding users' click behavior. First, we present two novel *rank-biased neural network* models (*RBNN* and *RBNN**) for click modeling. The key idea is to *deploy different weight matrices across different rank positions*. Second, we introduce a new method (*QD-DCCA*) for automatically learning the vector representations for both queries and documents within the same low-dimensional space, which provides high-quality inputs for *RBNN* and *RBNN**. Finally, a series of experiments are conducted on two different real query logs to validate the effectiveness and efficiency of the proposed neural click models. The experiments demonstrate that: (1) The proposed models can achieve substantially improved performance over the state-of-the-art baseline on two datasets across multiple metrics. By incorporating rank-specific weight matrices, *RBNN* and *RBNN** are more capable of dealing with the *position-bias* problem. (2) The input representations of queries, documents and context information significantly affect the performance of neural click models. Thanks to the application of *QD-DCCA*, not only *RBNN* and *RBNN** but also the baseline method exhibit enhanced performance. Furthermore, the training cost under the proposed models is greatly reduced.

KEYWORDS

Click modeling, deep learning, recurrent neural networks

*Corresponding author.
†Work done prior to joining Amazon.

CHIIR '19, March 10–14, 2019, Glasgow, United Kingdom

ACM ISBN 978-1-4503-6025-8/19/03...$15.00
https://doi.org/10.1145/3295750.3298920

ACM Reference Format:
Hai-Tao Yu, Adam Jatowt, Roi Blanco, Joemon M. Jose, and Ke Zhou. 2019. A Rank-biased Neural Network Model for Click Modeling. In *2019 Conference on Human Information Interaction and Retrieval (CHIIR '19), March 10–14, 2019, Glasgow, United Kingdom.* ACM, New York, NY, USA, 9 pages. https://doi.org/10.1145/3295750.3298920

1 INTRODUCTION

Query logs capture and store interactions between search engines and their users and comprise a source of rich information regarding the ways in which users express their information needs, seek and select desired information units. The benefits of utilizing the knowledge embedded in query logs have been clearly demonstrated across many studies [1, 3, 37], particularly due to the enormous volume of search requests submitted nowadays (e.g., Google processes over 3.5 billion searches per day[1]). In this work we focus on *click models, which simulate how users interact with a search engine result page* (SERP). A successful click model is valuable for *enhanced interface design, as well as for collecting more reliable feedback information.* The applications of click models include, but are not limited to, predicting user click behavior, inferring the perceived relevance of documents, improving ranking functions by incorporating inferred signals as features in learning to rank functions and simulating real users' click behavior at a very low cost in terms of human annotations [35]. Moreover, one can predict the degree of a user's satisfaction by constructing a click model [20, 32, 39, 46] based on a large amount of click data. However, how to effectively model user search behavior and how to decode the feedback information hidden in query logs are still open research problems.

The theory of *probabilistic graphical models* [28] provides a unified framework for many traditional click models like [8, 15, 40, 41]. Search behavior is interpreted as a sequence of observed events (e.g., *click* and *skip*) and hypothesized hidden events (e.g., *examination* and *satisfaction*), where each event is represented by a binary random variable, either observed or latent. These click models capture the structural dependencies among predefined events by associating either a probability or a conditional probability to each configuration of a subset of the variables. Typically, a set of hard-coded rules (e.g., the *examination hypothesis* [13, 36]) must be satisfied in such models. *Learning* consists in finding the optimal setting of model parameters, such as maximizing the likelihood of observed events in the training data (e.g., [15]) or searching for a maximum a posteriori solution (e.g., [8]). Given an estimation of model parameters, the process of *inference* consists in finding values of the target variables that maximize the joint likelihood of the graphical

[1] http://www.internetlivestats.com/google-search-statistics/

model given a set of observed random variables as an input. Within this common learning/inference framework, the wide choice of *hypothesized events* and *dependency-rules allows* for the design of many types of click models. Unfortunately, this kind of model suffer from the following shortcomings. The hypothesized events and dependency-rules, which lie at the heart of typical click models, are essentially explicit simplifications of real search behavior. It becomes then unfeasible to capture and model more complex patterns, e.g., multiple levels of non-linear combinations that can be achieved by higher capacity learning models like neural networks [31]. Moreover, the rules and events have to be set manually, and different click models tend to use different sets of rules.

To cope with the aforementioned issues, some recent works have proposed a different breed of click models [4, 5, 33, 45] that appeal to *neural networks*. These are referred to as *neural click models* to differentiate them from the aforementioned traditional click models. Thanks to the advantage of neural networks in representing both linear and non-linear relationships and the ability of learning these relationships directly from the training data, it becomes possible to discover intricate patterns underlying users' search behavior. Due to the fact that users' search behavior can be affected by various factors [43], another compelling advantage is the decrease in effort required for manually designing rules for describing dependencies among events, for instance the Recurrent Neural Network (RNN) deployed by [5, 45] for click prediction.

Despite the success achieved by the state-of-the-art neural click models, they still have significant limitations. First, the advantages of neural click models arise from the power of composition and depend on a distributed representation [22] having an appropriate compositional structure [31]. However, for most of the prior neural click models, the vector representations of queries and documents rely on manually crafted features (e.g., Zhang et al. [45]). Although the automatic way for generating vector representations introduced by Borisov et al. [5] relies on simple so-called *click patterns*, the length of an input document vector is set to $10,240$, and to $1,024$ for a query vector. Consequently, the vectors are neither interpretable nor directly comparable between queries and documents (e.g., the difficulty in computing the cosine similarity between queries and documents as an indicator of relevance). Moreover, the high-dimensionality of input vectors does not only greatly impact the efficiency (shown in Table 4), but can also be rather restrictive for deploying more complex functions (e.g., multiple bilinear transformations via tensors) to learn the intricate dependencies underlying users' search behavior. Second, when dealing with sequence information, RNN relies on a single, shared *input weight matrix* and *hidden-to-hidden weight matrix* for every step of the sequence. This might be rather ineffective in dealing with *position-bias*, which is a fundamental problem when decoding users' clicks. The aforementioned limitations motivated us to explore more effective neural network models for predicting users' click behavior. The main contributions of this paper are as follows:

1. We present a novel method called *QD-DCCA* for automatically learning vector representations of both queries and documents in the same low-dimensional latent space. Consequently, the problem of manually designing feature vectors is then naturally circumvented. Moreover, the aforementioned non-comparability and high-dimensionality issues become addressed. The experimental results show that *QD-DCCA* not only facilitates improving the performance, but also greatly helps to reduce the training time.

2. We propose two novel rank-biased neural click models by deploying different weight matrices across different rank positions. The ability of capturing more complex rank-specific dependencies behind users' search behavior is thus enhanced. The experimental results show that *RBNN* and $RBNN^*$ achieve significantly improved performance compared to prior neural click models in tasks of both click prediction and relevance prediction.

The remainder of the paper is as follows. In §2, we survey the traditional approaches and methods based on neural networks for click modeling. In §3, we formulate the framework for click modeling based on distributed representations, and we introduce two rank-biased neural click models. A series of experiments are conducted and discussed in §4. Finally, we conclude the paper in §5.

2 RELATED WORK

In this section we first give a brief survey of the traditional click models.[2] Then, we detail how the neural networks are deployed for interpreting users' search behavior. Following the work by Chen et al. [9], in this paper we use *query session* to refer to the search behaviors related to a single query.

2.1 Traditional Click Modeling

The so-called *position bias* [10, 18, 26] is a common issue in the task of users' search behavior modeling. It refers to a phenomenon where users tend to click on documents at higher positions of a ranked list, even if such documents provide less relevant information than the ones at lower positions. The *examination hypothesis* [13, 36] has been applied to cope with the position bias. It assumes that a click depends on both the relevance and examination and if a surrogate of a retrieved document is examined, then only its relevance determines whether a user clicks or not. The position bias is then reflected via the probability of user examining document at a given rank position, which merely depends on the rank. Follow-up studies have further extended the capabilities of the examination hypothesis. Specifically, cascade model [13] assumes that a user examines search results sequentially and stops examining once a relevant document is clicked. The probability of examination in the cascade model depends on the rank of the target document and on the relevance of all the documents ranked above. Another popular click model, dynamic Bayesian network model [8], distinguishes between the perceived relevance (the relevance of the snippet presented by a search engine) and the actual relevance (the relevance of the landing page). The authors of dynamic Bayesian network model argue that a user can not examine the content of a document until she clicks on the corresponding URL. Therefore, the decision to click on a document is determined based on its perceived relevance rather than based on its actual relevance.

Recent click models have built on more complex assumptions by incorporating additional knowledge or data about user behavior to better understand users' click behavior. For example, a number of studies [12, 24] tried to improve click models by exploring the *intent diversity*. Instead of exploring users' click behaviors based on individual queries, Zhang et al. [44] proposed to characterize

[2] For a detailed review, please refer to the recent work by Chuklin et al. [11].

user behavior at a task level, which involved multiple queries and browsing actions that users performed to satisfy their search intents. Huang et al. [25] explored how to use mouse movements and page scrolls to facilitate the detection of users' examination events. Their experimental results demonstrated that such additional data can improve the performance of click models in predicting user click behavior. Another line of work to enhance click models is to use document features [36, 40, 45, 47]. A significant advantage of these feature-based models is that they can predict click behavior for unseen query-document pairs.

2.2 Neural Networks for Click Modeling

Recently, *deep learning* techniques have attracted great attention as they yield state-of-the-art performance in many fields [31], such as image recognition and natural language processing. Deep learning techniques are also becoming popular as an alternative framework for parsing user search behavior. A number of neural click models, e.g., [4, 5, 33, 45], have been then proposed. Particularly, the search behavior is interpreted as a sequence of *vector states* and *learning* consists in finding the optimal setting of a set of weight matrices that maximize a particular objective function.

RNN is a popular neural network architecture for sequence modeling, which has been employed for click models. It processes a sequence of search results one result at a time, and maintains a hidden vector that implicitly abstracts the historical information. Each time a new hidden vector is derived and used to perform predictions. Regarding the input vector representation for items like query and document, most studies resort to manually designed features. For example, Zhang et al. [45] used three groups of features, *ad features, user features* and *sequential features.* Borisov et al. [5] proposed several heuristics to initialize the vector representations of queries and documents. Specifically, the click information per query session are aggregated by associating a value to each click pattern in a query session.

Our model differs from the aforementioned neural click models in two key aspects. First, we present a novel way of automatically learning the input vector representations of queries and documents. Second, we propose two new rank-biased neural network architectures for click modeling. To the best of our knowledge, this paper is the first to enhance the performance of neural click models by improving the input vector representations and incorporating rank-specific weight matrices.

3 PROPOSED METHOD

In this section we first formulate how a query session is generated. Then the rank-biased neural click models are explained. Finally, a novel way of automatically learning vector representations for queries and documents is introduced.

3.1 A General Framework

Fig. 1 describes a general framework for abstracting users' search behavior. The search process is depicted as follows: Initially, the input query represents the underlying information needs of a user. After submitting the query, she will get a list of ranked results. We assume that she sequentially examines this result list from top to bottom. The user state represents the internal mental state of a user with respect to the searched task and is updated at each rank

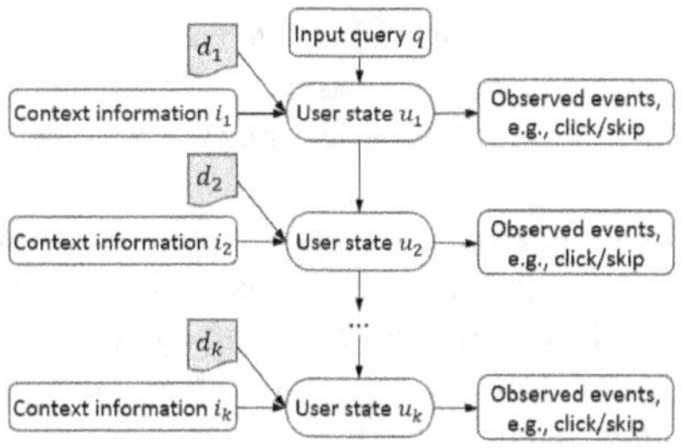

Figure 1: The search process at the level of query session.

position based on the examined document, the context information and the previous state. For example, she would summarize useful information based on the current document and the previously examined content, adjust her information need due to the amount of elapsed time, etc. According to the specific user state, she decides to click or skip a document. In this work, we assume that the user sequentially examines the documents in a query session.

3.2 Rank-biased Neural Click Models

In this section, we present two novel neural click models by modifying the standard RNN's architecture in order to effectively cope with biased user clicks. The main components of a standard RNN are two weight matrices, i.e., the *input weight matrix* and the *recurrent weight matrix.* As mentioned before, in the context of click modeling, many prior studies (e.g., [13, 18, 26]) have demonstrated the impact of position bias. To cope with this issue, our key idea is to deploy a specific weight matrix at a particular rank position to determine the transition of either input or historical information, hence the name *Rank-biased Neural Network* model (RBNN). Empirically, we have observed that the efficiency is not greatly impacted when using rank-specific weight matrices (discussed in §4.4.4), which also reveals the generalization ability of the proposed methods when dealing with larger query sessions.

Specifically, we represent the items involved in the search process on a SERP as real-valued vectors. Corresponding to the formulation given in Fig. 1, $q \in R^{h\times 1}$, $d \in R^{h\times 1}$, $i \in R^{s\times 1}$ and $u \in R^{m\times 1}$ are used to denote the vector representations of a query, a document, context information and a user state, respectively. A subscript is added to indicate the rank position in the query session if needed. $b \in R^{2\times 1}$ is used to denote the behavior state. Since we only consider the events of click and skip w.r.t. a document, b is restricted to: $b_j \in [0, 1]$ and $b_1 + b_2 = 1$. In Fig. 2, we illustrate the structure of the proposed RBNN for click modeling.

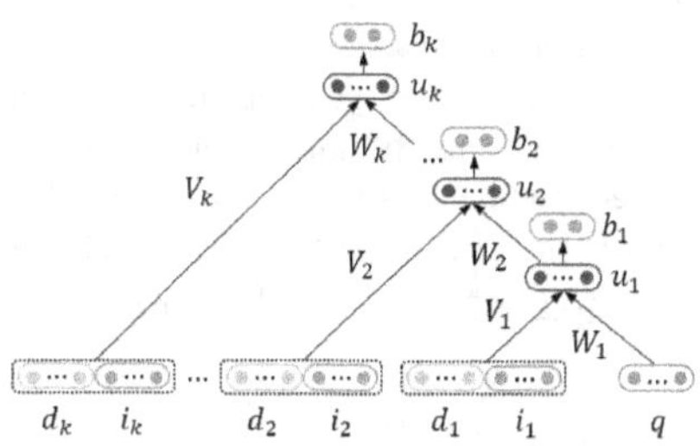

Figure 2: The rank-biased neural click model.

Under the RBNN click model, the generation of a query session is described as: For each query session, the input query q carries the initial information need. After examining the first document, d_1, the user state u_1 is updated as in Eq-1, which leads to the consequent behavior state b_1 as given by Eq-3. The user continues examining documents at lower positions. In particular, after examining a document d_k $(k > 1)$, the user state u_k is updated as in Eq-2, where the previous user state u_{k-1} is taken into account. The resulting behavior state b_k is generated in the same way as in Eq-3.

Particularly, given the query q, the first document d_1 and the context information i_1, the initial user state u_1 is obtained as

$$u_1 = f(W_1 q + V_1 [\begin{smallmatrix} d_1 \\ i_1 \end{smallmatrix}] + l) \quad (1)$$

where $W_1 \in R^{m \times h}$ and $V_1 \in R^{m \times (h+s)}$ are weight matrices. $l \in R^{m \times 1}$ is a bias vector. f is an element-wise nonlinearity function, e.g., *tanh*. Different from u_1, a subsequent user state, say u_k $(k > 1)$, is obtained as,

$$u_k = f(W_k u_{k-1} + V_k [\begin{smallmatrix} d_k \\ i_k \end{smallmatrix}] + p) \quad (2)$$

where both $W_k \in R^{m \times m}$ and $V_k \in R^{m \times (h+s)}$ are weight matrices, and $p \in R^{m \times 1}$ is a bias vector. The behavior state b_k is computed as

$$b_k = g(Y u_k + e) \quad (3)$$

where $Y \in R^{2 \times m}$ is the behavior prediction matrix. $e \in R^{m \times 1}$ is the bias vector and g is the softmax function.

Furthermore, to examine the effect of using rank-specific weight matrices, we explore different settings. One is using the same input weight matrix (i.e., V_1, ..., V_{10} are identical) and different recurrent weight matrices. The corresponding click model is denoted as *RBNN*. The second one uses both different input weight matrices and different recurrent weight matrices as shown in Fig. 2, the corresponding click model is denoted as *RBNN**.

Compared with the standard RNN used in [5, 45] and the recursive neural network [17, 38], the key characteristic of the proposed neural networks (*RBNN* and *RBNN**) is the configuration of rank-specific weight matrices. Note that using the same input weight matrix and recurrent weight matrix, would mean that *RBNN* and *RBNN** become the standard recursive neural network. Going further, by adding one more hidden vector upon the input query vector, *RBNN* and *RBNN** then become the standard RNN.

3.3 Parameter Learning

At each rank position k, the real behavior state y_k is encoded as a one-hot representation of size 2. One entry represents that the corresponding document is skipped, the other represents the event of being clicked. We want to minimize the cross-entropy error between the predicted behavior state distribution b_k and the real behavior distribution y_k. The loss function w.r.t. the model parameters $\theta = \{\{W_i\}_{i=1}^{k}, \{V_j\}_{j=1}^{k}, Y, l, p, e\}$ for a query session is,

$$L(\theta) = \sum_k \sum_j y_{k,j} \log b_{k,j} + \lambda \|\theta\|^2 \quad (4)$$

We skip the details on computing derivatives w.r.t. θ, which can be easily obtained based on the built-in automatic differentiation support of many deep learning toolkits[3]. During the training process, the parameter matrices are initialized using the *Xavier* strategy [16]. For the optimization, the *ADAM* algorithm [27] (with default values of $\beta_1 = 0.9$, $\beta_2 = 0.999$ and $\epsilon = 10^{-8}$) is deployed. We also use the gradient clipping technique to alleviate the exploding gradient problem (with the threshold of 1).

3.4 Input Vector Representations

In this section, we first describe how to represent the context information and we next present a novel way of learning vector representations for queries and documents.

3.4.1 Representations of Context Information. Regarding the representation of context information, we consider three different settings. The first setting (denoted as CI-1) is that *no dynamic context information is added.* This setting helps to mimic the *online case,* under which it is hard to obtain much information, e.g., whether a document is skipped or not. The second setting (denoted as CI-2) is the same as in [5], namely, *a binary vector of size 1:* if a user clicked on the previous document, the value is 1, otherwise 0 denoting the case of skipping the previous document. The third setting (denoted as CI-3) is a vector of size 4. The four entries denote *the position of the current document, the distance to the last click, the click status of the previous document and the number of prior clicks within this query session,* respectively. We investigate the effects of different settings in §4.4.3.

3.4.2 Learning Representations for Queries and Documents. Inspired by the *Set3* strategy by Borisov et al. [5], a query is initially represented with a vector of size 1,024, where each entry denotes the number of times a particular click pattern was observed from training query sessions initiated by this query. For a document, it is represented with a vector of size 10,240. Each entry in the vector denotes the number of times a particular click pattern was observed from query sessions containing the document d at a particular rank.

In contrast, in this work we consider learning representations of queries and documents from a bipartite graph in which each node holds metadata that accounts for the input representation. Given a set of query sessions, we build *an undirected unweighted bipartite graph* $\mathcal{G}$ composed of nodes representing queries and nodes representing documents. An edge is added for each query-document pair within a given query session. The underlying intuition is that since a document returned by a search engine appears in a top slot, it tends to include certain relevant information. Partially inspired by the recent techniques of *multi-view representation learning* [2, 42], we assume that queries and documents in the graph belong to different embedding spaces $\mathcal{Q}$ and $\mathcal{D}$, which might be either homogeneous or heterogeneous. We want to learn a common latent space that merges the information given the initial *views* of queries and documents based on deep neural networks. Specifically, we define the objective function as:

$$\arg \max_{\mathcal{M}_Q, \mathcal{M}_D} \sum_{e_{ij} \in \mathcal{G}} \frac{< \mathcal{M}_Q(q_i), \mathcal{M}_D(d_j) >}{\| \mathcal{M}_Q(q_i) \| \| \mathcal{M}_R(d_j) \|} \quad (5)$$

[3]Theano 0.8.2 is used in this work.

where $\mathcal{M}_Q$ and $\mathcal{M}_D$ denote the mapping functions achieved by multi-layer networks for queries and documents, respectively. $\mathcal{M}_Q(q_i)$ and $\mathcal{M}_D(d_j)$ are the mapped vectors in common latent space. $e_{ij} \in \mathcal{G}$ denotes the edge between q_i and d_j. The key idea is to maximize the cosine similarities of the mapped vectors of queries and documents co-occurring frequently via non-linear mapping (note that the projected vectors of queries/documents sharing many co-connected documents/queries in the bipartite graph will be close to each other). Given the training set of query sessions, the steps of learning the target representations are as follows: **Step-1**: Build the undirected unweighted bipartite graph $\mathcal{G}$. **Step-2**: Generate the initial query and document representations based on the *Set*3 strategy. **Step-3**: Train the deep neural network model by optimizing the objective function Eq. 5. **Step-4**: Once the training process is finished, the desired representations for queries and documents are just the outputs of $\mathcal{M}_Q$ and $\mathcal{M}_D$, respectively. We refer to this method as *QD-DCCA*, namely, learning representations for queries and documents based on deep canonical correlation analysis. In the experiments we selected the widths of the hidden layers to be [800, 500] (query-side) and [5000, 2500] (document side), respectively. The dimension of the joint latent space is set to 100. For the optimization procedure, the *ADAM* algorithm is deployed via TensorFlow r0.12 (the gradient clipping threshold is 1, the batch-size is 100, and the number of epochs is 3). It should be noted that: the initial input representations of queries and documents are not restricted to the ones obtained via *Set*3. Other embedding algorithms, such as network-embedding [19, 34] and *doc2vec* [30] given the text of queries and documents can be used.

4 EXPERIMENTS

In this section we investigate the following key research questions: **RQ-1**: Do the rank-biased neural click models have better performance than the prior neural click models when predicting clicks? **RQ-2**: Can the rank-biased neural click models achieve better performance than the prior neural click models when estimating the relevance of documents? **RQ-3**: How do the input vector representations of queries and documents affect the performance of a neural click model? **RQ-4**: Is *RBNN** that builds on both different input weight matrices and different recurrent weight matrices superior to *RBNN* using rank-specific recurrent weight matrices? **RQ-5**: To what extent does the input context information affect the performance of a neural click model?

4.1 Data Set

We make use of a query log spanning 7 days (April 1-7, 2013) collected from a major web search engine, hereinafter referred to as Data-A. The associated search activities include the anonymized user ID, requesting time, query string, the result list shown to a user, the corresponding clicks, etc. To avoid over-representing performance on a particular data collection, we employ another query log with a similar size (cf. Table 1). Specifically, the initial 3, 000, 000 query sessions extracted from the Yandex query log published as part of the Web Search Click Data (WSCD) workshop in 2012[4] are used. This dataset is referred to as Data-B. Although the data is fully anonymized, it includes human-assessed binary relevance labels

[4]http://imat-relpred.yandex.ru/en/datasets

for a set of query-document pairs. Each query log is split into the training set and the test set with a 3 : 1 ratio. Table 1 shows a basic summary of Data-A and Data-B.

Table 1: The basic summary of adopted datasets.

	Data-A	Data-B
Size of query session	8	10
Query sessions	3, 116, 864	3, 000, 000
Click count	1, 876, 535	3, 682, 814
Unique queries	1, 446, 022	1, 124, 074
Unique documents	10, 740, 851	6, 966, 325
Human-judged query-document pairs	None	41, 275

4.2 Evaluation Tasks

We consider two evaluation tasks, *click prediction* and *relevance prediction*. Following [5, 8, 15], for the test set, a query session is filtered if it includes a query-document pair that is not observed in the training set. The click prediction task refers to predicting user clicks on search engine results. We report two commonly used evaluation metrics *log-likelihood* and *conditional perplexity*:

Log-Likelihood. The metric of log-likelihood evaluates a click model's performance by looking at the likelihood of held-out test data. For each query session in the testing data $s \in S_{test}$, the likelihood of this session under a click model M is computed as $L(s) = P_M(C_1^s, ..., C_n^s)$, where $C_1^s, ..., C_n^s$ are the click events observed in s. Assuming the independence of query sessions, the log-likelihood of M averaged over S_{test} is given as

$$LL(M) = \frac{1}{|S_{test}|} \sum_{s \in S_{test}} \log P_M(C_1^s, ..., C_n^s) \quad (6)$$

where $|S_{test}|$ is the total number of test query sessions. The higher log-likelihood a model has, the better performance it achieves.

Conditional Perplexity According to [11], the conditional perplexity (denoted as C-perplexity for short) of a model at a particular rank k is given as

$$p_k = 2^{-\frac{1}{N} \sum_{j=1}^{N} (\delta[C_k^j = 1] \log_2^{q_k^j} + \delta[C_k^j = 0] \log_2^{(1-q_k^j)})} \quad (7)$$

where N is the total number of test query sessions, C_k^j is a binary value that indicates an observed click on the k-th position of the j-th query session, and δ is the indicator function (i.e., [true]=1 and [false]=0). q_k^j is the predicted probability of a click on the k-th position of the j-th query session given the status of the previous clicks in the same query session. The final C-perplexity of a click model is computed by averaging C-perplexity across all rank positions. C-perplexity measures how "surprised" the model is on observing the clicks in test data. The lower C-perplexity a model achieves, the better its performance is. *The key difference between C-perplexity and perplexity* [15] is that when computing perplexity, the click probability at a particular rank is independent of the clicks in the current session, which involves marginalizing over all possible assignments for the previous clicks (please refer to §5.2.1 in [11] for more explanation). Therefore, we use C-perplexity since the entries of the input vector of context information (e.g., CI-2 and CI-3), such as the previous click and the distance to last click, correspond to a single assignment rather than all possible assignments.

The relevance prediction task is defined as ranking documents by their predicted relevance to a query. For Data-A, which has no human-assessed relevance labels, the logged user clicks are regarded as binary relevance annotations following [40]. Particularly, if a document is clicked, it is viewed as relevant, otherwise, it is non-relevant. For a test query-document pair in Data-B, if it has a human generated relevance label showing the document is relevant, then the document is considered relevant. Otherwise, it is treated as not relevant. For estimating the relevance of a document d with respect to a query q, we use the click probability on d when d appears on the first rank position following [5]. We evaluate relevance using **nDCG** [6] and **nERR** [7].

4.3 State-of-the-art Baseline

The neural networks adopted in [5, 45] belong to the same class, namely, recurrent neural networks. The work by Borisov et al. [5] proposed a neural click model, which outperforms not only the traditional click models (e.g., *UBM* [15] and *DBN*[8]), but also the neural click model based on the standard RNN that is used by [45].

In the following experiments, we then use as the key baseline the neural click model based on the Long Short-Term Memory (LSTM) network [23] (i.e., a variant of RNN), which achieves the best performance in [5]. It is referred to as *LSTM-C*. Following the setting in [5], for *LSTM-C*, the input representations of queries and documents are obtained using the *Set*3 strategy. To clearly demonstrate the effects of different representations of queries and documents on the performance of a neural click model, we introduce the baseline *LSTM-C*$^+$ as a variant of *LSTM-C*. Specifically, for *LSTM-C*$^+$, the input vector representations of queries and documents are obtained via our proposed method *QD-DCCA*. To conduct a fair comparison, we use the same training setting following [5] for each neural click model. In particular, the size of the hidden layer is 256, and the batch-size is 64. The number of epochs over the training data is 3. The context information is represented using the way of CI-2 (different settings are investigated in §4.4.3).

4.4 Experimental Results

In this section, we first investigate the effectiveness of the proposed click models. We then examine the effects of incorporating different kinds of context information. Finally, we describe the efficiency of different neural click models.

Table 2: The click prediction performance. The best result of each metric is indicted in bold. Differences among all pairs of neural click models are statistically significant based on the paired t-test with $p < 0.001$.

Click model	Data-A		Data-B	
	Log-likelihood	C-perplexity	Log-likelihood	C-perplexity
LSTM-C	-2.9288	1.4479	-4.2034	1.5269
LSTM-C$^+$	-2.8954	1.4419	-4.1662	1.5236
RBNN	-1.2185	1.1852	**-2.8058**	**1.3437**
RBNN*	**-1.1499**	**1.1751**	-2.9678	1.3627

4.4.1 Click Prediction Task. Table 2 shows the performance of the four neural click models for predicting clicks based on both Data-A and Data-B. At first glance, Table 2 reveals that all the click models exhibit a better performance on Data-A than that on Data-B. This largely results from the query log differences (cf. §4.1). This issue is not further explored in-depth and we focus on click modeling itself. From Table 2, we can see that *LSTM-C*$^+$ shows a better performance than *LSTM-C* on both Data-A and Data-B, especially in terms of Log-likelihood. The only difference between *LSTM-C* and *LSTM-C*$^+$ is the input representations of queries and documents. Specifically, For *LSTM-C*, these representations are generated based on click-patterns (cf. §3.4.2). In contrast, *LSTM-C*$^+$ builds upon the deliberately processed representations of queries and documents via the method *QD-DCCA*. The key difference is that when optimizing w.r.t. the co-occurrence of query-document pairs implying what documents have been retrieved and ranked high, the mapped representations of queries and documents by *QD-DCCA* carry enhanced information for estimating the relevance between a query and a document. Consequently, it becomes easier for *LSTM-C*$^+$ to capture the underlying intricate dependencies for click prediction, since relevance is a key factor for predicting the click of a particular rank position. On one hand, this largely explains why *LSTM-C*$^+$ outperforms *LSTM-C*. On the other hand, it demonstrates the effect of input representations of queries and documents on click modeling, which provides the answer to RQ-3.

A closer look at Table 2 reveals that the rank-biased neural click models *RBNN* and *RBNN** greatly outperform *LSTM-C* and *LSTM-C*$^+$ on both Data-A and Data-B. For example, the improvements by *RBNN** over *LSTM-C* and *LSTM-C*$^+$ are 60.74% and 60.24% in terms of Log-likelihood, 20.58% and 20.25% in terms of C-perplexity on Data-A, respectively. Note that the advantage of *RBNN* and *RBNN** over *LSTM-C*$^+$ completely stems from the neural network's structure, since they use the same input representations. The advantage of *RBNN* and *RBNN** over *LSTM-C* comes from two aspects. One is the neural network's structure. The other is the input representations of queries and documents. In other words, rank-specific weigh matrices are adopted by *RBNN* and *RBNN** rather than the same weigh matrices as adopted by *LSTM-C* and *LSTM-C*$^+$ for each rank position. Therefore, *RBNN* and *RBNN** are more effective in decoding users' sequential click behavior, especially in coping with the problem of *position bias*. This provides the answer to RQ-1. The only difference between *RBNN* and *RBNN** is that *RBNN* relies on the same input weight matrix, while *RBNN** resorts to rank-specific input weight matrices. From Table 2, we can observe that *RBNN* and *RBNN** show different performance on Data-A and Data-B. Namely, *RBNN** outperforms *RBNN* on Data-A but slightly underperforms *RBNN* on Data-B. Besides the straightforward explanation of the dataset differences, another plausible reason is that the effect of input weight matrix on click prediction is relatively small. The above results provide the answer to RQ-4, namely *RBNN** is superior to *RBNN*.

In addition, we further examine the performance of each neural click model across different rank positions. Particularly, Fig. 3 illustrates the C-perplexity variation of each neural click model at different ranks based on Data-A and Data-B, where the x-axis indicates the rank, and the y-axis represents the C-perplexity value. The same legend is used for Fig. 3(a) and Fig. 3(b).

From Fig. 3, we can observe that all the models achieve better performance at lower ranks than that at the first rank position,

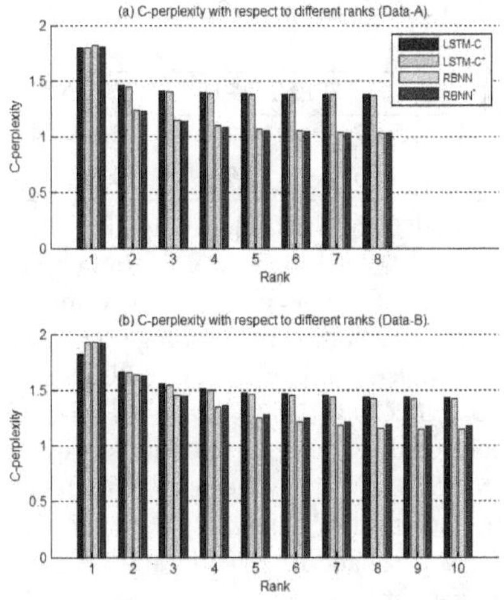

Figure 3: C-perplexity variation of each neural click model.

which is consistent with the previous reports [5]. This reveals the effect of rank positions on the performance of a neural click model. By comparing *LSTM-C* and *LSTM-C*$^+$ in both Fig. 3(a) and Fig. 3(b), we see that they show slightly different performance (except the case at the first rank position over Data-B). Moreover, they achieve slightly better performance with the increase of rank. In contrast, the performance variation of the rank-biased neural click models *RBNN* and *RBNN** is more obvious with the increase of rank. The most possible reason is the deployment of rank-specific matrices, which enables our models to more effectively capture the dependencies at different ranks.

4.4.2 Relevance Prediction Task. Before describing the performance on relevance prediction, we emphasize the difference between click prediction and relevance prediction tasks. For click prediction, the prediction of lower positions are dependent on historical information of the previous rank positions. For example, the current hidden vector state depends on the previous hidden vector state(s) within all the click models being studied. In particular, the dependency exists across the training phase and testing phase. However, the relevance prediction of a document w.r.t. a query is independent from other documents during the testing phase. Thus, this helps to understand the possible inconsistent performance of a neural click model on two different tasks across different datasets.

Table 3 shows the performance of the four neural click models for relevance prediction based on both Data-A and Data-B. From Table 3, we observe that all click models except *RBNN* exhibit a better relevance prediction performance on Data-B than that on Data-A. Besides the possible reasons of query log differences and different search behaviors of users from each query log, another plausible reason is the aforementioned task difference. A closer look at Table 3 indicates that *LSTM-C*$^+$ outperforms significantly *LSTM-C* for relevance prediction on both Data-A and Data-B in terms of both metrics. This is mainly because the input representations of queries and documents for *LSTM-C*$^+$ carry superior information (over the ones generated the *Set*3 strategy adopted by *LSTM-C*) in estimating the relevance between queries and documents, which is explained in §4.4.1. Benefiting from this advantage, it is easier for

Table 3: The relevance prediction performance. The best result of each metric is indicted in bold. Differences among all pairs of neural click models are statistically significant based on the paired t-test with $p < 0.001$.

	Metric	*LSTM-C*	*LSTM-C*$^+$	*RBNN*	*RBNN**
Data-A	nDCG@5	0.3894	0.5188	0.4248	**0.7538**
	nDCG@8	0.5688	0.6784	0.6154	**0.8360**
	nERR@5	0.2808	0.5049	0.4122	**0.7533**
	nERR@8	0.3510	0.5654	0.4842	**0.7844**
Data-B	nDCG@5	0.4418	0.5457	0.0765	**0.8784**
	nDCG@10	0.6720	0.7185	0.4434	**0.9301**
	nERR@5	0.5058	0.5244	0.0727	**0.8752**
	nERR@10	0.5731	0.5767	0.2025	**0.8918**

LSTM-C$^+$ to learn the underlying complex dependencies during the training procedure and achieve better performance for the relevance prediction. This also demonstrates the strong effect of input representations of queries and documents on relevance prediction. Going further, by comparing the performance of *LSTM-C*$^+$, *RBNN* and *RBNN** against that of *LSTM-C* (except the case that *RBNN* underperforms *LSTM-C* over Data-B), it is reasonable to say that the input representations of queries and documents has a big impact the performance of relevance prediction. This again provides the answer to RQ-3. Moreover, this also demonstrates the effectiveness of the proposed embedding method *QD-DCCA*.

Given the same input representations of queries and documents, *LSTM-C*$^+$, *RBNN* and *RBNN** exhibit different performances. In particular, *RBNN* underperforms *LSTM-C*$^+$ on both Data-A and Data-B across different metrics. *RBNN** outperforms *LSTM-C*$^+$ on both Data-A and Data-B across different metrics. This indicates the different effects of deploying rank-specific weight matrices. In view of the difference between *RBNN* and *RBNN**, it is reasonable to say that using rank-specific input weight matrices helps to predict the relevance between a query-document pair. This provides the answer to RQ-4. Furthermore, if we perform a joint analysis over both Table 2 and Table 3, we can observe that *RBNN** outperforms *LSTM-C*$^+$ on two tasks across different datasets and evaluation metrics. Without using rank-specific input weight matrices, i.e., *RBNN** turns into *RBNN*, and the performance on relevance prediction decreases. Under *RBNN**, we only use the input weight matrix at the first rank position (i.e., V_1) when computing the relevance value. This indicates the flexibility of using rank-specific input weight matrices, which enables us to deal with different tasks.

To summarize, *the input vector representations of queries and documents greatly impact the performance of click modeling.* The method in §3.4.2 provides an effective way for learning high-quality representations of queries and documents, especially when devising neural click models. Moreover, *the rank-biased neural click models RBNN and RBNN** *are more effective in tasks of both click prediction and relevance prediction than neural click models without using rank-specific weight matrices.* This echoes the findings in the previous works [13, 18, 26], which demonstrate the great effect of position bias in decoding users' search behaviors.

4.4.3 The Effects of Context Information. We examine how the neural click models (*LSTM-C*, *LSTM-C*$^+$, *RBNN* and *RBNN**) vary when we use different context information, namely CI-1, CI-2 and

CI-3, respectively. For *LSTM-C* and *LSTM-C*$^+$, refer to Fig.2(b) of [5] on how to concatenate the vector of context information.

Based on Data-A, Fig. 4 illustrates how the performance of *LSTM-C*, *LSTM-C*$^+$, *RBNN* and *RBNN** differs when we change the context information. The results based on Data-B which exhibit a similar variation are not shown due to space limitation. Specifically, Figs. 4(a)-4(d) share the same legend and the same x-axis that represents the three types of representations of context information, and the y-axes represents the metric values, respectively.

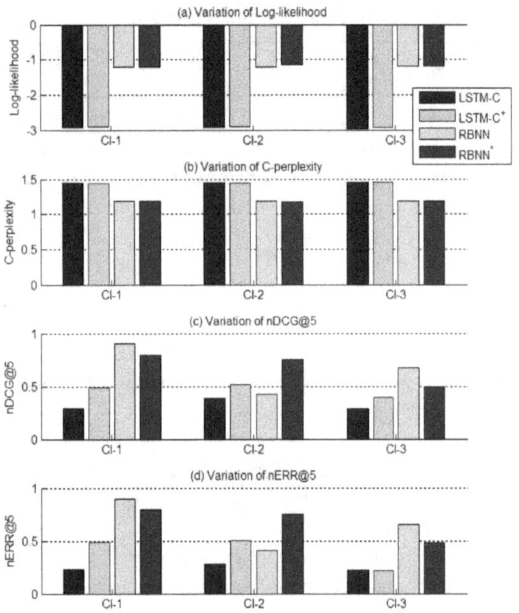

Figure 4: Performance variation of each neural click model.

Figs. 4(a)-4(b) reveal that although we use different context information, the performance variations in terms of Log-likelihood and C-perplexity are quite small for all the neural click models. In contrast, in Figs. 4(c)-4(d), we can observe clear performance variations in terms of nDCG@5 and nERR@5. However, the performance variations among the four neural click models are not consistent. For example, *RBNN* achieves better performance without context information (i.e., CI-1) than that by using more context information, e.g., CI-3. On the other hand, *LSTM-C*$^+$ achieves comparable performance given either CI-1 or CI-2. Yet *LSTM-C*$^+$ shows a decreased performance given CI-3. For this kind of performance variation, a plausible reason is that not all of the pre-defined context information is useful, some of them might hurt the performance. In other words, *we should examine the adopted context information during the development of neural click models, otherwise, the performance might be negatively impacted.* This provides the answer to RQ-5.

4.4.4 Efficiency. In our study, we have also evaluated the overhead of *LSTM-C*, *LSTM-C*$^+$, *RBNN* and *RBNN** by measuring the training time. Table 4 illustrates the training time required by each neural click model over both Data-A and Data-B. The comparison is conducted using Python 2.7.12 on an IMac (Intel Core i7, 4GHz, 32 GB of RAM).

Table 4: Training efficiency (hours).

	LSTM-C	*LSTM-C*$^+$	*RBNN*	*RBNN**
Data-A	5.47	1.11	**0.43**	0.57
Data-B	28.56	1.47	**0.87**	2.43

We can observe that *LSTM-C* requires significantly more training time than *LSTM-C*$^+$, *RBNN* and *RBNN**. In fact, it still requires relatively more time (1.23 hours on Data-A and 7.72 hours on Data-B) even after accelerating the training process via a GPU configuration (the detailed configuration is: GPU:GeForce GTX 1080, CPU:Intel-Xeon E5-2630 v4@2.20GHz). This is largely because of the high-dimensional vector representations of queries and documents input to *LSTM-C*. Given the size k of a query session, the length of a query vector is 2^k, and $k \cdot 2^k$ for a document vector. For instance, they are 1,024 and 10,240 on Data-B, respectively. Therefore, the large weight matrices to be learned by *LSTM-C* greatly degrade its efficiency. One more point regarding the structure of *LSTM-C* is that a zero-vector with the same length of a query vector is added to each document. Though its effectiveness on the final performance is not explored in-depth by [5], it at least increases the training time. Thanks to the method *QD-DCCA* (cf. §3.4.2), we are able to obtain high-quality low-dimensional representations of queries and documents while at the same time enhancing the efficiency of *LSTM-C*$^+$, *RBNN* and *RBNN**. This also provides the answer to RQ-3 from the perspective of efficiency.

5 CONCLUSIONS AND FUTURE WORK

In this paper, we propose two novel rank-biased neural click models (*RBNN* and *RBNN**). The key novelty is to deploy different weight matrices across different rank positions aiming to effectively deal with the problem of position bias. Moreover, a novel method *QD-DCCA* is introduced to automatically learn low-dimensional representations for queries and documents. Based on a series of experiments on two different datasets, we have shown that the proposed models, *RBNN* and *RBNN** lead to not only substantially improved performance, but also to highly enhanced efficiency when compared to the state-of-the-art baseline method. The representations learned by *QD-DCCA* are helpful to improve the performance of the proposed neural click models and the baseline method. Since high-quality input vector representations are necessary to any kind of neural click models, we believe that the method *QD-DCCA* is a better choice for newly devised neural click models when learning representations of queries and documents.

Even though the proposed methods achieved relatively enhanced performance, the following practical issues are still worth exploring in the future. First, it is interesting to investigate the effect of extending the context information with more complex signals (e.g., using eye-tracking [18, 21] or cursor movements [14, 29]) on the proposed neural click models. Second, the setting of using different input weight matrices but the same recurrent weight matrix has not been explored. Finally, it is also interesting to investigate the differences among the rank-specific weight matrices, which helps to design improved methods for dynamically determining the span of rank positions that share the same weight matrix.

6 ACKNOWLEDGMENTS

We would like to thank Anjie Fang for his invaluable help during this work. This research has been supported by JSPS KAKENHI Grant Number JP17K12784.

REFERENCES

[1] Jae-wook Ahn, Peter Brusilovsky, and Shuguang Han. 2015. Personalized Search: Reconsidering the Value of Open User Models. In *Proceedings of the 20th International Conference on Intelligent User Interfaces.* 202–212.

[2] Galen Andrew, Raman Arora, Jeff Bilmes, and Karen Livescu. 2013. Deep Canonical Correlation Analysis. In *Proceedings of the 30th ICML.* 1247–1255.

[3] Ricardo Baeza-Yates and Alessandro Tiberi. 2007. Extracting semantic relations from query logs. In *Proceedings of the 13th KDD.* 76–85.

[4] Afroze Ibrahim Baqapuri and Ilya Trofimov. 2014. Using Neural Networks for Click Prediction of Sponsored Search. *CoRR* abs/1412.6601 (2014).

[5] Alexey Borisov, Ilya Markov, Maarten de Rijke, and Pavel Serdyukov. 2016. A Neural Click Model for Web Search. In *Proceedings of the 25th WWW.* 531–541.

[6] Chris Burges, Tal Shaked, Erin Renshaw, Ari Lazier, Matt Deeds, Nicole Hamilton, and Greg Hullender. 2005. Learning to rank using gradient descent. In *Proceedings of the 22nd ICML.* 89–96.

[7] Olivier Chapelle, Donald Metlzer, Ya Zhang, and Pierre Grinspan. 2009. Expected reciprocal rank for graded relevance. In *Proceedings of the 18th CIKM.* 621–630.

[8] Olivier Chapelle and Ya Zhang. 2009. A Dynamic Bayesian Network Click Model for Web Search Ranking. In *Proceedings of the 18th WWW.* 1–10.

[9] Weizhu Chen, Dong Wang, Yuchen Zhang, Zheng Chen, Adish Singla, and Qiang Yang. 2012. A Noise-aware Click Model for Web Search. In *Proceedings of the 5th WSDM.* 313–322.

[10] Ye Chen and Tak W. Yan. 2012. Position-normalized Click Prediction in Search Advertising. In *Proceedings of the 18th KDD.* 795–803.

[11] Aleksandr Chuklin, Ilya Markov, and Maarten de Rijke. 2015. *Click Models for Web Search.* Vol. 7:3. Synthesis Lectures on Information Concepts, Retrieval, and Services.

[12] Aleksandr Chuklin, Pavel Serdyukov, and Maarten de Rijke. 2013. Using Intent Information to Model User Behavior in Diversified Search. In *Proceedings of the 35th ECIR.* 1–13.

[13] Nick Craswell, Onno Zoeter, Michael Taylor, and Bill Ramsey. 2008. An Experimental Comparison of Click Position-bias Models. In *Proceedings of the 1st WSDM.* 87–94.

[14] Fernando Diaz, Qi Guo, and Ryen W. White. 2016. Search Result Prefetching Using Cursor Movement. In *Proceedings of the 39th SIGIR.* 609–618.

[15] Georges E. Dupret and Benjamin Piwowarski. 2008. A User Browsing Model to Predict Search Engine Click Data from Past Observations. In *Proceedings of the 31st SIGIR.* 331–338.

[16] Xavier Glorot and Yoshua Bengio. 2010. Understanding the difficulty of training deep feedforward neural networks. In *AISTATS*, Vol. 9. 249–256.

[17] Christoph Goller and Andreas Küchler. 1996. Learning task-dependent distributed representations by backpropagation through structure. In *Proceedings of ICNN-96.* 347–352.

[18] Laura A. Granka, Thorsten Joachims, and Geri Gay. 2004. Eye-tracking Analysis of User Behavior in WWW Search. In *Proceedings of the 27th SIGIR.* 478–479.

[19] Aditya Grover and Jure Leskovec. 2016. Node2Vec: Scalable Feature Learning for Networks. In *Proceedings of the 22nd KDD.* 855–864.

[20] Fan Guo, Chao Liu, Anitha Kannan, Tom Minka, Michael Taylor, Yi-Min Wang, and Christos Faloutsos. 2009. Click Chain Model in Web Search. In *Proceedings of the 18th WWW.* 11–20.

[21] Jacek Gwizdka and Yinglong Zhang. 2015. Differences in Eye-Tracking Measures Between Visits and Revisits to Relevant and Irrelevant Web Pages. In *Proceedings of the 38th SIGIR.* 811–814.

[22] G. E. Hinton, J. L. McClelland, and D. E. Rumelhart. 1986. Parallel Distributed Processing: Explorations in the Microstructure of Cognition, Vol. 1. Chapter Distributed representations, 77–109.

[23] Sepp Hochreiter and Jürgen Schmidhuber. 1997. Long Short-Term Memory. *Neural Computation* 9, 8 (1997), 1735–1780.

[24] Botao Hu, Yuchen Zhang, Weizhu Chen, Gang Wang, and Qiang Yang. 2011. Characterizing Search Intent Diversity into Click Models. In *Proceedings of the 20th WWW.* 17–26.

[25] Jeff Huang, Ryen W. White, Georg Buscher, and Kuansan Wang. 2012. Improving Searcher Models Using Mouse Cursor Activity. In *Proceedings of the 35th SIGIR.* 195–204.

[26] Thorsten Joachims, Laura Granka, Bing Pan, Helene Hembrooke, and Geri Gay. 2005. Accurately Interpreting Clickthrough Data As Implicit Feedback. In *Proceedings of the 28th SIGIR.* 154–161.

[27] Diederik P. Kingma and Jimmy Ba. 2015. Adam: A Method for Stochastic Optimization. In *ICLR.*

[28] Daphne Koller and Nir Friedman. 2009. *Probabilistic Graphical Models: Principles and Techniques.* The MIT Press.

[29] Dmitry Lagun, Mikhail Ageev, Qi Guo, and Eugene Agichtein. 2014. Discovering Common Motifs in Cursor Movement Data for Improving Web Search. In *Proceedings of the 7th WSDM.* 183–192.

[30] Quoc Le and Tomas Mikolov. 2014. Distributed Representations of Sentences and Documents. In *Proceedings of the 31st ICML.* 1188–1196.

[31] Yann LeCun, Yoshua Bengio, and Geoffrey Hinton. 2015. Deep learning. *Nature* 521 (2015), 436–444. https://doi.org/10.1038/nature14539

[32] Chao Liu, Fan Guo, and Christos Faloutsos. 2010. Bayesian Browsing Model: Exact Inference of Document Relevance from Petabyte-Scale Data. *ACM Transactions on Knowledge Discovery from Data* 4, 4 (2010), 19:1–19:26.

[33] Qiang Liu, Feng Yu, Shu Wu, and Liang Wang. 2015. A Convolutional Click Prediction Model. In *Proceedings of the 24th CIKM.* 1743–1746.

[34] Bryan Perozzi, Rami Al-Rfou, and Steven Skiena. 2014. DeepWalk: Online Learning of Social Representations. In *Proceedings of the 20th KDD.* 701–710.

[35] Filip Radlinski, Madhu Kurup, and Thorsten Joachims. 2008. How Does Clickthrough Data Reflect Retrieval Quality?. In *Proceedings of the 17th CIKM.* 43–52.

[36] Matthew Richardson, Ewa Dominowska, and Robert Ragno. 2007. Predicting Clicks: Estimating the Click-through Rate for New Ads. In *Proceedings of the 16th WWW.* 521–530.

[37] Fabrizio Silvestri. 2010. Mining Query Logs: Turning Search Usage Data into Knowledge. *Foundations and Trends in Information Retrieval* 4, 1-2 (2010), 1–174.

[38] Richard Socher, Cliff Chiung-Yu Lin, Andrew Ng, and Christopher D Manning. 2011. Parsing Natural Scenes and Natural Language with Recursive Neural Networks. In *Proceedings of the 28th ICML.* 129–136.

[39] Dong Wang, Weizhu Chen, Gang Wang, Yuchen Zhang, and Botao Hu. 2010. Explore Click Models for Search Ranking. In *Proceedings of the 19th CIKM.* 1417–1420.

[40] Hongning Wang, ChengXiang Zhai, Anlei Dong, and Yi Chang. 2013. Content-aware Click Modeling. In *Proceedings of the 22nd WWW.* 1365–1376.

[41] Hongning Wang, ChengXiang Zhai, Feng Liang, Anlei Dong, and Yi Chang. 2014. User Modeling in Search Logs via a Nonparametric Bayesian Approach. In *Proceedings of the 7th WSDM.* 203–212.

[42] Weiran Wang, Raman Arora, Karen Livescu, and Jeff Bilmes. 2015. On Deep Multi-View Representation Learning. In *Proceedings of the 32nd ICML.* 1083–1092.

[43] Yisong Yue, Rajan Patel, and Hein Roehrig. 2010. Beyond Position Bias: Examining Result Attractiveness As a Source of Presentation Bias in Clickthrough Data. In *Proceedings of the 19th WWW.* 1011–1018.

[44] Yuchen Zhang, Weizhu Chen, Dong Wang, and Qiang Yang. 2011. User-click Modeling for Understanding and Predicting Search-behavior. In *Proceedings of the 17th KDD.* 1388–1396.

[45] Yuyu Zhang, Hanjun Dai, Chang Xu, Jun Feng, Taifeng Wang, Jiang Bian, Bin Wang, and Tie-Yan Liu. 2014. Sequential Click Prediction for Sponsored Search with Recurrent Neural Networks. In *Proceedings of the 28th AAAI.* 1369–1375.

[46] Yuchen Zhang, Dong Wang, Gang Wang, Weizhu Chen, Zhihua Zhang, Botao Hu, and Li Zhang. 2010. Learning Click Models via Probit Bayesian Inference. In *Proceedings of the 19th CIKM.* 439–448.

[47] Zeyuan Allen Zhu, Weizhu Chen, Tom Minka, Chenguang Zhu, and Zheng Chen. 2010. A Novel Click Model and Its Applications to Online Advertising. In *Proceedings of the 3rd WSDM.* 321–330.

Interplay of Documents' Readability, Comprehension and Consumer Health Search Performance Across Query Terminology

Carla Teixeira Lopes
INEST TEC/Faculdade de Engenharia da Universidade do Porto
ctl@fe.up.pt

Cristina Ribeiro
INEST TEC/Faculdade de Engenharia da Universidade do Porto
mcr@fe.up.pt

ABSTRACT

Because of terminology mismatches, health consumers frequently face difficulties while searching the Web for health information. Difficulties arise in query formulation but also in understanding the retrieved documents. In this work we analyze how documents' readability affects users' comprehension and how both affect the retrieval performance, measured in different ways. In addition, we analyze how performance measures relate with each other. For this purpose we have conducted a laboratory user study with 40 participants. We found that readability is essential for a document to be at least partially relevant and that it becomes even more important if the document has medico-scientific terminology. Moreover, the relevance of a document to a specific user highly depends on its comprehension. In lay queries we found the medical accuracy of users' answers is related to the session's relevance assessments. This shows that users can, at least in part, relate their relevance assessments with the medical accuracy of the documents. On the other hand, this relationship does not exist with medico-scientific queries.

CCS CONCEPTS

• **Information systems** → **Personalization**; **Retrieval effectiveness**; *Query suggestion*; • **Applied computing** → **Consumer health**;

KEYWORDS

Consumer health information search; readability; comprehension; evaluation; medical accuracy; user study

ACM Reference Format:
Carla Teixeira Lopes and Cristina Ribeiro. 2019. Interplay of Documents' Readability, Comprehension and Consumer Health Search Performance Across Query Terminology. In *2019 Conference on Human Information Interaction and Retrieval (CHIIR '19), March 10–14, 2019, Glasgow, United Kingdom.* ACM, New York, NY, USA, 9 pages. https://doi.org/10.1145/3295750.3298927

ACM ISBN 978-1-4503-6025-8/19/03...$15.00
https://doi.org/10.1145/3295750.3298927

1 INTRODUCTION

There are obvious mismatches between the terminology used by consumers and the one used in health documents and standard medical vocabularies [3, 25]. This makes searching for health information difficult for health consumers. Difficulties emerge when users are formulating the queries and, for this reason, some works propose and evaluate strategies to translate lay terms to medico-scientific ones [15] and others present query suggestion systems [16, 17, 26].

While these systems might help users reach topically relevant documents, studies have shown that the average user also experiences difficulty in understanding the retrieved results [5]. For this reason, the assistance provided by search engines to consumers cannot be limited to the query formulation stage. Search engines should also assist users understanding the retrieved information. The readability of documents is a characteristic that might influence users' comprehension.

Another important issue in consumer health search is the evaluation of its performance. In this domain, traditional measures based on topical relevance are important but should be combined with measures that assess utility such as the medical accuracy of the knowledge obtained during the search session and users' satisfaction with it. Ideally, this evaluation should take into account users, tasks, search applications and underlying information retrieval systems in a holistic perspective assuring that global aspects can be assessed [1].

In this work we study the interplay between the readability of documents, their comprehension, and aspects related to the evaluation of the retrieval performance, namely, sessions' precision, sessions' medical accuracy and tasks' motivational relevance. The latter relates user's goals and motivations with the information objects [21]. We want to know how readability affects comprehension and how both affect the retrieval performance. In addition, we want to understand how different evaluation measures relate to each other. We will do this analysis across query terminology (lay and medico-scientific) using a previously proposed system that suggests alternative queries using these terminologies. A description of this system and its effects can be found in previous works [12, 13].

2 RELATED WORK

Readability is the ease with which someone can read a certain text. It depends highly on the vocabulary and syntax of the text and popular readability metrics are based on characters, syllables and word counts. For example, the Simple Measure of Gobbledygook (SMOG) readability metric considers the number of polysyllables per sentence. The Flesch-Kincaid one is based on a weighted combination of the number of words and number of syllables in a sentence. The Gunning-Fog uses sentence length and frequency of complex words. All these metrics indirectly assess the educational grade level necessary to understand a document and a higher score indicates that the text is more difficult to read.

Several works report high scores of readability metrics when applied to health contents on the Web, which may be an obstacle for some users, particularly to those with lower literacy. Friedman et al. [5] assessed the readability level of 55 websites on breast, colon, and prostate cancers using SMOG, Flesch-Kincaid and Flesch Reading Ease metrics. Authors concluded that cancer information on the Internet is accessible to people having at least a college level, excluding a segment of the population that is at risk of cancer. Similar conclusions were found by these authors in a study conducted 2 years later [6] with a larger sample of websites (100) and the same readability metrics. Also focused on cancer, Hoppe [7] assesses text from the National Cancer Institute's website and concludes that text is written at a level between the 10th and 12th grade, much above the 7th-grade reading level, which is the average American reading level identified by the United States Department of Health and Human Services. Walsh et al. [24] also found that health information available on the Web exceeds the 7th-grade reading level. In their work, authors used SMOG, Gunning-Fog and Flesch-Kincaid to assess 100 health articles randomly collected from consumer-oriented websites of reputable American associations.

Towards the simplification of health contents, researchers have worked to find text features that raise difficulty so that barriers to reading can be lowered and understanding of information increased [9, 10]. First, authors systematically manipulated the sentence structure, noun phrase complexity and function word density and assessed difficulty by means of questions posed to the users [10]. Although these changes improved on the perceived difficulty of text, they were insufficient to simplify text and improve understanding. On a later work, Leroy and other authors developed algorithms that automatically identify difficult sections in text and provide easier alternatives [9]. Term familiarity was estimated using term frequencies in Google Web Corpus and alternatives were synonyms, hypernyms, definitions and semantic types extracted from WordNet, the Unified Medical Language System (UMLS), and Wiktionary. With this strategy, authors found strong beneficial effects of the simplification on both perceived and actual difficulty of the text. Still in 2013, Leroy et al. [11] also evaluated the simplification of text through lexical simplification and coherence enhancement. Lexical simplification reduced the perceived difficulty of texts but negatively impacted the flow of the text. Coherence enhancement reduced the actual difficulty of the text.

Readability has also been used to improve search engine results. Collins-Thompson et al. [23] proposed models and algorithms to estimate user's reading level, document's reading level and to rerank results based on the reading levels. Their work shows the importance of finding results at an appropriate reading level. Tan et al. [22] reach a similar conclusion modelling text readability (or text comprehensibility, as the authors call it) and building user profiles. Muresan et al. [18] concluded that a higher readability has positive effects on retrieval performance.

Other researchers use readability metrics as a proxy to comprehension. Zuccon [27], for example, estimates understandability based on readability metrics computed for each retrieved document, and proposes understandability-biased evaluation measures based on rank-biased precision to evaluate information retrieval systems for consumer health search. He concludes that considering both understandability and topicality in the evaluation of retrieval systems leads to conclusions that differ from those obtained when considering topicality alone. Palotti et al. [19] use readability metrics and medical lexical aspects to infer understandability and combine it with relevance in a learning to rank approach. Authors concluded that this approach promotes documents that are at the same time topically relevant and understandable.

3 USER STUDY

Three research questions, all focused on both lay and medico-scientific queries, drove this study:

(1) How does documents' readability affect users' comprehension and the precision, medical accuracy and motivational relevance of the session?
(2) How does comprehension affect the precision, medical accuracy and motivational relevance of the session?
(3) How are precision, medical accuracy and motivational relevance related?

Note that although sometimes understandability or comprehension is used as a synonym of readability, in this work, readability is different of comprehension. Readability is a characteristic of the text, independent of the user and comprehension depends on both the text and the user. A certain text may be comprehended by some and not be comprehended by others.

The interdependencies that we analyzed in lay and medico-scientific terminologies are depicted in Figure 1.

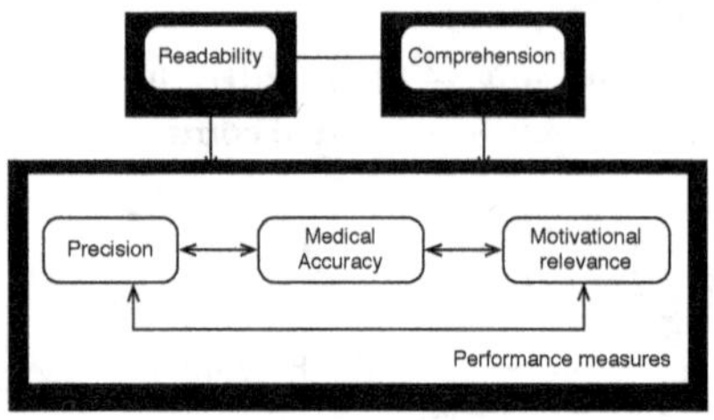

Figure 1: Analyzed interdependencies.

To answer these questions we conducted a laboratory user study with forty information science undergraduate students (25 females; 15 males) with a mean age of 22.25 years (sd=6.42).

We defined 8 information needs based on questions submitted to the health category of Yahoo! Answers, where all require finding a treatment for a particular disease or condition. Researchers formulated medico-scientific and lay queries for each information need and, using Google as a black-box search engine, collected the top-30 results. The selected information needs (IN) are:

- About 3 days ago, I started having a burning feeling every time I urinated. How should I treat this?
- For the past 5 days my head has been very itchy and I don't have lice. What can I do to stop the itching?

- I have high uric acid (8.0 mg/dL) with reference units 3.6 - 7.7. How can I lower my uric acid level?
- I am suffering with an inflammation on my lips and mouth area for more than a year. I have difficulties eating. What can I do to treat it?
- My father got bit by a dog and is in the hospital with a bone infection. How is this treated?
- I frequently get heartburn even when I stay away from spicy stuff. What can I do to prevent it?
- I have been noticing lots of hair coming out from my head. Usually I only comb my hair once a day. What can I do to stop losing my hair?
- I'm on the computer all day so I type a lot and use the mouse. My right pointing finger is starting to give me some joint pain. How I can treat my finger?

Users had to assess, in a 3-value scale, the relevance and comprehension of the top-30 documents retrieved by one of the queries defined for each information need. For relevance, the three values were "not relevant", "partially relevant" and "totally relevant", denoted by 0, 1 and 2, respectively. For comprehension, the three values were "not understood", "Partially understood" and "Totally understood", denoted by 0, 1 and 2, respectively. As this assessment was an initial task of an academic assignment, they had an additional stimulus to do it carefully. Assessments were done in a custom designed system. Each user assessed every information need, that is, 8 sets of documents.

In a post-search questionnaire users evaluated their feeling of success with the task in a scale of 1 (lowest level of success) to 5 (highest level of success). This information was used to assess motivational relevance that expresses the "relation between the intents, goals, and motivations of a user, and texts retrieved by a system" [21]. According to Saracevic [21], "satisfaction, success, accomplishment, and the like are criteria for inferring motivational relevance".

In this same questionnaire, users had to write an answer to the information need that drove the task. A medical doctor evaluated this answer in relation to the correct and incorrect content it possessed. Answer's correctness was evaluated in a scale of 0 (inappropriate answer) to 2 (appropriate answer). The 1 was used for answers with "some value". In terms of answer's incorrectness, user's answer was classified with 0 (all or almost all content is incorrect), 1 (some incorrect content) or 2 (no incorrect content). These values were added into a single variable called "medical accuracy" that, therefore, varies between 0 (lowest accuracy) and 4 (highest accuracy).

To evaluate the reliability of the medical assessments, a second medical doctor judged 30% of the answers and we estimated the inter-rater reliability through the weighted Cohen's Kappa, an adaptation of Cohen's Kappa to ordinal scales that treats disagreements differently [2]. The measured weighted Cohen's Kappa, with squared weights, for the correctness ratings is 0.68 (95% CI: [0.54, 0.77]), indicating a substantial agreement [8]. For the incorrectness ratings, this measure is 0.7 (95% CI: [0.48, 0.84]), also pointing to a substantial agreement. These inter-rater reliability results assure the quality of the initial ratings.

The readability of documents was evaluated using the SMOG metric where a higher score indicates that the text is more difficult to read. To compute this metric we used a web service[1] after extracting the main content of the documents. We chose this metric because it was recommended as a measure of readability in consumer-oriented healthcare documents [4]. To evaluate precision, we have used individual relevance assessments and Graded Average Precision (GAP), a measure proposed by Robertson et al. [20] that is based on the probabilistic model and generalizes average precision to the case of multi-graded relevance.

4 DATA ANALYSIS

Whenever possible we applied a parametric test instead of a non-parametric one due to the former's greater statistical power. The selection of the hypothesis test depends on the number of groups to be compared and on the scale of the variable that is being compared. In situations where ordinal variables are involved, we employed the Mann-Whitney test and used the W letter to indicate the test value. When more than two groups are being compared we initially applied the one way ANOVA or the Kruskal-Wallis test (KW), if the ANOVA assumptions are not verified, to investigate if there were significant differences between the groups and, if so, we either applied the Tukey's test or we did a pairwise comparison. In the pairwise comparison we applied the Bonferroni correction, dividing α by the total number of comparisons to minimize the type I error. These comparisons allowed us to detect where the differences are located. Henceforward, a * signs a result statistically significant at $\alpha = 0.05$ and a ** signs a result statistically significant at $\alpha = 0.01$.

4.1 Readability impact

4.1.1 On Comprehension. Figure 2 shows that in medico-scientific queries the comprehension increases with documents' readability, i.e., as SMOG gets lower. In fact, in these queries, we found statistically significant differences in readability between all levels of comprehension (Table 1). In lay queries we found the readability of the documents does not affect the comprehension so much. Surprisingly, as seen in Table 1, we even found that documents "totally understood" are significantly harder to read than documents "partially understood".

Table 1: Significant differences in the mean SMOG between comprehension levels.

	Lay queries	Medico-scientific queries
$SMOG_0 > SMOG_1$	-	W=353147.5, p = 8.71e-08**
$SMOG_0 > SMOG_2$	-	W = 449795, p < 2.2e-16**
$SMOG_1 < SMOG_2$	W=1890011, p =1.1e-04**	-
$SMOG_1 > SMOG_2$	-	W=2177938, p = 3.08e-08**

$SMOG_n$ is the SMOG at comprehension level n.

4.1.2 On Precision. To analyze how the readability of the documents affects precision we do not use graded precision but compare the readability score of the documents with their relevance assessments. The mean SMOG by relevance level and type of query is plotted in Figure 3. This figure shows that, in both types of queries,

[1] https://github.com/ipeirotis/ReadabilityMetrics

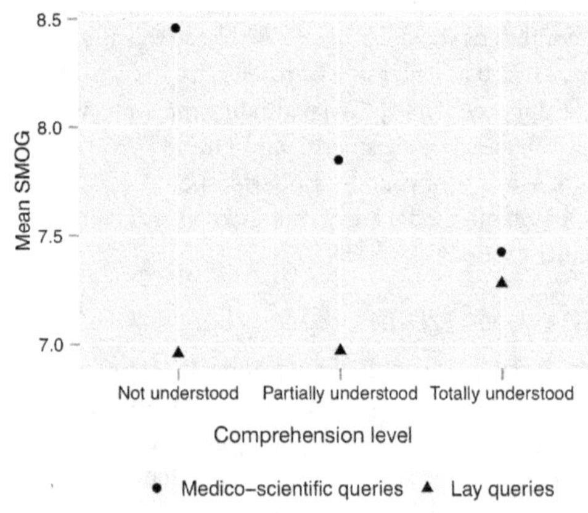

Figure 2: Mean SMOG by comprehension level and type of query.

easier to read documents tend to be associated with higher relevance scores. Table 2 shows the significant differences that were found in the mean SMOG between not relevant documents and the others. Since we are performing multiple comparisons, we applied the Bonferroni correction, dividing α by the number of tests performed in each type of query, i.e., 3. These results show that a low readability (that corresponds to a higher SMOG) can be considered an obstacle for a document's relevance, disregarding the type of terminology.

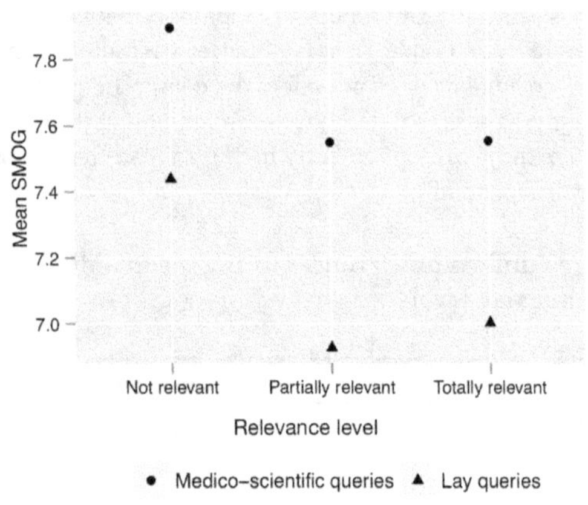

Figure 3: Mean SMOG by relevance level and type of query.

4.1.3 *On Medical accuracy.* Figure 4 shows that, with some exceptions, documents that are harder to read (higher SMOG) tend o be associated with answers with higher medical accuracy. Answers with the highest level of medical accuracy (4) stand out as an exception, with a lower mean SMOG (mean=7.39, sd=0.09) than answers with a medical accuracy of 3 (mean=7.69, sd=0.06). We

Table 2: Significant differences in the mean SMOG between levels of relevance.

	Lay queries	Medico-scientific queries
$SMOG_0 > SMOG_1$	W = 1492732, p = 3.967e-15**	W = 1206654, p = 4.522e-08**
$SMOG_0 > SMOG_2$	W = 1300120, p = 3.489e-08**	W = 1266217, p = 5.693e-09**

SMOG$_n$ is the SMOG at comprehension level n.

found significant statistical differences in the mean SMOG between levels of medical accuracy in each query type (for lay queries, F(4)= 4.264, p=0.0019**; for medico-scientific queries, KW χ^2 = 49.65 , p=4.27e-10**).

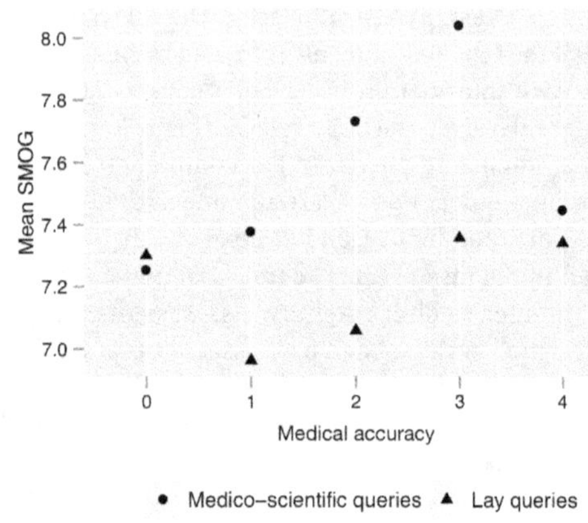

Figure 4: Mean SMOG by answer's medical accuracy and type of query.

Table 3 presents the significant results of the pairwise comparisons in each type of query. In lay queries we used Tukey's HSD test and in medico-scientific queries we used several Wilcoxon tests with the Bonferroni correction. We found that, with both types of queries, documents associated with sessions with a medical accuracy of 3 are more complex (higher SMOG mean) than documents of sessions with a medical accuracy of 1 and 2. With medico-scientific queries, they are also more complex than documents of sessions with a medical accuracy of 0. Moreover, sessions with a medical accuracy of 2 are associated with less readable documents than sessions with a medical accuracy of 0 and 1.

4.1.4 *On Motivational Relevance.* In Figure 5 we plotted the mean SMOG by motivational relevance and query type. As can be seen, in medico-scientific queries less readable documents are associated with sessions with lowest satisfaction rates (1 and 2). In lay queries this only happens with the first level of motivational relevance. In sessions where users feel "completely satisfied", documents are less readable than those in previous levels of satisfaction. In medico-scientific queries we detected no significant differences in the mean SMOG between levels of satisfaction with the task but we found them in lay queries (F(4)=5.91, p=9.7e-05**).

Table 3: Mean SMOG significant differences between levels of medical accuracy by types of query.

	Lay queries	Medico-scientific queries
$SMOG_0 < SMOG_2$		W = 213191.5, p = 0.0021*
$SMOG_0 < SMOG_3$		W = 123912, p = 4.964e-06**
$SMOG_1 < SMOG_2$		W=656522, p = 1.28e-05**
$SMOG_1 < SMOG_3$	(0.071; 0.717), p=0.0078**	W=382476.5, p = 2.282e-10**
$SMOG_2 < SMOG_3$	(0.023; 0.572), p=0.026*	W=873451.5, p = 0.0011**

SMOG$_n$ is the SMOG at medical accuracy level n.

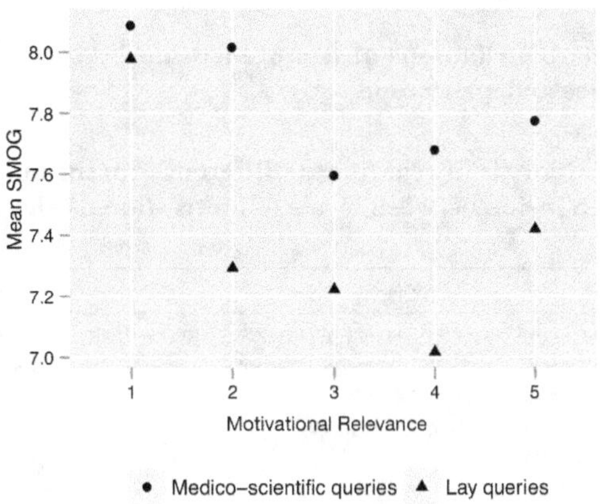

Figure 5: Mean SMOG by motivational relevance and type of query.

We can see in Table 4 that documents associated with sessions where users feel "completely unsatisfied" are less readable than the ones of sessions associated with levels 3 and 4 of motivational relevance. Moreover, this also happens with documents of sessions where the users feel "completely satisfied" (level 5) when compared with documents of sessions where users feel "satisfied" (level 4).

Table 4: Significant differences in the SMOG metric between levels of motivational relevance in lay queries.

$SMOG_1 > SMOG_3$	$SMOG_1 > SMOG_4$	$SMOG_5 > SMOG_4$
(-1.459; -0.051) p=0.029*	(-1.657; -0.264) p=0.001**	(0.055; 0.751) p=0.014*

SMOG$_n$ is the SMOG at motivational relevance level n.

4.2 Comprehension Impact

4.2.1 On Precision. We can see, in Figure 6, that comprehension and relevance are simultaneously high or low, in both types of queries. With lay queries we found that "totally relevant" documents have a comprehension median higher than the other documents (Table 5). With medico-scientific queries, as the relevance of the documents increases, so does their comprehension. As can be seen in Table 5 all these differences are statistically significant. In line with the previous results, the comprehension median is higher in lay queries in every level of relevance: 0 (W = 1991875, p<2.2e-16**), 1 (W = 987763, p<2.2e-16**) and 2 (W = 908917, p = 5.161e-14**).

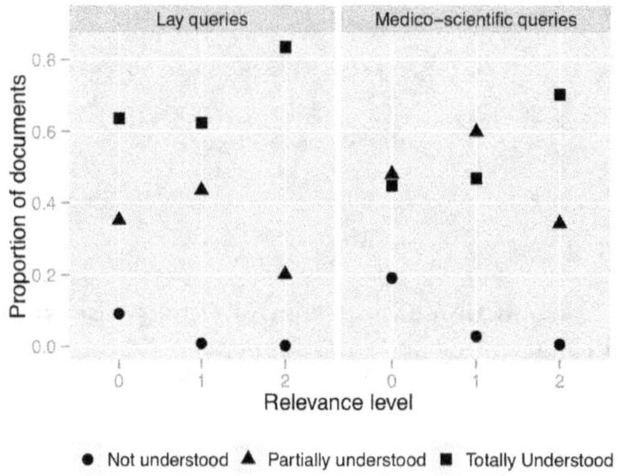

Figure 6: Proportion of documents by comprehension, relevance level and query type.

Table 5: Significant differences in the comprehension median between relevance levels.

	Lay queries	Medico-scientific queries
$Comp_0 < Comp_1$		W = 965872, p = 1.023e-08**
$Comp_0 < Comp_2$	W=906232.5, p < 2.2e-16**	W=765754.5, p < 2.2e-16**
$Comp_1 < Comp_2$	W=614633.5, p < 2.2e-16**	W=654833.5, p < 2.2e-16**

Comp$_n$ is Comprehension at relevance level n.

4.2.2 On Medical accuracy. Relating comprehension with medical accuracy we observe different behaviors in lay and medico-scientific queries. In lay queries the tendency shows that, as the accuracy of the answer improves, the global comprehension of the documents of that session also increases. As can be seen in Figure 7, in this type of queries, higher levels of medical accuracy have more "totally understood" and less "partially understood" documents. Using the Kruskal-Wallis test we detected significant differences on the median of comprehension between levels of medical accuracy (KW $\chi^2(4)$ = 41.59, p=2.026e-08**).

With further analysis (Table 6) we concluded that the comprehension in the lowest levels of medical accuracy (0 and 1) with lay queries is lower than the comprehension in the levels 2 and 4 of medical accuracy. This means that, when medical terminology is not an issue, comprehension may be a decisive factor to the accuracy of the knowledge obtained from a session.

In medico-scientific queries the reality is different and we found that some of the lower levels of medical accuracy, namely 0 and 1, are associated with documents that are comprehended better than

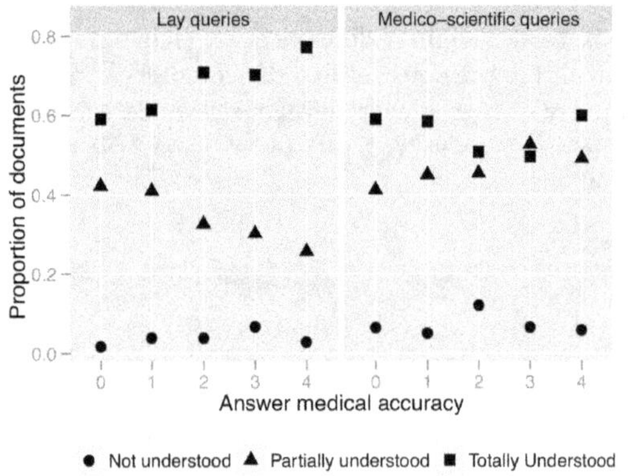

Figure 7: Proportion of documents by comprehension, level of medical accuracy and query type.

Table 6: Significant differences in the comprehension median between medical accuracy levels.

	Lay queries	**Medico-scientific queries**
$Comp_0 < Comp_2$	W = 269071.5, p = 0.0002384**	
$Comp_0 < Comp_4$	W = 75189.5, p = 2.511e-07**	
$Comp_1 < Comp_2$	W = 610154.5, p = 3.858e-05**	
$Comp_1 < Comp_4$	W = 170947.5, p = 3.684e-08**	
$Comp_0 > Comp_2$		W = 267363, p = 0.00019**
$Comp_0 > Comp_3$		W = 166383, p = 0.0006**
$Comp_1 > Comp_2$		W = 794181.5, p = 3.452e-05**
$Comp_1 > Comp_3$		W = 493273, p = 0.00053**

$Comp_n$ **is Comprehension at medical accuracy level n.**

the ones of higher levels of medical accuracy, namely 2 and 3. These differences are statistically significant as can be seen in Table 6. This makes us conjecture that, when medico-scientific terminology is used in documents, comprehension is not so preponderant to the answers' medical accuracy. Users may understand documents a little worse but still be able to assimilate the main message.

4.2.3 On Motivational Relevance. Figure 8 shows that the comprehension and the feeling of success in the search task are simultaneously high or low. In both types of queries we detected significant differences in the median of comprehension between levels of motivational relevance (lay - KW $\chi^2(4) = 121.47$, p<2.2e-16**; medico-scientific - KW $\chi^2(4) = 164.95$, p<2.2e-16**). As shown in Table 7, a set of Wilcoxon tests with the Bonferroni correction allowed us to conclude that, in medico-scientific queries, the comprehension significantly grows as we move from lower levels to higher levels in the motivational relevance scale. In lay queries, this also happens with the exception of the comparison of the 2nd level with the 3rd and the 4th levels.

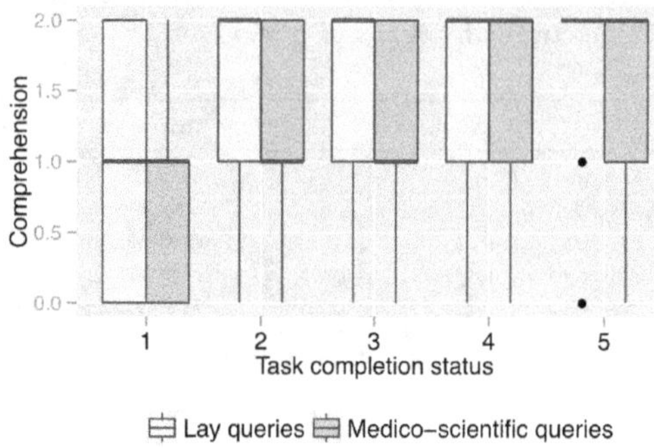

Figure 8: Distributions of comprehension by motivational relevance and query type.

Table 7: Statistically significant differences in the median of comprehension between levels of motivational relevance.

	Lay queries	Medico-scientific queries
$Comp_1 < Comp_2$	W = 11676.5, p=7.391e-07**	W = 5119.5, p=2.106e-06**
$Comp_1 < Comp_3$	W = 66599.5, p=2.279e-09**	W = 26407.5, p=1.526e-10**
$Comp_1 < Comp_4$	W = 89145.5, p=1.23e-14**	W = 32663.5, p=3.76e-14**
$Comp_1 < Comp_5$	W= 20048, p<2.2e-16**	W = 6652.5, p<2.2e-16**
$Comp_2 < Comp_3$	-	W = 187861, p=0.0007877**
$Comp_2 < Comp_4$	-	W = 239695.5, p=1.406e-09**
$Comp_2 < Comp_5$	W= 63345.5, p=3.12e-07**	W = 49552.5, p<2.2e-16**
$Comp_3 < Comp_4$	W = 1600860, p=1.384e-07**	W = 1622274, p=6.437e-08**
$Comp_3 < Comp_5$	W = 356269.5, p=4.38e-15**	W = 340579.5, p<2.2e-16**
$Comp_4 < Comp_5$	W= 573607, p=6.649e-07**	W = 535750.5, p=2.475e-09**

$Comp_n$ **is Comprehension at motivational relevance level n.**

4.3 Relation between precision, medical accuracy and motivational relevance

4.3.1 Relation of Precision with Medical accuracy. Figure 9 shows the distributions of GAP by medical accuracy and query type. We cannot detect a clear pattern of association between answer's medical accuracy and GAP. Within medico-scientific queries, we could not detect significant differences in the mean GAP between levels of medical accuracy. On the other hand, we detected them in sessions with lay queries (F(4)=2.767, p=0.029*). Tukey's HSD test allowed us to conclude that answers with the lowest medical accuracy (0) are associated with sessions with lower mean GAP than sessions of answers with a medical accuracy of 1 ((0.025, 0.41), p=0.017*) and 3 ((0.009, 0.372), p=0.033*).

4.3.2 Relation of Precision with Motivational Relevance. Globally, and as expected, the median of GAP and the the degree of satisfaction with the session tend to be directly associated (Figure 10). In lay queries we found significant differences between levels of motivational relevance (F(4)=6.65, p=5.78e-05**). In Table 8 we present the significant differences found, i.e., sessions where users feel "unsatisfied" (2) have a lower mean GAP than sessions with higher feeling of success. In medico-scientific queries we found no significant differences between levels of motivational relevance.

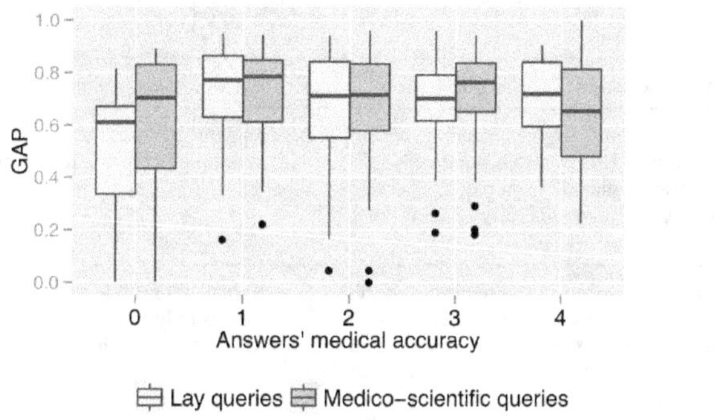

Figure 9: Distributions of GAP by answer's medical accuracy and query type.

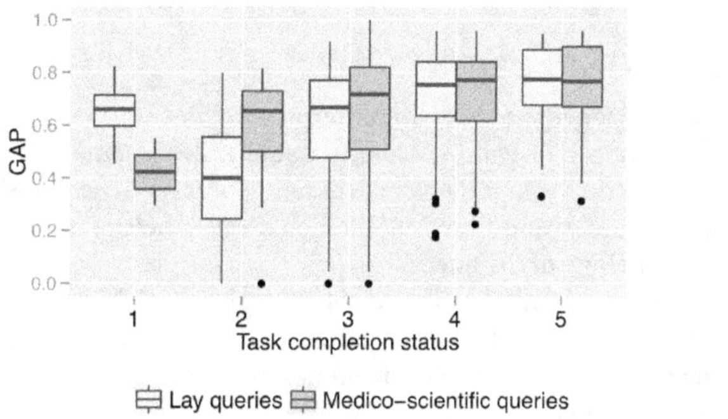

Figure 10: Distributions of GAP by motivational relevance and query type.

Table 8: Significant differences in GAP between levels of motivational relevance in lay queries.

$GAP_2 < GAP_3$	$GAP_2 < GAP_4$	$GAP_2 < GAP_5$
(0.0198; 0.4155) p=0.023*	(0.118; 0.505) p=0.00016**	(0.1278; 0.5713) p=0.0002**

GAP_n is the GAP at motivational relevance level n.

4.3.3 *Relation of Medical Accuracy with Motivational Relevance.*

The median of the medical accuracy is almost always 2, independently of the motivational relevance and query type. The only exception lays in the most successful search tasks with lay queries where the median of medical accuracy is 3 (Figure 11). We did not find any significant differences between the medians of medical accuracy between levels of motivational relevance in any of the types of query.

5 DISCUSSION

The relations between the analyzed dimensions are summarized in Table 9. Low readability can be an obstacle to document's relevance,

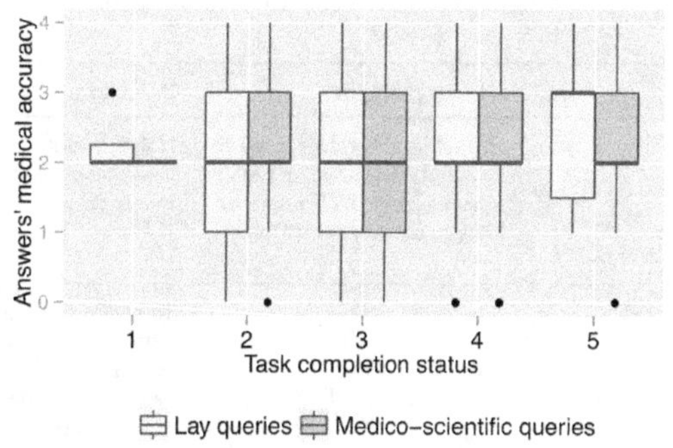

Figure 11: Distributions of medical accuracy by motivational relevance and query type.

agreeing with Muresan et al. [18] who concluded that a higher readability has positive effects on retrieval performance.

Readability is more important for comprehension in documents with medico-scientific terminology. In documents retrieved with lay queries this is less important and we even found cases where less readable documents were better understood than documents easier to read. This suggests that the presence of medical-scientific terminology is a greater obstacle to comprehension than traditional parameters used in readability formulas (e.g.: number of words per sentence or number of syllables per word). This supports the need for systems that assist health consumers through medical annotations like the one built by Lopes and Sousa [14].

About medical accuracy, we observed that lay sessions with almost maximum accuracy (3) are associated with documents less readable than the ones of sessions with medical accuracy of 1 and 2. In medico-scientific queries, this relation is more systematic. These results suggest that documents with more accurate medical contents are significantly harder to read, creating an obstacle to low literacy users.

Regarding the motivational relevance, with lay queries, we found that sessions where users feel "completely unsatisfied" have less readable documents than sessions where they are "unsatisfied" or "neutral". Although documents' lack of readability may be an obstacle to, at least, some success in the task, this is not true in the highest level of motivational relevance. In fact, we found that, with lay queries, sessions where users feel "completely satisfied" have documents harder to read than sessions where they feel "satisfied" and "neutral".

Through the relation between precision and comprehension we can see the relevance of a document highly depends on its comprehension. Looking into the relationship of precision with medical accuracy we observe that, in lay queries, users relevance assessments are related to the medical accuracy of their answers. The number of relevant documents or the degree of documents' relevance affect users' answers. Since we found no significant differences in medico-scientific queries, we can speculate that, with this type of queries, either relevance assessments are less related with the accuracy of the documents' contents, or users assess documents by an estimate of their relevance to others.

Table 9: Statistical significant relationships between analyzed dimensions. L = lay; MS = medico-scientific.

	Comprehension	Precision	Med. accuracy	Motivational relevance
Readability	Readability not so crucial to comprehension as in professional queries [L]. Comprehension increases with readability [MS].	Not relevant documents are less readable than partially and totally relevant ones [L&MS].	Highest levels of med. accuracy associated with less readable documents [L]. As the medical accuracy of the session increases, the readability of their documents decreases [MS].	Less readable documents are associated with sessions where the user feels "unsatisfied" [L].
Comprehension	-	Totally relevant documents are better understood than less relevant documents [L]. Relevance systematically increases with comprehension [MS].	Comprehension in the lowest levels of medical accuracy is lower than comprehension in higher levels of medical accuracy [L]. Lowest levels of medical accuracy are associated with higher comprehension than higher levels of medical accuracy [MS].	Comprehension grows as we move from lower levels to higher levels in the motivational relevance scale [L&MS].
Precision	-	-	Sessions with the lowest medical accuracy have lower GAP than sessions with a medical accuracy of 1 and 3 [L].	Sessions where users feel "unsatisfied" have lower precision than sessions with higher feeling of success [L].
Med. Accuracy	-	-	-	No relationship found [L&MS].

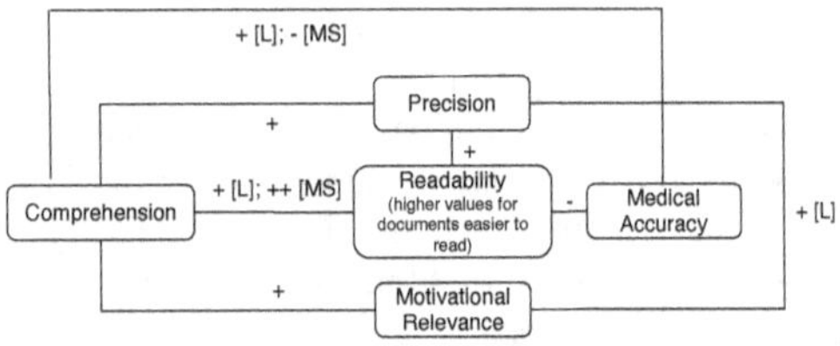

Figure 12: Summary of direct (+ and ++) and inverse (-) associations in lay (L) and medico-scientific (MS) queries.

This can happen, for example, if a user assesses a document as relevant when the content seems related to the topic but they cannot understand it or use it for their own benefit. Finally, in the last cell of the "precision" row of Table 9, we can see that, in lay sessions, the users' feeling of success is related with session's precision. The considerations presented for the absence of relationship between precision and medical accuracy may also explain why no relation was found between precision and motivational relevance in medico-scientific queries.

The relation between comprehension and medical accuracy in lay queries indicates that, when medical terminology is not a question, comprehension may be an important factor to the accuracy of the obtained knowledge. In medico-scientific queries, the opposite finding let us say that, when medico-scientific terminology is used in documents, comprehension is not so preponderant to the answers' medical accuracy. Either the users understand documents worse but are still able to assimilate at least part of the contents, or the higher accuracy of medico-scientific documents, when compared with lay documents, compensates users' lower comprehension of these documents. With respect to motivational relevance, comprehension is an important and influent factor.

Figure 12 provides a quick overview on our main findings, illustrating the direct and inverse associations found between the variables under study.

6 CONCLUSION

In this paper we study the interplay between aspects of the information retrieval experience, namely, documents' readability, documents' comprehension, sessions' precision, sessions' medical accuracy and tasks' motivational relevance, considering the terminology of the query.

This analysis allows us to conclude that readability is essential for a document to be at least partially relevant; that it becomes even more important if the document has medico-scientific terminology and that it is crucial in the lower satisfaction levels but not in the higher ones. This information is valuable both to search engines and to health websites. Search engines can explore this, incorporating readability in their ranking algorithm, not only in searches associated with lay queries but also in search performed by consumers using professional queries. Through past behaviors it should not be difficult to predict if the user is a professional or a consumer. Search engines should be aware that the relevance of a document depends highly on its comprehension and that unsuccessful tasks have lower precision than more successful ones. Health websites that want to provide information to consumers should also be aware that, if they need to use medico-scientific terminology, they need, at least, to simplify the remaining contents. A conjecture that is also worth mentioning is that the more accurate documents are, the harder they are to read.

In lay queries we found the medical accuracy of users' answers is related to the session's relevance assessments. This shows that users can, at least in part, relate their relevance assessments with the medical accuracy of the documents. On the other hand, in medico-scientific queries we expect this relationship to be weaker. In lay queries, comprehension is more crucial to the accuracy of the resulting knowledge than in medico-scientific queries. In the latter, either the user understands documents worse but is still able to assimilate at least part of the content, or the higher accuracy of medico-scientific documents, when compared with lay documents, compensates users' lower comprehension.

ACKNOWLEDGMENTS

This work was partially funded by Fundação para a Ciência under the grant SFRH/BD/40982/2007 and by project "NORTE-01-0145-FEDER-000016" (NanoSTIMA) that is financed by the North Portugal Regional Operational Programme (NORTE2020), under the PORTUGAL 2020 Partnership Agreement, and through the European Regional Development Fund (ERDF).

REFERENCES

[1] Maristella Agosti, Richard Berendsen, Toine Bogers, Martin Braschler, Paul Buitelaar, Khalid Choukri, Giorgio M. Di Nunzio, Nicola Ferro, Pamela Forner, Allan Hanbury, Karin F. Heppin, Preben Hansen, Anni Järvelin, Birger Larsen, Mihai Lupu, Ivano Masiero, Henning Müller, Simone Peruzzo, Vivien Petras, Florina Piroi, Maarten de Rijke, Giuseppe Santucci, Gianmaria Silvello, and Elaine Toms. 2012. *PROMISE Retreat Report: Prospects and Opportunities for Information Access Evaluation.* Technical Report. PROMISE network of excellence, grant agreement no. 258191.

[2] Jacob Cohen. 1968. Weighted kappa: Nominal scale agreement provision for scaled disagreement or partial credit. *Psychological Bulletin* 70, 4 (1968), 213–220. http://psycnet.apa.org/doiLanding?doi=10.1037%2Fh0026256

[3] Johanna Eerola and Pertti Vakkari. 2008. How a general and a specific thesaurus cover expressions in patients' questions and physicians' answers. *Journal of Documentation* 64, 1 (2008), 131–142.

[4] P. R. Fitzsimmons, B. D. Michael, J. L. Hulley, and G. O. Scott. 2010. A readability assessment of online Parkinson's disease information. *The Journal of the Royal College of Physicians of Edinburgh* 40, 4 (Dec. 2010), 292–296. https://doi.org/10.4997/jrcpe.2010.401

[5] Daniela B. Friedman, Laurie Hoffman-Goetz, and Jose F. Arocha. 2004. Readability of cancer information on the internet. *Journal of Cancer Education* 19, 2 (2004), 117–122. https://doi.org/10.1207/s15430154jce1902_13

[6] Daniela B. Friedman, Laurie Hoffman-Goetz, and Jose. F. Arocha. 2006. Health literacy and the World Wide Web: comparing the readability of leading incident cancers on the Internet. *Medical informatics and the Internet in medicine* 31, 1 (March 2006), 67–87. http://view.ncbi.nlm.nih.gov/pubmed/16754369

[7] Ian C. Hoppe. 2010. Readability of patient information regarding breast cancer prevention from the Web site of the National Cancer Institute. *Journal of Cancer Education* 25, 4 (Dec. 2010), 490–492. http://view.ncbi.nlm.nih.gov/pubmed/20238201

[8] J. Richard Landis and Gary G. Koch. 1977. The Measurement of Observer Agreement for Categorical Data. *Biometrics* 33, 1 (1977), 159–174. https://www.jstor.org/stable/2529310

[9] Gondy Leroy, James E. Endicott, David Kauchak, Obay Mouradi, and Melissa Just. 2013. User evaluation of the effects of a text simplification algorithm using term familiarity on perception, understanding, learning, and information retention. *Journal of Medical Internet Research* 15, 7 (2013), e144. https://doi.org/10.2196/jmir.2569

[10] Gondy Leroy, Stephen Helmreich, and James R. Cowie. 2010. The influence of text characteristics on perceived and actual difficulty of health information. *International Journal of Medical Informatics* 79, 6 (June 2010), 438–449.

[11] Gondy Leroy, David Kauchak, and Obay Mouradi. 2014. A user-study measuring the effects of lexical simplification and coherence enhancement on perceived and actual text difficulty. *International Journal of Medical Informatics* 82, 8 (Aug. 2014), 717–730.

[12] Carla Teixeira Lopes and Cristina Ribeiro. 2013. Measuring the value of health query translation: An analysis by user language proficiency. *Journal of the American Society for Information Science and Technology* 64, 5 (May 2013), 951–963. https://doi.org/10.1002/asi.22812

[13] Carla Teixeira Lopes and Cristina Ribeiro. 2015. Effects of Terminology on Health Queries: An Analysis by User's Health Literacy and Topic Familiarity. *Advances in Librarianship* 39 (2015), 145–184. https://doi.org/10.1108/S0065-283020150000039013

[14] Carla Teixeira Lopes and Hugo Sousa. 2019. Assisting Health Consumers While Searching the Web Through Medical Annotations. In *Proceedings of the 2019 Conference on Human Information Interaction & Retrieval.* ACM, New York, NY, USA. https://doi.org/10.1145/3295750.3298941

[15] Wen-Hsiang H. Lu, Ray Shih-Jui, Yi-Che C. Chan, and Kuan-Hsi H. Chen. 2006. Overcoming terminology barrier using Web resources for cross-language medical information retrieval.. In *AMIA Annual Symposium proceedings.* American Medical Informatics Association (AMIA), Maryland, USA, 519–523. http://view.ncbi.nlm.nih.gov/pubmed/17238395

[16] Gang Luo. 2009. Design and Evaluation of the iMed Intelligent Medical Search Engine. In *Proceedings of the 2009 IEEE International Conference on Data Engineering (ICDE'09).* IEEE Computer Society, Washington, DC, USA, 1379–1390. https://doi.org/10.1109/icde.2009.10

[17] Gang Luo, Chunqiang Tang, Hao Yang, and Xing Wei. 2008. MedSearch: a specialized search engine for medical information retrieval. In *CIKM'08: Proceedings of the 17th ACM Conference on Information and Knowledge Mining.* ACM, New York, NY, USA, 143–152. https://doi.org/10.1145/1458082.1458104

[18] Gheorghe Muresan, Michael Cole, Catherine L. Smith, Lu Liu, and Nicholas J. Belkin. 2006. Does Familiarity Breed Content? Taking Account of Familiarity with a Topic in Personalizing Information Retrieval. In *Proceedings of the 39th Annual Hawaii International Conference on System Sciences, 2006. HICSS'06.*, Vol. 3. IEEE, New York, NY, USA, 53c. https://doi.org/10.1109/hicss.2006.130

[19] Joao Palotti, Lorraine Goeuriot, Guido Zuccon, and Allan Hanbury. 2016. Ranking Health Web Pages with Relevance and Understandability. In *Proceedings of the 39th International ACM SIGIR Conference on Research and Development in Information Retrieval (SIGIR'16).* ACM, New York, NY, USA, 965–968. https://doi.org/10.1145/2911451.2914741

[20] Stephen E. Robertson, Evangelos Kanoulas, and Emine Yilmaz. 2010. Extending average precision to graded relevance judgments. In *Proceeding of the 33rd international ACM SIGIR conference on Research and development in information retrieval (SIGIR '10).* ACM, New York, NY, USA, 603–610. https://doi.org/10.1145/1835449.1835550

[21] Tefko Saracevic. 1996. Relevance reconsidered. In *Information science: Integration in perspectives. Proceedings of the Second Conference on Conceptions of Library and Information Science.* Royal School of Librarianship, Copenhagen, 201–218.

[22] Chenhao Tan, Evgeniy Gabrilovich, and Bo Pang. 2012. To Each His Own: Personalized Content Selection Based on Text Comprehensibility. In *Proceedings of the Fifth ACM International Conference on Web Search and Data Mining (WSDM'12).* ACM, New York, NY, USA, 233–242. https://doi.org/10.1145/2124295.2124325

[23] Kevyn C. Thompson, Paul N. Bennett, Ryen W. White, Sebastian de la Chica, and David Sontag. 2011. Personalizing Web Search Results by Reading Level. In *Proceedings of the 20th ACM International Conference on Information and Knowledge Management (CIKM'11).* ACM, New York, NY, USA, 403–412. https://doi.org/10.1145/2063576.2063639

[24] Tiffany M. Walsh and Teresa A. Volsko. 2008. Readability assessment of internet-based consumer health information. *Respiratory Care* 53, 10 (Oct. 2008), 1310–1315. http://view.ncbi.nlm.nih.gov/pubmed/18811992

[25] Q. Zeng, S. Kogan, N. Ash, R. A. Greenes, and A. A. Boxwala. 2002. Characteristics of consumer terminology for health information retrieval. *Methods of Information in Medicine* 41, 4 (2002), 289–298. http://view.ncbi.nlm.nih.gov/pubmed/12425240

[26] Qing T. Zeng, Jonathan Crowell, Robert M. Plovnick, Eunjung Kim, Long Ngo, and Emily Dibble. 2006. Assisting consumer health information retrieval with query recommendations. *Journal of the American Medical Informatics Association* 13, 1 (2006), 80–90. https://doi.org/10.1197/jamia.m1820

[27] Guido Zuccon. 2016. Understandability Biased Evaluation for Information Retrieval. In *Advances in Information Retrieval*, Nicola Ferro, Fabio Crestani, Marie-Francine Moens, Josiane Mothe, Fabrizio Silvestri, Giorgio M. Di Nunzio, Claudia Hauff, and Gianmaria Silvello (Eds.). Lecture Notes in Computer Science, Vol. 9626. Springer International Publishing, Cham, 280–292. https://doi.org/10.1007/978-3-319-30671-1_21

"Enslaved to the Trapped Data": A Cognitive Work Analysis of Medical Systematic Reviews

Ian A. Knight
School of Computer Science
University of Nottingham
Nottingham, UK
ian.knight1@nottingham.ac.uk

Max L. Wilson
Mixed Reality Lab
University of Nottingham
Nottingham, UK
max.wilson@nottingham.ac.uk

David F. Brailsford
School of Computer Science
University of Nottingham
Nottingham, UK
david.brailsford@nottingham.ac.uk

Natasa Milic-Frayling
School of Computer Science
University of Nottingham
Nottingham, UK
natasa.milic-frayling@nottingham.ac.uk

ABSTRACT

Systematic reviews are a comprehensive and parameterised form of literature review, found in most disciplines, that involve exhaustive analyses and rigorous interpretation of prior literature. Performing systematic reviews, however, can involve repetitive and laborious work in order to reach reliable standards. Strict guidelines and availability of published reviews make the task amenable to computerised assistance and automation using text mining, information extraction, and machine learning techniques. However, it is unclear which aspects of this Work Task are best suited for such support. This paper describes a three-month ethnographic study and Cognitive Work Analysis of the systematic reviews performed by a medical research group. Our findings show that the IR aspects of systematic reviews involve many tasks at two separate levels: 1) taxonomic organisation of documents and sub-document elements in relation to topic queries and domain-specific resources, and 2) extraction methods for structured summaries from the classified resources. This provides the basis for future work designing search tools with localised optimization and subtask automation to support specific phases of the process.

CCS CONCEPTS

• **Human-centered computing** → *Ethnographic studies*; • **Information systems** → Information extraction; Summarization.

KEYWORDS

Work task; Systematic review; Cognitive work analysis

ACM Reference Format:
Ian A. Knight, Max L. Wilson, David F. Brailsford, and Natasa Milic-Frayling. 2019. "Enslaved to the Trapped Data": A Cognitive Work Analysis of Medical Systematic Reviews. In *2019 Conference on Human Information Interaction and Retrieval (CHIIR '19), March 10–14, 2019, Glasgow, United Kingdom.* ACM, New York, NY, USA, 10 pages. https://doi.org/10.1145/3295750.3298937

CHIIR '19, March 10–14, 2019, Glasgow, United Kingdom

ACM ISBN 978-1-4503-6025-8/19/03...$15.00
https://doi.org/10.1145/3295750.3298937

1 INTRODUCTION

A Systematic Review, as a formal approach to literature review, is a Recall-oriented task [19], that appears in most disciplines. In their extreme forms, within evidence based medicine and legal e-discovery [29], *all* relevant documents *must* be found to be confident that decisions are being made in the light of all possible data, *and* that no data is missed. As an activity, a systematic review is usually performed by experts, under very tightly controlled parameters that have been prescribed as the task was assigned. In practice, however, systematic reviews might be spread across multiple people as a collaborative search activity [16], and is typically performed across a complex multi-stage process [22]. Further, multiple people with different skills and expertise often take different roles at different stages. Systematic reviews must be rigorously performed and are currently laborious and repetitive. First, they must be sufficiently inclusive and comprehensive to include all relevant research, and second, researchers must then find, comprehend, extract, and integrate the data from within the search results.

We aimed to reveal the full nature of the Systematic Reviews, as a Work Task [24], or indeed as a series of multiple Work Tasks. Our research questions were as follows:

RQ1 What is the nature of the work task, and its sub-tasks?
RQ2 What opportunities exist to support the work task with search systems?

In contrast to published protocols on how systematic reviews *should* be performed, this paper's main contribution lies in presenting a detailed Cognitive Work Analysis [39] of actual working practices around systematic reviews (Section 4), based on a focused-ethnography study [28]. Our results lay the foundations for future research into the design of search systems that support this high-recall collaborative work task.

2 RELATED WORK

We begin by contextualising Systematic Reviews as a Work Task, which Järvelin and Ingwersen define as the larger task involving information use, that typically creates the information need that leads to information seeking [24]. We then highlight the benefit of exploring a medical case study as context for our research.

2.1 Systematic Reviews as a Work Task

Systematic reviews involve a well established process [21], applied in most research disciplines, including our own community (e.g., Kelly & Sugimoto's systematic review of IIR Evaluation [26]). Brereton *et al.* [7] acknowledge 10 stages of a systematic review that span the planning, execution, and documentation of systematic reviews: 1) plan research questions, 2) specify review protocol, 3) validate review protocol, 4) identify relevant research, 5) select primary studies, 6) assess study quality, 7) extract required data, 8) synthesize data, 9) write review report, 10) validate report. In comparison to a literature review, a systematic review is designed to 1) parameterise a literature review space to define what will be included and excluded, 2) survey *all* the available research that meets those criteria, 3) synthesise the studies' combined data (e.g., through meta-analysis), and 4) present quantifiable recommendations based on the synthesised data [17]. While a literature review might outwardly look for possible extant literature that relates by any one criteria, a systematic review looks inwardly to find all the literature that matches all the prespecified criteria, to the exclusion of results that only partially meet the criteria.

Brereton *et al.* applied their 10 stages to software engineering literature, and dicovered that poor quality abstracts and lack of infrastructure make such reviews difficult. Thus, they need to be adapted to suit different domains. Athukorala *et al.*, for example, found that literature searching was a highly collaborative experience for the computer scientists they studied [3]. Papaioannou *et al.* studied the different search tactics used by social scientists in systematic reviews, noting that beyond reference lists, checking and expert contacts were needed to reach rigorous standards [31]. More recently, Booth performed an in depth systematic review of methodologies used in *qualitative* systematic reviews [6], noting the data extraction of comparable specific detail as an open challenge.

The stages of the systematic review task lend themselves to different roles, similar to the Prospector and Miner proposed by Golovchinsky *et al.* [16], where one person's role is to find sources of information, and another person's role is to extract data from them. In 2005, Harris studied the crucial role that a medical research librarian plays in the process, in collaboration with researchers on a project [20]. Similarly, Beverley *et al.* studied 11 different roles that may be performed by an information specialist in healthcare literature reviews [5]. It could be argued that Systematic Reviews are made up of a series of Work Tasks, such as selecting primary studies, reviewing papers, etc.; however, as our results further highlight below, each of the stages are closely integrated and depend on shared document artefacts.

2.2 Case Study: Medical Systematic Reviews

While systematic reviews are recognised across disciplines, in medical research and practice, systematic reviews represent work tasks of significant importance. "Evidence-based medicine" is the practice of ensuring that the therapies proposed by clinicians to their patients are those best supported by existing medical evidence [32]. To do this, medical practitioners must constantly study medical literature in order to continually update and revise their practice in the light of new evidence. Often there is a delay between new research being published and clinicians updating their methods, leading to a so-called "evidence-practice gap" [18]. Narrowing this gap is a significant challenge for medical practitioners. Indeed, '*It is unlikely that all [medical practitioners] will have the time, skills and resources to find, appraise, and interpret this evidence and to incorporate it into healthcare decisions.*' [21, Sec. 1.2.1]. Systematic reviews are a key approach to overcoming this problem. By providing practitioners with summarised data,systematic reviews narrow the evidence-practice gap by removing the need for individual clinicians to do their own literature reviews; they can instead refer to the systematic review performed by other experts.

2.3 Systematic Review Tools

An important challenge and a limitation of systematic reviews is their currency—i.e., the extent to which they reflect the most up-to-date research. The highly rigorous nature of systematic review production makes the review-writing process a very time-consuming one. There can be a gap of anywhere between 2.5 and 6.5 years between new research being published and that research being incorporated into a review [25], and there is also commonly at least a year between completing the literature search and publishing the final review [10], meaning that systematic reviews are often out of date from the moment they are written, or missing key evidence.

Not surprisingly then, much research (including the background motivation of our own work) is focused on identifying opportunities for tool provision for this work task [3]. Fabbri *et al.* [12], for example, have produced a tool for text mining content from found relevant papers, and visualising the results for the systematic reviewer. It is hoped that replacing human effort with machine effort during systematic review production will vastly reduce this latency, improving the relevance of the systematic reviews thus produced [10, 37]. Across the tasks, the challenge lies in identifying ways of automating elements of the review writing process while still maintaining the high standards of impartiality required in a systematic review [4, 38]. Currently, this impartiality is ensured by never relying solely on automated systems for any part of the review production process. Most stages of the process involve two or more workers operating in tandem, and it is recommended that replacing a *single* worker with an automated system should still ensure unbaised outputs [30]. Current systematic review support tools are largely designed, therefore, as decision support tools rather than as tools to replace humans altogether (e.g., [14, 27]).

3 FOCUSED-ETHNOGRAPHY STUDY

In this section, we describe our method for investigating systematic reviews, and introduce the context of our case study.

3.1 Methodology and Setting

A three-month ethnographic study was designed to understand the work of a medical research group involved in producing systematic reviews. While ethnographic studies may take years to conduct, studies of shorter duration can be sufficient to understand the environment, systems and practices and to provide the foundations for more in-depth studies [8]. Such shorter studies are particularly appropriate for *design ethnography*, the application of ethnographic methods to systems design. They enable designers to account for the *social characteristics* of the system being studied, rather than focusing solely on the functional characteristics [9]. The aim of our study was to provide as complete picture of the group's work as possible, revealing both the movement of artefacts between participants and the tight interdependence of sub-tasks.

Because systematic reviews are particularly important in medical research and practices (Section 2) we sought to engage a research group that is actively contributing to the Cochrane Collaboration.[1] The Cochrane Collaboration is an international organisation founded in 1993 to establish standards for the production of medical systematic reviews and make them widely available [21].

We approached the international Cochrane Schizophrenia Group (CSzG)[2] and conducted the study at their headquarters in the Institute of Mental Health at the University of Nottingham. Most systematic reviews produced by the group are written by volunteers who engage on a temporary basis. The core group retains a small number of editors who coordinate the writing process and select the topics for systematic reviews. The group's headquarters occupies part of a shared office in the Institute of Mental Health, alongside a number of other mental health-related research groups, that provides a working space for local volunteer reviewers. These individuals and their roles are described in detail below.

3.2 Data Collection and Analysis

One of the authors spent three months working full-time at the group's office, integrated with the review team. The author assisted with the data extraction for systematic reviews, while observing and interviewing selected members of the group. The data was collected through informal discussions and *ad hoc* interviews throughout January to March 2018. In particular, we followed four participants who play key roles in the group: The group's Coordinating Editor (P1) and Information Specialist (P2), the director of a consultancy firm Review Solutions (P3), and a Medical Student who was engaged in producing a systematic review for their dissertation (P4). The gathered data included field observation notes, interview recordings and transcripts, screenshots of computer-based work, and examples of physical artefacts produced during the group's work.

In order to gain an in-depth understanding of the group's processes and roles, we analysed the data using Cognitive Work Analysis (CWA) [39], a framework developed to model complex sociotechnical systems. It is *formative*, describing a system in terms of 'constraints on action' rather than prescribing a specific workflow. Thus the method is well aligned with our intent to understand the requirements for the enhancement of the computerised support.

CWA is made up of five sub-analyses (termed *phases*), that are conducted in a recommended order to capture multiple facets of work:1) Work Domain Analysis (WDA), 2) Control Task Analysis (ConTA), 3) Strategies Analysis (SA), 4) Social Organisation and Cooperation Analysis (SOCA), and 5) Worker Competencies Analysis (WCA). Each phase builds on the results of the previous phases to construct a complete picture of the system under analysis. Analysis was performed in the first instance by the lead author, whose findings were then checked and discussed by the others.

A recent extension of CWA proposes modifying the phases for team-based Computer-Supported Collaborative Work [1]. However, that technique is more suited for same-time same-place collaboration [2]. We discovered early in our study that the team's multistage process was set up and managed so that the work is more *social* [11] than collaborative [16], and so we proceeded with the original CWA approach [39].

4 FINDINGS

In this section we present the findings of the ethnographic study through the lens of the five CWA phases. We group our findings thematically to include the nature of group work and characteristics of the work processes, referring to the key work tasks we uncovered and discussing specific work tasks by considering the relevant CWA phases in sequence.

In our discussion we adopt the following terminology: a *report* refers to an individual document presenting data of interest (e.g., a journal article); a *study* is a collection of all reports related to the same underlying clinical trial; and a *review* designates a systematic review summarising several studies.

4.1 Nature of the Group's Work

We begin with a broad description of the group's work based on the first two phases of CWA, the later phases being better suited to discussion of specific tasks, and then define the Work Tasks and analyze them in depth.

4.1.1 Work Domain. The first phase of CWA is the Work Domain Analysis (WDA) that focuses on the physical and environmental constraints of the system used by CSzG. This analysis is important because a system's function is constrained not just by the tasks that must be performed, but also by the environment they must be performed in. The results of the WDA are summarized in Table 1. In general, the CSzG group produces and publishes medical systematic reviews relating to the treatment of schizophrenia. Their work involves a mix of physical and digital artefacts. They use face-to-face and virtual communication, both constrained by their shared office space. The workers make use of physical artefacts and face-to-face communications wherever possible, but certain interactions are required to take place via computer.

4.1.2 Control Tasks. During the Control Task Analysis (ConTA) we identified distinct Work Tasks that are performed to complete the systematic reviews. We organise our findings based on prominent aspects of the Work Tasks that are of interest to our research. The summary of identified Work Tasks is presented in Table 2. ConTA aims to describe all the tasks performed within a system, taking no considerations of *how* they are done or by *whom*. In the later stages of our analysis it became apparent that, in practice, several of the lower level tasks are combined to form a few larger tasks. We broadly group these individual tasks under two processes: a "Search and De-duplication Process", and a "Data Extraction Process". Some tasks occur in both processes while others are specific to only one.

[1] https://cochrane.org
[2] https://schizophrenia.cochrane.org

Table 1: Work Domain Analysis of CSzG

Abstraction level	Domain description
Functional purposes *Objectives & external limits*	Review production; Review dissemination; Use time & money efficiently; Cochrane Handbook
Abstract functions *Fundamental laws, principles, values*	Impartiality; Transparency; Rigour; Comprehensiveness; Uniqueness; Work-hours per review; Qualification of reviewers
Generalised functions *Functions enabling fulfilment of purposes*	Intra-team communication; Recording past reviews; Peer review; Screening; Data extraction; Meta-analysis; Study de-duplication; Translation of non-English documents
Physical functions *Capabilities & limits of physical objects*	Word processing; Highlighting of text; Annotation of text; Search for studies/reports; Record data; Question asking; Computer networking
Physical forms *Physical artefacts and tools*	PDF documents; Printed documents; Data extraction forms; Pens & highlighters; Post-it (sticky) notes; Skype; WeChat; MS Word; MS Excel; MS Access; MeerKat; Review Manager; RevMan HAL; Information specialist; Editors; Reviewers; Review Solutions consultancy; Chinese government firewall

Table 2: Key Work Tasks in CSzG

Work Task	Description
Register update and maintenance	Updating the study-based register; Refining the ontology used to code the register's contents.
Reviewer training	Providing training, as a service, for new reviewers, teaching skills needed to conduct a systematic review.
Study de-duplication	Determining which individual research reports describe the same underlying study in the database.
Screening	Determining the relevance of provided studies.
Data extraction	Obtaining required qualitative and quantitative data from relevant studies.
Review compilation	Entering results of data extraction into RevMan; Writing conclusions.

In brief, the Search and De-duplication process involves the group's information specialist, who manages the group's database of schizophrenia-related studies and performs the actual work of searching it for studies relevant to a review. The Data Extraction process takes place during the production of an actual review, and involves extracting data from medical research reports provided by the information specialist and recording them.

4.1.3 Cooperative, but individual. Before proceeding to describe these two processes, we first give a general account of the social and organisational characteristics of the group. We identified three broad classes of worker within the group: *Editors*, *Authors*, and *Trials Search Coordinators*. Referring to the list of participants earlier, P1 is an Editor, P2 is a Trials Search Coordinator, and both P3 and P4 would be considered Authors (as would our researcher).

A key research question for us was about the possible *cooperative* nature of systematic review production. Social Organisation and Cooperation Analysis of CSzG's work indicated that the group's work does not fit conventional notions of collaborative or cooperative work. There were no organised teams of individuals conducting exactly the same tasks at the same time. Data extraction, for example, seems a suitable candidate for cooperative work. Instead, by the formal protocols, it was required to be performed individually in order to avoid bias. This makes the CSzG work more *coordinated* than cooperative or collaborative [33]. That said, Authors would often confer with others outside of their own review, in order to get or provide help and advice, particularly their associated Editors. In this sense, the work of producing a systematic review is more social [11] than collaborative, especially for specific tasks. In principle, several of the tasks could benefit from the development of systems to improve collaboration, but they would have to be carefully assessed to ensure that no biases are introduced into the end product. This finding highlights the importance of access permissions in collaborative search [16].

Cooperation *was*, however, observed in two cases: processing reports written in Mandarin and quality assurance at the end of the extraction process. In the first case the group had to work with reports published in Mandarin. As there are many studies in Schizophrenia research published in non-English languages, for an English-speaking research group the data in them are '*locked behind a language barrier*' (P1). For that reason, CSzG works with a Chinese consultancy firm (Review Solutions, RS) to extract data from Mandarin-language reports, translate them into English, and provide them to reviewers. That requires close communication between the study author, the consultancy's director based in the CSzG office (P3), and the consultancy staff assigned to perform the data extraction. This communication is complicated by the fact that all the RS staff except for the RS Director are based in China and work remotely. The second case of cooperation was observed at the end of the data extraction task. In principle, this task is conducted by two reviewers entirely separately, who then come together to discuss the extracted data, check one another's results, and agree on the final data to be included in the review.

4.2 Search and De-duplication Process

The first stages of a systematic review involve conducting the literature search, screening the results to filter out non-relevant reports, and grouping relevant reports that relate to the same clinical trial. In CSzG these tasks are conducted by the group's information specialist (P2), as part of the Search and De-duplication Process. We note that this set up represents a significant departure from the traditional systematic review methodology. We defer providing more details and commenting on the implications until the discussion.

4.2.1 Strategies for Search and De-duplication. The Strategies Analysis phase of CWA is concerned with describing the different possible approaches to completing the control tasks identified during ConTA. The Search and De-duplication Process, in particular, involves three control tasks: Register Update and Maintenance, Screening, and Study De-duplication.

The CSzG strategy for Register Update and Maintenance is thoroughly described in [34], as the group has pioneered this methodology. In CSzG, the group's information specialist (P2) runs a monthly literature search using a previously-approved search protocol, performs initial screening of the results to ensure they relate to schizophrenia, and records them in a database along with their broad PICO[3] characteristics and their full text in PDF form:

> *So, to have this register updated, we've used 70 different databases, like your medical databases. [...] We have MEDLINE, Embase. We do the searches in 10 databases every month. It's automatically done, the majority of it, and I receive the records. I screen them to see if they are randomised, if they [say] schizophrenia. If so, I am adding to our database and I extract those metadata, that I told you. Which is participants, are they schizophrenia? Age group, and do they have a special problem, like depression and schizophrenia? Then, what are the interventions and what are the outcomes? (P2)*

The search strategy employed by the group is fixed, in compliance with the requirements for rigorous and reproducible search results imposed by the Cochrane Handbook (e.g., [21, Sec. 6.1.1.2]). These regulations prevent the group from utilising more interactive or exploratory search strategies. In principle, the regular literature search strategy could be enhanced, but any changes to the methodology would have to be carefully studied to ensure that the required degree of transparency and reproducibility is retained.

Screening is the task of filtering out results of the literature search that are non-relevant. Diagrams illustrating strategies for screening are shown in Figure 1. The general method for screening a particular report involves comparing the PICO characteristics of that report to the PICO characteristics of the systematic review. In the case of the current process, this is performed more generally, as described in the quote above: any report of a randomised controlled trial relating to schizophrenia is deemed relevant at this stage and included in the database. Reports are labelled in the database according to an informal taxonomy defined by the group itself, which consists of standardised names and spellings of drugs, outcome measures, and other data of interest. This enhances later retrieval of documents.

Finally, the de-duplication task is that of identifying which individual reports returned in the search results relate to the same underlying clinical trial. This is important, because often several publications will be made from the same original study, but, '*Duplicate publication can introduce substantial biases if studies are inadvertently included more than once in a meta-analysis.*' [21, Sec. 7.2.2] Only one feasible strategy for study de-duplication was identified, shown in Figure 2.

4.2.2 Social Organisation and Worker Competencies. The fourth and fifth phases of CWA describe how workers are organised within the system being analysed, and what skills and abilities those workers require to perform their tasks. Conventionally in a medical

[3]An acronym referring to the four major categories of qualitative data extracted from a study: **P**atient, **I**ntervention, **C**ontrol, **O**utcome.

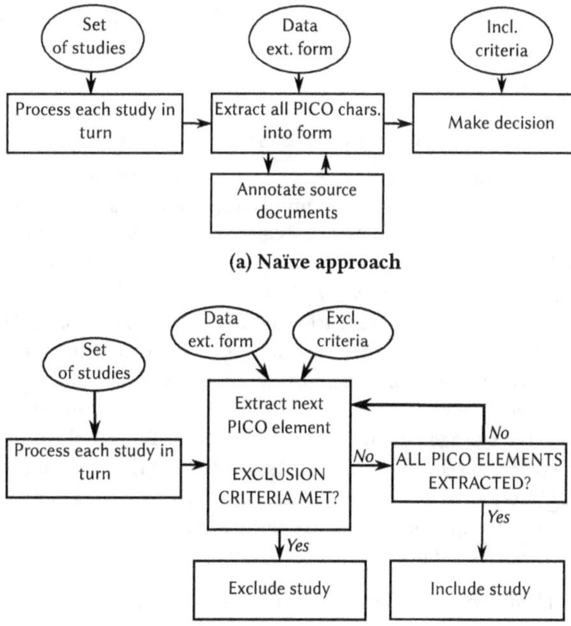

(a) Naïve approach

(b) Iterative approach

Figure 1: Strategies Analysis for Screening

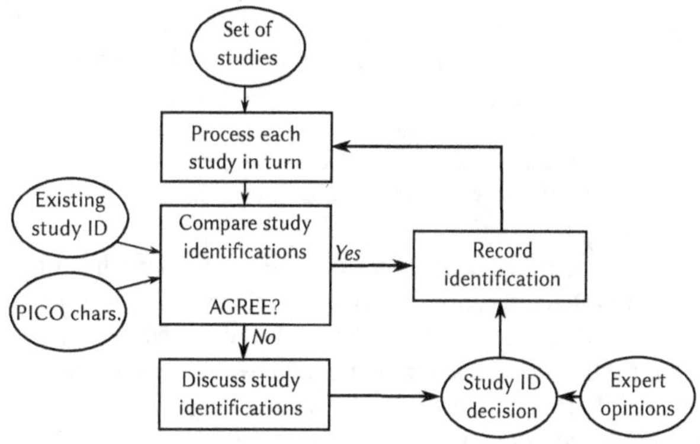

Figure 2: Strategies Analysis for Study De-duplication

systematic review, the responsibility for the described control tasks would be the responsibility of an Author, with the search task supported by a Trials Search Coordinator [21, Sec. 6.1.1.1]. In the CSzG, however, these tasks are allocated to a single person, the information specialist. As will be described below, Authors still engage with some parts of the Search and De-duplication Process, but only at a later stage, and only in a confirmatory capacity.

Worker Competency Analysis typically breaks down the individual behaviours (required to perform a control task) into three categories: *skill-based* behaviours which are at the fundamental level and considered almost instinctive; *rule-based* behaviours which involve execution of learned sets of rules; and *knowledge-based* behaviours which require critical thinking and debate on the part of the actor in order to undertake the execution. Among the identified tasks, by far most complex is de-duplication, requiring a high degree of knowledge-based behaviours. Screening is rule-based, as the actor simply compares extracted PICO characteristics against those of the study.

4.3 Data Extraction Process

The Data Extraction Process seemed particularly demanding to those involved in the corresponding tasks. The Coordinating Editor (P1) described systematic reviewers as being *'enslaved to the trapped data'*, with reviewers *'chiselling the mine'* to get at the data they needed. Both qualitative and quantitative data are extracted from the studies under review. The qualitative data consist of PICO characteristics describing the study in terms of the drugs that were involved, the number of patients studied, and similar, while the quantitative data include the actual results of the study in terms of measured changes in outcomes. As shown in Table 2, this process involved the control tasks of Screening, Study De-duplication, Data Extraction, and Review Compilation. This process is almost exclusively performed by Authors, with advice from Editors or a Trials Search Coordinator when requested.

4.3.1 Data Extraction Strategies. The first two control tasks are also carried out during Search and De-duplication as described in the previous section. The strategies remain the same, but the goals are slightly different. Study de-duplication is only conducted to verify the decision of the information specialist to include the study in the review, rather than to conduct the search from scratch. De-duplication decisions are in fact constantly up for debate, and may be changed at any time with a sufficient justification:

> *[...] whatever conclusion [we reach], we [re]apply on our register. So, whatever exists in our register is the accumulation of all of the efforts that have been done by reviewers, editors, me, people who have realised there is an error and report it. Whoever reports any error, I just correct it here. (P2)*

Screening, on the other hand, is more precise here than during Search and De-duplication, involving consideration of more detailed characteristics and inclusion criteria. The author embedded in the group participated in a systematic review where one study was excluded because its outcomes were not specific enough to be clearly related to the purpose of the review:

> *So, if you look in diagnosis, it doesn't really specify if the patients had aggression. It was just an exacerbation of schizophrenia. So we were like, "You can't say psychosis induced aggression." (P4)*

It is the screening during the data extraction process that revealed the naive screening strategy shown in Figure 1a. This approach was adopted by a first-time review author with minimal training in systematic review production, who commented,

> *[...] although I've done this one a bit more fully, [P1] said usually what happens is, with the excluded ones, they fill in the things until it gets excluded, and then they stop filling it in [...] So, technically I could have stopped there and it would have been fine. (P4)*

The author's inexperience led her to obtain the vast majority of the study's characteristics and only then make a decision to exclude it from the review.

The *control task* of Data Extraction is only performed during this process. This task requires the majority of the effort during the Data Extraction Process, and consists of identifying all of the qualitative and quantitative data contained in the studies processed for the systematic review, and recording them. Strategies for this task are shown in Figure 3. In the group, the preferred practice is to print physical copies of the reports in a study, along with a data extraction form, and to use these as reference materials for data extraction rather than working with digital media.

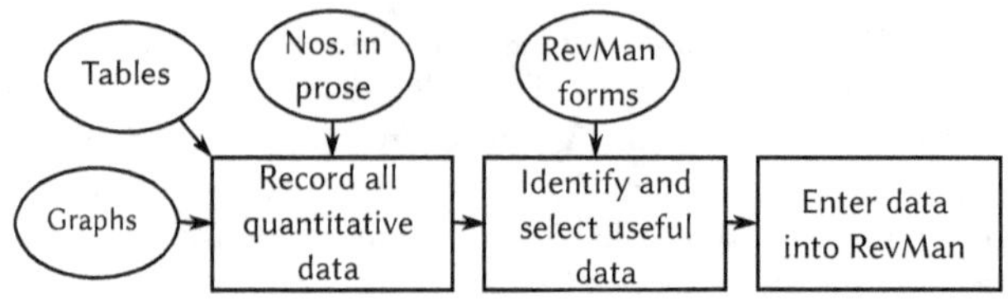

(a) Naïve strategy

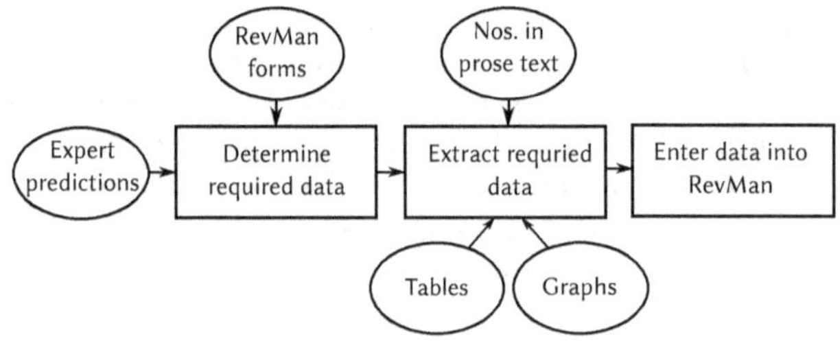

(b) Expert strategy

Figure 3: Strategies Analysis for Data Extraction

Data are first extracted into a specially-designed data extraction form (see Figure 4 in the appendix for an example), and then entered into the review writing software. The data extraction form specifies precisely which qualitative data are required for the review, and the task consists simply of filling in this form with evidence drawn from the study. Quantitative data extraction is more complicated that this, however. Only certain data are actually required to support the meta-analysis, but an inexperienced reviewer will not know in advance which data these are. Referring back to the review author, she experienced exactly this problem:

> P4 *[Entering the extracted data] was the longest part, because so much had to get deleted, ultimately [...] So, a lot of the stuff that [report authors] put isn't needed [for the review], and so they put in baseline figures and we don't use those. Skewed data goes.*
>
> Int. *Okay, so you've pulled out all the numbers?*
>
> P4 *Yes, you've pulled out absolutely everything.*
>
> Int. *Then when you go to enter it, you find that you don't actually need all of the numbers.*
>
> P4 *Yes, it takes a lot of careful checking.*

The data are simply extracted onto sheets of paper (Figure 5) and then entered later into the review writing software. In principle it should be possible for a more experienced review author to predict which quantitative data are going to be needed for a particular review and only extract those, hence the alternative strategy shown in Figure 3b.

A vital part of all strategies for data extraction is the annotation of the source documents to indicate the location of the evidence for the data in the forms. This annotation may take the form of highlighting sentences or phrases (see Figure 6), or by placing small numbered marks in the forms that are then referred back to. These annotations serve to make it much easier for other reviewers to verify that the extracted data are correct.

> *Yes, so, [P1] makes [the data extraction form], he had to be like, 'Yes, highlight where you've got things from, annotate where you've got the things from.' [...] [In] a lot of them I put asterisks, numbers, just to know that I can go back and see exactly where I've got the stuff from. (P4)*

It should be noted that this reliance on using physical artefacts for data extraction may not be a widely adopted practice across systematic reviewers. There are different software solutions available to support systematic reviewers in extracting and storing data,[4] but flexibility in the process and the data means that the group prefers to work on paper. The variability of data, types of data, and formats of presentation mean that paper adds flexibility in a way that is often complex to record in digital forms. The most obvious example of flexibility requirements is collaboration with Review Solutions to extract data from Mandarin-language studies prevents the use of many of these tools. The director of Review Solutions commented,

> *The reason we haven't used [Covidence] is because my team is mostly based in China, and the government has a firewall, which makes [...] Covidence incredibly slow. [...] There's another tool—Apparently, it's more powerful than Covidence; it's called Distiller [...] but then we had the same trouble. Sometimes we simply can't even get on to the website. (P3)*

4.3.2 Social Organisation and Worker Competencies. Social Organisation and Cooperation Analysis for Data Extraction uncovered a range expertise levels amongst review authors, from fully-qualified medical doctors, to medical students, to entirely non-medical workers such as the embedded researcher from our team. In addition to these differing levels of domain expertise, authors also possessed varying levels of expertise in the systematic review process. As such, the authors had and required varying levels of training in data extraction.

It quickly became apparent that this variance in expertise was not an obstacle to the production of systematic reviews of an appropriate quality. The group's coordinating editor *prefers* to make use of less-qualified people to conduct reviews, citing the use of full time fully-paid medical doctors as '*a waste of NHS money*'. Training is provided by the coordinating editor on an informal basis, but there is also a lot of "learning on the job":

> P4 *At the beginning, I was really overwhelmed. I did not understand how I was going to be able to do this in such a short time period. [...] I don't really like to make a big thing of asking help all the time [...] [but] as soon as you start doing it, it gets easier and easier [...]*
>
> Int. *Okay, so a lot of learning by example, would that be fair?*
>
> P4 *Yes, and then also [P1] gave loads of advice, but we've also got [P3] here [...] she's done some stuff and then [P2] is really good at all the search stuff, and even then the people that come in and out. A lot of the time they'll literally just pop in, I'll ask them a question, and they'll disappear. I have no idea who they are, but they were very helpful.*

The coordinating editor described his own role in the process as to be '*breathing down the neck*' of the reviewers to guide them in how to write their reviews to an appropriate standard. He also runs an annual training seminar on how to conduct systematic reviews, but it was not possible to observe this during the study.

Data extraction is conventionally organised to involve two separate review authors working in tandem. The recommended method is for each author to separately conduct data extraction for the studies in the review, and for them to then come together and compare results [21, Sec. 7.6.2]. In this way, the authors can check each others' work to improve accuracy of data extraction. In practice, this may not always be performed "by the book"; in the systematic review we participated in, data extraction had been completed by the first author (P4), who then gave their results to the embedded researcher and simply asked them to '*double check*' the data.

In terms of worker competencies, de-duplication and screening remain much the same as they were described previously. Screeing becomes more knowledge-based in this process, however, because the decisions to be made are more complex. Data extraction itself requires a wide mix of skill- and knowledge-based behaviours: certain PICO elements can be identified almost by "pattern matching" on the part of the review author, while other data require much interpretation of the source document before they can be successfully extracted, especially when it comes to extracting qualitative data.

5 DISCUSSION

This section draws together an initial set of conclusions from the CWA analysis, organised according to our research questions.

5.1 Key Tasks (RQ1)

Broadly, we would typically classify the systematic review task as one involving Exploratory Search [40], well beyond the query-response paradigm. *Exploration*, however, is actively discouraged in favour of comprehensive review of results, by creating *processes* that make it impartial and procedural.

5.1.1 Pre-Search Problem. The first stage of their processes involved the procedural retrieval and pre-categorisation of new literature into a purpose built taxonomy, which is performed entirely separately from an ongoing systematic review task. By creating subscriptions to digital libraries, and performing pre-determined manuals searches, the team reviews all new publications for how they relevant to their expertise, and classifies the results for future reviews. This represents an information monitoring task, and is perhaps an ideal opportunity for more advanced Slow Search [35] systems. Further, this pre-search stage involves document inspection and judging relevance of a straight list of results, which is not unlike a standard, yet comprehensive, version of a very straight information retrieval task.

The larger *work task* of this phase is to classify of results into different parts of the taxonomy, designed to make subsequent search tasks more procedural. Indeed, the work is a lot like those performed to create a TREC test collection. However, in this case they are creating an intermediary search system, such that people performing systematic reviews further down the process do not actually explore the literature available in digital libraries, but retrieve pre-classified data from pre-defined queries.

[4]Covidence was mentioned by P3 [https://www.covidence.org/home]

5.1.2 Search Problem. Once a systematic review begins, the work is still executed in separate phases, often by different people. One stage involves the more exploratory *searching*, and the other involves more investigative *inspection* of results.

The first phase involves the identification, only, of search queries for a systematic review. This activity focuses on identifying the queries that are relevant, in order to meet the requirements of the systematic review. This may involve interactive querying and making relevance judgements of result sets, but it rarely involves what we would often consider a core part of the information retrieval process: finding information.

The second phase of the systematic review involves almost no searching at all, and instead involves the comprehensive analysis of the results returned from the queries built (by another person) in the first phase. This person cannot, or should not, seek more results or explore related terminology, they must simply examine the results provided to them by the intermediary search system. In the examples from our observations, a study that included symptoms of acute exacerbation was not included, because it was not specifically controlling for *aggression* as a variable. Indeed, the reports produced as a result of the systematic review are expected to identify works that are excluded; these results are *found*, judged as *relevant*, but not *included* in the review. These findings help to elaborate on part of the *Collaborative Search role* that Golovchinsky *et al.* referred to as a Prospector [16].

5.1.3 Post-Search Problem. The role of a Miner [16] in our case study, has to make very detailed relevance judgements based upon a key challenge: Data Extraction. Here, the quantitative data must be examined by the main systematic reviewer to determine precisely which reported outcomes are usable or not. Qualitative data extraction was observed to be generally an exercise in pattern matching, and most of the data extraction involved simply searching for key words or phrases in the text that indicated a sentence contained PICO data. For future systems, automated quantitative data extraction could prove to be a hard challenge, as the data needed for the review may only consist of one or two rows of a single table in an entire report, and at present the reviewers must do a lot of manual work to identify exactly what is needed.

The heterogeneous nature of the group's document collection also makes the work of data extraction harder; there were a variety of document types in the corpus, ranging from journal articles to conference abstracts to doctoral theses. There were also a variety of qualities of PDF documents, some of which have very unreliably transcribed text which will make automated extraction inconsistent and more prone to errors. These challenges are similar to those identified by Brereton *et al.* [7].

5.2 HCIR Opportunities (RQ2)

Our investigation identified a series of opportunities for HCIR systems to support systematic reviews through automation of tasks that were described as laborious and repetitive. One initial observation is that this multi-stage process may be facilitated better by systems that, overall, model search stages explicitly [22, 23]. The breadth of expertise observed in those conducting systematic reviews indicates that great care must be taken when designing any technologies for systematic review automation to enable as many people as possible to participate in the review production process, particularly in data extraction. There is already interest in enabling less-exprienced volunteers to participate in certain stages of review production (e.g., [36]), and so care should be taken when developing new systems to ensure they are usable by novice reviewers.

In the pre-search stage, systematic review process might be best supported by tools designed for taxonomy management, than for exploratory search. This role involves work more like a librarian, cataloguing data for their team, than a reviewer/searcher.

In the main systematic review stage, the work is more focused on result-dataset comprehension task, such that tools could better support a searcher in knowing a) what portion of the available results they have retrieved, and b) how they relate to parts of the taxonomy. One tool that made developments in this area was Querium [15], which made efforts to help searchers understand the relationships between each of their queries, returned results, and the full dataset.

The post-search data extraction problem is one that is more closely related to automatic summarisation. In practical terms, a tool for systematic review data extraction would need to be capable of coping with arbitrary document layouts and PDF qualities, for example. More importantly, however, the data extraction problem is a varied and interactive task involving retrieving data from within documents, rather than documents themselves. Given what was observed of people using paper artefacts, this task could benefit from, e.g., interactive machine learning interfaces like Cueflik [13], that would allow searchers to dynamically specify the types of data they are intending to extract for the systematic review.

6 CONCLUSIONS

In this paper we have presented a Cognitive Work Analysis, based on a novel focused-ethnography study of Medical Systematic Reviewing, as a rich and well-structured case study of such a Work Task. In its premise, we might consider Systematic Reviews to involve Exploratory Search activities. In practice, however, we find that well structured systematic review processes can involve a series of constrained search tasks, performed by different people, none of which involves exploratory search as we would normally describe it. Systematic Reviews, in our case study, were facilitated by a pre-search task that categorised new documents asynchronously from any actual systematic review. Notably, all subsequent people in the process work with these pre-classified documents without broadly searching online digital libraries for new documents. Perhaps the most exploratory actions are taken by a different person who identifies and then dictates the queries that will be used by the main systematic reviewer, but does very little exploring of the actual results. This final stage is then largely a data extraction task rather than a search task, reviewing a potentially large linear list of results. We find that most of these processes are purposefully delineated such that collaboration is coordinated by process, rather than performed as a synchronised co-located activity. There are opportunities, however, to support each of the subtasks involved in systematic reviews with different types of search tools. Alternatively, a system designed to support individuals in achieving the entire process alone would likely benefit from facilitating the separation of processes observed in our case study.

ACKNOWLEDGMENTS

This work was supported by the Engineering and Physical Sciences Research Council [grant number EP/M000877/1]. We would like to thank all of our study participants for taking the time to talk to us and explain their work, and the Cochrane Schizophrenia Group for affording us valuable desk space. We are also very grateful to our anonymous reviewers for their feedback and suggestions.

Data access: Due to concerns over preserving the anonymity of our participants, supporting data cannot be made publicly available.

REFERENCES

[1] Maryam Ashoori and Catherine Burns. 2013. Team Cognitive Work Analysis: Structure and Control Tasks. *Journal of Cognitive Engineering and Decision Making* 7, 2 (2013), 123–140. https://doi.org/10.1177/1555343412445577

[2] Maryam Ashoori, Catherine M. Burns, Barbara d'Entremont, and Kathryn Momtahan. 2014. Using team cognitive work analysis to reveal healthcare team interactions in a birthing unit. *Ergonomics* 57, 7 (2014), 973–986.

[3] Kumaripaba Athukorala, Eve Hoggan, Anu Lehtiö, Tuukka Ruotsalo, and Giulio Jacucci. 2013. Information-seeking Behaviors of Computer Scientists: Challenges for Electronic Literature Search Tools. In *Proceedings of the 76th ASIS&T Annual Meeting: Beyond the Cloud: Rethinking Information Boundaries (ASIST '13)*. American Society for Information Science, Silver Springs, MD, USA, Article 20, 11 pages. http://dl.acm.org/citation.cfm?id=2655780.2655800

[4] Elaine Beller, Justin Clark, Guy Tsafnat, Clive Adams, Heinz Diehl, Hans Lund, Mourad Ouzzani, Kristina Thayer, James Thomas, Tari Turner, Jun Xia, Karen Robinson, Paul Glasziou, and founding members of the ICASR group. 2018. Making progress with the automation of systematic reviews: Principles of the International Collaboration for the Automation of Systematic Reviews (ICASR). *Systematic Reviews* 7, 1 (2018), 77–84. https://doi.org/10.1186/s13643-018-0740-7

[5] C.A. Beverley, A. Booth, and P.A. Bath. 2003. The role of the information specialist in the systematic review process: a health information case study. *Health Information & Libraries Journal* 20, 2 (2003), 65–74. https://doi.org/10.1046/j.1471-1842.2003.00411.x

[6] Andrew Booth. 2016. Searching for qualitative research for inclusion in systematic reviews: a structured methodological review. *Systematic Reviews* 5, 1 (04 May 2016), 74. https://doi.org/10.1186/s13643-016-0249-x

[7] Pearl Brereton, Barbara A. Kitchenham, David Budgen, Mark Turner, and Mohamed Khalil. 2007. Lessons from applying the systematic literature review process within the software engineering domain. *Journal of Systems and Software* 80, 4 (2007), 571 – 583. https://doi.org/10.1016/j.jss.2006.07.009 Software Performance.

[8] Andy Crabtree. 2003. *Designing Collaborative Systems: A Practical Guide to Ethnography*. Springer-Verlag, London.

[9] Andrew Crabtree, Mark Rouncefield, and Peter Tolmie. 2012. *Doing Design Ethnography*. Springer-Verlag, London.

[10] Julian H. Elliott, Tari Turner, Ornella Clavisi, James Thomas, Julian P.T. Higgins, Chris Mavergames, and Russell L Gruen. 2014. Living Systematic Reviews: An Emerging Opportunity to Narrow the Evidence-Practice Gap. *PLoS Medicine* 11, 2 (2014), 1–6. https://doi.org/10.1371/journal.pmed.1001603

[11] Brynn M. Evans and Ed H. Chi. 2010. An elaborated model of social search. *Information Processing & Management* 46, 6 (2010), 656–678.

[12] Sandra Fabbri, Elis Hernandes, Andre Di Thommazo, Anderson Belgamo, Augusto Zamboni, and Cleiton Silva. 2013. Using Information Visualization and Text Mining to Facilitate the Conduction of Systematic Literature Reviews. In *Enterprise Information Systems*, José Cordeiro, Leszek A. Maciaszek, and Joaquim Filipe (Eds.). Springer Berlin Heidelberg, Berlin, Heidelberg, 243–256.

[13] James Fogarty, Desney Tan, Ashish Kapoor, and Simon Winder. 2008. CueFlik: interactive concept learning in image search. In *Proceedings of the sigchi conference on human factors in computing systems*. ACM, 29–38.

[14] Allison Gates, Cydney Johnson, and Lisa Hartling. 2018. Technology-assisted title and abstract screening for systematic reviews: A retrospective evaluation of the Abstrackr machine learning tool. *Systematic Reviews* 7 (2018), 45. https://doi.org/10.1186/s13643-018-0707-8

[15] Gene Golovchinsky, Abdigani Diriye, and Tony Dunnigan. 2012. The future is in the past: designing for exploratory search. In *Proceedings of the 4th Information Interaction in Context Symposium*. ACM, 52–61.

[16] Gene Golovchinsky, Pernilla Qvarfordt, and Jeremy Pickens. 2008. Collaborative information seeking. *Information Seeking Support Systems* (2008), 47–48.

[17] David Gough, Sandy Oliver, and James Thomas. 2017. Introducing Systematic Reviews. In *An Introduction to Systematic Reviews* (2nd ed.), David Gough, Sandy Oliver, and James Thomas (Eds.). Sage, London, 1–18.

[18] Jeremy M. Grimshaw, Martin P. Eccles, John N. Lavis, Sophie J. Hill, and Janet E. Squires. 2012. Knowledge translation of research findings. *Implementation Science* 7, 1 (2012), 50–67. https://doi.org/10.1186/1748-5908-7-50

[19] Maura R Grossman, Gordon V Cormack, and Adam Roegiest. 2016. TREC 2016 Total Recall Track Overview.. In *TREC*.

[20] Martha R. Harris. 2005. The librarian's roles in the systematic review process: a case study. *Journal of the Medical Library Association* 93, 1 (2005), 81.

[21] Julian P.T. Higgins and Sally Green (Eds.). 2011. *Cochrane Handbook for Systematic Reviews of Interventions, Version 5.1.0.* http://handbook-5-1.cochrane.org

[22] Hugo C Huurdeman and Jaap Kamps. 2014. From multistage information-seeking models to multistage search systems. In *Proceedings of the 5th Information Interaction in Context Symposium*. ACM, 145–154.

[23] Hugo C Huurdeman, Max L Wilson, and Jaap Kamps. 2016. Active and passive utility of search interface features in different information seeking task stages. In *Proceedings of the 2016 ACM on Conference on Human Information Interaction and Retrieval*. ACM, 3–12.

[24] Kalervo Järvelin and Peter Ingwersen. 2004. Information Seeking Research Needs Extension towards Tasks and Technology. *Information Research: An International Electronic Journal* 10, 1 (2004), n1.

[25] Siddhartha R. Jonnalagadda, Pawan Goyal, and Mark D. Huffman. 2015. Automating data extraction in systematic reviews: a systematic review. *Systematic Reviews* 4, 1 (2015), 78. https://doi.org/10.1186/s13643-015-0066-7

[26] Diane Kelly and Cassidy R. Sugimoto. 2013. A systematic review of interactive information retrieval evaluation studies, 1967–2006. *Journal of the American Society for Information Science and Technology* 64, 4 (2013), 745–770. https://doi.org/10.1002/asi.22799

[27] Svetlana Kiritchenko, Berry De Bruijn, Simona Carini, Joel Martin, and Ida Sim. 2010. ExaCT: Automatic extraction of clinical trial characteristics from journal publications. *BMC Medical Informatics and Decision Making* 10 (2010), 56. https://doi.org/10.1186/1472-6947-10-56

[28] Hubert Knoblauch. 2005. Focused Ethnography. *Forum Qualitative Sozialforschung / Forum: Qualitative Social Research* 6, 3 (2005). https://doi.org/10.17169/fqs-6.3.20

[29] Douglas W. Oard, Jason R. Baron, Bruce Hedin, David D. Lewis, and Stephen Tomlinson. 2010. Evaluation of information retrieval for E-discovery. *Artificial Intelligence and Law* 18, 4 (01 Dec 2010), 347–386. https://doi.org/10.1007/s10506-010-9093-9

[30] Alison O'Mara-Eves, James Thomas, John McNaught, Makoto Miwa, and Sophia Ananiadou. 2015. Using text mining for study identification in systematic reviews: a systematic review of current approaches. *Systematic Reviews* 4, 1 (2015), 5–27. https://doi.org/10.1186/2046-4053-4-5

[31] Diana Papaioannou, Anthea Sutton, Christopher Carroll, Andrew Booth, and Ruth Wong. 2010. Literature searching for social science systematic reviews: consideration of a range of search techniques. *Health Information & Libraries Journal* 27, 2 (2010), 114–122. https://doi.org/10.1111/j.1471-1842.2009.00863.x

[32] David L. Sackett. 1997. Evidence-based medicine. *Seminars in Perinatology* 21, 1 (1997), 3–5. https://doi.org/10.1016/S0146-0005(97)80013-4

[33] Chirag Shah. 2009. Toward collaborative information seeking (CIS). (2009). arXiv:0908.0709

[34] Farhad Shokraneh and Clive Elliott Adams. 2017. Study-based registers of randomized controlled trials: Starting a systematic review with data extraction or meta-analysis. *BioImpacts* 7, 4 (2017), 209–217. https://doi.org/10.15171/bi.2017.25

[35] Jaime Teevan, Kevyn Collins-Thompson, Ryen W White, Susan T Dumais, and Yubin Kim. 2013. Slow search: Information retrieval without time constraints. In *Proceedings of the Symposium on Human-Computer Interaction and Information Retrieval*. ACM, 1.

[36] James Thomas, Anna Noel-Storr, Ian Marshall, Byron Wallace, Steven McDonald, Chris Mavergames, Paul Glasziou, Ian Shemilt, Annelise Synnot, Tari Turner, and Julian Elliott. 2017. Living systematic reviews: 2. Combining human and machine effort. *Journal of Clinical Epidemiology* 91 (2017), 31–37. https://doi.org/10.1016/j.jclinepi.2017.08.011

[37] Guy Tsafnat, Paul Glasziou, Miew Keen Choong, Adam Dunn, Filippo Galgani, and Enrico Coiera. 2014. Systematic review automation technologies. *Systematic Reviews* 3, 1 (2014), 74–89. https://doi.org/10.1186/2046-4053-3-74

[38] Alexander Tsertsvadze, Yen Fu Chen, David Moher, Paul Sutcliffe, and Noel McCarthy. 2015. How to conduct systematic reviews more expeditiously? *Systematic Reviews* 4, 1 (2015), 160–166. https://doi.org/10.1186/s13643-015-0147-7

[39] Kim J. Vicente. 1999. *Cognitive Work Analysis: Towards safe, productive, and healthy computer-based work*. Lawrence Erlbaum Associates, Mahwah, NJ.

[40] Ryen W White and Resa A Roth. 2009. Exploratory search: Beyond the query-response paradigm. *Synthesis lectures on information concepts, retrieval, and services* 1, 1 (2009), 1–98.

A EXAMPLES OF PHYSICAL ARTEFACTS

In this appendix we show some examples of the physical artefacts referred to in Section 4.

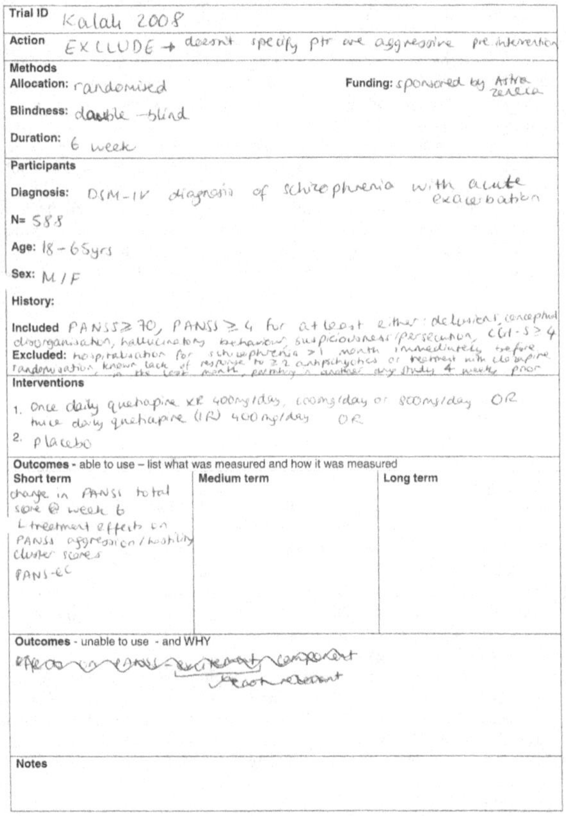

Trial ID Kalali 2008

Action EXCLUDE + doesn't specify ptr are aggressive pre intervention

Methods

Allocation: randomised

Funding: sponsored by Astra Zeneca

Blindness: double-blind

Duration: 6 week

Participants

Diagnosis: DSM-IV diagnosis of schizophrenia with acute exacerbation

N= 588

Age: 18-65yrs

Sex: M/F

History:

Included PANSS≥70, PANSS≥4 for at least either: delusions, conceptual disorganisation, hallucinatory behaviour, suspiciousness/persecution, CGI-S>4

Excluded: hospitalisation for schizophrenia >1 month immediately before randomisation, known lack of response to ≥2 antipsychotics or treatment with clozapine in the last month, participating in another study 4 weeks prior

Interventions

1. Once daily quetiapine XR 400mg/day, 600mg/day or 800mg/day OR twice daily quetiapine (IR) 400mg/day OR

2. placebo

Outcomes - able to use – list what was measured and how it was measured

Short term	Medium term	Long term
change in PANSS total score @ week 6 L treatment effects on PANSS aggression/hostility cluster scores PANSS-EC		

Outcomes - unable to use - and WHY

Notes

Figure 4: Example data extraction form

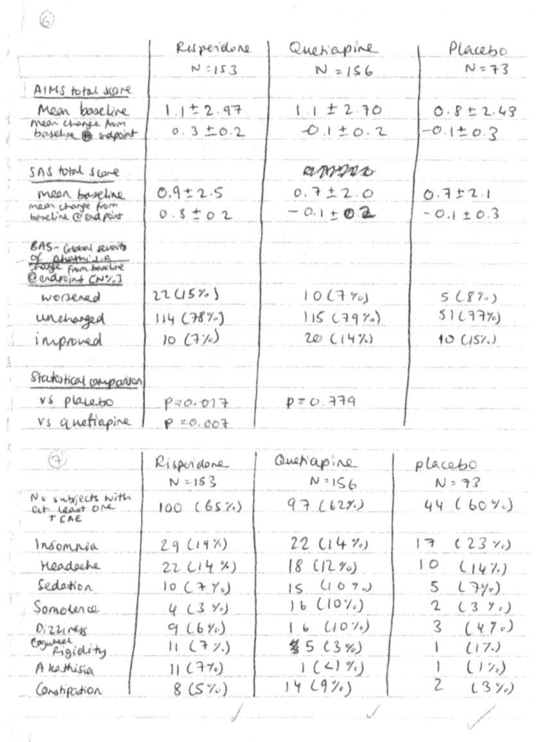

(6)

	Risperidone N=153	Quetiapine N=156	Placebo N=73
AIMS total score			
Mean baseline	1.1±2.97	1.1±2.70	0.8±2.48
mean change from baseline @ endpoint	0.3±0.2	-0.1±0.2	-0.1±0.3
SAS total score			
mean baseline	0.9±2.5	0.7±2.0	0.7±2.1
mean change from baseline @ end point	0.8±0.2	-0.1±0.2	-0.1±0.3
BAS - Global assessment of akathisia change from baseline @ endpoint (N%)			
worsened	22 (15%)	10 (7%)	5 (8%)
unchanged	114 (78%)	115 (79%)	51 (77%)
improved	10 (7%)	20 (14%)	10 (15%)
Statistical comparison			
vs placebo	p=0.017	p=0.779	
vs quetiapine	p=0.007		

(7)

	Risperidone N=153	Quetiapine N=156	placebo N=73
No subjects with at least one TEAE	100 (65%)	97 (62%)	44 (60%)
Insomnia	29 (19%)	22 (14%)	17 (23%)
Headache	22 (14%)	18 (12%)	10 (14%)
Sedation	10 (7%)	15 (10%)	5 (7%)
Somnolence	4 (3%)	16 (10%)	2 (3%)
Dizziness	9 (6%)	16 (10%)	3 (4%)
Cogwheel Rigidity	11 (7%)	5 (3%)	1 (1%)
Akathisia	11 (7%)	1 (<1%)	1 (1%)
Constipation	8 (5%)	14 (9%)	2 (3%)

Figure 5: Example quantitative data extraction

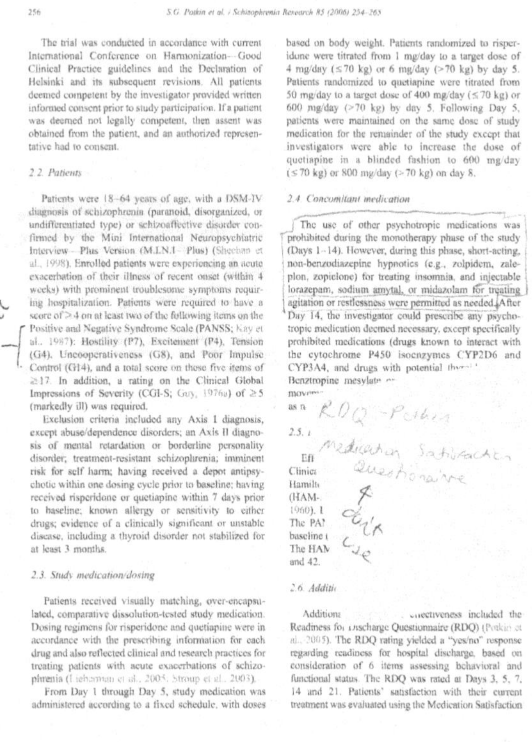

256 S.G. Potkin et al. / Schizophrenia Research 85 (2006) 254–265

The trial was conducted in accordance with current International Conference on Harmonization—Good Clinical Practice guidelines and the Declaration of Helsinki and its subsequent revisions. All patients deemed competent by the investigator provided written informed consent prior to study participation. If a patient was deemed not legally competent, then assent was obtained from the patient, and an authorized representative had to consent.

2.2. Patients

Patients were 18–64 years of age, with a DSM-IV diagnosis of schizophrenia (paranoid, disorganized, or undifferentiated type) or schizoaffective disorder confirmed by the Mini International Neuropsychiatric Interview—Plus Version (M.I.N.I—Plus) (Sheehan et al., 1998). Enrolled patients were experiencing an acute exacerbation of their illness of recent onset (within 4 weeks) with prominent troublesome symptoms requiring hospitalization. Patients were required to have a score of ≥4 on at least two of the following items on the Positive and Negative Syndrome Scale (PANSS; Kay et al., 1987): Hostility (P7), Excitement (P4), Tension (G4), Uncooperativeness (G8), and Poor Impulse Control (G14), and a total score on these five items of ≥17. In addition, a rating on the Clinical Global Impressions of Severity (CGI-S; Guy, 1976a) of ≥5 (markedly ill) was required.

Exclusion criteria included any Axis 1 diagnosis, except abuse/dependence disorders; an Axis II diagnosis of mental retardation or borderline personality disorder; treatment-resistant schizophrenia; imminent risk for self harm; having received a depot antipsychotic within one dosing cycle prior to baseline; having received risperidone or quetiapine within 7 days prior to baseline; known allergy or sensitivity to either drugs; evidence of a clinically significant or unstable disease, including a thyroid disorder not stabilized for at least 3 months.

2.3. Study medication/dosing

Patients received visually matching, over-encapsulated, comparative dissolution-tested study medication. Dosing regimens for risperidone and quetiapine were in accordance with the prescribing information for each drug and also reflected clinical and research practices for treating patients with acute exacerbations of schizophrenia (Lieberman et al., 2005; Stroup et al., 2003).

From Day 1 through Day 5, study medication was administered according to a fixed schedule, with doses based on body weight. Patients randomized to risperidone were titrated from 1 mg/day to a target dose of 4 mg/day (≤70 kg) or 6 mg/day (>70 kg) by day 5. Patients randomized to quetiapine were titrated from 50 mg/day to a target dose of 400 mg/day (≤70 kg) or 600 mg/day (>70 kg) by day 5. Following Day 5, patients were maintained on the same dose of study medication for the remainder of the study except that investigators were able to increase the dose of quetiapine in a blinded fashion to 600 mg/day (≤70 kg) or 800 mg/day (>70 kg) on day 8.

2.4. Concomitant medication

The use of other psychotropic medications was prohibited during the monotherapy phase of the study (Days 1–14). However, during this phase, short-acting, non-benzodiazepine hypnotics (e.g., zolpidem, zaleplon, zopiclone) for treating insomnia, and injectable lorazepam, sodium amytal, or midazolam for treating agitation or restlessness were permitted as needed. After Day 14, the investigator could prescribe any psychotropic medication deemed necessary, except specifically prohibited medications (drugs known to interact with the cytochrome P450 isoenzymes CYP2D6 and CYP3A4, and drugs with potential thyr... Benztropine mesylate ... movem... as n...

2.5. ...

Eff... Clinic... Hamilt... (HAM-... 1960). ... The PA... baseline ... The HAM... and 42.

2.6. Additi...

Addition... ...ectiveness included the Readiness for Discharge Questionnaire (RDQ) (Potkin et al., 2005). The RDQ rating yielded a "yes/no" response regarding readiness for hospital discharge, based on consideration of 6 items assessing behavioral and functional status. The RDQ was rated at Days 3, 5, 7, 14 and 21. Patients' satisfaction with their current treatment was evaluated using the Medication Satisfaction

Figure 6: Example page from annotated report

Online Hate Ratings Vary by Extremes: A Statistical Analysis

Joni Salminen
Qatar Computing Research Institute, HBKU; and Turku School of Economics
Doha, Qatar
jsalminen@hbku.edu.qa

Hind Almerekhi
Hamad Bin Khalifa University
Doha, Qatar
hialmerekhi@hbku.edu.qa

Ahmed Mohamed Kamel
Cairo University
Cairo, Egypt
ahmedm.kamel@pharma.cu.edu.eg

Soon-gyo Jung
Qatar Computing Research Institute, HBKU
sjung@hbku.edu.qa

Bernard J. Jansen
Qatar Computing Research Institute, HBKU
Doha Qatar
bjansen@hbku.edu.qa

ABSTRACT

Analyzing 5,665 crowd ratings on 1,133 social media comments, we find that individuals tend to agree on the extremes of a hate rating scale more than in the middle when evaluating the hatefulness of online comments. The agreement is higher for less hateful comments and lowest on moderately hateful comments. The results have implications for researchers developing machine learning models for online hate processing, as the extreme classes are likely to require fewer annotations for reaching statistical stability. Our findings suggest that the models developed in this domain should consider the distributions of hate ratings rather than average hate scores.

CCS CONCEPTS

• Applied computing → Law, social and behavioral sciences → Sociology

KEYWORDS: Online hate, toxicity, ratings; interpretation; crowdsourcing

ACM Reference format:

Joni Salminen, Hind Almerekhi, Ahmed Mohamed Kamel, Soon-Gyo Jung, Bernard J. Jansen. 2019. Online Hate Ratings Vary by Extremes: A Statistical Analysis. In *Proceedings of ACM SIGIR Conference on Human Information Interaction and Retrieval (CHIIR'19) March 10–14, 2019, Glasgow, United Kingdom.* ACM, New York, NY, USA, 5 pages. DOI: https://doi.org/10.1145/3295750.3298954

1 INTRODUCTION

Online hate research is important because hate has become commonplace in many social networks, communities, and websites [11, 13, 16]. Overall, online hate has a detrimental effect on the health of online communities [12], degrading the user experience of all users and specifically vulnerable groups [10].

For these reasons, researchers are working continuously to improve automatic methods for online hate processing, including detection, classification, manipulation, and moderation [16]. A major part of this work is the creation of training data that will be used to train the algorithms to better detect and score online comments for the hatefulness of their content.

However, interpretation of hatefulness varies among individuals [19], hindering the use of approaches that assign one hate score to an online comment. Thus, the distribution of online hate ratings is important for the creation of better models for online hate processing.

In this research, we pursue two research questions that relate to the nature of online hate ratings:

- **RQ1:** Are crowd raters agreeing more on comments that are considered as either very hateful or very little hateful, compared to moderately hateful comments?
- **RQ2:** Are crowd raters more likely to agree when a comment is more hateful or less hateful on average?

To answer these questions, we collect data from a crowdsourcing platform and conduct a statistical analysis.

2 RELATED LITERATURE

The high prevalence of online hate has urged research in detecting, classifying, and scoring hateful comments [16]. Typically, these efforts involve machine learning trained with crowdsourced ratings [21]. An example is Perspective API, a tool by Alphabet for scoring toxicity of online comments, that is trained using crowd annotators [9]. In previous research, toxicity has been seen conceptually equivalent to online hate [16].

However, the major issue in the existing approaches is that they consider hate as an aggregate value (e.g., a comment is "0.85 hateful") rather than the empirical distribution of the ratings. A notable exception is Wulczyn et al. [22] that utilizes empirical distribution, however, only using binary ratios (e.g., the comment is "[0.8] toxic and [0.2] non-toxic"). Previous research has shown many sources for the variation of interpretation for online hate. For example, the hate interpretation may depend on the context [2], such as community norms and specific use of language [15], so

CHIIR '19, March 10–14, 2019, Glasgow, United Kingdom

ACM ISBN 978-1-4503-6025-8/19/03...$15.00
https://doi.org/10.1145/3295750.3298954

that the same language is perceived hateful in one context and non-hateful in another context.

Moreover, the interpretation of hatefulness varies by the individual raters, and there is also evidence suggesting that people from different countries perceive hatefulness of the same online comments differently [19].

3 METHOD

3.1 Data collection

Similar to Chatzakou et al. [3], we use a dictionary-based method to retrieve hateful comments. To build a dictionary, we compiled the list of hate words by using a two-staged process: (1) first, we searched for lists of profanity and/or swear words available online, finding four lists that appeared valid for our purpose[1].

Second, (2) we expanded these lists by identifying more hateful words using 500 randomly sampled comments from the online comments dataset collected by Salminen et al. [18], which originates from a YouTube channel of a major online news and media company. We added the identified hateful words and phrases in our hate keyword dictionary.

Searching with the dictionary, we retrieved a random sample of 1,133 comments from the said dataset that contain hateful language. With these comments, we proceed to crowdsourcing. We set up a data collection task on CrowdFlower (currently called Figure Eight), asking the crowd workers to rate the hatefulness in each comment, with the options Very hateful (4), Moderately hateful (3), Slightly hateful (2), or Not hateful at all (1). Hatefulness was defined as follows: *"Hateful comment is something that aims to hurt another person or contains bad language."*

A total of 5,665 ratings were collected, so that each of the 1,133 YouTube comments was rated by 5 reviewers. We undertook several measures to ensure the quality of work inputs:

- **Max Judgments Per Rater:** *50 judgments*, to limit the impact of individual raters' bias on the results.
- **Minimum Time:** *25 seconds*, a page has 5 comments and we expect it would take a rater at least 5 seconds to read and rate each.
- **Quality Level:** *Level 2 ("Higher Quality")*, consisting of a smaller group of more experienced, higher accuracy raters on CrowdFlower.
- **Judgments Per Row:** *5 judgments*, to get more information on the preferences, as is suggested for more subjective crowd classification tasks [1, 17].
- **Price per Judgment:** *4 cents USD*, a 33% increase in the price suggested by CrowdFlower.

3.2 Interrater agreement

The interrater agreement was first calculated using Krippendorff's alpha (K alpha) that is a good measure of agreement when an ordinal scale is used for rating. K alpha can take a value that from 0 to 1, with 0 indicating perfect disagreement and 1 perfect agreement. However, the values of K alpha tend to show less agreement than percentage agreement (PA), since K alpha corrects for the expected agreement by chance. This is problematic when the expected agreement due to chance is high, as this may bias the calculation of K alpha [8]. This phenomenon is known as Krippendorff's alpha paradox [6].

Thus, an additional measure was used, namely, Gwet's AC2, that can be used in the presence of high expected agreement by chance, as it does not assume independence between raters [7]. Like K alpha, Gwet's AC2 can range from 0 to 1, with higher values indicating higher agreement between the raters.

3.3 Analytical approach

RQ1: The average hatefulness score (AHS) for each comment was calculated by averaging the ratings for the five raters. A threshold was then identified and used to separate the comments into lower and upper extremes and moderate hatefulness groups.

The data was divided into three groups based on the 25th percentile and the 75th percentile. Comments with a score below the 25th percentile or above 75th percentiles were identified as extremes. K alpha and PA were calculated for each of the three groups. Scores were compared between the three groups as well as to the overall K alpha of the whole data.

Bootstrapping (with 1,000 resamples) was used to obtain the 95% confidence interval (Bias corrected and accelerated) for K alpha and PA for each of the three groups, as and well as for the overall score. For Gwet's AC2, bootstrapping was not needed, as the metric incorporates the standard error for the coefficient that can be used to calculate the 95% confidence interval.

RQ2: We used an approach similar to RQ1 to compare the agreement for more hateful comments to the agreement for less hateful comments. The toxicity score that captures the degree of online hate in a comment was calculated for each comment. The median toxicity score (50% percentile) was used to classify the data into more hateful (upper 50%) and less hateful (lower 50%) comments. Agreement was calculated for each group (more hateful vs. less hateful) and scores were compared between the groups. Bootstrapping was used to obtain the 95% confidence interval for K alpha and PA.

4 RESULTS

4.1 Descriptive statistics

Table 1 shows the agreement measures for all rated comments. The overall agreement among participants is only 22.6%. The overall K alpha is 0.55, which is considered moderate. Gwet's AC2 is 0.369, which is also considered moderate.

Table 1: Measures of interrater agreement across all comments (n = 1133)

Measure	Results [95% CI]
Krippendorff's alpha	0.55 [0.48 – 0.62]
Percentage agreement (%)	22.6 [20.21 – 25.15]
Gwet's AC2	0.369 [0.344 -0.394]
Toxicity score (median [IQR])	2 [1.2 – 3]

[1] http://www.bannedwordlist.com/lists/swearWords.txt; https://github.com/LDNOOBW/List-of-Dirty-Naughty-Obscene-and-Otherwise-Bad-Words/blob/master/en; https://www.frontgatemedia.com/a-list-of-723-bad-words-to-blacklist-and-how-to-use-facebooks-moderation-tool/; http://onlineslangdictionary.com/lists/most-vulgar-words/

4.2 RQ1: Extreme vs. medium perceptions

The median toxicity score is 2, which means that 50% of the comments have an AHS lower than 2, while the remaining 50% have an average hatefulness score greater than 2. The interquartile range is 1.2 – 3, implying that 25% of the comments have an AHS below 1.2, while 25% have an AHS greater than 3.

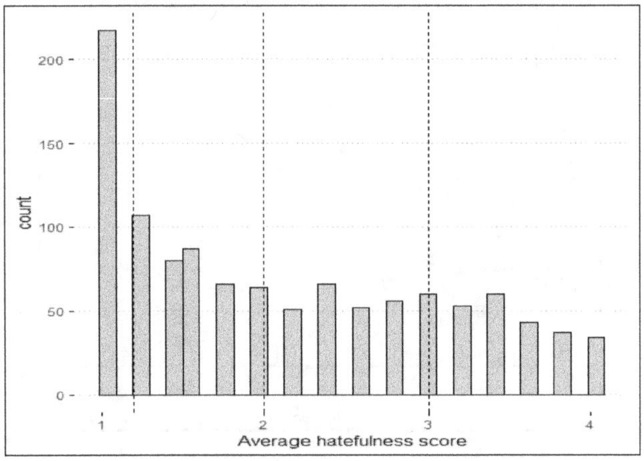

Figure 1: Distribution of average hatefulness score

From Figure 1, we can see that the AHS is right-skewed. Thus, interquartile range (IQR) is a good option to separate the comments into three groups, based on the 25th and 75th percentiles. Values below the 25th percentile or above the 75th percentile are identified as lower and upper extremes, respectively. Table 2 compares agreement measures across moderately and extremely hateful comments.

Table 2: Agreement across groups (95% CI)

Group	K alpha	PA	AC2
Lower extreme (N = 324)	0 [0 – 0.46]	66 [61.42 – 71.6]	0.85 [0.82 – 0.88]
Moderate (N = 582)	0.08 [0 – 0.18]	0.86 [0.17 – 1.72]	0.25 [0.22 – 0.29]
Upper extreme (N = 227)	0.02 [0 – 0.15]	14.98 [10.57 – 19.38]	0.76 [0.73 – 0.79]

K alpha and PA were calculated for each of the three groups. Bootstrapping (using 1000 resamples as recommended by Efron [5]) was used to calculate the 95% confidence interval.

Results for K alpha show some conflicts with the percentage agreement measure. The K alpha for the extreme two groups was very low compared to PA. This can be explained by examining the distribution of ratings for the three groups (see Table 3).

Table 3 shows that most raters in Group 1 rated the comment as either 1 (n = 1513, 93.4%) or 2 (n = 107, 6.6%). The same was true for Group 3 where most raters rated the comments as either 3 (n = 347, 30.57%) or 4 (n = 712, 62.73%). This makes K alpha a less reliable indicator in such a case, since it compares the observed agreement to the expected agreement by chance (which will be very high in these two cases). This will result in a lower K alpha than expected. Thus, PA and AC2 are more appropriate measures to answer the first research question.

Table 3: Distribution of reviews across the three groups

Group	1	2	3	4
Lower extreme	1513 (93.4%)	107 (6.6%)	0 (0%)	0 (0%)
Moderate	1082 (37.18%)	691 (23.75%)	347 (30.57%)	328 (11.27%)
Upper extreme	16 (1.41%)	60 (5.29%)	347 (30.57%)	712 (62.73%)

Results in Table 2 show that PA was highest for the lower extreme group (PA = 66%, 95% CI = 61.42 – 71.6). This means that PA in the lower extreme is 66%. The 95% confidence interval 61.42% - 71.6% means that 95% of the intervals constructed will contain the true agreement score.

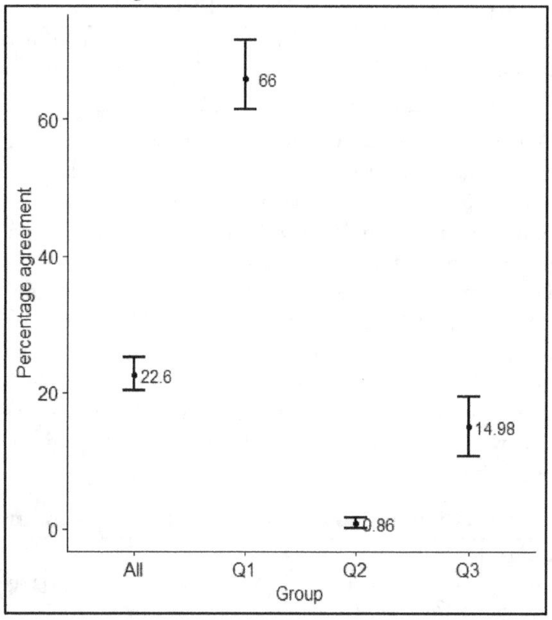

Figure 2: Percentage agreement across the whole data and per group

The PA in the upper extreme was 14.98% (95% CI = 10.57 – 19.38) which is relatively low compared to the lower extreme but high when compared to the comments with moderate hatefulness (Group 2) where the agreement was nearly zero (PA = 0.86, 95% CI = 0.17 – 1.72). Results from AC2 were in line with PA, showing the highest agreement for the lower extreme. The agreement is lower in the upper extreme than in the lower extreme, while the moderate hatefulness group showed the lowest AC2.

These findings show that raters agree most when they review comments that are in the *lower extreme*. They agree to a lower extent when the comment is in the *upper extreme*, and they rarely agree when the comment has *moderate hatefulness*.

Results from Figure 2 show that confidence intervals do not overlap, which indicates that the differences in PA between groups are statistically significant. Group 1 (least toxic comments) had the highest PA. Group 3 (most toxic comments) had the second highest, while moderately toxic comments had the lowest PA.

These results show that extreme hatefulness have more agreement than medium hatefulness perceptions.

4.3 RQ2: More vs. less hateful comments

We first identify the threshold for more and less hateful comments. The median toxicity score was 2 (Table 1), which means that comments with an AHS below 2 were considered as less hateful while comments with an AHS above 2 were considered as more hateful comments.

Using these thresholds, we compare agreement across more and less hateful comments

Table 4: Agreement across more and less hateful comments (95% CI)

Group	K alpha	PA	Gwet's AC2
More hateful (N =621)	0.17 [0.07 – 0.27]	7.62 [5.27 – 9.96]	0.88 [0.79 – 0.83]
Less hateful (N =512)	0.10 [0 – 0.23]	34.9 [30.76 – 39.37]	0.41 [0.37 – 0.46]

Agreement was calculated for each of the two groups. Bootstrapping (with 1000 resamples) was used to calculate the 95% confidence interval for K alpha and PA. The same issue that we identified with K alpha in RQ1 was identified for less hateful comments, since a few comments were rated as either as 3 or 4, while the majority were rated as 1 or 2. This increases the expected agreement and lowers the K alpha of less hateful compared to the more hateful group. The distribution of responses, however, shows that the agreement is much higher among less hateful comments, since only a small number of responses were 3 and 4, while the majority were 1 and 2 (75.62% and 14.43%, respectively).

Table 5: Distribution of reviews across the two groups

Group	1	2	3	4
Less hateful	2348 (75.62%)	448 (14.43%)	263 (8.47%)	46 (1.48%)
More hateful	263 (10.27%)	410 (16.02%)	893 (34.88%)	994 (38.83%)

Results (Table 4) show that the PA was higher for the less hateful comments (34.9%, 95% CI = 30.76 – 39.37). The PA for more hateful comments was 7.62% (95% CI = 5.27 – 9.96) which is low compared to less hateful comments.

Results for Gwet's AC2, as with the previous research question, were in concordance with PA. They show that the interrater reliability was higher for less hateful comments compared to more hateful comments.

Figure 3 shows that the 95% confidence intervals do not overlap for both groups, which indicates that the difference in PA between both groups is statistically significant. The previous findings show that raters agree more when they review comments that are less hateful compared to when they review comments that are more hateful.

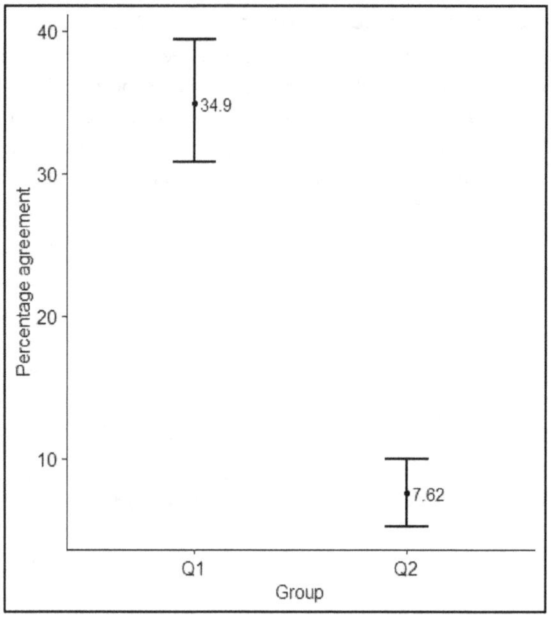

Figure 3: Percentage agreement among less and more hateful comments

5 DISCUSSION

Crowd raters tend to agree most when reviewing comments that are perceived as less hateful. In contrast, the agreement is smaller when the comment is more hateful, and the agreement is lowest for comments with moderate hatefulness. Overall, crowd raters agree more on comments that are less hateful (based on their avg. hatefulness) than on comments that are more hateful (based on their avg. hatefulness).

Thus, the general tendency inclines to be that it is easier for human raters to agree that a comment is either very hateful or not at all hateful, but harder to agree on the middle ground. We explain the results through previous research. Online hatefulness has been found to be a phenomenon that is divisive [4], with difficulties in maintaining and assessing grey areas. Partly, this originates from the subjective nature of online hate [19], and partly due to sarcastic use of language [14] that some individuals can interpret more easily than others. In addition, the interpretation of humor varies, so that a joke that is amusing to one is offensive to another one.

The implication of our findings for researchers developing machine learning models for automatic hate processing are two-fold: (1) *extreme classes are likely to require fewer annotations to reach statistical stability than medium-level hateful comments, because they are more easily agreed upon*; (2) *the variation of hate interpretation among individuals suggests that the machine learning models dealing with online hate should consider empirical distributions of hate ratings rather than averages.* While previous work has done limited advance in this aspect [22], more granular incorporation of hate interpretation distributions is needed, as well as considering individual-level features [20] that impact the hate interpretation of a user.

REFERENCES

[1] Alonso, O. 2015. Practical Lessons for Gathering Quality Labels at Scale. *Proceedings of the 38th International ACM SIGIR Conference on Research and Development in Information Retrieval* (New York, NY, USA, 2015), 1089–1092.

[2] Balbi, S. et al. 2018. Combining different evaluation systems on social media for measuring user satisfaction. *Information Processing & Management*. 54, 4 (2018), 674–685.

[3] Chatzakou, D. et al. 2017. Hate is Not Binary: Studying Abusive Behavior of #GamerGate on Twitter. *Proceedings of the 28th ACM Conference on Hypertext and Social Media* (New York, NY, USA, 2017), 65–74.

[4] Del Vicario, M. et al. 2016. Echo Chambers: Emotional Contagion and Group Polarization on Facebook. *Scientific Reports*. 6, (Dec. 2016), 37825. DOI:https://doi.org/10.1038/srep37825.

[5] Efron, B. 1982. *The jackknife, the bootstrap, and other resampling plans*. Siam.

[6] Feng, G.C. 2013. Underlying determinants driving agreement among coders. *Quality & Quantity*. 47, 5 (2013), 2983–2997.

[7] Gwet, K.L. 2008. Computing inter-rater reliability and its variance in the presence of high agreement. *British Journal of Mathematical and Statistical Psychology*. 61, 1 (May 2008), 29–48. DOI:https://doi.org/10.1348/000711006X126600.

[8] Gwet, K.L. 2011. On the Krippendorff's alpha coefficient. *Manuscript submitted for publication. Retrieved October*. 2, (2011), 2011.

[9] Hosseini, H. et al. 2017. Deceiving Google's Perspective API Built for Detecting Toxic Comments. *arXiv:1702.08138 [cs]*. (Feb. 2017).

[10] Hosseinmardi, H. et al. 2015. Analyzing Labeled Cyberbullying Incidents on the Instagram Social Network. *Social Informatics* (Dec. 2015), 49–66.

[11] Kwon, K.H. and Gruzd, A. 2017. Is offensive commenting contagious online? Examining public vs interpersonal swearing in response to Donald Trump's YouTube campaign videos. *Internet Research*. 27, 4 (Jun. 2017), 991–1010. DOI:https://doi.org/10.1108/IntR-02-2017-0072.

[12] Li, C. et al. 2019. Community detection using hierarchical clustering based on edge-weighted similarity in cloud environment. *Information Processing & Management*. 56, 1 (2019), 91–109.

[13] Mohan, S. et al. 2017. The Impact of Toxic Language on the Health of Reddit Communities. *SpringerLink* (May 2017), 51–56.

[14] Rajadesingan, A. et al. 2015. Sarcasm detection on twitter: A behavioral modeling approach. *Proceedings of the Eighth ACM International Conference on Web Search and Data Mining* (2015), 97–106.

[15] Saleem, H.M. et al. 2017. A Web of Hate: Tackling Hateful Speech in Online Social Spaces. *arXiv:1709.10159 [cs]*. (Sep. 2017).

[16] Salminen, J. et al. 2018. Anatomy of Online Hate: Developing a Taxonomy and Machine Learning Models for Identifying and Classifying Hate in Online News Media. *Proceedings of The International AAAI Conference on Web and Social Media (ICWSM 2018)* (San Francisco, California, USA, Jun. 2018).

[17] Salminen, J. et al. 2018. Inter-rater agreement for social computing studies. *Proceedings of The Fifth International Conference on Social Networks Analysis, Management and Security (SNAMS - 2018)* (Valencia, Spain, Oct. 2018).

[18] Salminen, J. et al. 2018. Neural Network Hate Deletion: Developing a Machine Learning Model to Eliminate Hate from Online Comments. *Lecture Notes in Computer Science (LNCS 11193)* (St. Petersburg, Russia, Oct. 2018).

[19] Salminen, J. et al. 2018. Online Hate Interpretation Varies by Country, But More by Individual: A Statistical Analysis Using Crowdsourced Ratings. *Proceedings of The Fifth International Conference on Social Networks Analysis, Management and Security (SNAMS - 2018)* (Valencia, Spain, Oct. 2018).

[20] Sánchez, P. and Bellogín, A. 2019. Building user profiles based on sequences for content and collaborative filtering. *Information Processing & Management*. 56, 1 (2019), 192–211.

[21] Sood, S.O. et al. 2012. Automatic identification of personal insults on social news sites. *Journal of the American Society for Information Science and Technology*. 63, 2 (Feb. 2012), 270–285.

[22] Wulczyn, E. et al. 2017. Ex Machina: Personal Attacks Seen at Scale. *Proceedings of the 26th International Conference on World Wide Web* (Republic and Canton of Geneva, Switzerland, 2017), 1391–1399.

Assisting Health Consumers While Searching the Web Through Medical Annotations

Carla Teixeira Lopes
INEST TEC/Faculdade de Engenharia da Universidade do Porto
ctl@fe.up.pt

Hugo Sousa
Faculdade de Engenharia da Universidade do Porto
ei11083@fe.up.pt

ABSTRACT

Health consumers usually face difficulties on their online searches, mainly because of the differences between terminologies used by laypeople and health professionals. This work presents a tool, HealthTranslator, available as a Google Chrome extension that intends to reduce this terminological gap while users are searching the Web for health information. HealthTranslator automatically annotates medical concepts in web documents, providing additional information, such as concept definition, related concepts and links to external references. The solution was evaluated regarding its: (a) performance - the document processing is done gradually, typically from the top to the bottom of the document and performance was not an issue raised by the users; (b) concept coverage - the solution was compared to a similar extension performing in English recognizing significantly more concepts. A comparison with a corpus of Portuguese documents manually annotated with medical concepts showed an average F-measure between 27% and 33%, depending on the type of concepts being recognized; (c) users' receptivity to HealthTranslator and its usability - many aspects were surveyed on a user study. In general, the extension has a good acceptance and users find it useful.

CCS CONCEPTS

• **Information systems → Web searching and information discovery**; **Users and interactive retrieval**; *Information extraction*; • **Computing methodologies → Natural language processing**; • **Applied computing → Consumer health**; • **Human-centered computing** → User studies;

KEYWORDS

Consumer health information retrieval; Medical concept annotation; Health terminologies.

ACM Reference Format:
Carla Teixeira Lopes and Hugo Sousa. 2019. Assisting Health Consumers While Searching the Web Through Medical Annotations. In *2019 Conference on Human Information Interaction and Retrieval (CHIIR '19), March 10–14, 2019, Glasgow, United Kingdom.* ACM, New York, NY, USA, 5 pages. https://doi.org/10.1145/3295750.3298941

ACM ISBN 978-1-4503-6025-8/19/03...$15.00
https://doi.org/10.1145/3295750.3298941

1 INTRODUCTION

With the rise of digital technologies and the Web in particular, the way we search for information was revolutionised, including in healthcare. The actual paradigm is to provide more autonomy to the health consumers, also called consumer engagement.

Searching online for health related information is rising [5]. A survey from 2013 shows that, in the United States of America, 72% of the Internet users looked for health information online in the previous year [3]. A similar survey conducted in the European Union in 2014 found that 59% of the respondents have searched for health information in the previous year [1].

Although most users find their health searches successful because they consider the retrieved information reliable [5], research studies show issues regarding these searches, such as query formulation problems [6] and poor consumer's information retrieval performance [8]. One of the reasons for these problems relies on the significant mismatch between terminologies used by laypeople and health professionals, leading also to a bad comprehension of health related content by laypeople [8].

In 2006, a system provides definitions mined from the Web to unfamiliar terms [2]. One year later, a prototype translator was presented, which replaces terms by their lay terminology and generates explanations, through the Unified Medical Language System (UMLS) and Open Access Collaborative Consumer Health Vocabulary (CHV) [9]. In 2010, the system was improved with syntactic simplification, resulting in better performance [4]. A different system, created in 2014, named Medical Translator[1] is a Chrome extension that provides a definition of medical jargon on web pages, redirecting users to the company's website whenever a drug is recognized.

In this context, we believe it is possible to help laypeople overcome the gap that may exist between their terminology and the one used in web documents when they seek for health information, in their native language or in a language they feel comfortable with, such as English. Our goal is to contribute to a better understanding of health information by laypeople. In this work we develop and evaluate a tool, HealthTranslator[2], presented as a Google Chrome extension, as this is the currently most used browser.

2 HEALTHTRANSLATOR

The extension recognizes medical concepts in web documents. The recognized concepts are highlighted as seen in Figure 1. When hovering a recognized concept, a tooltip is displayed with a definition, possible synonyms in different terminologies and a link to access concept details, as seen in Figure 2. The details' window displays

[1] https://bit.ly/2RzJ0TY
[2] http://hugosousa.github.io/HealthTranslatorClient/

the semantic type(s) of the concept, a definition, external references and related concepts, as seen in Figure 3. The semantic types are always included but the other fields may be unavailable.

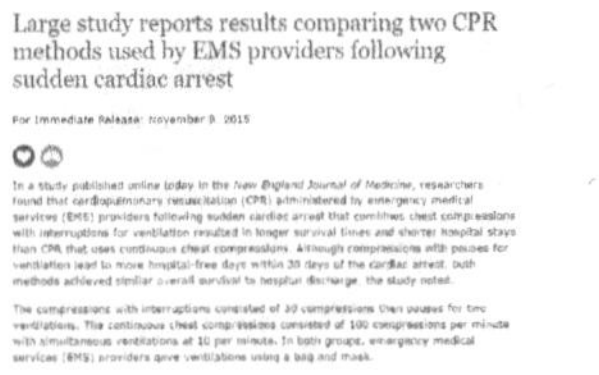

Figure 1: Page processed by the extension.

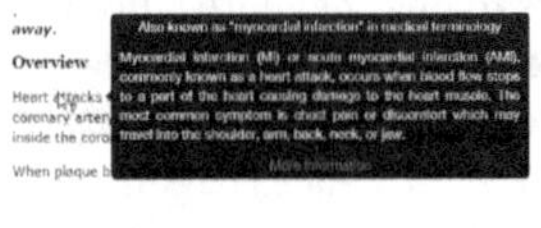

Figure 2: Hovering a recognized concept.

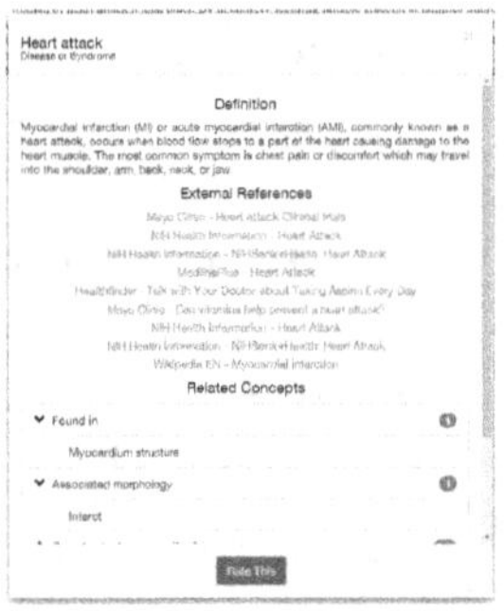

Figure 3: Details of a concept.

Users can rate the displayed information of a concept. The rating panel can be accessed from the details' window, if the user has not previously rated it. Users can suggest new concepts in any web page. A concept is only successfully suggested if it does not yet exist in the database and was not previously suggested by the same user.

The extension provides a settings page where user's preferences can be defined. Settings can be divided in three main sections: (a) Filtering, where users can exclude concepts that do not have a definition or that only exist in CHV and select which semantic types to recognize; (b) Language, where users can choose which languages the extension should work with and display the information; (c) Styling, where the concept highlighting colour can be changed. The user can also check the state of the system and its response times.

2.1 Concept recognition

Given the available resources and the existing Named Entity Recognition (NER) approaches, we opted for a dictionary based approach for concept recognition. The system is thus based on different resources. For English we used SNOMED CT for its comprehensive nature and CHV, all in the UMLS. In Portuguese, all the Portuguese vocabularies of UMLS were used (WHOPOR, MSHPOR, MDRPOR, LNC-PT-BR, ICPCPOR), as well as a Portuguese translation of CHV.

A REST service in the server is responsible for processing the text of the web page, tokenizing the text and recognizing medical concepts. It receives as input the string to be processed, the language of the string, a settings list and returns the recognized concepts with the respective HTML to be changed on the client side, with the synonyms in different terminologies and definition.

The input string is initially tokenized, using OpenNLP with pre-trained models for Portuguese and English. Then, the tokens are matched against the dictionary entries with a look-ahead of five tokens. That means that if there is a string 'A B C', and a forward threshold of two tokens is set, the lookup would be done for the strings 'A', 'A B', 'B', 'B C' and 'C', allowing the recognition of concepts with multiple words. The longest concept is the one recognized by the system, that is, if 'A' and 'A B' are medical concepts, 'A B' will be the recognized one. The token is skipped if the length of the first token is less than three characters, if the first token is a stopword or if it is a punctuation mark.

The dictionary entry comparison is performed with a case insensitive matching. Although other strategies with "LIKE" SQL operator were tried, including stemming words, the performance was not satisfactory.

2.2 Concept annotation

The definitions of the concepts were extracted from Wikipedia, a rich resource of content directed to the laypeople where about half of the medical content is updated by healthcare professionals [7].

Regarding the external references, we selected information sources mostly directed to laypeople. Some of the websites, such as MedlinePlus and healthfinder.gov, were accessed through their API and others, such as the National Institutes of Health website, required web scraping. Concerning the Portuguese language, a Portuguese dictionary of medical terms was selected, as well as a question and answer website, named Médico Responde, both requiring web scraping to analyze if results are returned for the searched concept.

The gathering of definitions was divided in two rounds. First, we performed a lookup by Concept Unique Identifier (CUI) in UMLS. If the lookup finished with a single result, it was inserted in the database; otherwise, it was written on a file for disambiguation on the second round. The second round consists of picking the concepts in the disambiguation file and lookup for its preferred string.

For the English language, we used the DBpedia Lookup service. This is a service of DBpedia, an ontology based on Wikipedia. The main advantage of DBpedia Lookup when compared with the MediaWiki API is that disambiguation pages are not retrieved. The lookup strategy is also different. A field named 'short abstract' is extracted from DBpedia Lookup, while on MediaWiki API we decided to retrieve the two first sentences. We could not adapt DBpedia Lookup to perform in Portuguese, so we used MediaWiki API in this language.

A REST service returns the details of a concept. It receives the CUI, the language of the concept, the user's identifier and a flag indicating if English external references should be included. It retrieves the details of the concept, including the semantic type(s), definition, external references, related concepts and indicates if the user has previously rated that concept. The related concepts are filtered by the type of relationships, as not all of them are interesting from a layperson point of view.

The information provided for a given concept is related to its CUI, e.g. 'hypertension' and 'high blood pressure' are two different strings but both will present the same information.

3 EVALUATION

To evaluate HealthTranslator we compare its average processing time with an existing similar English tool. We also assess its recognition coverage. In English we do a comparison with the existing English tool and, in Portuguese, we built an annotated corpus, used as ground-truth, and compared those annotations with the ones provided by HealthTranslator using precision, recall and F-measure.

To assess the receptivity of the users to this tool and its usability, we also conducted an user study with a within-subject design where users had two different search tasks, one conducted with the extension and the other without it.

3.1 Performance

One hundred documents were randomly selected from a collection of medical documents[3]. HealthTranslator presents significantly higher average processing times (2,722.69 ms) when compared with Medical Translator (112.90 ms). This happens because Medical Translator uses local processing as it is based on a significantly smaller dictionary. The processing strategy of both systems is similar, although Medical Translator only looks for three words forward, while HealthTranslator looks for five tokens ahead. Thus, the major delay of our solution is due to request delays over the network. We also believe that the computer's processor acts as a system bottleneck, as it easily reaches 100% usage. However, in general, users did not complain about the time taken to recognize concepts, as the annotation is done gradually, typically from the top to the bottom of the document.

3.2 Recognition Coverage

3.2.1 English. We compared the annotations of HealthTranslator with the ones of Medical Translator in the collection that was used to evaluate the performance. As a concept can be expressed by several strings (e.g. 'hypertension' and 'high blood pressure') and can appear multiple times in a document, we compared the number of unique strings and total concepts.

As seen in Figures 4 and 5, HealthTranslator recognizes a higher number of total concepts and unique strings in web pages when using with the semantic types selected by default in the extension's settings (henceforth named 'default semantic types'). Smaller differences were due to concepts not belonging to the default semantic types.

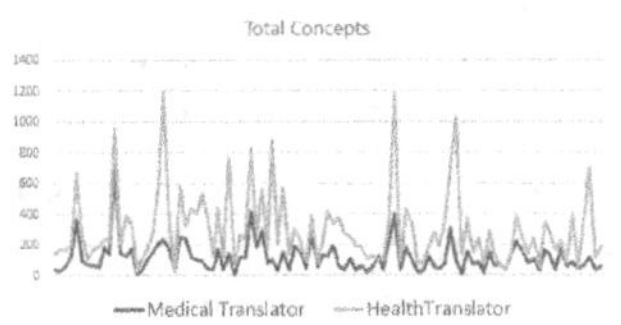

Figure 4: Total Concepts.

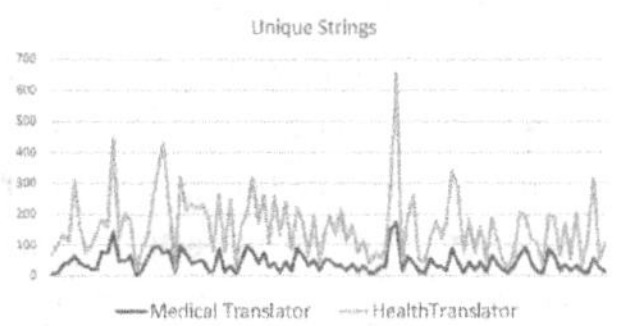

Figure 5: Unique Strings.

In average, HealthTranslator provides a definition for 80% of the recognized unique concepts (not to be confused with unique strings). In order to directly compare concept coverage, the terms in the Medical Translator's vocabulary were checked in the HealthTranslator's database. It was observed that from the 4,636 unique terms of Medical Translator, about 74% would be detected by HealthTranslator, independently of the semantic types. If the default semantic types are taken into account, about 64% of the terms would be recognized.

[3]https://bit.ly/2r7IVsm

Table 1: Annotation metrics, unique concepts and definitions provided by HealthTranslator with default and all semantic types. Standard deviation in parenthesis.

	Default Semantic Types	All Semantic Types
Precision	0.406 (0.208)	0.261 (0.129)
Recall	0.255 (0.190)	0.581 (0.182)
F-score	0.269 (0.150)	0.332 (0.149)
Unique Concepts	22.26 (19.94)	108.08 (90.98)
Definitions (%)	75.00 (11.13)	71.55 (6.42)

3.2.2 Portuguese. We do not know any comparable system performing in Portuguese or a corpus annotated with medical concepts. Thus, we decided to build an annotated corpus that we make available to the public[4]. The documents were randomly selected from a collection of medical documents[5]. Thirty-eight documents were successfully annotated by health professionals and laypeople. Laypeople should be able to perform a good quality annotation of medical concepts; even if they do not understand the concept, it is usually distinguishable by the context. Ten persons with bachelor or master's degree were invited to the laypeople group. The health professionals group is composed by five doctors and nurses. The annotation process is split in two phases. Each document was annotated by a layperson and by a health professional. Only consensual concepts are included in the final corpus.

The manually annotated corpus was then compared with HealthTranslator's annotations in two scenarios, as presented in Table 1: (a) with the default semantic types and (b) with all the semantic types. Although we obtained relatively low F-measure values, when compared with other state-of-art biomedical NER tools, it is important to note the broad range of the medical domain and the ambiguity of what a "medical concept" is. Tools with significantly higher F-measure values work with specific corpus, such as only recognizing diseases or species. HealthTranslator recognizes several concepts that were not annotated in the corpus, which decreases precision, and consequently, F-measure. We do not believe that all the spurious concepts are real false positives, as the content is mostly health related; the agreement strategy used to build the manually annotated corpus might be very conservative. It is also observable a clear increase of recall when all the semantic types are accepted but the F-measure remains stable, which confirms that although there are more matching concepts, there is also an increase of false positives.

Table 1 also shows the increase of unique recognized concepts when the accepted semantic types also increase. A high percentage of the concepts present a definition, even when all the semantic types are accepted.

3.3 Users' Receptivity and Usability

To evaluate users' receptivity to the extension and its usability, we conducted a user study. Twenty persons participated in it, with ages between 21 and 35 years old. Nineteen have or are currently finishing a bachelor or master's degree and one holds a PhD. The

[4]https://github.com/HugoSousa/HealthTranslator-Corpus
[5]https://bit.ly/2Il65zt

experiment was conducted with Portuguese speakers, as one of the differentiating features of HealthTranslator is the support of this language. All of the participants were proficient in English and could perform their searches in both languages.

After a brief presentation of the extension, users were faced with two set of questions and were asked to search for the answers online. One of the sets included questions related to asthma and the other questions related to nutrition. Questions were extracted from knowledge questionnaires previously translated and validated in the Portuguese population. Regarding the usage of the extension, a within-subject design was used. Half of the users performed the asthma task with the extension turned on and the nutrition task with the extension turned off (vanilla system) and vice-versa for the remaining half. While the extension was active, no restrictions were imposed on its use what means that the extension could not be used at all. Later on, the users were asked to provide feedback about the usage of the extension.

Only 5% of the respondents said they would not use the extension in their daily lives. However, the manual mode would be preferred in that case, as users only want to process pages of their choice. Although 70% of the users responded the extension might reduce the time of searching for health-related information, we found no significant differences between the time searching with the extension and without it. The remaining 30% state it does not interfere with the time.

It was observed that users do not frequently explore concept details. We think one of the main reasons is the slowness of this process, which can be largely improved. When asked about the speed of the gathering of details, the answers were a mix of positive and negative feedback. The majority of the users (53%) answered fast and 42% answered slow in a scale of 1 (very slow) to 4 (very fast). It can also be due to the information displayed, which may not be valuable enough for a better comprehension of the concept by the user.

Most users (75%) state the extension does not make them lose their focus on their task, while the remaining say it affects it sometimes. A large proportion of users (20%) did not find any wrong concept and 45% affirm they were not aware of it. As it is almost certain that some were presented during their searches, this makes us believe that the extension makes the users focus on the important concepts and corroborates the opinion of users regarding the focus on their tasks. 10% affirm they saw many false positives and 25% a few false positives.

Concerning the definitions, 55% of the users state they found a few missing/wrong definitions. The remaining found none. In general, when asked if the extension eases the comprehension of the information found online, 80% agree and the remaining 20% affirm it does not affect it.

Users were asked to rate the usefulness of the extension's features as seen in Figure 6. The presentation of a definition is the most consensual one, having only positive feedback. Providing synonyms in different terminologies is the second most appreciated feature, although some users do not find it useful. This shows that the preferred features are displayed by hovering a concept and why the users do not explore concept details so frequently. Providing related concepts and external references are relatively similar.

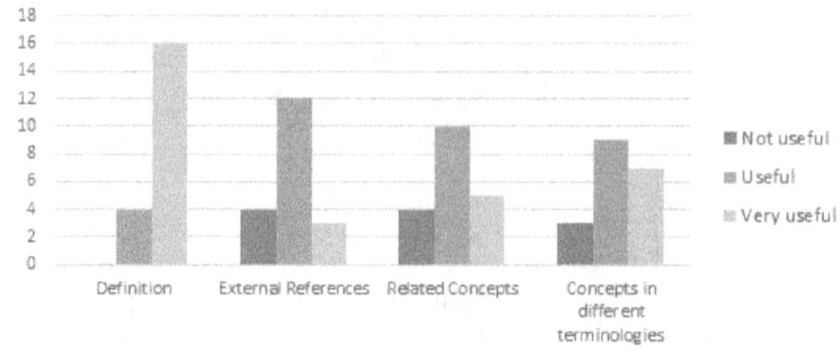

Figure 6: Rating of the usefulness of extension's features.

Opinions regarding suggesting new concepts and rating concept information were also gathered. Both features were found relevant by the majority of the users, 85% in the suggestion feature and 90% in the rating feature.

Most users find the extension user-friendly and easy to use (95%). Regarding the intrusiveness, 15% find it intrusive. Some users stated that it is somehow intrusive aesthetically, as the recognized concepts are noisy, especially on false positive cases. Another issue may be related to the automatic execution mode of the extension during the experiment, which might be changed in a real context. The look-and-feel of the extension received mostly positive feedback (90% of the users). Some users complained that the default colour can be confused with the browser "Find" option.

4 CONCLUSIONS

This article presents and evaluates a Chrome extension that aims to help laypeople search for health-related information on the Web. The proposed solution is novel because: (a) it is targeted for web documents instead of scientific literature or Electronic Health Records, the former presenting a larger diversity of content and context; (b) it mixes approaches included in previously referred solutions, such as definitions, terminology synonyms and external references, but also related concepts; (c) it aims language modularity. Portuguese and English are initially supported as proof of concept, but it should be easy to add new languages. It is not currently known any similar system to perform in Portuguese. This is one of the most spoken languages in the world, meaning that our results can be generalized to a substantial number of users.

When compared with the only tool with similar goals that we have found, HealthTranslator has higher processing time due to the use of a larger dictionary but, as annotation is done gradually, users have not complained about this. On the other hand, HealthTranslator has a better coverage in the English language, also supports the Portuguese language and provides more than a single definition for each concept.

Regarding the utility of the extension, results show that: (a) 80% of the users agree that the extension eases the comprehension of health-related content; (b) 75% of the users affirm the extension does not make them lose focus on their search tasks and (c) 95% of the users stated they would eventually use the extension in their daily lives.

ACKNOWLEDGMENTS

Project "NORTE-01-0145-FEDER-000016" (NanoSTIMA), financed by the North Portugal Regional Operational Programme (NORTE2020), under the PORTUGAL 2020 Partnership Agreement, and through the European Regional Development Fund (ERDF).

REFERENCES

[1] European Commission. 2014. *European Citizens' Digital Health Literacy.* Technical Report. European Commission. https://doi.org/10.2759/86596

[2] Noemie Elhadad. 2006. Comprehending technical texts: predicting and defining unfamiliar terms., In AMIA Annual Symposium. *AMIA ... Annual Symposium proceedings. AMIA Symposium*, 239–243. http://view.ncbi.nlm.nih.gov/pubmed/17238339

[3] Susannah Fox and Maeve Duggan. 2013. *Health Online 2013.* Technical Report. Pew Research Center's Internet & American Life Project, Washington, D.C.

[4] Sasikiran Kandula, Dorothy Curtis, and Qing Zeng-Treitler. 2010. A Semantic and Syntactic Text Simplification Tool for Health Content. In *AMIA Annu Symp Proc.* American Medical Informatics Association, 4720 Montgomery Lane, Suite 500 Bethesda, Maryland 20814, 366–370.

[5] The Harris Poll. 2011. The Growing Influence and Use Of Health Care Information. (2011). http://www.theharrispoll.com/health-and-life/The_Growing_Influence_and_Use_Of_Health_Care_Information_Obtained_Online_.html

[6] Elaine G. Toms and Celeste Latter. 2007. How consumers search for health information. *Health informatics journal* 13, 3 (01 Sept. 2007), 223–235. https://doi.org/10.1177/1460458207079901

[7] Vinod G. V. Vydiswaran, Qiaozhu Mei, David A. Hanauer, and Kai Zheng. 2014. Mining consumer health vocabulary from community-generated text. In *AMIA Annu Symp Proc.* American Medical Informatics Association, 4720 Montgomery Lane, Suite 500 Bethesda, Maryland 20814, 1150–1159.

[8] Q. Zeng, S. Kogan, N. Ash, R. A. Greenes, and A. A. Boxwala. 2002. Characteristics of consumer terminology for health information retrieval. *Methods of information in medicine* 41, 4 (2002), 289–298. http://view.ncbi.nlm.nih.gov/pubmed/12425240

[9] Qing Zeng-Treitler, Sergey Goryachev, Hyeoneui Kim, Alla Keselman, and Douglas Rosendale. 2007. Making texts in electronic health records comprehensible to consumers: a prototype translator. In *AMIA Annu Symp Proc.* American Medical Informatics Association, 4720 Montgomery Lane, Suite 500 Bethesda, Maryland 20814, 846–850.

Design Issues in Automatically Generated Persona Profiles:

A Qualitative Analysis from 38 Think-Aloud Transcripts

Joni Salminen
Qatar Computing Research Institute, HBKU; and Turku School of Economics
Doha, Qatar
jsalminen@hbku.edu.qa

Sercan Şengün
Northeastern University
Boston, Massachusetts, USA
s.sengun@northeastern.edu

Soon-gyo Jung
Qatar Computing Research Institute, HBKU
Doha Qatar
sjung@hbku.edu.qa

Bernard J. Jansen
Qatar Computing Research Institute, HBKU
bjansen@hbku.edu.qa

ABSTRACT

Increased access to data and computational techniques enable innovations in the space of automated customer analytics, for example, automatic persona generation. Automatic persona generation is the process of creating data-driven representations from user or customer statistics. Even though automatic persona generation is technically possible and provides advantages compared to manual persona creation regarding the speed and freshness of the personas, it is not clear (a) what information to include in the persona profiles and (b) how to display that information. To query into these aspects relating information design of personas, we conducted a user study with 38 participants. In the findings, we report several challenges relating to the design of automatically generated persona profiles, including usability issues, perceptual issues, and issues relating to information content. Our research has implications for the information design of data-driven personas.

KEYWORDS

User study, personas, automatically generated personas, data-driven personas, information design

ACM Reference format:

Joni Salminen, Sercan Şengün, Soon-Gyo Jung, Bernard J. Jansen. 2019. Design Issues in Automatically Generated Personal Profiles: A Qualitative Analysis from 38 Think-Aloud Transcripts. In *Proceedings of ACM SIGIR Conference on Human Information Interaction and Retrieval (CHIIR'19) March 10–14, 2019, Glasgow, United Kingdom.* ACM, New York, NY, USA, 5 pages. DOI: https://doi.org/10.1145/3295750.3298942

1 INTRODUCTION

Increased access to data and computational techniques [20, 24] enable innovations in the space of automated customer analytics.

ACM ISBN 978-1-4503-6025-8/19/03...$15.00
https://doi.org/10.1145/3295750.3298942

A potent example is automatic persona generation (APG) [1, 2] that creates data-driven representations from user or customer statistics, such as YouTube video views or in-house customer relationship management (CRM) data.

Even though automatic persona generation offers advantages relative to manual persona creation, such as the speed and freshness [1], automatically generating personas via an online system poses various challenges.

For example, two important problems emerge for information design: (a) it is not clear what information should be included in the persona profiles and (b) how to display that information to the end users of personas. To provide insights into these aspects relating to the end users of personas, we conducted a user study with 38 participants in a large non-profit organization.

2 RELATED LITERATURE

Personas are an interactive design technique [9] and an alternative form of analytics [6], with wide-ranging application in software development [18], marketing [21], and other fields. A persona simplifies numerical data into an easily understandable representation: another human being [17]. Personas enhance the communication of user data within an organization, so that content, marketing, or product decisions can be made while keeping end users in mind [10].

However, a drawback of personas relates to their creation. The traditional way of creating personas involves lengthy and costly manual work [7]. In addition, the resulting personas can quickly stale as shifts in the underlying customer base take place, especially in the fast-moving online content industry [23]. Even when user behavior is changing slowly, the validity of the generated personas should be regularly reviewed.

To solve the shortcomings of traditional persona generation, researchers have suggested automatic persona generation, which is defined as a methodology for automatically creating personas from online analytics data [1, 3]. These automatically generated personas are (1) rapidly created, within a matter of hours, (2) behaviorally accurate, as they are inferred from users' interaction patterns with online products, and (3) periodically updated through API-supported data collection and re-computation [14].

The methodology of APG (1) retrieves data on demographic segments' interaction with online products (e.g., video views), (2) generates a segment-content matrix using the interactions as elements, (3) applies non-negative matrix factorization to detect latent behavioral patterns, (4) associates the behavioral patterns with demographic data, (5) applies topic modeling to classify the content, and (6) outputs rich persona profiles by dynamically adding characteristics, such as names, photos, and descriptive quotes obtained from social media [1, 3, 14].

Even though automatically generated personas can address many shortcomings of traditional persona creation, they are not entirely immune to the general challenges of persona creation. For example, the risk of information inconsistency from unrelated datasets [4] still exists. Moreover, it is possible that end users perceive automatically generated personas as confusing [22] or lacking credibility [7]. As perceptual challenges have been found to be associated with the application and use of personas within real organizational use cases [13, 19], clarifying end user perceptions toward automatically generated personas is a priority matter for both research and practice.

3 METHOD

3.1 Data Collection

We conducted an eye-tracking user study, in which we showed automatically generated persona profiles to the end users of the persona generation system. We wanted to track both the visual engagement (eye-tracking) as well as the qualitative feedback from the end users. This manuscript focuses only on reporting the findings from analyzing the qualitative feedback.

Figure 1 shows an example of the personas shown to the end users, with the following information sections in the persona profile: Topics of Interest, Quotes, Most Viewed Contents, and Audience Size, along with basic information of the persona, including picture, name, age, gender, and location. This information pieces are defined in related work [21].

Figure 1: Example of the personas. Another persona, "Anar", was also shown to control for gender effects.

Our participants for this study were digital content creators from a major non-profit organization. This organization was chosen because they utilize personas to achieve their goals for external stakeholder communication, and the people in the organization generally have a satisfactory baseline knowledge of the persona technique.

There were 38 participants (27 males and 16 females). The average age of participants was 34 (min. 21; max. 57; std. 9.6) years old. The participants were selected to reflect the staff within the organization and interested in the organization's users. Forming a diverse pool of individuals, the participants came from a variety of job positions, ranging from data analysts, engineers, editors, social media, copy writers, and content specialists. The participants' experience with personas was 1.9 (*Slightly experienced*), with a minimum of 1 (*Not experienced at all*), a maximum of 4 (*Highly experienced*).

The participants were not financially compensated. The experiment took place in the participant's workplace. The sessions lasted approximately thirty minutes per participant. We instructed all participants in the same way about the usage of the devices and the procedure. For each treatment, the participants were presented a scenario prior to engaging with the persona profile. The scenario involved creating digital content for the user group that the persona represents (i.e., a marketing video that would interest the persona). The participants were encouraged to think aloud [12] when viewing the persona profiles. We made voice recordings and transcribed these recordings for the qualitative analysis.

3.2 Data Analysis

The qualitative analysis of the transcripts was performed by two of the researchers.

The first researcher conducted an exploratory analysis on the transcripts and, during that process, created a codebook [11] that guided the qualitative coding of the second researcher. The second researcher used this codebook to identify passages from the transcriptions that related to the code categories. The passages belonging to a category were stored in a database and manually analyzed for meaning. The identified passages were also coded as negative or positive for sentiment.

The following section presents the findings by category and by participant group. Table 1 gives a summary of the results.

4 FINDINGS

4.1 Findings by Category

Negative Emotional Response: This category was used when the participants voiced an emotion with negative sentiment. *Confusion* was used when the participant was unsure about what to do next or what the presented information meant (e.g., "Honestly I just want to have an idea, when we have quotes, how am I expected to react?" –P33).

Disapproval was used when the participant was criticizing the way the personas were presented (e.g., "That's a lot of things to read." –P17; "There's a lot of uncertainty." –P26). *Negativity* was used as a stronger version of *Disapproval*, wherein the participant was put off by the persona (e.g., "It's scary!" –P3; "I think this is a horrible presentation [...]" –P33).

Table 1: Frequencies of coded instances. Counts refer to the number of coded passages in the transcribed text that belong to the category. Negative and Positive Emotional Responses show the totals, the categories below them show the breakdown.

Category	Code	Count		% of Total Codes	
Negative Emotional Response	Confusion	66		14.2%	
	Disapproval	24		5.2%	
	Negativity	10		2.1%	
Positive Emotional Response	Appreciation	30		6,4%	
		Positive	**Negative**	**Positive**	**Negative**
Persona Perception	Authenticity	25	7	5.4%	1.5%
	Credibility	22	48	4.7%	10.3%
	Similarity	4	6	0.9%	1.3%
Information Elements of Persona Profile	Audience Size	3	13	0.6%	2.8%
	Basic Information	18	38	3.9%	8.2%
	Picture	23	8	4.9%	1.7%
	Quotes	9	32	1.9%	6.9%
	Topics of Interest	8	32	1.7%	6.9%
	Most Viewed Content	10	15	2.1%	3.2%
User Interface	Colors	3	2	0.6%	0.4%
	Scrolling	-	10	-	2.1%
NOTE: We did not code instances with neutral sentiment.					

Positive Emotional Response: This category was used to mark the segments that had positive remarks about the presentation of personas in general (e.g., "Their names are very interesting." –P9; "[The personas] had background, education, where they come from, the demographics and stuff. I think it gives interest and not interested things, I think they cover a lot of the important things." –P29).

Persona Perceptions: This category was used when the participants commented on the personas as if they were real people and compared the personas to themselves. These codes were marked as negative or positive.

Authenticity was used when personas were viewed as real people (e.g., positive: "Alright, I think I know Anar pretty well." –P16; negative: "He is a real person but he is a predator." –P19). *Credibility* was used when participants commented on the consistency of the shown information (e.g., positive: "I found this profile more coherent [...]" –P7; negative: "I don't believe this guy is actually American, (...) there is something wrong because he's writing in British English here." –P6).

Finally, *Similarity* was used when the participants relate to the personas on a personal level whether negatively or positively (e.g., positive: "[...] In fact we can be born in the same place and have different lives." –P21; negative: "I don't agree with his opinions, and I don't belong to his group." –P12).

Information Elements of Persona Profile: This category collects the remarks made about specific sections of the persona profile, including (a) Audience Size, (b) Basic Information, (c) Picture, (d) Quotes, (e) Topics of Interest, and (f) Most Viewed Content. Typically, each section is presented as a box in the persona profile page (see Figure 1).

By calculating a positive-to-negative mention ratio (Equation 1), it is possible to sort the information in the order of perceptual preference by the participants.

$$ratio_{positive\ to\ negative} = n_{positive\ comments} / n_{negative\ comments} \quad (1)$$

Audience Size was the weakest section ($r_{p/n}$ = 0.23), with most of its segment overlapping with confusion (e.g., "Audience size is not clear, I guess it's about how much this persona covers, the audience represented by this persona, I'm not sure." –P13; "What does this mean, audience size? How many are watching?" –P17; "Audience size is a bit vague." –P30). The other ratios are: *Topics of Interest* ($r_{p/n}$ = 0.25), *Quotes* ($r_{p/n}$ = 0.28), *Basic Information* ($r_{p/n}$ = 0.47), *Most Viewed Content* ($r_{p/n}$ = 0.67), and *Picture* ($r_{p/n}$ = 2.88).

Some information was considered redundant: "Why do I need to know 'less interested' [topics of interest]?" (P16). Some information was considered unclear based on its headings, e.g. it was unclear for participants whether *Quotes* were from the persona or about the persona, thereby suggesting that more precise phrasing need to be used (e.g., "Quotes by persona").

User Interface: This category contains the remarks of the participants relating to the issues of user interface and user experience. Mainly, these remarks were agglomerated under two categories: *Colors* and *Scrolling*. The scrolling codes refer to in-page scrollbars. These appear in the persona profile elements such as *Quotes* and *Most Viewed Content*.

In almost all cases, participants did not notice that the section was scrollable and those who did were unimpressed by this functionality (e.g., "Oh, there are more videos here. I didn't realize." –P10; "Okay, I see. [reading] I did not scroll down the last time. I can scroll down, I did not see this." –P13; "I don't really like this scrolling." –P1). All codes regarding scrolling were negative. *Colors*, on the other hand, had both positive and negative comments ($r_{p/n}$ = 1.5). These comments refer to personal preferences and taste (e.g., "Now the green colour is so bright that I'm wondering if it's more distracting." –P15 vs. "The higher education in topics of interest popped up because of the green." –P32).

4.2 Findings by Participant Group

To compare the participants (P), we divided them into two groups, according to their job roles (see Table 2).

Table 2: Participants by Gender and Profession.

Research Professional (n = 26; 68%)		Marketing Professional (n = 12; 32%)	
Male	Female	Male	Female
n = 18; 69%	n = 8; 31%	n = 6; 50%	n = 6; 50%

By calculating a ratio of all positive comments to negative comments by profession (see Equation 2), it is possible to see that marketing professionals (trΣp/Σn = 0.51) were slightly more positive than research professionals (trΣp/Σn = 0.49).

$$\text{total ratio}_{\text{all positive to all negative codes}} = \text{tr}\ \Sigma p/\Sigma n = n_{\text{positive comments}} / n_{\text{negative comments}} \qquad (2)$$

Moreover, there is a difference of style between the criticism of research and marketing professionals. The research professionals are more likely to comment on *how the information is presented* (e.g., "Usually in the description you provide the exact age, not 40-something." –P12; "Because the labels for me, they seem not correlative with the title of the video." –P5), whereas marketing professionals are more focused on *making generalized inferences from the information provided* (e.g., "I think what I wanted was basic information, which was there, like age, the gender, and stuff like that." –P27; "Yeah, he gives enough information about his most interested." –P28).

Another difference comes from the unpacking of the persona information. For example, the persona contains this information: "works in production [...] interested in research." Many participants from the research profession tried to unpack this information: "So he works in a production field. I actually don't know what production is." –P16; "I don't know what it means production." –P13; "Works in the production field. Not sure what that means." –P22; "I don't know what production field means." –P15; "Works production field. It's not clear what kind of production." –P18; "I don't know what research means here, but I guess it's documentary." –P10; "So, research is a strange, very generic topic. Because in my mind research is something very particular, like scientific research, but it could be other research." –P16. In contrast, no participant from the marketing profession commented similarly on these pieces of information.

Participants from the marketing profession are more likely to understand the personas through narratives pieced together from selective information on the screen. Some examples are: "[...] it showed me Yvette is in the US, she reads these publications, and she's interested in these topics [...]"–P30; "He's a layman, an everyday man, a common man." –P33; "[...] she works in the medical field, but she's looking at videos on Arab language, literacy around the world, so I don't know, I didn't see the connection." –P38.

5 DISCUSSION

Our findings show that automatically generated personas are predominantly perceived authentic (i.e., as real people), despite them being created automatically from data. In this regard, automatically generated personas are similar to manually created personas [9]. This implies that various technologies used for data-driven persona generation, having been developed for over a decade [15], have developed into maturity.

However, it also turns out that data-driven personas inherit the same challenges as traditionally created personas. Most notably, like manually created personas, lack of credibility [7] remains challenging for automatically generated personas, as we found a number of negative mentions about credibility.

Regarding the APG approach, results show that the information regarding *Audience Size* was found to be confusing, indicating potential adverse effects when including numerical information in persona profiles (or when not defining the information content properly). Confusion has also been associated with personas in previous research [22].

Also, both *Quotes* and *Topics of Interest* sections included a high ratio of negative mentions. The main reason was due to the perceived inconsistency, highlighting, yet again, a classical persona creation problem [4]: ensuring that different information elements are presented in a way that end users would perceive as consistent and coherent.

Picture and *Authenticity* were the only categories that had more positive than negative mentions. Interestingly, apart from *Most Viewed Content* that contained thumbnails of videos, the persona picture is the only element with visual information. Previous research asserts that visual information is deemed as more trustable and persuasive by the viewers for digital documents [8] and in cases where the visual and textual information conflict, the visual information was selected as the cannon [5]. The fact that *Authenticity* and *Picture* are the only categories with more positive than negative mentions also suggests a relationship between these two information elements.

The observed interface issues related to the choice of scrolling and the use of dual scroll bars. However, in general, presentation of personas in an interactive system as opposed to the traditional paper format [16] posed no notable usability issues.

6 CONCLUSION

Automatically generated personas, although utilizing efficient computational techniques and quantitative data, are not immune to the perceptual challenges observed in previous persona research. However, the manipulability of the automatic persona generation system also enables low-barrier experimentation with solutions to these problems. Therefore, future research should investigate solutions to the observed persona challenges, particularly relating to credibility, information definitions, and consistency of information elements.

REFERENCES

[1] An, J. et al. 2018. Customer segmentation using online platforms: isolating behavioral and demographic segments for persona creation via aggregated user data. *Social Network Analysis and Mining.* 8, 1 (2018). DOI:https://doi.org/10.1007/s13278-018-0531-0.

[2] An, J. et al. 2018. Imaginary People Representing Real Numbers: Generating Personas from Online Social Media Data. *ACM Transactions on the Web (TWEB).* 12, 3 (2018).

[3] An, J. et al. 2017. Personas for Content Creators via Decomposed Aggregate Audience Statistics. *Proceedings of Advances in Social Network Analysis and Mining (ASONAM 2017)* (Sydney, Australia, Aug. 2017).

[4] Bødker, S. et al. 2012. Personas, people and participation: challenges from the trenches of local government. (2012), 91.

[5] Burgoon, J.K. et al. 2003. Trust and deception in mediated communication. *System Sciences, 2003. Proceedings of the 36th Annual Hawaii International Conference on* (2003), 11–pp.

[6] Chapman, C.N. et al. 2008. Quantitative Evaluation of Personas as Information. *Proceedings of the Human Factors and Ergonomics Society Annual Meeting.* 52, 16 (Sep. 2008), 1107–1111. DOI:https://doi.org/10.1177/154193120805201602.

[7] Chapman, C.N. and Milham, R.P. 2006. The Personas' New Clothes: Methodological and Practical Arguments against a Popular Method. *Proceedings of the Human Factors and Ergonomics Society Annual Meeting.* 50, 5 (Oct. 2006), 634–636. DOI:https://doi.org/10.1177/154193120605000503.

[8] Cho, C.H. et al. 2009. Media richness, user trust, and perceptions of corporate social responsibility: An experimental investigation of visual web site disclosures. *Accounting, Auditing & Accountability Journal.* 22, 6 (2009), 933–952.

[9] Cooper, A. 1999. *The Inmates Are Running the Asylum: Why High Tech Products Drive Us Crazy and How to Restore the Sanity.* Sams - Pearson Education.

[10] Dantin, U. 2005. Application of personas in user interface design for educational software. *Proceedings of the 7th Australasian conference on Computing education-Volume 42* (2005), 239–247.

[11] DeCuir-Gunby, J.T. et al. 2011. Developing and using a codebook for the analysis of interview data: An example from a professional development research project. *Field methods.* 23, 2 (2011), 136–155.

[12] Fonteyn, M.E. et al. 1993. A description of think aloud method and protocol analysis. *Qualitative health research.* 3, 4 (1993), 430–441.

[13] Howard, T.W. 2015. Are Personas Really Usable? *Commun. Des. Q. Rev.* 3, 2 (Mar. 2015), 20–26. DOI:https://doi.org/10.1145/2752853.2752856.

[14] Jung, S.-G. et al. 2017. Persona Generation from Aggregated Social Media Data. *Proceedings of the 2017 CHI Conference Extended Abstracts on Human Factors in Computing Systems* (New York, NY, USA, 2017), 1748–1755.

[15] McGinn, J.J. and Kotamraju, N. 2008. Data-driven persona development. *Proceedings of the SIGCHI Conference on Human Factors in Computing Systems* (2008), 1521–1524.

[16] Nielsen, L. et al. 2015. A Template for Design Personas: Analysis of 47 Persona Descriptions from Danish Industries and Organizations. *Int. J. Sociotechnology Knowl. Dev.* 7, 1 (Jan. 2015), 45–61. DOI:https://doi.org/10.4018/ijskd.2015010104.

[17] Nielsen, L. and Storgaard Hansen, K. 2014. Personas is applicable: a study on the use of personas in Denmark. *Proceedings of the SIGCHI Conference on Human Factors in Computing Systems* (2014), 1665–1674.

[18] Pruitt, J. and Grudin, J. 2003. Personas: Practice and Theory. *Proceedings of the 2003 Conference on Designing for User Experiences* (New York, NY, USA, 2003), 1–15.

[19] Rönkkö, K. et al. 2004. Personas is Not Applicable: Local Remedies Interpreted in a Wider Context. *Proceedings of the Eighth Conference on Participatory Design: Artful Integration: Interweaving Media, Materials and Practices - Volume 1* (New York, NY, USA, 2004), 112–120.

[20] Saggi, M.K. and Jain, S. 2018. A survey towards an integration of big data analytics to big insights for value-creation. *Information Processing & Management.* 54, 5 (2018), 758–790.

[21] Salminen, J. et al. 2018. From 2,772 segments to five personas: Summarizing a diverse online audience by generating culturally adapted personas. *First Monday.* 23, 6 (Jun. 2018).

[22] Salminen, J. et al. 2018. "Is More Better?": Impact of Multiple Photos on Perception of Persona Profiles. *Proceedings of ACM CHI Conference on Human Factors in Computing Systems (CHI2018)* (Montréal, Canada, Apr. 2018).

[23] Widyantoro, D.H. et al. 1999. An adaptive algorithm for learning changes in user interests. *Proceedings of the eighth international conference on Information and knowledge management* (1999), 405–412.

[24] Zerbino, P. et al. 2018. Big Data-enabled Customer Relationship Management: A holistic approach. *Information Processing & Management.* 54, 5 (2018), 818–846.

A Study of Academic Search Scenarios and Information Seeking Behaviour

Orland Hoeber
Department of Computer Science
University of Regina
Regina, SK, Canada
orland.hoeber@uregina.ca

Dolinkumar Patel
Department of Computer Science
University of Regina
Regina, SK, Canada
drp901@uregina.ca

Dale Storie
Dr. John Archer Library
University of Regina
Regina, SK, Canada
dale.storie@uregina.ca

ABSTRACT

An important contribution in the development of interactive information retrieval as a research discipline has been the specification of information seeking models. A variety of such models have been documented, some of which apply generally to a broad set of search settings, and others which are specific to settings such as academic search. Within the domain of academic search, it is unclear to what extent searchers employ the strategies specified in such models when faced with different types of information needs (ranging from fact verification to knowledge discovery). Using an online questionnaire that presented four different academic search scenarios, we collected data on the self-reported likelihood of researchers (professors, graduate students) to use specific strategies from each of five different information seeking models. Preliminary analysis of data from a pilot study (n=10) has revealed differences in which of the strategies are employed depending on the type of search scenario as well as the level of expertise of the searcher.

KEYWORDS

academic search, information needs, information seeking strategies, survey

ACM Reference Format:
Orland Hoeber, Dolinkumar Patel, and Dale Storie. 2019. A Study of Academic Search Scenarios and Information Seeking Behaviour. In *2019 Conference on Human Information Interaction and Retrieval (CHIIR '19), March 10–14, 2019, Glasgow, Scotland UK.* ACM, New York, NY, USA, 5 pages. https://doi.org/10.1145/3295750.3298943

1 INTRODUCTION

As online digital libraries become the default starting point for conducting academic searches, it is becoming increasingly important to study how strategies from the different types of information seeking models are employed amid the variety of information needs that lead one to conduct such searches. Studies of information seeking and information searching behaviour provide important insight into how and why existing academic search tools are used, as well as guidance in the development of new approaches that may better support the academic searcher.

A number of information seeking models, strategies, processes, and behaviours have been documented in the research literature [4, 6]. Among these, we have selected five that we have found to be useful across the wide variety of academic search tasks and settings: the lookup-based retrieval model [3], the dynamic (berrypicking) model [3], Vakkari's three-stage model of information seeking [11], exploratory search [12], and Meho and Tibbo's [8] model of information seeking behaviour. In this paper, we operationalize these models as specific information seeking strategies that may be employed by the searcher.

Recent studies on academic search behaviour have revealed important insight into how specific strategies are employed and how the academic experience of the searcher may impact the strategies used. Athukorala et al. [1] studied the search behaviours of computer science researchers, with a focus on their reasons or purposes for searching for academic resources and the specific literature navigation techniques (forward chaining, backward chaining, journal browsing) used for these different purposes. Niu and Hemminger [9] found a variety of factors that affect the information behaviours (searching, using, collecting) of academic scientists, with the level of academic position/appointment being the most important for separating the individual differences among the participants. Similarly, Hsin et al. [7] found that the experience of the researcher affected the searching strategies and the sources for finding academic literature.

Following the call from Savolainen [10], this research seeks to test hypotheses regarding the correspondence between specific models of information seeking and various search scenarios. In particular, we hypothesize that the type of information need characterized within specific search scenarios (fact verification, knowledge enhancement, knowledge acquisition, and knowledge discovery) influences the extent to which specific strategies from the various different models of information seeking are employed. This research takes a decidedly different approach than prior work on academic search; our goal here is not to develop new models or approaches, but instead assess the applicability of existing models in relation to a range of increasingly complex information needs. This research is situated specifically in the context of information searching behaviour and strategies, acknowledging that this is only part of the broader information behaviour within the academic practice of scholars [5].

Combining prior research that showed differences attributed to the experience of the researcher, and our specific interest in studying the relationship between the type of information seeking

CHIIR '19, March 10–14, 2019, Glasgow, Scotland UK

ACM ISBN 978-1-4503-6025-8/19/03...$15.00
https://doi.org/10.1145/3295750.3298943

scenario and the information seeking model employed, our research was guided by the following three research questions:

> **RQ1:** What information seeking strategies do experienced researchers (University Professors) employ when faced with different types information seeking scenarios?
> **RQ2:** What information seeking strategies do novice researchers (University Graduate Students) employ when faced with different types information seeking scenarios?
> **RQ3:** How do the types of strategies employed differ between experienced and novice academic searchers?

2 INFORMATION SEEKING MODELS

Amid the large variety of information seeking models, we have selected five that represent a broad range of behaviours (from simple to complex) that may be employed to find relevant articles in an academic search context.

The lookup-based retrieval model [3] follows a simple pattern of formulating a query to describe the information need, and then viewing the search results and select documents of interest. It is the dominant model in many search engines, and is well-suited to fact-finding [12].

The dynamic (berrypicking) model [3] specifies a process wherein the searcher starts with a vague information need, which evolves over time as searches are conducted and the searcher learns more about the topic. In addition to traditional lookup retrieval, searchers using this model may also follow citations, browse within a journal or conference proceedings, or search the works of specific authors as part of the learning process.

Vakkari's three-stage model of information seeking [11] classifies search tasks into three stages: pre-focus, focus formulation, and post-focus. The pre-focus stage deals with the initiation of the search and undertaking a broad exploration of the topic. In the focus formulation stage, searchers refine their goals and explore these in detail. In the post-focus stage, searchers collect, synthesize, and make use of the results of their search.

Exploratory search exemplifies the interactive nature of some search process. Searchers start with a vague or under-defined search goal, and seek to develop knowledge and understanding by interactively querying the data to isolate potentially important subsets that are relevant. Such processes are often employed when the information need is open-ended and multi-faceted [12], or when the task is complex in nature [2].

Meho and Tibbo's model of the information-seeking behaviour [8] was developed to describe the specific needs of social scientists, although we contend that the general features apply more broadly to academic search across disciplines. The search process happens within four interconnected stages: searching, accessing, processing, ending.

3 METHODOLOGY

Four different information seeking needs of increasing complexity were formulated as retrospective academic search scenarios (see Table 1). These were used as the basis for an online questionnaire, where they were presented to participants in a random order. For each scenario, a set of statements that described strategies specific to each of the five information seeking models were presented to the participants (Look-up: 3 strategies; Dynamic: 5 strategies; Vakkari: 6 strategies; Exploratory: 5 strategies; Meho & Tibbo: 13 strategies). These statements were written in plain language, describing the core features of the specific information seeking models. A 5-point Likert scale was used to measure participants' likelihood of using these strategies for the given scenario (1: extremely likely; 2: somewhat likely; 3: neutral; 4: somewhat unlikely; 5: extremely unlikely). For each scenario, we also asked participants to consider prior similar searches, and report on their success in completing such searches, their confidence in the results of such searches, and the usefulness of their preferred academic search tool for such searches. This same online questionnaire collected demographic, career, and academic search experience information.

Participants for this pilot study were recruited from faculty members and graduate students in the Faculty of Science at our University via email recruitment letters distributed by the Graduate Coordinators in each of the six departments. The study procedures and participant recruitment practices were approved by our University's Research Ethics Board. All data collected was anonymous.

Fact Verification Suppose you are writing a paper in which you need to look-up or verify a specific fact (e.g., the date of an event, the correct spelling of someone's name, the details of a specific research paper). Think of the most recent time this situation came up. The rest of the questions on this page are in relation to this specific type of search scenario.
Knowledge Enhancement Suppose you are writing a paper in which you need to enhance your existing knowledge on a topic. That is, you already know a lot about the topic, but want to see if there are any new developments or literature in other venues that you haven't previously considered. Think of the most recent time this situation came up. The rest of the questions on this page are in relation to this specific type of search scenario.
Knowledge Acquisition Suppose you are planning on conducting a new study that is related to your previous research. As a result, you wish to acquire new knowledge on this topic, but you already know some basic things. Think of the most recent time this situation came up. The rest of the questions on this page are in relation to this specific type of search scenario.
Knowledge Discovery Suppose you are planning on initiating a new study on a topic that is not related to your previous research. You wish to discover new knowledge on this topic, and have limited prior information beyond your desire to learn about it. Think of the most recent time this situation came up. The rest of the questions on this page are in relation to this specific type of search scenario.

Table 1: Four increasingly complex information seeking scenarios within academic search.

Scenario	Participant Type	Success	Confidence	Usefulness	Look-up	Dynamic	Vakkari	Exploratory	Meho & Tibbo
Fact Verification	Professor	2.0	2.0	1.5	1.7	2.6	2.9	3.2	2.4
	Student	2.3	3.0	2.8	1.3	2.1	1.6	1.7	2.0
Knowledge Enhancement	Professor	2.0	2.0	1.8	1.5	2.7	2.8	3.0	2.4
	Student	2.7	2.3	2.8	1.6	2.1	1.8	1.7	2.0
Knowledge Acquisition	Professor	2.5	2.5	1.8	1.7	2.1	2.3	2.8	2.4
	Student	2.7	3.0	2.7	1.5	1.9	1.7	1.5	1.9
Knowledge Discovery	Professor	2.5	2.5	1.8	2.5	2.2	2.0	1.9	2.1
	Student	2.7	2.7	2.5	1.8	2.0	1.7	1.3	2.2

Table 2: Average scores for each scenario and participant type. For success, confidence, and usefulness, lower scores reflect stronger agreement. For the five models of information seeking, lower scores reflect a higher likelihood of using the approaches in the models. All scores were measured on a 5-point Likert scale.

At the end of the questionnaire, participants were given an opportunity to follow a link to a secondary questionnaire that collected names and contact information to be used in a draw for one of five $20 gift cards. The entire study was designed to take between 25-35 minutes to complete.

4 DATA ANALYSIS

A total of 12 participants completed the study over a three-week period around the start of our academic semester. Two participants (Master's level graduate students) reported being novice at conducting academic searches in their domain. These were excluded from this analysis to avoid the confounding factors of how true novices conduct academic searches. All other participants reported being proficient or expert at conducting academic searches within their research area.

Given that one's self-reported proficiency is influenced by their overall experience, we used the participants' role/position at the university to categorize the participants in one of two groups: professors (n=4) and graduate students (n=6). While we collected different career levels for the professors and different education levels of the graduate students, with the small number of participants, further categorization would have resulted in very small numbers of participants for each group.

The data was analyzed for each of the search scenarios independently. The scores for each of the strategies specific to each of the five information seeking models (Look-up, Dynamic, Vakkari, Exploratory, Meho & Tibbo) were aggregated, with the average reported for each of the two participant groups (Professors and Students). The distributions over each level in the five-point Likert scale were used to create stacked bar chart visualizations. The average scores for the success, confidence, and usefulness measures were also calculated per participant group.

5 RESULTS

The results of this study are summarized in Table 2. The participants indicated a general likelihood for using the strategies in the information seeking models, with no average score dropping below a value of 3 (neutral in the Likert scale). This may be due to the overlap in basic search strategies across all of the models. A more detailed picture can be seen by studying the distributions of the likelihood of using strategies associated with each of the information seeking models, as illustrated in the series of graphs in Table 3. The findings for each of the information seeking scenarios are discussed below.

Fact Verification. For this scenario, both professors and students show a preference for using the look-up model, as one would expect. The students also indicated that they would likely use more advanced approaches such as Vakkari's model and exploratory search, whereas the professors indicated that using some of the strategies associated with these models would be unlikely. The professors indicated a higher degree of success, confidence, and usefulness of search tools than the students. The willingness of students to employ strategies in addition to those in the simple look-up model may be due to their lack of knowledge and expertise; even for fact verification, they may feel the need to conduct a deep search.

Knowledge Enhancement. The results for this scenario had a similar pattern to that of fact verification, both for professors and students. The look-up model was the dominant model for professors, although some of the basic features of the other strategies were also likely to be used. The students indicated the likelihood of using advanced approaches, and the divergence in success, confidence, and usefulness from that of professors remained.

Knowledge Acquisition. This scenario was one in which participants were asked to consider how they acquire new knowledge in an area where they have a basic understanding. The professors reported lower scores in terms of success and confidence, which were close to those reported by the students. However, the professors reported a higher degree of usefulness of their search tools compared to the students, perhaps due to their more extensive experience with such tools. In terms of the models, the students continued to report that they were likely to use a broad range of strategies from the various models. While the strategies in the look-up model remained strong, the professors also indicated that some strategies from the dynamic model and Vakkari's model would likely be used.

Knowledge Discovery. The scenario of discovering new knowledge presented the most challenging information need in this study.

	Professor	Student
Fact Verification	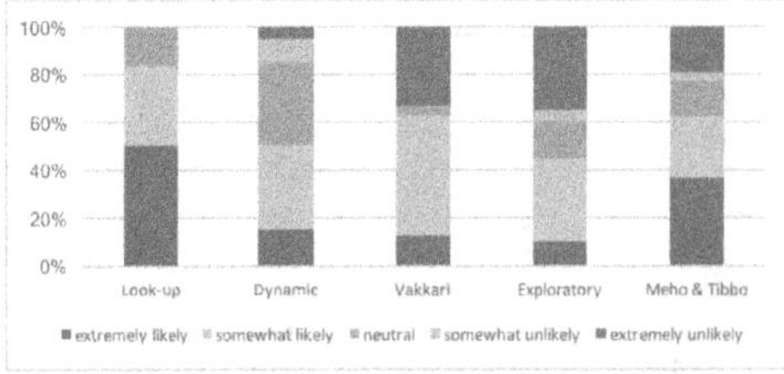	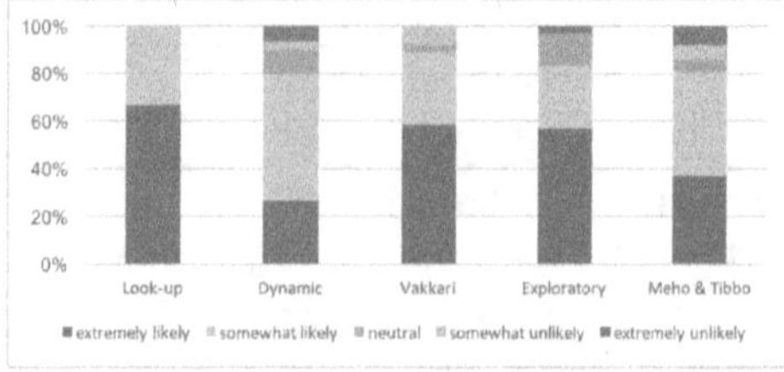
Knowledge Enhancement	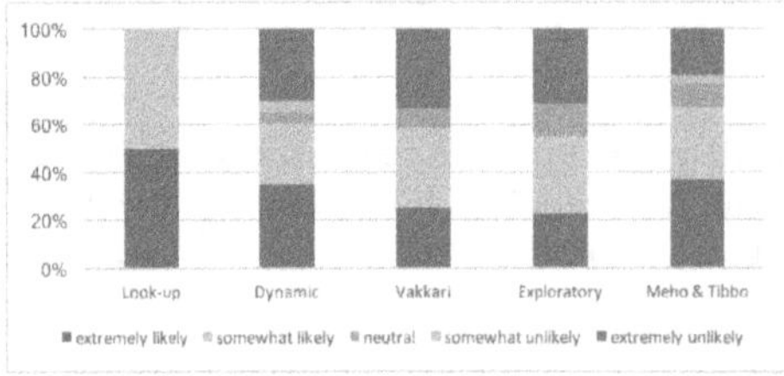	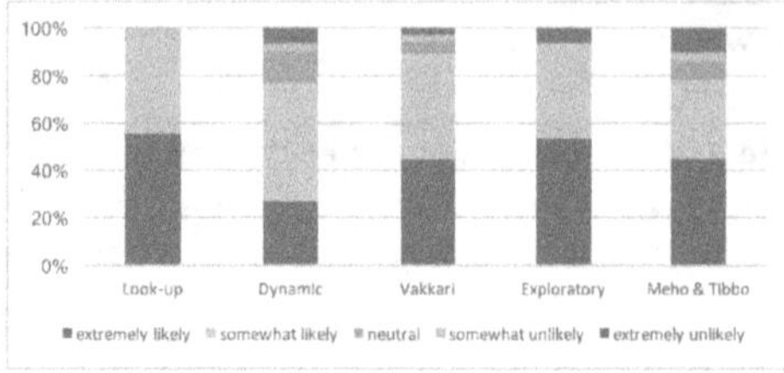
Knowledge Acquisition	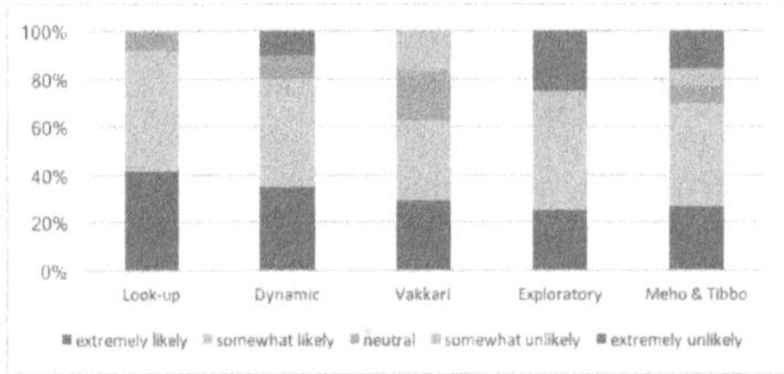	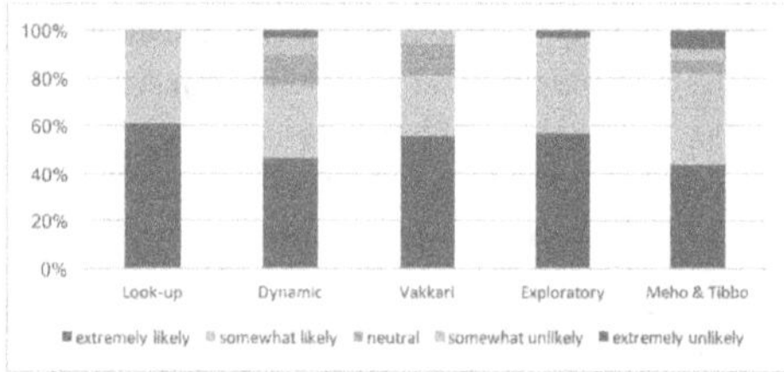
Knowledge Discovery	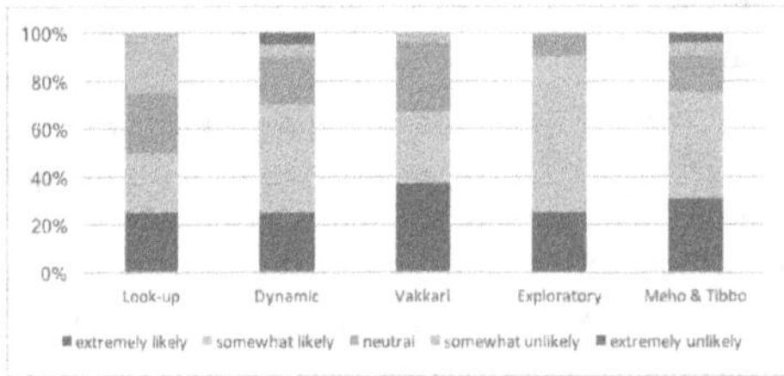	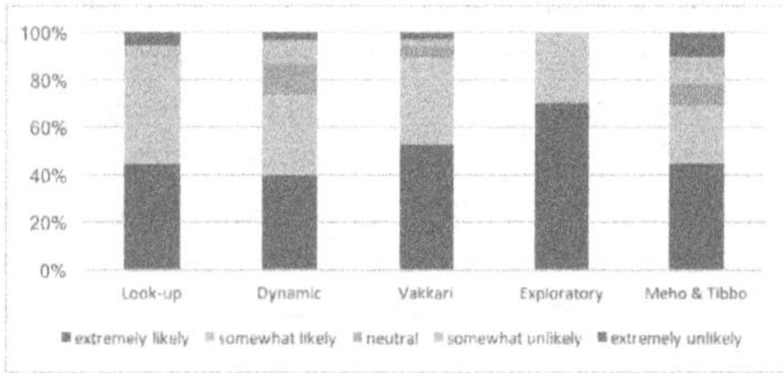

Table 3: Distribution of responses regarding the likelihood of employing specific strategies from each information seeking model for each scenario and participant type.

The pattern of success, confidence, and usefulness between professors and students was consistent with the knowledge acquisition scenario. However, here we see some differences in the models employed compared to the other scenarios. For professors, using strategies from the look-up model became less likely; instead they indicated that it is more likely that they would use strategies from exploratory search and Vakkari's model. A similar pattern held for the students.

6 CONCLUSIONS & FUTURE WORK

Even with just ten participants, this pilot study has shown that there are differences in how professors and students conduct academic searches, as well as the likelihood of using different information seeking strategies depending on the complexity of the information seeking scenario. The differences based on prior academic search experience is consistent with prior research. What is novel in this study is the comparison of various strategies from different information seeking models in increasingly complex scenarios. However, the small sample size and lack of statistical analysis limit the generalizability of the findings.

These results motivate us to continue this research, with a plan of recruiting participants across all other faculties at our University. Doing so will not only allow us to continue to compare professor and student information seeking behaviour, but also study whether the behaviour is different in fundamentally different research disciplines (e.g., natural science, social science, health) or methods (e.g., qualitative, quantitative, mixed). Such results may provide motivation for the refinement of existing and development of new academic search tools that can help guide inexperienced searchers (graduate students) to perform as if they were experienced searchers (professors).

ACKNOWLEDGMENTS

We acknowledge the support of the Natural Sciences and Engineering Research Council of Canada (NSERC), through the Discovery Grant held by the first author (RGPIN-2017-06446).

REFERENCES

[1] Kumaripaba Athukorala, Eve Hoggan, Anu Lehtiö, Tuukka Ruotsalo, and Giulio Jacucci. 2013. Information-seeking behaviors of computer scientists: Challenges for electronic literature search tools. In *Proceedings of the ASIS&T Annual Meeting*. Article 20: 1–11.

[2] Ahmed Hassan Awadallah, Ryen W White, Patrick Pantel, Susan T Dumais, and Yi-Min Wang. 2014. Supporting Complex Search Tasks. In *Proceedings of the ACM International Conference on Information and Knowledge Management*. 829–838.

[3] Marcia J Bates. 1989. The design of browsing and berrypicking techniques for the on-line search interface. *Online Review* 13, 5 (1989), 407–431. https://doi.org/10.1108/eb024320

[4] Nicholas J. Belkin. 2015. People, Interacting with Information. *ACM SIGIR Forum* 49, 2 (2015), 13–27. https://doi.org/10.1145/2766462.2767854

[5] Nancy Falciani-White. 2017. Information behaviors of elite scholars in the context of academic practice. *Journal of Documentation* 73, 5 (2017), 953–973.

[6] Marti Hearst. 2009. *Search User Interfaces.* Cambridge University Press, Cambridge, UK.

[7] Ching-Ting Hsin, Ying-Hsueh Cheng, and Ching-Chung Tsai. 2016. Searching and sourcing online academic literature: Comparisons of doctoral students and junior faculty in education. *Online Information Review* 40, 7 (2016), 979–997.

[8] Lokman I. Meho and Helen R. Tibbo. 2003. Modeling the Information-Seeking Behavior of Social Scientists: Ellis's Study Revisited. *Journal of the American Society for Information Science and Technology* 54, 6 (2003), 570–587.

[9] Xi Niu and Bradley M. Hemminger. 2012. A Study of Factors That Affect the Information-Seeking Behavior of Academic Scientists. *Journal of the American Society for Information Science and Technology* 63, 2 (2012), 336–353.

[10] Reijo Savolainen. 2017. Contributions to Conceptual Growth: The Elaboration of Ellis's Model for Information-Seeking Behavior. *Journal of the Association for Information Science and Technology* 68, 3 (2017), 594–608.

[11] Pertti Vakkari. 2003. Task-based information searching. *Annual Review of Information Science and Technology* 37, 2 (2003), 413–464. https://doi.org/10.1002/aris.1440370110

[12] Ryen W White and Resa A Roth. 2009. *Exploratory Search: Beyond the Query-Response Paradigm.* Morgan & Claypool Publisher, San Rafael, CA. https://doi.org/10.2200/S00174ED1V01Y200901ICR003

Studying Politicians' Information Sharing on Social Media

Florian Meier
Science, Policy and Information Studies
Department of Communication and Psychology
Aalborg University Copenhagen
Denmark
fmeier@hum.aau.dk

David Elsweiler
Information Science Group
I:IMSK
University of Regensburg
Germany
david.elsweiler@ur.de

ABSTRACT

In this study, we pair different perspectives on information sharing held by the information behaviour and computational social science communities. By reflecting on different conceptual models of sharing (two-actor vs three-actor model) and applying methods from social network analysis and text mining, we investigate the influence that different user interface features (retweeting and quote retweeting) have on politicians' sharing behaviour during an election campaign on the social media platform Twitter. Amongst other results, our analyses show that the two features are used quite differently with the quote RT feature promoting non-partisan interaction, which leads to a more civilized discourse with opponents and support for colleagues.

ACM Reference Format:

Florian Meier and David Elsweiler. 2019. Studying Politicians' Information Sharing on Social Media. In *2019 Conference on Human Information Interaction and Retrieval (CHIIR '19), March 10–14, 2019, Glasgow, Scotland Uk.* ACM, New York, NY, USA, 5 pages. https://doi.org/10.1145/3295750.3298944

1 INTRODUCTION

In the information behaviour (IB) literature, information sharing has typically played second fiddle to information seeking in terms of the amount of research performed. When sharing has been studied, the focus has often been on sharing information in work and academic settings [31], where people have been shown to share information they believe others might find useful or solve someone else's information need [25]. In leisure situations people share content for different but diverse reasons including the belief that it might simply make the receiver feel better [9, 20]. Other notable contexts studied include when teams of users share information to collaboratively achieve a common information seeking goal [26] and the implicit (sometimes undesired) sharing of information when asking another person for assistance [5].

We investigate aspects of information sharing less well studied in our community, focusing on the behaviour of politicians on Twitter during an election campaign. In such a political context, the motivation for sharing information is complex and potentially less altruistic than other examples in the IB literature. Politicians are known to share information to promote their message, set their agenda [7], communicate their views on specific issues [14], engage in political debate [6] or simply to endorse partisans [18]. On the other hand, information can be shared to depict rivals in a negative light [13] or to "challenge the other's side narrative" [28]. We study information sharing on Twitter, which is an interesting medium to study for many reasons: (i) Twitter provides a platform for politicians to not only communicate with voters, but also to engage with rivals and colleagues. We investigate whether differences can be observed in the way politicians share their own party's information compared to information from other parties. (ii) Twitter has several features, which allow information to be shared. We examine how politicians make use of these to understand whether different features promote different types of sharing or sharing with divergent intentions. Specifically we compare retweeting (RT) (where users forward content to their own followers) and quote RTing (qRT), where users additionally have the option to comment on the previously published content. (iii) Twitter has been studied in relation to the much publicized issue of the filter bubble, where individuals primarily receive information confirming their own views [3, 6]. Politicians' sharing behaviour on Twitter, depending on what they share and who ultimately receives the shared content, has the potential to defuse or compound the filter bubble [12]. We provide yet more evidence that the qRT feature, recently introduced on Twitter, promotes non-partisan interactions.

CHIIR '19, March 10–14, 2019, Glasgow, Scotland Uk

ACM ISBN 978-1-4503-6025-8/19/03...$15.00
https://doi.org/10.1145/3295750.3298944

2 RELATED WORK

Before presenting our analyses, we first review how information sharing has been studied in the IB community and continue to summarize literature relating to information sharing in the computational social sciences (CSS). Lastly, we look specifically at information sharing in political elections. Despite these areas being highly topically related, there has been little interaction between the communities involved. One aim here is to build links between the domains.

2.1 Information Sharing

Although recognised as a key information behaviour, in the literature information sharing has received far less research attention than information seeking [23]. Important theoretical and empirical contributions, however, have been made. Rioux focuses on the importance of the receiver's need, referring to information acquisition and sharing as 'a set of combined behaviors and processes whereby encountered information gets shared when this information might solve someone else's information need' [25]. Sonnenwald, on the other hand, emphasizes the interaction between sender and receiver, defining IS as providing information "to others, either pro-actively or upon request, such that the information has an impact on another person's (or persons') image of the world" [27]. Other work highlights (i) collaboration, (ii) mutual benefits and (iii) supported relationships, viewing the behaviour as the information exchange between two groups of actors (receivers and givers) to achieve individual or common interests [2, 20].

Tinto and Ruthven focus on sharing in leisure situations, revealing numerous factors that influence what information is shared and why [9]. Most participants considered sharing happy information important to their friendships and the act of sharing was shown to enhance the sharer's happiness. The literature, therefore, emphasises that information sharing is an inherently social activity and shows that the act of sharing is often more important than the content of the information and its immediate utility for resolving needs [20]. Thus, information sharing in the IB literature has considered two sets of actors, senders and receivers, and has focused either on the needs of the receiver or the relationship between these actors.

2.2 Information sharing in the computational social sciences

In the computational social sciences (CSS) sharing information has been investigated differently.[1] Social networks have been studied to ascertain how far and how quickly information diffuses in different settings [15] or determine if the future popularity of content can be predicted [8] and which factors contribute to this [16]. Others have studied user motivations when utilising specific SN features, such as RTing. Similar to the IB literature, these studies reveal that information is shared not only to propagate content perceived to be interesting and relevant, but for other diverse reasons ranging from promoting a specific message to enhancing one's personal reputation, to acts of friendship [4]. Not only can a RT indicate agreement with a Tweet's content, but it can represent an endorsement of or support for the author; a point confirmed by a meta-review of 100+ articles, which also suggests that author endorsement is particularly pronounced when sharing political opinions [21, 33]. These analyses, therefore, go beyond the IB studies to discuss an additional actor – the creator of the information.

Despite RTing being commonly viewed as a positive interaction, recent work has questioned this assertion by showing that RTs can, in some cases, be used to criticise or contradict the original Tweet [13]. Sarcastic humor or criticism of a Tweet is particularly common when it is retweeted out of temporal context, that is after some time has elapsed [13]. As the qRT feature has only recently been added to Twitter, the feature has been subject to less research, but one study examining usage in political discourse revealed: (i) qRTing facilitates better diffusion of information and offers potential for reducing polarization along party lines and, thus, diffuses ideological filter bubbles, (ii) qRTing facilitates a more civilized discourse with valuable discussions and fewer insults shared among disputants [12]. The qRT feature has been seen as a good means to engage members of ideologically differently positioned groups by mentioning them in the comment [28]. Whether exposure to opposing

[1]We emphasise that we define information sharing as encountered information that is forwarded to other actors and not as posting (personal) information on SM platforms as interpreted in [30].

Party	RT Count	RT Ratio	Quote RT Count	Quote RT Ratio
AfD	1639	8.24	398	9.12
CDU	2886	14.50	703	16.11
CSU	304	1.53	78	1.79
Left	4052	20.36	671	15.38
FDP	409	2.06	173	3.96
Greens	6086	30.58	1199	27.47
SPD	4525	22.74	1142	26.17
Total	19901	100%	4364	100%

Table 1: Overview of the number of RTs and qRTs per party

views drives discussion and thus limits political polarization on SM remains, however, unclear. Recent work shows that exposure to opposing views does not dissolve the filter bubble and may even increase the echo chamber effect [1].

As the role of Twitter in elections has grown in importance [24] – political candidates and parties have come to embrace interactive digital media as an integral part of their campaigns [10, 29] – investigations of Twitter's role in elections have also increased. Jungherr systematically reviewed 127 such articles [17]. One area studied is how political parties and candidates use Twitter to set their agenda and compete for votes by using hashtags, @mentions and RTing [17]. Multiple studies have found RTing among politicians to be an interaction that almost always occurs within parties and leads to high network polarisation by political orientation [6, 18, 19]. The extent of polarization varies highly depending on time periods and topics [3] e.g. polarisation is most pronounced when elections near but reduces after the vote [11, 12].

The reviewed research reveals different aspects, which can be studied in more detail and presents opportunities to bridge the gap between the IB and computational social science communities. Concretely, here, we collect a large longitudinal dataset of prominent politicians' Tweets during an election year and study:

- Differences in information sharing with RTs and qRTs.
- Differences between the features used when information from within and outwith the party is shared.
- Differences between how information is shared within and outwith the temporal context it was created.
- Differences in language use in comments for qRTs within and outwith the party.

In doing so we not only shed light on politicians' varying motivations for sharing information during elections but, moreover add the idea of a three-actor model of information sharing, as well as methods of social network analysis (SNA) to the IB discourse.

3 DATA-SET AND METHODS

From Jan 1st to Sept 24th (election day), 2017, we stored the Tweets posted by close to 1000 of the most prominent German politicians and political candidates active on Twitter. The sample reflects not only party size, but politician Twitter activity. To investigate sharing behaviour, we analyse 19901 RTs and 4364 qRTs. Table 1 gives an overview of how each party contributes to the dataset. Politicians' Twitter traces allow us to study sharing activities in two network layers (RTs & qRTs). Together the layers create a multi-relational network, in which each node belongs to each layer [11]. Nodes represent politicians from one of the seven biggest parties who have a Twitter account and used one or both sharing features. Both

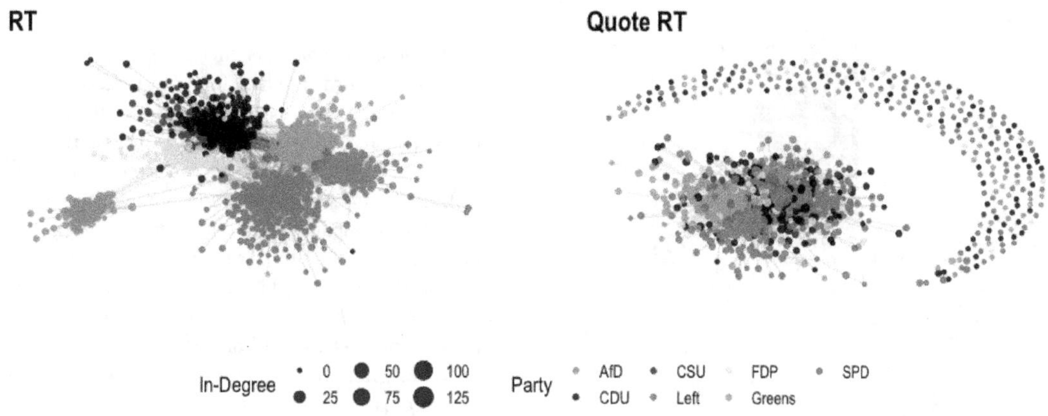

Figure 1: Network visualizations of the RT and qRT layers.

the RT and qRT layers are directed and weighted. A politician p_1 has a directed link to politician p_2 when they RT or qRT the other. The weight of the edge is equivalent to the frequency of the interaction. We use network- and node-level measures to asses how sharing behaviour on the platform differs between parties and features (see Table 2). Of the 934 politicians, $N_{RT} = 918$ used the RT feature to form $E_{RT} = 7602$ connections, whereas only $N_{qRT} = 666$ use the qRT feature to form $E_{qRT} = 2542$ connections among politicians.

4 RESULTS

4.1 Comparing the RT and Quote-RT Layers

Our data confirm that while RTing is a more popular information sharing feature generally, politicians were much more likely to use the qRT feature to propagate content from other parties. Of 19901 RTs only 5.91% occur across party lines , whereas almost a third of qRTs (29.38%) are used to share information created by politicians from other parties.

Measure	Retweet Layer	Quote-Retweet Layer
Nodes (N)	934 (918)	934 (666)
Edges (E)	7602	2542
Transitivity (C)	0.26	0.13
Reciprocity (r)	0.24	0.12
Modularity (Q)	0.74	0.45

Table 2: Network measures for the RT and qRT layers.

Figure 1 visualizes the RT and qRT network layers plotted using the force directed Fruchterman-Reingold algorithm, which pulls related nodes closer and pushes different nodes further apart. The RT layer exhibits clear polarization along party lines. CSU and CDU are exceptions, which is unsurprising given their strong political alliance. Politicians from the right-wing AfD party form a cluster far from the graph's centre as few other party members interact with them. In fact 99% of AfD's RTs were by their own members. The visual impression of polarization in the RT layer is corroborated by the modularity value $Q_{RT} = 0.74$, which quantifies network polarization by setting the density of 'edges within communities' in relation to the density of 'edges between communities' [22]. Q is bounded $[-1, 1]$ whereby $Q = 1$ represents complete polarization. The RT layer also has a high level of reciprocity (bounded $[-1, 1]$) among nodes which, in a directed layer, is the probability of a politician p_1 being connected to a politician p_2, and p_2 also being connected to p_1. Simply put, reciprocity measures mutual RTing, which is much higher in the RT layer ($r_{RT} = 0.24$) than in the qRT layer ($r_{qRT} = 0.12$).

The qRT layer has many satellite nodes that do not connect to other nodes. These represent politicians who use the RT feature to share posts but never qRT. In the qRT layer there is less evidence of clear party clusters with the nodes from different parties blending together, indicating increased cross-party interaction. Again, the modularity value supports this impression ($Q_{qRT} = 0.45$). That is, there are still signs of party-based polarization, but they are much less pronounced than in the RT layer (Q_{RT}).

Thus, our data confirm that RTing is mostly used to share Tweets sent by own party members, whereas the possibility of adding comments to a Tweet seems to increase the likelihood that politicians will share other parties' content. Below we present further analyses of the features to determine how and perhaps why they are used.

4.2 Sharing out of temporal context

While RTs are typically associated with endorsement, late or out-of-context RTs are sometimes used to mock the original author [13]. In our case, one would expect antagonism to be most prominent in cross-party RTs, thus, if the claim in [13] holds, one would expect the RT-repsonse-time for cross-party RTs to be longer than partisan RTs. Figure 2, which visualises the distribution of the RT-response-time (x-axis) for both feature and relation types, does not suggest this to be the case. To asses whether there is a significant difference in the RT-response-time for RTs across or within parties we bootstrapped the difference of the means for the two groups

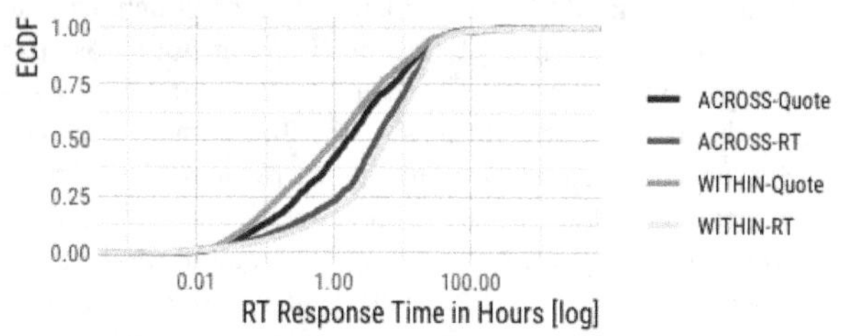

Figure 2: RT-response-time for both features and relation types in hours.

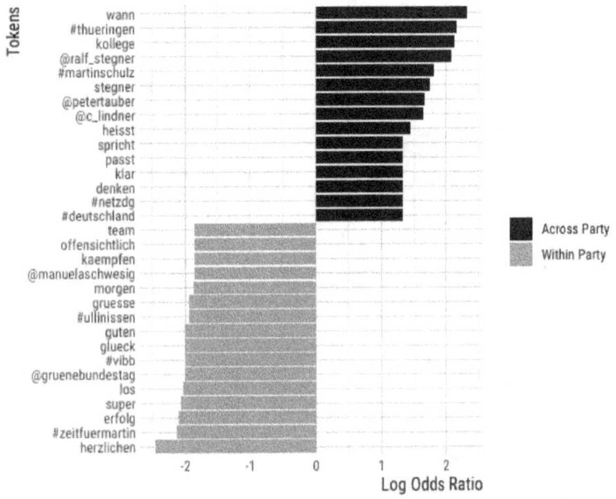

Figure 3: The 15 most distinctive words observed in quotes on RTs across and within party lines.

to check whether the 95% confidence interval contains the null effect (i.e. $CI \leq 0$). The confidence interval of the difference of bootstrapped means contains the null effect for both the RT (95% CI [-2.18,97.5]) and qRT (95% CI [-4.18,3.65]). Thus, no significant difference is found between within and outwith temporal context sharing. Figure 2 does, however, reveal that the time between a Tweet being posted and further interaction is shorter for qRTs ($qRTAcrossMedian = 1.55h$ vs $WithinMedian = 1.01h$) than for regular RTs ($RTAcrossMedian = 3.98h$ vs $WithinMedian = 5.37h$). This underlines that RT and qRT are used differently and if the thesis that sharing older content is more likely to be critical, this suggests that qRTing is less confrontational than we predicted. To investigate this further we next examine the text used in cross and within party qRTs.

4.3 Examining qRT comments

Using the same bootstrapping approach as above, we statistically compare properties of the quote text across and within parties. Comments on cross-party qRTs are significantly longer both in the number of characters ($AcrossMean = 70.94$ vs $WithinMean = 59.08$; 95% CI [9.67,13.99]) and tokens ($AcrossMean = 10.31$ vs $WithinMean = 8.29$; 95% CI [1.72,2.33]). Surprisingly, there are no differences in the number of hashtags ($AcrossMean = 0.58$ vs $WihtinMean = 0.61$), @mentions ($AcrossMean = 0.24$ vs $Within\text{–}Mean = 0.29$) or URLs ($AcrossMean = 0.02$ vs $WithinMean = 0.04$).

We use the log odds ratio to identify words which are likely to appear in within party (Within qRTing) but not across party (Across qRTing) comments and vice-versa.[2] Figure 3 shows the 15 most distinctive words for these cases. Tokens were derived by splitting on whitespace and removing stopwords. Users sharing cross-party Tweets tend to refer to other politicians when commenting either by directly using the @mention notation (@ralf_stegner, @petertauber, @c_lindner), a hashtag (#martinschulz) or simply their lastname (Stegner). We expected qRTing would be used to criticise or antagonise. It is, therefore, surprising that the first somewhat critical words are first found at rank 66 (*Schade*/Shame!) and 83 (Problem) for cross-party quoting. On the other hand, comments on Tweets shared by politicians in the same party, show many positive and supportive words e.g. *herzlichen* (happy), *Erfolg* (success), *super*, *Glück* (luck) or *guten* (good). Moreover, tokens used to support the campaign e.g. #zeitfuermartin or the word *kämpfen* (to fight) are among the most distinctive words for within party quoting. The most probable bi-grams within party are also very positive *Herzlichen Glückwunsch* (congratulations, −2.16) and *Vielen Dank* (many thanks, −1.24). Although few critical words being identified in the uni-gram analysis, the bi-gram with the highest log odds ratio for cross-party quotes is *fake news*, which is about three times (2.92) more likely to be observed in a quote for an across-party share.

Applying a basic, yet state of the art sentiment analysis approach for short, informal texts [32], reveals little difference in sentiment between the within and across party qRTs. We found neither evidence for cross-party comments being more negative nor within-party being more positive, which is partly explained by the classification of most comments as neutral. Further inspection revealed that approval, endorsement and support are sometimes expressed using emojis (e.g. , , or), which are not detected by this basic approach. About 3% of qRT comments contained approval expressing emojis. For expressing disagreement emoji use is less pronounced. Only 4 comments contained the thumbs-down emoji. Our analyses indicate that, in line with Garimella et al.'s thesis, qRTing promotes a civilized form of communication with little in the way of strong criticism for opponents and lots of praise for colleagues [12].

5 SUMMARY AND CONCLUSIONS

We have studied politicians' information sharing behaviour on Twitter by comparing their use of the RT and qRT features. In doing so we pair research from the IB and CSS communities. In particular, we extend the two-actor model commonly applied in IB by adding a further actor – the original creator of the information.

Applying methods prevalent in SNA we are able to identify that the qRT feature leads to less polarized interaction and has the potential to minimize the echo chamber effect, which supports findings from an earlier study by Garimella, Weber and De Choudhury [12]. Moreover, we examined Tweets shared out of temporal context to establish if – as past work has suggested [13] – they are more critical or offensive. Our analyses provide no evidence for this sentiment drift phenomenon, but we do observe distinct differences in the time-periods between the creation and sharing of Tweets shared via the RT and qRT features. qRTs occur much sooner than RTs. Although this finding does not contradict the standard assumption that sharing Tweets is a positive interaction or endorsement, it shows a certain bias with respect to the speed with which information is diffused. Finally, based on the literature, we assumed that in a political discourse the possibility of adding comments to a RT would lead to the feature being used for criticism or even insults. The results of various text mining analyses, however, do not support this assumption. Indeed, we observed the civilized discourse with opponents and support for colleagues, again supporting previous findings of [12].

[2] To remove noise we only include terms which appear at least 10 times in the dataset.

REFERENCES

[1] Christopher A. Bail, Lisa P. Argyle, Taylor W. Brown, John P. Bumpus, Haohan Chen, M. B. Fallin Hunzaker, Jaemin Lee, Marcus Mann, Friedolin Merhout, and Alexander Volfovsky. 2018. Exposure to opposing views on social media can increase political polarization. *PNAS* 115, 37 (2018), 9216âĂŞ–9221.

[2] X. Bao and F. Bouthillier. 2007. Information sharing: As a type of information behaviour. In *Proc. of ACAIS'07.* 1–14.

[3] Pablo Barberá, John T. Jost, Jonathan Nagler, Joshua A. Tucker, and Richard Bonneau. 2015. Tweeting From Left to Right: Is Online Political Communication More Than an Echo Chamber? *Psychological Science* 26, 10 (2015), 1531–1542.

[4] Danah boyd, Scott Golder, and Gilad Lotan. 2010. Tweet, Tweet, Retweet: Conversational Aspects of Retweeting on Twitter. In *In Proc. of HICSS'10.* IEEE, Washington, DC, USA, 1–10.

[5] Elfreda A. Chatman. 1996. The impoverished life-world of outsiders. *Journal of the American Society for Information Science* 47, 3 (1996), 193–206.

[6] Michael Conover, Jacob Ratkiewicz, Matthew Francisco, Bruno Goncalves, Filippo Menczer, and Alessandro Flammini. 2011. Political Polarization on Twitter. In *Proc. of ICWSM'11.* The AAAI Press, Washington.

[7] Bethany A. Conway, Kate Kenski, and Di Wang. 2015. The Rise of Twitter in the Political Campaign: Searching for Intermedia Agenda-Setting Effects in the Presidential Primary. *Journal of Computer-Mediated Communication* 20, 4 (2015), 363–380.

[8] Wei Feng and Jianyong Wang. 2013. Retweet or Not?: Personalized Tweet Reranking. In *Proc. of WSDM'13.* ACM, New York, NY, USA, 577–586.

[9] Tinto Fiona and Ruthven Ian. 2015. Sharing happy information. *JASIST* 67, 10 (2015), 2329–2343.

[10] Deen Freelon. 2017. Campaigns in control: Analyzing controlled interactivity and message discipline on Facebook. *Journal of Information Technology & Politics* 14, 2 (2017), 168–181.

[11] David Garcia, Adiya Abisheva, Simon Schweighofer, Uwe Serdült, and Frank Schweitzer. 2015. Ideological and Temporal Components of Network Polarization in Online Political Participatory Media. *Policy & Internet* 7, 1 (2015), 46–79.

[12] Kiran Garimella, Ingmar Weber, and Munmun De Choudhury. 2016. Quote RTs on Twitter: Usage of the New Feature for Political Discourse. In *Proc. of WebSci'16.* ACM, New York, NY, USA, 200–204.

[13] Pedro Guerra, Roberto Nalon, Renato Assunção, and Wagner Meira Jr. 2017. Antagonism Also Flows Through Retweets: The Impact of Out-of-Context Quotes in Opinion Polarization Analysis. In *Proc. of ICWSM'17.* The AAAI Press, Washington.

[14] Jeff Hemsley and Sam Jackson. 2018. Political Issues That Spread: Understanding Retweet Behavior During the 2016 U.S. Presidential Election. In *Proc. of SMSociety'18.* ACM, New York, NY, USA, 305–309.

[15] Nathan Oken Hodas and Kristina Lerman. 2012. How Visibility and Divided Attention Constrain Social Contagion. In *Proc. of SOCIALCOM-PASSAT'12.* IEEE, 249–257.

[16] Liangjie Hong, Ovidiu Dan, and Brian D. Davison. 2011. Predicting Popular Messages in Twitter. In *Proc. of WWW '11.* ACM, New York, NY, USA, 57–58.

[17] Andreas Jungherr. 2016. Twitter use in election campaigns: A systematic literature review. *Journal of Information Technology & Politics* 13, 1 (2016), 72–91.

[18] Haiko Lietz, Claudia Wagner, Arnim Bleier, and Markus Strohmaier. 2014. When Politicians Talk: Assessing Online Conversational Practices of Political Parties on Twitter. In *Proc. of ICWSM'14.* The AAAI Press, Washington.

[19] Avishay Livne, Matthew Simmons, Eytan Adar, and Lada Adamic. 2011. The Party Is Over Here: Structure and Content in the 2010 Election. In *Proc. of ICWSM'11.* The AAAI Press, Washington.

[20] Catherine C. Marshall and Sara Bly. 2004. Sharing Encountered Information: Digital Libraries Get a Social Life. In *Proc. of JCDL '04.* ACM, New York, NY, USA, 218–227.

[21] Panagiotis Metaxas, Eni Mustafaraj, Kily Wong, Laura Zeng, Megan O'Keefe, and Samantha Finn. 2015. What Do Retweets Indicate? Results from User Survey and Meta-Review of Research. In *Proc. of ICWSM'15.* The AAAI Press, Washington.

[22] M. E. J. Newman. 2006. Modularity and community structure in networks. *Proceedings of the National Academy of Sciences* 103, 23 (2006), 8577–8582.

[23] Ola Pilerot. 2012. LIS research on information sharing activities – people, places, or information. *Journal of Documentation* 68, 4 (2012), 559–581.

[24] Lee Rainie, Aaron Smith, Kay Lehman Schlozman, Henry Brady, and Sidney Verba. 2012. Social media and political engagement. *Pew Internet & American Life Project* 19 (2012).

[25] Kevin Rioux. 2005. Information Acquiring-and-Sharing. In *Theories of Information Behavior*, Karen E. Fisher, Sanda Erdelez, and Lynne McKechnie (Eds.). ASIST Information Today Inc., Medford, New Jersey, 169–173.

[26] Chirag Shah. 2014. Collaborative Information Seeking. *JASIST* 65, 2 (2014), 215–236.

[27] Diane H Sonnenwald. 2006. Challenges in Sharing Information Effectively: Examples from Command and Control. *Information Research: an International Electronic Journal* 11, 4 (2006), n4.

[28] Leo Graiden Stewart, Ahmer Arif, A. Conrad Nied, Emma S. Spiro, and Kate Starbird. 2017. Drawing the Lines of Contention: Networked Frame Contests Within #BlackLivesMatter Discourse. *PACMHCI* 1, CSCW (2017), 96:1–96:23.

[29] J. Stromer-Galley. 2014. *Presidential campaigning in the Internet age.* Oxford University Press, New York, NY.

[30] Sue Yeon Syn and Sanghee Oh. 2015. Why do social network site users share information on Facebook and Twitter? *Journal of Information Science* 41, 5 (2015), 553–569.

[31] S. Talja. 2002. Information sharing in academic communities:Types and levels of collaboration in information seeking and use. In *The New Review of Information Behaviour Research: Proc. of ISIC'02.* 143âĂŞ–160.

[32] Mike Thelwall, Kevan Buckley, Georgios Paltoglou, Di Cai, and Arvid Kappas. 2010. Sentiment Strength Detection in Short Informal Text. *JASIST* 61, 12 (2010), 2544–2558.

[33] I. Weber, V. R. K. Garimella, and A. Batayneh. 2013. Secular vs. Islamist polarization in Egypt on Twitter. In *Proc. of ASONAM'13.* ACM, New York, NY, USA, 290–297.

Variations in Assessor Agreement in Due Diligence

Adam Roegiest and Anne McNulty
Kira Systems
Toronto, Canada
{adam.roegiest,anne.mcnulty}@kirasystems.com

ABSTRACT

In legal due diligence, lawyers identify a variety of topic instances in a company's contracts that may pose risk during a transaction. In this paper, we present a study of 9 lawyers conducting a simulated review of 50 contracts for five topics. We find that lawyers agree on the general location of relevant material at a higher rate than in other assessor agreement studies, but they do not entirely agree on the extent of the relevant material. Additionally, we do not find strong differences between lawyers who have differing levels of due diligence expertise.

If we train machine learning models to identify these topics based on each user's judgments, the resulting models exhibit similar levels of agreement between each other as to the lawyers that trained them. This indicates that these models are learning the types of behaviour exhibited by their trainers, even if they are doing so imperfectly. Accordingly, we argue that additional work is necessary to improve the assessment process to ensure that all parties agree on identified material.

CCS CONCEPTS

• **Information systems → Information extraction**; • **Human-centered computing →** *User studies*;

KEYWORDS

Due diligence, user study, legal retrieval, assessor agreement

ACM Reference Format:
Adam Roegiest and Anne McNulty. 2019. Variations in Assessor Agreement in Due Diligence. In *2019 Conference on Human Information Interaction and Retrieval (CHIIR '19), March 10–14, 2019, Glasgow, United Kingdom.* ACM, New York, NY, USA, 5 pages. https://doi.org/10.1145/3295750.3298945

1 INTRODUCTION

Assessor agreement in Information Retrieval has traditionally been quite low but its effects on system evaluation have been relatively minimal [2, 17, 18]. In legal electronic discovery ("eDiscovery"), agreement has been higher and variation has attributed more to assessor rather than topical variance [6, 11]. In contrast, due diligence [14], where lawyers review a company's contracts during a merger or acquisition and find the potentially problematic passages, assessor disagreement could yield a potentially over-inclusive report, which would waste senior lawyer time, or miss crucial information, which could lead to a bad deal. Accordingly, understanding how assessor behaviour differs in the due diligence context from other IR contexts allows us to determine the extent to which we can rely on previous results for solutions in due diligence.

This work presents a study we conducted consisting of 9 of our in-house legal professionals, of which four have a high degree of due diligence experience and the remainder have a lower level of experience. The participants were required to find and highlight the five common due diligence topics in 50 short contracts (c.f. Section 3). While this does not necessarily match the scale of actual due diligence projects, it should provide a reasonable barometer of agreement, especially when given the high-costs associated with document review. Furthermore, these participants form what we might think of as an "optimistic" estimate of agreement as they are all familiar with our internal definitions of these topics rather than each reflecting a different institution's conception.

Using these participant annotations, we examine the coarse-grained agreement measures (e.g., Cohen's κ [4] and relevant overlap [18]) that rely on simple overlap of annotations to determine relevance. Such coarse-grained measures may omit valuable information as one participant may highlight more information than another. This type of disagreement (i.e., amount of content), if present, potentially exemplifies differences in assessing strategy that could have non-trivial ramifications (e.g., longer highlights may obfuscate important details). Accordingly, we compare and contrast these coarse-grained agreement measures with measures, influenced by plagiarism detection [12], that account for the amount of (non-)overlapping material between annotations from different participants.

In real-world due diligence, lawyers are often required to review thousands of contracts in very little time which is often not practical. Accordingly, the use of machine learning to train models to identify relevant material is becoming increasingly desirable. Given that premise, we might wonder how users and machine learning models would agree. Following Roegiest et al. [14], we train models for each participant's assessments on a topic. As it is prohibitively too expensive to get participants to review new documents, we use the models as imperfect proxies and have them annotate 20 additional documents. After comparing the agreement of the models on these new documents, we conclude with some thoughts on how to improve model agreement.

CHIIR '19, March 10–14, 2019, Glasgow, United Kingdom

ACM ISBN 978-1-4503-6025-8/19/03...$15.00
https://doi.org/10.1145/3295750.3298945

2 RELATED WORKS

Voorhees' work [18] into assessor agreement at TREC has led to many subsequent investigations about task specific agreement. Despite the fact that the TREC assessors came from similar backgrounds, Voorhees found that relevant assessments overlapped between 0.42 to 0.49 of the time on the TREC 4 collection. In spite of the high disagreement, Voorhees found that system evaluation and rankings were generally robust to changes in assessors. This result has been replicated by different authors [2, 17]. Assessor agreement can be affected by many different factors [1, 8, 19, 22, 24], of which Kinney et al.'s [8] and Al-Harbi and Smucker's [1] finding that assessing instructions may have some affect on behaviour is most applicable to this work.

In legal contexts, assessor agreement becomes important when we consider the fact that there can be repercussions when disagreement occurs (e.g., not returning material because one lawyer believes it not to be relevant may result in monetary penalties). Accordingly, there have been a number of studies into agreement in legal contexts, specifically eDiscovery [3, 6, 7, 20, 21, 23, 24]. Oard and Webber [11] found that Cohen's κ ranged from 0.31 to 0.59 in electronic discovery contexts and that the variability in agreement was generally smaller among assessors than topics. Outside of electronic discovery context, we know of no other studies in legal contexts that examines assessor agreement.

3 STUDY METHODOLOGY

The high-level procedure for our study was for a participant to annotate 50 documents for 5 common due diligence topics ("Change of Control", "Assignment", "Indemnity", "Exclusivity", and "Most Favoured Nation"). We note that participants were restricted to one of two assessing strategies but since our focus is on participants' due diligence experience, we omit details and analysis of the different strategies for future work. Participants were asked not to go back and alter any previous annotations they had made. The annotation process was conducted using in our in-house platform [15]. [1]

Participants were solicited from our in-house team of annotators and from other lawyers in our organization. In total, we had 9 respondents, four of which had previously had substantial experience with due diligence review. All annotators were at least familiar with the topics and generally found them easy according to self-report on a 5-point Likert scale. Additionally, one of the authors conducted a full-scale review of the document set to provide a baseline for performance and ensure that the documents were representative of the task. This annotator is referred to as the "Gold" annotator while all others are identified in aggregate as Lo(w) experience or Hi(gh) experience annotators.

While all participants were familiar with the topics they were asked to annotate, we provided additional fine-grained details about what should and should not be annotated in the course of their review. An example for the "Indemnity" topic can be seen in Figure 1. This reflects the real-world scenario where a senior lawyer will dictate what is and is not relevant for a particular review. We note that there has been evidence that instruction length can have non-trivial effects on assessing behaviour [1]. Such trends do not seem to hold in legal domains as more and less detailed instructions do not appear to produce substantial differences in assessor behaviour [24]. As none of our topic descriptions are particularly long nor extremely detailed, we do not believe this had a substantial effect on our results.

5) Indemnity
- include positive obligations to indemnify/hold harmless as well as indemnification procedures
- generally you will be highlighting entire indemnity sections
- exclude separate survival provisions referencing indemnities
- exclude separate defined terms relating to indemnities (but include if embedded in the provision)

Figure 1: Example of the additional instructions supplied to annotators as part of the study. They were expected to be otherwise familiar with the topic.

	T1	T2	T3	T4	T5
Gold	77 (490)	29 (353)	49 (533)	81 (1404)	9 (352)
A	63 (554)	39 (361)	45 (504)	67 (1662)	6 (395)
B	60 (521)	33 (521)	35 (420)	53 (1879)	11 (360)
C	75 (491)	56 (282)	47 (470)	72 (1528)	11 (322)
D	59 (574)	33 (498)	36 (530)	52 (2020)	6 (391)
E	71 (532)	34 (522)	38 (639)	37 (1826)	12 (490)
F	69 (520)	34 (464)	46 (517)	83 (1476)	9 (409)
G	64 (555)	30 (514)	40 (396)	70 (1639)	6 (448)
H	55 (515)	38 (619)	42 (622)	79 (1209)	9 (538)
I	74 (497)	41 (420)	35 (348)	69 (1592)	6 (452)

Table 1: Number of annotations and the average number of characters in an annotation for each of the five topics for the annotation task.

As can be seen in Table 1, by and large, all of the annotators identified a similar number of instances of each topic. There does appear to be a trend to either have more, shorter annotations or fewer, longer annotations. Some participants tend to follow this pattern quite rigidly (e.g., D), while others (e.g., E) fluctuate from topic to topic.

3.1 Evaluation Measures

Following Voorhees [18], we report Recall, Precision, and Overlap for pairwise comparisons between annotators, where we switch off the roles as primary (gold standard) and secondary annotator. We note that we only compare our Gold annotator against every one else (i.e., the Gold annotator is only ever used as the primary annotator) since any other comparisons may not be valid as Gold had unrestricted review capabilities. We also report Cohen's κ [4, 10] as it is a long standing measure of inter-annotator agreement. Following Landis and Koch [9], we consider any $0.6 < \kappa < 0.8$ to indicate substantial agreement. For these basic measures, we consider binary relevance to be a function of simple annotation overlap (i.e., any overlap indicates a true positive).

Binary overlap is not particularly nuanced, as a small annotation overlapping a large annotation does not account for the parts that do not overlap. To account for these nuances, we borrow from plagiarism detection [12] and consider macro-averaged Recall and

[1] The data for this study is being released under a restricted usage agreement available at science.kirasystems.com.

Pri.	Sec.	Recall	Precision	Cohen's κ	Overlap
Gold	Lo	0.75 (0.03)	0.84 (0.08)	0.67 (0.05)	0.61 (0.06)
Gold	Hi	0.71 (0.03)	0.82 (0.07)	0.67 (0.05)	0.61 (0.05)
Lo	Lo	0.81 (0.04)	0.93 (0.02)	0.74 (0.04)	0.68 (0.04)
Hi	Lo	0.89 (0.02)	0.81 (0.02)	0.76 (0.02)	0.70 (0.02)
Hi	Hi	0.82 (0.03)	0.87 (0.04)	0.77 (0.04)	0.70 (0.05)

Table 2: Mean and standard deviation of various binary relevance measures (i.e., span overlaps or not). The top lines represent when our Gold standard annotator is used to evaluate all other annotators. The remainder specify when each experience level is used as the primary annotator and evaluates another annotator as secondary assessor.

Pri.	Sec.	gRecall	gPrecision	gOverlap
Gold	Lo	0.71 (0.04)	0.73 (0.11)	0.61 (0.08)
Gold	Hi	0.69 (0.04)	0.73 (0.11)	0.66 (0.08)
Lo	Lo	0.75 (0.05)	0.82 (0.04)	0.64 (0.06)
Hi	Lo	0.79 (0.02)	0.78 (0.02)	0.69 (0.04)
Hi	Hi	0.77 (0.04)	0.80 (0.04)	0.70 (0.07)

Table 3: Mean and standard deviation when we take into account the granularity of the annotated spans. gRecall and gPrecision are the macro-averaged versions by Potthast et al. [12] that take into account overlap length of annotations.

Precision, gRecall and gPrecision, which account for the amount of overlap (or lack thereof) between annotations. Similarly, we can extend simple Overlap to gOverlap, such that we divide the length of the intersection of annotated text by the length of the union of all annotated text.

For the sake of brevity, we report measures with respect to meaningful combinations of Gold, Hi(gh) experience, and Lo(w) experience assessors. Since we are averaging over assessor pairs and topics, we use a fixed-effects model [5] to appropriately weight differences in mean and variance across the pairs of assessors and topics. For the purposes of our evaluation, the Pri(mary) assessor is the gold standard for evaluation and the Sec(ondary) assessor is the one being evaluated.[2]

4 BINARY AGREEMENT

In Table 2, we see that there is substantial agreement among annotators using binary measures, with annotations overlapping more often than not. Our κ and Overlap values are higher than those reported in the literature [3, 16, 18], which may be due to the fact that these are not strictly topical in nature. Namely, "Change of Control" has a precise legal meaning; whereas, identifying that a document is about "black bear attacks," or "fantasy football gambling at Enron" may be more open to interpretation. It has been argued [7, 11] that, in the eDiscovery context, it is often human error, rather than differences of opinion, that causes variations in assessments. It is worth noting that Wakeling et al. [19] found similar levels of agreement when examining agreement in real-world search topics (i.e., issued by real users rather than constructed for a particular task), which indicates that agreement we have observed may be due to real-world nature of our topics.

The participants achieve Precision on par with previous studies [6, 18] but Recall is higher than that reported by Voorhees and others [16, 18]. The disparity between what our study and other legal contexts have observed [3, 16] stems from the task itself. Namely, eDiscovery requires retrieval from a much larger document collection and so increases difficulty in achieving high Recall and Precision. While our values may be in-line with previous results, they are still quite low from a practical standpoint. Being overly inclusive means burdening a costly senior lawyer with additional review or missing a potentially important but cleverly hidden piece of information. Both issues could have consequences for the lawyer who led the review.

Similar to Bailey et al. [2], we do find some assessing differences between our more and less experienced annotators. When we compare High and Low experience assessors, there is higher Recall at the expense of Precision, which we may expect given that highly experienced lawyers would have more refined conceptions of the topics than less experienced ones. Interestingly, when compared to the Gold assessor, there do not appear to be meaningful differences between the levels of experience but this may be due to the study design and time constraints. When comparing agreement among the different experience levels, we do not observe a meaningful difference in κ or Overlap. This appears to support the finding of Kinney et al. [8] that background experience may not have substantive impact on assessor agreement.

5 GRANULAR AGREEMENT

The more granular measures of agreement are our mechanism for examining the nuances in the amount of material annotated by annotators. As seen in Table 3, gRecall and gPrecision are noticeably decreased from their equivalents in Table 2. This appears to indicate that even though users agree on the general area of relevant information in documents (as corroborated by the discussion in the previous section), they do not agree on the amount or exact context. Further evidence of this can be seen by the generally same levels of gOverlap and Overlap but higher variance. It is reasonable to expect this would only occur when the granularity of the annotation is the main source of disagreement rather than general area.

There is also a general increase in variation for the granular measures when compared to their coarse counterparts. From this we may infer that the granular measures may provide us with a more in-depth picture into how participants agree with each other. In particular, if we care about the amount of information annotated then there will be decidedly more disagreement between some assessors than Table 2 would lead us to believe. This is of particular importance since, in the real-world, these annotations would be used to generate a report on whether or not a transaction (e.g., merger, acquisition) is worthwhile. For example, if a senior lawyer expects concise annotations to expedite report generation then we would suggest that the annotating lawyer likely target that goal rather than try to capture surrounding context. While the surrounding context may be helpful to the more junior lawyer, it would likely distract the senior lawyer from their task.

[2]Note that these measures are symmetric and switching who is the Primary only flips Recall and Precision.

	T1		T2		T3		T4		T5	
	P	R	P	R	P	R	P	R	P	R
Gold	0.82	0.83	0.78	0.60	0.72	0.66	0.77	0.83	1.00	0.33
Lo	0.83	0.93	0.80	0.78	0.68	0.50	0.78	0.90	0.85	0.21
Hi	0.81	0.94	0.80	0.78	0.63	0.44	0.76	0.89	0.96	0.29

Table 4: Average P(recision) and R(ecall) for Gold, Low experience, and High experience models trained by 5-fold cross validation evaluated against the training user.

Pri.	Sec.	Cohen's κ	Overlap	gOverlap
Gold	Lo	0.64 (0.08)	0.59 (0.08)	0.65 (0.10)
Gold	Hi	0.69 (0.09)	0.64 (0.10)	0.67 (0.11)
Lo	Lo	0.70 (0.04)	0.64 (0.04)	0.70 (0.05)
Hi	Lo	0.74 (0.02)	0.68 (0.03)	0.71 (0.03)
Hi	Hi	0.72 (0.05)	0.66 (0.07)	0.69 (0.07)

Table 5: Mean and standard deviation of the agreement measures between the results of applying machine learning models trained by each annotator's assessments on 20 previously unseen documents.

In spite of these differences, the large scale trends appear to be the same as the previous section. Accordingly, the binary measures may be a suitable measure for assessing general assessor quality. The more granular measures may be more useful when attempting to match assessing styles between lawyers to mitigate any subsequent disagreement on the amount of material highlighted.

6 LEARNING RESULTS

In our study, it was feasible, if time consuming, to review the 50 documents for 5 fields. In practice, where there are thousands of contracts, the costs of having lawyers review documents is not feasible. Accordingly, we can take the annotations provided by our participants and train a user-specific machine learning model for each topic to identify instances in unseen documents. Following Roegiest et al. [14], we trained a Conditional Random Field ("CRF") for each participant and each topic. We generated each model's Precision and Recall with respect to its training assessor and report the aggregates across experience level in Figure 4.[3] The models trained by highly experienced lawyers do not appear to be substantially more accurate than those trained by the less experienced ones. Interestingly, our Gold assessor does not appear to produce a substantially superior model and goes to show that these models are imperfect copies of the underlying assessor. With more examples, this may be partially mitigated but how much is unknown.

We then ran those CRFs on 20 previously unseen documents. Figure 5 depicts κ, Overlap, and gOverlap when comparing model annotations across experience levels. When compared to Figures 2 and 3, we find that generally agreement is in accord with the annotator-level agreement. Though we do find increased variation compared to previous results. What we might infer from this is that, on average, the models produce roughly the same annotations as their training users might have. But the models have the potential to magnify the differences in their trainer's conception of relevance. To this end, two participants were able to annotate the 20 documents themselves and they achieved average κ values of 0.56 and 0.67 with respect to their models, lower than we might desire but not surprising given the above. Such a result further reinforces the idea that the models generated are imperfect copies.

Ideally, we would like the models trained on annotations to be generalizable such that another user would find them useful. While the models achieve what is considered substantial agreement [9], we are still not quite there in light of the results above. Part of the reason for this may be due to an insufficient amount of training data, but may also result from the restriction that participants could not go back and refine their opinion on previously judged documents and, thus, fix errors. All participants stated that this deviated from their general reviewing routine. Further exploration is necessary to determine whether a less restrictive annotation strategy would produce a better model and higher agreement. Alternatively, it may be the case, as Roegiest et al. [13] suggest, that combining annotations from multiple users could yield a more effective model and we leave this for future work.

[3]The performance of T5 ("Most Favoured Nation") is low due to the relatively few examples in the 50 study documents.

7 CONCLUSION

We have presented a study of assessor agreement when annotating passages in documents for the due diligence context. We have found that legal professionals tend to agree with each other more than assessors did in previous studies. However, this agreement diminishes when we account for the length of the annotated material. Indeed, there is more variability in agreement when accounting for amount than would be suggested by presence of any annotation overlap. In spite of this, the variability observed tends to be less than that found in other legal contexts indicating that perhaps the topics are sufficiently well understood. This suggests that the differences in assessing behaviour are what remain. While some small differences in agreement exist between more and less experienced users, there is no strong evidence that one is inherently better than the other. We place the caveat that our results form an "optimistic" estimate of agreement as the participants are familiar with internal definitions of these topics. Accordingly, we might reasonably expect more disagreement between professionals from different institutions.

When using the annotations rendered by users to train a machine learning model, we find that the resulting models exhibit similar levels of agreement as the constituent users. This has interesting implications as it means that presenting the annotations of one user's model to another will likely yield similar disagreement to presenting the trainer's annotations. Such an implication means that we need to be careful and ensure that when training such models, the annotations should target as close as possible to a "reasonable" interpretation of relevance.

ACKNOWLEDGMENTS

The authors would like to thank our in-house team of legal professionals, whose participation made this study possible. The authors would also like to thank Karen Anello for finding and organizing the documents that were used in this study.

REFERENCES

[1] Aiman L. Al-Harbi and Mark D. Smucker. 2014. A Qualitative Exploration of Secondary Assessor Relevance Judging Behavior *(IIiX '14).*

[2] Peter Bailey, Nick Craswell, Ian Soboroff, Paul Thomas, Arjen P. de Vries, and Emine Yilmaz. 2008. Relevance Assessment: Are Judges Exchangeable and Does It Matter *(SIGIR '08).*

[3] Thomas Barnett and Svetlana Godjevac. 2011. Faster, better, cheaper legal document review, pipe dream or reality?. In *Proc. ICAIL DESI IV Workshop.*

[4] Jacob Cohen. 1960. A Coefficient of Agreement for Nominal Scales. *Educational and Psychological Measurement* 20, 1 (1960).

[5] Gordon V. Cormack and Thomas R. Lynam. 2006. Statistical Precision of Information Retrieval Evaluation *(SIGIR '06).*

[6] Maura R Grossman and Gordon V Cormack. 2010. Technology-assisted review in e-discovery can be more effective and more efficient than exhaustive manual review. *Rich. JL & Tech.* 17 (2010).

[7] Maura R. Grossman and Gordon V. Cormack. 2011. Inconsistent Assessment of Responsiveness in E-Discovery: Difference of Opinion or Human Error?. In *Proc. ICAIL DESI IV Workshop.*

[8] Kenneth A. Kinney, Scott B. Huffman, and Juting Zhai. 2008. How Evaluator Domain Expertise Affects Search Result Relevance Judgments *(CIKM '08).*

[9] J. Richard Landis and Gary G. Koch. 1977. The Measurement of Observer Agreement for Categorical Data. *Biometrics* 33, 1 (1977).

[10] Christopher D. Manning, Prabhakar Raghavan, and Hinrich Schütze. 2008. *Introduction to Information Retrieval.* Cambridge University Press.

[11] Douglas W Oard and William Webber. 2013. Information retrieval for e-discovery. *Foundations and Trends® in Information Retrieval* 7, 2–3 (2013).

[12] Martin Potthast, Benno Stein, Alberto Barrón-Cedeño, and Paolo Rosso. 2010. An evaluation framework for plagiarism detection. In *COLING '10.*

[13] Adam Roegiest, Gordon V. Cormack, Charles L.A. Clarke, and Maura R. Grossman. 2015. Impact of Surrogate Assessments on High-Recall Retrieval *(SIGIR '15).*

[14] Adam Roegiest, Alexander K. Hudek, and Anne McNulty. 2018. A Dataset and an Examination of Identifying Passages for Due Diligence. In *Proc. SIGIR 2018.*

[15] Adam Roegiest and Winter Wei. 2018. Redesigning a Document Viewer for Legal Documents. In *Proc. CHIIR 2018.*

[16] Herbert L. Roitblat, Anne Kershaw, and Patrick Oot. 2010. Document Categorization in Legal Electronic Discovery: Computer Classification vs. Manual Review. *J. Am. Soc. Inf. Sci. Tec.* 61, 1 (2010).

[17] Andrew Trotman and Dylan Jenkinson. 2007. IR evaluation using multiple assessors per topic. In *Proc. ADCS '07.*

[18] Ellen M Voorhees. 2000. Variations in relevance judgments and the measurement of retrieval effectiveness. *Information processing & management* 36, 5 (2000).

[19] Simon Wakeling, Martin Halvey, Robert Villa, and Laura Hasler. 2016. A Comparison of Primary and Secondary Relevance Judgements for Real-Life Topics *(CHIIR '16).*

[20] Jianqiang Wang and Dagobert Soergel. 2010. A user study of relevance judgments for E-Discovery. *Proc. Am. Soc. Info. Sci. Tech.* 47, 1 (2010).

[21] William Webber. 2011. Re-examining the effectiveness of manual review. In *Proc. SIGIR 2011 SIRE Workshop.*

[22] William Webber, Praveen Chandar, and Ben Carterette. 2012. Alternative Assessor Disagreement and Retrieval Depth *(CIKM '12).*

[23] William Webber and Jeremy Pickens. 2013. Assessor Disagreement and Text Classifier Accuracy *(SIGIR '13).*

[24] William Webber, Bryan Toth, and Marjorie Desamito. 2012. Effect of Written Instructions on Assessor Agreement *(SIGIR '12).*

Answer Interaction in Non-factoid Question Answering Systems

Chen Qu, Liu Yang, W. Bruce Croft
University of Massachusetts Amherst
{chenqu,lyang,croft}@cs.umass.edu

Falk Scholer
RMIT University
falk.scholer@rmit.edu.au

Yongfeng Zhang
Rutgers University
yongfeng.zhang@rutgers.edu

ABSTRACT

Information retrieval systems are evolving from document retrieval to answer retrieval. Web search logs provide large amounts of data about how people interact with ranked lists of documents, but very little is known about interaction with answer texts. In this paper, we use Amazon Mechanical Turk to investigate three answer presentation and interaction approaches in a non-factoid question answering setting. We find that people perceive and react to good and bad answers very differently, and can identify good answers relatively quickly. Our results provide the basis for further investigation of effective answer interaction and feedback methods.

KEYWORDS

User Interaction; Answer Interaction; Answer Presentation; Non-factoid Question Answering; Information-seeking

ACM Reference Format:
Chen Qu, Liu Yang, W. Bruce Croft, Falk Scholer, and Yongfeng Zhang. 2019. Answer Interaction in Non-factoid Question Answering Systems. In *2019 Conference on Human Information Interaction and Retrieval (CHIIR '19), March 10–14, 2019, Glasgow, Scotland Uk.* ACM, New York, NY, USA, 5 pages. https://doi.org/10.1145/3295750.3298946

1 INTRODUCTION

Classic information retrieval (IR) systems aim to return a list of relevant documents on a search engine result page (SERP). This type of presentation is often described as "ten blue links", because users typically need to click on the ranked results and be redirected to the documents. Modern search engines have paid attention to search results diversification [3, 21] and heterogeneous content presentation [29]. Recently, several works have focused on retrieving extractive answers instead of documents [11, 18, 35, 37, 38]. Industrial examples include Google's *featured snippets*,[1] which display a potential answer extracted from the top search result.

If search engines can return a list of potential answers rather than documents, it is essential to study the most effective way to present these answers and interact with users. Specifically, this research question should be emphasized in non-factoid question answering (QA) systems. This is because non-factoid QA poses unique challenges to answer presentation and interaction as it requires several answer sentences or passages, instead of simple entity-based answers as in factoid QA.

User interaction with SERPs has been widely studied using search logs that contain clicks and query reformulations [2, 23]. Furthermore, other works focus on interaction and feedback methods for document retrieval by studying real users instead of search logs [12, 13]. However, fine-grained presentation and interaction processes with answers have rarely been investigated in previous work. Additional information is needed from observing what constitutes a good answer when users provide fine-grained and precise feedback, instead of simply indicating whether the answer is relevant or not. We believe that studying fine-grained user interaction and feedback can lead to more effective answer finding, as well as having an impact on the design of conversational search systems.

In this work, we investigate three answer presentation and interaction approaches (Line by Line, Passage Highlight, and Passage Highlighting with Suggested Words) to understand how people perceive good and bad answers. The Line by Line setting reveals a potential answer passage one line at a time and observes people's reactions as they go through the passage. The Passage Highlight setting presents the full passage, and instructs users to highlight important words that make them believe the passage is a good or bad answer. The third setting is built upon the second one, and includes some suggested words emphasized with special styles. We hired crowdsourcing workers from Amazon Mechanical Turk (MTurk)[2] to conduct the experiments. Based on these fine-grained experiments, we find that people perceive good answers and bad answers very differently, which could lead to more effective relevance feedback schemes. For example, people do not hesitate to rate a bad answer, but they can be severe on the answer quality judgments even in some cases where the passage is the answer. Another finding is that people's initial impressions of answer quality are usually correct, and they become more and more confident about answer quality as they go through the answer. In addition, we investigate the relation between answer quality and QA text similarity and find that they are not always correlated.

Our contributions can be summarized as follows. (1) We conduct one of the first fine-grained analyses on answer presentation and interaction in a non-factoid QA setting. (2) We provide an empirical analysis to answer an important research question: is answer quality related to QA text similarity? Our findings can be used to design a more interactive IR system that emphasizes answer retrieval. In addition, our work also has implications for conversational search, since it is essentially a multi-turn interaction process.

2 RELATED WORK

User Interaction and Relevance Feedback. Relevance feedback [4, 8, 12, 15, 39] is an important and early interactive method in IR systems. In practice, pseudo-relevance feedback (PRF) [6, 14, 16]

[1] https://support.google.com/webmasters/answer/6229325

[2] https://www.mturk.com/

CHIIR '19, March 10–14, 2019, Glasgow, Scotland Uk

ACM ISBN 978-1-4503-6025-8/19/03...$15.00
https://doi.org/10.1145/3295750.3298946

is widely used. It assumes that top-ranked documents are relevant and thus can be used for query expansion. In contrast to PRF, some approaches focus on explicit interactions with the user [1, 7, 13, 17]. This work builds on these early papers and focuses on explicit and fine-grained user interaction with answers. Our methods could be especially useful when the interaction bandwidth is limited, such as in mobile search and conversational search.

Answer Retrieval. IR systems are evolving from document retrieval to answer retrieval. Substantial work has been done in factoid QA [9, 22, 34, 37, 38], community QA [10, 24, 24, 25, 32, 33], and non-factoid QA [5, 11, 18, 35]. All these works focus on finding effective methods for answer retrieval. However, even the most effective method can occasionally fail to find the answers. In that case, it is essential to employ user interaction and feedback methods to retrieve the answer in an iterative manner. In this work, we study answer presentation and interaction techniques in a non-factoid QA setting, as an essential complement to answer retrieval models.

Information-seeking Conversations. An information-seeking conversation typically involves multiple turns of interaction and information exchange between an information seeker and provider. Radlinski and Craswell [20] described a theoretical framework for conversational search and desirable properties in such systems. In addition, several works [19, 26, 27, 30, 31] observed and studied information-seeking conversations between humans and addressed different facets of such interactions. Finally, conversational recommendation [40] and response ranking [36] have been explored under this multi-turn interaction setting.

3 OUR APPROACH

3.1 Overview

We conduct an observational study of how people perceive answer quality under different interactive settings. This can help us identify effective methods for answer presentation and interaction. In this task, people are given a question and a short passage. The passage may or may not be a good answer to the question.[3] We present the answer passage in three ways, namely, Line by Line, Passage Highlight, and Passage Highlighting with Suggested Words. These settings are designed to obtain fine-grained user feedback to test various answer presentation and interaction methods.

3.2 Line by Line

In this setting, the answer passage is presented line by line. One line is typically one sentence. At each line, we instruct the annotators to give a rating of how confident they are that the passage is or contains a good answer to the question. This rating is based on the current line and previous lines. Lines that follow the current line are hidden. The confidence rating is provided on a scale of -2 to 2:

- -2: Confident this passage is not an answer to the question.
- -1: Believe that this passage might not be an answer.
- 0: Not sure yet.
- 1: Believe that the passage might be an answer to the question.
- 2: Confident this passage is an answer to the question.

This setting is designed to observe the evaluation of answer quality as people go through a potential answer.

[3] "Good" refers to good quality. Verifying the facts in the passages is not required.

3.3 Passage Highlight

In this setting, we present the full answer passages and instruct the annotators to highlight positive and negative words or phrases in the passage (sentences are not encouraged). The *positive words* are those that help to convince the annotators that the passage is a good answer. For example, these words may present a specific answer or introduce key arguments. In contrast, the *negative words* make the annotators feel the answer is of bad quality. For example, these words can be indicators of irrelevant issues, or may reveal that the answer providers are uncertain about their answers. Annotators are instructed to highlight complete words only. At least one highlight for each passage needs to be made for a successful submission. Figure 5 gives an illustration for the highlighting interface.[4] In addition, annotators are asked to give a rating on overall answer quality. The answer quality can be chosen on a scale of 0 to 2:

- 0: It is not an answer to the question.
- 1: It is an answer to the question, but not of good quality.
- 2: It is a good answer to the question.

This setting is designed to obtain fine-grained feedback on answer quality evaluation and observe rating agreement.

The main challenge of this setting is to quantify annotators' agreement on highlights. Although the annotators are instructed to highlight whole words only, they sometimes highlight partial words. So first, the character-level highlights need to be transformed into word-level highlights. Then a *consistency rule* is applied to highlight all occurrences of a word if this word is highlighted by the annotator. This rule is not applicable to stop words. Then the next step is transforming the highlighted passage into a string by denoting the highlighted words as "1" with others as "0". In this way the agreement of highlights can be cast into a string similarity problem. The overlap coefficient [28] is used to tackle this problem:

$$\text{overlap}(H_1, H_2) = \frac{|H_1 \cap H_2|}{\min(|H_1|, |H_2|)} \quad (1)$$

where H_1 and H_2 are string representations of highlights from two annotators. This method can compute agreement among multiple annotators. However, since complete agreement with more than two annotators is rare due to the open style of the task, only pairwise agreement is computed. The largest value among all pairwise agreements is considered as the agreement for this QA pair. We adopt this setting because perceptions and highlights of answer key words are highly subjective.

3.4 Passage Highlighting with Suggested Words

This setting is very similar to the previous setting. The only difference is that we mark some suggested words in the passage for the annotators' reference. These suggested words are marked in bold font and blue color to draw user attention. Figure 5 gives an example of the highlighting interface. The suggested words meet one of the following criteria: (1) Words that start with a capital letter, such as acronyms or proper nouns. Words that start a sentence have been excluded. (2) Words that have the top five tf-idf value in this passage. Idf values are computed with a Wikipedia dump (date: 20180520). The annotators understand that they do not have to keep to the suggested words. This setting is designed to compare reactions with and without the suggested words.

[4] The words in blue are marked for the next setting. They are in black in this setting.

4 EXPERIMENTS

4.1 Data Preparation

We sampled 200 QA pairs from nfL6,[5] a non-factoid community QA dataset. A question typically comes with multiple answers provided by the community, with one of them selected as the accepted answer. Our sampled data contains 100 questions, and each question has a good answer and a bad answer. The good answers are the accepted answers of the questions. To match a bad answer to each question, we first use BM25 to collect a small pool of candidate answers for each question and then use a BLSTM model [5] to rerank. We set a criterion that all the answers can be naturally split into four sentences so that the answers would have appropriate lengths, and to work with a fixed number of lines in the Line by Line setting.

4.2 MTurk Setup

We employed crowdsourcing workers (turkers) through Amazon Mechanical Turk (MTurk) to annotate the QA pairs. The three settings are conducted separately. Each QA pair receives annotations from three different turkers. Turkers conduct annotation in the form of assignments, which contain instructions, annotation examples, quiz questions on the instructions, and five QA pairs to annotate (with a combination of good and bad answers). We only use annotations from turkers who have passed the quiz test in the analysis. In addition, the turkers are required to have a HIT (Human Intelligence Task) approval rate of 95% or higher, a minimum of 1,000 approved HITs, and be located in US, Canada, Australia or Great Britain. The turkers are paid $0.5/assignment.

4.3 Line by Line

Figure 1a presents the distribution of confidence ratings from line 1 to line 4 for good answers. The most common confidence rating for line 1 and line 2 is 1. The most common rating gradually shifts to 2 at line 3 and line 4. The distribution of ratings consistently moves up to 2 from line 1 to line 4. Figure 1b presents the distribution of confidence ratings from line 1 to line 4 for bad answers. The most common confidence rating is always -2 through line 1 to line 4. The number of -2 ratings gradually increases as the passage is revealed to the turkers. These indicate that, *for good answers, the turkers have a sense that the answers might be good at the beginning, but they hesitate to make confident ratings until the latter half of the passage is revealed. In contrast, for bad answers, most of the turkers are able to determine the answer quality from the beginning.*

We also use a χ^2 test to evaluate the difference of confidence ratings between the previous line (expectation) and the current line (observation). We observe the same patterns for good answers and bad answers: the shifts of confidence ratings from line 1 $\rightarrow$ 2 and line 2 $\rightarrow$ 3 are statistically significant with p-value <0.01, while line 3 $\rightarrow$ 4 shows an insignificant difference. This indicates that *some people can determine answer quality quickly while others are slower, but they can make a decision before the last line is revealed.*

Figure 2 presents the majority of confidence ratings for all questions. The rating leaps from 1 to 2 between line 2 and line 3 for good answers. The rating remains at -2 throughout the passage for bad answers. This result double confirms the conclusions above.

[5] https://ciir.cs.umass.edu/downloads/nfL6/

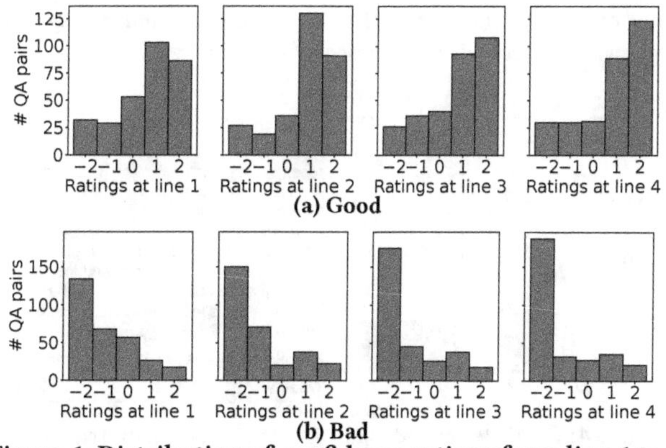

(a) Good

(b) Bad

Figure 1: Distribution of confidence ratings from line 1 to 4

In addition to the overall analysis presented above, we also focus on the level of individual QA pairs. Since each QA pair is annotated by three different turkers, we take the majority vote of the ratings at each line as the final rating. We plot the rating trends of individual QA pairs for a better illustration in Figure 3. We only plot the most commonly observed trends with more than two occurrences (in blue or red) to reduce noise. For example, if four QA pairs have the same trend of "0 $\rightarrow$ 1 $\rightarrow$ 2 $\rightarrow$ 2", we consider the occurrence of this trend as four. These common trends constitute about half of total trends. We also plot the remaining trends in gray to show that infrequent trends can be very diverse. The line widths are set to the square root of the trend occurrences to demonstrate trend frequency, while avoiding lines being too wide.

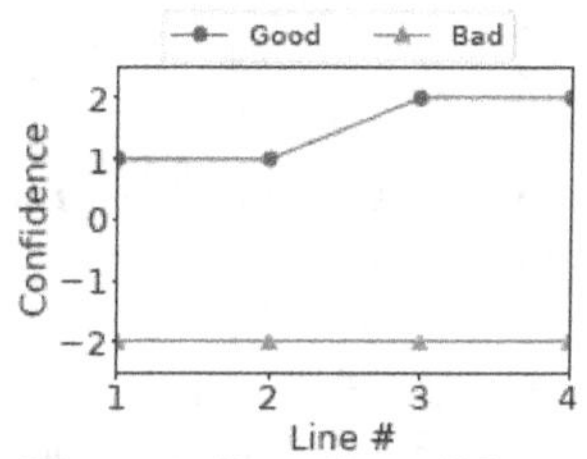

Figure 2: Overall confidence

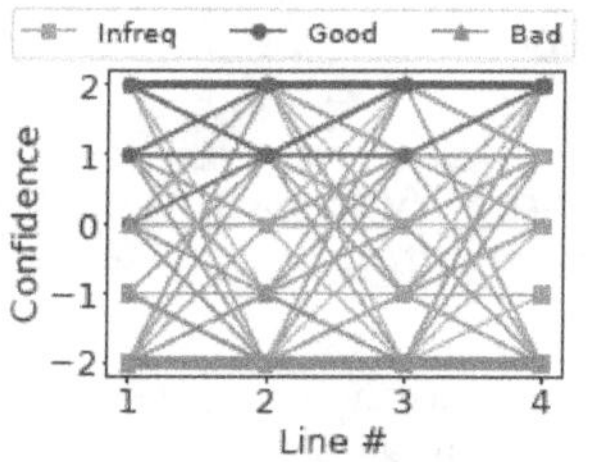

Figure 3: Common trends

As presented in the figure above, the common answer quality ratings start at (0, 1, 2) and converge to 2 for good answers. For bad answers, common ratings start at (0, -1, -2) and converge to -2. In addition, a large portion of good answers have consistent ratings of 2 at all lines. Similarly, a very common trend for bad answers is -2 at all lines. These observations indicate that *initial impressions of answer quality are usually correct, because good answers have positive ratings and bad answers have negative ratings from the very beginning. In addition, people become more and more confident about answer quality as they go through the answer.*

4.4 Passage Highlight

Turkers are instructed to rate the answer quality after highlighting the passage. Figure 4 presents the histogram of rated answer quality. We observe that turkers typically rate 1 or 2 for good answers and 0 for bad answers. This indicates that *turkers do not hesitate to rate a bad answer, but they can be severe on the answer quality judgments even in some cases where the passage is the answer.*

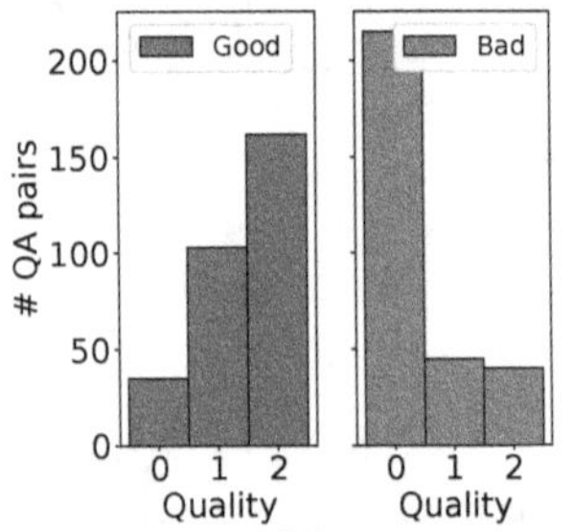

Figure 4: Confidence ratings for the second setting

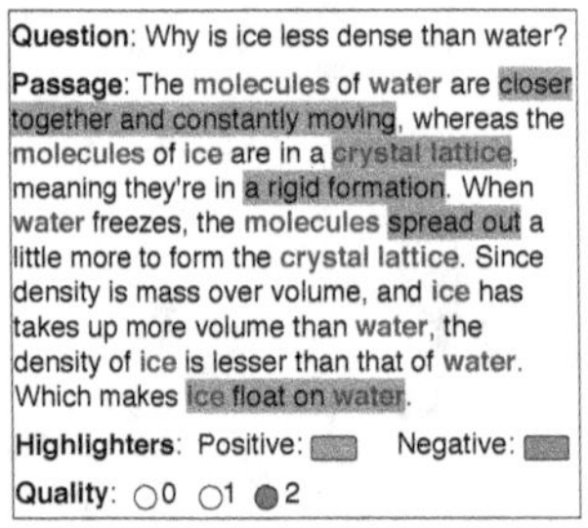

Figure 5: An illustration of the highlighting interface

On average, turkers highlight 7.57 words in good answers and 6.35 words in bad answers. In addition, the consistency rule adds about 0.5 words in both cases. Figure 6 presents the agreement of highlights in four different cases: positive highlight on good answers, positive highlight on bad answers, negative highlight on good answers, and negative highlight on bad answers.

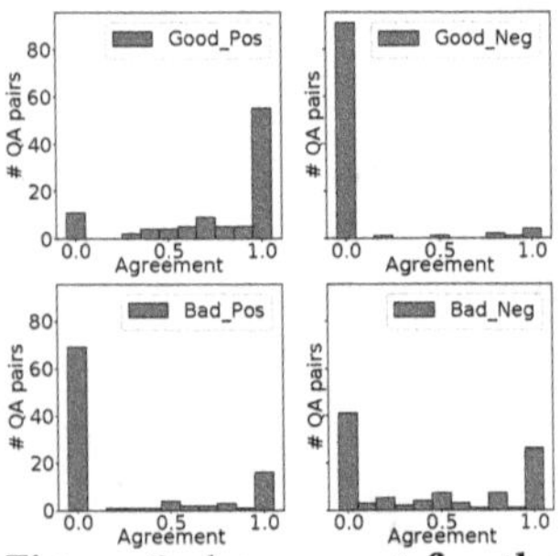

Figure 6: Agreement for the second setting

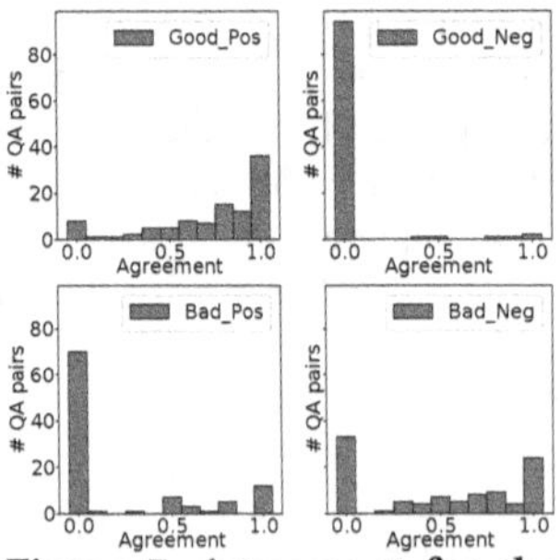

Figure 7: Agreement for the third setting

We notice the low agreement in Figures "Good_Neg" and "Bad_Pos". This can be accounted for by the fact that turkers rarely use negative highlights for good answers or positive highlights for bad answers. When one or both turkers in an agreement pair do not use a certain type of highlight (positive or negative), the agreement is 0 (turkers need to make at least one highlight, but they do not have to use both types of highlights). Therefore, we focus on positive highlights on good answers and negative highlights on bad answers. In the former case, more than half of the QA pairs achieve complete agreement, which means one turker's annotation is either exactly the same with or a subset of the other's. In the latter case, the agreement is fuzzy but it shows a total agreement in about 30% of the QA pairs. The results indicate that *people tend to get good agreement on what makes a good answer good. In contrast, when deciding what makes a bad answer bad, people tend to have more diverse opinions while still managing to achieve some agreement.*

4.5 Passage Highlighting with Suggested Words

In this setting, the distributions of answer quality ratings are very similar to the last setting, where the suggested words are unmarked.

We mark an average of 9.48 suggested words in special styles. The average number of highlighted words by turkers is 6.98 for good answers and 6.06 for bad answers, slightly smaller than the last setting. Overall, the agreement for the last setting (Figure 6) is more polarized while the agreement for this setting (Figure 7) has some distribution weight in the middle. These results indicate that some turkers may consider it unnecessary to highlight the marked words even when they believe the words are positive or negative.

One of the goals of this setting is to observe turkers' behavior under the impact of suggested words. This could be done by quantifying the agreement between highlights and suggested words with overlap coefficient. Figure 8 and 9 shows the results for Passage Highlight and Passage Highlighting with Suggested Words settings. They indicate that *turkers tend to base their decision more on the suggested words when these words are marked in special styles. This suggests that marking important words in answers could influence peoples' decision making process in answer quality evaluation.*

4.6 Answer Quality vs. QA Text Similarity

Some QA systems use the text similarity of questions and answers to perform answer retrieval [5, 35]. However, we show that answer quality is not the same as QA text similarity. We take the majority vote of overall ratings for each QA pair as the final answer quality rating. The rating data comes from the third setting (data from the second setting also gives a very similar result). To compute the text similarity between the question and answer in a QA pair, we obtain the tf-idf representations and the aggregated word embedding representations (the sum of the word embeddings in a passage). Then we calculate the cosine similarity for both representations respectively and compute their harmonic mean as the QA similarity measure. We plot the histogram of QA text similarity under each quality level in Figure 10.

We observe from the figure that the QA text similarity is relatively low in general for non-factoid QA. We further make three observations: (1) Quality level 2 has some high similarity values (such as 0.7 and 0.8), which are rare in quality level 1 and 0. (2) Quality level 0 has more low similarity (such as 0) QA pairs than the other two. (3) All three quality levels have large numbers of medium level similarities. These results indicate that *QA text similarity does not necessarily capture answer quality. They can be positively correlated when it comes to very similar or very different QA pairs. However, text similarity cannot determine answer quality effectively if the QA pair has medium level similarity.* For example, the QA pair shown in Figure 5 only has a text similarity of 0.56, but received quality level 2 ratings from all three turkers. We plan to investigate this in more detail in future work.

5 CONCLUSIONS

In this paper, we studied three different fine-grained answer presentation methods in a non-factoid QA setting. We also discovered that QA text similarity does not necessarily capture answer quality in this setting. Our findings are based on crowdsourcing and thus need to be generalized with caution. Our findings can be used in designing a more interactive IR system that emphasizes answer retrieval. Future work will include verifying our findings and exploring other answer interaction methods in a conversational setting.

ACKNOWLEDGMENTS

This work was supported in part by the Center for Intelligent Information Retrieval, NSF IIS-1715095 and ARC DP180102687. Any opinions, findings and conclusions or recommendations expressed in this material are those of the authors and do not necessarily reflect those of the sponsor.

REFERENCES

[1] IJsbrand Jan Aalbersberg. Incremental Relevance Feedback. In *SIGIR'92*, 1992.
[2] Eugene Agichtein, Eric Brill, Susan Dumais, and Robert Ragno. Learning User Interaction Models for Predicting Web Search Result Preferences. In *SIGIR'06*, 2006.
[3] Rakesh Agrawal, Sreenivas Gollapudi, Alan Halverson, and Samuel Ieong. Diversifying Search Results. In *WSDM'09*, 2009.
[4] Elinor Brondwine, Anna Shtok, and Oren Kurland. Utilizing Focused Relevance Feedback. In *SIGIR'16*, 2016.
[5] Daniel Cohen and W. Bruce Croft. End to End Long Short Term Memory Networks for Non-Factoid Question Answering. In *ICTIR'16*, 2016.
[6] Kevyn Collins-Thompson and Jamie Callan. Estimation and Use of Uncertainty in Pseudo-relevance Feedback. In *SIGIR'07*, 2007.
[7] W. Bruce Croft and Roger. H. Thompson. I^{3}R: A new approach to the design of document retrieval systems. *JASIS*, 1987.
[8] Fernando D. Diaz. Improving Relevance Feedback in Language Modeling with Score Regularization. In *SIGIR'08*, 2008.
[9] Mohit Iyyer, Jordan Boyd-Graber, Leonardo Claudino, Richard Socher, and Hal DaumÃĽ III. A Neural Network for Factoid Question Answering over Paragraphs. In *EMNLP'14*, 2014.
[10] Peter Jansen, Mihai Surdeanu, and Peter Clark. Discourse Complements Lexical Semantics for Non-factoid Answer Reranking. In *ACL*, 2014.
[11] Mostafa Keikha, Jae Hyun Park, W. Bruce Croft, and Mark Sanderson. Retrieving Passages and Finding Answers. In *ADCS'14*, 2014.
[12] Diane Kelly and Nicholas J. Belkin. Reading Time, Scrolling and Interaction: Exploring Implicit Sources of User Preferences for Relevance Feedback. In *SIGIR'01*, 2001.
[13] Jürgen Koenemann and Nicholas J. Belkin. A Case for Interaction: A Study of Interactive Information Retrieval Behavior and Effectiveness. In *CHI'96*, 1996.
[14] Victor Lavrenko and W. Bruce Croft. Relevance Based Language Models. In *SIGIR'01*, 2001.
[15] Yuanhua Lv and ChengXiang Zhai. Adaptive Relevance Feedback in Information Retrieval. In *CIKM'09*, 2009.
[16] Yuanhua Lv and ChengXiang Zhai. Positional Relevance Model for Pseudo-relevance Feedback. In *SIGIR'10*, 2010.
[17] Robert N Oddy. *Information Retrieval through Man-Machine Dialogue*. MCB UP Ltd, 1977.
[18] Jae Hyun Park and W. Bruce Croft. Using Key Concepts in a Translation Model for Retrieval. In *SIGIR'15*, 2015.
[19] Chen Qu, Liu Yang, W. Bruce Croft, Johanne R. Trippas, Yongfeng Zhang, and Minghui Qiu. Analyzing and Characterizing User Intent in Information-seeking Conversations. In *SIGIR'18*, 2018.
[20] Filip Radlinski and Nick Craswell. A Theoretical Framework for Conversational Search. In *CHIIR'17*, 2017.
[21] Rodrygo L. T. Santos, Craig Macdonald, and Iadh Ounis. Search Result Diversification. *Found. Trends Inf. Retr.*, 2015.
[22] Aliaksei Severyn and Alessandro Moschitti. Learning to Rank Short Text Pairs with Convolutional Deep Neural Networks. In *SIGIR'15*, 2015.
[23] Craig Silverstein, Hannes Marais, Monika Henzinger, and Michael Moricz. Analysis of a Very Large Web Search Engine Query Log. *SIGIR Forum*, 1999.
[24] Mihai Surdeanu, Massimiliano Ciaramita, and Hugo Zaragoza. Learning to Rank Answers on Large Online QA Collections. In *ACL:HLT'08*, 2008.
[25] Mihai Surdeanu, Massimiliano Ciaramita, and Hugo Zaragoza. Learning to Rank Answers to Non-factoid Questions from Web Collections. *Comput. Linguist.*, 2011.
[26] Paul Thomas, Daniel McDuff, Mary Czerwinski, and Nick Craswell. MISC: A Data Set of Information-seeking Conversations. In *CAIR'17*, 2017.
[27] Johanne R. Trippas, Damiano Spina, Lawrence Cavedon, Hideo Joho, and Mark Sanderson. Informing the Design of Spoken Conversational Search: Perspective Paper. In *CHIIR'18*, 2018.
[28] M.K. Vijaymeena and K. Kavitha. A Survey on Similarity Measures in Text Mining. *Machine Learning and Applications: An International Journal*, 2016.
[29] Yue Wang, Dawei Yin, Luo Jie, Pengyuan Wang, Makoto Yamada, Yi Chang, and Qiaozhu Mei. Beyond Ranking: Optimizing Whole-Page Presentation. In *WSDM'16*, 2016.
[30] Mei-Mei Wu and Ying-Hsang Liu. Intermediary's information seeking, inquiring minds, and elicitation styles. *Journal of the American Society for Information Science and Technology*, 2003.
[31] Mei-Mei Wu and Ying-Hsang Liu. On intermediaries' inquiring minds, elicitation styles, and user satisfaction. *Journal of the American Society for Information Science and Technology*, 2011.
[32] Xiaobing Xue, Jiwoon Jeon, and W. Bruce Croft. Retrieval Models for Question and Answer Archives. In *SIGIR'08*, 2008.
[33] Liu Yang, Minghui Qiu, Swapna Gottipati, Feida Zhu, Jing Jiang, Huiping Sun, and Zhong Chen. CQArank: Jointly Model Topics and Expertise in Community Question Answering. In *CIKM'13*, 2013.
[34] Liu Yang, Qingyao Ai, Jiafeng Guo, and W. Bruce Croft. aNMM: Ranking Short Answer Texts with Attention-Based Neural Matching Model. In *CIKM'16*, 2016.
[35] Liu Yang, Qingyao Ai, Damiano Spina, Ruey-Cheng Chen, Liang Pang, W. Bruce Croft, Jiafeng Guo, and Falk Scholer. Beyond Factoid QA: Effective Methods for Non-factoid Answer Sentence Retrieval. In *ECIR'16*, 2016.
[36] Liu Yang, Minghui Qiu, Chen Qu, Jiafeng Guo, Yongfeng Zhang, W. Bruce Croft, Jun Huang, and Haiqing Chen. Response ranking with deep matching networks and external knowledge in information-seeking conversation systems. In *SIGIR '18*, 2018.
[37] Scott Wen-tau Yih, Ming-Wei Chang, Chris Meek, and Andrzej Pastusiak. Question Answering Using Enhanced Lexical Semantic Models. In *ACL'13*, 2013.
[38] Lei Yu, Karl Moritz Hermann, Phil Blunsom, and Stephen Pulman. Deep Learning for Answer Sentence Selection. In *NIPS'14*, 2014.
[39] ChengXiang Zhai and John Lafferty. Model-based Feedback in the Language Modeling Approach to Information Retrieval. In *CIKM'01*, 2001.
[40] Yongfeng Zhang, Xu Chen, Qingyao Ai, Liu Yang, and W. Bruce Croft. Towards conversational search and recommendation: System ask, user respond. In *CIKM '18*, 2018.

A ADDITIONAL FIGURES

We include some additional figures to illustrate our findings from above. Figures 8 and 9 shows the agreement between turkers' annotations and the suggested words. The two figures correspond to the Passage Highlight and Passage Highlighting with Suggested words settings respectively. In addition, we plot the histogram of QA text similarity under each quality level in Figure 10.

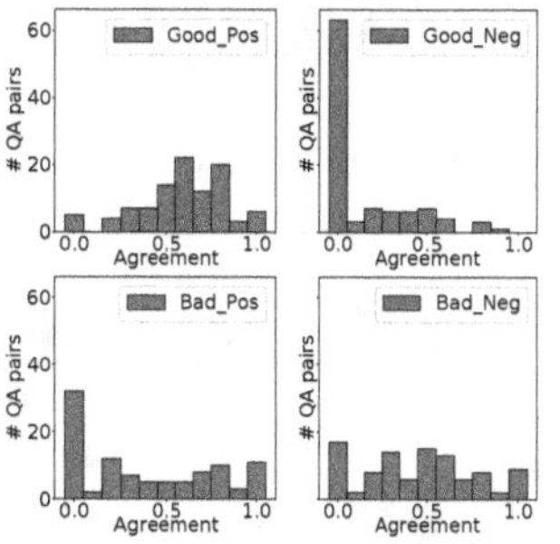

Figure 8: Suggestion overlap for the second setting

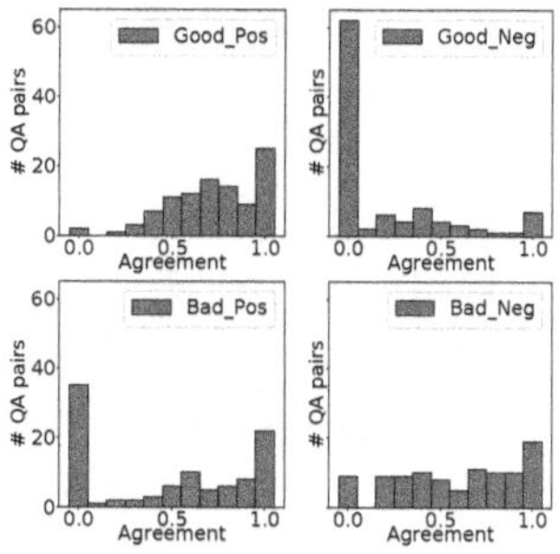

Figure 9: Suggestion overlap for the third setting

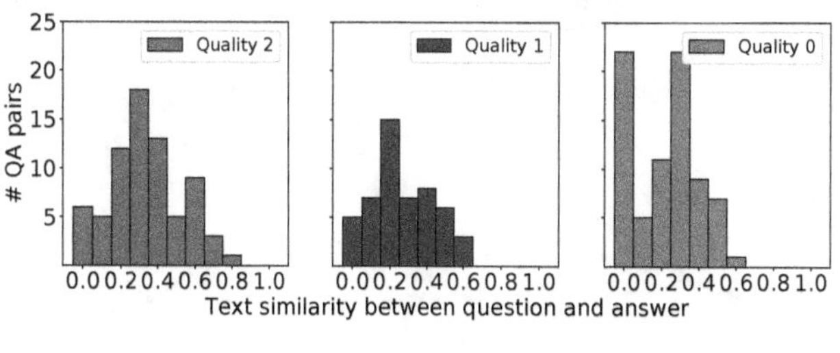

Figure 10: QA text similarity under each quality level

Stimulating Photo Curation on Smartphones

Xenia Zürn
University of Technology Sydney,
Eindhoven University of Technology
z.xenia@gmail.com

Mendel Broekhuijsen
Eindhoven University of Technology,
University of Technology Sydney
mendel@mendeldesign.nl

Doménique van Gennip
University of Technology Sydney,
Eindhoven University of Technology
domenique.vangennip@uts.edu.au

Saskia Bakker
University of Technology Sydney,
Eindhoven University of Technology
s.bakker@tue.nl

Annemarie Zijlema
University of Technology Sydney,
Eindhoven University of Technology
afzijlema@hotmail.com

Elise van den Hoven
University of Technology Sydney,
Eindhoven University of Technology,
University of Dundee
elise.vandenhoven@uts.edu.au

ABSTRACT

Personal photo collections have grown due to digital photography and the introduction of smartphones, and photo collections have become harder to manage. Deleting photos appears to be difficult and the task of curation is often perceived as not enjoyable. The lack of curation can make it harder to retrieve photos when people need them for various reasons, such as individual reminiscing, shared remembering or self-presentation. In this study we investigate how we can stimulate people to organise their photo collections on their smartphones. Ten participants evaluated and qualitatively compared four applications with different characteristics regarding voting on and deleting photos. We found that voting on photos is easier and more enjoyable in comparison to deleting photos, that participants showed reminiscence while organising, that deleting can be frustrating, that participants have different preferences for sorting and viewing photos and that voting could make deleting and retrieving easier.

CCS CONCEPTS

- Information systems~Users and interactive retrieval
- Human-centered computing~Interaction design
- Human-centered computing~Smartphones

KEYWORDS: Photo Curation, Smartphone, Interaction Design, Design Research

ACM Reference format:
Xenia Zürn, Mendel Broekhuijsen, Doménique van Gennip, Saskia Bakker, Annemarie Zijlema, Elise van den Hoven. 2019. Stimulating Photo Curation on Smartphones. In *Proceedings of ACM Conference on Human Information Interaction and Retrieval (CHIIR'19). March 10–14, 2019, Glasgow, Scotland UK.* ACM, NY, NY, USA, 9 pages. https://doi.org/10.1145/3295750.3298947

CHIIR '19, March 10–14, 2019, Glasgow, Scotland Uk

ACM ISBN 978-1-4503-6025-8/19/03...$15.00
https://doi.org/10.1145/3295750.3298947

INTRODUCTION

Over the past decades, personal photo collections have grown in size due to the rise of digital photography and reduced cost of storage [1,18,30]. The way people interact with personal photos has changed since the introduction of digital photography and especially camera phones that further increased the size of personal photo collections [14,22–24]. Due to their ever-expanding volume, it is increasingly difficult to manage personal photo collections [30]. People find deleting their photos difficult and would rather keep most of them [e.g.,15,18,29]. Moreover, the sheer number of photos makes curation a daunting task. People seem to be discouraged to curate their collections due to a perceived lack of expertise and time to manage a large collection [18,28,30]. People also suffer from a lack of motivation because curation is considered to be a chore, which is neither creative nor rewarding [26]. As a consequence, people experience difficulties retrieving valuable photos from their collections [30].
The study of people's curation activities of personal photos, as presented in this paper, is part of the research area 'Personal Information Management' (PIM). PIM involves the study of managing personal information, which besides photos includes emails, bookmarks and personal files [e.g.,3,11,17], and differs from other information management practices in that people have to curate for their future selves [2]. The curation of personal information is a pro-active activity and therefore often postponed or ignored [16].
This paper discusses a comparison study of four mobile applications that help to prune one's photo collections. We focus on the smartphone because for many people it has become their primary device for photo activities [14,22–24]. However, curating on smartphones is still rare and open for further investigation [33]. Following Broekhuijsen et al. in their PhotoUse model [5], we focus on organising (i.e., tagging, moving, categorizing, naming, captioning, archiving, and deleting) within the broader activity of curation. The present study took the challenge to leverage interaction design as a means to stimulate people to organise their photo collections on smartphones. Hereby, we investigate how voting on photos rather than deleting these could stimulate the organisation of personal collections.

RELATED WORK

This section describes research from Human-Computer Interaction and Computer-Supported Collaborative Work that relates to interaction with and curation of digital photo collections using mobile devices.

In a study by Ott, Hebecker, and Wakes [25] three interaction concepts, aimed at engaging people with their personal digital photos, were evaluated. The authors had difficulty in identifying specific design factors that focus on entertainment and play. While their study focused on management and presentation of personal digital photographs, it did not address the user experience of organising photos as we do in this paper.

There are a few examples that focus on group curation, but do not address the organisation of personal collections [e.g.,6,21,27]. GrayArea by Bergman et al. [1] is an example that is more closely related to the practices of deleting unwanted files in personal digital collections. It introduces a new kind of deleting of files called demoting, temporary hiding it from view instead of throwing it away, using the metaphor of storing physical items in an attic. Although not intended for just photos, it helps us to reflect on the way we interact with digital information. Demoting can be seen as organising in phases because it formalises a process where people do not delete photos right away, but place them in a digital attic for later disposal.

The related work makes clear that the design of photo use devices leaves room to explore how we can decrease mental effort of making organisational decisions while organising our personal digital collections. Because organising is usually perceived as a daunting but relatively unrewarding task, we believe that applications that support organising should not only reduce the mental effort of the activity but also enhance the experience itself. Organising photos is usually performed during leisure time and we argue that an efficient and pleasant experience may motivate people to drive improvements in the organisational state of personal photo collections.

STUDY

This study qualitatively compares four smartphone applications to explore how interaction design elements support and stimulate the organisation of personal photos. As described above, existing applications are limited in use because there is significant mental effort [15,18,29] in organising photo collections and a lack of enjoyment in the organising task itself [26]. Therefore, we compare two existing smartphone applications designed for viewing, selecting, and deleting one's photos and complement these with two applications designed to decrease effort and to increase enjoyment while organising.

Voting application

Decisions to delete photos are hard because these are irreversible, thus we reason that merely voting on photos could make the organisation task easier. We designed the Voting application in which users vote photos up or down using swiping gestures. Because swiping gestures can increase enjoyment and can positively influence reuse intentions [7,9], we implemented the swiping gesture for decision making in the Voting application. The Voting application has some conceptual overlap with the Photo-triage application by Drucker et al. [10]. In the Voting application (Figure 1A), participants can swipe right or press the 'up arrow button' to vote photos up (Figure 1C) and swipe left or press the 'down arrow button' to vote photos down (Figure 1B). Photos are 'down voted' or 'up voted' instead of kept or deleted.

A B C

Figure 1. Upvoting and downvoting photos with the Voting application. 1A: main view with downvote and upvote buttons; 1B: downvote a photo; 1C: upvote a photo.

Dilemma Voting application

Showing digital content in a random manner can evoke serendipity [19]. People are willing to give up direct control over what they see in return for the enjoyment of surprising interactions [31]. Frohlich et al. [13] suggest that serendipitous browsing should be stimulated since the most powerful instances of reinterpretation occur after seeing a photo in an unexpected manner. They also suggest that seeing a photo in an unexpected juxtaposition with other photos might trigger reinterpretation. To see whether random display of photos in unexpected juxtapositions while organising can increase enjoyment, we designed the Dilemma Voting application. This application (Figure 2A) asks a participant to choose between two random photos by tapping the most valued photo. While pressing a photo, a 'flash dot' is shown on the pressed photo (Figure 2B).

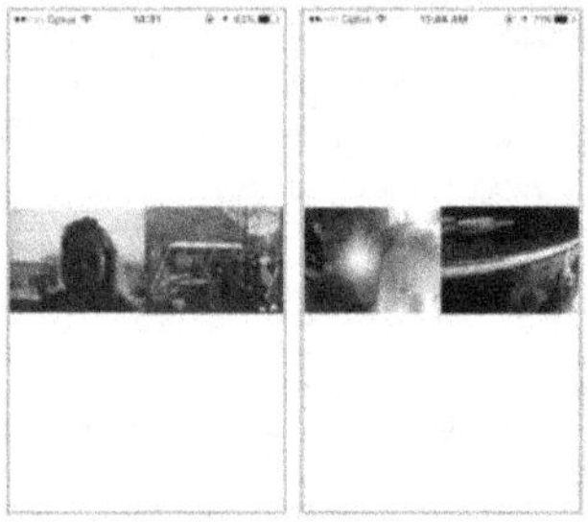

A B

Figure 2. Upvoting and downvoting photos with the Dilemma Voting application. 2A: main view; 2B: showing a flash dot (in this case on the left photo) when upvoting a photo by touching it.

After that, two new random photos are shown. In order to decrease mental effort, photos are 'downvoted' or 'upvoted' instead of kept or deleted.

Next to the two designed apps we described above, we used two commercially available applications during the study: 1) the default Photos application on Apple iOS9, allowing a comparison to the status quo, and 2) the application Pare Down [12]. The latter is very similar to our own Voting application, however, instead of voting photos up or down, photos are kept or deleted. As part of this study, we invite participants to comment on an idea for the visualisation of the voting data, which we call the Voted Gallery, because only voting on photos does not make a photo collection more manageable, if the voting metadata is not put to good use.

Voted Gallery

The Voted Gallery has features similar to a typical camera roll view on smartphones, showing thumbnails of the photos in chronological order. People prefer this way of viewing photos on their smartphones because it provides an overview and context for the photos [28,33]. Moreover, other studies found that people use context (i.e. event-based browsing) and thumbnail view in order to retrieve photos [18,30] and that this way of viewing can help to make decisions on what to keep [32]. The Voted Gallery differs from the camera roll view because it displays thumbnails of upvoted photos bigger and downvoted photos smaller. The size of the thumbnails correspond with the number of upvotes or downvotes, which could be helpful for people to find the valued photos among their collections, also echoing Petrelli and Whittaker's suggestion that a "distinction between an implicit favourite and the rest of a collection could promote new and engaging ways of revisiting" [26, p.167].

Participants

Participants were recruited from the personal and professional network of the researchers, and invited to participate via email. They were required to own a smartphone containing at least 600 digital photos. Ten people participated (7 women), aged 22-55 (M=28.9, SD=8.9). Six participants were native English speakers and the other four had comparable language skills.

Procedure

Participants were asked to bring 600 most recent (unsorted) photos from their smartphone photo collection. After participants signed a consent sheet, a subset of 150 photos were selected by the researcher and uploaded to the smartphone that was used for this study (Apple iPhone 5). After a short explanation of the smartphone application, the participants used the smartphone application for ten minutes, or until all photos were sorted. This process was repeated for all four applications, using a new set of 150 photos from the participant for each application. For each participant, the order of using the applications was randomised. Afterwards, a semi-structured interview probed participants for their experiences while using the applications and asked them to compare the applications. To stimulate the conversation but not miss out on unprompted ideas, we introduced the Voted Gallery after ranking the applications and after probing participants for the perceived usefulness of voting applications. Each session lasted for about 1.5 hours. Interviews were transcribed and selectively coded. We used thematic analysis to interpret the data and find common themes [4].

FINDINGS

Our analysis led to themes regarding the experience of voting and deleting, game elements, reminiscence, sorting preferences, combining voting and deleting, and how people's associations influence curation practices. In this section we will elaborate on these themes.

As expected, we found that voting on photos is easier and more enjoyable in comparison to deleting photos. Participants regarded deleting photos as something practical that needs to be done and therefore not that enjoyable. Voting on photos is regarded more positive. Also, as P3 and P7 illustrate, the limited impact of errors in voting makes that voting on photos is more enjoyable in comparison to deleting photos: *"I think deleting is something practical, that's something you do when [...] memory is full, I have to delete photos. Upvoting is something you do because you want to do it and not because it's practical."* (P7). And P3: *"[The Voting application] I found sort of enjoyable, [Pare Down] I also found enjoyable [...] but it felt like it was a bit sort of cutthroat because I was actually deleting things."*

A more enjoyable organising experience was also supported through the game elements of curiosity, discovery and challenge [20]. Participants' curiosity arose while using the swiping applications and the Dilemma Voting application while exploring their photo collection. Challenge, "the experience of suspense transforming into ecstatic release once some obstacle is overcome" [20, p.3], was observed by participants when using the Dilemma Voting application to choose between two photos. As P10 said: *"Quick, show me what's next, what's next, what's next! It's good fun,"* and P1: *"I also enjoyed picking, even though it was frustrating."*

We noted that participants showed signs of positive reminiscence during and after using the applications. This implies that organising photos is not only a way to improve reminiscence due to a better organised photo collection but that reminiscence also takes place while organising: *"I enjoyed the experience of [using the Voting application]. I found it fun, I really liked the fact that it allowed you to revisit those memories and I think that that in itself is a really nice experience, I want to do it again,"*(P3).

Nine participants considered the standard application to be the least enjoyable to use. They felt too much of a barrier to delete photos, which annoyed or even frustrated the participants: *"It really annoys me that when you bin it and then it asks you 'are you sure you want to delete this photo?' again. So it's twice you have to hit it,"*(P2).

Some participants liked the Dilemma Voting application for its approach to photo sorting, since one photo provides the reference for the other photo. However, others found the Dilemma Voting application not useful for sorting photos because it did not cater to their preferred way of sorting photos. This led to suggestions that the Dilemma Voting application would be more useful if it only rates photos of the same event or category, or to compare duplicates. As P4 put it: *"So if I had a hundred photos [of a party] and I compared a lot of them during the night [using the Dilemma Voting application] and after I would have them ranked, I would create an album with that and post it on Facebook or Instagram."*

Voting between two photos indeed posed a dilemma at times: *"Sometimes I felt like I was having to leave a very nice photo behind and sometimes I was having to pick a not so nice photo,"* (P3). Participants compared the content of the photos instead of comparing the quality of the photos. This also highlights that the photos were seen as representative of participants' associations: *"This isn't fair. I've got a beautiful family moment [versus] my boyfriend looking like a dog... I can't compare them!"* (P1).

Several participants considered voting on photos prior to deleting photos valuable. They saw how the Voting application in combination with the Voted Gallery could help them to make deleting decisions. Moreover, three participants mentioned that they would be interested to see how they would rank their photos over time: *"Then I can actually see over time which photos I actually do like as opposed to me telling myself I like them. It's like the coat hanger trick when you're sorting through all your extra clothes. You hang it backwards and when you wear it, you turn it back the normal way. So at the end, you can actually see which clothes you wear and [which to] get rid of,"* (P1). Furthermore, participants mentioned that the Voted Gallery could help them to find photos and show photos to friends. This is in line with other studies suggesting that creating an attractive presentation of one's favourite photos in order to share them is a key motivation to organise photos [25,28].

DISCUSSION & CONCLUSION

The present study indicates that people have different desires at different moments regarding the organisation of photos on their smartphone. For example, some people preferred the Dilemma Voting application and others the Voting application in order to organise their photos. People would also like to view photos in the Voted Gallery differently, since they would like to use it for different reasons (e.g., deleting versus showing photos to others). This is also in line with a study by Cosley et al. in which users pointed out that they would like to have control over when and how they view memory triggers [6]. Furthermore, we noticed that participants reminisce while organising and that some participants were quite frustrated about deleting photos with the default iOS application. Thus, we believe that multiple options to organise photo collections should be provided in order to fit more users. For example, the reminiscence experience and its occurrence during organising should be considered in future designs.

In this study, participants brought a copy of their photos and might therefore not have been hesitant to delete their photos during the organising task. Although we asked whether they would perform differently on their own phone or without a backup, the current findings are indicative only. Participants used the four applications with a new set of photos for each application. We did this because the participants could experience serendipity in each of the applications and would not get bored with viewing each set of photos four times. However, the photos in each set differ and thus might evoke different emotions, which could have influenced the experience of using the applications.

In this study we investigated the use of four applications within a lab setting, with each application only used for about ten minutes. We gained insights about which aspects of the applications could stimulate organisation of personal photo collections. However, the only way to validate the theoretical assumptions and test if these aspects really stimulate organisation, the applications would need to be developed further and tested long-term. It would be worthwhile to evaluate an application that uses a voting system in combination with our Voted Gallery concept to see if our design assumptions still hold in everyday use and to what extent it will stimulate organisation photo collections. For example, voting on photos might increase people's awareness of the photos they do not value enough to keep, which could reduce the perceived effort of deleting those photos and contribute to the overall value of their photo collections.

The results presented in this paper support using a voting system for organising our personal digital photo collections on smartphones. The results indicate that a voting system could support the deleting of photos and also could improve retrieving of our photo collections. Furthermore, we found that a voting system, introduction of a Voted Gallery, implementation of the swiping gesture and randomness in displaying photos can increase the enjoyment of the organising practice and therefore could stimulate curation of our personal digital photo collections. Despite the small sample size, we believe our findings provide valuable insights for the design of novel photo organising applications on smartphones.

ACKNOWLEDGMENTS

We thank all the participants for their contribution to our study. This research was supported by STW VIDI grant number 016.128.303 of The Netherlands Organisation for Scientific Research (NWO), awarded to Elise van den Hoven. The study was approved by the UTS Research Ethics Committee under REF ETH16-855.

REFERENCES

[1] Ofer Bergman, Simon Tucker, Ruth Beyth-Marom, Edward Cutrell, and Steve Whittaker. 2009. It's Not That Important: Demoting Personal Information of Low Subjective Importance Using GrayArea. In *Proceedings of the SIGCHI Conference on Human Factors in Computing Systems* (CHI '09), 269–278. DOI: https://doi.org/10.1145/1518701.1518745

[2] Ofer Bergman and Steve Whittaker. 2016. *The Science of Managing our Digital Stuff.* MIT Press, Cambridge, MA. DOI: https://doi.org/10.1002/asi.23870.

[3] Richard Boardman and M. Angela Sasse. 2004. "Stuff Goes into the Computer and Doesn't Come Out" A Cross-tool Study of Personal Information Management. In *Proceedings of the SIGCHI conference on Human factors in computing systems (CHI'04).* ACM Press, Vienna, Austria, 583-590. DOI: https://doi.org/10.1.1.115.3372.

[4] Virginia Braun and Victoria Clarke. 2006. Using thematic analysis in psychology. Qualitative Research in Psychology 3, 2: 77–101. DOI: https://doi.org/10.1191/1478088706qp063oa

[5] Mendel Broekhuijsen, Elise van den Hoven, and Panos Markopoulos. 2017. From PhotoWork to PhotoUse: exploring personal digital photo activities. Behaviour & Information Technology 36, 7: 754–767. DOI: https://doi.org/10.1080/0144929X.2017.1288266

[6] Frederik Brudy, Steven Houben, Nicolai Marquardt, and Yvonne Rogers. 2016. CurationSpace: Cross-Device Content Curation Using Instrumental Interaction. In *Proceedings of the 2016 ACM International Conference on Interactive Surfaces and Spaces (ISS '16),* 159–168. DOI: https://doi.org/10.1145/2992154.2992175

[7] Ben C F Choi, Samuel N Kirshner, and Yi Wu. 2016. Swiping vs. Scrolling in Mobile Shopping Applications. In HCI in Business, Government, and Organizations: eCommerce and Innovation, 177–188.

[8] Dan Cosley, Kathy Akey, Brian Alson, Jonathan Baxter, Mark Broomfield, Soyoung Lee, and Chethan Sarabu. 2009. Using Technologies to Support Reminiscence. In *Proceedings of the 23rd British HCI Group Annual Conference on People and Computers: Celebrating People and Technology (BCS-HCI '09),* 480–484.

[9] Xue Dou and S Shyam Sundar. 2016. Power of the Swipe: Why Mobile Websites Should Add Horizontal Swiping to Tapping, Clicking, and Scrolling Interaction Techniques. International Journal of Human–Computer Interaction 32, 4: 352–362. DOI: https://doi.org/10.1080/10447318.2016.1147902

[10] Steven Drucker, Curtis Wong, Asta Roseway, Steve Glenner, and Steve De Mar. 2003. Photo-triage: Rapidly annotating your digital photographs. Tech. rep., Microsoft Research Technical Report, MSR-TR-2003-99.

[11] David Elsweiler and Ian Ruthven. 2007. Towards task-based personal information management evaluations. In *Proceedings of the 30th annual international ACM SIGIR conference on Research and development in information retrieval.* ACM Press, Amsterdam, the Netherlands, 23-30. DOI: https://doi.org/10.1145/1277741.1277748.

[12] Fly Soup. 2014. Pare Down. Retrieved from https://itunes.apple.com/nl/app/pare-down-photo-album-editor/id914281628?mt=8

[13] David M Frohlich, Steven Wall, and Graham Kiddle. 2013. Rediscovery of Forgotten Images in Domestic Photo Collections. Personal Ubiquitous Comput. 17, 4: 729–740. DOI: https://doi.org/10.1007/s00779-012-0612-4

[14] Lisa Gye. 2007. Picture This: the Impact of Mobile Camera Phones on Personal Photographic Practices. Continuum 21, 2: 279–288. DOI: https://doi.org/10.1080/10304310701269107

[15] Nancy Van House and Elizabeth F Churchill. 2008. Technologies of memory: Key issues and critical perspectives. Memory Studies 1, 3: 295–310. DOI: https://doi.org/10.1177/1750698008093795

[16] William Jones. 2007. Personal Information Management. *Annual Review of Information Science and Technology (ARIST),* 41, 1, 453-504. DOI: https://doi.org/10.1002/aris.2007.1440410117.

[17] William Jones, Ammy Jiranida Phuwanartnurak, Rajdeep Gill and Harry Bruce. 2005. Don't take my folders away! Organizing personal information to get things done. *CHI'05 extended abstracts on Human factors in computing systems.* ACM Press, Portland, Oregon USA, 1505-1508. DOI: https://doi.org/10.1145/1056808.1056952.

[18] David Kirk, Abigail Sellen, Carsten Rother, and Ken Wood. 2006. Understanding Photowork. In *Proceedings of the SIGCHI Conference on Human Factors in Computing Systems (CHI '06),* 761–770. DOI: https://doi.org/10.1145/1124772.1124885

[19] Tuck Leong, Steve Howard, and Frank Vetere. 2008. Choice: Abidcating or Exercising? *In Proceedings of the SIGCHI Conference on Human Factors in Computing Systems (CHI '08),* 715–724. DOI: https://doi.org/10.1145/1357054.1357168

[20] Craig A Lindley and Charlotte C Sennersten. 2008. Game Play Schemas: From Player Analysis to Adaptive Game Mechanics. Int. J. Comput. Games Technol. 2008: 8:1--8:7. DOI: https://doi.org/10.1155/2008/216784

[21] Andrés Lucero, Jussi Holopainen, and Tero Jokela. 2011. Pass-them-around: Collaborative Use of Mobile Phones for Photo Sharing. In Proceedings of the SIGCHI Conference on Human Factors in Computing Systems (CHI '11), 1787–1796. DOI: https://doi.org/10.1145/1978942.1979201

[22] Effie Le Moignan, Shaun Lawson, Duncan A Rowland, Jamie Mahoney, and Pam Briggs. 2017. Has Instagram Fundamentally Altered the "Family Snapshot"? In Proceedings of the 2017 CHI Conference on Human Factors in Computing Systems (CHI '17), 4935–4947. DOI: https://doi.org/10.1145/3025453.3025928

[23] Susan Murray. 2008. Digital Images, Photo-Sharing, and Our Shifting Notions of Everyday Aesthetics. Journal of Visual Culture 7, 2: 147–163. DOI: https://doi.org/10.1177/1470412908091935

[24] Virginia Nightingale. 2007. The Cameraphone and Online Image Sharing. Continuum 21, 2: 289–301. DOI: https://doi.org/10.1080/10304310701278157

[25] Claudia Ott, Ralf Hebecker, and Sarah Wakes. 2012. Picture the Space: Three Concepts for Management and Presentation of Personal Digital Photographs. In Proceedings of the 13th International Conference of the NZ Chapter of the ACM's Special Interest Group on Human-Computer Interaction (CHINZ '12), 1–8. DOI: https://doi.org/10.1145/2379256.2379258

[26] Daniela Petrelli and Steve Whittaker. 2010. Family Memories in the Home: Contrasting Physical and Digital Mementos. Personal Ubiquitous Comput. 14, 2: 153–169. DOI: https://doi.org/10.1007/s00779-009-0279-7

[27] Martin Porcheron, Andrés Lucero, and Joel E Fischer. 2016. Co-curator: Designing for Mobile Ideation in Groups. In Proceedings of the 20th International Academic Mindtrek Conference (AcademicMindtrek '16), 226–234. DOI: https://doi.org/10.1145/2994310.2994350

[28] Kerry Rodden and Kenneth R Wood. 2003. How Do People Manage Their Digital Photographs? In Proceedings of the SIGCHI Conference on Human Factors in Computing Systems (CHI '03), 409–416. DOI: https://doi.org/10.1145/642611.642682

[29] Steve Whittaker. 2013. Personal information management: From information consumption to curation. Annual Review of Information Science and Technology 45, 1: 1–62. DOI: https://doi.org/10.1002/aris.2011.1440450108

[30] Steve Whittaker, Ofer Bergman, and Paul Clough. 2010. Easy on That Trigger Dad: A Study of Long Term Family Photo Retrieval. Personal Ubiquitous Comput. 14, 1: 31–43. DOI: https://doi.org/10.1007/s00779-009-0218-7

[31] John Williamson and Lorna M Brown. 2008. Flutter: Directed Random Browsing of Photo Collections with a Tangible Interface. In Proceedings of the 7th ACM Conference on Designing Interactive Systems (DIS '08), 147–155. DOI: https://doi.org/10.1145/1394445.1394461

[32] Maria K Wolters, Elaine Niven, and Robert H Logie. 2014. The Art of Deleting Snapshots. In CHI '14 Extended Abstracts on Human Factors in Computing Systems (CHI EA '14), 2521–2526. DOI: https://doi.org/10.1145/2559206.2581287

[33] Xenia Zürn, Koen Damen, Fabienne van Leiden, Mendel Broekhuijsen, and Panos Markopoulos. 2018. Photo Curation Practices on Smartphones. In Proceedings of ACE 2017: 14th International Conference on Advances in Computer Entertainment Technology, 406–414. DOI: https://doi.org/10.1007/978-3-319-76270-8_28

The Effects of Working Memory during Search Tasks of Varying Complexity

Bogeum Choi, Robert Capra, Jaime Arguello
University of North Carolina at Chapel Hill
{choiboge,rcapra,jarguello}@unc.edu

ABSTRACT

We report on a study that evaluated the effects of working memory and task complexity on participants' perceptions, behaviors, and outcomes. Twenty-four participants performed two search tasks of varying complexity and completed a psychometric test to measure working memory ability. Our results found several important trends. First, task complexity had an effect on participants' perceptions about temporal demand and satisfaction with the time spent on the task. Second, participants with higher working memory exerted more search effort (e.g., issued more queries). Third, participants with higher working memory had better outcomes, particularly during more complex tasks. Finally, while participants with lower working memory exerted less effort (engaged in satisficing behaviors) and had weaker outcomes, working memory did not affect participants' post-task perceptions about workload and satisfaction. We discuss implications of our results for developing search tools to support users with varying levels of working memory.

KEYWORDS

Working memory; task complexity; search behavior

ACM Reference Format:

Bogeum Choi, Robert Capra, Jaime Arguello. 2019. The Effects of Working Memory during Search Tasks of Varying Complexity. In *2019 Conference on Human Information Interaction and Retrieval (CHIIR '19), March 10–14, 2019, Glasgow, Scotland Uk.* ACM, New York, NY, USA, 5 pages. https://doi.org/10.1145/3295750.3298948

1 INTRODUCTION

In recent years, there has been a growing interest in better understanding how characteristics of individual users can influence search behaviors and outcomes. Studies have considered personality traits such as need for cognition (i.e., a person's disposition to engage with cognitively demanding activities) [32], as well as cognitive abilities such as perceptual speed [8, 28], visualization ability [8], visual memory [28], and working memory [16–18]. The end goal of this body of research is to better understand how search systems can best support users with different cognitive profiles.

We report on a laboratory study ($N = 24$) that investigated the effects of working memory and task complexity on participants' perceptions, behaviors, and outcomes. Participants in the study completed two *comparative tasks* of varying levels of complexity. Each task asked the participant to compare a set of items (or alternatives) along a set of dimensions (or attributes). To complete each task, participants were instructed to: (1) use a custom-built search engine to find information for all items and dimensions given in the task description, (2) enter information into a table consisting of items (rows) and dimensions (columns), (3) make a final item selection, and (4) provide a justification/explanation for their choice. Our manipulation of task complexity involved varying the number of items and dimensions participants were explicitly asked to consider as part of the comparative task (i.e., 2×2 vs. 4×4).

Our study investigated the following three research questions:

RQ1: What are the effects of working memory and task complexity on participants' post-task perceptions about their performance? Specifically, we focused on participants' perceived levels of workload and satisfaction with their task outcomes and strategies.

RQ2: What are the effects of working memory and task complexity on participants' search behaviors? Specifically, we focused on measures associated with the amount of search effort and the pace of interaction.

RQ3: What are the effects of working memory and task complexity on participants' search outcomes? Specifically, we focused on participants' ability to address all combinations of items/dimensions associated with the task and the justification length.

2 RELATED WORK

Our research builds on prior studies on the effects of working memory and task complexity on search behaviors and outcomes.

Working Memory: Working memory is defined as someone's ability to hold information in short-term memory and to work with information that is no longer perceptually present [13]. Working memory is said to be a core executive function that is critical for making sense of anything that unfolds over time (e.g., inferring relations between items and ideas) [13]. In this respect, working memory impacts higher-level cognitive skills such as reasoning [5, 23], reading comprehension [12, 24] and problem-solving [19, 31].

Several studies have considered the impact of working memory on search behaviors. Gwizdka [16, 17] investigated the effects of working memory (WM) and task complexity on participants' behaviors while interacting with two different search interfaces. Both interfaces returned a ranked list of search results, but one interface (the *overview* interface) also presented tag clouds with clickable terms for users to filter the search results. In less demanding situations (i.e., during simple tasks using the *overview* system), high-WM participants completed tasks faster than low-WM participants. Conversely, in more demanding situations (i.e., during complex tasks using the baseline system), high-WM participants expended more effort than low-WM participants. In a later study, Gwizdka [18] compared the search behaviors of high- and low-WM

ACM ISBN 978-1-4503-6025-8/19/03...$15.00
https://doi.org/10.1145/3295750.3298948

participants while performing complex search tasks. While high- and low-WM participants had similar completion times, high-WM participants performed more actions and spent more time reading content pages (especially towards the end of the search session). Consistent with previous findings [16, 17], these results suggest that low-WM participants may be more likely to engage in satisficing behaviors during mentally demanding tasks.

Prior studies have also compared the search behaviors of dyslexic and non-dyslexic searchers [14, 25]. While dyslexia is a heterogeneous condition, evidence suggests a strong correlation between dyslexia and lower phonological working memory (i.e., the ability to hold words in short-term memory) [6, 7, 11, 25, 26]. MacFarlane *et al.* [25] examined the search behaviors of dyslexic and non-dyslexic students, and found that non-dyslexic students examined more documents and judged a greater percentage of documents as non-relevant. In other words, non-dyslexic students were more "selective" in their relevance judgments. Additionally, Fourney et al. [14] compared relevance judgments from dyslexic versus non-dyslexic study participants, and found that relevance judgments from dyslexic participants had a greater central tendency (i.e., were less bi-modal). Consistent with MacFarlane *et al.* [25], non-dyslexic participants were more "selective" in their relevance judgments.

Task Complexity: Task complexity has been defined and manipulated from different perspectives [29]. Campbell [9] characterized task complexity in terms of: (1) the number of required outcomes, (2) the number possible paths to the outcomes, (3) the level of uncertainty about the paths, and (4) the degree of interdependence between the paths. Jansen [21] proposed that search task complexity can be viewed through the lens of *cognitive complexity*, which relates to the amount of mental effort and learning required to complete the task. Jansen *et al.* [21] and Kelly *et al.* [22] used Anderson and Krathwohl's taxonomy of learning outcomes [2] to develop tasks of varying complexity levels. Using this framework, studies have found that more cognitively complex tasks have greater levels of expected pre-task difficulty [10, 20, 22], experienced post-task difficulty [3, 10, 20, 22], search effort [3, 10, 20–22], and greater diversity of query reformulation strategies [30].

In this paper, we used comparative tasks, which fall under *analyze* tasks (intermediate complexity) within the cognitive complexity framework. Our manipulation of task complexity involved increasing the number of items and dimensions for participants to consider (2×2 vs. 4×4). Based on Campbell's view of task complexity [9], our 4×4 tasks had more outcomes, more paths to the outcomes, and possibly more interdependence between paths.

3 USER STUDY

To investigate our three research questions, we conducted a laboratory study with 24 participants (18 females). Participants were recruited using an opt-in mailing list of employees at our university. Participants were asked to complete two comparative tasks that involved using a web search engine to find information. A comparative task is one that involves comparing a set of items across a set of dimensions. For example, a comparative "car shopping" task might require comparing different models across dimensions such as price, safety features, and fuel efficiency. During each comparative task, participants were given specific items and dimensions to consider. To complete each task, participants were required to complete two sub-tasks. First, participants were asked to search for information in order to complete a table of *n* rows (items) and *n* columns (dimensions). Second, participants were asked to make a final item selection and write a justification for their choice based on the information found during their search.

Independent Variables: The study involved two independent variables: working memory and task complexity. Working memory was a between-subjects factor. As described below, we measured working memory capacity using the "operation-word-span" (OSPAN) test [27]. To study the effects of working memory (WM), participants were split into low- and high-WM groups using a median split. Task complexity was a within-subjects variable. We manipulated task complexity by varying the number of items and dimensions for participants to consider as part of the task. Simple tasks required comparing 2 items along 2 dimensions (i.e., a 2×2 table), and complex tasks required comparing 4 items along 4 dimensions (i.a., a 4×4 table). Each participant completed one simple and one complex task.

Protocol: First, the study moderator provided a general description of the study. Then, participants signed a consent form and completed a brief demographics questionnaire. To complete the tasks, participants were given access to a custom-built search engine to find information and a Microsoft Word document to enter their response. These two interfaces were displayed side-by-side. The custom-build search engine used the Bing Web Search API to retrieve results from the open web. The Word document provided a set of instructions and an empty table for participants to enter their response (i.e., a 2×2 or 4×4 table, depending on the task complexity condition). Header cells (top row and first column) in the given table contained the specific items and dimensions associated with the task. The custom-built search engine logged all user interactions on the search engine results page (SERP).

During each task, participants were instructed to find as much information as they thought was necessary to make an informed item selection. Participants were also asked to produce a written justification upon making a final decision. For each task, they were given 20 minutes with a 2-minute warning. Participants completed a post-task questionnaire after each task. After completing both tasks, participants were administered a working memory test that lasted 10-15 minutes. Participants were compensated $15 USD for participating in the study. The study took about 60 minutes.

Working Memory Test: To measure working memory capacity, we used the computerized "operation-word-span" (OSPAN) test [27] distributed with the "CogLab in a CD" textbook by Francis et al. [15]. The OSPAN test measures an individual's ability to recall words displayed in sequence while concurrently completing simple secondary tasks. Participants complete 15 trials of varying lengths. During each trial, the participant is shown a sequence of words and is then asked to recall the words in their original order from a grid display. Additionally, during each trial, participants complete simple math problems between each word shown in sequence (e.g., "Is (4/2)-1=1?"). The final score is equal to the sum of sequence lengths of all trials perfectly recalled.

Task Complexity Manipulation: Our manipulation of task complexity involved varying the number of items and dimensions associated with the task (simple = 2×2, complex = 4×4). To study the effect of task complexity, we developed four search tasks that varied across two levels of complexity (simple vs. complex) and two topics (dogs breeds to consider for adoption vs. methods to quit smoking). Each participant was exposed to both task complexity levels and both task topics. The presentation order of task complexity and task topic was counter-balanced (i.e., the 4 possible orderings were repeated 6 times across our 24 participants). All task descriptions involved a scenario in which participants were asked to look for information for a friend. For example, our simple (2 × 2) "dog breed" task asked: "A friend of yours has recently decided to get a dog for companionship. Your friend works during the day and lives in an apartment complex. Now you are trying to help your friend make a decision. How do: (a) Pug and (b) Bichon Frise dog breeds differ as a choice for your friend in terms of (a) the ability to be left alone during the day, and (b) the need for outdoor activity?"

We chose to use comparative tasks for several reasons. First, comparative tasks are likely to involve working memory. A searcher must identify different items, search for information about specific items and dimensions, and compare information across the items and dimensions. This process requires processing new information while retaining prior information. Second, working memory is often considered in terms of the number of discrete units of information over which one can distribute attention and maintain an active state [4]. Therefore, we thought that increasing the number of elements to consider could increase memory load. Finally, the ability to structure comparative tasks as a table allowed us to measure search outcomes in a straightforward way (e.g., by considering the percentage of completed cells).

Post-task Questionnaire (RQ1): After each task, participants completed a 9-item questionnaire that measured workload and satisfaction with their performance. To measure workload, we included four items from the NASA-TLX questionnaire [1]: (1) mental demand, (2) temporal demand, (3) performance, and (4) effort. Additionally, we included five questions about participants' satisfaction with their performance: (5) whether they found enough information, (6) satisfaction with the time spent on the task, (7) satisfaction with the amount of information found, (8) satisfaction with the quality of information found, and (9) satisfaction with the chosen search strategy. Participants responded to all items using a 5-point scale. For all workload items except for "performance", high response values indicate high levels of workload. For all satisfaction items, high values indicate high levels of satisfaction.

Behavioral Measures (RQ2): To investigate the effects on participants' search behaviors, we computed four behavioral measures: (1) number of queries issued, (2) number of SERP clicks, (3) average time to first SERP click after a query submission (in seconds), and (4) average time (in seconds) between subsequent search actions (i.e., queries and clicks).

Outcome Measures (RQ3): As previously mentioned, to complete the task, participants were required to fill a $n \times n$ table, make an item recommendation, and provide a written justification. These notes were considered as an external representation of participants' search performance other than behavioral measures. To investigate the effects on participants' search outcomes, we considered two measures. First, our *coverage* measure considered the percentage of the $n \times n$ table that was *not* left blank. Second, we considered the final justification length (in words) as a rough indicator of the justification's quality (i.e., depth and/or breadth).

4 RESULTS

Effects on Post-Task Perceptions (RQ1): In RQ1, we investigate the effects of working memory and task complexity on participants' post-task perceptions about workload and satisfaction. As shown in Table 1, mixed-effects ANOVAs found a significant main effect of task complexity on two measures: (1) temporal demand and (2) satisfaction with the time spent on the task. For complex tasks, participants reported greater levels of temporal demand and lower levels of satisfaction with the time spent on the task. No other main and interaction effects were significant.

Table 1: Mean (SD) of post-task measures according to task complexity (*p<.05).

category	item	simple	complex	$F(1, 22)$	p-value
workload	mental	2.58 (1.412)	2.88 (1.412)	1.286	.269
	temporal	2.54 (1.414)	3.38 (1.135)	5.670	.026*
	performance	3.96 (0.806)	3.63 (0.770)	2.514	.127
	effort	3.04 (1.268)	3.29 (1.197)	0.584	.453
satisfaction	enough info	3.96 (1.042)	3.46 (1.250)	2.760	.111
	time spent	3.92 (1.100)	3.12 (1.154)	5.954	.023*
	info amount	3.83 (1.167)	3.42 (1.176)	1.916	.180
	info quality	3.79 (1.179)	3.50 (1.180)	1.469	.238
	strategies	4.17 (0.761)	3.83 (0.816)	2.200	.152

Effects on Search Behaviors (RQ2): In RQ2, we investigate the effects of working memory and task complexity on participants' search behaviors. As shown in Table 2, mixed-effects ANOVAs found a significant main effect of working memory on all four behavioral measures: (1) number of queries, (2) number of clicks, (3) avg. time to the first SERP click, and (4) avg. time between search actions. High-WM participants performed more actions and searched at a faster pace than low-WM participants.

Table 2: Mean (SD) of behavioral measures according to working memory group (*p<.05).

measure	low-WM	high-WM	$F(1, 22)$	p-value
queries	5.33 (3.595)	7.71 (4.298)	5.479	.029*
clicks	7.79 (5.013)	11.75 (5.252)	7.257	.013*
time to 1st click	12.58 (11.716)	6.98 (2.824)	5.063	.035*
time between events	56.67 (31.857)	38.47 (14.962)	5.355	.030*

Effects on Search Outcomes (RQ3): In RQ3, we investigate the effects of working memory and task complexity on participants' search outcomes. As shown in Table 3, mixed-effects ANOVAs found the following effects. First, working memory had a significant main effect on the length of participants' justifications. High-WM participants produced significantly longer justifications than low-WM participants.

Second, task complexity had a significant main effect on the extent to which participants completed the corresponding $n \times n$ table. Simple tasks had higher levels of *coverage* than complex tasks. In other words, participants were less successful in adding information to every cell in the table during more complex tasks.

Finally, working memory and task complexity had a significant interaction effect on the length of participants' justifications ($F(1, 22) = 5.713, p = 0.026$). As shown in Figure 1, high-WM participants produced longer justifications for both simple and complex tasks. However, the difference was *greater* for complex tasks.

Table 3: Mean (SD) of search outcome measures according to working memory group and task complexity (*p<.05).

working memory (WM)	low-WM	high-WM	$F(1, 22)$	p-value
coverage	0.93 (0.11)	0.96 (0.10)	0.882	0.358
justification length	32.50 (29.21)	60.79 (28.04)	9.079	.006*
task complexity	**simple**	**complex**	**$F(1, 22)$**	**p-value**
coverage	1.00 (0.00)	0.89 (0.14)	12.942	.002*
justification length	50.83 (28.42)	42.46 (34.83)	1.714	.204

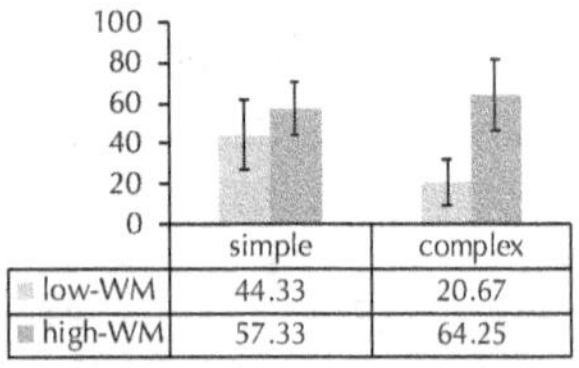

Figure 1: Means and 95% confidence intervals of justification lengths (words) according to working memory group and task complexity.

5 DISCUSSION AND CONCLUSION

In this study, we examined the effects of working memory and task complexity on participants' post-task perceptions (RQ1), search behaviors (RQ2), and search outcomes (RQ3). In this section, we summarize our findings, compare them to those from prior studies, and discuss their implications.

RQ1: Task complexity had an effect on temporal demand and satisfaction with the time spent on the task. As expected, participants reported greater temporal demand and lower satisfaction for complex versus simple tasks. This serves as a manipulation check that our complex tasks required greater effort (as measured by temporal demand). Interestingly, working memory did not have a significant effect on any of our RQ1 measures.

RQ2: Working memory had a significant effect on several behavioral measures. Participants in the high working memory group performed more search actions (e.g., queries and clicks) and worked at a faster pace (e.g., took less time between subsequent actions) than participants in the low working memory group.

RQ3: In terms of search outcomes, we found three important trends. First, task complexity had an effect on participants ability to fully complete the $n \times n$ table of items and dimensions. As expected, participants were less able to complete the table for complex versus simple tasks. This serves as a second sanity check that our manipulation of adding more items/dimensions increased the task's complexity. Second, working memory had an effect on participants' justification length. Participants in the high working memory group produced longer justifications than participants in the low working memory group. Finally, task complexity and working memory had a significant effect on participants' justification length. High-WM participants produced *even longer* justifications than low-WM participants for complex tasks versus simple tasks.

Participants in our study were asked to write justifications based on information found regarding items and dimensions. In this respect, we treated longer justifications as better outcomes (i.e., more depth and/or breadth). Our RQ2 and RQ3 results suggest that high-WM participants exerted more effort (i.e., performed more search actions) and achieved better outcomes (i.e., produced longer justifications) than low-WM participants. Furthermore, in terms of the justification length, this trend was more pronounced for complex tasks. Specifically, for complex tasks, high-WM participants produced justifications more than twice as long as those from low-WM participants. Interestingly, low-WM participants produced shorter justifications for complex versus simple tasks.

Our results suggest that low-WM participants were more likely to engage in satisficing behaviors, especially during more complex tasks. These results are largely consistent with prior studies, which found that low-WM participants were more likely to satisfice in challenging situations [16–18]. Also, our findings resonate with prior studies on the search behaviors of dyslexic users [14, 25]. In those studies, dyslexic participants were less "selective" than non-dyslexic participants in producing relevance judgments, possibly because they were less able to apply specific decision criteria and more likely to satisfice.

Interestingly, our RQ1 results are *inconsistent* with our RQ2 and RQ3 results. While high-WM participants exerted more effort (RQ2) and had better outcomes (RQ3), both participant groups reported *similar* levels of workload and satisfaction. In terms of workload, these results suggest that high-WM participants exerted more effort *without* perceiving greater levels of workload than low-WM participants. In terms of satisfaction, these results suggest that low-WM participants may have had a *lower* threshold for satisfaction with their performance. In other words, while low-WM participants exerted less effort and produced weaker justifications, they reported comparable levels of satisfaction as high-WM participants.

Implications: Our results have implications for designing systems that provide support and scaffolding for searchers with different working memory abilities. First and foremost, our results suggest that working memory plays an important role in performing comparative tasks, which are fairly common in everyday life (e.g., shopping). In our study, high-WM participants exerted more search effort and had better outcomes than low-WM participants. Future work should develop tools to support users (especially low-WM users) with comparative search tasks. Second, our results suggest that not all comparative tasks are equal. The number of items/dimensions being considered can impact the task's complexity. Our results suggest that low-WM users may need even *more* support with complex comparative tasks in order to achieve better outcomes. Finally, our results suggest that low-WM users may have lower expectations about task outcomes and may therefore not *perceive* a need for support. While there were differences in performance between low- and high-WM participants, both groups reported similar levels of satisfaction. In this respect, low-WM users may benefit more from support systems that are readily available, visually salient, and possibly proactive.

Future work: Further research is needed to better understand the exact functions of working memory that are most crucial during the search process (e.g., planning, regulating, inferring relations between concepts and ideas, recognizing/addressing knowledge gaps, etc.). A deeper understanding of these functions may inform the design of tools to provide support and scaffolding for searchers with varying levels of working memory ability.

Acknowledgements: This work was supported in part by NSF grants IIS-1552587 and IIS-1451668. Any opinions, findings, conclusions, and recommendations expressed in this paper are those of the authors and do not necessarily reflect the views of the NSF.

REFERENCES

[1] National Aeronautics and Space Administration Human Systems Integration Division. 2016. TLX NASA Ames. (2016).
[2] Lorin W. Anderson and David R. Krathwohl. 2001. *A taxonomy for learning, teaching, and assessing: A revision of Bloom's taxonomy of educational objectives.*
[3] Jaime Arguello. 2014. Predicting Search Task Difficulty. In *ECIR*. Springer, 88–99.
[4] Alan Baddeley. 2010. Working memory. *Current biology* 20, 4 (2010), R136–R140.
[5] Pierre Barrouillet and Jean-Francois Lecas. 1999. Mental models in conditional reasoning and working memory. *Thinking & Reasoning* 5, 4 (1999), 289–302.
[6] Harald Beneventi, Finn Egil Tønnessen, and Lars Ersland. 2009. Dyslexic children show short-term memory deficits in phonological storage and serial rehearsal: an fMRI study. *International Journal of Neuroscience* 119, 11 (2009), 2017–2043.
[7] Virginia W Berninger, Wendy Raskind, Todd Richards, Robert Abbott, and Pat Stock. 2008. A multidisciplinary approach to understanding developmental dyslexia within working-memory architecture: Genotypes, phenotypes, brain, and instruction. *Developmental neuropsychology* 33, 6 (2008), 707–744.
[8] Kathy Brennan, Diane Kelly, and Jaime Arguello. 2014. The effect of cognitive abilities on information search for tasks of varying levels of complexity. In *IIiX*. ACM, 165–174.
[9] Donald J Campbell. 1988. Task complexity: A review and analysis. *Academy of management review* 13, 1 (1988), 40–52.
[10] Robert Capra, Jaime Arguello, Anita Crescenzi, and Emily Vardell. 2015. Differences in the use of search assistance for tasks of varying complexity. In *SIGIR*. ACM, 23–32.
[11] Ravit Cohen-Mimran and Shimon Sapir. 2007. Deficits in working memory in young adults with reading disabilities. *Journal of communication disorders* 40, 2 (2007), 168–183.
[12] Meredyth Daneman and Patricia A Carpenter. 1980. Individual differences in working memory and reading. *Journal of verbal learning and verbal behavior* 19, 4 (1980), 450–466.
[13] Adele Diamond. 2013. Executive functions. *Annual review of psychology* 64 (2013), 135–168.
[14] Adam Fourney, Meredith Ringel Morris, Abdullah Ali, and Laura Vonessen. 2018. Assessing the Readability ofWeb Search Results for Searchers with Dyslexia. In *SIGIR*. ACM.
[15] Greg Francis, Angie MacKewn, and Danalee Goldthwaite. 2004. *CogLab on a CD.* Wadsworth Publishing Company.
[16] Jacek Gwizdka. 2009. What a difference a tag cloud makes: effects of tasks and cognitive abilities on search results interface use. *Information Research: An International Electronic Journal* 14, 4 (2009), n4.
[17] Jacek Gwizdka. 2013. Effects of Working Memory Capacity on Users' Search Effort. In *MIDI*. ACM, 11:1–11:8.
[18] Jacek Gwizdka. 2017. I Can and So I Search More: Effects Of Memory Span On Search Behavior. In *CHIIR*. ACM, 341–344.
[19] David Z. Hambrick and Randall W. Engle. 2003. *The Role of Working Memory in Problem Solving.* Cambridge University Press. 176–206 pages.
[20] Xiao Hu and Noriko Kando. 2017. Task complexity and difficulty in music information retrieval. *JASIST* 68, 7 (2017), 1711–1723.
[21] Bernard J Jansen, Danielle Booth, and Brian Smith. 2009. Using the taxonomy of cognitive learning to model online searching. *Information Processing & Management* 45, 6 (2009), 643–663.
[22] Diane Kelly, Jaime Arguello, Ashlee Edwards, and Wan-ching Wu. 2015. Development and evaluation of search tasks for IIR experiments using a cognitive complexity framework. In *ICTIR*. ACM, 101–110.
[23] Patrick C Kyllonen and Raymond E Christal. 1990. Reasoning ability is (little more than) working-memory capacity?! *Intelligence* 14, 4 (1990), 389–433.
[24] Cindy Lustig, Cynthia P May, and Lynn Hasher. 2001. Working memory span and the role of proactive interference. *Journal of Experimental Psychology: General* 130, 2 (2001), 199.
[25] Andrew MacFarlane, A Albrair, CR Marshall, and George Buchanan. 2012. Phonological working memory impacts on information searching: an investigation of dyslexia. In *IIiX*. ACM, 27–34.
[26] James Smith-Spark, John Fisk, Angela Fawcett, and Roderick Nicolson. 2003. Investigating the central executive in adult dyslexics: Evidence from phonological and visuospatial working memory performance. *European Journal of Cognitive Psychology* 15, 4 (2003), 567–587.
[27] Marilyn L Turner and Randall W Engle. 1989. Is working memory capacity task dependent? *Journal of memory and language* 28, 2 (1989), 127–154.
[28] Lauren Turpin, Diane Kelly, and Jaime Arguello. 2016. To Blend or Not to Blend?: Perceptual Speed, Visual Memory and Aggregated Search. In *SGIR*. ACM, 1021–1024.
[29] Barbara Wildemuth, Luanne Freund, and Elaine G. Toms. 2014. Untangling search task complexity and difficulty in the context of interactive information retrieval studies. *Journal of Documentation* 70, 6 (2014), 1118–1140.
[30] Barbara Wildemuth, Diane Kelly, Emma Boettcher, Erin Moore, and Gergana Dimitrova. 2018. Examining the impact of domain and cognitive complexity on query formulation and reformulation. *IP&M* 54, 3 (2018), 433 – 450.
[31] Jennifer Wiley and Andrew F Jarosz. 2012. How working memory capacity affects problem solving. In *Psychology of learning and motivation*. Vol. 56. Elsevier, 185–227.
[32] Wan-Ching Wu and Diane Kelly. 2014. Online search stopping behaviors: An investigation of query abandonment and task stopping. *ASIST* 51, 1 (2014), 1–10.

Generating Tasks for Study of Struggling Search

Luyan Xu
DEKE lab
Renmin University of China
Beijing, China
xuluyan@ruc.edu.cn

Xuan Zhou
School of Data Science & Engineering
East China Normal University
Shanghai, China
zhou.xuan@outlook.com

ABSTRACT

Interactive information-seeking systems are designed to help users with their struggling during the searching for complex fact checking tasks, where a searcher may have clear information needs but experience difficulty in collecting required information. However, evaluation and comparison of such systems requires a large number of such tasks, which are difficult to collect or make up. To the best of our knowledge, there has not been a commonly used task set for evaluating struggling search of this kind. This paper proposes a convenient method to generate complex fact checking tasks. Each of the generated task has a clearly defined goal, which however takes an average searcher a significant amount of effort to reach. We conducted lab user studies to verify the feasibility of this method. The results confirmed its feasibility and efficiency.

CCS CONCEPTS

• **Human-centered computing → Human computer interaction (HCI); User studies;**

KEYWORDS

task design; struggling search; user behavior analysis

ACM Reference Format:
Luyan Xu and Xuan Zhou. 2019. Generating Tasks for Study of Struggling Search. In *2019 Conference on Human Information Interaction and Retrieval (CHIIR '19), March 10–14, 2019, Glasgow, United Kingdom.* ACM, New York, NY, USA, 4 pages. https://doi.org/10.1145/3295750.3298949

1 INTRODUCTION

Recently, there have been many studies on creating "difficult" tasks to understand information-seeking behaviors or evaluate the function of information seeking systems.

Researchers in the sense-making find that searchers will suffer difficulty when there is an information gap between what they know and what they want to know [13], as they could hardly describe their questions clearly or find a way get close to the answer. This shed lights on the task generation method that the information points or the task solving strategy should not be directly given by the task (i.e. not tasks of strong problem solving [11]). On the contrary, the task description needs to be ill-structured, somehow implicit and vague, and information points need to be inferred and collected from some fragmentary information, which may spread over a number of documents.

Based on these theories, tasks generated by existing methods can be roughly divided into two categories. One type is situation-imitated and tries to simulate a mission or a problem in real life scenes [2, 8]. For example, "You once heard that Dave Matthews Band owns a studio in Virginia but you don't know the name of it. The studio is located outside of Charlottesville and it's in the mountains. What is the name of the studio?" [2]. Tasks of this kind imitate people's fragmented information (memory) about one objective, by setting up virtual scenes(a virtual need) and persuading searchers to imagine themselves in it. The other type is open-ended and usually asks searchers to gather and structure information about specific topics [4, 14]. For example, "Write a paper about president Obama's family history". As it is open-ended, searchers tend to explore a wide range of resources to obtain a relatively complete picture about the topic.

The limitations of the two types of tasks are apparent. Generation of the first type of tasks is demanding – construction of real-life situations requires researchers' extensive experience and fertile imagination, and there is no common pattern to follow. Therefore, it is infeasible to obtain sufficient such tasks for large scale experimental study. For the second type of tasks, the lack of clear objectives makes evaluation difficult – each searcher can set his / her own objective for an open-ended task, while each of the objectives can be valid according to the context or the personal experience of the searcher; without a common objective, it will be difficult to compare searchers' performance objectively

In this paper, we propose a scalable method to generate difficult search tasks on Wikipedia. We implemented the method into a task generation tool on XOWA[1], an open-source offline Wikipedia application. We conducted a user study, in which users were asked to generate and evaluate tasks using our tool (i.e. the tool is open-sourced online[2]). The results showed that each of generated tasks elicited multiple rounds of interactions and most of the tasks took searchers significant amount of effort to complete(i.e. the tasks could be found online[3])

2 RELATED WORK

Many studies have been focused on the design of "difficult" tasks. Researchers in the sense-making find that searchers will suffer difficulty when there is an information gap between what they know and what they want to know [13], as they could hardly describe

CHIIR '19, March 10–14, 2019, Glasgow, United Kingdom

ACM ISBN 978-1-4503-6025-8/19/03...$15.00
https://doi.org/10.1145/3295750.3298949

[1] http://xowa.org
[2] https://github.com/we-take-it-easy/xowa
[3] https://bitbucket.org/ielool/strugglingsearch/

their questions clearly or find a way get close to the answer. This shed lights on task generation that the information points or the task solving strategy should not be directly given by the task (i.e. not tasks of strong problem solving [11]). According to [16], a viable method for setting information-seeking experiments is trying to stimulate real-life situations.

Based on these theories, some researchers construct "difficult" tasks by imitating people's problems in real-life scenes [1, 2]. Others imitate the open-ended missions such as write a paper or make a travel plan under certain circumstances [9, 14]. A few studies extract independent examples of difficult tasks from user logs and focus on how task difficulty is reflected on behavioral signals [2, 12].

Previous researchers generate or find tasks for a small-sized experiment. Based on their studies, we provide an easy-to-use task generation module that could generate tasks for large-scale experimental study.

3 TASK GENERATION

In this section, we describe in details how our method generates search tasks on wikipedia.

3.1 The Intuition

The basic idea is to utilize "paraphrases", which is abundant in common writings. When composing a wikipeida article, an author tends to describe a thing or concept from multiple perspectives, to help reader understand. This naturally results in paraphrases. For instance, a statement following a causative sentence connector, such as "that is to say", "in plain English", is likely to be a paraphrase, which repeats the former sentence in a more colloquial way. If we remove these statements, it is unlikely to cause information loss. After removed, they can in theory be recovered by a human who has read through the previous contents. Usually, such a paraphrase is a declarative statement. It is normally straight forward to turn it into a question, with the statement as the answer.

For example, in Figure 1, we can remove the sentence “In other words, ‘bourgeois’ parties taken together now had more than half the seat” and turn it into the question “In 1917, did the 'bourgeois' take more than half the seats in Finnish parliamentary election?". Since we have removed the original sentence from the text, the answer will not be directly identifiable. A searcher may identify text segments such as "Finnish parliamentary election in 1917" using a conventional search engine. However, to understand what “bourgeois" is in the context and how it is related to the election, the searcher may be forced to explore Wikipedia a bit further, to acquire additional knowledge.

> **Parliamentary elections** were held in the Grand Duchy of Finland on 1 and 2 October 1917. The general voter turnout was higher than in previous elections. The Social Democrats lost the absolute majority that they had had in the previous two elections (although they, like the other parties, had increased their number of votes in absolute terms). In other words, the "bourgeois" (non-socialist) parties taken together now had more than half the seats.

Figure 1: Example in Wikipedia.

This inspires us to generate search tasks through the following steps:

(1) Identify a paraphrasing sentence;
(2) Remove it from the document;
(3) Induce an informational question from the sentence.

Since a paraphrasing sentence usually lacks accurate description of information, the task generated based on it simulates a real-life situation, where people have incomplete prior knowledge or means to meet their information need. Sometimes, a searcher can quickly identify the original document through a search engine. However, it normally takes him / her efforts to infer the correct answer. Some scenarios may force him / her to look for further information in other documents. In some cases, it is not even easy to identify the original document, as the exact keywords in the removed sentence do not recur in the document. As a result, exploratory actions will be required. The searcher may have to start from some arbitrary documents that seem relevant, navigate the url graph, and reason about the possible answer. If the searcher is unfamiliar with the topic, learning has to be conducted, as answering the question requires comprehension of the background knowledge. As the removed sentence contains only redundant information, in theory the searcher should be able to find the answer in the end, while the difficulty may vary from case to case.

3.2 Task Generation Process

To identify paraphrases in Wikipedia, we used several causative sentence connectors – "in other words", "that is to say", "in plain English", "namely", etc. Most of the time, the sentences following these connectors are intended to rephrase the previous contents in more colloquial expressions. There are of course many other types of paraphrases in Wikipedia. Since it is not the purpose of this paper to exhaust all types of paraphrases and discuss their difference in task generation. We limit our study to the quality of the tasks generated by this general approach.

3.2.1 The Toolkit. As shown in Figure 2A, we developed a task generation toolkit on XOWA, an open-source offline Wikipedia application. It has the same interface as the online Wikipedia (Figure 2D). We looked up the wikipedia index using the causative connectors as queries in Solr[4]. For each connector, we obtained the Top-50 search results. The IDs and titles of the resulting documents are passed to our toolkit (Figure 2A). Then, a human worker processes each document following instructions in the toolkit: first, he finds the paraphrasing sentence following the connector; second, he makes up a question which can be answered by the paraphrasing sentence; then, he deletes the sentence from the offline wikipedia. All the questions generated in the process, as well as the answers and deleted sentences are stored in a database, so that they can quickly be retrieved and recovered.

3.2.2 Task Generating Experiments. With this toolkit, we conducted a task generation experiment in the lab. We explained the the task generation module, the procedure and the possible use of these tasks to 10 volunteers (i.e. 5 female and 5 male, ages between 22 to 29) and asked them each to create 4 tasks following the instructions.

During the lab experiment, we found that not all the cases can be turned into qualified search tasks. Some candidate sentences

[4] http://lucene.apache.org/solr/

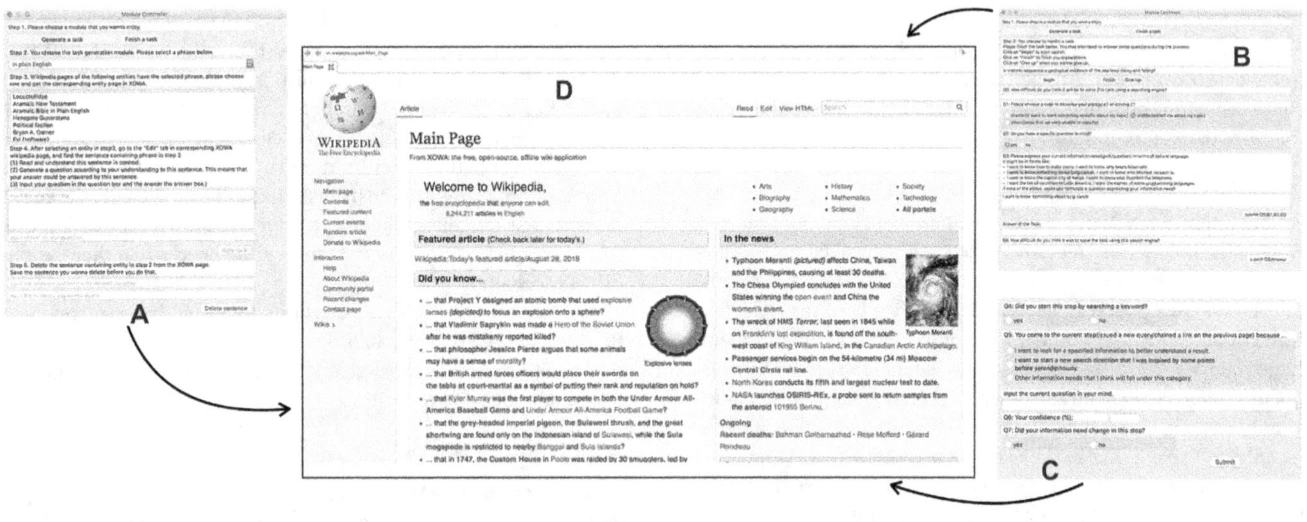

Figure 2: Interface of the interactive searching system. (A): a module controller for generating tasks, users follow instructions in the controller to generate a task, the instructions are illustrated step by step in 3.2.1; (B): a questionnaire recording users' pre-task and post-task feedback about task difficulty; (C): a questionnaire recording users' step feedback, questions are illustrted in Table 1; (D): interface of the offline wikipedia system, users could search and edit the wiki dump through this interface

are actually not paraphrases. For example, "in other words" can also be the name of a song. Some sentences are too short or too common-sense to induce "difficult" tasks. In such a case, the worker can skip the documents and proceed with the next ones. Using our toolkit, a task can be generated within a few minutes. In the end, we collected 40 tasks.

4 USER STUDY

We evaluated the quality of generated tasks through user behavior analysis. We implemented a logging system in XOWA to track the explicit user behaviors such as searching and chaining, etc. We also designed a questionnaire based on the criteria of [6, 15] to collect implicit feedback.

4.1 Participants

In the experiment, we recruited another 16 volunteers (all are Ph.D. and M.Sc. students), in which 7 are female and 9 are male. Their ages ranged from 22 to 29, and all had experience in using search engines. Each volunteer was asked to finish 5 out of the 40 tasks generated in the previous experiment.

4.2 Information Collection

Our logging system records searchers' interactions by a system log and a video log. The system log contains the history of each user's queries and visited pages, the backward/forward navigation actions, and the user's dwelling time on each page. The video log can tell us more about user's detailed behaviors on each page, such as using ctrl+f to search for certain terms or highlighting a few lines of text for focused reading. Referring to the experience of the previous works on information seeking [5, 7], our analysis mainly considered the following measures: task completion time, number of visited pages, number of searches, number of backward and forward actions, and dwelling time on each page.

The questions in our questionnaire were divided into four parts, as illustrated in Table. 1. The pre-task and post-task questions and

Table 1: Task Questionnaire Items

Expected Task Difficulty (pre-task)	How difficult do you think it will be to solve this task using a search engine? 0% (very easy) – 50% (mediate) – 100% (very hard)
Initial Status (pre-task)	Which case could best describe your current task solving status? directed ("I want to learn something specific about it") undirected ("tell me about my task") unknown (ones that we were unable to classify) Is the current goal clear or vague? clear/vague Can you describe your current question/goal in terms of natural language?
Step Feelings During Process	Did your information goal change in the current step? Can you describe your current question in mind in terms of natural language? Currently, how much confidence do you have in solving the task? 0% (no confidence) to 100% (full of confidence)
Experienced Task Difficulty (post-task)	How difficult do you think it was to solve this task using a search engine? 0% (very easy) – 50% (mediate) – 100% (very hard)

questions about initail states (in Figure 2B) should be answered before and after the task conduction respectively. Questions about behaviors (in Figure 2C) should be answered by the searchers every time they finish an operation on wikipedia. The time spent on filling questionnaires was not included in task completion time.

Before the experiment, each participant was taught about precautions during the experiments, such as task descriptions, experimental processes, features of the offline search engine and how to use it. Users were told that they cannot use external search engines (e.g. google, etc.), but only our experimental search engine. They can do any operations (e.g. browsing, searching, highlighting, etc.) to collect information. An exploration process will end if user is confident about his / her answer or gives up, or the user was idle for more than 30 minutes.

5 TASK FILTERING

We obtained 79 task solving cases containing 869 interaction steps. Among the interaction steps, there are 192 search steps and 677 page loading steps (chaining, backward / forward). Based on the collected information, we primarily measured the difficulty of the tasks from three dimensions: the number of interactions (e.g. the number of issued queries, the visited pages, etc.) a searcher took to finish a task; the time a searcher spends to understand certain information points about the task; a searcher's subjective experience about whether he / she felt struggling in the task solving process.

1. Searching and chaining Based on our collected user behaviors, we found that a searcher needs to interact with wikipedia for 11 times on average to complete a task, including about 3 times of search and 8 to 9 times of page browsing. In only 10% (8 out of 79) of the cases, the tasks could be solved within 5 steps (we found that these tasks are similar to information look-up tasks, of which the answers are directly mentioned in other pages). In 71% of the cases (56 out of 79), a task could be solved in more than 9 interaction steps. These are different from simple look-up tasks, as searchers could not locate required information through a one-shot query [3]. Instead, they needed to issue multiple queries to explore the information space or change search direction. They often chained links on the result pages to search for more clues, and took backward / forward actions to review related information.

2. Browsing According to the previous study [10], a searcher spends on average less than 70 seconds locating information on a wikipedia page. Based on this finding, we used 70 seconds as the dwell-time threshold to distinguish between learning and quick browsing. In the 677 single page-loading steps we collected, around 26% (177 out of 677 steps) lasted over 70 seconds, and around 4% (25 out of 677) lasted more than 180 seconds. The video logs show that in these cases searchers would highlight sentences or use "ctrl+f" to refind information. Thus, we can confirm that the searchers were trying to understand the content of the articles in a deeper sense. Some pages were revisited by searchers. We observed a significant difference between the dwell time on first-visit and revisit. This is consistent to the phenomena in exploratory search, in which searchers tend to firstly perform some exploratory browsing [16] to locate a page and then turn back to carefully review it for a deeper understanding. Based on this criteria, we further filtered 19 tasks, in which exploratory behaviors were supposed to be carried out.

3. Cognitive-level Evolvements. Based on the results on the questionnaire, we found that searchers mainly felt struggling in two circumstances. When issuing the first query, in 65% of the cases (51 out of 79), searchers felt "undirected". They said that after seeing the tasks they were either totally unfamiliar with the domain of the task or unsure about their goals. While some could extract a concrete query from the question as the starting point, they were still unsure about whether the query can lead they to the answers. Besides, users could meet difficulties during browsing and navigating that they need to chain and follow the clues they find, but sometimes the clues just break off and they need to start again. Before conducting search, all the searchers judged that the tasks were difficult (i.e., pre-task difficulty measures of all the 40 tasks were above 50%). For half of the tasks, the searchers did not change attitude about their difficulty after finishing the tasks(i.e., their post-task difficulty measures were still larger than 50%). This is consistent with the findings about pre- and post- task difficulty in [6]. On average, a searcher's search direction changed for 3 times for each task. Their confidence for solving the task were influenced when their search direction changes.

Considering the three dimensions together, we can conclude that at least 19 out of the 40 tasks are difficult search tasks that can potentially make searchers struggle (these qualified tasks could be found in the online repository [5]).

6 CONCLUSION

According to our study, utilizing paraphrases in wikipedia to generate difficult search tasks appears to be a promising method. On the one hand, a task can be generated quickly, within a few minutes. This makes it an efficient and scalable approach. On the other hand, tasks generated by this method are in general difficult. In most cases, it takes a searcher several rounds of interactions and a significant amount of dwell time to solve a task, and they often feel struggling. While there are also simple look-up tasks, they can be filtered out through a post-processing step, e.g., manual verification. We expect that these tasks will help us gain more insights about users' struggles in information seeking.

REFERENCES

[1] Mikhail Ageev, Qi Guo, Dmitry Lagun, and Eugene Agichtein. 2011. Find it if you can: a game for modeling different types of web search success using interaction data. In *SIGIR*. 345–354.
[2] Anne Aula, Rehan M Khan, and Zhiwei Guan. 2010. How does search behavior change as search becomes more difficult?. In *CHI*. 35–44.
[3] Marcia J Bates. 1984. The fallacy of the perfect thirty-item online search. *RQ* (1984), 43–50.
[4] William R Hersh. 2002. TREC 2002 Interactive Track Report.. In *TREC*.
[5] Christine Jenkins, Cynthia L Corritore, and Susan Wiedenbeck. 2003. Patterns of information seeking on the Web: A qualitative study of domain expertise and Web expertise. *IT & Society* 1, 3 (2003), 64–89.
[6] Diane Kelly, Jaime Arguello, Ashlee Edwards, and Wan-ching Wu. 2015. Development and evaluation of search tasks for IIR experiments using a cognitive complexity framework. In *ICTIR*. ACM, 101–110.
[7] Diane Kelly and Nicholas J Belkin. 2004. Display time as implicit feedback: understanding task effects. In *SIGIR*. 377–384.
[8] Bill Kules and Robert Capra. 2008. Creating exploratory tasks for a faceted search interface. *HCIR* (2008), 18–21.
[9] Bill Kules, Robert Capra, Matthew Banta, and Tito Sierra. 2009. What do exploratory searchers look at in a faceted search interface?. In *JCDL*. 313–322.
[10] Chao Liu, Ryen W White, and Susan Dumais. 2010. Understanding web browsing behaviors through Weibull analysis of dwell time. In *SIGIR*. 379–386.
[11] Allen Newell, Herbert Alexander Simon, et al. 1972. *Human problem solving*. Vol. 104. Prentice-Hall Englewood Cliffs, NJ.
[12] Daan Odijk, Ryen W White, Ahmed Hassan Awadallah, and Susan T Dumais. 2015. Struggling and success in web search. In *CIKM*. 1551–1560.
[13] Peter Pirolli and Stuart Card. 2005. The sensemaking process and leverage points for analyst technology as identified through cognitive task analysis. In *ICIA*, Vol. 5. 2–4.
[14] Martin Potthast, Matthias Hagen, Michael Völske, and Benno Stein. 2013. Exploratory Search Missions for TREC Topics. *EuroHCIR* 1033 (2013), 7.
[15] Daniel E Rose and Danny Levinson. 2004. Understanding user goals in web search. In *WWW*. 13–19.
[16] Ryen W White and Resa A Roth. 2009. Exploratory search: Beyond the query-response paradigm. *Synthesis lectures on information concepts, retrieval, and services* 1, 1 (2009), 1–98.

[5] https://bitbucket.org/ielool/strugglingsearch/

Lessons Learned from Users Reading Highlighted Abstracts in a Digital Library

Dagmar Kern, Daniel Hienert
GESIS - Leibniz Institute for the Social Science
Cologne, Germany
dagmar.kern@gesis.org,daniel.hienert@gesis.org

Katrin Angerbauer
VISUS, University of Stuttgart
Stuttgart, Germany
katrin.angerbauer@visus.uni-stuttgart.de

Tilman Dingler
University of Melbourne
Melbourne, Australia
tilman.dingler@unimelb.edu.au

Pia Borlund
Oslo Metropolitan University
Oslo, Norway
pia.borlund@oslomet.no

ABSTRACT

Finding relevant documents is essential for researchers of all disciplines. We investigated an approach for supporting searchers in their relevance decision in a digital library by automatically highlighting the most important keywords in abstracts. We conducted an eye-tracking study with 25 subjects and observed very different search and reading behavior which lead to diverse results. Some of the participants liked that highlighted abstracts accelerate their relevance decision, while others found that they disturb the reading flow. What many agree on is that the quality of highlighting is crucial for trust and system credibility.

CCS CONCEPTS

• **Human-centered computing** → **User studies**; • **Applied computing** → *Digital libraries and archives*;

KEYWORDS

highlighting, reading behavior, user study, relevance judgment

ACM Reference Format:
Dagmar Kern, Daniel Hienert, Katrin Angerbauer, Tilman Dingler, and Pia Borlund. 2019. Lessons Learned from Users Reading Highlighted Abstracts in a Digital Library. In *2019 Conference on Human Information Interaction and Retrieval (CHIIR '19), March 10–14, 2019, Glasgow, Scotland Uk.* ACM, New York, NY, USA, 5 pages. https://doi.org/10.1145/3295750.3298950

1 INTRODUCTION

Digital environments have generally changed reading behavior. People very often only browse or scan documents and web pages, look for keywords, read more selectively and spend less time on in-depth reading [12]. This also applies for the document triage process in digital libraries [4]. During this process, a user first decides if a given document is relevant to her information need. Most often this relevance judgment is based on the title and the abstract of a document [4, 11, 15]. Considering the importance of the abstract on the relevance judgment and the changed reading behavior, we present an approach to support keyword spotting by highlighting the most important keywords in abstracts.

Highlighting search terms in search results is already a common practice in web search and digital libraries to directly show users in which part of the document the search term has been found. In the research literature, one can find more specific approaches like dynamic highlighting of sentences based on their accordance with their salience [18], highlighting of whole sentences containing conceptual keywords [5], highlighting of automatically generated search query terms that were used to find a recommended document [2], or different highlighting of keywords in abstracts that relate to predefined concepts [17]. In our previous work, we explored the use of highlighting and other keyword summary visualizations to prime readers a priori to support reading comprehension and improve subjective impressions for which we found highlighting to be most effective [1, 7]

Eye-tracking data of a user can provide a lot of information about the search and reading behavior as well as the relevance judgment [8, 9, 13]. Therefore, we conducted a user study utilizing an eye tracker to find answers to the following research questions: (R1) How do key-term-highlighted abstracts support users in their document relevance decision? (R2) What effects have key-term-highlighted abstracts on the reading behavior?

2 KEY-TERM-HIGHLIGHTED ABSTRACTS

We tested the effect of key-term highlighted abstracts with the digital library system Sowiport. Sowiport [10] was a digital library for social science information with 9.7 million bibliographic records, full texts, and research projects[1]. Sowiport showed results to a search query in a ranked result list and provided a detailed view page for each result on demand with more metadata about the selected article. This included in most cases a German or English abstract. Figure 1 shows a detailed view page with a key-term-highlighted abstract.

CHIIR '19, March 10–14, 2019, Glasgow, Scotland Uk

ACM ISBN 978-1-4503-6025-8/19/03...$15.00
https://doi.org/10.1145/3295750.3298950

[1]Sowiport was discontinued at the end of 2017

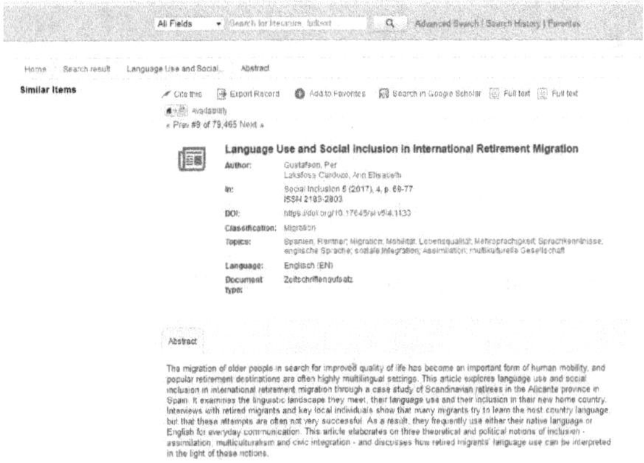

Figure 1: Detailed view page of Sowiport.

2.1 Approach

To identify the relevant key-terms we used the term-frequency inverse document frequency (tf-idf) measure. The corpora used to train the tf-idf models consisted of approximately 10,000 English and 21,000 German full texts on topics of social science. These texts were obtained via the Social Science Open Access Repository (SSOAR)[2] to train our German and English tf-idf models. Stop words were filtered in both languages. Furthermore, we considered only nouns and adjectives for scoring and thus highlighting, as we considered them to be the most informative content words. The preprocessing of the abstract (tokenization and part of speech-tagging) and the scoring was done during run-time. To calculate the scores of the abstracts' terms the preprocessed sentences were passed to the pre-trained models. The number of terms highlighted in the abstract was determined in relation to the abstract's length. We set the number of terms to be highlighted to ten percent. If a term occurred multiple times, it was highlighted in every occurrence.

2.2 Implementation

For the highlighting, the documents of the corpora and the abstracts were preprocessed with TreeTagger [16] to obtain the lemmas and the corresponding inflected forms of the words as well as their parts of speech. To model the corpora and to calculate the tf-idf models and to do the scoring of the abstracts' tf-idf values we used the gensim library [14] for Python. For the presentation of the highlighted key-terms we used basic HTML and CSS and modified their background color. Through a config file, we could easily turn on or off the highlighting functionality for the abstracts.

3 EVALUATION

We conducted an eye-tracking study with 25 participants to examine what effect highlighting of the most important keywords in abstracts has on the relevance decision and reading behavior in the digital library Sowiport.

[2]https://www.gesis.org/ssoar/home/, SSOAR provides an Open Archives Initiative Protocol for Metadata Harvesting (OAI-PMH) interface for metadata access

3.1 Experimental Setup

The study took place in our usability lab in single sessions under controlled conditions without distraction. Participants were seated alone in the usability lab in front of a 22-inch monitor. The SMI iView RED 250 mobile eye tracker was attached to the lower frame of it. The monitor and the eye tracker were connected to a laptop that ran the eye tracking software. The eye gazes were recorded with a sampling rate of 60Hz. The participant used a keyboard and a mouse to interact with the system. The experimenter sat next to the usability lab in an observation room in front of a monitor showing the screen the participant saw. The experimenter captured everything on the participant's screen and the gaze behavior with the capturing software Camtasia[3] to be able to conduct a stimulated recall interview after the task performance.

3.2 Participants

As the digital library comprised documents in the field of social science, we needed participants with a background in social science or a similar field of study. We recruited participants through mailing lists and posters at the local university. Thirty participants took part in our study. Due to technical problems with the eye tracker we had to exclude the results of 5 participants from the data analysis. Sixteen of the remaining participants were female and nine male. Their age ranged from 23 to 45 years (mean: 28.6, SD: 4.12). Fourteen hold a Bachelor degree, ten a Master degree and one was a postdoctoral researcher. Twenty-four of them had a background in Sociology while one was a psychologist.

3.3 Simulated Work Tasks

As we were interested in how the highlighting influenced users' usual information seeking behavior in a digital library, we created two simulated work task scenarios (according to [3]), which the participants had to perform.

Task A: "Please use Sowiport to find publications on a topic you are well familiar with, for example, your main research topic. Please bookmark (using browser bookmarks) documents that seem to be useful to you."

Task B: "Please use Sowiport to find publications on a topic you are not familiar with, but you are interested in learning more about it. Please bookmark (using browser bookmarks) all documents that seem to be useful to you." The simulated work tasks provide context for realistic searching and form the basis for reliable reading and relevance assessment behavior.

3.4 Methodology

Data collection took place from August 2017 to January 2018 at our research institute. We invited participants to single sessions. We followed a within-subject design approach with the highlighting and simulated work tasks (A and B) being the independent variables in two conditions: (1) abstracts with key-term-highlights (named highlighting) and (2) abstracts without key-term-highlights (named non-highlighting). The condition sequence was counterbalanced among participants.

[3]https://www.techsmith.com/video-editor.html

	highlighting		Task A		Task B		more-readers		less-readers	
	non-highlighting	highlighting	non-highlighting	highlighting	non-highlighting	highlighting	non-highlighting	highlighting	non-highlighting	highlighting
Number of examined documents	284	265	178	112	106	153	118	132	166	133
(1) Average fixation time a on word in abstract	13.38 (14.01)	13.02 (12.4)	12.44 (14.45)	13.19 (12.10)	14.96 (13.17)	12.89 (12.66)	**21.63 (16.36) ***	15.81 (12.25) *	7.52 (7.99)	10.25 (11.97)
(2) Relevance judgment	3.86 (1.29)	3.63 (1.38)	4.01 (1.21)	3.68 (1.44)	3.59 (1.39)	3.6 (1.33)	3.53 (1.48)	3.59 (1.47)	**4.09 (1.9) ***	3.68 (1.28) *
(3) Ratio bookmarked and examined documents	**0.82 (0.44) ***	0.73 (0.44) *	**0.88 (0.42) ***	0.71 (0.46) *	0.72 (0.46)	0.75 (0.43)	0.74 (0.55)	0.68 (0.47)	**0.87 (0.33) ***	0.78 (0.41) *
(4) Jumps in abstract	0.50 (0.50) *	**0.68 (0.47) ***	0.55 (0.5) *	**0.68 (0.47) ***	0.43 (0.5) *	**0.68 (0.46) ***	0.46 (0.50) *	**0.62 (0.49) ***	0.53 (0.50) *	**0.74 (0.44) ***
(5) Sequentially read	0.79 (0.41)	0.73 (0.44)	0.76 (0.43)	0.74 (0.44)	**0.84 (0.37) ***	0.73 (0.44) *	0.87 (0.34)	0.85 (0.36)	**0.73 (0.44) ***	0.62 (0.48) *
(6) Percentage read	0.44 (0.4)	0.48 (0.42)	0.39 (0.4)	0.52 (0.44)	0.53 (0.4)	0.44 (0.40)	0.67 (0.39)	0.63 (0.4)	0.27 (0.3)	0.33 (0.38)

Table 1: Results for each dependent variable separated by the different subgroups, *p<0.05.

3.5 Procedure

All participants followed the same procedure: after greeting the participant, the experimenter explained the purpose of the study and asked to sign a consent form as well as to fill out a demographic survey. The experimenter provided a short introduction to Sowiport and gave the participant time to familiarize with the system. Afterwards, the eye tracker was calibrated and the first task was given. The participant was asked to read the instruction carefully. Then, she started searching for documents. There was no announced time-constraint so that the participant searched until she considered the information need was satisfied. After the search in the highlighting condition, the participants filled out a questionnaire to provide feedback on the highlighting. Afterwards, the stimulated recall interview took place. For each bookmark or closed detailed view page, the experimenter asked how useful this document was to solve the task and why. The second run with the other condition and the other task was conducted following the same procedure as in the first run. In the end, the participant filled out the post-questionnaire asking which of the two conditions she would prefer and which advantages and disadvantages she saw in the highlighting. We thanked the participants by compensating their effort with 30€. Altogether, one session took about 2 hours.

4 RESULTS

Altogether, the 25 participants judged the relevance of 912 documents. To be able to answer our research questions we focused on the detailed view pages that had an abstract because only those were different in the highlighting and non-highlighting conditions. From these documents, we further looked at just the documents which had at least one fixation in the abstract because in the other cases the other metadata was responsible for the relevance decision like the title or author and not the abstract. That left us with 549 abstracts for analysis. A total of 265 abstracts were with highlighting and 284 were without highlighting. On average, each participant looked at 10.6 (SD=3.34) detailed view pages in the highlighting condition and 11.36 (SD=5.23) detailed view pages in the non-highlighting condition. To determine the statistical significance of our results, we conducted Wilcoxon Signed Rank tests with $\alpha = 0.05$. Table 1 shows an overview of the results, which we will report on in the following.

4.1 Dependent variables

Our analysis is based on the following dependent variables: (1) Average fixation time on a word in abstract: value calculated by dividing the fixation time per abstract by the number of words in the abstract. In doing so, we address the different abstract lengths. (2) Relevance judgment of document: For each bookmarked or rejected document participants judged how useful the document for their task was on a Likert-style scale from 1 (not at all useful) to 5 (very useful). (3) Ratio between documents bookmarked and documents examined. (4) Jumps in abstract: For each document, we identified if a user jumped between different parts of the abstract (boolean value). (5) Sequentially read: whether the abstract or part of the abstract had been sequentially read (boolean value). (6) Percentage read of the abstract: How much of the abstract relative to its length had been read. This value is calculated by the number of rows a participant had read and the abstract's total number of rows.

4.2 Data recording and preparation

Sowiport has a logging component which logs every user action within the whole session. These are user actions like typed-in search query, the resulting list of search results, which detailed view has been shown, which link has been clicked, etc. Additionally to the logging data, we recorded the eye gaze data and used the SMI analyzing software BeGaze to calculate the fixation times on the abstract. To be able to do that we had to draw for every abstract the Area of Interest on the detailed view page. Through questionnaires, we collected the subjective assessments. The audio recording of the stimulated recall interview had been transcribed.

4.3 How do key-term-highlighted abstracts support users' document relevance decision?

4.3.1 Average fixation time on word in abstract. When we started with our research, we assumed that the key-term-highlights allow users to skim the text faster and to extract the gist of the text just by reading the highlighted terms. We thought that based on that, they could decide faster if a document is relevant or not. However, the results do not confirm our assumption. We did not find any significant differences regarding the average fixation time comparing the documents in the highlighting and non-highlighting condition. We wanted to know if there is a factor that influences this result in any way. Therefore we looked at different subgroups. First, we checked if the task might play a role, but again there are no significant differences in the highlighting condition, but we found significant differences in the non-highlighting condition. Participants were quicker in their relevance decision when looking for documents to a familiar topic (task A) (mean: 12.44, SD: 14.45) than while looking for documents to an unfamiliar topic (mean: 14.96, SD: 13.17) (p=0.022). Secondly, we divided the group of participants into those who read much of the abstract (more-readers (n=13) read on average >=33% of the abstract) and those who read little of the abstract (less-readers (n=12) read on average <33% of the abstract). More readers spent significantly less time reading the abstract in the highlighting condition (mean: 15.81, SD:12.25) than in the non-highlighting condition (mean: 21.63, SD: 16.36) (p=0.003). The results of the less-readers were not statistically significant.

4.3.2 Relevance judgment of document. There were no significant differences comparing highlighting vs. non-highlighting. When looking at the two tasks, it is remarkable that participants judged the relevance of bookmarked documents in the non-high-lighting with task A (familiar topic) higher (mean 4.01, SD:1.21) than with task B (mean 3.59, SD: 1.39) (p=0.008). We found that less-readers judged the relevance of bookmarked documents higher in the non-high-lighting condition (mean: 4.09, SD: 1.9) than in the highlighting condition (mean: 3.68, SD: 1.28) (p= 0.004).

4.3.3 Bookmarked documents. Here, we found significant differences in the highlighting and non-highlighting condition. Participants bookmarked more documents in the non-highlighting condition (mean: 0.82, SD: 0.44) than in the highlighting condition (mean: 0.73, SD: 0.44) (p=0.033). This is also true for task A (familiar topic) and the less-readers.

4.4 What effects have key-term-highlighted abstracts on the reading behavior in digital libraries?

4.4.1 "Jumps" in abstract. The highlights affected the reading behavior in so far that participants jumped more in the abstracts in the highlight condition (mean: 0.68, SD: 0.47) than in the non-highlighting condition (mean: 0.5, SD: 0.50) (p<0.0001). This is also evident in all subgroups. This result is not surprising as the idea of highlights is to guide the user's attention to the highlighted terms. In analyzing the gaze behavior of all participants, however, we observed that there were three different types of interactions: (1) participants first skimmed the highlighted terms and then decided to read more or not, (2) participants started reading the abstract and after a while stopped sequential reading and checked the remaining highlighted key-terms, and (3) the highlighted key-terms were fully ignored by participants.

4.4.2 Sequentially read. Most often jumps were combined with sequential reading. Participants read significantly more sequentially in the non-highlighting condition than in the highlighting condition while performing task B (unfamiliar topic) (non-highlighting mean: 0.84, SD:0.37, highlighting mean: 0.73, SD: 0.37, p=0.04) and when they were part of the subgroup less-readers (non-highlighting mean: 0.74, SD:0.44, highlighting mean: 0.62, SD: 0.49, p=0.041).

4.4.3 Percentage read. We could not find any significant differences in the amount of text participants read in the highlighting and non-highlighting condition for all subgroups. There were, however, significant differences in the non-highlighting condition considering each subgroup: participants read more of the abstract while searching for a document on an unfamiliar (task B) (mean: 0.53, SD:0.4) than on a familiar topic (task A) (mean 0.39, SD: 0.39) (p=0.003). More-readers read more from the abstract (mean: 0.67, SD: 0.39) than less-readers (mean: 0.27, SD: 0.33) (p<0.0001) and in this case, this was also true for the highlighting condition.

4.5 Subjective Feedback

In the post-questionnaire, we asked participants which version of the system they preferred. The answers were almost equally distributed (14 in favor of highlighting condition vs. 11 preferring non-highlighting). Answers given to 7-point-Likert-style scales revealed that the highlighting distracted participants rather less while reading the abstract (mean: 2.88, SD: 1.87, 1=not at all distracting to 7=very distracting) but the usefulness of the highlighting was rated mediocre (mean: 4.12, SD: 0.94, 1=not at all useful to 7=very useful to 1=not at all useful). Participants mentioned three main benefits of the highlighting: "faster relevance decision" (n=5), "quick overview" (n=5) and "relevant keywords at a glance" (n=4). The three most often stated disadvantages of the systems were: "Disturb the reading flow" (n=8), "wrong/unimportant keywords were highlighted" (n=6), "risk of overlooking important terms when they are not highlighted" (n=4).

4.6 Discussion and Conclusion

To summarize the insights from our experiment: (1) Highlighting not being beneficial for all: for some of the participants, highlights had a positive effect on relevance judgment and reading behavior but not for all. If a digital library plans to offer such a function, we recommend an opt-out option. (2) Task A vs. Task B: With the simulated work tasks A and B we intended to evoke a similar search behavior for both conditions. However, the comparison of the dependent variables of task A and task B in the non-highlighting conditions revealed that there were already some differences in search behavior (see table 1). (3) Versatile search and reading behavior: we observed very different search and reading behavior in both conditions. Some participants used a lot of search queries, visited a high number of detailed view pages, took their time for solving the tasks and read the abstract carefully. Others finished their tasks quite soon with only using a few search terms. Most often they just skimmed the abstract or ignored it at altogether. This is also reflected in the rather large standard deviation of our results (see 1). (4) Quality of highlighting: The quality of the highlighted keywords is crucial and needs to be very high so that users can trust that really the most important keywords are highlighted.

In future work, we plan to analyze the seeking and reading behavior further (similar as proposed in [6]) to find similar searching or reading patterns that give us more indications for which user group or which task a simple key-term-highlighting based on tf-idf might be helpful for supporting document relevance judgment. We further intend to address the quality issue by investigating different approaches to highlighting most important keywords.

5 ACKNOWLEDGEMENTS

We thank the participants of our study.

REFERENCES

[1] Katrin Angerbauer, Tilman Dingler, Dagmar Kern, and Albrecht Schmidt. 2015. Utilizing the Effects of Priming to Facilitate Text Comprehension. In *Proceedings of the 33rd Annual ACM Conference Extended Abstracts on Human Factors in Computing Systems (CHI EA '15)*. ACM, New York, NY, USA, 1043–1048. https://doi.org/10.1145/2702613.2732914

[2] Daniel Billsus, David M. Hilbert, and Dan Maynes-Aminzade. 2005. Improving Proactive Information Systems. In *Proceedings of the 10th International Conference on Intelligent User Interfaces (IUI '05)*. ACM, New York, NY, USA, 159–166. https://doi.org/10.1145/1040830.1040869

[3] Pia Borlund. 2003. The IIR evaluation model: a framework for evaluation of interactive information retrieval systems. *Information Research. An International Electronic Journal* 8, 3 (2003).

[4] George Buchanan and Fernando Loizides. 2007. Investigating Document Triage on Paper and Electronic Media. In *Research and Advanced Technology for Digital Libraries*, László Kovács, Norbert Fuhr, and Carlo Meghini (Eds.). Springer Berlin Heidelberg, Berlin, Heidelberg, 416–427.

[5] Ed H. Chi, Michelle Gumbrecht, and editor="Jacko Julie A. Hong, Lichan". 2007. Visual Foraging of Highlighted Text: An Eye-Tracking Study. In *Human-Computer Interaction. HCI Intelligent Multimodal Interaction Environments*. Springer Berlin Heidelberg, Berlin, Heidelberg, 589–598.

[6] Michael J. Cole, Jacek Gwizdka, Chang Liu, Ralf Bierig, Nicholas J. Belkin, and Xiangmin Zhang. 2011. Task and user effects on reading patterns in information search. *Interacting with Computers* 23, 4 (2011), 346–362. https://doi.org/10.1016/j.intcom.2011.04.007

[7] Tilman Dingler, Dagmar Kern, Katrin Angerbauer, and Albrecht Schmidt. 2017. Text Priming - Effects of Text Visualizations on Readers Prior to Reading. In *Human-Computer Interaction – INTERACT 2017*, Regina Bernhaupt, Girish Dalvi, Anirudha Joshi, Devanuj K. Balkrishan, Jacki O'Neill, and Marco Winckler (Eds.). Springer International Publishing, Cham, 345–365.

[8] Laura A. Granka, Thorsten Joachims, and Geri Gay. 2004. Eye-tracking Analysis of User Behavior in WWW Search. In *Proceedings of the 27th Annual International ACM SIGIR Conference on Research and Development in Information Retrieval (SIGIR '04)*. ACM, New York, NY, USA, 478–479. https://doi.org/10.1145/1008992.1009079

[9] Jacek Gwizdka. 2014. Characterizing Relevance with Eye-tracking Measures. In *Proceedings of the 5th Information Interaction in Context Symposium (IIiX '14)*. ACM, New York, NY, USA, 58–67. https://doi.org/10.1145/2637002.2637011

[10] Daniel Hienert, Frank Sawitzki, and Philipp Mayr. 2015. Digital library research in action–supporting information retrieval in sowiport. *D-Lib Magazine* 21, 3/4 (2015).

[11] Joseph W Janes. 1991. Relevance judgments and the incremental presentation of document representations. *Information Processing & Management* 27, 6 (1991), 629–646.

[12] Ziming Liu. 2005. Reading behavior in the digital environment: Changes in reading behavior over the past ten years. *Journal of documentation* 61, 6 (2005), 700–712.

[13] Keith Rayner. 1998. Eye movements in reading and information processing: 20 years of research. *Psychological bulletin* 124, 3 (1998), 372.

[14] Radim Řehůřek and Petr Sojka. 2010. Software Framework for Topic Modelling with Large Corpora. In *Proceedings of the LREC 2010 Workshop on New Challenges for NLP Frameworks*. ELRA, Valletta, Malta, 45–50. http://is.muni.cz/publication/884893/en.

[15] Tefko Saracevic. 1969. Comparative effects of titles, abstracts and full texts on relevance judgments. *Proceedings of the American Society for Information Science* 6, 1 (1969), 293–299.

[16] H. Schmid. 1999. *Improvements in Part-of-Speech Tagging with an Application to German*. Springer Netherlands, Dordrecht, 13–25".

[17] Chih-Hsuan Wei, Hung-Yu Kao, and Zhiyong Lu. 2013. PubTator: a web-based text mining tool for assisting biocuration. *Nucleic acids research* 41, W1 (2013), W518–W522.

[18] Qian Yang, Gerard de Melo, Yong Cheng, and Sen Wang. 2017. HiText: Text Reading with Dynamic Salience Marking. In *Proceedings of the 26th International Conference on World Wide Web Companion (WWW '17 Companion)*. International World Wide Web Conferences Steering Committee, Republic and Canton of Geneva, Switzerland, 311–319. https://doi.org/10.1145/3041021.3054168

From Bubbles to Lists: Designing Clustering for Due Diligence

Winter Wei, Adam Roegiest and Mary Mikhail
Kira Systems
Toronto, Canada
{winter,adam.roegiest,mary.mikhail}@kirasystems.com

ABSTRACT

In due diligence, lawyers are tasked with reviewing a large set of legal documents to identify documents and portions thereof that may be problematic for a merger or acquisition. In an effort to aid users to review more efficiently, we sought to determine how document-level clustering may help users of a due diligence system during their workflow.

Following an iterative design methodology, we conducted several user studies with different versions of a document-level clustering feature consisting of three distinct phases and 27 users. We found that the interface should adapt to a user's understanding of what "similar documents" means so that trust can be established in the feature. Furthermore, the ability to negotiate with the underlying algorithm is facilitated by the establishment of trust. Finally, while the usage of this feature may be influenced by a user's role, it remains primarily a project management tool.

ACM Reference Format:
Winter Wei, Adam Roegiest and Mary Mikhail. 2019. From Bubbles to Lists: Designing Clustering for Due Diligence. In *2019 Conference on Human Information Interaction and Retrieval (CHIIR '19), March 10–14, 2019, Glasgow, United Kingdom.* ACM, New York, NY, USA, 5 pages. https://doi.org/10.1145/3295750.3298951

1 INTRODUCTION

When conducting due diligence, lawyers seek to find and determine the risk in a target company's legal documents (e.g., contracts, employment agreements, leases), often through extraction and analysis of passages from these documents. As there is usually time pressure to review the document collection as quickly as possible, there is no time to explore the collection. Rather lawyers attempt to find the hypothetical "needle(s) in the haystack" that may compromise the deal. Traditionally, these collections are compiled from several sources and so a project manager's job of estimating the amount of work required by the number of documents and assigning documents to lawyers becomes complex. This assignment process is often done "without rhyme or reason" and so may not leverage a particular lawyer's special capabilities. Risks and action items are identified after lawyers review and extract information from documents.

CHIIR '19, March 10–14, 2019, Glasgow, United Kingdom

ACM ISBN 978-1-4503-6025-8/19/03...$15.00
https://doi.org/10.1145/3295750.3298951

Despite of the lack of visibility into what may be relevant or important in this approach, it remains the most common way of working among most law firms. As pointed out by Russell et al. [15], sense makers tend to choose the lowest-cost method when facing a one-off task with limited time. Accordingly, we sought to provide lawyers with a feature that would allow them to quickly identify these risks and actions items without requiring extensive review of a document collection. One obvious technique to aid in this task would be clustering, such that anomalous/risky documents would ideally be identified as outliers (i.e., ungrouped documents). This resulted in the prototype featured in Figure 1, where the red bubble denotes the outlier group.

This prototype quickly proved to be confusing and a potential hindrance to the users we interviewed. They could find no discernible reason for how and why documents were (not) grouped together when using the feature. This led to a series of prototypes over three distinct phases spanning 8 months and 27 users (e.g., senior partner, junior associates), and marked the transition from a risk identification tool to a project management tool. Overall, we investigated the following research questions:

(1) What is the most appropriate representation for document-level clustering to help users make sense of the collection, while achieving their goals in the due diligence context?
(2) What does it mean for a user to "trust" the clustering algorithm? Should we focus on transparency of information, or a representation that meets their expectations?
(3) What are our users' mental models when it comes to "similar documents"? How do we design an experience to match their mental models?
(4) How would users' expectations of the clustering results and their inclination to negotiate with the clusters be influenced by their particular roles in a due diligence project?

While not all of these questions were answered to complete satisfaction, we found that aligning the interface to the terminology used by lawyers helps to build trust and an inherent understanding of why an algorithm behaves as it does. Once trust is established, users are more likely to want to negotiate with the algorithm to correct mistakes. This willingness appears to be beneficial since it is a lower cost activity than not using the feature.

2 RELATED WORK

There has been extensive work into data visualization techniques at-large, Bilal et al. [2] and Kucher and Keren [8] provide good overviews of the most recent developments and best practices. Chuang et al. [4] emphasized the importance of facilitating interpretations and trust when designing for model-driven visualizations. Kang et al. [1] suggest that visualization tools for domain experts should allow considered augmentation of the visualization

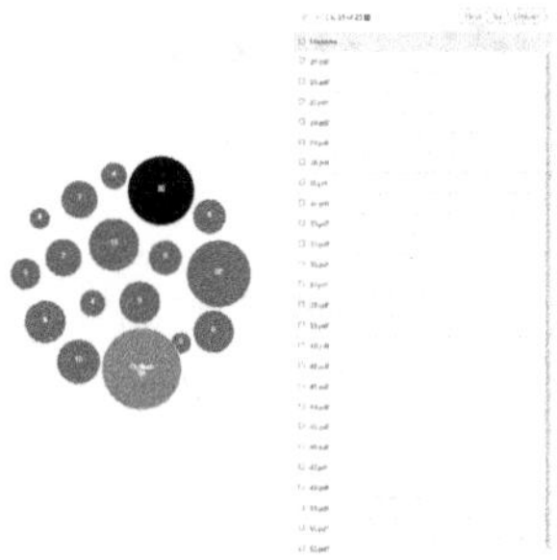

Figure 1: An example of our initial clustering prototype based primarily on the belief that users would want to examine groups of similar documents and the outlier (red bubble) documents.

such that users do not draw invalid conclusions. Along those lines, Russell et al. found that certain types of representation and manipulation were preferable to others for some tasks as they would have a lower cost [14]. As project managers often have to make sense of an unknown collection, Sarrafzadeh et al.'s suggestion that hierarchical visualizations can be better at providing an overview in uncertain situations [16] is an apt one for due diligence.

In the legal domain, while there are existing studies that examine the information seeking behaviour of lawyers, they mostly focus on case law [9] and academic lawyers [10] whose main tasks and therefore information seeking behaviour are different than those of transaction and corporate lawyers. As such, the design implications of visualization in the legal domain in existing literature have largely revolved around email collections and how to view the different relationships (e.g., email threads, social networks, etc) for the purposes of electronic discovery [3, 17, 18]. While such results may be useful in some diligence contexts (e.g., involving email), the results are not generally useful as the end goals between due diligence and electronic discovery do not necessarily align.

3 PHASE ONE

This phase represented our initial prototype (Figure 1), which was developed largely using our intuition about what users would want (i.e., risk identification). Accordingly, our hypotheses were that:

(1) Dissimilar documents would be prioritized for review, as we assumed they were anomalous documents.
(2) Reviewing documents that are similar would make review faster.
(3) Visualization is desirable in providing a high level overview to the structure of the document collection [6].

3.1 Methodology

We tested our initial prototype (Figure 1) with a selected group of interested users that all found the feature confusing. To determine what caused this confusion, we conducted a round of generative research [7] by interviewing 5 senior partners to understand their current workflos and goals. As part of this process, we presented them with several abstract visualizations (Figure 2) for different scenarios and asked what they might prefer. Following this round, we conducted several rounds of paper-prototyping and think-aloud studies to determine which interface may be of the most use. These

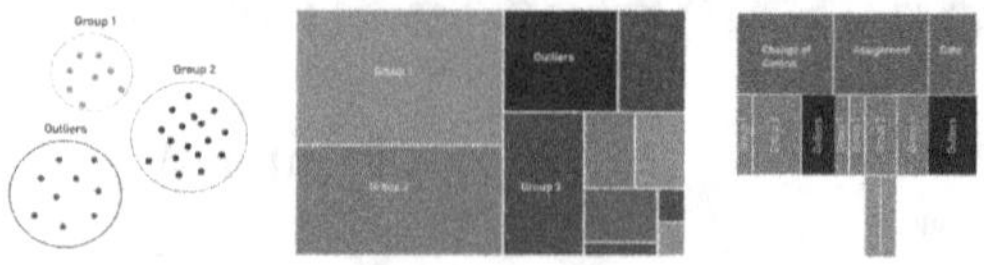

Figure 2: Examples of the various cluster visualizations that were presented to senior partners during a user study. From left to right: circle clusters, treemaps, icicle diagrams.

sessions tested 7 different designs with 16 legal professionals, including senior partners, project managers, and associates. Additional feedback was collected from in-house legal professionals to determine out how they might use such a feature.

3.2 Results

We find that for due diligence, abstract visualizations, like that in Figure 1, did not yield something lawyers can easily interpret. As one user opined, *"The Coca-Cola bubbles are more trouble than its worth, I like percentage, number and name but no bubbles."* Lawyers, when facing a tight deadline, tend not to find non-structured or non-hierarchical interfaces useful. They effectively want "just the facts" and this desire must be facilitated by the system and tool builders. As Tesler's Law of Conservation of Complexity [12] states that the complexity of a system is constant, the onus is upon the system builders to facilitate that desire at their expense and not the user's.

One aspect of user behaviour that became apparent in this phase is that users are not readily willing to trust an opaque algorithm. Fundamentally, they did not want to have to spend the time understanding how and why a cluster is formed. Users frequently expressed opinions such as *"At least highlight the provision that made it an outlier. There's gotta be a punchy way of explaining why something is an outlier,"* and *"I don't know what the computer is looking at, I'm hesitant to trust it. I don't know how it's grouping."* These attitudes highlight that "trust" and "transparency" are needed to achieve buy-in from users.

We believe the lack of trust in our original prototype stemmed from several factors. The first was that the visualization itself was overly simplistic and did not facilitate an understanding of why documents were grouped as they were. Secondly, our definitions of "outlier" differed from theirs in that we saw them as "documents that are not similar enough;" whereas, they define them to be "documents that should be similar but are not." Due to the above, we believe that we were not able to convey the appropriate information to the users and that this lack of knowledge transfer led to their dissatisfaction. Indeed, it has been shown [5] that humans will avoid algorithms when they have seen them "fail" to produce their desired outcome. Finally, our hypothesis that risky documents would be dissimilar ones did not bear fruit. Risk, as it turns out, can manifest in several different ways (e.g., unfavourable terms shared across multiple documents) rather than a single document not looking like others.

3.3 Design Implications

Based on the results of this first phase, our subsequent designs focused on aligning the interface and algorithms with the mental

Figure 3: A screenshot of our clustering user interface for Phase Two. This showed the four different classes of similarity that we determined users were interested in.

models of the users. Instead of a one-size-fits-all clustering technique, we would seek to use several to identify near duplicates, documents that are "Based on a Form," documents that have otherwise "Similar Content" (e.g., specific types of leases), and documents that do not have a home elsewhere ("Ungrouped"). These categories are drawn from interviewees' own words to provide familiarity and align with their underlying goals more so than technical jargon or elaborate descriptions and justifications. This is similar to the findings of Attfield and Bandford [3] that, in electronic discovery, identifying and specifying the different classes of relevant and irrelevant material was a prerequisite for success.

During this phase, we rapidly designed and prototyped different variations of two major design paradigms to test the coarse grain effect of the designs. We started with representing a cluster of documents as a deck of cards with descriptive information on the card thumbnails, and soon discovered from user testing that it introduced more cognitive load as the card paradigm was not used to represent document collections in other parts of the user interface. This led to a quick decision to change the representation of document collections to lists, which conforms more to users' mental models. We found that users were quicker in identifying what they were looking at and making sense of the document collections.

This phase also made it clear that users need to be able to test actual working prototypes to discover how well their needs are met. Accordingly, in all subsequent phases, we encouraged users to use their own data, when possible, or to use data provided by us that simulates a due diligence collection.

4 PHASE TWO

Our main goal for this phase was to validate the effectiveness of the design and algorithmic changes made based upon our discoveries in Phase One. These changes are shown in Figure 3. In our testing for this phase, we sought to investigate the following:

(1) Increased algorithmic accuracy is essential to establish trust and increase likelihood of using the feature.
(2) Different categories imply different levels of similarity (e.g., near duplicates are more similar than "Similar Content" documents).
(3) That additional metadata is needed for understanding why documents are grouped together as filenames do not convey sufficient context.
(4) This feature is most likely to be used by project managers, and functionality should be optimized for their tasks.

4.1 Methodology

This prototype feature was provided to three users, who ran 10s to 100s of documents through it. A short survey was also sent to them to provide consistent feedback. In particular, we asked about the number and type of documents, their general impressions, how accurate they found each category, whether they might use this feature day to day, and in what capacity. We allowed them to define their own task goals to get a sense of the real-world applicability.

4.2 Results

From post-test interviews, we found an increased level of trust in, and understanding of, the feature. Users were able to understand the meaning behind the categories and subsequently form concrete ideas about what to expect. However, users felt there was some ambiguity between "Near Duplicates" and "Based on a Form" as they could imagine scenarios where there may be overlap that this design did not allow. We also discovered in the interviews that users would like the ability to correct/negotiate with the algorithm by moving documents from one cluster to another.

The metadata we provided in this phase (i.e., document title, parties in the document, and document date) proved to be a boon for users towards understanding why documents were grouped together. However, the paginated card view made observing the relationships between documents in a cluster hard for users, which increased sensemaking cost. Accordingly, the ability of project managers to assign users to review documents was hindered because they could not get a sense of what was in a particular cluster.

4.3 Design Implications

Based on our findings in this phase, we moved forward with three major changes. The first was to merge the "Near Duplicates" and "Based on a Form" categories into a new "Similar Structure and Content" category. The second was to provide a list view to allow users to view-at-a-glance all documents and document metadata for a cluster, which had the intended goal of reducing sensemaking cost. Finally, we added the ability to move documents between groups, create groups, and delete groups. We refer to these abilities in aggregate as "negotiation," since the movement of documents affects how subsequently added documents may be clustered.

5 PHASE THREE

In this final phase, we had what we believed to be a mostly robust solution (Figure 4). To verify this, we investigated the following hypotheses:

(1) The role of the users (e.g., project manager vs. reviewer) would influence their expectation on document grouping and the usefulness of this feature.
(2) The more users need to negotiate, the less likely they will use this feature as the cost of the tasks increases.
(3) Document title is the most helpful meta data for users make sense of the group without having to read each document.

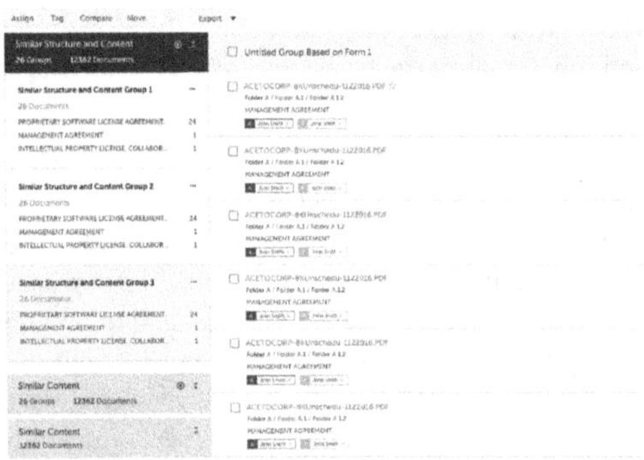

Figure 4: The final clustering user interface showing the list of documents and document metadata in the same view as the group they belong to.

5.1 Methodology

We asked 8 users (6 project managers, 2 reviewers) from 3 firms to test our new interface. We asked users to conduct three tasks (i.e., examine categories, perform a self-assigned task, negotiate) in a think-aloud fashion and interviewed them afterwards to validated our hypotheses. Unlike the previous phase, we had them use a simulated diligence collection of 103 documents to expedite the testing process and ensure all users had a consistent experience.

5.2 Results

One of our primary findings in this phase is that user roles *may* influence how they interact with the similarity categories but is not an absolute. Only one of the reviewers said that they would use "Similar Structure and Content" clusters to identify near duplicates. Similarly, only a slight majority of the project managers said they would use "Similar Content" to assign users to review documents. At best, these trends encourage us to continue to investigate how role influences the usage of this feature once it is deployed.

Contrary to our hypothesis, negotiation appears to be a useful ability for project managers. We posit that this may be due to the fact that clusters can act as "starting points" for assigning reviewers. Traditionally project managers will assign documents to users based upon the unreliable folder structure present in their document collections. Thus, starting with an "almost correct" cluster and negotiating may result in a net gain as they are able to assign documents to users in a more efficient manner.

From this phase and the previous phase, we noticed a trend to want to assign users to documents that are not necessarily similar but are *related* (e.g., amendments, signed versions). While at a high-level, these documents may be similar (e.g., referring to the same contract or deal) they textually look and feel different. Handling these cases is not something the feature currently does. It also highlights that there is no definitive analysis that one can conduct on due diligence document collections.

6 DISCUSSION

6.1 Matching Representation to Mental Models

Our study has demonstrated that effective designs should reflect users' mental models for due diligence as has been shown for UX design at large [11, 13]. Designers should take the time through generative research to understand their users' jargon, concepts, and goals. Furthermore, we have found that to provide an accurate and useful representation, we must first understand how our mental models and that of our users differ. While we may use the same words, they have different meanings. Accordingly, our different similarity categories evolved from our growing understanding of the different similarity-based tasks our users would like to undertake.

6.2 Adapting Interface Based on Tasks

In due diligence, the tantamount goal is to identify whether a particular transaction would put a client at risk. This is a high-stress situation for all involved and users are generally less likely to tolerate sensemaking tasks that require high costs. Efficiency then becomes a primary motivator for lawyers which means that they are more inclined to prefer obviously structural visual representations (e.g., *"This format isn't helpful since circles are misleading. Bars are more simple and straight-forward"*). Once we realized that the the primary task for clustering would be for time and project management, it was much easier to refine the design to meet those needs in a way that was clear to lawyers.

6.3 Trust and negotiation

Throughout the first phase, users continually expressed the idea that they could not "trust" a black-box algorithm. We later determined that this appeared to be a result of a gap between their mental model and how we were representing the data. Once we were able to align our representation to their model, users were more willing to tolerate the algorithm even if they still did not know how it worked. Consequently, they were willing to tolerate mistakes from the algorithm when given the option to negotiate with it and potentially correct those mistakes. Thus, even when the algorithm does not meet their expectations out-of-the-box, they are able to correct it in a meaningful way with low cost.

7 CONCLUSION

This paper has presented an overview of our user-centric approach to designing a document-level clustering tool for due diligence. We have shown that aligning a tool to the intended mental model and tasks of envisioned users is crucial for establishing trust. Furthermore, we have found that when trust is established, users are more willing to tolerate and accommodate flaws in the feature. It becomes more efficient to negotiate with the feature than it does not to use it. While our study is relatively small, we have found that involving users early in the design process and iterating will yield a substantially better product than delivering only an end product that was developed in relative isolation. Further work will be done as additional feedback is gathered after the feature launch. We anticipate that much of our subsequent work will continue to refine the design to further increase trust in and utility of the feature.

ACKNOWLEDGMENTS

The authors would like to thank all of the users and members of our Legal Knowledge Engineering team who took time out of their busy schedules to help facilitate this work.

REFERENCES

[1] Youn ah Kang, John Stasko, and Senior Member. 2012. Examining the Use of a Visual Analytics System for Sensemaking Tasks: Case Studies with Domain Experts. (2012).

[2] Bilal Alsallakh, Luana Micallef, Wolfgang Aigner, Helwig Hauser, Silvia Miksch, and Peter Rodgers. 2016. The State-of-the-Art of Set Visualization. *Computer Graphics Forum* 35, 1 (2016).

[3] Simon Attfield and Ann Blandford. 2010. Discovery-led refinement in e-discovery investigations: sensemaking, cognitive ergonomics and system design. *Artif. Intell. Law* 18, 4 (2010).

[4] Jason Chuang, Daniel Ramage, Christopher D. Manning, and Jeffrey Heer. 2012. Interpretation and trust: Designing model-driven visualizations for text analysis. In *SIGCHI '12*.

[5] Berkeley J. Dietvorst, Joseph P. Simmons, and Cade Massey. [n. d.]. Algorithm Aversion: People Erroneously Avoid Algorithms After Seeing Them Err. ([n. d.]).

[6] Stephen Few and Perceptual Edge. 2007. Data visualization: past, present, and future. *IBM Cognos Innovation Center* (2007).

[7] Erika Hall. 2013. *Just Enough Research*. A Book Apart.

[8] K. Kucher and A. Kerren. 2015. Text visualization techniques: Taxonomy, visual survey, and community insights. In *2015 IEEE Pacific Visualization Symposium (PacificVis)*.

[9] Gloria J Leckie, Karen E Pettigrew, and Christian Sylvain. 1996. Modeling the information seeking of professionals: A general model derived from research on engineers, health care professionals, and lawyers. *The Library Quarterly* 66, 2 (1996), 161–193.

[10] Stephann Makri, Ann Blandford, and Anna L Cox. 2008. Investigating the information-seeking behaviour of academic lawyers: From EllisâĂŹs model to design. *Information Processing & Management* 44, 2 (2008), 613–634.

[11] Jakob Nielsen. 2010. Mental Models. (2010). https://www.nngroup.com/articles/mental-models/

[12] Don Norman. 2011. *Living with Complexity*. The MIT Press.

[13] Don Norman. 2013. *The Design of Everyday Things*. Basic Books.

[14] Daniel M. Russell, Malcolm Slaney, Yan Qu, and Mave Houston. 2006. Being literate with large document collections: Observational studies and cost structure tradeoffs. (2006).

[15] Daniel M. Russell, Mark J. Stefik, Peter Pirolli, and Stuart K. Card. [n. d.]. Proceedings of InterCHI 1993 ABSTRACT The Cost Structure of Sensemaking. ([n. d.]).

[16] Bahareh Sarrafzadeh, Alexandra Vtyurina, Edward Lank, and Olga Vechtomova. 2016. Knowledge Graphs versus Hierarchies: An Analysis of User Behaviours and Perspectives in Information Seeking. In *CHIIR*.

[17] Mithileysh Sathiyanarayanan and Cagatay Turkay. 2017. Challenges and Opportunities in using Analytics Combined with Visualisation Techniques for Finding Anomalies in Digital Communications. In *ICAIL DESI VII Workshop*.

[18] David van Dijk, David Graus, Zhaochun Ren, Hans Henseler, and Maarten de Rijke. 2015. Who is Involved? Semantic Search for E-Discovery. In *ICAIL DESI VI Workshop*.

Privacy Nudging in Search: Investigating Potential Impacts

Steven Zimmerman, Alistair Thorpe, Chris Fox, Udo Kruschwitz
University of Essex
Colchester, United Kingdom
{szimme,athorpe,foxcj,udo}@essex.ac.uk

ABSTRACT

From their impacts to potential threats, privacy and misinformation are a recurring top news story. Social media platforms (e.g. Facebook) and information retrieval (IR) systems (e.g. Google), are now in the public spotlight to address these issues. Our research investigates an approach, known as Nudging, applied to the domain of IR, as a potential means to minimize impacts and threats surrounding both matters. We perform our study in the space of health search for two reasons. First, encounters with misinformation in this space have potentially grave outcomes. Second, there are many potential threats to personal privacy as a result of the data collected during a search task. Adopting methods and a corpus from previous work as the foundation, our study asked users to determine the effectiveness of a treatment for 10 medical conditions. Users performed the tasks on 4 variants of a search engine results page (SERP) and a control, with 3 of the SERP's being a Nudge (re-ranking, filtering and a visual cue) intended to reduce impacts to privacy with minimal impact to search result quality. The aim of our work is to determine the Nudge that is least impactful to good decision making while simultaneously increasing privacy protection. We find privacy impacts are significantly reduced for the re-ranking and filtering strategies, with no significant impacts on quality of decision making.

KEYWORDS

Information Retrieval; Interactive Studies; Privacy; Information Filtering

ACM Reference Format:
Steven Zimmerman, Alistair Thorpe, Chris Fox, Udo Kruschwitz. 2019. Privacy Nudging in Search: Investigating Potential Impacts. In *2019 Conference on Human Information Interaction and Retrieval (CHIIR '19), March 10–14, 2019, Glasgow, Scotland Uk.* ACM, New York, NY, USA, 5 pages. https://doi.org/10.1145/3295750.3298952

1 INTRODUCTION

Specific to the domain of IR, users encounter misinformation for various reasons, including IR system and individual biases [16, 19, 32], which raises ethical concerns [3, 21]. These biases may prevent users from finding the most correct and accurate information [22, 32, 33]. User biases often prevent viewing beyond the first 2 results [12, 20] or consideration of additional sources [11]. Users searching in the domain of health and medical information are not exempt from these biases [1, 22, 34], which is perhaps more problematic than a user seeking information to help decide what movie to see.

Concurrently, there are privacy concerns within IR systems, including collection and inference of personal health data [10] and other demographics [2, 26, 30, 31]. Furthermore, the data collected through websites a user visits via an IR system (e.g. Google), is often collected by means of 3rd party tracking, which raises many additional threats to personal privacy [5, 6, 35]. Personal data collected via tracking cookies and query logs allow for targeted advertising [28] and a personalized experience [24], however this data collection has many potential harms [18]. There are effective tools available to identify and potentially block trackers [5, 35].

Nudging [25] is one possible approach to address problems around misinformation and privacy. Nudges are appealing as they have low cognitive cost and permit freedom of choice due to the guiding philosophy of libertarian paternalism [25], with a tradeoff of ethical concerns due to non-transparent agendas [9]. Nudging is grounded in the "2 system" theory of decision making [13, 14, 27]. Regardless of the ethical [9] and underlying theoretical [8] concerns around Nudging, it is an effective approach to individual and societal change [25], so much so that government administrations have formed Nudge units[1]. In the domain of IR, Nudging towards healthier food options [4] and healthier information consumption [7] have been considered[2]. Given the climate surrounding privacy and misinformation, it is plausible a business model or government policy emerges to address both privacy and misinformation, using Nudging as the approach. It is thus important to understand possible implications of such an approach.

To assess possible impacts of Nudging in health search, we use an existing set of fact-based search tasks (10 total) [22], which are based upon findings from Cochrane Medical Reviews. Participants were tasked with making a decision on a set of 10 search tasks to determine if the provided medical treatment was *helpful, not helpful* or *inconclusive* for a given medical problem. Search tasks include the question: *"Do probiotics help treat eczema?"*.

2 QUESTIONS AND HYPOTHESES

Our guiding question is *"To what extent do user behaviors change in relation to their information biases when presented a privacy protecting Nudge?"*, which leads to many underlying questions and hypotheses. Our immediate research goal is to find the optimal Nudge approach that increases privacy protection and minimizes

CHIIR '19, March 10–14, 2019, Glasgow, Scotland Uk

ACM ISBN 978-1-4503-6025-8/19/03...$15.00
https://doi.org/10.1145/3295750.3298952

[1] examples: in the UK under David Cameron and in Obama Administration in the USA.
[2] SafeSearch, a filtering tool on many search engines, is a Nudge when the default is set to on (e.g. Bing). Its default setting has the intent of reducing risk of seeing offensive results, users have freedom of choice to shut it off, the default is low cost to the user, and it requires effort to change the setting. As most users keep the default, the goal of reducing visits to offensive material is thus achieved.

negative impacts to decisions and cognitive load for information seeking tasks in a SERP (specifically health search). Our initial focus is 1) to determine what negative effects may occur in regards to decision making in a system that nudges users towards privacy and 2) to determine if privacy impacts are reduced. Due to the difficulty of objectively measuring privacy impacts, we use the number of 3rd party trackers as a proxy.

Using the results viewed by users and the linked 3rd party trackers (using the Ghostery tracking detection tool), we calculate the average number of encounters with 3rd party trackers for each search task. Our study makes use of the number of trackers to drive the 3 Nudge approaches: re-ranking, filtering and stoplight cues (see Section 3.5.1). The stoplight approach is inspired through findings in nutrition studies that encourage healthier eating behavior [17, 23, 29], which show much better results and satisfaction by users as compared to a nutrition table [7].

We expect that all 3 interfaces will have a significant impact on encounters with 3rd party trackers (a reduction), given most users do not consider many results [12] and red lights are effective at producing the desired outcome [17, 29]. Simulations on our test corpus show precision at rank 10 will be 2-3% lower than our baseline SERP, and therefore expect some negative impacts on decisions. Time taken to complete a search task is linked to cognitive load [15], and cognitive load is expected to be increased for all three interfaces, for several reasons. First, source bias [11] of users certainly exists, and would likely result in increased time as many popular websites (e.g. Newspapers such as the New York Times and the Guardian, Medical sites including WebMD.com) are heavily reliant on 3rd party trackers, and thus will likely not appear in the first 10 results of re-ranking and filtering approaches, with users visiting many more websites they have not heard of. Additionally, while the stoplight is likely to be more efficient than a nutrition label approach [23], the stoplight SERP is visually busier than the ranking, filtering and baseline approaches, therefore we expect users to take longer in their decisions (potentially more-so when seeing this SERP for the first time).

3 METHODS

We use the methods developed by Podacar et al. [22] as the starting point for our study, as their work has many desirable qualities. One quality being their study and ours are both within-group designs that manipulate results in a SERP. Another quality being search tasks with clear definitive answers that are likely interesting to university participants. Furthermore, our study is interested in search tasks where concerns around ethics and biases are strong; health search has both types of concerns and the tasks covered by [22] are about health.

Unlike our study, which considers impacts on decisions due to *privacy* Nudging, their study looked at the impacts on decisions due to *quality* of results. Specifically, they biased results such that users had 8 of first 10 results correct or incorrect, and either the first or third result being correct. Their study, like ours, was a within-group design, with each participant seeing 4 variants plus a control variant (5 total), with 2 search tasks assigned to each variant.

The section headings used below match the phrasing used in Podacar et al. [22] to allow the reader to directly compare key differences from their work, we do not include headings where there were no differences.

3.1 Overview

We had one independent variable, being the SERP (and underlying system biased results) for users to make decisions. A baseline SERP with results biased in a manner similar to modern search engines (discussed further below), 3 privacy SERPs with results biased in a manner expected to reduce 3rd party privacy impacts and a control with no results (like [22]). We consider the dependent variables *correct* and *harmful* decisions as defined by [22], where Pogacar et al. defined *correct* to be a user decision that matched the Cochrane review and *harmful* as a decision that was opposite the Cochrane review (e.g. decision is *harmful* if a user decides the treatment is *helpful*, while the Cochrane review says the treatment is *not helpful*). Additionaly, we also look at the average number of privacy impacting trackers and the time taken per search task.

3.2 Search Results

We desired a baseline ranking of results that closely matched results for live search engines (e.g. WebMD.com often ranks high in medical search). From the baseline ranking, we then manipulated results based upon the 3rd party trackers found for each webpage.

For the baseline ranking, we use the rank score of the webpage as it was found in live search systems (see Section 3.3 for annotation details). Using the rank score, we then apply an inverse cumulative distribution function (CDF) to the set of documents assigned to a given medical question to produce the final baseline ranking. Use of the inverse CDF in this manner places a much higher probability of a webpage found at Google rank 3 to appear for a participant than a webpage found at Google rank 27. The inverse CDF allows for natural randomness of result ranking for each participant, as would be seen in a commercial search engine[3]. We use the findings that 80.69% of results for medical queries are *correct* in the top 10 results [34] as a guideline to tune the ranking of the experimental corpus.

For the biasing of results for the 3 privacy nudges, we first retrieve all documents for the search task a participant is on, then perform baseline ranking, then retrieve the number of 3rd party trackers for each result. For the re-ranking Nudge, we re-order the results based on the number of privacy trackers, with rank 1 being associated with fewest trackers and rank N being associated with most trackers. For the filtering Nudge, we keep the original baseline ranking then remove any result above the median number of trackers. Should the user shut off the filter (or other Nudge), the results return to the baseline. For the stoplight approach, we keep the baseline ranking and then associate each result with a color, anything below the median number of trackers receives green, above the median but below the top quartile is given yellow, and anything in the top quartile is assigned red (for highest concern).

3.3 Documents and Snippets

We begin with the documents already published by [22] and find 55 were no longer available. These documents were excluded from the

[3]Anecdotally, we found this behavior in Bing going back and forth between page 1 and 2 of results, in other words the results were changed without re-running a query.

study as we would not be able to retrieve 3rd party tracking data for them. This produced some challenges, particularly in regards to the filtering approach, where for instance only 4 documents would appear to the user for some tasks had we used only the original annotations [22][4]. Furthermore, we wanted baseline results to closely match the findings of [34], therefore we gathered additional documents.

For the expansion of the corpus, we used Bing, Yahoo and Google, as did the original authors. We also used a VPN set to the Toronto area of Canada (location near original authors) and ran searches using incognito browsing to minimize any potential of personalization of results. We contacted the authors to determine search terms they used and followed their instructions. Due to time constraints, we only went through the first 30 results in each search engine. We recorded the rank of each *correct* result found in the top 30 results. Anything beyond rank 30 was recorded as 31, as were incorrect results. These rankings were assigned to all documents in the original and expanded corpus, we then created a weighted ranking based on the market share of each of the 3 search engines in July 2018[5]. As did [22], two authors on this paper confirmed the correctness of all webpages added. Altogether, 95 documents were added (93 correct and 2 incorrect).

We noticed some inconsistencies in the snippets of the original corpus in addition to the T9 and T10 matters [22] discussed, specifically that many snippets were longer than 2 sentences. To address all issues, we collected the first two sentences for task T9 and T10. For all other tasks, we ran the Python NLTK sentence splitter over the snippets to ensure only 2 sentences were visible for each result.

Lastly, we needed a privacy marker. For this, we used the Ghostery[6] privacy tracking tool to determine the number of trackers for each article in our corpus[7]. Our updated corpus had 19-24 documents per search task, using standard settings of 10 results per page.

3.4 Dependent Variables

We consider four dependent variables to help determine the most effective Nudge, which include the fraction of *correct* decisions [22], the fraction of *harmful* decisions [22], the *average # of privacy trackers encountered* and the *time to complete a search task*.

For a privacy protective search system, minimization of the average number of trackers is one possible objective, and thus is used as one dependent variable. Though a future study could look at cross website trackers encountered (e.g. Facebook tracker), we assume independence for our research (e.g. 3 trackers on website X will not be found on any other website).

Multiple methods to measure cognitive load exist [15], however we only consider the time it takes (in seconds) to complete a task. Future research would take a more in-depth focus on cognitive measures.

3.5 Study Design

Once ethics approval was granted by the university, we ran participants in the following manner. Once signing consent, participants went through a 10x10 Graeco-Latin square fully balanced design (built in similar manner to [22]). We placed the demographic survey after the main experiment, where participants were debriefed with correct information about each medical treatment.

3.5.1 User Interface. The SERP is standard search interface modeled after popular search engines (see Appendix A for screenshots), we also provide medical definitions and decision options like [22], with some differences worth noting. A sticky panel was used at the top of the page to allow for definitions to be visible during the scroll of results. The definitions of medical treatment efficacies were kept in this sticky panel at the top right. A decision button was added in this sticky panel, in addition to the button at the bottom of the results page. We also added a message to users to let them know they could click on links, based on feedback from pilot participants, even then, several users did not click on any links. In the top left of the sticky panel was a hamburger icon, commonly seen in websites and search engines (e.g. Bing), to change settings. The only setting users could change was privacy protection, which allowed the user to turn the Nudge off (default is on, except for baseline). For the stoplight interface, a mouse-over tool tip is provided which gives users definitions: (Privacy risk where Red = much above normal, Yellow = above normal, Green = below normal.).

In the results page, the filtering and re-ranking results appeared exactly the same visually as the baseline SERP. For the stoplight approach, a round light was added just to the left of the result link, that would change color based on the privacy score (see Section 3.2) and had a letter "P" for privacy in the center. We also provided pagination for any results beyond the first 10 results available. This was done in order to allow users access to all possible results if they wished to go to extra pages and ensured that if users were to shut off the filtering Nudge then all results would be available[8].

3.6 Participants

We recruited 40 participants via a university experiment recruitment list server[9]. All participants provided consent to use their non-identifying data. We provided a debriefing survey of the privacy interfaces and also gave information about Cochrane Reviews and the answers from their findings. Participants were paid £10 or given course credit. 39 students (all undergraduates) and 1 non-student participated, of which 29 were females and 11 were male. The average reported age was 21.3 years. The average time for experiment completion was 40 minutes. 14 reported English as the primary language at home[10].

[4]For examaple, Only 8 of the 16 documents from Task 9 were still available online for our research.

[5]Market share based on results from http://gs.statcounter.com/search-engine-market-share/ for desktop in Canada (Accessed August 2018).

[6]https://www.ghostery.com/ (Accessed August 2018)

[7]The documents used in our study as well as the 3rd party tracking scores collected and code for experiments is available at `https://github.com/stevenzim/chiir-2019`.

[8]One might argue that filtering is not a Nudge, however the low cost option remains available to turn off filtering, thus filtering in this manner is a Nudge.

[9]These participants and results are different from the original conference submission. We found an error in the Graeco-Latin square design that required us to run an entirely new set of participants.

[10]We note the majority of students are non-native English speakers. As a whole, native English speakers made more harmful decisions (22%) compared to non-native English speakers (15%). Correct decisions were similar for native and non-native speaking groups, 47% and 45% respectively.

3.7 Statistical Significance and Modeling

In all models, the independent variable was the type of interface. All models were controlled for repeated entries of participants and search tasks. Logistic regression was used for analysis of decision making variables (correct, harmful) while analysis of variance (ANOVA) was used for privacy and cognitive impacts.

4 RESULTS

Our study considers the effects of the independent variable of a privacy protective search system on 4 dependent variables. The participants interacted with a controlled SERP (either a baseline or privacy Nudge variant) or a control question with no search results available to assist with their decision.

Table 1 provides the percentage of correct and harmful decisions for 40 participants. A direct comparison of the user decisions to [22] shows the control performs worse for our participants. Comparisons of the user decisions for the 3 Nudge SERPs against the baseline SERP indicate that harmful decisions are reduced for all approaches, however the effects on decision making are not found to be significant for any Nudge SERP variant compared to baseline.

Independent Variables	Correct	Harmful
Baseline SERP	49%	18%
Privacy Nudge - Ranking SERP	49%	16%
Privacy Nudge - Stoplight SERP	54%	15%
Privacy Nudge - Filtering SERP	50%	14%
Control	29%	26%

Table 1: Impacts on decisions. While minor variations exist when comparing the decisions of baseline SERP with decisions of the three privacy SERPs, none of the differences indicate statistical significance. For the control, we find values indicating worse performance than participants in the study performed by [22].

With respect to the impacts of the 3 Nudge approaches on reductions of encounters with privacy trackers, Table 2 shows significant effects for both the re-ranking and filtering approaches as compared with the baseline. Their are no significant differences when comparing the stoplight approach with baseline in our sample (N=40).

We have also performed analysis[11] on the time taken for each task as a measure of possible cognitive impacts [15] due to variances between the SERPs. The mean time in seconds to complete a search task for the 4 SERPs are: baseline = 117 sec., filtering = 99 sec., reranking = 99 sec. and stoplight = 108 sec. The confidence intervals for re-ranking and filtering are identical, while these approaches shift below the stoplight and baseline approaches, our sample does not provide any statistical significance.

It is also noteworthy that not a single participant changed the setting of the Nudge. In other words, the default was kept by all users, and the goal of significantly reducing privacy impacts was achieved for 2 of the 3 Nudges.

[11]Table excluded due to space limitations.

Independent Variables	Avg # 3rd Party Trackers Encountered	Lower 95%	Upper 95%
Baseline SERP	6.11	5.25	6.97
Filtering SERP	2.27	1.41	3.13
Ranking SERP	1.93	1.07	2.79
Stoplight SERP	6.64	5.78	7.50

Table 2: Confidence intervals are calculated with one-way analysis of variance. Interfaces have a significant effect on the average number of 3rd party trackers encountered during a search task, $F(3, 316) = 32.30$, $p < .0001$. When comparing the individual Privacy Nudge approaches with the baseline SERP, non-overlapping confidence intervals for the ranking and filtering approaches confirm $p < .05$.

5 DISCUSSION AND CONCLUSIONS

The results from our work suggest re-ranking and filtering are the most promising approaches to move forward if the goal is to minimize impacts on decisions and maximize privacy protection from 3rd party tracking. This finding is guided by analysis showing significant reductions in privacy tracking encounters but no significant difference between the performance of decisions made for fact-based search tasks with these approaches when compared to the baseline approach. Government policy and laws in the health domain (e.g. HIPPA in USA) suggest that maximization of privacy is a goal; in the domain of search, both the re-ranking and filtering approaches appear to have maximal effect.

While the nutrition literature has found stoplight approaches to be highly promising when compared to other nutrition label approaches, no significant effect was found with any of the dependent variables. Though the percentage of correct decisions is highest for the stoplight approach, power analysis indicates we would need an infeasible number of participants (6000+) to demonstrate an effect. Most surprising of all, participants did not reduce the amount of encounters with privacy trackers with this approach compared to baseline. Why this occurs is a very interesting question to ponder for future work. Future work might also consider different approaches inspired by the less promising labels from the nutrition literature, which might be more effective in an IR system. Also, considerations of different proxies for privacy should be made. Though we have expanded the corpus beyond what was provided in previous work, a key limitation is the small number of documents, future work would consider a larger corpus (such as using results via the Bing API), a similar study in a live environment could produce different results. We also recognize that our study would benefit from a between-group design with a larger sample, however resource limitations were a major consideration in our design.

ACKNOWLEDGMENTS

This work was supported by the Economic and Social Research Council grant number ES/M010236/1 and The Human Rights Big Data and Technology (HRBDT) Project.

REFERENCES

[1] Ahmed Allam, Peter Johannes Schulz, and Kent Nakamoto. 2014. The Impact of Search Engine Selection and Sorting Criteria on Vaccination Beliefs and Attitudes: Two Experiments Manipulating Google Output. *Journal of Medical Internet research* 16, 4 (2014).

[2] Bin Bi, Milad Shokouhi, Michal Kosinski, and Thore Graepel. 2013. Inferring the demographics of search users: Social data meets search queries. In *Proceedings of the 22nd international conference on World Wide Web.* ACM, 131–140.

[3] Fernando Diaz. 2016. Worst Practices for Designing Production Information Access Systems. In *ACM SIGIR Forum*, Vol. 50. ACM, 2–11.

[4] David Elsweiler, Christoph Trattner, and Morgan Harvey. 2017. Exploiting food choice biases for healthier recipe recommendation. In *Proceedings of the 40th Annual International ACM SIGIR Conference on Research and Development in Information Retrieval.* ACM, 575–584.

[5] Steven Englehardt and Arvind Narayanan. 2016. Online tracking: A 1-million-site measurement and analysis. In *Proceedings of the 2016 ACM SIGSAC Conference on Computer and Communications Security.* ACM, 1388–1401.

[6] Steven Englehardt, Dillon Reisman, Christian Eubank, Peter Zimmerman, Jonathan Mayer, Arvind Narayanan, and Edward W Felten. 2015. Cookies that give you away: The surveillance implications of web tracking. In *Proceedings of the 24th International Conference on World Wide Web.* International World Wide Web Conferences Steering Committee, 289–299.

[7] Norbert Fuhr, Anastasia Giachanou, Gregory Grefenstette, Iryna Gurevych, Andreas Hanselowski, Kalervo Jarvelin, Rosie Jones, YiquN Liu, Josiane Mothe, Wolfgang Nejdl, Isabella Peters, and Benno Stein. 2017. An Information Nutritional Label for Online Documents. In *ACM SIGIR Forum*, Vol. 51. ACM, 46–66.

[8] Gerd Gigerenzer and Henry Brighton. 2009. Homo heuristicus: Why biased minds make better inferences. *Topics in cognitive science* 1, 1 (2009), 107–143.

[9] Ralph Hertwig and Till Grüne-Yanoff. 2017. Nudging and boosting: Steering or empowering good decisions. *Perspectives on Psychological Science* 12, 6 (2017), 973–986.

[10] Eric Horvitz and Deirdre Mulligan. 2015. Data, privacy, and the greater good. *Science* 349, 6245 (2015), 253–255.

[11] Samuel Ieong, Nina Mishra, Eldar Sadikov, and Li Zhang. 2012. Domain bias in web search. In *Proceedings of the fifth ACM international conference on Web search and data mining.* ACM, 413–422.

[12] Thorsten Joachims, Laura Granka, Bing Pan, Helene Hembrooke, and Geri Gay. 2005. Accurately Interpreting Clickthrough Data As Implicit Feedback. In *Proceedings of the 28th Annual International ACM SIGIR Conference on Research and Development in Information Retrieval (SIGIR '05).* ACM, 154–161.

[13] Daniel Kahneman. 2011. *Thinking, Fast and Slow.* Macmillan.

[14] Daniel Kahneman and Amos Tversky. 1984. Choices, values, and frames. *American psychologist* 39, 4 (1984), 341.

[15] Diane Kelly, Jaime Arguello, Ashlee Edwards, and Wan-ching Wu. 2015. Development and evaluation of search tasks for IIR experiments using a cognitive complexity framework. In *Proceedings of the 2015 international conference on the theory of information retrieval.* ACM, 101–110.

[16] Jon Kleinberg, Sendhil Mullainathan, and Manish Raghavan. 2016. Inherent trade-offs in the fair determination of risk scores. *arXiv preprint arXiv:1609.05807* (2016).

[17] Ninya Maubach, Janet Hoek, and Damien Mather. 2014. Interpretive front-of-pack nutrition labels. Comparing competing recommendations. *Appetite* 82 (2014), 67–77.

[18] Jonathan R Mayer and John C Mitchell. 2012. Third-party web tracking: Policy and technology. In *2012 IEEE Symposium on Security and Privacy.* IEEE, 413–427.

[19] Alamir Novin and Eric Meyers. 2017. Making Sense of Conflicting Science Information: Exploring Bias in the Search Engine Result Page. In *Proceedings of the 2017 Conference on Conference Human Information Interaction and Retrieval.* ACM, 175–184.

[20] Bing Pan, Helene Hembrooke, Thorsten Joachims, Lori Lorigo, Geri Gay, and Laura Granka. 2007. In Google We Trust: Users' Decisions on Rank, Position, and Relevance. *Journal of computer-mediated communication* 12, 3 (2007), 801–823.

[21] Eli Pariser. 2011. *The filter bubble: What the Internet is Hiding From You.* Penguin UK.

[22] Frances A Pogacar, Amira Ghenai, Mark D Smucker, and Charles LA Clarke. 2017. The Positive and Negative Influence of Search Results on People's Decisions about the Efficacy of Medical Treatments. In *Proceedings of the ACM SIGIR International Conference on Theory of Information Retrieval.* ACM, 209–216.

[23] Michael Siegrist, Rebecca Leins-Hess, and Carmen Keller. 2015. Which front-of-pack nutrition label is the most efficient one? The results of an eye-tracker study. *Food Quality and Preference* 39 (2015), 183–190.

[24] Jaime Teevan, Susan T Dumais, and Eric Horvitz. 2005. Personalizing search via automated analysis of interests and activities. In *Proceedings of the 28th annual international ACM SIGIR conference on Research and development in information retrieval.* ACM, 449–456.

[25] Richard H Thaler and Cass R Sunstein. 2009. *Nudge: Improving Decisions about Health, Wealth, and Happiness.* Penguin.

[26] Zeynep Tufekci. 2015. Facebook said its algorithms do help form echo chambers, and the tech press missed it. *New Perspectives Quarterly* 32, 3 (2015), 9–12.

[27] Amos Tversky and Daniel Kahneman. 1974. Judgment under Uncertainty: Heuristics and Biases. *Science* 185, 4157 (1974), 1124–1131.

[28] Blase Ur, Pedro Giovanni Leon, Lorrie Faith Cranor, Richard Shay, and Yang Wang. 2012. Smart, useful, scary, creepy: perceptions of online behavioral advertising. In *Proceedings of the eighth symposium on usable privacy and security.* ACM, 4.

[29] Erica Van Herpen and Hans CM Van Trijp. 2011. Front-of-pack nutrition labels. Their effect on attention and choices when consumers have varying goals and time constraints. *Appetite* 57, 1 (2011), 148–160.

[30] Ingmar Weber and Carlos Castillo. 2010. The demographics of web search. In *Proceedings of the 33rd international ACM SIGIR conference on Research and development in information retrieval.* ACM, 523–530.

[31] Ingmar Weber, Venkata Rama Kiran Garimella, and Erik Borra. 2012. Mining Web query logs to analyze political issues. In *Proceedings of the 4th Annual ACM Web Science Conference.* ACM, 330–334.

[32] Ryen White. 2013. Beliefs and biases in web search. In *Proceedings of the 36th international ACM SIGIR conference on Research and development in information retrieval.* ACM, 3–12.

[33] Ryen W White. 2016. *Interactions with search systems.* Cambridge University Press.

[34] Ryen W White and Ahmed Hassan. 2014. Content bias in online health search. *ACM Transactions on the Web (TWEB)* 8, 4 (2014), 25.

[35] Zhonghao Yu, Sam Macbeth, Konark Modi, and Josep M Pujol. 2016. Tracking the trackers. In *Proceedings of the 25th International Conference on World Wide Web (WWW 2016).* International World Wide Web Conferences Steering Committee, 121–132.

A APPENDIX - SCREENSHOTS

Figure 1: For all SERP's, users had the ability to switch on or off the privacy settings (settings in upper left). Task description and definitions were provided (center top) and decision definitions (top right). 10 results were available per page.

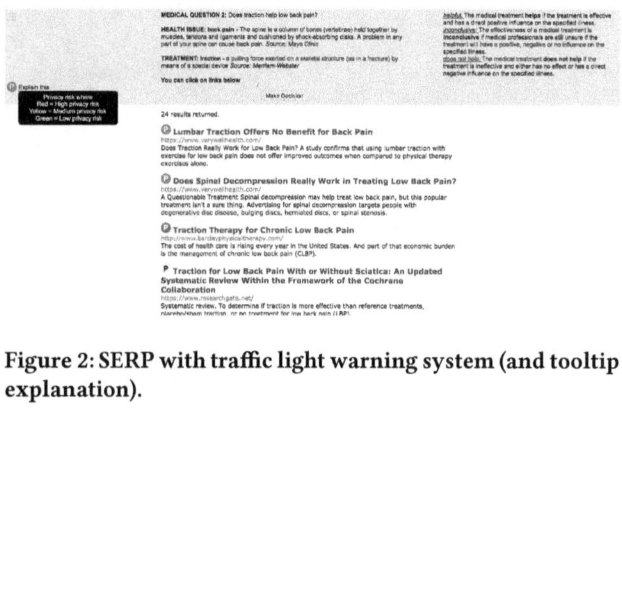

Figure 2: SERP with traffic light warning system (and tooltip explanation).

Holes in the Outline: Subject-dependent Abstract Quality and its Implications for Scientific Literature Search

Chien-yu Huang and Arlene Casey
University of Edinburgh
s1771650@sms.ed.ac.uk; A.J.Casey@sms.ed.ac.uk

Dorota Głowacka and Alan Medlar
University of Helsinki
glowacka@cs.helsinki.fi; alan.j.medlar@helsinki.fi

ABSTRACT

Scientific literature search engines typically index abstracts instead of the full-text of publications. The expectation is that the abstract provides a comprehensive summary of the article, enumerating key points for the reader to assess whether their information needs could be satisfied by reading the full-text. Furthermore, from a practical standpoint, obtaining the full-text is more complicated due to licensing issues, in the case of commercial publishers, and resource limitations of public repositories and pre-print servers.

In this article, we use topic modelling to represent content in abstracts and full-text articles. Using Computer Science as a case study, we demonstrate that how well the abstract summarises the full-text is subfield-dependent. Indeed, we show that abstract representativeness has a direct impact on retrieval performance, with poorer abstracts leading to degraded performance. Finally, we present evidence that how well an abstract represents the full-text of an article is not random, but is a consequence of style and writing conventions in different subdisciplines and can be used to infer an "evolutionary" tree of subfields within Computer Science.

CCS CONCEPTS

• **Information systems** → *Document structure*; *Document collection models*;

KEYWORDS

scientific literature search, topic models, term taxonomy

ACM Reference Format:
Chien-yu Huang and Arlene Casey and Dorota Głowacka and Alan Medlar. 2019. Holes in the Outline: Subject-dependent Abstract Quality, and its Implications for Scientific Literature Search. In *2019 Conference on Human Information Interaction and Retrieval (CHIIR '19), March 10–14, 2019, Glasgow, United Kingdom.* ACM, New York, NY, USA, 5 pages. https://doi.org/10.1145/3295750.3298953

1 INTRODUCTION

In scientific literature search abstracts are frequently used as the primary source for indexing and as snippet text that is displayed with search results. The reasons for this are twofold. First, readers assume that abstracts convey sufficient information about the paper to decide whether or not to read the full article. Second, abstracts often form part of a document's metadata (along with article title and author names), which is more readily accessible to search engines and researchers. Full-text documents are hard to obtain due to the need for commercial licenses and, in the case of public repositories such as arXiv, due to resource limitations (e.g. bandwidth costs). Given that the use of abstracts is common in Information Retrieval (IR), the idea that an abstract could have limitations in terms of representing the content of the full-text has implications for experimental results and scientific literature search engine design. Retrievability bias is known to be impacted by factors such as document representations [28]. Differences between abstracts and full-texts could therefore erroneously rank inferior documents higher in search results than more relevant ones. From the perspective of user experience, such ranking issues could undermine users' opinion of the search system if the top ranked search results are not the most relevant documents. Additionally, if the abstract is inaccurate, then this can mislead users into making incorrect choices when considering the relevance of items in the search listing [27].

Our research seeks to understand to what extent the abstract represents the full-text of Computer Science (CS) papers and to investigate the impact abstract representativeness has on retrieval performance. We used topic modelling to represent content in articles and individual sections within each article, allowing us to quantify any discrepancies between the two. We show that how well an abstract represents the full-text is subfield-dependent, with abstracts from theoretical CS subfields being the least representative of the full-text. We further demonstrate that rankings based on abstracts are a poor substitute for rankings of full-texts, with retrieval performance degrading with less representative abstracts. Finally, we present evidence suggesting that the degree to which an abstract represents the full-text is not random and can be used to infer an "evolutionary" tree of subfields within Computer Science.

2 BACKGROUND

Using Topic Models to Represent Content Topic modelling is an unsupervised learning method for understanding the content in collections of documents. It models text collections as a mixture of topics, with each topic corresponding to a distribution over the vocabulary [2]. Probabilistic topic models are generative processes that specify how documents are created and are typically based on Latent Dirichlet Allocation (LDA) [3].

There are numerous applications of topic models in scientific literature analysis and representation, such as exploring how ideas develop over time [5, 20] and mapping publications of authors of a specific nationality [24]. Topic models have also been used extensively in IR, for example, in exploratory search to assess relevance [18] and to derive search queries [19]. These works differ from our

CHIIR '19, March 10–14, 2019, Glasgow, United Kingdom

ACM ISBN 978-1-4503-6025-8/19/03...$15.00
https://doi.org/10.1145/3295750.3298953

research as they look to classify topics between documents, not differences within documents. Syed *et al.* [26] suggest that the semantics used in condensing information into an abstract may lead to topics in the abstract not present in the full-text. However, others have argued that topic models are an appropriate representation of content even considering this issue [8].

Article Section Content There are many studies comparing bibliographic records and article sections with full-text documents. In IR, for example, while naïve full-text search can improve recall, it tends to do so at the expense of precision [7, 17, 21]. This result, however, can be improved upon by augmenting abstract search with partial information from the full-text (section or paragraph-level) to achieve both high precision and recall [12, 14]. Complementary to these findings, in the biosciences it has been shown that different article sections besides the abstract can provide better representations of certain biological concepts [23]. Indeed, clinical decisions based solely on abstracts have worse patient outcomes than when doctors have access to complete articles [15], which might be due to information content being highest in results sections [22].

In this study, we show that different subfields of CS vary in the degree to which abstracts and other sections represent the full-text of the article. Furthermore, the patterns of section-wise representativeness capture the domain structure of the field. Our findings are supported by studies of language and conventions for academic writing. Several studies have highlighted that style and expectations of content differ across disciplines [9, 25]. Harmon and Gross [6] suggest how article content type may influence abstracts, comparing an article from an established theoretical field with one describing a new approach. In the former, "how it was done" would not be included in the abstract. Recent research has shown that article content is influenced by the maturity of the academic field [11], which may explain why we find differences between theoretical and (more modern) applied subfields.

3 METHODS

To perform our study, we used topic modelling to summarise the content of full-text articles and individual sections. We used the Kullback-Leibler (KL) divergence of topic distributions to quantify how well each article section represents the full-text.

3.1 Data Preprocessing

Our data set was composed of Computer Science papers downloaded from arXiv (http://www.arxiv.org) that included LaTeX source files. The data set contained 35,137 articles covering a 9 year period from 2007 to mid-2015. We used arXiv instead of a pre-existing test collection because we needed access to the full-text from a comprehensive number of CS subfields. We removed papers from the categories *General Literature* and *Other Computer Science.* These two categories were vague and contained few articles (46 and 214, respectively). Articles can be associated with multiple arXiv categories, although a majority (67%) are only associated with one.

Articles were split into sections by parsing the source files for section commands and abstract environments. We extracted on average 6.7 sections per article ($SD = 2.7$). We wanted to categorise sections into abstract, introduction, background, related work, methods, results, discussion, conclusions and back matter. Back matter includes acknowledgements and funding information, that were categorised to allow for an accurate count of uncategorised sections, but was otherwise excluded from further analysis. We ordered all section headings by decreasing frequency and manually categorised all unambiguous headings with a frequency greater than 1. This procedure categorised 53% of section headings. While the proportion of classified headings appears quite low, 35% of headings only occurred once. Each article had on average 3.3 categorised sections ($SD = 1.2$). Articles can contain an arbitrary number of sections associated with the same category. Some articles, for example, had multiple results sections.

We performed some limited preprocessing of full-text articles and separate sections for topic modelling: LaTeX markup was removed using the detex program, all punctuation and numbers were removed, and characters were made lower case.

3.2 Topic Models

We used the MALLET toolkit [16] to generate probabilistic topic models. We inferred 100 topics for the corpus of full-text documents. Then, we reused this model to predict the topic distributions for each separate section. As stated previously, some articles contained multiple sections devoted to the same category, e.g. results split into multiple sections. In these cases, we created a composite results section by performing an element-wise summation of the topic distributions and normalising the resultant vector.

3.3 Measuring Representativeness

Each full-text article is associated with 1 – 8 separate sections. We wanted to estimate the extent to which each section represented the complete article. For this purpose we used the KL divergence [13], which for discrete probability distributions is:

$$D_{KL}(P\|Q) = \sum_i P(i) \log_2 \left(\frac{P(i)}{Q(i)} \right) \quad (1)$$

where, in our case, P and Q are the topic distributions for the full-text and a given article section, respectively. KL divergence is usually defined with the natural logarithm, however, here we use base 2 for ease of interpretation. KL divergence is a measure of the difference between two probability distributions, where $D_{KL}(P\|Q)$ is the amount of information lost when Q is used to approximate P. In this instance, the higher the KL divergence, the worse the abstract represents the full-text.

3.4 Generating Search Queries

We needed to generate search queries to examine how retrieval is impacted as a result of using abstracts in place of full-text documents. Our goal was to generate queries such that each one disproportionately favoured documents in one arXiv category over all the others. To do this, we extracted abstracts from our arXiv corpus and used collocation detection to identify n-grams of length 2, 3 and 4. Each abstract was labelled with an arXiv category. In cases where an abstract was associated with more than one category, we randomly selected one. We converted each document into a bag-of-words and trained a multi-class support vector machine (SVM) to predict the arXiv category based on the article title and abstract text [4]. The SVM was not used to make predictions, but instead used to identify

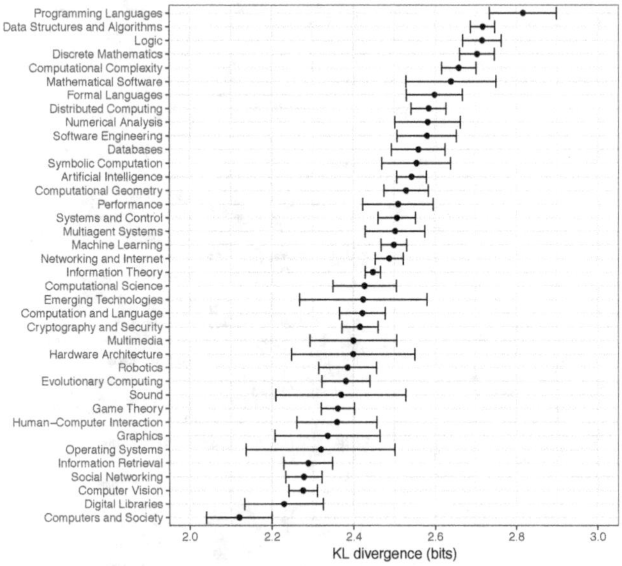

Figure 1: Mean KL divergence between topic distributions from abstract and full-text document. Error bars show 95% confidence interval. arXiv categories are ordered by mean KL divergence.

the top 100 discriminatory features for each arXiv category, i.e. those with the highest coefficients. These top ranked features were used as search queries. We stemmed all search queries and filtered out those that appeared in multiple categories. If, after stemming, a single arXiv category contained duplicate queries, all but one were removed. Finally, poor queries were manually removed, e.g. "paper considers" is not specific to any particular subject, but happens to be strongly associated with the *Information Theory* category in our corpus. This procedure produced a total of 1,257 search queries, an average of 33.1 search queries per arXiv category ($SD = 14.5$).

4 RESULTS

In this study, we were concerned with whether abstract representativeness, as measured by the KL divergence between abstract and full-text topic distributions (from now on simply KL divergence), varies across subjects and to what degree it affects retrieval performance.

4.1 Abstract Representativeness is Subfield-dependent

How well an article's abstract represents the full-text in terms of its topic content is subfield-dependent. Furthermore, similar subfields appear to exhibit similar levels of average KL divergence.

Figure 1 shows the mean KL divergence per arXiv category with error bars showing the 95% confidence interval. Categories are ordered by mean KL divergence. Categories at the top of the plot with higher average KL divergence are generally mathematical subjects (e.g. *Programming Languages*, *Logic* and *Discrete Mathematics*), whereas categories at the bottom with lower KL divergence are more likely to be social science-influenced subjects (*Computers and Society*, *Digital Libraries*, *Human-Computer Interaction*). For some categories, the 95% confidence interval appears quite wide with respect to the range of KL divergences. Higher variances are generally due to lower article counts. The smallest arXiv categories, *Operating Systems*, *Sound* and *Emerging technologies*, had among the widest confidence intervals and contained the fewest articles (106, 116 and 141 articles, respectively).

One possible alternative explanation for the differences between arXiv categories could be the abstract length. If, for example, articles in a given category tend to have shorter abstracts due to academic convention, then this could lead to greater KL divergences. However, this is not the case: abstract length is uncorrelated with KL divergence between abstract and full-text topic distributions ($R^2 = 0.003, p < 2.2 \times 10^{-16}$).

4.2 Abstract Representativeness is Correlated with Retrieval Performance

Representativeness, measured using KL divergence, is negatively correlated with retrieval performance. We retrieved documents with our generated search queries (see Section 3.4) from a full-text database and an abstract database (containing abstracts and article titles) using the Okapi BM25 algorithm [10]. The top 100 search results from the full-text database was used as the ground truth to calculate precision@100 for the abstract database. Figure 2 shows how mean precision@100 varies with the mean KL divergences for each arXiv category.

In general, abstracts have *higher* precision than full-texts when using an external (i.e. expert-derived) definition of relevance (see Section 2 for references). Here, however, we are concerned with how well abstracts represent the content of the full-text and are less interested in the absolute precision scores, than the relative differences in precision between subfields. Indeed, the average precision is negatively correlated with KL divergence ($R^2 = 0.3811, p = 3.65 \times 10^{-5}$). This suggests that users running queries in different subfields could have considerably different experiences of the search process with different levels of incongruence between abstract and full-text rankings.

4.3 Section-wise Representativeness Captures Domain Structure

While we have shown that the average representativeness of an abstract is subfield-dependent (Section 4.1) and that this is important from an IR perspective (Section 4.2), we also wanted to investigate whether these differences were random or indicative of the underlying structure of the field.

For each arXiv category, we calculated the average KL divergence for all 8 article sections and normalised the resulting vector. Next, we performed hierarchical clustering using complete linkage clustering with Euclidean distance as the distance metric. Figure 3 shows a heatmap and dendrogram of the results. Lighter colours indicate higher average KL divergence between article sections and full-text documents (we additionally clustered article sections, but omitted the dendrogram from the figure for clarity).

The dendrogram in Figure 3 appears to reflect the structure of Computer Science, dividing it into two main subtrees containing applied (top) and theoretical (bottom) subfields. Theoretical subfields

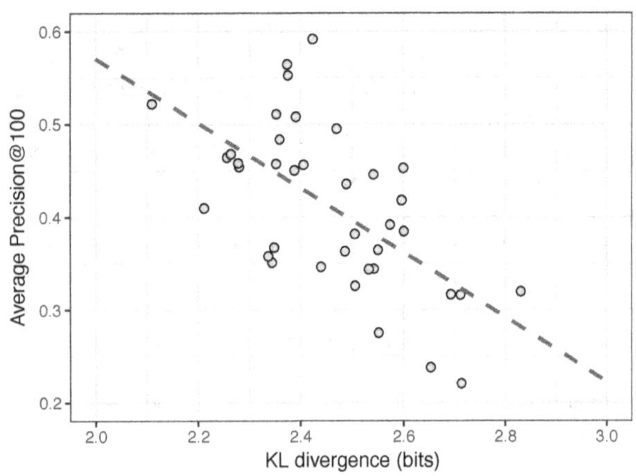

Figure 2: There is a negative correlation between mean precision@100 and mean KL divergence between abstract and full-text topic distributions for queries derived from arXiv categories (R^2 = 0.38).

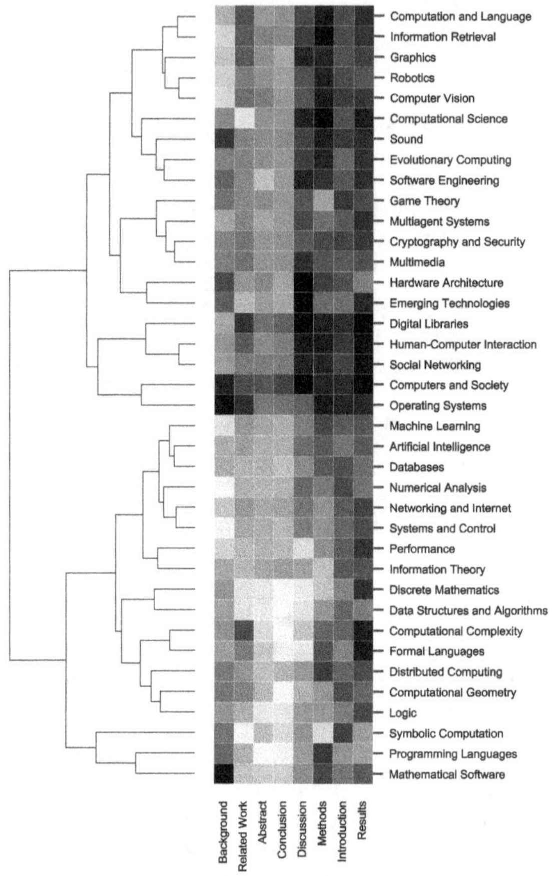

Figure 3: A heatmap and dendrogram showing the relatedness of subfields in Computer Science from the perspective of section-article representativeness. Lighter colours correspond to higher KL divergence between topic distributions from a given section and the full-text.

are distinguished by having higher KL divergences in their abstract, conclusion, background and related work sections (lighter colours). In contrast, the methods and results sections in applied subfields are closer in topic content to the complete document (darker colours).

The groupings identified in Figure 3 are generally reasonable and errors either reflect biases in the data set or appear concordant with wider confidence intervals from Figure 1. In the theoretical subtree, there are groupings for programming languages, mathematics and theoretical topics with direct applications (e.g. *Machine Learning*, *Information Theory*, etc.). In the applied subtree, there are groupings for social sciences (e.g. *Human-Computer Interaction*), applied Machine Learning (e.g. *Information Retreival*), multiagent systems and hardware. *Networking and Internet* seems to have been placed incorrectly in the same subtree as *Machine Learning*, however, this reflects bias in the arXiv data set as ~23% of networking articles are co-associated with *Information Theory*. Finally, *Operating Systems* and *Graphics* appear to be placed erroneously, but this is probably due to having very few articles associated with them and therefore higher uncertainty with respect to the KL divergence.

5 DISCUSSION AND CONCLUSIONS

Our study shows that how well an abstract represents the full-text of an article is subfield-dependant. We used Computer Science as a case study to show that this subfield-dependence is not random, but reflects the structure of computing as a discipline. Given that different fields are known to follow their own idiosyncrasies in terms of style and writing conventions, it seems plausible that content placement would evolve in a similar manner. Understanding differences in content placement and knowing when to read beyond the abstract is useful knowledge for academics undertaking search in unfamiliar subject domains, which is known to be challenging [1]. IR systems that selectively index article sections exist (e.g. [12]), but, to the best of our knowledge, do not account for subfield differences.

More importantly, we showed that for subfields with less representative abstracts, the differences between search rankings from abstracts and full-texts can be significant. From the perspective of scientific literature search, this suggests that users searching in theoretical subfields would see a greater disconnect between their expectations of results (based on reading abstracts) and their actual experience (reading the full-text) compared to applied subfields. For more complex searches involving both applied and theoretical aspects, search quality could be biased towards the papers from applied subfields. This is particularly worrying as theoretical topics are harder to understand and searching for unfamiliar topics is already challenging.

One limitation of our work may be in using papers from arXiv, as quality can vary widely on pre-print servers, and how well they are written could be an influencing factor. In future work we want to understand whether other variables influence section representativeness and design a user study to understand its impact in real-world information retrieval settings.

REFERENCES

[1] Kumaripaba Athukorala, Eve Hoggan, Anu Lehtiö, Tuukka Ruotsalo, and Giulio Jacucci. 2013. Information-seeking behaviors of computer scientists: Challenges for electronic literature search tools. In *Proceedings of the 76th ASIS&T Annual Meeting: Beyond the Cloud: Rethinking Information Boundaries*. American Society for Information Science, 20.

[2] David M Blei. 2012. Probabilistic topic models. *Commun. ACM* 55, 4 (2012), 77–84.

[3] David M Blei, Andrew Y Ng, and Michael I Jordan. 2003. Latent dirichlet allocation. *Journal of machine Learning research* 3, Jan (2003), 993–1022.

[4] Chih-Chung Chang and Chih-Jen Lin. 2011. LIBSVM: a library for support vector machines. *ACM transactions on intelligent systems and technology (TIST)* 2, 3 (2011), 27.

[5] David Hall, Daniel Jurafsky, and Christopher D Manning. 2008. Studying the history of ideas using topic models. In *Proceedings of the conference on empirical methods in natural language processing*. Association for Computational Linguistics, 363–371.

[6] Joseph E Harmon and Alan G Gross. 2010. *The Craft of Scientific Communication*. University of Chicago Press.

[7] Bradley M Hemminger, Billy Saelim, Patrick F Sullivan, and Todd J Vision. 2007. Comparison of full-text searching to metadata searching for genes in two biomedical literature cohorts. *Journal of the American Society for Information Science and Technology* 58, 14 (2007), 2341–2352.

[8] Germán Hurtado Martín, Steven Schockaert, Chris Cornelis, and Helga Naessens. 2011. Finding similar research papers using language models. In *2nd Workshop on Semantic Personalized Information Management: Retrieval and Recommendation (SPIM-2011)*. University College Ghent, 106–113.

[9] Ken Hyland. 2015. Genre, discipline and identity. *Journal of English for Academic Purposes* 19 (2015), 32–43.

[10] K Sparck Jones, Steve Walker, and Stephen E. Robertson. 2000. A probabilistic model of information retrieval: development and comparative experiments. *Information processing & management* 36, 6 (2000), 779–840.

[11] David Jurgens, Srijan Kumar, Raine Hoover, Dan McFarland, and Dan Jurafsky. 2018. Measuring the Evolution of a Scientific Field through Citation Frames. *Transactions of the Association for Computational Linguistics* 6 (2018), 391–406.

[12] Noriko Kando. 1999. Text structure analysis as a tool to make retrieved documents usable. In *Proceedings of the 4th International Workshop on Information Retrieval with Asian Languages*. 126–135.

[13] Solomon Kullback and Richard A Leibler. 1951. On information and sufficiency. *The annals of mathematical statistics* 22, 1 (1951), 79–86.

[14] Jimmy Lin. 2009. Is searching full text more effective than searching abstracts? *BMC bioinformatics* 10, 1 (2009), 46.

[15] Alvin Marcelo, Alex Gavino, Iris Thiele Isip-Tan, Leilanie Apostol-Nicodemus, Faith Joan Mesa-Gaerlan, Paul Nimrod Firaza, John Francis Faustorilla, Fiona M Callaghan, and Paul Fontelo. 2013. A comparison of the accuracy of clinical decisions based on full-text articles and on journal abstracts alone: a study among residents in a tertiary care hospital. *BMJ Evidence-Based Medicine* 18, 2 (2013), 48–53.

[16] Andrew Kachites McCallum. 2002. Mallet: A machine learning for language toolkit. (2002).

[17] Emma Jean McKinin, MaryEllen Sievert, E Diane Johnson, and Joyce A Mitchell. 1991. The Medline/full-text research project. *Journal of the American Society for Information Science* 42, 4 (1991), 297–307.

[18] Alan Medlar and Dorota Glowacka. 2017. Using Topic Models to Assess Document Relevance in Exploratory Search User Studies. In *Proceedings of the 2017 Conference on Conference Human Information Interaction and Retrieval*. ACM, 313–316.

[19] Alan Medlar, Kalle Ilves, Ping Wang, Wray Buntine, and Dorota Glowacka. 2016. Pulp: A system for exploratory search of scientific literature. In *Proceedings of the 39th International ACM SIGIR conference on Research and Development in Information Retrieval*. ACM, 1133–1136.

[20] Michael Paul and Roxana Girju. 2009. Topic modeling of research fields: An interdisciplinary perspective. In *Proceedings of the International Conference RANLP-2009*. 337–342.

[21] Jung Soon Ro. 1988. An evaluation of the applicability of ranking algorithms to improve the effectiveness of full-text retrieval. I. On the effectiveness of full-text retrieval. *Journal of the American Society for Information Science* 39, 2 (1988), 73–78.

[22] Martijn J Schuemie, Marc Weeber, Bob JA Schijvenaars, Erik M van Mulligen, C Christiaan van der Eijk, Rob Jelier, Barend Mons, and Jan A Kors. 2004. Distribution of information in biomedical abstracts and full-text publications. *Bioinformatics* 20, 16 (2004), 2597–2604.

[23] Parantu K Shah, Carolina Perez-Iratxeta, Peer Bork, and Miguel A Andrade. 2003. Information extraction from full text scientific articles: where are the keywords? *BMC bioinformatics* 4, 1 (2003), 20.

[24] Arho Suominen and Hannes Toivanen. 2016. Map of science with topic modeling: Comparison of unsupervised learning and human-assigned subject classification. *Journal of the Association for Information Science and Technology* 67, 10 (2016), 2464–2476.

[25] John Swales. 1990. *Genre analysis: English in academic and research settings*. Cambridge University Press.

[26] Shaheen Syed and Marco Spruit. 2017. Full-text or abstract? Examining topic coherence scores using latent dirichlet allocation. In *Data Science and Advanced Analytics (DSAA), 2017 IEEE International Conference on*. IEEE, 165–174.

[27] Andrew Turpin, Falk Scholer, Kalvero Jarvelin, Mingfang Wu, and J Shane Culpepper. 2009. Including summaries in system evaluation. In *Proceedings of the 32nd international ACM SIGIR conference on Research and development in information retrieval*. ACM, 508–515.

[28] Colin Wilkie and Leif Azzopardi. 2017. Algorithmic Bias: Do Good Systems Make Relevant Documents More Retrievable?. In *Proceedings of the 2017 ACM on Conference on Information and Knowledge Management*. ACM, 2375–2378.

Take One for the Team:

Social-emotional Interactions and Outcomes on Social Question and Answers Sites

Sei-Ching Joanna Sin
Wee Kim Wee School of Communication and Information
Nanyang Technological University
Singapore
joanna.sin@ntu.edu.sg

Xinran Chen
Wee Kim Wee School of Communication and Information
Nanyang Technological University
Singapore
chen0872@ntu.edu.sg

ABSTRACT

With a process- and interaction-focus, this study posited that the nature and flow of users' interactions on a social question & answer (SQA) thread can impact their collaborative information seeking outcomes. Interaction Process Analysis (IPA) was applied to investigate the types and outcomes of users' social-emotional interactions. Over 1,000 Stack Overflow postings were manually coded; Chi-square tests and logistic regressions were used for analysis. The study found that over half of the sample included IPA social-emotional acts. Interestingly, *Disagrees*, an act in IPA's negative social-emotional area, was the most frequently found category. *Disagrees* exhibited a significant negative relationship with the post-level outcome, post score, but a significant positive main effect and an interaction effect with a thread-level outcome, view count. The study identified two tension points: (1) potential benefits for the group of collaborative information seekers, at the slight expense of the individual who performed the negative social-emotional act; and (2) strains between the instrumental vs. social aspects of SQA. Research and practical implications of the findings were discussed.

CCS CONCEPTS

• Human-centered computing → Empirical studies in collaborative and social computing • Information systems → Collaborative search

KEYWORDS

Social question and answers, User interactions, Collaborative information seeking, Affective information behavior, Interaction Process Analysis

CHIIR '19, March 10–14, 2019, Glasgow, United Kingdom

ACM ISBN 978-1-4503-6025-8/19/03...$15.00
https://doi.org/10.1145/3295750.3298955

ACM Reference format:

Sei-Ching Joanna Sin and Xinran Chen. 2018. Take One for the Team: Social-emotional Interactions and Outcomes on Social Question and Answers Sites. In *CHIIR '19: 2019 Conference on Human Information Interaction & Retrieval March 10–14, 2019, Glasgow, United Kingdom.* ACM, NY, NY, USA, 5 pages. https://doi.org/10.1145/3295750.3298955

1 Introduction

Social question & answer (SQA) sites have become a prime space of collaborative information seeking and exchange [3,7,23]. Sites such as Stack Exchange (SE), Yahoo! Answers and Quora have attracted sizable use and traffic. Stack Overflow, a prominent community within SE for programming questions, has 9.5 million users and garners 10 million visits per day [29]. Despite the potentials of SQA platforms, a daunting problem remains: Some questions received no answers; others received only low-quality responses [4,14,24]. These unsatisfactory query outcomes highlight the need to better understand what actions and mechanisms can help users obtain successful query outcomes.

SQA research has contributed to examining different predictors of query success (e.g., user characteristics, textual features of posts). However, research gaps exist regarding users' turn-by-turn interactions [13,26]. Less is known about the nature and flows of users' interactions within a SQA thread, and how these interactions affect query outcomes. Furthermore, while social and emotional connections are an integral part of human interaction, it has been pinpointed that the affective aspects of online discussion have not received sufficient attention [22]. Currently, it is not clear whether social and emotional aspects of users' interactions on SQA would make a difference. This gap warrants attention, as recent literature has underscored that need to investigate affective factors [10,17,18]. Studies in these underexplored areas will help identify effective (and detrimental) user-to-user social-emotional interaction behaviors, which can inform SQA users training and system design.

2 Framework and Research Questions

This study focused on processes and interactions, which have been identified as important in information behavior and information retrieval literature [8,9,31,32]. We posit that the back and forth between users on a SQA thread is akin to the query reformulation stage of information search and retrieval.

Scholars have developed frameworks and empirical studies to reveal the changes in a variety of information behavior throughout the search process. For example, changes in the choice of sources, search terms, search tactics, and relevance judgment criteria have been identified. Also observed are changes in users' feelings during the search process [11,20,28,30,33]. These studies demonstrate the rich insights that process-focused research brings. Applying this process focus to the SQA context, we hypothesized that how users interact with each other on a SQA thread may impact the success or failure of that thread. In addition to investigating user-system interactions and user-information interactions, studying user-user interactions on SQA platforms will bring additional perspectives and fresh insights into collaborative information behaviors.

This study built on Interaction Process Analysis (IPA), a prominent framework developed by Robert Bales for studying small-group interactions [1]. IPA has been applied in studying computer-mediated communication, including social media such as blogs [21], microblogs [12,34] and online health community [15]. However, IPA research on SQA interactions is nascent, with the few existing studies focusing only on bivariate relationships [27] or a single post-level outcome [25]. Different from previous studies, this study investigated both post-level and thread-level outcomes. It also investigated a different aspect of IPA: the IPA social-emotional areas.

Specifically, this exploratory study applied IPA to investigate the social-emotional aspects of the interaction process, when users work on the same question together through a SQA platform. The emphasis is on the use and impact of social-emotional acts (e.g., shows solidarity, agreement, or antagonism) in a primarily instrumental information environment, in this case, SQA communities that focus on factual answers. Would users' social-emotional acts contribute to query success in such communities, or would a functional, no-frills approach work better? Specifically, the study investigated three research questions (RQs), as follows:

RQ1: What types of IPA social-emotional acts were used?

RQ2: Do different IPA social-emotional acts yield different post scores?

RQ3: Do different share of IPA social-emotional acts in a thread yield different thread-level outcomes, specifically, obtaining accepted answers and garnering views?

3 Research Methods

3.1 Data collection and coding methods

This study analyzed postings on Stack Overflow, including questions, answers, and comments. Postings data were retrieved from the official data dump released by SE. The study randomly sampled 150 questions published on the same date (February 1, 2016). All answers and comments posted to the sampled questions within a one-month period were then retrieved. This yielded 150 threads, with a total of 1,007 postings (150 questions, 203 answers, and 654 comments).

Content analysis was conducted by two coders to manually identify the IPA social-emotional acts. The coding scheme consisted of the six IPA social-emotional acts put forth by Bates: (1) shows solidarity (e.g., raises other's status); (2) shows tension release (e.g., jokes, shows satisfaction); (3) agrees; (4) disagrees; (5) shows tension; and (6) shows antagonism [1]. Each SQA posting was coded on the presence or absence of each of the six social-emotional IPAs. The coding yielded a data frame of 1,007 rows (postings) and 6 columns (the six IPA acts). Cell values were either 0 (absence of the corresponding IPA act) or 1 (presence of the corresponding IPA act). The intercoder percentage agreements of the six IPAs ranged from 94% to 99%, which suggest an acceptable intercoder reliability level.

3.2 Data analysis methods

Descriptive statistics were used for RQ1; inferential statistics were used for RQ2 and RQ3. The distributions of the outcome variables (post scores and view counts) were not normal. They were thus discretized into dichotomous variables (high/low level) using the mean scores as cut-off points. Chi-square tests were used to examine the relationships between IPA social-emotional acts and post scores (RQ2). Chi-square test is a non-parametric test for analyzing the association between two categorical variables. For data that did not meet the chi-square assumptions (e.g., expected cell counts should be greater than five), the Monte Carlo simulation option of R's [19] chisq.test function was used to compute the p-values [6].

The relationships between IPA social-emotional acts and thread-level outcomes (RQ3) were analyzed using logistic regressions, a technique for examining the relationships between several categorical or continuous predictors with a dichotomous outcome variable. Potential confounding variables—including the length of the thread and the extent to which a question asker participated in his/her own thread (operationalized as the percentage of postings in the thread that was created by the question askers) [26]—were included as control variables. In summary, the logistic regression test included eight variables: six explanatory variables (six IPA social-emotional acts) and two control variables (number of postings in the thread and the question asker's share of participation). In addition to testing the main effects of IPA social-emotional acts as indicated above, another logistic regression test was conducted to examine potential interaction effects between IPA acts and the question asker's share of participation. The analyses were conducted with R [19].

4 Findings

4.1 Sample characteristics

The 1,007 postings from 150 threads came from 477 users. On average, the number of postings in each thread was 6.71 (SD = 4.11). The longest thread included 19 postings. Overall, the question askers (i.e., the original posters, hereafter referred to as *OPs*) shown notable presence. OPs on average contributed to 47.43% of the postings in their own threads. However, OPs' share ranged from 14.29% to 100% (SD = 18.38%). These large variations suggest that this variable warrants attention. More than half of the threads (n = 83, 55.3%) have at least one IPA social-emotional acts.

Regarding post-level outcomes, post score reflects how other users rated a particular posting. Post score was directly obtained from the official data dump released by SE. SE computed post score using the following formula: the number of upvotes a post received – the number of downvotes a post received. (The specific breakdown of the number of upvotes and number of downvotes were not available in the data dump.) The post scores of this sample ranged from -7 to 8 (M = 0.38, SD = 1.03). Regarding thread-level outcomes, view count of the posts ranged from 24 to 4,419 (M = 436.77). The variations in view count are large (SD = 673.09). Out of 150 threads, 71 (47.3%) have accepted answers.

4.2 Use of IPA social-emotional acts (RQ1)

At the post level, among the 1,007 posts, Disagrees was the most frequently found acts (n = 59, 5.9%). This is followed by Shows tension release (n = 48, 4.8%), Agrees (n = 14, 1.4%), Shows solidarity (n = 11, 1.1%), Shows tension (n = 5, 0.5%), and Shows antagonism (n = 1, 0.1%). Figure 1 shows the presence (circles) or absence (small x) of the social-emotional acts as interactions unfolded from the first postings to the last postings of a thread. The position of a posting in the thread was identified by its timestamp. Figure 1 indicates that two negative acts, Shows tension (the fifth row in Figure 1) and Shows antagonism (the last row in Figure 1), appeared relatively early. In contrast, Tension release (the second row of Figure 1), was more spread out across the thread.

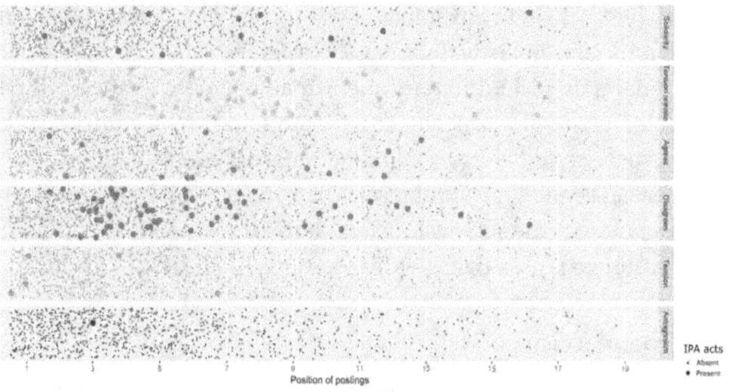

Figure 1: Presence or absence of the six social-emotional acts as interactions unfolded

4.3 IPA social-emotional acts and post-level outcome (RQ2)

The Chi-square tests found two significant relationships between post scores and IPA social-emotional acts. First, postings with Disagrees was found with a lower post score, $\chi^2(1, N = 1007)$ = 6.90, p = .009, Cramer's V = .08. Interestingly, the presence of Shows tension release, a category under the positive social-emotional area of IPA, was found to associate with a lower post score, $\chi^2(1, N = 1007) = 3.89$, $p = .049$, Cramer's $V = .06$.

4.4 IPA social-emotional acts and thread-level outcomes (RQ3)

RQ3 examined the thread-level relationships between IPA social-emotional acts and outcomes. Seven of the 150 threads included missing data; they were removed from this analysis. The boxplots in Figure 2 show the percentage share of IPA social-emotional acts at the thread level.

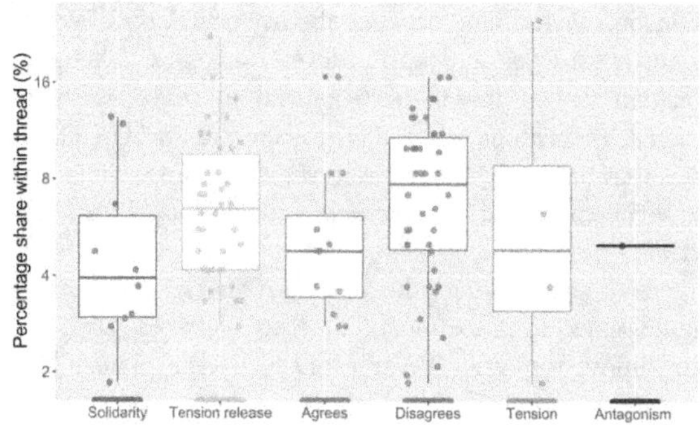

Figure 2: Boxplots: Percentage share of social-emotional acts

4.4.1 Obtaining an accepted answer. The share of Shows tension release yielded a significant positive relationship (Odds ratio [OR] = 1.14, p = .010) in the main-effects only analysis (Nagelkerke R^2 = 0.178), while the main and interaction effects analysis found no significant predictors. Given that Shows tension release was significant in the main-effects analysis, we further investigated whether tension release occurred before or after the posting of the answer that was ultimately accepted, as well as who (OP or non-OP) expressed tension release. Among the threads that have an accepted answer, tension release from OPs came overwhelming (94.7%) after the accepted answer was posted. This suggests that the OPs took the efforts to share their feelings in writing (instead of only clicking to upvote or accept an answer, as recommended by Stack Overflow). In contrast, tension release from non-OPs was more spread out. Among non-OP, 18.2% of the tension release occurred before the accepted answer was posted, 54.5% were after. Notably, about 27% of the tension release occurred in the postings that were ultimately selected as an accepted answer.

4.4.2 View count. The main and interaction effects analysis on view count (Nagelkerke R^2 = 0.177) found two significant relationships. First, there was a main effect of Disagrees on view count (OR = 1.49, p = .037). Second, the above main effect was modified by a significant interaction between Disagrees and the share of OP's participation (OR = 0.99, p = .041). Interestingly, the main effect itself suggested a positive relationship. That is, a higher share of disagreement was associated with more views. This relationship was modified by the share of OP's participation, as follows. The 'higher disagreement, higher view count' relationship mentioned above occurred mainly in threads where non-OPs provided a larger share of postings. Conversely, for threads in which the OP has a larger share of postings, a higher percentage of disagreement in the thread tended to end up with lower view counts.

5 Discussion

This study examined the use of social-emotional acts in a sample of 1,007 postings from Stack Overflow, a programming community that focuses on factual answers. Over half of the threads included at least one IPA social-emotional acts. Notably, significant relationships were found between the use of IPA social-emotional acts and post-level and thread-level outcomes. The research implication is that it will be beneficial to study user's social-emotional interactions when they collaborate on SQA platforms. Studies that model SQA query success, for example, may include user social-emotional interaction variables in their features selection.

Interestingly, among the six IPA social-emotional acts, Disagrees emerged as the most frequently observed category. This finding differs from prior IPA research such as Savolainen [21] and Maloney-Krichmar [15], in which disagreement was found to be rare. A possible reason is that the above studies are on health-related communities, such as slimming blogs [21] and a health support community for people with knee injury [15]. While informational support is a focus of health-related communities online, emotional support is also hypothesized to be a considerable component [5]. It is possible that users may avoid casting negative comments towards other users when it comes to matters of health. For less emotionally laden topics such as computer programming, users may feel less inhibited from expressing disagreement.

The principal purpose of Stack Overflow is functional: to answers programming questions. While Disagrees belongs to the negative social-emotional area of IPA, it may still serve instrumental functions. For example, agreement and disagreement on social media can contribute to collective sensemaking [16]. Disagreement may prompt individuals to reflect on the topic, which may subsequently lead to better understanding [2]. The potential positive impacts of disagreement not withstand, findings from RQ2 and RQ3 suggest that Disagrees is not only a double-edged sword, it also brings differential benefits and harm to different parties. Specifically, RQ2 found that postings expressing disagreement tended to end up with lower post scores, suggesting that this social-emotional act is still less welcomed by SQA users. In sum, the benefits of disagreement are not reaped by the user who performed such acts. Rather, the benefits are gained at the thread level by a broader group. Particularly, findings of RQ3 indicated that benefits manifested as a thread garnering more views (suggesting that more people can learn from the thread or that the thread was consulted/used more frequently), especially when the OP was not dominating the interaction in his/her thread.

The above findings have research and practical implications. SQA platform designers may explore what system features and community norms can be introduced to reward users (especially non-OPs) who provide constructive disagreement. Regarding practical implications for users, the findings suggest that strategic use of social-emotional acts such as Shows tension release may be beneficial to thread-level outcomes. For OPs, it seems prudent to refrain from crowding their own threads, especially when notable disagreement exists in the thread. This may help avoid giving an impression of acting too pushy or aggressive. In terms of research implications, the contrasting outcomes at the post-level and thread-level suggest that it is valuable to investigate different types of outcomes at different units of analysis.

We identified two tension points from the findings. First, there is a tension between individual and group outcomes (e.g., positive outcomes for the group of users who are interested in a topic, but not for the individual who performed the social-emotional act). Second, the findings hint at possible tensions between the instrumental and social aspects of SQA (e.g., inspiring a better understanding of a topic through disagreements, but also possibly evoking negative feelings among users). The impacts of such tensions will be fascinating to explore.

Given the current exploratory study has found complex relationships between social-emotional acts and SQA outcomes, we proposed the following future work. The first is to verify whether similar patterns are found in large samples and different SQA communities. Particularly, in the current study, two negative acts—Shows tension and Shows antagonism—were rarely used. This may have made it difficult for the present study to detect their impacts. Analysis of large samples may provide more insights into their effects. Also, the relationship between Shows tension release and obtaining an accepted answer (RQ3) suggests possible interactions effects between IPA social-emotional acts and the position of a posting in the interaction sequence. Further analysis may apply social sequence analysis [e.g., 26] or Markov chain [e.g., 33] to examine how social-emotional acts are sequenced, and investigate whether different sequences of social-emotional acts yield different query outcomes. Last but not least, to understand why certain social-emotional acts contribute to query success or failure, qualitative data collection methods such as interviews and focus groups can be conducted. These will allow researchers to directly ask users how they react to different interaction acts, as well as the reasoning behind their reactions.

6 Conclusion

This exploratory study investigated users' social-emotional interactions on a SQA community that focuses on factual answers. Social-emotional acts, particularly Shows tension release and Disagrees, were found to exhibit significant and complex relationships with query outcomes at the post-level and thread-level. The tensions between individual users and groups and between the instrumental and social aspects of SQA warrant investigations. Further explorations on the nature, tension points, and impacts of users' interaction on SQA platforms will ultimately contribute towards better user experience and successful outcomes on SQA.

ACKNOWLEDGMENTS

This work was supported by the Singapore Ministry of Education Academic Research Fund (RG58/14).

REFERENCES

[1] R.F. Bales, 1951. *Interaction Process Analysis: A Method for the Study of Small Groups.* Addison-Wesley Press, Cambridge, MA.

[2] I. Bråten and J.L.G. Braasch, 2018. The Role of Conflict in Multiple Source Use. In *Handbook of Multiple Source Use,* J.L.G. Braasch, I. Bråten and M.T. Mccrudden Eds. Routledge, New York, 184-202.

[3] S. Chirag, 2014. Collaborative Information Seeking. *Journal of the Association for Information Science and Technology 65,* 2, 215-236.

[4] A.Y.K. Chua and S. Banerjee, 2015. Answers or No Answers: Studying Question Answerability in Stack Overflow. *Journal of Information Science 41,* 5, 720-731.

[5] D.N.S. Coulson, 2005. Receiving Social Support Online: An Analysis of a Computer-Mediated Support Group for Individuals Living with Irritable Bowel Syndrome. *CyberPsychology & Behavior 8,* 6, 580-584.

[6] A.P. Field, J. Miles, and Z. Field, 2012. *Discovering Statistics using R.* Sage, London.

[7] R. Gazan, 2011. Social Q&A. *Journal of the American Society for Information Science and Technology 62,* 12, 2301-2312.

[8] P. Hansen and K. Järvelin, 2005. Collaborative Information Retrieval in an Information-Intensive Domain. *Information Processing & Management 41,* 5, 1101-1119.

[9] D. Kelly, 2009. Methods for Evaluating Interactive Information Retrieval Systems with Users. *Foundations and Trends in Information Retrieval 3,* 1-224.

[10] S. Kim, J.S. Oh, and S. Oh, 2007. Best-Answer Selection Criteria in a Social Q&A Site from the user-Oriented Relevance Perspective. *Proceedings of the American Society for Information Science and Technology 44,* 1, 1-15.

[11] C.C. Kuhlthau, 1991. Inside the Search Process: Information Seeking from the User's Perspective. *Journal of the American Society for Information Science 42,* 5, 361-371.

[12] J.-S. Lin and J. Peña, 2011. Are You Following Me? A Content Analysis of TV Networks' Brand Communication on Twitter. *Journal of Interactive Advertising 12,* 1, 17-29.

[13] Z. Liu and B.J. Jansen, 2013. Question and Answering Made Interactive: An Exploration of Interactions in Social Q&A. In *Proceedings of the 2013 International Conference on Social Intelligence and Technology.* IEEE Computer Society, Washington, DC, 1-10.

[14] Z. Liu and B.J. Jansen, 2017. Identifying and Predicting the Desire to Help in social Question And Answering. *Information Processing & Management 53,* 2, 490-504.

[15] D. Maloney-Krichmar and J. Preece, 2005. A Multilevel Analysis of Sociability, Usability, and Community Dynamics in an Online Health Community. *ACM Transactions on Computer-Human Interaction 12,* 2, 201-232.

[16] L. Mamykina, D. Nakikj, and N. Elhadad, 2015. Collective Sensemaking in Online Health Forums. In *Proceedings of the Proceedings of the 33rd Annual ACM Conference on Human Factors in Computing Systems,* ACM, 2702566, 3217-3226.

[17] D. Nahl and D. Bilal, 2007. *Information and Emotion: The Emergent Affective Paradigm in Information Behavior Research and Theory.* Information Today, Medford.

[18] N. Novielli, F. Calefato, and F. Lanubile, 2014. Towards Discovering the Role of Emotions in Stack Overflow. In *Proceedings of the Proceedings of the 6th International Workshop on Social Software Engineering,* ACM, 2661689, 33-36.

[19] R Core Team. (2018). R: A Language and Environment for Statistical Computing. R Foundation for Statistical Computing, Vienna, Austria, https://www.R-project.org/

[20] S.Y. Rieh and H. Xie, 2006. Analysis of Multiple Query Reformulations on the Web: The Interactive Information Retrieval Context. *Information Processing & Management 42,* 3, 751-768.

[21] R. Savolainen, 2011. Asking and Sharing Information in the Blogosphere: The Case of Slimming Blogs. *Library & Information Science Research 33,* 1, 73-79.

[22] R. Savolainen, 2015. The Role of Emotions in online Information Seeking and Sharing: A Case Study of Consumer Awareness. *Journal of Documentation 71,* 6, 1203-1227.

[23] C. Shah, S. Oh, and J.S. Oh, 2009. Research Agenda for Social Q&A. *Library and Information Science Research 31,* 4, 205-209.

[24] C. Shah, M.L. Radford, L.S. Connaway, E. Choi, and V. Kitzie, 2012. "How Much Change Do You Get From 40$?" – Analyzing and Addressing Failed Questions on Social Q&A. *Proceedings of the American Society for Information Science and Technology 49,* 1, 1-10.

[25] S.-C.J. Sin, C.S. Lee, and X. Chen, 2018. Rewarding, but Not for Everyone: Interaction Acts And Perceived Post Quality on Social Q&A sites. In *Proceedings of the The 20th International Conference on Asia-Pacific Digital Libraries, ICADL 2018, University of Waikato, Hamilton, New Zealand* (2018), 1-5.

[26] S.-C.J. Sin, C.S. Lee, and Y.-L. Theng, 2016. Social Q&A Question-and-Comments Interactions and Outcomes: A Social Sequence Analysis. In *the Proceedings of the 18th International Conference on Asia-Pacific Digital Libraries, ICADL 2016, Tsukuba, Japan.* Springer International Publishing, Cham, 325-338.

[27] S.-C.J. Sin, C.S. Lee, and Y.-L. Theng, 2018. Tracing Social Question and Answer Users' Interaction Patterns. In *Proceedings of the The 81st Annual Meeting of the Association for Information Science & Technology, Vancouver, Canada* (2018), 1-2.

[28] A. Spink, 1997. Study of Interactive Feedback During Mediated Information Retrieval. *Journal of the American Society for Information Science 48,* 5, 382-394.

[29] Stack Exchange. (2018). All sites, https://stackexchange.com/sites?view=list#traffic

[30] P. Vakkari, 2001. A Theory of the Task-Based Information Retrieval Process: A Summary and Generalisation of a Longitudinal Study. *Journal of Documentation 57,* 1, 44-60.

[31] P. Vakkari, 2003. Task-based information Searching. *Annual Review of Information Science and Technology 37,* 1, 413-464.

[32] T.D. Wilson, 1999. Models in Information Behaviour Research. *Journal of Documentation 55,* 3, 249-270.

[33] I. Xie and S. Joo, 2010. Transitions in Search Tactics During the Web-based Search Process. *Journal of the American Society for Information Science and Technology 61,* 11, 2188-2205.

[34] X. Zhang, W. Tao, and S. Kim, 2014. A Comparative Study on Global Brands' Micro Blogs between China and USA: Focusing on Communication Styles and Branding Strategies. *International Journal of Strategic Communication 8,* 4, 231-249.

Exploring Language Style in Chatbots to Increase Perceived Product Value and User Engagement

Ela Elsholz, Jon Chamberlain, Udo Kruschwitz
School of Computer Science and Electronic Engineering, University of Essex
Colchester, Essex, UK
ela.elsholz@posteo.de, [jchamb|udo]@essex.ac.uk

ABSTRACT

Chatbots that can automatically answer customer requests have become a common feature on e-commerce Web sites. There are many factors that might affect overall customer satisfaction with such services. We explore how adding language style to e-commerce chatbots can be used to increase user satisfaction, perceived product value, user interest in a product, and user engagement with a chatbot service. We conducted an experimental pilot study, where two chatbots were used to sell theatre tickets: one communicating in modern English and one in a Shakespearean-style dialect. 169 participants interacted with a randomly-assigned version of the chatbot. The results indicate that the bot talking in modern English showed a significantly higher user satisfaction, whereas the Shakespearean-styled chatbot showed higher user engagement and perceived product value. It was also found that the modern chatbot version was more often referred to as being 'easy to use', whereas the Shakespearean chatbot version was more often referred to as being 'fun to use'.

CCS CONCEPTS

• **Information systems** → **Chat**; **Electronic commerce**; • **Human-centered computing** → *Usability testing*; *Natural language interfaces*;

KEYWORDS

Chatbots, Dialogue system, Styled conversational interface, Conversational agent, Language style transfer, Shakespeare

ACM Reference Format:
Ela Elsholz, Jon Chamberlain, Udo Kruschwitz. 2019. Exploring Language Style in Chatbots to Increase Perceived Product Value and User Engagement. In *2019 Conference on Human Information Interaction and Retrieval (CHIIR '19), March 10–14, 2019, Glasgow, Scotland Uk.* ACM, New York, NY, USA, 5 pages. https://doi.org/10.1145/3295750.3298956

1 INTRODUCTION

Conversational approaches to information interaction are not at all new, e.g. [3, 5], but they have attracted renewed interest in recent years, e.g. [8, 11]. As a result, chatbots are becoming ever more popular [17]. With the increasing integration of chatbots into daily life, their personalisation is starting to play an important role. Google has recently published a chatbot that can hardly be distinguished from a human.[1] In fact, several studies indicate that users prefer personalised chatbots [1, 9]; however, while the style of the conversation in dialogue systems has been the centre of research attention [18], to the best of our knowledge no studies to date have explored the impact of applying different language styles to chatbot responses on user satisfaction and engagement. As language style is a key component to the way chatbots communicate with users, it may influence a user's experience, and possibly even influence a user's attitude towards a product or service. This study is a first step to addresses this lack of research.

2 RELATED WORK

A chatbot service can be defined as 'a computer software program which interacts with a user through natural language dialogue and provides some form of service' [14]. For the purpose of this study, we simply refer to the term 'chatbot' for all forms of dialogue systems. Such systems can be traced back more than 50 years to *ELIZA* [19], which simulates a psychotherapy session. Although the algorithm is very simple, and the bot responds with a limited, predefined set of answers, it was reported that users felt emotionally touched when interacting with the system. Other example systems followed, e.g. *ALICE* [13]. Currently, *Mitsuku*[2] appears to be one of the most successful chatbots, having won the *Loebner prize* multiple times (in 2013, 2016, 2017).[3]

A large share of *task-oriented* chatbots can be found in the field of e-commerce, where chatbots offer customer services. Ikea's chatbot 'Anna' informs customers about furniture sizes and delivery options. Royal Mail customers can use a dialogue interface to ask for updates of their current parcel status. In fact, rapid developments in AI over the last few years have manifested in a new dimension of possible features in chatbots [7]. In particular, the personalisation of chatbots is gaining momentum. Studies indicate that users prefer personalised chatbots with human-like character traits [1, 9]. Personalisation begins by simply giving a chatbot a name or adding a picture to the dialogue and goes as far as to reacting to user emotions. Kuligowska [9] studied the impact that different aspects of personalisation in e-commerce chatbots have on user experience and satisfaction. It turned out that adding a picture which represents the chatbot as a person – be it a human or a comic figure image – has a positive effect on users' experience and satisfaction. They found that personalisation of chatbots also affects the length of the

CHIIR '19, March 10–14, 2019, Glasgow, Scotland Uk

ACM ISBN 978-1-4503-6025-8/19/03...$15.00
https://doi.org/10.1145/3295750.3298956

[1] https://www.wired.com/story/google-duplex-phone-calls-ai-future/
[2] https://www.pandorabots.com/mitsuku/
[3] http://www.aisb.org.uk/events/loebner-prize

conversation and the user's choice of words. Generally, Kuligowska reported that personalised chatbots were rated higher than neutral ones. This offers a good starting point for further explorations.

A key way to personalise a chatbot is by altering its language style. This is the area that we are interested in. Language style transfer can be achieved through different methods ranging from rule-based, e.g. [20], to the application of deep neural networks, e.g. [2, 4, 6, 15, 16]. Io and Lee demonstrate research gaps for chatbots applied in commercial settings [7]. We use these findings as a motivation to start exploring how applying language style to e-commerce chatbots affects customer experience and their attitude towards a presented product.

The research question we address is *How does adding language style to an e-commerce chatbot affect user satisfaction, user interest in a product, perceived product value and user engagement?*

Perceived value in our context is defined as the price a customer is willing to pay for a product. It is assumed that these are indicators that can be correlated with profit.

3 METHOD

A ticket selling scenario was created where theatre tickets for a Shakespeare play were sold by two differently styled chatbots. One chatbot communicates in modern English (our baseline), whereas the second chatbot in a Shakespearean manner. The functionality of both chatbots was identical, however the responses were differently styled renditions of the same response sentence.[4]

Subjects were assigned one of the chatbots randomly and asked to use the chatbot service to book a ticket for a play at a fictional Shakespeare theatre. The booking of the ticket took place in an imaginary setup, so no real booking happened. Before and after the booking, the participants were asked to fill in a questionnaire. Figure 1 shows a screenshot of the implemented chatbot with a booking dialogue example shown from an interaction with the Shakespearean dialect version. Here is a specific example of the same response in two different styles:

> *Modern English*: 'Type the requested number of tickets again. Only the number, please. I am handsome, but a simple bot. Thanks for your understanding.'
> *Shakespearean-styled*: 'Could thou say again the ticket number only? Handsome I am, though but a simple servant bot. Pray take my gratitude for thy understanding.'

Both systems are based on a rule-based approach that uses regular expression matching and slot filling. A rule-based system was deemed easier to control than a trained system avoiding issues such as unnecessary language generation errors when trying to explore the link between independent variable (the language style) and dependent variables (user satisfaction, user engagement, user interest in a presented product, and perceived product value). The system nevertheless does allow some flexibility in the interaction. For example, if a user tries to involve the chatbot in casual conversation, the chatbot will go into *'chatmode'* and will defer the booking process until input is detected that is interpreted as a valid filler for one of the slots. Chatmode is initiated in two ways. Firstly, if the user enters a specific keyword or phrase unrelated to the booking process, for example "love", or "what is your name", the chatbot will reply with something related to the keyword. Secondly, if a user enters an input that cannot be matched by the slot filling three times in a row, it will respond by a Shakespeare quote. Chatmode stops when a slot-relevant input is entered.

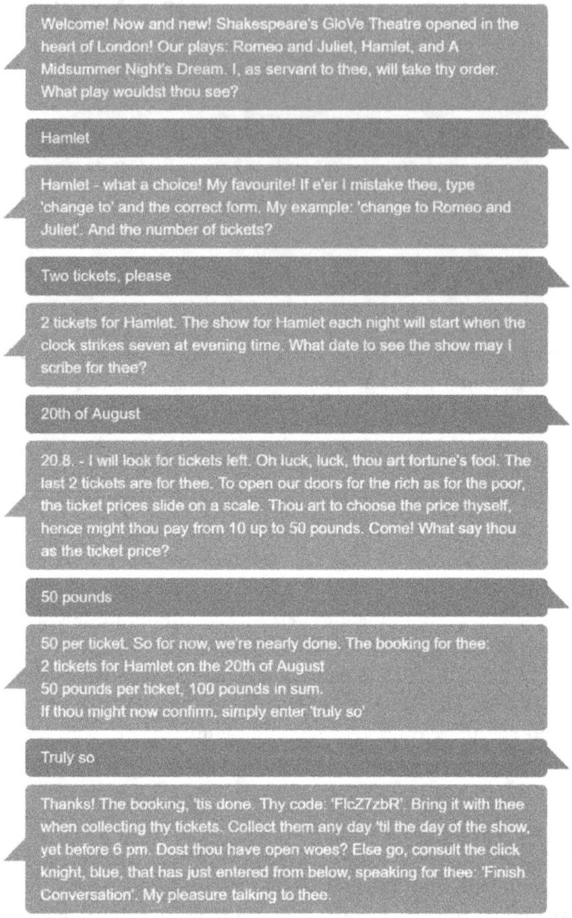

Figure 1: Example booking dialogue with Shakespearean-styled dialect chatbot version

3.1 Participants

169 subjects (111 female, 58 male) were recruited via the crowdsourcing platform *Figure Eight*.[5] Crowdsourcing falls under the category of *convenience sampling*, a form of *non-probability sampling* [12]. It is the most common sampling type in many research areas including IIR [10]. Convenience sampling generally does not exclude bias and therefore generalisations made on the basis of the results must be exercised with caution [10]. Users were allocated to one system at random and were unaware of the underlying research question.

[4] The conversion of style was performed manually by Ela Elsholz by consulting the online Shakespeare translation tool https://www.sparknotes.com/shakespeare/ and attempting to replicate the metre, rhythm and humour whilst preserving the meaning. Translations were proofread by an additional annotator before a final, agreed version being used for the chatbot.

[5] https://www.figure-eight.com/

Dependent variable	Mean (Var) *BotMod*	Mean (Var) *BotShake*
Overall user rating	6.07 (1.90)	5.61 (2.73)
Usability	6.35 (1.62)	6.09 (1.70)
Price willing to pay (in £)	35 (190)	41 (862)
Interest in visiting the theatre	5.82 (1.71)	5.46 (2.30)
Interest in visiting a Shakespeare play	5.62 (1.84)	5.30 (2.16)
Change of interest (post-task - pre-task)	0.35 (0.60)	0.18 (0.66)
Time with bot (min)	2.4 (1.53)	3.6 (8.08)
Non-task related inputs (per user)	0.16 (0.87)	1.01 (19.5)

Table 1: Mean and variance for all dependent variables (Interest in visiting the theatre and visiting a Shakespeare play are judgements obtained in the post-task questionnaire)

3.2 Questionnaires

There were two questionnaires, a pre-task questionnaire before the interaction with the chatbot system and a post-task questionnaire thereafter (see Appendix A for screenshots). The pre-task questionnaire captured demographic data about the user as well as their theatre habits. Additionally, a question was added about how high subjects estimate the ticket price for a professional theatre production in London to be. This question was added as a baseline to test that there were no significant differences between the two user groups, of which one group used only the modern chatbot and the other only the Shakespearean, before the chatbot experience.

For most of the questions a seven-point Likert-type scale – ranging from 1: 'not at all' to 7: 'very much so' – was used. One open question in form of a comment was included in the questionnaire to enhance a qualitative analysis of the user experience.

To test for differences between the two systems (the system using modern language, *BotMod*, and the system that uses Shakespearean style, *BotShake*) we applied significance tests to the results obtained for each dependent variable over the two user samples.

4 RESULTS

4.1 Quantitative Analysis

Table 1 illustrates the main results which we will now discuss in more detail (median scores left out for brevity).

User satisfaction. With a median score being greater or equal to 6 (7-point Likert-like scale), both bots show a high user rating of general bot experience and its usability[6]. We found that the modern chatbot had a higher user rating and reached a higher usability score (both at $p<0.05$, unpaired two-sample two-tailed Mann-Whitney U-test).

Perceived product value. Users stated how much they would be willing to pay for a ticket at the showcase theatre. The mean of this ticket price was £35 for the modern and £41 for the Shakespearean version although the difference is not statistically significant.

User interest in the product. Marginal differences were found regarding users' interest in visiting the showcase theatre between the users of the different bot versions, the interest in visiting a Shakespeare performance as well as the change in interest of visiting a Shakespeare performance from before to after using the bot.

User engagement. It was found that users spent more time with the Shakespearean chatbot version ($p<0.05$, unpaired two-sample two-tailed Mann-Whitney U-test). Also, more non-task related user inputs were recognized in conversations with this chatbot ($p<0.05$, unpaired two-sample two-tailed Mann-Whitney U-test).

Testing user groups for bias. The two user groups where investigated for bias in their theatre habits and price estimation of theatre tickets. This information was collected in a pre-task questionnaire, such that no experiment-related difference had occurred between the user groups so far. No significant difference can be found between the two user groups regarding their theatre habits or pre-task price estimation before using the chatbot.

4.2 Qualitative Analysis

The qualitative analysis was based on the user comments regarding the bot experience in the post-task questionnaire. Analysing all user comments, six general comment topics were categorised: 'works well', 'easy', 'difficult', 'fun', 'don't like bot', 'concept'. Ela Elsholz labelled each comment manually (without knowledge of which system produced this comment) to determine whether it can be assigned to one or more of these categories. It was then investigated whether there was a significant difference in frequency for each comment category between the two bots using z-tests. Table 2 gives an overview of the test results.

category	total	*BotMod*	*BotShake*	p-value
works well	19	12	7	0.25
easy	47	33	14	0.001 **
difficult	8	0	8	not applicable
fun	41	13	28	0.004 **
don't like bot	7	1	6	not applicable
concept	34	18	16	0.79

Table 2: Results for frequency of certain concepts in user comments (in some cases no z-test could be applied due to data sparsity).

It was found that users' comments regarding the modern-language bot version were more often related to the 'easy' category ($p<0.05$, unpaired two-sample two-tailed z-test), while comments on the Shakespearean-styled version were more frequently related to the 'fun' category ($p<0.05$, unpaired two-sample two-tailed z-test).

5 DISCUSSION

The purpose of this research was to investigate the effects of adding language style to e-commerce chatbots. The main focus has been to answer the research question: How does adding language style to an e-commerce chatbot affect *user satisfaction, user interest in a product, perceived product value* and *user engagement*?

By using the Shakespearean chatbot experiment, a difference in user satisfaction and user engagement was found between the

[6]Usability in the context of this research is the subjective rating given by the user of how easy the system was to use to perform the task.

test user groups, of which one used the modern and the other the Shakespearean chatbot. User satisfaction was found to be higher for the modern bot, whereas user engagement turned out to be higher for the Shakespeare bot.

The results of the qualitative analysis showed that the modern bot was described by more users to be *'easy to use'*, while the Shakespearean chatbot was more often described as *'fun to use'*. Also, the usability was rated higher for the modern chatbot implying that the test users preferred a fast and easy booking over an entertaining one; however, test users were recruited through the platform *Figure Eight* and participated in the experiment to earn money. Moreover, they were paid per experiment, not per time. Therefore *Figure Eight* users might show a stronger tendency to prefer a fast and easy process than an average customer in a daily life setting. Further experiments would be needed to see whether this preference can be generalised to a larger population.

Although the Shakespearean chatbot achieved a lower user rating, the ticket price users stated they would be willing to pay (as a proxy for user interest in the product) was on average higher. Although the difference was marginal, this can be interpreted as an indication that a more elaborate presentation might give the impression a product is worth more and hence users might be willing to pay more.

The user engagement was evaluated by measuring the time spent with the bot and counting non-task related user inputs in a conversation. That Shakespearean bot users spent more time in the booking dialogue can also be traced back to the fact that the chatbot responses were harder to understand as the qualitative analysis showed that the Shakespearean bot was more often described as difficult to use. However, more users of the Shakespearean bot group engaged in non-task related inputs than in the modern bot group. This can be interpreted as evidence that the Shakespearean styling of the bot increased users' interest in engaging the chatbot in conversation. In other words, users were more engaged with the bot in the conversation. Surprisingly few conversations contained non-task related user inputs (20 out of 169). While designing the bot, it was expected that more users would try to challenge the bot or experiment with how it reacts to different inputs. That this was not the case could possibly be traced back to the fact that *Figure Eight* users took part in the experiment to earn money. Also, the design of the bot could play a role as the questions provided by the bot to fill the slots were very straightforward and might not have invited users to engage in a more open dialogue. Finally, the test users were informed before the experiment that their conversation was to be recorded. They might, therefore, have been eager to complete the experiment properly and did not want to risk making a mistake by entering non-task relevant inputs. Again, to find out whether the results in user engagement can be generalised over a larger population further experiments with other test user groups would be necessary.

In addition to this, the results were found using an artificial booking setup. It can therefore only be speculated how far those results could be reproduced in a real world booking scenario. The setup also contained elements that evidently confused the test users, like the self-assessment of ticket prices and lack of information about seating. Also, some users had to repeat the date several times, as shows were booked out for their inputs or, in some cases, because their input date format was not recognised.

In the study, only one particular language style was investigated. It might be more a question of whether users like a Shakespearean dialect or find it annoying, artificial or hard to understand. The experimental results might be very different when adding another style. In addition, the findings from using the simple user interface of the experiment may not necessarily be generalisable to other dialogue systems, where the complexity of the task and range of potential responses mask the benefit of a stylised responder.

It can also be said that our baseline system, the modern chatbot, can be regarded as having a language style itself. It talked in a lively fashion, showing humour and tried to personally engage with the user. We deliberately decided to choose this as a baseline rather than a neutral version (aka an NLP interface to a database) based on Kuligowska's findings that personalised e-commerce chatbots were preferred over neutral ones [9].

There are many other issues arising from this line of research. For example, Google's recently published chatbot service[7] that adopts human behaviour by adding common speech pausing into the conversation raises ethical questions about whether chatbots are becoming too human, opening up discussion over whether it must be marked clearly that one is talking to a human or using an automatic interface. Another highly debated application of chatbot that has emerged in recent years is the use of chatbots in social media like on Facebook and Twitter – also called *Twitterbots*. These chatbots deliver advertising or purposefully influence political debates.[8] [9] There is certainly plenty of scope for further research.

6 CONCLUSION

We explored how adding language style to an e-commerce chatbot might affect overall user satisfaction, perceived product value, user interest in a product, and user engagement with the service. To do this we constructed a specific scenario of a ticket selling application. We found that adding Shakespearean language to an e-commerce chatbot increased user engagement (significantly) as well as perceived product value (though in this case only marginally). At the same time user satisfaction decreased. It was also found that the Shakespearean bot was more frequently described as *'fun'* in user comments, while the modern bot was referred to as *'easy'*. Those findings imply that in some e-commerce settings, it could be useful to accept a loss in user satisfaction to increase the perceived product value and user engagement.

Independent of which language style was used, both bot versions resulted in very high user acceptance and user satisfaction. Considering that both chatbot versions contained some degree of personality and language style, it may be promising to further investigate means of automatic style transfer. Applications of automatic style transfer are broad, and include adapting to the language styles of users. With the growing number of chatbots being applied to household devices, their personalisation will likely become more important.

[7] https://www.wired.com/story/google-duplex-phone-calls-ai-future/
[8] https://www.politico.com/story/2016/10/chatbots-are-invading-politics-229598
[9] https://politibot.io/this-is-how-politibot-platform-works/

REFERENCES

[1] R. E. Banchs. 2017. On the construction of more human-like chatbots: Affect and emotion analysis of movie dialogue data. In *2017 Asia-Pacific Signal and Information Processing Association Annual Summit and Conference (APSIPA ASC)*. 1364–1367. https://doi.org/10.1109/APSIPA.2017.8282245

[2] K. Carlson, A. Riddell, and D. N. Rockmore. 2017. Zero-Shot Style Transfer in Text Using Recurrent Neural Networks. *CoRR* abs/1711.04731 (2017). arXiv:1711.04731 http://arxiv.org/abs/1711.04731

[3] A. De Roeck, U. Kruschwitz, P. Neal, P. Scott, S. Steel, R. Turner, and N. Webb. 1998. YPA - an intelligent directory enquiry assistant. *BT Technology Journal* 16, 3 (1998), 145–155.

[4] Z. Fu, X. Tan, N. Peng, D. Zhao, and R. Yan. 2017. Style Transfer in Text: Exploration and Evaluation. *CoRR* abs/1711.06861 (2017). arXiv:1711.06861 http://arxiv.org/abs/1711.06861

[5] J. Glass, G. Flammia, D. Goodine, M. Phillips, J. Polifroni, S. Sakai, S. Seneff, and V. Zue. 1995. Multilingual spoken-language understanding in the MIT Voyager system. *Speech Communication* 17, 1 (1995), 1 – 18.

[6] M. Han, O. Wu, and Z. Niu. 2018. Unsupervised Automatic Text Style Transfer Using LSTM. In *Natural Language Processing and Chinese Computing*, Xuanjing Huang, Jing Jiang, Dongyan Zhao, Yansong Feng, and Yu Hong (Eds.). Springer International Publishing, Cham, 281–292.

[7] H. N. Io and C. B. Lee. 2017. Chatbots and conversational agents: A bibliometric analysis. In *2017 IEEE International Conference on Industrial Engineering and Engineering Management (IEEM)*. 215–219. https://doi.org/10.1109/IEEM.2017.8289883

[8] H. Joho, L. Cavedon, J. Arguello, M. Shokouhi, and F. Radlinski. 2017. First International Workshop on Conversational Approaches to Information Retrieval (CAIR'17). In *Proceedings of the 40th International ACM SIGIR Conference on Research and Development in Information Retrieval (SIGIR '17)*. ACM, New York, NY, USA, 1423–1424.

[9] K. Kuligowska. 2015. Commercial Chatbot: Performance Evaluation, Usability Metrics and Quality Standards of Embodied Converstational Agents. *Professionals Center for Business Research* 2 (2015). https://papers.ssrn.com/sol3/papers.cfm?abstract_id=2569637

[10] D. Kelly. 2009. Methods for Evaluating Interactive Information Retrieval Systems with Users. *Foundations and Trends in Information Retrieval* 3, 1–2 (2009), 1–224. https://doi.org/10.1561/1500000012

[11] F. Radlinski and N. Craswell. 2017. A Theoretical Framework for Conversational Search. In *Proceedings of the 2017 Conference on Conference Human Information Interaction and Retrieval (CHIIR '17)*. ACM, 117–126.

[12] M. Schonlau, R. D. Fricker, and M. N. Elliott. 2002. *Conducting Research Surveys via E-mail and the Web*. Santa Monica, CA: RAND Corporation.

[13] B.A. Shawar and E. Atwell. 2002. *A comparison between Alice and Elizabeth chatbot systems*. University of Leeds, School of Computing research report 2002.19. http://eprints.whiterose.ac.uk/81930/ Shawar, BA and Atwell, E (c) 2002, University of Leeds. Reproduced with permission from the copyright holders.

[14] B. A. Shawar and E. Atwell. 2007. Different Measurements Metrics to Evaluate a Chatbot System. In *Proceedings of the Workshop on Bridging the Gap: Academic and Industrial Research in Dialog Technologies (NAACL-HLT-Dialog '07)*. Association for Computational Linguistics, Stroudsburg, PA, USA, 89–96. http://dl.acm.org/citation.cfm?id=1556328.1556341

[15] B. A. Shawar and E. Atwell. 2016. Stylistic Transfer in Natural Language Generation Systems Using Recurrent Neural Networks. In *Proceedings of EMNLP 2016 Workshop on Uphill Battles in Language Processing: Scaling Early Achievements to Robust Methods*. Association for Computational Linguistics, 43–47.

[16] T. Shen, T. Lei, R. Barzilay, and T. Jaakkola. 2017. Style Transfer from Non-Parallel Text by Cross-Alignment. In *Advances in Neural Information Processing Systems 30*, I. Guyon, U. V. Luxburg, S. Bengio, H. Wallach, R. Fergus, S. Vishwanathan, and R. Garnett (Eds.). Curran Associates, Inc., 6830–6841. http://papers.nips.cc/paper/7259-style-transfer-from-non-parallel-text-by-cross-alignment.pdf

[17] A. Shevat. 2017. *Designing Bots*. O'Reilly.

[18] P. Thomas, M. Czerwinski, D. McDuff, N. Craswell, and G. Mark. 2018. Style and Alignment in Information-Seeking Conversation. In *Proceedings of the 2018 Conference on Human Information Interaction & Retrieval (CHIIR '18)*. ACM, New York, NY, USA, 42–51.

[19] J. Weizenbaum. 1983. ELIZA - A Computer Program For the Study of Natural Language Communication Between Man And Machine (Reprint). *Commun. ACM* 26 (01 1983), 23–28.

[20] W. Xu, A. Ritter, W. B. Dolan, R. Grishman, and C. Cherry. 2012. Paraphrasing for style. In *24th International Conference on Computational Linguistics - Proceedings of COLING 2012: Technical Papers*. 2899–2914.

A APPENDIX - QUESTIONNAIRES

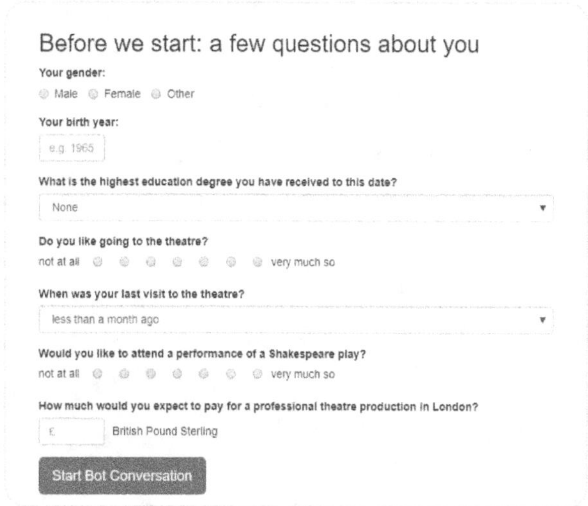

Figure 2: Pre-task questionnaire.

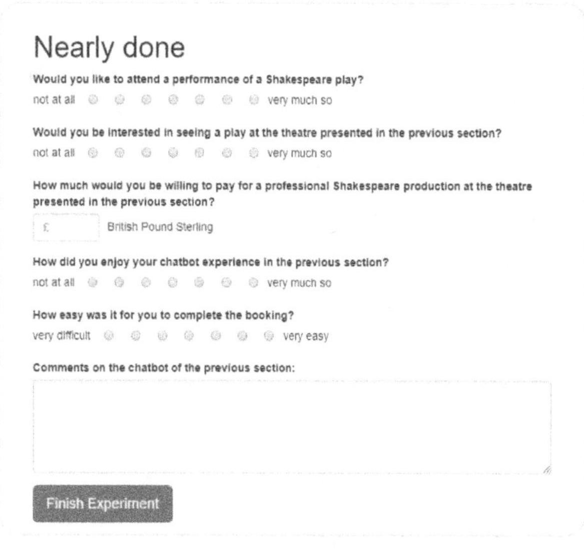

Figure 3: Post-task questionnaire.

How Relevance Feedback is Framed Affects User Experience, but not Behaviour

Dhruv Tripathi
University of Edinburgh
s1756548@sms.ed.ac.uk

Alan Medlar
University of Helsinki
alan.j.medlar@helsinki.fi

Dorota Głowacka
University of Helsinki
glowacka@cs.helsinki.fi

ABSTRACT

Retrieval systems based on machine learning require both positive and negative examples to perform inference, which is usually obtained through relevance feedback. Unfortunately, explicit negative relevance feedback is thought to have poor user experience. Instead, systems typically rely on implicit negative feedback. In this study, we confirm that, in the case of binary relevance feedback, users prefer giving positive feedback (and implicit negative feedback) over negative feedback (and implicit positive feedback). These two feedback mechanisms are functionally equivalent, capturing the same information from the user, but differ in how they are framed. Despite users' preference for positive feedback, there were no significant differences in behaviour. As users were not shown how feedback influenced search results, we hypothesise that previously reported results could, at least in part, be due to cognitive biases related to user perception of negative feedback.

CCS CONCEPTS

• **Information systems → Relevance assessment**;

KEYWORDS

relevance feedback, negative relevance feedback, user studies, experimental design, scientific literature search

ACM Reference Format:

Dhruv Tripathi, Alan Medlar, and Dorota Głowacka. 2019. How Relevance Feedback is Framed Affects, User Experience, but not Behaviour. In *2019 Conference on Human Information Interaction and Retrieval (CHIIR '19), March 10–14, 2019, Glasgow, United Kingdom.* ACM, New York, NY, USA, 5 pages. https://doi.org/10.1145/3295750.3298957

1 BACKGROUND

Traditional information retrieval (IR) systems present users with search results ranked by their relevance to a search query. IR systems tend to assume that users have specific search goals in mind and sufficient domain knowledge to formulate appropriate queries. In many situations, however, users have difficulty expressing their information needs [6]. In exploratory search, for example, users are characterised as attempting to learn or discover new information and may struggle to achieve their search goals without additional support [1, 2, 16, 17].

To support users, IR systems can use feedback mechanisms to supplement the traditional query interface. Relevance feedback (RF) is a mechanism by which users flag search results that are relevant to the current search [9, 13, 14]. By doing so, users can refine the scope of their search without explicitly describing what information they are seeking. Instead, the IR system infers which documents would satisfy the user based on those documents previously identified as relevant [12].

Traditionally, RF was used for query expansion: identifying new terms that could be included or reweighted in the search query [5]. Query expansion can be achieved by finding terms that are over-represented in relevant documents compared to background term frequencies in the corpus. However, it was demonstrated early on that using additional information from non-relevant documents improved performance [11]. What constitutes non-relevance differs from system to system. Non-relevant documents can be those that were *a*) assessed by the user and explicitly marked as non-relevant (explicit negative feedback) or *b*) assumed to be non-relevant because they were not marked as relevant (implicit negative feedback). In the latter case, there is no guarantee that users have assessed, or even seen, those documents assumed to be non-relevant.

In this study we are interested in non-relevant documents and negative feedback for two main reasons. First, retrieval systems are increasingly based on machine learning algorithms that require both positive and negative examples to perform inference (e.g. [3, 15, 18, 22]). Indeed, such systems assume that RF categorizes documents into relevant and non-relevant sets, whether users are doing so explicitly or not [8, 10]. Second, RF-based systems typically require an initial search query before any relevance judgments can be made. If we assume the query is at least broadly related to the user's information needs and that relevant documents are more likely to be ranked highly, then negative feedback should provide more information to the system than positive feedback [7, 12]. Indeed, we would argue that IR systems should be designed to optimise the quality of negative feedback.

It is therefore unfortunate that negative relevance feedback (NRF) - the explicit flagging of non-relevant documents - is thought to have a poor user experience in comparison to RF. Belkin *et al.* report that users worry about the unintended consequences of using NRF. That negative assessments could erroneously lower the ranking of relevant documents [4]. Ruthven and Lalmas suggest that this concern could be because the potential "harm" caused by negative feedback is unknowable: relevant documents that are missed out on are not presented to the user [19]. The effect of improper positive assessments, however, can be observed and corrected in subsequent iterations. Further criticisms of NRF include higher cognitive load,

CHIIR '19, March 10–14, 2019, Glasgow, United Kingdom

ACM ISBN 978-1-4503-6025-8/19/03...$15.00
https://doi.org/10.1145/3295750.3298957

unfamiliarity and general dislike [4, 13]. Indeed, when users have the opportunity to use NRF, it is either underutilised or not used at all [4, 21].

It is unclear, however, whether user experience of NRF is genuinely negative. The suggestion that the outcome of NRF is less observable than PRF is inaccurate. Any feedback, whether positive or negative, has an impact on which search results are shown to the user. As there is only a finite number of search results per page, there will always be results that do not get ranked sufficiently high and the "harm" of not seeing them is unknown in both cases. Other problems with NRF could merely be side-effects of user study or system/interface design. For example, while NRF is found to be more cognitively demanding, NRF is often implemented in addition to RF (users can give both positive and negative feedback). With respect to underutilisation of NRF, Belkin *et al.* [4] observed that some participants felt under time pressure to complete the experiment and consequently were less inclined to use NRF because it was unfamiliar. In real life, users have time to become comfortable with new interfaces, but in experimental settings may only get a single opportunity to perform their search task. Furthermore, past work does not make a distinction between the *mechanism* of negative assessment and its *implementation* in IR systems, where user experience can be impacted by other factors (interface, ranking algorithm, etc.). Indeed, Dunlop showed that NRF implementation is often inconsistent with our logical expectations of how it should operate, suggesting that our understanding of the user experience for NRF might be based on broken implementations [7].

In this study, users performed a categorisation task: they had to flag search results as either *relevant* or *not relevant* to a search query provided as part of the experiment. Participants were told that flagged documents could only be relevant (not relevant) and that unflagged documents were *de facto* not relevant (relevant). The experiments were designed to ensure there would be relevant, not relevant and ambiguous search results for each search query. Crucially, participants are performing the exact same task whether giving positive or negative feedback: categorising search results into two distinct sets. The only thing that changes is the set (relevant or not relevant) that flagging identifies. We show that how the feedback mechanism is framed (explicit positive/implicit negative versus implicit positive/explicit negative) has a significant impact on user experience, however, user behaviour and which documents are identified as relevant are indistinguishable from one another.

2 USER STUDY

2.1 Search System

Users were placed in a scientific literature search scenario, where documents are displayed in a list-like interface and relevance feedback is given per document. The interface to the system is shown in Figure 1. Each search task is limited to a single results page (users never see how their feedback influences search results in subsequent iterations). Instructions are displayed at the top of the page. Documents are presented in a list with a button next to each document for relevance feedback. Each search task shows 10 documents with 2-3 documents visible without scrolling (dependent on abstract length). A brief questionnaire at the bottom of the page was used to record immediate impressions of the current task. Search

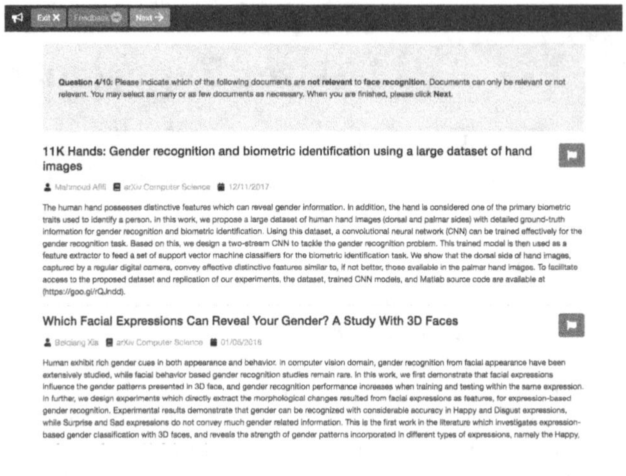

Figure 1: Screenshot of the search interface. Instructions for the search task are displayed at the top of the page. Documents can be flagged by clicking the icon in the right-hand margin. The Next icon takes the user to the next search task.

results were retrieved from a database of 170,367 Computer Science articles from arXiv (downloaded June 2018) using Okapi BM25 [20].

2.2 Study Design

We designed a within-subjects study where participants performed 10 search tasks. Each task required participants to either flag documents that were relevant to the stated search query (RF) or documents that were not relevant (NRF). An expert researcher from the machine learning domain designed five search queries well covered by our dataset. While the displayed documents were retrieved using these queries, participants were shown a different, related query (Table 1). For example, when presented with documents retrieved using the query "gender recognition", participants were asked to mark documents related to "face recognition". This was to ensure that search results contained a mixture of relevant, non-relevant and ambiguous documents.

Participants performed assessments for each query twice: once to provide positive relevance feedback and once to provide negative relevance feedback. They were told explicitly that documents could only be relevant or not relevant. We included instructions at the top of each page using the same template for each search task:

> *"Question 1/10: Please indicate which of the following documents are* ***relevant/not relevant*** *to* ***search query****. Documents can only be relevant or not relevant. You may select as many or as few documents as necessary. When you are finished, please click Next."*

To avoid order effects, the 5 search queries were randomised and then repeated in the same order. This ensured queries were spaced out as much as possible: the first query being repeated as the sixth query, the second query as the seventh, etc. Whether the first search task was to mark documents as relevant or not relevant was randomised and then alternated for the remainder of the experiment. Finally, the order of the top ranking search results shown to the user were randomised.

True search query	Stated search query
gender recognition	face recognition
sentiment analysis	twitter sentiment analysis
wireless sensor networks	wireless energy efficiency
fake news twitter	fake news detection
deep learning medicine	clinical applications of deep learning

Table 1: List of search queries together with what participants were told the queries were. Stated queries differed to ensure search results were a mixture of relevant, ambiguous and irrelevant documents.

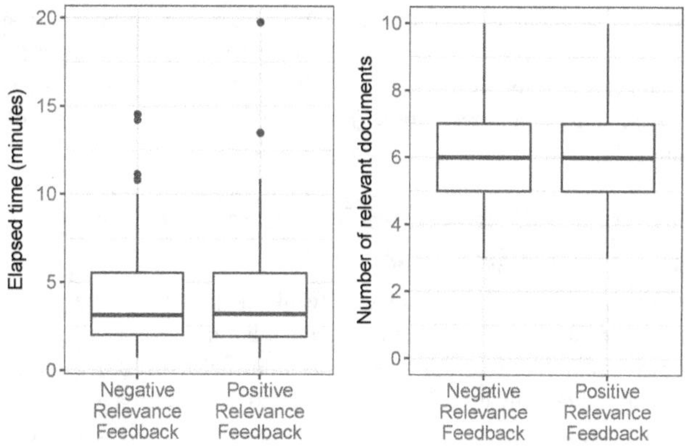

(a) Elapsed time **(b) Relevant documents**

Figure 2: Boxplots showing interaction data collected from search tasks using positive and negative relevance feedback. Subplot a shows the number of relevant documents is independent of feedback mechanism. Subplot b shows the same for the time taken to complete each search task.

2.3 Measures and Procedure

Prior to each experiment, users were shown how to complete search tasks via an instructional video. Participants were not informed that they would repeat each query with a different relevance feedback mechanism in the second half of the experiment.

Studies were conducted in a soundproof room in order to avoid distractions. The experiment was performed on a MacBook Air laptop with a 13 inch screen. There were no time limits to complete the experiments. At the beginning of the study, participants completed a consent form and a short questionnaire about their background. Participants then performed the 10 search tasks. Each search task contained the same instructional text (stated previously) at the top of the page and a short intermediate questionnaire at the bottom. The intermediate questionnaire asked users to assess their knowledge of the stated query and their level of comfort giving positive or negative relevance feedback depending on the current search task. After the final task users answered a questionnaire related to their overall assessment of the search tasks and different methods of relevance feedback.

To conclude the study, we conducted a semi-structured interview inquiring about each participants personal experience during the experiment. Each experiment lasted on average ~50 minutes in total and each participant was compensated with £10.

3 RESULTS

We recruited 24 participants (16 male and 8 female) between the ages of 18 and 35. The male to female ratio of 2:1 reflects the sex distribution in Computer Science in our institution. A majority of participants were finishing MSc students (22) in addition to 2 PhD students. All participants were proficient in English and had knowledge of artificial intelligence and machine learning. All participants reported experience with scientific literature search engines. Four participants were excluded from further study: 2 were pilot experiments and a further 2, based on post-experimental interviews, appeared to have misunderstood the instructions.

3.1 Negative Relevance Feedback Feels Unnatural

Users were asked to rate how natural/comfortable they found using positive or negative relevance feedback on a 5 point Likert scale at the end of each search task. We used ordinal logistic regression to understand whether there was a statistically significant difference between feedback mechanisms (ordinal R package, version 2015.6.28). Ordinal logistic regression is similar to multinomial logistic regression with the exception that the response variable is ordered, as in Likert scale responses. We controlled for the search query and accounted for repeated measures by including the participant as a random effect in the model. We performed a likelihood ratio test (LRT) comparing the full model with a reduced model that did not include a feedback mechanism term. There was a significant difference between positive and negative relevance feedback mechanisms based on users' perception of how natural or comfortable it felt ($LRT = 5.399; p = 0.02$). Users preferred giving positive over negative relevance feedback by a factor of 2.05 (95% CI [1.11, 3.78]). This finding was confirmed in the post-experiment questionnaire, where a majority of users (14/20) stated explicitly that they preferred giving positive over negative relevance feedback (14 positive relevance feedback, 4 negative relevance feedback, 2 no preference).

One possible explanation for positive relevance feedback feeling more natural is that negative relevance feedback is more cognitively demanding. However, only a slim majority of participants (12/20) felt this way. Seven participants felt the opposite, stating that positive relevance feedback was more demanding and 1 participant said that both modes felt the same.

3.2 Negative Relevance Feedback Feels Slower

A slim majority of participants (12/20) stated in the post-experiment questionnaire that performing positive relevance feedback felt faster than giving negative relevance feedback (5 thought negative relevance feedback faster, 3 thought neither was faster).

Figure 2a shows boxplots for the time taken to complete each search task. Users giving positive relevance feedback took on average 4.2 minutes per search task ($SD = 3.1$), whereas those giving negative relevance feedback took an average of 4.0 minutes

($SD = 2.7$). Repeated measures ANOVA found no significant difference between the time taken to perform the search task and the feedback mechanism ($F(1, 179) = 0.31; p = 0.578$). Indeed, positive relevance feedback was not significantly faster for the 12 people that said it was ($F(1, 107) = 0.006; p = 0.941$).

3.3 Users Disagree on Relevance, but are Highly Self-consistent

Whether using positive or negative feedback, participants identified the same number of relevant documents. Figure 2b shows boxplots for the number of relevant documents identified using both positive and negative relevance feedback. Users identified on average 5.87 relevant documents ($SD = 1.552$) using positive relevance feedback, and an average of 6.02 relevant documents ($SD = 1.58$) using negative relevance feedback. Repeated measures ANOVA found no significant difference between the number of relevant documents and the feedback mechanism ($F(1, 179) = 0.648; p = 0.422$).

In general, users identified the same documents as relevant whether using positive or negative feedback. Different users, however, thought different documents were relevant. Figure 3 is a graphical representation of document relevance across all experiments. Each search task is shown as a grid of documents (rows) and participants (columns). For each document we identified whether participants' feedback was consistent between positive and negative feedback, i.e. whether documents that received positive feedback did not receive negative feedback. If documents were identified as relevant to the query with both positive and negative relevance feedback, it is coloured purple. If neither method found the document to be relevant, it is coloured white. If it was relevant only with positive feedback, then it is red, and only with negative feedback, blue. Rows are sorted by inter-participant agreement (users agreeing on document relevance) and columns are sorted by intra-participant agreement (consistency of feedback for a single participant).

Users are highly self-consistent. Irrespective of whether they use positive or negative relevance feedback, users tend to come to the same relevance judgments. Indeed, 89.7% of squares in Figure 3 are coloured either purple (relevant with both feedback mechanisms) or white (relevant in neither). Despite participants' feedback being self-consistent, relevance feedback between participants tended to disagree depending on search task. We therefore believe that users made genuine relevance judgments and were not simply looking for matching keywords in the snippet text for each document.

3.4 Qualitative Feedback Reveals Mixed Feelings

The post-experimental interviews revealed a complex picture of how participants felt about different methods of relevance feedback. Several participants reported that negative relevance feedback made intuitive sense: "No problems using negative feedback ... We can save time by removing documents which are completely non-relevant" [Participant 9]. Others, however, did not like giving negative feedback. One participant said "it is a bit weird and unnatural. The idea of flagging is to get things which are relevant because when you search for something you want relevant results" [P11]. Another participant commented that negative feedback was "more taxing because it required a deeper understanding of the topics" [P8]. Almost half of respondents, however, reported that after a few search tasks they felt more comfortable giving negative feedback despite their initial misgivings.

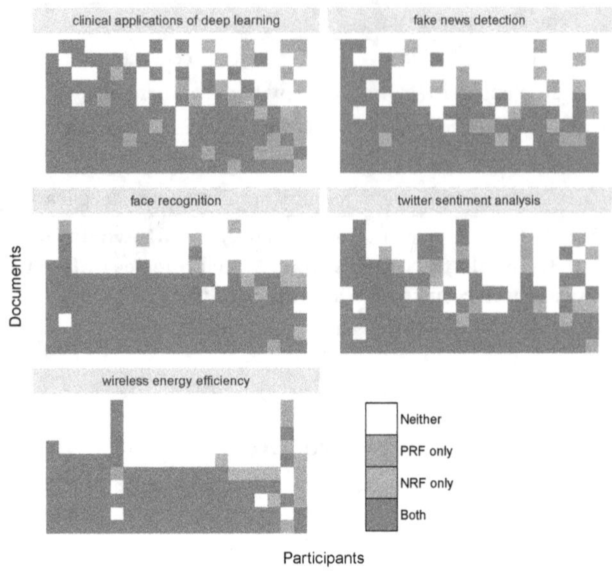

Figure 3: Visualisation of relevance feedback consistency. Each search query is shown as a grid of documents (rows) and participants (columns). Purple and white squares show documents where positive and negative feedback agree.

Irrespective of feedback mechanism, majority of participants claimed to have difficulties marking ambiguous documents and split evenly on whether ambiguous documents were better reported as relevant or not relevant. In the case of ambiguous documents, 75% of participants said they made the relevance judgments based solely on the search query. We assume that this strategy relates to the semantic meaning of search query terms and not exact keyword matches.

4 DISCUSSION AND CONCLUSIONS

While users tend to prefer positive relevance feedback over negative feedback, they performed consistently with both methods in terms of finding relevant documents and the time taken. First, implicit negative feedback appears to give the same results as explicit negative feedback, validating an assumption made by machine learning-based systems. Second, while giving negative feedback had a worse user experience than positive feedback, in our experiments it was exactly the same categorisation task, just framed in a different manner. Neither feedback mechanism could be objectively better or worse than the other, which is supported by users' behaviour. Therefore, any differences in experience can only be explained as the effect of cognitive biases. Retrieval systems might be able to improve user experience of negative feedback by presenting it using an intuitive analogy, e.g. pruning away bad things, to overcome these biases. As most systems only use positive feedback, this could lead to novel search systems. To conclude, negative feedback may have a worse user experience, but it is all in our heads.

REFERENCES

[1] Kumaripaba Athukorala, Dorota Głowacka, Giulio Jacucci, Antti Oulasvirta, and Jilles Vreeken. 2016. Is exploratory search different? A comparison of information search behavior for exploratory and lookup tasks. *Journal of the Association for Information Science and Technology* 67, 11 (2016), 2635–2651.

[2] Kumaripaba Athukorala, Alan Medlar, Antti Oulasvirta, Giulio Jacucci, and Dorota Glowacka. 2016. Beyond Relevance: Adapting Exploration/Exploitation in Information Retrieval. In *Proceedings of the 21st International Conference on Intelligent User Interfaces*. ACM, 359–369.

[3] Khadidja Belattar and Sihem Mostefai. 2013. CBIR using relevance feedback: comparative analysis and major challenges. In *Computer Science and Information Technology (CSIT), 2013 5th International Conference on*. IEEE, 317–325.

[4] Nicholas J Belkin, J Perez Carballo, S Lin, SY Park, SY Rich, P Savage, C Sikora, H Xie, C Cool, and James Allan. 1998. Rutgers' TREC-6 interactive track experience. In *TREC*. 221–229.

[5] Claudio Carpineto and Giovanni Romano. 2012. A survey of automatic query expansion in information retrieval. *ACM Computing Surveys (CSUR)* 44, 1 (2012), 1.

[6] Sudatta Chowdhury, Forbes Gibb, and Monica Landoni. 2011. Uncertainty in information seeking and retrieval: A study in an academic environment. *Information Processing & Management* 47, 2 (2011), 157–175.

[7] Mark D Dunlop. 1997. The effect of accessing nonmatching documents on relevance feedback. *ACM Transactions on Information Systems (TOIS)* 15, 2 (1997), 137–153.

[8] Dorota Glowacka and John Shawe-Taylor. 2010. Content-based image retrieval with multinomial relevance feedback. In *Proceedings of 2nd Asian Conference on Machine Learning*. 111–125.

[9] Donna Harman. 1992. Relevance feedback revisited. In *Proceedings of the 15th annual international ACM SIGIR conference on Research and development in information retrieval*. ACM, 1–10.

[10] Sayantan Hore, Lasse Tyrvainen, Joel Pyykko, and Dorota Glowacka. 2014. A reinforcement learning approach to query-less image retrieval. In *International Workshop on Symbiotic Interaction*. Springer, 121–126.

[11] Eleanor Ide. 1971. New experiments in relevance feedback. *The SMART retrieval system: Experiments in automatic document processing* (1971), 337–354.

[12] Maryam Karimzadehgan and ChengXiang Zhai. 2010. Exploration-exploitation tradeoff in interactive relevance feedback. In *Proceedings of the 19th ACM international conference on Information and knowledge management*. ACM, 1397–1400.

[13] Diane Kelly and Xin Fu. 2006. Elicitation of term relevance feedback: an investigation of term source and context. In *Proceedings of the 29th annual international ACM SIGIR conference on Research and development in information retrieval*. ACM, 453–460.

[14] Diane Kelly and Jaime Teevan. 2003. Implicit feedback for inferring user preference: a bibliography. In *Acm Sigir Forum*, Vol. 37. ACM, 18–28.

[15] Mohammed Lamine Kherfi and Djemel Ziou. 2006. Relevance feedback for CBIR: a new approach based on probabilistic feature weighting with positive and negative examples. *IEEE Transactions on Image Processing* 15, 4 (2006), 1017–1030.

[16] G. Marchionini. 2006. Exploratory search: from finding to understanding. *Commun. ACM* 49, 4 (2006), 41–46.

[17] Alan Medlar and Dorota Glowacka. 2018. How Consistent is Relevance Feedback in Exploratory Search?. In *Proceedings of the 27th ACM International Conference on Information and Knowledge Management*. ACM, 1615–1618.

[18] A. Medlar, K. Ilves, P. Wang, W. Buntine, and D. Glowacka. 2016. PULP: A System for Exploratory Search of Scientific Literature. In *Proceedings of the 39th International ACM SIGIR Conference on Research and Development in Information Retrieval*. ACM, 1133 – 1136.

[19] Ian Ruthven and Mounia Lalmas. 2003. A survey on the use of relevance feedback for information access systems. *The Knowledge Engineering Review* 18, 2 (2003), 95–145.

[20] K. Sparck Jones, S. Walker, and S. E. Robertson. 2000. A probabilistic model of information retrieval: Development and comparative experiments. *Info. Proc. & Manag.* 36, 6 (2000), 779–840.

[21] Amanda Spink, Dietmar Wolfram, Major BJ Jansen, and Tefko Saracevic. 2001. Searching the web: The public and their queries. *Journal of the American society for information science and technology* 52, 3 (2001), 226–234.

[22] Xiang Sean Zhou and Thomas S Huang. 2003. Relevance feedback in image retrieval: A comprehensive review. *Multimedia systems* 8, 6 (2003), 536–544.

Challenges and Supports for Accessing Open Government Datasets

Data Guide for Better Open Data Access and Uses

Fanghui Xiao
University of Pittsburgh
Pittsburgh, PA
fax2@pitt.edu

Daqing He
University of Pittsburgh
Pittsburgh, PA
dah44@pitt.edu

Yu Chi
University of Pittsburgh
Pittsburgh, PA
yuc73@pitt.edu

Wei Jeng
National Taiwan University
Taipei, Taiwan
wjeng@ntu.edu.tw

Christinger Tomer
University of Pittsburgh
Pittsburgh, PA
ctomer@pitt.edu

ABSTRACT

The importance of open government data is often associated with increased public trust, civic engagement, and accountable administrations. While there is a myriad of benefits, the existing literature suggests that many open government datasets lack accessibility and usability for diverse users. This study seeks to explore what contextual information users require when they access these datasets. Using mixed methods, we aim to discover the challenges of accessing data, and the necessary contextual information needed by the users to overcome these challenges. As the outcome of this study, we propose a framework called "Data Guides", which is composed of the identified important contextual information. In future work, we will test the effectiveness of the Data Guide in aiding users' accessing and understanding open government data.

CCS CONCEPTS

• **Information systems** → *Users and interactive retrieval*;

KEYWORDS

Open government data (OGD), structured data, accessibility, understandability, contextual information, Data Guides

ACM Reference Format:

Fanghui Xiao, Daqing He, Yu Chi, Wei Jeng, and Christinger Tomer. 2019. Challenges and Supports for Accessing Open Government Datasets : Data Guide for Better Open Data Access and Uses. In *2019 Conference on Human Information Interaction and Retrieval (CHIIR '19), March 10–14, 2019, Glasgow, Scotland Uk,* Jennifer B. Sartor, Theo D'Hondt, and Wolfgang De Meuter (Eds.). ACM, New York, NY, USA, 5 pages. https://doi.org/10.1145/3295750.3298958

ACM ISBN 978-1-4503-6025-8/19/03...$15.00
https://doi.org/10.1145/3295750.3298958

1 INTRODUCTION

While the Internet and communication technology facilitates data sharing, there are numbers of online open data for general public or parties with commercial interests to access or consume. Many of those datasets are shared and managed by governments at various levels. Open Government Data (OGD) is available to anyone to access, reuse, and distribute without copyright restrictions[6, 13]. Being recognized as treasured resources for enhancing policy transparency and government accountability, OGD has been widely accessed for many projects aiming for both economic and social development [2, 11, 12]

However, there are challenges in accessing OGD. In 2012, Zuiderwijk et al. [17] reviewed existing literatures and found that "difficult to access" is a major impediment to OGD. At that time, the results were mainly attributed to the limited openness of the data (e.g., access to the data is restricted to a particular group of users), emphasizing more on the publishers' side. With the open data related policies and rules being developed since then, which contributed an increasing number of datasets available online, the accessibility barriers become more about locating and making use of the appropriate datasets. Thus the issues are discussed more from users' perspectives. For example, through working on Globe Open Data Index (GODI) 2016/2017, LÃďmmerhirt et al. [9] identified three critical barriers, and the most important one is about findability : "data is hard to find." Some example difficulties are: citizens have to check many different websites to find all the data they need; users have to try many queries to access the needed dataset due to bad naming or website indexing. Koesten et al. [8] also pointed out that finding datasets in many practical situations are not always straightforward and may need the datasets from different sources.

Unlike online webpages, datasets contain various forms of data often without sufficient contextual information. Therefore, conventional content indexing methods used in web search engines do not always work for the datasets [8].

Furthermore, although many datasets could come with certain metadata schema, which provides limited capabilities of text description, these structured descriptions presented in a metadata schema often suffer problems such as lacking detail descriptions, containing irrelevant elements for access, or missing certain important elements[4, 17, 18]. This is because metadata is mainly created for collection management or long-term preservation, which often is not fully associated with supporting access for a particular user.

Besides the above general challenges to access datasets, accessing OGD also has some unique difficulties. Users who want to access OGD can be an individual citizen who just wants to know more about the public work in her neighborhood, or a commercial startup company aims to build real-time traffic alert Apps on mobile devices. The former user would mostly be a user with little technology capabilities or data literacy[4], whereas the latter user could be an expert on data manipulation or analysis. Both groups of users should be supported in their access to OGD, which presents interesting, important and open challenges to the designers and managers of OGD repositories.

In addition to the challenge of accessibility, understandability is also one of the major difficulties for OGD users. For example, Zuiderwijk et al. [17] and Janssen et al. [4] pointed out that the main reasons that cause the difficulties of understanding OGD include lacking of information to interpret data, lacking of explanation for the meaning of data, and lacking of knowledge to make sense of data. If users cannot make sense of data, they would not be able to evaluate the data; let alone using the data they found.

Existing literatures suggest that guidance and help with understanding the content within OGD (e.g., descriptions of categories, what data is present, and so on) are important supports for improving the accessibility and understandability [13, 15]. For example, within the context of land use, Verburg et al. [14] stated that it is essential to have clear and extended documentation to help users understand the data they are engaging with. Janssen et al. [4] pointed out "an infrastructure is necessary which helps users to make sense of data." Koesten et al. [8] found out more detailed information on *how the original data was collected* can aid users in making decisions of trusting in the data. These studies emphasized the importance of providing information and context surrounding OGD. Therefore, we believe that a more detailed document beyond metadata should be utilized to help users in their access to and make use of the OGD.

However, what exactly the information should be included in the documentation is unrevealed. There has no systematic investigation on the specific elements in the documentation. In this paper, we call this type of documentation *Data Guide*, and we aim to examine the necessity of the Data Guide, and to explore the important content components for the Data Guide. Specifically, the research questions are: RQ1: what are the specific challenges when users accessing OGD? RQ2: what information should be included in the Data Guide to enable users better access and use OGD?

2 RESEARCH METHODS

An iterative exploratory-sequential mixed-method design is adopted in this research project. A semi-structured interview was conducted first to obtain deeper insights into the users' needs. Then, the results of the interview, the sense-making theories [1, 3, 10, 16] as well as the framework of human structured-data[8] were adopted to guide the development of the questionnaire. Finally, the instrument was disseminated to collect the perspectives of the OGD users.

There are two reasons that motivated us to start our study with an interview. Firstly, the qualitative approach can improve our understandings of the specific challenges that the users might encounter and the supports they expect for overcoming the challenges

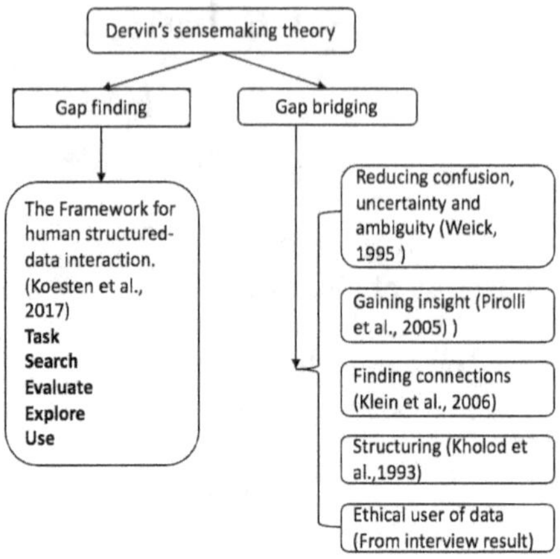

Figure 1: The main structure of the questionnaire

when accessing OGD. Secondly, as there is little research on systematically investigating contextual information for helping the accessibility and understandability of open data, we lacked sufficient guidance to frame a larger-scale quantitative survey. We therefore combining the results of semi-structured interviews with sense-making theories and a framework of human structured-data interaction to construct a theoretical basis for a web-based questionnaire survey.

Overall, the theories and framework guide us to build the structure of questions, and the interview results provide the options of each question. The structure of Gap finding and Gap bridging in the questionnaire was designed, as shown in Figure 1, and we will illustrate the design process in the following sections.

2.1 Questionnaire Design

The questionnaire includes four sections: the challenges of accessing OGD (Gap finding), the expected contextual information (Gap bridging), participants' data literacy skill, and their demographic information. The motivations for this design are several folds. Firstly, we adopted Dervin's sense-making theory as the fundamental theory, in which she claimed that one needs to identify the gap (i.e., gap finding) and make use of the corresponding bridge to achieve the outcome of moving to the other end of the gap via the bridge (i.e., gap bridging) [3]. We believe that accessing a relevant dataset to satisfy one's particular need follows a similar process too. Besides, we collected the participants' data literacy skill and the demographic information to investigate whether these factors would affect users' access to data. In this preliminary paper, the analysis focused on the questions of gap finding and gap bridging, while the data of the other two sections will be analyzed in the future.

After completing the interviews, we performed an initial comparative analysis to examine transcripts for the interviews. First, we identified the challenges and useful elements that brought up by interviewees, and then the information was coded into different categories (see Table 1 & Table 2, 2nd Column).

2.1.1 Questions regarding Gap Finding. To bridge the users' gaps in accessing data, we investigated what their gaps are first. Koesten et al. [8] conducted a study to see the information seeking behaviors of people searching for the sources of structured data online, including the behaviors of data search and the identification of relevant datasets. According to the findings, they, ultimately, proposed a framework for human structured-data interaction that concludes the whole process of users interacting with OGD. Therefore, we adopted this framework to design questions to learn the difficulties during the entire processes of accessing data. Based on the framework for human structured-data interaction and the interview results, we identified 9 challenges that were presented in the questionnaire. We also have open-ended questions to ask if they have other ideas, but no other challenges were brought up, so we assume the options we provided are sufficient. (see Table 1):

Table 1: Gap finding questions and corresponding options

Perspectives	Options
Search	A. Forming queries for searching
Evaluate	B. Finding the content-relevant datasets C. Finding the usable datasets
Explore	D. Knowing what data is about in the datasets that I found E. Inferring deeper information according to the dataset that I found F. Interpreting the visualizations that websites provide G. Trusting the credibility
Use	H. Using the tools or functions within the portals that are provided for users using data, such as analyzing data or visualizing data I. Using the data to my work

2.1.2 Questions regarding Gap Bridging. Next, we began to find out the useful information to bridge the gaps. Alsufiani et al. [1] examined the different sensemaking theories that proposed by different scholars, including reducing confusion, uncertainty and ambiguity [16], gaining insight [10], finding connections [7], structuring [1], and gap-finding & gap-bridging [3]. They proved that sensemaking involves all these processes. Therefore, we adopted these theories to design the questions regarding gap bridging. In addition, 12 elements were collected from the interview results and were proposed in the questionnaire.

For both Gap Finding and Gap Bridging questions, we employed typical five-level Likert scores, from *Not at all challenge/important* (score 1) to *Extremely challenge/important* (score 5).

2.2 Data Collection

The participants of our study mainly came from users population of a regional data center in the northeast region of the US. The data center serves mainly to local communities, and currently hosts hundreds of datasets (such as transportation and environment data) from the local county, other public-sector agencies, academic institutions, and nonprofit organizations.

We adopted the snowball sample method for recruiting participants with the experience of using open data. We made initial contacts with users who are qualified and willing to participant the interviews and the questionnaire. Then, these participants recommended their colleagues or other suitable people to be the new subjects. In total, we interviewed 14 users (9 females and 5 males, 3 researchers, 3 data scientists, 6 librarians, 1 educator, and 1 business people, age from 18 to 45 years old), and collected 14 valid

Table 2: Gap Bridging questions and corresponding options.

Reducing confusion, uncertainty and ambiguity. Weick [16]	A. Data collection and creation process B. More detailed description of the dataset C. Information about the publisher D. Additional information, such as tips, tricks, and cautionary notes
Gaining insight. Pirolli and Card [10]	A. The publisher's purposes for collecting and publishing the datasets B.Examples of how the data has been used C. Potential uses of a dataset
Finding connections. Klein et al. [7]	A.The relationships (scenario-based connections) with other datasets within the same data center in the datasets that I found B. Cross-linking to other sites' data that related to the data that you are looking at
Structuring. Alsufiani et al. [1]	A. Database schema with a dataset or a database B. The governance history of data formats
Ethical use of data (From interview results)	How to cite the dataset that you want to use

responses to our questionnaire (3 females and 11 males, 6 students, 3 researchers, 2 developers, 1 librarian, and 1 data analyst, age from 18 to 45 years old) by the end of September 21, 2018.

3 RESULT ANALYSIS

In total, we distributed 36 invitations of the questionnaire, and received 14 valid responses, with a response ratio of 38.9%. Because we focus on a special group of people, who are the users of the local OGD site, the initial contact size was limited, so the final sample size is small despite we actually had a pretty high response rate. Reviewing the current positions of the participants, we found that four of them are data scientists who may search or use data frequently, but the rest may not access data very often in their work. Therefore, it is reasonable to think that our participants are similar to general dataset search users, who have the information needs for accessing or using datasets, but do not have much experience with dataset search

3.1 Top challenges of accessing OGD

Table 3 presents the five most challenging processes. The most difficult one is *inferring deeper information.* Also, our results, such as *Finding the usable/content-relevant datasets,* and *Using the data to my work* are consistent with Koesten et al. study in 2017[8]. They learned that people have difficulties in finding datasets, and lack of the information for evaluating the fitness of use, or the information that helps interpret data out of context. This finding would help data portals learn more about their users' difficulties, and then develop training or tools to help users overcome these challenges.

3.2 The important components of a Data Guide

In the questionnaire, we asked the question *What are the following statements describing the next action(s) you would probably take when you cannot understand a dataset? (Select all that apply).* All 14 participants chose answer *Look for related documentations within data portals.* This result further confirms the need that mentioned

Table 3: The top five challenging process

Processes	Mean	Mode	SD
Inferring deeper information according the dataset that I found	3.7	4	0.9
Using the data to my work	2.9	3	1.0
Finding the usable datasets	2.9	2	1.1
Finding the content-relevant datasets	2.8	2	1.1
Knowing what data is about in the datasets that I found	2.7	3	1.0

in the previous literatures that a clear and extended documentation to help users understand the data they are engaging with.

Table 4 presents the important elements that participants selected for conquering their difficulties. *More detailed description of the data* has been recognized as the most essential element (Mean=4.1, Mode=5, SD=0.9). In fact, some elements are almost equally important, such as *Examples, Potential uses, and Data collection and creation process.* Additionally, we built the connections between the challenges and the supportive elements (see Figure2).

Table 4: The important contextual information

Elements	Mean	Mode	SD
More detailed description of the dataset, such as data metrics	4.1	5	0.9
Additional information, such as tips, tricks, and cautionary notes	3.6	3	0.9
Database schema	3.5	3	1.2
Examples of how the data has been used	3.4	4	1.2
Potential uses of a dataset	3.4	4	1.3
Data collection and creation processes	3.4	4	1.1
How to cite the dataset that you want to use	3.4	3	1.2
Cross-linking to other sites' data that related to the data that you are looking at	3.4	3	1.2
The relationships (scenario-based connections) with other datasets within the same data portal	3.1	2	1.3
The publisher's purposes for collecting and publishing the datasets	2.9	2	1.3
Information about publishers	2.4	2	1.0
The governance history of data formats	2.1	2	0.9

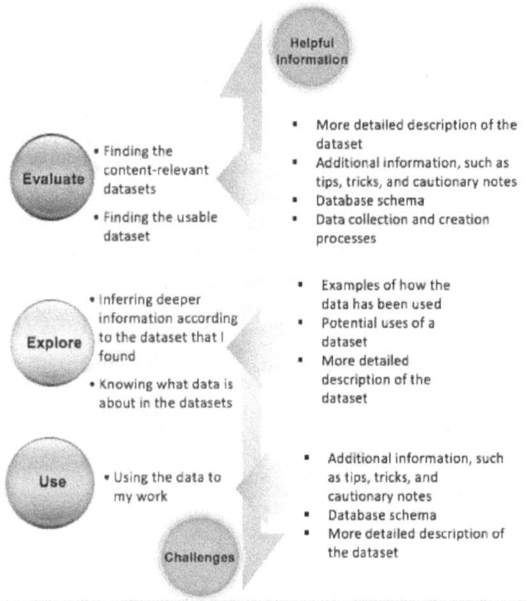

Figure 2: The connections between the challenges and the contextual information

4 DISCUSSION

Components of a "Data Guide". Based on the survey and interview results, we propose the best practices for composing a Data Guide for OGD platforms with twelve preferred components: 1) detailed information of data collection and creation processes, 2) more detailed description of the dataset, 3) information about publishers, 4) additional information such as tips and cautionary notes, 5) data publishers' purposes for collecting and publishing the datasets, 6) examples of how the data has been used, 7) potential uses of a dataset, 8) the relationships (scenario-based connections) with other datasets within the same data portal, 9) cross-linking to other sites' data that related to the data that a user is looking at, 10) database schema, 11) the way to cite the dataset, and 12) the governance history of data formats. It is worth noting that these guidelines were confirmed with the real-world OGD users' perception.

Managerial Implications. Not surprisingly, participants from different perspectives reported what they value more differently. For instances, we found that researchers indicated that 1) detailed information of data collection and creation processes are critical since it can help evaluate the trustworthiness of a certain dataset. These findings are aligned with the prior work based on research data [5]. In contrast, the participants who reported as developers in the interview paid more attention to 12) the governance history of data formats and 10) database schema. We thus encourage data publishers and data portals to consider distributing more contextual information by following the Data Guide along with their data publishing process. However, to avoid the OGD users being overwhelmed by too much information appending to a Data Guide itself, we suggest the components in the Data Guide to be presented optionally and can be manipulated by individual users, e.g., they could collapse and expand some certain components.

Increasing the opportunities of accessing OGD. For the online dataset search, especially numerical data, the related descriptive information is usually insufficient. From this perspective, this Data Guide will enhance the search engines' performance in datasets search by providing the related contextual information.

5 CONCLUSION & FUTURE WORK

In this study, we examined the challenges for users to access open government data (OGD), and we also collected the important contextual information that could facilitate users in their accessing to OGD. The results of the study help us to design a basic framework, which we called Data Guides, to help users.

For future work, we have a short-term and a long-term plan. Our short-term plan includes increasing our sample size and conducting further analysis on whether there are associations between users' perceived challenges and their perceived data literacy skills, as well as between users' occupations and their needs for ODG. For the longer-term goal, we aim to validate and improve the Data Guide by working with professionals affiliated with OGD centers.

ACKNOWLEDGEMENT

This work was partially supported from the Young Scholar Fellowship Program by Ministry of Science and Technology (MOST) in Taiwan, under Grant MOST107-2636-H-002 -002.

REFERENCES

[1] Kholod Alsufiani, Simon Attfield, and Leishi Zhang. 2017. Towards an instrument for measuring sensemaking and an assessment of its theoretical features. In *Proceedings of the 31st British Computer Society Human Computer Interaction Conference*. BCS Learning & Development Ltd., 86.

[2] Ahmad Assaf, Raphaël Troncy, and Aline Senart. 2015. HDL-Towards a Harmonized Dataset Model for Open Data Portals.. In *USEWOD-PROFILES@ ESWC*. 62–74.

[3] Brenda Dervin. 1999. Chaos, order and sense-making: A proposed theory for information design. *Information design* (1999), 35–57.

[4] Marijn Janssen, Yannis Charalabidis, and Anneke Zuiderwijk. 2012. Benefits, adoption barriers and myths of open data and open government. *Information systems management* 29, 4 (2012), 258–268.

[5] Wei Jeng, Eleanor Mattern, Daqing He, and Liz Lyon. 2016. Unpacking the "Black Box": A Preliminary Study of Visualizing Humanists and Social Science Scholars' Data and Research Processes. *Proceedings of iConference* (2016).

[6] Maxat Kassen. 2013. A promising phenomenon of open data: A case study of the Chicago open data project. *Government Information Quarterly* 30, 4 (2013), 508–513.

[7] Gary Klein, Brian Moon, and Robert R Hoffman. 2006. Making sense of sensemaking 1: Alternative perspectives. *IEEE intelligent systems* 4 (2006), 70–73.

[8] Laura M Koesten, Emilia Kacprzak, Jenifer FA Tennison, and Elena Simperl. 2017. The Trials and Tribulations of Working with Structured Data:-a Study on Information Seeking Behaviour. In *Proceedings of the 2017 CHI Conference on Human Factors in Computing Systems*. ACM, 1277–1289.

[9] Danny LÄd'mmerhirt, Oscar Montiel, and Mor Rubinstein. 2017. The State of Open Government Data in 2017. (2017).

[10] Peter Pirolli and Stuart Card. 2005. The sensemaking process and leverage points for analyst technology as identified through cognitive task analysis. In *Proceedings of international conference on intelligence analysis*, Vol. 5. McLean, VA, USA, 2–4.

[11] Jeffrey Thorsby, Genie NL Stowers, Kristen Wolslegel, and Ellie Tumbuan. 2017. Understanding the content and features of open data portals in American cities. *Government Information Quarterly* 34, 1 (2017), 53–61.

[12] Barbara Ubaldi. 2013. Open government data: Towards empirical analysis of open government data initiatives. *OECD Working Papers on Public Governance* 22 (2013), 0–1.

[13] Nataša Veljković, Sanja Bogdanović-Dinić, and Leonid Stoimenov. 2014. Benchmarking open government: An open data perspective. *Government Information Quarterly* 31, 2 (2014), 278–290.

[14] Peter H Verburg, Kathleen Neumann, and Linda Nol. 2011. Challenges in using land use and land cover data for global change studies. *Global Change Biology* 17, 2 (2011), 974–989.

[15] Pieter Verdegem and Gino Verleye. 2009. User-centered E-Government in practice: A comprehensive model for measuring user satisfaction. *Government information quarterly* 26, 3 (2009), 487–497.

[16] Karl E Weick. 1995. *Sensemaking in organizations*. Vol. 3. Sage.

[17] Anneke Zuiderwijk, Marijn Janssen, Sunil Choenni, Ronald Meijer, and Roexsana Sheikh Alibaks. 2012. Socio-technical Impediments of Open Data. *Electronic Journal of e-Government* 10, 2 (2012).

[18] Anneke Zuiderwijk, Keith Jeffery, and Marijn Janssen. 2012. The potential of metadata for linked open data and its value for users and publishers. *JeDEM-eJournal of eDemocracy and Open Government* 4, 2 (2012), 222–244.

Investigating the Impacts of Expectation Disconfirmation on Web Search

Jiqun Liu
School of Communication & Information
Rutgers University
New Brunswick, NJ, USA, 08901
jl2033@scarletmail.rutgers.edu

Chirag Shah
School of Communication & Information
Rutgers University
New Brunswick, NJ, USA, 08901
chirags@rutgers.edu

ABSTRACT

Expectation disconfirmation refers to the situation where a user's perceived performance of a system disconfirms her original expectation. Previous information systems studies have demonstrated that expectation disconfirmation can significantly affect a system user's behavior and experience. Inspired by this finding, we go beyond the traditional approach that focuses on the final post-search perception and study the expectation disconfirmation problem in Web search. Our study investigates *task difficulty expectation disconfirmation* and demonstrates that: (1) unexpectedly difficult task can significantly decrease a user's perceived level of search success and increase the perceived time pressure; (2) the size and direction of task difficulty expectation disconfirmation are significantly associated with Web search behavior; (3) it is possible to predict the state of expectation disconfirmation (especially the negative, unexpectedly difficult cases) based on search behavioral features. This study demonstrates the value of integrating expectation disconfirmation approach with interactive IR research and thus may encourage future researchers to further explore the effects of other aspects of users' expectations and post-search perceptions.

CCS CONCEPTS

• **Information systems → Users and interactive retrieval.**

KEYWORDS

Expectation disconfirmation; task difficulty; interactive IR

ACM Reference Format:
Jiqun Liu and Chirag Shah. 2019. Investigating the Impacts of Expectation Disconfirmation on Web Search. In *2019 Conference on Human Information Interaction and Retrieval (CHIIR '19), March 10–14, 2019, Glasgow, United Kingdom.* ACM, New York, NY, USA, 5 pages. https://doi.org/10.1145/3295750.3298959

1 INTRODUCTION

When interacting with information retrieval (IR) systems, users often engage in a series of information searching activities with various goals and expectations which emerge from characteristics of their search tasks at hand. As a result, users' search behaviors often vary significantly across tasks of different types [11]. In particular, users tend to work harder (e.g., formulate more queries, visit more web pages) and seek available help(s) when they encounter an unexpected difficult task [2, 13]. To embrace a deeper understanding of task-based information searching, we need to investigate both users' expectations (prior to search) and perceptions (after search) of search task features (cf. [10]), especially task difficulty.

The size and direction of the discrepancy between pre-use expectation and post-use perception has been demonstrated to be predicative of information systems users' satisfaction and continuance intention [3, 6, 15]. Specifically, according to the Expectation Confirmation Theory (ECT) [15], when a system outperforms the user's original expectations (which means the expectation disconfirmation is *positive*), the user is more likely to be satisfied with the performance of the system. In contrast, when the expectation disconfirmation is *negative*, the user is more likely to be dissatisfied and thus may discontinue his or her usage of the system or affordance. In the context of Web search, the framework of ECT may serve as a new approach towards explaining Web search behavior.

There are several task-related features that are closely related to users' expectations and perceptions (e.g., task difficulty, topic familiarity, task familiarity). Among these subjective task features, task difficulty is arguably one of the most widely studied features in task-based information seeking and retrieval research (e.g. [1, 2, 8, 12]). It is worth noting that in the context of search, the difficulty of a task is closely associated with *the difficulty of using an IR system(s) to complete the task*. Specifically, for example, finding useful knowledge for writing an economics research paper could be a difficult intellectual task if the person only have a regular search engine. However, this task may not be difficult anymore if the person could get supports from an advanced retrieval system dedicated to economics literature. Thus, both the expectation and perception of task difficulty are partially determined by the system that can be used in performing the task. In this sense, employing the ECT approach can help reveal the connections among task difficulty expectation, task difficulty perception, and search interactions.

Most of the existing research on the behavioral effect of task difficulty mainly focuses on the final state of perceived task difficulty (i.e. post-search measurement of difficulty) in their analyses (e.g., [11–13]). In the light of the ECT framework and the associated findings from empirical studies, we take a step forward by exploring the behavioral impacts of users' expectation-perception discrepancies with respect to task difficulty (i.e., Δ *task difficulty*) in Web search. Based on the existing measurements employed in

CHIIR '19, March 10–14, 2019, Glasgow, United Kingdom

ACM ISBN 978-1-4503-6025-8/19/03...$15.00
https://doi.org/10.1145/3295750.3298959

ECT studies [3], in this study, we measured task difficulty expectation disconfirmation using the difference between post-search measurement of perceived task difficulty and pre-search measurement of expected task difficulty (given the task description) (i.e. Δ *task difficulty = post-search task difficulty - pre-search task difficulty*).

In addition to the evidences from ECT-based studies, there are two reasons that motivated us to examine Δ task difficulty in the context of Web search: (1) Δ task difficulty may serve as a (simplified) representation of the extent to which a user is mentally prepared for a potentially difficult task. Specifically, if Δ task difficulty<0, it may suggest that the user is mentally well-prepared and may perform well in search. However, if Δ task difficulty≥0, then the user may be barely prepared or not mentally prepared at all for a potentially difficult task. As a result, the user may need to break his or her established search strategies, work harder on the task, and seek additional supports from the system. (2) For recommendations design, it is critical to predict the negative states of task difficulty expectation disconfirmation (in this case, Δ task difficulty≥0) based on users' search behaviors and provide appropriate recommendations to support users' information searching activities. In this study, we seek to answer three research questions:

- **RQ1**: What are the effects of task difficulty expectation disconfirmation (Δ task difficulty) on users' perceived levels of search success and time pressure?
- **RQ2**: How is a user's search behavior associated with task difficulty expectation disconfirmation?
- **RQ3**: To what extent can we predict the state of task difficulty expectation disconfirmation from search behaviors?

The study designed to answer the RQs above has several contributions: (1) It demonstrates that task difficulty expectation disconfirmation can significantly affect a user's search experience and is closely associated with multiple aspects of Web search behavior; (2) It indicates the predicative power of search behavior models in predicting the state of task difficulty expectation disconfirmation and thus can help IR systems determine the appropriate timing and situation for offering recommendations and supports; (3) It highlights the value of integrating the ECT framework with interactive IR research and may encourage future researchers to further explore other aspects of users' expectations and perceptions of systems performance, such as perceived knowledge gain and ease of use. The study design is explained in the following section.

2 METHOD

To answer the aforementioned RQs, we collected data through a controlled lab study where we assigned two search tasks for each of the 40 participants and measured their perceptions of task difficulty and search experience in pre- and post-search questionnaires. The behavioral data were collected via a browser plugin.

Search tasks and participants. To effectively control the task context, we designed four work tasks within the domain of journalism: Copy editing (CPE), Story pitch (STP), Relationships (REL), and Interview preparation (INT). Each work task contextualized a corresponding search task. These tasks were constructed based on a modification of Li and Belkin [10]'s faceted classification scheme and the facet values of the four tasks were varied as indicated in Table 1. Also, we recruited 40 undergraduate students majoring in journalism from a major U.S. research university as study participants. To ensure that the participants have similar levels of familiarity with the assigned journalism tasks, we only selected upper-division undergraduate students who have taken either one journalism writing or reporting course. More detailed descriptions regarding the tasks and participants are reported in [16].

Table 1: Task characteristics.

Work task	Search task	Goal	Product
CPE	find authoritative webpages to confirm/disconfirm a given statement.	Specific	Factual
STP	find webpages that contain interesting facts about a given topic.	Amorphous	Factual
REL	find webpages that explain the relationships between two given facts.	Amorphous	Intellectual
INT	identify authoritative webpages and relevant facts about an interviewee.	Amorphous	Intellectual

Study procedure. The controlled lab study consisted of three sessions: pre-search survey session, search session, and post-search survey and interview session. In the pre-search survey session, participants were asked to complete a demographic questionnaire and a task-based questionnaire which asks questions about their work task familiarity, topic familiarity, and expected task difficulty. After that, each participants were assigned two search tasks and they had up to 20 minutes to complete each search task. Participants' search actions (e.g., timestamp, query, URLs, page type, clickthrough) were recorded by a Firefox browser plugin and Morae. The task types were rotated for different participants. After completing the task-based search session, participants were asked to answer questions about their perceived task difficulty, level of search success, and time pressure. The questions and scales corresponding to different task-related features (from both pre- and post-search questionnaires) are provided in the Table 2. Also, we invited participants to participate in a post-search semi-structured individual interview where we asked them to further elaborate on their search strategies and experiences.

Data analysis. Given the three RQs proposed above, our data analysis can be segmented into three parts: To answer RQ1 (the effects of Δ task difficulty on search experience), we regress perceived level of search success and time pressure (time condition) respectively on Δ task difficulty. We also include task familiarity and topic familiarity in the regression models as controlled variables, aiming to clear out the potential mixed effects from these two contextual variables. Since both search success and time condition were measured using Likert scales (which means they are ordinal variables), we use *Ordered Probit Model* for regression analyses [4]. To answer RQ2 (the relationships between search behavior and Δ task difficulty), we conduct *Kendall Rank Correlation Analysis* on each behavior-Δ task difficulty pairs. Specifically, we include three categories of search behavior features that have been applied in a variety of task-based IR studies (e.g., [5, 11, 14]), including:

- **Query behavior**: query length, query reformulation (generalization, specialization, repeat, new, word substitution).
- **Clicking and browsing**: # all actions (query+click+bookmark), # clicks, # unique URLs, # content pages visited (including repeatedly visited pages).

Table 2: Task-related features

Variables	Questions and Scales
Task familiarity	How much experience do you have with this kind of assignment? 1 (not at all)-7 (extremely) - pre-search
Topic familiarity	How familiar are you with the topic of this assignment? 1 (not at all) - 7 (extremely) - pre-search
Expected difficulty	(Given the task description) How difficult do you think it will be to find the information for this assignment? 1 (not at all) - 7 (extremely) - pre-search
Perceived difficulty	How difficult was it to find the information you need for this assignment 1 (not at all) - 7 (extremely) - post-search
Search success	How successful do you think you were in gathering the information to complete this assignment 1 (not at all) - 7 (extremely) - post-search
Time condition	Did you have enough time to complete the assignment successfully? 1 (far too little), 2 (too little), 3 (barely enough), 4 (enough), 5 (more than enough) - post-search

- **Dwell time and display time features**: dwell time on all content pages, mean dwell time on each content page, dwell time before saving the first useful web page, dwell time on search engine result page (SERP), display time on all content pages, mean display time on each content page.

Note that regarding dwell time and display time features, dwell time on a content page refers to the amount of time that a user actually spent on reading the page. In contrast, display time measures how long a page has been kept open during web search [5, 14].

To answer RQ3 (predicting the direction of Δ task difficulty), we consider two different situations: positive state (Δ task difficulty<0) and negative state (Δ task difficulty ≥0) of expectation disconfirmation. Then, we employ multiple classifiers (e.g., Logistic regression, Naive Bayes, Random forest, SVM) to predict and differentiate these two states based on the behavioral features identified above.

3 RESULTS

In the controlled lab study, we collected search behavior data from 693 query segments that were generated in 80 task/search sessions by 40 participants. The length of a session ranges from 2 to 29 queries, with an average of 8.66 queries. All of our analyses are conducted at session level and the results are explained as follows.

RQ1: the effects of Δ task difficulty on users' perceptions of search success and time pressure. As it is shown in Table 3, when Δ task difficulty (post-search task difficulty - pre-search task difficulty) increased, participants perceived a higher level of task difficulty which might significantly surpass their original expected level of difficulty. Consequently, their perceived level of search success decreased and the perceived time pressure significantly increased given the predefined time limit. It is worth noting that these impacts are still statistically significant when we include expected task difficulty, topic familiarity, task familiarity, and task type as controlled variables in the ordered probit regression model, indicating that the negative effects of Δ task difficulty on the perceptions of search success and time pressure are robust and it is not very likely that these effects are caused by other task features.

To answer RQ1, We define search success and time condition as dependent variables and run two separate ordered probit regression models (see Table 3). The result presented in Table 3 echoes the findings in previous ECT-based information systems studies (e.g., [3, 15]) as it empirically confirms the effects of task difficulty expectation disconfirmation on search experience in Web search. RQ2 takes a step forward by exploring the connections between Δ task difficulty and Web search behaviors.

RQ2: the relationships between Web search behaviors and Δ task difficulty. To understand why task difficulty expectation

Table 3: Ordered probit regression model: odds ratios.

	Search success	Time condition
Δ task difficulty	**.470*****	**.398*****
expected difficulty	**.463*****	**.482*****
goal: amorphous	2.046	2.907
product: intellectual	**.277***	.387
topic familiarity	.960	.997
task familiarity	1.188	1.038

Note: *:<.05, **:<.01, ***:<.001. Statistically significant odds ratios are boldfaced. The first column presents all independent variables. Odds ratio<1 indicates negative effect; odds ratio>1 indicates positive effect.

Table 4: Kendall rank correlation analysis: Kendall's tau.

Behavioral features	Within-session/mean	Whole-session/sum
# all actions	**.248****	**.194***
# clicks	.110	**.203***
# unique URLs	-.026	.134
# pages visited	.056	.144
dwell time on content page	.037	**.331*****
dwellcontent to first save	.039	**.271*****
dwell time on SERP	.022	.039
display time content page	**.218****	**.271****
query refo: generalization	**.234****	**.236****
query refo: specialization	.002	.149
query refo: new	-.043	-.010
query refo: repeat	-.004	-.077
query refo: wordSubstitute	-.011	-.025

Note: *:<.05, **:<.01, ***:<.001. Statistically significant correlations (measured by Kendall's tau coefficient) are boldfaced.

disconfirmation can significantly affect search experience, it is critical to investigate the relationship between Web search behavior and Δ task difficulty and to understand how participants reacted to different levels of Δ task difficulty at behavioral level.

When conducting behavioral analysis at task/session level, some existing studies only compute the average value (per query segment) for each behavioral feature, such as average dwell time on each query segment, average number of content pages visited (e.g. [14]). In this paper, query segment is defined as *a search session segment which starts from one issued query and ends at the next query*. To obtain a more comprehensive picture of participants' Web search behaviors, this study follows Liu et al [12]'s approach and calculates both whole-session (i.e. sum/total values for the entire task session) and within-session (i.e. average values per query segment) for each behavioral feature introduced in the previous Method section.

According to the results in Table 4, in general, when Δ task difficulty increased and the expectation disconfirmation tended to be negative, participants usually worked significantly harder on their search tasks by increasing their total actions, clicking more pages, and spending more time on reading content pages. This may be because when participants encountered an unexpected difficult task, they tended to increase their resource input (e.g., time, cognitive resource) in order to maintain their regular or average level of knowledge gain or search performance. Another possible reason is that participants were struggling to find satisfactory search strategies and results when the tasks were more difficult than they thought. Consequently, they had to be more active in searching information and trying various alternative search tactics.

In addition to the general trend discussed above, participants also formulated significantly more broad, generalized queries when Δ task difficulty increased. This may be because when encountering an unexpected difficult task, participants often found it difficult to formulate longer, more specific queries to accurately locate useful information. In other words, unexpectedly difficult task might lead to the increase of perceived uncertainty in selecting query terms and determining directions for search [9]. As a result, participants tended to "take a step back" by formulating short and broad queries and constantly seeking new viable search paths. With respect to the types of behavioral features, our result suggests that compared to the within-session average values, the totalities of different types of search actions generated in the whole session can better represent Δ task difficulty in Web search.

RQ3: predicting the state of task difficulty expectation disconfirmation. The results in Table 4 empirically confirm the connections between explicit search behaviors and implicit Δ task difficulty and also naturally lead to another question: to what extent can we predict the direction or state of task difficulty expectation disconfirmation based on search behavioral features? and more importantly, to what extent can we predict the negative state of expectation disconfirmation (Δ task difficulty≥0) and determine the right time to provide useful system recommendations?

To address these questions, based on the original definition of expectation disconfirmation [15], we first identify two states of task difficulty expectation disconfirmation for constructing prediction task: positive disconfirmation (i.e. Δ task difficulty<0) and negative disconfirmation (i.e. Δ task difficulty≥0). Based on this classification, our dataset contains 47 positive cases and 33 negative cases. Given the nature of RQ3, we focus on two measures when comparing the performances of the classifiers: (1) *the overall accuracy* of predicting the state of Δ task difficulty; (2) *the precision of predicting the negative disconfirmation cases* where timely system supports are badly needed. In prediction analysis, we adopt multiple classifiers (see Table 5) and compare them with the baseline (ZeroR). We use 80% data for training the models and 20% data for testing.

We use both whole-session and within-session behavioral features in building prediction models. The result in Table 5 demonstrates that the best classifiers/performers built on search behavioral features clearly outperform the baseline model in both overall accuracy and the precision of predicting negative cases. As our response to RQ3, this result illustrates the potential of search behavioral models in predicting the state of Δ task difficulty and empirically proves that it is possible to predict the direction or state of expectation disconfirmation based on explicit search behaviors and thereby to determine the right time to provide apt supports for users.

Table 5: Predicting the state of expectation disconfirmation.

Classifier	Accuracy	Precision
Logistic Regression	.575	.462
Naive Bayes	.625	.552
K-nearest Neighbors	.600	.520
Support Vector Machine	.550	.412
Multilayer Perceptron	.513	.412
Random Forest	**.638**	.577
Decision Tree	.625	**.636**
ZeroR (baseline)	.587	.000

Note: ZeroR (baseline) model simply labels all cases with the most frequent label (in our dataset, positive label). The best performers in each column are boldfaced.

4 DISCUSSION AND CONCLUSION

This study investigates the expectation disconfirmation problem in Web search and tests its effects on behavior and experience. Specifically, in this work we focus on *task difficulty expectation disconfirmation* and address three logically connected research questions.

With respect to the RQ1, our results show that the increase in Δ task difficulty can significantly decrease participants' perceived level of search success and also increase their perceived time pressure. This results confirm the effects of expectation disconfirmation identified in previous classical research (e.g., [3, 15]) in the context of Web search. Regarding RQ2, our results show that Δ task difficulty is positively correlated with several aspects of search behaviors, indicating that when participants encountered an unexpectedly difficult task, they tended to work harder and constantly try various alternative search tactics. Built upon our response to the RQ2, in RQ3, we test the predicative power of search behavioral models in predicting the state of Δ task difficulty. The results indicate that the best classifiers/performers built upon search behavioral features clearly outperform the baseline model (ZeroR) in both the overall accuracy and the precision of predicting negative cases. The RQ2 and RQ3 jointly reveal the connections between task-related expectation, task perception, and search behavior. In particular, the answer to RQ3 demonstrates that the prediction models built on behavioral signals can to some extent predict the negative disconfirmation cases. Therefore, it is possible for IR systems to leverage this knowledge and offer proactive supports for the users who encounter unexpected difficult tasks and obstacles [17].

As always, there are limits to our study as well as needs for future efforts. This study only focused on task difficulty expectation disconfirmation and left out other aspects of users' expectations, such as expected ease of use and knowledge gain [18]. However, this research illustrates a promising direction of applying ECT framework in understanding the effects of expectation disconfirmation and may encourage future research to explore other aspects of expectations and perceptions in users' interactions with IR systems. In addition, the findings reported here need to be tested on other datasets collected from both lab and naturalistic settings. Based on larger scale datasets and additional fine-grained behavioral features (e.g., cursor movement features [7]), it seems realistic to believe that we will eventually be able to predict various aspects of expectation disconfirmation in search interaction and to proactively provide users with timely system recommendations and supports.

5 ACKNOWLEDGEMENTS

This work is supported by the National Science Foundation (NSF) grant IIS-1717488. It also uses dataset generated as a part of the NSF grant IIS-1423239.

REFERENCES

[1] Jaime Arguello. 2014. Predicting search task difficulty. In *European Conference on Information Retrieval.* Springer, 88–99.

[2] Anne Aula, Rehan M Khan, and Zhiwei Guan. 2010. How does search behavior change as search becomes more difficult?. In *Proceedings of the SIGCHI Conference on Human Factors in Computing Systems.* ACM, 35–44.

[3] Anol Bhattacherjee. 2001. Understanding information systems continuance: an expectation-confirmation model. *MIS Quarterly* (2001), 351–370.

[4] William H Greene. 2003. *Econometric analysis.* Pearson Education.

[5] Daniel Hienert, Matthew Mitsui, Philipp Mayr, Chirag Shah, and Nicholas J Belkin. 2018. The Role of the Task Topic in Web Search of Different Task Types. In *Proceedings of the 2018 Conference on Human Information Interaction&Retrieval.* ACM, 72–81.

[6] Mohammad Alamgir Hossain and Mohammed Quaddus. 2012. Expectation–confirmation theory in information system research: A review and analysis. In *Information systems theory.* Springer, 441–469.

[7] Jeff Huang, Ryen W White, and Susan Dumais. 2011. No clicks, no problem: using cursor movements to understand and improve search. In *Proceedings of the SIGCHI conference on human factors in computing systems.* ACM, 1225–1234.

[8] Jeonghyun Kim. 2006. Task difficulty as a predictor and indicator of web searching interaction. In *CHI'06 Extended Abstracts on Human Factors in Computing Systems.* ACM, 959–964.

[9] Carol C Kuhlthau. 1993. A principle of uncertainty for information seeking. *Journal of Documentation* 49, 4 (1993), 339–355.

[10] Yuelin Li and Nicholas J Belkin. 2008. A faceted approach to conceptualizing tasks in information seeking. *Information Processing & Management* 44, 6 (2008), 1822–1837.

[11] Jingjing Liu, Michael J Cole, Chang Liu, Ralf Bierig, Jacek Gwizdka, Nicholas J Belkin, Jun Zhang, and Xiangmin Zhang. 2010. Search behaviors in different task types. In *Proceedings of the 10th Annual Joint Conference on Digital Libraries.* ACM, 69–78.

[12] Jingjing Liu, Jacek Gwizdka, Chang Liu, and Nicholas J Belkin. 2010. Predicting task difficulty for different task types. In *Proceedings of the 73rd ASIS&T Annual Meeting on Navigating Streams in an Information Ecosystem-Volume 47.* American Society for Information Science, 16.

[13] Jingjing Liu, Chang Liu, Michael Cole, Nicholas J Belkin, and Xiangmin Zhang. 2012. Exploring and predicting search task difficulty. In *Proceedings of the 21st ACM International Conference on Information and Knowledge Management.* ACM, 1313–1322.

[14] Matthew Mitsui, Jiqun Liu, Nicholas J Belkin, and Chirag Shah. 2017. Predicting Information Seeking Intentions from Search Behaviors. In *Proceedings of the 40th International ACM SIGIR Conference on Research and Development in Information Retrieval.* ACM, 1121–1124.

[15] Richard L Oliver. 1980. A cognitive model of the antecedents and consequences of satisfaction decisions. *Journal of Marketing Research* (1980), 460–469.

[16] Eun Youp Rha, Matthew Mitsui, Nicholas J Belkin, and Chirag Shah. 2016. Exploring the relationships between search intentions and query reformulations. *Proceedings of the Association for Information Science and Technology* 53, 1 (2016), 1–9.

[17] Chirag Shah. 2018. Information Fostering-Being Proactive with Information Seeking and Retrieval: Perspective Paper. In *Proceedings of the 2018 Conference on Human Information Interaction&Retrieval.* ACM, 62–71.

[18] Ran Yu, Ujwal Gadiraju, Peter Holtz, Markus Rokicki, Philipp Kemkes, and Stefan Dietze. 2018. Predicting User Knowledge Gain in Informational Search Sessions. *arXiv preprint arXiv:1805.00823* (2018).

Exploring Email Triage: Challenges and Opportunities

Bahareh Sarrafzadeh*
University of Waterloo
Waterloo, Canada
bsarrafz@uwaterloo.ca

Ahmed Hassan Awadallah, Milad Shokouhi
Microsoft
Redmond, WA, USA
{hassanam,milads}@microsoft.com

ABSTRACT

Despite the centrality of email in the daily routines of knowledge workers, fundamental aspects of its usage are still poorly understood. We are particularly interested in understanding one aspect of email management, *email triage*, the process of going through unhandled email and deciding what to do with them. In this paper we investigate the email triage behavior by presenting interview and survey results that characterize user behavior and needs. The results highlight current challenges and enhance our understanding of how the triage process can be more effectively supported.

ACM Reference Format:
Bahareh Sarrafzadeh and Ahmed Hassan Awadallah, Milad Shokouhi. 2019. Exploring Email Triage: Challenges and Opportunities. In *2019 Conference on Human Information Interaction and Retrieval (CHIIR '19), March 10–14, 2019, Glasgow, United Kingdom.* ACM, New York, NY, USA, 5 pages. https://doi.org/10.1145/3295750.3298960

1 INTRODUCTION

Email usage has significantly evolved beyond *communication* to encompass other areas like *task management, archiving*, etc. [10, 17]. Despite people's reliance on email, especially in work settings, fundamental aspects of its usage are still not well understood.

Email *triage* is the process of going through unhandled email and deciding what to do with it. This paper looks at an important aspect of email management, namely how people triage their messages and what support is needed to design the next-generation of email clients to empower users to better triage large volumes of emails. In fact, the high volume of emails has prompted users to engage in email triage, where users must quickly decide which messages to read and how to act. Triage is important for *task management* and *productivity* as it is one of the main activities to deal with Email Overload [7, 14]. Similar to *search*, the triage process requires the user to go through a list of emails and judge their utility. While in search the goal is usually finding a single item matching the user's query, in triage, the user is making a decision about every email as she comes across it. When messages are opened and handled, they are usually classified as whether they require a reply (immediate or postponed [6]), and whether they should be filed outside the inbox, deleted or left in the inbox [2, 9, 11, 17].

Email triage can quickly become a serious problem for users as the number of unhandled emails grows.[1] This problem arises because existing email clients do not provide users with an effective means for performing email triage. In this paper, we shed more light on how people handle email triage. We perform a qualitative study with face-to-face interviews and a survey to better understand how people triage their emails. In addition to understanding the process of triage, we study strategies people use for triage, challenges facing them and opportunities for improving email clients or building intelligent assistant capabilities to better support email triage.

Previous work studied several aspects of email including email usage, overload and triage. Siu et al. [13] studied email use in the context of everyday work practices. Venolia et al. [14] identified five major activities surrounding how people use email. In particular, they highlighted two activities: keeping up with the flow of incoming messages and triaging existing messages. Dabbish et al. [6] showed that people defer responding to 37% of messages that need a reply. Previous work also studied a variety of factors that made an email important [14]. Dabbish et al [6] studied how users make decisions about triaging their emails, finding that factors such as social information predicted a user's action on a message. Following up on "social importance of emails" several systems have extracted different social features (e.g. known contacts, relationship between sender and recipients, sent to user directly vs distribution lists, etc.) and suggested to re-order messages based on such features [18].

Neustaedter et al. [11] studied triage patterns and found people either use a single pass or multiple passes to triage their emails. Balter [1] found that the majority of participants in their study scanned the inbox an average of 2.3 times before selecting a message to read. Past research (e.g. [4, 8]) has also shown people employ a variety of strategies to ensure important information is not missed, messages that require a response are handled as quickly as possible and tasks, associated with these messages, are carried out efficiently.

We build on this existing body of knowledge by providing insights on how people interlace email triage and management with their day-to-day work processes.

2 STUDY METHODOLOGY

Our study of email triage took place in two stages. First, we conducted a series of contextual interviews with fifteen information workers (4 females) in a large US-based technology company. Second, we distributed a survey to different mailing lists within this company and collected 91 responses (response rate: 9.1%, completion rate: 97.8%). These respondents were distributed across a wide age range, ranging from under 20 to more than 60, and 37% of them

*Work done while at Microsoft.

[1] Whittaker and Sidner [17] coined the term "email overload" to describe the problem of people struggling to keep up with the rate of incoming messages.

CHIIR '19, March 10–14, 2019, Glasgow, United Kingdom

ACM ISBN 978-1-4503-6025-8/19/03...$15.00
https://doi.org/10.1145/3295750.3298960

were females. Participants in both stages ranged in their job roles from product managers and software developers to sales people and administrative assistants. All participants used Microsoft Outlook on a daily basis while some of them used other email clients as well.

2.1 Interview

Interviews were scheduled for 30 minutes in the participant's office where they had access to their mailbox. Part of the interview was conducted as a contextual inquiry, where the participants were asked to look through their mailbox and share some information about any emails that they had triaged on the day of interview and *had to leave for later to deal with* and contrast them with the ones they acted on immediately.[2] We were mostly interested in learning about the emails, the senders, whether they were handled immediately or left for later and how and when they were handled.

For the remainder of the interview, the participants were asked a variety of questions, such as how many emails they receive daily, what kind of email management strategies do they usually employ (e.g. whether they use folders, maintain a clean inbox, have many unread emails), how frequently they need to attend to their mailbox to go through their emails and how this process looks like.

Interviews were all transcribed and analyzed using open coding and affinity diagramming. Several main themes were identified that combine different aspects of triage activity, namely: *How*, *Why* and *When* does triage happen? The first theme is concerned with the characteristics of a triage session (How), while the second theme looks at the external factors that motivates triage (Why) and the frequency of triage sessions (When) for an individual.

2.2 Survey

Inspired by the insights from the interviews we designed a survey to first, verify the discovered trends with a larger audience and second, collect statistics on different email management and triage activities. Responses from survey participants were analyzed to identify common email management and triage characteristics. As in the interview, respondents came from a diverse set of roles. Multi-tasking on different projects was a common trend among them, with 54% working on at least 3 projects and the majority have been working at this company for more than 5 years (55%).

3 CHARACTERIZING TRIAGE

Using our interview and survey data we observed two broad themes regarding the triage process: (a) session-level triage strategies and (b) message-level decision making process for triage.

3.1 Triage strategies

In our survey, we revisited some of the questions from Neustaedter et al.'s study [11], conducted in 2005, including "Do people triage email sequentially or by priority"; "Do people triage email with a single pass or with multiple passes?"; "In each of these strategies, which emails are handled first?". Similar to Neustaedter et al., we found that more users tend to triage emails sequentially than by priority (48% vs 41%), contrasting with 30% and 19% figures reported in [11]. Additionally, we observed that slightly over half of our survey respondents use a multi-pass approach for triaging their messages while 46% perform a single pass only. While this observation is in line with the multi-pass strategy dominating the single-pass strategy reported by [11] (47% versus 17%), we find the difference more marginal in our data.

Finally, we also observe that users tend to handle emails that are easy to delete or archive first (corresponding to 46% of all responses), followed by emails that are important to one's work (28%) and email from important senders (20%). Looking more closely at the follow-up passes during a multi-pass triage, we observe a shift in the types of messages that get higher priorities starting from emails that are important to one's work (36%), followed by emails from important senders and emails that are easy to delete or archive (28% each).

> "in my first pass I try to get rid of things that don't require a response or aren't relevant to my project; second pass is everything that does require a response or further reading; it's either a reply I can write right now and then archive it or it is something that requires me to go do something in the world and come back to it."[P13]

3.2 Decision Making Process

We identified three steps the user goes through to decide how to handle an email: prioritization, deferral and strategy to facilitate revisiting.

Prioritization. During a triage session, users need a fast way to identify messages that require an action from their side (e.g. need a response) from messages that can safely be archived or deleted without negatively impacting their work. Previous work on email suggests that individuals prioritize some messages for attention over others when scanning their inbox [1, 13–15].

During our interviews we noticed that participants take into account different factors to make decisions about each message. They reported that the decision making process happens quickly and on the fly and it is highly subjective and requires the full context of an individual:

> "It does matter who is on the email or who sent it. And I guess that calculus just happens quickly or subconsciously when you are going through your emails. And then there is the other piece that if there is a specific ask to you. e.g. Hey .., what are your thoughts on this?"[P11]

Most of our participants mentioned different strategies they use to be able to quickly identify the emails that are more likely to require their attention: setting rules to highlight emails with their names mentioned [P4, P11], using conditional formatting to be able to distinguish between emails that have multiple recipients versus emails that are sent to them only [P2, P4, P9], the emails on which they appear on the To line versus the CC line [P4], etc.

Deferral. Once the user decides whether the message needs her attention or not, she has to decide whether to take an immediate action or defer dealing with the email [3, 9]. During a Triage session, users commonly defer emails until later to manage overflow [12, 13]. Previous work [12] has discussed several factors that impact the decision of whether the message is deferred including: time or effort needed, urgency, sender and workload.

In our interviews, we found that if handling an email is easy or quick, the importance or the relevance of the email to one's work,

[2] The participants were asked not to share any confidential information and use general terms to describe the content of those emails.

or the prominence of the sender has very little impact on choosing to defer the email to a later time:

> " When I get emails from my students I can answer quickly. Because there are no strategic considerations! If I don't know the answer I still reply quickly and say I need to think about it." [P10]

Similarly in our survey, the most salient factors that led to handling emails right away were: "email is asking a question that I immediately know the answer to" (87.7%) followed by the "urgency of the email" (86%). "The organizational rank of the sender" and "handling the email right away requires less time and effort than leaving it for later and setting reminders to go back to it" were reported as the next two factors by 52.6% and 51% of respondents respectively. An interesting observation is the trade-off between the cost of deferring emails for a later time and the cost of handling an email right away that often leads to context switching and interruptions to the main task or activity at hand:

> "Emails that I'm able to handle right away, I make sure that I do. It would be much more of a mental load if I leave them for later and then I have to track them and remember to go back to them." [P4]

To better understand deferral decisions, we asked our survey respondents how much time they think was needed to handle their deferred email. Responses indicate that more than 75% of deferred messages needed less than 30 minutes to be handled; with 27% needing less than 15 minutes. This finding suggests that individuals are willing to incur the cost of leaving emails for later in order to save on the cost of interruption to their current task at hand as soon as handling the message cannot be done instantly.

Strategies to Facilitate Revisiting. If the user decides to defer dealing with the message, she may opt to take an action to facilitate getting back to it. Previous work has found that how messages are managed is inextricably linked to how users expect to be able to find them in the future [5, 16]. In fact, two main types of email management strategies were identified [10, 17]: *preparatory organization* and *opportunistic management.* While in the former approach the user deliberately creates manual folder structures or tags that anticipate the context of retrieval, the latter approach shifts the burden to the time of retrieval. Similarly, during triage, a user can engage in a preparatory process- ranging from flagging or marking emails as unread to creating tasks and ToDo items in calendars, planners or other tools. On the contrary, the user may rely on an opportunistic approach to handle messages once more time or information is available. Both of these approaches have important productivity implication since preparatory strategies are costly to perform, whereas, relying on opportunistic approaches might lead the user to re-triage the messages again to remember about the intended action or whether or not they can be handled at this time. Our survey data indicates that only 18% of respondents stated that they did not need to use a preparatory strategy to track their pending items and revisit to take care of them at a later time. Among the other group, 32% marked pending emails as unread, 18% flagged them and 2% moved them to a specific folder. The remaining 30% described a mixed strategy including leaving it open in a separate tab, setting a task, reminder or a to-do item in the email client or an external tool, keeping it in inbox (for those that frequently clean up their inbox), assigning a category or relying on memory.

4 TRIAGE CONTEXT

Past research [11, 14] suggests that triage is primarily performed when people arrive at work first thing in the morning, return from a meeting or receive an important email. Alongside these findings, our interviews also indicate that different contextual factors influence the frequency of triage sessions in a day and whether or not people use dedicated sessions to triage their emails.

> "obviously when I first get into work there's the initial what's in my inbox? and then some things I'll just leave for a couple of hours if it's not urgent. [...] some things might get pushed to lunchtime but generally by lunchtime I've looked at all the mails and tried to action on them" [P5]

We also note the close ties between flow and triage activities, as reported by Siu et al. [13]. To elaborate, while some users dedicate some time at the beginning or the end of the day to triaging their emails, the majority of interactions with email in the middle of the day are part of what Venolia et al. [14] labels as *flow.*

> "I come in in the morning and I clean up my inbox. And then throughout the day I see if there are important things to handle. Then after lunch I review things again so I can stay caught up. And then I go to that mode that if something is very important I deal with it now.And then I do the check again when I get home at night."[P3]

We find that a better understanding of the factors motivating triage activities can provide insights to explain how frequently users interlace email triage with their day-to-day ongoing work processes. We can classify these motivating factors into two main themes: (1) Task management and (2) Emotional aspects of Triage.

Task Management. Siu et al [13] proposed a model of *situated email interaction* which describes the majority of these email interactions in terms of a user's short-term attention and task management objectives. In fact, since timely email management is often task critical, users maintain an awareness of their inbox even when processing email is not the primary activity [14]. Similarly, in our interviews the need to triage emails was mainly motivated by the need for effective task management. Most participants mentioned different types of tasks, related to their roles, that come in through emails, and directly impact their work.

> "[my email management strategy is] a little bit of everything. Being a Product Manager, makes email a lot of what I do. And I have to be very organized and on top of things. I have folders for my projects. I leave things in inbox as indication of I still need to deal with them."[P4]

The prominence of triage for task management highlights *deferral* as a particularly salient aspect of process. Alongside our interview data, our survey responses indicate that deferral is indeed common, with 77% of respondents had at least 1 deferred email on the day they responded to the survey, 75% of respondents mentioned they defer at least 1 email every day, among them 44% deferred at least 5 emails every day. As well, we found that 75% of deferred emails required the user to perform some task, which highlights the role of task management as an external factor motivating triage and rationalizes commonality of deferral.

Emotional Aspects of Triage. While email is increasingly used for task management, the fundamental messaging metaphor of most email clients is not optimized for this purpose [2]. Email users clearly feel overwhelmed and daunted by the time it takes to deal with all the work coming in through this medium [17]. As well, the accumulation of messages in the inbox is identified as a key cause of stress and of the sense of *overload* [9].

The literature on email management and inbox triage suggests that the sense of e-mail overload is a subjective reaction by users to increases in inbox size, number of unread messages, and response times. As the messages accumulate, users' perception that they can effectively handle the message load is diminished.

Our interview data suggest that users' email management strategies, the frequency of triage sessions and how emails are handled during triage are in part a means to cope with the sense of overload and maintaining one's desired state of inbox. We note that the feelings of being overloaded or stressed is even more intensified for individuals who collaborate across different timezones:

> "It's very stressful when I wake up in the morning. Because Europe is 8-9 hours ahead and they have done a lot of work and they were asking questions and sending emails. Which is different from when I'm in the same time zone, where the flow is more continuous over the day."[P10]

Another related motivating factor for triage activity is maintaining a consistent email management persona. Users were traditionally categorized based on their email management strategies and how frequently they filed emails [10, 17]. Fisher et al. [8] presented some quantitative results on email overload and proposed to categorize users based on their sensibilities towards email organization and how they *feel* about it. Our survey data suggests that the individuals can associate themselves with a common email management strategy, and that these management personas are somewhat equally distributed with 34% self-identify as "pilers, I don't really use folders"; 43% as "0-inbox, I tend to move messages away from the Inbox" and 23% as "0-unread, I normally don't have many unread messages in my Inbox".

> "Somehow I'm programmed to achieve inbox zero and with too many emails coming in that's a lot of stress." [P6];

We note that the users that self-identify as 0-inboxers or 0-unreads (as opposed to pilers) [9], do strive to dedicate more time to triage their emails and maintain their sense of "being organized" with their mailbox as perceived by them. This in turn helps with coping with the feelings of 'being overloaded' or stress [16].

5 DISCUSSION AND DESIGN IMPLICATIONS

Our study of email triage revisited some of the prior findings regarding session-based triage strategies, while providing more insights about how emails are handled during these triage sessions and what factors impact the frequency and time of these sessions.

With respect to *Triage Strategies*, similar to Neustaedter et al. [11], we find that more people triage emails sequentially than by priority, that a multi-pass strategy is more common than a single pass and that the first pass is mostly used to handle emails that are easy to delete or archive. As well, during a triage session, a user needs to go through a decision making process to identify (a) messages that require an action, (b) whether a message can be dealt with right away or deferred to a later time and (c) whether a preparatory strategy can facilitate revisiting a deferred message.

Prior work [12] has identified the main factors affecting the decision to defer acting on an email; such as the time and effort needed to handle a message, the user's workload and the urgency of the message were the most prominent. Our survey and interview data indicates that, among these factors, *effort* is the most salient one (corresponding to 88% of the cases where an email was handled immediately based on our survey data). In fact, for emails that are *easy* to handle, the importance of emails to one's work or the importance of sender, are not really impacting the deferral decision.

A very interesting observation during our interviews, which was later confirmed by our survey data, was the trade-off between **(a) Deferral Cost**, that is, deferring an email which minimizes the interruption to one's work but then adds a "tracking cost" to ensure timely handling of the email at a later time, versus **(b) Interruption Cost**, that is, handling an email right away which often requires "context switching" to eliminate the "tracking cost". While both of these decisions have major productivity consequences, our survey data indicates the threshold for eliminating (b) while incurring (a) is as low as "email needs less than 30 minutes to be handled". That is for all those emails where users preferred to incur the "deferral and tracking cost", 75% needed less than 30 minutes to handle and 27% needed less than 15 minutes to handle. That is, any email with expected effort exceeding 30 minutes is relatively likely to be differed, which may explain the commonality of deferral among the majority (71%) of our survey respondents. This highlights the potential for features that allow users to handle their deferred emails better in email clients and intelligent assitants.

We identified both preparatory and opportunistic strategies for revisiting and handling the messages that are deferred during triage. More work is needed to quantify whether or not preparatory strategies result in any gain in productivity and the efficiency of managing pending tasks. Nevertheless, we observe that users do utilize different preparatory strategies to manage their emails for effective task management as well as a means to cope with the sense of overload. In particular, our survey data shows that only 18% of respondents expressed no need for preparatory strategies.

Finally, our survey data shows that users are able to associate themselves with different email management persona (e.g. piler versus 0-inbox) and these persona (that can be learned by tracing users action logs) correspond to different frequencies of dedicated triage sessions throughout the day. We argue that the next generation of email clients can use these signals to infer when the user is in triage mode and hence need support with annotating, scheduling or flagging emails to ensure a timely and convenient handling of deferred emails.

6 CONCLUSION

In this work, through contextual interviews and a survey, we sought to understand how people interlace email triage and management with their day-to-day work processes, what strategies are employed to ensure tasks are handled efficiently, interruptions to other tasks are minimized and important information is not missed. We also identified the main challenges that are encountered during triage activities which can critically affect productivity at the work place. Our findings suggest that individuals actively engage in a complex decision making process while utilizing a mix of preparatory and opportunistic strategies to facilitate task management and as a coping mechanism to deal with the feelings of being overloaded or stressed. One promising implication for the next generation of email clients is using *mixed initiative* approaches that provide the right kind of balance, that is, sufficiently automated to reduce the cost of preparatory email management strategies, while preserving an essential level of interaction between the users and their emails.

REFERENCES

[1] Olle Bälter and Candace L Sidner. 2002. Bifrost Inbox Organizer: Giving users control over the inbox. In *Proceedings of the second Nordic conference on Human-computer interaction*. ACM, 111–118.

[2] V. Bellotti, N. Ducheneaut, M. Howard, and I. Smith. 2003. Taking Email to Task: The Design and Evaluation of a Task Management Centered Email Tool. In *Proc. SIGCHI.* 345–352.

[3] Victoria Bellotti, Nicolas Ducheneaut, Mark Howard, Ian Smith, and Rebecca E Grinter. 2005. Quality versus quantity: E-mail-centric task management and its relation with overload. *Human–Computer Interaction* 20, 1-2 (2005), 89–138.

[4] R. Capra, J. Khanova, and S. Ramdeen. 2013. Work and personal e-mail use by university employees: PIM practices across domain boundaries. *Journal of the Association for Information Science and Technology* 64, 5, 1029–1044.

[5] M.E. Cecchinato, A. Sellen, M. Shokouhi, and G. Smyth. 2016. Finding email in a multi-account, multi-device world. In *Proc. SIGCHI.* 1200–1210.

[6] L. A. Dabbish and R. E. Kraut. 2006. Email overload at work: An analysis of factors associated with email strain. In *Proc. CSCW.* 431–440.

[7] Mark Dredze, Hanna M Wallach, Danny Puller, Tova Brooks, Josh Carroll, Joshua Magarick, John Blitzer, Fernando Pereira, et al. 2008. Intelligent Email: Aiding Users with AI.. In *AAAI.* 1524–1527.

[8] D. Fisher, A. J. Brush, E. Gleave, and M. Smith. 2006. Revisiting Whittaker & Sidner's "email overload" ten years later. In *Proc. CSCW.* 309–312.

[9] Y.M. Kalman and G. Ravid. 2015. Filing, piling, and everything in between: The dynamics of E-mail inbox management. In *J. Assoc. Inf. Sci. Technol.* 2540–2552.

[10] Wendy E. Mackay. 1988. More Than Just a Communication System: Diversity in the Use of Electronic Mail. In *Proc. CSCW.* 344–353.

[11] Carman Neustaedter, A. J. Bernheim Brush, and Marc A. Smith. 2005. Beyond "from" and "Received": Exploring the Dynamics of Email Triage. In *Proc.SIGCHI.* 1977–1980.

[12] B. Sarrafzadeh, A. Awadallah Ch. Lin, Ch. Lee, M. Shokouhi, and S. Dumais. 2019. Characterizing and Predicting Email Deferral Behavior. In *Proc. WSDM.*

[13] Nelson Siu, Lee Iverson, and Anthony Tang. 2006. Going with the Flow: Email Awareness and Task Management. In *Proc. CSCW.* 441–450.

[14] L. Cadiz J. Venolia, G. Dabbish and A. Gupta. 2001. *Supporting Email Workflow.* Vol. 2088.

[15] Jaclyn Wainer, Laura Dabbish, and Robert Kraut. 2011. Should I Open This Email?: Inbox-level Cues, Curiosity and Attention to Email. In *Proc. SIGCHI.* 3439–3448.

[16] S. Whittaker, T. Matthews, J. Cerruti, H. Badenes, and J. Tang. 2011. Am I wasting my time organizing email?: A study of email refinding. In *Proc. SIGCHI.* 3449–3458.

[17] Steve Whittaker and Candace Sidner. 1996. Email overload: exploring personal information management of email. In *Proceedings of the SIGCHI conference on Human factors in computing systems.* ACM, 276–283.

[18] Yiming Yang, Shinjae Yoo, Frank Lin, and Il-Chul Moon. 2010. Personalized email prioritization based on content and social network analysis. *IEEE Intelligent Systems* 25, 4 (2010), 12–18.

Clarifying False Memories in Voice-based Search

Johannes Kiesel
Bauhaus-Universität Weimar
Weimar, Germany
johannes.kiesel@uni-weimar.de

Arefeh Bahrami
Bauhaus-Universität Weimar
Weimar, Germany
arefeh.bahrami@uni-weimar.de

Benno Stein
Bauhaus-Universität Weimar
Weimar, Germany
benno.stein@uni-weimar.de

Avishek Anand
L3S Research Center
Hannover, Germany
anand@l3s.de

Matthias Hagen
Martin-Luther-Universität
Halle-Wittenberg
Halle, Germany
matthias.hagen@informatik.
uni-halle.de

ABSTRACT

Queries containing false memories (i.e., attributes the user misremembered about a searched item) represent a challenge for search systems. A query with a false memory will match inadequate results or even no result, and an automatic query correction is necessary to satisfy the user expectations. For voice-based search interfaces, which aim at a natural, dialog-based search experience, a sensible answer to this kind of unintentionally ill-posed queries is even more crucial. However, the usual solutions in display-based interfaces for queries without matches (e.g., suggesting to drop some query terms) cannot really be transferred to the voice-based setting. Based on the assumption that false memory queries *could* be identified—a research problem in its own right—, we present the first user study on how voice-based search systems may communicate the respective corrections to a user. Our study compares the user satisfaction in a voice-based search setting for three kinds of false memory clarifications and a baseline case where the system just answers "I don't know." Our findings suggest that (1) users are more satisfied when they receive a clarification that and how the system corrected a false memory, (2) users even prefer failed correction attempts over no such attempt, and (3) the tone of the clarification has to be considered for the best possible user satisfaction as well.

ACM Reference Format:
Johannes Kiesel, Arefeh Bahrami, Benno Stein, Avishek Anand, and Matthias Hagen. 2019. Clarifying False Memories in Voice-based Search. In *2019 Conference on Human Information Interaction and Retrieval (CHIIR '19), March 10–14, 2019, Glasgow, United Kingdom.* ACM, New York, NY, USA, 5 pages. https://doi.org/10.1145/3295750.3298961

1 INTRODUCTION

Re-finding and known-item search are common retrieval tasks. But the longer an item was not accessed, the more the memory declines [4, 6, 7]. This decline may even lead to *false memories* (i.e., misremembered "properties" the desired item actually does not have). Queries containing such false memories will match no or only inadequate results, leaving the user at a loss when the retrieval system does not detect and correct the false memory.

When systems correct a user request, the user should be made aware of this to avoid confusion—a particular challenge for the new and promising technology of personal voice assistants. While such assistants are specifically useful for re-finding and known-item searches when not sitting at a computer (e.g., at a dinner table, what was that movie with actor X?), every additional information the system wants to transmit means the user has to listen for their answer for a longer time. Given a retrieval system that could identify and correct false memories, we carry out a user-centric study to broaden our understanding of how to best clarify false memories in voice-search setups (e.g., it was a movie with actor Y, not X!).

With this first study on the topic of false memory clarifications in voice-based search, we address the following research questions.

RQ I Does language fluency affect user satisfaction?
RQ II Do wrong clarifications degrade user satisfaction?
RQ III How to best clarify false memories?

To answer these questions, we conducted a user study in which the 12 participants had to find answers for various information needs using a voice assistant despite false "memories" in the need descriptions. We tested different ways in which a system could respond after it detected a false memory and had the users rate on 5-point Likert scales whether the assistant was helpful, behaved as expected, was easy to understand, and was pleasant to use. As data, we collected 672 judgments as well as background information and general comments from the participants (cf. Section 3), which we use for an empirical analysis of the research questions (cf. Section 4).

Our key findings are, among others, that for voice-based search (1) automatic corrections of false memories should be made clear to the user to increase user satisfaction, (2) users even prefer a failed attempt to correct a false memory over no such attempt under certain circumstances, and (3) the tone in which the correction is clarified impacts the user satisfaction as well. The results of our study can directly be employed in the design and evaluation of search-related voice-based interfaces. In addition, they open the door for more focused research on query corrections—not just false memories—in the future.

CHIIR '19, March 10–14, 2019, Glasgow, United Kingdom

ACM ISBN 978-1-4503-6025-8/19/03...$15.00
https://doi.org/10.1145/3295750.3298961

Scenario: You try to remember the title of a controversial book that came out in the 1990s and claimed scientific evidence that whites are genetically superior to blacks. You think its title was like "The *something* Factor."

Interaction start: Alexa. Explore!
What is the title of the book from the 1990s that claimed superiority of Whites and is called "The *something* Factor" ?

Post-interaction questions:

The system...	Agree		Neutral		Disagree	Don't know
...was helpful	☐	☐	☐	☐	☐	☐
...behaved as I expected	☐	☐	☐	☐	☐	☐
...was easy to hear/understand	☐	☐	☐	☐	☐	☐
...was pleasant to use	☐	☐	☐	☐	☐	☐

Figure 1: Example task. Participants started with "Alexa, Explore!" and read the question. The highlight shows the seeked item's attributes—one of which is misremembered. After the interaction, the participants rated the system.

2 RELATED WORK

We briefly review the related work on clarifying queries and re-finding / known-item search (the user has previously accessed the item in case of re-finding but not necessarily in known-item search).

Query Clarification. Clarifying a user's query (intent) has been studied extensively in the context of web search interfaces [3, 18] but voice-based systems lead to different interaction patterns [20]. Voice-based search systems are characterized as mixed-initiative systems between users and memory-equipped agents [16, 17, 22], but focused studies on the respective user interaction were lacking for quite some time [1, 15, 16]. Trippas et al. [19] were among the first who found that query refinement / clarification plays a crucial role in voice-based search (at least 25% of the interactions in their study are clarifications) while Braslavski et al. [5] studied human strategies to clarify questions on a question answering platform.

In a previous study [12], we analyzed clarifications in voice-based search for ambiguous queries (where several interpretations of the query seem plausible, in contrast to false memories where no interpretation matches the query without assuming an error). We found that clarifications do not decrease the user satisfaction and that the level of English proficiency of the participants played a major role in their perception of the (English) system.

Re-finding and Known Items. Blanc-Brude and Scapin [4] found that re-finding personal documents comes with the problem of memory decline and false memories (e.g., wrongly associated keywords after some weeks). Similar memory decline can be observed for email re-finding [6, 7] while re-finding in web search is often used to continue a previous, not too long ago session [21].

To study re-finding / known-item search without large-scale logs, different approaches tried to generate known-item queries automatically [2, 8, 13] or in human-computation games [14]. But these approaches fail to capture realistic known-item searches with false memories [10, 11]. Hagen et al. [9] thus crawled a set of 2,755 known-item intents (movies, books, etc.) from Yahoo! Answers and found that about 10% contain false memories. The information needs in our user study are inspired by these cases.

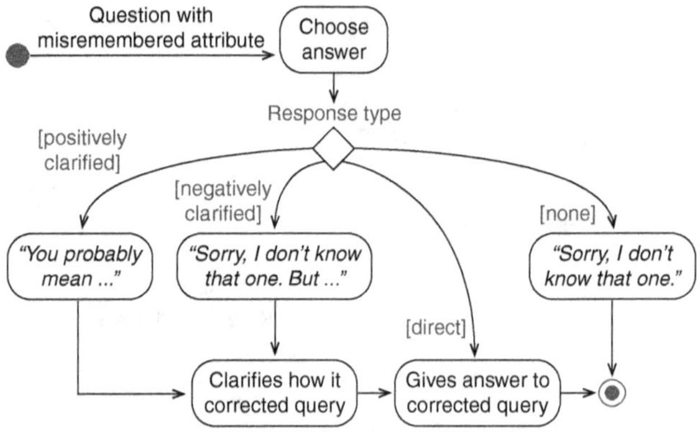

Figure 2: The four response types of our study with the corresponding Alexa reaction.

3 USER STUDY

In order to analyze clarifications of false memories in voice queries, we conducted a user study in which participants had to query a voice assistant in short information-seeking tasks. The task descriptions we provided, however, contained a wrong information to simulate the participant having a false memory (cf. Figure 1).

3.1 Setup

For the study, each participant had to (1) fill out a privacy-related consent form, (2) provide basic and study-related background information, (3) read the provided instructions, (4) complete two small "tutorial" tasks (off the record), (5) complete the 14 main tasks, and (6) give comments and suggestions (optional).

For each of the 14 tasks, a participant received a print-out as shown in Figure 1 and was seated in front of an Amazon Echo voice assistant. Each task contains a question that the user should read aloud to the voice assistant. The question fits the information need that is described in the scenario and always contains three attributes that specify the searched item. The tasks are based on real information needs from the false memory needs collected by Hagen et al. [9]. We rewrote the needs to short questions that are easy to speak aloud. We made sure that, due to the misremembered attribute, no answer exists that matches all three attributes. Note that the participants did not know which attribute is wrong.

To analyze how to cope with false memories in voice-based search, the voice assistant—controlled by us—responded in the following different ways to a participant's question (also cf. Figure 2):

none (2 tasks with this type in the study) It does not try to provide an answer but responds "Sorry, I don't know that one"—a standard line of Amazon's voice assistant in case no answer is found.

direct (4 tasks) It responds with an answer to a question where one attribute is modified. In accordance with best practices for voice-interface design, the response includes the attributes of the question.[1] We chose the system to mention the modified instead of the original attribute to hint at the modification.

negativeley clarified (4 tasks) It responds like for *none*, but then continues with a clarification how it modified one attribute to get

[1] developer.amazon.com/docs/custom-skills/voice-design-best-practices-legacy.html

to a question where it found an answer, and then answers this modified question like for *direct*.

positively clarified (4 tasks) It responds like for *negatively clarified*, but starts with the more positive suggestion "You probably mean ..." instead of the failure-implying "I don't know."

As computationally resolving false memories is error-prone, we test the response types with attribute modifications (all but *none*) both for correct modifications of the misremembered attribute and for modifications of an actually correctly remembered attribute (2 tasks each). To signal the participant a correct modification, the instructor gave the participants a short thumb up gesture, which should simulate an "Oh yes!"-moment. However, if the instructor shows thumb down, the participant had to modify the question themselves until they got the desired answer. Participants where instructed before they started the tasks to modify questions in such a case by dropping a single attribute.

After each task, the participant had to rate their experience with the system on four metrics (cf. Figure 1). The whole setup was verified by one of our university's privacy officers before execution.

For the study, we avoided voice recognition errors, which occur frequently in today's voice interfaces, by using a tightly fit interaction model and pre-formulated questions. In detail, the assistant's recognition model was trained to listen for the different questions of the known tasks, complete or with one attribute dropped. This setup allowed for an excellent speech recognition. This is important, as our study would otherwise be outdated quickly by the current rapid advancements in speech recognition quality. To avoid order-biases, we randomized the task-order for each participant.

3.2 Participants

After a small pilot study (not considered in the results), we recruited 12 different participants from our university for the main study. The participants were between 18–30 (6 participants) and 31–49 years old (6). Furthermore, 7 were male and 5 were female. Participants had an intermediate (5 participants) or proficient (7) English level. Finally, 2 participants stated to never use voice assistants, whereas 9 use them rarely and 1 uses them frequently.

3.3 Data

The 12 participants took between 20 and 26 minutes for completing the study. Each participant finished 14 tasks for a total of 168 interaction phases. For each phase, we collected 4 ratings in post-interaction questionnaires, totaling in 672 ratings.

4 RESULTS

The research questions we raised in the introduction all focus on user satisfaction, which we measure by participant ratings of the system's effectiveness (did it answer the question?), predictability (did it behave as expected?), clarity (was it easy to hear and understand?), and pleasantness of use. In order to allow for a direct comparison with our previous study [12], we analyze the participants' ratings using graphical plots and statistical testing like we did there. We always use Fisher's exact test for statistical testing as it is most-suited for the small size of our study.

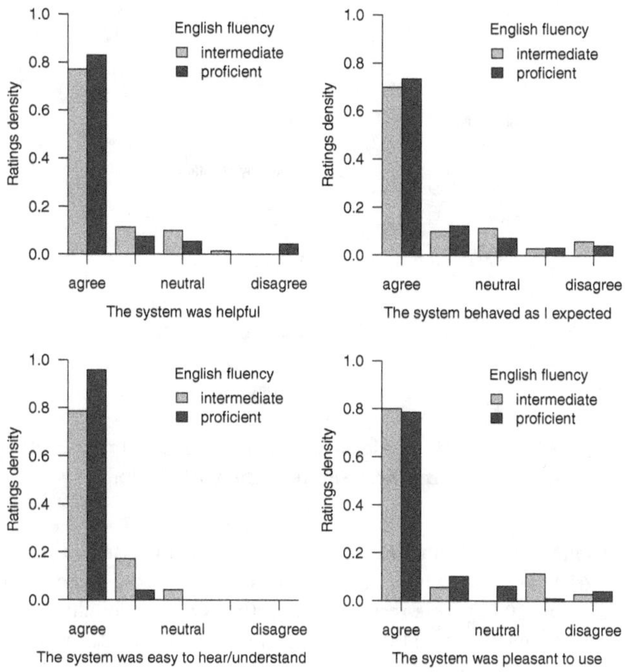

Figure 3: Overall ratings by English fluency.

4.1 Does language fluency affect satisfaction?

Since query corrections may arise unexpectedly, it can be difficult to make it clear to the user what happened, especially in voice interfaces and (as one would assume) even more so when the user is less fluent in the spoken language. Figure 3 illustrates the ratings of the participants for the four study questions according to the participant's fluency of English. Based on previous results [12], we expected that participants that are less fluent in English would find the system less pleasant to use. However, while there is a significant difference ($p < 0.01$), there is no correlation between fluency and pleasantness ratings (Pearson's $r = 0.05$). Moreover, as the figure suggests, there is no significant difference in perceived effectiveness and predictability ($p > 0.05$). Therefore, for the response types we tested, English fluency seems to be not too much of an issue, even though we measured significant differences with respect to the perceived clarity ($p < 0.01$, $r = 0.28$). We believe that this difference to previous results stems from the fact that we did not use response types in which participants needed to formulate their own replies, which is much harder for users that are less fluent.

4.2 Do wrong corrections degrade satisfaction?

Query corrections can have a severe impact on a user's perception of the system, and thus it is natural to ask under what circumstances their gain outweighs their cost. While query corrections in case of false memories may allow the system to give an answer at all, users might get annoyed by unmotivated and especially unhelpful modifications to their query. As Figure 4 shows, the participants were, for some response types, more pleased with a system that corrected their query even if it did not help them with their information need. For *positively clarified* corrections, this result is significant

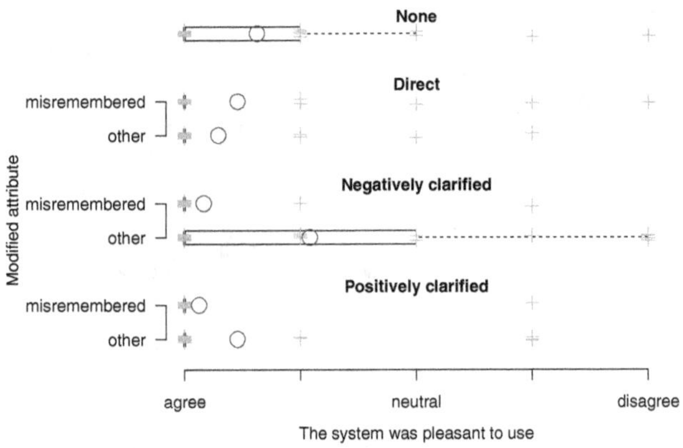

Figure 4: Box plot, single ratings (+), and mean (○) pleasantness by response method and modified attribute.

despite the small sample size for both the general case and when restricted to tasks where the misremembered attribute is modified (both $p < 0.05$). This result suggests that systems should try to correct queries, even at the risk of picking the wrong attribute.

4.3 How to best clarify corrections?

Once the system identifies a potential correction, the question arises how to clarify that and/or the fact that results were retrieved for a correction to the user—or whether to clarify all. While much more ways of explanation are imaginable, we here focus on two of the most basic parameters to explanations: should corrections be clarified at all and does the tone of the correction matter?

For the case that the system modifies an attribute that was actually remembered correctly, Figure 4 shows a clear difference between the two response types that clarify the correction, where the positive one (which is worded more like a suggestion than a correction) was rated as more pleasant on average. This is intuitive as a wrong suggestion (as in *positively clarified*) is not as harsh as a wrong correction (as in *negatively clarified*). Moreover, while only three participants gave a rating between neutral and disagree for *positively clarified* (cf. Figure 4), seven participants did so for *negatively clarified*. In fact, four participants fully disagreed that the latter was pleasant to use, but none did so for *positively clarified*. However, due to the small sample size, this difference is not statistically significant ($p > 0.05$) and should be validated in future studies. Still, our results suggest that the tone of the correction should be taken into account to maximize user satisfaction.

For the case that the modified attribute is the misremembered one, Figure 5 displays the participants' ratings in detail. As can be seen, the response types that clarify the corrections receive better ratings in both predictability and pleasantness. Furthermore, two participants specifically made a comment that the explanations were useful and that they would wish for such a functionality in the real assistant. Even though this result is not statistically significant for our small sample size ($p > 0.05$), the distribution of ratings and informal feedback nevertheless suggests that explanations of the query corrections are well-received and to some degree expected, even if today's assistants do not yet contain this functionality.

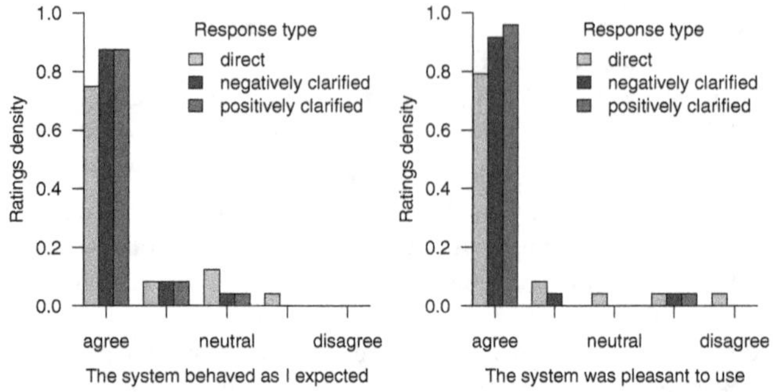

Figure 5: Ratings for predictability and pleasantness when the misremembered attribute is corrected.

5 CONCLUSION

We present the first user study on how voice-based search systems may communicate false memory corrections to their users. We identified three key research questions for false memory clarification regarding adaptations to the user's language level, possible costs of query corrections, and optimal clarification phrasing. Our findings are—among others—that (1) clarifications usually raise user satisfaction; (2) a failed correction, where the system assumes the false memory in the wrong attribute and modifies what was actually correct, is preferable over no correction, and (3) the tone of the clarifications impacts user satisfaction as well, with a positive tone achieving a higher user satisfaction. Unlike previous research [12], we did not find that the user's language fluency has a large impact on their experience. We attribute this to the fact that our participants did not really need to formulate own queries.

All these findings speak in favor of more conversation-oriented interfaces. Participants were the most satisfied with the system that kept the conversation going, by offering a clarification in the positive tone of a polite suggestion. Moreover, in this case participants where also more forgiving to failed corrections, which is especially important as the correction of false memory queries is a difficult task and current systems fail to achieve satisfiable performance yet.

However, the limitations of the study have to be considered for further interpretation. Our participants do not constitute a representative sample of voice assistant users. Therefore a large-scale study (e.g., using crowdsourcing) should be conducted to improve the confidence in the results of our preliminary study. Furthermore, while the false memories used in the study are based on "real" false memories of information seekers, they are not the false memories of the participants. Therefore, real users with false memories may react differently. Especially, they may not accept so easily that they misremembered something. In this regard, our setup mirrors the case where all users directly accept their error.

Our findings open the door for more focused research on query corrections and false memory clarifications in voice-based search. Specifically, more ways of clarification should be investigated in the future, with "positively clarified" as the new baseline. For example, the system might ask the user whether they may have erred on some attribute in the question. Finally, to maximize user satisfaction, experiments with several positive response types could be conducted to find a set of suitable response phrases for alternation.

REFERENCES

[1] James Allan, W. Bruce Croft, Alistair Moffat, and Mark Sanderson. 2012. Frontiers, challenges, and opportunities for information retrieval: Report from SWIRL 2012. *SIGIR Forum* 46, 1 (2012), 2–32.

[2] Leif Azzopardi, Maarten de Rijke, and Krisztian Balog. 2007. Building simulated queries for known-item topics: An analysis using six european languages. In *Proceeding of SIGIR 2007*, pages 455–462.

[3] Sumit Bhatia, Debapriyo Majumdar, and Prasenjit Mitra. 2011. Query suggestions in the absence of query logs. In *Proceedings of SIGIR 2011*, pages 795–804.

[4] Tristan Blanc-Brude and Dominique L. Scapin. 2007. What do people recall about their documents?: Implications for desktop search tools. In *Proceedings of IUI 2007*, pages 102–111.

[5] Pavel Braslavski, Denis Savenkov, Eugene Agichtein, and Alina Dubatovka. 2017. What do you mean exactly?: Analyzing clarification questions in CQA. In *Proceedings of CHIIR 2017*, pages 345–348.

[6] David Elsweiler, Mark Baillie, and Ian Ruthven. 2008. Exploring memory in email refinding. *ACM Transactions on Information Systems.* 26, 4 (2008), 1–36.

[7] David Elsweiler, Mark Baillie, and Ian Ruthven. 2011. What makes re-finding information difficult? A study of email re-finding. In *Proceedings of ECIR 2011*, pages 568–579.

[8] David Elsweiler, David E. Losada, José Carlos Toucedo, and Ronald T. Fernández. 2011. Seeding simulated queries with user-study data for personal search evaluation. In *Proceedings of SIGIR 2011*, pages 25–34.

[9] Matthias Hagen, Daniel Wägner, and Benno Stein. 2015. A corpus of realistic known-item topics with associated web pages in the ClueWeb09. In *Proceedings of ECIR 2015*, pages 513–525.

[10] Claudia Hauff, Matthias Hagen, Anna Beyer, and Benno Stein. 2012. Towards realistic known-item topics for the ClueWeb. In *Proceedings of IIiX 2012*, pages 274–277.

[11] Claudia Hauff and Geert-Jan Houben. 2011. Cognitive processes in query generation. In *Proceedings of ICTIR 2011*, pages 176–187.

[12] Johannes Kiesel, Arefeh Bahrami, Benno Stein, Avishek Anand, and Matthias Hagen. 2018. Toward voice query clarification. In *Proceesings of SIGIR 2018*, 1257–1260.

[13] Jinyoung Kim and W. Bruce Croft. 2009. Retrieval experiments using pseudo-desktop collections. In *Proceedings of CIKM 2009*, pages 1297–1306.

[14] Jinyoung Kim and W. Bruce Croft. 2010. Ranking using multiple document types in desktop search. In *Proceedings of SIGIR 2010*, pages 50–57.

[15] J Lai and N Yankelovich. 2006. Speech Interface Design. (12 2006).

[16] Ewa Luger and Abigail Sellen. 2016. "Like having a really bad PA": The gulf between user expectation and experience of conversational agents. In *Proceedings of CHI 2016*, pages 5286–5297.

[17] Filip Radlinski and Nick Craswell. 2017. A theoretical framework for conversational search. In *Proceedings of CHIIR 2017*, pages 117–126.

[18] Fabrizio Silvestri. 2009. Mining query logs: Turning search usage data into knowledge. *Foundations and Trends in IR* 4, 1–2 (2009), 1–174.

[19] Johanne R Trippas, Damiano Spina, Lawrence Cavedon, Hideo Joho, and Mark Sanderson. 2017. How do people interact in conversational speech-only search tasks: A preliminary analysis. In *Proceedings of CHIIR 2017*, pages 325–328.

[20] Johanne R Trippas, Damiano Spina, Lawrence Cavedon, Hideo Joho, and Mark Sanderson. 2018. Informing the design of spoken conversational search. In *Proceedings of CHIIR 2018*, pages 32-41.

[21] Sarah K. Tyler and Jaime Teevan. 2010. Large scale query log analysis of re-finding. In *Proceedings of WSDM 2010*, pages 191–200.

[22] Alexandra Vtyurina, Denis Savenkov, Eugene Agichtein, and Charles LA Clarke. 2017. Exploring conversational search with humans, assistants, and wizards. In *Proceedings of CHI 2017*, pages 2187–2193.

How Sensitivity Classification Effectiveness Impacts Reviewers in Technology-Assisted Sensitivity Review

Graham McDonald, Craig Macdonald, Iadh Ounis
University of Glasgow, Glasgow, Scotland, UK
firstname.lastname@glasgow.ac.uk

ABSTRACT

All government documents that are released to the public must first be manually reviewed to identify and protect any *sensitive* information, e.g. confidential information. However, the unassisted manual sensitivity review of born-digital documents is not practical due to, for example, the volume of documents that are created. Previous work has shown that sensitivity classification can be effective for *predicting* if a document contains sensitive information. However, since all of the released documents must be manually reviewed, it is important to know if sensitivity classification can *assist* sensitivity reviewers in making their sensitivity judgements. Hence, in this paper, we conduct a digital sensitivity review user study, to investigate if the accuracy of sensitivity classification effects the number of documents that a reviewer correctly judges to be sensitive or not (reviewer accuracy) and the time that it takes to sensitivity review a document (reviewing speed). Our results show that providing reviewers with sensitivity classification predictions, from a classifier that achieves 0.7 Balanced Accuracy, results in a 38% increase in mean reviewer accuracy and an increase of 72% in mean reviewing speeds, compared to when reviewers are not provided with predictions. Overall, our findings demonstrate that sensitivity classification is a viable technology for assisting with the sensitivity review of born-digital government documents.

1 INTRODUCTION

Government documents must be manually reviewed to identify any *sensitive* information, e.g. personal or confidential information, before they can be released to the public, e.g. through the UK Freedom of Information Act [6] (FOIA). In the UK, the sensitivity review of paper documents requires an exhaustive manual review, usually by expert sensitivity reviewers, of *all* of the documents that are released.

However, this human-only sensitivity review process is not practical for the sensitivity review of born-digital documents, due to the volume of digital documents that are created and the lack of structure in the collections that are to be reviewed [25]. Therefore, it has been widely recognised that a technology-assisted review (TAR) approach to the sensitivity review of digital government documents is both necessary and unavoidable [1, 12, 21].

CHIIR '19, March 10–14, 2019, Glasgow, Scotland Uk

ACM ISBN 978-1-4503-6025-8/19/03...$15.00
https://doi.org/10.1145/3295750.3298962

The automatic classification of sensitive information [17, 18] is one emerging technology that has the potential to be the basis for technology-assisted sensitivity review (TASR). However, although it is generally accepted that some form of TASR is necessary [2], it is also accepted that: (1) *all* government documents will continue to be manually sensitivity reviewed for the foreseeable future [25]; (2) governments will not be able to recruit enough reviewing resources [25]. One of the roles of sensitivity classification in TASR will, therefore, be to provide the reviewers with useful information that can assist them in making accurate reviewing decisions more quickly. Moreover, this, in-turn, could potentially enable governments to increase the reviewing resources by recruiting more less-experienced (less expensive) reviewers and assisting them to conduct accurate sensitivity reviewing.

In this work, we conduct a within-subject controlled user study to investigate if providing reviewers with automatic sensitivity classification predictions helps them to perform sensitivity review. The study participants each reviewed three *batches* of government documents to identify two FOIA sensitivities [7], namely *international relations* and *personal information*. Each batch of documents had an associated *effectiveness* level of sensitivity classification predictions, either *None*, *Medium* or *Perfect* predictions. The study evaluates how the effectiveness (accuracy) of sensitivity classification predictions affects the number of documents that a reviewer correctly judges to contain, or to not contain, sensitive information (reviewer accuracy) and the length of time that it takes for a reviewer to sensitivity review a document (reviewing speed).

Our findings show that automatic sensitivity classification, with an effectiveness close to that of the sensitivity classifiers from the literature (e.g. from McDonald *et al.* [17, 18]), can result in significant improvements in the accuracy of sensitivity reviewers, compared to when no predictions are provided (+38%). Moreover, we find that providing reviewers with sensitivity classification predictions results in a statistically significant 72% increase in the mean reviewing speed of reviewers (repeated measures ANOVA ($p < 0.05$)).

The contributions of this paper are two-fold: Firstly, we present the first examination of the benefits of automatic sensitivity classification predictions for human sensitivity reviewers; Secondly, our study shows that sensitivity classification is a valuable technology for TASR, and can significantly increase the speed and accuracy of reviewers when they sensitivity review born-digital documents.

2 RELATED WORK

The need for automatic tools to identify sensitive information has been recognised by governments for a number of years [1, 12, 26, 27]. However, although there is a substantial amount of literature on masking personal information, e.g. [13, 24], it is only relatively recently that research has advanced in the field of sensitivity classification that we address in this work, i.e. classifying FOIA sensitivities.

Table 1: The distribution of classification predictions for classification accuracy treatments (batches).

Classification	TP	FN	FP	TN	Sensitive	Not Sensitive	Total	BAC
None	-	-	-	-	5	15	20	-
Medium	3	2	3	12	5	15	20	0.7
Perfect	5	0	0	15	5	15	20	1.0

McDonald et al. [18] was the first work to investigate automatically classifying FOIA exemptions. In [18], the authors showed that text classification [23] is a viable approach for developing sensitivity classification. The authors achieved a Balanced Accuracy (BAC) [5] of 0.73 when classifying individual FOIA exemptions. When classifying two FOIA exemptions as a single category of information (on a different collection), McDonald et al. [17] achieved 0.71 BAC. The sensitivity classifiers of [17, 18] both achieved ~0.7 BAC. Therefore, in this study, we evaluate if sensitivity classification that achieves 0.7 BAC is sufficiently effective to assist sensitivity reviewers to make accurate reviewing decisions faster.

As previously mentioned in Section 1, all digital government documents will continue to be manually reviewed for the foreseeable future. Therefore, sensitivity classification must be deployed within a TAR framework. TAR is notably associated with e-discovery [22]. In e-discovery, the human reviewers typically only review the documents that are predicted to be relevant [8]. In that context, TAR has been shown to be more effective and more efficient than human only review [14]. However, in sensitivity review, *all* of the documents that are to be released must first be manually reviewed. Therefore, there is a need for studies to investigate how sensitivity classification can be of benefit to sensitivity reviewers when all of the relevant and non-relevant documents will be reviewed.

Berardi et al. [3] evaluated how sensitivity classification could be deployed within TASR to increase the overall accuracy of a human review, when there are insufficient available reviewing resources. Berardi et al. [3] built on the work of McDonald et al. [18] and showed that ranking the classified documents by the *Utility* [4], or expected increase in the overall classification effectiveness, that would be achieved if a mis-classified document was corrected, resulted in substantial improvements in overall classification effectiveness (+ 14% F_2) when only part of the collection was reviewed. Differently from the work of Berardi et al. [3], in this paper, we investigate if sensitivity classification can *assist* reviewers to make accurate sensitivity reviewing decisions more quickly.

3 EXPERIMENTAL METHOD

To investigate if sensitivity classification increases the number of correct sensitivity judgements (reviewer accuracy) and the speed at which reviewers sensitivity review digital documents (reviewing speed), we investigate four research questions, as follows:

- **RQ1**: Does providing reviewers with sensitivity classification predictions increase reviewer accuracy?
- **RQ2**: Does the reviewer accuracy increase as the sensitivity classifier's accuracy increases?
- **RQ3**: Does providing reviewers with sensitivity classification predictions increase reviewing speed?
- **RQ4**: Does the reviewing speed increase as the sensitivity classifier's accuracy increases?

We conducted a controlled user study under laboratory conditions. Participants, i.e. *reviewers*, reviewed 3 *batches* of documents to identify any documents that contained sensitive information

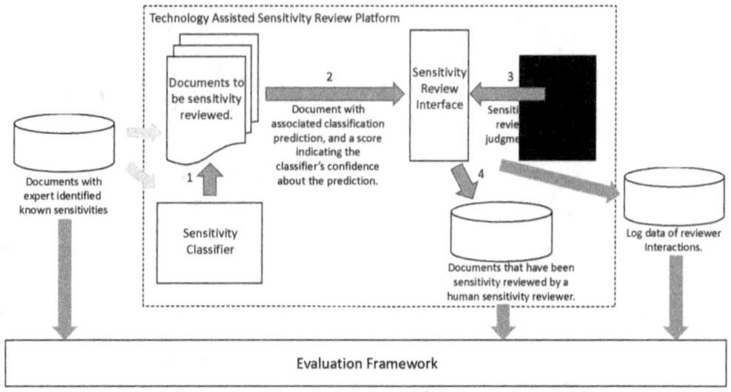

Figure 1: A platform for evaluating the benefits of providing reviewers sensitivity classification predictions in TASR.

relating to either of two UK FOIA sensitivities [7], namely: international relations; and personal information. Each batch of documents had an associated *treatment* of sensitivity classification predictions. **Test Collection and Expert judgements**: The sixty documents used in this study are from a collection of 4000 government documents that contain real sensitivities. We obtained *gold standard* ground truth sensitivity judgements for the collection prior to the start of the study by having *expert* sensitivity reviewers from UK government departments sensitivity review the documents. **Experimental Design**: The study was a within-subject design, where each participant was exposed to all of the conditions being evaluated. Participants were asked to review 3 batches of 20 documents. Each batch of documents had an associated treatment of classifier effectiveness, either *None* (i.e. no classification predictions were provided), *Medium* (i.e. the accuracy of the classification predictions was 0.7 BAC) or *Perfect* (i.e. the classification predictions agreed with the expert reviewers gold standard and, therefore, had an accuracy of 1.0 BAC).

Using the expert sensitivity reviewers' gold standard judgements, we randomly sampled documents from the collection to fit the distributions of sensitive and not-sensitive documents presented in Table 1 (25% sensitive, 75% not sensitive). For batches with *Medium* classification effectiveness (0.7 BAC), 3 documents had True Positive (TP) predictions, 2 documents had False Negative (FN) predictions, 3 documents had False Positive (FP) predictions and 12 documents had True Negative (TN) predictions (*sensitive* is the positive class).

Participants reviewed 3 batches of documents each (1**None*, 1**Medium*, 1**Perfect*), i.e. 60 documents each. To control for learning effects and fatigue, we counterbalanced the allocation of batches, i.e. we permuted the order in which batches were reviewed by different reviewers. Documents within a batch were presented in random order, consistently between reviewers. Participants were advised to proceed linearly through the batch, however, they were able to re-visit documents and change any previously made judgements. For each document, a participant recorded whether the document was "*Not Sensitive*" or contained either "*Section 27*" (international relations), "*Section 40*" (personal information) or "*Both*" sensitivities. **Reviewing Interface and Logging**: Figure 1 presents the four steps of the TASR process (within the dashed box). In Step 1, a sensitivity classifier predicts which of the documents that are to be reviewed contain sensitive information. In Step 2, the documents and associated sensitivity predictions are displayed to a reviewer via a reviewing interface. In Step 3, the reviewer reads, and reviews, each document in-turn to judge whether the document is sensitive or not. In our study, we evaluate how the effectiveness of sensitivity

Figure 2: Reviewing Interface Information Panel: Reviewers can view the classification prediction (Sensitive or Not Sensitive), record sensitivity judgements and pause the system.

classification predictions affect Step 3 of the TASR process. In step 4, the sensitivity reviewed documents, their sensitivity judgements and the reviewers' actions are logged for analysis.

Figure 2 presents the information panel of the reviewing interface. When participants review a document, the panel presents the current document's classification prediction (Sensitive or Not Sensitive). The document to be reviewed is displayed below the panel in Figure 2. Therefore, when reviewing a document, the reviewers are presented with the classification prediction before they actually review the document. As can be seen in Figure 2, participants recorded a sensitivity judgement by selecting one of the four radio buttons at the left of the panel. Participants were also asked to provide a short comment about their decision. For documents that were judged to be sensitive, participants were asked to highlight any sensitive text within the document. A simple mouse-click and drag functionality facilitated the highlighting of sensitive text.

As can be seen from Figure 2, we provided the participants with a button to pause the system. Participants could use this button at any time, for example to have a comfort break or ask a question, this helped to ensure that we recorded accurate timings of when participants were focused on the reviewing task. The interface logged a timestamped record of when a participant loaded a document, saved a judgement, paused or restarted the system.

Participants, Incentives and Training: We recruited eight participants for the study from a well-known international university. Since participants were to identify information relating to personal information or international relations sensitivities, we limited participants to those whose main subject of education was politics or international law (to ensure that the participants had a good knowledge of the FOIA and were familiar with the concepts that they were being asked to review). Additionally, all of the subjects had spoken English for at least 10 years. Full ethical approval for the study was obtained from our organisation's ethics IRB.

At the beginning of the study, there was a 1 hour training session where participants were provided with training on the reviewing interface and the sensitivities that they were being asked to identify. Participants were provided with the same training manual that the expert sensitivity reviewers used. The 1 hour training session included a presentation of the manual and examples of sensitive and not-sensitive documents. Moreover, participants were given time to review a batch of 8 practice documents, and discuss their reviewing decisions with the study coordinator, before the study began.

Participants were remunerated £7.50 per hour. In total, including training times, each participant took between 10-12 hours, split over 2 sessions, to complete the study. In line with the findings of [19], participants were advised to take frequent short breaks.

Evaluation and Metrics: We compare the reviewers performance for each of the classification treatments. We report the mean performance (calculated over all reviewers) for each classification treatment, *None*, *Medium* and *Perfect*, in terms of the number of documents that a reviewer correctly judges to contain, or to not contain, sensitive information (reviewer accuracy) and the length of time that it takes to sensitivity review a document (reviewing speed).

When evaluating the reviewer accuracy, we use the expert sensitivity reviewers' judgements as a ground truth. We select BAC and F_2 as our metrics, since these measures are particularly suited to identifying sensitivity [16]. More specifically: BAC provides an easily interpretable accuracy score (0.5 indicates random) for both classes when the classes are imbalanced; and F_2 accounts for the fact that, in sensitivity review, there are greater consequences from miss-classifying a sensitive document than a non-sensitive one.

When evaluating the participants' reviewing speeds, we use Normalised Processing Speed (NPS) [11] to control for the effects of varying reading speeds and document lengths. NPS is calculated as $\frac{|d|}{exp(\log(time)+\mu-\mu_\alpha)}$, where $|d|$ is the document length and $\log(time)$ is the natural logarithm of the time taken to review d, μ_α is the mean $\log(time)$ for the reviewer who reviewed d, calculated over a particular treatment condition, and μ is the global mean $\log(time)$ calculated for all reviewers over all documents.

When presenting our results in Section 4, we plot the mean participant score (e.g. for BAC or NPS) and 95% confidence intervals. We use the Cousineau and Morey [9, 15, 20] method to calculate confidence intervals. Importantly, this enables the reader to use the *rule of eye* to evaluate the significance of the results from the plots, i.e. we can expect $p < 0.01$ for non-overlapping intervals and $p < 0.05$ when two intervals overlap by <50%. To calculate statistical significance, we use a one-way repeated measures univariate ANOVA in pair-wise comparisons between treatment conditions, e.g. *Medium* vs. *Perfect*. We select $p < 0.05$ as our significance threshold.

4 RESULTS

To answer the research questions that we presented in Section 3, we compare the mean reviewer performance, in terms of reviewer accuracy and reviewing speed, for each of the classification levels *None*, *Medium* and *Perfect*. Firstly, we evaluate if providing reviewers with sensitivity classification predictions increases reviewer accuracy. Figure 3 presents the mean reviewer accuracy in terms of Balanced Accuracy (BAC) for each of the classification treatments, while Figure 4 presents the analogous reviewer accuracy in terms of F_2.

From Figure 3, we note that there is a clear and steady improvement in mean participant BAC scores as the effectiveness of the classifier increases, from 0.5 BAC when there are no classification predictions to 0.69 BAC (+38%) for medium classification effectiveness and 0.8 BAC when the classification predictions agree perfectly with the expert ground truth. Importantly, 0.5 BAC indicates that, on average, without classification predictions the participants' judgements were effectively random. This is indicative of the difficulty of the sensitivity reviewing task, and underlines why government departments have typically employed expert sensitivity reviewers.

Additionally from Figure 3, we note that for the *Medium* classification effectiveness treatment, the mean participant performance is

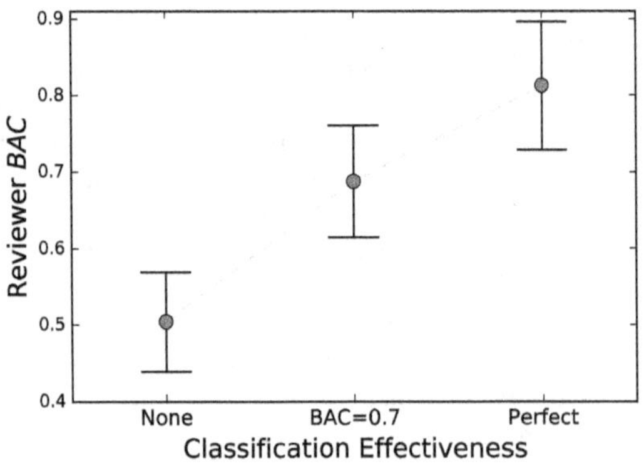

Figure 3: Mean reviewer Balanced Accuracy (BAC).

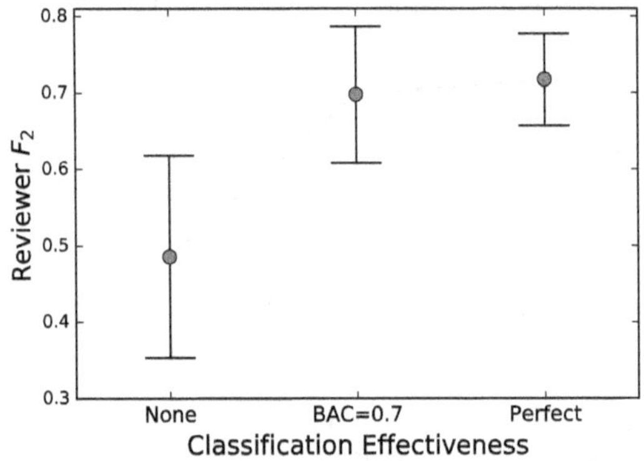

Figure 4: Mean reviewer accuracy in terms of F_2.

almost equivalent to the level of classification effectiveness (participants = 0.69 BAC, classifier = 0.7 BAC). However, the participants only achieved an accuracy of 0.8 BAC when they were provided with perfect classification predictions. This shows that even when the classifier agrees perfectly with the expert ground truth, reviewers still disagree with the classifier. Indeed, none of the participants in our study completely agreed with the *Perfect* classifier.

From Figure 4, we note that, in terms of F_2, the increase in reviewer accuracy is notably greater between the *None* and *Medium* classification than between the *Medium* and *Perfect* classification. The ANOVA test of mean reviewer accuracy between no classification and *Medium* classifier effectiveness shows significant improvements, both in terms of BAC $[F(1,7) = 23.528, p = 0.002]$ and F_2 $[F(1,7) = 7.936, p = 0.026]$. However, comparing the reviewer accuracy improvements between the *Medium* and *High* classifier effectiveness, the ANOVA test shows significant improvements in terms of BAC $[F(1,7) = 6.377, p = 0.040]$ but not in terms of F_2 $[F(1,7) = 0.560, p = 0.479]$. The main increase in reviewer accuracy between the *Medium* and *Perfect* classification are a result of more True Negative judgements since the BAC score, which accounts for True Negatives, significantly increased, while there was no significant increase in F_2, which does not consider True Negatives.

In response to **RQ1**, we conclude that providing reviewers with sensitivity classification predictions does increase the reviewer accuracy. In response to **RQ2**, we conclude that the reviewer accuracy does indeed increase as the classifier accuracy increases. However, in our study, there appears to be diminishing gains in reviewer accuracy as the classification accuracy increases towards perfect. We will investigate this further as future work.

Turning our attention to reviewing speed, Figure 5 presents the participants' mean NPS, in words per minute (wpm). As can be seen

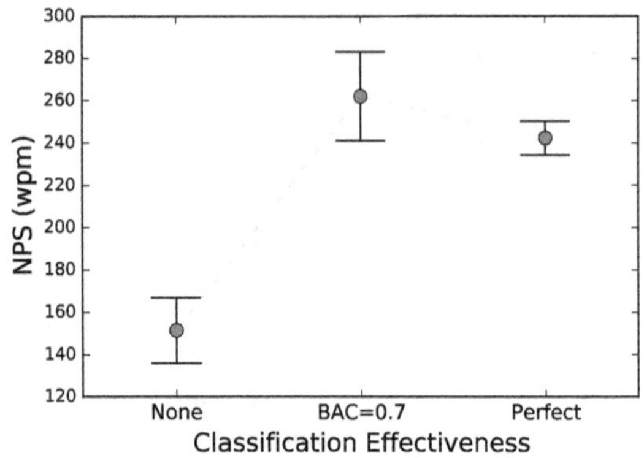

Figure 5: Mean reviewer Normalised Processing Speed (NPS).

from Figure 5, the mean NPS of reviewers when no classification predictions are provided is 151 wpm. Providing reviewers with classification predictions (0.7 BAC) results in a mean NPS increase of 72% to 260 wpm. The one-way ANOVA between *None* and *Medium* shows that this is a significant result, $[F(1,7) = 79.549, p = 0.0001]$.

Interestingly, we note from Figure 5 that the mean reviewing speed is slightly less when the classifier predictions are *Perfect*, 260 wpm (0.7 BAC) vs 244 wpm (perfect). The one-way ANOVA between *Medium* and *Perfect* classification shows that this decrease is not significant ($[F(1,7) = 4.210, p = 0.079]$). Therefore, the significant gains in reviewing speeds compared with no classification predictions are sustained over both levels of classification accuracy. In response to **RQ3**, we conclude that providing reviewers with sensitivity classification predictions does increase the average reviewing speed. In response to **RQ4**, we conclude that the average reviewing speed does increase between no classification and *Medium* classification. However, in our study, reviewing speeds did not increase when the classifier's accuracy increased from *Medium* to *Perfect*.

In summary, the results of our study show that providing reviewers with sensitivity classification predictions can increase the accuracy and speed of the reviewers. We argue that, our findings show that sensitivity classification with an accuracy of 0.7 BAC is sufficiently effective to assist reviewers in making sensitivity reviewing decisions. Importantly, our findings suggest that governments may be able to increase the volume of digital documents that can be reviewed, while maintaining high levels of reviewing accuracy, if they increase the number of reviewers by recruiting less experienced reviewers (at less expense than expert reviewers) and assisting them with automatic sensitivity classification predictions. This, in turn, would enable the expert reviewers to focus on reviewing the more *high risk* documents or disputed reviews.

5 CONCLUSIONS

In this work, we conducted a within-subject digital sensitivity review user study under laboratory conditions, to evaluate the benefits of automatic sensitivity classification predictions for sensitivity reviewers. We found that providing reviewers with sensitivity classification predictions resulted in significant improvements in the number of correct sensitivity judgements made by the reviewers in our study (+38% BAC) and their reviewing speed (+72% NPS), according to a repeated measures ANOVA, $p < 0.05$. Our findings provide evidence that a sensitivity classifier that achieves 0.7 BAC is sufficiently effective to assist reviews in making accurate sensitivity judgements faster when reviewing born-digital documents.

REFERENCES

[1] Sir Alex Allan. 2014. Records Review. Cabinet Office, UK Government. https://www.gov.uk/government/publications/records-review-by-sir-alex-allan

[2] Sir Alex Allan. 2015. Government Digital Records and Archives Review. Cabinet Office, UK Government. https://www.gov.uk/government/publications/government-digital-records-and-archives-review-by-sir-alex-allan

[3] Giacomo Berardi, Andrea Esuli, Craig Macdonald, Iadh Ounis, and Fabrizio Sebastiani. 2015. Semi-Automated Text Classification for Sensitivity Identification. In *Proc. CIKM.*

[4] Giacomo Berardi, Andrea Esuli, and Fabrizio Sebastiani. 2012. A Utility-theoretic Ranking Method for Semi-automated Text Classification. In *Proc. SIGIR.*

[5] Kay Henning Brodersen, Cheng Soon Ong, Klaas Enno Stephan, and Joachim M Buhmann. 2010. The balanced accuracy and its posterior distribution. In *Proc. ICPR.*

[6] c. 36. 2000. Freedom of Information Act 2000. https://www.legislation.gov.uk/ukpga/2000/36/contents. (2000).

[7] c. 36. 2000. Freedom of Information Act 2000, Part 2, Exempt Information. https://www.legislation.gov.uk/ukpga/2000/36/part/II. (2000).

[8] Gordon V Cormack and Maura R Grossman. 2014. Evaluation of machine-learning protocols for technology-assisted review in electronic discovery. In *Proceedings of the 37th Annual International ACM SIGIR Conference on Research and Development in Information Retrieval.*

[9] Denis Cousineau. 2005. Confidence intervals in within-subject designs: A simpler solution to Loftus and Masson's method. *Tutorials in quantitative methods for psychology* 1, 1 (2005), 42–45.

[10] Geoff Cumming and Robert Maillardet. 2006. Confidence intervals and replication: where will the next mean fall? *Psychological methods* 11, 3 (2006), 217.

[11] Tadele T Damessie, Falk Scholer, and J Shane Culpepper. 2016. The influence of topic difficulty, relevance level, and document ordering on relevance judging. In *Proc. ADCS.*

[12] DARPA. 2010. New technologies to support declassification. (2010). http://fas.org/sgp/news/2010/09/darpa-declass.pdf.

[13] Benjamin Fung, Ke Wang, Rui Chen, and Philip S Yu. 2010. Privacy-preserving data publishing: A survey of recent developments. *ACM Computing Surveys (CSUR)* 42, 4 (2010), 14.

[14] Maura R Grossman and Gordon V Cormack. 2010. Technology-assisted review in e-discovery can be more effective and more efficient than exhaustive manual review. *Rich. JL & Tech.* 17 (2010), 1.

[15] Geoffrey R Loftus and Michael EJ Masson. 1994. Using confidence intervals in within-subject designs. *Psychonomic bulletin & review* 1, 4 (1994), 476–490.

[16] Graham McDonald, Nicolás García-Pedrajas, Craig Macdonald, and Iadh Ounis. 2017. A Study of SVM Kernel Functions for Sensitivity Classification Ensembles with POS Sequences. In *Proc. SIGIR.*

[17] Graham McDonald, Craig Macdonald, and Iadh Ounis. 2017. Enhancing Sensitivity Classification with Semantic Features Using Word Embeddings. In *Proc. ECIR.*

[18] Graham McDonald, Craig Macdonald, Iadh Ounis, and Timothy Gollins. 2014. Towards a Classifier for Digital Sensitivity Review. In *Proc. ECIR.*

[19] Linda McLean, Maureen Tingley, Robert N Scott, and Jeremy Rickards. 2001. Computer terminal work and the benefit of microbreaks. *Applied ergonomics* 32, 3 (2001), 225237.

[20] Richard D Morey. 2008. Confidence intervals from normalized data: A correction to Cousineau (2005). *reason* 4, 2 (2008), 61–64.

[21] Michael S Moss and Tim J Gollins. 2017. Our Digital Legacy: an Archival Perspective. *Journal of Contemporary Archival Studies* 4, 2 (2017), 3.

[22] Douglas W Oard, William Webber, et al. 2013. Information retrieval for e-discovery. *Foundations and Trends® in Information Retrieval* 7, 2–3 (2013), 99–237.

[23] Fabrizio Sebastiani. 2002. Machine Learning in Automated Text Categorization. *ACM Comput. Surv.* 34, 1 (2002), 147.

[24] Latanya Sweeney. 2002. k-anonymity: A model for protecting privacy. *International Journal of Uncertainty, Fuzziness and Knowledge-Based Systems* 10, 05 (2002), 557–570.

[25] The National Archives. 2016. The Application of Technology-Assisted Review to Born-Digital Records Transfer, Inquiries and Beyond. (2016). http://www.nationalarchives.gov.uk/documents/technology-assisted-review-to-born-digital-records-transfer.pdf

[26] E Dale Thompson and Michelle L Kaarst-Brown. 2005. Sensitive information: A review and research agenda. *Journal of the Association for Information Science and Technology* 56, 3 (2005), 245–257.

[27] Alistair G Tough. 2018. The Scope and Appetite for Technology-Assisted Sensitivity Reviewing of Born-Digital Records in a Resource Poor Environment. *Handbook of Research on Heritage Management and Preservation* (2018).

Computational Surprise, Perceptual Surprise, and Personal Background in Text Understanding

Xi Niu
University of North Carolina at Charlotte
Charlotte, North Carolina
xniu2@uncc.edu

Fakhri Abbas
University of North Carolina at Charlotte
Charlotte, North Carolina
fabbas1@uncc.edu

ABSTRACT

The concept of surprise has special significance in information retrieval in attracting user attention and arousing curiosity. In this paper, we introduced two computational measures of calculating the amount of surprise contained in a piece of text, and validated with the perceived surprise by users with different background knowledge expertise. We utilized a crowdsourcing approach and a lab-based user study to reach a large amount of users. The implication could be used to propose or refine future computational approaches to better predict human feeling of surprise triggered by reading a body of text.

CCS CONCEPTS

• **Information systems → Users and interactive retrieval**;

KEYWORDS

surprise; computational approach; personalization; crowdsourcing

ACM Reference Format:
Xi Niu and Fakhri Abbas. 2019. Computational Surprise, Perceptual Surprise, and Personal Background in Text Understanding. In *2019 Conference on Human Information Interaction and Retrieval (CHIIR '19), March 10–14, 2019, Glasgow, United Kingdom.* ACM, New York, NY, USA, 5 pages. https://doi.org/10.1145/3295750.3298963

1 INTRODUCTION

Emotions play an important role in effective understanding of text, and therefore have attracted the interest of researchers in information retrieval. Recently there is growing research interest in sentiment analysis, which uses computational approaches to detect sentiments, emotions, feelings, or attitudes in a given body of text. While sentiment analysis is understanding the text authors' emotions, IR researchers also care about the readers' feelings that could be triggered by reading a piece of text, in order to better serve the retrieval purpose.

Among different kinds of emotions, surprise has special significance in information retrieval because natural human information discovery processes are full of surprises, from finding a bizarre movie at Netflix to discovering X-rays in scientific breakthroughs. Previous studies have shown that surprising or unexpected discovery attracts user attention and may arouse pleasant feelings, such as interest, like, and curiosity (e.g., [5, 6]). The explanation is in neuro-science, where it is believed seeking surprise is a human trait. Only the surprising signal at one stage is transmitted to the next stage [8]. Hence, human sensory cortex has adapted to predict and downplay the expected regularities of the world [4, 7], focusing instead on events that are unpredictable or surprising. However, compared to some other user feelings such as relevance, interest, and satisfaction, surprise has not received much attention in IR community, probably due to the vague and elusive nature of the feeling. Surprise by nature contradicts intention and control, which are incompatible with modern IR approaches that highly rely on computing.

In this paper, we introduce our effort in constructing computational measures of surprise and validating them with user perceptions. We call the former computational surprise and the latter perceptual surprise. We also examine the personalization factor of background knowledge expertise and its relationship with perceptual surprise with the hypothesis that it is harder to surprise a knowledgeable person. We use a corpus of health news as the experiment dataset to investigate those research problems. The contribution of this research is three-fold. Most importantly, the research compares computational surprise by machine and perceptual surprise by human. The implication could be used to refine the future computational approaches to better predict human feeling of surprise. Second, taking the individual background knowledge into consideration contributes to better understanding of the personalization factor for surprise, which further informs the construction of computational models of surprise. Third, this study also contributes a human-labeled text corpus collected from a crowdsourcing platform and a lab-based user study. As we know, so far such kind of datasets that contain human annotations and evaluations on surprise is not available.

2 COMPUTATIONAL MEASURES OF SURPRISE

We have introduced our surprise definition and various computational measures in our previous papers [removed for review]. Below is a brief summary of our previous work that is needed in this study.

We have defined that the amount of surprise as the distance to the expectation, represented as in Equation 1:

$$surprise = dist(expectation) \quad (1)$$

CHIIR '19, March 10–14, 2019, Glasgow, United Kingdom

ACM ISBN 978-1-4503-6025-8/19/03...$15.00
https://doi.org/10.1145/3295750.3298963

Through this equation, we have converted the problem of modeling surprise to a problem of modeling expectation. Based on this definition, we will briefly summarize two of our proposed measures, as documented in [removed for review].

2.1 Topic-MI and Theme-KL

In our first approach, we view each news article as "a bag of co-occurring topics", where topics are the labels assigned to an article by experts or users. The expectation of seeing an article is modeled as the expected likelihood of a particular bag of co-occurring topics in the corpus, represented as the multiplication of the individual likelihood of each topic contained in the article, i.e., p(t_1)*p(t_2)...*p(t_n). The actual or observed likelihood for an article, however, is the joint likelihood of the topic combination, i.e., p(t_1, t_2,...,t_n). The difference between the observed likelihood and the expected likelihood reflects the amount of surprise, represented as the negative of the log ratio to discount the very large difference, as in Equation 2:

$$s_1 = -log_2 \frac{p(t_1, t_2, ..., t_n)}{p(t_1)p(t_2)...p(t_n)} \quad (2)$$

where s_1 represents the surprise score of the article calculated by this method. This surprise calculation is a variation of an established metric in text mining field called Mutual Information (MI) [3]. For later reference, we label method as Topic-MI.

Going deeper or more fine-grained than topics, in second approach, we view each article as "a bag of co-occurring latent themes". Probabilistic topic modeling [1] is a set of algorithms that discover the latent themes that run through words and how these themes are connected. LDA (Latent Dirichlet Allocation) [2] is a popular example of these algorithms and is applied in this study. According to LDA, each article is generated by choosing the latent themes z_i probabilistically and then for each latent theme choosing the word w_i probabilistically, represented as:

$$p(d) = \Pi_{i=1}^{k} p_\alpha(z_i) \Pi_{j=1}^{\theta} p_\beta(w_j|z_i) \quad (3)$$

where p_α is the distribution of the latent themes in an article, z_i is the latent theme i, $p_\beta$is the distribution of the words for the latent theme z_i, and w_j is the word *j*. In fact, the generative model is the likelihood of observing such an article with *k* latent themes. We apply this model such that the expected likelihood of seeing a typical article will be the likelihood of observing an "average" article by averaging the distributions of all articles in the main topic that this article addresses. Each individual article's divergence from this expectation is that article's degree of surprise. We use the Kullback Leibler (KL) divergence as the divergence measure. The surprise score s_2 is calculated as Equation 4, where p_α is the distribution of the latent themes in an article, *q* is the distribution of a typical article, and *i* is the index of the latent themes. We label this approach as Theme-KL.

$$s_2 = KL(p_\alpha, q) = \sum_{i=1}^{k} p_{\alpha_i} log_2 \frac{p_{\alpha_i}}{q_i} \quad (4)$$

2.2 Topic-MI and Theme-KL on the Health News Corpus

To apply Topic-MI and Theme-KL, we have scraped the health news articles from Medical News Today (MNT) since its launch in 2003 to the present. The corpus contains 268,850 articles, classified into 135 health topics, such as diabetes, heart disease, anxiety, women's health, by health professionals working with MNT. Most articles have multiple topic labels.

For the Topic-MI approach, these 135 topic labels were leveraged as the topics (t_i) as in Equation 2. The value of s_1 for each article was calculated using Python's *math* and *sklearn* packages. For the Theme-KL approach, a high efficiency topic modeling tool, *gensim*, a Python library, was used for the LDA analysis and calculating s_2 for each article.

To demonstrate the computational result of the surprise scores, let us take the topic *cancer* as an example. Figure 1 presents the cumulative distribution of the Z-scores of s_1 and s_2 respectively of the 27,760 articles that invovle the topic *cancer*. For the s_1 distribution in Figure 1(a), a Z-score at the right side (above the average 0, highlighted in gray) indicates a topic combination with cancer potentially surprising, co-occurring less often than expected by chance. One such example is the combination of *cancer, veterinary, drug resistance*, and *public health*, as shown as one example in Table 1. For the s_2 distribution in Figure 1(b), a Z-score at the right side indicates a larger divergence from an average article. This suggests a potentially surprising latent theme distribution, such as an article talking about a new brochure that helps patients understand clinical trials, as shown in the example table (Table 1). Both curves are roughly parallel to a normal distribution, suggesting that most articles are centered around the average level of surprise. The distribution for the Topic-MI approach is skewed to the higher end whereas that of the Theme-KL approach to the lower end, implying the Topic-MI approach is more generous in giving high scores whereas the Theme-KL approach is more selective in identifying highly surprising articles. Table 1 lists some examples of the most and the least surprising articles based on s_1 and s_2. We will validate these scoring mechanisms with user perceived surprise.

3 HUMAN PERCEPTION COLLECTION

No matter which approach (Topic-MI or Theme-KL) we use, the surprise is a "database" surprise obtained through mining a large corpus, which represents the society's collective knowledge. However, for individuals, their feelings of surprise are different because of their background difference. We will use an interactive process to gather information about user background and their perceptual amount of surprise to investigate how the same amount of "database" surprise is felt by different people with different backgrounds. Our assumption is that it is harder to surprise a knowledgeable person than a novice. For example, a news article about male breast cancer would be surprising to most of people but not necessarily so for those who know that it is not only women who can develop breast cancer and males can too.

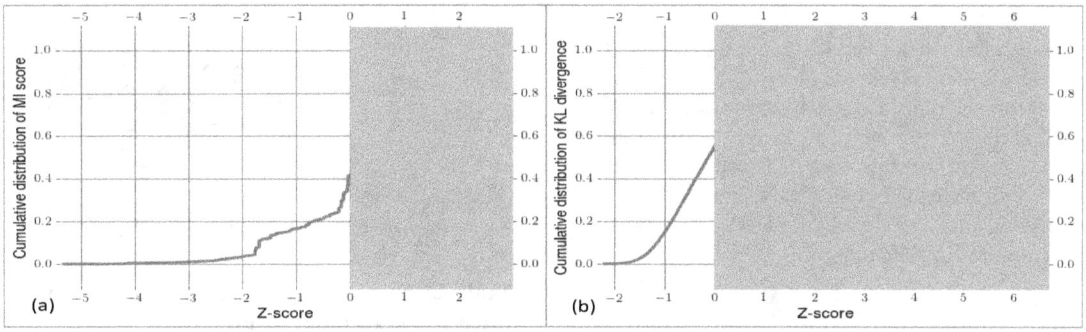

Figure 1: Topic-MI (a) and Theme-KL (b) distributions for all the *cancer* articles

Table 1: Article examples based on s_1 and s_2

Example Article Titles for the MI Approach	**Topic Labels**	s_1	**Z-score**
Are routine pelvic exams 'more harm than good' for healthy women?	Cancer, Women's Health, Infectious Disease	5.13	2.47
Hospital for humans to offer radiotherapy for animals criticized	Cancer, Veterinary, Drug Resistance, Public Health	5.10	2.46
Father's Day gift: encourage dad to go for prostate screening	Cancer, Prostate Cancer, Urology, Men's Health	-12.02	-4.13
University of Southern California study explains major cause of drug-resistance in chronic myeloid leukemia	Cancer, Drug Resistance, Lymphoma	-12.44	-4.29
Example Article Titles for the KL Approach	**Topic Labels**	s_2	**Z-score**
Fostering cancer research - Miss America, Dan Haney and Randy 'Duke' Cunningham win awards	Cancer	2.18	6.70
New brochure helps cancer patients understand clinical trials	Cancer	2.10	6.33
New 'targeted' treatments improve colon cancer survival rates	Cancer, Colorectal Cancer, Gastrointestinal	0.21	-2.10
Enzyme responsible for brain tumors discovered	Cancer, Biology, Neurology	0.21	-2.11

* the gray area indicates surprising articles whereas the white area indicates non-surprising ones

3.1 The Crowdsourcing Approach

To reach a large amount of users, we used Amazon Mechanical Turk[1] (MTurk), the well-known crowdsourcing platform. We posted 500 human intelligence tasks (HITs). Each HIT presented a health news article to the recruited workers. The workers needed to offer their ratings on 5-point Likert scales on three questions: 1) how surprising they think the article is, 2) how much they like the article, and 3) how familiar they are with the topics contained in the article. The surprise ratings are the core information we want to collect from the workers. The reason to have this "like" question is that we need to understand whether the encountered surprise is favored by the person. Favorable surprise instead of random or negative surprise is the further target of our future computational approaches or machine learning models. There are many implementation ways to collect the information about a person's background knowledge. In this study, we have adopted a simple way of asking their familrity on the article topics, for the proof-of-concept purpose.

For the 500 HITs, we hand-selected 500 articles with varying scores of s_1 and s_2 from five popular health topics: *Diabetes, Depression, Nutrition, Cancer,* and *Children's Health.* For each topic, we hand-selected 100 articles with the focus on everyday reading, avoiding those research-oriented articles with chemistry symbols or medical terminologies. Although we selected five topics, most of the 500 articles also contain other topics outside the five topics. For each HIT, we have recruited three different workers. Therefore, we have collected 1,500 (500 x 3) cases of user ratings.

3.2 Lab-Based User Study

To supplement the user ratings collected from MTurk, we have made use of the user ratings collected from one of our previous user studies [removed for review]. The procedure is summarized briefly in below. Thirty graduate students were recruited into our lab for a one-hour study. None of them had completed any formal medical education. After the introduction and obtainment of consent, each participant was recommended 50 - 100 articles with varying scores of s_1 and s_2. These articles were separated into 10 sessions. They were encouraged to click on whatever articles they would like to read. For each clicked article, they were required to provide their ratings on 5-point Likert-scales on same three questions as in the crowdsourcing study: whether the article content is surprising, whether they like the article, and how familiar they are with the topics contained in the article. As the result, we have collected 497 cases of user ratings.

[1]https://www.mturk.com/

4 RESULTS

For the 1,997 cases combined, the distribution of the surprise, like, and familiarity ratings are presented in Figure 2. The surprise ratings are rather evenly distributed across the five categories. As to the like ratings, users are very generous in giving their ratings, with 4 as the most frequent rating. In terms of the self-reported familiarity level on the main topic of the article, most of them rated themselves as having a medium familiarity level. The familiarity ratings follow a normal distribution.

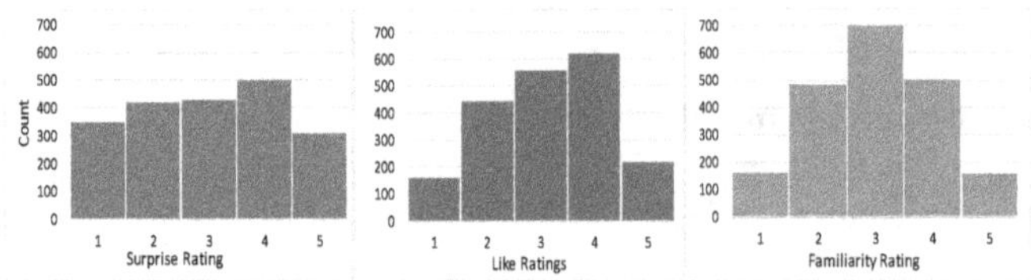

Figure 2: The distribution of the surprise ratings, like ratings, and familiarity ratings

4.1 Computational Surprise vs. Perceptual Surprise

Pairwise Pearson correlations between s_1, s_2, and the surprise ratings are summarized in Table 2. The non-significant correlation between s_1 and s_2 (r = 0.13, p = 0.2054) suggests that the two approaches do not agree with each other in calculating the amount of surprise an article contains. However, the correlations between s_1 and the surprise ratings as well as s_2 and the surprise ratings are both significant (r = 0.46, p < 0.0001; r = 0.33, p = 0.0107), meaning both computational approaches are able to capture what the users think surprising to some degree, but in different aspects. MI-Topic is better aliened with what users think, given s_1's higher correlation coefficient.

When we manually checked into the contents of the surprising articles identified by each approach, we found that the Topic-MI approach is to find the articles with rare topic co-occurrence whereas the the Theme-KL approach was good at finding "atypical" articles, such as ones on government policy, insurance, academic conference announcements, etc. Such atypical content was captured as peripheral latent themes.

We are also interested in the correlation between the computational surprise and the perceived favorable surprise, implemented as the sum of the surprise rating and the like rating. The reason is that favorable surprise, not negative surprise or random surprise, is the ultimate goal for the future retrieval models. As shown in Table 3, both correlation coefficients drop compared to Table 2, with one remains statistically significant and the other not. This means that although our computational approaches are able to find surprising contents, but not necessarily favorable surprising contents by users. Future work needs to construct separate computational models of "favor", as the content-based or collaborative filtering algorithms used in recommender systems, before applying the computational approaches of surprise, in order to restrict the search for surprise in the space of what users favor.

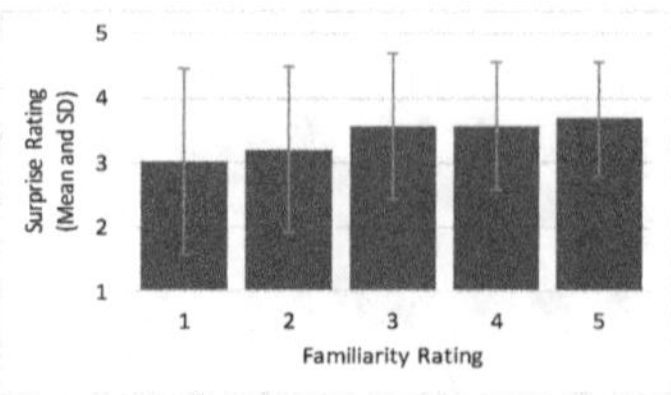

Figure 3: Surprise ratings vs. familiarity ratings

Table 2: Pearson correlation between computational surprise and perceptual surprise

	s_1	s_2	surprise rating
s_1	1		
s_2	0.13	1	
surprise rating	0.46*	0.33*	1

Notes: * denotes statistical significance at 0.05 level.

Table 3: Pearson correlation between computational surprise and perceived favorable surprise

	s_1	s_2
surprise rating + like rating	0.28*	0.17

Notes: * denotes statistical significance at 0.05 level.

4.2 Perceptual Surprise vs. Topic Familiarity

Since each news article has a main topic, on which the user has indicated their familiarity level. The articles' surprise ratings grouped by user familiarity levels are presented in Figure 3. Unexpectedly, the participants with the highest familiarity level have provided the highest average surprise rating whereas those who barely know about a topic have offered the lowest average surprise ratings. ANOVA test shows there is significant difference among these different familiarity groups (F(4, 1992) = 2.84, p = 0.0230). The standard deviations, as shown in the error bars in Figure 3, are generally decreasing from the familiarity group 1 through the group 5. The decreasing variance suggests that people with the familiarity level of 5 are more consistent in offering their ratings. The finding is different from our expectation that it would be more difficult to surprise the knowledgeable. On the contrary, the users who know more are in fact more generous in giving high ratings of surprise. It could be that those knowledgeable users are more certain about what they know and they do not know, and therefore more capable of recognizing surprise when seeing them.

5 CONCLUSION AND FUTURE WORK

We have evaluated whether the computational surprise aligns with the perceived surprise by users with different background. As the result, we find that although the two computational surprise measures do not correlate, they each moderately correlate with the user perceived surprise, capturing different aspects of what users think surprising. We unexpectedly find that the knowledgeable users perceive more surprise than the novice users, probably because they are more capable of recognizing surprise. Future work includes in constructing machine learning models, leveraging s_1, s_2, and topic familiarity as features, to predict what text will trigger the readers' feeling of surprise.

REFERENCES

[1] David M Blei. 2012. Probabilistic topic models. *Commun. ACM* 55, 4 (2012), 77–84.

[2] David M Blei, Andrew Y Ng, and Michael I Jordan. 2003. Latent dirichlet allocation. *Journal of Machine Learning Research* 3, Jan (2003), 993–1022.

[3] Gerlof Bouma. 2009. Normalized (pointwise) mutual information in collocation extraction. *Proceedings of the Conference of the German Society for Computational linguistic and Language Technology,(GSCL)* (2009), 31–40.

[4] Valentin Dragoi, Jitendra Sharma, Earl K Miller, and Mriganka Sur. 2002. Dynamics of neuronal sensitivity in visual cortex and local feature discrimination. *Nature neuroscience* 5, 9 (2002), 883–891.

[5] Kazjon Grace, Mary Lou Maher, David Wilson, and Nadia Najjar. 2017. Personalised specific curiosity for computational design systems. In *Design Computing and Cognition'16*. Springer, 593–610.

[6] Luís Macedo and Amílcar Cardoso. 2005. The role of surprise, curiosity and hunger on exploration of unknown environments populated with entities. In *Proceedings of the Portuguese Conference on Artificial Intelligence*. 47–53.

[7] Bruno A Olshausen and David J Field. 1996. Emergence of simple-cell receptive field properties by learning a sparse code for natural images. *Nature* 381, 6583 (1996), 607.

[8] Rajesh PN Rao and Dana H Ballard. 1999. Predictive coding in the visual cortex: a functional interpretation of some extra-classical receptive-field effects. *Nature neuroscience* 2, 1 (1999), 79–87.

Relevance-driven Clustering for Visual Information Retrieval on Twitter

Mohamed Reda Bouadjenek
University of Toronto
Toronto, Ontario M5S 3G8, Canada
mrb@mie.utoronto.ca

Scott Sanner
University of Toronto
Toronto, Ontario M5S 3G8, Canada
ssanner@mie.utoronto.ca

ABSTRACT

Geo-temporal visualization of Twitter search results is a challenging task since the simultaneous display of all matching tweets would result in a saturated display. In such settings, clustering search results can assist users to scan only a few coherent groups of related tweets rather than many individual tweets. However, in practice, the use of unsupervised clustering methods such as k-means does not necessarily guarantee that the clusters themselves are relevant. Therefore, we develop a novel method of relevance-driven clustering for visual information retrieval to supply users with highly relevant clusters representing different information perspectives of their queries. We specifically propose a Visual Twitter Information Retrieval (Viz-TIR) tool which based on a fast greedy algorithm that optimizes an approximation of an expected F1-Score metric to generate these clusters. We demonstrate its effectiveness w.r.t. k-means and a baseline method that shows all top matching results on a scenario related to searching natural disasters in US-based Twitter data. Our demo shows that Viz-TIR is easy to use and more precise in extracting geo-temporally coherent clusters given search queries in comparison to k-means, thus aiding the user in visually searching and browsing social network content. Overall, we believe this work enables new opportunities for the synthesis of information retrieval as well as combined relevance and display-aware optimization techniques to support query-adaptive visual information exploration interfaces.

Keywords: Visual Search Interfaces; Relevance-driven Clustering.

ACM Reference format:
Mohamed Reda Bouadjenek and Scott Sanner. 2019. Relevance-driven Clustering for Visual Information Retrieval on Twitter. In *Proceedings of 2019 Conference on Human Information Interaction and Retrieval, Glasgow, United Kingdom, March 10–14, 2019 (CHIIR '19)*, 5 pages.
DOI: https://doi.org/10.1145/3295750.3298914

1 INTRODUCTION

Traditional search engines such as Google or Bing display search results in a vertical list of textual summaries. However, this display mode is certainly not adapted for search results over Twitter content, since related tweets are often geographically and temporally localized. Moreover, given the massive volume of available information in Twitter, displaying all relevant tweets for a given query prevents the visual extraction of relevant information as it results in a saturated and unreadable display [1–3]. In such settings, standard clustering methods such as k-means [4] can be used to address this issue, based on the assumption that documents in the same cluster behave similarly with respect to information needs. This is known as the *cluster hypothesis* [5–8]. While the approach of query-specific clustering has been widely explored in the information retrieval literature [9–14], all methods tend to use unsupervised clustering methods such as k-means that do not necessarily guarantee that the clusters themselves are relevant. Therefore, the development of novel visual interfaces based on relevance-driven clustering is necessary to supply the users with highly relevant clusters representing different information perspective of their queries. In this work, we propose a Visual Twitter Information Retrieval (Viz-TIR) tool for relevance-driven and display-aware clustering and presentation of Twitter search results based on timestamp, location, and text content of tweets.

To make the task of clustering in visual information retrieval more concrete, we introduce an example scenario. Consider the case of searching a multiyear Twitter corpus for content related to natural disasters. As shown in Figure 1(a), a typical visual approach would be to provide all matching tweets in an interactive visual interface. Clearly in this case, displaying all matching tweets simultaneously results in a saturated and unreadable display that will take the user a large amount of time to sift through. To ease the task of browsing search results, a clustered results display like that shown in Figure 1(b) can be used to restrict the displayed information to highly relevant clusters that cover a large fraction of

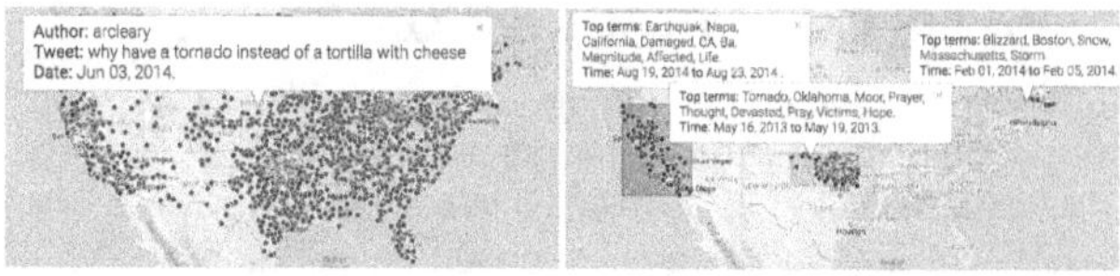

(a) Baseline display showing all results. (b) Visually clustered results display.

Figure 1: (a) An interface for visual information retrieval showing all geolocated tweets that match a query related to natural disasters in a multiyear Twitter corpus, where *all* matching tweets are shown. (b) A clustered version of the same search results showing three clusters (i.e., bounding boxes) of tweets, in this case corresponding to three well-defined natural disasters: (i) a blizzard in Boston in February 2014, (ii) a tornado in Oklahoma in May 2013, and (iii) an earthquake in California in August 2014.

CHIIR '19, March 10–14, 2019, Glasgow, United Kingdom

ACM ISBN 978-1-4503-6025-8/19/03.
DOI: https://doi.org/10.1145/3295750.3298914

relevant content. Hence it is critically important to define a clustering objective that optimizes for relevance, coverage, and visually coherent presentation of the clustered search results.

To the best of our knowledge, Viz-TIR is the first tool to address relevance-driven clustering of search results in Visual Information Displays for social media, and moreover, to do so as the direct optimization of spatial, temporal, and content-based cluster parameters w.r.t. surrogates of F1-Score to balance cluster precision and recall.

2 VizTIR CORE DESCRIPTION

In this section, we first define the mathematical notation used in this paper, then we proceed to propose Expected F1-Score (EF1) as a clustering objective well-suited to our task. Finally, we briefly describe a fast greedy relevance-driven clustering algorithm for optimizing EF1 that drives our real-time Viz-TIR interface.

2.1 Mathematical Notation

Throughout this paper we use the following mathematical notation:

- An tweet j has three types of associated metadata: (i) textual content, which is composed of a set of terms of size n, (ii) a timestamp t_e, which may represent the creation date of j, and (iii) a position coordinates (x_e, y_e).
- Three variables $I(j)$, $B(j)$ and $S(j)$ are associated with each tweet j: $I(j)$ refers to whether a tweet j is selected; $B(j)$ is a Boolean random variable indicating the relevance of a tweet j; $S(j)$ is a probabilistic score indicating the relevance of a tweet j w.r.t. a query. $B(j)$ follows a *Bernoulli* distribution with parameter $S(j)$, and hence, the expectation of $B(j)$ is $S(j)$, i.e., $\mathbb{E}_{\mathbb{S}}[B(j)] = S(j)$.
- GC is the global set of tweets with total size $|GC| = m$.
- The set of tweets selected to match a user query is labeled E with $E \subseteq GC$; we use E^* to refer to further subsets of tweets of clusters, i.e., $E^* \subseteq E$. Note that the size of E can be represented as the sum of $I(j)$ among the global collection GC. Therefore, we have $|E| = \sum_{j=1}^{m} I(j)$.
- We label the set of ground truth relevant tweets as the relevant set RS consisting of $|RS|$ elements. Note that $|RS|$ is equal to the sum of $B(j)$ among the global collection GC. Therefore, we have $|RS| = \sum_{j=1}^{m} B(j)$.

2.2 Deriving Expected F1-Score (EF1)

We adopt the Boolean relevance framework standard in information retrieval [15]. Thus, we assume that any information element j has a ground truth relevance assessment $B(j)$ available at evaluation time. Because clusters are equivalent to Boolean retrieval (they either select or do not select elements) and we have a probabilistic estimate of relevance $S(j)$, we propose to evaluate *expected* variants of standard precision, recall, and F1-score. While both precision and recall can be trivially optimized through pathological solutions (maximizing recall would select all information elements while maximizing precision would select the single highest probability information element), expected F1-score is a non-pathological objective that balances both expected precision and recall.

Recalling our previous definitions, given a set of selected information elements E and a relevant set RS, by rearranging and cancelling terms, the F1-Score of E can be expressed as follows:

$$F1(E) = \frac{2 \times \sum_{j \in E} B(j)}{|E| + |RS|} = \boxed{\frac{2 \times \sum_{j=1}^{m} B(j)I(j)}{\sum_{j=1}^{m} I(j) + \sum_{j=1}^{m} B(j)}} \quad (1)$$

Taking a 1st order Taylor expansion, we have the following expectation approximation $\mathbb{E}(X/Y) \approx \mathbb{E}(X)/\mathbb{E}(Y)$ for two dependent random variables X and Y [16]. Hence, given that $B(j)$ is a Boolean random variable, we define an *approximated expected recall* as:

$$EF1(E) = \mathbb{E}_{\mathbb{S}}[\square] \approx \frac{2 \times \sum_{j=1}^{m} \mathbb{E}_{\mathbb{S}}[B(j)]I(j)}{\sum_{j=1}^{m} I(j) + \sum_{j=1}^{m} \mathbb{E}_{\mathbb{S}}[B(j)]} = \frac{2 \times \sum_{j=1}^{m} S(j)I(j)}{\sum_{j=1}^{m} I(j) + \sum_{j=1}^{m} S(j)} \quad (2)$$

2.3 Greedy relevance-driven clustering

Now we greedily optimize $EF1(E)$. In this work, we assume that three types of clustering "parameters" are used to optimize clusters: Keywords, Time, and Space. A cluster is generated by *conjoining* these three selection parameters. In the following, we describe how to greedily optimize each of these selection parameters by iterative pruning, how to combine them for producing relevance-driven clusters, and finally, how to generate multiple relevant clusters.

2.3.1 Greedy Keyword Selection algorithm. Given a set of information elements matching a user query, the Greedy Keyword Selection algorithm aims to select a set of keywords in order to exclude a subset of tweets containing these keywords for the purpose of maximizing the EF1-Score. Formally, the algorithm aims to select an optimal subset of k terms $T_k^* \subset T_E$ (where $|T_k^*| = k$ and T_E are terms of the initial set of elements) to exclude tweets containing these keywords for optimizing the EF1-score. This is achieved by building T_k^* in a greedy manner by choosing the next optimal term t_k^* given the previous set of optimal term selections $T_{k-1}^* = \{t_1^*, \ldots, t_{k-1}^*\}$ (with $T_0^* = \emptyset$) using the following criterion:

$$t_k^* = \underset{t_k \notin T_{k-1}^*}{\arg\max}[EF1(E^* \text{ that don't contain } \{t_1^*, \ldots t_k^*\})] \quad (3)$$

where E^* is a subset of the initial tweet set E that don't contain the keywords $\{t_1^*, \ldots t_k^*\}$.

2.3.2 Greedy Time Selection algorithm. The idea behind the time-based greedy selection algorithm is as simple as finding a time window range $[t_{start}, t_{end}]$ for *temporal coherency* of clusters, which allows to select a subset of tweets $E^* \subseteq E$ falling in that time window, with E^* having the highest EF1-Score. Formally, given a list of elements $E = \{j_{t_1} \leq \cdots \leq j_{t_n}\}$, where "$\leq$" specifies the timestamp order, we propose to use *binary partitioning search* (BPS) to find the best set that optimizes EF1.

2.3.3 Greedy Spatial Selection algorithm. It is critical to main *visual coherency* of clusters and bounding boxes are one way to visually bound regions that facilitate direct optimization. The aim of the spatial greedy selection algorithm is to return coordinates $[(x_{min}, y_{min}), (x_{max}, y_{max})]$ representing the EF1-Score maximizing bounding box represented by the lower and upper bound coordinates – respectively (x_{min}, y_{min}) and (x_{max}, y_{max}). This 2D

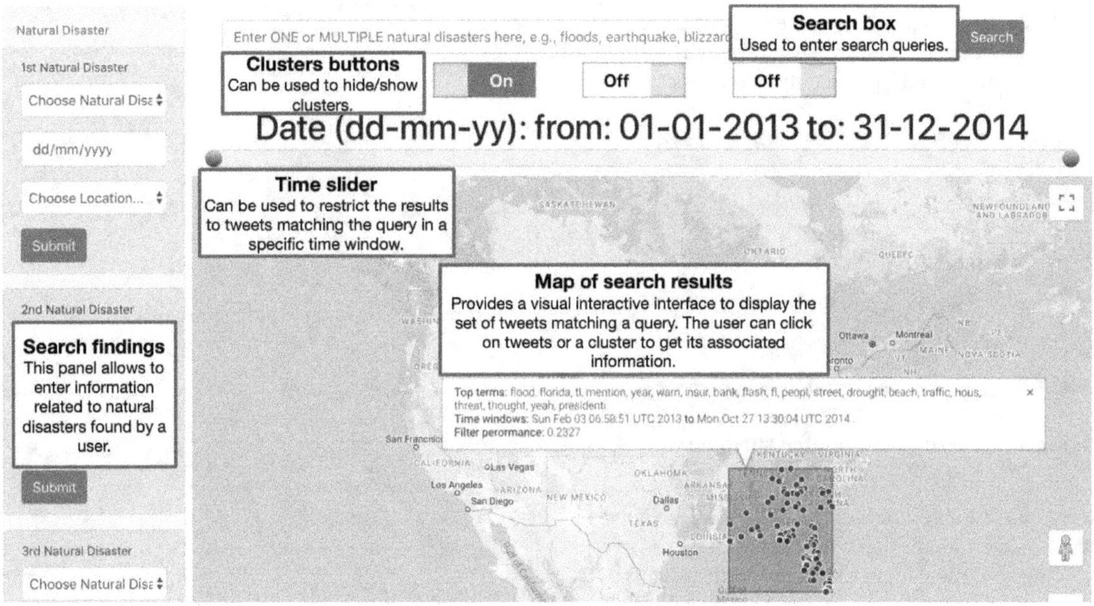

Figure 2: Main interface of the demonstration.

problem is similar to the previous one dimensional problem of finding the best time window. Therefore, we propose to sequentially apply a BPS on the x-axis to determine (x_{min}, x_{max}), then on the y-axis to determine (y_{min}, y_{max}).

2.3.4 Relevance-driven clustering algorithm. To obtain a cluster combining the above selection parameters, we propose a greedy algorithm, which at each iteration applies all the above selection algorithms and chooses the one that improves the most EF1. The selected cluster is updated with its new setting and the iteration continues. Iterations terminate when no selection algorithm can unilaterally improve EF1 and the final cluster is returned.

2.3.5 Multiple Cluster Selection Wrapper. In practice a single cluster chosen by the previously described algorithm will narrow the user in a single "information perspective". However, there will likely be multiple perspectives and so the user should have a choice of multiple clusters. Consider Figure 1: this actually shows three different spatial bounding boxes corresponding to three different events provided by three clusters. Here, we provide a greedy approach for providing a ranked list of clusters. The algorithm itself is quite simple: after the first cluster is produced, all selected tweets in that cluster have their scores $S(j)$ zeroed out. The relevance-driven clustering algorithm is then run again, where it will inherently focus on a different content set.

3 DEMONSTRATION OVERVIEW

The demonstration will be illustrated using a scenario related to finding natural disasters discussed in a collection of tweets. We used Twitter data crawled using the Twitter Streaming API for two years spanning 2013 and 2014 [17] with the following restrictions intended for user experimentation: (i) the dataset was restricted to users located within the US, (ii) non-English tweets were filtered out, (iii) only the tweets related to 12 natural disasters were kept – tweets related to other natural disasters were removed. These natural disasters are temporally, and geographically disjoint – a storm, a hurricane, a drought, two floods, two earthquakes, two tornadoes, and three blizzards. Finally, (iv) false positive tweets mentioning natural disaster keywords but not related to a particular natural disaster were intentionally included. The final dataset contains 39,486 tweets with 5,075 relevant natural disaster tweets.

As shown in Figure 2, the demonstration's main user interface allows users to enter a search query with search results then shown on an interactive map used to browse the results. The user can interact with the map by panning and zooming and also by clicking on tweets and clusters to view their content (for clusters, we display a summary in terms of selected keywords). Also, the user will be able to use a time slider bar to restrict the results to tweets in a specific time window.

In the scenario of this demonstration, the user will experience finding three different natural disasters using three different algorithms. In addition to Viz-TIR, two different algorithms are used to show the effectiveness of Viz-TIR, including: (i) a baseline method which displays all tweets that match a query (see Figure 3) and (ii) X-Means [18] (an extension of k-means, which tries to automatically determine the number of clusters) – a baseline method for clustering the top relevant results (see Figure 5). At each step, the user will be asked to enter information related to each natural disaster they may identify, including the type of the natural disaster, its location (US state), and the date on which they think the disaster first occurred.

In this demonstration, a user can perform interactive searches such as the following example search scenarios:

Baseline scenario: A user may search for information on natural disaster events. Using the query box, the user enters the keyword "earthquake". As shown in Figure 3, the baseline algorithm shows all tweets that match the query on the map using circles with a color range corresponding to the probability of relevance.

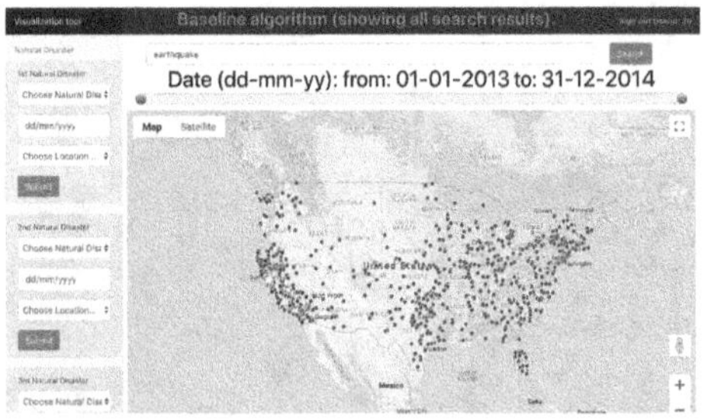

Figure 3: All results that match the query.

As shown in Figure 4, the user can restrict the list of tweets shown to a specific time window with the time slider; here a cluster of tweets appears indicating an earthquake in California during August 2014. The user may click on tweets to learn more about that event.

Figure 4: Sub-set of the results that match the query.

Clustering scenarios: The scenario using k-means or EF1 is similar. For example, the user may search multiple natural disasters using the multi-term query "earthquake, blizzard, tornado". As shown in Figures 5 and 6, clusters will appear for both algorithms, which show different clustered information perspectives. The user can then click on a cluster to get a summary description.

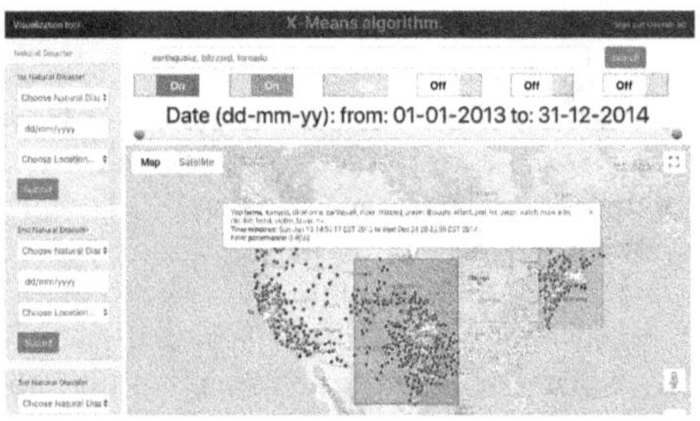

Figure 5: Clustered results using X-Means.

User Study: To determine whether our proposed relevance-driven EF1 optimization approach to clustering improves human search task performance in the Viz-TIR visual search interface (in comparison to k-means clustering and the non-clustering baseline), we performed an evaluation of 24 users who were given the task of searching for natural disasters in the previously described data. An analysis of their performance is provided in Figure 7, which shows that on average, users have higher recall on natural disaster types and locations as well as lower error estimating the time of the disaster using EF1 clustering in comparison to other methods.

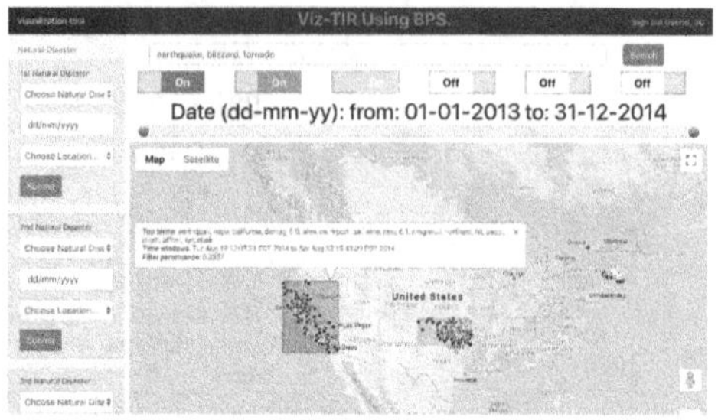

Figure 6: Compact clustered results using EF1 (Viz-TIR).

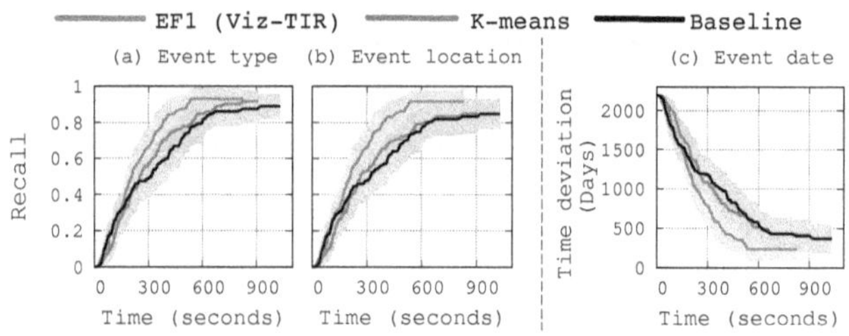

Figure 7: The performance of the algorithms measured using cumulative recall for the type and location of the natural disasters and the absolute error in the dates of the disasters.

4 SUMMARY AND FUTURE WORK

In this paper, we have developed Viz-TIR, a tool to visually search Twitter content through spatial, temporal, and content-based clustering. Viz-TIR formulates clustering as a relevance-driven optimization problem w.r.t. a user-provided query. In particular, Viz-TIR leverages a fast greedy optimization algorithm to maximize an approximation of the expected F1-Score metric to generate multiple clusters for visual display. We provide a demonstration use case that compares Viz-TIR with two baselines over 2 years of Twitter content for finding information related to natural disasters.

Important areas of future work include consideration of the role of (pseudo-)relevance and other explicit or implicit feedback methods to create a tighter and more responsive user interaction loop. Furthermore, in combination with user studies and consideration of human factors, future work should also consider novel application-specific objectives, e.g., in specific visualization frameworks or based on a ranking theory of results presentation (e.g., using size or color for visual ranking emphasis).

Acknowledgement: We would like to thank Yihao Du for running the user study.

REFERENCES

[1] T. von Landesberger, A. Kuijper, T. Schreck, J. Kohlhammer, J.J. van Wijk, J.-D. Fekete, and D.W. Fellner. Visual analysis of large graphs: State-of-the-art and future research challenges. *Computer Graphics Forum*, 30(6):1719–1749, 2011.

[2] Shixia Liu, Weiwei Cui, Yingcai Wu, and Mengchen Liu. A survey on information visualization: recent advances and challenges. *The Visual Computer*, 30(12):1373–1393, Dec 2014.

[3] Guo-Dao Sun, Ying-Cai Wu, Rong-Hua Liang, and Shi-Xia Liu. A survey of visual analytics techniques and applications: State-of-the-art research and future challenges. *Journal of Computer Science and Technology*, 28(5):852–867, Sep 2013.

[4] Stuart P. Lloyd. Least squares quantization in pcm. *IEEE Transactions on Information Theory*, 28:129–137, 1982.

[5] Christopher D. Manning, Prabhakar Raghavan, and Hinrich Schütze. *Introduction to Information Retrieval.* Cambridge University Press, New York, NY, USA, 2008.

[6] N. Jardine and C.J. van Rijsbergen. The use of hierarchic clustering in information retrieval. *Information Storage and Retrieval*, 7(5):217 – 240, 1971.

[7] Ellen M. Voorhees. The cluster hypothesis revisited. In *Proceedings of the 8th Annual International ACM SIGIR Conference on Research and Development in Information Retrieval*, SIGIR '85, pages 188–196, New York, NY, USA, 1985. ACM.

[8] C. J. Van Rijsbergen. *Information Retrieval.* Butterworth-Heinemann, Newton, MA, USA, 2nd edition, 1979.

[9] Oren Kurland. Re-ranking search results using language models of query-specific clusters. *Inf. Retr.*, 12(4):437–460, August 2009.

[10] Oren Kurland and Eyal Krikon. The opposite of smoothing: a language model approach to ranking query-specific document clusters. *Journal of Artificial Intelligence Research*, 41:367–395, 2011.

[11] Or Levi, Ido Guy, Fiana Raiber, and Oren Kurland. Selective cluster presentation on the search results page. *ACM Trans. Inf. Syst.*, 36(3):28:1–28:42, February 2018.

[12] Fiana Raiber and Oren Kurland. Exploring the cluster hypothesis, and cluster-based retrieval, over the web. In *Proceedings of the 21st ACM International Conference on Information and Knowledge Management*, CIKM '12, pages 2507–2510, New York, NY, USA, 2012. ACM.

[13] Ismail Sengor Altingovde, Rifat Ozcan, Huseyin Cagdas Ocalan, Fazli Can, and Özgür Ulusoy. Large-scale cluster-based retrieval experiments on turkish texts. In *Proceedings of the 30th Annual International ACM SIGIR Conference on Research and Development in Information Retrieval*, SIGIR '07, pages 891–892, New York, NY, USA, 2007. ACM.

[14] Xiaoyong Liu and W. Bruce Croft. Cluster-based retrieval using language models. In *Proceedings of the 27th Annual International ACM SIGIR Conference on Research and Development in Information Retrieval*, SIGIR '04, pages 186–193, New York, NY, USA, 2004. ACM.

[15] Ricardo A Baeza-Yates and Berthier Ribeiro-Neto. *Modern Information Retrieval.* Addison-Wesley Longman Publishing Co., Inc., 2 edition, 2010.

[16] G.M.P. van Kempen and L.J. van Vliet. Mean and variance of ratio estimators used in fluorescence ratio imaging. *Cytometry*, 39(4):300–305, 2000.

[17] Zahra Iman, Scott Sanner, Mohamed Reda Bouadjenek, and Lexing Xie. A longitudinal study of topic classification on twitter. In *ICWSM*, pages 552–555, 2017.

[18] Dan Pelleg and Andrew W. Moore. X-means: Extending k-means with efficient estimation of the number of clusters. In *Proceedings of the Seventeenth International Conference on Machine Learning*, ICML '00, pages 727–734, San Francisco, CA, USA, 2000. Morgan Kaufmann Publishers Inc.

The Semantic Snake Charmer Search Engine

A Tool to Facilitate Data Science in High-tech Industry Domains

Corrado Grappiolo
Emile van Gerwen
ESI-TNO
Eindhoven, The Netherlands
corrado.grappiolo@tno.nl
emile.vangerwen@tno.nl

Jack Verhoosel
Data Science department TNO
Soesterberg, The Netherlands
jack.verhoosel@tno.nl

Lou Somers
Océ Technologies
Venlo, The Netherlands
lou.somers@oce.com

ABSTRACT

The booming popularity of data science is also affecting high-tech industries. However, since these usually have different core competencies — building cyber-physical systems rather than e.g. machine learning or data mining algorithms — delving into data science by domain experts such as system engineers or architects might be more cumbersome than expected.

In order to help domain experts to delve into data science we designed the Semantic Snake Charmer (SSC), a domain knowledge-based search engine for Jupyter Notebooks. SSC is composed of three modules: (1) a human-machine cooperative module to identify internal documentation which contains the most relevant domain knowledge, (2) a natural language processing module capable of transforming relevant documentation into several semantic graph types, (3) a reinforcement-learning based search engine which learns, given user feedback, the best mapping between input queries and semantic graph type to rely on.

We believe SSC can be a fundamental asset to allow the easy landing of data science in industrial domains.

CCS CONCEPTS

• **Information systems → Search interfaces**; **Collaborative search**; **Personalization**; • **Computing methodologies → Information extraction**; **Semantic networks**;

KEYWORDS

Reinforcement Learning; Natural Language Processing; Semantic Graph; Search Engine; Document Classification; Human-computer Collaboration

ACM Reference Format:
Corrado Grappiolo, Emile van Gerwen, Jack Verhoosel, and Lou Somers. 2019. The Semantic Snake Charmer Search Engine: A Tool to Facilitate Data Science in High-tech Industry Domains. In *2019 Conference on Human Information Interaction and Retrieval (CHIIR '19), March 10–14, 2019, Glasgow, Scotland Uk.* ACM, New York, NY, USA, 5 pages. https://doi.org/10.1145/3295750.3298915

ACM ISBN 978-1-4503-6025-8/19/03.
https://doi.org/10.1145/3295750.3298915

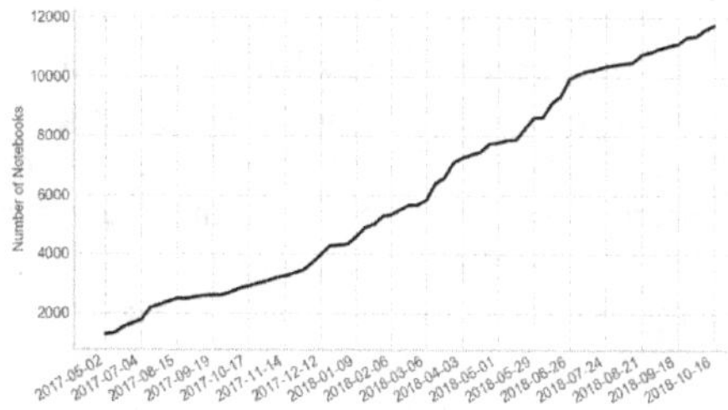

Figure 1: Rising of popularity of Jupyter Notebooks at Océ Technologies

1 INTRODUCTION

Data science is an interdisciplinary field that uses scientific methods, processes and algorithms to extract knowledge and insights from data in various forms, both structured and unstructured [4]. The analytical aspect of data science can be realised from simple statistical analysis up to the most advanced machine learning techniques. No matter how sophisticated the analysis is, a data scientist must write/use/combine algorithms written in programming languages. Python [6] is one of the most used programming language in data science, being it easy to learn, it can be used for quick prototyping, and its vast utility library makes it possible to combine already existing algorithms. Jupyter [15] is a browser-based interactive environment extensively used in data science in combination with Python. It allows to create so-called notebooks composed of cells, each cell containing code snippets, which can be executed in a more agile way than, for instance, by writing purely procedural code.

Data science is adopted by high-tech industries to enhance their insights and provide servicing to their customers, e.g. predictive maintenance based on logged data. With this respect, Figure 1 depicts the trend in Jupyter Notebooks being used for analysing machine data, on a daily bases, at Océ Technologies [20], one of the leading digital printing manufacturers in the world. As it can be seen, in just 17 months, the number of available Jupyter Notebooks has increased nearly twelve-fold. The amount of data that is at the disposal of experts is often overwhelming. For instance, a chemical engineer may want to exclude all test prints from her data analysis. To do so, she needs to step into the control engineering domain, which has its own data streams and associated ontologies. In other words, for effective data analysis in one disciple, a multi-disciplinary understanding of the data is required. The knowledge is somewhere, the question is how to find it.

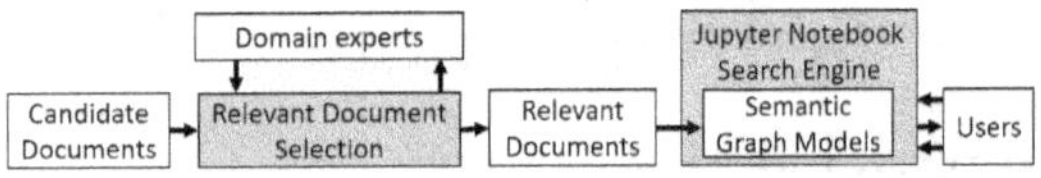

Figure 2: The Semantic Snake Charmer design diagram. The grey boxes correspond to the two adaptive components.

In order to facilitate domain experts in answering data scientific questions we designed the Semantic Snake Charmer (SSC) [22], a domain knowledge-based Jupyter notebook search engine. Given input queries, SSC returns code snippets and related Jupyter notebooks internally created at Océ Technologies. SSC contains semantic graphs with domain concepts and their relations that are used to guide the search process. The graphs are constructed via natural language processing algorithms from a corpus of text documents. For these algorithms to work properly, it is important to identify a corpus of text documents that well represent the domain. For that identification process, we use a human-machine cooperative algorithm. Summarizing, our SSC is based on three interconnected modules: (1) collaborative human-machine relevant document selection component, (2) a semantic graph extractor, and (3) a reinforcement learning-based search engine which learns, given user feedback, the best mapping between input queries and semantic graph type to rely on. The graph-based search, essentially, corresponds into expanding the input query with terms neighbouring the original one in the semantic graph, in order to obtain a more semantically generic search of code snippets. A summary of the Semantic Snake Charmer structure is depicted in Figure 2. A fundamental property of the Semantic Snake Charmer is that two of its modules – relevant document selection and search engine – are adaptive based on either domain expert knowledge (for the former) and user feedback (the latter). This allows SSC to maintain up-to-date representations of domain knowledge and to provide the continuously more accurate results. We believe that SSC would speed up the process of promoting data science in high-tech industries and life-long learning by domain experts.

2 RELATED WORK

McCallum et al. [11] built a search engine for computer science papers, their domain-specific scenario. They relied on Bayesian inference to build a hierarchy of document categories and on reinforcement learning to build the crawler. We differ from them as we build knowledge from an industrial domain, hence much more specific and narrow, and rely on semantic graphs for knowledge representation. Diligenti et al. [5], instead, attempted the creation of a search engine based on contextual graphs and subsequent crawling. We share the same idea of graph-based search and document vectorisation, although we rely on the doc2vec [17] algorithm whilst they rely on term frequency inverse document frequency (TF-IDF). Moreover, and most importantly, our graphs represent domain knowledge and not the dataset to be crawled. Chau and Chen [2] focus on topic-specific search engines and study the use of machine learning approaches to filter out irrelevant documents from a set of documents collected from the Web. Our work shares the same principle, namely the need for specific search engines. However, our need for relevant document selection is not occurring at the crawling phase, rather at the construction of domain knowledge. Finally, Oyama et al. [12] attempt solving the problem of domain-specific searches by augmenting queries with domain-specific words, and subsequently relying on universal search engines. Although we share the same idea of query augmentation, our approach does not rely on universal search engines, also because the data in our possess is stored at Océ Technologies' premises.

3 RELEVANT DOCUMENT SELECTION

In machine learning terms, the relevant document selection module is essentially a classifier. The module is implemented as a web-browser interface via Flask [18] as back-end and React [8] as front-end. Given a set of candidate documents, which we assume are selected by the domain expert from a vast repository, the classifier first performs document vectorisation, and subsequently feeds the vectorised document to a two-class classifier, where the classes are "relevant" and "not relevant" documents with respect to the domain at hand. The classification results are then presented to the expert-user, see Figure 3a. The classifier's labels are presented as gray boxes; the expert-user can correct them, in which case they become highlighted in green or red, for "relevant" and "not relevant" corrections respectively. The expert-user can also observe each single document by clicking the "eye" button at the right-hand side of each row. Once the expert-user is satisfied with the classification and its corrections, she can then click the bottom-right "update" button, which will send the feedback information to the classifier and submit the relevant documents to the module in charge of extracting the semantic graphs. As we do not expect the expert would review all selected documents – this would make the need for a classifier pointless – in this current version of SSC we assume that the lack of expert feedback corresponds to a classification agreement. The bottom-left "visualisation" button in Figure 3a allows to depict the document landscape via dimensionality reduction – see Figure 3b. Finally, the "cog" button on the top-right corner of Figure 3a leads to Figure 3c, where it is possible to observe the historical performance of the default classifier accuracy and compare it with other available ones. The "manage classifiers" at the bottom-right corner of the page would allow the expert-user to upload new classifiers, set a new default classifier, and so on.

In order to establish an initial version of the document classifier, we conducted a quick supervised learning investigation. We asked two domain experts to initially analyse 84 Portable Document Format (PDF) documents, uniformly sampled from a corpus of 6000, and to classify them as either being "relevant" or "not relevant". The rationale for such a small labelled dataset is that we cannot expect having experts classifying a much bigger number of documents. Moreover, the adaptation feature of the module would make it incrementally learning from new classification tasks.

After selecting accuracy [14] as optimisation metric, we embarked a quick exploration of possible algorithms combinations, based on 10-fold cross validation (70 training-test and 14 validation-set documents). The best results – average accuracy score 0.92, standard deviation 0.034 – was obtained by a doc2vec embedding network with 75 output neurons and window size 50 words, followed by a 1-Nearest neighbour classifier.

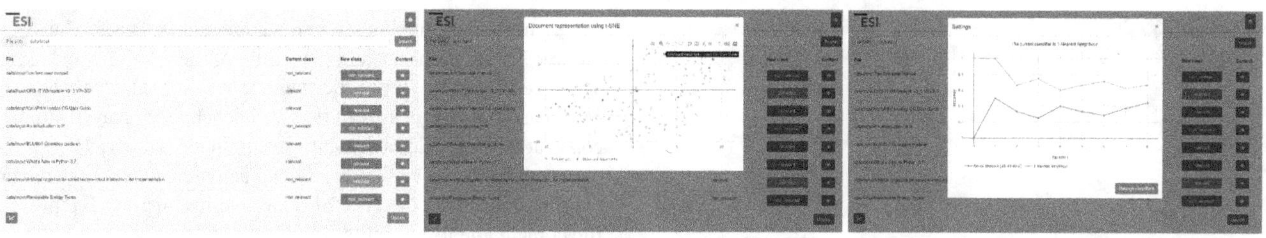

(a) Document classification. (b) Document classification landscape. (c) Document classification performance.

Figure 3: Overview of the three main interfaces of the Semantic Snake Charmer's document classifier module. The document names are fictional.

4 SEMANTIC GRAPH CONSTRUCTION

The second module of the Semantic Snake Charmer takes the corpus of documents from the Relevant Document Selection module and extracts a semantic graph from it. We have implemented a number of algorithms for this task:

- **structure-based algorithm:** the algorithm, instead of relying on domain-relevant documents, takes the names of folders and files containing tables with log-data of the specific domain and extracts relations between them. Specifically, the algorithm extracts *hasFolder*, *hasTableName* and *hasColumnName* relations between the names of these folders and files. In addition, the algorithm splits names into multiple parts based on capitals within the names and extracts a *isPartOfName* relation between these parts. Last but not least, the algorithm identifies generic parts in names and extracts a *isSuperClassOf* relation between them, e.g: Id $\rightarrow$ *isSuperClassOf* $\rightarrow$ sheetId
- **open information extraction:** this algorithm uses Stanford CoreNLP's DepParse annotator [10] to extract entities and relations from a corpus of documents. The annotator uses part of speech tags and dependencies parsing based on grammar and language constructs. Each document from the set of relevant documents is converted into a plain text one and the text is tokenized into sentences with the Python NLTK package [16]. Each sentence is cleaned using Python's language detection package [3] and only sentences with 5 words or larger are considered to get only proper English sentences. Each $(entity, \ relation, \ entity)$ triple found by OpenIE was added to the semantic model;
- **Hearst patterns:** the algorithm [7] uses the well-known patterns defined by Hearst to find hyponym relations between generic and specific entities. Examples of Hearst patterns in text are language constructs *like, such as, including, for example* and *other.* The generic entity can be found in a sentence before these constructs and the specific entities after these constructs. Each $(generic, \ specific)$ tuple found in the relevant documents was added as a $(generic, \ superclass, \ specific)$ triple to the semantic model;
- **word co-occurrences:** the algorithm finds tuples of words in a sentence that are close to each other. The algorithm, based on Python's SciKit-learn text feature extraction implementation [13] to find N-grams in the sentence and filters the N-grams on a distance window of maximum 3 words. The algorithm also maintains a count on the number of co-occurrences per tuple and an English stop-word vocabulary to filter on the large amount of word co-occurrences. Each remaining tuple is added to the semantic model with a co-occurrence relation.

The resulting semantic graphs are stored in a Neo4j database [9].

5 JUPYTER NOTEBOOK SEARCH ENGINE

The third module of the Semantic Snake Charmer is the actual search engine. Figure 4 depicts the schematics of the engine. The search relies on the four semantic graph models introduced in Section 4 to enhance the input query of a user. The enhancement, essentially, corresponds to locate, in each semantic graph, the nodes corresponding to the query words, and subsequently extract a limited number of neighbours for each node. In this way we aim to expand the specific query in order to retrieve Jupyter notebooks covering semantically similar topics. The enrichment is then achieved via querying the models in the Neo4j database.

The graph search task of Figure 4 is implemented via Elastic Search [1], which relies on a database of indexed Jupyter notebooks updated on daily basis. The Graph Search task retrieves the notebooks by text matching and is done five times: one for each semantic graph model's enhanced query, and one based on a plain query. The final step of the search engine corresponds to the aggregation of results. This is done in order to (1) remove repeated results returning from the five search strategies and (2) to order the results so that those considered being the most relevant ones are presented first. The former is trivially implemented. The latter corresponds to a decision making problem. We attempted its solution by interpreting the search task as a contextual multi-armed bandit problem [19], where the state corresponds to the input query, the action space

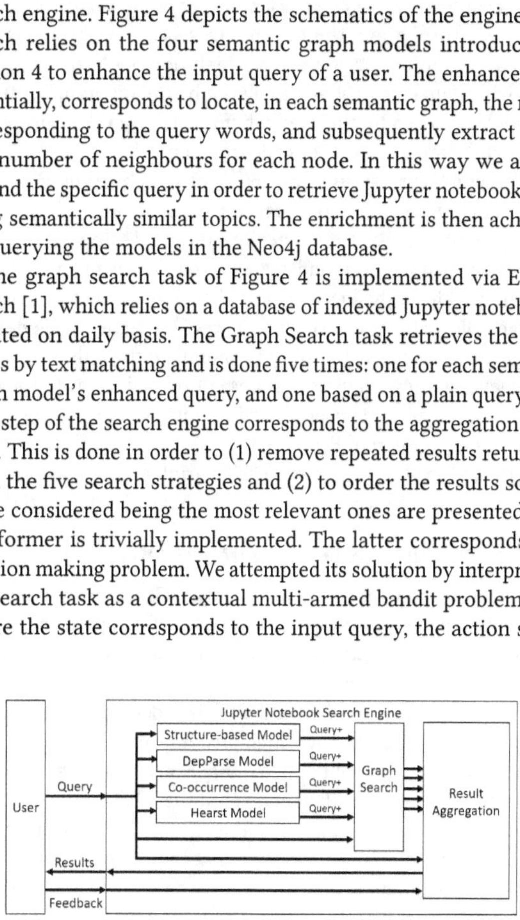

Figure 4: Details of the Jupyter notebook search engine

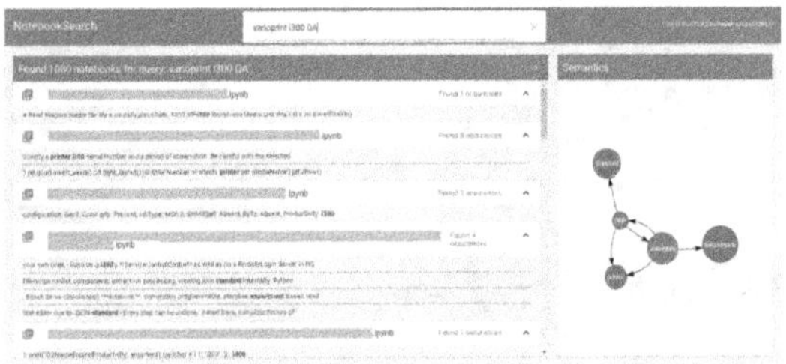

Figure 5: Snapshot of the Snake Charmer. Filesystem paths have been occluded for privacy reasons.

Figure 6: Access point of Semantic Snake Charmer.

to the five search strategies, and the reward signal to the Jupyter notebook the user considers the most appropriate. We define the latter as the Jupyter notebook the user chooses among the results to copy its content by keeping track of any copy command performed by the user throughout the search. The search engine keeps track which search approach returned which notebook; the user feedback helps penalising the use of a search strategy which returned notebooks ignored by the user, whom instead scrolls through the results and eventually copies code from a notebook far away from top and which corresponds to a different search strategy.

To conclude this Section, Figure 5 presents a snapshot of the search engine in function. The web-interface, implemented via React, returns notebooks and presents code snapshots which highlight, in bold font, the keywords used during the search. The web-interface allows the user to observe part of the semantic model used during the search which also corresponds to the enhanced query. We believe that by showing a glimpse of related terms to the input query could inspire the user to further improve her searches. Such situation can be seen in Figure 5: the user searched for "varioprint i300 QA", but the bold items are "i300", "printer", "standard" and "experiment" (VarioPrint is a printer model of Océ Technologies [21]).

6 ONGOING AND FUTURE WORK

The current version of the Semantic Snake Charmer is deployed at Océ Technologies as internal search engine for Jupyter notebooks through a notebook extension that adds a search button to every notebook – see Figure 6.

Given the current configuration of the document classification module – see Section 3 – we attempted a second supervised learning task. We asked one of the two initial experts to classify 140 new PDF documents and we then compared the labels returned by the document classifier. We obtained a remarkable classification accuracy of 0.77, especially considering that the classifier was trained on only 70 documents.

Concerning the semantic graph construction module, the four algorithms considered generate graphs of various quality. The structure-based approach produces a semantic graph that is a good representation of the domain in question, but is therefore also very specific for the terms used in the names of these logfiles and folders. The OpenIE approach produces entity-relationships between concepts based on part of speech tags and dependency parsed language constructs. This yields a semantic graph that contains a lot of redundant concepts based on nouns and adjective modifier dependencies. On the other hand, the type of relationships fairly well represents the domain and its concepts. The Hearst patterns approach extracts a semantic graph with only a few concepts and relationships, but the semantic graph shows a very good precision with respect to the domain to be represented. Finally, the word co-occurrence approach yields a lot of entities with possible relationships, but does not give any indication of the exact meaning of these relationships. Thus, neither of the algorithms seem to extract a semantic graph that is a very good representation of the Océ Technologies domain. For the search problem at hand this does not constitute a big issue, since the semantic graph is used to guide the end-user towards alternative directions in his search and the contextual multi-armed bandit implementation of the search engine would allow to learn the best mapping between queries and results.

We believe that the design of SSC is future-proof: more document classifiers can be plugged in, more/less NLP approaches to extract semantic graphs can be added/removed from the search engine, with the only consequence that the action space of the multi-armed bandit solver would change. The subsequent phase of our work will correspond in heavily promoting the use of the Semantic Snake Charmer within Océ Technologies in order to gather as many searches as possible, for validation purposes and, intuitively, to take into consideration other modelling approaches in any of the three SSC modules.

7 CONCLUSIONS

Data science is an extremely popular discipline which is also entering high-tech industries. However, domain experts are not data scientists. Re-using data science assets built by their peers greatly improves their capabilities and efficiency. In addition, non-disciplinary domain experts need expertise from other domains to effectively find, interpret, and analyse the data. Cross-domain sharing of knowledge leverages the data science virtues. We presented the Semantic Snake Charmer (SSC), a web-browser based search engine for Jupyter notebooks – arguably the most consolidated data science framework – with the aim to facilitate domain experts in answering their data scientific questions. SSC is composed of three main modules: (1) a human-machine cooperative module to identify industry internal documentation which contain the most relevant domain knowledge, (2) an automatic natural language processing module capable of transforming relevant documentation into several semantic graph types, (3) a reinforcement-learning based search engine which learns, given user feedback, the best mapping between input queries and semantic graph type to rely on. SSC is currently deployed at Océ Technology. We are confident that its popularity in use would soon grow together with the experience in data science of domain experts. SSC is designed to learn from experts, to represent their domain knowledge, and to adapt to the queries it receives.

ACKNOWLEDGMENTS

The research is carried out as part of the ITEA3 14035 REFLEXION project under the responsibility of the Embedded Systems Innovation by TNO (ESI) with Océ Technologies as carrying industrial partner. The REFLEXION research is supported by the Netherlands Organisation for Applied Scientific Research TNO and Netherlands Ministry of Economic Affairs. The authors thank Koen Kanters for his work in building the Semantic Snake Charmer.

REFERENCES

[1] Elasticsearch BV. Accessed: 2018-10-19. Elastic Search Framework. https://www.elastic.co/.

[2] Michael Chau and Hsinchun Chen. 2008. A machine learning approach to web page filtering using content and structure analysis. *Decision Support Systems* 44, 2 (2008), 482–494.

[3] Michal Mimino Danilak. Accessed: 2018-10-19. Langdetect library. https://pypi.org/project/langdetect/.

[4] Vasant Dhar. 2013. Data Science and Prediction. *Commun. ACM* 56, 12 (Dec. 2013), 64–73. https://doi.org/10.1145/2500499

[5] Michelangelo Diligenti, Frans Coetzee, Steve Lawrence, C Lee Giles, Marco Gori, et al. 2000. Focused Crawling Using Context Graphs.. In *VLDB*. 527–534.

[6] Python Software Foundations. Accessed: 2018-10-19. Python Programming Language. https://www.python.org/.

[7] Marti A Hearst. 1992. Automatic acquisition of hyponyms from large text corpora. In *Proceedings of the 14th conference on Computational linguistics-Volume 2*. Association for Computational Linguistics, 539–545.

[8] Facebook Inc. Accessed: 2018-10-19. React Library. https://reactjs.org//.

[9] Neo4j Inc. Accessed: 2018-10-19. Neo4j Graph Database. https://neo4j.com/.

[10] Christopher D. Manning, Mihai Surdeanu, John Bauer, Jenny Finkel, Steven J. Bethard, and David McClosky. 2014. The Stanford CoreNLP Natural Language Processing Toolkit. In *Association for Computational Linguistics (ACL) System Demonstrations*. 55–60. http://www.aclweb.org/anthology/P/P14/P14-5010

[11] Andrew McCallum, Kamal Nigam, Jason Rennie, and Kristie Seymore. 1999. A machine learning approach to building domain-specific search engines. In *IJCAI*, Vol. 99. Citeseer, 662–667.

[12] Satoshi Oyama, Takashi Kokubo, and Toru Ishida. 2004. Domain-specific web search with keyword spices. *IEEE Transactions on knowledge and data engineering* 16, 1 (2004), 17–27.

[13] F. Pedregosa, G. Varoquaux, A. Gramfort, V. Michel, B. Thirion, O. Grisel, M. Blondel, P. Prettenhofer, R. Weiss, V. Dubourg, J. Vanderplas, A. Passos, D. Cournapeau, M. Brucher, M. Perrot, and E. Duchesnay. 2011. Scikit-learn: Machine Learning in Python. *Journal of Machine Learning Research* 12 (2011), 2825–2830.

[14] David Martin Powers. 2011. Evaluation: from precision, recall and F-measure to ROC, informedness, markedness and correlation. (2011).

[15] Jupyter Project. Accessed: 2018-10-19. Jupyter Project. http://jupyter.org/.

[16] NLTK Project. Accessed: 2018-10-19. NLTK Library. https://www.nltk.org/.

[17] Radim Rehurek and Petr Sojka. 2010. Software framework for topic modelling with large corpora. In *In Proceedings of the LREC 2010 Workshop on New Challenges for NLP Frameworks*. Citeseer.

[18] Armin Ronacher. Accessed: 2018-10-19. Flask Microframework. http://flask.pocoo.org/.

[19] Richard S Sutton, Andrew G Barto, et al. 1998. *Reinforcement learning: An introduction*. MIT press.

[20] Océ Technologies. Accessed: 2018-10-19. https://www.oce.com/.

[21] Océ Technologies. Accessed: 2018-10-19. Océ VarioPrint i-series. https://www.oce.com/products/varioprint-i-series/.

[22] Semantic Snake Charmer Demonstration Video. Accessed: 2018-10-19. http://www.esi.nl/research/research-in-projects/reflexion.dot.

Answering Comparative Questions: Better than Ten-Blue-Links?

Matthias Schildwächter
University of Hamburg, Germany

Alexander Bondarenko
Martin Luther University of Halle-Wittenberg, Germany

Julian Zenker
University of Hamburg, Germany

Matthias Hagen
Martin Luther University of Halle-Wittenberg, Germany

Chris Biemann
University of Hamburg, Germany

Alexander Panchenko
University of Hamburg, Germany

ABSTRACT

We present CAM (comparative argumentative machine), a novel open-domain IR system to argumentatively compare objects with respect to information extracted from the Common Crawl. In a user study, the participants obtained 15% more accurate answers using CAM compared to a "traditional" keyword-based search and were 20% faster in finding the answer to comparative questions.

KEYWORDS

HCI, Comparative Question Answering, Keyword Search, Natural Language Processing

ACM Reference Format:
Matthias Schildwächter, Alexander Bondarenko, Julian Zenker, Matthias Hagen, Chris Biemann, and Alexander Panchenko. 2019. Answering Comparative Questions: Better than Ten-Blue-Links?. In *2019 Conference on Human Information Interaction and Retrieval (CHIIR '19), March 10–14, 2019, Glasgow, United Kingdom.* ACM, New York, NY, USA, 5 pages. https://doi.org/10.1145/3295750.3298916

1 INTRODUCTION

Everyone faces choice problems on a daily basis. Besides choosing what to wear or what to have for lunch, people compare all kinds of options: cameras to buy, universities to study at, or even programming languages to use. Question answering platforms like Quora, Reddit, or StackExchange are packed with comparative questions like "How does X compare to Y with respect to Z?". An informed choice then is often based on an objective argumentation why to favor one of the candidates (e.g., comparing important aspects).

Specific product comparison systems, such as Compare.com or Check24, allow to compare any subset of objects in narrow domains such as cameras. Other systems like WolframAlpha aim at providing comparative functionality across domains, but also often only use some (limited) structured database while ignoring the rich textual content available on the web. Somewhat surprising, no system is currently able to satisfy comparative information needs for the general domain with sufficient coverage and explanations. No available system is able to support comparisons on a broad range of object types with arguments about relative qualities or even supporting objective arguments about the best choice. Indeed, web search engines are able to directly answer many factoid questions but do not treat comparative questions any special beyond returning default search results. Advanced question answering systems, such as IBM's Watson [6], answer factoid questions very well, but do not really handle comparative questions of everyday users.

We present CAM (comparative argumentative machine), a system that aims at solving the shortcomings mentioned above. CAM is a tool for answering comparative general-domain questions based on information extracted from the web-scale Common Crawl.[1]

ACM ISBN 978-1-4503-6025-8/19/03.
https://doi.org/10.1145/3295750.3298916

2 RELATED WORK

Commercial systems like GoCompare, Compare.com, Diffen.com, and Versus.com offer high-precision comparison capabilities based on well-curated structured data sources focusing on single domains. But their low coverage in other than their focus domains rules out answering most of the comparative questions found on portals like Quora or Yahoo! Answers—that themselves form a good source of (argumentative) comparisons and results.

Previous text-based comparison approaches have mostly focused on the biomedical domain. Fiszman et al. [7] collected sentences comparing drug therapies using manually crafted patterns to recognize the subjects of comparison and the comparison direction. They reached a very high precision at moderate recall. On a set of full-text articles on toxicology, Park and Blake [13] succeeded in training a highly precise Bayesian Network for identifying comparative sentences relying on lexical clues and dependency parsers. More recently, Gupta et al. [9] described a system based on manually collected patterns on the basis of lexical matches and dependency parses in order to identify comparison targets and to classify the type of comparison into the classes given by Jindal and Liu [11]: gradable vs. non-gradable and superlative comparisons.

Building a general-domain argumentative comparison facility comes with the additional challenge of argument mining from user-generated content [15]. Text is typically noisy, misses argument structures and contains poorly formulated claims. On the other hand, specialized jargon and idiosyncrasies of a platform can be utilized [4] (e.g., hashtags for mining argumentative tweets).

Aker et al. [1] confirmed the findings of Stab and Gurevych [17] that information from dependency parsers does not help to find the (general) argument structure in persuasive essays and Wikipedia articles while simpler structural features such as punctuation are more effective. Daxenberger et al. [3] noted that claims across different domains share lexical clues and further stated that current

[1] **Demo, API & code: http://ltdemos.informatik.uni-hamburg.de/cam/**

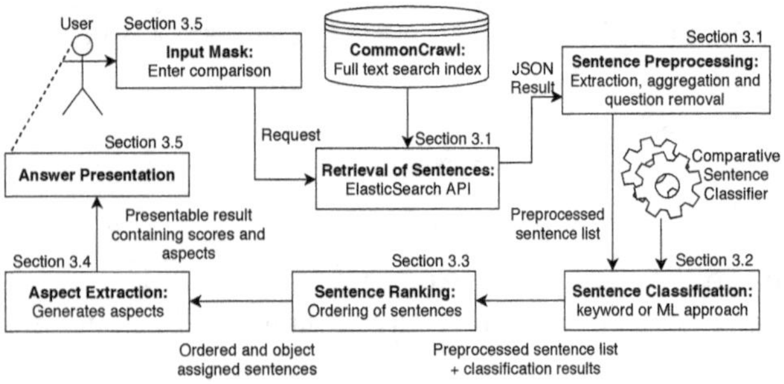

Figure 1: Design of the CAM system.

datasets are too small for recent DNN-based classifiers resorting to traditional feature engineering for argument mining.

Some argument mining systems work on larger corpora of user-generated content to find the most relevant argument for a given claim [10] or to oppose different argumentative viewpoints [19]. Web-scale systems for comparing query results [18] or for retrieving single arguments matching a user query [16] form the inspiration for our new CAM system (comparative argumentative machine).

3 THE CAM SYSTEM DESIGN

To ensure a wide coverage, a comparative answer of our CAM system for two objects is based on argumentative structures extracted from web-scale text resources. The system looks for textual structures asserting that one of the compared objects is superior to the other, that they are equal, or that they are not comparable. A comparison of two objects o and o' in the CAM sense is defined as "o ? o' w.r.t. $a_i, \ldots, a_j \in$ a", where ? is in $\{>, <, =, \neq\}$ and $\text{a} = \{a_1, \ldots, a_k\}$ is the set of comparison aspects of o and o'. We thus focus on mining sentences like "*Python=o* is better than *Matlab=o'* for *web development=a_i*."

The design of our CAM system is shown in Figure 1. It consists of the following generic stages, which are further described in details: (1) retrieval of relevant sentences, (2) classification of comparative sentences, (3) ranking of the comparative sentences, (4) extraction of object aspects, and (5) presentation of the answer.

3.1 Sentence Retrieval

Our CAM system uses an Elasticsearch full text index of a linguistically pre-processed corpus [12] containing 14.3 billion English sentences from the Common Crawl. To retrieve textual argumentative structures relevant to a comparative user input, the index is queried for sentences matching the input objects and containing comparison aspects; sentences without aspects are used as a fall-back. Questions are removed from the initial retrieval results since they usually do not help in returning an argumentative answer.

3.2 Sentence Classification

We use a classifier to distinguish between four classes: the first object from the user input is better / equal / worse than the second one ($>, =, <$) w.r.t. a comparison aspect, or no comparison is found ($\neq$). The classifier uses the text between both objects to identify the "polarity" and is inspired by the best model reported by Franzek et al. [8]: XGBoost [2] using word frequencies as representations, which achieves a high F1 score of 0.92 for $\neq$, a good F1 of 0.74 for $>$ but a rather low F1 of 0.46 for $<$. We identified the main issue in missing negation handling, for which we added a simple keyword-based heuristic to our CAM system inverting common negations.

3.3 Sentence Ranking and Object Comparison

To rank comparative sentences (category $>$ or $<$), we score them by combining the classifier confidence and the Elasticsearch score[2] according to the following heuristic s:

$$s = \begin{cases} \alpha + e + e_{max}, & \text{if confidence} \geq \gamma, \\ (\alpha + e) \cdot \delta, & \text{otherwise,} \end{cases}$$

where e is the Elasticsearch score of the sentence, e_{max} is the maximum Elasticsearch score of any comparative sentence retrieved for the user input, and $\alpha = w_{a_i} e_{max}$ if the user-specified aspect a_i is present in the sentence and $\alpha = 0$ otherwise. For the α aspect boost, the weights w_{a_i} are specifiable in the user interface. Confidently classified sentences obtain a boost of e_{max} while scores of low confidence sentences are decreased by a factor of δ; we set $\gamma = 0.8$ and $\delta = 0.1$ in our experiments.

For scoring a CAM output "$o > o'$ w.r.t. a", we sum up the s-scores of all sentences *supporting* the statement. To this end, we have developed a heuristic to include two directions of comparison and thus taking into account that a statement like "Python is better than Matlab" (class $>$) is also supported by "Matlab is worse than Python" (class $<$); important factors being the object ordering and the polarity.

3.4 Aspect Extraction

In addition to user-specified comparison aspects, CAM generates up to ten supplementary aspects (even when no comparison aspect at all was provided by the user). We use three different methods for aspect mining: (1) searching for comparative adjectives and adverbs; (2) searching for phrases with comparative adjectives / adverbs and a preposition like *to*, *for*, etc. (e.g., "*quicker to* develop code" or "*better for* scientific computing"); (3) searching for specific hand-crafted patterns like "because of higher *speed*", "since it has more *options*", "as we have proven its *resilience*" or "reason for this is the *price*". An extracted aspect is assigned to the object with the higher co-occurrence frequency (cf. Figure 2 for examples).

3.5 CAM User Interface

The user interface consists of a question input form (Figure 3) and an answer presentation component (Figure 2). The input interface allows to submit a comparative question in the form of two compared objects and their aspects. The answer presentation summarizes the sentences retrieved from the Common Crawl providing decision-making support for the informed choice.

Input Form. The input form is divided into three parts (cf. Figure 3). On the top, the user enters two comparison target objects. In the middle, the interface allows to add an arbitrary number of aspects and assign them a weight indicating their importance (1 to 5; used to boost the scores of the sentences containing the aspect). On the bottom, one of the three different search models can be selected: *Default* is based on keyphrases like "better than" or "faster

[2]https://www.elastic.co/guide/en/elasticsearch/guide/current/scoring-theory.html

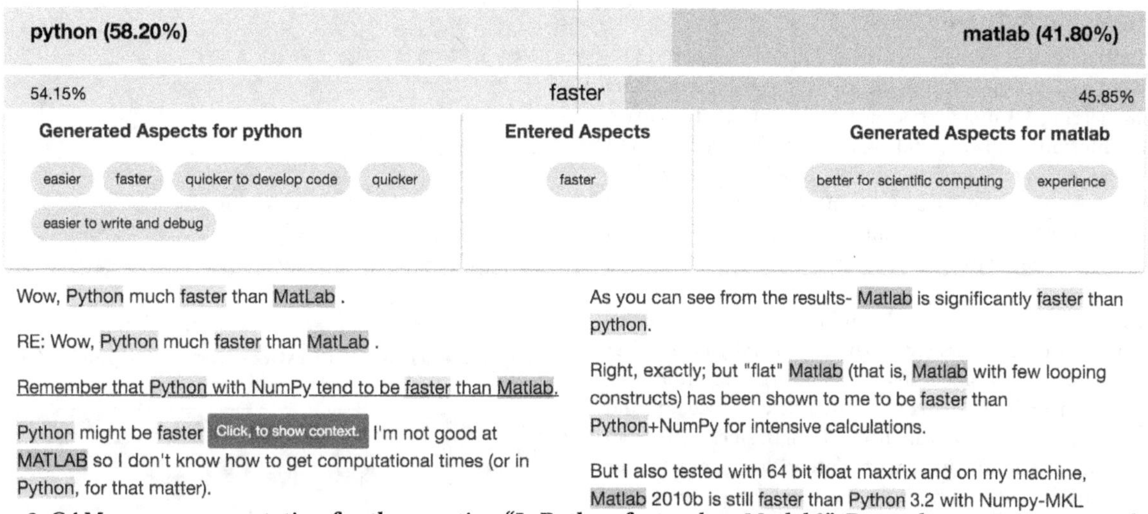

Figure 2: CAM answer presentation for the question "Is Python faster than Matlab?". Pro and con sentences are shown.

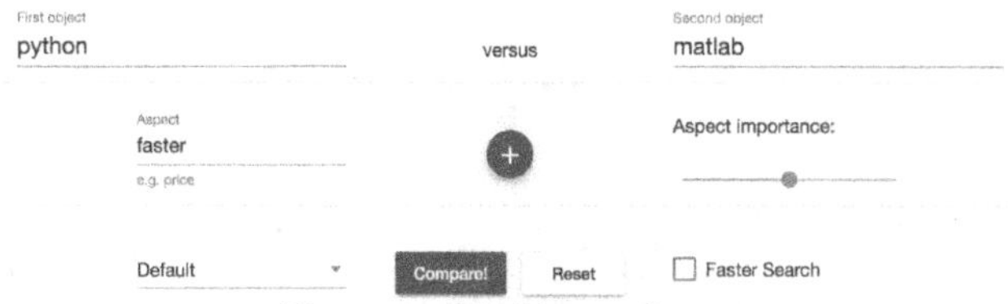

Figure 3: CAM input form.

than" to find comparative sentences; *BoW* is built upon the word frequency-based XGBoost classifier described above, and *Infersent* uses sentence embeddings. The *Faster Search* option limits the number of queried fall-back sentences to 500 in order to speed up the answer construction.

Answer Presentation. On the top of the comparative answer presentation (cf. Figure 2), different score bars are given. The overall score distribution allows the user to grasp a general impression for the entered comparative question while the aspect-specific score bars show the distribution for the individual user-specified aspects.

Additionally, up to ten automatically generated aspects are presented in a clickable manner to allow the user to only display result sentences for such aspects (disjunctive filter interpretation). The user-specified aspects are used on both result sentence sides while the generated aspects only filter the corresponding column.

The objects in the displayed sentences are highlighted with their respective colors from the score bars, while the aspect highlighting uses different colors. Clicking on a result sentence reveals its Common Crawl context—by default the ±3 sentences around it, with the possibility of expanding to the whole original document.

4 EVALUATION

We compare our new CAM system to a keyword-based search in two user studies with 14 and 9 participants on 34 comparison topics.

4.1 Experimental Setup

The 34 topics (two compared objects + one aspect) for our studies were created from comparative Quora questions containing the phrase "better than" and also being present on comparison pages like Diffen.com and DifferenceBetween.net. For each topic, we manually double-checked that the underlying corpus of our CAM system and the keyword-based search (i.e., the 14.3 billion Common Crawl sentences) allows to answer the comparison; we only included topics with at least 20 support sentences. One of the topics for instance has *mp3* and *wma* as objects and *compression ratio* as the aspect. Given the ground truth answer *worse*, a study participant should answer that mp3 is worse than wma with respect to compression ratio. To clarify potential ambiguities or subjectivities, descriptions for the participants were added to the topics (e.g., to inform a potential music afficionado who might claim a worse compression rate being better since it might come with an improved sound quality).

In a **Group A** setup, we focus on the question whether users are faster answering correctly when using the CAM system. A G*Power analysis [5] did output a required sample size of 272 comparisons to be a able to measure a statistically significant difference in answer times. We thus decided to engage 14 participants on all 34 topics (477 comparisons). Each participant uses both experimental systems alternatingly (CAM / keyword-based search). Since every participant should work on each topic just once with one of the systems but not the other, we randomly split the 34 topics into two groups (one for each system). To avoid any order bias, the topics of each group were presented in random order.

The participants were informed that they should give an answer as quickly as possible; the whole study took about one hour per participant and ended with a questionnaire. We measured the time for different phases (e.g., the time needed to enter a query and the time needed to determine an answer) and the correctness of a participant's answer with respect to manually derived gold labels.

In a **Group B** setup, we focussed on collecting some more "natural" feedback using a less forced study environment. We had 9 different participants (not from Group A) who were allowed to just "play" with the systems for any and as many of our 34 comparison topics as they liked. In total, 85 comparisons were performed.

4.2 Study Participants

Among the 14 Group A participants, 9 were male (5 female), 13 indicated 18–24 as their age (1 was in the 25–34 range), 8 participants had an Engineering & Computer Science background (3 from Arts, Culture & Entertainment, 1 from Law & Public Policy, 2 selected "other") with 9 having a Bachelor's degree. The participants characterized themselves as having a proficient (nine) or intermediate (five) English level. Seven participants stated to use comparison websites rarely or never (once a year or less), whereas five used them once a month and two even once a week.

Group B consisted of five female and four male participants, 1 participant was 13–17 years old, 2 participants fell in the 18–24 age range, 5 in the 25–34 range, and one in 35–44. This group was dominated by an Engineering & Computer Science background (five out of nine); one from Education, one from Business, one from Arts, Culture & Entertainment, and one "other" background. Four participants already had a Master's degree, two were students, one had a Bachelor's degree, one a doctorate degree, and one selection of "other". Six participants rated their English level as proficient and three as intermediate. Five participants stated they used comparison websites rarely or never, whereas two used them once a month and two even once a week or more.

4.3 Results and Discussion

A Shapiro-Wilk test [14] verified the visual assumption of a log-normal distribution ($\alpha = 0.05$) of the different measured times for CAM usage and keyword-based search. Therefore, t-tests were used to check whether the null hypothesis of same answer determination times or same total times can be rejected.

Figure 4 shows the time distributions of Group A. **Until typing** indicates the participants being about 19% faster starting to enter a query with the CAM system (in Group B, the CAM users were even about 25% faster). **Typing** is the time from the first key stroke until the query is submitted. The Group A participants again were faster with the CAM interface (about 24% on average); the Group B participants needed about twice as long, being slightly faster with the CAM system. The **loading** phase measures the time the system needs to show the answer (from sending the query until the result is presented). On average, keyword-based search loads slightly faster than CAM since CAM uses a keyword-based search subroutine with some further post-processing.

Most importantly, the time the users need to give their answer (**determination** in Figure 4) shows that the Group A participants were significantly faster when using the CAM system (about 39% difference). In Group B, the participants were slower in general, but interestingly they were also slightly slower using CAM than keyword-based search. One potential reason is that the participants explored the new CAM interface more even providing verbal feedback during their work (remember that Group B was allowed to "play" with the systems).

For the overall task (**total** in Figure 4), Group A was significantly faster when using the CAM interface while the more exploratory Group B was overall slower but with no substantial advantage for either system. Our main focus in a Group B was on observing participants behavior which is why they were allowed to test, play with and comment on the systems while using them.

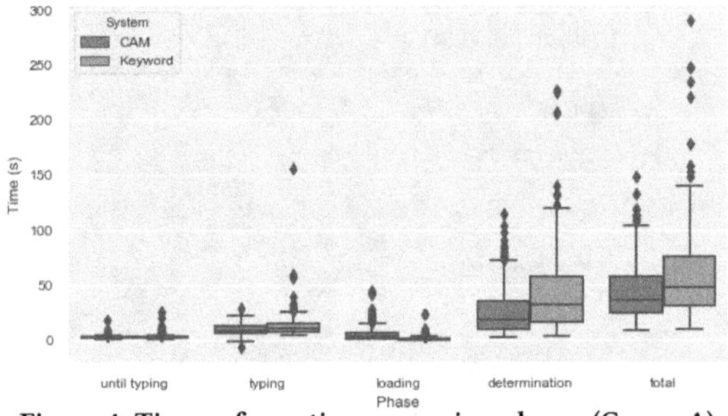

Figure 4: Times of question answering phases (Group A).

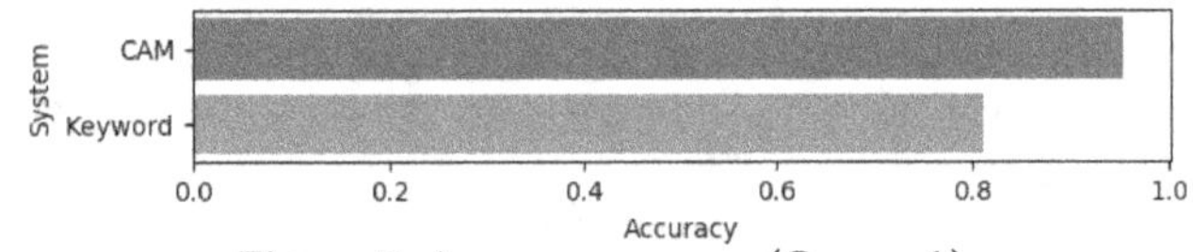

Figure 5: Answer accuracy (Group A).

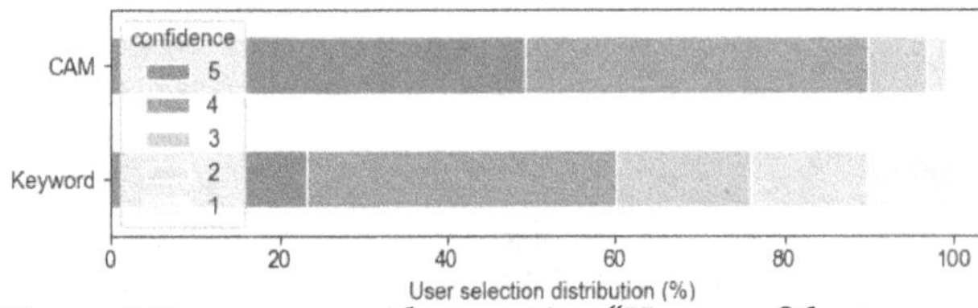

Figure 6: Responses on the question "How confident are you that the determined answer is correct?" (Group A).

Besides statistically significant quicker answers, the Group A participants also made fewer errors using the CAM system (cf. Figure 5). The average CAM accuracy in Group A is 95% (9 of 14 participants reached 100%), whereas for the keyword-search it is 81% (with a best result of 94%). The Group B participants also were more accurate using CAM (84%) than using keyword-based search (75%).

In the evaluation questionnaire, we asked the participants to rate the system features on the scale from 1 (very negative) to 5 (very positive). The question "How convenient was it to use the CAM system?" and the statement "Learning the usage of CAM is..." achieved values between 4 and 5 for both groups, which is very positive. In addition, the participants of both groups on average were almost one point more confident that an answer determined by CAM was correct than for keyword-based search (cf. Figure 6 for Group A; 5 being the highest confidence).

5 CONCLUSION

Our new CAM system helps users to faster and more confidently find answers on comparative questions compared to a keyword-based search. Moreover, a summary provided in the answer serves to support a decision-making process. While the objects of comparison and the important aspects have still to be stated explicitly, this gives rise to comparative question handling in search engines once respective questions can be identified automatically. A demo of our CAM system is online[3] and available as open source.[4]

[3] http://ltdemos.informatik.uni-hamburg.de/cam/
[4] https://github.com/uhh-lt/cam

ACKNOWLEDGMENTS

This work has been supported by the Deutsche Forschungsgemeinschaft (DFG) within the project "Argumentation in Comparative Question Answering (ACQuA)" (grant BI 1544/7-1 and HA 5851/2-1) that is part of the Priority Program "Robust Argumentation Machines (RATIO)" (SPP-1999).

REFERENCES

[1] Ahmet Aker, Alfred Sliwa, Yuan Ma, Ruishen Lui, Niravkumar Borad, Seyedeh Ziyaei, and Mina Ghobadi. 2017. What works and what does not: Classifier and feature analysis for argument mining. In *Proceedings of ArgMining@EMNLP 2017*. 91–96.

[2] Tianqi Chen and Carlos Guestrin. 2016. XGBoost: A scalable tree boosting system. In *Proceedings of KDD 2016*. 785–794.

[3] Johannes Daxenberger, Steffen Eger, Ivan Habernal, Christian Stab, and Iryna Gurevych. 2017. What is the essence of a claim? Cross-domain claim identification. In *Proceedings of EMNLP 2017*. 2055–2066.

[4] Mihai Dusmanu, Elena Cabrio, and Serena Villata. 2017. Argument mining on Twitter: Arguments, facts and sources. In *Proceedings of EMNLP 2017*. 2317–2322.

[5] Franz Faul, Edgar Erdfelder, Albert-Georg Lang, and Axel Buchner. 2007. G* Power 3: A flexible statistical power analysis program for the social, behavioral, and biomedical sciences. *Behavior Research Methods* 39, 2 (2007), 175–191.

[6] David A. Ferrucci, Eric W. Brown, Jennifer Chu-Carroll, James Fan, David Gondek, Aditya Kalyanpur, Adam Lally, J. William Murdock, Eric Nyberg, John M. Prager, Nico Schlaefer, and Christopher A. Welty. 2010. Building Watson: An overview of the DeepQA project. *AI Magazine* 31, 3 (2010), 59–79.

[7] Marcelo Fiszman, Dina Demner-Fushman, François-Michel Lang, Philip Goetz, and Thomas C. Rindflesch. 2007. Interpreting comparative constructions in biomedical text. In *Proceedings of BioNLP@ACL 2007*. 137–144.

[8] Mirco Franzek, Alexander Panchenko, and Chris Biemann. 2018. Categorization of comparative sentences for argument mining. *CoRR* abs/1809.06152 (2018). http://arxiv.org/abs/1809.06152

[9] Samir Gupta, A. S. M. Ashique Mahmood, Karen Ross, Cathy H. Wu, and K. Vijay-Shanker. 2017. Identifying comparative structures in biomedical text. In *Proceedings of BioNLP@ACL 2017*. 206–215.

[10] Xinyu Hua and Lu Wang. 2017. Understanding and detecting supporting arguments of diverse types. In *Proceedings of ACL 2017 (Volume 2: Short Papers)*. 203–208.

[11] Nitin Jindal and Bing Liu. 2006. Mining comparative sentences and relations. In *Proceedings of AAAI 2006*. 1331–1336.

[12] Alexander Panchenko, Eugen Ruppert, Stefano Faralli, Simone Paolo Ponzetto, and Chris Biemann. 2018. Building a web-scale dependency-parsed corpus from CommonCrawl. In *Proceedings of LREC 2018*.

[13] Dae Hoon Park and Catherine Blake. 2012. Identifying comparative claim sentences in full-text scientific articles. In *Proceedings of DSSD@ACL 2012*. 1–9.

[14] Samuel Sanford Shapiro and Martin B. Wilk. 1965. An analysis of variance test for normality (complete samples). *Biometrika* 52, 3/4 (1965), 591–611.

[15] Jan Snajder. 2017. Social media argumentation mining: The quest for deliberateness in raucousness. *CoRR* abs/1701.00168 (2017). http://arxiv.org/abs/1701.00168

[16] Christian Stab, Johannes Daxenberger, Chris Stahlhut, Tristan Miller, Benjamin Schiller, Christopher Tauchmann, Steffen Eger, and Iryna Gurevych. 2018. ArgumenText: Searching for arguments in heterogeneous sources. In *Proceedings of NAACL 2018 (Demonstrations)*. 21–25.

[17] Christian Stab and Iryna Gurevych. 2014. Identifying argumentative discourse structures in persuasive essays. In *Proceedings of EMNLP 2014*. 46–56.

[18] Jian-Tao Sun, Xuanhui Wang, Dou Shen, Hua-Jun Zeng, and Zheng Chen. 2006. CWS: A comparative web search system. In *Proceedings of WWW 2006*. 467–476.

[19] Henning Wachsmuth, Martin Potthast, Khalid Al Khatib, Yamen Ajjour, Jana Puschmann, Jiani Qu, Jonas Dorsch, Viorel Morari, Janek Bevendorff, and Benno Stein. 2017. Building an argument search engine for the web. In *Proceedings of ArgMining@EMNLP 2017*. 49–59.

Coagmento v3.0: Rapid Prototyping of Web Search Experiments

Diana Soltani
Department of Computer Science
Rutgers University
New Brunswick, New Jersey
diana.soltani@rutgers.edu

Matthew Mitsui
School of Comm. and Information
Rutgers University
New Brunswick, New Jersey
mmitsui@rutgers.edu

Chirag Shah
School of Comm. and Information
Rutgers University
New Brunswick, New Jersey
chirags@rutgers.edu

ABSTRACT

As understanding of web search behavior grows, researchers rapidly develop new study designs to capture and understand search behavior. Researchers have restricted time in which to design a study, develop a collection tool, collect data, analyze it, and report new insights. In particular, sufficient time and development skills are often required to create a tool that meets the needs of any particular web search behavior study. Coagmento is a tool that is developed for facilitating many of the needs for designing and running a lab study, from executing a session flow to collecting log data. By streamlining the programming of unique parts for a specific study, Coagmento helps researchers tailor various parts of running a user study, lowering the barrier for designing and conducting lab study experiments. One-click interactions with a graphical user interface permit researchers to operate through a web-based administrative service to generate stages, search tasks, and questionnaires for their interactive information retrieval studies. In this demonstration, Coagmento provides a solution to increase efficiency in the production of laboratory experiments for web search behavior.

CCS CONCEPTS

• **Information systems** → **Task models**; *Search interfaces*; Test collections; • **Human-centered computing** → *Open source software*;

KEYWORDS

collaborative information seeking, human-computer interaction, information retrieval, user studies, task-model studies, web search behavior

ACM Reference Format:

Diana Soltani, Matthew Mitsui, and Chirag Shah. 2019. Coagmento v3.0: Rapid Prototyping of Web Search Experiments. In *2019 Conference on Human Information Interaction and Retrieval (CHIIR '19), March 10–14, 2019, Glasgow, United Kingdom.* ACM, New York, NY, USA, 5 pages. https://doi.org/10.1145/3295750.3298917

1 BACKGROUND

Interactive Information Retrieval (IIR) - as a research discipline - broadly refers to research studying people's search behaviors in electronic environments to determine predictable or distinguishable patterns between behaviors, different types of users, and/or the tasks that drive users' searches. IIR researchers define the environmental or user characteristics they wish to study, for instance a search task's complexity [3] or the time constraint experienced by a user when searching [6]. Researchers manipulate that independent variable and observe how these changes affect behaviors. Researchers in IIR have studied diverse aspects of the user or task context. Researchers have studied changes in behavior for general web searching [5, 24] and also domain-specific searches [18, 25]. They have also studied constructs such as general topic familiarity [14], users' engagement with a task [7], and even search task determinability [4], among others.

Despite this diversity in research agendas, the necessary mechanisms to support such studies share several commonalities. For one, the studies often passively collect the searching behavior of participants - for instance, their clicks on links, queries issued to search engines, and time spent on content pages [3, 4, 17]. They also often explicitly collect questionnaire information from their users, tailored to the specific design of their study. Such questions may elicit information about general demographics [28] or about their field of expertise [22] or their general search expertise. Researchers may also ask participants before they begin searching about their general familiarity with the topic [14]. After the task, researchers may ask participants about the difficulties searchers faced [17], about how engaged they were with the task [7], or even about their intentions for a specific query [19].

When a researcher has a new research question, she carefully designs components of her respective study. She determines how much passive data to collect, what questionnaires to create, what tasks should be assigned to searchers, the order in which tasks should be presented, and the logical flow of these items from start to finish. This conceptual design is a given overhead cost for any new study. Generally, the flow from research question to research product proceeds as follows: determining the research questions, designing the study, developing a data collection tool, collecting data, analyzing it, and reporting new insights. Substantial overhead exists in developing the collection tool, yet despite the diversity in studies, IIR studies follow similar patterns. Figure 1 represents a common workflow for participants in IIR studies, followed by past and recent research efforts [7, 13, 19]. Study participants often engage in a linear flow of stages. Stages may contain questionnaires and/or a prompt of the participant's designated search task. There is currently no tool that acknowledges these common study design patterns and leverages this insight to expedite the process of creating a study. Coagmento serves as an appropriate solution in this regard. Once a study has been designed, Coagmento allows

CHIIR '19, March 10–14, 2019, Glasgow, United Kingdom

ACM ISBN 978-1-4503-6025-8/19/03.
https://doi.org/10.1145/3295750.3298917

researchers to quickly create and manipulate these common constructs of IIR studies through a graphical user interface, expediting the creation of a novel study. This saves a considerable amount of time with easy access for study creation, consequently allowing researchers to focus less attention on programming the study and more attention on design and analysis. Particularly, this system is useful for researchers beginning research in IIR as well as managing portions of the development that requires substantial effort otherwise. In this paper, we will present a version of Coagmento that helps support this prototyping, additionally discussing its implications for future research in IIR.

2 WHAT IS COAGMENTO?

2.1 Coagmento in the Past

Coagmento originally debuted in 2008 as a tool to collect data for collaborative information seeking. It followed the work of pre-existing tools to support collaborative information seeking such as Ariadne [27], Cerchiamo [8], CoSearch [2], and SearchTogether [23]. Subsequent versions since 2008 have been demonstrated at various venues (e.g., [10, 21]). Coagmento has been used in several versions and in several studies to passively collect searching and browsing behaviors like described above. For instance, Hendahewa and Shah [12] examined users in a traditional lab setting to predict from behavior how well a person will perform in the future in a session-based Web search task. González-Ibáñez et al. [9] used Coagmento to examine the relationship between mood and information seeking behaviors. Knight et al. [15] deployed it in a larger scale laboratory study of over 1,000 users to study searchers' assessments of expertise and document trust. Mitsui et al. [19] used it to compare searchers' observed behaviors to the information seeking intentions they reported for a given moment. Most versions focused on collecting information related to user search behavior on the general web and specialized web-based portals such as digital libraries (e.g., [26]). As of recently, researchers using Coagmento were required to modify its source code as per their study design [21].

In light of the needs specified in the Introduction, the newest version of Coagmento - presented here - facilitates the prototyping of a working web search behavior study and data collection tool with little programming intervention. First, this workflow allows for a rapid prototyping of user studies. Since several IIR studies follow similar templates, creating similar studies should require minimal effort. Second, a interface-based approach to creating a study lowers the learning curve to create one. Researchers who are generally interested in IIR but have little programming experience have a more accessible method for realizing their research agendas. Through a graphical user interface (GUI), Coagmento allows researchers to operate and manage a web-based administrative service to generate web-search studies. Our work aims to allow researchers to explore their research in a time-effective and cost-effective manner.

2.2 Administrative Tools

Coagmento is a web-based application that allows for users to set up their own custom studies with minimal programming. Given that a researcher has already designed a new IIR study on paper, Coagmento facilitates the management of task design, participant workflow design, questionnaire creation, participant registration, and communication with participants. In particular, it offers a GUI-based administration tool with the following support, to help create web search behavior studies.

2.2.1 Task Representation. One central unit of analysis in IIR studies is the *task*. It is believed that tasks vary along several important measurable characteristics - such as the topic, task type, and task complexity - that influence behavior. Tasks may vary categorically - e.g., having a "well-defined" or "ill-defined" goal [16] - or even numerically - being increasingly or decreasingly complex. Coagmento allows administrators to first create the task prompt that will be shown to study participants (e.g., "You are a student in an undergraduate history course. Please bookmark 5 pages on World War II."). Administrators can further define how these tasks should be characterized. Administrators are not limited to varying tasks' goal or complexity but may define new categories, such as the task's determinability, the task product, or the topic, to fit the needs of a study. A task presented to a participant may subsequently be characterized by multiple attributes simultaneously (e.g., specific goal + factual product + medium complexity).

2.2.2 Task Assignment by Rotation. Not every user should be exposed to identical tasks in identical order. More generally, it is often desired to expose different participants to different conditions to determine the effect of that condition (as independent variable) on search and browsing behaviors (as dependent variables). A Coagmento administrator can specifically determine which task each participant is exposed to. If study participants are only required to search on one task, the task that participant is exposed to can be manipulated. If a single participant must search on multiple tasks sequentially, the order of these tasks can also be altered per participant to reduce ordering effects.

This is performed by designating participants to a row in an assignment table, with each row specifying the configuration for a study participant. Such a table can be manually created by the user. We also provide a Latin square algorithm [1] to automatically generate such a table. Given a number of columns n, the algorithm generates and rearranges a n x n table to equally expose each participant to different conditions. This is a common method to counteract ordering effects such as participant fatigue or learning effects [11]. The user may opt to use the provided algorithm or add, remove, or reorder rows in the participant assignment table as needed (or do both in parallel).

2.2.3 Questionnaires. Often, qualitative self-reported data is collected from participants during the course of IIR or web search studies. It is elicited from basic demographic questionnaires, questionnaires about a participant's search expertise or domain expertise [17], and pre-task and post-task questionnaires about anticipated or experienced task difficulty or topic familiarity, respectively. Coagmento provides a dedicated tool for creating questionnaires. It supports a variety of common question types: Likert scale, multiple choice, numerical, and open-ended text. It provides configuration options per question, such as optional help text, validation options, and text formatting. Administrators may create, edit, and save questionnaires for later reuse. Questionnaires and their respective answers are loaded and saved to Coagmento's MySQL database.

Figure 1: An example study setup which includes a demographic questionnaire, task, and pretask/posttask questionnaires; this linear flow of stages can be easily replicated by Coagmento.

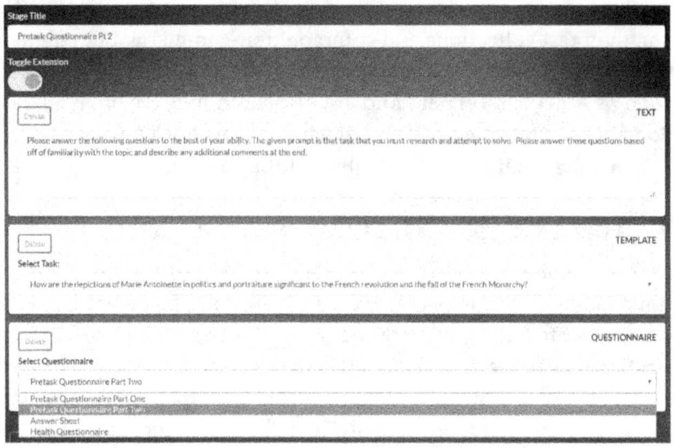

Figure 2: Example stage editor. Each section represents a component of the stage. Components are draggable for rearrangement. A previewing exists to examine the participant's point of view of the stage.

Rendering questionnaires - both for editing and displaying to participants - is supported through formBuilder[1], an external JavaScript library. The support provided by Coagmento and formBuilder allows for easy and efficient questionnaire creation, removal, and editing.

Questionnaires are not tied to any particular stage of the study. Some questionnaires should be asked per user (e.g., demographics), and some should be asked for each task a user conducts (e.g., task difficulty). As explained next, the placement of each questionnaire can be controlled by the user. This similarly applies to visible components of the study, as each visible component in the study is treated as a "widget".

2.2.4 Stages. Figure 1 demonstrates one common type of study flow. A participant logs into Coagmento and is welcomed by the system, answers a demographic questionnaire, engages with pretask materials, conducts the search task provided by the researchers, engages with posttask materials, and concludes participation in the study. This is one basic flow, and some modifications to this design are also common. Participants may engage in multiple series of pretask-task-posttask episodes. Alternatively, they may engage in several Google-a-day tasks before concluding with one general postsearch questionnaire. Coagmento has the ability to support all of these linear stage flows and more. And again, it can support these quite effortlessly through the GUI. Generally speaking, each can be composed of one or more of the following components:

- Static text - e.g., "Welcome..."
- Task prompt - e.g., "You are enrolled in a Japanese history course... Please bookmark 5 pages on..."
- Questionnaire - e.g., demographic questionnaire or posttask questionnaire
- Resource files - e.g., a training video/PDF

Each of these is a potential "widget" in a stage. A welcome stage may only include static text, while a demographic questionnaire stage may omit any task prompts or resource files. If a stage requires a questionnaire or a task, the creator references a previously created item. Figure 2 shows an administrator creating a task stage, additionally selecting the previously made "Pretask Questionnaire Part One". Lastly, administrators can rapidly edit and reorder stages in a drag-and-drop fashion. They may also toggle whether the Chrome extension should actively record search behavior. Admins can also preview a stage as it would be presented to a study participant.

2.2.5 User Management. Coagmento administrators can control login permissions of users. Participants by default cannot log in unless granted access, preventing premature login until the participant meets a requirement - such as meeting the administrator face-to-face before conducting the study. Upon first login, participants are designated to one of the task rotations described above. Coagmento also provides a method for creating e-mail templates to communicate with participants. For instance, one template may be introductory instructions for navigating to the physical laboratory to conduct the study or to provide instructions on payment collection. In Coagmento's current state, researchers must manually send out these e-mail to participants.

A fresh installation of Coagmento has a default administrative user with default credentials that can be modified. Multiple administrative accounts can be created so that collaborating researchers can create components of the study. For debugging purposes, a Coagmento user may also create user accounts with random user names and credentials.

2.2.6 Chrome Extension Interface. Coagmento is additionally comprised of a Chrome extension that collects information pertaining to a participant's web interactions, such as querying to search engines, clicking results, and spending time on pages. The browser plug-in includes a Chrome menu button with popup menu and a right-click context menu for saving bookmarks and page text snippets [20].

[1] https://formbuilder.readthedocs.io/en/latest/

2.2.7 Setup. Coagmento's backend primarily comprises of PHP, built on Laravel [2] to create a RESTful framework. If programming is required, Laravel's standard structure is highly supported by online tutorials. The front-end is largely custom HTML, CSS, and JavaScript, and the Chrome Extension is also custom. While these help support the rendering of a specific study, most other components of the study are otherwise not hard coded. Task stage layout, stage order, task prompts, questionnaires, and answers are manipulated, saved, and retrieved as records to and from a MySQL database. Out of the box, configuration of the database is largely handled in advance, with the final setup only requiring a single command ('php artisan migrate'). Coagmento can be run locally on a laptop but is intended to run on a remote server so that participants may access it via the web.

3 CONCLUSION

Coagmento provides a platform for IIR researchers to rapidly prototype a study with a button-guided interface. Coagmento provides a plethora of tools to create a tailored research design and collect searcher data. Creation of questionnaires, tasks, and stages can all be done on Coagmento's GUI. Some features can be enabled or disabled according to the design specification. While the above demonstration largely advocated for Coagmento's support for laboratory-based studies, it can in theory be applied to naturalistic settings where participants remotely install Coagmento on their personal computers, and it has been applied accordingly in practice. In short, Coagmento can help rapidly create old and new study designs, expediting the research pipeline in the field of IIR.

For the current suite of features described, Coagmento requires no programming interventions to create a customized web search behavior study. Installation of Coagmento is required on the server where data will be stored, and installation of the Chrome extension is required on study participants' machines (or a laboratory machine). Configuring Coagmento for one's study largely requires manipulations through 1) configuration files or 2) the graphical user interface. In a few cases, the Coagmento code base may require programmer intervention. This is necessary if a researcher wants to develop a novel Chrome extension data collection tool - e.g., if the researcher wants to clean and collect Quora or Spotify API calls or wants to embed an external recommender system into the extension.

In Coagmento's current form, the code base only supports the creation of a single study. A researcher who wants to run multiple studies will need to copy multiple instances of the code base and reconfigure one for each study instance. An extension to the work presented here is to treat each study as an object and to design Coagmento as a factory that can create, moderate, and run studies simultaneously. On a related note, a small future extension to Coagmento is a suite of visualizations to monitor the progress of the completion of a study (e.g., # of completed users and # open registrations). Lastly, while Coagmento currently supports only the designed rotation of tasks (viz., Latin square) between participants, it should eventually support the rotation of other components as well, such as the rotation of questions within a questionnaire and the configuration of other environmental factors, such as controlling whether there is a time constraint as in previous studies [6].

Future work on Coagmento includes the implementation of data collection from external devices such as Electroencephalogram (EEG), eye tracking, and mobile devices. These have become popular methods of data collection for recent research in IIR. Coagmento should allow researchers to toggle whether (and which) physiological data collection tools are being used, as well as whether the participant is using a mobile or desktop/laptop device. At minimum, it should support the most commonly used models and operating systems. Another future direction is to manage interactions with common test collections and common non-commercial IR engines. IIR researchers often use standard non-commercial search engines such as Indri[3] or Terrier[4] and create search indexes on available domain-specific or general Web document corpora. One last feature is to manage more of the data itself through the GUI.

4 WHAT'S IN THE DEMONSTRATION?

In this demonstration, we will present the front-end administrative functionality of Coagmento. We will show conference participants how to create a basic study flow such as the one in Figure 1, demonstrating how to create tasks, questionnaires, and stages in the proper order, as well as how to register and run participants. We will also assist interested individuals with installing Coagmento locally on their machines to test the system independently. Additionally, we will present and describe basic portions of the code base to individuals interested in replicating, recreating, or extending Coagmento. The code is available for open source on GitHub[5].

ACKNOWLEDGMENTS

Work on Coagmento is supported through the National Science Foundation (NSF) grant IIS-1717488.

REFERENCES

[1] [n. d.]. Latin Squares - Williams Design. http://statpages.info/latinsq.html
[2] Saleema Amershi and Meredith Ringel Morris. 2008. CoSearch: A System for Co-located Collaborative Web Search. In *Proceedings of CHI '08*. ACM, New York, NY, USA, 1647–1656. https://doi.org/10.1145/1357054.1357311
[3] Jaime Arguello. 2014. Predicting Search Task Difficulty. In *Proceedings of the 36th European Conference on IR Research on Advances in Information Retrieval - Volume 8416 (ECIR 2014)*. Springer-Verlag New York, Inc., New York, NY, USA, 88–99. https://doi.org/10.1007/978-3-319-06028-6_8
[4] Rob Capra, Jaime Arguello, and Yinglong Zhang. 2017. The effects of search task determinability on search behavior. In *Advances in Information Retrieval - 39th European Conference on IR Research, ECIR 2017, Proceedings (Lecture Notes in Computer Science (including subseries Lecture Notes in Artificial Intelligence and Lecture Notes in Bioinformatics))*. Springer Verlag, Germany, 108–121. https://doi.org/10.1007/978-3-319-56608-5_9
[5] Marc-Allen Cartright, Ryen W. White, and Eric Horvitz. 2011. Intentions and Attention in Exploratory Health Search. In *Proceedings of the 34th International ACM SIGIR Conference on Research and Development in Information Retrieval (SIGIR '11)*. ACM, New York, NY, USA, 65–74. https://doi.org/10.1145/2009916.2009929
[6] Anita Crescenzi, Diane Kelly, and Leif Azzopardi. 2015. Time Pressure and System Delays in Information Search. In *Proceedings of the 38th International ACM SIGIR Conference on Research and Development in Information Retrieval (SIGIR '15)*. ACM, New York, NY, USA, 767–770. https://doi.org/10.1145/2766462.2767817
[7] Ashlee Edwards and Diane Kelly. 2017. Engaged or Frustrated?: Disambiguating Emotional State in Search. In *Proceedings of the 40th International ACM SIGIR*

[2] https://laravel.com/

[3] https://www.lemurproject.org/indri/
[4] http://terrier.org/
[5] https://github.com/InfoSeeking/Coagmento/tree/study

Conference on Research and Development in Information Retrieval (SIGIR '17). ACM, New York, NY, USA, 125–134. https://doi.org/10.1145/3077136.3080818

[8] Gene Golovchinsky, John Adcock, Jeremy Pickens, Pernilla Qvarfordt, and Maribeth Back. 2008. Cerchiamo: a collaborative exploratory search tool. *Proceedings of CSCW* (2008), 8–12.

[9] Roberto González-Ibáñez, Chirag Shah, and Natalia Cordova-Rubio. 2011. Smile! Studying expressivity of happiness as a synergic factor in collaborative information seeking. *Proceedings of the American Society for Information Science and Technology* 48, 1 (2011), 1–10. https://doi.org/10.1002/meet.2011.14504801171

[10] Roberto González-ibáñez and Chirag Shah. 2011. Coagmento: A System for Supporting Collaborative Information Seeking. *The74th Annual Meeting of the American Society for Information Science and Technology ASIST 2011* (2011).

[11] Paul Grau. 2017. Balanced Latin Squares in Python âĂŞ Paul Grau âĂŞ Medium. https://medium.com/@graycoding/balanced-latin-squares-in-python-2c3aa6ec95b9

[12] Chathra Hendahewa and Chirag Shah. 2017. Evaluating User Search Trails in Exploratory Search Tasks. *Inf. Process. Manage.* 53, 4 (July 2017), 905–922. https://doi.org/10.1016/j.ipm.2017.04.001

[13] Hugo C. Huurdeman, Max L. Wilson, and Jaap Kamps. 2016. Active and Passive Utility of Search Interface Features in Different Information Seeking Task Stages. In *Proceedings of the 2016 ACM on Conference on Human Information Interaction and Retrieval (CHIIR '16)*. ACM, New York, NY, USA, 3–12. https://doi.org/10.1145/2854946.2854957

[14] Diane Kelly and Colleen Cool. 2002. The Effects of Topic Familiarity on Information Search Behavior. In *Proceedings of the 2Nd ACM/IEEE-CS Joint Conference on Digital Libraries (JCDL '02)*. ACM, New York, NY, USA, 74–75. https://doi.org/10.1145/544220.544232

[15] Simon Knight, Bart Rienties, Karen Littleton, Matthew Mitsui, Dirk Tempelaar, and Chirag Shah. 2017. The relationship of (perceived) epistemic cognition to interaction with resources on the internet. *Computers in Human Behavior* 73, Supplement C (2017), 507 – 518. https://doi.org/10.1016/j.chb.2017.04.014

[16] Yuelin Li and Nicholas J. Belkin. 2008. A faceted approach to conceptualizing tasks in information seeking. *Information Processing and Management* 44, 6 (2008). Adaptive Information Retrieval.

[17] Chang Liu, Jingjing Liu, Michael Cole, Nicholas J. Belkin, and Xiangmin Zhang. [n. d.]. Task difficulty and domain knowledge effects on information search behaviors. *Proceedings of the American Society for Information Science and Technology* 49, 1 ([n. d.]), 1–10. https://doi.org/10.1002/meet.14504901142 arXiv:https://onlinelibrary.wiley.com/doi/pdf/10.1002/meet.14504901142

[18] Mihai Lupu. 2012. Patent Information Retrieval: An Instance of Domain-specific Search. In *Proceedings of the 35th International ACM SIGIR Conference on Research and Development in Information Retrieval (SIGIR '12)*. ACM, New York, NY, USA, 1189–1190. https://doi.org/10.1145/2348283.2348536

[19] Matthew Mitsui, Jiqun Liu, Nicholas J. Belkin, and Chirag Shah. 2017. Predicting Information Seeking Intentions from Search Behaviors. In *Proceedings of the 40th International ACM SIGIR Conference on Research and Development in Information Retrieval (SIGIR '17)*. ACM, New York, NY, USA, 1121–1124. https://doi.org/10.1145/3077136.3080737

[20] Matthew Mitsui, Jiqun Liu, and Chirag Shah. 2018. Coagmento: Past, Present, and Future of an Individual and Collaborative Information Seeking Platform. In *Proceedings of the 2018 Conference on Human Information Interaction & Retrieval (CHIIR '18)*. ACM, New York, NY, USA, 325–328. https://doi.org/10.1145/3176349.3176896

[21] Matthew Mitsui, Jiqun Liu, and Chirag Shah. 2018. The Paradox of Personalization: Does Task Prediction Require Individualized Models?. In *Proceedings of the 2018 Conference on Human Information Interaction & Retrieval (CHIIR '18)*. ACM, New York, NY, USA, 277–280. https://doi.org/10.1145/3176349.3176887

[22] Sophie Monchaux, Franck Amadieu, Aline Chevalier, and Claudette MarinâĹŽâĹ. 2015. Query strategies during information searching: Effects of prior domain knowledge and complexity of the information problems to be solved. *Information Processing & Management* 51, 5 (2015), 557 – 569. https://doi.org/10.1016/j.ipm.2015.05.004

[23] Meredith Ringel Morris and Eric Horvitz. 2007. SearchTogether: An Interface for Collaborative Web Search. In *Proceedings of the 20th ACM UIST Symposium (UIST '07)*. ACM, New York, NY, USA, 3–12. https://doi.org/10.1145/1294211.1294215

[24] Kira Radinsky, Krysta M. Svore, Susan T. Dumais, Milad Shokouhi, Jaime Teevan, Alex Bocharov, and Eric Horvitz. 2013. Behavioral Dynamics on the Web: Learning, Modeling, and Prediction. *ACM Trans. Inf. Syst.* 31, 3, Article 16 (Aug. 2013), 37 pages. https://doi.org/10.1145/2493175.2493181

[25] Georg P. Schoenherr and Ryen W. White. 2014. Interactions Between Health Searchers and Search Engines. In *Proceedings of the 37th International ACM SIGIR Conference on Research & Development in Information Retrieval (SIGIR '14)*. ACM, New York, NY, USA, 143–152. https://doi.org/10.1145/2600428.2609602

[26] Chirag Shah and Roberto González-Ibáñez. 2012. Spatial context in collaborative information seeking. *Journal of Information Science* 38, 4 (2012), 333–349.

[27] Michael B. Twidale, David M. Nichols, and Chris D. Paice. 1997. Browsing is a collaborative process. *Information Processing & Management* 33, 6 (1997). https://doi.org/10.1016/S0306-4573(97)00040-X

[28] Ingmar Weber and Carlos Castillo. 2010. The Demographics of Web Search. In *Proceedings of the 33rd International ACM SIGIR Conference on Research and Development in Information Retrieval (SIGIR '10)*. ACM, New York, NY, USA, 523–530. https://doi.org/10.1145/1835449.1835537

The CLARIAH Media Suite: A Hybrid Approach to System Design in the Humanities

Liliana Melgar-Estrada
University of Amsterdam
The Netherlands
melgar@uva.nl

Marijn Koolen
KNAW Humanities Cluster
The Netherlands
marijn.koolen@di.huc.knaw.nl

Kaspar Beelen
University of Amsterdam
The Netherlands
k.beelen@uva.nl

Hugo Huurdeman
University of Amsterdam
The Netherlands
h.c.huurdeman@uva.nl

Mari Wigham
Netherlands Institute for Sound and Vision
The Netherlands
mwigham@beeldengeluid.nl

Carlos Martinez-Ortiz
Netherlands eScience Center
The Netherlands
c.martinez@esciencecenter.nl

Jaap Blom
Netherlands Institute for Sound and Vision
The Netherlands
jblom@beeldengeluid.nl

Roeland Ordelman
University of Twente
The Netherlands
roeland.ordelman@utwente.nl

ABSTRACT

The practices of digital humanists are evolving, highly diversified and experimental. There is also a lack of agreement about whether or not digital humanists should have data and programming skills. Thus, their underlying needs for higher levels of flexibility and transparency may be contradicted by their explicit requests for user-friendly graphic user interfaces (GUIs), creating challenges for designing information systems in the digital humanities. This paper describes the experience of designing the Media Suite, which provides access to important Dutch audiovisual collections and is part of the Dutch infrastructure for digital humanities. We outline a solution to the conflicting needs of scholars, by combining a semi-traditional GUI with Jupyter Notebooks. This solution tackles the needs of both novice and advanced users in digital research methods in the humanities. This demonstration paper explains how the Media Suite and the Jupyter notebooks work together, and elaborates on the rationale behind the design choices. We also outline the implications this hybrid and extensible approach has for interface design for the information science and scholarly community.

CCS CONCEPTS

• **Human-centered computing** → *Command line interfaces*; *Graphical user interfaces*;

KEYWORDS

Complex Tasks; Research Information Systems; Digital Humanities

ACM Reference Format:

Liliana Melgar-Estrada, Marijn Koolen, Kaspar Beelen, Hugo Huurdeman, Mari Wigham, Carlos Martinez-Ortiz, Jaap Blom, and Roeland Ordelman. 2019. The CLARIAH Media Suite: A Hybrid Approach to System Design in the Humanities. In *2019 Conference on Human Information Interaction and Retrieval (CHIIR '19), March 10–14, 2019, Glasgow, United Kingdom.* ACM, New York, NY, USA, Article 4, 5 pages. https://doi.org/10.1145/3295750.3298918

ACM ISBN 978-1-4503-6025-8/19/03.
https://doi.org/10.1145/3295750.3298918

1 INTRODUCTION

The emergence of *Digital Humanities* is tied to an increasing data-driven approach to scholarship, in which the so-called *fourth paradigm* in science [7] meets the humanities, challenging their established epistemologies and methods [9]. Digital humanists address research questions by identifying patterns in textual and audio-visual sources (for example, by massively analyzing topics in digitized newspapers or color patterns in films [1]) or by extracting structured data from historical records to reconstruct objects, places, or events from the past.[2] Hence, information systems are no longer used only for searching for information sources, but for the direct analysis, manipulation and experimentation with humanities sources.

In this paper, we introduce a hybrid and extensible solution to the design of information systems to support digital humanists, combining a more traditional search interface with Jupyter Notebooks,[3] a flexible system for interactive data science.

2 BACKGROUND

2.1 The infrastructure project

The Dutch CLARIAH infrastructure project[4] aims to build the Dutch part of the European infrastructures DARIAH[5] (Digital Research Infrastructure for the Arts and Humanities) [5], and CLARIN[6] (Common Language Resources and Technology Infrastructure) [10]. The main target user groups of the CLARIAH infrastructure are humanities and social sciences scholars interested in Dutch history and society—taking into account that most sources are in Dutch language. All tools developed in the infrastructure are open source, to benefit the broader digital humanities community, as well as software developers. CLARIAH consists of three working groups centered around data types and the needs of scholars working with them: 1. textual data (linguists), 2. structured data (socio-economic historians), and

[1] E.g. *Mining Shifting Concepts Through Time* project (https://www.esciencecenter.nl/project/mining-shifting-concepts-through-time-shico) and the *Sensoring Moving Image Archive* project (http://sensorymovingimagearchive.humanities.uva.nl/)
[2] E.g. in the projects *Golden agents* (https://www.huygens.knaw.nl/golden-agents/?lang=en) and *Time machine* (https://timemachine.eu/)
[3] http://jupyter.org/
[4] https://www.clariah.nl.
[5] https://www.dariah.eu/
[6] https://www.clarin.eu/

3. audio-visual data (media historians and oral historians). This paper focuses on the third group, which includes a diverse group of scholars from disciplines such as media studies (including film and television studies), oral and political history.

2.2 User requirements

Following the steps for user-centered software design indicated by Toms [20], we evaluated first the requirements of this user group in different ways: via naturalistic observations, personal interviews, design sessions, and workshops (partly described in [12]). We found that, beyond generic functionality such as searching and browsing, the most important scholarly requirements were:

(a) Access to the original sources. Due mostly to copyright and privacy, most of the relevant collections (e.g., the Dutch television archive, or collections of oral history interviews) had previously only been made partially available. The scholars wanted access to the actual media content, and to the complete archival metadata, to preserve the principles of (meta)data transparency (respecting the original metadata from the providers as much as possible), and provenance (mostly for "traceability" to the original source).

(b) *Flexible* and *user-friendly* interfaces that support most phases in the process of simultaneous exploration and analysis of very complex and big, mixed media collections (e.g., the Dutch newspaper archive together with the Dutch television and radio archive).

The first prototype of the so-called "Media Suite," (Section 5.1), appeared after the initial requirements analysis phase.

3 PROBLEM DESCRIPTION

Large-scale infrastructure projects in the humanities and social sciences, such as the aforementioned DARIAH, CLARIN, or the Australian NuHi,[7] aim to provide solutions for preservation and access to collections and data necessary for scholarly research [22].

One of the main challenges of building these infrastructures is catering to methodologically diverse humanities disciplines [9], while at the same time supporting individual research projects which use specific methods. This is what van Zundert [22] has called "the generalization paradox." The requirements in Section 2.2 lead to different types of challenges in designing the infrastructure for the audio-visual group: data governance, sustainable development, user-friendliness, and the need for personalized work spaces [13].

Another important challenge is supporting the scholars' diverse information and data skills. Most scholars only had experience with using graphic user interfaces (GUI), but some used programming and command line tools for data manipulation. This diversity is not uncommon, because, even though the humanities started to experiment with computational approaches in the 1940s [11], the training in data-related work of humanists differs greatly between disciplines and institutions [15]. Besides, it is not yet agreed whether or not digital humanists should have coding skills [15]. Thus, we were faced with another paradox: most users request a low-complexity, user-friendly GUI-based environment, but their underlying needs

[7]https://huni.net.au/

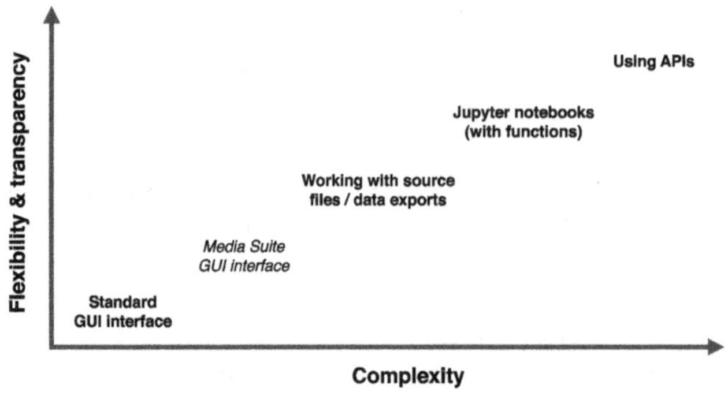

Figure 1: Degree of flexibility vs complexity in data provision for scholarly work.

require more exposure and transparency of the metadata (requirement *a)* above), as well as flexible querying and data manipulation (requirement *b)*). We refer to this as the "flexibility vs. complexity" paradox. Figure 1 indicates that the simpler the system (e.g., a standard GUI), the less flexible and transparent it is for scholarly work. While the most flexible and transparent way to manipulate the data (i.e., using APIs directly) would represent a high level of complexity for those less familiar with the "literacy of code" [23]. There is also evidence that just providing APIs for working with cultural heritage data may not be enough for humanists [5], for the same reasons mentioned above. Therefore, none of the pre-existing infrastructure service models (atomic services like CLARIN [10], or GUI-based VREs like CENDARI [2]) alone seemed to meet the needs of scholars working with audio-visual data. We concluded that we had to implement a hybrid solution, which combines a GUI with support for programmatic access to the APIs.

4 RELATED WORK

There is a growing interest among scientists and data scientists in using Jupyter Notebooks. Querying the Scopus database with the term "Jupyter notebooks," with no restrictions, shows an increasing number of publications either using or referring to them since 2015. But this is mostly the case in scientific domains where, as [18] illustrates, they have become "a robust tool for scientists to share code, associated computation, and documentation," properly aligned with the FAIR principles (Findable, Accessible, Interopeable, Reusable) for scholarly digital research objects [25]. Jupyter Notebooks are also used in industry, for example, at Netflix, where they have become "the de facto standard for quick prototyping and exploratory analysis."[21]. However, except for presentations at some conferences[8], their use in the humanities disciplines is scarcely reported.

[8]See for example the workshop at the Benelux 2018 Conference: http://2018.dhbenelux.org/workshops/#delpher)

Figure 2: Example of transparency features in the MS.

Figure 3: Example of a parameterizable Jupyter notebook that complements the MS.

5 IMPLEMENTATION APPROACH

5.1 The Resulting GUI

The Media Suite[9] is a virtual research environment (VRE) [4] where access to data and tools is authorized using a federated authentication mechanism. The indexes are built on Elasticsearch[10], offering the following features accessible via the GUI:

(1) *A metadata inspector,* which shows the metadata completeness of the different collections and completeness analysis features (e.g., per metadata field, or for data enrichments), Figure 2.
(2) *Traditional Boolean and faceted search and browsing features.*[11] We augmented this with flexible metadata selection possibilities per provider (e.g., the creation of custom facets for searching).
(3) *Basic visualizations* for data exploration, such as time lines of number of hits per year;
(4) *Personal work space and "user projects"*, [12] which allow users to create their own project spaces to store collections of bookmarks, saved queries, and user annotations created by the annotation tool included in the Media Suite [1];
(5) *Automatic enrichment services and data.* Currently, this includes automatic speech recognition (ASR), both for bulk processing and indivisual collections [14];
(6) *Basic export facilities* of user bookmarks and annotations.

5.2 Beyond the GUI: Jupyter notebooks

To move beyond the GUI, and so overcome the "flexibility vs complexity paradox", we integrate Jupyter Notebooks, a web-based UI for interactively writing and running code as well as visualizing outputs, into the research environment. Jupyter Notebooks are applications to create and share documents that contain live code, equations, visualizations and narrative text. They allow users to run Python (and use about 40 more programming languages) in a web browser, and surround their code with cells that include narrative text in Markdown [16].

For the Media Suite, a cloud-based service for the notebooks was offered. This service: (1) facilitates their use, since users do not have to install any extra software to run the notebooks, and (2) adds more security, since the notebooks become available only to users who have passed the authentication step of the Media Suite. Based on user needs elicited via the different studies described in the previous section, we populated the notebooks with different pre-built functions. These allow the users to specify parameters in the code and accept input values at runtime [21]. We then prepared queries and visualizations to enable our users to fulfill some of the tasks that the Media Suite could not handle.

The functions that we included originated from our analysis of scholarly tasks. These were meant either to:

(1) *Extend existing GUI functionality.* For this purpose, we created different notebooks, which used the same name of the GUI features that they extend. For example, the MS offers an "inspector" tool for analyzing the metadata completeness of certain fields (Figure 2), but this can be done only for one field per collection in the GUI. The function integrated in the complementary "inspector" notebook allows for combining more than one metadata field from various collections (Figure 3). Because users may not know the technical labels of the metadata fields that should be used in the notebooks, the MS provides a "metadata dictionary," where the definitions of the metadata fields are included (Figure 2).
(2) *Add new functionalities.* For example, the Media Suite offers the time-labeled, automatic speech recognition (ASR) transcripts of one important part of the Netherlands Institute for Sound and Vision (NISV) collection, which can be searched, and used as interactive transcripts for the fragment-level navigation of individual resources. However, processing pipelines that take speech transcripts as input to analyse occurrences of named entities or to generate visualisations (e.g., word clouds) by applying natural language processing (NLP) tools, are not yet implemented, or are not feasible to implement given the flexibility that is required and the existence of libraries that are freely available. The "Analysis" notebook offers this flexibility: by using the *annotation* and *search APIs* in the notebook, the users can get the ASR transcripts for

[9]http://mediasuite.clariah.nl/
[10]https://www.elastic.co/products/elasticsearch
[11]Recent developments also include the simultaneous querying of Sparql end-points
[12]Some parts, like collaborative projects, are work in progress

their bookmarked resources, and generate word frequencies and related visualizations based on their analysis since the notebook has an integrated NLP toolkit.[13]

(3) *Experiment with new Media Suite functionalities.* Besides extending the Media Suite, the *extension* role of the notebooks facilitates the task of co-developing (experimenting and testing new functionalities with scholars), e.g., word clouds in this case, before actually implementing them in the GUI.

(4) *Provide dynamic collection overviews.* Finally, they also provide dynamic collection overviews that can be usefully deployed for both scholars and institutional archivists to answer questions such as: how many hours of television do we have in the archive? Are speech transcripts available for all news programmes? What percentage of the material is already digital? Are documentaries longer now than they were in the 70's? We further describe these and other advantages of the notebooks from an archival and scholarly perspective in Wigham et al. [24].

5.3 Initial Evaluation

The resulting hybrid version combining GUI and Jupyter Notebooks was informally evaluated during the first CLARIAH media studies Summer School, where circa forty scholars worked on eight group research projects using the Media Suite[14]. The scholars received explanation of the notebooks in a workshop, and had the opportunity to try out some examples during their working sessions, assisted by data scientists or developers, who also had knowledge of the collections. More formal evaluations are planned.

6 DEMONSTRATION OVERVIEW

We will demonstrate the combination of the Media Suite (MS)'s GUI and the Jupyter notebooks in this way:

(1) Via a walk-through of the GUI. We introduce the data that are available, and functionalities described in Section 5.1. Next, we illustrate how the MS's GUI works via a scholarly use case selected for the purpose, of a scholar investigating the representation of refugees in the Dutch mainstream media (radio, television, and newspapers). We show how the MS supports the different stages of scholarly work ([3, 12]), from collection overview and *Data criticism*, [6, 8] to then gathering a representative sample (i.e. a corpus), to the analysis (e.g. manual annotation) of that sample, concluding with further analysis and synthesis (exporting and interpreting the resulting corpus and their annotations).

(2) Via a walk-through of the Jupyter notebooks. First, we explain the service model (authentication and APIs), then show the types of notebooks that we offer, the specific functions that we have pre-built in the notebooks and how users can customize and extend them.

(3) Finally, we illustrate how the MS's GUI and the notebooks complement each other, which focuses attention on two scholarly tasks. First, *Data criticism* occurs when scholars are looking for overviews of the collection and need to observe the completeness of the collections' metadata. We show what levels of this type of preliminary analysis are supported by the MS GUI, and how the dedicated notebook for this task makes the analysis more complete and flexible. This illustrates the purpose of `Extending` existing functionality via the notebooks. Second, *Preliminary data analysis* occurs when scholars are looking for patterns in the portions of the collection(s) that they have selected. This illustrates the purpose of `Adding` new functionality via the notebooks.

7 DISCUSSION: EXPECTED IMPACT

A large part of the work of the digital humanities scholar depends on data manipulation (almost 80 percent of the work is data preparation [17]). This includes a wide variety of tasks that cannot be executed within the confines of a GUI. Therefore, some scholars view these interfaces as "golden cages", where rich data is only partially unlocked via pre-determined functionalities and pre-selected interactions. Certainly, the intrinsic value of these interfaces in the humanities is that they facilitate wider access and "close reading" [19] the resources, supporting user annotations, as well as collaboration. But, designing systems in a digital humanities context has an inherently experimental nature, and an intrinsic instability as scholarly methods are gradually changing. There is a call for system design in the humanities to be open and transparent, that is, where the "source code" can be the subject of analysis and critique. As van Zundert [22] indicated, "especially now that more digital tools are getting integrated into the methodology of humanities, the adequacy and validity of analyses depend to a certain extent on an adequate understanding of such specific rules." In this sense, Jupyter Notebooks allow testing and experimentation, with full potential for encouraging transparency in reading and sharing the code that builds some of the parts of the GUI. Moreover, the notebooks provide an extensible and more interactive research environment since the code represents open building blocks that users can reuse and or reconfigure. This hybrid solution allows a shift in scholarly practice by lowering the threshold for transparency of method and data processes. The challenges for system design are important, since we assume that as demand for this transparency grows in digital scholarship, hybrid and extensible solutions to the design of GUIs like the one we proposed here will be more needed. We anticipate that the creation of prepared functions in the notebooks will require a more direct connection between data scientists and traditional scholars for creating meaningful and common (yet parameterizable) functions that can support them in their data-related tasks. Finally, the hybrid solution we propose makes scholars more compelled to deal with the trade-offs between flexibility and complexity in system design.

8 ACKNOWLEDGEMENTS

The research for this paper was made possible by the CLARIAH-CORE project (www.clariah.nl) financed by NWO. The work described is the result of the collaboration between software developers and scholars of CLARIAH WP5.[15] We specifically acknowledge the contributions of Jonathan Blok and Willem Melder to this work.

[13]NLTK, see http://www.nltk.org/

[14]https://clariah.github.io/mediasuite-blog/blog/2018/10/01/Clariah-Media-Studies-Summer-School-report

[15]People involved are listed here: http://mediasuite.clariah.nl/documentation/faq/who-develops

REFERENCES

[1] Jaap Blom, Marijn Koolen, Liliana Melgar Estrada, Peter Boot, Ronald Haentjens Dekker, Christian Olesen, Susan Aasman, Norah Karrouche, and Rob Wegter. 2017. A Demonstration of Scholarly Web Annotation Support Using the W3C Annotation Data Model and RDFa. http://easychair.org/smart-program/BIGVID2017/2017-11-24.html

[2] Nadia Boukhelifa, Mike Bryant, Nataša Bulatović, Ivan Čukić, Jean-Daniel Fekete, Milica Knežević, Jörg Lehmann, David Stuart, and Carsten Thiel. 2018. The CENDARI Infrastructure. *Journal on Computing and Cultural Heritage* 11, 2 (April 2018), 1–20. https://doi.org/10.1145/3092906 arXiv: 1612.05239.

[3] Marc Bron, Jasmijn van Gorp, and Maarten de Rijke. 2016. Media studies research in the data-driven age: How research questions evolve. *Journal of the Association for Information Science and Technology* 67, 7 (2016), 1535–1554. https://doi.org/10.1002/asi.23458 jasist2015-bron-media.pdf.

[4] Christopher Brown. 2013. Implementing a virtual research environment (VRE). https://www.jisc.ac.uk/guides/implementing-a-virtual-research-environment-vre

[5] Jennifer Edmond, Vicky Garnett, and Agiatis Benardou. 2014. *So we've built it, but have they come? Investigating barriers and opportunities for API usage among the AHSS community.* Workshop Europeana Cloud WP1. Europeana Professional, The Hague, Netherlands. http://pro.europeana.eu/europeana-cloud/about-europeana-cloud

[6] Frederick W. Gibbs. 2016. New Forms of History: Critiquing Data and Its Representations. *The American Historian* (Feb. 2016). http://tah.oah.org/february-2016/new-forms-of-history-critiquing-data-and-its-representations/

[7] Tony Hey, Stewart Tansley, and Kristin Tolle. 2009. *The Fourth Paradigm: Data-Intensive Scientific Discovery.* https://www.microsoft.com/en-us/research/publication/fourth-paradigm-data-intensive-scientific-discovery/

[8] Rik Hoekstra and Marijn Koolen. 2018. Data Scopes: towards Transparent Data Research in Digital Humanities – DH2018. Mexico. https://dh2018.adho.org/en/data-scopes-towards-transparent-data-research-in-digital-humanities/

[9] Rob Kitchin. 2014. Big Data, new epistemologies and paradigm shifts. *Big Data & Society* 1 (Sept. 2014), 1–12. http://eprints.maynoothuniversity.ie/5364/

[10] Steven Krauwer and Erhard Hinrichs. 2014. The CLARIN Research Infrastructure: Resources and Tools for e-Humanities Scholars. http://dspace.library.uu.nl/handle/1874/307981

[11] Gerhard Lauer. 2014. Challenges for the Humanities: Digital Infrastructures. In *Facing the Future : European Research Infrastructures for the Humanities and Social Sciences*, Adrian Duşa, Dietrich Nelle, Günter Stock, and Gert G. Wagner (Eds.). Scivero Verlag, Berlin. https://edoc.bbaw.de/frontdoor/index/index/docId/2327

[12] Liliana Melgar Estrada, Marijn Koolen, Hugo Huurdeman, and Jaap Blom. 2017. A process model of time-based media annotation in a scholarly context. In *CHIIR 2017: ACM SIGIR Conference on Human Information Interaction and Retrieval.* Oslo.

[13] Roeland Ordelman, Carlos Martínez Ortíz, Liliana Melgar Estrada, Marijn Koolen, Jaap Blom, Willem Melder, Jasmijn van Gorp, Victor De Boer, Themistoklis Karavellas, Lora Aroyo, Thomas Poell, Norah Karrouche, Eva Baaren, Johannes Wassenaar, Oana Inel, and Julia Noordegraaf. 2018. Challenges in Enabling Mixed Media Scholarly Research with Multi-media Data in a Sustainable Infrastructure – DH2018. Mexico. https://dh2018.adho.org/en/challenges-in-enabling-mixed-media-scholarly-research-with-multi-media-data-in-a-sustainable-infrastructure/

[14] Roeland J.F. Ordelman and Adrianus J. van Hessen. 2018. Speech Recognition and Scholarly Research: Usability and Sustainability. In *CLARIN 2018 Annual Conference*, Inguna Skadina and Maria Eskevich (Eds.). 163–168.

[15] James O'Sullivan, Diane Jakacki, and Mary Galvin. 2015. Programming in the Digital Humanities. *Digital Scholarship in the Humanities* 30, suppl_1 (2015), i142–i147. https://doi.org/10.1093/llc/fqv042

[16] Fernando Perez and Brian E. Granger. 2015. Project Jupyter: Computational Narratives as the Engine of Collaborative Data Science. https://blog.jupyter.org/project-jupyter-computational-narratives-as-the-engine-of-collaborative-data-science-2b5fb94c3c58

[17] Gil Press. 2016. Cleaning Big Data: Most Time-Consuming, Least Enjoyable Data Science Task, Survey Says. https://www.forbes.com/sites/gilpress/2016/03/23/data-preparation-most-time-consuming-least-enjoyable-data-science-task-survey-says/

[18] Bernadette M. Randles, Irene V. Pasquetto, Milena S. Golshan, and Christine L. Borgman. 2018. Using the Jupyter Notebook as a Tool for Open Science: An Empirical Study. *arXiv:1804.05492 [cs]* (2018). http://arxiv.org/abs/1804.05492 arXiv: 1804.05492.

[19] Kathryn Schulz. 2011. The mechanic muse - what is distant reading? *The New York Times* (June 2011). http://www.nytimes.com/2011/06/26/books/review/the-mechanic-muse-what-is-distant-reading.html

[20] Elaine G. Toms. 2009. User-Centered Design of Information Systems. https://doi.org/10.1081/E-ELIS3-120043525

[21] Michelle Ufford, Matthew Seal, and Kyle Kelley. 2018. Beyond Interactive: Notebook Innovation at Netflix. https://medium.com/netflix-techblog/notebook-innovation-591ee3221233

[22] Joris van Zundert. 2012. If You Build It, Will We Come? Large Scale Digital Infrastructures as a Dead End for Digital Humanities. *Historical Social Research / Historische Sozialforschung* 37, 3 (141) (2012), 165–186. http://www.jstor.org/stable/41636603

[23] Joris van Zundert and Ronald Haentjens Dekker. 2017. Code, scholarship, and criticism: When is code scholarship and when is it not? *Digital Scholarship in the Humanities* 32, suppl_1 (2017), i121–i133. https://doi.org/10.1093/llc/fqx006

[24] Mari Wigham, Liliana Melgar Estrada, and Roeland Ordelman. 2018. Jupyter Notebooks for generous archive interfaces. In *IEEE Big Data 2018: 3rd Computational Archival Science (CAS) Workshop.* Seattle, WA. https://dcicblog.umd.edu/cas/ieee-big-data-2018-3rd-cas-workshop/

[25] Mark D. Wilkinson, Michel Dumontier, IJsbrand Jan Aalbersberg, Gabrielle Appleton, Myles Axton, Arie Baak, Niklas Blomberg, Jan-Willem Boiten, Luiz Bonino da Silva Santos, Philip E. Bourne, Jildau Bouwman, Anthony J. Brookes, Tim Clark, Mercè Crosas, Ingrid Dillo, Olivier Dumon, Scott Edmunds, Chris T. Evelo, Richard Finkers, Alejandra Gonzalez-Beltran, Alasdair J. G. Gray, Paul Groth, Carole Goble, Jeffrey S. Grethe, Jaap Heringa, Peter A. C. 't Hoen, Rob Hooft, Tobias Kuhn, Ruben Kok, Joost Kok, Scott J. Lusher, Maryann E. Martone, Albert Mons, Abel L. Packer, Bengt Persson, Philippe Rocca-Serra, Marco Roos, Rene van Schaik, Susanna-Assunta Sansone, Erik Schultes, Thierry Sengstag, Ted Slater, George Strawn, Morris A. Swertz, Mark Thompson, Johan van der Lei, Erik van Mulligen, Jan Velterop, Andra Waagmeester, Peter Wittenburg, Katherine Wolstencroft, Jun Zhao, and Barend Mons. 2016. The FAIR Guiding Principles for scientific data management and stewardship. *Nature* 3 (March 2016), 160018. https://doi.org/10.1038/sdata.2016.18

A Visual Approach to Query Formulation for Systematic Search

Tony Russell-Rose
UXlabs Ltd
3000 Cathedral Hill,
Guildford, Surrey, UK
tgr@uxlabs.co.uk

Jon Chamberlain
School of Computer Science and
Electronic Engineering,
University of Essex
Colchester, Essex, UK
jchamb@essex.ac.uk

Farhad Shokraneh
The Institute of Mental Health,
University of Nottingham
Nottingham, UK
farhadshokraneh@gmail.com

ABSTRACT

Knowledge workers (such as healthcare information professionals, patent agents and legal researchers) need to create and execute search strategies that are accurate, repeatable and transparent. The traditional solution offered by most database vendors is to use proprietary line-by-line 'query builders'. However, these offer limited support for error checking or query optimisation, and their output can often be compromised by errors and inefficiencies. Using the healthcare domain for context, we demonstrate a new approach to search strategy formulation in which concepts are expressed as objects on a two-dimensional canvas, and relationships are articulated using direct manipulation. This approach eliminates many sources of syntactic error, makes the query semantics more transparent, and offers new ways to optimise, save and share search strategies and best practices.

CCS CONCEPTS

• **Information systems** → **Query representation**; **Search interfaces**; *Expert search*; • **Computing methodologies** → *Representation of Boolean functions*;

KEYWORDS

healthcare information retrieval, boolean, systematic search, search visualisation, systematic review

ACM Reference Format:
Tony Russell-Rose, Jon Chamberlain, and Farhad Shokraneh. 2019. A Visual Approach to Query Formulation for Systematic Search. In *2019 Conference on Human Information Interaction and Retrieval (CHIIR '19), March 10–14, 2019, Glasgow, United Kingdom.* ACM, New York, NY, USA, 5 pages. https://doi.org/10.1145/3295750.3298919

1 INTRODUCTION

Medical knowledge is growing so rapidly that it is difficult for healthcare professionals to keep up. As the volume of published studies increases each year [14], the gap between research knowledge and professional practice grows ever wider [2]. Healthcare information professionals play a key role in closing this gap by synthesising the complex, incomplete and at times conflicting findings of biomedical research into a form that can readily inform healthcare decision making [5]. The systematic literature review process relies on the painstaking and meticulous searching of multiple databases using complex Boolean search strategies that often consist of hundreds of keywords, operators and ontology terms [12]. An example from the CLEF 2017 eHealth Lab dataset[1] is shown in Figure 1 (titled 'Galactomannan detection for invasive aspergillosis in immunocompromised patients').

1 "Aspergillus"[MeSH]
2 "Aspergillosis"[MeSH]
3 "Pulmonary Aspergillosis"[MeSH]
4 aspergill*[tiab]
5 fungal infection[tw]
6 (invasive[tiab] AND fungal[tiab])
7 1 OR 2 OR 3 OR 4 OR 5 OR 6
8 "Serology"[MeSH]
9 Serology"[MeSH]
10 (serology[tiab] OR serodiagnosis[tiab] OR serologic[tiab])
11 8 OR 9 OR 10
12 "Immunoassay"[MeSH]
13 (immunoassay[tiab] OR immunoassays[tiab])
14 (immuno assay[tiab] OR immuno assays[tiab])
15 (ELISA[tiab] OR ELISAs[tiab] OR EIA[tiab] OR EIAs[tiab])
16 immunosorbent[tiab]
17 12 OR 13 OR 14 OR 15 OR 16
18 Platelia[tw]
19 "Mannans"[MeSH]
20 galactomannan[tw]
21 18 OR 19 OR 20
22 11 OR 17 OR 21
23 7 AND 22

Figure 1: An example Boolean search strategy

The choice of search strategy plays a vital role in ensuring that the review process is sufficiently exhaustive and that the outcome is not biased by easily accessible studies [10]. In addition, the strategy needs to be transparent and repeatable, so that others may replicate the methodology. However, systematic literature reviews can take years to complete [2], with new research findings may be published in the interim, leading to a lack of currency and potential for inaccuracy [23]. Moreover, there are often mistakes in search strategies reported in the literature that prevent them from being executed in their published form. In one study of 63 MEDLINE strategies, at least one error was detected in over 90%, including

[1]https://sites.google.com/site/clefehealth2017/task-2, accessed 10 October 2018.

CHIIR '19, March 10–14, 2019, Glasgow, United Kingdom

ACM ISBN 978-1-4503-6025-8/19/03.
https://doi.org/10.1145/3295750.3298919

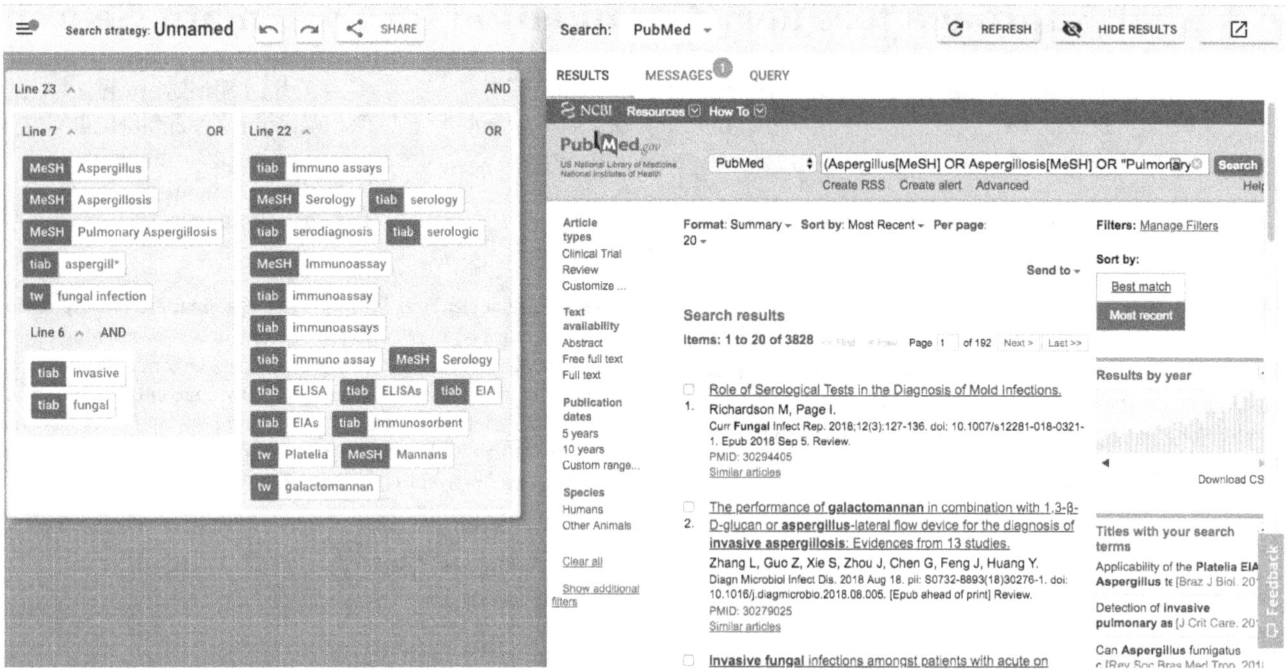

Figure 2: Screenshot of the 2dSearch application showing the query canvas (left) and the search results pane (right).

spelling errors, truncation errors, logical operator error, incorrect query line references, redundancy without rationale, etc. [5].

One study showed the average time spent on a systematic literature search was 26.9 hours (median: 18.5 hours), depending on the information professional's experience, most of which is spent on developing the search strategies and translating them into a compatible format for each search interface [4]. Unfortunately, these search strategies, as part of research methods, are getting lost in the process of reporting. This loss undermines the two principles of replicability and reproducibility of systematic reviews [7, 13, 15]. Although because of space limitation some journals have to accept the search strategies as external supplementary files, this practice is not strategic in terms of storage and data linkage [17], and these appendices are becoming inaccessible as the time passes [6]. Despite valuable efforts to save and share these search strategies in an online static database and update them [22], it is not widely resourced or updated so the information professionals end up creating and recreating search strategies for the same concepts. These requirements are considered valuable in multiple professional contexts in which complex Boolean search is a common task, such as media monitoring, recruitment (sourcing) [18], patent search and legal research [20].

Our proposed approach (called 2dSearch[2]) offers a radical alternative to conventional 'advanced search'. Instead of entering Boolean strings into one-dimensional search boxes, queries are formulated by combining objects on a two-dimensional canvas. The use of a visual approach eliminates many sources of syntactic error, makes the query semantics more transparent, and offers further opportunities for query refinement and optimisation.

In this paper, we describe related work and explain how 2dSearch supports and extends their key design principles and insights. We then explore the application in more detail, reviewing the support it offers for search strategy formulation, optimisation, sharing and re-use. Finally, we discuss some of the implementation details along with opportunities for commercial impact and further work.

2 RELATED WORK

The application of data visualisation to search query formulation can offer significant benefits, such as fewer zero-hit queries, improved query comprehension and better support for exploration of an unfamiliar database [9]. An early example of such an approach is that of Anick et al. [1], who developed a system that could parse natural language queries and represent them as movable tiles on a two-dimensional canvas. The user was able to re-arrange the tiles to reformulate the expression, and to activate or deactivate alternative elements to optimise the query. In addition, the system offered support for integration with thesauri and it displayed the number of hits in the lower left corner of each tile.

In subsequent work, Fishkin and Stone [8] investigated the application of direct manipulation techniques to the problem of database query formulation, using a system of 'lenses' to refine and filter the data. Lenses could be combined by stacking them and applying a suitable operator, or combined to create compound lenses, and hence support the encapsulation of queries of arbitrary complexity. Influential work by Jones [11] proposed an approach in which concepts are expressed using a Venn diagram notation combined with integrated query result previews. Queries could be formulated

[2] https://2dsearch.com

by overlapping objects within the workspace to create intersections and disjunctions, and subsets could be selected to facilitate execution of subcomponents of an overall query.

A further example is that of Yi et al. [24], who developed a system based around a 'dust and magnet' metaphor, in which dimensions of interest within the data could be represented as 'magnets' on a visual canvas, and the relationships between points in the data could be understood by observing the effect of the 'magnetic forces' on individual 'data particles'. More recently, Nitsche and Nürnberger [16] developed a system based around a radial interface in which queries and results could be integrated and collectively manipulated. The concept utilised a pseudo-desktop metaphor in which objects of interest clustered toward the centre. Query objects could be entered directly onto this canvas, and their proximity to the centre and to other objects was used as a relevance cue, influencing the selection and position of search results.

2dSearch adopts and extends many of the design principles and insights embodied in this work, for example:

- Boolean expressions can be formulated as a objects on a canvas, and arranged by direct manipulation;
- Query elements can be individually invoked or interrogated to facilitate exploration;
- By nesting aggregate structures, it is possible to create queries of arbitrary complexity;
- Interaction and animation can be used to communicate meaning and structure;
- Real-time feedback is fundamental to effective query optimisation.

3 DESIGN CONCEPT

3.1 Query formulation

At the heart of 2dSearch is a graphical editor which allows the user to formulate search strategies using a visual framework in which concepts are expressed as objects on a two-dimensional canvas. Concepts can be simple keywords or attribute:value pairs representing controlled vocabulary terms (e.g. Mesh terms) or database-specific search operators (e.g. field codes and other commands). They can be combined using Boolean (and other) operators to form higher-level groups and then iteratively nested to create expressions of arbitrary complexity.

The application itself consists of two panes (see Figure 2): a query canvas on the left and a search results pane on the right (which can be resized or detached in a separate tab or window). The canvas itself can be resized or zoomed, and features an 'overview' widget which allows the user to view or navigate to elements that may be outside the current viewport. Adopting design cues from Google's Material Design language[3], a sliding menu is offered on the left, providing file I/O and other options. This is complemented by a navigation bar across the top which provides support for common document-level functions such as naming and sharing search strategies.

Although 2dSearch supports the creation of complete strategies from a blank canvas, its function and value are most readily understood by reference to an example (i.e. text-based) search strategy,

[3]https://material.io

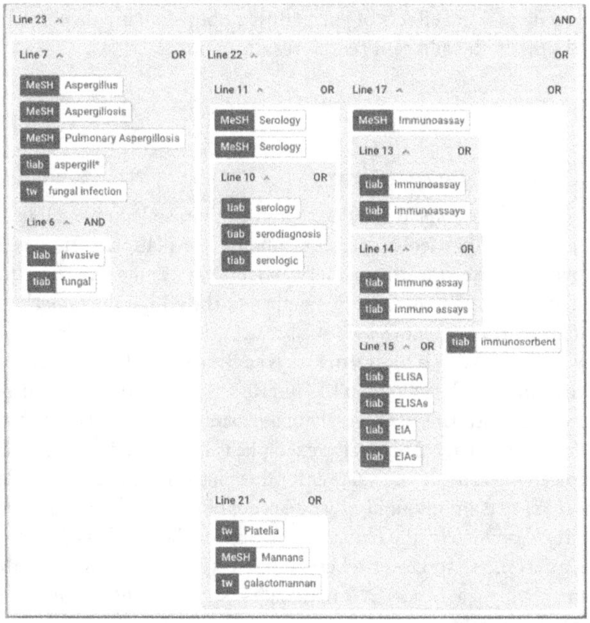

Figure 3: Visualising a text-based search strategy

such as that shown in Figure 1. A trained professional may be able to mentally 'parse' the sequence of commands shown and interpret the general approach, but without associated documentation it is difficult to understand exactly what the searcher intended. Moreover, it is difficult to optimise, debug or re-use strategies expressed in this form.

However, when this strategy is opened using 2dSearch, its structure becomes much more apparent (see Figure 3). It can be seen that the overall expression consists of a conjunction of two disjunctions (Lines 7 and 22), the first of which articulates variations on the fungal infection concept, while the latter contains various nested disjunctions to capture the diagnostic test (serology) and associated procedures. Evidently, the line numbers themselves are somewhat arbitrary in this context, having served an original purpose analogous to that of line numbering in first generation BASIC. However, by displaying them as nested groups with transparent structure, 2dSearch offers support for abstraction, in which lower-level details can be hidden and higher-level structure revealed. Moreover, it is now possible to give meaningful names to sub groups, so that they can be saved and re-used as modular components.

Although visualisation of search strategies in this manner can offer immediate utility, the true value of the approach is not so much in the *information* design, but in the *interaction* design. For example, to edit the expression, the user can move terms from one block to another using direct manipulation, and create new groups simply by combining terms. They can also cut, copy, delete, and lasso multiple objects. If they want to understand the effect of one block in isolation, they can execute it individually. Conversely, if they want to remove one element from consideration, they can temporarily disable it. It is also possible edit the content inline, interchanging Mesh terms with keywords and field tags as required.

In each case, the effects of each editing operation are displayed in real time in the adjacent search results pane.

3.2 Query execution

2dSearch functions as a meta-search engine, so is in principle agnostic of any particular search technology or platform. In practice however, to execute a given query and retrieve results, the semantics of the canvas content must be mapped to the API of the underlying database. This is achieved via an abstraction layer or set of 'adapters' for common search platforms such as Bing, Google, PubMed, etc. These are user selectable in the interface via a drop-down control.

Search platforms vary widely in the extent to which they support complex querying. Google, for example, is limited in its support for Boolean querying, so an adapter for this platform has been provided more for reasons of familiarity and proof of concept than long-term utility. Conversely, the true value of approaches such as 2dSearch becomes more apparent when coupled with databases that offer more sophisticated search functionality, such as PubMed and other specialist databases.

It is common for healthcare information professionals to want to search more than one database, particularly when undertaking a systematic literature review [19]. In practice, this requires a process of 'translation' of the search strategy to match the syntax of the target database and the search operators it supports. For a relatively simple query this may not be a major undertaking, particularly if such operators form a relatively small proportion of the overall search strategy. However, the user still has to understand which elements are platform-specific, identify the closest equivalent in the other database and manually edit their query, all of which is laborious and time consuming [3].

Since 2dSearch uses a visual framework that is database-agnostic, it raises the prospect of a universal language for search strategy formulation, in which information needs can be articulated in a generic manner, and the task of mapping to the semantics of an underlying database can be delegated to platform-specific adapters. Evidently, this is an ambitious goal, since some search strategies will always require human judgement for accurate translation [3]. However, a significant proportion of the translation process is routine in nature and is thus amenable to some form of automated support [19].

2dSearch already provides elementary support for search strategy translation in the form of a 'Messages' tab on the results pane. This serves a similar purpose to a console or messages pane in a software IDE, alerting the user to compilation issues and offering advice, fixes and workarounds. For example, if the user tries to execute a query string using Bing containing operators specific to Google, an alert is shown and the unknown operators are listed in the 'Messages' tab. In due course, this mechanism could be extended to offer a greater degree of interactive support for the translation of strategies across databases. Moreover, 2dSearch also offers the potential for search strategy optimisation through the elimination of redundant structure (eg. spurious brackets or duplicate elements) and comparison of canonical representations.

4 IMPLEMENTATION

2dSearch is implemented as a web app using Vue.js[4] and other Javascript libraries. User authentication is provided via Auth0[5] and persistence of search strategies and other user data is implemented using MongoDB.[6] Query suggestions are provided via an NLP services API which utilises various Python NLP libraries (for user authentication, word embedding, keyword extraction, etc.) and SPARQL endpoints (for linked open data ontology lookup)[21]. The NLP API is deployed via Digital Ocean[7], and the production instance of the 2dSearch client is deployed via Heroku.[8]

2dSearch offers utility to anyone who needs to create search strategies that are comprehensive, repeatable, and transparent. This includes applications in digital libraries, healthcare, legal research, media monitoring, patent search and recruitment/sourcing [19]. In practice, many of these would entail the development of additional, specialist adapters to support custom database integration. However, the profession for whom the benefit may be greatest is (arguably) healthcare information professionals, due to the strict governance and reporting requirements of systematic literature review. In this context, our current integration with PubMed offers immediate utility, particularly with its ability to visualise, save and share components as reusable, executable building blocks, and the potential for semi-automated strategy translation and optimisation.

5 SUMMARY AND FURTHER WORK

2dSearch is a framework for search strategy formulation in which queries are expressed by combining objects on a two-dimensional canvas. Transforming logical structure into visual layout provides a more direct mapping between the underlying semantics and the physical appearance. This helps to eliminate syntax errors, makes the query semantics more transparent and offers new ways to optimise, save and share search strategies.

We currently provide adapters for Google, Google Scholar, Bing and PubMed, the latter of which offers immediate utility to anyone wishing to search MEDLINE in a systematic manner. In due course, other adapters will be provided, but in the short term we would hope to engage in a formal, user-centric evaluation of 2dSearch, particularly in relation to traditional 'line-by line' query builders. We are currently engaging in an outreach programme with the healthcare information community and we welcome feedback of any sort. We hope to work with domain experts in building repositories of curated (or user generated) content in the form of best practice examples and templates.

Adopting a database-agnostic approach presents challenges, but it also offers the prospect of a universal framework for search strategy formulation in which information needs can be articulated in a generic manner and the task of mapping to the semantics of an underlying database can be delegated to platform-specific adapters. If that transpires to be a practicable proposition, then such a development could have profound implications for the way in which professional search skills are taught, learnt and applied.

[4]https://vuejs.org
[5]https://auth0.com
[6]https://www.mongodb.com
[7]https://www.digitalocean.com
[8]https://www.heroku.com

REFERENCES

[1] P. G. Anick, J. D. Brennan, R. A. Flynn, D. R. Hanssen, B. Alvey, and J. M. Robbins. 1990. A Direct Manipulation Interface for Boolean Information Retrieval via Natural Language Query. In *Proceedings of the 13th Annual International ACM SIGIR Conference on Research and Development in Information Retrieval (SIGIR '90)*. ACM, New York, NY, USA, 135–150. https://doi.org/10.1145/96749.98015

[2] H. Bastian, P. Glasziou, and I. Chalmers. 2010. Seventy-Five Trials and Eleven Systematic Reviews a Day: How Will We Ever Keep Up? *PLoS Med* 7, 9 (2010). https://doi.org/10.1371/journal.pmed.1000326

[3] W. M. Bramer, M. L. Rethlefsen, J. Kleijnen, and O. H. Franco. 2017. Optimal Database Combinations for Literature Searches in Systematic Reviews: A Prospective Exploratory Study. *Systematic Reviews* 6, 245 (2017). https://doi.org/10.1186/s13643-017-0644-y

[4] K. Bullers, A. M. Howard, A. Hanson, W. D. Kearns, J. J. Orriola, R. L. Polo, and K. A. Sakmar. 2018. It Takes Longer Than You Think: Librarian Time Spent on Systematic Review Tasks. *Journal of the Medical Library Association (JMLA)* 106, 2 (2018), 198–207. https://doi.org/10.5195/jmla.2018.323

[5] J. H. Elliott, T. Turner, O. Clavisi, J. Thomas, J. P. T. Higgins, C. Mavergames, and R. L. Gruen. 2014. Living Systematic Reviews: An Emerging Opportunity to Narrow the Evidence-Practice Gap. *PLoS Med* 11, 2 (18 Feb. 2014). https://doi.org/10.1371/journal.pmed.1001603

[6] E. Evangelou, T. A. Trikalinos, and J. P. Ioannidis. 2005. Unavailability of Online Supplementary Scientific Information From Articles Published in Major Journals. *FASEB Journal: Official publication of the Federation of American Societies for Experimental Biology* 19, 14 (2005), 1943–4. https://doi.org/10.1096/fj.05-4784lsf

[7] C. M. Faggion Jr, R. Huivin, L. Aranda, N. Pandis, and M. Alarcon. 2018. The Search and Selection for Primary Studies in Systematic Reviews Published in Dental Journals Indexed in MEDLINE Was Not Fully Reproducible. *Journal of Clinical Epidemiology* 98 (2018), 53–61. https://doi.org/10.1016/j.jclinepi.2018.02.011

[8] K. Fishkin and M. C. Stone. 1995. Enhanced Dynamic Queries via Movable Filters. ACM Press, 415–420.

[9] Joseph H. Goldberg and Uday N. Gajendar. 2008. Graphical condition builder for facilitating database queries. *U.S. Patent No. 7,383,513. 3* (2008).

[10] P. Hemingway and N. Brereton. 2009. What is a Systematic Review? http://www.bandolier.org.uk/painres/download/whatis/Syst-review.pdf

[11] S. Jones. 1998. Graphical Query Specification and Dynamic Result Previews for a Digital Library. In *Proceedings of the 11th Annual ACM Symposium on User Interface Software and Technology (UIST '98)*. ACM, New York, NY, USA, 143–151. https://doi.org/10.1145/288392.288595

[12] S. Karimi, S. Pohl, F. Scholer, L. Cavedon, and J. Zobel. 2010. Boolean Versus Ranked Querying for Biomedical Systematic Reviews. *BMC Med Inform Decis Mak* 10, 58 (2010). https://doi.org/10.1186/1472-6947-10-58

[13] J. B. Koffel and M. L. Rethlefsen. 2016. Reproducibility of Search Strategies Is Poor in Systematic Reviews Published in High-Impact Pediatrics, Cardiology and Surgery Journals: A Cross-Sectional Study. *PloS One* 11, 9 (2016). https://doi.org/10.1371/journal.pone.0163309

[14] Z. Lu. 2011. PubMed and Beyond: A Survey of Web Tools for Searching Biomedical Literature. *Database* 2011 (2011). https://doi.org/10.1093/database/baq036

[15] M. M. Mullins, J. B. DeLuca, N. Crepaz, and C. M. Lyles. 2014. Reporting Quality of Search Methods in Systematic Reviews of HIV Behavioral Interventions (2000-2010): Are The Searches Clearly Explained, Systematic and Reproducible? *Research Synthesis Methods* 5, 2 (2014), 116–30. https://doi.org/10.1002/jrsm.1098

[16] M. Nitsche and A. Nürnberger. 2006. QUEST: Querying Complex Information by Direct Manipulation. *In: Yamamoto S. (eds) Human Interface and the Management of Information. Information and Interaction Design. HIMI 2013. Lecture Notes in Computer Science* 8016 (2006).

[17] A. Price, S. Schroter, M. Clarke, and H. McAneney. 2018. Role of Supplementary Material in Biomedical Journal Articles: Surveys of Authors, Reviewers and Readers. *BMJ Open* 8, 9 (2018). https://doi.org/10.1136/bmjopen-2018-021753

[18] T. Russell-Rose and J. Chamberlain. 2016. Searching for talent: The information retrieval challenges of recruitment professionals. *Business Information Review* 33, 1 (2016), 40–48. https://doi.org/10.1177/0266382116631849

[19] T. Russell-Rose and J. Chamberlain. 2017. Expert Search Strategies: The Information Retrieval Practices of Healthcare Information Professionals. *JMIR Med Inform* 5, 4 (02 Oct 2017), e33. https://doi.org/10.2196/medinform.7680

[20] T. Russell-Rose, J. Chamberlain, and L. Azzopardi. 2018. Information Retrieval in the Workplace: A Comparison of Professional Search Practices. *Information Processing & Management* 54, 6 (2018), 1042–1057. https://doi.org/10.1016/j.ipm.2018.07.003

[21] T. Russell-Rose and P. Gooch. 2018. 2dSearch: A Visual Approach to Search Strategy Formulation. In *Proceedings of DESIRES: Design of Experimental Search Information REtrieval Systems* (28-31 August 2018) *(DESIRES 2018)*.

[22] A. A. Saleh, M. A. Ratajeski, and J. Ladue. 2014. Development of a Web-based Repository for Sharing Biomedical Terminology From Systematic Review Searches: A Case Study. *Medical Reference Services Quarterly* 33, 2 (2014), 167–78. https://doi.org/10.1080/02763869.2014.897518

[23] H. Tang and J. H. K. Ng. 2006. Googling for a Diagnosis—Use of Google as a Diagnostic Aid: Internet Based Study. *BMJ* 333, 7579 (2006), 1143–1145. https://doi.org/10.1136/bmj.39003.640567.AE

[24] J. S. Yi, R. Melton, J. Stasko, and J. A. Jacko. 2005. Dust & Magnet: Multivariate Information Visualization Using a Magnet Metaphor. *Information Visualization* 4, 4 (Oct. 2005), 239–256. https://doi.org/10.1057/palgrave.ivs.9500099

Analysing Qualitative Data

You Asked Them, Now What to Do with What They Said

Rebekah Willson
Department of Computer & Information Sciences
University of Strathclyde
Glasgow, Scotland
rebekah.willson@strath.ac.uk

ABSTRACT

This half-day tutorial is for researchers who are relatively new to qualitative research; it will include discussion and provide hands-on experience of analysing qualitative data. The tutorial will begin with a discussion about qualitative research and data and then discuss some major qualitative data analysis methodologies, centring on thematic analysis. The focus of the tutorial will be on how to systematically use these data analysis methodologies to deal with qualitative data from interviews, surveys, and other textual sources. Tutorial participants will be provided with example an example interview and provided with opportunities to try out coding (a main method of qualitative data analysis) and discuss ways that they might be able to make use of these approaches in their own research.

KEYWORDS

Qualitative data; Data analysis; Thematic analysis

ACM Reference format:

Rebekah Willson. 2019. Analysing Qualitative Data: You Asked Them, Now What to Do with What They Said. In *Proceedings of the ACM SIGIR Conference on Human Information Interaction and Retrieval (CHIIR'19). ACM, Glasgow, Scotland, UK,* ACM, New York, NY, USA, 3 pages.
DOI: https://doi.org/10.1145/3295750.3298933

1 Introduction

One of the ways to "understand how people interact with information and the consequences of those interactions" - part of the scope for the CHIIR 2019 conference - is to speak directly with the people using and interacting with that information. Qualitative data is not only able to get at how people think and feel and understanding, but it also provides in-depth and weighty data that would not otherwise be available. However, counting instances or utterances can result in missing much of the richness that comes from speaking to people, including unanticipated answers and broader meanings.

ACM ISBN 978-1-4503-6025-8/19/03.
https://doi.org/10.1145/3295750.3298964

In order to fully make use of qualitative data - which is challenging to gather and messy to analyse - this tutorial will explore the use of coding to analyse qualitative data. This includes an in-depth discussion of qualitative data analysis methodologies and the provision of a hands-on opportunity to try out one analytical methodology. At the beginning of the tutorial, participants will be given a portion from an interview for analysis. They will be asked to read the section at the start of the tutorial with the knowledge that the tutorial will end with them coding the interview in pairs or small groups. This interview will be referred to throughout the tutorial and will provide a concrete reference for the concepts discussed, in addition to examples from the presenter.

2 Deductive and Inductive Approaches

Qualitative data analysis can be approached deductively or inductively. Mostly commonly associated with the scientific method, deduction begins with a theory and seeks evidence to test that theory (in order to confirm or disconfirm). A deductive (or 'top down') approach is particularly useful for phenomena that have been previously researched and/or theorized. It is also particularly useful in mixed methods research, where quantitative and qualitative research are used in the same study. Induction begins with evidence and seeks to build theories, explanations, or interpretations that explain the particular aspects of evidence [7]. This is done by developing concepts - including categories or themes, statements of relationship, and theories - based on a close examination of the data [7]. These developments move from the concrete (explanations of particular events) to the abstract (theories that explain the data) [7]. Abstraction is a key feature of induction. An inductive (or 'bottom up') approach, as it is exploratory, is particularly useful for phenomena that have little previous research and that are not well understood. The focus of inductive analysis is using evidence to create theories means that the understandings and explanations of the data are grounded in the data.

For many researchers, induction is a different approach to research that may not fit with their understanding of the scientific method. So, how does one ensure that the data is accurately represented? If all you have are the words people say, how is it more than just subjective analysis? These questions and concerns will be addressed by discussing the nature of qualitative research. Part of the answer is acknowledging that by speaking to people, we get a different type of data that is different and challenging to analyse. Dealing with textual data is not the same as dealing with numerical data and, therefore, the same rules cannot be applied. Part of the answer is that there are rigorous methodologies for qualitative data analysis that, when followed, lead to high quality data analysis, which are discussed in a later section.

3 Qualitative Codes and Coding

Central to this tutorial is a discussion about what codes and coding are and what they involve. It is important to have these discussions not only because coding is one of the main methods of analysis of textual data, but also because they are frequently used with little discussion of what codes refer to or what the process of coding actually entails. Codes will be described as concepts, which are identified through explicit criteria, and coding as the process of generating concepts, ideas, and categories from data, which are identified and then arranged in a systematic way [2]. Coding identifies interesting aspects of the data – events, behaviour, features, processes – and then provides those aspects with labels [2]. These labels are the beginnings of codes. In working with the data, the labels are combined to include similar instances or separated to ensure the descriptions are differentiated [2]. Codes begin to take shape. Through the process, notes – often referred to as a codebook – should be kept that include codes, their definitions, and criteria for inclusion and exclusion. This codebook will evolve over time. Codebooks will be described and an example of what codebooks look like will be presented from the presenter's own research.

The iterative nature of coding will be discussed. Typically, two rounds of coding take place. The tutorial will discuss both initial and focused coding. Initial coding is done to make sense of the data, going through a transcript line-by-line and identifying as many concepts as possible [2]. The focal point is on identifying actions [4] and answering questions such as what is going on? How is it taking place? What is meaning? [2]. Throughout initial coding, repeated concepts emerge, as well as variations; coding should take place until nothing new emerges [2].

Next, focused coding will be discussed. Focused coding is moving from identifying concepts in a line-by-line fashion and beginning to refining and integrating codes identified [2]. The codes should be unique and have explanatory power. In examining the results of initial coding, important concepts can be identified, and broader and more abstract concepts will emerge. By iteratively examining the codes, links and relationships also begin to become clear [2]. As the level of abstraction increases, codes can them be grouped into themes, or recurring ideas that pervade the data set. Themes are the overarching ideas that encompass what the data tells us. Tutorial participants will be given examples of the process of both initial and focused coding.

An important part of coding is the rigour involved in the process. Discussions will take place about the quality of data analysis requiring iterative analyses, looking for negative cases, data triangulation, and the use of evidence to support explanations and theories [6]. In particular, inter-coder reliability will be discussed, which is the process of comparing the coding done by individuals. Coders work together and discuss codes and put together a common codebook. Coders then work on their own and compare their coding agreement. A reliability coefficient of .60 is acceptable for qualitative data analysis [6].

4 Qualitative Data Analysis Methodologies

After codes and coding are discussed, different qualitative data analysis methodologies will be presented. There are many different ways to approach qualitative data analysis. However, what they share is a framework that guides the researcher through the process of analysis. Like statistical tests, different approaches are used for different types of data and with different approaches to the data. When these data analysis methodologies are followed, high quality data analysis takes place. Several commonly used qualitative data analysis methodologies will be presented, including qualitative content analysis [5, 6], grounded theory [4], and thematic analysis [1, 3]. Different qualitative research methodologies are suited to either deductive or inductive approaches, which will be discussed.

4.1 Thematic Analysis

While several different methodologies will be presented, the focus will be on thematic analysis. Thematic analysis, which can be approached deductively or inductively, is a "method for identifying, analysing and reporting patterns (themes) within data" and that provides interpretation of that data [3, p. 79]. Braun and Clark [3] have described this method in detail, which they have encapsulated in 6 steps:

1. Familiarize yourself with your data
2. Generating initial codes
3. Searching for themes
4. Reviewing themes
5. Defining and naming themes
6. Producing the report [p. 87]

While these steps involve complicated action, they are clear and straightforward, making thematic analysis a useful methodology to begin using for qualitative data analysis. The discussion of thematic analysis will end with an example of how data can be analysed using thematic analysis, talking through each step of the process and how decisions were made. This example will serve as a guide for participants when trying hands-on coding.

5 Hands-On Coding

The last hour and a half of this tutorial will be a chance for participants to analyse qualitative data in pairs or small groups. Participants will be given the opportunity to code the published article they received at the beginning of the tutorial using thematic analysis. Using the thematic analysis guidelines outlined by Braun and Clark [3], tutorial participants will have 45-60 minutes to inductively code the data. This will be followed by a discussion of what themes were identified, what worked well during the analysis process, challenges in carrying out qualitative coding, questions about the process, and considerations for use in participants' own research.

6 Facilitator

Dr Rebekah Willson is a lecturer in information science in the Department of Computer and Information Science at the University of Strathclyde. Dr Willson's research focuses on information behavior. Her previous research projects have involved university students' information retrieval in online catalogues, digital humanists' use of technology in their work, pre-school children's use of technology at home and school, grape growers' and wine producers' use of information, and early career academics' information behaviour as they transition in the workplace. Trained in a variety of research methods, Dr Willson has undertaken quantitative, qualitative, and mixed-method research projects, specializing in inductive research projects using constructivist grounded theory methodology.

REFERENCES

[1] L. Ayres (2008). Thematic Coding and Analysis. *The SAGE Encyclopedia of Qualitative Research Methods.* DOI:https://doi.org/10.4135/9781412963909.n451

[2] L. Benaquisto (2008). Codes and Coding. *The SAGE Encyclopedia of Qualitative Research Methods.* DOI:https://doi.org/10.4135/9781412963909.n48

[3] V. Braun and V. Clarke (2006). Using thematic analysis in psychology. *Qualitative Research in Psychology* 3(2), 77–101. DOI:https://doi.org/10.1191/1478088706qp063oa

[4] K. Charmaz (2006). Constructing grounded theory: A practical guide through qualitative analysis. Sage Publications Inc, Thousand Oaks, CA.

[5] J. Drisko and T. Maschi, 2015 Qualitative content analysis. In *Content Analysis.* Oxford University Press. DOI:https://doi.org/10.1093/acprof:oso/9780190215491.001.0001

[6] H. Julien (2008). Content Analysis. *The SAGE Encyclopedia of Qualitative Research Methods,* 121–122. DOI:https://doi.org/10.4135/9781412963909.n65

[7] J. Preissle (2008). Analytic Induction. *The SAGE Encyclopedia of Qualitative Research Methods.* DOI:https://doi.org/10.4135/9781412963909.n10

Workshop on Barriers to Interactive IR Resources Re-use (BIIRRR 2019)

Toine Bogers
Aalborg University Copenhagen
Denmark
toine@hum.aau.dk

Samuel Dodson
University of British Columbia
Canada
dodsons@mail.ubc.ca

Luanne Freund
University of British Columbia
Canada
luanne.freund@ubc.ca

Maria Gäde
Humboldt-Universität zu Berlin
Germany
maria.gaede@ibi.hu-berlin.de

Mark Hall
Martin-Luther-Universität
Halle-Wittenberg
Germany
mark.hall@informatik.uni-halle.de

Marijn Koolen
Royal Netherlands Academy of Arts and Sciences
Netherlands
marijn.koolen@di.huc.knaw.nl

Vivien Petras
Humboldt-Universität zu Berlin
Germany
vivien.petras@ibi.hu-berlin.de

Nils Pharo
Oslo Metropolitan University
Norway
nils.pharo@oslomet.no

Mette Skov
Aalborg University
Denmark
skov@hum.aau.dk

CCS CONCEPTS

• **Information systems → Users and interactive retrieval**; • **General and reference →** *Empirical studies*; *Evaluation*;

KEYWORDS

IIR, re-use, secondary use, research design

ACM Reference Format:
Toine Bogers, Samuel Dodson, Luanne Freund, Maria Gäde, Mark Hall, Marijn Koolen, Vivien Petras, Nils Pharo, and Mette Skov. 2019. Workshop on Barriers to Interactive IR Resources Re-use (BIIRRR 2019). In *2019 Conference on Human Information Interaction and Retrieval (CHIIR '19), March 10–14, 2019, Glasgow, United Kingdom.* ACM, New York, NY, USA, 4 pages. https://doi.org/10.1145/3295750.3298965

1 DESCRIPTION

What would be the equivalent of a re-usable TREC test collection for the interactive information retrieval (IIR) community? The goal of the BIIRRR 2019 workshop is to answer this question by continuing existing community-driven efforts to design and implement a platform for the collection, organization, maintenance, and sharing of resources for IIR experimentation. These efforts developed out of discussions at the CHIIR 2017 workshop on Supporting Complex Search Tasks (SCST 2017) [1] and were expanded upon during the BIIRRR workshop at CHIIR 2018 [2, 3].

The IR community has a strong tradition of making research data of system-based experimentation available for re-use, as exemplified by the development of test collections and shared tasks in large-scale initiatives such as TREC, CLEF, NTCIR, and FIRE. These efforts have had significant benefits for the IR community, in particular enabling the re-use of aspects of the test collections or shared tasks in other IR research. Comparable efforts have been undertaken to bring this paradigm to IIR research, such as the TREC Interactive and Session tracks, the INEX Interactive track, and the Interactive Social Book Search track. The high degree of variation between IIR studies, however, has meant that none of these have achieved similar degrees of standardisation and re-use. It seems that the traditional shared task structure is not successful in inducing re-use in IIR. Instead the equivalent type and level of re-use is more likely to be achieved through increased sharing of research designs, enabling better comparability, more transparent reporting, and greater methodological standards and rigour.

As stated above, IIR research exhibits a large variety of research designs and methods[11]. This methodological diversity and richness needs to be investigated to identify ways of representing these research materials and also to develop an understanding of how and when researchers currently re-use or would like to find and re-use materials. The workshop environment is the most appropriate venue to gather information and input from the IIR community regarding the kind of methods used, their experiences with both re-using materials and making materials available for re-use, and ideas on how to move towards increased sharing and re-use. The organizers already represent a wide range of IIR research perspectives, but to achieve the goal of encouraging re-use a high degree of community input and commitment is needed.

The goal of of the 2nd edition of the BIIRRR workshop is to provide an interactive forum to address relevant questions around re-use of IIR materials. At the BIIRRR 2018 workshop a number of high-level focus areas were identified [3]. To make further progress on these issues, the focus of the 2019 edition will be on the following five topics:

- **Terminology** The terms used in IIR studies, their definitions, and origins.

CHIIR '19, March 10–14, 2019, Glasgow, United Kingdom

ACM ISBN 978-1-4503-6025-8/19/03.
https://doi.org/10.1145/3295750.3298965

- **Research design** The overall research design structures and patterns employed and their potential for re-use.
- **Methodology** General and specific methodologies employed in IIR studies, their origins, and their re-use.
- **Resources** Existing resources re-used as part of IIR studies, how to find them, and issues with re-using them.
- **Reporting** What and how to document aspects of IIR studies to maximise the potential for re-use.

BIIRRR 2019 will provide a highly interactive venue to address these topics, combining short paper presentations with breakout groups. For the presentations we invite short contributions in which authors analyze one of their previously published IIR studies in the context of the five topics listed above. The contributions will be presented in themed sessions in the morning to introduce ideas and potential pitfalls for re-use. The afternoon will then pick up these ideas and discuss them in more depth in breakout groups based around the five themes. The workshop will conclude with a reporting and discussion session as well as planning future activities. This interactive format has proven to be very fruitful in the past at the SCST 2017 and BIIRRR 2018 workshops, acting as the springboard for publications, tools, and funding proposals.

2 RELATED EFFORTS

There have been several successful gatherings directed toward addressing the need for considering how to collect, organize, maintain, and share research resources for conducting IIR experiments. IIR campaigns on this topic include the TREC Interactive Track (1997–2002) [12], the INEX Interactive Track (2004–2010) [13, 14], the Cultural Heritage in CLEF (CHiC) Interactive Task (2013) [15], and the interactive Social Book Search (iSBS) task (2014-2016) [7–9] which provided great insight into the challenges and opportunities for long-term, re-usable IIR research materials.

While these demonstrate the ongoing interest in standardising the evaluation of IIR studies [11], they also show that establishing and maintaining a collaborative platform for the re-use of IIR research instruments is still an open issue. This is due to the complexity of IIR studies, which require a combination of system- and user-centered evaluation approaches [10]. In addition to the tasks and document collections that are needed and provided in most shared tasks, participants, search contexts, tasks, processes, systems, data sets, and evaluation measures all need to be modeled to enable re-use for IIR studies. Building on this work, a subset of this workshop's organizers are currently in the process of analyzing past IIR studies (published at IIiX and CHIIR) for re-use, from which an initial analysis has been submitted as a short paper to CHIIR 2019.

There have been efforts to collect and make available some of these IIR research components. The Repository of Assigned Search Tasks (RepAST)[1] collects, analyzes, and shares search tasks taken from publications of IIR studies. RepAST contains bibliographic data and abstracts from approximately 750 published papers, as well as a list of author-identified search task types (e.g., complex, simple, subject, known-item, factual), and the full text of any assigned search tasks reported in the papers [5]. As such, RepAST serves as a library of tasks. Members of the IIR community are encouraged to compare and contrast task descriptions as well as reuse the tasks in the collection. While RepAST is valuable, it has been underutilized to date, likely due to a lack of awareness.

Issues related to re-use have also been discussed at various workshops, including the Supporting Complex Search Tasks (SCST) workshops in 2015 and 2017 [1, 6], which were organized based on the experiences of running the iSBS shared task. In particular, the discussions at the popular SCST 2017 workshop (co-located with CHIIR 2017) identified a strong desire within the IIR community to address the issues around re-use. This led to the BIIRRR 2018 workshop at CHIIR 2018, which focused exclusively on the re-use issue and was very productive, resulting in the publication of a research paper [3], as well as a grant proposal, and spawned several informal follow-up meetings. It also served as a starting point for a concrete, community-driven effort focused on the challenges and opportunities for designing and implementing a platform for the collection, organization, maintenance, and sharing of resources for IIR experimentation. The BIIRRR 2019 workshop aims to build upon the organisers' experience in running highly interactive workshops that produce concrete outcomes for the IIR community—at least one of this workshop's organisers was involved in each of the previous workshops. The goal is to provide a forum for exchanging experiences with undertaking and documenting IIR studies and then discussing how these can be structured in a platform for IIR re-use.

3 CALL FOR PAPERS

In order to incorporate the community's experience we invite original contributions in the form of *experience papers* that detail methodological and re-use aspects of previously published or in-press IIR studies. Rather than focus on research questions and results, *experience papers* should focus on the following aspects of IIR studies, which are generally under-reported in scientific publications:

- **Terminology** What terminology did you use to describe the different components of the study? Why did you choose this terminology? How did you develop this terminology?
- **Methodology** What overarching and specific methodologies did you employ in the study? How did you decide which methodologies to employ? Examples of overarching methodologies include qualitative/quantitative/mixed methods, theory/practice/design, distant/close reading, big data/small data. Specific methods include, for instance, log studies, eye tracking, A/B testing, and simulated work tasks.
- **Research designs** What research design(s) did you use? Which (aspects) of these have the potential to be re-used? To capture the variation within the IIR field, we use the broad definition of research designs from Cheek [4]: *"the way in which a research idea is transformed into a research project or plan that can then be carried out in practice by a researcher or research team".*
- **Re-use** What previously created materials did you re-use? This can cover all aspects, such as research designs, software, interfaces, data, scales, and specific survey questions. How did you decide what to re-use? How did you discover the materials that you re-used? Which problems did you encounter searching for them?

[1] https://ils.unc.edu/searchtasks/search.php

- **Documentation** What aspects of your study could be re-used and how have you documented and represented them to enable re-use? What aspects were fully documented in your publication? What aspects do you feel should be documented outside the main publication?

We invite contributions from both early career and established academics to develop a well-rounded picture of the challenges and rewards of sharing and re-using aspects of IIR studies at different stages in the academic career path.

3.1 Important dates

- **First call for participation:** November 19, 2018
- **Submission deadline:** January 18, 2019
- **Notification of acceptance:** February 4, 2019
- **Camera-ready deadline:** February 18, 2019
- **Workshop at CHIIR 2019:** March 14, 2019

4 WORKSHOP ACTIVITIES

Like the 2018 edition, BIIRRR 2019 will be a highly interactive, full-day workshop, which will combine accepted presentations, discussion lead-ins, and break-out discussions. We will start the day with a full round of introductions of all participants, asking them to identify their interest in the workshop. The morning program will contain up to 10 presentations of accepted *experience papers*, divided over two paper sessions, organized to elicit more interaction and discussion. Each paper session will contain up to five papers and will follow the same format: each paper will be presented (10 minutes), followed by brief clarifying questions (3 minutes) about it while the next presenter sets up. During the last 20 minutes of the session, the session moderator will introduce and moderate a panel discussion among the presenters to probe the experiences and interplay of the presented work and positions. Each presenter will be asked in advance to prepare at least one question about the other papers. The afternoon is organized around two break-out sessions dedicated to discussion of the five workshop themes introduced in Section 3. The workshop will close with a concrete mission statement and a clear plan for future work in this area.

The workshop targets a broad audience of researchers at any level of their academic careers, working in IIR as well as related fields dealing with heterogeneous research designs. In order to achieve this, we plan to directly target experienced researchers in the field and encourage them to submit their own work and also get their doctoral and post-doctoral researchers to contribute. We expect around 10-15 paper submissions, and have room to accept 8-10. To enable an interactive workshop where everyone is involved, we aim to have 25-30 participants with breakout groups of 6-8 people—thereby broadening the scope compared to the 2018 edition of the BIIRRR workshop.

4.1 Tentative workshop program

The workshop is planned as a **full-day** workshop with a tentative program shown below:

- **Introduction**
  - Short introductions by participants (all participants)
  - Introduction of workshop purpose, goals and planned activities (workshop leads)
  - Presentation of analysis of IIR research at previous IIiX and CHIIR conferences (workshop leads)
- **Paper session 1**
  - Presentation of 4-5 experience papers with 10 mins for presentation and 3 mins for clarification questions
  - Panel discussion between the paper presenters and the audience about the sessions' experience papers
- **Coffee break**
- **Paper session 2**
  - Presentation of 4-5 experience papers with 10 mins for presentation and 3 mins for clarification questions
  - Panel discussion between the paper presenters and the audience about the sessions' experience papers
- **Lunch break**
- **Break-out session 1**
  - Introduction to break-out round 1
  - Break-out discussions round centered around the five workshop themes
  - Feedback round: feedback from each break-out group (all participants)
- **Coffee break**
- **Break-out session 2**
  - Introduction to break-out round 2
  - Break-out discussions round centered around the five workshop themes
  - Feedback round: feedback from each break-out group (all participants)
- **Closing**
  - Summary of insights (workshop leads)
  - Discussion & task assignment for next steps (all participants)
  - Collaborative composition & publication of closing statement (workshop leads)

The break-out discussions will have smaller groups, organized around the five workshop themes. We will gauge interest in the different themes from the workshop participants before the start of the workshop and this, together with the interests identified in the short introductions by all participants, will be used to assign participants to the break-out discussions. This should allow us to ensure that each break-out group represents different experience levels and also research backgrounds, with the aim of ensuring that the results from the break-out groups' discussions are as representative as possible.

Written comments and minutes for the workshop will be solicited through a shared document, which will be continuously updated throughout the workshop and which will be available from the workshop website. Via this document, Twitter, and other available social media channels, interested IIR researchers may participate remotely if they cannot attend the workshop in person.

5 DESIRED OUTCOMES & CONTINUING ACTIVITIES

The 2018 edition of the BIIRRR workshop defined five working areas to move the discussion on IIR resource re-use forward [3], one of them being a discussion of the aspects of research designs—more broadly the diversity of methodological approaches employed by the community. BIIRRR 2019 is designed around developing specific requirements and activities to move this area forward.

One of the main outcomes of BIIRRR 2019 will therefore be a set of requirements on *terminology*, *methodology*, and *research designs* that will be developed in the breakout groups, drawing on the experience paper presentations, the results of the IIR re-use survey conducted in the context of BIIRRR 2018, and an ongoing analysis of IIR studies. The focus of the outcome is on producing concrete requirements that can directly feed into the development of the so-called *iRepository*—a long-term repository of research designs and components used in IIR research. The aim is not to produce a definitive, final set of requirements, but an initial set of requirements that form the baseline from which to develop and then further evolve the *iRepository*.

The second outcome will be a set of principles around the themes of *re-use* and *documentation*, which will provide specific guidelines on how the requirements for the three themes listed above are to be integrated into the iRepository to enable realistic re-use. The two outcomes will be published in a short report on the workshop website, followed by a more detailed SIGIR Forum publication, to ensure wide-spread dissemination within the IR community and to encourage engagement with the development of the iRepository.

The central aspect of these two initial outcomes is that they will enable follow-up events to have a solid foundation from which to continue, rather than having to re-invent the wheel each time. As part of this—and to ensure that the workshop's momentum is maintained—we propose setting up a public mailing list. This will not only allow the discussions to continue after the workshop completes, it will also enable researchers who could not attend the workshop to engage in the discussion, increasing the likelihood that the workshop achieves its aims.

In addition to these short-term outcomes, a community-wide repository requires a certain amount of discussion and coordination of all its development. To achieve this, we envision a more extensive activity, such as a Dagstuhl-style seminar, which will provide the time to discuss the requirements and solutions in more detail. In parallel to that, smaller hackathon-style events could be organized that focus on developing technical solutions for aspects of the problem. From our experience with the BIIRRR 2018 outcomes, these tend to form organically around existing conferences in the field, and the aim here is to increase the structure and planning of these events to encourage wider participation.

Finally, as part of this workshop, participants will also be invited to commit to participating in or leading some of the iRepository development activities. The aim of this is to encourage wider community participation in this process, but also to enable participants to organically form into interest groups with a view towards potential grant applications in their area of interest, as was an unplanned—but very welcome—outcome of the BIIRRR 2018 workshop.

To achieve these outcomes, wide dissemination to the community is a key activity, in particular to maintain momentum directly after the workshop. We propose to provide more dissemination activities on the workshop website directly after its completion. The main focus of this will initially be a short statement of intent that is produced and discussed at the end of the workshop and published within a few days of the workshop. This statement of intent will not be comprehensive, but indicate the direction of the initiative and providing a point of reference that participants can state their commitment to. This will be followed by the more extensive report and SIGIR Forum contribution described above. Long-term we are aiming for an article in an appropriate journal to articulate our vision, detail the knowledge gained from the BIIRRR 2018 survey, workshop outcomes, results of the IIR study re-use analysis, and the concrete, practical frameworks developed based on the workshops' results.

REFERENCES

[1] Nicholas Belkin, Toine Bogers, Jaap Kamps, Diane Kelly, Marijn Koolen, and Emine Yilmaz. 2017. Second Workshop on Supporting Complex Search Tasks. In *Proc CHIIR 2017*. ACM, New York, NY, 433–435.

[2] Toine Bogers, Maria Gäde, Luanne Freund, Mark Hall, Marijn Koolen, Vivien Petras, and Mette Skov. 2018. Workshop on Barriers to Interactive IR Resources Re-use. In *Proc CHIIR 2018*. ACM, New York, NY, 382–385.

[3] Toine Bogers, Maria Gäde, Mark Hall, Luanne Freund, Marijn Koolen, Vivien Petras, and Mette Skov. 2018. Report on the Workshop on Barriers to Interactive IR Resources Re-use (BIIRRR 2018). *SIGIR Forum* 52, 1 (Aug. 2018), 119–128.

[4] Julianne Cheek. 2008. Research design. In *The SAGE Encyclopedia of Qualitative Research Methods*, Lisa M. Given (Ed.). SAGE.

[5] Luanne Freund and Barbara M. Wildemuth. 2014. Documenting and studying the use of assigned search tasks: RepAST. *Proceedings of the American Society for Information Science and Technology* 51, 1 (2014), 1–4.

[6] Maria Gäde, Mark M. Hall, Hugo Huurdeman, Jaap Kamps, Marijn Koolen, Mette Skove, Elaine Toms, and David Walsh. 2015. Report on the First Workshop on Supporting Complex Search Tasks. *SIGIR Forum* 49, 1 (June 2015), 50–56.

[7] Maria Gäde, Mark Michael Hall, Hugo C. Huurdeman, Jaap Kamps, Marijn Koolen, Mette Skov, Toine Bogers, and David Walsh. 2016. Overview of the SBS 2016 Interactive Track. In *Working Notes of the CLEF 2016 Conference (CEUR Workshop Proceedings)*, Krisztian Balog, Linda Cappellato, Nicola Ferro, and Craig Macdonald (Eds.), Vol. 1609. CEUR-WS.org, 1024–1038.

[8] Maria Gäde, Mark Michael Hall, Hugo C. Huurdeman, Jaap Kamps, Marijn Koolen, Mette Skov, Elaine Toms, and David Walsh. 2015. Overview of the SBS 2015 Interactive Track. In *Working Notes of the CLEF 2015 Conference (CEUR Workshop Proceedings)*, Linda Cappellato, Nicola Ferro, Gareth J. F. Jones, and Eric SanJuan (Eds.), Vol. 1391. CEUR-WS.org.

[9] Mark Michael Hall, Hugo C. Huurdeman, Marijn Koolen, Mette Skov, and David Walsh. 2014. Overview of the INEX 2014 Interactive Social Book Search Track. In *Working Notes of the CLEF 2014 Conference (CEUR Workshop Proceedings)*, Linda Cappellato, Nicola Ferro, Martin Halvey, and Wessel Kraaij (Eds.), Vol. 1180. CEUR-WS.org, 480–493.

[10] Diane Kelly. 2009. Methods for Evaluating Interactive Information Retrieval Systems with Users. *Foundations and Trends in Information Retrieval* 3, 1–2 (2009), 1–224.

[11] Diane Kelly and Cassidy R Sugimoto. 2013. A Systematic Review of Interactive Information Retrieval Evaluation Studies, 1967–2006. *Journal of the American Society for Information Science and Technology* 64, 4 (2013), 745–770.

[12] Paul Over. 2001. The TREC Interactive Track: An Annotated Bibliography. *Information Processing & Management* 37, 3 (2001), 369–381.

[13] Nils Pharo, Thomas Beckers, Ragnar Nordlie, and Norbert Fuhr. 2011. Overview of the INEX 2010 Interactive Track. In *INEX '10: Proceedings of the Ninth International Workshop of the Initiative for the Evaluation of XML Retrieval*, Shlomo Geva, Jaap Kamps, Ralf Schenkel, and Andrew Trotman (Eds.). Springer, Berlin, Heidelberg, 227–235.

[14] Anastasios Tombros, Birger Larsen, and Saadia Malik. 2005. The Interactive Track at INEX 2004. In *INEX '04: Proceedings of the Third International Workshop of the Initiative for the Evaluation of XML Retrieval*, Norbert Fuhr, Mounia Lalmas, Saadia Malik, and Zoltán Szlávik (Eds.). Springer, Berlin, Heidelberg, 410–423.

[15] Elaine G. Toms and Mark M. Hall. 2013. The CHiC Interactive Task (CHiCi) at CLEF 2013. In *Working Notes of the CLEF 2013 Conference (CEUR Workshop Proceedings)*, Pamela Forner, Roberto Navigli, Dan Tufis, and Nicola Ferro (Eds.), Vol. 1179. CEUR-WS.org.

Second Workshop on Evaluation of Personalisation in Information Retrieval (WEPIR 2019)

Gareth J. F. Jones
ADAPT Centre, School of Computing
Dublin City University
Dublin 9, Ireland
Gareth.Jones@dcu.ie

Nicholas J. Belkin
School of Communication & Information
Rutgers University,
New Brunswick, NJ, USA
belkin@rutgers.edu

Séamus Lawless
ADAPT Centre, School of Computer Science & Statistics
Trinity College Dublin
Dublin, Ireland
seamus.lawless@scss.tcd.ie

Gabriella Pasi
Department of Informatics, Systems & Communication
University of Milano-Bicocca
Milan, Italy
pasi@disco.unimib.it

ABSTRACT

The second WEPIR 2019 workshop brings together researchers with different backgrounds interested in continuing to explore and advance the evaluation of personalisation in information retrieval. The workshop builds on the first WEPIR workshop held at CHIIR 2018, and will focus on further developing a common understanding of the challenges, requirements and practical limitations of meaningful evaluation of personalisation in information retrieval. In particular, the planned outcome of the workshop is to progress the work from WEPIR 2018 towards the development of concrete proposals for novel and innovative methodologies to support evaluation of personalised information retrieval from both the perspectives of the user experience in interactive search settings, and of user models for personalised information retrieval and their algorithmic incorporation in the search process.

CCS CONCEPTS

• **Information systems → Users and interactive retrieval**; **Personalization**; **Task models**; **Evaluation of retrieval results**; *Web searching and information discovery*; *Search interfaces*; *Retrieval tasks and goals*;

KEYWORDS

information retrieval, personalisation, user models, interaction, evaluation

ACM Reference Format:

Gareth J. F. Jones, Nicholas J. Belkin, Séamus Lawless, and Gabriella Pasi. 2019. Second Workshop on Evaluation of Personalisation in Information Retrieval (WEPIR 2019). In *2019 Conference on Human Information Interaction and Retrieval (CHIIR '19), March 10–14, 2019, Glasgow, Scotland Uk*. ACM, New York, NY, USA, Article 4, 4 pages. https://doi.org/10.1145/3295750.3298966

ACM ISBN 978-1-4503-6025-8/19/03.
https://doi.org/10.1145/3295750.3298966

1 INTRODUCTION

One of the key goals of information retrieval research is to advance the development of search applications which enable searchers to satisfy their information needs more effectively and efficiently. Given that the information need underlying their engagement with a search application relates to a personal need for information, it makes intuitive sense that in addition to the searcher's stated search request, a search application should make use of all available information about the searcher and the context in which the search is being carried out in order to return content most likely to be useful or relevant to this user.

Information relating to the user of a search application can be gathered from logs of their previous search activities, and also from monitoring their other online activities with various applications and their context. A user can also be requested to explicitly provide information to complete a personal profile. Given the very large amounts of information available from these different sources, an important research question is how to utilize it within the search process [3]. It might for example be used to populate personal profiles of characteristics and interests or more general user models, which can then be used within a personalised information retrieval application to return documents more likely to be relevant to the user than those returned by an equivalent, but not personalised search application.

There are many ways in which personal information might be modelled and represented within some form of user model and how this model might be used within the information retrieval process. In order to determine how best to implement a personalised information application, carefully planned evaluation strategies are required. These need to consider both the algorithmic aspects of the information retrieval process, and also the user-centered or interactive elements of search and the user experience of using a search application.

Evaluating the use of personalisation models in classic "single" shot information retrieval settings could amount to simply incorporating alternative personalisation models into the process for a given query. However, much more interesting is the incorporation of personalisation in session based settings incorporating multiple queries expressing the evolution of an information need as the searcher progresses through the session, and further the use of personalisation across multiple sessions where the user model is updated in response to developments in the searcher's interests. Evaluation in this setting is a highly complex problem.

The first WEPIR workshop at CHIIR 2018 brought together a group of interested researchers to open a broad discussion of the issues relating to the evaluation of personalised information retrieval applications within the CHIIR community. The WEPIR 2019 workshop will seek to extend the discussions from WEPIR 2018, as summarised in the WEPIR 2018 report in SIGIR Forum [6], to move towards more concrete proposals for evaluation methodologies, metrics, etc.

2 BACKGROUND

Prior to the WEPIR 2018 workshops, a number of current and earlier initiatives and workshops have focused on topics relevant to WEPIR. While each of these has aspects relevant to WEPIR 2019, none of them directly addresses the focus of WEPIR or encompasses the scope of this workshop.

The key relevant activity exploring this topic from the perspective of the user is the Interactive Track at the TREC conferences, which ran for twelve years [5], and is of relevance to this workshop for several reasons. One is that it developed methods for evaluating various aspects of system performance over entire search sessions, a crucial aspect of evaluation of personalisation. Another is that one of the main findings of this track was the difficulty, perhaps impossibility, of applying the general TREC/Cranfield evaluation model to the dynamic situation of interactive information retrieval, again, a key aspect of the personalisation situation.

More recently the TREC Session Track held from 2010 to 2014, sought to provide test collections and evaluation measures for studying information retrieval over user sessions with multiple stages of query reformulation rather than one-time queries. This track introduced modified evaluation metrics for session based search [7], but had the limitation that the information need was assumed to remain static for a query across the session.

The 2012 NII-Shonan Seminar on Whole-Session Evaluation of Interactive Information Retrieval Systems [2], and the 2013 Dagstuhl Seminar on Evaluation Methodologies in Information Retrieval [1], each addressed evaluation issues relevant to this workshop, including evaluation measures for entire search sessions, and user modeling for evaluation, but stopped short of the problem of evaluation of personalisation of information retrieval.

The recent interest in conversational information retrieval is also related to the topic of this workshop. The International Workshop on Conversational Approaches to Information Retrieval held at SIGIR 2017 and SIGIR 2018 addressed some personalisation issues, including system adaptation and clarification dialogues, but discussion of evaluation of such techniques was minimal.

Introduced at CLEF 2017, the Personalised Information Retrieval (PIR-CLEF) task is seeking to develop a framework for the repeatable evaluation of algorithms for personalised search, and for the evaluation of user models [8][9]. PIR-CLEF 2017 and PIR-CLEF 2018 introduced a benchmark task that provided user data gathered during a single search session. These data relate to various activities undertaken during their search session by each participant, including details of relevant documents as marked by the searchers [10]. PIR-CLEF 2019 will continue to explore this task while seeking to expand its activities to take in datasets from other tasks for which personalisation of the search process is important.

Unlike the information retrieval research community, the User Modeling research community has traditionally not had a significant focus on comparative evaluation or shared evaluation tasks. However, this situation is changing with the emergence of the EvalUMAP workshop series exploring the evaluation of user modeling, adaptation and personalisation which began at the UMAP 2016 conference [4], and is currently being held on an annual basis.

The first WEPIR 2018 workshop featured an invited keynote, a small number of short paper presentations, a panel and an extended session of breakout groups which focused on the topics of: *measurement, understanding* and *context* [6]. The workshop attracted more than 20 participants from diverse backgrounds who engaged very actively in lively discussions throughout the day. There was a strong consensus at the end of the meeting that it would be valuable to hold a further workshop focusing on this topic.

3 WORKSHOP FORMAT

WEPIR 2019 will focus on establishing and exploring proposals for methodologies and metrics for the evaluation of personalised information retrieval. As outlined above, this will build on the successful WEPIR 2018 workshop held at CHIIR 2018.

WEPIR 2019 is a full day workshop with the following components:

- One invited talk by Professor Ian Ruthven
- Presentations of papers submitted in response to an open call for research and position papers. Papers will be presented as short oral and/or poster format. The number of oral presentations will be limited to at most four to allow for the maximum of time for interactive activities, with other papers being presented as posters.
- Working groups focusing on relevant topics for the evaluation of personalised information retrieval including experimental protocols, test collection development, evaluation metrics.
- Consolidation session: integration of the activities of the working groups, and proposal of agreed framework or frameworks for the evaluation of personalised information retrieval.

4 CALL FOR CONTRIBUTIONS

An open Call for Contributions to the workshop was made to relevant mailing lists. Since the focus of WEPIR 2019 is primarily on exchange of ideas and development of new research activities, only short paper contributions were sought in the form of 2 or 4 page papers in the standard ACM conference format.

Topics for contributions include but not are not limited to:

- task design for evaluation of personalised information retrieval
- test collections for personalised information retrieval
- evaluation metrics for personalised information retrieval

- protocols for evaluation of interactive personalised information retrieval
- user modeling for personalised information retrieval
- search algorithms for personalised information retrieval

Submitted contributions were selected for inclusion in the workshop on the basis of reviews by an invited programme committee of relevant international experts.

5 ORGANISERS

The organisers of the workshop have a broad range of relevant expertise in the topics of the workshop including benchmark evaluation task development, interactive information retrieval, search algorithm design, user modeling, and personalised information retrieval, as well as extensive experience in organising and running successful workshops.

Gareth Jones is Professor of Computing in the School of Computing, and a Principal Investigator in the ADAPT Research Centre, Dublin City University, Ireland, His research focuses on multiple topics in information retrieval including adaptive search, multimedia information retrieval (particularly for spoken content), multilingual information retrieval, interactive and algorithm search for lifelogging, A particular focus in much of this work has been the development of evaluation frameworks including task design, test collection specification and construction, and the introduction of new task specific evaluation metrics. With Gabriella Pasi he is currently leading the PIR-CLEF Lab for the comparative evaluation of personalisation algorithms in information retrieval. PIR-CLEF was introduced at CLEF 2017, and is running again as a lab at CLEF 2019. He is co-founder of the MediaEVal multimedia benchmark evaluation initiative, and since 2002 has coordinated a variety of benchmark tasks at CLEF, FIRE, NTCIR and TRECVid. He regularly serves on of programme committees leading conferences in information retrieval, multimedia, natural language processing and human-computer interaction. He served as Programme co-Chair for CIKM 2010 amd ECIR 2011, and as General co-Chair for SIGIR 2013 and CLEF 2017.

Nicholas Belkin is a Distinguished Professor in the Department of Library and Information Science at Rutgers University. He was the initiator of the Interactive Track in TREC, and variously chaired and participated in that Track for its twelve years. He was also a key participant in the TREC Session Track, devising the task classification system used in that Track. He was the organizer of the NII Shonan Seminar on Evaluation of Whole Session Information Retrieval, and of the Dagstuhl Seminar on Interactive Information Retrieval. His research group has been engaged in studies of personalization of interactive information retrieval since 2010, with funding from the US Institute for Museum and Library Services, the US National Science Foundation, and Google. His proposal that the best criterion for evaluation of interactive information retrieval is usefulness, rather than relevance, has been adopted, and validated, by several different research groups throughout the world. Professor Belkin holds the ACM SIGIR Salton Award, the ASIS&T Award of Merit, and has been the Chair of the ACM SIGIR, and the President of the ASIS&T.

Seámus Lawless is Assistant Professor in the Knowledge and Data Engineering Group in the School of Computer Science and Statistics at Trinity College Dublin. He is also a Funded Investigator in the ADAPT Centre for Digital Content and Media Innovation. His research interests are in the areas of information retrieval, information management and digital humanities with a particular focus on adaptivity and personalisation. The common focus of this research is the application of technology to support enhanced, personalised access to knowledge. He was General co-Chair of the 23rd Conference on User Modelling, Adaptation and Personalization (UMAP 2015) and of CLEF 2017. He is a co-organiser of the EvalUMAP Workshop series beginning at UMAP 2016 focusing on "Comparative evaluation in user modeling, adaptation and personalization".

Gabriella Pasi is Full Professor at the University of Milano-Bicocca, Italy, where she leads the Information Retrieval Lab within the Department of Informatics, Systems and Communication, of which she is the Head. Her research activities mainly concern the modelling and design of flexible and context-aware systems for the management and access to huge collections of documents (such as Information Retrieval Systems and Recommender Systems). With Gareth Jones she led the introduction of the PIR-CLEF initiative for the evaluation of Personalised Search at CLEF 2017, and is again co-chairing the PIR-CLEF lab at CLEF 2019. She has contributed to the organization of several international events, in both roles of General and Program Chair (e.g. for ECIR 2018). She is Associate Editor or member of the Editorial Board of several International Journals in her domains of expertise.

6 ACKNOWLEDGEMENTS

This work was partially supported by Science Foundation Ireland as part of the ADAPT Centre (Grant No. 13/RC/2106) (www.adaptcentre.ie), and by the US National Science Foundation under grant IIS-1423239.

REFERENCES

[1] Maristella Agosti, Norbert Fuhr, Elaine Toms, and Perti Vakkari. 2014. *Evaluation methodologies in information retrieval.* Dagstuhl Seminar 13441. Schloss Dagstuhl - Leibniz-Zentrum fuer Informatik, Schloss Dagstuhl, Germany.

[2] Nicholas J. Belkin, Susan Dumais, Noriko Kando, and Mark Sanderson. 2016. *Whole-session evaluation of interactive information retrieval systems.* NII Shonan Meeting Report 2012-7. National Institute of Informatics, Japan, Tokyo, Japan.

[3] Paul N. Bennett, Filip Radlinski, Ryen W. White, and Emine Yilmaz. 2011. Inferring and Using Location Metadata to Personalize Web Search. In *Proceedings of the 34th International ACM SIGIR Conference on Research and Development in Information Retrieval (SIGIR 2011).* ACM, Beijing, China, 135–144.

[4] Owen Conlan, Liadh Kelly, Kevin Koidl, Seamus Lawless, Killian Levacher, and Athanasios Staikopoulos (Eds.). 2016. *EvalUMAP2016: Towards Comparative Evaluation in the User Modelling, Adaptation and Personalization.* Halifax, Canada.

[5] Susan Dumais and Nicholas J. Belkin. 2005. The TREC interactive tracks: Putting the user into search. In *TREC. Experiment and evaluation in information retrieval,* Ellen M. Voorhees and Donna K. Harman (Eds.). MIT Press, Cambridge, MA, 123 – 152.

[6] Gareth J. F. Jones, Nicholas J. Belkin, Seamus Lawless, and Gabriella Pasi. 2018. Report on the CHIIR 2018 Workshop on Evaluation of Personalisation in Information Retrieval (WEPIR 2018). *SIGIR Forum* 52, 1 (2018), 129–134.

[7] Evangelos Kanoulas, Ben Carterette, Paul D. Clough, and Mark Sanderson. 2011. Evaluating Multi-query Sessions. In *Proceedings of the 34th International ACM SIGIR Conference on Research and Development in Information Retrieval (SIGIR 2011).* ACM, Beijing, China, 1053–1062.

[8] Gabriella Pasi, Gareth J. FJones, Keith Curtis, Stefania Marrara, Camilla Sanvitto, Debasis Ganguly, and Procheta Sen. 2018. Overview of the CLEF 2018 Personalised Information Retrieval Pilot Lab (PIR-CLEF 2018). In *Proceedings of CLEF 2018.* Springer, Avignon, France.

[9] Gabriella Pasi, Gareth J. F.Jones, Stefania Marrara, Camilla Sanvitto, Debasis Ganguly, and Procheta Sen. 2017. Overview of the CLEF 2017 Personalised Information Retrieval Pilot Lab (PIR-CLEF 2017). In *Proceedings of CLEF 2017*. Springer, Dublin, Ireland.

[10] Camilla Sanvitto, Debasis Ganguly, Gareth J. F.Jones, and Gabriella Pasi. 2016. A Laboratory-Based Method for the Evaluation of Personalised Search. In *Proceedings of The Seventh International Workshop on Evaluating Information Access (EVIA 2016)*. Tokyo, Japan.

Exploring User Experience on Mobile Library Service by Cognitive Mapping

Yaming Fu
Department of Information Studies
University College London
London, United Kingdom
yaming.fu.17@ucl.ac.uk

ABSTRACT

The ubiquitous application of mobile web technology is having a significant impact on education and is changing the way of learning and teaching. With this evolving technological change, new ways of exploring information behaviour and user experience with mobile devices are needed.

This research aims to explore user experience (UX) by using an innovative ethnographic approach, cognitive mapping, trying to investigate this issue from an interpretivist viewpoint. A triangulation of log analysis, cognitive mapping and semi-structured interview is adopted to gain a comprehensive view of how users interact with mobile technology with a specific look into their experience on using the mobile library service.

KEYWORDS

User experience; Information behaviour; Cognitive mapping; Mobile library service

ACM Reference Format:

Yaming Fu. 2019. Exploring User Experience on Mobile Library Service by Cognitive Mapping. In *2019 Conference on Human Information Interaction and Retrieval (CHIIR '19), March 10–14, 2019, Glasgow, United Kingdom.* ACM, New York, NY, USA, 4 pages. https://doi.org/10.1145/3295750.3298968

1 INTRODUCTION AND MOTIVATION

Technology advancement always has a great impact on the way of teaching and learning, bringing revolutionary changes to education world [18]. Mobile web technology, from its advent, brought new possibilities in the way of accessing, seeking, using and sharing information and this also brought changes to the way library promoting their resources and services. The concept "mobile library service" was raised up with the mobile web technology development, meaning the online library service that can be accessed via mobile devices [21]. Previous research around the topic of mobile library service focused on assessing users' acceptance on using mobile devices to work by adopting theoretical frameworks like Technology Acceptance Model (e.g: [2]) or on the implementation and construction of certain mobile service (e.g: [9, 14]). While it has been indicated that the way people use their mobile devices is shifting from merely communicating to exploring, reading, sharing and learning, as well as producing digital contents [8]. In the mobile environment, the user's context is dynamic. There are constant changes in the characteristics of users at different times, different locations, facing different tasks with a specific demand. The changing information behaviour with mobile technology and their user experience should be looked into in order to understand the users in the mobile age. Therefore, this research is aiming to fill the gap to look into how users' information behaviour changes with the mobile devices, what is their experience on such technological shift in the library context and what are their expectations on the future mobile library service development.

In the library context, UX is not a new area of study. Most of the library UX study focus on improving the effectiveness of library website interface and task design to meet users' search goals and perform a better task on the library websites [5]. When Don Norman, the pioneer of UX research, published his work *'Living with Complexity'* in 2011, a complexity nature of design and user experience was uncovered [20]. UX in the library is more than just the usability of web-based services, but should be a comprehensive and systemic concept in all aspects of library service design. Therefore, rather than only focusing on the library system, some of the libraries started to adopt ethnographic techniques to learn about their users. Many of the early works on using ethnographic concepts in learning UX in the library context were from libraries in USA and Canada and their pioneer works led to more user-centered research in libraries that look beyond the system, and focus more on people [19]. In UK, ethnographic methods started gaining popularity in the late 2000s. In 2009, for example, the library of the University of Loughborough in UK conducted an observational study to explore students' activities took place in library learning space [7].

It gives inspiration to this research to adopt an ethnographic technique, cognitive mapping, to investigate UX and look beyond the system, trying to explore a new way of understanding human information behavior and UX with technologies.

2 RESEARCH QUESTIONS

The goal of this research is to investigate information behaviours and user experiences in the context of mobile library services, in order to learn about library users in the mobile age and to better understand their changing habits triggered by technological shifts. The research engages libraries with a deeper understanding around explicit goals to update their mobile services. Therefore, the research questions are as follows:

CHIIR '19, March 10–14, 2019, Glasgow, United Kingdom

ACM ISBN 978-1-4503-6025-8/19/03.
https://doi.org/10.1145/3295750.3298968

RQ1: What information behaviours and user experiences do individual evidence when using library service on their mobile devices?

RQ2: What do students do now and what would they like to be able to do in the future as technologies and possibilities evolve with mobile library service?

RQ3: How can the library improve its service with mobile technologies to better support students' mobile learning behavior?

3 METHODOLOGIES

This research adopts an interpretivist framework. The research explores subjective experience, seeking to understand the meanings of and reasons behind user behaviours. Qualitative data is the main resource of the research, aiming to discover the inner experience of people [10]. Meeting the research aim, a triangulation of methods, including log analysis, cognitive mapping and semi-structured interview is employed, which gives validation to the research outcomes [13].

3.1 Cognitive Mapping

Cognitive mapping is a method derived from geography and psychology research and it is used to get a visual representation of the way users utilise or think about a particular resource or place [17]. The term "map" here does not refer to the 'pictorial graphic model', but means the process of forming the cognition of the outsider environment and the representation of such cognition Downs and Stea [11, p.313].

In the library context, cognitive mapping is known as one of the ways to get rich data in a short time. From the year 2000, this method started to be used in the context of academic libraries in studying the users' behaviour in the way they interact with the resources and services provided by physical or digital library [3, 12]. One of its successful applications is from the ERIAL Project (Ethnographic Research in Illinois Academic Libraries), where 137 students from five ERIAL campuses engaged in the study and drew their impressions of the library.

To conduct cognitive mapping, participants are asked to draw their opinions on a piece of paper using three different color pens in six minutes given in total. They are required to change the color of the pen in every two minutes to show the sequence and relative importance of their mind map stages.

A follow-up interview is often used as a complementary method with cognitive mapping to allow participants to explain their drawings and discuss the topic in detail. Through labelling the elements appeared on the drawing and discovering the reason behind the scene, researchers will get in-depth and sometimes unexpected answers and perspectives from participants [22].

3.2 Procedure

This research was conducted in three stages. In the first stage of research, a pilot study was carried out on a small scale of sample in order to test the research methods and give inspirations to the next stages design of research, especially the design of the cognitive mapping session and the interview questions. In addition, the pilot study gave clues on the sample choice in the formal stage of research.

In the second stage of research, log analysis will be used to analyse the backend data from library regarding users' current behavioural data on mobile devices. This part of data will give an overview of the current information behaviour statistics (e.g: user actions, devices usage, popular searches, sessions, etc.).

The third stage of research will be to conduct cognitive mapping and semi-structured interviews. This part of research is mainly to find out the UX aspect on mobile library service, aiming to find out the reasons behind their information behaviour, the way how mobile service changed their behaviour and experience and their expectations of its future development.

4 PROGRESS

Through the first year of research, a comprehensive review on the literature around information behavior and UX was achieved. The first stage of this study, the pilot study, was carried out and initial data was obtained and analysed.

In the pilot study, a small sample of six students studying in University College London from different cultural and academic backgrounds were recruited. Each session combined with a cognitive mapping and an interview lasting around 30 minutes in a study room with one student and the researcher.

Six cognitive maps were gathered and by analyzing the elements appeared on maps, 67 unique elements were identified. These elements were then grouped by themes into five categories. Through analyzing interview transcriptions by content analysis, 180 quotes were coded and then categorized into seven categories.

The comparison between the number of elements/quotes in the categories of cognitive maps and interviews is shown in Table 1.

Table 1: The comparison between the number of elements/quotes in the categories of cognitive maps and interviews

Category in maps	Number of elements	Category in interviews	Number of quotes
Expectations on mobile library service	18	Expectations on mobile library service	52
Mobile learning behaviour	9	Mobile learning behaviour	63
Library services	15	Library services	16
Library resources	10	Library resources	16
Others	15	Opinions on Cognitive mapping	15
		Library catalogue usage	12
		Experience on using library apps	6

During cognitive map drawing, students were given three different color pens to show their sequence of thinking and drawing.

Frequency/Position (F/P) index was created according to the frequency of the element and the position it appeared in the drawing (first, second or third). The index calculated in this way (frequency divided by the mean position of an element) can indicate the relative importance of each element [3]. The elements with the F/P index higher than 1 are shown in Table 2.

Table 2: Cognitive maps elements with F/P index higher than 1

Element	Frequency	Mean Position	F/P index
Library Resources			
"Explore" Search (library catalogue)	7	1.14	6.14
Books, articles, journals, archives, newspapers	6	1.16	5.17
Physical libraries	3	1.33	2.26
Book status track	5	2.4	2.08
Database (web of science, etc)	2	1	2
Library services			
User Log in	5	2	2.5
Wifi, eduroam	3	2	1.5
Expectations on mobile library service			
Accessibility	5	2.2	2.27
University logo	2	1	2
Playability, desirability, gamification	3	2	1.5
Information security (finger print, face id)	3	2.65	1.13
Mobile Learning behaviour			
Location: on the move	4	2	2

Previous findings in psychology research showed that people's brains store information in a hieratical structure [6]. Therefore, by revealing the sequence and the times of drawing a specific element, people's cognitive processes can be traced. As is shown in the table above, the library catalogue and different forms of library resources were the ones that were relatively important when they were thinking of the conception "mobile library service".

Students engaged in the pilot study showed certain mobile information behaviour, and they made use of their mobile device as one of the important information source regarding their study needs. The frequently used library resources include the library catalogue, different types of electronic resources, databases and several library online services, such as "book status track" (a function that can check the availability, borrowing status and the location of the books). They also made use of the functions from their mobile devices to support their study (e.g: dictionary apps and notes taker apps).

The contexts and needs of using mobile devices to support learning process are diverse, which is mostly caused by their learning habits. Some students prefer to read articles on the train; some tend to write essays on their mobile phone while taking the bus. This explains the concept of "contextualization of learning" by using mobile devices that gives learners mobility to learn regardless of context and platform [16, p.2]. It also suggests that combining functions on the mobile phones and providing mobile access to library resources are necessary to meet users' information behaviour under different contexts and improve digital learning environment.

Another finding from the pilot study is about their expectations on the future library service development with mobile technologies, which encompass four aspects-functions, customisation and personalisation, design and data protection concerns. First of all, they pointed out the functions they wish to use specifically with mobile device, for example, library room booking, reliable checking of availability of library study spaces and the library catalogue. Secondly, they also conveyed a strong desire in having a personalized system which could give them unique recommendations for resources and updates, like reading lists and book recommendations. Thirdly, the design aspect of the mobile library service was mentioned as well with a focus on improving the usability of such service on mobile devices (e.g: visual representation). Finally, students engaged expressed their concerns on the data protection and ethical issues of using the library system on mobile devices. They hope to enjoy the convenience afforded by such technology, with their personal information being protected at the same time. This finding reveals the factors that may influence the user experience on mobile library service. As is illustrated by Beauregard and Corriveau in their conceptual framework of UX, the interaction between user and product is an iterative process, in which users' perception and intention of one product are influenced by their previous knowledge, concerns, skills and personalities [4]. The four aspects of the expectation found in the pilot study is in line with the influential factors in the UX framework.

From the pilot study, the cultural factors influencing information behaviour and UX with international Chinese students were explored. Two Chinese students engaged in the study expressed their cross-cultural perspectives as international students from a Confucian culture background. From their drawings and interviews, they both put emphasis on the friendly and straightforward design of the mobile library service (as one of them drew the desired interface of a mobile library, see section of his drawing in Figure 1). Avoiding jargon, they stressed the importance of a straightforward expression of the interface and techniques to improve accessibility. Hughes has found that rather than the linguistic factors, it is the cultural background and past learning experience that have more impact on international students' wider educational experience [15]. Thus, exploring the cultural influential factors on international students and improving the university services based on that is essential for the globalization strategy. This pilot study identifies the sample choice for the formal data collection, which will be focused on international Chinese students.

Through the pilot study, an initial view of the current UX on mobile library service was obtained. The research method, cognitive mapping, combined with semi-structured interview, was found to be a good way of helping participants deliberate on the research topic and of gathering abundant visual data in a relatively short time.

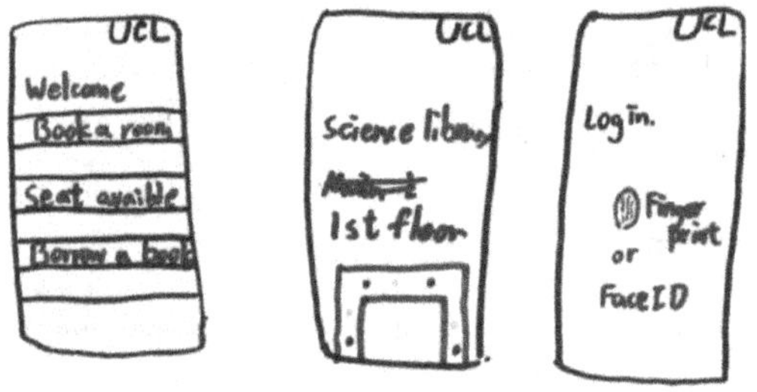

Figure 1: Part of the cognitive map by one Chinese student

5 FUTURE PLAN

The pilot study, as the first stage of research, tested the reliability and feasibility of the research methods and process design. The sample size and the specific user group for the formal data collection has been determined. A regional focus on international Chinese students studying in UK will be investigated. The rationale for this selection of sample is, on the one hand, two Chinese students engaged in the pilot study shared their UX with mobile technology from a specific cross-cultural viewpoint and this way of looking into UX has been overlooked; on the other hand, international Chinese student constitutes a considerable large number among the international students studying in UK [1], therefore learning their information behaviour and improving their experience studying abroad is of great value.

The next step of research is to analyse the backend data from the library of University College London. This part of data includes twelve months log data (October, 2017-October, 2018) from all students and it will show the behavioural characteristic of library users by the details of their user actions (what they did in the system), device usage (what devices and browsers used), facet usage, popular searches, sessions information (what country, where session took place) and other related information. Log analysis will be used to analyse this part of data. The finding on this stage will answer the RQ1 and guide the design of cognitive mapping and interview questions.

After finding out users' current behaviour, the last step is to explore the reasons behind this, and answer RQ2 and RQ3. This will be achieved by conducting cognitive mapping and interview sessions. Ultimately, a holistic view of users' information behaviour and UX on mobile library service with a specific cross-cultural perspective will be gained.

ACKNOWLEDGMENTS

This research is sponsored by China Scholarship Council (CSC)(File No.201808060180). The pilot study is supported and funded by UCL ChangeMakers (https://www.ucl.ac.uk/changemakers/). I would like to express my sincere gratitude to my PhD supervisors, Charlie Inskip and Elizabeth Lomas for their valuable support. Also, I want to give thanks to Margaret Stone (the Head of UCL Digital Libraries), Anne Binsfeld and Orla Delaney (my project team members) for their help on the project.

REFERENCES

[1] Higher Education Statistical Agency. 2018. Higher Education Student Statistics: UK, 2016/17. Retrieved December 9, 2018 from https://www.hesa.ac.uk/news/11-01-2018/sfr247-higher-education-student-statistics
[2] Noa Aharony. 2014. Mobile libraries: librarians' and students' perspectives. *College & Research Libraries* 75, 2 (2014), 202–217.
[3] Andrew Asher and Susan Miller. 2011. So you want to do anthropology in your library. *Or a practical guide to ethnographic research in academic libraries* (2011).
[4] Russell Beauregard and Philip Corriveau. 2007. User experience quality: a conceptual framework for goal setting and measurement. In *International Conference on Digital Human Modeling*. Springer, 325–332.
[5] Steven J Bell. 2014. Staying true to the core: Designing the future academic library experience. *portal: Libraries and the Academy* 14, 3 (2014), 369–382.
[6] Sariya Binsaleh and Muazzan Binsaleh. 2013. Mobile learning: What guidelines should we produce in the context of mobile learning implementation in the conflict area of the four southernmost provinces of Thailand. *Asian Social Science* 9, 13 (2013), 270.
[7] Joanna Bryant, Graham Matthews, and Graham Walton. 2009. Academic libraries and social and learning space: A case study of Loughborough University Library, UK. *Journal of Librarianship and Information Science* 41, 1 (2009), 7–18.
[8] Robin Canuel, Emily MacKenzie, Andrew Senior, and Nazi Torabi. 2017. Apps for academic success: Developing digital literacy and awareness to increase usage. *Education for Information* Preprint (2017), 1–18.
[9] Po-Sheng Chiu, Ying-Hung Pu, Tzung-Shi Chen, Yen-Hung Kuo, and Yueh-Min Huang. 2014. Design and development of a mobile library APP system. In *Educational Innovation through Technology (EITT), 2014 International Conference of*. IEEE, 43–48.
[10] Juliet Corbin, Anselm Strauss, et al. 2008. Basics of qualitative research: Techniques and procedures for developing grounded theory. (2008).
[11] Roger M Downs and David Stea. 1973. *Cognitive maps and spatial behavior: Process and products*. na.
[12] Lynda M Duke and Andrew D Asher. 2012. *College libraries and student culture: What we now know*. American Library Association.
[13] Raya Fidel. 2008. Are we there yet?: Mixed methods research in library and information science. *Library & Information Science Research* 30, 4 (2008), 265–272.
[14] Jingru Hoivik. 2013. Global village: mobile access to library resources. *Library Hi Tech* 31, 3 (2013), 467–477.
[15] Hilary Hughes. 2005. Actions and reactions: exploring international students' use of online information resources. *Australian Academic & Research Libraries* 36, 4 (2005), 169–179.
[16] JISC. 2011. Mobile learning-A practical guide for educational organisations planning to implement a mobile learning initiative. Retrieved December 9, 2018 from https://www.jisc.ac.uk/guides/mobile-learning
[17] Rob Kitchin, Scott Freundschuh, et al. 2000. *Cognitive mapping: Past, present, and future*. Vol. 4. Psychology press.
[18] Joan K Lippincott. 2010. A mobile future for academic libraries. *Reference services review* 38, 2 (2010), 205–213.
[19] Lynne EF McKechnie, Christopher M Dixon, Jana Fear, and Angela Pollak. 2013. Rules of (mis) conduct: User behaviour in public libraries. In *Proceedings of the Annual Conference of CAIS/Actes du congrès annuel de l'ACSI*.
[20] Donald A Norman. 2010. *Living with complexity*. MIT press.
[21] Lorraine Paterson and Boon Low. 2011. Student attitudes towards mobile library services for smartphones. *Library Hi Tech* 29, 3 (2011), 412–423.
[22] Andy Priestner and Matt Borg. 2016. *User experience in libraries: applying ethnography and human-centred design*. Routledge.

The Effect of Motivation on Web Search Behaviors of Health Consumers

Iman Tahamtan
School of Information Sciences
University of Tennessee
Knoxville, TN USA
tahamtan@vols.utk.edu

ABSTRACT

I aim to investigate how autonomous motivation versus controlled motivation affects Web search behaviors of health consumers, as well as their search effort and enjoyment. I will conduct a within-subject study to investigate the research questions. The design of the search tasks will be the key to whether participants are autonomously motivated to search or not. The design of the search tasks will be based on the Self-Determination Theory (SDT), a theory of motivation. The results of the experiment will enrich our understanding of how users within different motivational situations search online information.

CCS CONCEPTS

- **Information systems~Information retrieval**
- Information systems~Web and social media search
- **Applied computing~Consumer health**
- **Applied computing~Health informatics**
- Applied computing~Health care information systems

KEYWORDS

Motivation; Information need; Search behavior; Health information, Search effort, Search enjoyment

ACM Reference format:

Iman Tahamtan, 2019. The effect of motivation on web search behaviors of health consumers. In *Proceedings of Human Information Interaction and Retrieval (CHIIR'19), March 10-14, 2019, Glasgow, Scotland, UK. ACM, New York, NY, USA.* 4 pages. https://doi.org/10.1145/3295750.3298969

1 MOTIVATION

It is suggested that individuals may be motivated to engage in Web information search to satisfy their physiological, cognitive and affective needs. Satisfying these needs is the root of motivation to search information [1]. It is also noted that the degrees to which individuals' basic psychological needs of autonomy, competence, and relatedness are supported versus thwarted influences the type and strength of motivation [2] to search information [3-5]. If these needs are entirely met, people will be intrinsically motivated to search information.

ACM ISBN 978-1-4503-6025-8/19/03
https://doi.org/10.1145/ 3295750.3298969

Motivation is a component of human behavior that hasn't been explored as extensively as other factors in the information science literature [4] and when studied, has been examined under diverse labels such as information need [3]. Motivation has also been a missing component from the most models of credibility assessment of information, despite its importance [6].

Motivation is a multidimensional and fundamental component in human performance that is constituted by intrinsic (internal) and extrinsic (external) factors such as beliefs and subjective values [3]. The information science literature and theories, e.g. [7] and [8], haven't differentiated between different types of motivation to search - the searches driven by curiosity and thirst for knowledge (internally motivated) and searches driven by external factors (externally motivated) [5].

Motivated individuals tend to have higher interest, effort, engagement, and persistence in their activities that help them achieve better performance. For example, they may be more likely to pay attention to the content of the found information, and take time to learn about the search topic [9]. In my doctoral research proposal, I am aiming to use the self-determination theory (SDT), which is a theory of motivation, to investigate the effect of autonomous motivation versus controlled motivation on the search behaviors of health consumers, as well as their information search effort and enjoyment. Only a few studies have employed SDT in the information seeking literature [3-5], most of which have relied on self-reported data [5]. The effect of motivation on online information search is an important line of research that hasn't been explored before.

2 THEORETICAL FRAMEWORK

Unlike most motivation theories that suggest people are only more or less motivated, SDT suggests that people are motivated by different types of motivation, often simultaneously [10]. SDT differentiates the types of motivation based on the reasons that give rise to behavior: intrinsic motivation and extrinsic motivation [11]. Intrinsic motivation is engaging in a task or behavior for the rewards inside the task or behavior such the pleasure, enjoyment and satisfaction that the behavior provides. Extrinsic motivation is engaging in a task or behavior for the rewards outside the task or behavior such as receiving rewards, avoidance of punishment, gaining social approval, or achievement of a valued result [12].

SDT consists of six mini-theories, most importantly cognitive evaluation theory [13] and organismic integration theory. Cognitive evaluation theory explains that individuals have the psychological needs of autonomy (choices and control over actions), competence (feeling that we are able and effective in doing a task) and relatedness (the sense of positively connected to others) that must be satisfied for psychological interest, development and wellness. This theory explains how supporting these psychological needs lead to intrinsic motivation [10].

Organismic integration theory [14] differentiates the types of motivation along a regulation continuum which vary in the amount of autonomy that the person has: (1) external regulation, (2) introjected regulation, (3) identified regulation, and (4) integrated regulation which are the four subsets of extrinsic motivation and (5) intrinsic motivation (the highest level of autonomy). External regulation is the motivation to satisfy an external demand. Introjected regulation is evidenced when behavior is performed because of internal pressures such as obligation and guilt in a controlled fashion. Identified regulation is an autonomous form of extrinsic motivation, when individuals perform and engage in a behavior because they personally find it important [15]. Integrated regulation is also an autonomous form of extrinsic motivation in which identified regulations are congruent with the person's values and needs [15]. Extrinsically motivated behaviors vary in the degree to which they are controlled versus autonomous where external regulation has the lowest degree of autonomy and integrated regulation has the highest degree of autonomy. Meeting the psychological needs of competence, autonomy and relatedness will move individuals from external regulation towards the integrated regulation by facilitating the internalization of the values [10].

3 MOTIVAITON TO SEARCH

What makes SDT a proper theory to study motivations to search is that its components could be used to explain the triggers and drivers of information seeking [3]. For example, satisfying autonomy and competence will influence information search by increasing autonomous motivation [5].

3.1 Autonomous motivation to search

To the extent that participants' psychological needs are met, they will tend toward autonomous motivation to search [5]. When people are intrinsically motivated to search, they are fully autonomous, and motivation is fully internalized. Extrinsic motivation can also be autonomous when the external factor to search becomes a personally accepted or important goal (identified regulation) or when the search goals are so deeply internalized and are congruent with the personal values (integrated regulation). Extrinsic motivation of this type becomes so close to intrinsic motivation [10].

3.2 Controlled motivation to search

External regulation and introjected regulation are fully and moderately controlled (without autonomy), respectively. According to STD [10], external regulation in search will be evidenced, for example, when a student searches online information to complete an assignment to avoid teacher confrontation. Introjected regulation will be evidenced when individuals try their best to complete the search task to avoid the feeling of guilty or anxiety, or to prove that they can complete the search task (to attain pride) rather than accepting the task as one's own.

3.3 Related work

Among the few studies that have employed SDT in information science [3-5], it is found that autonomous motivation leads to higher levels of effort and enjoyment during information seeking than extrinsically motivated individuals [5]. Another study [4] indicated that students at external regulation engaged in research tasks to avoid negative consequences or to satisfy course requirements, while extrinsically motivated students who were closer to autonomous motivation (i.e. identified regulation) engaged in research to obtain skills necessary to be successful as students and in their future careers because they understand the benefits of obtaining research skills beyond the project at hand [4]. Another study found that autonomous information seeking is experienced as interesting and enjoyable because it is driven by personal interests and curiosity. However, information seeking that is driven by controlled motivation is found stressful because it aims at complying with internal demands and external requirements [16].

4 RESEARCH QUESTION

The following research questions will be addressed: RQ1: How does autonomous search tasks versus controlled search tasks influence Web search behaviors of health consumers? RQ2: How does autonomous search tasks versus controlled search tasks influence information search enjoyment and effort?

5 METHEDOLOGY

5.1 Participants

This will be a lab study in which 30 undergraduate students between the ages of 18-24 will be recruited through the university mailing system to complete two types of search tasks in Google: autonomous search task versus controlled search task. The design of the search tasks will be explained in the following section.

5.2 Search Tasks

In an experimental setting, people will generally be extrinsically motivated to search information compared to a natural setting where they could be both intrinsically or extrinsically motivated to search. Thus, the design of a search task is the key to whether or not participants are autonomously motivated to engage in search or not. Rather than focusing on rewards for motivating participants to complete a task, it is important to focus more on how to facilitate intrinsic motivation, for example, by developing more interesting tasks considering participants' viewpoint [17]. At present, there no published guidelines about how to design motivational search tasks. SDT has some practical solutions for designing motivational tasks [9] in experimental settings. The search task should have three features to produce enough variance in autonomous motivation: providing a meaningful rational (vs no rational), acknowledging the behavior's feeling (vs no acknowledgement), and choice and low controlling language (versus high controlling language) [18]. Designing the search tasks that satisfies the three psychological needs might relatively enhance extrinsic motivation from being controlled (external and introjected) to being autonomous (identified and integrated) which is close in quality to intrinsic motivation [19]. Autonomous tasks will be the two most interesting tasks, while controlled tasks (without autonomy) will be the least interesting tasks (evaluated by participants). Furthermore, the two most interesting tasks will be evaluate tasks and the two least interesting tasks will include remember tasks, because it is indicated that evaluate tasks are the most interesting and engaging tasks, while remember tasks are the least interesting tasks [20]. Another feature that will be included in the design of the search tasks is that the autonomous tasks will use realistic scenarios, known as *simulated work task* situations [21] while the controlled tasks will be *topic-based tasks*. Topic-based tasks are artificial, and subjects may not have context for executing the task. Subjects may be unmotivated to search for artificial tasks. Simulated work task provides context which may lead to perceiving the importance of the task [22]. To put the search task in a more focused context, the potential of SDT will be examined by exploring motivations for seeking health related information. The reason for choosing the medical domain is that many previous large-scale surveys have indicated that almost more than half of the people use the Web to find health information [23, 24]. This represents that most people are intrinsically motivated to search online information to improve their health [25].

5.3 Procedure

After signing the consent form, each participant will conduct two health related search tasks with autonomous support (AS) and two without AS (controlled) in Google. Information search enjoyment and effort questionnaires will be administered before the study and once at the end of the two AS search tasks and once at the end of the two without AS search tasks. Information search enjoyment and effort will be assessed using the subscales of interest/enjoyment and effort/importance in Intrinsic Motivation Inventory [11]. Participants' search behaviors (e.g. query characteristics, time spent on tasks and documents, etc.) will be recorded using Tobii eye tracker X-60 data logs. Participants will be asked to bookmark a webpage if they conceive it reliable and relevant to the search task. No task time limit will be imposed, because time pressure influences motivation [26]. Retrospective think-aloud (RTA) semi-structured interviews will be used to obtain participants' behaviors, thoughts and actions.

6 FUTURE PLANS

My previous background in medical library and information sciences has motivated me to investigate how consumers of health information search information on the Web and which factors influence their search behavior. I aim to present my work at the doctoral consortium at CHIIR 2019 to receive feedback from experts to improve my work and research design. One of my plans is to conduct a pilot study to investigate whether the designed search tasks with the mentioned features will produce enough variance in autonomous motivation to search. I would also like to see how consumers of health information evaluate the credibility of information when they are autonomously motivated to search versus when they are not. Another future plan is to look at how the search systems or medical websites (e.g. their interfaces) should be improved to increase the basic psychological needs during online information search.

ACKNOWLEDGMENTS

I would like to acknowledge the Student Travel Grant I received from the SIGIR to attend CHIIR 2019.

REFERENCES

[1] T. D. Wilson, "On user studies and information needs," Journal of documentation, vol. 37, no. 1, pp. 3-15, 1981.

[2] E. L. Deci, and R. M. Ryan, "Self-determination theory: A macrotheory of human motivation, development, and health," Canadian psychology/Psychologie canadienne, vol. 49, no. 3, pp. 182, 2008.

[3] R. Savolainen, "Self-determination and expectancy-value: Comparison of cognitive psychological approaches to motivators for information seeking about job opportunities," Aslib Journal of Information Management, vol. 70, no. 1, pp. 123-140, 2018.

[4] A. Dubnjakovic, "Information Seeking Motivation Scale development: a self-determination perspective," Journal of Documentation, vol. 73, no. 5, pp. 1034-1052, 2017.

[5] A. Dubnjakovic, "Antecedents and consequences of autonomous information seeking motivation," Library & Information Science Research, vol. 40, no. 1, pp. 9-17, 2018.

[6] M. J. Metzger, "Making sense of credibility on the Web: Models for evaluating online information and recommendations for future research," Journal of the Association for Information Science and Technology, vol. 58, no. 13, pp. 2078-2091, 2007.

[7] N. J. Belkin, "Anomalous states of knowledge as a basis for information retrieval," Canadian journal of information science, vol. 5, no. 1, pp. 133-143, 1980.

[8] C. C. Kuhlthau, "Inside the search process: Information seeking from the user's perspective," Journal of the American society for information science, vol. 42, no. 5, pp. 361-371, 1991.

[9] B. D. Jones, "Motivating students to engage in learning: The MUSIC model of academic motivation," International Journal of Teaching and Learning in Higher Education, vol. 21, no. 2, pp. 272-285, 2009.

[10] R. M. Ryan, and E. L. Deci, Self-determination theory: Basic psychological needs in motivation, development, and wellness: Guilford Publications, 2017.

[11] E. Deci, and R. M. Ryan, Intrinsic motivation and self-determination in human behavior: Springer Science & Business Media, 1985.

[12] R. M. Ryan, and E. L. Deci, "Self-determination theory and the facilitation of intrinsic motivation, social development, and well-being," American psychologist, vol. 55, no. 1, pp. 68, 2000.

[13] E. L. Deci, and R. M. Ryan, "The Empirical Exploration of Intrinsic Motivational Processes1," Advances in experimental social psychology, pp. 39-80: Elsevier, 1980.

[14] R. M. Ryan, J. P. Connell, and E. L. Deci, "A motivational analysis of self-determination and self-regulation in education," Research on motivation in education: The classroom milieu, vol. 2, pp. 13-51, 1985.

[15] C. F. Ratelle, F. Guay, R. J. Vallerand, S. Larose, and C. Senécal, "Autonomous, controlled, and amotivated types of academic motivation: A person-oriented analysis," Journal of educational psychology, vol. 99, no. 4, pp. 734, 2007.
[16] R. Savolainen, "Autonomous, controlled and half-hearted. Unemployed people's motivations to seek information about jobs," Information Research, vol. 13, no. 4, pp. p5-5. 1p., 2008.
[17] E. L. Deci, R. Koestner, and R. M. Ryan, "Extrinsic rewards and intrinsic motivation in education: Reconsidered once again," Review of educational research, vol. 71, no. 1, pp. 1-27, 2001.
[18] E. L. Deci, H. Eghrari, B. C. Patrick, and D. R. Leone, "Facilitating internalization: The self-determination theory perspective," Journal of personality, vol. 62, no. 1, pp. 119-142, 1994.
[19] D. Peters, R. A. Calvo, and R. M. Ryan, "Designing for Motivation, Engagement and Wellbeing in Digital Experience," Frontiers in Psychology, vol. 9, 2018.
[20] D. Kelly, J. Arguello, A. Edwards, and W.-c. Wu, "Development and evaluation of search tasks for IIR experiments using a cognitive complexity framework." pp. 101-110.
[21] P. Borlund, "The IIR evaluation model: a framework for evaluation of interactive information retrieval systems," Information Research. An International Electronic Journal, vol. 8, no. 3, 2003.
[22] D. Kelly, "Methods for evaluating interactive information retrieval systems with users," Foundations and Trends® in Information Retrieval, vol. 3, no. 1–2, pp. 1-224, 2009.
[23] F. Beck, J.-B. Richard, V. Nguyen-Thanh, I. Montagni, I. Parizot, and E. Renahy, "Use of the internet as a health information resource among French young adults: results from a nationally representative survey," Journal of medical Internet research, vol. 16, no. 5, 2014.
[24] B. Hasse, D. Nelson, and G. Kreps, "Trust and sources of health information," Arch Intern Med, vol. 165, pp. 2618-2624, 2005.
[25] M. S. Zanchetta, and S. L. Moura, "Self-determination and information seeking in end-stage cancer," Clinical journal of oncology nursing, vol. 10, no. 6, 2006.
[26] M. Touré-Tillery, and A. Fishbach, "How to measure motivation: A guide for the experimental social psychologist," Social and Personality Psychology Compass, vol. 8, no. 7, pp. 328-341, 2014.
[27] A. J. Flanagin, and M. J. Metzger, "The role of site features, user attributes, and information verification behaviors on the perceived credibility of web-based information," New media & society, vol. 9, no. 2, pp. 319-342, 2007.

A Reference-Dependent Model of Search Evaluation

Jiqun Liu
School of Communication and Information, Rutgers University
New Brunswick, New Jersey
jl2033@scarletmail.rutgers.edu

ABSTRACT

Most of the existing IR studies employed final values of search behavior measures in building evaluation metrics. However, according to the theories and empirical evidences from Behavioral Economics studies, in people's evaluations of actions and outcomes, the carriers of the values of different actions are gains and losses defined relative to a reference point, rather than the absolute final assets. Based on this idea, I will first explore how users' levels of search satisfaction are affected by the gains and losses defined relative to the pre-search expectations of system performance or reference levels in a controlled lab study. Then, based on the data collected from a field study, I will test the predicative power of my reference-dependent models (built upon Δ-value-based behavioral features given the corresponding reference points) in predicting user satisfaction in naturalistic settings, aiming to examine the extent to which the reference-dependent approach can approximate real users' search evaluations. The findings of this work can help us better understand the subjectivity, bias, and variation in users' evaluation of search experience and thus have implications for user modeling and system recommendations design.

CCS CONCEPTS

• **Information systems → Users and interactive retrieval.**

KEYWORDS

Reference dependence; search evaluation; interactive IR

ACM Reference Format:
Jiqun Liu. 2019. A Reference-Dependent Model of Search Evaluation. In *2019 Conference on Human Information Interaction and Retrieval (CHIIR '19), March 10–14, 2019, Glasgow, United Kingdom.* ACM, New York, NY, USA, 4 pages. https://doi.org/10.1145/3295750.3298970

1 INTRODUCTION

How users evaluate their search experience when interacting with information retrieval (IR) systems is a fundamental research problem in the area of Interactive Information Retrieval (IIR). In particular, *user satisfaction* as a major aspect of search experience can significantly affect search actions and judgments in online information seeking episodes and thus has been widely used as a ground truth for evaluating IR evaluation metrics of different types (including both behavior-based online metrics and annotation-based offline metrics) [5, 12]. Therefore, to embrace a deeper understanding of user characteristics in information interaction, it is critical to investigate how user satisfaction is affected by their interactions with IR systems and the associated outcomes.

Most of the existing IR studies employed final values of search behavior measures in building evaluation metrics. However, according to the theories and empirical evidences from Behavioral Economics studies, in real people (instead of "rational man")'s evaluations of actions and outcomes, the carriers of the values of different actions are gains and losses defined relative to a reference point, rather than the absolute final assets [18]. Given these findings, it is critical to explore (1) *how, if at all, are users' levels of search satisfaction affected by the gains and losses defined relative to the corresponding reference levels*, and (2) *to what extent can we infer user satisfaction based on a reference-dependent approach.*

CHIIR '19, March 10–14, 2019, Glasgow, United Kingdom

ACM ISBN 978-1-4503-6025-8/19/03.
https://doi.org/10.1145/3295750.3298970

2 MOTIVATION

A promising development in the modeling of search interaction and evaluation came from the application of classical economic theories. Specifically, for example, Azzopardi and his colleagues adopted models (e.g., Cobb-Douglas Production Function) from Microeconomics Theory to develop Search Economic Theory and empirically tested some of the connections between behavioral factors (e.g., number of queries issued, number of documents assessed) [2, 4]. With respect to evaluation, [3] designed and applied information-foraging-based measure in evaluating the utility of search engine result pages (SERPs). Built upon classical economic theories, these models use the final values of search behavior measures (e.g., total number of documents assessed within a query segment, number of queries issued within a task session) in developing behavioral features and evaluation metrics. Behind these measurements is the implicit assumption that individuals evaluate utility based on the final objective assets or outcomes associated with different actions and decisions (cf. expected utility theory [9]).

However, as one of the cornerstone of classical/rational economic models, the final-outcome-based objective preference and outcome evaluation assumption has been demonstrated to be problematic in a variety of *Behavioral Economics* studies (e.g., [10, 16–18]). Based on the evidences collected from a series of experiments, Tversky and Kahneman [17] rejected the expected utility approach which assumes that people evaluate the utility of an option based on the final outcome. Instead, they proposed a *Reference-Dependent Model* and argued that the carriers of the values of different actions are gains and losses defined relative to a reference point, rather than the absolute final assets. Therefore, people's preferences and result evaluations are essentially dynamic and relative rather than static and objective as they depend on their corresponding reference levels (which is often represented by status quo). This theory also helps explain another relevant phenomenon: *Framing Effect.*

Specifically, according to [18], the framing of options in evaluation can yield systematically different preferences. An individual's perception of a given option and the associated decision can be easily reversed with merely adjusting the reference point. Therefore, it is not appropriate to define and represent people's preferences using predefined indifference curves (cf. ordinal utility theory [6]). Also, Tversky and Kahneman [18] found that people are more sensitive to the gains and losses which are close to the reference point.

Furthermore, based on the idea of reference dependence, Tversky and Kahneman [18] also demonstrated that people tend to prefer avoiding losses to acquiring equivalent gains: it is better to not loss $5 than to find $5 (*Loss Aversion*). Consequently, when the outcome of an option is perceived as a loss, the decision maker's satisfaction level will drop quickly. Also, when an option consists of different facets and dimensions, people are more sensitive to the dimension in which they are losing relative to the reference point.

As one of the fundamental principle of behavioral economics, reference dependence (1) helps explain other associated "anomalies" (e.g., framing effects, loss aversion) which clearly violate the assumption of final-outcome-based evaluation and (2) speaks to the human bias in evaluation and decision making, which are not covered by the classical rational economic models. Inspired by the reference-dependent approach, in my dissertation work I will build a reference-dependent model of search evaluation and explore how the dynamic reference points affect users' evaluations of their search experience and performance. It is likely that the reference-dependent approach can offer search evaluation model a more realistic behavioral and psychological foundation.

3 RESEARCH QUESTIONS

In the light of the relevant theories and empirical evidences from behavioral economics research [10, 16–18], I will study the roles of reference level and the associated tendency, loss aversion, in users' search evaluation. Specifically, my dissertation study seeks to address the following research questions (RQs):

- **RQ1:** *To what extent, if at all, does the difference in reference level lead to the difference in user satisfaction?*
- **RQ2:** *Are users' levels of satisfaction more sensitive to losses than to gains given a reference level?*

RQ1 and RQ2 examine the effects of reference level and the tendency of loss aversion on user satisfaction. Given the existing evidences on the phenomenon of reference dependence from various behavioral economic experiments, we may find similar effects of reference level and loss aversion in the context of user search evaluation and IIR in general.

- **RQ3:** *To what extent, if at all, do different amounts of loss and gain cause different levels of cognitive load and stress?*

To explain the effect of reference dependence at cognitive level, Gonzalez et al. [8] ran fMRI tests and their neuro evidences demonstrate that without changing the nature of the options, the cognitive efforts or loads increased when a participant needed to select a option that was framed as a loss. I will take a step forward by investigating the effect of relevance dependence at both cognitive level (i.e. cognitive load) and emotional level (i.e. perceived stress), aiming to help explain how reference level affect user evaluation.

- **RQ4:** *To what extent can we predict a user's expectation disconfirmation state using the reference-dependent model?*
- **RQ5:** *To what extent can we predict a user's level of satisfaction in search interaction using the reference-dependent model?*

According to the Expectation Confirmation Theory (ECT) [15], when a system outperforms a user's expectations (which means the expectation disconfirmation state is *positive*), the user is very likely to be satisfied with the system performance. In contrast, when the expectation disconfirmation state is *negative*, the user is more likely to be dissatisfied and thus may discontinue the usage of the information system. In the reference-dependent framework, a user's pre-search expectation of system performance can be approximated by the reference level or status quo for search evaluation. Accordingly, the expectation disconfirmation state can be considered as the perceived result of search interaction (i.e. gain or loss). Predicting the expectation disconfirmation state from search behavioral signals can help explain the effect of reference level on users' evaluations. As a natural extension from RQ4, RQ5 directly speaks to the predicative power of search-behavioral-based reference-dependent model. When building reference-dependent models, I will use the *Δ values of different search behaviors* (i.e. the difference between each behavioral measurement and the corresponding reference point) as features and build prediction models based on several possible reference levels. Given the Δ-value-based measure, RQ5 essentially pushes us to investigate the extent to which we can infer the implicit user satisfaction based on a user's gains and losses over various dimensions of explicit search interaction.

4 METHODOLOGY

Given the nature of different research questions, my dissertation work consists of two different user studies. The first user study is a *controlled lab study* where I control task topic and cost-benefit scenarios (i.e. number of relevant results on predefined SERPs) in search evaluation, aiming to accurately examine the "clean effects" of reference level and loss aversion. The controlled lab study is designed to answer RQ1-3. The second study is a *field study* where I collect data on participants' search behavior and evaluation in naturalistic settings and test the predicative power of behavior-based reference-dependent model in predicting participants' expectation disconfirmation states and levels of search satisfaction (RQ4-5).

4.1 Controlled Lab Study

SERPs and cost-benefit scenarios. I will represent different levels of benefits by varying the amount of relevant results on a SERP consisting of 12 results in total (see the 12 scenarios in Figure 1). I include 12 text-only snippets (instead of 10 results) to make sure there is enough room for detecting the variations on both the gain (above) and loss (below) sides of the reference levels in search evaluation.

For each participant, each scenario has two different SERPs. Thus, each participant needs to evaluate 26 SERPs in total. The queries and search result snippets will be extracted from the results retrieved from Microsoft Bing API. I will prepare 26 different tasks with different topics to contextualize the 26 different SERPs in order to avoid learning effects. The relevance (highly relevant, somewhat relevant, not relevant) of each result snippet to the given task will be evaluated by at least two external assessors separately. To avoid

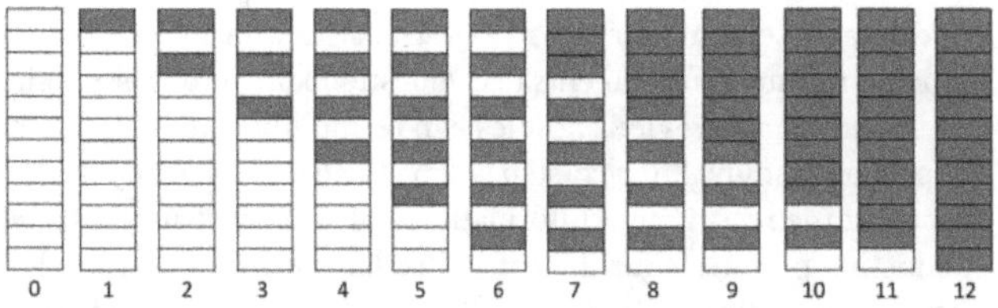

Figure 1: 13 SERPs (blue: relevant, white: non-relevant).

the potential ambiguity in relevance judgment, among the search result snippets which receive the same relevance rating from two assessors, I will only use the ones which are rated as either "highly relevant" or "not relevant". Also, I only use factual task here in order to make it clearer for relevance judgment. Since query length may affect users' judgments [19], all queries here will be the same in length (for example, 4 words). In Figure 1, for each condition, I mix the relevant and irrelevant results in SERPs (except the 0 condition) instead of aggregating relevant results altogether on the top as I want participants to be sensitive all the time to the relevant results. I control the ranking of the results instead of randomizing them in order to clear out the effect of ranking when analyzing the role of reference level. To make sure each SERP can create a unique, well-controlled cost-benefit scenario, I will ask participants to evaluate all result snippets on each SERP (so the total cost is controlled and the total benefit is manipulated by the scenarios).

Note that the search result snippets here are not clickable. The participants will be asked to evaluate the relevance of each result based on the snippet only. I make this decision in order to control the length of study within a reasonable amount of time. The sequence of the SERP scenarios will be rotated for each participant.

Participant and study procedure. I design two different reference levels here, *4 relevant results out of 12 results* and *8 relevant results out of 12 results*, aiming to make sure there are enough data points on both gain and loss sides of each reference level. The reference levels will be introduced as the average level of performance of the current system both at the beginning of study and in the side bar of the system during the study (see Figure 2). The number of relevant documents found will also be shown in the side bar. Participant can indicate their level of satisfaction on a continuum by dragging the slider. I adopt a *between-subjects design* here to avoid possible learning effect. This study only recruits undergraduate students who are native English speakers in order to control the possible effect of language and education level on snippet evaluation. I will recruit 60 participants and randomly assign them into the two reference level groups (30 participants for each group).

With respect to the study procedure, the study will start with a short survey asking questions about their backgrounds and demographic information. Then I will ask the participants to start the first session where they need to evaluate the first set of 13 SERPs (about 26 minutes). Then participants will take 2 minutes break (to mitigate fatigue) and continue with evaluating the other 13 SERPs in the second session. Participants will be asked to find as many relevant result snippets as they can. To answer RQ3, I will collect *Electroencephalogram (EEG)* data (using EEG headset) [1] and *Heart Rate* data (using BioPac) [7] to infer participants' cognitive load and perceived stress respectively.

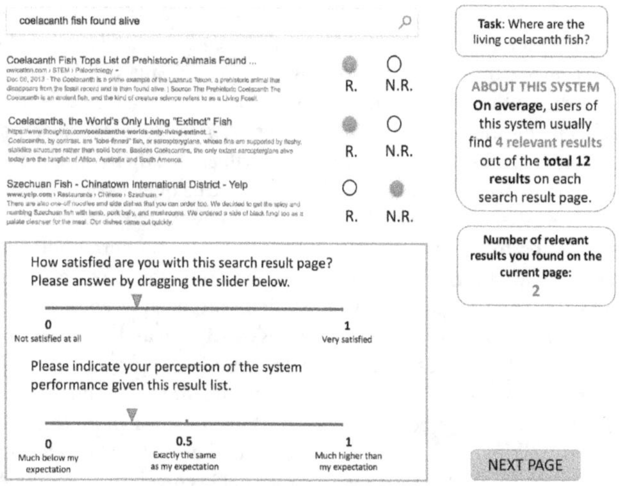

Figure 2: Mockup of the study system (Note that the real system will include 12 result snippets).

Data analysis. Before answering RQ1-3, I will test the correlation between the user-reported expectation disconfirmation state (below or above expectation) and the perceived result of SERP evaluation (loss or gain). A high correlation value would indicate that our manipulation of participants' reference levels is successful.

To answer RQ1, I will employ t-test or Mann-Whitney U test (depending on the data distribution) to compare the satisfaction levels of the participants from the two reference level groups under same SERP conditions. If there is a reference-dependent effect, then the differences in satisfaction rating between the groups should be statistically significant in all conditions (with the "4 out 12" group always higher than the "8 out 12" group). To answer the RQ2, in each reference level group, I will divide the dataset into two parts according to the result state (above or below the reference level) and run regression models (regress user satisfaction on evaluation result) on them separately. If there is a tendency of loss aversion, then the slope of the loss-side model should be greater than that of the gain-side model. To answer RQ3, I will test the difference in the electrical activity of the brain and heart rate between the two different reference-level groups within the same SERP scenarios.

4.2 Field Study

Participant and study procedure. To answer RQ4-5, in the field study, I will recruit 30 native English speakers to do seven-day Web search in naturalistic settings. Participants' search behavioral data will be collected via a Chrome browser plugin.

The field study will start with a pre-search interview session where I will ask questions about participants' daily work tasks and search tasks and also give participants a tutorial on installing and using the browser plugin. Then, the participants will do their regular Web search with the plugin turned on and annotate their search tasks at the end of each day (annotate the name of search task for the corresponding segments of search logs and offer task descriptions). To collect ground truth data for evaluating prediction models, when a participant searches on the Web with the browser plugin turned on, a pop-up window will show up at the end of each query segment. In this work, query segment is defined as *a search session segment which starts from one issued query and ends at the next query*. In the pop-up window, the participant will be asked to indicate their expectation disconfirmation state and satisfaction level using the sliders shown in Figure 2. To reduce participants' cognitive load in study participation, I will enable them to skip one questionnaire/pop-up window for every three query segments.

After the seven-day Web search in the wild, participants will be invited to a post-search individual interview where I will ask detailed questions on how they decide their pre-search expectations and search strategies and evaluate their search experiences.

Search behavioral measurements and data analysis. To measure the gains and losses in search interaction, I employ a variety of search behavioral measures here: (1) the benefit side of interaction, such as number of content pages that are read for more than 30 seconds (i.e. number of relevant pages), total dwell time on relevant pages. (2) the cost side of interaction, such as dwell time on SERP, dwell time on content page, number of search result snippets examined, number of content pages clicked and hovered by the mouse cursor, distance of cursor movement, time spent on formulating query. Given the query-level user satisfaction evaluation, all behavioral measures are calculated within query segments. To apply the reference-dependent approach, I design six "candidate reference levels" here and compute six sets of Δ-value-based features:

- average value of each search behavioral measure within the current search task (local reference level1);
- average value of each measure within the most recent search task + the current task (local reference level2);
- average value of each measure within the most recent search task of same type + the current task (local reference level3);
- average value of each measure within all search tasks from the same day (meso reference level);
- average value of each measure within the search tasks of same type from all past days (global reference level1);
- average value of each measure within the search tasks from all past days (global reference level2);

To answer RQ4-5, I will build six regression prediction models based on the six sets of Δ-value-based behavioral features to predict participants' perceived system performance and levels of search satisfaction within query segments. I will compare the prediction performances of different models in order to determine the best model which can approximate the reference level employed by participants in real-time search evaluation. Furthermore, this study will also compare the prediction performances of the models across different groups of participants (e.g., male and female) and tasks of different types (e.g., fact finding task and exploratory task), aiming to obtain a deeper understanding of the reference-dependent evaluation in different contexts. In addition, I will code and extract qualitative evidences from the transcripts of post-search interviews in order to better interpret the prediction models and results.

5 PROGRESS AND FUTURE PLAN

Previously, I have conducted a series of studies at both conceptual level and empirical level to explore the task and information seeking intention aspects of search interaction (e.g., [13, 14]) as well as the applicability of economic approach in modeling information seeking and search behaviors [11]. The search tasks, prediction models, and study instruments (e.g., questionnaire, browser plugin) developed in my previous studies can be modified and applied in the proposed study. My next step will be finalizing the study design, preparing the recruitment information and study instruments, and conducting pilot tests for the controlled lab study. A first round of pilot tests with five participants will be conducted to test the study instruments, procedure, and the predefined SERPs.

6 ACKNOWLEDGMENTS

I would like to thank my advisor, Dr. Chirag Shah. This work is supported by National Science Foundation grant IIS-1717488.

REFERENCES

[1] Pavlo Antonenko, Fred Paas, Roland Grabner, and Tamara Van Gog. 2010. Using electroencephalography to measure cognitive load. *Educational Psychology Review* 22, 4 (2010), 425–438.

[2] Leif Azzopardi. 2014. Modelling interaction with economic models of search. In *Proceedings of the 37th international ACM SIGIR conference on Research & development in information retrieval.* ACM, 3–12.

[3] Leif Azzopardi, Paul Thomas, and Nick Craswell. 2018. Measuring the utility of search engine result pages: an information foraging based measure. In *41st International ACM SIGIR Conference on Research and Development in Information Retrieval.*

[4] Leif Azzopardi and Guido Zuccon. 2016. An analysis of the cost and benefit of search interactions. In *Proceedings of the 2016 ACM International Conference on the Theory of Information Retrieval.* ACM, 59–68.

[5] Ye Chen, Ke Zhou, Yiqun Liu, Min Zhang, and Shaoping Ma. 2017. Meta-evaluation of Online and Offline Web Search Evaluation Metrics. SIGIR.

[6] James S Coleman and Thomas J Fararo. 1992. Rational choice theory. *Nueva York: Sage* (1992).

[7] Ashlee Edwards and Diane Kelly. 2017. Engaged or Frustrated?: Disambiguating Emotional State in Search. In *Proceedings of the 40th International ACM SIGIR Conference on Research and Development in Information Retrieval.* ACM, 125–134.

[8] Cleotilde Gonzalez, Jason Dana, Hideya Koshino, and Marcel Just. 2005. The framing effect and risky decisions: Examining cognitive functions with fMRI. *Journal of economic psychology* 26, 1 (2005), 1–20.

[9] John D Hey and Chris Orme. 1994. Investigating generalizations of expected utility theory using experimental data. *Econometrica: Journal of the Econometric Society* (1994), 1291–1326.

[10] Daniel Kahneman, Jack L Knetsch, and Richard H Thaler. 1991. Anomalies: The endowment effect, loss aversion, and status quo bias. *Journal of Economic Perspectives* 5, 1 (1991), 193–206.

[11] Jiqun Liu. 2017. Toward a unified model of human information behavior: an equilibrium perspective. *Journal of Documentation* 73, 4 (2017), 666–688.

[12] Mengyang Liu, Yiqun Liu, Jiaxin Mao, Cheng Luo, Min Zhang, and Shaoping Ma. 2018. "Satisfaction with Failure" or"Unsatisfied Success": Investigating the Relationship between Search Success and User Satisfaction. In *Proceedings of the 2018 World Wide Web Conference. Geneva, Switzerland.* 1533–1542.

[13] Matthew Mitsui, Jiqun Liu, Nicholas J Belkin, and Chirag Shah. 2017. Predicting Information Seeking Intentions from Search Behaviors. In *Proceedings of the 40th International ACM SIGIR Conference on Research and Development in Information Retrieval.* ACM, 1121–1124.

[14] Matthew Mitsui, Jiqun Liu, and Chirag Shah. 2018. How Much is Too Much?: Whole Session vs. First Query Behaviors in Task Type Prediction. In *Proceedings of ACM SIGIR.* ACM, 1141–1144.

[15] Richard L Oliver. 1980. A cognitive model of the antecedents and consequences of satisfaction decisions. *Journal of Marketing Research* (1980), 460–469.

[16] Amos Tversky and Daniel Kahneman. 1981. The framing of decisions and the psychology of choice. *science* 211, 4481 (1981), 453–458.

[17] Amos Tversky and Daniel Kahneman. 1991. Loss aversion in riskless choice: A reference-dependent model. *The Quarterly Journal of Economics* 106, 4 (1991), 1039–1061.

[18] Amos Tversky and Daniel Kahneman. 1992. Advances in prospect theory: Cumulative representation of uncertainty. *Journal of Risk and Uncertainty* 5, 4 (1992), 297–323.

[19] Wan-Ching Wu, Diane Kelly, and Kun Huang. 2012. User evaluation of query quality. In *Proceedings of the 35th international ACM SIGIR conference on Research and development in information retrieval.* ACM, 215–224.

The Impact of Dyslexia on the Information-Seeking Behaviour of Undergraduate Students

Lynne Cole
City, University of London, London
lynne.cole@city.ac.uk

ABSTRACT

This research aims to identify the impact of dyslexia on the information-seeking behaviour of undergraduate students within the context of preparation for a HE assignment by understanding the barriers to information-seeking and the workarounds employed. This will allow recommendations for support, through instruction and system design, to be made. A qualitative approach has been adopted to gain a rich, in-depth understanding of how dyslexia impacts information-seeking and naturalistic data has been collected. Participant captured screen recordings with follow up interviews have been collected and retrospective think aloud sessions are ongoing with undergraduate students with dyslexia. Initial findings suggest that dyslexia is causing barriers to information-seeking due to cognitive and affective challenges. Barriers identified from initial findings included difficulties attributed to spelling and memory difficulties which could manifest in the focus formulation phase of Kuhlthau's ISP and Bates' berrypicking model. Affective barriers relating to self-efficacy while information-seeking that could cause the information-seeker frustration were also found. There were indications that workarounds are being employed to try and overcome the difficulties to information-seeking caused by dyslexia, such as the use of query building aids, and the effectiveness of these workarounds for information-seekers with dyslexia will be investigated in future work.

CCS CONCEPTS

User Studies • People with disabilities

KEYWORDS

Information-seeking; dyslexia; undergraduates

ACM Reference format:

Lynne Cole. 2019. The Impact of Dyslexia on the Information-Seeking Behaviour of Undergraduate Students. In *2019 Conference on Human Information Interaction and Retrieval (CHIIR '19), March 10–14, 2019, Glasgow, United Kingdom.* ACM, New York, NY, USA, 4 pages.
DOI: https://doi.org/10.1145/3295750.3298971

CHIIR'19, March 10–14, 2019, Glasgow, United Kingdom.

ACM ISBN 978-1-4503-6025-8/19/03.
DOI: https://doi.org/10.1145/3295750.3298971

1 MOTIVATION

In the UK, 2-3% of the undergraduate population have dyslexia, which is a cognitive disability that manifests itself in difficulties in reading, writing and spelling skills [1]. How difficulties present themselves vary for each person but are persistent throughout life and can cause disengagement and underachievement within HE [1]. Information-seeking is an integral component of the skills undergraduate students require for success in HE and beyond, and requires complex cognitive skills [2]. The symptoms of dyslexia can cause difficulties with complex cognitive tasks that involve higher order cognitive and affective skills [1], such as those required for information-seeking. It is possible that without mastery of the necessary information-seeking skills, chances of success in HE and beyond are hindered. However, how dyslexia may impact upon information-seeking has not been widely studied previously.

Challenges faced by those with dyslexia within education include barriers to tasks that involve skills associated with reading, writing, spelling and verbal memory [1]. Information-seeking to prepare for assignments is a key element of success for undergraduate student studies [3] and the development of skills associated with information literacy [2] is a lifelong proficiency that is also of benefit and importance in the workplace. This demographic of undergraduate students encounter difficulties in educational tasks and the associated required skills due to problems with reading, writing, spelling and verbal memory caused by dyslexia; dyslexia may present unique barriers to information-seeking because information-seeking involves skills associated with reading, writing, spelling and verbal memory and these are competencies that can be problematic for those with dyslexia [4-9]. These difficulties may cause barriers to manifest themselves throughout the information-seeking process. Furthermore, disadvantages faced by students with dyslexia increase with the academic demand on them and the information skills required become more sophisticated and complex, hence, by targeting those with dyslexia at undergraduate stage, barriers to information-seeking that could impact upon wider information skills needed in the workplace can be identified and tackled.

In addition to cognitive barriers, dyslexia can present affective barriers to learning and education [10]. Self-efficacy has been shown to be problematic for learners with dyslexia [10] and has also been argued to be of importance with regards to the continuation of information-seeking in the face of setbacks [11, 12]. If the information seeker has low self-efficacy with regards to educational tasks that involve reading, writing and spelling then this may in turn impact upon self-efficacy in information-seeking, which involves those skills. If it is less likely that those with dyslexia will continue information-seeking when a barrier is encountered, it will be less likely that information-seeking is successful. These cognitive and affective challenges and the impact they have on information-seeking behaviour have not previously investigated holistically.

1.1 Related Work

The majority of the few previous studies investigating how those with dyslexia seek information have had a quantitative methodology. These studies considered how dyslexia may impact information retrieval and have shown that, due to difficulties faced, those with dyslexia do behave differently to their peers while interacting with online information systems [4 - 9]. However, this research seeks to expand on this understanding by considering why difficulties associated with dyslexia impact information-seeking.

Difficulties in reading [9] and verbal working memory [5] have been highlighted in previous studies. Berget, Mulvey and Sandnes [9] suggest that use of icons in replacement of text in online search systems are favoured by those with dyslexia, offering the some of the few recommendations for online information system design for those with dyslexia. Most recently, Morris *et at* [13] have investigated the needs of information searchers with dyslexia through a mixed methods approach. Interviews and then questionnaires were used to collate information from dyslexic information-seekers on where they felt they had difficulties during information-seeking. They have made further recommendations for design that will support those with dyslexia, including; the provision of voice input for search, specialised spelling support, features that could aid in the confirmation that the performed search is that which was intended and features to aid with document triage [13]. These are important developments in the process of understanding what barriers are faced by information-seekers with dyslexia. However, a full understanding of how and where weaknesses in phonological awareness, which impacts reading, writing, and spelling skills, and verbal memory present barriers throughout the information-seeking process for a task such as assignment preparation has not been developed. The naturalistic approach adopted for this project is unique in the field thus far and aims to contribute to understanding of how dyslexia impacts realistic information-seeking tasks rather than prescribed ones.

2 RESEARCH AIMS AND QUESTIONS

The research project seeks to address two research aims;

RA1) Understand the information-seeking behaviour of undergraduate students with dyslexia in the context of assignment preparation

RA2) Make recommendations to better support dyslexic information-seekers.

Recommendations will be made for **a)** those involved in the information-seeking instruction of dyslexic undergraduate students and **b)** for those involved in information search tool design.

In order to achieve this, four research questions have been identified;

RQ1) What barriers to information-seeking success do undergraduates with dyslexia face?

RQ2) What workarounds are being employed by undergraduates with dyslexia during information-seeking?

RQ3) How useful is current understanding of information-seeking behaviour, including associated models and frameworks, which have been developed in exclusion of those with cognitive disabilities, in the explanation of the information-seeking behaviour of undergraduate students with dyslexia?

RQ4) What are the implications of the identified barriers and workarounds for training and system design?

3 METHODS

After initially exploring the usefulness of a mixed methodological approach, a qualitative methodology has been adopted to facilitate a full exploration of the thoughts, behaviours and feelings of information-seekers with dyslexia. In order to investigate the information-seeking behaviour of undergraduate students with dyslexia, a naturalistic methodological approach [14] was designed so that the online information-seeking behaviours that were being demonstrated by participants as they completed an assignment could be captured, rather than a pre-determined information-seeking task. This research argues that it is important to understand the thoughts, behaviours and feelings of information-seekers with dyslexia as they seek information for the purpose of an assignment, as the completion of an assignment is a key element of an undergraduate student's studies that will require information-seeking.

So that barriers and workarounds could be identified, participant captured screen recordings were collected in the first stages of the research project: participants were asked to record their screens whenever they sought information for their assignment and were invited to a follow up interview. Self-captured screen recordings allow naturalistic information-seeking behaviour to be captured over the duration of a complex information-seeking task, such as the completion of an undergraduate assignment. Follow up interviews allowed the opportunity to explore how participants felt dyslexia impacted their information-seeking but the need to explore why the observable information-seeking behaviours were being exhibited in much fuller detail was identified. These interviews highlighted the need for the researcher to ask questions to explore what was happening on the screen during information-seeking and to explore in-depth how the symptoms of dyslexia were influencing the information-seeking behaviours. In response to this, through a process of reflection, an alternative data collection method was adopted.

Think aloud studies, where by the interface user is required to verbalise their cognitive processes as the information-seeking progresses, place an additional load on working memory [15] and, as such, would not be an appropriate in a study with participants that may suffer from working memory problems. However, a retrospective think-aloud (RTA) process does not interrupt the information-seeking process, but allows participants the opportunity to describe barriers encountered and any workarounds they may have employed during the session. Branch [16] found that this 'think after' process is best where there is a concern that the load of the cognitive process of the information-seeking may be too great for the participants. Thus, the naturalistic information-seeking behaviour of participants is still collected but a full exploration of the behaviours seen can be sought by exploring how dyslexic information-seekers experience barriers to information-seeking in the context of assignment preparation in the follow up interview session. RTA protocols are appropriate to this study as they have the advantage of being able to explore why things were done during an information-seeking session, including investigating whether the strategies adopted were found to be successful or otherwise, but whether there are more effective observation techniques is still being investigated.

4 PROGRESS MADE

An exploratory study was conducted at an alternative HE provider, a small College offering one BA (Hons) which is validated by the University of Gloucestershire. This took place between September 2015 and March 2016. 7 participants were recruited and asked to submit screen recordings of each time they sought information for an assignment of their choosing. Participants also had a follow up interview with the researcher.

For the second stage of the research, a call for participants was issued in May and again in September of 2017 to the above HE College, the University of Gloucestershire and City, University of London. 8 participants were recruited; 3 of these participants submitted participant captured screen recordings as well as attending RTA sessions. 13 RTA sessions have been held with these 8 participants. The research project is currently in the middle of this second stage and participants are still being recruited. Further calls for participants are in planning for the beginning of 2019.

4.1 Data Analysis Methods

For the exploratory study; each screen recording was viewed and when an interface action was visible on screen, this was noted down in a linear record of actions, along with a time marker. Then, to establish if unique barriers were being faced by those with dyslexia and the workarounds being employed, observed behaviours from the screen recordings were analysed in relation to current models of information-seeking. Finally, interview transcripts were thematically analysed using theory driven methods in relation to the information-seeking behaviours that had been identified. Findings from the screen recordings were then cross referenced with the themes extracted from the interview data. Data analysis for the RTA sessions is ongoing; Braun and Clarke's Thematic Analysis Approach [17] will be used to identify barriers and workarounds from the transcriptions. This data will be examined alongside the analysis of any screen recordings submitted and screen recordings of the information-seeking performed during the RTA session, analysis of which will follow the process outlined above.

5 INITIAL FINDINGS

The exploratory study highlighted areas where dyslexia may be causing barriers during information-seeking and provided initial examples of workarounds being used by participants. Explanations as to how cognitive and affective barriers were impacting the information-seeking process were sought by examining well cited information-seeking models and theories, including Kuhlthau [6] and Bates [13]. This served to identify where and how in the information-seeking process any unique barriers caused by dyslexia were manifesting themselves.

Barriers were seen within the focus formulation phase of the Information Search Process [11]. Keyword creation and modification appeared to be problematic, with three participants describing challenges experienced when creating search terms for their information-seeking. Reasons given for these difficulties included issues with spelling and recall of vocabulary. Vocabulary is stored in verbal memory, an area that those with dyslexia can face challenges in and P1 noted that it was 'hard when you can't find the information you want because of the wording and stuff...because you've got to do the proper wording, don't you and be more accurate.' This inability to recall vocabulary that would describe the search need was also observed when P3 stated that she was unable to get the online information system she was using to 'work' because she could not think of words to type as a search query that would return the results sought. The workaround that was observed, of the use of query building aids as an alternative to identifying and spelling appropriate search terms, will be further investigated to ascertain its effectiveness.

It was also found that incorporating newly found information into search strategies was a barrier for participants; a skill described by Bates' [18] berrypicking model in its description of evolving search. This would be understandable in the presence of working memory difficulties that would hinder the ability to incorporate new information into search strategies as information-seeking progresses. This was observed when P9 only used three very similar search terms in a 21-minute information-seeking session and stated that, 'you get stuck, just like in a search term, like I can't think what I can search around it...and I just end up with the same results over and over again'. In an evolving search [18], working memory would be used to hold information relating to the search while interacting with new information as it is found but this is something that P9 feels is challenging for her. This example also serves to highlight participants' frustration at failure to progress in their information-seeking. It was a common theme that participants felt that they did not have the skills necessary to perform successful searches for information and if participants do not believe that they can be successful in their information-seeking, then the likelihood that they will persevere in the face of challenges is diminished [19]. Dyslexia can cause low self-efficacy within educational contexts and how this may be impacting upon information-seeking will be fully explored in the main study.

6 FUTURE PLANS

In order to develop a full understanding of how dyslexia impacts the information-seeking behaviour of undergraduate students, a further 15 to 20 participants are to be recruited for RTA sessions. It is felt that this number of participants will allow a holistic picture of the information-seeking behaviour of undergraduate students with dyslexia to be captured and the point of theoretical saturation to be reached in the data collection. Participants will initially be sought from the HE establishments named above, with a call for participants being distributed in January 2019. If the required number of participants is not recruited, other Universities and dyslexia screening centres in the Southwest of England will be approached. It has proven challenging to recruit participants, with only one student responding to an email sent to all undergraduates at City, University of London and alternative strategies to recruit more participants are being investigated.

To understand the information-seeking behaviour of undergraduate students with dyslexia in the context of assignment preparation (RA1), a model of information-seeking behaviour for undergraduate students with dyslexia will be developed and a framework that shows where barriers to information-seeking have been identified, along with any workarounds employed will be created. This could be a variant on an existing model, such as Kuhlthau's [6] that demonstrates where barriers and workarounds exist, which will in turn allow recommendations for support (RA2) to be made.

The development of a model of the information-seeking behaviour of undergraduate students with dyslexia will be used to inform recommendations for the support of this group of information-seekers (RQ4). To support this demographic of students in their information-seeking through multiple, complementary interventions, recommendations for support made will be two-fold; for those involved in the information-seeking instruction and training of undergraduate students with dyslexia and those involved in online information system design. The creation of a model will also serve to answer RQ3, as whether current models and frameworks can be used to explain the behaviour observed in the research will be investigated.

The creation of a framework of barriers faced by this demographic of information-seeker, that also shows when and how workarounds are being employed, will serve to demonstrate how dyslexia as a cognitive disability can influence information-seeking behaviour (RQ1 and RQ2). By understanding at which points in the information-seeking process barriers are faced, the specific interactions with online information systems that are problematic can be used to influence system and instruction design (RQ4).

REFERENCES

[1] G. Reid. 2016. *Dyslexia.* (2nd Edition) Continuum Books, London

[2] CILIP. 2018. *What is information literacy* https://cilip.org.uk/page/informationliteracy?

[3] SCONUL. 2011. *The SCONUL Seven Pillars of Information Literacy. Core Model for Higher_Education.* http://www.sconul.ac.uk/sites/default/files/documents/coremodel.pdf

[4] A. MacFarlane, A. Al-Wabil, C.R. Marshall, A. Albriar, S.A. Jones and P. Zaphiris. 2010. The effect of dyslexia on information retrieval: a pilot study. *Journal or Documentation.* 66, 3, 307-326

[5] A. MacFarlane, A. Albriar, C.R. Marshall and G Buchanan. 2012. *Phonological working memory impacts on information searching: an investigation of dyslexia.* Paper presented at 4th Information Interaction in Context. 21-08-2012-24-08-2012, Nijmegen, Netherlands.

[6] A. MacFarlane, G. Buchanan, A. Al-Wabil, G, Andrienko, and N, Andrienko. 2017. *Visual Analysis of Dyslexia on Search. CHIIR 2017.* March 7 – 11 Oslo, Norway

[7] G. Berget, F.E. Sandnes. 2015. Searching databases without query building aids: implications for dyslexic users. *Information Research.* 20, 4

[8] G. Berget, F.E. Sandnes. 2015. Do autocomplete functions reduce the impact of dyslexia on information-searching behaviour? The case of Google. *Journal for the Association of Information Science and Technology. 67, 10, 2320-2328*

[9] G. Berget, F. Mulvey, F.E., Sandnes. 2016. Is visual content in textual search interfaces beneficial to dyslexic users? *International Journal of Human-Computer Studies.* 92,93, 17-29

[10] B. Pavey, M. Meehan and A. Waugh. 2010. *Dyslexia-Friendly Further and Higher Education.* Sage, London

[11] C. Kuhlthau. 1985. A Process Approach to Library Skills Instruction. *School Library Media Quarterly.* 13,1, 35-40

[12] T. D. Wilson. 1981. On user studies and information needs. *Journal of Documentation.* 37,1, 28-31

[13] M. R. Morris, Adam Fourney, Abdullah Ali and Laura Vonessen. 2018. *Understanding the Needs of Searchers with Dyslexia. CHI 2018* April 21-26, Montreal, Canada

[14] N.J Salkind. 2010. Naturalistic Enquiry. *Encyclopaedia of Research Design.* http://0-dx.doi.org.wam.city.ac.uk/10.4135/9781412961288.n262

[15] T.K Hoppmann. 2007. Examining the point of frustration. *The think aloud method applied to online search tasks. Qual Quant.* 43, 211-224

[16] J.L. Branch. 2000. Investigating the information-seeking processes of adolescents: the value of using think alouds and think afters. *Library and Information Science Research.* 22, 4, 371-392

[17] V. Braun and V. Clarke. 2012. Thematic Analysis in H. Cooper, P. Camic, D. long, A.T. Panter, D. Rindskopf and K. Sher (eds) *APA Handbook of Research Methods in Psychology.* 2, 57-71

[18] M. J. Bates. 1989. The design of browsing and berrypicking techniques for the online search interface. *Online Review.* 13,5, 407-424

[19] A. Bandura. 1993. Perceived Self-Efficacy in Cognitive Development and Functioning. *Educational Psychologist.* 28, 2, 117-148

Where to Go and What to Do

Towards Understanding Task-Based Information Behavior at Transitional Spaces

Melanie A. Kilian
2nd Year PhD
Supervisors: David Elsweiler, Bernd Ludwig
Information Science Group, University of Regensburg
Regensburg, Germany
Melanie.Kilian@ur.de

ABSTRACT

In public transitional spaces, such as airports, users are faced with diverse challenges regarding information interaction and use. These challenges arise due to the scheduled and/or location-dependent procedures users are required to perform. Understanding what these users need or desire in the context of such spaces, what information is on offer, both online and in situ, and how these aspects interrelate is important to facilitate the design of systems that are accepted by the users concerned. However, very little is known about human information behavior (HIB) in public transitional spaces. As a starting point to understand how behavior in such spaces relates to or differs from information behavior in other contexts, holistically, I will create an explanatory model of airport information behavior by conducting an exploratory grounded theory based field study and relating my findings to those of existing models.

KEYWORDS

information behavior; information needs; information tasks; models of information behavior; field study; grounded theory

ACM Reference Format:

Melanie A. Kilian. 2019. Where to Go and What to Do: Towards Understanding Task-Based Information Behavior at Transitional Spaces. In *2019 Conference on Human Information Interaction and Retrieval (CHIIR '19), March 10–14, 2019, Glasgow, Scotland Uk.* ACM, New York, NY, USA, 4 pages. https://doi.org/10.1145/3295750.3298972

1 MOTIVATION

Technological developments, such as ubiquitous mobile access to personalized information via smartphones, have changed the way we deal with information and information systems [19, 28] as well as how we perceive the real-world environment which surrounds us while we interact with information [20, 29]. Whereas we are increasingly able to adjust our homes and gadgets, such as phones, televisions, or even washing machines, to our information practices and patterns of information behavior and vice versa, information interaction in *public spaces* is often not under our control, especially in transitional spaces where we have to act upon scheduled and/or location-dependent procedures. This makes information behavior in the context of these places a worthwhile area of study.

Transitional spaces are, as Marc Augé put it, "to be passed through" [1, p. 104], meaning spaces, such as supermarkets, train stations, or airports. These are places where visitors primarily do not want to linger but are required to cross in order to meet their goals. "Successfully" managing the crossing of these public spaces depends very much on how the users cope with the information on offer, both online and in situ, to complete their tasks (e.g. reaching the right gate at the right time or killing time until a flight departure). Understanding what users need in such contexts, what information is on offer and how these aspects interrelate is important to facilitate the design of systems that adequately meet user needs.

Information science has a tradition of studying human information behavior (HIB) and there are many models that not only depict but also explain information-related human behavior by identifying contextual or other factors [6, p. 146]. Such models contribute to a broadening comprehension of HIB and can help improve our knowledge of information behavior in complex contexts. However, as these models were derived by studying people in very different situations, they may reach their descriptive and explanatory limits when it comes to information behavior in the context of public transitional spaces. Traditional HIB models typically focus on work or work-like tasks [6, p. 155] (e.g. writing a research report or preparing a large celebratory dinner for one's family). Other research has studied information behavior in leisure situations ranging from finding information in pursuit of a hobby requiring specialist skills or knowledge [16, 17] to casual-leisure tasks (e.g. killing time or watching television) and the associated information behavior [12, 13]. HIB in transitional spaces falls between these two cases as casual-leisure activities are often embedded in work-like tasks (e.g. window shopping to kill time until departure can only take place as long as the travellers' schedule allows it and only at places where they can still reach their gate in time; seating areas for relaxation or sockets to power smartphones for video streaming first have to be located). At the same time work-like tasks can arise from casual-leisure activities (e.g. air travel related questions can emerge while chattering to airport staff just for the fun of socializing; questions regarding which food may be packed in your carry-on baggage can come up while visiting eating places).

In addition to the uncertainty regarding the ability of existing models to explain user behavior at public transitional places holistically, there is indeed both a lot of general work that emphasizes the importance of contextual factors, such as time and location, regarding public or mobile information behavior [e.g. 9, 24] and

CHIIR '19, March 10–14, 2019, Glasgow, Scotland Uk

ACM ISBN 978-1-4503-6025-8/19/03.
https://doi.org/10.1145/3295750.3298972

several applied research to support in-situ information behavior in public spaces like airports [e.g. 2, 21]. Currently, however, we lack an appropriate framework that both describes and explains human information behavior and needs at public transitional places, especially in the light of actual information (systems) use.

Such a framework would be particularly useful given recent work underlining that the real-world adoption of technical systems in public spaces often fails due to lacking user acceptance normally because systems are implemented without researchers or practitioners appropriately considering a system's social or ethical consequences [3] or users' attitudes towards the system and its implications [22].

To form a better understanding of HIB in complex public contexts such as transitional spaces and thereby go to the limits of existing models, I have been investigating human information behavior and needs in transitional spaces, holistically. It is my aim to build a model that both describes and explains in-situ information behavior within such spaces, including a user's handling of information and information sources. In this exploration, information sources involve diverse information systems and channels including human sources. In doing so, I also examine how well existing models are able to describe or even explain information behavior in the context of such public spaces. This will ensure that the developed model is not isolated from previous research and that my contribution is able to reveal "docking points" as well as opportunities to integrate my model into other models.

My examination is based on airport scenarios as using airport information behavior as a domain is convenient for several reasons – first, due to the relatively complex and sequence-dependent air passenger ground handling services (e.g. check-in, baggage drop, security check, and boarding services for departing passengers) and the air travelers' need for both timely and location-based information that constitute the airport as a setting with a range of potential contextual factors on information behavior and needs, and secondly, due to the various activities that are performed by airport users – from solving air travel related work tasks, such as navigating to one's gate, to hedonistic or casual-leisure activities, such as going duty-free shopping, visiting eating places, or relaxing until departure.

2 RESEARCH QUESTIONS

With respect to the project goals, i.e. to build an explanatory model of information behavior in transitional spaces, the following research questions have been developed:

RQ1 – The What What various information behaviors do airport users exhibit? What various information needs (or tasks) do they have (to attend to)?

RQ2 – The How How do they carry out theses various information related behaviors and tasks? Meaning what sources of information or what additional strategies do they use in the context of which kind of information behavior and need (task)?

RQ3.1 – The Why Why do airport users behave as they do? More concretely put, how do airport users construct meaning of their information behaviors, needs (or tasks) and choices of information sources?

RQ3.2 – The Why From an expert perspective: Why do airport users behave as they do? More concretely put, how do airport information experts construct meaning of airport users' information behaviors, needs (or tasks) and choices of information sources?

RQ4 – The Systematic Review How well do exiting models of information behavior describe and explain HIB in public transitional spaces?

It is important to note that these research questions are open-ended and non-exhaustive as understanding airport information behavior holistically requires an exploratory iterative research approach, which is described in section 3.

In this study, the term "airport users" refers to the following groups of people:

passengers business and leisure air travelers, both departing and arriving

well wishers persons who accompany departing passengers

meeters & greeters persons who pick arriving passengers up

airport sightseers persons who visit the airport for entertainment

The in-situ information behavior and needs of these groups of people is the object of my investigation.

3 PLANNED AND ONGOING METHODOLOGY

3.1 General Method

This study is grounded in an exploratory qualitative research approach that makes use of grounded theory methodology to create a detailed model of airport information behavior out of rich naturalistic data. An exploratory as well as qualitative approach is expedient as I cannot build on existing models or studies of information behavior given the uncertainty as to their ability to explain airport information behavior holistically. Moreover, existing literature from fields of transportation research has focused on passenger requirements, flow models, and passenger experience on airports [e.g. 5, 14, 15, 18], but neglected the associated (information) behavior of passengers.

Employing a critical application of the grounded theory methodology introduced by Strauss and Corbin in 1990 and later adjusted by Corbin and once again by Charmaz [7, 10, 27] instead of other qualitative methodologies is premised on the goal of this study: My investigation targets an *understanding* of HIB in transitional spaces to finally model it rather than exclusively producing rich *descriptions.* The Ellis model [11] shows that grounded theory methodology is suitable for not only building a model of information behavior but a wide used and diverse applicable one [6, p. 152].

The naturalistic data driven approach of this study also contributes to the field of information science methodically as the examination of task-based information behavior within naturalistic field studies is rare according to Saastamoinen and Järvelin [26].

Finally, to meet the complexity and heterogeneity of the field under study and at the same time to take advantage of the diverse qualitative research methods, I will study my area of interest from two different perspectives, meaning I will investigate what I refer to as the (1) outsider view and the (2) insider view on information behavior in transitional spaces.

(1) The OUTSIDER VIEW constitutes the comprehension of airport information behavior (i.e. the What, How, and Why) from the standpoint of both airport information experts and the researchers involved in the study, meaning it represents the view of these two parties on airport users' in-situ information behavior.
(2) The INSIDER VIEW constitutes the comprehension of airport information behavior and needs from the standpoint of the various airport users.

Collecting data on both the insider and the outsider view is appropriate given the set goal of achieving a holistic understanding. First, it provides rich and heterogeneous qualitative data from different standpoints and therefore forms a more balanced portrayal of airport information behavior. Second, it provides the opportunity to validate the results on the basis of different data types. Third, this approach compensates for limitations the several qualitative methods I plan to use may have in isolation.

3.2 Investigating the Outsider View

The outsider view is investigated by means of theory-generating expert interviews [4] with Munich airport costumer service employees and nonparticipant observations [25] of airport users.

3.2.1 Expert Interview Study. SAMPLING APPROACH. The expert interview study pursues a systematic sampling rationale due to the heterogeneity of the field. Munich airport costumer service employees assist clients with airport-related questions or problems via different media channels (e.g. video chat counters, telephone, and Facebook) and therefore proved themselves as suitable candidates for the expert interview study. Participants were selected from this target population on the basis of defined properties, such as age and professional experience. Ethical standards regarding informed consent and data protection were met.

METHODS FOR DATA COLLECTION. The interviews were performed by means of an open interview style only loosely directed by an ad hoc semi-structured interview guide. All interviews were audio recorded. Whenever possible the interviews assumed the character of contextual inquiries to enable interviewers to observe how enquiries of airport users are resolved. Right after each interview so called postscripts were documented, whereby the interviewers noted incidents which occurred during the interviews.

METHODS FOR DATA TRANSCRIPTION. All expert interviews were transcribed by thoroughly trained student assistants that neither conducted the interviews nor met the interviewees to ensure unbiased transcript data production. To ensure high transcript data quality transcriptions were reviewed for accuracy. Software was used to facilitate the time-consuming task. The student assistants were guided by transcription rules to produce full and verbatim transcripts that capture specific elements of paralanguage.

METHODS FOR DATA ANALYSIS. Analysis of the transcribed data is planned to be associated by listening to the audio recording and performed via qualitative data analysis software. During the analysis I plan to employ defined grounded theory based techniques (e.g. memoing, open coding, and constant comparisons) in order to systematically produce a data-grounded theory based on the expert interview data.

3.2.2 Nonparticipant Observational Study. SAMPLING APPROACH. The sub-study is based on an event sampling approach [23] that guided me to record each visible and/or audible occurrence of information behavior during the observation sessions. Thereby, my notion of information behavior rested upon a broad definition of the term given by Case and Given [6, p. 6].

METHODS FOR DATA COLLECTION. To further investigate the outsider view nonparticipant, unobtrusive and semi-structured naturalistic observations were conducted. At a distance, I observed real-world events that occurred on selected public locations on the grounds of Munich airport and, in the meantime, noted each occurrence of information behavior for a selected time period. By observing in a public setting I was able to cover my investigation, thereby prevent the emergence of an observer effect and was still able to meet ethical standards.

METHODS FOR DATA TRANSCRIPTION. As video recording of relevant incidents was not practical due to data protection concerns, observational data collection *and* transcription had to take place simultaneously.

METHODS FOR DATA ANALYSIS. I plan to analyze the observational data by again applying the above mentioned grounded theory based techniques. Moreover, it will be essential to use this data as a complementary and validating source of information on the outsider view and therefore assess it in reference to the expert interview data.

3.3 Investigating the Insider View

The insider view is investigated by means of in-depth (grounded theory) interviews [8] with airport users and proposed participant observations [25] of airport users.

3.3.1 Airport User Interview Study. SAMPLING APPROACH. A partly systematic partly convenience sampling approach was employed within the scope of the airport user interviews. The target population consisted of in-situ airport users of Munich airport. Participants were chosen from this group on the basis of specific properties and recruited on the grounds of Munich airport. Ethical standards regarding informed consent and data protection were met.

METHODS FOR DATA COLLECTION. Interviews with airport users were conducted by thoroughly trained student assistants instructed by an ad hoc semi-structured interview guide that was tested along with the entire interview project for feasibility and adequacy in a pilot study at a comparable transitional space, a central station of a German city. All interviews were audio recorded. The context of the interviews was planned to vary regarding weekday, time of day, and location due to the heterogeneity of the field. Demographic information as well as memorable or promising incidents were documented in postscripts right after each interview.

METHODS FOR DATA TRANSCRIPTION. The transcription rationales regarding the airport user interviews correspond to those of the expert interviews.

METHODS FOR DATA ANALYSIS. The data will be analyzed according to the outsider view data and additionally used to validate and enrich the theory built on the basis of the outsider view data.

3.3.2 Participant Observational Study (planned). If data analysis does not lead to theoretical saturation [7, 10, 27] after analyzing and comparing the airport user interview data to the outsider view data, I plan to complement the insider view interview data by collecting additional participant observational data. The design of this study will depend on the outcome of the previous data analysis and will be clearer by the time of the CHIIR Doctoral Consortium. Currently, I plan to accompany designated types of air passengers from the starting point of their journey (e.g. their home or a train station) to the security check area (or from the immigration hall to the endpoint of their journey in the case of arriving passengers) and thereby collect data by means of moderate to active participant observations. This data will help me "to refine and fill out ... major categories" [7, p. 12] I elaborated thus far.

4 PROGRESS MADE AND FUTURE PLANS

Between December 12th, 2016 and January 25th, 2017 the following data was collected on the grounds of Munich airport:

(1) Eight expert interviews of which each lasted on average one hour and twenty minutes (minimum value 61 minutes, maximum value 91, median 77, mean 78)
(2) 378 minutes of nonparticipant observations with 132 occurrences of information behavior
(3) 133 airport user interviews with an average duration of eleven minutes (minimum value 3, maximum value 30, median 9, mean 11)

The sample of airport users is very heterogeneous regarding participants' demographic and travel-related properties.

Between December 12th, 2016 and November 20th, 2017 the gathered data was post-processed, meaning postscripts, overviews of participants' properties and primary data transcripts were prepared and repeatedly reviewed.

After several preliminary analyses of parts of the gathered data to guide sampling, the literature review, and the training of students in grounded theory based analysis, I started working intensely on analyzing the expert interview data in August, 2018. From the early phase of open coding I have already identified a preliminary set of airport information needs or tasks. These are based on various conceptual goals, such as wayfinding, fact/person finding, or information gathering. Whereas wayfinding and fact/person finding bear more upon work-like tasks, such as navigating to one's gate and ascertaining a relative's scheduled arrival gate, information gathering seems to often occur in the context of casual-leisure tasks, such as sight seeing and exploring the dining options of an airport. I plan to further elaborate and enrich these findings in the light of diverse information sources and strategies and moreover include a process-based perspective in my analysis agenda to avoid exclusively static statements and also consider dynamic entities.

Whereas **RQ1** to **RQ3** are explored by investigating the outsider and insider view on airport information behavior through complementary qualitative research methods, **RQ4** is planned to be addressed employing a systematic review of existing models of information behavior compared against the airport information behavior model I plan to generate on the basis of my studies. Therefore, it will be indispensable to initially elaborate inclusion and exclusion criteria for existing models of information behavior, search strategies for detecting relevant models and procedures of assessing them.

REFERENCES

[1] Marc Augé. 1995. *Non-Places.* Verso, New York, NY, USA.
[2] Kagonya Awori, Emme Clark, Andreia Gonçalves, Troy Effner, Justine Yang, Ian Oakley, and Nuno Nunes. 2012. Flytalk: Social Media to Meet the Needs of Air Travelers. In *CHI'12 Extended Abstracts on Human Factors in Computing Systems (CHI EA '12).* ACM, New York, NY, USA, 1769–1774.
[3] Gabriel Bartl, Lars Gerhold, and Matthias Wählisch. 2014. Towards a Theoretical Framework of Acceptance for Surveillance Systems at Airports. In *11th International Conference on Information Systems for Crisis Response and Management (ISCRAM '14).* Pennsylvania State University, State College, PA, USA, 299–303.
[4] Alexander Bogner and Wolfgang Menz. 2009. The Theory-Generating Expert Interview. In *Interviewing Experts.* Palgrave Macmillan, Basingstoke, UK, 43–80.
[5] Debra Burdette and Mark Hickman. 2001. Investigation of Information Needs of Departing Air Passengers. *TRR: Journal of the TRB* 1744 (Jan. 2001), 72–81.
[6] Donald O. Case and Lisa M. Given. 2016. *Looking for Information* (4 ed.). Emerald, Bingley, UK.
[7] Kathy Charmaz. 2006. *Constructing Grounded Theory.* Sage, Thousand Oaks, CA.
[8] Kathy Charmaz and Linda L. Belgrave. 2012. Qualitative Interviewing and Grounded Theory Analysis. In *The SAGE Handbook of Interview Research: The Complexity of the Craft* (2 ed.). Sage, Thousand Oaks, CA, USA, 347–365.
[9] Karen Church and Barry Smyth. 2009. Understanding the Intent Behind Mobile Information Needs. In *Proceedings of the 14th International Conference on Intelligent User Interfaces (IUI '09).* ACM, New York, NY, USA, 247–256.
[10] Juliet Corbin and Anselm Strauss. 2015. *Basics of Qualitative Research* (4 ed.). Sage, Thousand Oaks, CA, USA.
[11] David Ellis. 1989. A Behavioural Approach to Information Retrieval System Design. *Journal of Documentation* 45, 3 (Sept. 1989), 171–212.
[12] David Elsweiler, Stefan Mandl, and Brian Kirkegaard Lunn. 2010. Understanding Casual-Leisure Information Needs. In *Proceedings of the 3rd Symposium on Information Interaction in Context (IIiX '10).* ACM, New York, NY, USA, 25–34.
[13] David Elsweiler, Max L. Wilson, and Brian Kirkegaard Lunn. 2011. Understanding Casual-Leisure Information Behaviour. In *New Directions in Information Behaviour (Library and Information Science, Volume 1).* Emerald, Bingley, UK, 211–241.
[14] Tianlun Fei, Neil de Joux, Genovefa Kefalidou, Mirabelle D'Cruz, and Sarah Sharples. 2016. Towards Understanding Information Needs and User Acceptance of Mobile Technologies to Improve Passenger Experience in Airports. In *European Conference on Cognitive Ergonomics (ECCE '16).* ACM, New York, NY, 4 pages.
[15] Anna Harrison. 2015. *Principles of Experience Design for Airport Terminals.* Ph.D. Dissertation. Queensland University of Technology, Brisbane City, Australia.
[16] Jenna Hartel. 2003. The Serious Leisure Frontier in Library and Information Science: Hobby Domains. *Knowledge Organization* 30, 3-4 (Jan. 2003), 228–238.
[17] Jenna Hartel. 2005. Serious Leisure. In *Theories of Information Behavior.* Information Today, Medford, NJ, USA, 313–317.
[18] Tristan Kleinschmidt, Xufeng Guo, Wenbo Ma, and Prasad K. D. V. Yarlagadda. 2011. Including Airport Duty-Free Shopping in Arriving Passenger Simulation and the Opportunities this Presents. In *Proceedings of the Winter Simulation Conference (WSC '11).* WSC, San Marcos, TX, USA, 210–221.
[19] David M. Levy. 2016. *Scrolling Forward* (2 ed.). Skyhorse, New York, NY, USA.
[20] Ming-I Brandon Lin and Yu-Ping Huang. 2017. The Impact of Walking While Using a Smartphone on Pedestrians' Awareness of Roadside Events. *Accident Analysis & Prevention* 101 (April 2017), 87–96.
[21] Yilin Elaine Liu, Christina Harrington, Sarah Melgen, and Jon Sanford. 2016. GatePal - Universal Design for Airport Navigation to Allow Departing Travellers to Stay Informed. In *International Conference on Universal Access in Human-Computer Interaction (UAHCI '16).* Springer, Cham, Germany, 586–594.
[22] Emil Lundberg. 2017. *How to Compete Effectively with Self-Service Technologies.* Master's thesis. Uppsala University, Uppsala, Sweden.
[23] Dan McAdams. 2018. Observation, Case Studies, Archival Research, and Meta-analysis. In *Research Methods.* Oxford University Press, Oxford, UK, 227–251.
[24] David Nicholas, David Clark, Ian Rowlands, and Hamid R. Jamali. 2013. Information on the Go. *JASIST* 64, 7 (July 2013), 1311–1322.
[25] Mildred L. Patten and Michelle Newhart. 2018. *Understanding Research Methods: An Overview of the Essentials* (10 ed.). Routledge, Abingdon-on-Thames, UK.
[26] Miamaria Saastamoinen and Kalervo Järvelin. 2017. Search Task Features in Work Tasks of Varying Types and Complexity. *Journal of the Association for Information Science and Technology* 68, 5 (May 2017), 1111–1123.
[27] Anselm Strauss and Juliet Corbin. 1990. *Basics of Qualitative Research: Grounded Theory Procedures and Techniques.* Sage, Thousand Oaks, CA, USA.
[28] Kar Yan Tam and Shuk Ying Ho. 2006. Understanding the Impact of Web Personalization on User Information Processing and Decision Outcomes. *MIS quarterly* 30, 4 (Dec. 2006), 865–890.
[29] Matthew A. Timmis, Herre Bijl, Kieran Turner, Itay Basevitch, Matthew J. D. Taylor, and Kjell N. van Paridon. 2017. The Impact of Mobile Phone Use on Where We Look and How We Walk When Negotiating Floor Based Obstacles. *PLoS one* 12, 6 (June 2017), 20 pages.

Do Metrics Matter?

The Effect of Indicators on Scientific Search Behavior

Jacqueline Sachse
Department of Social Sciences
Humboldt-Universität zu Berlin
Berlin, Germany
jacqueline.sachse@hu-berlin.de

ABSTRACT

Scientific search engines enrich result lists with indicators of scientific quality, such as citation counts, in order to enhance user experience and improve performance. This dissertation project aims to study the effect of such integration of impact indicators in search result pages on relevance evaluation, considering both traditional citation-based and altmetric measures. The user behavior is analyzed with a combination of eye-tracking and think-aloud as well as a questionnaire. This paper describes the methodology of an experimental study designed to answer the question if the visibility of metrics alters the behavior during scientific literature search and if behavior varies depending on the kind of metric, specifically citation rate and altmetric score.

KEYWORDS

altmetrics; eye-tracking; indicators; information behavior; scientific search; search behavior

ACM Reference format:
Jacqueline Sachse. 2019. Do Metrics Matter? The Effect of Indicators on Scientific Search Behavior. In *Proceedings of 2019 Conference on Human Information Interaction and Retrieval (CHIIR '19), March 10–14, 2019, Glasgow, Scotland UK.* ACM, New York, NY, USA, 4 pages. https://doi.org/10.1145/3295750.3298973

1 MOTIVATION & RESEARCH QUESTIONS

Search engines play an essential role for researchers in finding scientific literature. In order to enhance user experience and improve performance, search results are enriched with indicators of scientific quality. Most common is the citation count, used for instance by Google Scholar, Web of Science and Scopus. Citation-based measures are established as a proxy of a work's impact and hence understood as an indicator of quality [11]. However, they are known to be prone to certain biases, such as biases against books or non-English publications, which correlates with a low coverage of publications in social sciences and humanities, thereby neglecting disciplinary differences in publication practices [1; 5; 21; 23; 26].

Approximately in the last decade, this and other criticism has led to the development of a group of social media metrics under the umbrella term of altmetrics. The term was coined in 2010 by Priem and colleagues [28], but still lacks a common definition [11]. Altmetrics count mentions of scholarly work in social media and online platforms, thus claiming to value underappreciated output (e. g. data sets) and to make forms of impact beyond academia visible. Although there is great uncertainty about what this impact could be and, accordingly, what altmetrics actually signify, there is a growing number of activities aiming at using altmetrics for evaluative purposes[1].

The interest in altmetrics is based on three main features attributed to them: societal impact, timeliness and filter function. It is argued that mentions in news or social media can indicate societal impact of research activities. Altmetrics are in this context rather understood as a complementary measure to traditional citation-based indicators. However, parallel to this notion, there is also the assumption that altmetrics can serve as a predictor for traditional metrics, since their data is available within a few days or weeks after publication compared to years it might take the first citation to appear. This is somehow contradictory, as altmetrics are expected to indicate both, the same as and different impact than traditional indicators. Aside from the specific kind of impact measured, altmetrics at least show that attention is devoted to a research output. This attention is considered to hint at some kind of importance, significance or relevance. Hence, it is argued that altmetrics can be used as a new way of filtering through the sheer endless amount of scientific literature, to create rankings of the most significant work in a field and to provide reading recommendations. Thus, altmetrics offer themselves as supplementary pieces of information to be used for relevance evaluation. As a result, search engines, such as Dimensions[2] or 1Findr[3], begin to introduce altmetrics to their interfaces. The hypothesis that altmetrics can fulfill a new filter function therefore becomes especially interesting from an information

ACM ISBN 978-1-4503-6025-8/19/03.
https://doi.org/10.1145/3295750.3298973

[1] For instance on the European level, the European Commission formed a high level *Expert Group on Altmetrics* (http://ec.europa.eu/transparency/regexpert/index.cfm?do=groupDetail.groupDetail&groupID=3393) and the EU *Expert Group on Indicators for Researchers' Engagement with Open Science and its Impacts* (https://ec.europa.eu/research/openscience/index.cfm?pg=altmetrics_eg).
[2] https://app.dimensions.ai/discover/publication
[3] https://1findr.1science.com/home/

science perspective. However, so far no research was conducted to study the effect of indicator integration into scientific search on user behavior, neither with traditional citation-based nor with altmetric measures.

Previous research on search behavior consistently showed that the position of a result within the result list is one of the strongest determinants to gain users' attention and clicks [9; 10; 15; 18; 27]. However, there are studies suggesting that the ranking bias can be weakened by several factors, such as a bias against ads [4; 6; 8; 12; 14] and relevance [12; 17; 19; 25; 29], both of which can encourage users to skip the first few results and to consider lower ranks as well. Considering the important role in research assessment and long history of citation-based measures as indicators of scientific quality, it appears probable that such indicators are another of those factors which can override the ranking influence, especially in the context of scientific search. Are indicators able to convince researchers of a paper's relevance? This itself is an interesting question, but the ongoing establishment of altmetrics yet adds another dimension to it: Does the pure presence of any number create a sense of objectivity that might be strong enough to bypass the ranking bias? Or is the effect pronounced dissimilarly for altmetrics and citations? Is the meaning inscribed in those indicators an influential factor, hinting at different value concepts of researchers?

As a conclusion of these considerations, part of my doctoral project aims at answering the following research questions:

RQ1: Does the visibility of metrics alter the behavior during relevance evaluation in scientific literature search?
RQ2: Does behavior vary when different metrics are provided?

These research questions are only the first part of a greater project with a broader question. The doctoral project as a whole focuses on the role of altmetrics in scientific valuation practices to answer questions such as: What role do altmetrics play within existing (e-)valuation practices? What new practices are or already have emerged through altmetrics? What potential is attributed to altmetrics, what skepticism do they have to face?

A promising approach towards an answer to these questions lies in a link between information science, which offers theories on and methods to study researchers' information behavior and interaction with altmetrics, and the sociology of valuation and evaluation, which provides key concepts for theorizing (e-)valuation practices. In order to make the broad questions of the role of altmetrics in scientific practices of valuation and evaluation manageable, I focus on concrete practices related to the before mentioned three features of altmetrics (filter function, societal impact and timeliness). As a result, my doctoral project follows a threefold approach.

Firstly, as argued above, the filter function of altmetrics is related to scientific literature search, i. e., relevance evaluation of academic publications. Secondly, societal impact adds a relatively new parameter to scientific core quality values. The question is if this concept is valued by researchers, and if altmetrics are perceived as adequate measures for this task. Thirdly, the possible use of altmetrics as predictors for citation rates leads to the question if users trust and value the competing indicators differently and how this affects their quality judgments and valorization of scientific work over time.

This paper focuses on the first part of the project, thus the filter function of altmetrics and the related practice of relevance evaluation in scientific literature search. The two questions I want to pursue in this first part are if indicators have the power to convince researchers of a paper's relevance and if this power is pronounced dissimilarly for altmetrics and citations.

2 METHODOLOGY

In part one of my doctoral project, in order to study the effect of different indicators on relevance evaluation during literature search, I conduct a laboratory eye-tracking experiment.

The competing situation of altmetrics and citations points to an experimental design, which allows a direct comparison of behavior with different kinds of metrics and without metrics. Although a laboratory observation always differs from the realistic situation, it enables full control over the independent variables and probably generates less distorted data than self-reporting in interviews or in a survey. Eye movements have been shown to strongly correlate with cognitive processes [16]. Hence, eye-tracking data can tell which parts of a page attention is given to, and in what order. Furthermore, think-aloud will serve as a useful supplement, because it provides insights into the motivations behind the attention.

The experiment follows a within-subject design and consists of three conditions: either an altmetric score, a citation count or no metric at all is presented with each search result on a search engine result page (SERP). In order to answer RQ1 the no-metric condition is compared to both metric conditions, regardless of altmetrics or citations. Furthermore, the no-metric condition serves as a comparison group to both metric conditions individually, and thus provides the baseline. Thus, the strength of the effect of the altmetric score can be compared to the effect of the citation count in order to examine RQ2.

2.1 Stimulus

Participants perform three searches for a given scenario, one per experimental condition. The scenario description also provides a query on which participants click to be directed to the SERP. A SERP contains ten results with links to a respective detail page. The pages are wireframes converted to HTML. No second result pages are provided and it is not possible to requery. A score is attached to each entry on the SERP (cf. Figure 1), except in the no-metric condition. These scores do not equal the result's real scores, but are oriented on a realistic scale for the specific result set. The search results shown in the SERP were retrieved from Google Scholar, excluding patents and citations. The ranking was not altered and is assumed to sufficiently reflect the results' relevance, although I am aware this is a potential point of critique. However, the results' "actual" relevance is only a vague concept, and compared to the ranking bias it is of minor importance. I intend to bypass the influence of the ranking bias by placing a few high scores on second, fifth and seventh ranks and let the other results show a comparably low score. This makes it possible to compare if the respective results receive more, less or equal visual attention and clicks depending on the experimental condition and thus allows to conclude, 1) if the visibility of metrics alters the behavior during relevance evaluation and, 2) if it is the certain type of indicator or the pure presence of any number that matters.

Figure 1: Search engine result page

2.2 Participants

When participants are acquired, they will initially not be informed about the specific aim of the experiment. More broadly, they will be invited to a general investigation of search behavior of researchers in their field with special focus on factors influencing the click decision.

Participants will be researchers of two distinct disciplines: Medicine and Social Sciences. These reflect two fields in which indicators are appreciated with different intensity. While the first focuses strongly on performance indicators, the latter has a more skeptical attitude and is typically disadvantaged in traditional bibliometric analyses due to an insufficient journal coverage, a stronger book culture and a higher tendency to publish in native languages compared to Medicine. I intend to acquire at least 60 participants, 30 per discipline.

2.3 Procedure

At the beginning of a session, participants sign a consent form and the eye-tracker is calibrated. After a training task, they spend a maximum of 15 minutes with each of three task. During the tasks, participants are encouraged to perform think-aloud. Participants are further instructed to choose three papers from the SERP and to put them in an order in which they would read them. After each task, they shortly perform a self-assessment regarding their topical familiarity and rate the task's level of difficulty, both performed on a 5-point Likert scale. When all tasks are completed, participants fill out a questionnaire about their familiarity with altmetrics and their personal attitude towards scholarly indicators as well as demographic information. Thus, a session will last no longer than 90 minutes. I intend to conduct the study in the iLab of the Berlin School of Library and Information Science.

2.4 Tasks

Literature search is usually performed at an early stage of the research process to gain an overview of a new topic [2; 3; 7; 13; 20; 22; 24; 30]. Hence, every task asks participants to become acquainted with a topic that is broad and easy enough to grasp for novices and only loosely related to participants' disciplines Medicine and Social Sciences (since otherwise it would pose the risk of participants becoming aware of the experimental conditions due to their expertise). Topics are 1) vegetarianism from a sociological perspective, 2) attitudes of athletes towards doping, and 3) use of big-data applications in health care. The order of tasks and experimental conditions will be randomized separately to exclude both task and order effects.

2.5 Data

The data from this experiment will be processed with regard to the following independent variables: Next to the experimental condition (no metric, altmetrics, citations), the participant's attitude towards scholarly indicators is crucial. This attitude, i. e. to what extent are citation counts and altmetrics considered useful for relevance evaluation, is gained from the questionnaire. Discipline, seniority and social media use are expected to be influencing this attitude.

The dependent variables can be grouped into three categories. Among the ones to capture attention are the fixation and click distribution and the ranks of those papers chosen for reading. Secondly, there are more subjective variables, such as the perceived task difficulty and the self-perception with regard to the usage of the indicators. The latter will be derived from the think-aloud data and the questionnaire. Lastly, there is a group of variables measuring the time and effort needed to fulfill the task, such as the scanpath length, task time or fixation duration. However, for now it remains unsure whether a longer time spent on a task necessarily indicates a negative impact of the condition. Fixation duration might increases when indicators are present because there is more information to process, but at the same time this allows a more thorough analysis of the result's relevance. Thus, the user might has a better experience despite a longer task time.

3 PROGRESS & FUTURE PLANS

The planning and preparation of the suggested eye-tracking experiment (i. e. stimuli-data gathering, design of the search engine, task creation, configuration of the eye-tracking software, laboratory set-up) is almost finished. After the pretests, I intend to perform the experiments in the second quarter of 2019 and estimate the data cleaning and analysis to take about half a year.

Although 60 participants is a comparably high count, laboratory studies do by nature range on a smaller scale than online studies. Therefore, I intend to transfer the experiment into an online environment. This would mean to give up eye-tracking and think-aloud data and to restrain to the less expressive data from click behavior. Nevertheless, it would be a great opportunity to gain more diverse participants from several disciplines and different countries, and to enrich and verify the in-depth data from the laboratory experiment by a large-scale online experiment. This way my doctoral project will contribute findings on the use of indicators for scientific literature search and influence on user behavior on the one hand, and the role of metrics, especially altmetrics, within scientific practices of valuation and evaluation on the other.

ACKNOWLEDGMENTS

This research has been funded under the research group grant "Reflexive Metrics" (FKZ 01PQ17002) by the German Federal Ministry of Education and Research (BMBF).

REFERENCES

[1] D.W. Aksnes and G. Sivertsen (2018). A criteria-based assessment of the coverage of Scopus and Web of Science. Proceedings of the 23rd International Conference on Science and Technology Indicators, 707–716.

[2] S. Antonijević and E.S. Cahoy (2014). Personal Library Curation: An Ethnographic Study of Scholars' Information Practices. Portal: Libraries and the Academy, 14(2), 287–306. DOI: https://doi.org/10.1353/pla.2014.0010.

[3] I Bøyum and S. Aabø (2015). The information practices of Business PhD students. New Library World, 116(3/4), 187–200. DOI: https://doi.org/10.1108/NLW-06-2014-0073.

[4] G. Buscher, S.T. Dumais and E. Cutrell (2010). The good, the bad, and the random: an eye-tracking study of ad quality in web search. Proceedings of the 33rd international ACM SIGIR conference on research and development in information retrieval, 42–49.

[5] D.A. Chavarro Bohórquez (2017). Universalism and Particularism: Explaining the Emergence and Development of Regional Indexing Systems (doctoral thesis). University of Sussex, Brighton, UK.

[6] S. Djamasbi, A. Hall-Phillips and R. Yang (2013). SERPs and Ads on Mobile Devices: An Eye Tracking Study for Generation Y. Universal Access in Human-Computer Interaction: User and Context Diversity, 259–268.

[7] J.T. Du and N. Evans (2011). Academic Users' Information Searching on Research Topics: Characteristics of Research Tasks and Search Strategies. The Journal of Academic Librarianship, 37(4), 299–306. DOI: https://doi.org/10.1016/j.acalib.2011.04.003.

[8] S.T. Dumais, G. Buscher and E. Cutrell (2010). Individual differences in gaze patterns for web search. Proceedings of the third symposium on information interaction in context, 185.

[9] L. Granka, T. Joachims and G. Gay (2004). Eye-Tracking Analysis of User Behavior in WWW Search. Proceedings of the 27th annual international ACM SIGIR conference on research and development in information retrieval, 478–479.

[10] Z. Guan and E. Cutrell (2007). An Eye Tracking Study of the Effect of Target Rank on Web Search. Proceedings of the SIGCHI conference on human factors in computing systems, 417–420.

[11] S. Haustein (2016). Grand challenges in altmetrics: heterogeneity, data quality and dependencies. Scientometrics. DOI: https://doi.org/10.1007/s11192-016-1910-9.

[12] G. Hotchkiss, S. Alston and G. Edwards (2005). Eye Tracking Study: An in depth look at interactions with Google using eye tracking methodology: Research white paper. Enquiro Search Solutions Inc.

[13] C.-T. Hsin, Y.-H. Cheng and C.-C. Tsai (2016). Searching and sourcing online academic literature: Comparisons of doctoral students and junior faculty in education. Online Information Review, 40(7), 979–997. DOI: https://doi.org/10.1108/OIR-11-2015-0354.

[14] B.J. Jansen, A. Brown and M. Resnick (2007). Factors relating to the decision to click on a sponsored link. Decision Support Systems, 44(1), 46–59. DOI: https://doi.org/10.1016/j.dss.2007.02.009.

[15] T. Joachims, L. Granka, B. Pan, H. Hembrooke and G. Gay (2005). Accurately Interpreting Clickthrough Data as Implicit Feedback. Proceedings of the 28th annual international ACM SIGIR conference on research and development in information retrieval, 154–161.

[16] M.A. Just, and P.A. Carpenter (1976). Eye fixations and cognitive processes. Cognitive Psychology, 8(4), 441–480. DOI: https://doi.org/10.1016/0010-0285(76)90015-3.

[17] M.T. Keane, M. O'Brien and B. Smyth (2008). Are people biased in their use of search engines? Communications of the ACM, 51(2), 49–52. DOI: https://doi.org/10.1145/1314215.1314224.

[18] K. Klöckner, N. Wirschum and A. Jameson (2004). Depth- and breadth-first processing of search result lists. Extended Abstracts on Human Factors in Computing Systems, 1539.

[19] L. Lorigo, M. Haridasan, H. Brynjarsdóttir, L. Xia, T. Joachims and G. Gay (2008). Eye tracking and online search: Lessons learned and challenges ahead. Journal of the American Society for Information Science and Technology, 59(7), 1041–1052. DOI: https://doi.org/10.1002/asi.20794.

[20] L.I. Meho and H.R. Tibbo (2003). Modeling the information-seeking behavior of social scientists: Ellis's study revisited. Journal of the American Society for Information Science and Technology, 54, 570–587.

[21] P. Mongeon and A. Paul-Hus (2016). The journal coverage of Web of Science and Scopus: a comparative analysis. Scientometrics, 106(1), 213–228.

[22] J. Murphy (2003). Information-seeking habits of environmental scientists: A study of interdisciplinary scientists at the Environmental Protection Agency in Research Triangle Park, North Carolina. Issues in Science and Technology Librarianship. DOI: https://doi.org/10.5062/F4PV6HBW.

[23] A.J. Nederhof (2006). Bibliometric monitoring of research performance in the social sciences and the humanities: A review. Scientometrics, 66(1), 81-100.

[24] D. Nicholas, I. Rowlands, P. Williams, D. Brown and D. Clark (2011). E-Journals: Their Use, Value and Impact – Final Report.

[25] M. O'Brien and M.T. Keane (2006). Modeling Result-List Searching in the World Wide Web: The Role of Relevance Topologies and Trust Bias. Proceedings of the 28th annual conference of the cognitive science society, 1881–1886.

[26] T.L.B. Ossenblok, T.C.E. Engels and G. Sivertsen (2012). The representation of the social sciences and humanities in the Web of Science-a comparison of publication patterns and incentive structures in Flanders and Norway (2005-9). Research Evaluation, 21(4), 280–290.

[27] B. Pan, H. Hembrooke, T. Joachims, L. Lorigo, G. Gay and L. Granka (2007). In Google We Trust: Users' Decisions on Rank, Position, and Relevance. Journal of Computer-Mediated Communication, 12(3), 801–823. DOI: https://doi.org/10.1111/j.1083-6101.2007.00351.x.

[28] J. Priem, D. Taraborelli, P. Groth and C. Neylon (2010). Altmetrics: A manifesto, 26 October 2010. http://altmetrics.org/manifesto

[29] S. Schultheiß, S. Sünkler and D. Lewandowski (2018). We still trust in Google, but less than 10 years ago: an eye-tracking study. Information Research, 23(3), paper 799.

[30] L. Westbrook (2003). Information needs and experiences of scholars in women's studies: Problems and solutions. College & Research Libraries, 64, 192–209.

Investigating Result Presentation in Conversational IR

Souvick Ghosh
School of Communication and Information (SC&I)
Rutgers University
New Brunswick, NJ
souvick.ghosh@rutgers.edu

ABSTRACT

Recent researches in conversational IR have explored problems related to context enhancement, question-answering, and query reformulations. However, very few researches have focused on result presentation over audio channels. The linear and transient nature of speech makes it cognitively challenging for the user to process a large amount of information. Presenting the search results (from SERP) is equally challenging as it is not feasible to read out the list of results. In this paper, we propose a study to evaluate the users' preference of modalities when using conversational search systems. The study will help us to understand how results should be presented in a conversational search system. As we observe how users search using audio queries, interact with the intermediary, and process the results presented, we aim to develop an insight on how to present results more efficiently in a conversational search setting. We also plan on exploring the effectiveness and consistency of different media in a conversational search setting. Our observations will inform future designs and help to create a better understanding of such systems.

CCS CONCEPTS

• **Information systems → Presentation of retrieval results; Specialized information retrieval; Multimedia and multimodal retrieval; Speech / audio search**; *Information retrieval*; *Users and interactive retrieval*; Retrieval tasks and goals;

KEYWORDS

Conversational Information Retrieval, Spoken Search, Information seeking, Result presentation

ACM Reference Format:
Souvick Ghosh. 2019. Investigating Result Presentation in Conversational IR. In *2019 Conference on Human Information Interaction and Retrieval (CHIIR '19), March 10–14, 2019, Glasgow, Scotland Uk.* ACM, New York, NY, USA, 4 pages. https://doi.org/10.1145/3295750.3298974

1 INTRODUCTION AND MOTIVATION

Information Retrieval systems consist of three components - the user (or the seeker), the knowledge resource, and an intermediary who act as a bridge between the information seeker and the knowledge resource. The major shortcomings of traditional information retrieval systems could be attributed to the following factors [2]: (1) The user may not know the exact nature of the information problem and what he needs to do to solve the problem [3]; (2) It is difficult for the user to find terms that are accurate in describing their information need. Also, they need to make sure that these terms appear in the documents in the knowledge resource (the database). Researches in IR acknowledged the above-mentioned limitations of traditional IR systems. The best way to automate the interactions between the user and the intermediary is through the use of dialogues. This allows the user to describe his information problem in natural language, which in turn allows for a better understanding of his knowledge gap (or information need). Additionally, the system can ask follow-up questions to resolve ambiguities and provide more fine-tuned answers to satisfy the information needs of the user. Conversational systems mimic the human-human interactions which occur between a human information seeker and provider (e.g., librarian).

The conversation between the user and system could be in the form of text (as in the case of chatbots) or audio (as in the case of personal assistants). The use of natural language dialogues, over multiple turns, is the reason why these systems are called "conversational." In other words, conversational search systems provide more human-like interaction [1] to the user who has the freedom to speak to the system (voice requests) instead of typing. Our research focuses on conversations which occur in the audio-only environment.

Recent advances in automatic speech recognition and natural language generation have made it easier to identify utterances and generate responses in natural language. As mobile devices became ubiquitous, users started to perform more searches on such devices with limited display capabilities (small or no screen), which warranted different strategies to respond and present the results. The audio channel allows the user to query by voice (asking questions in natural language) which is faster than typing. The system response is also over the audio channel. In situations like driving, cooking, or exercising [9], where traditional search (through typing) may be difficult or erroneous, the spoken system allows hands-free and eyes-free operation, and so, the user can multitask.

Conversational IR systems are also better suited for people with visual or manual impairment [9] or people with limited literacy skills. Although textual interfaces provide autocorrect suggestions, speaking to the system eliminates the need to the correct spelling of complex, difficult or foreign words. Also, by identifying the characteristics of voice (intensity, pitch, loudness), the system may be trained to tune the response based on the emotional state of the user. This could help in better assessing the information needs of the user in the context of his emotional state. However, it is challenging for the system to keep track of the context (as humans do) and

CHIIR '19, March 10–14, 2019, Glasgow, Scotland Uk

ACM ISBN 978-1-4503-6025-8/19/03.
https://doi.org/10.1145/3295750.3298974

maintain communication over multiple turns. This has limited the existing conversational IR systems to answer only factoid questions. As of now, traditional IR systems provide better support for complex queries and exploratory searches.

The limitations for audio-only search interfaces can be attributed to the transient and linear nature of speech, which requires information to be transmitted in smaller chunks (short audios or limited results) [10, 15] to prevent overloading the users' short-term memory [16]. Thus, conversational systems with only audio-support cannot present complex structures and hence, traditional text-based systems are preferred when the expected result is in the form of images, graphs, and videos. Traditional IR systems are also preferred in noisy environments, such as outdoors, where the environmental noise may superpose with the voice searches and responses, thus causing recognition and comprehension errors [16].

Lastly, the VARK model of education suggests that there are four primary types of learners: visual, auditory, reading/writing, and kinesthetic [7]. So, for educational and learning purposes, the preference of the search system will depend on the user's subjective preference for the learning medium. An ideal solution will be to use a multimodal interface which will support queries for human-computer dialogue and use visual displays for presenting visual objects and the results of complex queries.

2 RESEARCH QUESTIONS

Recent researches in conversational IR have explored problems related to context enhancement, question-answering, and query reformulations. However, very few researches have focused on result presentation over audio channels. The linear and transient nature of speech makes it cognitively challenging for the user to process a large amount of information. Presenting the search results (from SERP) is equally challenging as it is not feasible to read out the list of results. Hence, in this research, we propose to evaluate the users' preference of modalities when using conversational search systems. We also plan on exploring the effectiveness and consistency of different media in a conversational search setting.

The following research question guide the overall direction and objective of the research study:

RQ1: *How does the mode (text, audio) of result (information) presentation influence the users' experiences in a search task?*

RQ2: *Do the users prefer any specific modality over others for result presentation in a conversational search setting?*

RQ3: *Using an audio-only input channel, are the system responses and results presented, as perceived by the user, consistent across all the modalities?*

3 PROPOSED METHODOLOGY

We attempt to answer our research question(s) by conducting an empirical laboratory-based Wizard of Oz experiment. The study will help us to understand how results should be presented in a conversational search system. While the user will be allowed to present his query in only audio form, the results returned by the system could be in the form of text or audio replies. As we observe how users search using audio queries, interact with the intermediary, and process the results presented, we aim to develop an insight on how to present results more efficiently in a conversational search setting. Our observations will inform future designs and help to create a better understanding of such systems.

3.1 Observational Study

The study will contain several search sessions, using two entities or participants, the information seeker, and the intermediary. The seeker - who has no access to the internet or any other online or offline information source (apart from a spoken communication channel) and a non-networked computer - will be presented with an information need (through a simulated backstory and a search task). The intermediary – on the other end of the communication channel (audio only), with access to a networked computer but no knowledge of the backstory or the task assigned to the user – will attempt to help the seeker with the search task. The participants will need to understand and create models of each other, envision the limitations, and collaborate to complete the tasks. The seeker and the intermediary will be in different physical spaces and will not be able to see each other or communicate using gestures or otherwise. We have modeled our experiment to demonstrate that conversational search systems mirror the human-human interactions in real life. While the input (or query) method will be strictly spoken, the result may be presented in text, audio, or any other forms. The wizard represents future versions of conversational agents like Siri, Cortana, or Alexa, where the mode of result presentation is expected to influence the search experience of the user.

3.2 Recruitment

We plan on recruiting N = 48 users for our study. Although the age of the participants is not an influencing factor in our study, we will aim to keep the variance low by targeting students from a public university with similar search skills and experience. Also, we aim to have a balanced number of male and female participants. Participants will be required to be fluent speakers and listeners of North American English (as our system will rely on existing speech-to-text and text-to-speech systems) with some familiarity in using internet and search functions. Although previous studies [17] have shown that experienced and inexperienced users perform search differently, we target the users who are familiar with the basics of search systems. The novelty of conversational search systems acts as motivation in selecting experienced searchers for this study. The role of the seeker and intermediary will be randomly assigned to the participants.

3.3 Protocol

The user and the intermediary will be asked to complete different search tasks in a laboratory setting. The experiment will be a within-subjects design, in which the users will perform different search tasks using the three different systems, a baseline system, and two experimental systems. There will be a total of four tasks, the first being a warm-up task to familiarize the users with the system. The next three tasks will explore the three methods of result presentation: 1. the baseline or control system, where the result is presented as the intermediary retrieves it using a screen sharing mechanism; 2. the text-based system, where the response of the intermediary will be presented as text on the screen; and 3.

the spoken system, where the response of the intermediary will be converted back to speech using a text-to-speech synthesizer and presented over an audio-only channel. Three experimental systems will be used to evaluate the three methods of presenting the search results: the baseline system ($S_{baseline}$), the textual system(S_{text}), and the audio system (S_{audio}). The order of the task types and topics and the experimental system will be rotated for different users to prevent any learning effects. For all the three systems, the intermediary will help the seeker in resolving his information problem and will control how the responses are presented back to the participant. For each task, the user will be allowed a maximum of 15 minutes, after which he will be asked to fill up a questionnaire and move to the next task. Participants could leave at any time but to be compensated, they must either complete all the four tasks or spent at least two hours in the laboratory engaging with the intermediary or seeker to complete the task.

3.4 Tasks

We will create backstories or simulated search situations [4] to place the user in real-life information seeking situation. Such a situation comprises two parts: the backstory and the search task. The backstory provides context about the search task, creates an information need, and situates the user in the simulated task. This promotes a more natural search behavior [5]. According to Borlund [2003], the situation should have the following characteristics [17]: (1) realistic enough so that the user can relate himself to it; (2) topically interesting, and; (3) provide the imaginative context for the user to apply the situation.

The first task will be a warm-up task which will familiarize the participants with the search system, the search process, and the intermediary. The next three tasks will be assigned one after the other and will involve the use of the baseline or experimental systems. To prevent one task or system from influencing the next task-system combination, we plan on using a Graeco-Latin square design [13]. Table 1 shows the experimental design.

Table 1: Experimental Design using Graeco-Latin Square.

User	System/Task Order		
	1	2	3
1	$S_{baseline}$, T_A	S_{text}, T_B	S_{audio}, T_C
2	S_{audio}, T_B	$S_{baseline}$, T_C	S_{text}, T_A
3	S_{text}, T_C	S_{audio}, T_A	$S_{baseline}$, T_B

In the above table, we have presented a system-task block for three users, where the task categories are represented as $T_{A\text{-}C}$ and the systems are represented using $S_{baseline}$, S_{text}, and S_{audio}. There will be 16 similar blocks of three users for our proposed recruitment of 48 participants. By rotating the experimental systems and the tasks, we aim to prevent any task learning effects. Our tasks, which will aim to simulate naturalistic search behavior among experimental subjects, will be adopted from the literature [17]. The tasks, which have already been developed, range from high to moderate in difficulty and complexity (adapted from [17]) and are expected to initiate a multi-turn conversation between the seeker and the intermediary. Although we have avoided the details of the task in this paper, they range from various topics ranging from vacation planning to policy development.

3.5 Procedure

Once the participants report for the user study, they will be given a brief overview of the research procedure and objectives and the role which they are expected to assume during the search tasks. They will also be required to sign the consent form and fill up the pre-test questionnaire (details in the Data Collection section). They will be introduced to the baseline system and the two experimental systems and given a warm-up task to familiarize themselves with the functioning of the systems. The researcher will be available to assist the participants with understanding how each system works and will provide demonstrations if required. After the warm-up session, the participants will need to complete three search tasks in three consecutive sessions, using different systems, the order of which will be determined using the matrix presented in Table 1. The researcher or an expert searcher will play the role of the wizard. For each search session, the participant will have 15 minutes to complete the task, after which they will need to answer the post-task questionnaire (details in the Data Collection section). At the end of the study, the participants will be compensated for their time and effort, and the researchers will conduct a semi-structured interview to assess the experience of the participants. The entire study should not take more than two hours to complete.

4 DATA COLLECTION

We aim to collect different types of raw data during our study, like the users' background and demographic information, the details of the search session, and the pre-test and post-task questionnaire, and the exit interview to assess the users' search experience.

4.1 Pre-test

Before starting the search session, the registered participants will be asked to fill out a questionnaire on basic demographic and background information. The questionnaire will include basic profile (i.e., age, gender, and academic backgrounds), self-reported web search experience, search frequency, and search skills, and self-reported language proficiency. The participants will also be asked to report their frequency of use of intelligent personal assistants (Siri, Cortana, Amazon Alexa). For all the self-reported items, we will use a 5-point scale, where 1=novice and 5=expert.

4.2 During task

During each of the search tasks, we will record the screens and the audio channels of the seeker and the intermediary. Recording the intermediary's screen will provide us with the details of queries input in response to the seeker, the pages visited, and the amount of time spent on each page. Capturing the seeker's screen will help us in capturing the displayed results (for Systems 1 and 2). The audio channel will allow us to capture the interaction between the seeker and the intermediary.

4.3 Post-task

After each task, we will ask the participants (seekers) to answer questions about their search experience. We also plan on using a set of questions derived from the User Engagement Scale [11] to measure how the user engaged with the three systems. Our questions, measured on a five-point Likert-scale will aim to capture details on novelty, involvement, and feelings of reward, success, and engagement [11, 14]. These questions are relevant to the use of new technology and will be grouped in three categories: questions pertaining to the the users' task experience, system and search experience, and quality of information retrieved. The details of the post-task questionnaire has been avoided for space constraints. We plan on reverse-coding alternate questions to make sure that we can identify if the participants select random answers.

4.4 Exit Interview

At the end of the study, the participants will be asked to come for a brief in-person semi-structured interview, where they will be asked a few open-ended questions about their overall experiences. The questions (details avoided here) will try to assess the users' overall experience with the three prototypical systems and the tasks. The users will need to rank the systems and the tasks in order of preference, difficulty, comfort, helpfulness, engagement, convenience, and familiarity. The researchers will also provide clarifications if the users have any questions or comments about the study.

5 PROPOSED DATA ANALYSIS

Subjects will be asked to complete assessments of differentials on task, search experiences, and quality of information after every search session (post-task questionnaire). As the systems will be identical except in how the results are presented, the system-level differentials will allow us to process how the result presentation was perceived by the participants. The quality of information retrieved by the different systems may affect the perception of users towards them. As the three systems are similar in retrieval mechanisms used, any difference in the quality of information retrieved (as perceived by the users) would indicate the shortcoming of the modality in presenting results. The search tasks could also influence the experimental results. We will analyze the post-task responses to the search task to discern if they have any influence on the perception of the experimental systems. We evaluate factors like clarity, simplicity, interest, engagement, and success. We will need to run pilot tests to confirm that the tasks are of similar complexity levels. Otherwise, they will introduce unwanted task effects in the analysis. We plan on using Friedman Rank Sum Test for each differential for all the three systems. Multiway ANOVA could also be used instead. Bonferroni correction will be applied as required and post hoc tests will be done for differentials with significant differences. For identical systems, the sum of ranks should be the same for random samples. When the sum of ranks is different, Friedman Rank Sum Test calculates the chance of obtaining the observed sum. In the exit interview and questionnaire, we will ask participants to rank the tasks and the systems and explain the ordering (which could be used for qualitative assessment). By performing the Kruskal-Wallis test or one-way ANOVA, and relevant post hoc tests, we aim to determine if any of the systems or tasks were significantly different from others. Through our analysis, we aim to understand how the users perceive the different modalities of result presentation, if one of the modalities is preferred over the others, and if the results returned is consistent across all modalities.

6 PROGRESS AND FUTURE PLANS

So far, I have developed the backstories and the tasks. Also, the pre-search, pre-task and post-task questionnaires, and the exit interview questionnaires have been compiled for running pilot studies. In previous user studies [8, 12], I have explored the users' behavioral patterns for search tasks of different complexity levels. I have also explored the influence of information source on search behavior. The codebook and browser plugins developed in those studies will be modified and reused for the proposed study. An initial round of pilot tests will be performed with six or twelve participants to test the study design, instruments, and procedure. By interviewing the participants, we aim to obtain some insight into the potential glitches or shortcomings in the prototypical systems or procedure. A second round of pilot studies may be conducted with revisions, if necessary.

REFERENCES

[1] J Arguello, B Choi, and R Capra. 2017. Factors Affecting UsersâĂŹ Information Requests. In *SIGIR 1st International Workshop on Conversational Approaches to Information Retrieval (CAIR'17)*, Vol. 4.

[2] Grace M Begany, Ning Sa, and Xiaojun Yuan. 2015. Factors affecting user perception of a spoken language vs. textual search interface: a content analysis. *Interacting with Computers* 28, 2 (2015), 170–180.

[3] Nicholas J Belkin, Robert N Oddy, and Helen M Brooks. 1982. ASK for information retrieval: Part I. Background and theory. *Journal of documentation* 38, 2 (1982), 61–71.

[4] Pia Borlund. 2000. Experimental components for the evaluation of interactive information retrieval systems. *Journal of documentation* 56, 1 (2000), 71–90.

[5] Pia Borlund. 2002. Evaluation of interactive information retrieval systems. (2002).

[6] Pia Borlund. 2003. The IIR evaluation model: a framework for evaluation of interactive information retrieval systems. *Information Research. An International Electronic Journal* 8, 3 (2003).

[7] Neil D Fleming. 2001. *Teaching and learning styles: VARK strategies.* IGI Global.

[8] Souvick Ghosh, Manasa Rath, and Chirag Shah. 2018. Searching as Learning: Exploring Search Behavior and Learning Outcomes in Learning-related Tasks. In *Proceedings of the 2018 Conference on Human Information Interaction&Retrieval.* ACM, 22–31.

[9] Ido Guy. 2016. Searching by talking: Analysis of voice queries on mobile web search. In *Proceedings of the 39th International ACM SIGIR conference on Research and Development in Information Retrieval.* ACM, 35–44.

[10] Jennifer Lai and Nicole Yankelovich. 2002. Conversational speech interfaces. In *The human-computer interaction handbook.* L. Erlbaum Associates Inc., 698–713.

[11] Heather L O'Brien and Elaine G Toms. 2010. The development and evaluation of a survey to measure user engagement. *Journal of the American Society for Information Science and Technology* 61, 1 (2010), 50–69.

[12] Manasa Rath, Souvick Ghosh, and Chirag Shah. 2018. Exploring Online and Offline Search Behavior Based on the Varying Task Complexity. In *Proceedings of the 2018 Conference on Human Information Interaction&Retrieval.* ACM, 285–288.

[13] Jean Tague-Sutcliffe. 1992. The pragmatics of information retrieval experimentation, revisited. *Information Processing & Management* 28, 4 (1992), 467–490.

[14] Paul Thomas, Daniel McDuff, Mary Czerwinski, and Nick Craswell. 2017. MISC: A data set of information-seeking conversations. In *SIGIR 1st International Workshop on Conversational Approaches to Information Retrieval (CAIR'17)*, Vol. 5.

[15] Johanne R Trippas, Damiano Spina, Mark Sanderson, and Lawrence Cavedon. 2015. Results presentation methods for a spoken conversational search system. In *Proceedings of the First International Workshop on Novel Web Search Interfaces and Systems.* ACM, 13–15.

[16] Markku Turunen, Jaakko Hakulinen, Nitendra Rajput, and Amit A Nanavati. 2012. Evaluation of mobile and pervasive speech applications. *Speech in Mobile and Pervasive Environments* (2012), 219–262.

[17] Ryen W White, Joemon M Jose, and Ian Ruthven. 2006. An implicit feedback approach for interactive information retrieval. *Information processing & management* 42, 1 (2006), 166–190.

Examining and Supporting Laypeople's Learning in Online Health Information Seeking

Yu Chi*
4th year Ph.D. Student
School of Computing and Information
University of Pittsburgh
Pittsburgh, PA, USA
yuc73@pitt.edu

ABSTRACT

It has long been understood that knowledge acquisition is an important component in the information seeking process [2, 18]. Further, empirical studies have demonstrated that learning is a common phenomenon in information seeking [8, 10, 20]. However, for users, especially laypeople, who must gain knowledge through their interactions with a search engine, the current general-purpose search engine does not sufficiently support learning through search. Health information seeking (HIS, hereafter) is a domain-specific search [14], where users who possess higher knowledge tend to have better strategies and performances in solving their search tasks [3, 21]. While learning clearly plays an important role in the HIS process, there has been little research in this area. Little is known about the factors that might enhance or impede such learning during online HIS. Therefore, this project aims at examining health consumers, especially laypeople's search as learning behaviors and performances. A mixed method design will be adopted, consisting of experimental-based studies and interviews. So far, we have conducted 24 user studies and semi-structured interviews, investigating the source selection behaviors in the HIS tasks with increasing levels of learning goals. The results of this phase of the study will be used to guide the following analysis and predict laypeople's knowledge levels in the HIS process and provide corresponding support.

CCS CONCEPTS

• **Information systems** → *Users and interactive retrieval*;

KEYWORDS

search as learning; health information seeking; source selection; system design

ACM Reference Format:

Yu Chi. 2019. Examining and Supporting Laypeople's Learning in Online Health Information Seeking. In *2019 Conference on Human Information Interaction and Retrieval (CHIIR '19), March 10–14, 2019, Glasgow, Scotland, Uk.* ACM, New York, NY, USA, 4 pages. https://doi.org/10.1145/3295750.3298975

*This work is guided by my advisor: Dr. Daqing He, dah44@pitt.edu.

CHIIR '19, March 10–14, 2019, Glasgow, Scotland, Uk

ACM ISBN 978-1-4503-6025-8/19/03.
https://doi.org/10.1145/3295750.3298975

1 MOTIVATION

According to a national survey conducted by the Pew Research Center [5], 72% of Internet users in the USA have looked online for health information, many reporting that this information affected decisions they took about their health. However, not all online health consumers are equal.

In general, health information seeking (HIS) is a typical type of domain-specific search [14], in which high domain knowledge is required to conduct search successfully. Therefore, consumers who possess higher knowledge tend to have better strategies and higher success rates in solving HIS tasks [3, 21]. While, on the contrary, laypeople mostly rely on the general-purpose search engine as they are not familiar with domain-specific sources, but the lack of knowledge also restrains them from formulating the accurate queries[3, 21]. The current general-purpose search engine is not sufficient in supporting laypeople's health-related search.

The knowledge of a person is not fixed. Information seekers can gain domain-specific knowledge in their interactions with the online information sources. In information seeking behavior literature, learning has been primarily situated around the concept of knowledge acquisition, as stated in ASK (Anomalous State of Knowledge) model, in which Belkin [2] argued that information seeking is a process to resolve the anomaly between users' current states of knowledge and the problem they faced. Marchionini [18] claimed that beyond simple lookup search, people often engage in exploratory search tasks where learning and investigation could play essential roles. Besides, numerous empirical studies suggested that learning is a common phenomenon in people's search process [8, 20]. Learning can occur in a relatively long-duration search [20, 22]. It can take place in a single search session as well [6, 8, 12].

While an increasing population relies on online information seeking to solve their health-related questions, it is known that, in this kind of domain-specific information seeking, learning plays an important role as both a byproduct of the search process and as an influential factor determining the search performance [3, 21]. However, to the best of our knowledge, there is little existing work that combines learning and HIS. Therefore, our ***first motivation*** in this research project is to fill the gap of the literature to understand laypeople's behavior and performance from the perspective of learning achievement in HIS.

Additionally, in the assessment of performance, we are interested in how well the current HIS web environment can support laypeople in terms of learning. So we plan to examine the learning performance against the six cognitive levels in Bloom's taxonomy [1].

Bloom's Taxonomy[1] identified six levels of learning goals from lower to higher order of thinking skills. It is used in the search as learning studies for assessing the learning outcomes[8, 12, 23].

Our ***second motivation*** is to investigate the interplay between health consumers' behaviors and their learning outcomes. Previous work suggests that domain experts and novices behave differently in searching [21, 22], while on the other hand, there exist studies demonstrate one's knowledge level is predictable from her searching behaviors [17, 24]. So this motivated us to investigate the interplay between search behaviors and learning performances in the dynamic HIS interaction process. Is it possible to predict the laypeople's current learning performance based on the prior search behaviors? Besides, what following search behaviors will one adopt given the temporary learning performance? The goal is to alleviate the difficulties and provide the demanding facilities that would result in better search as learning experience in the design of the domain-specific search system.

In addition, our ***third motivation*** is inspired by the uniqueness of health information seeking. We are interested in examining whether searching for different health conditions, for example, acute vs. chronic or severe vs. mild conditions would influence the relationship between search behavior and learning performance.

In the most HIS tasks, health consumers', especially laypeople's domain knowledge is lack, so they are more likely to involve in search as learning process. A search system specifically supporting learning in the health-related domain is needed. Given the insufficient support for learning in the current search system, our final objective in this study is to provide design implications or improve ranking algorithm that enhances search as learning performance in the HIS process and evaluate its usability.

With more and more exploration in the search as learning research area, studying learning in the HIS is a promising research agenda. Overall, this research project aims to respond to an increasing demand for understanding the interplay between search as learning and health information seeking, and how the external factors such as health conditions would influence the behavior and the performance, thus providing demanding support.

2 RESEARCH QUESTIONS

Specifically, the research questions are defined as follows. Firstly, RQ1 and RQ2 are driven by the first motivation to understand the laypeople's behaviors and learning performance.

- RQ1: How do laypeople search to fulfill HIS information needs with different levels of learning goals?
- RQ2: To what extent, can web search support laypeople's search as learning for HIS information needs?

RQ3 is to examine the interplay between search behavior and learning performance, and it is broken down to two sub-questions.

- RQ3a: How does the former search behavior influence the learning performance at different stages of the HIS process? Does the influence vary when searching for different health conditions? If so, how?
- RQ3b: How does the temporal learning performance influence the following search behavior at different stages of the HIS process? Does the influence vary when searching for different health conditions? If so, how?

The answer to RQ1, RQ2, and RQ3 will help to design learning enhancing search systems. Therefore, the RQ4 is:

- RQ4: How can we support and enhance the search as learning in the system design? What is the usability of the support functions?

3 METHODOLOGY

We adopt a mixed method design of combining quantitative and qualitative approaches. Mixed methods research possesses the strengths that offset the weaknesses of both quantitative and qualitative research [9]. As shown in Figure 1, this research consists of three studies for the data collection: user study I and the semi-structure interview for collecting the data to answer RQ1, RQ2 and RQ3. Based on the results, user study II will be conducted to answer RQ4.

The major emphasis in the experimental-based user study is the behavioral data and the emphasis in the survey-based interview study is the subjective data. The data from these two studies will be compared with each other to identify agreements or divergences. The triangulation of the two separate studies helps to increase the validity as well as provide a better understanding of the research problem than either approach alone [13].

4 PROGRESS

To date, the data collection in the user study I and the semi-structured interview has been conducted. After initial data analysis, we have obtained following preliminary results.

4.1 Study 1: User Study I

We designed the controlled study around scenario-based health problems, and provided a live search system for the participants to search on. The study design was approved by the Human Research Protection Office (formerly IRB) of the University of Pittsburgh.

4.1.1 Health conditions and task design. We selected two health conditions with different severity levels: Severe Condition (SC) and Mild Condition (MC). SC was designed to be a more urgent and more complex health issue comparing to MC. This is because we want to explore whether health conditions with different severity levels would result in different search as learning behaviors and performances. As for the specific health issue, the former was multiple sclerosis and the latter was weight loss.

The design of the specific search task is guided by Table 1. The simulated tasks should be both close to real HIS information needs on the web and capable of reflecting learning with different levels of goals. Therefore, we map the classification of health search intentions established by Cartright et al. [4] through large-scale real search logs to three levels of Bloom's taxonomy [1]. Understand, analyze and evaluate represents three levels of six learning goals in Bloom's Taxonomy[1] from lower to higher order of thinking skills. Based on the mapping, we also propose specific search goals for each HIS intention. This framework was used to design the specific scenario-based search tasks in the user study I.

4.1.2 System and procedure. Upon arrival, the participants were asked to fill in a questionnaire about their background (e.g., age, education). Then they were introduced with our experimental search system, on which they could freely search, click and view webpages. The system is wrapped around Google search API, and it returns

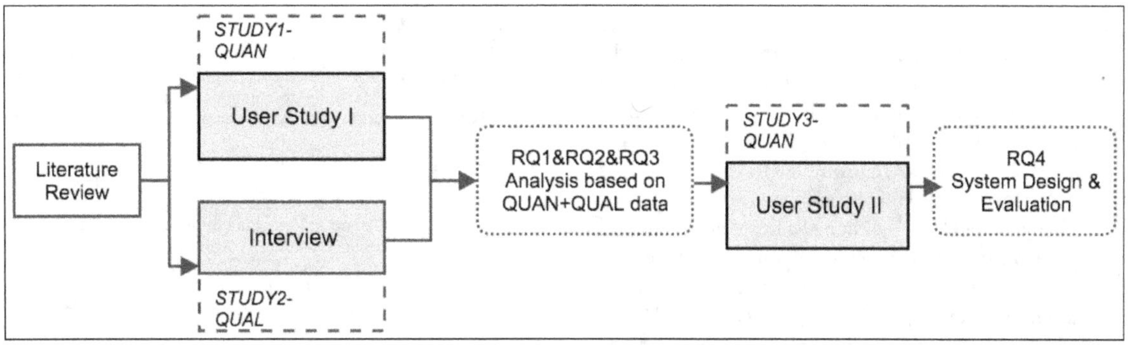

Figure 1: Data Collection Techniques and the Research Questions

Table 1: The Mapping Between Health Information Seeking Intentions and Depths of learning

Depths of Learning [1]	HIS Intentions [4]	Task Design Guidance
Understand	Evidence-based HIS	pursuit of details and relevance of signs and symptoms
Analyze	Hypothesis-based HIS	pursuit of content on one or more illnesses, and on the discrimination among different diseases under the uncertainty
Evaluate	Decision-based HIS	given specific situation of a condition, collect causes, treatments, tests and other information to make decision

Google search results with our behavioral logging functions for follow-up log analysis. During the introduction of our system, the participants were given a training task to get familiar with our system, and they were explicitly informed that their behaviors such as queries and clicks would be logged and analyzed afterward. Participants could highlight certain text in any webpage and click the "save to workspace" button to save it. They could save as many snippets as possible, which would be used for them to generate reports after the search. During the actual search, each participant were assigned to the two health conditions in different rotations to avoid sequential bias. The participants were given 21 minutes to complete the three subtasks with increasing levels of learning goal for each condition. The whole study took approximately 1.5 hours.

4.1.3 Participants and user study data. 24 college students (15 females and 9 males, 18-33 years old) were recruited as convenient samples from the University of Pittsburgh (17) and Carnegie Mellon University (7). 17 of them were undergraduates and the remaining were graduate. We applied two screening criteria to make sure all the participants were laypeople: 1) we excluded people from health or medicine related domains; and 2) we only recruited people who have conducted online health information seeking within the last 12 months [19]. Therefore, most of our participants have searched for health-related information very recently (in last week: n=15, 62.8%; last month: n=8, 33.3%; last six months: n=1, 4.2%). In total, we collected 48 complete search logs (144 search sessions) from 24 participants. Our data collection contains 5,298 clicked webpages, among which 965 (18.21%) were saved into the workspace.

4.1.4 Current findings: analysis of the source selection behavior. To start with RQ1 and RQ3, source selection during the whole HIS process has been examined. One preliminary study has been published in CHIIR'18 [7]. in which we examined what sources laypeople select (i.e., visit and adopt) to resolve their HIS needs, and how different health conditions affect the selection.

Source selection is found to vary in the information seeking process and would result in different learning outcomes [7, 16]. While, given the uniqueness of HIS, source selection becomes an even more important type of behavior. This is because health consumers may use the information found online to make critical health-related decisions. Besides, different types of online sources might serve different roles in the learning process, because understanding health-related information often requires users to master a certain amount of domain-specific knowledge, particularly when encountering the resources full with domain-specific terminologies. The selected online health information sources were classified on the website level as well as webpage level for the analysis. We plotted the source selection behavior in search tasks with different levels of learning goals, and found that, in both health conditions, the participants visited more sources in the tasks with higher levels of learning goals, especially in the evaluate task, but significant results were only found in the mild condition. We also analyzed the changes in the types of online sources. The results indicated the laypeople tend to select more health-specific webpage, such as WebMD.com, when they lack sufficient knowledge to solve their HIS task. Additionally, laypeople will select more diverse types of sources with the increase of the levels of the learning goals, i.e., in the evaluate tasks. Consequently, search engines are also employed more frequently in the higher learning level tasks.

However, the relationship between source selection and the learning performance remains unknown and will be further analyzed.

4.2 Study 2: Semi-structured interview

4.2.1 Interview Design. Though the user study collects some subjective data, such as self-assessment of their learning achievements, we conducted another survey-based study, where the participants could express opinions in their own words, and we could directly elicit their HIS experiences in the real practice. The goal of the interview was to learn about laypeople's own HIS process and the factors that may involve in the process. A semi-structured interview protocol guided the interviews, consisting of two sections. In the first section, the participants were asked to express their general views about online HIS, including the barriers they encountered.

After these general conversations, the interview processed to the section designed to elicit the participants' real HIS experiences based on the principles of Critical Incident Technique (CIT) [11]. If they were glad to share, they were prompted to start from their most impressive or most recent HIS experience.

To take full advantage of CIT, we designed a list of questions and prompts to help the participants to recall and unfold the incidents from memory. In general, the conversation was led by a list of questions: *"What motived your HIS? How did you search for it? Could you recall what kind of websites did you select, and Why? Did you encounter any difficulty? How did you feel before and after the search?"* and *"Did your HIS involve any decision-making activities and Why?"*

4.2.2 Current findings: characterizing the HIS process and discovering the barriers relates to learning. 24 interview audio clips were transcribed and the data analysis was conducted through conventional content analysis, an inductive process [15]. The Participants reported that knowledge plays a critical role in their HIS experience, as lack of knowledge is a major difficulty. Participants were asked to identify the major barriers they confronted when conducting online HIS. Among the 30 relevant comments, the most commonly reported barrier is the 1) "lack of knowledge" about the disease (18 out of 30), accounting for more than half of the comments. 7 comments were grouped into the criticism of the quality of the information from the Internet - 2) "hard to find credible source". The rest 5 comments reflected that the difficulties come from - 3) "intrinsic complexity of the health condition." Furthermore, we characterized the diverse online HIS process with four critical aspects: information needs, search starting-points, emotion changes, and decision-making. The study demonstrated the importance of studying learning in HIS process. Future analysis will investigate the learning goal in each incident shared by the participants, and the corresponding behaviors and search process.

5 FUTURE PLAN

The future research plan includes three main phases:

(i) So far, the initial data analysis only centered on the source selection behavior in response to HIS tasks with different levels of learning goals. For the next step, we plan to explore other types of search behaviors and assess the performance of the participants with the rich behavioral logs, as well as the questionnaire responses. We asked the participants to write a short summary in answer to the search tasks after each search session and they also self-assessed their knowledge levels. This data is available for the assessment of the participants' learning performance.

(ii) With the results and findings, we plan to upgrade the current search system with either ranking algorithm or design features in support of learning for HIS. For example, is it beneficial to recommend different types of learning sources to the consumers based on the prediction of her topic knowledge level? Also, is it worth to assess the severity of the health condition searched by the consumer and support the HIS accordingly?

(iii) After employing the upgraded system, We plan to design user study II and evaluate the usability of the system.

REFERENCES

[1] Lorin W Anderson, David R Krathwohl, Peter W Airasian, Kathleen A Cruikshank, Richard E Mayer, Paul R Pintrich, James Raths, and Merlin C Wittrock. 2001. A taxonomy for learning, teaching, and assessing: A revision of BloomâĂŹs taxonomy of educational objectives, abridged edition. *White Plains, NY: Longman* (2001).

[2] Nicholas J Belkin. 1980. Anomalous states of knowledge as a basis for information retrieval. *Canadian journal of information science* 5, 1 (1980), 133–143.

[3] Suresh K Bhavnani. 2002. Domain-specific search strategies for the effective retrieval of healthcare and shopping information. In *CHI'02 Extended Abstracts on Human Factors in Computing Systems*. ACM, 610–611.

[4] Marc-Allen Cartright, Ryen W White, and Eric Horvitz. 2011. Intentions and attention in exploratory health search. In *Proceedings of the 34th international ACM SIGIR conference on Research and development in Information Retrieval*. ACM, 65–74.

[5] Pew Reseach Center. 2013. Health Fact Sheet. *Pew Res. Cent. Internet Sci. Tech* (2013).

[6] Yu Chi, Shuguang Han, Daqing He, and Rui Meng. 2016. Exploring knowledge learning in collaborative information seeking process. In *CEUR Workshop Proceedings*, Vol. 1647.

[7] Yu Chi, Daqing He, Shuguang Han, and Jie Jiang. 2018. What Sources to Rely on:: Laypeople's Source Selection in Online Health Information Seeking. In *Proceedings of the 2018 Conference on Human Information Interaction&Retrieval*. ACM, 233–236.

[8] Kevyn Collins-Thompson, Soo Young Rieh, Carl C Haynes, and Rohail Syed. 2016. Assessing learning outcomes in web search: A comparison of tasks and query strategies. In *Proceedings of the 2016 ACM on Conference on Human Information Interaction and Retrieval*. ACM, 163–172.

[9] John W Creswell and Vicki L Plano Clark. 2017. *Designing and conducting mixed methods research*. Sage publications.

[10] Carsten Eickhoff, Jaime Teevan, Ryen White, and Susan Dumais. 2014. Lessons from the journey: a query log analysis of within-session learning. In *Proceedings of the 7th ACM international conference on Web search and data mining*. ACM, 223–232.

[11] John C Flanagan. 1954. The critical incident technique. *Psychological bulletin* 51, 4 (1954), 327.

[12] Souvick Ghosh, Manasa Rath, and Chirag Shah. 2018. Searching as Learning: Exploring Search Behavior and Learning Outcomes in Learning-related Tasks. In *Proceedings of the 2018 Conference on Human Information Interaction&Retrieval*. ACM, 22–31.

[13] Lisa Guion. 2002. Triangulation: Establishing the validity of qualitative studies. *University of Florida-IFAS Extension* (2002).

[14] Allan Hanbury. 2012. Medical information retrieval: an instance of domain-specific search. In *Proceedings of the 35th international ACM SIGIR conference on Research and development in information retrieval*. ACM, 1191–1192.

[15] Hsiu-Fang Hsieh and Sarah E Shannon. 2005. Three approaches to qualitative content analysis. *Qualitative health research* 15, 9 (2005), 1277–1288.

[16] Chang Liu and Xiaoxuan Song. 2018. How do Information Source Selection Strategies Influence Users' Learning Outcomes'. In *Proceedings of the 2018 Conference on Human Information Interaction&Retrieval*. ACM, 257–260.

[17] Jingjing Liu, Chang Liu, and Nicholas J Belkin. 2016. Predicting information searchers' topic knowledge at different search stages. *Journal of the Association for Information Science and Technology* 67, 11 (2016), 2652–2666.

[18] Gary Marchionini. 2006. Exploratory search: from finding to understanding. *Commun. ACM* 49, 4 (2006), 41–46.

[19] Susan L Perez, Debora A Paterniti, Machelle Wilson, Robert A Bell, Man Shan Chan, Chloe C Villareal, Hien Huy Nguyen, and Richard L Kravitz. 2015. Characterizing the processes for navigating Internet health information using real-time observations: a mixed-methods approach. *Journal of medical Internet research* 17, 7 (2015).

[20] Pertti Vakkari, Mikko Pennanen, and Sami Serola. 2003. Changes of search terms and tactics while writing a research proposal: A longitudinal case study. *Information processing & management* 39, 3 (2003), 445–463.

[21] Ryen W White, Susan T Dumais, and Jaime Teevan. 2009. Characterizing the influence of domain expertise on web search behavior. In *Proceedings of the second ACM international conference on web search and data mining*. ACM, 132–141.

[22] Barbara M Wildemuth. 2004. The effects of domain knowledge on search tactic formulation. *Journal of the american society for information science and technology* 55, 3 (2004), 246–258.

[23] Mathew J Wilson and Max L Wilson. 2013. A comparison of techniques for measuring sensemaking and learning within participant-generated summaries. *Journal of the American Society for Information Science and Technology* 64, 2 (2013), 291–306.

[24] Ran Yu, Ujwal Gadiraju, Peter Holtz, Markus Rokicki, Philipp Kemkes, and Stefan Dietze. 2018. Predicting User Knowledge Gain in Informational Search Sessions. *arXiv preprint arXiv:1805.00823* (2018).

Towards Non-Visual Web Search

Alexandra Vtyurina
University of Waterloo
Waterloo, Ontario, Canada
sasha.vtyurina@uwaterloo.ca

ABSTRACT

Speech-based user interfaces and, in particular, voice-activated digital assistants are gaining popularity. Assistants provide their users with an opportunity for hands-free interaction, and present an additional accessibility level for people who are blind. According to prior research, informational searches form a noticeable fraction of user interactions with the assistants. All major commercially available assistants handle factoid questions well by providing an answer that is quick, concise, and to-the-point. However, for complex information seeking intents, when a deeper exploration and multi-turn interaction may be required, the assistants often do not produce the desired results.

One of the main challenges for designing a voice-based web search system is the higher cognitive load for audio perception compared to visual perception. Additionally, close attention should be paid at differences in designing for different user groups, as their information seeking styles and design needs and may differ.

In this work, we discuss the challenges of designing systems for non-visual ad-hoc web search and exploration and outline a set of proposed experiments tackling various aspects of non-visual web search.

ACM Reference Format:
Alexandra Vtyurina. 2019. Towards Non-Visual Web Search. In *2019 Conference on Human Information Interaction and Retrieval (CHIIR '19), March 10–14, 2019, Glasgow, Scotland Uk.* ACM, New York, NY, USA, 4 pages. https://doi.org/10.1145/3295750.3298976

1 INTRODUCTION OR MOTIVATION

The popularity of speech-based interfaces has been growing in recent years with 20% of mobile search queries being issued over voice in 2014[1]. Similarly, voice-based digital assistants, such as Amazon Echo and Google Home, have been widely adopted with 24% of the US households owning a smart speaker in 2018.[2] People find voice assistants practical for their hands-free interaction model, which is valuable for when the user's hands are busy [17], or for dealing with other kinds of situationally-induced impairments [28]. While some sighted users consider digital assistants a source of entertainment [16, 17], many people who are blind also appreciate this technology for providing access to otherwise inaccessible applications and services [2].

According to prior research, voice-based assistants are mainly used for simple commands such as controlling a music player and checking the weather [18, 27]. However, a prominent portion of the user queries are informational in their nature [18]. While most commercially available digital assistants generally perform well in answering factoid questions, such as "When was Albert Einstein born?", more complex information seeking intents may not yield a satisfactory response. In the latter cases, the assistants often fall back on their screen-based counterparts (e.g. a phone app), showing the user the conventional web search results for the query. Such interaction model effectively forces the users to switch to a different device and modality, leaving them with little to no recourse.

Presenting search results over voice and building an interaction model that accommodates users at all stages of their search process poses a series of challenges. First of all, the sequential nature of the audio channel presents a higher cognitive load compared to visual displays. For example, the user can no longer "glimpse" at a page and get an overall impression about the relevance or trustworthiness of the results [1]. Additionally, voice interaction with digital assistants is often a secondary activity, meaning even less resources are left for performing the search [28].

Designing an interaction model that supports user needs at every step of the search process: query formulation, results exploration, and query reformulation, needs careful crafting. Radlinsky and Craswell [21] proposed a theoretical framework for a conversational search system, and Trippas et al. [26], as well as Thomas et al. [25] studied the process of audio-only web-based information seeking between two people. Additionally, different user groups, such as children, older adults, and people with disabilities exhibit different behaviour and require different features to support their needs [20, 30, 31], which must be considered in the proposed system design.

Finally, understanding user behaviour is an important aspect of a web search system. A large body of research has explored a variety of features signalling user (dis)satisfaction with the search process [3]. However, less is known about the users' behavioural patterns when performing voice-based web search [11, 15]. Studying user behaviour during voice search is necessary for optimizing how the system works, and making necessary adjustments for improved user experience.

In this work, we discuss the challenges presented when designing a non-visual voice-search system and propose a set of experiments aimed to build a knowledge base for further research in the area.

[1] https://googleblog.blogspot.com/2014/10/omg-mobile-voice-survey-reveals-teens.html
[2] https://www.nielsen.com/us/en/insights/news/2018/smart-speaking-my-language-despite-their-vast-capabilities-smart-speakers-all-about-the-music.html

CHIIR '19, March 10–14, 2019, Glasgow, Scotland Uk

ACM ISBN 978-1-4503-6025-8/19/03.
https://doi.org/10.1145/3295750.3298976

2 RESEARCH QUESTIONS

The main focus of our work is designing a voice-based interface for ad-hoc web search and exploration. In broad terms, we aim to answer the following research questions:

- **RQ 1**: What is the optimal way of presenting web search results over an audio channel without cognitively straining users?
- **RQ 2**: What features should a voice-based information seeking system possess to support users at all stages of the search process?
- **RQ 3**: What are the differences in requirements between user groups (blind and sighted people), and how should a proposed system adapt to them?
- **RQ 4**: What features of user behaviour can be leveraged to assess the user (dis)satisfaction of their search process?

3 PROPOSED METHODOLOGY

To address the questions outlined above, we plan to use a combination of different approaches such as laboratory studies, semi-structured interviews, longitudinal studies, and log analysis. We describe the proposed experiments in the following sections.

3.1 Audio Representation of Search Results

Speech comprehension as a secondary activity takes less cognitive effort compared to consuming information from a visual display [28]. Speech is therefore a preferred way of consuming information when performing another activity [23]. However, speech lacks in comparison to visual displays in one important aspect – it is sequential, and a user can no longer "glimpse" at a page. A mismatch between the linear representation of results and the spatial outline of the page results in an increased cognitive load [24]. Various methods have been developed to try and bring down the cognitive load for the users of voice interfaces, such as non-visual skimming [4], semantic page clustering [8], and approaches based on concurrent speech [9]. On the other hand, a large body of research is devoted to investigating the visual appearances of the web search results [12] and how they affect user interactions [7].

The optimal audio-based representation of the search results **(1)** should not put a cognitive strain on the user, making it possible to multi-task while performing the search, **(2)** should expose enough details, so that the user can identify similar results as relevant for their query, **(3)** should emphasize certain features so that a user can assess the trustworthiness of the source [1].

We will compare the different audio-based methods for presenting web search results in the following aspects:

- how cognitively taxing is a representation when search in the primary activity?
- how cognitively taxing is a representation when search is the user's secondary activity, with the varying complexity of the primary activity?
- how well can a user perform their primary activity while also engaged in the task of non-visual web search?
- how well can a user identify the list of relevant results?
- how well can a user identify the relevant and trustworthy results?

Overall, to answer RQ 1 we will conduct a laboratory study, where the participants will be invited to compare several audio-based representations of web search results. To compare how well the chosen representations are suited for different user groups we plan to seek participation from sighted and blind user populations. We plan to borrow the search tasks from similar research [25, 26], as well as asking the participants to perform the task on the topic that they are personally interested in. We will vary the participants' primary activity and measure their cognitive load using standard tools such as a NASA TLX questionnaire [10]. Finally, we will duplicate the task and compare the results chosen over the voice interface with the results chosen over a conventional interface. We will conclude by conducting a semi-structured interviews with the participants, which may provide us with an additional insight about the design of the system.

3.2 Interaction Model for Information-Seeking Conversations

The web search cycle can be split into four major steps: query formulation, search results exploration, query reformulation, and search results management [22]. A system for non-visual web search should provide adequate support for the users at every step, ensuring a clear and convenient access to all features offered by a search engine.

A conversation between a human and a computer is often compared and contrasted to a conversation between two people. When considering a task of finding information by talking to a voice-based digital assistant, it is worth considering the analog alternative – a conversation with a librarian. Research by Trippas et al. [26] and Thomas et al. [25] has explored the interactions between two people connected by an audio channel while performing a search task. We will start addressing the **RQ 2** by studying the functional patterns exhibited by the participants during their conversations in [25, 26].

The problem of developing an interaction model for search was also explored by Radlinsky and Craswell [21] who proposed a theoretical model for a conversational search system, outlining possible flow of an information seeking conversation. Specific areas, such as error recovery for a conversational system was extensively studied in a series of research by Dan Bohus [5]. Murad et al. [19] proposed a set of design guidelines for speech-based applications by examining twenty recent studies of voice interfaces and mapping GUI design principles to speech interfaces.

The pitfalls of existing digital voice assistants include not knowing the functionality of the system, and not knowing how to phrase commands [17]. In our previous work we also found that a successful speech-based system will support highly conversational interactions [29], whereas the work Kiesel et al. [14] found that users are not dissatisfied when a system clarifies user intents.

Backed by the substantial theoretical and practical findings outlined above we plan to design a voice-based interaction model for web search that paves a clear path for users to interact with search engine functions, and is conversational and proactive enough to not cause the user frustration.

3.3 Differences Between User Groups

Different user groups exhibit various behavioural patterns while interacting with voice-based digital assistants. Previous research has explored how children, older adults and people with various disabilities user voice assistants [2, 20, 30, 31]. In our work, we plan to focus on investigating two user groups: sighted and blind users.

Sighted and blind people search the web in a very different way due to the assistive technology [22]. However not all differences are caused by the use of assistive technology. People who have been blind for a prolonged period of time exhibit much higher listening rates compared to sighted people [6] and may benefit from being able to increase the speech rate of voice assistants. People who are blind are typically early adopters and proficient users of voice interfaces [20] and may have a different set of requirements for a voice-based search system. Additionally, voice-based search may act as a primary activity for people who are blind, which in its turn may further contribute to the discussed differences.

As such, enabling customizable settings, and exploring the space of an adaptive system for non-visual search will help address **RQ 3**. To fully understand how the two user groups approach the task of voice-based web search we plan to combine laboratory user studies with semi-structured interviews with the participants. While the laboratory studies will help understand the benefits and the shortcomings of a proposed system, the interviews will uncover the motives behind particular preferences of the users and help inform further design choices.

3.4 Inferring User Satisfaction

Finally, to address the **RQ 4**, we will explore the behavioural patterns exhibited by users that are reflective of user (dis)satisfaction with the system performance. We plan to take inspiration from the substantial body of research investigating user behaviour while performing web search [3], and discover similar features in voice user interactions.

Some signs of user frustration include enunciating when rephrasing [13] and adjacent repetitions [11]. An under-researched subject is the use of abusive language with assistants, which in some cases can be an indicator of an extreme dissatisfaction with the system performance.

Explicit relevance feedback in visual search interfaces is not often provided by people, as it requires an additional effort. However, voice medium is an extremely cheap way and requires little user effort. In this work, we plan to explore the space of soliciting explicit user relevance feedback, and investigating the optimal model for doing so without irritating the user.

User behaviour may be affected by multiple factors including a task choice, their motivation and interest, and the environment [12]. This may make the laboratory environment unsuited for a valid evaluation of user satisfaction. We plan to deploy our search system onto a smart speaker device and invite a number of users to use it over a period of several weeks. After the study period we will ask the participants about their experience by going through the interaction logs and discussing the general interaction patterns and exploring the signs of dissatisfaction. The collected logs and interview data will be used to assess the signals of user (dis)satisfaction and potential reasons behind it. This information can be further used to adjust the system behaviour on-the-go.

4 CONCLUSION

Voice-based digital assistants are growing in popularity and offer the advantages of hands-free interaction and multi-tasking. Informational searches constitute a noticeable portion of user interactions, but complex search intents are often not supported. This work discusses the challenges for creating a voice-based system for ad-hoc web search and outlines the set of proposed research experiments. The findings produced from the proposed experiments will add to the knowledge base for further research in the area.

REFERENCES

[1] Ali Abdolrahmani and Ravi Kuber. 2016. Should I trust it when I cannot see it?: Credibility assessment for blind web users. In *Proceedings of the 18th International ACM SIGACCESS Conference on Computers and Accessibility*. ACM, 191–199.

[2] Ali Abdolrahmani, Ravi Kuber, and Stacy M Branham. 2018. Siri Talks at You: An Empirical Investigation of Voice-Activated Personal Assistant (VAPA) Usage by Individuals Who Are Blind. In *Proceedings of the 20th International ACM SIGACCESS Conference on Computers and Accessibility*. ACM, 249–258.

[3] Eugene Agichtein, Eric Brill, and Susan Dumais. 2006. Improving web search ranking by incorporating user behavior information. In *Proceedings of the 29th annual international ACM SIGIR conference on Research and development in information retrieval*. ACM, 19–26.

[4] Faisal Ahmed, Yevgen Borodin, Andrii Soviak, Muhammad Islam, IV Ramakrishnan, and Terri Hedgpeth. 2012. Accessible skimming: faster screen reading of web pages. In *Proceedings of the 25th annual ACM symposium on User interface software and technology*. ACM, 367–378.

[5] Dan Bohus. 2007. *Error awareness and recovery in conversational spoken language interfaces*. Ph.D. Dissertation.

[6] Danielle Bragg, Cynthia Bennett, Katharina Reinecke, and Richard Ladner. 2018. A Large Inclusive Study of Human Listening Rates. In *Proceedings of the 2018 CHI Conference on Human Factors in Computing Systems*. ACM, 444.

[7] Georg Buscher, Susan T Dumais, and Edward Cutrell. 2010. The good, the bad, and the random: an eye-tracking study of ad quality in web search. In *Proceedings of the 33rd international ACM SIGIR conference on Research and development in information retrieval*. ACM, 42–49.

[8] Prathik Gadde and Davide Bolchini. 2014. From screen reading to aural glancing: towards instant access to key page sections. In *Proceedings of the 16th international ACM SIGACCESS conference on Computers & accessibility*. ACM, 67–74.

[9] João Guerreiro. 2016. Towards screen readers with concurrent speech: where to go next? *ACM SIGACCESS Accessibility and Computing* 115 (2016), 12–19.

[10] Sandra G Hart and Lowell E Staveland. 1988. Development of NASA-TLX (Task Load Index): Results of empirical and theoretical research. In *Advances in psychology*. Vol. 52. Elsevier, 139–183.

[11] Ahmed Hassan Awadallah, Ranjitha Gurunath Kulkarni, Umut Ozertem, and Rosie Jones. 2015. Characterizing and predicting voice query reformulation. In *Proceedings of the 24th ACM International on Conference on Information and Knowledge Management*. ACM, 543–552.

[12] Marti Hearst. 2009. *Search user interfaces*. Cambridge University Press.

[13] Jiepu Jiang, Wei Jeng, and Daqing He. 2013. How do users respond to voice input errors?: lexical and phonetic query reformulation in voice search. In *Proceedings of the 36th international ACM SIGIR conference on Research and development in information retrieval*. ACM, 143–152.

[14] Johannes Kiesel, Arefeh Bahrami, Benno Stein, Avishek Anand, and Matthias Hagen. 2018. Toward Voice Query Clarification.. In *SIGIR*. 1257–1260.

[15] Julia Kiseleva, Kyle Williams, Jiepu Jiang, Ahmed Hassan Awadallah, Aidan C Crook, Imed Zitouni, and Tasos Anastasakos. 2016. Understanding user satisfaction with intelligent assistants. In *Proceedings of the 2016 ACM on Conference on Human Information Interaction and Retrieval*. ACM, 121–130.

[16] Irene Lopatovska, Katrina Rink, Ian Knight, Kieran Raines, Kevin Cosenza, Harriet Williams, Perachya Sorsche, David Hirsch, Qi Li, and Adrianna Martinez. 2018. Talk to me: Exploring user interactions with the Amazon Alexa. *Journal of Librarianship and Information Science* (2018), 0961000618759414.

[17] Ewa Luger and Abigail Sellen. 2016. Like having a really bad PA: the gulf between user expectation and experience of conversational agents. In *Proceedings of the 2016 CHI Conference on Human Factors in Computing Systems*. ACM, 5286–5297.

[18] Rishabh Mehrotra, A Hassan Awadallah, AE Kholy, and Imed Zitouni. 2017. Hey Cortana! Exploring the use cases of a Desktop based Digital Assistant. In *SIGIR 1st International Workshop on Conversational Approaches to Information Retrieval (CAIR'17)*, Vol. 4.

[19] Christine Murad, Cosmin Munteanu, Leigh Clark, and Benjamin R Cowan. 2018. Design guidelines for hands-free speech interaction. In *Proceedings of the 20th International Conference on Human-Computer Interaction with Mobile Devices and Services Adjunct.* ACM, 269–276.

[20] Alisha Pradhan, Kanika Mehta, and Leah Findlater. 2018. Accessibility Came by Accident: Use of Voice-Controlled Intelligent Personal Assistants by People with Disabilities. In *Proceedings of the 2018 CHI Conference on Human Factors in Computing Systems.* ACM, 459.

[21] Filip Radlinski and Nick Craswell. 2017. A theoretical framework for conversational search. In *Proceedings of the 2017 Conference on Conference Human Information Interaction and Retrieval.* ACM, 117–126.

[22] Nuzhah Gooda Sahib, Anastasios Tombros, and Tony Stockman. 2012. A comparative analysis of the information-seeking behavior of visually impaired and sighted searchers. *Journal of the American Society for Information Science and Technology* 63, 2 (2012), 377–391.

[23] Andrew Sears, Min Lin, Julie Jacko, and Yan Xiao. 2003. When computers fade: Pervasive computing and situationally-induced impairments and disabilities. In *HCI International,* Vol. 2. 1298–1302.

[24] Tony Stockman and Oussama Metatla. 2008. The influence of screen-readers on web cognition. In *Proceeding of Accessible design in the digital world conference (ADDW 2008), York, UK.*

[25] Paul Thomas, Daniel McDuf, Mary Czerwinski, and Nick Craswell. 2017. MISC: A data set of information-seeking conversations. (2017).

[26] Johanne R Trippas, Damiano Spina, Lawrence Cavedon, and Mark Sanderson. 2017. How do people interact in conversational speech-only search tasks: A preliminary analysis. In *Proceedings of the 2017 Conference on Conference Human Information Interaction and Retrieval.* ACM, 325–328.

[27] Janice Y. Tsai, Tawfiq Ammari, Abraham Wallin, and Jofish Kaye. 2018. Alexa, play some music: Categorization of Alexa Commands. In *Voice-based Conversational UX Studies and Design Wokrshop at CHI.* ACM.

[28] Kristin Vadas, Nirmal Patel, Kent Lyons, Thad Starner, and Julie Jacko. 2006. Reading on-the-go: a comparison of audio and hand-held displays. In *Proceedings of the 8th conference on Human-computer interaction with mobile devices and services.* ACM, 219–226.

[29] Alexandra Vtyurina and Adam Fourney. 2018. Exploring the Role of Conversational Cues in Guided Task Support with Virtual Assistants. In *Proceedings of the 2018 CHI Conference on Human Factors in Computing Systems.* ACM, 208.

[30] Linda Wulf, Markus Garschall, Julia Himmelsbach, and Manfred Tscheligi. 2014. Hands free-care free: elderly people taking advantage of speech-only interaction. In *Proceedings of the 8th Nordic Conference on Human-Computer Interaction: Fun, Fast, Foundational.* ACM, 203–206.

[31] Svetlana Yarosh, Stryker Thompson, Kathleen Watson, Alice Chase, Ashwin Senthilkumar, Ye Yuan, and AJ Brush. 2018. Children asking questions: speech interface reformulations and personification preferences. In *Proceedings of the 17th ACM Conference on Interaction Design and Children.* ACM, 300–312.

Assessing Online Content Quality through User Surveys and Web Analytics

Jessica Muirhead
Centre for Digital Business
University of Salford, UK
j.muirhead@edu.salford.ac.uk

ABSTRACT

Improving the informativeness of online content can help organisations to reach a wider range of audiences and ensure that their information is accessible to as many people as possible. Whilst many studies focus on the technical aspects of system design, this research aims to identify the key characteristics of quality within informative websites, and provide practitioners with a technique to generate improved content through an action research approach.

CCS CONCEPTS

• **Information systems → Web searching and information discovery**; • **Human-centered computing →** *Empirical studies in interaction design; HCI design and evaluation methods*;

KEYWORDS

Action research; human-computer interaction; information quality; online content; web analytics

ACM Reference Format:
Jessica Muirhead. 2019. Assessing Online Content Quality through User Surveys and Web Analytics. In *2019 Conference on Human Information Interaction and Retrieval (CHIIR '19), March 10–14, 2019, Glasgow, United Kingdom.* ACM, New York, NY, USA, 4 pages. https://doi.org/10.1145/3295750.3298977

This doctoral research is being conducted by Jessica Muirhead, a 4th year part-time PhD student in the Centre for Digital Business, University of Salford, UK. The researcher is currently collecting data from a number of case websites using an action research methodology.

1 INTRODUCTION

Over the past two decades, the world wide web has changed the way we publish, seek and process information. Access to the Internet has become so ubiquitous that many organisations and public sector bodies are pushing a digital-first agenda, with preference given to interactions with service users over online formats rather than more traditional postal mail or telephone [13].

Publishing information online is only one part of the communication and dissemination process. A wide range of users need to be able to find, read and understand information in a one-way exchange to understand and interact with organisations.

CHIIR 19, March 10–14, 2019, Glasgow, UK

ACM ISBN 978-1-4503-6025-8/19/03.
https://doi.org/10.1145/3295750.3298977

Despite this shift towards online services, many academic studies focus on the *presentation* of content, rather than the information contained within [28]. Providing a quality website has been demonstrated by various studies [23, 27] to have a large impact on user satisfaction, thus becoming a strategic importance for many online services.

This study aims to identify the key information quality characteristics that impact upon website use, and provide a model for practitioners to assess their own content, providing suggestions for improvement. The idea for this study follows the researcher's ten-year experience working with UK digital agencies building online systems and websites for a range of clients. Even though many of the projects differed in scale, approach and industry domain, the same challenges have continued to reoccur. The improvement of online content is often an unknown area to practitioners, who often follow trends of guidelines and best practices [5], yet are unsure how to assess the actual performance with real users.

With the rise of user-generated content, especially within the age of social media, there has been an emergence of active users involved in producing and sharing their own content [30]. Rather than focus on this type of content, this study examines *engineered content*, online information that is provided by organisations and is 'generally considered to be more reliable and credible, with less author bias' [11].

Many authors have attempted to provide a complete framework for information quality evaluation through the analysis of *attributes* and *dimensions* [8, 9, 16, 20, 22, 33]. The majority of these frameworks are based on the enumeration of information quality dimensions provided by Wang and Strong [34]. Whilst this list provides a useful starting point for categorising the aspects of quality, it does not provide any contextual preferences for specific characteristics.

This research examines the key characteristics inherent in the online content provided on *informational* websites, enabling practitioners to enhance the effectiveness, accessibility and informativeness of such content through application of a documented technique.

2 RESEARCH AIM

To devise a technique to aid practitioners in the assessment and improvement of information quality within online content.

3 RESEARCH QUESTIONS

RQ1. How are content quality and website success related?
RQ2. How can practitioners improve the success of online content by considering information quality characteristics?

4 RESEARCH OBJECTIVES

RO1. To identify information characteristics inherent in online content.
RO2. To define a research model incorporating the relationship between content characteristics and information quality.
RO3. To determine the key characteristics that impact on the success of online content.
RO4. To create a technique to aid practitioners in the alteration of online content leading to increased user success.

5 METHODOLOGY

The development of the practitioner-focused technique is being conducted using an action research approach, with the researcher playing an active role in the development and refinement of content for a number of information-rich websites. Each case website is being studied through several cycles of quality refinement, with step-wise improvements in content being performed iteratively. Assessment of information quality is triangulated through the use of qualitative user feedback surveys, and quantitative web analytics that are already being collected by the partner organisations (see Figure 1). This allows for the concurrent identification of key quality characteristics, along with confirmation of their impact on user behaviour and perceptions. Using triangulation can help improve action research validity [6], whilst respecting that information quality criteria 'are often of subjective nature and can therefore not be assessed automatically' [25]. Each cycle of data collection forms a *benchmark* (see Figure 2), evaluating specific information quality criteria during a particular iteration of the online content. The relevance and salience of different aspects of user experience can change over time, demonstrating the importance of an iterative approach to capture the evolving state [21].

The selection of information quality characteristics to be analysed has been made using a systematised literature review, identifying and synthesising the various lists of attributes within information quality and human-computer interaction literature [2, 3, 7, 12, 14, 15, 17, 18, 26, 31, 32, 34, 36]. Many prior works have focused on the most frequently occurring terms [10, 17, 18], however this has not been demonstrated to lead to a maximal impact on content improvement. This research enables the domain-specific exploration of the characteristics with the most impact on online quality, with the resulting practitioner technique allowing for the identification of such terms within individual contexts.

5.1 User survey

The user survey has been developed based on prior works such as WebQual 4.0 [4], Aladwani & Palvia's web quality instrument [1], Knight's 80-element user perception survey [19] and Kandari et al.'s devices for website quality evaluation [17, 18].

The initial survey contains a number of Likert scale questions to rank the prevalence of characteristics within the users' experience of the site, as well as a selection of free-text questions to capture more qualitative data about the usefulness of the information for the users' task.

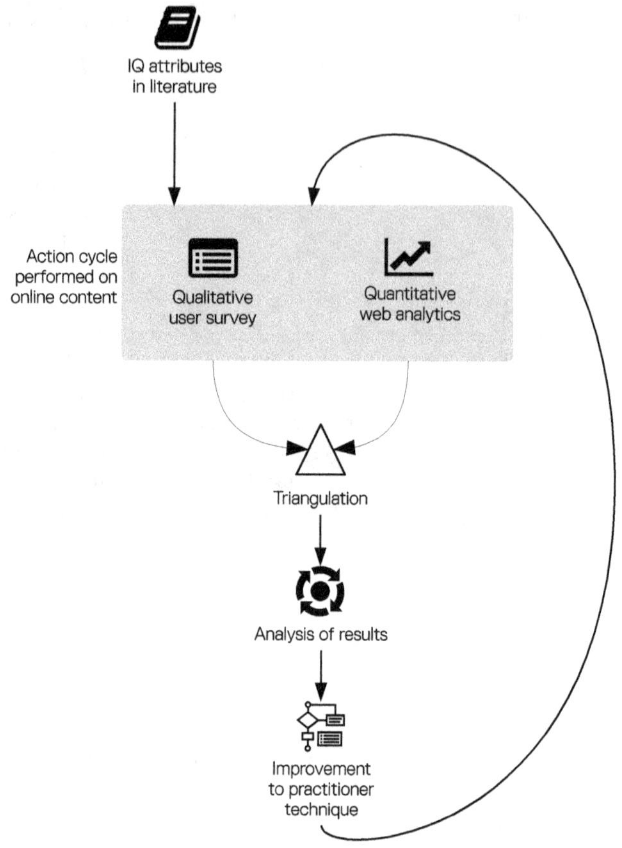

Figure 1: Data collection stages and triangulation to be performed at each iteration of content improvement of each case website.

5.2 Web analytics

The selection of web analytics tools has been modelled by researchers such as Nakatani & Chuang [24] to ensure appropriate data collection techniques, however this study has been guided by the data already available to the researcher through the partner organisations and collected through GDPR-compliant[1] channels. All usage data is anonymised, with aggregated user journey metrics used to confirm the selection of information quality characteristics through the qualitative surveys.

6 CASE WEBSITES

The researcher has arranged three informational websites to be studied as part of this project. Each website is independently evaluated against the information quality characteristics identified above, incorporating the contextual-specific nature of the content. The cases are based within different industries and are focused on providing access to large amounts of textual based content, making their analysis consistent even though there are differences in content, style and information density between the domains.

[1] General Data Protection Regulations, the May 2018 update to European Union data protection laws aimed at giving users more control over their personal and identifiable data.

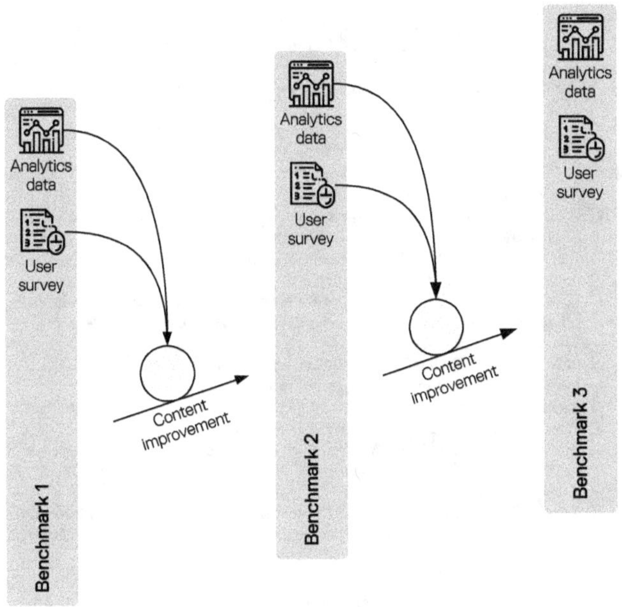

Figure 2: Iterative content improvement benchmarks with cycles applied to same case website.

The research participants are being recruited through three tracks:

(1) **Partner organisations**
By working with live websites, the researcher has negotiated access to both web content and existing stakeholders such as employees, focus groups and customer panels. As these participants are already actively involved in the improvement of the organisation's services, they have more background knowledge (are *expert* users) and have an interest in successful outcomes to the study.

(2) **Website advertisements**
Unobtrusive advertisements are placed on the case websites, to attract those users who may be frustrated with their experience or have an interest in improving the information available.

(3) **Direct recruitment**
During the later cycles of improvement on case websites, specific areas of content or characteristics may need to be re-evaluated. In order to conduct this study with a narrower focus, the researcher is directly recruiting participants with no prior domain experience to follow a task-based approach. These activities are guided through the use of *task scenarios* as 'grounded examples of specific experience' [29].

Each cycle involves a small number of participants (less than 10) to allow for the identification of a wider range of issues whilst ensuring the research is swift to provide an evolving content quality improvement.

The user survey and analytics do not capture background information about the user such as age, location, experience or familiarity with the website. These factors are unimportant to the overall task of creating an accessible information resource as many users have been recruited through self-selecting routes leading to a non-probabilistic sample of natural website users.

The study of a number of case sites reduces the reliance on the impact of quality cues such as 'overall organization, creator and readability as identifiers to evaluate the source' of information [35].

7 NEXT STEPS

The researcher is currently conducting cycles of action research on a number of case websites. This will be continued with further cycles until the key characteristics have been refined to a sufficient point that their improvement has limited impact on the analytics data.

Following the conclusion of the action research cycles, the researcher will use the key characteristics to define a technique for practitioner development of content quality, providing contextual and domain-specific advice. This will be validated by being applied to a further case project (yet to be determined).

8 CONTRIBUTIONS

The main output of this research will be the practitioner technique for improving website information quality. This will be a documented process outlining an iterative approach to content development focused on specific techniques appropriate to the context.

The application of a mixed methods approach involving user surveys and web analytics data is a novel contribution based on two separate areas of information quality literature. Through this research, the validity of this approach will be demonstrated, highlighting the possibility of combining both qualitative and quantitative data within further studies.

REFERENCES

[1] Adel M Aladwani and Prashant C Palvia. 2002. Developing and validating an instrument for measuring user-perceived web quality. *Information & management* 39, 6 (2002), 467–476.

[2] Janet E Alexander and Marsha Ann Tate. 1999. Web wisdom: how to evaluate and create information quality on the Web. (1999).

[3] Donald P Ballou and Harold L Pazer. 1985. Modeling data and process quality in multi-input, multi-output information systems. *Management science* 31, 2 (1985), 150–162.

[4] Stuart Barnes and Richard Vidgen. 2000. WebQual: an exploration of website quality. *ECIS 2000 Proceedings* (2000), 74.

[5] Susanne Bødker. 1998. Understanding representation in design. *Human-Computer Interaction* 13, 2 (1998), 107–125.

[6] Robert Davison, Maris G Martinsons, and Ned Kock. 2004. Principles of canonical action research. *Information systems journal* 14, 1 (2004), 65–86.

[7] William H DeLone and Ephraim R McLean. 1992. Information systems success: The quest for the dependent variable. *Information systems research* 3, 1 (1992), 60–95.

[8] Martin J Eppler and Peter Muenzenmayer. 2002. Measuring Information Quality in the Web Context: A Survey of State-of-the-Art Instruments and an Application Methodology. *Proceedings of the Seventh International Conference on Information Quality (ICIQ-02)* (2002), 187–196.

[9] Mouzhi Ge and Markus Helfert. 2007. A review of information quality research—develop a research agenda. In *Paper presented at the International Conference on Information Quality 2007.* Citeseer.

[10] Mouzhi Ge, Markus Helfert, and Dietmar Jannach. 2011. Information quality assessment: validating measurement dimensions and processes.. In *Proceedings of the European Conference of Information Systems (ECIS).*

[11] Carlisle E George and Jackie Scerri. 2007. Web 2.0 and User-Generated Content: legal challenges in the new frontier. *Journal of Information, Law and Technology* 2 (2007).

[12] Dale L Goodhue. 1995. Understanding user evaluations of information systems. *Management science* 41, 12 (1995), 1827–1844.

[13] Government Digital Service. 2017. Government Transformation Strategy. https://www.gov.uk/government/publications/government-transformation-strategy-2017-to-2020

[14] Layla Hasan and Emad Abuelrub. 2011. Assessing the quality of web sites. *Applied Computing and Informatics* 9, 1 (2011), 11–29.

[15] Matthias Jarke and Yannis Vassiliou. 1997. Data Warehouse Quality: A Review of the DWQ Project.. In *IQ*. 299–313.

[16] Beverly K Kahn, Diane M Strong, and Richard Y Wang. 2002. Information quality benchmarks: product and service performance. *Commun. ACM* 45, 4 (2002), 184–192.

[17] Jaikrit S Kandari, Erick C Jones, Fiona Fui-Hoon Nah, and Ram R Bishu. 2011. Information quality on the world wide web: A framework to measure and its validation. In *Proceedings of the 17th International Conference on Information Systems Analysis and Synthesis*.

[18] Jaikrit S Kandari, Erick C Jones, Fiona Fui-Hoon Nah, and Ram R Bishu. 2011. Information quality on the world wide web: development of a framework. *International Journal of Information Quality* 2, 4 (2011), 324–343.

[19] Shirlee-ann Knight. 2011. The combined conceptual life cycle model of information quality in user perceptions of IQ on the Web. *Proceedings of the 16th International Conference on Information Quality (ICIQ-11)* (2011), 570–590.

[20] Shirlee-ann Knight and Janice Burn. 2005. Developing a framework for assessing information quality on the World Wide Web. *Informing Science* 8 (2005).

[21] Sari Kujala, Virpi Roto, Kaisa Väänänen-Vainio-Mattila, Evangelos Karapanos, and Arto Sinnelä. 2011. UX Curve: A method for evaluating long-term user experience. *Interacting with Computers* 23, 5 (2011), 473–483.

[22] Yang W Lee, Diane M Strong, Beverly K Kahn, and Richard Y Wang. 2002. AIMQ: a methodology for information quality assessment. *Information & management* 40, 2 (2002), 133–146.

[23] Chang Liu and Kirk P Arnett. 2000. Exploring the factors associated with Web site success in the context of electronic commerce. *Information & management* 38, 1 (2000), 23–33.

[24] Kazuo Nakatani and Ta-Tao Chuang. 2011. A web analytics tool selection method: an analytical hierarchy process approach. *Internet Research* 21, 2 (2011), 171–186.

[25] Felix Naumann and Claudia Rolker. 2000. Assessment methods for information quality criteria. In *Proceedings of the fifth International Conference on Information Quality*.

[26] Jeff Offutt. 2002. Quality attributes of web software applications. *IEEE software* 19, 2 (2002), 25–32.

[27] Álvaro Rocha. 2012. Framework for a global quality evaluation of a website. *Online Information Review* 36, 3 (2012), 374–382.

[28] A Savoy and G Salvendy. 2008. Foundations of content preparation for the web. *Theoretical Issues in Ergonomics Science* 9, 6 (2008), 501–521.

[29] Alistair Sutcliffe. 2003. Symbiosis and synergy? scenarios, task analysis and reuse of HCI knowledge. *Interacting with Computers* 15, 2 (2003), 245–263.

[30] José Van Dijck. 2009. Users like you? Theorizing agency in user-generated content. *Media, culture & society* 31, 1 (2009), 41–58.

[31] Gisela von Dran, Ping Zhang, and Ruth Small. 1999. Quality websites: An application of the Kano model to website design. *AMCIS 1999 Proceedings* (1999), 314.

[32] Yair Wand and Richard Y Wang. 1996. Anchoring data quality dimensions in ontological foundations. *Commun. ACM* 39, 11 (1996), 86–95.

[33] Richard Y Wang. 1998. A product perspective on total data quality management. *Commun. ACM* 41, 2 (1998), 58–65.

[34] Richard Y Wang and Diane M Strong. 1996. Beyond accuracy: What data quality means to data consumers. *Journal of management information systems* 12, 4 (1996), 5–33.

[35] Yiwei Wang, Shawon Sarkar, and Chirag Shah. 2018. Juggling with Information Sources, Task Type, and Information Quality. In *Proceedings of the 2018 Conference on Human Information Interaction&Retrieval*. ACM, 82–91.

[36] Robert W Zmud. 1978. An empirical investigation of the dimensionality of the concept of information. *Decision sciences* 9, 2 (1978), 187–195.

Investigating the Effects of Popularity Data on Predictive Relevance Judgments in Academic Search Systems

Christiane Behnert
Department of Information
Hamburg University of Applied Sciences
Hamburg, Germany
christiane.behnert@haw-hamburg.de

ABSTRACT

The elements of a surrogate serve as clues to relevance. They may be seen as operationalized relevance criteria by which users judge the relevance of a search result according to their information need. In addition to short textual summaries, today's academic search systems integrate additional data into their search results presentation, for example, the number of citations or the number of downloads. This kind of data can be described as popularity data, serving as factors also incorporated in search engines' ranking algorithms. Past research shows that there are diverse criteria and factors involved in relevance judgements from the user perspective. However, previous empirical studies on relevance criteria and clues examined surrogates that did not include popularity data. The goal of my doctoral research is to gain significant knowledge on the criteria by which users in an academic search situation make relevance judgements based on surrogates that include popularity data. This paper describes the current state of the experimental research design and method of data collection.

CCS CONCEPTS

• Human-centered computing → User models; User studies; Empirical studies in HCI

KEYWORDS

Relevance behavior; predictive judgments; experimental design

ACM Reference format:

Christiane Behnert. 2019. Investigating the effects of popularity data on predictive relevance judgments in academic search systems. In *Proceedings of ACM SIGIR Conference on Human Information Interaction and Retrieval (CHIIR'19) March 10–14, 2019, Glasgow, United Kingdom.* ACM, New York, NY, USA, 4 pages.
DOI: https://doi.org/10.1145/3295750.3298978

ACM ISBN 978-1-4503-6025-8/19/03.
https://doi.org/10.1145/3295750.3298978

1 Research problem

The standard elements of a surrogate provide general information about a document retrieved by an Information Retrieval (IR) system. Today's academic search systems integrate additional data into their search results presentation. For example, Google Scholar's results include the number of citations or other versions of the particular work, and the ACM Digital Library provides the number of downloads for search results. This kind of data can be described as popularity data. Popularity data are factors for popularity based on the wisdom of crowds principle [24]. For instance, the more users judge a search result as relevant, the more popular the search result would be. Such popularity factors are also integrated into relevance ranking algorithms [17]. In the library context, popularity data would be, for example, the number of circulations, or the number of copies held by the library [5].

The elements of a surrogate (i.e., metadata and additional information such as popularity data) serve as clues to relevance since they provide a significant proportion of the information by which users judge the relevance of the result according to their information need. These relevance clues build the foundation for the criteria that users employ in the process of relevance judgment, that is, clues may be seen as operationalized relevance criteria. Past research shows that there are diverse criteria and factors involved in relevance judgments from the user perspective [e.g., 3, 13, 20, 21]. Empirical studies on relevance criteria and clues are based on search results that, at that time, usually did not include additional data in general or popularity data in particular. The goal of my doctoral research is to gain significant knowledge about the criteria by which users make relevance judgments of surrogates when the surrogates include popularity data. The focus is on academic search systems and user behavior in an academic search situation.

2 Related research

The related work is synthesized according to three topics: (a) relevance criteria and clues to relevance, (b) document representations as objects of investigations in relevance criteria studies, and (c) user models of relevance criteria.

2.1 Relevance criteria

In the 1990's, a shift from a system-oriented view towards a user-oriented view on relevance in IR occurred, which is mirrored by studies on relevance criteria that were undertaken at this time (see [14]). Saracevic [22] synthesizes what we have learned from decades of relevance research. He provides an overview of twenty-one "observational, empirical, or experimental" studies on relevance clues and criteria, including the influential work by Barry and Schamber [3]. They had analyzed criteria according to which users judge the relevance of a document. Among other studies [4, 8, 10, 11, 16, 25], their results show that several criteria beyond topical relevance are involved in relevance judgments, for example, validity, recency, availability, and credibility of the information source.

With respect to the dynamic nature of the Web and its exponential growth, credibility and quality are both significant factors to filter and judge information retrieved by Web search engines [20]. Credibility, in particular, can be considered in terms of cognitive authority [31], which is highly subjective: A person is not only an expert but a cognitive authority as well, when his or her statements of knowledge are accepted by others as truth – the information is trustworthy – while he or she would also influence other people's thoughts. Assessments of an author's cognitive authority are based on his or her present reputation and accomplishments [18]. Thus, in an academic context, information about an author's impact is helpful for users making relevance judgments. A similar finding was reported by Wang and Soergel [30], as their results suggest a need for providing information about the status or impact of authors and publishers as part of the search results' presentations.

2.2 Document representations as objects of investigation in studies on relevance criteria

Rieh [19] distinguishes between predictive and evaluative relevance judgments within the information search process, i.e., judgments based on the search result and judgments made based on the full-text document. Past studies on relevance criteria involving predictive relevance judgments are, for example, the study on document representations and clues by Barry [2], the study on document information elements by Wang [29] and Wang and Soergel [30], and the study on individual criteria in the process of judging abstracts by Tang & Solomon [26]. Overall findings suggest that titles and abstracts provide most of the relevance clues [22], which confirms the great importance of topicality and content-related criteria.

In Web search, snippets and hyperlinks may be seen as website surrogates. For example, Savolainen and Kari [23] conducted a study on selection behavior based on hyperlinks. Rieh [19] investigated how users decide on what website to look. Her study focused on information quality and cognitive authority as factors influencing web search behavior. In another study by Papaeconomou, Zijlema and Ingwersen [15], participants' eye movements were recorded to explore the "relevance hot spots" of Web pages applied during the judgment process, while Balatsoukas and Ruthven [1] investigate relevance criteria in judgment process on Google also applying an eye-tracking approach. However, those studies were not set in an academic search context, i.e., did not investigate predictive judgments in academic search systems.

As mentioned above, today's academic web search engines and other academic information systems integrate popularity data into their search results representations. At the time of the previous research reported above, such data were not parts of the search results, or did not focus on an academic context. However, more recently published research on relevance criteria that involve surrogates in academic search systems as objects of investigation [6, 27, 28] lack enrichment with additional data such as popularity data.

To the best of my knowledge, no studies on the relevance of surrogates containing this type of data in an academic context, while at the same time taking into account the user perspective, have been published to date.

2.3 User models on relevance criteria

Saracevic [22] states that "All IR and human information behavior models have relevance at their base either explicitly or as an invisible hand – in effect they are relevance models" (p. 40). Although these models may incorporate relevance and relevance judgments, they do not demonstrate the criteria and factors involved in the judgment process. Models that intend to do so are (a) the Document selection model for academic users in agricultural economics [30], initially developed by Wang [29], and (b) the Model of judgment of information quality and cognitive authority by Rieh [19]. While Wang studied the cognitive processes and document information elements that affect users in their decision making, Rieh's model focuses on two criteria particularly salient in Web search, namely, information quality, and cognitive authority.

Again, additional or popularity data as described above were not elements of the search results that the participants in their studies had judged.

To sum up, the results of the literature review revealed a gap in research on relevance criteria employed by users of academic search systems with regard to popularity data.

3 Research questions

The overall purpose of this research is to gain significant knowledge on the criteria by which users of academic search systems judge the relevance of a search result. The goal is to develop a user model on predictive relevance judgments in academic information systems. An initial version of this user model has been developed based on the results of the literature review, which helped me to narrow my research focus onto relevance criteria based on popularity data and, thus, to concretize my research questions. The model explicitly distinguishes between relevance clues, relevance criteria and relevance factors and, thus, offers a systematic representation of the influencing variables on the predictive relevance judgment process in academic search systems. In this model, popularity data are presented as dynamic, user-independent elements of a surrogate because they bear information that may change over time and are independent of the user in his or her particular information search situation. Following this definition, the research questions were formulated as follows:

RQ I: Which dynamic, user-independent elements of the surrogate influence how people searching for information judge the relevance of a search result?

RQ II: Which of these elements influence the relevance decision to what extent?

RQ III: How are the criteria derived from these elements weighted against each other?

4 Methodology

The research goal is pursued in five steps: (1) an extensive literature review of related research, (2) the development of an initial user model of relevance criteria which allows to formulate hypotheses, (3) an empirical examination through an online experiment with human test persons, (4) the statistical data analysis, (5) the alteration of the initial user model after reflecting the results of the online experiment.

The research questions will be addressed by conducting a user study. The study applies an experimental design, where participants are asked to perform predictive relevance judgments of search results to given search tasks.

At the time of writing this proposal, I have designed the experiment with a first version of the data collection instrument, as described in the following sections.

4.1 Experimental research design

Much research on the concept of relevance, as well as the factors and criteria that may influence users' relevance judgments has been undertaken [e.g., 13, 21]. However, Buckland [9], claims relevance to be immeasurable "in the normative sense of formal and physical sciences such as mathematics and physics, based on formal conjecture and refutation" (p. 163), because of its subjective and dynamic nature. He argues that a relevant document "must be useful to an actual human being's mental activity" (p. 161).

One approach to studying relevance with regard to human behavior is to develop an experimental research design, as common in social science disciplines, e.g., psychology and education, where experiments are frequently conducted to study human behavior. Information Behavior and Interactive Information Retrieval research may strongly benefit from experiments to gain significant insights into search behavior and interaction between users and IR systems and to get more valid and reliable results [13].

In an experiment, a researcher aims to establish causality between variables (stimuli and effects). To test whether a causal conclusion can be derived, some manipulation of variables (stimuli) and control of conditions (e.g., randomization, counter-balancing) are required. Through this, variables can be isolated and studied systematically [12]. Thus, the factors or criteria involved in relevance judgments, i.e., variables, can be isolated and modelled, which in real-life situations would not be feasible.

Table 1: Levels of independent variables (IVs)

IV	Level A	Level B	Level C
No. of citations (work)	Low	High	Not provided
No. of citations (author)	Low	High	Not provided
Author impact	Low	High	Not provided
No. of downloads	Low	High	Not provided

To investigate the effects of popularity data (independent variables) on academic users' predictive relevance judgments (dependent variable), I developed a multifactorial within-subjects design. Since we assume that a variety of clues affects relevance judgments, a multifactorial design is needed to test a combination of factors. Table 1 provides an overview of the independent variables (IV). Each of the IV will be manipulated on three levels: (a) a low number, (b) a high number, (c) no information will be provided, leading to 81 experimental conditions (3x3x3x3=81).

4.2 Data collection

The online experiment will be conducted using the online survey tool EFS Survey (by Questback). Aside from a questionnaire to collect demographic data and information on search self-efficacy as well as experiences with academic search systems, study participants will judge nine search results to a total of nine search tasks (81 surrogates to test all experimental conditions), on a visual analogue scale with a slider from zero to 100. Within the task description, the concept of relevance is operationalized as usefulness, stating: "Please use the slider to judge how useful you think each search result is for answering the search task!"

Both surrogates and search tasks will be presented in a randomized order. The search tasks will be developed based on the concept of simulated work task situations [7]. Topics for search tasks will be information science related topics that participants from different academic backgrounds are assumed to be familiar with in order to understand the given task. Topics include, for example, the peer review process, alternative metrics with regard to social media, and Wikipedia.

So far, I selected search results from topically relevant information science sources for two tasks, i.e., review articles in ARIST and JASIS&T's Advances in Information Science. All search results are manually produced images inspired by the Google Scholar search results presentation design. Participants will not be able to click on links or even view the full text to avoid comparability issues and reducing the internal validity of the experiment.

Participants will be graduate students (Master or PhD level) or academic staff from different academic disciplines. As an incentive and as a thank you for participation, an Amazon gift voucher à 10 EUR will be sent to the participant after completing the questionnaire via e-mail.

5 Future plans

At the beginning of 2019, I will conduct a pilot study to confirm the validity of the experimental research design. Further, the preliminary results will verify preceding choices of type and number of independent variables, characteristics of the sample, presentation of surrogates, and measures for statistical analysis. If need be, the research design will be revised.

The size of the sample for the study itself is planned to be at least n=400 to get statistically significant and sound results. To establish the exact sample size needed, the software tool G*Power for statistical analysis will be used.

ACKNOWLEDGMENTS

This research is funded by a three-year Ph.D. scholarship from the Hamburg University of Applied Sciences, Germany. I thank my supervisors Prof. Dr. Ulrike Spree, Hamburg University of Applied Sciences, and Prof. Dr. Joachim Griesbaum, University of Hildesheim, Germany, for their ongoing support.

REFERENCES

[1] Balatsoukas, P. and Ruthven, I. 2012. An eye-tracking approach to the analysis of relevance judgments on the Web: The case of Google search engine. *Journal of the American Society for Information Science and Technology.* 63, 9 (Sep. 2012), 1728-1746. DOI:https://doi.org/10.1002/asi.22707.

[2] Barry, C.L. 1998. Document representations and clues to document relevance. *Journal of the American Society for Information Science.* 49, 14 (Jan. 1998), 1293–1303. DOI:https://doi.org/10.1002/(SICI)1097-4571(1998)49:14<1293::AID-ASI7>3.0.CO;2-E.

[3] Barry, C.L. and Schamber, L. 1998. Users' criteria for relevance evaluation: A cross-situational comparison. *Information Processing & Management.* 34, 2–3 (März 1998), 219–236. DOI:https://doi.org/10.1016/S0306-4573(97)00078-2.

[4] Bateman, J. 1998. Changes in Relevance Criteria: A Longitudinal Study. *Proceedings of the 61st ASIS Annual Meeting* (1998), 23–32.

[5] Behnert, C. and Lewandowski, D. 2015. Ranking search results in library information systems – Considering ranking approaches adapted from web search engines. *The Journal of Academic Librarianship.* 41, 6 (Nov. 2015), 725–735. DOI:https://doi.org/10.1016/j.acalib.2015.07.010.

[6] Beresi, U.C. et. al. 2010. Why did you pick that? Visualising relevance criteria in exploratory search. *International Journal on Digital Libraries.* 11, 2 (June 2010), 59–74. DOI:https://doi.org/10.1007/s00799-011-0067-7.

[7] Borlund, P. und Ingwersen, P. 1997. The development of a method for the evaluation of interactive information retrieval systems. *Journal of Documentation.* 53, 3 (Aug. 1997), 225–250. DOI:https://doi.org/10.1108/EUM0000000007198.

[8] Bruce, H.W. 1994. A cognitive view of the situational dynamism of user-centered relevance estimation. *Journal of the American Society for Information Science.* 45, 3 (Apr. 1994), 142–148. DOI:https://doi.org/10.1002/(SICI)1097-4571(199404)45:3<142::AID-ASI4>3.0.CO;2-6.

[9] Buckland, M.K. 2017. *Information and society.* MIT Press.

[10] Cool, C. u. a. 1993. Characteristics of texts affecting relevance judgments. *Proceedings of the 14th Annual National Online Meeting, New York, May 4 - 6, 1993* (1993), 77–84.

[11] Howard, D.L. 1994. Pertinence as reflected in personal constructs. *Journal of the American Society for Information Science.* 45, 3 (1994), 172–185. DOI:https://doi.org/10.1002/(SICI)1097-4571(199404)45:3<172::AID-ASI7>3.0.CO;2-V.

[12] Kelly, D. 2009. Methods for evaluating interactive information retrieval systems with users. *Foundations and Trends® in Information Retrieval.* 3, 1–2 (2009). DOI:https://doi.org/10.1561/1500000012.

[13] Kelly, D. and Cresenzi, A. 2016. From design to analysis: Conducting controlled laboratory experiments with users. *Proceedings of the 39th International ACM SIGIR Conference on Research and Development in Information Retrieval - SIGIR '16* (New York, New York, USA, 2016), 1207–1210.

[14] Mizzaro, S. 1997. Relevance: The whole history. *Journal of the American Society for Information Science.* 48, 9 (Sep. 1997), 810–832. DOI:https://doi.org/10.1002/(SICI)1097-4571(199709)48:9<810::AID-ASI6>3.0.CO;2-U.

[15] Papaeconomou, C. et. al. 2008. Searchers' relevance judgments and criteria in evaluating web pages in a learning style perspective. *Proceedings of the second international symposium on Information interaction in context - IIiX '08* (New York, New York, USA, 2008), 123–132.

[16] Park, T.K. 1993. The nature of relevance in Information Retrieval: An empirical study. *The Library Quarterly.* 63, 3 (July 1993), 318–351.

[17] Plassmeier, K. et. al. 2015. Evaluating popularity data for relevance ranking in library information systems. *Proceedings of the 78th ASIS&T Annual Meeting* (2015).

[18] Rieh, S.Y. 2009. Credibility and cognitive authority of information. *Encyclopedia of Library and Information Sciences.* CRC Press. 1337–1344.

[19] Rieh, S.Y. 2002. Judgment of information quality and cognitive authority in the Web. *Journal of the American Society for Information Science and Technology.* 53, 2 (Jan. 2002), 145–161. DOI:https://doi.org/10.1002/asi.10017.

[20] Rieh, S.Y. and Belkin, N.J. 1998. Understanding judgment of information quality and cognitive authority in the WWW. *Proceedings of the 61st ASIS Annual Meeting* (1998), 279–289.

[21] Saracevic, T. 2007. Relevance: A review of the literature and a framework for thinking on the notion in information science. Part III: Behavior and effects of relevance. *Journal of the American Society for Information Science and Technology.* 58, 13 (Nov. 2007), 2126–2144. DOI:https://doi.org/10.1002/asi.20681.

[22] Saracevic, T. 2016. The Notion of relevance in information science: Everybody knows what relevance is. But, what is it really?. Morgan & Claypool.

[23] Savolainen, R. and Kari, J. 2006. User-defined relevance criteria in web searching. *Journal of Documentation.* 62, 6 (Nov. 2006), 685–707. DOI:https://doi.org/10.1108/00220410610714921.

[24] Surowiecki, J. 2005. *The wisdom of crowds.* Anchor Books.

[25] Tang, R. and Solomon, P. 1998. Toward an understanding of the dynamics of relevance judgment: An analysis of one person's search behavior. *Information Processing & Management.* 34, 2–3 (March 1998), 237–256. DOI:https://doi.org/10.1016/S0306-4573(97)00081-2.

[26] Tang, R. and Solomon, P. 2001. Use of relevance criteria across stages of document evaluation: On the complementarity of experimental and naturalistic studies. *Journal of the American Society for Information Science and Technology.* 52, 8 (Jan. 2001), 676–685. DOI:https://doi.org/10.1002/asi.1116.

[27] Taylor, A. 2013. Examination of work task and criteria choices for the relevance judgment process. *Journal of Documentation.* 69, 4 (July 2013), 523–544. DOI:https://doi.org/10.1108/JD-12-2011-0054.

[28] Taylor, A. 2012. User relevance criteria choices and the information search process. *Information Processing & Management.* 48, 1 (Jan. 2012), 136–153. DOI:https://doi.org/10.1016/j.ipm.2011.04.005.

[29] Wang, P. 1994. *A cognitive model of document selection of real users of information retrieval systems.* University of Maryland; College of Library and Information Science.

[30] Wang, P. and Soergel, D. 1998. A cognitive model of document use during a research project. Study I. Document selection. *Journal of the American Society for Information Science.* 49, 2 (1998), 115–133. DOI:https://doi.org/10.1002/(SICI)1097-4571(1998)49:2<115::AID-ASI3>3.0.CO;2-1.

[31] Wilson, P. 1983. Second-hand knowledge: An inquiry into cognitive authority. Greenwood Press.

Collaborative Information Seeking in Tourism

A Study of Young Chinese Leisure Tourists Visiting Australia

Mouda Ye
School of Information Technology & Mathematical Sciences
University of South Australia
Adelaide, Australia
mouda.ye@mymail.unisa.edu.au

ABSTRACT

People often travel in groups where information seeking occurs throughout the whole course of travel before various decisions can be made. This grounded-theory-based study investigates how small groups of young Chinese leisure tourists conduct collaborative information seeking (CIS) to support their joint decision-making as travelling to Australia. Most of existing literature in CIS are limited to workplace contexts. In addition, previous studies often failed to include the outcome of information seeking to better understand collaboration as a process of joint decision-making. This study aims to develop new models and theories of tourist CIS, propose appropriate methods to study CIS in leisure contexts and provide practical implication regarding the design of CIS tools and systems for tourists. The research contributes to existing understandings of CIS by exploring the understudied leisure context, investigating it in a broader framework of joint decision-making, and looking at a comprehensive project where CIS occurs instead of individual information seeking tasks.

CCS CONCEPTS

• **Information systems~Collaborative search** • Human-centered computing~Empirical studies in HCI

KEYWORDS: Collaborative information seeking; Information seeking; Decision-making; Tourism

ACM Reference format:

Mouda Ye. 2019. Collaborative Information Seeking in Tourism: A Study of Young Chinese Leisure Tourists Visiting Australia. In *Proceedings of the 2019 ACM SIGIR Conference on Human Information Interaction and Retrieval (CHIIR'19), March 10-14, 2019, Glasgow, UK.* ACM, NY, NY, USA, 4 pages. https://doi.org/10.1145/3295750.3298979

1 MOTIVATION

Considering the intangibility of tourism products, the high customer commitment and emotional significance, extensive information search is generally conducted by tourists before purchase decisions can be made [40]. For tourists, gathering and organising travel information is a complex task [17]. Tourism can be regarded as an 'information-intensive activity'; information needs arise spontaneously across the stages of destination selection, itinerary planning and travelling in the destination, and these needs seem especially pertinent for free and independent travellers who organise their trips by themselves instead of booking a package through tour operators or travel agencies [30]. Accordingly, information seeking occurs throughout the whole course of travel.

People rarely travel on their own, and whom they travel with shapes the scheduled trip significantly [41]. Recent survey has shown that in 2016, 45% of the visitors to South Australia were accompanied by their friends or family [39]. Under such circumstances, members of a tourist group would need to exchange ideas, make compromises and reach a shared understanding and joint decisions when various information needs arise across all stages of their trips. A thorough understanding of CIS is therefore needed.

CIS can be seen as the combination of the "information-seeking activities performed by actors to inform their collaborative work" and the "collaborative-grounding activities involved in making this information part of the actors' shared understanding of their work" [13]. CIS has been examined under various contexts, such as research [21, 42], military [29], healthcare [12, 32], design [1, 4, 28], patent application [9], and education [15, 16, 20, 37], to name a few. Yet tourism, as a frequently-raised example of CIS context [11, 25, 34, 35, 38], has not been thoroughly examined. On multiple facets including motivations and outcomes, CIS differs across contexts [8]. It is therefore not perfectly plausible to adapt theories derived from other contexts to tourism, especially given the complexity and multidimensionality of tourist information seeking [17, 30]. To develop new theories and models of CIS in the tourism context, naturalistic inquiry from the real-life situations appears beneficial.

Collaboration is "a process of joint decision-making among key stakeholders of a problem domain" [7], information sought during this process contributes to effective decisions [23]. However, within existing literature on CIS, decision-making has been neglected largely. It has been pointed out that recognition of information needs and the outcome of CIS remained unexplored within CIS literature [14]. In the model of collaborative information behaviour by Karunakaran, Reddy and Spence [19], problem formulation and information use were excluded from the scope of CIS; CIS contains only "retrieve, share, search" of information [19]. This model was proposed for organisations and

ACM ISBN 978-1-4503-6025-8/19/03.
https://doi.org/10.1145/3295750.3298979

hence might not be as suitable for tourism. In the context of tourism, recognition of information needs and utilisation of the information obtained towards purchase are crucial to tourist behaviour studies, as it informs practitioners on when and how to provide information by tourist preference. It is also difficult to separate them; trip planning and travelling is typically an "ongoing process" [3] where the actions of seeking and obtaining information are often directed by their information needs and highly related to the following decisions they will make during the rest of their travel. It is then important to take a holistic look at these stages. Therefore, to add to the existing understanding of CIS in tourism, the framework of joint decision-making in tourist behaviour studies is introduced [31]. Theories in tourist decision-making typically position information seeking between the recognition of problem and purchase decisions [22].This allows the study to investigate CIS in a more holistic point of view and to produce more informative outcomes for the tourism industry and academia.

Considering the insufficient understanding of tourist CIS and its outcomes, this study proposes to investigate tourist CIS using the case of free and independent young Chinese leisure travellers to Australia. The case was chosen for its significance to Australian tourism economy, its tremendous growth potential as well as the fact that characteristics of Chinese tourists' information behaviour have not been well understood by either Australian tourism industry or academia.

2 RESEARCH QUESTIONS

Based on the gaps in the current research discussed above and the scope of CIS defined in this study, the following research questions are raised.

Main research question: How do small groups of Chinese leisure tourists conduct CIS to inform their joint decision-making as travelling to Australia?

Sub research questions:

1. *What are the motivations for small groups of young Chinese tourists to conduct CIS during joint decision-making process while visiting Australia?*

   Previous research on CIS seldom identified motivations in the situations where collaboration occurred [34]. A study in healthcare noted "lack of immediate accessible information", "complexity of information needs", and "lack of expertise" as triggers of CIS [32]. Studies on tourist behaviour have partially confirmed that CIS took place during tourist joint decision-making process [18], but have not investigated the motivations behind it.

2. *How do small groups of young Chinese tourists visiting Australia conduct CIS for visiting Australia?*

   Prior research indicated that CIS is more than the sum of each member's individual information seeking behaviour [33]. It may involve, e.g. the occurrences of sharing, sense-making, different levels of decision-making, within-group discussions, and interactions between people and their environments during such process. It is also important that information seeking activities carried by members or subgroups of could inform the outcome of the group [13].

3. *How does CIS contribute or influence the joint decision-making process?*

   Research has suggested various internal and external influencing factors of tourist decision-making [5, 26]. It remains unclear, though, the way in which information seeking influences the final decisions made, let alone on a group level.

4. *Do small groups of young Chinese tourists visiting Australia conduct CIS differently when planning their trip and travelling at the destination? What are the differences?*

   With new information needs arise during the travel [30] together with the change of spatial context [6, 36], information behaviour patterns might not stay consistent across different sessions of the travel.

Relevant concepts addressed in the research questions are mapped to identify the focus of this study. Figure 1 illustrates such a research framework. Given the absence of the widely accepted and effective existing theories or models to explain tourist collaborative information seeking, this study is bound to be exploratory and below is not a conceptual framework on which data collection instruments will be based or against which future data analysis will tested, but rather an illustration of the area being addressed in this study.

As shown in the framework, motivators of CIS marks the start of collaborative information seeking during the process of joint decision-making. This might not be the same as that during individual tourism information search and will be explored in the empirical study (relevant to sub research question 1). CIS is understood as the combination of information seeking and collaborative grounding as proposed by Hertzum [13]. Based on this understanding the characteristics of CIS in tourism is investigated (relevant to sub research question 2). Tourist joint decision marks the outcome and closure of collaborative information seeking and this study looks at how the latter contribute to joint decision-making for tourist (relevant to sub research question 3). At last the changes of behavioural characteristics as the trips progress are studied (relevant to sub research question 4).

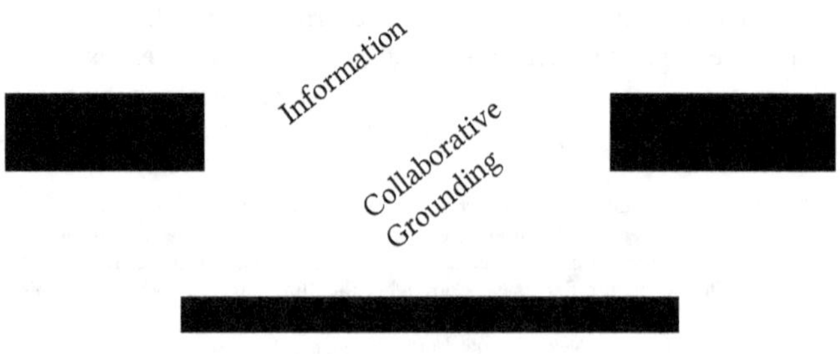

Figure 1 Research framework

3 METHODOLOGY

The study was deemed qualitative, due to the experiential and contextual nature of the required data to answer the research questions. Given the lack of a well-developed model or conceptual framework of CIS in tourism and yet limited understanding of CIS behaviour in general, the study employs the grounded theory [2] methods aiming to develop a refined conceptual framework for CIS in tourism. Following a grounded theory method, the propositions and conceptual framework emerge from the data as the study proceeds. Previously, the grounded theory approach has been successfully applied in several CIS studies [10, 24, 29, 32, 37, 43].

I intend to recruit 30 groups of Chinese free and independent leisure tourists travelling from China to Australia during the year 2018 and 2019. Theoretical sampling techniques [2] will be applied in this study for maximum theory development. The initial acquisition of participants for the field study would be made through recruitment advertisements posted on the Australia destination webpages of several China's largest online travelling communities including Mafengwo.com, Qyer.com and on Australia destination forum threads on China's largest online travel agency website Ctrip.com. If not enough participants are obtained from this channel, purposeful sampling will be conducted through personal networks of the researcher combined with the snowballing sampling technique to acquire participants from the under-represented demographic groups. During the process of study, additional participants may be acquired to reach variation and saturation of the sample.

Before taking part in the study, the participants will be made available an information sheet explaining the purpose, procudures, data use and storage, and expected outcomes of the study. Formal written consent will then be obtained from the participants. A demographic questionnaire will be completed by each participant upon comencement of data collection. Each participant will then be interviewed before and after their trip to Australia. Multiple interview sessions are designed to capture nuances of dynamic and ongoing CIS during joint decision-making processes in their journey, i.e. from the planning to trip excursion. During their holidays, they will be encouraged to submit eletronic diaries [9, 27] to document their CIS activities while travelling. Figure 2 summarises the data collection procedures.

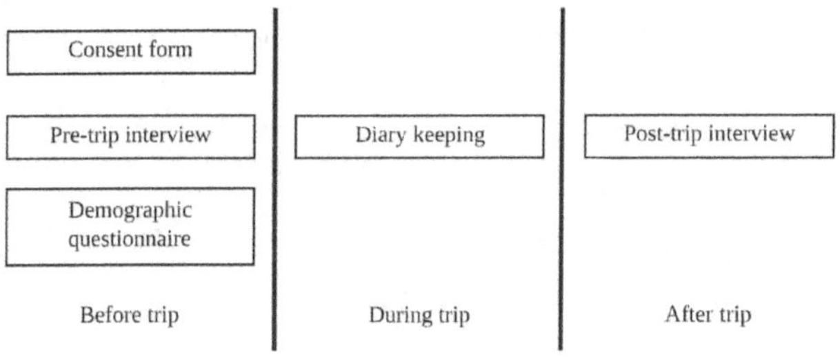

Figure 2 Data collection process

Coding of the gathered data will start from open coding, leading to axial and then selective coding, following the procedures proposed by Strauss and Corbin [2]. Gathered data would constantly be compared with relevant literature and previous data to synthesise new concepts and determine further sampling and instruments.

4 PROGRESS MADE

To test the methodology and instruments, I conducted a pilot study from June to September during 2018. Data was collected from twelve (12) individuals across five travel groups. The participants consist of six (6) males and six (6) females, aged ranging from 25 to 35. At least one traveller from each travel group participated in two interview sessions and kept diaries during their holiday, from which I was able to obtain data regarding the actions and thoughts of their travel mates. So far, I have conducted 14 interview sessions and received 26 diary entries.

Data from the pilot study reflected tourists' broad and complex information needs before and during their trip in an ongoing and dynamic process. Themes and categories have been extracted from the gathered data to answer the research questions. For example, regarding my first research question "What are the motivations for small groups of young Chinese tourists to conduct CIS during joint decision-making process while visiting Australia?", I have discover several dimensions of motivation including gathering rich information, shaping specific information needs, sharing information seeking workload, accommodating each member's preferences and opinions, and sense of participation.

5 FUTURE PLANS

My next steps will be thoroughly organise and analyse the obtained data from the pilot study. Upon finishing the pilot study, I will be able to further revise my instruments and data collection methods. So far, my observation of the data shows that diary entries from the participants are not providing enough details concerning their CIS activities. To ease the trouble of documenting information seeking experiences in long paragraphs, I intend to develop a template based on the diaries received from pilot study as future diary instrument. Participants will then be able to complete a semi-structured diary form to report their involvements of CIS during their travel. Other modifications will be made based on closer review of the pilot study. Once the research design is finalised, I will continue recruiting participants and collecting data until theoretical saturation is achieved. Data analysis will be carried out along the data collection process.

ACKNOWLEDGMENTS

The work presented here is supported by Australian Research Council (ARC). Grant ID: DE170100572

REFERENCES

[1] Bruce, H. et al. 2003. A comparison of the collaborative information retrieval behaviour of two design teams. *The New Review of Information Behaviour Research.* 4, 1 (2003), 139–153.

[2] Corbin, J. and Strauss, A. 2008. *Basics of Qualitative Research: Techniques and Procedures for Developing Grounded Theory.* SAGE Publications, Inc.

[3] Decrop, A. and Snelders, D. 2004. Planning the summer vacation: An

Adaptable Process. *Annals of Tourism Research.* 31, 4 (Oct. 2004), 1008–1030. DOI:https://doi.org/10.1016/J.ANNALS.2004.03.004.

[4] Fidel, R. et al. 2004. A multidimensional approach to the study of human-information Interaction: A case study of collaborative information retrieval. *Journal of the American Society for Information Science and Technology.* 55, 11 (2004), 939–953. DOI:https://doi.org/10.1002/asi.20041.

[5] Gilbert, D.C. 1991. An examination of the consumer behaviour process related to tourism. *Progress in tourism, recreation and hospitality management.* 3, (1991), 78–105.

[6] González-Ibáñez, R. et al. 2012. Time and space in collaborative information seeking: The clash of effectiveness and uniqueness. *Proceedings of the ASIST Annual Meeting.* (2012). DOI:https://doi.org/10.1002/meet.14504901080.

[7] Gray, B. 1989. *Collaborating: Finding common ground for multiparty problems.* Jossey-Bass San Francisco, CA.

[8] Hansen, P. et al. eds. 2015. *Collaborative Information Seeking: Best Practices, New Domains and New Thoughts.* Springer International Publishing.

[9] Hansen, P. and Järvelin, K. 2005. Collaborative Information Retrieval in an information-intensive domain. *Information Processing and Management.* 41, (2005), 1101–1119. DOI:https://doi.org/10.1016/j.ipm.2004.04.016.

[10] Haseki, M. et al. 2012. Time as a trigger of interaction and collaboration in research teams. *Proceedings of the ACM 2012 conference on Computer Supported Cooperative Work Companion - CSCW '12* (New York, New York, USA, 2012), 95.

[11] Hearst, M.A. 2014. What's missing from collaborative search? *Computer.* 47, 3 (2014), 58–61. DOI:https://doi.org/10.1109/MC.2014.77.

[12] Hertzum, M. 2010. Breakdowns in collaborative information seeking: A study of the medication process. *Information Processing and Management.* 46, 6 (2010), 646–655. DOI:https://doi.org/10.1016/j.ipm.2009.10.005.

[13] Hertzum, M. 2008. Collaborative information seeking: The combined activity of information seeking and collaborative grounding. *Information Processing and Management.* 44, 2 (Mar. 2008), 957–962. DOI:https://doi.org/10.1016/j.ipm.2007.03.007.

[14] Hertzum, M. 2017. Collaborative information seeking and expertise seeking: different discourses about similar issues. *Journal of Documentation.* 73, 5 (2017), 858–876. DOI:https://doi.org/10.1108/JD-04-2016-0053.

[15] Hyldegård, J. 2009. Beyond the search process - Exploring group members' information behavior in context. *Information Processing and Management.* 45, (2009), 142–158. DOI:https://doi.org/10.1016/j.ipm.2008.05.007.

[16] Hyldegård, J. 2006. Collaborative information behaviour-exploring Kuhlthau's Information Search Process model in a group-based educational setting. *Information Processing and Management.* 42, (2006), 276–298. DOI:https://doi.org/10.1016/j.ipm.2004.06.013.

[17] Imazu, M. et al. 2011. Effect of explicit roles on collaborative search in travel planning task. *Information Retrieval Technology* (2011), 205–214.

[18] Jenkins, R.L. 1978. Family Vacation Decision-Making. *Journal of Travel Research.* 16, 4 (Apr. 1978), 2–7. DOI:https://doi.org/10.1177/004728757801600401.

[19] Karunakaran, A. et al. 2013. Toward a model of collaborative information behavior in organizations. *Journal of the American Society for Information Science and Technology.* 64, 12 (Dec. 2013), 2437–2451. DOI:https://doi.org/10.1002/asi.22943.

[20] Leeder, C. and Shah, C. 2016. Collaborative information seeking in student group projects. *Aslib Journal of Information Management.* 68, 5 (2016), 526–544.

[21] Luo, A. and Olson, J.S. 2006. Informal Communication in Collaboratories. *CHI'06 Extended Abstracts on Human Factors in Computing Systems* (Montréal, 2006), 1043–1048.

[22] Mathieson, A. and Wall, G. 1982. *Tourism: Economic, Physical and Social Impacts.* Longman.

[23] Mishra, J.L. 2014. Factors affecting group decision making: An insight on information practices by investigating decision making process among Tactical Commanders. *Proceedings of ISIC, the Information Behaviour Conference* (Leeds, 2014).

[24] Mohammad Arif, A.S. et al. 2015. Understanding tourists' collaborative information retrieval behavior to inform design. *Journal of the Association for Information Science and Technology.* 66, 11 (2015), 2285–2303. DOI:https://doi.org/10.1002/asi.23319.

[25] Morris, M.R. 2008. A Survey of Collaborative Web Search Practices. *Proceedings of the SIGCHI Conference on Human Factors in Computing Systems (CHI)* (New York, New York, USA, 2008), 1657--1660.

[26] Moutinho, L. 1987. *Consumer Behaviour in Tourism.*

[27] Narayan, B. and Spink, A. 2009. Building an integrated model of information behavior through information journals. *Proceedings of the American Society for Information Science and Technology.* (2009). DOI:https://doi.org/10.1002/meet.2008.1450450332.

[28] Poltrock, S. et al. 2003. Information Seeking and Sharing in Design Teams. *Proceedings of the ACM conference on supporting group work (GROUP'03)* (2003), 239–247.

[29] Prekop, P. 2002. A qualitative study of collaborative information seeking. *Journal of Documentation.* 58, 5 (2002), 533–547. DOI:https://doi.org/10.1108/00220410210441000.

[30] Prestipino, M. 2004. Supporting Collaborative Information Spaces for Tourists. *Szwillus (Hrsg.): Mensch & Computer Allgegenwärtige Interaktion. München: Oldenbourg Verlag* (2004).

[31] van Raaij, W.F. and Francken, D.A. 1984. Vacation decisions, activities, and satisfactions. *Annals of Tourism Research.* (1984). DOI:https://doi.org/10.1016/0160-7383(84)90098-7.

[32] Reddy, M.C. and Spence, P.R. 2008. Collaborative information seeking: A field study of a multidisciplinary patient care team. *Information Processing and Management.* 44, 1 (2008), 242–255. DOI:https://doi.org/10.1016/j.ipm.2006.12.003.

[33] Shah, C. 2012. *Collaborative Information Seeking: The Art and Science of Making the Whole Greater than the Sum of All.* Springer-Verlag Berlin Heidelberg.

[34] Shah, C. 2014. Collaborative information seeking. *Journal of the Association for Information Science and Technology.* 65, 2 (2014), 215–236. DOI:https://doi.org/10.1002/asi.22977.

[35] Shah, C. 2014. Evaluating collaborative information seeking – synthesis, suggestions, and structure. *Journal of Information Science.* 40, 4 (2014), 460–475. DOI:https://doi.org/10.1177/0165551514530651.

[36] Shah, C. and González-Ibáñez, R. 2012. Spatial context in collaborative information seeking. *Journal of Information Science.* 38, 4 (2012), 333–349. DOI:https://doi.org/10.1177/0165551512438356.

[37] Shah, C. and Leeder, C. 2016. Exploring collaborative work among graduate students through the C5 model of collaboration: A diary study. *Journal of Information Science.* 42, 5 (2016), 609–629. DOI:https://doi.org/10.1177/0165551515603322.

[38] Soulier, L. et al. 2016. MineRank: Leveraging users' latent roles for unsupervised collaborative information retrieval. *Information Processing and Management.* (2016). DOI:https://doi.org/10.1016/j.ipm.2016.05.002.

[39] South Australian Tourism Commission 2017. *The International Market Place: Results for Year Ending December 2016.*

[40] Swarbrooke, J. and Horner, S. 2007. Models of the purchase decision-making process. *Consumer Behaviour in Tourism.* Elsevier. 69–80.

[41] Swarbrooke, J. and Horner, S. 2007. Motivators. *Consumer Behaviour in Tourism.* Elsevier. 53–61.

[42] Talja, S. 2002. Information sharing in academic communities: Types and levels of collaboration in information seeking and use. *New Review of Information Behavior Research.* 3, 1 (2002), 143–159.

[43] Tao, Y. and Tombros, A. 2017. How collaborators make sense of tasks together: A comparative analysis of collaborative sensemaking behavior in collaborative information-seeking tasks. *Journal of the Association for Information Science and Technology.* 68, 3 (2017), 609–622. DOI:https://doi.org/10.1002/asi.23693.

Interacting with Heterogeneous Information Ecologies: Challenges and Opportunities for Students in Diverse and Distributed Learning Environments

Samuel Dodson
iSchool
University of British Columbia
Vancouver, Canada
dodsons@mail.ubc.ca

ABSTRACT

The rise of heterogeneous information leads to questions of how people find, manage, and use information in increasingly fragmented ecologies. The extent to which interactive technologies can be re-designed to help people thrive in these environments should be explored. A two-phase study is proposed to investigate the effects of heterogeneous information on undergraduates' interactions with their information ecologies. Phase one will examine how students interact with the elements of their information ecologies. Phase two will explore how tools can be re-designed to help students more cohesively weave elements of their information ecologies together. An Activity Theoretical approach to these questions will be taken by examining the relationships between people, information, and tools.

CCS CONCEPTS

• **Information systems** → *Users and interactive retrieval*; *Multimedia and multimodal retrieval*;

KEYWORDS

Activity Theory; Information Ecology; Personal Information Management.

ACM Reference Format:

Samuel Dodson. 2019. Interacting with Heterogeneous Information Ecologies: Challenges and Opportunities for Students in Diverse and Distributed Learning Environments. In *2019 Conference on Human Information Interaction and Retrieval (CHIIR '19), March 10–14, 2019, Glasgow, United Kingdom.* ACM, New York, NY, USA, 4 pages. https://doi.org/10.1145/3295750.3298967

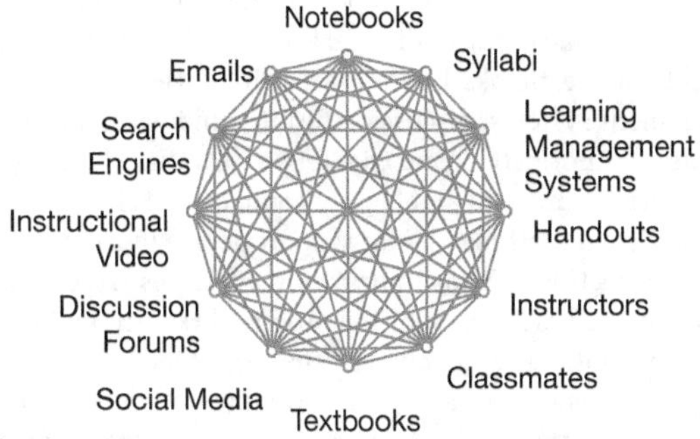

Figure 1: Students' information ecologies are made up of diverse and distributed information, people, and tools. Ecologies are dynamic, and may change through the addition, subtraction, or alteration of elements.

1 MOTIVATION

How do individuals interact with information, tools, and people within their increasingly diverse and distributed information ecologies? While the research literature has shown that the amount of available information can be overwhelming [1, 14] and difficult to manage [18, 41], existing work has primarily focused on text-based information. This emphasis overlooks the heterogeneity of information, and the difficulty people have constructing and sustaining networks of information, people, and tools. For example, information is often divided up by the tools used to create or consume content (e.g., email clients, image viewers, video players, web browsers, word processors, etc.), leading to the breaking up of information ecologies by media type rather than weaving elements together through spatial, semantic, or social relationships [2, 3]. The proposed research will investigate the ways in which information ecologies are both enriched *and* fragmented by diverse and distributed information, people, and tools, and explore the means by which people are adapting their information practices to these challenges.

Students experience breakdowns in their information ecologies that need to be repaired in order for them to engage in learning activities, including, but not limited to, note taking, homework, and preparing for exams [11]. Information ecologies are systems of interdependent elements (e.g., information, people, practices, tools, and values) that support human information interaction [31]. The proposed research will draw this metaphor out further by examining the nature of elements within these information ecologies. The breakdowns in information ecologies caused by heterogeneous information have been under-explored in the research literature. Heterogeneous information refers to distinctions between not only the type of media information is communicated through but also the material and social aspects of information. Breakdowns can prevent individuals from taking control of their learning, and may

CHIIR '19, March 10–14, 2019, Glasgow, United Kingdom

ACM ISBN 978-1-4503-6025-8/19/03.
https://doi.org/10.1145/3295750.3298967

lead to a culture of distrust in authoritative and credible sources or a filtering of information that does not conform to beliefs or expectations [32].

Students face challenges when using heterogeneous information on a daily basis as part of their learning activities. The proposed research will investigate how undergraduates interact with their information ecologies, which increasingly draw on information communicated through multiple media types and are mediated by an assortment of educational technologies. For example, students in flipped classrooms, a popular pedagogical approach [33], watch instructional video before class and work with their peers and instructors in hands-on problem-solving activities in class. While instructional video plays an important role in flipped classrooms, students continue to use traditional learning objects, such as syllabi, handouts, and textbooks. Educational technologies, such as learning management systems, discussion forums, and wikis, are also part of students' information ecologies (Figure 1). These heterogeneous sources are fragmented and loosely connected [11].

Re-designed tools may better support people by enabling meaningful connections across information ecologies. To explore this hypothesis, the first phase of the proposed research will provide a rich description of the current state of students' information ecologies, focusing on the degree of fragmentation in information ecologies and how students find, manage, and use their information ecologies. In the second phase, the solution space will be examined by re-designing and evaluating tools to address the tensions and challenges identified in the first phase. A lab-based evaluation will test the feasibility of the re-designed tools in helping people cohesively connect their information ecologies.

1.1 Scenario: Students' Information Ecologies

A scenario, based on interviews [11, 17] conducted with undergraduates as part of the ViDeX project,[1] may provide more insight into how and why students' interact with their information ecologies:

> Emily is a second-year undergraduate majoring in engineering, and is taking a flipped class on electromagnetics. She watches an instructional video before each class. Emily bookmarks information in the video that she finds confusing and would like to re-watch, and writes notes in her spiral notebook that she thinks may be useful when doing homework and studying for exams. She also writes notes in her notebook when reading her textbook, because she likes to keep all her annotations and notes in one place. Emily has access to the class discussion forum, but she does not like how difficult it is to keep up to date with new posts and replies. She is especially frustrated by how infrequently her instructor replies to posts. Consequently, Emily prefers to message her classmates on social media, where they share answers to the latest assignment by uploading snapshots of their homework with their cellphones. When she finishes her homework, Emily uploads it to the learning management system for grading. Emily knows the information she needs is available to her, but it is not easy to access, in part, because she cannot search across all the elements of her information ecology. This situation contributes to Emily's frustration that she cannot make sense of all the information that she could benefit from.

This scenario demonstrates the multiplicity of media, people, and tools that students interact with in their day-to-day learning activities and emphasizes the difficulties they face in searching, managing, and using their information ecologies.

2 RESEARCH QUESTIONS

The proposed research explores how students interact with and sustain their information ecologies by asking:

(1) What elements—information, people, and tools—constitute students' information ecologies, and what relationships exist between these elements?
(2) What tensions and breakdowns exist within students' information ecologies?
(3) How do students adapt and design their information practices when interacting with heterogeneous information?
(4) How can tools support more cohesive and connected information ecologies for students?

The research questions, methods, and analysis are informed by Activity Theoretical methods [20]. Activity Theory (AT) provides concepts that will be useful when making sense of students' learning activities, motivations, and tensions.[2] AT is a theoretical perspective that acknowledges that learning is actively constructed, involves interdependencies between information, people, and tools, and is pursued within spaces that in turn structure our activities.

A deeper understanding of the problem space is needed to inform the design of technologies with students' lived experiences in mind. I am motivated to contribute to critical discussions about how people manage diverse, distributed, conflicting information and weave heterogeneous information together when making decisions based on the material, cognitive, and social aspects of information.

3 PREVIOUS WORK

The proposed work builds upon the human-computer interaction and information retrieval research literature. There has been a substantial amount of interest in students' information practices; however, most research has not focused on heterogeneous information, people, and tools. Students' personal information management of text-based information, including activities for "finding, keeping, organizing, and maintaining information" [18], has been studied [29]. Similarly, students' annotation [25, 26, 43], clipping [27], and note taking [28, 34, 35] practices have been investigated. Scholars have explored these practices—annotation, for example—in non-text media; however, non-text-based works also focus on medium-specific information interactions, such as video [10, 12, 30]. While the research literature helps to explain why and how students interact with a specific medium, it is unclear how information practices translate to information ecologies comprised of audio, images, text, *and* video, resulting in calls to study how people interact with information across media [22, 39]. Now is the time to pursue

[1] See http://videx.ece.ubc.ca/research.

[2] See Kaptelinin and Nardi [19] for a review of AT.

this research agenda given how students are increasingly using heterogeneous information.

Improving search across information ecologies may help address the fragmentation problem [2, 13], but cross-media search remains a challenge. Searching across information ecologies requires techniques for representing and comparing the various types of media that comprise information ecologies. The dominant text-based approaches are not especially well-suited for audiovisual information and queries [24]. Video, for example, is a challenging medium to search given its streams of aural and visual information. The visual stream is comprised of a series of frames to be grouped into scenes, key frames to be selected, and people, places, and things within frames to be identified [37]. The aural stream of video also needs to be processed, often using speech recognition. There has been considerable effort to represent these information streams [38, 42]. How can advancements in federated and multimedia search be applied to context of the proposed research?

More than the content of information objects can be used to weave elements of information ecologies together. In addition to representing the content of objects, attempts have been made to represent how information objects are used [23, 36]. There have been attempts to incorporate interaction histories [40] to signal which parts of an object has (or has not) received attention in the past. Brown and Duguid [5], for example, argue that interaction histories provide traces that can be used for deciding how to interact with information. Interaction histories, such as shared annotations [28], can be found in some digital reading environments, and are beginning to appear in some video players, which display the most viewed [21] and annotated [8, 12] intervals of content. In the context of the proposed research, when made aware of the activities of other students, such as where in video they have highlighted, tagged, and written notes, students' information interaction can inform subsequent information use. More work is needed to explore the effects of guiding peoples' attention through interaction histories. The value of pre-existing annotations, for example, remains unclear. Shared highlights have been found to have no clear positive effect on reading comprehension [6, 7], but may support other learning processes and outcomes.

4 METHODS

The proposed research will be conducted as a two-phase study to investigate undergraduates' information practices (RQs 1–3) and how tools can help address the challenges students face in interacting with heterogeneous information (RQ4). In working towards the research questions, the proposed research will take a design-based research approach [4] by deploying ViDeX [15], a video player designed for active viewing [9]. Both phases of the proposed work will recruit students enrolled in courses using ViDeX.

In the first phase, students will be interviewed about the nature of their information ecologies, obtaining descriptions of the relationships between information, tools, and people using information world mapping (IWM)—an arts-based technique for eliciting visual representations of these relationships [16]. Throughout the semester, data will also be logged by ViDeX as students interact with instructional video, providing a second-by-second record of activity. The analysis of the log data will identify patterns of information interaction which will complement the qualitative analysis of the interview transcripts. The combination of IWM and log data analysis will allow for the triangulation of multiple sources of data.

In the second phase, ViDeX will be re-designed to introduce new tools for addressing the tensions and breakdowns identified in the first phase of the study. For example, class materials may be woven with other elements of students' information ecologies, such as information snippets from the discussion forum, textbook, and instructional video that may otherwise remain unused fragments. Interaction histories [40] may also be displayed to guide students' information interaction and use. To evaluate the re-designed ViDeX, a lab-based study will be conducted.

5 PROGRESS MADE & FUTURE PLANS

Through my collaborations with the other members of the ViDeX team, I have begun to understand how students interact with heterogeneous information. In a study—the primary source for the earlier scenario—we explored students' note taking practices in flipped classrooms [11]. We found that students wove information from their information ecologies into their notebooks, which acted as a tapestry of diverse and distributed information.

I have also explored how video-based highlights, notes, and tags can be shared as interaction histories [8], and have found that annotations clustered around the same intervals of instructional video. This is evidence that students identified the same content as important or confusing, suggesting that students' may benefit from seeing each other's annotations. Future work could explore how students may use shared annotations when working towards different tasks, such as viewing video to prepare for class, homework, or exams, and how these traces could be connected to other information in students' ecologies.

A goal of the proposed work is to explore how the design of practices and systems can be improved through a perspective that is sensitive to the interactions within information ecologies, and how educational technologies can support students in weaving information, people, and tools together.

I plan to defend my dissertation proposal in the spring of 2019. The first phase of the proposed research will begin by the summer of 2019, and a manuscript dissertation will be defended by the 2020/2021 academic year. This dissertation will act as the basis for the development of educational technologies and other tools for bringing together diverse and distributed information.

6 CONCLUSION

Our lives are increasingly dependent upon an ability to find, manage, and use information. While there has been considerable attention paid to information overload, individuals now interact with diverse and distributed information, people, and tools. This demands renewed scholarly focus on shifts in information diversity and dispersion, not only information volume. The proposed work will investigate both the problem and solution spaces, aiming to make practical and theoretical contributions. Practically, the proposed work will act as a design guideline for educational technologies and other information systems. Theoretically, the proposed work will further develop the concept of heterogeneous information by describing the challenges and opportunities people face when interacting with contemporary information ecologies. A deeper understanding of these tensions and breakdowns is needed to inform the design of technologies with individuals' lived experiences in mind. Managing information ecologies is a critical, transferable skill that requires improved support, as it is crucial to learning and participating in contemporary society.

REFERENCES

[1] David Bawden and Lyn Robinson. 2009. The dark side of information: Overload, anxiety and other paradoxes and pathologies. *Journal of Information Science* 35, 2 (2009), 180–191.

[2] Ofer Bergman, Ruth Beyth-Marom, and Rafi Nachmias. 2006. The Project Fragmentation Problem in Personal Information Management. In *Proceedings of the SIGCHI Conference on Human Factors in Computing Systems*. ACM, New York, NY, 271–274.

[3] Richard Boardman and M Angela Sasse. 2004. "Stuff Goes Into the Computer and Doesn't Come Out": A Cross-Tool Study of Personal Information Management. In *Proceedings of the SIGCHI Conference on Human Factors in Computing Systems*. ACM, New York, NY, 583–590.

[4] Ann L Brown. 1992. Design Experiments: Theoretical and Methodological Challenges in Creating Complex Interventions in Classroom Settings. *The Journal of the Learning Sciences* 2, 2 (1992), 141–178.

[5] John Brown and Paul Duguid. 2000. *The social life of information.* Harvard Business School Press, Boston, MA.

[6] Samuel Dodson, Luanne Freund, and Rick Kopak. 2017. Do highlights affect comprehension? Lessons from a user study. In *Proceedings of the 2017 Conference on Conference Human Information Interaction and Retrieval*. ACM, New York, NY, 381–384.

[7] Samuel Dodson, Luanne Freund, and Rick Kopak. 2018. The role of pre-existing highlights in reader-text interactions and outcomes.. In *Proceedings of the 18th ACM/IEEE Joint Conference on Digital Libraries*. ACM, New York, NY, 17–20.

[8] Samuel Dodson, Luanne Freund, Dongwook Yoon, Matthew Fong, Rick Kopak, and Sidney Fels. 2018. Video-Based Consensus Annotations for Learning: A Feasibility Study.. In *Proceedings of the 81st ASIS&T Annual Meeting*. ASIS&T, Silver Spring, MD, 792–793.

[9] Samuel Dodson, Ido Roll, Matthew Fong, Dongwook Yoon, Negar M Harandi, and Sidney Fels. 2018. Active viewing: A framework for understanding student engagement with educational videos. In *Proceedings of the Fifth Annual ACM Conference on Learning at Scale*. ACM, New York, NY, 24:1–24:4.

[10] Samuel Dodson, Ido Roll, Matthew Fong, Dongwook Yoon, Negar M. Harandi, and Sidney Fels. 2018. Active viewing: A study of video highlighting in the classroom. In *Proceedings of the 2018 Conference on Human Information Interaction & Retrieval*. ACM, New York, NY, 237–240.

[11] Samuel Dodson, Dongwook Yoon, Negar M Harandi, Ido Roll, Matthew Fong, and Sidney Fels. [n. d.]. Weaving Together Media, Technologies, and People: Students' Information Practices in Flipped Classrooms. ([n. d.]).

[12] Brian Dorn, Larissa B Schroeder, and Adam Stankiewicz. 2015. Piloting TrACE: Exploring spatiotemporal anchored collaboration in asynchronous learning. In *Proceedings of the 18th ACM Conference on Computer Supported Cooperative Work & Social Computing*. ACM, New York, NY, 393–403.

[13] Susan Dumais, Edward Cutrell, J J Cadiz, Gavin Jancke, Raman Sarin, and Daniel C Robbins. 2003. Stuff I've Seen: A System for Personal Information Retrieval and Re-Use. In *Proceedings of the 26th Annual International ACM SIGIR Conference on Research and Development in Information Retrieval*. ACM, New York, NY, 72–79.

[14] Martin J Eppler and Jeanne Mengis. 2004. The concept of information overload: A review of literature from organization science, accounting, marketing, MIS, and related disciplines. *The Information Society* 20, 5 (2004), 325–344.

[15] Matthew Fong, Samuel Dodson, Xueqin Zhang, Ido Roll, and Sidney Fels. 2018. ViDeX: A platform for personalizing educational videos. In *Proceedings of the 18th ACM/IEEE Joint Conference on Digital Libraries*. ACM, New York, NY, 331–332.

[16] Devon Greyson, Heather O'Brien, and Jean Shoveller. 2017. Information world mapping: A participatory arts-based elicitation method for information behavior interviews. *Library & Information Science Research* 39, 2 (2017), 149–157.

[17] Negar M Harandi, Farshid Agharebparast, Luis Linares, Samuel Dodson, Ido Roll, Matthew Fong, Dongwook Yoon, and Sidney Fels. 2018. Student Video-Usage in Introductory Engineering Courses. *Proceedings of the Canadian Engineering Education Association (CEEA)* (2018), 80:1–80:8.

[18] William Jones. 2008. *Keeping found things found: The study and practice of personal information management.* Morgan Kaufmann Publishers, Amsterdam, The Netherlands.

[19] Victor Kaptelinin and Bonnie A Nardi. 2006. *Acting with technology: Activity theory and interaction design.* MIT Press, Cambridge, MA.

[20] Victor Kaptelinin, Bonnie A Nardi, and Catriona Macaulay. 1999. The activity checklist: A tool for representing the "space" of context. *Interactions* 6, 4 (1999), 27–39.

[21] Juho Kim, Philip J Guo, Carrie J Cai, Shang-Wen Daniel Li, Krzysztof Z Gajos, and Robert C Miller. 2014. Data-driven interaction techniques for improving navigation of educational videos. In *Proceedings of the 27th Annual ACM Symposium on User Interface Software and Technology*. ACM, New York, NY, 563–572.

[22] Tibor Koltay. 2011. The media and the literacies: Media literacy, information literacy, digital literacy. *Media, Culture & Society* 33, 2 (2011), 211–221.

[23] Richard Kopak, Luanne Freund, and Heather L O'Brien. 2011. Digital information interaction as semantic navigation. In *Innovations in Information Retrieval: Perspectives for Theory and Practice*, Allen Foster (Ed.). Facet Publishing, London, England, 117–134.

[24] Gary Marchionini. 2008. Human–information interaction research and development. *Library & Information Science Research* 30, 3 (2008), 165–174.

[25] Catherine C Marshall. 1997. Annotation: From Paper Books to the Digital Library. In *Proceedings of the Second ACM International Conference on Digital Libraries*. ACM, New York, NY, 131–140.

[26] Catherine C Marshall. 1998. Toward an ecology of hypertext annotation. In *Proceedings of the Ninth ACM Conference on Hypertext and Hypermedia*. ACM, New York, NY, 40–49.

[27] Catherine C Marshall and Sara Bly. 2005. Saving and using encountered information: Implications for electronic periodicals. In *Proceedings of the SIGCHI Conference on Human Factors in Computing Systems*. ACM, New York, NY, 111–120.

[28] Catherine C Marshall and A J Bernheim Brush. 2004. Exploring the relationship between personal and public annotations. In *Proceedings of the 4th ACM/IEEE-CS Joint Conference on Digital Libraries*. ACM, New York, NY, 349–357.

[29] Diane Mizrachi and Marcia J Bates. 2013. Undergraduates' personal academic information management and the consideration of time and task-urgency. *Journal of the Association for Information Science and Technology* 64, 8 (2013), 1590–1607.

[30] Xiangming Mu. 2010. Towards effective video annotation: An approach to automatically link notes with video content. *Computers & Education* 55, 4 (2010), 1752–1763.

[31] Bonnie Nardi and Vicki O'Day. 1999. *Information ecologies: Using technology with heart.* MIT Press, Cambridge, MA.

[32] Safiya Noble. 2018. *Algorithms of Oppression: How Search Engines Reinforce Racism.* New York University Press, New York, NY.

[33] Jacqueline O'Flaherty and Craig Phillips. 2015. The use of flipped classrooms in higher education: A scoping review. *The Internet and Higher Education* 25 (2015), 85–95.

[34] Kenton O'Hara, Fiona Smith, William Newman, and Abigail Sellen. 1998. Student readers' use of library documents: Implications for library technologies. In *Proceedings of the SIGCHI Conference on Human Factors in Computing Systems*. ACM, New York, NY, 233–240.

[35] Jennifer Pearson, George Buchanan, Harold Thimbleby, and Matt Jones. 2012. The digital reading desk: A lightweight approach to digital note-taking. *Interacting with Computers* 24, 5 (2012), 327–338.

[36] David A Shamma, Ryan Shaw, Peter L Shafton, and Yiming Liu. 2007. Watch what I watch: Using community activity to understand content. In *Proceedings of the International Workshop on Workshop on Multimedia Information Retrieval*. ACM, New York, NY, 275–284.

[37] Alan F Smeaton. 2004. Indexing, browsing, and searching of digital video. *Annual Review of Information Science and Technology* 38, 1 (2004), 371–407.

[38] Yaxiao Song, Gary Marchionini, and Chi Young Oh. 2010. What are the most eye-catching and ear-catching features in the video?: Implications for video summarization. In *Proceedings of the 19th International Conference on World Wide Web*. ACM, New York, NY, 911–920.

[39] Sue Thomas, Chris Joseph, Jess Laccetti, Bruce Mason, Simon Mills, Simon Perril, and Kate Pullinger. 2007. Transliteracy: Crossing divides. *First Monday* 12, 12 (2007).

[40] Alan Wexelblat and Pattie Maes. 1999. Footprints: History-rich tools for information foraging. In *Proceedings of the SIGCHI Conference on Human Factors in Computing Systems*. ACM, New York, NY, 270–277.

[41] Steve Whittaker. 2011. Personal Information Management: From Information Consumption to Curation. *Annual Review of Information Science and Technology* 45, 1 (2011), 1–62.

[42] Barbara M Wildemuth, Gary Marchionini, Todd Wilkens, Meng Yang, Gary Geisler, Beth Fowler, Anthony Hughes, and Xiangming Mu. 2002. Alternative surrogates for video objects in a digital library: Users' perspectives on their relative usability. In *International Conference on Theory and Practice of Digital Libraries*. Springer, Berlin, Germany, 493–507.

[43] Sacha Zyto, David Karger, Mark Ackerman, and Sanjoy Mahajan. 2012. Successful classroom deployment of a social document annotation system. In *Proceedings of the SIGCHI Conference on Human Factors in Computing Systems*. ACM, New York, NY, 1883–1892.

Author Index

www.ingramcontent.com/pod-product-compliance
Lightning Source LLC
LaVergne TN
LVHW080006210926
848481LV00011B/2957
* 9 7 8 1 4 5 0 3 6 7 3 8 7 *